IF FOUND, please notify and arrange return to owner. This text is an important study guide for the owner's cost/managerial accounting and quantitative method classes or continuing professional education.

Name of Accounting Student
  or Practitioner   _____

Address   _____

City, State, Zip   _____

Telephone   (_____)_____

Additional copies of *Managerial Accounting Objective Questions and Explanations* are available for $14.95 direct from:

   Accounting Publications, Inc.
   P.O. Box 12848, University Station
   Gainesville, Florida 32604
   (904) 375-0772

Other similar study manuals:

   Auditing & EDP Objective Questions and Explanations $14.95
   Business Law/Legal Studies Objective Questions and Explanations 14.95
   Federal Tax Objective Questions and Explanations 14.95
   Financial Accounting Objective Questions and Explanations 14.95

Also available are:

   CIA Examination Review Volume I Outlines and Study Guides, 3rd ed. $21.95
   CIA Examination Review Volume II Problems and Solutions, 3rd ed. 21.95
   CIA 1990 Updating Edition 15.95
   All three CIA books for $49.90 (save $9.95)

   CMA Examination Review Volume I Outlines and Study Guides, 4th ed. 23.95
   CMA Examination Review Volume II Problems and Solutions, 4th ed. 23.95

Order forms for these and all of our other publications are provided at the back of this book.

All mail orders must be prepaid and are shipped postpaid, i.e., our prices include postage and handling. Shipping charges will be added to telephone orders, and to library and company orders which may be on account. Please add applicable sales tax for shipments **within** Florida. All payments must be in U.S. funds and payable on a U.S. bank. Please call or write for prices and availability of all foreign country shipments. The book(s) will usually be shipped on the day after your order is received. Allow 10 days for delivery. Please contact us if you do not receive your shipment within 2 weeks.

Accounting Publications, Inc. guarantees an immediate, complete refund on all direct-mail orders if a resalable text is returned within 30 days.

REVIEWERS AND CONTRIBUTORS

Yasemin A. Birgil, M.S., is a Ph.D. candidate in the Department of Management and Administrative Sciences, University of Florida. Ms. Birgil reviewed many of the linear programming questions in the Second Edition.

Maria Bolanos, B.A.Ed., University of Florida, is our production manager. She coordinated and supervised the production staff and reviewed the entire text.

Grady M. Irwin, J.D., University of Florida Holland Law Center, has taught in the University of Florida College of Business. Mr. Irwin provided first drafts of many answer explanations as well as extensive editorial assistance throughout the project.

John F. Rebstock, CIA, is a graduate of the School of Accounting at the University of Florida. He has passed the CPA exam and is a CMA candidate. Mr. Rebstock reviewed the entire edition and prepared the page layout.

A PERSONAL THANKS

This manual would not have been possible without the extraordinary efforts and dedication of Ann Finnicum, Doña Kochman, Sherry Nobles, Louann Sammons, and Connie Steen, who typed the entire manuscript and all revisions, as well as prepared the camera-ready pages.

The authors also appreciate the proofreading assistance of Kim Allen, Nanci Chertoff, Kim Cornell, Laura David, Brian Fowler, Robert Francis, David Hepburn, Kim Iley, Windy Kemp, Andy Mason, Michael McLamb, Sean Menendez, Leslie O'Donnell, Douglas O'Dowd, Ketan Patel, Chris Powell, Caroline Roche, Evan Rothman, Dee Sanchez, Tim Szczepanski, and Marie Wilker, and the production assistance of Windy Kemp and Carol Marr.

The authors also appreciate the editorial and reviewing assistance of Kim Allen, Kim Cornell, Gillian Hillis, Douglas O'Dowd, Ketan Patel, and Marie Wilker.

Finally, we appreciate the encouragement, support, and tolerance of our families throughout this project.

Third Edition

MANAGERIAL ACCOUNTING

Objective Questions and Explanations

by

Irvin N. Gleim
Ph.D., CPA, CIA, CMA

and

Terry L. Campbell
DBA, CPA, CMA, CCA

ABOUT THE AUTHORS

Irvin N. Gleim is Professor Emeritus in the Fisher School of Accounting at the University of Florida and is a member of the American Accounting Association, American Business Law Association, American Institute of Certified Public Accountants, Association of Government Accountants, Florida Institute of Certified Public Accountants, Institute of Internal Auditors, Institute of Certified Management Accountants, and the National Association of Accountants. He has had articles published in the *Journal of Accountancy, The Accounting Review,* and *The American Business Law Journal* and is author/coauthor of numerous accounting and aviation books and CPE courses. He has enjoyed over 20 years as accounting professor at Pittsburg State University, Illinois State University, and the University of Florida.

Terry L. Campbell is a member of the faculty of the Department of Accounting and MIS at Pennsylvania State University. He is a member of the American Accounting Association, American Institute of Certified Public Accountants, American Institute of Decision Sciences, Florida Institute of Certified Public Accountants, American Economic Association, National Association of Business Economists, National Association of Accountants, and the Institute of Certified Management Accountants. His primary academic and research areas of interest include decision support systems, management accounting, information systems, management of accounting practices, applied microeconomic analysis to CPA firms' practice management, accounting education in the 21st century, and CPA practice management issues.

Accounting Publications, Inc.
P.O. Box 12848
University Station
Gainesville, Florida 32604

Library of Congress Catalog Card No. 88-71872
ISBN 0-917537-28-9

Copyright © 1988
Accounting Publications, Inc.

Second Printing: July 1990

ALL RIGHTS RESERVED. No part of this material may be reproduced in any form whatsoever without express permission from Accounting Publications, Inc.

ACKNOWLEDGMENTS

The authors appreciate and thank the American Institute of Certified Public Accountants for permission to use Uniform Certified Public Accountant Examination questions, copyright © 1969, 1970, 1971, 1972, 1973, 1974, 1975, 1976, 1977, 1978, 1979, 1980, 1981, 1982, 1983, 1984, 1985, 1986, 1987, and 1988 by the American Institute of Certified Public Accountants.

The authors also appreciate and thank the Institute of Internal Auditors, Inc. for permission to use the Institute's Certified Internal Auditor Examination questions, copyright © 1975, 1976, 1977, 1978, 1979, 1980, 1981, 1982, 1983, 1984, 1985, 1986, 1987, and 1988 by The Institute of Internal Auditors, Inc.

The authors also appreciate and thank the Institute of Certified Management Accountants of the National Association of Accountants for permission to use problem materials from past CMA examinations, copyright © 1972, 1973, 1974, 1975, 1976, 1977, 1978, 1979, 1980, 1981, 1982, 1983, 1984, 1985, 1986, 1987, and 1988 by the National Association of Accountants.

This publication is designed to provide accurate and authoritative information with regard to the subject matter covered. It is sold with the understanding that the publisher is not engaged in rendering legal, accounting, or other professional service.

If legal advice or other expert assistance is required, the services of a competent professional person should be sought.

(From a declaration of principles jointly adopted by a Committee of the American Bar Association and a Committee of Publishers.)

PREFACE FOR ACCOUNTING STUDENTS

The purpose of this study manual is to help you understand managerial accounting concepts and procedures, and their applications. In turn, these skills will enable you to perform better on your undergraduate examinations, as well as look ahead to (and prepare for) professional examinations.

One of the major benefits of this study manual is comprehensive coverage of managerial accounting topics. Accordingly, when you use this study manual to help prepare for managerial accounting courses and examinations, you are assured of covering virtually all topics that can reasonably be expected to be studied in typical college or university cost/managerial accounting courses.

The question-and-answer format is designed and presented to facilitate effective study. Students should be careful not to misuse this text by referring to the answers before independently answering each question.

The majority of the questions in this book are from past CIA, CMA, and CPA examinations. Although a citation for the source of each question is provided, some have been modified to accommodate changes in professional pronouncements, to clarify questions, and/or to emphasize a managerial accounting concept or its application. In addition, hundreds of publisher-written questions test areas covered in current textbooks but not directly tested on accounting certification examinations.

Note that this study manual should not be relied upon to prepare for the professional examinations. You should utilize review manuals specifically developed for each examination. *CIA Examination Review, CMA Examination Review,* and *CPA Examination Review* are up-to-date manuals that comprehensively cover all material necessary for successful completion of each examination. Further description and an order form for these other books are provided on pages 649 through 652.

Thank you for your interest in this study manual. We deeply appreciate the many letters and suggestions received from accounting students and educators during the past years, as well as from CIA, CMA, and CPA candidates. Please send us your suggestions, comments, and corrections concerning this manual. The last two pages have been designed to help you note corrections and suggestions throughout your study process.

Please read the first three chapters carefully. They are very short but nevertheless very important.

Good Luck on Your Exams,

Irvin N. Gleim
Terry L. Campbell
July 15, 1988

PREFACE FOR ACCOUNTING PRACTITIONERS

The first purpose of this study manual is to permit you to assess your technical proficiency concerning cost and managerial accounting and related special skills such as quantitative methods, planning, and control. The second purpose is to facilitate your review and update of cost accounting concepts with our compendium of nearly 2,000 objective questions. The third purpose is to provide CPE credit for your self-assessment and review/update study effort.

This new approach to CPE is both interactive and intense. You should be continuously challenged to answer each question correctly. When you answer a question incorrectly or have difficulty, you should pursue a complete understanding by reading the answer explanation and consulting reference sources as necessary.

Most of the questions in *Managerial Accounting Objective Questions and Explanations* were taken from various professional examinations, but many have been revised, adapted, etc., to provide broader and up-to-date coverage of the managerial accounting body of technical knowledge. While some are from the CPA exam, many are from the CIA and CMA exams. Thus, you have an opportunity to consider the appropriateness of pursuing these other accounting certifications. In addition, hundreds of publisher questions cover material not directly tested on the accounting certification examinations. Also, this book contains multiple-choice questions developed from essay questions/computational problems that appeared on the CIA, CMA, and CPA exams.

Finally, we ask for any supplemental comments, reactions, suggestions, etc. that you may have as you complete our CPE program. Please attach them to the Course Evaluation (handwritten notes are fine). The last two pages of this study book have been designed to help you note corrections and suggestions throughout your study process.

Chapters One through Three of *Managerial Accounting Objective Questions and Explanations* are directed primarily to accounting students. Those practitioners interested in multiple certification, however, may find the discussion of the CIA and CMA certification programs in Chapter Three to be useful. If, as you work through this study book and take the open-book CPE final exams, you find you need to refer to a cost or quantitative methods textbook, Chapter One contains a list of current titles. You should be sure to read carefully the "Introduction: How to Use This CPE Program" in the accompanying *Managerial Accounting CPE* book.

Thank you for your interest, and we look forward to hearing from you.

Best Wishes in Your CPE Endeavors,

Irvin N. Gleim
Terry L. Campbell
July 15, 1988

TABLE OF CONTENTS

	Page
Preface for Accounting Students	v
Preface for Accounting Practitioners	vi
1. How to Use This Book	1
2. Objective Questions Answering Technique	21
3. The CIA, CMA, and CPA Certification Programs	25

PART I: COST ACCOUNTING

4. Cost Accounting Terminology and Overview	43
5. Job Order Costing	71
6. Process Costing	109
7. Spoilage, Waste, and Scrap	141
8. Joint Products and By-Products	161
9. Service Cost Allocations	189
10. Absorption and Variable Costing	203

PART II: PLANNING AND CONTROL

11. Cost/Volume/Profit Analysis	223
12. Budgeting	289
13. Standard Costs	315
14. Responsibility Accounting	399

PART III: NONROUTINE DECISIONS AND QUANTITATIVE METHODS

15. Nonroutine Decisions	427
16. Capital Budgeting	467
17. Inventory Planning and Control	515
18. Probability and Statistics	535
19. Regression Analysis	573
20. Linear Programming	599
21. Other Quantitative Approaches	625

Index	657

CONTRIBUTING PROFESSORS

We are especially grateful to the following professors who submitted questions for the Third Edition. Their participation has made *Managerial Accounting Objective Questions and Explanations* truly a community project. We welcome further submissions of questions, either for the Fourth Edition of *Managerial Accounting Objective Questions and Explanations* or for future editions of our other Objective Question and Explanation books.

Ahadiat, N.	Southern Illinois University
Boze, K.	University of Alaska at Fairbanks
Collier, H.	California State University at San Bernardino
Ferry, J.W.	Pittsburg State University
Gruber, R.	University of Wisconsin at Whitewater
Mayne, F.	University of Texas at El Paso
McCarthy, L.J.	Slippery Rock University
Romal, J.B.	SUNY College at Fredonia
Skender, C.J.	North Carolina State University
Wagner, C.	Mankato State University
Wilson, A.	Auburn University

CHAPTER ONE
HOW TO USE THIS BOOK

Our Use of "Modules"	3
Sources of Objective Questions	3
Identification of the Source of Each Question	4
Order of Questions in Each Module	4
Answer Explanations Alongside the Questions	4
Uniqueness of Objective Questions	5
Using Objective Questions to Study	5
Preparing for Essay Questions and Computational Problems	6
Abbreviations Used in This Book	7
Module Cross-References to Cost/Managerial and Quantitative Methods Textbooks	7

This chapter explains how and why this study manual was written. More importantly, it directs you on how to use it efficiently and effectively.

The format and content of this study manual are innovative in the accounting text market. The first purpose is to provide accounting students with a well-organized, comprehensive compendium of objective questions covering the topics taught in typical undergraduate cost/managerial and quantitative method undergraduate courses. The second purpose is to provide accounting professionals with a comprehensive presentation of diagnostic objective questions for both self-diagnostic use and/or review of basic level cost/managerial accounting standards and procedures, including quantitative methods.

This study manual consists solely of objective questions and answer explanations, with the exception of the first three chapters:

1. How to Use This Book
2. Objective Questions Answering Technique
3. The CIA, CMA, and CPA Certification Programs

The chapter titles and organization of this study manual are based on the organization of the following current cost/managerial and quantitative method textbooks.

Cost/Managerial Accounting

Deakin and Maher, *Cost Accounting,* Second Edition, Richard D. Irwin, Inc., 1987.

DeCoster and Schaefer, *Management Accounting: A Decision Emphasis,* Fourth Edition, John Wiley & Sons, Inc., 1988.

Dominiak and Louderback, *Managerial Accounting,* Fifth Edition, Kent Publishing Company, 1988.

Engler, *Managerial Accounting,* Richard D. Irwin, Inc., 1988.

Fischer and Frank, *Cost Accounting: Theory and Applications,* South-Western Publishing Co., 1985.

Garrison, *Managerial Accounting: Concepts for Planning, Control, Decision Making,* Fifth Edition, Business Publications/Richard D. Irwin, Inc., 1988.

Hartley, *Cost and Managerial Accounting,* Second Edition, Allyn and Bacon, Inc., 1986.

Hirsch and Louderback, *Cost Accounting: Accumulation, Analysis and Use,* Second Edition, Kent Publishing Company, 1986.

Horngren and Foster, *Cost Accounting: A Managerial Emphasis,* Sixth Edition, Prentice-Hall, Inc., 1987.

Kellough and Leiminger, *Cost Accounting: Concepts and Techniques for Management,* West Publishing Co., 1984.

Moore, Anderson, Jaedicke, *Managerial Accounting,* Seventh Edition, South-Western Publishing Co., 1988.

Moriarity and Allen, *Cost Accounting,* Second Edition, John Wiley & Sons, Inc., 1987.

Morse, Davis, Hartgraves, *Management Accounting,* Second Edition, Addison-Wesley Publishing Co., Inc., 1988.

Morse and Roth, *Cost Accounting: Processing, Evaluating, and Using Cost Data,* Third Edition, Addison-Wesley Publishing Co., Inc., 1986.

Moscove, Crowningshield, Gorman, *Cost Accounting with Managerial Applications,* Fifth Edition, Houghton Mifflin Company, 1985.

Polimeni, Fabozzi, Adelberg, *Cost Accounting: Concepts and Applications for Managerial Decision Making,* Second Edition, McGraw-Hill Book Company, 1986.

Rayburn, *Principles of Cost Accounting: Managerial Applications,* Third Edition, Richard D. Irwin, Inc., 1986.

Ricketts and Gray, *Managerial Accounting,* Houghton Mifflin Company, 1988.

Smith, Keith, Stephens, *Managerial Accounting,* McGraw-Hill, Inc., 1988.

Usry, Hammer, Matz, *Cost Accounting: Planning and Control,* Ninth Edition, South-Western Publishing Co., 1988.

Warren and Fess, *Managerial Accounting,* Second Edition, South-Western Publishing Co., 1988.

Quantitative Methods

Anderson and Lievano, *Quantitative Management: An Introduction,* Second Edition, Kent Publishing Co., 1986.

Bierman, Bonini, Hausman, *Quantitative Analysis for Business Decisions,* Seventh Edition, Richard D. Irwin, Inc., 1986.

Budnick, Mojena, Vollmann, *Principles of Operations Research for Management,* Second Edition, Richard D. Irwin, Inc., 1988.

Davis and McKeown, *Quantitative Models for Management,* Second Edition, Kent Publishing Company, 1984.

Levin, Rubin, Stinson, *Quantitative Approaches to Management,* Sixth Edition, McGraw-Hill Book Company, 1986.

Markland and Sweigart, *Quantitative Method for Management Decisions,* John Wiley & Sons, Inc., 1987.

Undoubtedly, some textbooks have been inadvertently omitted from the above lists, for which we apologize. The last section in this chapter (see page 7) contains the tables of contents of each of these textbooks, with cross-references to modules in this study manual.

OUR USE OF "MODULES"

Each chapter of this book is divided into subtopics (i.e., groups of questions) to assist your study program. We call these subtopics "modules."

Choosing modules and arranging questions within these subtopics was difficult. As a result, there is some overlapping of topics and questions. We wanted the number of questions to be large enough for comprehensive coverage without becoming overwhelming. We defined each module to be narrow enough to cover a single topic but broad enough so the questions are not redundant.

SOURCES OF OBJECTIVE QUESTIONS

Past CIA, CMA, and CPA examinations are the primary sources of questions in this study manual. Additionally, your authors have prepared questions (coded in this text as "Publisher") based upon the content of the cost/managerial accounting and quantitative method textbooks listed above. These "Publisher" questions were developed to review topics not adequately covered by questions from the other sources.

The source of each question appears in the first line of its answer explanation, in the column to the right of the question. Summary of sources:

CIA	Certified Internal Auditor Examination
CMA	Certified Management Accountant Examination
CPA	Uniform Certified Public Accountant Examination
Publisher	Your authors
(Professor name)	Professor who contributed question

New to this Objective Question and Explanation series are multiple-choice questions developed from longer computational problems and essay questions that appeared for the most part on the CPA exam, but also some from the CIA and CMA exams. The fact situations of these longer problems are presented (with the source identified), and then a series of author-developed multiple-choice questions. Questions generated in this manner allow you to gain experience with longer, more involved problems while retaining the advantages of answering multiple-choice questions.

IDENTIFICATION OF THE SOURCE OF EACH QUESTION

After each source code (except Publisher), codes for the following information are given:

> Month and year (e.g., 588)
> Exam part (see below)
> Question number (see below)

Roman numerals signify the parts of the CIA exam, e.g., I, II, III, IV. Arabic numerals signify the parts of the CMA exam, e.g., 1, 2, 3, 4, 5. The parts of the CPA exam covered in this book are coded as follows:

> P - Practice I
> Q - Practice II
> T - Theory

Examples of complete source codes and their meanings:

(CIA 588 IV-5)	CIA exam, May 1988, Part IV, question 5
(CMA 1287 3-20)	CMA exam, December 1987, Part 3, question 20
(CPA 1188 Q-2)	CPA exam, November 1988, Practice II section, question 2
(Publisher)	Prepared by your authors
(C. Wagner)	Professor who contributed question

ORDER OF QUESTIONS IN EACH MODULE

Within each module, the multiple-choice questions are presented in a sequence moving from the general to the specific, elementary to advanced, etc. to provide an effective learning sequence. Duplicate questions and redundant explanations have been kept to a minimum.

In future editions we hope to include selected questions prepared by your own professor, whose name we will insert in the place of "Publisher."

ANSWER EXPLANATIONS ALONGSIDE THE QUESTIONS

Our more efficient format presents the objective questions and their answer explanations side by side. The answer explanations are to the right of each question. The example is question number 29 from Chapter 6, "Process Costing."

29. Kew Co. had 3,000 units in work-in-process at April 1 which were 60% complete as to conversion cost. During April, 10,000 units were completed. At April 30, 4,000 units remained in work-in-process which were 40% complete as to conversion cost. Direct materials are added at the beginning of the process. How many units were started during April?

    a. 9,000.
    b. 9,800.
    c. 10,000.
    d. 11,000.

The correct answer is (d). *(CPA 586 Q-25)*
REQUIRED: The number of units started in April.
DISCUSSION: Set up a physical flow formula and calculate the unknown.

BWIP + Started = Completed + EWIP
3,000 + x = 10,000 + 4,000
Units Started = 11,000

Chapter 1: How to Use This Book

The format in this study manual (illustrated on the previous page) is designed to facilitate your study of objective questions, their answers, and the answer explanations. The intent is to save you time and effort by eliminating the need to turn pages back and forth from questions to answers.

Be careful, however. You must exercise restraint against misusing this format by consulting the answers before you have answered the questions. Misuse of the readily available answers will give you a false sense of security and result in your performing poorly on examinations. The best way to use this study manual is to cover up the answer explanations with a sheet of paper as you read and answer each question. As a crucial part of the learning process, you must honestly commit yourself to an answer before looking at the answer explanation. Whether you are right or wrong, your memory of the correct answer will be reinforced by this process.

UNIQUENESS OF OBJECTIVE QUESTIONS

The major advantage of objective questions is their ability to cover (i.e., to study or to test) a large number of topics with little time and effort when compared to essay questions or computational problems.

A multiple-choice question is actually four or five statements, of which all but one are incorrect given the facts of the question. The advantage of multiple-choice questions over true-false questions is that they require more analysis and result in a lower score for those with little or no knowledge. Random guessing on questions with four answer choices results in an expected grade of 25%. Random guessing on a true-false test results in an expected grade of 50%.

Students and practitioners both like multiple-choice questions. Because they present alternative answers and only one alternative must be selected, they are relatively easy to answer. Professors like objective questions because they are easy to grade and because much more material can be tested in the same period of time.

USING OBJECTIVE QUESTIONS TO STUDY

Testing experts are increasingly favoring multiple-choice questions as a valid means of testing various levels of knowledge. For example, 60% of each part of the current CPA examination consists of objective questions, and in 1994 the percentage will increase to about 85%. Using objective questions to study for these professional certification examinations and undergraduate examinations is an important tool in obtaining good grades. The following suggestions can be used as a guideline for your study purposes in conjunction with any of our Objective Question and Explanation books (see our order form on page 652).

1. Locate the chapter and module that contain questions on the topic you are currently studying. The end of Chapter 1 has cross-references to the tables of contents of most textbooks.
2. Work through a series of questions, one or more modules at a time.
    a. Cover the answers and explanations as you work the questions.
    b. Circle the answer you think is correct.
    c. Check your answer.

3. **DO NOT CONSULT THE ANSWER OR ANSWER EXPLANATIONS ON THE RIGHT SIDE OF EACH PAGE UNTIL AFTER YOU HAVE CHOSEN AND WRITTEN DOWN AN ANSWER.**

   a. It is crucial that you cover the answer explanations and intellectually commit yourself to an answer. This method will help you understand the concept much better, even if you answered the question incorrectly.

4. Study the explanations to each question you answered incorrectly. In addition to learning and understanding the concept tested, analyze WHY you missed the question. Did you misread the question? Misread the requirement? Make a computational error? Not know the concept tested? Now you can identify your weaknesses in answering multiple-choice questions and take corrective action (before you take a test).

   a. Studying the important concepts that we provide in our answer explanations will help you understand the principles to the point that you can answer that question (or any other like it) successfully.

5. Prepare a summary analysis of your work on each module (topic). It will show your weaknesses (areas needing more study) and also your strengths (areas of improvement). You can improve your performance on objective questions both by increasing your percentage of correct answers and by decreasing the time spent per question. Here are sample column headings for the summary analysis:

Date	Module	Time to Complete	Number of Questions	Minutes Per Question	Number Correct	Percent Correct

The **Gleim Series** of Objective Question and Explanation books really works! You can pretest yourself before class to see if you are strong or weak in the assigned area. You can retest after class to see if you really understand the material. The questions in these books cover **all** topics in your related courses, so you will encounter few questions on your exams for which you will not be well prepared. Furthermore, each book covers the material generally taught in two or three courses, so your cost per course is nominal.

PREPARING FOR ESSAY QUESTIONS AND COMPUTATIONAL PROBLEMS

Do not overemphasize studying objective questions to the extent of neglecting essay questions and computational problems. Remember, currently 40% of each part of the CPA exam and about 50% of each part of the CIA and CMA exams are essay questions or computational problems. Exception: Part IV of the CIA exam is now entirely multiple choice. Thus, a complete study program must include working essay questions and computational problems as well as objective questions under exam conditions.

When working cost/managerial and quantitative method essay questions and/or computational problems, survey the question/problem and set a time budget, e.g., 10, 15, or 20 minutes. Then complete the question or problem in the budgeted time. Question/problem answering strategies for essay questions and computational problems are discussed and illustrated in our CIA, CMA, and CPA review texts.

Chapter 1: How to Use This Book

ABBREVIATIONS USED IN THIS BOOK

ARR	Accounting rate of return	FC	Fixed cost
BE	Breakeven	FG	Finished goods
BEP	Breakeven point	IRR	Internal rate of return
BWIP	Beginning work-in-process	LP	Linear programming
CGM	Cost of goods manufactured	NPV	Net present value
CGS	Cost of goods sold	NRV	Net realizable value
CM	Contribution margin	O/H	Overhead
CMR	Contribution margin ratio	PV	Present value
CVP	Cost/volume/profit	UCM	Unit contribution margin
EOQ	Economic order quantity	VC	Variable cost
EWIP	Ending work-in-process	WIP	Work-in-process
EUP	Equivalent units of production		

MODULE CROSS-REFERENCES TO COST/MANAGERIAL AND QUANTITATIVE METHODS TEXTBOOKS

The next 13 pages contain the tables of contents of current cost/managerial and quantitative methods textbooks, with cross-references to the related modules in this study manual. Occasionally, the cross-reference is to *Auditing & EDP Objective Questions and Explanations* or *Financial Accounting Objective Questions and Explanations,* which are study manuals similar to this book. They are available from Accounting Publications, Inc. (see page 652). The texts are listed in alphabetical order by the (first) author. As you study a particular chapter in your managerial accounting or quantitative methods textbook, you can easily determine which module(s) to study in this manual. You should review all questions in the module.

COST/MANAGERIAL ACCOUNTING

DeCoster and Schaefer, *Management Accounting: A Decision Emphasis,* **Fourth Edition, John Wiley & Sons, Inc., 1988.**

Part One - Accounting Data for Decision Making
    Chapter 1 - The Planning and Control Process for Decision Making - 4.1, 4.5
    Chapter 2 - Determining Cost Behavior Patterns - 4.3, 4.4, 11.3, 19.3
    Chapter 3 - Cost/Volume/Profit Interactions for Operating Decisions - 11.1 to 11.9
Part Two - Systems for Product Costing
    Chapter 4 - Cost Flows for Product Costing - 4.2, 5.1 to 5.6
    Chapter 5 - Variable Historical Costing for Recording Past Costs - 6.1 to 6.8
    Chapter 6 - Variable Standard Costing for Cost Efficiency - 6.1 to 6.8, 13.1 to 13.8
Part Three - Absorbtion Costing Systems and Cost Allocations
    Chapter 7 - Absorption Costing - 5.3, 10.2
    Chapter 8 - The Allocation of Indirect Costs - 9.1, 9.2
Part Four - The Use of Data in Making Decisions
    Chapter 9 - Revenue and Pricing Decisions - 11.1 to 11.6, 13.5
    Chapter 10 - Production Decisions - 17.1 to 17.4
    Chapter 11 - Long-Range Decisions - 16.1 to 16.8
Part Five - Planning and Control Systems for Decision Implementation
    Chapter 12 - Budgeting: A Systematic Approach to Planning - 12.1, 12.2
    Chapter 13 - Budgetary Control, Responsibility Accounting, and Their Behavioral Implications - 12.1, 12.2, 14.1
    Chapter 14 - Measurement of Divisional Performance - 14.1 to 14.3

Deakin and Maher, *Cost Accounting,* Second Edition, Richard D. Irwin, Inc., 1987.

    Chapter 1 - Cost Accounting: Its Nature and Usefulness - 4.1
    Chapter 2 - Cost Concepts and Behavior - 4.1 to 4.6
Part One - Cost Accounting Systems
    Chapter 3 - Accounting for Cost Flows: Cost Accumulation - 4.2 to 4.4, 5.2
    Chapter 4 - Cost Allocation Concepts - 4.2 to 4.5
    Chapter 5 - Job Costing - 5.1 to 5.6
    Chapter 6 - Process Costing - 6.1 to 6.8, 7.1 to 7.4
    Chapter 7 - Allocating Service Department Costs - 9.1 to 9.2
    Chapter 8 - Allocating Joint Costs - 8.1 to 8.7
    Chapter 9 - Variable Costing - 10.1 to 10.3
Part Two - Differential Costs for Decision Making
    Chapter 10 - Cost Estimation - 4.3, 11.3, 19.3
    Chapter 11 - Cost-Volume-Profit Analysis - 11.1 to 11.9
    Chapter 12 - Differential Cost Analysis - 15.1 to 15.3
    Chapter 13 - Multiple-Product Decisions - 11.7
    Chapter 14 - Inventory Management Costs - 17.1 to 17.4
    Chapter 15 - Capital Investment Cash Flows - 16.1 to 16.8
    Chapter 16 - Capital Investment Models - 16.1 to 16.8
Part Three - Cost Data for Performance Evaluation
    Chapter 17 - The Master Budget - 12.1 to 12.2
    Chapter 18 - Using the Budget for Performance Evaluation and Control - 12.1 to 12.2
    Chapter 19 - Cost Variances - 13.1 to 13.8
    Chapter 20 - Standard Cost Systems - 13.1 to 13.8
    Chapter 21 - Mix, Yield, and Revenue Variances - 13.5
    Chapter 22 - Decentralization and Performance Evaluation - 14.1 to 14.3
    Chapter 23 - Transfer Pricing - 14.2
Part Four - The Impact of Uncertainty on Cost Analysis
    Chapter 24 - Decision Making Under Uncertainty - 18.1 to 18.6
    Chapter 25 - The Variance Investigation Decision - 13.1, 13.8, 18.5
    Chapter 26 - The Economics of Information - N/A

Dominiak and Louderback, *Managerial Accounting,* Fifth Edition, Kent Publishing Company, 1988.

    Chapter 1 - Introduction - 4.1
Part One - Volume/Cost/Profit Analysis and Decision Making
    Chapter 2 - Profit Planning - 11.1
    Chapter 3 - Analyzing Cost Behavior - 4.3, 11.3, 19.3
    Chapter 4 - Additional Aspects of Volume/Cost/Profit Analysis - 11.2, 11.4 to 11.9
    Chapter 5 - Short-Term Decisions and Accounting Information - 11.1, 11.2
Part Two - Budgeting
    Chapter 6 - Operational Budgeting - 12.1, 12.2
    Chapter 7 - Financial Budgeting - 12.1, 12.2
    Chapter 8 - Capital Budgeting, Part I - 16.1 to 16.8
    Chapter 9 - Capital Budgeting, Part II - 16.1 to 16.8
Part Three - Control and Performance Evaluation
    Chapter 10 - Responsibility Accounting - 14.1
    Chapter 11 - Divisional Performance Measurement - 14.1 to 14.3
    Chapter 12 - Control and Evaluation of Cost Centers - 14.1 to 14.3
Part Four - Product Costing
    Chapter 13 - Introduction to Product Costing: Job Order Costing - 5.1 to 5.6
    Chapter 14 - Standard Costing: Absorption and Variable - 13.1 to 13.8
    Chapter 15 - Process Costing and the Cost Accounting Cycle - 6.1 to 6.8
Part Five - Special Topics
    Chapter 16 - Quantitative Methods and Managerial Accounting - 19.1 to 19.5, 20.1 to 20.4, 21.1 to 21.6
    Chapter 17 - Statement of Cash Flows
           - *Financial Accounting Objective Questions and Explanations,* Chap. 22
    Chapter 18 - Analyzing Financial Statements
           - *Financial Accounting Objective Questions and Explanations,* Chap. 26

Engler, *Managerial Accounting,* **Richard D. Irwin, Inc., 1988.**

    Chapter 1 - The Nature and Objectives of Managerial Accounting - 4.1
Part I - Essentials of Managerial Accounting
    Chapter 2 - Cost Definitions and Behavior - 4.2 to 4.5
    Chapter 3 - Job Order Costing - 5.1 to 5.6
    Chapter 4 - Process Costing - 6.1 to 6.8
    Chapter 5 - Cost Behavior and Cost Estimation - 4.3, 11.3, 19.1 to 19.5
    Chapter 6 - Cost, Volume, and Profit -- Analysis and Relationships - 11.1 to 11.9
Part II - Planning and Control
    Chapter 7 - The Master Budget - 12.1 to 12.2
    Chapter 8 - Standard Costs and Performance Evaluation - 13.1 to 13.8
    Chapter 9 - Flexible Budgeting and Manufacturing Overhead Analysis - 12.1 to 12.2, 13.4
    Chapter 10 - Contributor Approach to Segment Reporting - 10.1, 14.1
    Chapter 11 - Selecting Relevant Data for Decision Making - 15.1 to 15.3
    Chapter 12 - Capital Budgeting - 16.1 to 16.8
    Chapter 13 - Income Tax Effects on Capital Budgeting Decisions - 16.4 to 16.8
    Chapter 14 - Decentralized Operations and Transfer Pricing - 14.1 to 14.3
Part III - Additional Selected Topics
    Chapter 15 - Selected Quantitative Methods for Managers - 19.1 to 19.5, 20.1 to 20.4, 21.1 to 21.6
    Chapter 16 - Statement of Changes in Financial Position
        - *Financial Accounting Objective Questions and Explanations,* Chap. 22
    Chapter 17 - Analysis of Financial Statements
        - *Financial Accounting Objective Questions and Explanations,* Chap. 26

Fischer and Frank, *Cost Accounting: Theory and Applications,* **South-Western Publishing Co., 1985.**

Chapter 1 - Role of Cost Accounting in Decision Making - 4.1
Chapter 2 - Cost Concepts and Behavior; Job Order and Process Costing - 5.1 to 5.6, 6.1 to 6.8
Chapter 3 - Determining the Relationship of Costs to Volume - 18.1 to 18.6
Chapter 4 - Cost-Volume-Profit Analysis - 11.1 to 11.9
Chapter 5 - Extensions of Cost-Volume-Profit Analysis - 11.1 to 11.9, 20.1 to 20.4
Chapter 6 - Implementing Cost and Revenue Analysis - 10.1 to 10.3
Chapter 7 - Basics of Capital Budgeting - 16.1 to 16.8
Chapter 8 - Special Issues in Capital Budgeting - 16.1 to 16.8
Chapter 9 - Standard Costs - 13.1 to 13.8
Chapter 10 - Special Issues in Standard Costing - 7.1 to 7.4, 13.1 to 13.8
Chapter 11 - Process Costing - 6.1 to 6.8
Chapter 12 - Allocation of Joint Costs and Common Costs - 8.1 to 8.7, 9.1 to 9.2
Chapter 13 - Profit Planning and Budgeting - 12.1 to 12.2
Chapter 14 - Segmental Analysis and Transfer Pricing - 14.1 to 14.3
Chapter 15 - Operations Research Techniques and Managerial Accounting - 17.1 to 17.4, 19.1 to 19.5, 21.3, 21.4

Garrison, *Managerial Accounting: Concepts for Planning, Control, Decision Making,* **Fifth Edition, Business Publications/Richard D. Irwin, Inc., 1988.**

    Chapter 1 - Managerial Accounting - A Perspective - 4.1
Part One - The Foundation: Cost Terms, Cost Behavior, and Systems Design
    Chapter 2 - Cost Terms, Concepts, and Classifications - 4.2 to 4.5
    Chapter 3 - Systems Design: Job Order Costing - 5.1 to 5.6
    Chapter 4 - Systems Design: Process Costing - 6.1 to 6.8
    Chapter 5 - Cost Behavior: Analysis and Use - 4.3, 11.3, 19.3
Part Two - The Central Theme: Planning and Control
    Chapter 6 - Cost/Volume/Profit Relationships - 11.1 to 11.9
    Chapter 7 - Segmented Reporting and the Contribution Approach to Costing - 10.1, 14.1
    Chapter 8 - Profit Planning - 12.1, 12.2
    Chapter 9 - Control through Standard Costs - 13.1 to 13.8
    Chapter 10 - Flexible Budgets and Overhead Analysis - 12.1, 12.2
    Chapter 11 - Control of Decentralized Operations - 14.1 to 14.3

Part Three - The Capstone: Using Cost Data in Decision Making
    Chapter 12 - Pricing of Products and Services - 14.1 to 14.3
    Chapter 13 - Relevant Costs for Decision Making - 15.1 to 15.3
    Chapter 14 - Capital Budgeting Decisions - 16.1 to 16.8
    Chapter 15 - Further Aspects of Investment Decisions - 16.1 to 16.8
Part Four - Selected Topics for Further Study
    Chapter 16 - Service Department Cost Allocations - 9.1, 9.2
    Chapter 17 - "How Well Am I Doing?" - Financial Statement Analysis
        - *Financial Accounting Objective Questions and Explanations,* Chap. 26
    Chapter 18 - "How Well Am I Doing?" - Statement of Cash Flows
        - *Financial Accounting Objective Questions and Explanations,* Chap. 22

Hartley, *Cost and Managerial Accounting,* Second Edition, Allyn and Bacon, Inc., 1986.

Part One - Introductory Materials
    Chapter 1 - The Role of Cost and Managerial Accounting - 4.1
    Chapter 2 - Cost Behavior, Systems, and Reporting - 4.2 to 4.5
Part Two - Systems to Support Reporting Functions
    Chapter 3 - Job Order Systems - 5.1 to 5.6
    Chapter 4 - Process Cost Accounting - 6.1 to 6.8
    Chapter 5 - Standard Cost Systems - 13.1 to 13.8
    Chapter 6 - Standard Cost Systems: Additional Topics - 13.1 to 13.8
    Chapter 7 - Variable (Direct) Costing System - 10.1 to 10.3
    Chapter 8 - Spoilage and the Cost Accounting System - 7.1 to 7.4
    Chapter 9 - Allocation of Indirect Costs - 9.1, 9.2
    Chapter 10 - Accounting for Joint Costs - 8.1 to 8.7
    Chapter 11 - Cost Accounting Applied to Nonmanufacturing Costs - 13.1
Part Three - Topics in Support of Decision Making and Control
    Chapter 12 - Master Budget - 12.1 to 12.2
    Chapter 13 - Cost-Volume-Profit Analysis - 11.1 to 11.9
    Chapter 14 - Concept of Relevant Data - 18.5
    Chapter 15 - Capital Budgeting - 16.1 to 16.8
    Chapter 16 - Advanced Considerations in Capital Budgeting - 16.1 to 16.8
Part Four - Topics in Support of Control
    Chapter 17 - Control: Basic Concepts and Systems - 13.1
    Chapter 18 - Variances from Standards: Alternatives and Significance - 13.6 to 13.8
    Chapter 19 - Evaluating Performance in a Decentralized Organization - 14.1
    Chapter 20 - Transfer Pricing - 14.2, 14.3
Part Five - Quantitative Support Topics
    Chapter 21 - Planning Aids - Spreadsheets and Decision Support Systems - N/A
    Chapter 22 - Planning Aids - Linear Programming and Inventory Models - 17.1 to 17.4, 20.1 to 20.4
    Chapter 23 - Regression Analysis - 19.1 to 19.5
    Chapter 24 - Learning Curves - 21.4
    Chapter 25 - Decision Making Under Uncertainty and Information Economics - 18.1 to 18.6

Hirsch and Louderback, *Cost Accounting: Accumulation, Analysis and Use,* Second Edition, Kent Publishing Company, 1986.

Part One - Cost Accounting for Planning and Decision Making
    Chapter 1 - Introduction - 4.1
    Chapter 2 - Cost/Volume/Profit Analysis - 11.1 to 11.9
    Chapter 3 - Cost Estimating and Forecasting - 4.3, 11.3, 19.3
    Chapter 4 - Tactical Decision Making - 11.1, 15.1 to 15.3, 18.5
Part Two - Product Costing
    Chapter 5 - Product Costing: Job Order Costing - 5.1 to 5.6
    Chapter 6 - Process Costing - 6.1 to 6.8
    Chapter 7 - Standard Costs and Variances - 13.1 to 13.8
    Chapter 8 - Standard Costing - 13.1 to 13.8
    Chapter 9 - Joint Products and By-Products - 8.1 to 8.7
    Chapter 10 - Spoilage, Lost Units, and Scrap - 7.1 to 7.4
    Chapter 11 - Variable Costing - 10.1 to 10.3
    Chapter 12 - Cost Allocation - 9.1, 9.2

Chapter 1: How to Use This Book   11

Part Three - Budgeting and Control
    Chapter 13 - Budgeting: General and Behavioral Aspects - 12.1, 12.2
    Chapter 14 - Budgeting: Analytical and Technical Aspects - 12.1, 12.2
    Chapter 15 - Capital Budgeting Decisions - 16.1 to 16.8
    Chapter 16 - Capital Budgeting: Complexities - 16.1 to 16.8
Part Four - Divisional Performance Evaluation
    Chapter 17 - Decentralization: Measures of Performance - 14.1 to 14.3
    Chapter 18 - Transfer Pricing - 14.1 to 14.3
    Chapter 19 - Performance Analysis: Other Concepts - 14.1 to 14.3
Part Five - Key Areas for Further Study
    Chapter 20 - Variance Investigation and Reporting - 13.1, 13.8, 18.5
    Chapter 21 - Inventory Control - 17.1 to 17.4
    Chapter 22 - The Learning Effect - 21.4

Horngren and Foster, *Cost Accounting: A Managerial Emphasis*, Sixth Edition, Prentice-Hall, Inc., 1987.
Part One - Cost Accounting Fundamentals
    Chapter 1 - The Accountant's Role in the Organization - 4.1
    Chapter 2 - An Introduction to Cost Terms and Purposes - 4.1 to 4.6   → Ch 2-3
    Chapter 3 - Cost-Volume-Profit Relationships - 11.1 to 11.9   → Ch 2-3
    Chapter 4 - Job, Process, and Operational Systems - 5.1 to 6.8
Part Two - Budgets and Standards as Keys to Planning and Control
    Chapter 5 - Master Budget and Responsibility Accounting - 12.1 to 12.2, 14.1 to 14.3   → CH.6
    Chapter 6 - Flexible Budgets and Standards: Part I - 12.1 to 12.2, 13.1 to 13.8
    Chapter 7 - Flexible Budgets and Standards: Part II - 12.1 to 12.2, 13.1 to 13.8
    Chapter 8 - Income Effects of Alternative Product-Costing Methods - 10.1 to 10.3
Part Three - Cost Information for Various Decision and Control Purposes
    Chapter 9 - Relevance, Pricing, and the Decision Process - 15.1 to 15.3
    Chapter 10 - Determining How Costs Behave - 4.3, 11.3, 19.1 to 19.5
    Chapter 11 - Systems Choice: Discretionary and Nonmanufacturing Costs
        - *Auditing & EDP Objective Questions and Explanations*, Chap. 8
Part Four - Cost Allocation and Accumulation
    Chapter 12 - Cost Allocation: Part I - 9.1 to 9.2
    Chapter 13 - Cost Allocation: Part II - 9.1 to 9.2
    Chapter 14 - Cost Allocation: Joint Products and Byproducts - 8.1 to 8.7
    Chapter 15 - Process Costing - 6.1 to 6.8
    Chapter 16 - Spoilage, Waste, Reworked Units, and Scrap - 7.1 to 7.4
    Chapter 17 - Nonmanufacturing Job Costing, Process Costing, Operation Costing, and JIT
        Costing - 5.1, 6.1 to 6.8
Part Five - Decision Models and Cost Information
    Chapter 18 - Decision Models, Uncertainty, and the Accountant - 15.1 to 15.3, 18.1 to 18.6
    Chapter 19 - Capital Budgeting and Cost Analysis - 11.1 to 11.9, 16.1 to 16.8
    Chapter 20 - Capital Budgeting: A Closer Look - 16.1 to 16.8
    Chapter 21 - Operations Management and the Accountant (I): Materials and Inventory - 17.1 to 17.4
    Chapter 22 - Operations Management and the Accountant (II): Linear Programming - 20.1 to 20.4
Part Six - More on Cost Behavior and Analysis
    Chapter 23 - Cost Behavior and Regression Analysis - 19.1 to 19.5
    Chapter 24 - Variances: Mix, Yield, and Investigation - 13.1 to 13.8
Part Seven - Cost Accounting, Systems Choice, and Management Control
    Chapter 25 - Systems Choice: Decentralization and Transfer Pricing
        - *Auditing & EDP Objective Questions and Explanations*, Chap. 8
    Chapter 26 - Systems Choice: Performance Measurement and Executive Compensation
        - *Auditing & EDP Objective Questions and Explanations*, Chap. 8
    Chapter 27 - Accounting Systems and Internal Control
        - *Auditing & EDP Objective Questions and Explanations*, Chap. 8
    Chapter 28 - Cost Accounting in Professional Examinations
        - *Auditing & EDP Objective Questions and Explanations*, Chap. 3

Kellough and Leiminger, *Cost Accounting: Concepts and Techniques for Management,* **West Publishing Co., 1984.**

Chapter 1 - The Role of Accounting in the Management System - 4.1
Chapter 2 - Introduction to Cost Terminology, Behavior, and Estimation Methods - 4.1 to 4.5
Chapter 3 - Cost Accounting Cycle and Job Order Costing - 5.1 to 5.6
Chapter 4 - Process Costing - 6.1 to 6.8
Chapter 5 - Additional Process Costing Topics - 7.1 to 7.4
Chapter 6 - Special Cost Allocation Problems - 8.1 to 8.7, 9.1 to 9.2
Chapter 7 - Budgeting: The Key to Planning and Control - 12.1 to 12.2
Chapter 8 - Standards and Standard Costing - 13.1 to 13.8
Chapter 9 - Additional Standard Costing Topics - 13.1 to 13.8
Chapter 10 - Productivity Measurement and Cost Accounting - 13.1 to 13.8
Chapter 11 - Direct (Variable) Costing - 10.1 to 10.3
Chapter 12 - Cost-Volume-Profit Relationships - 11.1 to 11.9
Chapter 13 - The Product Mix Problem: A Linear Programming Solution - 20.1 to 20.4
Chapter 14 - The Uses of Cost in Making Non-Routine Decisions - 15.1 to 15.3
Chapter 15 - Capital Budgeting and Capital - 16.1 to 16.8
Chapter 16 - Additional Capital Budgeting Topics - 16.1 to 16.8
Chapter 17 - Management Information Systems
 - *Auditing & EDP Objective Questions and Explanations,* Chap. 8
Chapter 18 - Performance Measurement and Evaluation in Divisionalized Organizations - 14.1 to 14.3
Chapter 19 - Transfer Pricing in Divisionalized Organizations - 14.2
Chatper 20 - Use of Cost in Inventory Decisions - 17.1 to 17.4
Chapter 21 - Cost Estimation Using Linear Regression - 19.1 to 19.5
Chapter 22 - Learning Curves and Cost Analysis - 21.4

Moore, Anderson, Jaedicke, *Managerial Accounting,* **Seventh Edition, South-Western Publishing Co., 1988.**

Part 1 - Introduction
    Chapter 1 - Managerial Accounting and the Management Process - 4.1
    Chapter 2 - Cost Concepts, Classifications, and Income Statement - 4.1 to 4.6
Part 2 - Cost Determination and Control
    Chapter 3 - Job Order or Special Project Costing - 5.1 to 5.6
    Chapter 4 - A Process Cost System - 6.1 to 6.8
    Chapter 5 - Materials and Labor Cost Control - 13.1 to 13.8, 17.1 to 17.4
    Chapter 6 - Overhead Cost Control - 13.4
    Chapter 7 - Cost Behavior and Estimation - 4.3, 11.3, 18.5
Part 3 - Profit Planning
    Chapter 8 - Cost, Volume, Profit Relationships - 11.1 to 11.9
    Chapter 9 - Variable Costing - 10.1 to 10.3
    Chapter 10 - Budgeting for Operations - 12.1 to 12.2
    Chapter 11 - Financial Budget and Other Budgeting Approaches - 12.1
Part 4 - Analysis and Decision Making
    Chapter 12 - Accounting Data for Managerial Decisions - 15.1 to 15.3
    Chapter 13 - Capital Investment Decisions - I - 16.1 to 16.8
    Chapter 14 - Capital Investment Decisions - II - 16.1 to 16.8
    Chapter 15 - Managerial Control and Decision Making in Decentralized Operations - 9.1 to 9.2, 15.1 to 15.3
Part 5 - Interfaces of Financial and Managerial Accounting
    Chapter 16 - Price Level and Foreign Exchange Problems - N/A
    Chapter 17 - Analysis of Financial Statements
            - *Financial Accounting Objective Questions and Explanations,* Chap. 26
    Chapter 18 - Tracing the Flow of Net Working Capital and Cash
            - *Financial Accounting Objective Questions and Explanations,* Chap. 22

Moriarity and Allen, *Cost Accounting,* Second Edition, John Wiley & Sons, Inc., 1987.

Part 1 - Introduction
    Chapter 1 - The Cost Accounting Environment - 4.1
    Chapter 2 - Introduction to Cost Accounting: The Basics - 4.2
    Chapter 3 - Estimates Cost Behavior - 4.3, 11.3, 19.3
    Chapter 4 - Cost/Volume/Profit Analysis - 11.1 to 11.9
Part 2 - Planning and Budgeting
    Chapter 5 - Profit Planning: Short-Term Decisions, Multiple Products - 13.6 to 13.8
    Chapter 6 - Preparation of the Master Budget - 12.1, 12.2
    Chapter 7 - Inventory Control -
    Chapter 8 - Capital Budgeting - 16.1 to 16.8
    Chapter 9 - Capital Budgeting: Additional Considerations - 16.8
    Chapter 10 - PERT/Cost Budgeting - 21.3
Part 3 - Accumulating Product Costs
    Chapter 11 - Allocating Costs - 8.1 to 8.7
    Chapter 12 - Assigning Service Center Costs - 9.1, 9.2
    Chapter 13 - Allocating Joint Production Costs - 8.1 to 8.7
    Chapter 14 - Job Costing - 5.1 to 5.6
    Chapter 15 - Process Costing - 6.1 to 6.8
    Chapter 16 - Process Costing with Spoilage and Rework - 7.1 to 7.4
    Chapter 17 - Absorption versus Direct Costing - 10.1 to 10.3
Part 4 - Measuring and Evaluating Performance
    Chapter 18 - Standard Costs and Variance Analysis - 13.1 to 13.8
    Chapter 19 - More on Variance Analysis - 13.1 to 13.8
    Chapter 20 - Reacting to Variance - 13.2 to 13.6
    Chapter 21 - Measuring Segment Performance - 9.1 to 9.2, 13.1 to 13.8
Part 5 - Government Regulations
    Chapter 22 - Cost Accounting for Government Contracts - N/A

Morse, Davis, Hartgraves, *Management Accounting,* Second Edition, Addison-Wesley Publishing Co., Inc., 1988.

Part 1 - Essential Elements of Management Accounting
    Chapter 1 - Accounting and Management - 4.1
    Chapter 2 - Basic Cost Concepts - 4.2 to 4.5
    Chapter 3 - Cost Behavior Analysis - 4.3, 11.3, 19.3
    Chapter 4 - Cost/Volume/Profit Analysis - 11.1 to 11.9
    Chapter 5 - Relevant Costs for Management Decisions - 15.1 to 15.3
Part 2 - Planning and Control
    Chapter 6 - Operating Budgets - 12.1, 12.2
    Chapter 7 - Responsibility Accounting and Flexible Budgets - 14.1 to 14.3
    Chapter 8 - Performance Evaluation of Standard Cost Centers - 13.1 to 13.8
    Chapter 9 - Control of Decentralized Operations - 14.1 to 14.3
    Chapter 10 - Inventory Valuation Approaches and Segment Reporting - 17.1 to 17.4
Part 3 - Product Costing and Cost Allocation
    Chapter 11 - Product Costing - 5.1 to 5.6, 6.1 to 6.8
    Chapter 12 - The Assignment of Common Costs - 9.1, 9.2
Part 4 - Selected Topics for Further Study
    Chapter 13 - Relevant Costs for Quantitative Models - 17.2, 20.1 to 20.4, 21.1
    Chapter 14 - Capital Budgeting - 16.1 to 16.5
    Chapter 15 - Impact of Taxes on Capital Budgeting and Other Management Decisions
        - *Federal Tax Objective Questions and Explanations*, Chaps. 18 and 19
    Chapter 16 - Financial Statement Analysis and the Statement of Resource Flows
        - *Financial Accounting Objective Questions and Explanations*, Chaps. 22 and 26
    Chapter 17 - The Impact of Changing Prices
        - *Financial Accounting Objective Questions and Explanations*, Chap. 23

Morse and Roth, *Cost Accounting: Processing, Evaluating, and Using Cost Data*, Third Edition, Addison-Wesley Publishing Co., Inc., 1986.

    Chapter 1 - Introduction - 4.1 to 4.6
Part 1 - Processing Cost Data with Actual and Normal Cost Systems
    Chapter 2 - Product Costing Concepts - 4.2 to 4.4
    Chapter 3 - Actual and Normal Job-Order Costing - 5.1 to 5.6
    Chapter 4 - Actual and Normal Process Cost Systems - 6.1 to 6.8, 7.1 to 7.4
    Chapter 5 - Costing Joint Products and By-Products - 8.1 to 8.7
    Chapter 6 - Allocating Service Department and Other Indirect Costs - 9.1 to 9.2
Part 2 - Evaluating and Using Cost Data for Planning
    Chapter 7 - Estimating Costs from Accounting Data - 19.1 to 19.5
    Chapter 8 - Cost-Volume-Profit Analysis - 11.1 to 11.9
    Chapter 9 - The Contribution Income Statement and Variable Costing - 10.1 to 10.3
    Chapter 10 - The Master Budget - 12.1 to 12.2
Part 3 - Evaluating and Using Cost Data for Performance Evaluation
    Chapter 11 - Responsibility Accounting for Cost Centers - 14.1 to 14.3
    Chapter 12 - Responsibility Accounting for Revenue and Profit Centers - 14.1 to 14.3
    Chapter 13 - Responsibility Accounting for Investment Centers - 14.1 to 14.3
    Chapter 14 - Standard Cost Systems - 13.1 to 13.8
Part 4 - Selected Topics for Further Study
    Chapter 15 - Special Decisions in Short-Range Planning - 15.1 to 15.3
    Chapter 16 - Capital Budgeting I - 16.1 to 16.8
    Chapter 17 - Capital Budgeting II - 16.1 to 16.8
    Chapter 18 - Inventory Planning and Control Systems - 17.1 to 17.4
    Chapter 19 - Quality Control and Variance Analysis - 13.1 to 13.8
    Chapter 20 - Special Considerations in Payroll Accounting - 5.5
    Chapter 21 - Transfer Pricing - 14.2

Moscove, Crowningshield, Gorman, *Cost Accounting with Managerial Applications*, Fifth Edition, Houghton Mifflin Company, 1985.

Part One - Development and Operation of Cost Accounting Systems that Provide Decision-Making Information to Management
    Chapter 1 - Introduction to Management Accounting and Basic Concepts - 4.1
    Chapter 2 - Accounting Procedures for Manufacturing Firms - 4.1 to 4.6
    Chapter 3 - Job-Order and Process Cost Accounting Systems - 5.1 to 5.6, 6.1 to 6.8
    Chapter 4 - Process Cost Accounting System: Inventories of Work in Process - 5.4, 6.4
    Chapter 5 - Process Cost Accounting System: Costing Multiple Products - 6.5 to 6.7
Part Two - The Analysis of Costs Associated with Manufacturing Activities
    Chapter 6 - Introduction to Internal Control Systems: Materials Control and Costing - 6.8, 13.1, 13.2
    Chapter 7 - Labor Control and Costing - 6.8, 13.1, 13.3
    Chapter 8 - Indirect Manufacturing Costs I: Budgeting and Applying Indirect Manufacturing Costs - 5.3, 6.8, 13.1, 13.4
    Chapter 9 - Indirect Manufacturing Costs II: Recording Indirect Manufacturing Costs, and Variance Analysis - 5.3, 5.5, 6.8, 13.4, 13.7
Part Three - Cost Accounting Techniques to Aid Managerial Planning, Control, and Decision Making
    Chapter 10 - Standard Cost Accounting Systems: Basic Concepts and Variance Analysis - 13.1 to 13.8
    Chapter 11 - Standard Cost Accounting Systems: Recording Standard Costs and Variances for Managerial Information - 13.1 to 13.8
    Chapter 12 - Direct (Variable) Costing for Internal Reporting to Management - 10.1 to 10.3
    Chapter 13 - Analyzing Cost Behavior Within Accounting Systems - 11.3, 19.3
    Chapter 14 - Cost-Volume-Profit Analysis for Effective Managerial Planning, Control, and Decision-Making - 11.1 to 11.9
Part Four - The Role of Accounting Systems in Managerial Applications of Accounting Data
    Chapter 15 - Comprehensive Budgeting: An Integral Part of an Accounting System - 12.1, 12.2
    Chapter 16 - Responsibility Accounting Systems and Reporting to Management - 14.1
    Chapter 17 - Accounting Systems for Analyzing Profit Performance - 14.2, 14.3
    Chapter 18 - Accounting Systems for Distribution Cost Analysis and Control - 9.1, 9.2
    Chapter 19 - Accounting Systems to Aid Special, Nonrecurring Managerial Decisions - 15.1 to 15.3
    Chapter 20 - Accounting Systems for Capital Expenditures Budgeting - 16.1 to 16.8
Part Five - The Use of Quantitative Methods in Accounting Systems
    Chapter 21 - Linear Programming for Managerial Decision Making - 20.1 to 20.4
    Chapter 22 - Statistics, Probability, and Sampling in Business Decision Making - 18.1 to 18.6
    Chapter 23 - Inventory Planning - 17.1 to 17.4
    Chapter 24 - Regression and Correlation Analysis in Business Decision Making - 19.1 to 19.5
    Chapter 25 - Performance Evaluation and Review Technique (PERT) - 21.3

Chapter 1: How to Use This Book   15

**Polimeni, Fabozzi, Adelberg, *Cost Accounting: Concepts and Applications for Managerial Decision Making*,
Second Edition, McGraw-Hill Book Company, 1986.**

    Chapter 1 - The Nature, Concepts, and Classification of Cost Accounting - 4.1 to 4.6
Part 1 - Product Costing
    Chapter 2 - Product Cost Accumulation Systems, External Financial Statements,
        and Internal Reports - 4.1
    Chapter 3 - Costing and Control of Materials and Labor - 5.2
    Chapter 4 - Costing and Control of Factory Overhead - 5.2, 5.3
    Chapter 5 - Job Order Cost System - 5.1 to 5.6
    Chapter 6 - Process Cost I: Nature and Characteristics - 6.1 to 6.8
    Chapter 7 - Process Cost II: Expanded Concepts - 7.1 to 7.4, 9.1, 9.2
    Chapter 8 - Joint Product and By-Product Costing - 8.1 to 8.7
    Chapter 9 - Standard Cost I: Establishment of Standards - 13.1
    Chapter 10 - Standard Cost II: Computation and Analysis of Variances - 13.2 to 13.8
    Chapter 11 - Standard Cost III: Journal Entries and Disposition of Variances - 13.7
    Chapter 12 - Direct and Absorption Costing - 10.1 to 10.3
Part 2 - Performance Evaluation and Managerial Decision Making
    Chapter 13 - Master Budget: Its Nature, Development, and Behavioral Aspects - 12.1 to 12.2
    Chapter 14 - Relevant Costs and Revenues in Short-Term Decision Making - 15.1 to 15.3
    Chapter 15 - Break-even Analysis and Cost/Volume/Profit Analysis - 11.1 to 11.9
    Chapter 16 - Capital Budgeting I - 16.1 to 16.8
    Chapter 17 - Capital Budgeting II - 16.1 to 16.8
    Chapter 18 - Quantitative Techniques for Long-Term and Short-Term Decision Making I - Chaps. 16-21
    Chapter 19 - Quantitative Techniques for Long-Term and Short-Term Decision Making II - Chaps. 16-21
    Chapter 20 - Quantitative Techniques for Long-Term and Short-Term Decision Making III - Chaps. 16-21
    Chapter 21 - Decentralized Operations and Responsibility Accounting - 14.1 to 14.3
    Chapter 22 - Performance Measurement I: Responsibility Center Performance Evaluation - 14.1 to 14.3
    Chapter 23 - Performance Measurement II: Gross Profit Analysis - 13.5
    Chapter 24 - Performance Measurement III: Transfer Pricing - 14.2

Rayburn, *Principles of Cost Accounting: Managerial Applications*, Third Edition, Richard D. Irwin, Inc., 1986.

Part 1 - Basic Cost Accounting Concepts
    Chapter 1 - The Role of Cost Accounting in Planning and Control - 4.1
    Chapter 2 - Basic Cost Concepts and Manufacturing Statements - 4.2
    Chapter 3 - Costing Materials and Quantitative Models for Materials Planning and Control - 17.1 to 17.4
    Chapter 4 - Learning Curve Theory and Labor Accounting - 21.4
    Chapter 5 - Cost Behavior and Cost Estimation Methods with Regression Analysis - 4.3, 11.3, 19.1 to 19.5
    Chapter 6 - Allocating Overhead Costs and Variance Analysis - 9.1, 9.2, 13.4
Part 2 - Product Cost Accumulation Procedures
    Chapter 7 - Process Costing - Weighted Average and FIFO Costing - 6.1 to 6.8
    Chapter 8 - Process Costing - Addition of Material and Lost Units - 7.1 to 7.4
    Chapter 9 - Joint Product and By-Product Costing - 8.1 to 8.7
Part 3 - Planning and Control of Costs with Standards
    Chapter 10 - Standard Costs for Material and Labor - 13.1 to 13.3
    Chapter 11 - Standard Costs for Factory Overhead and Variance Analysis - 13.4 to 13.8
Part 4 - Cost Analysis for Decision Making
    Chapter 12 - Cost-Volume-Profit Analysis - 11.1 to 11.9
    Chapter 13 - Variable Costing - 10.1 to 10.3
    Chapter 14 - Decision Models and Cost Analysis Under Uncertainty - 15.1 to 15.3
Part 5 - Budgeting and Capital Investment Decisions
    Chapter 15 - The Budgeting Process - 12.1, 12.2
    Chapter 16 - Cash, Administrative, and Marketing Budgets, and Forecasted Statements - 12.1, 12.2
    Chapter 17 - Behavioral Factors in Accounting Control - 14.1
    Chapter 18 - Capital Budgeting and Cost Analysis - 16.1 to 16.8
Part 6 - Quantitative Models for Planning and Control
    Chapter 19 - Gantt Charts, PERT, and Decision Tree Analysis - 21.3
    Chapter 20 - Linear Programming and the Cost Accountant - 20.1 to 20.4
Part 7 - Performance Evaluation and Pricing Analysis
    Chapter 21 - Marketing Cost Analysis - 13.5
    Chapter 22 - The Use of Costs in Pricing Decisions - 10.1 to 10.3
    Chapter 23 - Segment Analysis - 14.1 to 14.3
    Chapter 24 - Transfer Pricing in Multidivisional Companies - 14.1 to 14.3

Ricketts and Gray, *Managerial Accounting*, Houghton Mifflin Company, 1988.

Part 1 - Fundamentals of Managerial Accounting
    Chapter 1 - Accounting and the Management Process - 4.1
    Chapter 2 - Cost Classification and Flow - 4.3 to 4.5
    Chapter 3 - Cost Behavior and Estimation - 4.3, 11.3, 18.5
Part 2 - Cost Accounting Systems
    Chapter 4 - Job Order Costing - 5.1 to 5.6
    Chapter 5 - Process Costing - 6.1 to 6.8
Part 3 - The Role of the Accountant in Managerial Planning Decisions
    Chapter 6 - Cost-Volume-Profit Analysis - 11.1 to 11.9
    Chapter 7 - Planning the Master Budget - 12.1 to 12.2
    Chapter 8 - Relevant Costs and Management Decisions - 15.1 to 15.3
Part 4 - The Role of Accounting in Managerial Control Decisions
    Chapter 9 - Responsibility Accounting: Segmented Reporting and Direct Costing - 14.1 to 14.3
    Chapter 10 - Standard Costs: Direct Materials and Direct Labor - 13.1 to 13.3
    Chapter 11 - Flexible Budgets and Manufacturing Overhead Costs - 12.1 to 12.2, 13.1, 13.4
    Chapter 12 - Performance Measurement: Revenue Centers and Profit Centers - 9.1 to 9.2, 13.1
    Chapter 13 - Performance Measurement: Investment Centers - 9.1 to 9.2, 13.1
Part 5 - Advanced Topics in Managerial Accounting
    Chapter 14 - Introduction to Capital Expenditure Analysis - 16.1
    Chapter 15 - Further Topics in Capital Expenditure Analysis - 16.1 to 16.8
    Chapter 16 - Cost Allocation - 9.1 to 9.2
    Chapter 17 - Analysis of Financial Statements
          - *Financial Accounting Objective Questions and Explanations*, Chap. 26
    Chapter 18 - Statement of Cash Flows
          - *Financial Accounting Objective Questions and Explanations*, Chap. 22

Smith, Keith, Stephens, *Managerial Accounting*, McGraw-Hill, Inc., 1988.

Part One - Management Accounting and Key Underlying Concepts
    Chapter 1 - Management Accounting: An Introduction - 4.1 to 4.6
    Chapter 2 - An Introduction to Cost Accounting Systems - 4.1 to 4.6, 5.1, 6.1
    Chapter 3 - Analysis of Cost Behavior: Variable, Fixed, and Mixed - 4.3, 4.5
Part Two - Cost-Volume-Profit Analysis and Short-Run Decisions
    Chapter 4 - The Contribution Margin Approach to Cost-Volume-Profit Analysis: Part I - 11.1 to 11.9
    Chapter 5 - The Contribution Margin Approach to Cost-Volume-Profit Analysis: Part II - 11.1 to 11.9
    Chapter 6 - Relevant Information for Special Decisions - 15.1 to 15.3
Part Three - Applying the Concept of Relevance to Long-Run Decisions
    Chapter 7 - Capital Budgeting: An Introduction to the Discounted and Nondiscounted Cash-Flow Methods - 16.1 to 16.8
    Chapter 8 - Capital Budgeting: Tax Considerations - 16.4 to 16.8
Part Four - The Planning and Control of Operations in the Short Run
    Chapter 9 - The Master Budget - 12.1 to 12.2
    Chapter 10 - The Flexible Budget, Standard Costs, and Variance Analysis - 12.1 to 12.2, 13.1 to 13.8
    Chapter 11 - Responsibility Centers, Service Department Cost Allocations, Transfer Pricing, and Return on Investment - 9.1 to 9.2, 14.1 to 14.3, 16.5 to 16.8
Part Five - The Extremes of Product Costing: Job Order Costing and Process Costing
    Chapter 12 - Process Costing Methods Part I: Job Order Costing - 5.1 to 5.6
    Chapter 13 - Process Costing Methods Part II: Process Costing - 6.1 to 6.8
Part Six - Using Financial Statements
    Chapter 14 - Financial Statement Analysis and Interpretation
          - *Financial Accounting Objective Questions and Explanations*, Chap. 26
    Chapter 15 - The Statement of Cash Flows
          - *Financial Accounting Objective Questions and Explanations*, Chap. 22

Chapter 1: How to Use This Book

Usry, Hammer, Matz, *Cost Accounting: Planning and Control,* Ninth Edition, South-Western Publishing Co., 1988.

Part 1 - Costs: Concepts and Objectives
    Chapter 1 - The Management Concept and the Function of the Controller - 4.1 to 4.6
    Chapter 2 - Cost Concepts and the Cost Accounting Information System - 4.1 to 4.6
Part 2 - Cost Accumulation Process
    Chapter 3 - Job Order Costing - 5.1 to 5.6
    Chapter 4 - Process Costing: Cost of Production Report - N/A
    Chapter 5 - Process Costing: Average and FIFO Costing - 6.1 to 6.8
    Chapter 6 - Costing By-Products and Joint Products - 8.1 to 8.7
Part 3 - Planning and Control of the Elements of Cost
    Chapter 7 - Materials: Controlling and Costing - 13.1 to 13.2, 13.4 to 13.8
    Chapter 8 - Materials: Quantitative Models for Planning and Control - 17.1 to 17.4
    Chapter 9 - Labor: Controlling and Accounting for Costs - 13.1, 13.3 to 13.8
    Chapter 10 - Labor: Accounting for Labor -- Related Costs - 13.3
    Chapter 11 - Cost Behavior Analysis - 19.1 to 19.5
    Chapter 12 - Factory Overhead: Planned, Actual, and Applied; Variance Analysis - 13.1, 13.4 to 13.8
    Chapter 13 - Factory Overhead: Departmentalized - 9.1 to 9.2
    Chapter 14 - Factory Overhead: Responsibility Accounting and Reporting - 14.1 to 14.3
Part 4 - Budgeting and Standard Costing
    Chapter 15 - Budgeting: Profits, Sales, Costs, and Expenses - 12.1 to 12.2
    Chapter 16 - Budgeting: Capital Expenditures, Research and Development Expenditures, and Cash; PERT/Cost;
        The Flexible Budget - 12.1 to 12.2, 15.1 to 15.3, 16.1 to 16.8, 21.3
    Chapter 17 - Standard Costing: Setting Standards and Analyzing Variances - 13.1 to 13.8
    Chapter 18 - Standard Costing: Incorporating Standards into the Accounting Records - 13.1 to 13.8
Part 5 - Analysis of Costs and Profits
    Chapter 19 - Direct Costing and the Contribution Margin - 10.1 to 10.3
    Chapter 20 - Break-Even and Cost-Volume-Profit Analysis - 11.1 to 11.9
    Chapter 21 - Differential Cost Analysis - 11.5, 15.1 to 15.3
    Chapter 22 - Linear Programming for Planning and Decision Making - 20.1 to 20.4
    Chapter 23 - Capital Expenditures: Planning, Evaluating, and Controlling - 16.1 to 16.8
    Chapter 24 - Capital Expenditures Evaluation: Considering Uncertainty - 18.1 to 18.6
    Chapter 25 - Marketing Cost and Profitability Analysis - N/A
    Chapter 26 - Profit Performance Measurements; Intracompany Transfer Pricing; Product Pricing
        Methods - 9.1 to 9.2, 13.1 to 13.8

Warren and Fess, *Managerial Accounting,* Second Edition, South-Western Publishing Co., 1988.

Part 1 - Fundamentals of Managerial Accounting
    Chapter 1 - Nature of Managerial Accounting - 4.1
Part 2 - Managerial Accounting Concepts and Systems
    Chapter 2 - Cost Concepts and Classifications - 4.1 to 4.6
    Chapter 3 - Accounting Systems for Manufacturing Enterprises: Job Order Cost Systems - 5.1 to 5.6
    Chapter 4 - Process Cost System - 6.1 to 6.8
Part 3 - Planning and Control
    Chapter 5 - Cost Behavior and Cost Estimation - 18.1 to 18.6, 19.1 to 19.5
    Chapter 6 - Cost-Volume-Profit Analysis - 11.1 to 11.9
    Chapter 7 - Profit Reporting for Management Analysis - 9.1 to 9.2, 13.1
    Chapter 8 - Budgeting - 12.1 to 12.2
    Chapter 9 - Standard Cost Systems - 13.1 to 13.8
Part 4 - Accounting for Decentralized Operations
    Chapter 10 - Responsibility Accounting for Cost and Profit Centers - 14.1 to 14.3
    Chapter 11 - Responsibility Accounting for Investment Centers; Transfer Pricing - 9.1 to 9.2, 14.1 to 14.3
Part 5 - Analysis for Decision Making
    Chapter 12 - Differential Analysis and Product Costing - 11.5, 15.1 to 15.3
    Chapter 13 - Capital Investment Analysis - 16.1 to 16.8
    Chapter 14 - Quantitative Techniques for Controlling Inventory and Making Decisions Under
        Uncertainty - 17.1 to 17.4, 18.1 to 18.6
Part 6 - Financial Analysis for Management USC
    Chapter 15 - Financial Statement Analysis and Annual Reports
        - *Financial Accounting Objective Questions and Explanations,* Chap. 26
    Chapter 16 - Statement of Cash Flows
        - *Financial Accounting Objective Questions and Explanations,* Chap. 22
Part 7 - Modern Uses of Managerial Accounting
    Chapter 17 - Nonprofit Organizations - N/A
    Chapter 18 - Trends in Managerial Accounting - 4.1, 4.6

QUANTITATIVE METHODS

Anderson and Lievano, *Quantitative Management: An Introduction,* **Second Edition, Kent Publishing Co., 1986.**

    Chapter 1 - Introduction - N/A
Section One - Mathematical Programming
    Chapter 2 - Linear Programming: Formulation and Graphical Method - 20.1 to 20.2
    Chapter 3 - Linear Programming: The Simplex Method - 20.4
    Chapter 4 - The Transportation Problem - 20.1
    Chapter 5 - The Assignment Problem - 20.1
Section Two - Operations Models
    Chapter 6 - Inventory Models: Part I - 17.1 to 17.4
    Chapter 7 - Inventory Models: Part II - 17.1 to 17.4
    Chapter 8 - Queuing Models - 21.2
    Chapter 9 - Project Management: CPM and PERT - 21.3
Section Three - Probabilistic Models
    Chapter 10 - Decision Theory - 18.1 to 18.6
    Chapter 11 - Markov Chains - 21.1
    Chapter 12 - Simulation - 21.1
Section Four - Advanced Topics
    Chapter 13 - Goal Programming - 20.1
    Chapter 14 - Integer Programming - 20.1
    Chapter 15 - Dynamic Programming - 20.1
    Chapter 16 - Network Optimization Methods - 21.3
    Chapter 17 - Branch-and-Bound Methods - N/A
    Chapter 18 - Heuristics in Management Science - N/A

Bierman, Bonini, Hausman, *Quantitative Analysis for Business Decisions,* **Seventh Edition, Richard D. Irwin, Inc., 1986.**

Part 1 - Models and Decision Making
    Chapter 1 - Introduction to Quantitative Analysis - 21.1
    Chapter 2 - Introduction to Model Building - 21.1
Part 2 - Probability
    Chapter 3 - Basic Probability Concepts - 18.1, 18.5
Part 3 - Decision Analysis
    Chapter 4 - Decision Making Under Uncertainty - 18.1 to 18.6
    Chapter 5 - Decisions and Revision of Probabilities - 18.6
    Chapter 6 - Decision Theory - 18.2
    Chapter 7 - Utility as a Basis for Decision Making - 18.4
    Chapter 8 - Decision Theory and Classical Statistics - 18.6
    Chapter 9 - The Normal Probability Distribution and the Value of Information - 18.6
    Chapter 10 - Revision of Normal Probabilities By Sampling - N/A
    Chapter 11 - Game Theory - N/A
Part 4 - Mathematical Programming
    Chapter 12 - Introduction to Linear Programming - 20.1, 20.2
    Chapter 13 - Linear Programming: The Simplex Method - 20.3, 20.4
    Chapter 14 - Linear Programming: The Dual Problem and Sensitivity Analysis - 20.3, 20.4, 2l.1
    Chapter 15 - Linear Programming: Special Topics - 20.1
    Chapter 16 - Integer Programming and Branch and Bound Procedures - 20.1
Part 5 - Deterministic and Probabilistic Models
    Chapter 17 - Inventory Control with Constant Demand - 17.1 to 17.4
    Chapter 18 - Inventory Control with Reordering and Uncertain Demand - 17.1 to 17.4
    Chapter 19 - Inventory Control with Uncertainty and No Reordering - 17.1 to 17.4
    Chapter 20 - Waiting Lines: Queuing Theory - 21.2
    Chapter 21 - Simulation - 21.1
    Chapter 22 - PERT (Program Evaluation and Review Technique) - 21.3
    Chapter 23 - Markov Processes - 21.1
    Chapter 24 - Dynamic Programming - 20.1

Chapter 1: How to Use This Book

Budnick, Mojena, and Vollmann, *Principles of Operations Research for Management,* **Second Edition, Richard D. Irwin, Inc., 1988.**

Chapter 1 - The Process of Operations Research/Management Science - N/A
Chapter 2 - Classical Deterministic Models -
Chapter 3 - Linear Programming: The Model and its Applications - 20.1
Chapter 4 - Linear Programming: Geometric and Computerized Solutions - 20.2 to 20.4
Chapter 5 - Linear Programming: Postoptimality Analysis and the Dual Problem - N/A
Chapter 6 - Linear Programming: The Simplex Method - 20.4
Chapter 7 - Transportation and Assignment Models - 20.1
Chapter 8 - Integer and Zero-One Programming - 20.1
Chapter 9 - Multicriteria Mathematical Programming - 20.1, 21.5
Chapter 10 - Network Models - 21.3
Chapter 11 - Project Scheduling - 21.1 to 21.3
Chapter 12 - Dynamic Programming and Sequential Decisions - 20.1
Chapter 13 - Decision Analysis - 18.1 to 18.6
Chapter 14 - Markov Processes - 21.1
Chapter 15 - Inventory Models - 17.1 to 17.4
Chapter 16 - Queuing Models - 21.2
Chapter 17 - Simulation - 21.1
Chapter 18 - Management Science in Perspective - 4.1

Davis and McKeown, *Quantitative Models for Management,* **Second Edition, Kent Publishing Company, 1984.**

Chapter 1 - Introduction to Modeling and Management Science - N/A
Chapter 2 - Introduction to Linear Programming Models - 20.1
Chapter 3 - Linear Programming: Model Formulations - 20.1, 20.2
Chapter 4 - The Simplex Method - 20.3, 20.4
Chapter 5 - Sensitivity Analysis and Duality - 20.3, 20.4
Chapter 6 - PERT/CPM Network Models - 21.3
Chapter 7 - LP Network Models - N/A
Chapter 8 - Multicriteria Models and Methods - N/A
Chapter 9 - Integer Programming - 20.1
Chapter 10 - Dynamic Programming - 20.1
Chapter 11 - Inventory Models - 17.1 to 17.4
Chapter 12 - Decision Models - 18.1 to 18.6
Chapter 13 - Queuing Analysis: Waiting-Line Problems - 21.2
Chapter 14 - Simulation - 21.1
Chapter 15 - Markov Processes - 21.1
Chapter 16 - Implementation - N/A

Levin, Rubin, and Stinson, *Quantitative Approaches to Management,* **Sixth Edition, McGraw-Hill Book Company, 1986.**

Chapter 1 - Introduction: Quantitative Methods and Their Supporting Information Systems - N/A
Chapter 2 - Review of Probability Concepts - 18.1 to 18.6
Chapter 3 - Forecasting - 19.1 to 19.4
Chapter 4 - Decision Making Using Probabilities I - 18.2
Chapter 5 - Decision Making Using Probabilities II - 18.4 to 18.6
Chapter 6 - Inventory I: Order Quantity Models - 17.1, 17.2
Chapter 7 - Inventory II: Reordering, Backorders, Discounts, Material Requirements Planning - 17.3, 17.4
Chapter 8 - Linear Programming I: Graphic Methods - 20.1, 20.2
Chapter 9 - Linear Programming II: The Simplex Method - 20.3, 20.4
Chapter 10 - Linear Programming III: Economic and Operational Issues: Duality, Infeasibility, Unboundedness, Degeneracy, Right-Hand-Side Ranging, Changes in Objective Function Coefficients, Linear Programming Applications, Use of the Computer in Linear Programming - N/A
Chapter 11 - Networks I: Special Purpose Algorithms - N/A
Chapter 12 - Networks II: PERT/CPM, Minimal Tree, Maximal Flow, and Dynamic Progression - 20.1, 21.3
Chapter 13 - Integer Programming, Branch-and-Bound Method, Goal Programming, Heuristics - 20.1
Chapter 14 - Simulation - 21.1
Chapter 15 - Waiting Lines - 21.2
Chapter 16 - Markov Analysis - 21.1
Chapter 17 - Management Science: Yesterday, Today, Tomorrow - N/A

Markland and Swelgert, *Quantitative Methods for Management Decisions,* John Wiley & Sons, Inc., 1987.

Chapter 1 - Introduction - 21.1
Chapter 2 - Probability Concepts - 18.1
Chapter 3 - Probability Distribution - 18.3
Chapter 4 - Decision Theory and Utility Theory - 18.6
Chapter 5 - Forecasting - 19.1 to 19.5
Chapter 6 - Introduction to Linear Programming and Model Formulation - 20.1 to 20.4
Chapter 7 - Graphical Solution of Linear Programming Problems - 20.2
Chapter 8 - The Simplex Method - 20.3, 20.4
Chapter 9 - Postoptimality Analysis - N/A
Chapter 10 - Goal Programming - 20.1
Chapter 11 - Transportation, Transshipment, and Assignment Problems - 20.1
Chapter 12 - Network Models - 21.3
Chapter 13 - PERT/CPM - 21.3
Chapter 14 - Integer Programming Models - 20.1
Chapter 15 - Inventory Analysis: Deterministic Models - 17.1 to 17.4
Chapter 16 - Inventory Analysis: Probabilistic Models - 17.1 to 17.4
Chapter 17 - Line Models - 21.2
Chapter 18 - Computer Simulation - N/A
Chapter 19 - Other Quantitative Models - 21.1 to 21.6
Chapter 20 - Implementation and Integration of Management Science Techniques in the Decision Framework - 15.1 to 15.3

CHAPTER TWO
OBJECTIVE QUESTIONS ANSWERING TECHNIQUE

> *Multiple-Choice Questions on Professional Certification Exams* 23
> *True-False Questions* 23

You need a personalized control system **(technique)** for answering objective questions, essay questions, and computational problems. The objective is to obtain complete, correct, and well-presented solutions. Because this study manual is limited to objective questions, this chapter only discusses the objective question answering technique. Developing answers to computational problems and essay questions is discussed and illustrated in our CIA, CMA, and CPA review texts.

The following series of steps is suggested for answering multiple-choice questions. The important point is that you need to devote attention to and develop YOUR OWN TECHNIQUE for objective questions (and for computational problems and essay questions, which are beyond the scope of this study manual).

Personalize and practice your **objective question answering technique** on questions in this study manual. Modify the following suggested steps to suit your individual skills and ability.

1. First cover the answer choices! They are a distraction. Almost everyone is focused on answers, and reads the answers intentionally or unintentionally unless they are covered. This may result in misreading the question requirements to suit a particular answer.

2. Proceed methodically, question by question, in the order presented.

    a. Begin with the requirement(s).

    b. Note **exceptions**, e.g., "Which of the following is **not** an appropriate application of queuing theory?"

    c. When more than one question are based on one fact situation, understand the requirements of all the questions **before** beginning to work the first question.

        1) Often it is better to work questions either simultaneously or in a different sequence.

    d. Underline key words and important data. Make notes and do computations in the margin as appropriate. If you use scratch paper, label your solutions so you can relocate them if you need to review them.

3. Determine the correct answer **before** uncovering the answer choices. After you uncover the answers:

    a. Consider each answer carefully.

    b. Treat each answer as a true-false question. Consider marking a "T" or "F" next to each answer as you analyze it.

4. Write the correct (or best guess) answer on the examination itself, not on a separate answer sheet (if one exists).

   a. Note that most examinations do not penalize guessing since the score is determined by the number of correct responses.

      1) When guessing is not penalized, you should answer every question.

   b. When a subtraction is made for incorrectly answered questions (in contrast to unanswered questions), guessing is penalized.

      1) When guessing is penalized, you should evaluate the cost/benefit of the penalty as it relates to how unsure you are of the answer.

5. If you need to skip a question temporarily, mark the question with a big "X". This may be advisable if a question requires too much time.

   a. Go back to each of the unanswered questions and do the best you can within your time budget.

6. After answering all the questions in a question set, record your answers on the separate answer sheet (if one exists).

   a. Double check your work.

   b. If you lose the proper sequence, many of your answers may be wrong.

   c. Do not wait until the end of the examination session, since you may not have enough time.

7. Budget your time carefully.

   a. Before beginning a series of multiple-choice questions, write the starting time on the exam booklet near the first multiple-choice question.

   b. Compute the minutes allowed for each multiple-choice question after you have allocated exam time to all of the overall questions on the exam; e.g., if the first overall question consists of 20 individual multiple-choice questions and is allocated 30 minutes on the exam, you would want to spend a little over 1 minute per individual multiple-choice question (always budget extra time for transferring answers to answer sheets, interruptions, etc.).

   c. As you work through the individual multiple-choice questions, check your time; e.g., assuming the above time allocation of 30 minutes for 20 questions, if you have worked five multiple-choice questions in 6 or 7 minutes, you are fine, but if you spent 10 minutes on five questions, you need to speed up.

MULTIPLE-CHOICE QUESTIONS ON PROFESSIONAL CERTIFICATION EXAMS

Every part of the CIA, CMA, and CPA exams begins with a series of multiple-choice questions.

Each of the five sections on the CPA exam has 60 multiple-choice questions, which constitute 60% of the score on each of the four parts of the exam (Practice consists of two, 4½-hour sessions -- See the next chapter for a more complete discussion of the CIA, CMA, and CPA programs).

The number of multiple-choice questions and percentage of the score for each part of the CIA and CMA exams for the five most recent examinations are presented below. Computations of the percentages are based on estimated time allowances and approximate the relative weight assigned to the questions.

On the CIA exam:	May 1990	Nov. 1989	May 1989	Nov. 1988	May 1988
Part I	50 - 50%	50 - 50%	50 - 50%	50 - 50%	50 - 50%
Part II	50 - 50%	50 - 50%	50 - 50%	50 - 50%	50 - 50%
Part III	50 - 50%	50 - 50%	50 - 50%	50 - 50%	50 - 50%
Part IV	50 - 100%	70 - 100%	70 - 100%	70 - 100%	70 - 100%

On the CMA exam:	June 1990	Dec. 1989	June 1989	Dec. 1988	June 1988
Part 1	30 - 30%	30 - 30%	30 - 30%	30 - 30%	30 - 30%
Part 2 (all essay)	--	--	--	--	--
Part 3	30 - 30%	30 - 30%	30 - 30%	30 - 30%	30 - 30%
Part 4	30 - 30%	30 - 30%	30 - 30%	30 - 30%	30 - 30%
Part 5	30 - 30%	30 - 30%	30 - 30%	30 - 30%	30 - 30%

TRUE-FALSE QUESTIONS

True-false questions are not widely used on examinations because they encourage guessing and result in a 50% expected score given no knowledge.

Remember, a multiple-choice question is really four or five true-false questions. Treat them that way and use the true-false questions for practice. The answering strategy for true-false questions is largely the same as discussed above for multiple-choice questions. The general rule is if any part of a statement is false, the entire statement is false.

CHAPTER THREE
THE CIA, CMA, AND CPA CERTIFICATION PROGRAMS

Overview of Accounting Certification Programs	*25*
Rationale for Accounting Certification Programs	*27*
Examination Content for CIA, CMA, and CPA Exams	*27*
Exam Schedules and Future Dates	*31*
Examination Pass Rates	*32*
Factors Contributing to the Confusion About CPA Exam Pass Rates	*33*
Reasons for Low Pass Rates	*34*
Sponsoring Organizations	*34*
Cost to Obtain and Maintain Professional Certification	*35*
Education and Experience Requirements	*35*
Continuing Professional Education (CPE) Requirements	*35*
When to Sit for the Exams	*36*
How to Register and Apply for the CIA Exam	*36*
Special Student Examination Fee for the CIA Exam	*37*
How to Apply and Register for the CMA Exam	*37*
Special Student Examination Fee for the CMA Exam	*38*
How to Obtain CIA and CMA Examination Review	*38*
Other Certification Programs	*39*
Individual State CPA Requirements	*40*

The purpose of this chapter is to describe the three primary accounting certification examinations and the CIA, CMA, and CPA designations. You should become conversant with these programs and their requirements very early in your accounting career so you can "look ahead" to all three accounting examinations. If you are a student, the best time to prepare for these exams is now. A secondary benefit will be good grades; i.e., the high standards of these examinations will force you to work hard, learn much, and do well in your courses. If you are a practitioner, you should consider these examinations as professional development opportunities rather than examinations or tests.

Page 42 in this chapter can be photocopied to send for application and registration forms and additional information for the CIA and CMA programs. While all are nationally uniform examinations, application for the CPA exam must be made through your individual state board of accountancy. The addresses of the 54 state boards of accountancy (one for each state plus the District of Columbia, Guam, Puerto Rico, and the U.S. Virgin Islands) appear on page 41.

OVERVIEW OF ACCOUNTING CERTIFICATION PROGRAMS

The CPA (Certified Public Accountant) exam is the grandfather of all the professional accounting examinations. Its origin was in the 1896 public accounting legislation of New York. In 1916 the American Institute of CPAs (AICPA) began to prepare and grade a uniform CPA exam. It is currently used to measure the technical competence of those applying to be licensed as CPAs in all 50 states, Guam, Puerto Rico, the Virgin Islands, and the District of Columbia. Over 140,000 candidates sit for the two CPA exams each year.

CIA, CMA, CPA EXAMINATION SUMMARY

	CIA	CMA	CPA
Sponsoring Organization	Institute of Internal Auditors 249 Maitland Avenue P.O. Box 1119 Altamonte Springs, FL 32701 (407) 830-7600 (800) CIA-DESK	National Association of Accountants 10 Paragon Drive Montvale, NJ 07645-1959 (201) 573-6300 (800) 562-4262	American Institute of Certified Public Accountants 1211 Ave. of the Americas New York, NY 10036 (212) 575-6495
Passing Score	75%	70%	75%
Average Pass Rate by Exam Part	45%	45%	30%
Year Examination Was First Administered	1974	1972	1916
Major Exam Sections and Length	I. Theory and Practice of Internal Auditing (3½ hours) II. Theory and Practice of Internal Auditing (3½ hours) III. Management, Quantitative Methods, and Information Systems (3½ hours) IV. Accounting, Finance, and Economics (3½ hours)	1. Economics, Finance, and Management (4 hours) 2. Financial Accounting and Reporting (4 hours) 3. Management Reporting, Analysis, and Behavioral Issues (4 hours) 4. Decision Analysis and Information Systems (4 hours)	1. Auditing (3½ hours) 2. Business Law (3½ hours) 3. Accounting Theory (3½ hours) 4. Accounting Practice (9 hours)
Length of Exam	14 hours	16 hours[1]	19½ hours[2]
Candidates Sitting for Exam:			
1974	654	633	72,052*
1975	719	723	80,433*
1976	1,099	1,037	86,464*
1977	1,227	2,046*	93,148*
1978	2,091	2,355*	104,791*
1979	2,250	2,734*	113,629*
1980	2,653	3,301*	120,937*
1981	3,137	3,790*	128,793*
1982	4,989*	4,538*	138,677*
1983	4,070*	4,578*	142,564*
1984	3,610*	4,934*	137,918*
1985	3,574*	4,734*	139,454*
1986	3,534*	4,711*	139,647*
1987	3,408*	4,557*	136,997*
1988	3,531*	4,595*	139,117*
1989	3,892*	4,879*	142,114*

[1] Reflects change from 5-part to 4-part exam in December 1990.
[2] To change to 2-day, 15½ hours in May 1994.

* Total number of candidates sitting for two examinations; many are repeaters.

Other professional accounting-related designations include: CBA (Chartered Bank Auditor), CDP (Certificate in Data Processing), CFA (Chartered Financial Analyst), CISA (Certified Information Systems Auditor), Enrolled Agent (one enrolled to practice before the IRS).

Copyright © 1990 Accounting Publications, Inc.

The CIA (Certified Internal Auditor) and CMA (Certified Management Accountant) examinations are neophytes when compared to the CPA exam. The CMA exam was first administered in 1972, and the first CIA exam was in 1974. Why were these certification programs begun? Generally, the requirements of the "CPA" designation instituted by the boards of accountancy, especially the necessity for public accounting experience, led to development of the CIA and CMA programs.

Certification is important to professional accountants because it provides

1. Participation in a recognized professional group.
2. An improved professional training program arising out of the certification program.
3. Recognition among peers for attaining the professional designation.
4. An extra credential for the employment market/career ladder.
5. The personal satisfaction of attaining a recognized degree of competency.

These reasons hold particularly true in the accounting field due to the wide recognition given to the CPA designation. Accountants (and even accounting students) are frequently asked if they are CPAs when people learn they are accountants. Thus, there is considerable pressure for accountants to become "certified."

A new development is multiple certification, which is important for the same reasons as initial certification. The table of selected CIA, CMA, and CPA examination data (presented on the opposite page) provides an overview of the three accounting examinations.

RATIONALE FOR ACCOUNTING CERTIFICATION PROGRAMS

The primary purpose of the CIA, CMA, and CPA examinations is to measure the technical competence of candidates. This includes technical knowledge, ability to apply such knowledge with good judgment, and comprehension of professional responsibility. Additionally, the nature of these examinations (low pass rate, broad and rigorous coverage, etc.) has several very important effects.

1. Candidates are forced to learn all of the material that should have been presented and learned in a "good" accounting educational program.
2. Relatedly, candidates must integrate the topics and concepts which are presented in individual courses in accounting educational programs.
3. The content of each examination provides direction to accounting education programs; i.e., what is tested on the examinations will be taught to students.

EXAMINATION CONTENT FOR CIA, CMA, AND CPA EXAMS

The content of each of these examinations is specified by their governing boards by means of lists of topics to be tested. In all three review manuals -- CIA, CMA, and CPA -- the material tested is subdivided into subtopics or modules. A module is a more manageable study unit than the overall parts of each exam. The listings of topics on pages 28 through 31 provide an overview of the content of the three examinations.

THE CIA EXAMINATION*

Part I   THEORY AND PRACTICE OF INTERNAL AUDITING
- Nature of Internal Auditing
- Administration of the Internal Audit Department
- Administration of the Audit Assignment
- Internal Control

Part II   THEORY AND PRACTICE OF INTERNAL AUDITING, CONTINUED
- Audit Evidence
- EDP Auditing
- Statistical Sampling
- Audit Communications
- Ethics
- Fraud

Part III   MANAGEMENT, QUANTITATIVE METHODS, AND INFORMATION SYSTEMS
- Management Behavior
  - Nature and Theories of Management
  - Planning
  - Organization Theory
  - The Directing Process
  - The Controlling Process
- Quantitative Methods
- Management Information Systems
- Current Related Topics

Part IV   ACCOUNTING, FINANCE, AND ECONOMICS
- Management Accounting
- Financial Accounting
- Finance
- Economics

*These are the modules in the Third Edition of *CIA Examination Review* by Irvin N. Gleim.

1. The CIA exam lasts 14 hours (four 3½-hour parts) in contrast to the 19½ hours (four varying-length parts) of the CPA exam and the 16 hours (four 4-hour parts) of the CMA exam.

2. The first two parts of the CIA exam focus on the theory and practice of internal auditing. The body of knowledge of internal auditing consists of

   a. The typical undergraduate auditing class (as represented by auditing texts, e.g., Arens and Loebbecke, Taylor and Glezen, etc.).

   b. Textbooks on internal auditing, e.g., Sawyer and Sumners, *The Practice of Modern Internal Auditing,* and Atkisson, Brink, and Witt, *Modern Internal Auditing*.

   c. Various IIA (Institute of Internal Auditors) pronouncements, e.g., IIA Code of Ethics, Standards for the Professional Practice of Internal Auditing, and Statement of Responsibilities of Internal Auditing.

3. Thus, 50% of the CIA exam tests only one topic: internal auditing.

4. The remaining 50% of the exam (7 hours) covers seven topics with 120 multiple-choice questions and about 4 essay questions.

a. Since management cannot personally observe the functioning of all officers, employees, and specialized functions (finance, marketing, operations, etc.), each has its own special point of view, only internal auditing is in a position to take a total company point of view.

b. Thus, Parts III and IV of the CIA exam assure that internal auditors are conversant with topics, methodologies, and techniques ranging from individual and organizational behavior to economics, both macro and micro.

5. Note that Parts I, II, and III consist of 50 multiple-choice questions that constitute 50% of the grade. Part IV has 70 multiple-choice questions and no essay questions.

THE CMA EXAMINATION*

Part 1: ECONOMICS, FINANCE, AND MANAGEMENT
    Microeconomics
    Macroeconomics and International Economics
    Institutional Environment of Business
    Working Capital Policy and Management
    Long-term Finance and Capital Structure
    Organization and Management Theory
    Communication

Part 2: FINANCIAL ACCOUNTING AND REPORTING
    Financial Statements
    Reporting Requirements
    Analysis of Accounts and Statements
    External Auditing

Part 3: MANAGEMENT REPORTING, ANALYSIS, AND BEHAVIORAL ISSUES
    Cost Measurement
    Planning
    Control and Performance Evaluation
    Behavioral Issues

Part 4: DECISION ANALYSIS AND INFORMATION SYSTEMS
    Decision Theory and Operational Decision Analysis
    Investment Decision Analysis
    Quantitative Methods for Decision Analysis
    Information Systems
    Internal Auditing

*From the ICMA's Content Specification Outlines.

1. The ICMA decided in January 1990 to convert the CMA exam from a 5-part, 2½-day, 17½-hour exam to a 4-part, 2-day, 16-hour exam beginning December 1990. As this book goes to press, we are in the process of redoing *CMA Examination Review* to reflect those changes. Thus, the module listing above is the ICMA's, as we have not finalized our modular organization to reflect the new CMA exam format.

2. Each of the four parts of the CMA exam will be 4 hours long, resulting in 16 total hours versus 14 hours for the CIA exam and 19½ hours for the CPA exam.

3. The CMA exam provides expanded and more rigorous coverage of CIA Parts III and IV.

4. The CMA examination has broader coverage than the CPA examination in several areas. For example,

   a. The management information systems area of EDP is tested more extensively on the CMA exam.

   b. SEC Financial Reporting Releases and Cost Accounting Standards Board pronouncements are covered on the CMA exam but not on the CPA exam.

   c. Topics like economics, finance, and management on Part 1 of the CMA exam are covered lightly, if at all, on the CPA exam.

   d. The CMA examination tests internal auditing to a far greater degree than does the CPA exam.

   e. The CMA exam tests business ethics, but not business law.

5. About 30% of each part of the CMA exam consists of multiple-choice questions.

6. CMA questions are generally more analysis oriented than CPA questions. On the CPA exam, the typical requirement is the solution of an accounting problem, e.g., consolidated worksheet, funds statement, etc. The CMA exam generally has an additional requirement to analyze the impact of the data in the accounting presentation or to explain how the accounting data are used.

THE CPA EXAMINATION*

ACCOUNTING THEORY
   General Concepts, Principles, Terminology, and Other Professional Standards
   Measurement, Valuation, Realization, and Presentation of Assets
   Valuation, Recognition, and Presentation of Liabilities
   Ownership Structure, Presentation, and Valuation of Equity Accounts
   Measurement and Presentation of Income and Expense Items
   Other Financial Topics
   Cost Accumulation, Planning, and Control
   Not-for-Profit and Governmental Accounting

BUSINESS LAW
   The CPA and the Law
   Business Organizations
   Contracts
   Debtor-Creditor Relationships
   Government Regulation of Business
   Uniform Commercial Code
   Property

ACCOUNTING PRACTICE
   Presentation of Financial Statements or Worksheets
   Measurement, Valuation, Realization, and Presentation of Assets
   Valuation, Recognition, and Presentation of Liabilities
   Ownership Structure, Presentation, and Valuation of Equity Accounts
   Measurement and Presentation of Income and Expense Items
   Other Financial Topics
   Cost Accumulation, Planning, and Control
   Not-for-Profit and Governmental Accounting
   Federal Taxation - Individuals, Estates, and Trusts
   Federal Taxation - Corporations, Partnerships, and Exempt Organizations

AUDITING
   Professional Responsibilities
   Internal Control
   Evidence and Procedures
   Reporting
   Other Reporting Considerations

*From the AICPA Content Specification Outlines.

1. The schedule for the CPA exam is

Accounting Practice, Part I	Wednesday	1:30 - 6:00	4½ hours
Auditing	Thursday	8:30 - 12:00	3½ hours
Accounting Practice, Part II	Thursday	1:30 - 6:00	4½ hours
Business Law	Friday	8:30 - 12:00	3½ hours
Accounting Theory	Friday	1:30 - 5:00	3½ hours

   Only one grade is given for the Practice section since it is treated as one part, even though it is 9 hours long. Practice and Theory cover the same general topics, except that Federal Income Taxation is tested only in Practice.

2. In addition to multiple-choice questions, the Practice section of the CPA exam consists of typical "accounting problems." The other sections contain multiple-choice questions and essay questions rather than computational problems.

3. Currently, 60% of each section of the CPA exam consists of multiple-choice questions, largely due to advice from testing experts indicating that the testing quality of multiple-choice questions can be defended statistically. The AICPA is planning to increase objective question coverage to 85% beginning in May 1994 in conjunction with a reorganization of the CPA exam into a 4-part, 2-day examination.

EXAM SCHEDULES AND FUTURE DATES

The CPA exam schedule is presented above. The exam is generally given during the first week of May and November. Future CPA exam dates are

1990	1991	1992
November 7, 8, 9	May 8, 9, 10	May 6, 7, 8
	November 6, 7, 8	November 4, 5, 6

The CIA exam is given the Thursday and Friday following the CPA examination. Parts I and II are given Thursday morning and afternoon, respectively. Parts III and IV are on Friday morning and afternoon, respectively. Morning exams are from 8:30 to 12:00, and afternoon exams are from 1:30 to 5:00. Future CIA exam dates are

1990	1991	1992
November 15, 16	May 9, 10	May 14, 15
	November 14, 15	November 12, 13

The CMA exam is offered in the second week of June and December. Parts 1, 3, and 5 are scheduled Wednesday, Thursday, and Friday from 1:30 p.m. to 5:00 p.m. Parts 2 and 4 are scheduled Thursday and Friday mornings from 8:30 to 12:00. Future CMA exam dates are

1990	1991	1992
December 13, 14	June 13, 14	June 11, 12
	December 12, 13	December 10, 11

Note that all three examinations can be taken within a 6-week period, which is ideal owing to the great amount of overlap of the material tested. The formats of the three exams are very similar, which also contributes to the synergy of preparing for and taking all 3 exams together.

EXAMINATION PASS RATES

The pass rates on the CIA and CMA exams are about the same, which is about 50% higher than the pass rate on the CPA exam. Nationally, the pass rate on the CPA exam is about 30% on each of the four parts. The pass rates on the CIA and CMA exams average about 45% per part (see the tables below and on the next page).

Note that the average pass rate on the CIA exam has decreased over time but it is expected to stabilize at 45+%. The higher pass rates on the CIA and CMA exams reflect the added maturity of these participants, who are about 10 years older on average than CPA candidates. Also, the CIA and CMA programs permit you to take as few as one or two parts, respectively, in contrast to the CPA exam, on which you must do well on all parts at once.

Unfortunately, a great deal of confusion surrounds CPA exam pass rates. CPA pass rates are reported by individual state boards of accountancy, not nationally. There is considerable variation in the pass rate from state to state, even though the national rate is fairly constant. Nationally, about 10% pass all four parts on the first sitting even though the pass rate on each part is about 30%. Approximately 20% of all candidates sitting for each CPA exam successfully complete the exam (this includes those passing the entire exam on one sitting and those passing their final parts for successful completion). Over 80% of "serious" CPA candidates eventually complete the CPA exam.

PASS RATES ON THE CIA EXAMINATION

MO/YR	TOTAL SITTING	Part I No.	Part I %	Part II No.	Part II %	Part III No.	Part III %	Part IV No.	Part IV %
5/85	1,797	1,080	46.9%	1,105	46.7%	826	44.4%	891	49.4%
11/85	1,777	1,045	47.6%	1,055	47.3%	829	44.4%	815	47.1%
5/86	1,681	968	45.0%	964	45.3%	832	59.9%	789	47.7%
11/86	1,853	1,111	44.6%	1,107	46.6%	850	43.5%	865	44.9%
5/87	1,698	961	47.8%	949	48.6%	831	44.6%	804	40.2%
11/87	1,710	922	45.1%	918	43.1%	832	44.7%	848	45.5%
5/88	1,755	994	42.8%	976	44.0%	877	43.4%	875	45.6%
11/88	1,776	1,073	44.4%	1,051	42.5%	811	44.1%	853	41.4%
5/89	1,835	1,079	40.1%	1,077	40.1%	868	42.3%	819	42.3%
11/89	2,057	1,292	42.1%	1,280	42.0%	1,074	42.2%	1,058	42.2%

PASS RATES ON THE CMA EXAMINATION

Examination Part	DEC. 1986	JUNE 1987	DEC. 1987	JUNE 1988	DEC. 1988	JUNE 1989	DEC. 1989
Part 1 Economics and Business Finance	40%	43%	48%	47%	46%	46%	43%
Part 2 Organization and Behavior, Including Ethical Considerations	44%	30%	48%	43%	39%	43%	33%
Part 3 Public Reporting Standards, Auditing, and Taxes	50%	44%	38%	46%	40%	48%	37%
Part 4 Internal Reporting and Analysis	39%	36%	40%	34%	44%	50%	46%
Part 5 Decision Analysis, Including Modeling & Information Systems	46%	39%	46%	39%	47%	47%	37%
Weighted average for entire examination	44%	38%	44%	42%	43%	47%	39%
All five parts passed in one sitting	21%	11%	21%	12%	17%	22%	14%
Completed examination by taking parts omitted or failed in earlier years	44%	42%	49%	41%	46%	46%	38%
No. of candidates completing examination	398	362	419	326	385	412	339
No. of successful candidates since inception of the program	7,683	8,045	8,464	8,790	9,175	9,587	9,926

FACTORS CONTRIBUTING TO THE CONFUSION ABOUT CPA EXAM PASS RATES

1. There is confusion between pass rates and condition rates. While 75% is the passing grade for each part, "conditional" status is assigned to candidates who pass some, but not all, parts. The combined pass and condition rate is therefore higher than the pass rate, usually more than twice as high.

2. Relatedly, the qualifications and the requirements for conditional status vary from state to state (see Individual State CPA Requirements on page 41), which impedes the comparability of condition rates from state to state.

3. Confusion also exists between pass rates of first-time candidates, and of all CPA candidates. While the pass rate on each section of the exam is 30%, the percentage of those who pass all four sections of the exam on the first sitting is only about 10% nationally.

4. Further confusion arises from the different reporting methods by the few states that do disclose pass rates. For example, Florida releases detailed grade analyses of only first-time candidates; Illinois computes the percentage of CPA candidates who successfully complete the exam; and Colorado computes a cumulative success rate for each examination.

5. Finally, many schools and CPA review courses advertise the quality of their program by reporting pass rates. Obviously the best rates are emphasized. Thus, a reported percentage may be that for first-time candidates, all candidates, candidates passing a specific section of the examination, candidates completing the examination, or even candidates successfully completing the exam after a specified number of sittings.

Note that the CIA and CMA programs have done away with these problems by publicly disclosing their pass rates on a national basis.

REASONS FOR LOW PASS RATES

Although a very high percentage of serious candidates successfully complete each of the examinations, the 30% CPA pass rate and the 45% CIA and CMA pass rates warrant an explanation. First, the pass rates are low (relative to bar and medical exams) because the examination reflects the high standards of the accounting profession, which contribute greatly to the profession's reputation and also attract persons with both competence and aspiration. On the other hand, entrance to accounting educational programs is unrestricted compared to entrance requirements of law and medical schools.

Second, the pass rates are low because most accounting educational programs are at the undergraduate rather than graduate level. Undergraduate students are generally less mature and career-oriented than graduate students. Undergraduates generally look on their program as a number of individual courses required for graduation rather than as an integrated program to prepare them for professional practice. Your authors encourage accounting undergraduates to take their accounting programs very seriously by looking ahead to the requirements of professional practice and the CIA, CMA, and CPA exams. Accounting practitioners should pursue these certification programs as professional development.

Third, the pass rates are low because accounting programs and curricula at most colleges and universities are not given the budgetary priority they deserve. Accounting faculties are generally understaffed for the number of accounting majors, the number of accounting courses, the nature of accounting courses (problem-oriented vs. descriptive), etc., relative to other faculties. Additionally, accounting curricula generally have not expanded commensurate to the expanding body of accounting knowledge.

SPONSORING ORGANIZATIONS

The CPA designation is controlled by the individual boards of accountancy in the 50 states, Guam, Puerto Rico, the Virgin Islands, and the District of Columbia. Fortunately, all boards of accountancy use the Uniform Certified Public Accountant Examination, which is prepared and graded by the examinations division of the American Institute of Certified Public Accountants (AICPA). For information on taking the examination, write to the board of accountancy for your state; the addresses are provided in the table on page 41.

> The American Institute of CPAs
> 1211 Avenue of the Americas
> New York, NY 10036
> (212) 575-6945

The CIA certification program is sponsored by the Institute of Internal Auditors, which was organized to develop the professional status of internal auditing.

> The Institute of Internal Auditors
> 249 Maitland Avenue
> P.O. Box 1119
> Altamonte Springs, FL 32701
> (407) 830-7600

Chapter 3: The CIA, CMA, and CPA Certification Programs

The National Association of Accountants (NAA) was conceived as an educational organization to develop the individual management accountant professionally and to provide business management with the most advanced techniques and procedures. The Institute of Certified Management Accountants (ICMA) was formed in 1972 by the NAA to offer and administer the CMA examination.

        Institute of Certified Management Accountants
        10 Paragon Drive
        Montvale, NJ 07645-1759
        (201) 573-6300

COST TO OBTAIN AND MAINTAIN PROFESSIONAL CERTIFICATION

The cost to take the CIA exam is a $50 registration fee plus $50 per part examination fee, which totals $250 (assuming you pass all parts the first time you take them). Full-time students can save 50%. See the discussion on page 37. A $20 per year record-keeping fee is charged to maintain CPE records (see below). Membership in the Institute of Internal Auditors is not required.

Membership in the National Association of Accountants is required in order to take the CMA exam. The general NAA membership fee is $115. There is also a $50 per part examination fee. Full-time students may take the CMA examination one time at a reduced fee of $25 per part. See the discussion on page 38.

The cost of the CPA exam varies by state. The table on page 41 lists the examination fee in each state. Additionally, most states require an annual fee to maintain the CPA certificate and/or license.

EDUCATION AND EXPERIENCE REQUIREMENTS

Both the CIA and CMA programs require the equivalent of a baccalaureate degree from an accredited college or university. Both, however, encourage college seniors to apply and take the exam prior to graduation. They also have alternative means of satisfying the education requirement, e.g., satisfactory performance on the Graduate Record Exam, holding a CPA certificate, etc.

Additionally, 2 years of work experience are required prior to the issuance of the CIA or CMA certificate. The experience requirement is broadly interpreted. Government work, public accounting, and other accounting/auditing experience are accepted. The CIA program accepts a graduate degree as 1 year of the 2-year experience requirement.

CONTINUING PROFESSIONAL EDUCATION (CPE) REQUIREMENTS

The IIA, ICMA, and most State Boards of Accountancy have CPE requirements. The IIA and ICMA refer to it as CPD (continuing professional development). The purpose is to promote the development and maintenance of accounting and auditing proficiency for those who have passed initial certification examinations.

For CIAs wishing to have a current CPD listing, the IIA requires 100 CPD hours every 3 years, beginning January 1, 1982. Annual reports on forms sent to CIAs by the IIA must be completed each March in sufficient detail to facilitate verification. Documentation must be kept for 1 year after filing. There is a $20 yearly record-keeping fee. Formal educational programs can qualify for as much as 100% of the CPD requirement. Published writing or oral presentations may each amount to as much as 50%. Participation as an officer, director, governor, committee member, or equivalent in professional organizations, when the participation contributes to the CIA's professional development, may constitute up to 25%.

The ICMA requires 90 CPE hours every 3 years, and annual reporting in July. There is no annual CMA fee; only NAA membership is required. Educational subject matter need only be related to the efficient and effective functioning of management accounting, so management, marketing, behavioral topics, etc. qualify. In addition to professional education seminars, credit toward the CMA's requirements for CPE can be earned through serving as a teacher, home-study courses, employer training programs (but not on-the-job training), technical speeches, publications, and by examination. Fifteen hours of CPE credit is awarded for CMAs who successfully complete a selected section of the June CMA exam on an open-book basis (there is a $75 grading charge).

CPE requirements for CPAs are mandated by individual state boards, which generally require documentation and restrict the nature of the courses allowed. Frequently, a portion of the CPE for CPAs must be earned in accounting or auditing topics. See the table on page 41.

WHEN TO SIT FOR THE EXAMS

Sit for all three examinations as soon as you can. Both the CIA and CMA exams can be taken by students in their senior year and offer a 50% reduction in fees to full-time students (see pages 37 and 38). In many states, you may also take the CPA exam in your last quarter or semester. If you are graduating in June, you may take the CPA exam the first week of May, the CIA exam the second week of May, and the CMA exam the second week of June. Your preparation program for all three exams is quite synergistic and not appreciably more work than preparing for just the CPA exam.

HOW TO REGISTER AND APPLY FOR THE CIA EXAM

First, you are required to **register** for the exam. WRITE FOR YOUR REGISTRATION MATERIALS TODAY (a form is provided on page 42) -- it only takes a few minutes.
The registration form requires employment and education data (see the discussion on page 35). An official transcript (or photocopy of a diploma) providing proof of graduation and a character reference from a CIA or supervisor are also required. The registration fee is $50. The registration form requires knowledge of and adherence to the CIA Code of Ethics (which is reproduced on the reverse side of the registration form). You must register by the end of March for the May exam, and by September 30 for the November sitting.

Second, it is necessary to **apply** each time you wish to sit for the examination. The exam application is very simple (it takes about two minutes to complete). The application fee for each part of the exam is $50. The first time you sit for the exam, you are required to take at least two parts; thereafter you may take one to four parts (you would only take four parts on reexamination if you had failed all parts taken on the initial sitting). Your exam application must be received 45 days prior to the exam, i.e., at the end of March for the May exam.

Finally, remember that you have six consecutive exams, including the one in which the first part is passed, to pass all four parts. You are not required to sit each time an exam is given, but the six-exam period is not extended. If you do not pass all four parts in the six-exam period, you lose credit for the parts passed and you must re-register and start the process again.

SPECIAL STUDENT EXAMINATION FEE FOR THE CIA EXAM

Senior accounting students are eligible for reduced fees (one-half price). The one-time registration fee is $25 (instead of $50), with an additional fee of $25 (instead of $50) per part. Use the form on page 42. The eligibility requirements are that the student must

1. Be a full-time student as defined by the institution in which the student is enrolled (usually a minimum of 12 semester hours for undergraduates and 9 semester hours for graduate students). Students who need fewer hours to fulfill graduation requirements in the final semester will be considered full-time.

2. Register in the certification program of The Institute of Internal Auditors while enrolled in school -- undergraduate students during their final year, graduate students during the year their degree is awarded.

3. Participate in the first Certified Internal Auditor Examination scheduled following registration acceptance. Candidates must take at least two parts of the first examination following registration acceptance. The remaining two parts must be taken at the next examination date in order to be eligible for the reduced examination fee on those parts.

HOW TO APPLY AND REGISTER FOR THE CMA EXAM

First, you are required to **apply** both for membership in the NAA and for admission into the CMA program. Thus, two applications are required if you are not already an NAA member. WRITE FOR YOUR APPLICATION MATERIALS TODAY (a form is provided on page 42) -- it only takes a few minutes. The CMA program application form requires education, employment, and reference data (see the discussion on page 35). You must provide two references: one from your employer and the second from someone other than a family member or fellow employee. Character reference forms will be sent by the ICMA with your application forms. An official transcript providing proof of graduation is also required. There is no application fee other than NAA membership. This application must be filed by March 1 or September 1, respectively, prior to the scheduled exam.

Second, it is necessary to **register** each time you wish to sit for the examination. The exam registration is very simple (it takes about 2 minutes to complete). The registration fee for each part of the exam is $50. Each time you sit for the exam, you are required to take at least two parts (unless you have only one part remaining). Your exam **registration** is due March 1 and September 1 for new applicants, April 1 and October 1 for continuing candidates. Prior to these dates, the ICMA will send you a registration form for the closest CMA exam.

Finally, remember that you have six consecutive exams, starting with the one in which the first part is passed, to pass all five parts. You are not required to sit each time an exam is given, but the six-consecutive-exam period is not extended if you skip one or more sittings.

SPECIAL STUDENT EXAMINATION FEE FOR THE CMA EXAM

Seniors or graduate students carrying 6 hours or more may, during any term, take the examination one time for $25 per part (instead of the regular $50). The procedure is to apply and register at the same time (use the form on page 42). This requires completion and submittal of

1. A completed and signed Confirmation of Student Status form.
2. The standard ICMA application form.
3. A completed examination registration form.
4. A check for $20.00 (NAA membership) plus $25.00 per part for the number of parts to be taken.

Note that the examination fee will be forfeited if no part is taken at the first scheduled examination after registration. A Student Performance Award is presented to the student applicant with the highest scores who passes all parts on the first sitting.

HOW TO OBTAIN *CIA* and *CMA EXAMINATION REVIEW*

CIA Examination Review and *CMA Examination Review* have similar formats and approaches. Each has four important introductory chapters:

1. The CIA or CMA Program: An Overview
2. CIA or CMA Exam: Preparation, Administration, and Grading
3. Preparing to Pass the CIA or CMA Exam
4. Writing the CIA or CMA Examination

Each text then has a chapter for each part of that exam, and each chapter is subdivided into 4 to 9 modules or subtopics. Each module in Volume I (22 in *CIA Examination Review* and 33 in *CMA Examination Review*) contains a comprehensive, easy-to-study outline of the subject matter. Volume II for each manual is divided into those same study modules and contains

1. Multiple-choice questions from recent examinations,
2. Essay questions/computational problems from recent examinations,
3. The IIA or ICMA answers for the multiple-choice questions,
4. One- or two-paragraph explanations of the multiple-choice questions and answers, and
5. The IIA or ICMA suggested solution for each essay question/computational problem, following a one- or two-paragraph commentary on the solutions approach.

Each review manual is a set of two 8½ x 11-inch paperbacks, presented in easy-to-read type styles and spacing. They may be used with or without any other study materials or review courses. The primary objective of each is to provide you with a two-volume, complete, efficient, inexpensive, and effective study program. Each set is all you should need to obtain the knowledge and the confidence to pass the CIA or CMA examination.

Order *CIA Examination Review* and/or *CMA Examination Review* directly from Accounting Publications, Inc. in Gainesville, Florida. Please submit requests to your school's and/or your employer's librarian to acquire these texts. Orders from individuals must be prepaid. Accounting Publications guarantees immediate, complete refund on all mail orders if a resalable text is returned within 30 days. An order form is provided on page 652.

OTHER CERTIFICATION PROGRAMS

Certificate in Data Processing (CDP) -- administered by the Institute for Certification of Computer Professionals (ICCP). The ICCP represents a number of professional computer-related societies, of which the Data Processing Management Association (DPMA) is probably the most closely aligned to the CDP program.

The CDP exam is 300 minutes in length. Its five 60-minute sections test

1. Data Processing Equipment
2. Computer Programming and Software
3. Principles of Management
4. Accounting and Quantitative Methods
5. Systems Analysis and Design

Write to the ICCP for information and an application form:

> Institute for Certification of Computer Professionals
> 35 East Wacker Drive
> Chicago, IL 60601
> (312) 782-9437

Certified Information Systems Auditor (CISA) -- In 1976 the EDP Auditors Association (EDPAA) formed the EDP Auditors Foundation to support research and educational activities. The first examination was administered in 1981. The CISA examination is given once each year. The major topics and their approximate percentage of the test are

Application Systems Controls	20%
Data Integrity Review	12%
Systems Development Life	5%
Application Development Review	9%
Maintenance Review	12%
General Operational Procedures	14%
Security Review	5%
Systems Software Review	6%
Acquisition Review	3%
Data Processing Resource Management Review	5%
Information Systems Audit	9%
	100%

The test application, administration, etc. is done by ETS in Princeton, New Jersey. Write to the EDP Auditors Foundation for a CISA Bulletin of Information and application form. You need their bulletin to apply for the examination because item 16 on the application requires you to affirm your acceptance of the test conditions, procedures, rules, etc. in the Bulletin of Information.

EDP Auditors Foundation, Inc.
373 South Schmale Road
Carol Stream, IL 60187
(312) 682-1200

Other professional accounting-related designations include CBA (Chartered Bank Auditor), CFA (Chartered Financial Analyst), and Enrolled Agent (one enrolled to practice before the IRS).

INDIVIDUAL STATE CPA REQUIREMENTS

Even though there is a Uniform CPA Examination, there is no national CPA certificate. Candidates must comply with the requirements of a specific state to receive a CPA certificate. The following comments and the table of individual state requirements (taken from *CPA Examination Review*) are general and subject to revision, exceptions, interpretations, etc.

1. **Education.** Most jurisdictions require a college degree or equivalent. Many states allow candidates to take the exam in their last quarter or semester. Two jurisdictions do not presently require any college education, and five jurisdictions require only 2 years of college. Some jurisdictions accept experience in lieu of education.

2. **Application Dates.** Many candidates are precluded from sitting for the exam because they fail to apply within the stated registration period.

3. **Exam Fee.** The fees listed on the accompanying table are for first-time candidates. The fee for reexamination candidates is usually less than for first-time candidates. Conditional candidates' fees are often based on the sections remaining.

4. **Conditional Requirements.** Conditional status is granted to candidates who pass some, but not all, sections. Conditional candidates are only required to take the remaining sections of the exam. The notation "2 or P, 50" means that to receive conditional status, candidates must pass two sections or Practice and not receive a grade lower than 50% on the sections failed.

5. **Life of Conditional Status.** Most states limit the length of conditional status. If candidates do not successfully complete the remaining sections within the time limit, they must retake all four sections, i.e., start over. The notation "3Y" means 3 years, and "6NE" means the next six exams.

6. **Experience Requirements.** Most states have experience requirements, with many exceptions, substitutes, etc. For example, many states allow substitution of postgraduate study for a portion or all of the experience requirements. Almost all states allow some form of experience other than public accounting.

7. **Continuing Education Requirements.** There is a substantial movement toward requiring CPAs to undertake continuing professional education. The requirements are generally specified as a number of hours per year(s), e.g., 120 hours every 3 years. The hour requirement is classroom hours, not college credit hours.

8. **Citizenship and Residency.** (Not listed on the accompanying table.) About one-half of the jurisdictions require U.S. citizenship or intent to apply for U.S. citizenship. Most jurisdictions have a residency requirement. Some require candidates to be a legal resident of the state, others require employment in the state, and others accept either.

9. Contact your state board to confirm the data appearing on the opposite page or for an interpretation of your specific situation.

CPA REQUIREMENTS BY STATE

Residency: If required, R indicates residency requirement.

Ethics test: If required, E indicates separate ethics test.

Certificate separate from license to practice: Indicated by an "X."

Education required to take exam: HS = high school; B = bachelors; B-A = bachelors with accounting major; + = hours in excess of bachelors.

Experience required for certificate (or license if not separate from certificate): Years correspond to education levels just to left. Asterisk means <u>additional</u> education beyond bachelors will apply toward experience requirement.

Condition requirement: Number of parts to pass, or P for practice, followed by minimum grade on other parts, if any.

Application deadlines: New candidates, followed by repeat candidates.

Exam fee: For all four parts, usually less if conditioned.

CPA REQUIREMENTS BY STATE

NOTE: The information below continuously changes. Contact your State Board for complete up-to-date requirements.

STATE BOARD • Address	Telephone #	Residency	Ethics	Separate Certificate	Education	Experience	Application Deadline First Time	Application Deadline Re-Exam	Condition Requirements	Exam Fee
AK P.O. Box D • Juneau, AK • 99811	(907) 465-2580	R	E		2/B/BA	4/3/2	60 days	60 days	2 or P	$70
AL 20 Com. Row • 529 S. Perry St. • Montgomery, AL • 36104	(205) 834-7651	--	E		B	2	2/28; 8/31	3/31; 9/30	2 or P	$150
AR 1515 W. 7th Street, Suite 320 • Little Rock, AR • 72202	(501) 682-1520	R	--	X	B-A	0	60 days	30 days	2 or P, 50	$125
AZ 3110 N. 19th Avenue • Suite 140 • Phoenix, AZ • 85015	(602) 255-3648	R	E		B-A	2*	2/28; 8/31	2/28; 8/31	2 or P	$100
CA 2135 Butano Drive • Suite 112 • Sacramento, CA • 95825	(916) 920-7121	--	E		2/B-A	4/3*	3/1; 9/1	3/1; 9/1	2 or P	$75
CO 1525 Sherman St., Room 617 • Denver, CO • 80203-1760	(303) 866-2869	--	E		B-A	1	3/1; 9/1	3/1; 9/1	2 or P	varies
CT 30 Trinity Street • Hartford, CT • 06106	(203) 566-7835	R	E		B-A	3*	60 days	60 days	2 or P, 50	$100
DC 614 N Street, N.W. • Room 923 • Washington, DC • 20001	(202) 727-7468	R	--	X	B-A	0	90 days	60 days	2 or P	$100
DE P.O. Box 1401 • Dover, DE • 19903	(302) 738-6065		E	X	2-A	0	3/1; 9/1	3/1; 9/1	2 or P, 75	$125
FL 4001 NW 43rd St. • Suite 16 • Gainesville, FL • 32606	(904) 336-2165	--	E		B/+30	0	2/1; 8/1	3/1; 9/1	2 or P, 50	$125
GA 166 Pryor Street, S.W. • Atlanta, GA • 30303	(404) 656-3941	--	--		B-A	2, 1	2/1; 8/1	3/1; 9/1	2, 40	$125
GU P.O. Box P • Agana, Guam • 96910	(671) 646-6987	R	--		B-A	2*	60 days	60 days	2 or P, 50	$35
HI P.O. Box 3469 • Honolulu, HI • 96801	(808) 548-7471	--	E		B/+30	2	3/1; 9/1	3/1; 9/1	2 or P, 50	$100
IA 1918 S.E. Hulsizer Avenue • Ankeny, IA • 50021	(515) 281-4126	R	E	X	HS/B-A	3/0	2/28; 8/31	2/28; 8/31	2 or P	$90
ID 500 S. Tenth Street • Suite 104 • Boise, ID • 83720	(208) 334-2490	R	E		B-A	1	3/1; 9/1	3/1; 9/1	2 or P, 50	$100
IL 10 Admin. Bldg • 506 S. Wright St. • Urbana, IL • 61801	(217) 333-1565	--	--	X	4-A	0	3/1; 9/1	3/1; 9/1	2 or P	$180
IN 1021 State Office Building • Indianapolis, IN • 46204	(317) 232-3898	R	E		B-A	3*, I	3/1; 9/1	3/1; 9/1	2, 50	$135
KS 900 S.W. Jackson Street • Topeka, KS • 66612	(913) 296-2161	--	E	X	B-A	0	3/15; 9/15	3/15; 9/15	2, 50	$120
KY 332 W. Broadway • Suite 310 • Louisville, KY • 40202	(502) 588-3037	R	E		B-A	2*	3/1; 9/1	3/1; 9/1	2 or P, 50	$100
LA 1515 WTC • 2 Canal Street • New Orleans, LA • 70130	(504) 566-1244	R	--	X	B-A	0	3/1; 9/1	3/1; 9/1	2, 50	$100
MA 100 Cambridge St. • Room 1514 • Boston, MA • 02202	(617) 727-1753	--	--		B	3*	42 days	42 days	2 or P, 50	$130
MD 501 St. Paul Street • Room 902 • Baltimore, MD • 21202	(301) 333-5322	--	E		B-A	0	60 days	60 days	2 or P, 50	$70
ME State House Station 35 • Augusta, ME • 04333	(207) 289-3671	R	--		B	2*	4/15; 10/1	4/15; 10/1	2 or P	$80
MI P.O. Box 30018 • Lansing, MI • 48090	(517) 373-0682	--	--		B-A	2*	60 days	60 days	2 or P, 50	$115
MN Metro Square Bldg • Fifth Floor • St. Paul, MN • 55101	(612) 296-7937	--	E		HS/2/B/BA	5/3/1/0	60 days	60 days	2, 50	$115
MO P.O. Box 613 • Jefferson City, MO • 65102	(314) 751-2334	R	E	X	B-A	0	3/1; 9/1	3/1; 9/1	2 or P	$100
MS P.O. Box 55447 • Jackson, MS • 39216	(601) 981-3773	R	--	X	B	0	3/15; 9/15	3/15; 9/15	2 or P, 45	$92
MT 1424 9th Avenue • Helena, MT • 59620-0407	(406) 444-3739	--	E	X	B-A	0	3/15; 9/15	3/15; 9/15	2 or P, 50	$100
NC P.O. Box 12827 • Raleigh, NC • 27605	(919) 821-2443	R	E		B-A	2*	2/28; 8/31	2/28; 8/31	2 or P	$125
ND Box 8104 • University Station • Grand Forks, ND • 58202	(701) 777-3869	R	E		HS/B-A	4/0	3/15; 9/15	3/15; 9/15	2 or P	$112.50
NE P.O. Box 94725 • Lincoln, NE • 68509	(402) 471-3595	R	E	X	B	0	3/31; 9/30	3/31; 9/30	2 or P, 50	$120
NH 2½ Beacon Street • Concord, NH • 03301-4447	(603) 271-3286	R	--		B	2*	4/1; 10/1	4/1; 10/1	2, 50	$125
NJ 1100 Raymond Blvd • Room 507-A • Newark, NJ • 07102	(201) 648-3240	R	--		B-A	2*	3/1; 9/1	3/1; 9/1	2 or P, 50	$100
NM 4125 Carlisle Boulevard, N.E. • Albuquerque, NM • 87107	(505) 841-6524	R	E	X	B-A	0	3/1; 9/1	3/1; 9/1	2	$125
NV One E. Liberty Street • Suite 311 • Reno, NV • 89501	(702) 786-0231	R	E		B-A	2	3/1; 9/1	3/1; 9/1	2 or P, 35	$120
NY Cultural Ed. Center • Room 3011 • Albany, NY • 12230	(518) 474-3836	--	--		HS/B-A	2*	90 days	60 days	2 or P	$245
OH 65 S. Front Street • Suite 222 • Columbus, OH • 43215	(614) 466-4135	R	E		B-A	2*	3/1; 9/1	4/1; 10/1	1, 40	$120
OK 6600 N. Harvey, Ste 130, Bldg #6 • Ok. City, OK • 73116	(405) 521-2397	R	--		HS/B-A	3/0	60 days	60 days	2 or P	$100
OR 403 Labor & Industries Building • Salem, OR • 97310	(503) 378-4181	--	E		B-A	/2*	3/1; 9/1	3/1; 9/1	2 or P, 50	$75
PA P.O. Box 2649 • Harrisburg, PA • 17105-2649	(717) 783-1404	R	--		B-A	2*	2/15; 8/15	2/15; 8/15	1, 20	$80
PR Box 3271 • San Juan, Puerto Rico • 00904	(809) 722-2122	R	--		HS/B/B-A	6/4/0, I	60 days	60 days	2	$50
RI 100 N. Main Street • Providence, RI • 02903	(401) 277-3185	--	E		B-A	2*	45 days	45 days	2 or P	$125
SC 800 Dutch Square Blvd • Ste 260 • Columbia, SC • 29210	(803) 737-9266	R	E		B-A	2	3/15; 9/15	3/15; 9/15	2 or P, 40	$100
SD 1509 S. Minnesota Ave. • Ste 1 • Sioux Falls, SD • 57105	(605) 339-6746	--	E	X	B-A	0	50 days	50 days	2 or P, 50	$165
TN 1808 West End Bldg • 10th Floor • Nashville, TN • 37219	(615) 741-2550	R	E	X	B-A	0	3/1; 9/1	3/1; 9/1	2 or P	$75
TX 1033 LaPosada • Suite 340 • Austin, TX • 78752-3892	(512) 451-0241	--	E		2/B-A	6/2*	2/28; 8/31	2/28; 8/31	2	$100
UT 160 E 300 St., S • Box 45802 • Salt Lake City, UT • 84145	(801) 530-6628	R	E	X	B-A/+30	0	60 days	60 days	2 or P, 50	$165
VA 3600 West Broad Street • Richmond, VA • 23230	(804) 367-8505	--	E	X	B-A	0	60 days	60 days	2 or P, 50	$90
VI 1-B King St. • Christiansted, St. Croix • Vir. Is. • 00820	(809) 773-0096	R	--		HS/B/B-A	6/3/2	3/15; 9/15	3/15; 9/15	2	$100
VT 26 Terrace Street • Montpelier, VT • 05602	(802) 828-2363	R	E		2-A	2	4/1; 10/1	4/1; 10/1	2 or P	$100
WA 210 E. Union Street • Box 9131 • Olympia, WA • 98504	(206) 753-2585	--	E	X	B-A	0	3/1; 9/1	3/1; 9/1	2 or P, 75	$125
WI P.O. Box 8935 • Madison, WI • 53708	(608) 266-3020	R	E		B-A	3	3/1; 9/1	3/1; 9/1	2, 50	$102.50
WV 204 L&S Bldg • 812 Quarrier St. • Charleston, WV • 25301	(304) 348-3557	R	E		B-A	0	3/1; 9/1	3/1; 9/1	1	$40
WY Barrett Building • Third Floor • Cheyenne, WY • 82002	(307) 777-7551	R	E	X	B-A	0	3/15; 9/15	3/15; 9/15	2 or P	$159

TO: CIA Program
        Institute of Internal Auditors
        Post Office Box 1119
        Altamonte Springs, FL 32701

FROM: _____
        _____
        _____
        _____

Please send me information about the CIA program, including application and registration forms complete with instructions.

        _____ I am a full-time student and would like the appropriate materials for taking the CIA exam at the special student rate.

- -

TO: Institute of Certified Management Accountants
        Dept. IG - 10 Paragon Drive
        Montvale, NJ 07645-1759

FROM: _____
        _____
        _____
        _____

Please send me information about the CMA program, including application and registration forms complete with instructions

        _____ I am a full-time student and would like the appropriate materials for taking the CMA exam at the special student rate.

CHAPTER FOUR
COST ACCOUNTING TERMINOLOGY AND OVERVIEW

4.1 Cost vs. Managerial Accounting	(18 questions)	43
4.2 Cost of Goods Manufactured	(14 questions)	48
4.3 Variable vs. Fixed Costs	(18 questions)	52
4.4 Product vs. Period Costs	(19 questions)	57
4.5 Other Cost Definitions	(30 questions)	62
4.6 Cost Accounting Standards Board (CASB)	(3 questions)	70

The purpose of this chapter is to present introductory definitional material which usually appears in the first chapter or two of most basic cost/managerial accounting texts. Some of the questions presuppose knowledge of topics appearing in subsequent chapters, but they are nonetheless included to supplement an introduction to the "basics" of cost/managerial accounting. The "management process" and "control loop" are also covered because of the relationship of cost/managerial accounting to the planning and control functions of management.

The following abbreviations are used in this chapter:

CGM -- Cost of goods manufactured
CGS -- Cost of goods sold (cost of sales)
BWIP -- Beginning work-in-process (manufacturing account)
EWIP -- Ending work-in-process (manufacturing account)

4.1 Cost vs. Managerial Accounting

1. Managerial accounting differs from financial accounting in that financial accounting is

  a. More oriented toward the future.
  b. Primarily concerned with external financial reporting.
  c. Concerned with nonquantitative information.
  d. Heavily involved with decision analysis and implementation of decisions.
  e. None of the above.

The correct answer is (b). *(Publisher)*
REQUIRED: The concept that applies more to financial than to managerial accounting.
DISCUSSION: Financial accounting is primarily concerned with historical accounting, i.e., traditional financial statements, and with external financial reporting to creditors and shareholders. Managerial accounting deals primarily with the planning and control of organizational operations, considers nonquantitative information, and is usually less precise.
Answers (a), (c), and (d) are incorrect because each describes a characteristic of managerial accounting.

Module 4.1: Cost vs. Managerial Accounting

2. In a broad sense, cost accounting can be defined within the accounting system as

   a. Internal and external reporting that may be used in making nonroutine decisions and in developing plans and policies.
   b. External reporting to government, various outside parties, and stockholders.
   c. Internal reporting for use in management planning and control, and external reporting to the extent its product-costing function satisfies external reporting requirements.
   d. Internal reporting for use in planning and controlling routine operations.

The correct answer is (c). *(Publisher)*
REQUIRED: The definition of cost accounting within the accounting system.
DISCUSSION: Cost accounting is a combination of 1) managerial accounting in the sense that its purpose can be to provide internal reports for use in planning and control, and in making nonroutine decisions, and 2) financial accounting since its product costing function satisfies external reporting requirements for reporting to shareholders, government, and various outside parties.
Answer (a) is incorrect because cost accounting is concerned with more than just reporting to be used in making nonroutine decisions. Answer (b) is incorrect because cost accounting also provides information for internal reporting. Answer (d) is incorrect because this is an aspect of managerial accounting.

3. If a distinction is made between cost accounting and managerial accounting, managerial accounting is more oriented toward

   a. Valuation of inventory.
   b. Analysis of variances including spoilage.
   c. Financial reporting to third parties.
   d. The planning and controlling aspects of the management process.

The correct answer is (d). *(Publisher)*
REQUIRED: How managerial accounting differs from cost accounting.
DISCUSSION: Managerial accounting is concerned with the planning and control aspects of the organization's operations.
Answers (a) and (b) are incorrect because cost accounting emphasizes accounting for costs incurred in the manufacturing process, i.e., historical or past costs. Answer (c) is incorrect because cost accounting helps generate the inventory figures that are used in the financial statements, which in turn become the basis for financial reporting to third parties.

4. Management accountants help develop and maintain reporting systems that are aligned with organizational structures and that provide useful information on an organization's performance. Management decision processes fall into three categories. These three categories are

   a. Nonrepetitive, nonprogrammed, and nonstrategic.
   b. Repetitive, nonprogrammed, and strategic.
   c. Repetitive, nonprogrammed, and nonstrategic.
   d. Nonrepetitive, nonprogrammed, and strategic.
   e. Repetitive, programmed, and strategic.

The correct answer is (b). *(CMA 1286 5-1)*
REQUIRED: The three categories of management decision processes.
DISCUSSION: Decision making can be classified variously. For example, repetitive decisions concern routine, programmable, day-to-day matters, e.g., the automatic reordering of stock when it reaches a predetermined level. Nonprogrammed decisions involve the shorter-term, tactical implementation of the strategic decisions. Strategic decisions concern setting long-term goals and objectives and making other overall ongoing decisions for the entity.

5. The basic management process does not include

   a. Planning.
   b. Organizing.
   c. Rationalizing.
   d. Directing.
   e. Controlling.

The correct answer is (c). *(Publisher)*
REQUIRED: The function not a part of the basic management process.
DISCUSSION: Planning involves setting standards and defining goals. Organizing is the development of the entity's personnel structure to achieve the goals set by the planners. Directing is the process of managing the organization and its operations to achieve goals. Controlling is the process that provides feedback of actual results to be compared with those planned. Planning, organizing, directing, and controlling are all parts of the basic management process. Rationalizing is the process of ascribing to one's behavior, opinions, etc. motives that seem valid but are not the actual, possibly subconscious causes.

Module 4.1: Cost vs. Managerial Accounting

6. The control loop in a management system contains four sequential steps, including

1) Implementing a program of corrective action.
2) Analyzing and comparing actual performance with the standards.
3) Measuring actual performance.
4) Establishing standards of performance.

The proper sequence of these activities is

a. 3, 4, 1, 2.
b. 4, 3, 2, 1.
c. 4, 2, 3, 1.
d. 3, 4, 2, 1.

The correct answer is (b). *(Publisher)*
REQUIRED: The appropriate sequence of steps in a management control loop.
DISCUSSION: A management control loop involves

1) Establishing standards for performance,
2) Measuring the actual performance,
3) Analyzing performance and comparing it with standards, and
4) Implementing a program of corrective action.

7. Budgeting is which step in the control loop process?

a. Constructing and implementing a program of corrective action.
b. Analyzing and comparing actual performance with standards.
c. Measuring the actual performance.
d. Establishing standards of performance.

The correct answer is (d). *(Publisher)*
REQUIRED: The function of budgeting in the management control loop.
DISCUSSION: Budgeting is the formal quantification of management's plans. Budgets are usually expressed in quantitative terms and are used to motivate management and evaluate its performance in achieving goals. In this sense, "standards" are established.
Answers (a), (b), and (c) are incorrect because each is a step in the control loop that follows setting standards (the budget).

8. In a management control system, feedback is critical. Feedback

a. Compares actual performance with standard results.
b. Is based on historical data.
c. Is a process of reviewing and revising the standards.
d. Is the program of corrective action.

The correct answer is (a). *(Publisher)*
REQUIRED: The definition of feedback in a control system.
DISCUSSION: Management cannot evaluate its progress toward objectives without comparing actual results with standards. This comparison is feedback. Analyzing variances from standard costs is an example of feedback.
Answer (b) is incorrect because feedback is based on standard (estimated) costs rather than the actual (historical) costs. Answers (c) and (d) are incorrect because each process follows the comparison of actual performance with standards in the control loop.

9. What is meant by management by exception?

a. Management emphasizes activities responsible for production and sale of goods and/or services.
b. Management emphasizes providing other units of the enterprise with specialized service including advice and assistance.
c. Management attention is devoted primarily to activities that do not meet expectations.
d. Each manager cannot supervise more than six to eight people efficiently.
e. The less management involvement in activities, the more efficient the organization.

The correct answer is (c). *(Publisher)*
REQUIRED: The meaning of management by exception.
DISCUSSION: Management by exception focuses the attention of management on those areas in which results deviate from established standards. Thus, not all operations need to be reviewed, only those that deviate from planned or budgeted activity.
Answer (a) is incorrect because it defines line activity. Answer (b) is incorrect because it describes staff activity. Answer (d) is incorrect because it states the span-of-control principle. Answer (e) is incorrect because management is a necessary function within every organization.

10. When should management implement a different and/or more expensive accounting system?

   a. Only when the cost of the system exceeds the benefits.
   b. Only when management thinks it appropriate.
   c. Only when the board of directors dictates a change.
   d. Only when the benefits of the system exceed the cost.

The correct answer is (d). *(Publisher)*
   REQUIRED: The reason for using a different and/or more expensive accounting system.
   DISCUSSION: Changing to a different and/or more expensive accounting system requires cost/benefit analysis. Changes should be undertaken only if the benefits of the proposed change exceed its cost.
   Answer (a) is incorrect because it is economically irrational to implement a system in which the cost exceeds the benefits. Answers (b) and (c) are incorrect because each implies ignoring cost/benefit analysis and selecting an accounting system on other than an objective basis.

11. Cost/managerial accounting systems are goods in the economic sense and, as such, their benefits must exceed their costs. When managerial accounting systems change, which cost is frequently ignored?

   a. Educating users.
   b. Gathering data.
   c. Analyzing data.
   d. Training accounting staff.
   e. Preparing reports.

The correct answer is (a). *(Publisher)*
   REQUIRED: The cost typically ignored in cost/benefit analysis of proposed changes in accounting systems.
   DISCUSSION: Users, i.e., managers, must be both willing and able to use new accounting systems. Accordingly, they should be encouraged to participate in the design and implementation of the new system. If they do not, they may not understand or want to use the new information.
   Answers (b), (c), (d), and (e) are incorrect because each is a more direct cost of changing managerial accounting systems and is usually considered.

12. Management accountants generally exercise which type of authority?

   a. Company.
   b. Functional.
   c. Line.
   d. Staff.

The correct answer is (d). *(Publisher)*
   REQUIRED: The type of authority exercised by management accountants.
   DISCUSSION: Management accountants perform a staff function in that they provide data to managers and others without directing the decision-making process. They facilitate this process by acting in an advisory capacity.
   Answer (a) is incorrect because company authority is a nonsense term. Answer (b) is incorrect because functional authority is the right to command horizontally as well as downward. Answer (c) is incorrect because line authority includes the power to direct. Line personnel have operational responsibilities. Management accountants generally do not exercise such authority except over their respective staff subordinates.

13. What kind of authority is exercised over subordinates?

   a. Functional.
   b. Line.
   c. Company.
   d. Staff.

The correct answer is (b). *(Publisher)*
   REQUIRED: The term describing the authority exercised over subordinates.
   DISCUSSION: A distinction is made between "line" and "staff" authority. Line personnel are concerned with the production of goods and services that are going to be sold, rendered, etc. Staff personnel provide assistance to line personnel. Accordingly, their function is advisory rather than directive. Line managers exercise line authority over their subordinates. Staff managers also exercise line authority over their respective subordinates.
   Answer (a) is incorrect because functional authority is the right to command both horizontally and downward. Answer (c) is incorrect because company authority is a nonsense term. Answer (d) is incorrect because staff authority refers to advisory rather than authoritative capacity.

Module 4.1: Cost vs. Managerial Accounting

14. Controllers are generally not concerned with

   a. Preparation of tax returns.

   b. Reporting to government.

   c. Protection of assets.

   d. Investor relations.

   e. Planning and control.

The correct answer is (d). *(Publisher)*
REQUIRED: The activity with which controllers are usually not concerned.
DISCUSSION: Controllers are generally in charge of budgets, accounting, accounting reports, and related controls, as opposed to treasurers, who are generally involved with control over cash, receivables, short-term investments, financing, and insurance. Thus, treasurers rather than controllers are concerned with investor relations.
Answers (a), (b), (c), and (e) are incorrect because each is a typical controller responsibility.

15. The treasurer function is usually not concerned with

   a. Investor relations.

   b. Financial reports.

   c. Short-term financing.

   d. Cash custody and banking.

   e. Credit extension and collection of bad debts.

The correct answer is (b). *(Publisher)*
REQUIRED: The function usually not fulfilled by the treasurer.
DISCUSSION: Treasurers are generally concerned with investing cash and near-cash assets, the provision of capital, investor relations, insurance, etc. Controllers, on the other hand, are responsible for the reporting and accounting activities of an organization, including financial reporting.
Answers (a), (c), (d), and (e) are incorrect because each lies within the normal range of treasurer functions.

16. For which of the following purposes is feedback least likely to be used in control systems?

   a. Modifying goals.

   b. Altering predictions.

   c. Allocating costs to finished products.

   d. Changing the operating process.

   e. Changing the reward system for performance.

The correct answer is (c). *(Publisher)*
REQUIRED: A function least likely to be performed by feedback in control systems.
DISCUSSION: Feedback, one of the final steps in the control loop, involves comparing actual with budgeted performance. It is used for a variety of purposes such as changing goals and making predictions. Feedback has no impact on the allocation of cost to product. This is a function of cost accounting, whereas feedback is a function of planning and control.
Answers (a), (b), (d), and (e) are incorrect because each is an example of the effects of feedback.

17. The professional organization that represents management accountants in the United States is the

   a. American Institute of Certified Public Accountants (AICPA).

   b. Institute of Internal Auditors (IIA).

   c. Institute of Certified Management Accountants (ICMA).

   d. National Association of Accountants (NAA).

The correct answer is (d). *(Publisher)*
REQUIRED: The professional organization representing management accountants in the U.S.
DISCUSSION: The primary purpose of the NAA is to enhance the professionalism of management accountants. Membership is open to all persons interested in management accounting. Unlike the AICPA, which restricts membership to CPAs, the NAA does not require a member to have a CMA certificate.
Answer (a) is incorrect because the AICPA primarily represents the public accounting profession. Answer (b) is incorrect because the IIA represents internal auditors. Answer (c) is incorrect because the ICMA is a division of the NAA that administers the Certificate in Management Accounting (CMA) program.

18. The professional certification program most suited for one interested in a career in management accounting leads to which of the following designations?

   a. CDP.
   b. CIA.
   c. CISA.
   d. CMA.
   e. CPA.

The correct answer is (d). *(Publisher)*
REQUIRED: The professional certification program most appropriate for a career in management accounting.
DISCUSSION: The Certificate in Management Accounting (CMA) is offered by the National Association of Accountants through its Institute of Certified Management Accountants. The CMA certificate is awarded those who pass five, three-and-a-half hour examinations on economics and business finance; organization and behavior, including ethical considerations; public reporting standards, auditing, and taxes; internal reporting and analysis; and decision analysis, including modeling and information systems.
   Answer (a) is incorrect because a Certificate in Data Processing (CDP) is appropriate for those interested in data processing and is issued by the Institute for Certification of Computer Professionals. Answer (b) is incorrect because the Certified Internal Auditor (CIA) program is appropriate for internal auditors and is offered by the Institute of Internal Auditors. Answer (c) is incorrect because a Certified Information Systems Auditor (CISA) is a specialist in auditing EDP systems. The certificate is offered by the EDP Auditors Association. Answer (e) is incorrect because the Certified Public Accountant (CPA) certificate is appropriate for those going into public accounting and is offered through the various state boards of accountancy which use the AICPA uniform CPA examination.

4.2 Cost of Goods Manufactured

19. In a retailing enterprise, the income statement includes cost of goods sold. Cost of goods sold is, in effect, purchases adjusted for changes in inventory. In a manufacturing company, the purchases account is replaced by which account?

   a. Inventory.
   b. Cost of goods manufactured.
   c. Finished goods.
   d. Cost of sales.

The correct answer is (b). *(Publisher)*
REQUIRED: The account in a manufacturing company equivalent to purchases.
DISCUSSION: Instead of purchasing goods and services for resale, a manufacturing company manufactures goods and services for sale. Accordingly, the CGM account is similar to the purchases account. CGS is equal to the BI of finished goods plus CGM less the EI of finished goods. CGM includes the costs of labor, materials, and overhead for goods completed within the current period and transferred to finished goods inventory.
   Answers (a) and (c) are incorrect because both manufacturing and retailing companies have inventory accounts, e.g., finished goods, WIP, and raw materials. Answer (d) is incorrect because cost of sales is essentially purchases or CGM adjusted for changes in inventory.

20. The formula for cost of goods manufactured is

   a. Beginning inventory plus purchases minus ending inventory.
   b. Beginning work-in-process plus direct labor plus materials plus overhead minus ending work-in-process.
   c. Direct materials plus direct labor plus overhead applied.
   d. Direct materials plus direct labor plus overhead incurred plus beginning work-in-process.

The correct answer is (b). *(Publisher)*
REQUIRED: The formula for cost of goods manufactured.
DISCUSSION: CGM includes all the costs incurred (direct labor, materials, and overhead) in the current period plus the costs accumulated in BWIP, less the costs in EWIP.
   Answer (a) is incorrect because it is the formula for cost of sales for a retailing organization. Answer (c) is incorrect because it is the sum of the costs incurred in the present period. Answer (d) is incorrect because it is the total of costs in the manufacturing account that must be allocated between goods completed this period (CGM) and goods that remain in production (EWIP).

21. Which is the best explanation of traditional "cost accounting"?

   a. The entire general ledger and subsidiary ledgers and related journals, etc. of a manufacturer.

   b. The general ledger and subsidiary accounts and related records, etc. used to accumulate the cost of goods or services provided by an entity.

   c. The accounts used to determine the costs of goods sold by an entity.

   d. All of the journals, ledgers, records, and financial statements utilized by an enterprise to record, classify, summarize, and report economic activity of an enterprise.

The correct answer is (b). *(Publisher)*
REQUIRED: The best explanation of traditional "cost accounting."
DISCUSSION: Cost accounting includes all of the accounts and records used to accumulate the cost of goods and services provided by an entity. In a retail enterprise, the inventory accounts, i.e., accounts for the costs of goods purchased from others for resale, serve this function. In manufacturing companies, service enterprises, etc., goods and services are created by the enterprise rather than purchased from others. The accounting for the costs of these enterprises is a cost accounting system.
Answer (a) is incorrect because the entire general ledger and subsidiary ledgers serve many other financial accounting functions besides the accumulation of cost data. Answer (c) is incorrect because a retailer uses only inventory and CGS accounts to determine CGS. In a manufacturing company, other accounts are used in the costing system, such as WIP and FG. Answer (d) is incorrect because it describes the accounting system in general.

22. If BWIP is $90, and $100 of direct labor cost, $200 of overhead cost, and $250 of material cost are incurred during the period, what is the cost of goods manufactured if EWIP is $50?

   a. $440.

   b. $540.

   c. $590.

   d. $640.

The correct answer is (c). *(Publisher)*
REQUIRED: The CGM given BWIP, EWIP, direct labor, overhead, and material costs.
DISCUSSION: The total of the debits to the manufacturing account is $640 (BWIP $90, direct labor $100, overhead $200, and material $250). If there were no ending inventory (i.e., if all goods worked on were completed), the entire CGM during the period would be $640. However, the $50 of EWIP represents goods that were not completed. Thus, the CGM is $590 ($640 - $50).

23. Given that the total of the debits to the manufacturing account (including BWIP) was $740 during the period and the cost of goods manufactured was $630, what was the cost of incomplete goods (EWIP) at the end of the period?

   a. $0.

   b. $110.

   c. $240.

   d. $1,370.

The correct answer is (b). *(Publisher)*
REQUIRED: The cost of work-in-process at the end of the period.
DISCUSSION: Total manufacturing costs incurred including BWIP are given as $740. If no goods were completed during the period, the value of EWIP would be $740. Since the value of goods that were completed is given as $630, $110 ($740 - $630) must represent EWIP.

Module 4.2: Cost of Goods Manufactured

24. The cost of goods manufactured statement is

a. A summarized presentation of the details of transactions recorded in the manufacturing (work-in-process) account.

b. A reconciliation of the income statement and balance sheet of a manufacturing company.

c. A report of standard costs, variance analysis, and allocation of variances to inventory and cost of goods sold accounts.

d. The cost of goods sold for a manufacturing company.

The correct answer is (a). *(Publisher)*
REQUIRED: The composition of a cost of goods manufactured statement.
DISCUSSION: A CGM statement summarizes the activity accounted for in the manufacturing account. This includes all the manufacturing costs incurred (debited to the account) during the period, i.e., BWIP, materials, labor, and overhead. EWIP, the amount not transferred to finished goods, is deducted from the total manufacturing cost for the period (note this includes BWIP) to give CGM.
Answer (b) is incorrect because income statements and balance sheets are not reconciled. A balance sheet is a statement of financial position at a given date. Income statements are reports of inflows and outflows during a period. Answer (c) is incorrect because the CGM statement can be prepared even when standard costs are not used. Answer (d) is incorrect because the CGS for a manufacturing company is the CGM adjusted for the change in finished goods inventory.

25. Theoretically, cash discounts permitted on purchased raw materials should be

a. Added to other income, whether taken or not.

b. Added to other income, only if taken.

c. Deducted from inventory, whether taken or not.

d. Deducted from inventory, only if taken.

The correct answer is (c). *(CPA 586 T-10)*
REQUIRED: The treatment of cash discounts on purchases.
DISCUSSION: In theory, cash discounts on purchases should be treated as reductions in the invoiced prices of specific purchases so that goods available for sale reflects the purchase price net of the discounts. Any purchase discounts not taken are recorded as losses in the income statement. The net method is preferable to recording inventories and payables at gross amounts because the discounted amounts are the most accurate exchange prices. Moreover, since the return on taking cash discounts will usually exceed the firm's cost of capital, the net method is also preferable because it measures management's stewardship by recording as financing charges any discounts not taken.
Answers (a) and (b) are incorrect because cash discounts are never added to other income whether using the gross or net methods. Answer (d) is incorrect because it describes the gross method, which is theoretically inferior to the net method.

26. Paul Company has a recent gross profit history of 40% of net sales. The following data are available from Paul's accounting records for the three months ended March 31:

Inventory at January 1	$ 650,000
Purchases	3,200,000
Net sales	4,500,000
Purchase returns	75,000
Freight-in	50,000

Using the gross profit method, the estimated cost of goods sold for the three months ended March 31 should be

a. $1,800,000.

b. $2,700,000.

c. $3,775,000.

d. $3,825,000.

The correct answer is (b). *(CPA 1186 P-41)*
REQUIRED: The estimated cost of goods sold using the gross profit method.
DISCUSSION: By definition, gross profit is the excess of sales over the cost of goods sold. If the gross profit is 40% of net sales, cost of goods sold is 60% of net sales (100% - 40%). Therefore, the estimated cost of goods sold is $2,700,000 (60% x $4,500,000 net sales).

Module 4.2: Cost of Goods Manufactured

27. The following cost data were taken from the records of a manufacturing company:

Depreciation on factory equipment	$ 1,000
Depreciation on sales office	500
Advertising	7,000
Freight-out (shipping)	3,000
Wages of production workers	28,000
Raw materials used	47,000
Sales salaries and commissions	10,000
Factory rent	2,000
Factory insurance	500
Materials handling	1,500
Administrative salaries	2,000

Based upon the above information, the manufacturing costs incurred during the year was

a. $78,500.
b. $80,000.
c. $80,500.
d. $83,000.

The correct answer is (b). *(CIA 1185 IV-1)*
REQUIRED: The amount of manufacturing cost incurred during the year.
DISCUSSION: Manufacturing costs include direct labor, direct materials, and any other indirect costs (overhead) connected with production. Selling and administrative costs (e.g., depreciation on sales office, freight-out, sales salaries, and commissions, advertising, and administrative salaries) are not included. As computed below, manufacturing cost for the year is $80,000.

Production wages	$28,000
Raw materials	47,000
Factory rent	2,000
Factory insurance	500
Factory depreciation	1,000
Materials handling	1,500
	$80,000

28. Glen Company has the following data pertaining to the year ended December 31:

Purchases	$450,000
Beginning inventory	170,000
Ending inventory	210,000
Freight-in	50,000
Freight-out	75,000

How much is the cost of goods sold for the year?

a. $385,000.
b. $460,000.
c. $485,000.
d. $540,000.

The correct answer is (b). *(CPA 586 P-44)*
REQUIRED: The cost of goods sold for the year.
DISCUSSION: Freight-in is the cost of receiving inventory and is thus a product cost. Freight-out, however, is the cost of shipping products to customers and accordingly should be treated as a selling expense (period cost).

Beginning inventory		$170,000
Purchases	$450,000	
Freight-in	50,000	500,000
Goods available		$670,000
Ending inventory		(210,000)
Cost of goods sold		$460,000

29. What is the nature of the manufacturing or work-in-process account?

a. Inventory.
b. Cost of goods sold.
c. Productivity.
d. Nominal.

The correct answer is (a). *(Publisher)*
REQUIRED: The nature of the manufacturing account.
DISCUSSION: The manufacturing account is an inventory account, a work-in-process inventory. All the manufacturing costs charged to the manufacturing account this period and those remaining in the account from last period (BWIP) are allocated between goods that are completed and goods that are incomplete (EWIP). Note that this description excludes spoilage, a matter covered in Chapter Seven.

Answer (b) is incorrect because CGS is CGM adjusted for the change in finished goods inventory. Answer (c) is incorrect because productivity is a nonsense term in this context. Answer (d) is incorrect because, since the manufacturing account is an inventory account, it is a real rather than a nominal account.

Questions 30 through 32 are based on the following data pertaining to Lam Co.'s manufacturing operations:

Inventories	4/1	4/30
Direct materials	$18,000	$15,000
Work-in-process	9,000	6,000
Finished goods	27,000	36,000

Additional information for the month of April:

Direct materials purchased	$42,000
Direct labor payroll	30,000
Direct labor rate per hour	$ 7.50
Factory overhead rate per direct labor hour	10.00

30. For the month of April, prime cost incurred was

a. $75,000.
b. $69,000.
c. $45,000.
d. $39,000.

The correct answer is (a). *(CPA 587 Q-23)*
REQUIRED: The prime cost added to production during the period.
DISCUSSION: Prime costs consist of direct material and direct labor. Direct labor is given as $30,000. The direct materials must be determined from the change in direct material inventory, a decrease of $3,000 ($18,000 - $15,000), plus the $42,000 of purchases, or $45,000. Accordingly, the prime costs total $75,000 ($30,000 + $45,000).

31. For the month of April, conversion cost incurred was

a. $30,000.
b. $40,000.
c. $70,000.
d. $72,000.

The correct answer is (c). *(CPA 587 Q-24)*
REQUIRED: The conversion cost added to production during the period.
DISCUSSION: Conversion cost consists of direct labor and overhead. Direct labor is given as $30,000. Factory overhead is applied at the rate of $10.00 per direct labor hour. Given 4,000 direct labor hours ($30,000/$7.50) incurred in April, at $10.00 per hour, $40,000 of overhead was applied. Thus, the conversion costs for April total $70,000 ($30,000 + $40,000).

32. For the month of April, cost of goods manufactured was

a. $118,000.
b. $115,000.
c. $112,000.
d. $109,000.

The correct answer is (a). *(CPA 587 Q-25)*
REQUIRED: The cost of goods manufactured for the period.
DISCUSSION: Cost of good manufactured is the sum of BWIP, direct material used, direct labor incurred, and overhead applied, less EWIP.

BWIP (given)	$ 9,000
Material (from Q 30)	45,000
Direct labor (given)	30,000
Overhead applied (from Q 31)	40,000
	$124,000
Less EWIP (given)	(6,000)
Cost of goods manufactured	$118,000

4.3 Variable vs. Fixed Costs

33. A cost that remains unchanged on a per unit basis in a given time period despite changes in the level of activity should be considered

a. A prime cost.
b. An overhead cost.
c. A fixed cost.
d. A variable cost.

The correct answer is (d). *(CIA 1186 IV-9)*
REQUIRED: The unit cost that is unchanged despite changes in activity.
DISCUSSION: Variable costs are constant per unit but fluctuate in total in direct proportion to changes in total activity or volume (the rate of use of capacity).
Answer (a) is incorrect because prime costs are direct labor and direct materials costs. Answer (b) is incorrect because overhead is an indirect cost that may be variable or fixed. Answer (c) is incorrect because total fixed costs do not change within the relevant range. Hence, the per unit fixed cost declines as production increases.

Module 4.3: Variable vs. Fixed Costs

34. When cost relationships are linear, total variable costs will vary in proportion to changes in

a. Direct labor hours.
b. Total material cost.
c. Total overhead cost.
d. Volume of production.
e. Machine hours.

The correct answer is (d). *(CIA 976 IV-2)*
REQUIRED: The variable to which total variable costs are proportionate given linear cost relationships.
DISCUSSION: Variable costs vary in proportion to changes in the volume of production. Unit variable costs are assumed to remain the same per unit within the relevant range.
Answers (a) and (b) are incorrect because, even though direct labor hours and total material cost are components of total variable costs, neither is the independent variable to which total variable costs relate. Answer (c) is incorrect because total overhead cost contains both fixed costs and variable costs. Unit overhead costs vary with the volume of production. Answer (e) is incorrect because production levels may not always vary directly with machine hours; e.g., more spoilage may occur at lower or higher levels of utilization.

35. Which of the following best describes a fixed cost?

a. It may change in total when such change is unrelated to changes in production.
b. It may change in total when such change is related to changes in production.
c. It is constant per unit of change in production.
d. It may change in total when such change depends on production within the relevant range.

The correct answer is (a). *(CPA 576 T-21)*
REQUIRED: The statement that best describes a fixed cost.
DISCUSSION: A fixed cost remains unchanged in total for a given period despite fluctuations in activity. Note that per unit fixed costs do change as the level of activity changes. A fixed cost may change in total between different periods or when production is outside the relevant range.
Answer (b) is incorrect because a variable cost changes in relation to changes in production. Answer (c) is incorrect because it also describes a variable cost. Answer (d) is incorrect because fixed costs are fixed within the relevant range.

36. A company has always used the full cost of its product as the starting point in the pricing of that product. The price set by competitors and the demand for the company's only product, the Widget, have never been predictable. Lately, the company's market share has been increasing as it continues to lower its price, but total revenues have not changed significantly relative to the gain in sales volume. The likely reason for the stability of total revenues is

a. The variable cost component of the full cost.
b. The unstable contribution margin.
c. The fixed cost component of the full cost.
d. The drop in the incremental cost of the units in the increased sales volume.

The correct answer is (c). *(CIA 1184 IV-1)*
REQUIRED: The likely reason for stability of total revenue given full costing, a lower price, and greater volume.
DISCUSSION: Fixed costs remain fixed in total at different activity levels. Thus, unit fixed cost will vary inversely with the activity level. The use of full cost pricing would result in a lowering of total cost and a lower selling price. Total revenues could remain approximately the same as sales volume increases.
Answer (a) is incorrect because variable cost per unit remains the same at all activity levels. Answer (b) is incorrect because an unstable contribution margin would affect total revenues. Answer (d) is incorrect because the drop in the incremental cost is the result of the decline in unit fixed cost.

37. The term "relevant range" as used in cost accounting means the range over which

 a. Costs may fluctuate.
 b. Cost relationships are valid.
 c. Production may vary.
 d. Relevant costs are incurred.

The correct answer is (b). *(CPA 575 T-29)*
REQUIRED: The definition of relevant range as used in cost accounting.
DISCUSSION: The relevant range is the range of activity (production volume) within which variable unit costs are constant and fixed costs are constant in total. In this range the incremental cost of one additional unit of production is the same, i.e., the unit variable cost.
Answer (a) is incorrect because total cost fluctuates both within and outside the relevant range because variable costs vary. Answer (c) is incorrect because production levels may be above or below the relevant range; they are not confined to the relevant range. Answer (d) is incorrect because relevant costs are incurred at any level, not just within the relevant range.

38. Depreciation based on the number of units produced is classified as what type of cost?

 a. Out-of-pocket.
 b. Marginal.
 c. Variable.
 d. Fixed.

The correct answer is (c). *(CPA 1176 T-26)*
REQUIRED: The cost resulting from depreciation based on the number of units produced.
DISCUSSION: A variable cost is uniform per unit but, in total, fluctuates in direct proportion to changes in the related activity or volume. Thus, a per unit depreciation charge is a variable cost.
Answer (a) is incorrect because the purchase of an asset, not the subsequent depreciation, is an out-of-pocket cost. Answer (b) is incorrect because a marginal cost is incurred by producing and/or selling an additional or partial unit. Marginal costs include material, labor, etc. Answer (d) is incorrect because fixed costs do not fluctuate with activity levels; they are not based on the number of units produced.

39. When the number of units manufactured increases, the most significant change in average unit cost will be reflected as

 a. An increase in the nonvariable element.
 b. A decrease in the variable element.
 c. A decrease in the nonvariable element.
 d. An increase in the semivariable element.
 e. An increase in the variable element.

The correct answer is (c). *(CIA 976 IV-14)*
REQUIRED: The most significant change in average unit cost when the number of units manufactured increases.
DISCUSSION: As production increases or decreases, the most significant change in the average unit cost will occur in the fixed (nonvariable) cost element. When production increases, the average cost of the nonvariable element per unit will decrease because total fixed cost is constant.
Answer (a) is incorrect because the nonvariable fixed element varies indirectly with production level; fixed cost per unit decreases with an increase in the production level. Answers (b) and (e) are incorrect because the variable element per unit is assumed to remain constant for changes in the production level within the relevant range. Answer (d) is incorrect because the semivariable element decreases to the extent it consists of fixed costs and remains constant to the extent it includes variable costs.

Module 4.3: Variable vs. Fixed Costs

40. Depreciation based on the straight-line method is classified as what type of cost?

a. Out-of-pocket.

b. Marginal.

c. Variable.

d. Fixed.

The correct answer is (d). *(J.W. Ferry)*
REQUIRED: The classification of depreciation when it is based on the straight-line method.
DISCUSSION: By definition, a fixed cost is a cost that remains unchanged over a given time period regardless of the related level of production activity. Straight-line depreciation is thus properly classified as fixed since it is correlated with the passage of time, not the level of activity.
Answer (a) is incorrect because payment for an asset, not the subsequent depreciation, is an out-of-pocket cost. Answer (b) is incorrect because a marginal cost is incurred by producing and/or selling an additional or partial unit. Answer (c) is incorrect because variable costs fluctuate with activity levels. For example, depreciation based on the units-of-production method is a variable cost.

41. The term incremental cost refers to

a. The difference in total costs that results from selecting one choice instead of another.

b. The profit forgone by selecting one choice instead of another.

c. A cost which does not entail any dollar outlay but which is relevant to the decision-making process.

d. A cost which continues to be incurred even though there is no activity.

e. A cost common to all choices in question and not clearly or practically allocable to any of them.

The correct answer is (a). *(CMA 1277 5-1)*
REQUIRED: The definition of an incremental cost.
DISCUSSION: Incremental cost is the difference in total cost between two courses of action. Decremental costs is the term used when the difference is noted as a decline although incremental is the more common term. Incremental cost is also referred to as differential cost.
Answer (b) is incorrect because it is the definition of opportunity cost. Answer (c) is incorrect because it describes imputed cost. Answer (d) is incorrect because a fixed cost is incurred even though no output is produced. Answer (e) is incorrect because common or joint costs are not allocable among the possible choices.

42. If a predetermined overhead rate is not employed and the volume of production is increased over the level planned, the cost per unit would be expected to

a. Decrease for fixed costs and remain unchanged for variable costs.

b. Remain unchanged for fixed costs and increase for variable costs.

c. Decrease for fixed costs and increase for variable costs.

d. Increase for fixed costs and increase for variable costs.

The correct answer is (a). *(CPA 573 T-25)*
REQUIRED: The change in cost per unit given an increase in production volume with no predetermined overhead rate.
DISCUSSION: Total fixed costs do not vary, so fixed costs per unit decrease with increases in production volume. Not using predetermined overhead rates means the overhead rate is based on actual production and is therefore lowered as production levels increase. Total variable costs change in response to changes in production volume because they remain constant for each unit produced. Therefore, the variable costs per unit will remain unchanged.
Answers (b), (c), and (d) are incorrect because fixed unit costs decrease and variable unit costs remain unchanged with increases in production volume within the relevant range.

43. Within a relevant range, the amount of variable cost per unit

a. Differs at each production level.

b. Remains constant at each production level.

c. Increases as production increases.

d. Decreases as production increases.

The correct answer is (b). *(CPA 1180 T-34)*
REQUIRED: The amount of variable cost per unit within the relevant range.
DISCUSSION: In the relevant range, variable unit costs are assumed to be constant, and fixed costs are assumed to be constant in total.
Answers (a), (c), and (d) are incorrect because variable cost per unit remains constant within the relevant range, as opposed to total variable cost, which differs at each production level.

Module 4.3: Variable vs. Fixed Costs

44. Unit fixed costs

a. Are constant per unit regardless of units produced or sold.
b. Are determined by dividing total fixed costs by a denominator such as production or sales volume.
c. Vary directly with the activity level when stated on a per unit basis.
d. Include both fixed and variable elements.

The correct answer is (b). *(Publisher)*
REQUIRED: The correct statement about unit fixed costs.
DISCUSSION: A unit fixed cost is equal to total fixed costs divided by an appropriate denominator or activity level. The resulting average or unit fixed cost must be used with extreme caution in decision making.
Answer (a) is incorrect because it defines a variable cost. Answer (c) is incorrect because unit fixed costs vary inversely with activity. Answer (d) is incorrect because the question concerns only unit fixed costs.

45. When production levels are expected to decline within a relevant range, and a flexible budget is used, what effects would be anticipated with respect to each of the following?

	Fixed Costs per Unit	Variable Costs per Unit
a.	Increase	No change
b.	Increase	Increase
c.	No change	No change
d.	No change	Increase

The correct answer is (a). *(CPA 1187 T-47)*
REQUIRED: The effect of a production decline within a relevant range.
DISCUSSION: Within the relevant range, regardless of the budget method employed, a decrease in production will result in fewer units produced. This decrease results in higher fixed costs per unit since total fixed costs are assumed not to vary within the relevant range. However, variable costs are by definition constant per unit but fluctuate in total. Thus, there would be no change in per unit variable costs.

46. When production increases, variable manufacturing costs react in which of the following ways?

	Unit Variable Cost	Total Variable Cost
a.	Decrease	Decrease
b.	Remain same	Increase
c.	Remain same	Decrease
d.	Increase	Increase

The correct answer is (b). *(J.W. Ferry)*
REQUIRED: The reaction of variable costs to changes in production.
DISCUSSION: Variable manufacturing costs do not change per unit over the relevant range. However, total variable cost has a direct relationship with the activity level; the higher the activity level the larger the total variable cost.

47. Costs that increase as the volume of activity decreases within the relevant range are

a. Average costs per unit.
b. Average variable costs per unit.
c. Total fixed costs.
d. Total variable costs.

The correct answer is (a). *(CIA 1185 IV-8)*
REQUIRED: The costs that increase as the volume of activity decreases within the relevant range.
DISCUSSION: As production levels decrease, total fixed costs must be allocated over fewer units. This increase in average fixed costs per unit increases total average cost per unit.
Answers (b) and (c) are incorrect because average variable costs per unit and total fixed costs remain constant as the volume of activity decreases. Answer (d) is incorrect because total variable costs decrease as volume decreases.

48. The accountant's concept of marginal cost is similar to

a. Average cost.
b. Total cost.
c. Production cost.
d. Incremental unit cost.

The correct answer is (d). *(Publisher)*
REQUIRED: The accountant's concept of marginal cost.
DISCUSSION: Accountants are concerned with incremental unit cost, the cost to produce an additional unit, i.e., the variable cost. This is related to marginal cost because it is associated with a one-unit change in activity level. In other words, it is usually not practical to produce partial units.

49. The marginal cost of the economist is most closely associated with the accountant's

a. Unit fixed cost.
b. Unit variable cost.
c. Unit total cost.
d. Unit manufacturing cost.

The correct answer is (b). *(Publisher)*
REQUIRED: The accountant's measure most like the economist's marginal cost.
DISCUSSION: Marginal cost is associated with a one-unit change in the activity level. The accountant assumes that production of one additional unit would only require incurring costs directly related to it, i.e., the variable costs.
Answer (a) is incorrect because unit fixed cost represents total fixed cost divided by the activity level. Total fixed cost does not change with a change in production level. Answers (c) and (d) are incorrect because each includes both variable ad fixed cost elements. Unit fixed cost varies with the production level, but total fixed cost is constant.

50. Assuming all manufacturing costs for finished goods are known, which of the following statements explains why the accountant's unit cost used in inventory valuation for the annual financial statements would differ from the economist's marginal unit cost?

a. The company used LIFO or FIFO assumptions to compute inventory cost.
b. Accounting information that is based on historical manufacturing costs ignores current cost trends.
c. The economist's definition of marginal cost excludes a provision for profit per unit.
d. The manufacturing cost per unit reflected in financial statements includes an allocation of fixed costs.
e. The inventory cost per unit reflected in financial statements is only an approximation of the marginal manufacturing cost per unit.

The correct answer is (d). *(CIA 580 IV-5)*
REQUIRED: The difference between the economist's marginal cost and the accountant's unit cost.
DISCUSSION: The economist's marginal cost equals the cost to produce one additional unit; thus, no fixed costs are included in the computation. The accountant's unit cost for financial statement purposes includes an allocation of fixed costs.
Answer (a) is incorrect because the cost flow assumption is separate from the assumption of which costs are included. Answer (b) is incorrect because variable costs are stated at current period prices. Answer (c) is incorrect because both accountants and economists usually exclude profit from inventory unit costs. Answer (e) is incorrect because inventory unit costs include both fixed and manufacturing costs for financial reporting.

4.4 Product vs. Period Costs

51. Inventoriable (product) costs are

a. Manufacturing costs incurred to produce units of output.
b. All costs associated with manufacturing other than direct labor costs and raw material costs.
c. Costs that are associated with marketing, shipping, warehousing, and billing activities.
d. The sum of direct labor costs and all factory overhead costs.
e. The sum of raw material costs and direct labor costs.

The correct answer is (a). *(CMA 678 4-8)*
REQUIRED: The definition of costs which are inventoriable.
DISCUSSION: Inventoriable costs are incurred to produce units of output and are deferred to future periods to the extent output is not sold (kept on hand for sale in future periods). Inventoriable costs are expensed in the period the product is sold. Product costs and inventoriable costs are synonymous.
Answer (b) is incorrect because it defines factory overhead. Direct labor and raw material are also inventoriable costs. Answer (c) is incorrect because it defines selling expenses, which are recognized when incurred. Answer (d) is incorrect because inventoriable costs also include direct material costs. Answer (e) is incorrect because inventoriable costs also include factory overhead costs.

Module 4.4: Product vs. Period Costs

52. Which of the following is normally considered to be a product cost when using absorption costing?

a. Insurance on a factory building.
b. Selling expenses.
c. President's salary.
d. Miscellaneous expense.

The correct answer is (a). *(CIA 586 IV-1)*
REQUIRED: The item considered a product cost when using absorption costing.
DISCUSSION: Product costs are those that can be associated with the production of specific revenues during a period. Product costs include direct labor, direct materials, and overhead. Insurance on a factory building, which is an overhead expense, is therefore considered a product cost.
Answers (b), (c), and (d) are incorrect because they each relate to the period in which they were incurred rather than specific revenues (i.e., they are period costs).

53. Which of the following is not a characteristic of product costs?

a. Product costs include costs of the factors of production identifiable with the product.
b. Product costs do not include any fixed cost.
c. Product costs are expensed when the product is sold.
d. Product costs include direct materials, direct labor, and factory overhead.

The correct answer is (b). *(Publisher)*
REQUIRED: The incorrect statement about product costs.
DISCUSSION: Product costs are the costs of producing the product and are usually directly identifiable with it. Thus, product costs include the costs of the factors of production identifiable with the product, which usually include direct materials, direct labor, and factory (not general) overhead. Factory overhead includes both fixed and variable elements. Product costs are inventoried until the product is sold, at which time they are expensed.

54. Which of the following is a characteristic of period costs?

a. Period costs are not identifiable with a product and are not inventoried.
b. Period costs may be classified as revenue expenditures; they are charged to the income statement in the period when the costs are incurred.
c. Period costs may be classified as capital expenditures; they are initially recorded as assets and then charged to expense as used.
d. All of the above.

The correct answer is (d). *(Publisher)*
REQUIRED: The characteristic(s) of period costs in cost accounting.
DISCUSSION: Period costs are charged to expense as incurred and not to a particular product. They are not identifiable with a product and are not inventoried. Period costs may be classified as either revenue expenditures or capital expenditures. Revenue expenditures, e.g., advertising and officers' salaries, are charged to the income statement in the period the costs are incurred because they usually do not benefit future periods. Period costs classified as capital expenditures, e.g., depreciation, are initially recorded as assets and then charged to expense as they are consumed, used, or disposed of.

55. The Gray Company has a staff of five clerks in its general accounting department. The three clerks who work during the day perform sundry accounting tasks; the two clerks who work in the evening are responsible for (1) collecting the cost data for the various jobs in process, (2) verifying manufacturing material and labor reports, and (3) supplying production reports to the supervisors by the next morning. The salaries of these two clerks who work at night should be classified as

a. Period costs.
b. Opportunity costs.
c. Product costs.
d. Direct costs.

The correct answer is (a). *(CIA 585 IV-1)*
REQUIRED: The classification of clerks' salaries.
DISCUSSION: Clerks' salaries are a part of general overhead and are thus considered period costs. Period costs are charged to expense as incurred since they are not identifiable with any particular product.
Answer (b) is incorrect because opportunity cost is the contribution forgone by choosing one alternative over others. Answer (c) is incorrect because product costs are inventoriable and are charged to expense as sold. Answer (d) is incorrect because direct costs are identifiable and attributable to specific units of production.

Module 4.4: Product vs. Period Costs

56. The term "prime costs" refers to

a. Manufacturing costs incurred to produce units of output.

b. All costs associated with manufacturing other than direct labor costs and raw material costs.

c. Cost standards that are predetermined and should be attained.

d. The sum of direct labor costs and all factory overhead costs.

e. The sum of raw material costs and direct labor costs.

The correct answer is (e). *(CMA 678 4-7)*
REQUIRED: The definition of prime costs in cost accounting.
DISCUSSION: Prime costs are direct materials and direct labor. They are the directly identifiable elements of production costs and are directly traceable to the product.
Answer (a) is incorrect because it is the definition of product costs. Answer (b) is incorrect because it describes factory overhead. Answer (c) is incorrect because prime costs are actual costs incurred, not standard costs. Answer (d) is incorrect because it defines conversion costs.

57. Which of the following is an element of prime cost?

	Direct Materials	Indirect Materials
a.	Yes	No
b.	Yes	Yes
c.	No	Yes
d.	No	No

The correct answer is (a). *(CPA 584 T-37)*
REQUIRED: The item that is an element of prime costs.
DISCUSSION: Prime costs are direct materials and direct labor. They are directly identifiable with the product. Indirect materials are charged to overhead and thus are conversion costs.

58. A manufacturer of machinery currently produces equipment for a single client. The client supplies all required raw material on a no-cost basis. The manufacturer contracts to complete the desired units from this raw material. The total production costs incurred by the manufacturer are correctly identified as

a. Prime costs.

b. Conversion costs.

c. Variable production costs.

d. Factory overhead.

The correct answer is (b). *(CIA 1187 IV-2)*
REQUIRED: The classification of the total production costs incurred.
DISCUSSION: The basic components of manufacturing costs are direct materials, direct labor, and indirect manufacturing costs (factory overhead). The latter two elements are the costs of converting raw materials into finished products.
Answer (a) is incorrect because direct materials and labor are prime costs. Answer (c) is incorrect because it excludes fixed factory overhead. Also, direct materials is a variable cost of production. Answer (d) is incorrect because it excludes direct labor.

59. Certain workers are assigned the task of unpacking production materials received from suppliers. These workers place the material in a storage area pending subsequent use in the production process. The labor cost of such workers is normally classified as

a. Direct labor.

b. Direct materials.

c. Indirect labor.

d. Indirect materials.

The correct answer is (c). *(CIA 1187 IV-1)*
REQUIRED: The type of cost represented by the described labor.
DISCUSSION: Indirect labor consists of manufacturing labor wage costs not incurred for direct labor. Indirect labor costs are not reasonably traceable to particular products.
Answer (a) is incorrect because direct labor is traceable to particular products. Answers (b) and (d) are incorrect because the question concerns labor, not materials, costs.

Module 4.4: Product vs. Period Costs

60. Factory overhead
   a. Is a prime cost.
   b. Can be a variable cost or a fixed cost.
   c. Can only be a fixed cost.
   d. Includes all factory labor.

The correct answer is (b). *(CPA 1181 T-42)*
REQUIRED: The correct statement about factory overhead.
DISCUSSION: Factory overhead consists of all costs other than direct materials and direct labor that are associated with the manufacturing process. It includes both fixed and variable costs. All fixed costs are factory overhead because they are not incurred to produce specific output. Indirect material and indirect labor are variable components of factory overhead; they vary with the level of production.
Answer (a) is incorrect because direct materials and direct labor are prime costs. Answer (c) is incorrect because variable costs, e.g., supplies and indirect labor, are included in factory overhead. Answer (d) is incorrect because factory overhead includes only indirect labor.

61. Direct materials are a

	Conversion Cost	Manufacturing Cost	Prime Cost
a.	Yes	Yes	No
b.	Yes	Yes	Yes
c.	No	Yes	Yes
d.	No	No	No

The correct answer is (c). *(CPA 1181 T-46)*
REQUIRED: The classification of direct material cost.
DISCUSSION: Direct materials are a manufacturing cost and a prime cost. Direct materials constitute a directly identifiable element of the manufacturing costs which are inventoried. Direct materials and direct labor are also prime costs. Conversion cost consists of direct labor and factory overhead, but not direct materials (the direct materials are being converted).

62. Indirect materials are a

	Conversion Cost	Manufacturing Cost	Prime Cost
a.	Yes	Yes	Yes
b.	Yes	Yes	No
c.	No	Yes	Yes
d.	No	No	No

The correct answer is (b). *(J.W. Ferry)*
REQUIRED: The classification of indirect material cost.
DISCUSSION: Indirect materials are a manufacturing cost and a conversion cost. Indirect materials constitute a manufacturing cost which can not be directly identifiable to a specific unit of production and is therefore a part of manufacturing overhead. Conversion cost consists of direct labor and manufacturing overhead, but not direct materials (the direct materials are being converted). Prime cost consists of direct material and direct labor.

63. Prime cost and conversion cost share what common element of total cost?
   a. Direct labor.
   b. Direct materials.
   c. Variable overhead.
   d. Fixed overhead.

The correct answer is (a). *(CPA 1186 T-41)*
REQUIRED: The element of total cost that is common to both prime cost and conversion cost.
DISCUSSION: Prime costs are direct labor and direct materials. Conversion costs are direct labor and factory overhead. Thus, the element common to both is direct labor.
Answer (b) is incorrect because conversion cost does not include direct materials. Answers (c) and (d) are incorrect because prime costs do not include overhead.

64. Factory overhead includes
   a. All manufacturing costs.
   b. All manufacturing costs, except direct materials and direct labor.
   c. Indirect materials but not indirect labor.
   d. Indirect labor but not indirect materials.

The correct answer is (b). *(CPA 1179 T-35)*
REQUIRED: The definition of factory overhead.
DISCUSSION: Factory overhead consists of all costs other than direct materials and direct labor that are associated with the manufacturing process.
Answer (a) is incorrect because factory overhead does not include direct materials and direct labor. Answers (c) and (d) are incorrect because factory overhead includes both indirect labor and indirect materials.

Module 4.4: Product vs. Period Costs

65. The cost of fire insurance for a manufacturing plant is generally a

    a. Nonmanufacturing cost.
    b. Period cost.
    c. Semivariable cost.
    d. Conversion cost.

The correct answer is (d). *(CPA 585 T-37)*
REQUIRED: The classification of fire insurance for a manufacturing plant.
DISCUSSION: Fire insurance for a manufacturing plant is attributable to the products produced. The cost of the fire insurance is thus charged to manufacturing overhead, a conversion cost.
Answer (a) is incorrect because the insurance is a manufacturing cost. Answer (b) is incorrect because fire insurance is a product cost. Answer (c) is incorrect because insurance is usually a fixed cost.

66. Wages of the security guard for a small plant are an example of

	Indirect Labor	Fixed Factory Overhead
a.	No	No
b.	Yes	Yes
c.	Yes	No
d.	No	Yes

The correct answer is (b). *(CPA 1182 T-42)*
REQUIRED: The classification of wages of a security guard.
DISCUSSION: Wages for a security guard are not directly associated with production of a product. Hence, they are considered to be indirect labor. All indirect labor related to production is included in factory overhead.

67. The fixed portion of the semivariable cost of electricity for a manufacturing plant is a

	Conversion Cost	Product Cost
a.	No	No
b.	No	Yes
c.	Yes	Yes
d.	Yes	No

The correct answer is (c). *(CPA 584 T-39)*
REQUIRED: The classification(s) of fixed electricity cost for a manufacturer.
DISCUSSION: Electricity costs in a manufacturing plant are a part of manufacturing overhead. Manufacturing overhead is both a conversion cost and a product cost.

68. Which of the following are usually considered period costs?

	A	B	C	D
Direct labor			X	X
Direct materials		X		X
Sales materials	X	X	X	
Advertising costs	X	X		
Indirect factory materials				X
Indirect labor				X
Sales commissions	X	X	X	
Factory utilities		X		X
Administrative supplies expense	X	X	X	
Administrative labor	X	X	X	X
Depreciation on administration building	X	X	X	X
Cost of research on customer demographics	X	X	X	

    a. A.
    b. B.
    c. C.
    d. D.

The correct answer is (a). *(CIA 1187 IV-52)*
REQUIRED: The items usually considered period costs.
DISCUSSION: Period costs are charged to expense as incurred and not to a particular product. They are not identifiable with a product and are not inventoried. Period costs may be classified as either revenue expenditures or capital expenditures. Revenue expenditures, e.g., advertising and officers' salaries, are charged to the income statement in the period the costs are incurred because they usually do not benefit future periods. Period costs classified as capital expenditures, e.g., depreciation, are initially recorded as assets and then charged to expense as they are consumed, used, or disposed of. Accordingly, all the items listed are period costs except for the direct materials, direct labor, and the factory overhead items.
Answers (b), (c), and (d) are incorrect because direct labor, direct materials, and factory overhead (factory utilities, indirect labor, and indirect materials) are product costs.

69. Wages paid to a timekeeper in a factory are a

	Prime Cost	Conversion Cost
a.	Yes	No
b.	Yes	Yes
c.	No	No
d.	No	Yes

The correct answer is (d). *(CPA 586 T-41)*
REQUIRED: The classification of wages paid to a factory timekeeper.
DISCUSSION: Wages paid to timekeepers are indirect labor and considered to be conversion costs. Conversion costs consist of labor and overhead. Prime costs consist only of direct labor and direct material.

4.5 Other Cost Definitions

70. What is the term that means that all manufacturing costs (direct and indirect, variable and fixed) that contribute to the production of the product are assigned to output and inventories?

a. Job order costing.
b. Process costing.
c. Full or absorption costing.
d. Variable or direct costing.

The correct answer is (c). *(CPA 574 T-15)*
REQUIRED: The costing method that assigns all traceable costs to inventories.
DISCUSSION: Absorption costing (full costing) is the accounting method that considers all manufacturing costs as product costs. These costs include variable and fixed manufacturing costs whether direct or indirect.
Answers (a) and (b) are incorrect because they are different methods of accumulating costs. The issue in this question involves whether fixed overhead costs are expensed or inventoried. Answer (d) is incorrect because variable (direct) costing excludes fixed manufacturing costs as product costs (and expenses them as period costs).

71. What is the basic difference between direct costing and absorption costing?

a. Direct costing always produces less taxable earnings than absorption costing.
b. Direct costing recognizes fixed costs as period costs and absorption costing recognizes fixed costs as product costs.
c. Direct costing cannot use standards and absorption costing can.
d. Direct costing may be used only in situations in which production is essentially homogeneous, but absorption costing may be used under any manufacturing condition.

The correct answer is (b). *(CPA 578 T-36)*
REQUIRED: The basic difference between absorption costing and direct costing.
DISCUSSION: The essential distinction between absorption costing and direct costing lies in the treatment of fixed manufacturing costs. Absorption costing treats fixed manufacturing costs as product costs by allocating them to inventory and cost of goods sold. Direct costing treats all fixed manufacturing costs as period costs, expensing them as incurred.
Answer (a) is incorrect because earnings fluctuate based upon the relationship between production and sales, and direct costing could produce greater earnings when sales exceed production. Direct costing is generally not permitted for tax purposes. Answer (c) is incorrect because standard costs may be used with either absorption or direct costing. Answer (d) is incorrect because either absorption costing or direct costing can be used under any manufacturing condition.

72. To calculate the contribution margin, all of the following are deducted from revenue (sales price) except

a. Direct materials.
b. Direct labor.
c. Fixed factory overhead.
d. Variable factory overhead.
e. Variable general overhead.

The correct answer is (c). *(Publisher)*
REQUIRED: The element not subtracted from sales revenue to arrive at contribution margin.
DISCUSSION: The contribution margin is calculated by subtracting all variable costs from sales revenue. Variable costs include both manufacturing variable costs and variable selling and general costs. Hence, direct materials, direct labor, and variable factory overhead are deducted from revenue as well as the variable selling and general overhead items. Fixed costs (whether manufacturing or nonmanufacturing costs) are not deducted.

Module 4.5: Other Cost Definitions

73. The contribution margin and the gross margin are not synonymous. Select the false statement about them.

a. The contribution margin is calculated by subtracting all variable costs from sales revenue.

b. The gross margin concept is used by management accountants to aid management in answering "what if" questions.

c. The gross margin is calculated by subtracting all product costs from sales revenue.

d. None of the above.

The correct answer is (b). *(Publisher)*
REQUIRED: The false statement about the contribution margin and the gross margin.
DISCUSSION: The gross margin concept cannot be used by management in decision making because it includes an element of fixed costs. Such costs do not vary with changes in activity levels. The contribution margin concept, because it only uses variable costs, can be used for this purpose, e.g., in estimating the effects of changes in production volume.
Answers (a) and (c) are incorrect because the contribution margin is the result of deducting all variable costs from sales revenue, and the gross margin is the result of subtracting all product costs from revenue.

74. Meaningful comparisons of costs for different accounting periods are complicated by changes in

a. The prices of inputs.
b. Production technology.
c. The efficiency with which inputs are used.
d. Accounting systems.
e. All of the above factors.

The correct answer is (e). *(CIA 976 IV-1)*
REQUIRED: The change(s) affecting the comparison of costs for different accounting periods.
DISCUSSION: The ability to compare costs between accounting periods is affected whenever the determinants of costs change. Prices of inputs, production technology, the efficiency with which inputs are used, and accounting systems are some of the items used to determine costs. Therefore, changes in them undermine comparability of cost data.

75. The costs presented to management for an equipment replacement decision should be limited to

a. Relevant costs.
b. Standard costs.
c. Controllable costs.
d. Conversion costs.

The correct answer is (a). *(CPA 1180 T-45)*
REQUIRED: The costs considered in making an equipment replacement decision.
DISCUSSION: Relevant costs are those expected future costs that vary with the action taken. All other costs are assumed to be constant and thus have no effect on (are irrelevant to) the decision.
Answer (b) is incorrect because standard costs are predetermined for use in comparing actual costs and attainable costs. Answer (c) is incorrect because controllable costs are directly regulated by management at a given level of production within a given time span; e.g., fixed costs are not controllable. Answer (d) is incorrect because conversion costs are direct labor and factory overhead, the costs of "converting" raw materials into finished goods.

76. In deciding which of two new machines to purchase to replace an old machine, the management of Ashworth Company should consider as relevant

a. Historical costs associated with the old machine.
b. Future costs which will be classified as variable rather than fixed.
c. Future costs which will differ between the two choices.
d. Future costs which will be classified as fixed rather than variable.

The correct answer is (c). *(CPA 573 T-31)*
REQUIRED: The relevant costs when choosing which of two machines to purchase.
DISCUSSION: Relevant costs are the future costs which will differ between the two choices. All other costs are assumed to be constant and thus have no effect on the decision.
Answer (a) is incorrect because historical costs are sunk costs; i.e., they have been made in the past and will not affect the future. Answers (b) and (d) are incorrect because all future costs (both variable and fixed) must be considered.

Module 4.5: Other Cost Definitions

77. As part of the data presented in support of a proposal to increase the production of clock radios, the sales manager of Wittman Electronics reported the total additional cost required for the proposed increased production level. The increase in total cost is known as

a. Controllable cost.
b. Incremental cost.
c. Opportunity cost.
d. Out-of-pocket cost.

The correct answer is (b). *(CPA 573 T-19)*
REQUIRED: The term describing the additional cost incurred when production is increased.
DISCUSSION: The additional cost incurred because of increased production is referred to as incremental cost.
Answer (a) is incorrect because controllable costs are all costs likely to respond to the attention devoted to them by a specified manager. Answer (c) is incorrect because an opportunity cost is the profit forgone by making one decision instead of another. Answer (d) is incorrect because an out-of-pocket cost requires current or near-future outlays.

78. An opportunity cost is

a. The difference in total costs which results from selecting one choice instead of another.
b. The profit forgone by selecting one choice instead of another.
c. A cost that may be saved by not adopting an alternative.
d. A cost that may be shifted to the future with little or no effect on current operations.
e. A cost that cannot be avoided because it has already been incurred.

The correct answer is (b). *(CMA 1277 5-3)*
REQUIRED: The definition of an opportunity cost.
DISCUSSION: The term opportunity cost refers to the benefit (e.g., profit) forgone because of the choice of a given action. Opportunity costs are considered when determining the most profitable utilization of resources.
Answer (a) is incorrect because it refers to a differential or incremental cost. Answer (c) is incorrect because it is the definition of an avoidable cost. Answer (d) is incorrect because a postponable cost may be shifted to the future. Answer (e) is incorrect because a sunk cost has already been incurred.

79. Which of the following best describes an opportunity cost?

a. It is usually relevant, but is not part of traditional accounting records.
b. It is usually not relevant, but is part of traditional accounting records.
c. It is usually relevant, and is part of traditional accounting records.
d. It is usually not relevant, and is not part of traditional accounting records.

The correct answer is (a). *(CPA 1176 P-23)*
REQUIRED: The best description of an opportunity cost.
DISCUSSION: Opportunity cost is the benefit forgone by using a scarce resource for another purpose. Opportunity costs are relevant to (and should be considered in) every decision to use scarce resources, but they are not recorded in the accounting records. Only the actual cost of the resource is reflected.

80. The opportunity cost of making a component part in a factory with no excess capacity is the

a. Variable manufacturing cost of the component.
b. Fixed manufacturing cost of the component.
c. Total manufacturing cost of the component.
d. Cost of the production given up in order to manufacture the component.
e. Net benefit forgone from the best alternative use of the capacity required.

The correct answer is (e). *(CMA 1285 5-29)*
REQUIRED: The opportunity cost of making a part in a factory with no excess capacity.
DISCUSSION: An opportunity cost is the return from the next best opportunity that could have been selected for the use of scarce resources. It does not represent an actual receipt or disbursement of resources and is not recorded in the accounting records. If the part could be made using otherwise idle capacity, there would be no opportunity cost.
Answer (a) is incorrect because variable costs include actual outlays for raw materials, direct labor, and variable overhead. Answers (b) and (c) are incorrect because opportunity costs are not the actual costs incurred. Answer (d) is incorrect because an opportunity cost is a benefit, not a cost, forgone.

Module 4.5: Other Cost Definitions

81. The opportunity cost of making a component part in a factory with excess capacity for which there is no alternative use is

   a. The variable manufacturing cost of the component.
   b. The total manufacturing cost of the component.
   c. The total variable cost of the component.
   d. The fixed manufacturing cost of the component.
   e. Zero.

The correct answer is (e). (CMA 1285 5-30)
REQUIRED: The opportunity cost when no alternative use exists for excess capacity.
DISCUSSION: Opportunity cost is the benefit forgone by not selecting the next best use of scarce resources. The opportunity cost is zero when no alternative use is available.

82. An avoidable cost is

   a. A cost that may be saved by not adopting an alternative.
   b. The profit forgone by selecting one choice instead of another.
   c. A cost that does not entail any dollar outlay but is relevant to the decision-making process.
   d. A cost that continues to be incurred even though there is no activity.
   e. A cost common to all choices in question and not clearly or practically allocable to any of them.

The correct answer is (a). (CMA 1277 5-4)
REQUIRED: The definition of an avoidable cost.
DISCUSSION: An avoidable cost is a cost that may be saved (avoided) by not adopting a certain course of action.
Answer (b) is incorrect because an opportunity cost is a benefit forgone by making a given decision. Answer (c) is incorrect because it is the definition of imputed cost. Answer (d) is incorrect because a fixed cost is incurred even though no activity occurs. Answer (e) is incorrect because it describes a joint or common cost.

83. "Controllable costs" are

   a. Costs that management decides to incur in the current period to enable the company to achieve objectives other than the filling of orders placed by customers.
   b. Costs that are likely to respond to the amount of attention devoted to them by a specified manager.
   c. Costs that are governed mainly by past decisions that established the present levels of operating and organizational capacity and that only change slowly in response to small changes in capacity.
   d. Costs that fluctuate in total in response to small changes in the rate of utilization of capacity.
   e. Costs that will be unaffected by current managerial decisions.

The correct answer is (b). (CMA 678 4-12)
REQUIRED: The definition of controllable costs.
DISCUSSION: Controllable costs can be changed by action taken at the appropriate management level. All costs are controllable, but they are controlled at different management levels; e.g., the decision to build another plant is made at a higher level of management than the decision to buy office supplies.
Answer (a) is incorrect because it is the definition of discretionary costs. Answer (c) is incorrect because it is the definition of committed costs. Answer (d) is incorrect because variable costs respond to small changes in output. Answer (e) is incorrect because noncontrollable costs are unaffected by managerial decisions.

84. Controllable costs for responsibility accounting purposes are directly influenced only by

   a. A given manager within a given period.
   b. A change in activity.
   c. Production volume.
   d. Sales volume.

The correct answer is (a). (CPA 1181 T-51)
REQUIRED: The definition of controllable costs.
DISCUSSION: Controllable costs can be authorized by a given manager within a given period.
Answers (b) and (c) are incorrect because a change in activity or production volume influences variable costs. Answer (d) is incorrect because sales volume influences selling expenses, inventory level, profit, etc.

Module 4.5: Other Cost Definitions

85. The term "committed costs" refers to

a. Costs that management decides to incur in the current period to enable the company to achieve objectives other than the filling of orders placed by customers.

b. Costs that are likely to respond to the amount of attention devoted to them by a specified manager.

c. Costs that are governed mainly by past decisions that established the present levels of operating and organizational capacity and that only change slowly in response to small changes in capacity.

d. Costs that fluctuate in total in response to small changes in the rate of utilization of capacity.

e. Amortization of costs that were capitalized in previous periods.

The correct answer is (c). *(CMA 678 4-10)*
REQUIRED: The definition of "committed costs" in cost accounting.
DISCUSSION: Committed costs cannot be reduced to zero, even for short periods, without affecting profitability or long-range goals. Examples of committed costs include depreciation on buildings and equipment, salaries of key management personnel, and insurance.
Answer (a) is incorrect because such costs are discretionary. Answer (b) is incorrect because it is the definition of controllable costs. Answer (d) is incorrect because variable costs respond to small changes in output. Answer (e) is incorrect because it describes depreciation and depletion.

86. The term "discretionary costs" refers to

a. Costs that management decides to incur in the current period to enable the company to achieve objectives other than the filling of orders placed by customers.

b. Costs that are likely to respond to the amount of attention devoted to them by a specified manager.

c. Costs that are governed mainly by past decisions that established the present levels of operating and organizational capacity and that only change slowly in response to small changes in capacity.

d. Amortization of costs that were capitalized in previous periods.

e. Costs that will be unaffected by current managerial decisions.

The correct answer is (a). *(CMA 678 4-11)*
REQUIRED: The definition of discretionary costs.
DISCUSSION: Discretionary costs arise from annual decisions by management (e.g., advertising, R&D). They are short-term costs in that they can be changed from year to year. It is also possible to reduce discretionary costs for a short period without affecting long-range goals.
Answer (b) is incorrect because it is the definition of controllable costs. Answer (c) is incorrect because such costs are committed costs. Answer (d) is incorrect because depreciation and depletion represent the amortization of previously capitalized costs. Answer (e) is incorrect because noncontrollable costs are not affected by managerial decisions.

87. An imputed cost is

a. The difference in total costs that results from selecting one choice instead of another.

b. A cost that may be shifted to the future with little or no effect on current operations.

c. A cost that cannot be avoided because it has already been incurred.

d. A cost that does not entail any dollar outlay but which is relevant to the decision-making process.

e. A cost that continues to be incurred even though there is no activity.

The correct answer is (d). *(CMA 1277 5-5)*
REQUIRED: The definition of an imputed cost in cost accounting.
DISCUSSION: An imputed cost requires no dollar outlay but should be considered in decision making. An example of an imputed cost is the profit lost as a result of being unable to fill orders because the inventory level is too low.
Answer (a) is incorrect because it defines incremental costs. Answer (b) is incorrect because such costs are postponable. Answer (c) is incorrect because sunk costs have already been incurred. Answer (e) is incorrect because costs incurred when there is no activity are fixed.

Module 4.5: Other Cost Definitions

88. A sunk cost
    a. May be saved by not adopting an alternative.
    b. May be shifted to the future with little or no effect on current operations.
    c. Cannot be avoided because it has already been incurred.
    d. Does not entail any dollar outlay but is relevant to the decision-making process.
    e. Is common to all choices in question and not clearly or practically allocable to any of them.

The correct answer is (c). *(CMA 1277 5-2)*
  REQUIRED: The definition of a sunk cost in cost accounting.
  DISCUSSION: A sunk cost has already been incurred and therefore cannot be avoided. Because sunk costs are the result of past decisions, they are irrelevant to future decisions.
  Answer (a) is incorrect because it is the definition of an avoidable cost. Answer (b) is incorrect because such costs are postponable. Answer (d) is incorrect because it describes an imputed cost. Answer (e) is incorrect because it is the definition of a joint or common cost.

89. In making an equipment replacement decision, both the historical cost and the book value of the equipment to be replaced would represent
    a. Sunk costs.
    b. Fixed costs.
    c. Semi-variable costs.
    d. Opportunity costs.

The correct answer is (a). *(CIA 1186 IV-2)*
  REQUIRED: The cost represented by the historical cost and the book value.
  DISCUSSION: A sunk cost, such as the historical cost of the equipment, has already been incurred and cannot be avoided. It is irrelevant to and unaffected by future decisions.
  Answer (b) is incorrect because a fixed cost is one that does not vary within the relevant range of activity. Answer (c) is incorrect because semi-variable costs contain both fixed and variable elements. Answer (d) is incorrect because opportunity costs represent the profit forgone by making one decision rather than another.

90. Which of the following is one of the purposes of standard costs?
    a. To simplify costing procedures and expedite cost reports.
    b. To replace budgets and budgeting.
    c. To serve as a basis for product costing for external reporting purposes.
    d. To eliminate having to account for underapplied or overapplied factory overhead at the end of the period.

The correct answer is (a). *(CPA 1175 T-15)*
  REQUIRED: The statement giving a purpose of standard costs.
  DISCUSSION: A standard cost system differentiates the expected cost from the actual cost, thus identifying deviations from expected results on a routine basis. One of the purposes of standard costs is to simplify costing procedures and expedite cost reports.
  Answer (b) is incorrect because standard costs are used to prepare budgets. Answer (c) is incorrect because standard costs cannot be used for external reporting if large variances exist. Answer (d) is incorrect because the standard costs assist in determining the over- and underapplied overhead.

91. Common costs are those incurred
    a. By every department in an organization.
    b. To produce two or more inseparable products.
    c. Routinely in the industry in which the company operates.
    d. To produce common products beyond their split-off point.

The correct answer is (b). *(Publisher)*
  REQUIRED: The definition of common costs in cost accounting.
  DISCUSSION: Common costs are incurred in the production of two or more inseparable products (e.g., costs of refining petroleum into gasoline, diesel fuel, kerosene, lubricating oils, etc.) up to the point at which the products become separable (the split-off point).
  Answers (a) and (c) are incorrect because there is no term to describe costs incurred by every department or that are common to an industry. Answer (d) is incorrect because common costs (joint costs) are incurred up to the split-off point, not beyond.

92. Out-of-pocket costs

a. Are not recoverable.
b. Are under the influence of a supervisor.
c. Require expenditure of cash.
d. Are committed and unavoidable.

The correct answer is (c). *(Publisher)*
REQUIRED: The definition of out-of-pocket costs.
DISCUSSION: Out-of-pocket costs require negative cash flows (expenditures).
Answer (a) is incorrect because many out-of-pocket costs can be recovered over time; e.g., spending $10,000 on a machine may produce a cash flow of $4,000 for five years. Answer (b) is incorrect because costs under the influence of a supervisor are controllable costs. Answer (d) is incorrect because committed and unavoidable costs are sunk costs.

93. Differential costs

a. Are avoidable by changing a course of action.
b. Vary with changes in operations.
c. Include direct labor and direct material but not overhead.
d. Include direct labor and overhead but not direct material.

The correct answer is (b). *(Publisher)*
REQUIRED: The definition of differential costs.
DISCUSSION: Costs that change as a result of changes in operations or objectives are differential costs. It is synonymous with incremental costs.
Answer (a) is incorrect because, when a course of action is changed, the differential costs usually become committed costs and are unavoidable. Answer (c) is incorrect because direct labor and direct material are prime costs. Answer (d) is incorrect because direct labor and overhead are conversion costs.

94. Even if demand for the product is 20,000 units in the next quarter, the company will still have 40 percent idle capacity. The company can use this idle capacity to produce 6,000 units of a different product B, which it can sell for $7 per unit. The incremental variable cost of producing a unit of B is $6. Present fixed costs that will be allocated to B amount to $10,000. To decide whether to produce B, the company should use

a. Differential cost analysis.
b. Information economics.
c. Regression analysis.
d. Markov chain analysis.

The correct answer is (a). *(CIA 1186 IV-22)*
REQUIRED: The method to determine if idle capacity should be used for a special order.
DISCUSSION: Nonroutine decisions involve such questions as whether to make or buy or accept a special order. These decisions should be made in part on the basis of relevant costs. Analysis of differential costs is therefore essential. Costs that vary with changes in operations or objectives are differential (incremental) costs.
Answer (b) is incorrect because it concerns cost/benefit analysis of obtaining information for decision making. Answer (c) is incorrect because regression analysis attempts to find an equation describing the change in a dependent variable related to a change in an independent variable. Answer (d) is incorrect because Markov analysis is useful when a problem involves a variety of states of nature, and the probability of moving from one state to another is dependent only upon the current state.

95. Joint costs are those costs

a. Of products requiring the services of two or more processing departments.
b. Of a product from a common process that has relatively little sales value and only a small effect on profit.
c. Of production that are combined in the overhead account.
d. That are incurred to produce two or more products, each of relatively significant value, from a common process.

The correct answer is (d). *(Publisher)*
REQUIRED: The definition of joint costs in cost accounting.
DISCUSSION: Joint costs are the common costs of producing two or more inseparable products up to the point at which they become separable (the split-off point). The products are then sold as identifiably separate products or processed further.
Answer (a) is incorrect because the costs accumulated in prior processing steps are considered raw material costs for purposes of subsequent processing. Answer (b) is incorrect because common products with relatively little sales value are byproducts, e.g., woodchips from a saw mill. When byproducts only contribute a small amount of profit, no joint cost is allocated to them. Answer (c) is incorrect because indirect costs are combined in the overhead account.

Module 4.5: Other Cost Definitions

96. Cost is the amount measured by the current monetary value of economic resources given up or to be given up in obtaining goods and services. Costs may be classified as unexpired or expired. Which of the following costs is not always considered to be expired immediately upon being recognized?

 a. Cost of goods sold.
 b. Sales salaries.
 c. Depreciation expense for plant machinery.
 d. Loss from bankruptcy of a major debtor not provided for in the annual adjustment.

The correct answer is (c). *(C. Wagner)*
REQUIRED: The cost not always considered expired when recognized.
DISCUSSION: Unexpired costs are assets and apply to the production of future revenues. Expired costs, which are those not applicable to production of future revenues, are deducted from current revenues or, in very few cases, charged against retained earnings. Depreciation expense for plant machinery is a component of factory overhead that reflects the reclassification of a portion of the machinery cost to product (inventory) cost. This portion of inventory cost is an unexpired cost until the product is sold. At that time it becomes part of cost of goods sold (an expense).
Answers (a), (b), and (d) are incorrect because each is an expired cost (expense or loss).

97. The product cost determined in a conventional standard cost accounting system is a(n)

 a. Direct cost.
 b. Fixed cost.
 c. Joint cost.
 d. Expected cost.

The correct answer is (d). *(CPA 571 T-34)*
REQUIRED: The cost determined by a conventional standard cost system.
DISCUSSION: Standard costs are expected costs. Normally, the standard costs established are those expected to be actually incurred, not those reflecting an ideal efficiency level.
Answer (a) is incorrect because direct costs are traceable to a particular activity. Answer (b) is incorrect because product costs generally include both fixed and variable costs. Answer (c) is incorrect because joint or common cost is the cost of producing two or more inseparable products.

98. The perpetual inventory method differs from the periodic in that the former

 a. Includes only variable manufacturing costs in the product cost calculation.
 b. Requires a physical inventory count to determine amounts of inventories used and/or remaining.
 c. Maintains a continuous record of transactions affecting the inventory balances.
 d. Includes manufacturing and nonmanufacturing costs in inventory.

The correct answer is (c). *(Publisher)*
REQUIRED: A difference between the perpetual and periodic inventory methods.
DISCUSSION: Perpetual inventory records provide for continuous recordkeeping of the quantities of inventory (and possibly unit costs and/or total costs). Perpetual inventory records can be maintained either in units or in units and dollars. This method requires a journal entry every time items are added to or taken from inventory.
Answer (a) is incorrect because it describes variable costing. Answer (b) is incorrect because the periodic inventory system relies on physical counts to determine quantities. Answer (d) is incorrect because only manufacturing costs are included in inventory.

99. Of most relevance in deciding how indirect costs should be assigned to products is the degree of

 a. Avoidability.
 b. Causality.
 c. Controllability.
 d. Linearity.

The correct answer is (b). *(CPA 571 T-36)*
REQUIRED: The most relevant factor in assigning indirect costs to products.
DISCUSSION: Indirect costs, e.g., factory overhead, cannot be readily identified with a unit of production. The best method of assigning these indirect costs (overhead) is based upon what causes the cost. Machine hours and labor costs (or hours) are common allocation bases because of their substantial effect on indirect costs (e.g., depreciation, fringe benefits).
Answers (a) and (c) are incorrect because avoidability and controllability of costs have to do with responsibility accounting rather than with assigning costs to production. Answer (d) is incorrect because a linear relationship is only assumed in cost/volume/profit analysis.

4.6 Cost Accounting Standards Board (CASB)

100. The Cost Accounting Standards Board (CASB) was established by

a. The Accounting Principles Board (APB).
b. The General Accounting Office (GAO).
c. The Financial Accounting Standards Board (FASB).
d. The U.S. Congress.
e. The Securities and Exchange Commission (SEC).

The correct answer is (d). *(CMA 1274 3-22)*
REQUIRED: The source of authority for the Cost Accounting Standards Board (CASB).
DISCUSSION: The CASB was established by the U.S. Congress in 1970 to develop cost accounting standards which applied to defense contractors and subcontractors. Other government agencies also use the standards, however. The CASB was eliminated in 1980, but the standards remain in effect.
Answers (a) and (c) are incorrect because they are private sector organizations concerned with financial accounting and reporting issues. Answer (b) is incorrect because the GAO is the audit agency of the Congress. Answer (e) is incorrect because the SEC is a government agency concerned with public disclosure of financial and other data by publicly held companies.

101. The cost standards issued by the Cost Accounting Standards Board (CASB)

a. Were ratified directly by vote of both Houses of Congress.
b. Required consensus from industry to make the standard legal.
c. Became law after 60 days from the date of publication in the Federal Register for the second time provided Congress did not enact a resolution in opposition.
d. Became law once they were approved by the CASB.
e. Were suggested guidelines that companies were asked to adopt and follow.

The correct answer is (c). *(CMA 1274 3-24)*
REQUIRED: The correct statement about cost standards issued by the Cost Accounting Standards Board (CASB).
DISCUSSION: CASB standards became effective 60 days from the date of the second publication in the Federal Register provided Congress did not react negatively by enacting an opposing resolution. This procedure gave various constituencies the opportunity to respond through the political process.
Answer (a) is incorrect because Congress delegated cost accounting standard setting to the CASB. Answers (b) and (e) are incorrect because industry must comply with CASB standards as required by law. Answer (d) is incorrect because the standards had a 60-day waiting period before taking effect.

102. The Cost Accounting Standards Board's (CASB) purpose was to

a. Develop accounting principles and standard practices for industry.
b. Develop uniform cost accounting standards to be used in pricing, administration, and settlement of negotiated defense contracts and subcontracts with relevant federal agencies.
c. Work in conjunction with the Securities and Exchange Commission (SEC) in examining registration forms and statements filed by corporations.
d. Administer all contracts and subcontracts with federal agencies.
e. Aid the Financial Accounting Standards Board (FASB) in establishing accounting standards.

The correct answer is (b). *(CMA 1274 3-23)*
REQUIRED: The purpose of the Cost Accounting Standards Board (CASB).
DISCUSSION: The CASB was established by the U.S. Congress in 1970 to develop uniform cost accounting standards to be used in the pricing, administration, and settlement of defense contracts and subcontracts with relevant federal agencies. The standards also apply to all negotiated procurement contracts which are in excess of $100,000. Although the Board was disbanded in 1980, the standards remain in effect.
Answer (a) is incorrect because the CASB did not develop accounting principles or set standards other than for defense and procurement contracts. Answer (c) is incorrect because the CASB had no connection with the SEC and did not examine registration statements. Answer (d) is incorrect because the CASB did not administer the contracts. Answer (e) is incorrect because the CASB did not aid the FASB and it only applied to cost accounting standards.

CHAPTER FIVE
JOB ORDER COSTING

5.1 When to Use Job Order Costing	(9 questions)	72
5.2 Cost Flow Between Accounts	(11 questions)	74
5.3 Application of Overhead	(40 questions)	77
5.4 Work-in-Process Account Calculations	(21 questions)	89
5.5 Journal Entries	(12 questions)	96
5.6 Comprehensive	(27 questions)	100

    Job order costing is frequently presented before process costing in textbooks. The major distinction between the two procedures is that job order costing requires that a subsidiary ledger be maintained for the manufacturing (work-in-process) and finished goods inventory accounts to keep track of specifically identifiable batches of goods or projects. In process costing, there is no need for subsidiary ledgers because only one homogeneous product must customarily be accounted for. Use of the just-in-time (JIT) manufacturing methods often discussed in contemporary textbooks would not mitigate the need for cost accumulation and cost allocations.

    Questions on the basic flow of costs and cost data are given in Module 5.2 without dollar amounts and are repeated in Module 5.5 with dollar amounts to reinforce understanding of the flow of costs through the manufacturing account.

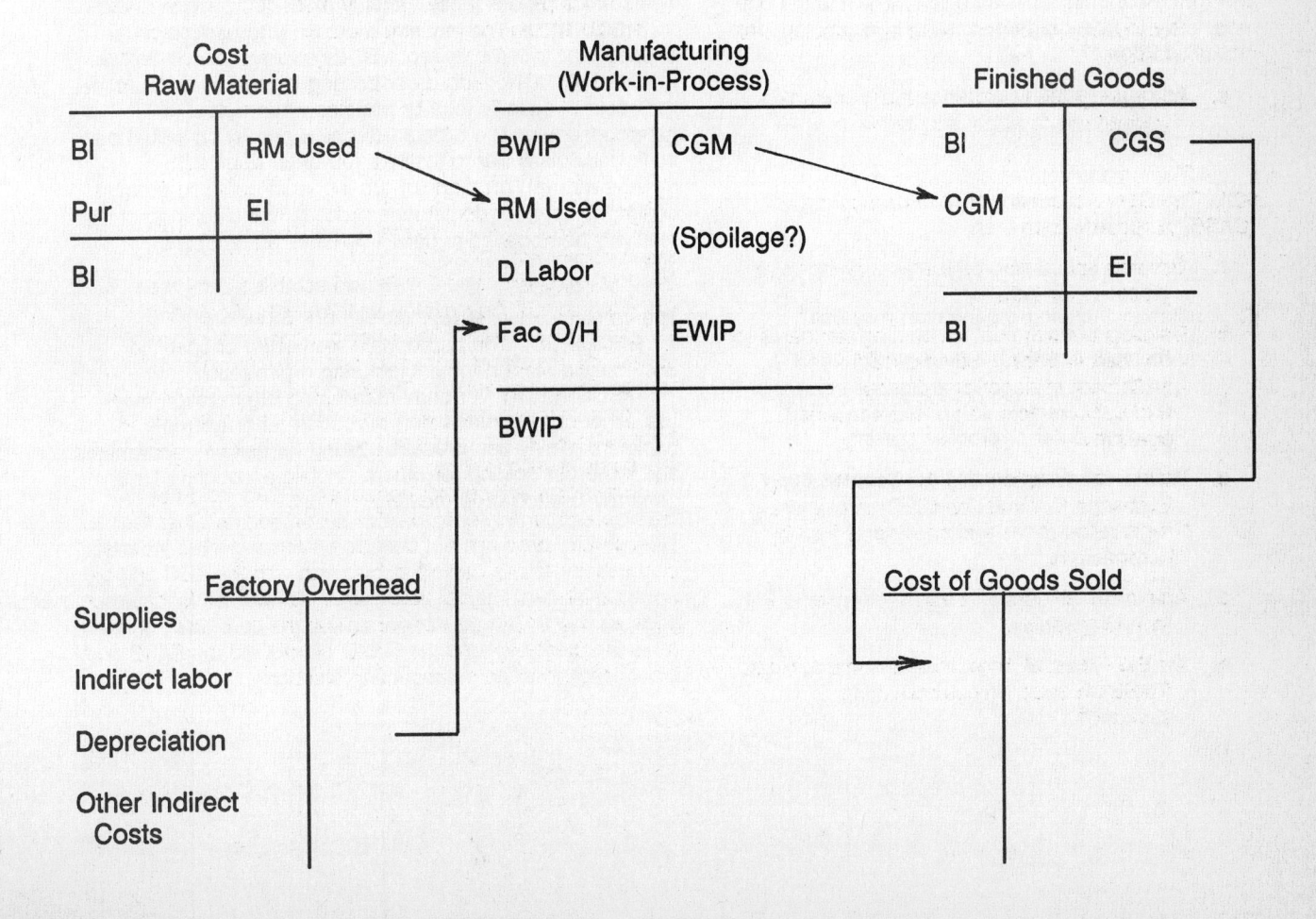

Cost Raw Material		Manufacturing (Work-in-Process)		Finished Goods	
BI	RM Used	BWIP	CGM	BI	CGS
Pur	EI	RM Used		CGM	
BI		D Labor	(Spoilage?)		EI
		Fac O/H	EWIP	BI	
		BWIP			

Factory Overhead
Supplies
Indirect labor
Depreciation
Other Indirect Costs

Cost of Goods Sold

5.1 When to Use Job Order Costing

1. What is the best cost accumulation procedure to use when many batches, each differing as to product specifications, are produced?

   a. Job order.
   b. Process.
   c. Actual.
   d. Standard.

The correct answer is (a). *(CPA 581 T-44)*
REQUIRED: The cost accumulation method suitable for batches of different products.
DISCUSSION: The job order cost system of accounting is appropriate when producing products with individual characteristics and/or when identifiable groupings are possible, e.g., batches of certain styles or types of furniture. The unique aspect of job order costing is the identification of costs to specific units or a particular job.
Answer (b) is incorrect because process costing should be used to accumulate costs when products are homogeneous and/or when groupings are not easily identifiable. Answers (c) and (d) are incorrect because each is a method of charging costs. Either method may be used with job order or process costing.

2. Job order costs are most useful for

   a. Determining inventory valuation using LIFO.
   b. Estimating the overhead costs included in transfer prices.
   c. Controlling indirect costs of future production.
   d. Determining the cost of a specific project.
   e. Determining labor cost involved in production.

The correct answer is (d). *(CIA 578 IV-1)*
REQUIRED: The most appropriate use of job order costs.
DISCUSSION: Job order costs are used in determining the costs of a specific, clearly identifiable job or project. In contrast, process costing averages the costs of all production.
Answers (a), (b), (c), and (e) are incorrect because each is equally applicable to either job order costing or process costing.

3. From the industries listed below, which is the one most likely to use job order costing in accounting for production costs?

   a. Automobile manufacturer.
   b. Specialty print shop.
   c. Paint manufacturer.
   d. Oil refinery.

The correct answer is (b). *(CIA 1187 IV-4)*
REQUIRED: The industry most likely to use job order costing.
DISCUSSION: Job order costing is used to account for the costs of specific jobs or projects when output is heterogeneous. The orders filled by a print shop would be sufficiently dissimilar to justify a job order approach.
Answers (a), (c), and (d) are incorrect because process costing is used for continuous process manufacturing of relatively homogeneous units (oil, paint, automobiles).

4. A nonmanufacturing organization may use

   a. Job order costing but not process costing.
   b. Process costing but not job order costing.
   c. Either job order or process costing.
   d. Neither job order costing nor process costing.

The correct answer is (c). *(CPA 1181 T-44)*
REQUIRED: The appropriate method(s) of cost accumulation in a nonmanufacturing organization.
DISCUSSION: A nonmanufacturing organization may use either cost accumulation procedure. For example, banks frequently use process costing for certain departments and job order costing for others. Public accounting firms generally use job order costing.

Module 5.1: When to Use Job Order Costing 73

5. Job order cost accounting systems and process cost accounting systems differ in the way

   a. Manufacturing costs are assigned to production runs and the number of units for which costs are averaged.

   b. Orders are taken and the number of units in the orders.

   c. Product-profitability is determined and compared with planned costs.

   d. Manufacturing processes can be accomplished and the number of production runs that may be performed in a year.

The correct answer is (a). *(CIA 1186 IV-4)*
REQUIRED: The way job order and process cost accounting systems differ.
DISCUSSION: A cost system accounts for the costs of manufacturing inventoriable output. The objective is to determine the portion of manufacturing cost to be expensed (because the output was sold) and the portion to be deferred (because the output was still on hand). Process costing is used for continuous process manufacturing of units that are relatively homogeneous (e.g., oil refining, automobile production lines, etc.). Job order costing is used to account for the cost of specific jobs or projects when output is heterogeneous. The difference is often overemphasized. Job order costing simply requires subsidiary ledgers (to keep track of the specific jobs) for the same work-in-process (manufacturing) account and finished goods inventory account that are basic to process costing.
Answer (b) is incorrect because how orders are taken is irrelevant. Answer (c) is incorrect because profit is determined in the same way in both systems. Answer (d) is incorrect because the cost system is not necessarily related to the manufacturing processes.

6. In job order costing, the basic document to accumulate the cost of each order is the

   a. Invoice.
   b. Purchase order.
   c. Requisition sheet.
   d. Job cost sheet.

The correct answer is (d). *(CPA 580 T-42)*
REQUIRED: The basic document to accumulate the cost of each order in job order costing.
DISCUSSION: The job cost sheet, or job order sheet, is used to accumulate product costs in a job order costing system. Materials, labor, and overhead are the costs accumulated.
Answer (a) is incorrect because an invoice shows the price and quantity of the product purchased or sold. Answer (b) is incorrect because the purchase order states the specifications, quantities, and prices of items to be purchased. Answer (c) is incorrect because a requisition sheet is an internal document used by production to request materials or other resources from another department or division.

7. How does a job order cost accounting system differ from a process cost accounting system?

   a. Subsidiary ledgers for the work-in-process (manufacturing) and finished goods inventories are necessary in job order costing.

   b. The procedure to apply overhead to product cost is different.

   c. Both the timing and nature of entries to transfer cost from the work-in-process account to the finished goods inventory account are different.

   d. Most of the journal entries which require debits and/or credits to the work-in-process account are different.

The correct answer is (a). *(Publisher)*
REQUIRED: A difference between a job order system and process costing.
DISCUSSION: Job order systems are used to account for manufacturing processes that produce distinctly different products or groups of products. By contrast, process costing is suitable to production of a homogeneous product. Given identifiable different products, costs need to be collected separately for each product or groups of products. Accordingly, while the same general ledger accounts are used for both cost systems, subsidiary ledgers are maintained in job order costing for the WIP and FG inventory accounts so the costs associated with individual products and groups of products may be separately accounted for.
Answers (b), (c), and (d) are incorrect because procedures with regard to the general ledger accounts are the same.

8. When switching to a just-in-time (JIT) system, the level of inventory maintained by an organization is expected to
   a. Increase.
   b. Decrease.
   c. Remain the same.
   d. Increase rapidly and then decrease.

The correct answer is (b). *(Publisher)*
REQUIRED: The characteristic of inventory in a JIT system of operation.
DISCUSSION: By definition, in a JIT system, items are produced immediately as needed (or just in time) for the next step in the production line. These systems consequently maintain a minimal amount of raw materials, work-in-process or finished goods in comparison with other manufacturing systems.

9. In a JIT costing system, factory overhead applied should be charged to
   a. Raw materials.
   b. Cost of goods sold.
   c. Finished goods.
   d. Work-in-process.

The correct answer is (b). *(Publisher)*
REQUIRED: The account that factory overhead applied is charged to in JIT systems.
DISCUSSION: In a JIT system of production, there typically are no work orders. Thus, items such as direct labor and factory overhead cannot be easily charged to specific jobs. Usually, direct labor and factory overhead are expensed directly to cost of goods sold. At year-end adjusting entries are required to properly allocate direct labor and factory overhead to the remaining work in process and finished goods.
Answer (a) is incorrect because overhead is not debited to raw materials. Answers (c) and (d) are incorrect because factory overhead applied is not charged directly to these accounts. They are only adjusted to include their share of factory overhead at the end of a period.

5.2 Cost Flow Between Accounts

10. What is the nature of the manufacturing (work-in-process) account?
    a. It is neither a real nor a nominal account.
    b. It is an inventory account indicating the beginning and ending inventory of goods being processed.
    c. It is a hybrid account, i.e., both a real and a nominal account.
    d. It is a nominal account to which indirect costs are charged as incurred and credited as these costs are charged to production.

The correct answer is (b). *(Publisher)*
REQUIRED: The nature of the manufacturing (work-in-process) account.
DISCUSSION: The manufacturing account is an inventory account to which materials, labor, and overhead costs are charged as they are incurred in the production process. The sum of these costs plus the cost of BWIP is the total production cost to be accounted for in any one period. These costs are allocated to goods completed during the period, i.e., to finished goods or EWIP. Additionally, the manufacturing account may be credited for abnormal spoilage.
Answers (a) and (c) are incorrect because the work-in-process account is an inventory or real account. Answer (d) is incorrect because it describes the factory overhead account.

11. The debits in the work-in-process account are BWIP, labor, material, and overhead. The account should be credited for production that is completed and sent to finished goods inventory. The balance in the account is
    a. Zero.
    b. EWIP, which is a credit.
    c. EWIP, which is a debit.
    d. Total production costs to be accounted for.

The correct answer is (c). *(Publisher)*
REQUIRED: The composition of the balance of the work-in-process account after the account is credited for goods produced during the period.
DISCUSSION: The sum of the debits to WIP equals total production costs to be accounted for. Ignoring possible spoilage, production consists either of goods that have been completed or those still in process. Accordingly, after the account is credited for the cost of goods completed and transferred to the FG inventory, the debit balance in the account is EWIP.
Answer (a) is incorrect because there is a zero balance only if there is no EWIP. Answer (b) is incorrect because the EWIP may be credited to balance the account (i.e., bring the account to a zero balance), but EWIP will never have a credit balance. Answer (d) is incorrect because total production costs to be accounted for include finished goods as well as EWIP.

Module 5.2: Cost Flow Between Accounts

12. What is the journal entry to record the purchase of materials on account?

a.	Raw material inventory	XX	
	Accounts payable		XX
b.	Accounts payable	XX	
	Raw material inventory		XX
c.	Accounts receivable	XX	
	Accounts payable		XX
d.	Cash	XX	
	Accounts receivable		XX

The correct answer is (a). *(Publisher)*
REQUIRED: The journal entry to record the purchase of materials on account.
DISCUSSION: The correct entry to record a purchase of materials on account is to increase the appropriate asset and liability accounts. Materials are charged to an inventory; the corresponding liability is accounts payable. The asset account(s) could be stores control and/or supplies or a number of other accounts. Also, subsidiary ledgers may be utilized to account for various individual items (a perpetual inventory system). The term "control" implies that a subsidiary ledger is being used.
Answer (b) is incorrect because it is the entry to record the return of materials to suppliers. Answer (c) is incorrect because it is an entry to reclassify credit balances in accounts receivable as liabilities or debit balances in accounts payable as assets. Answer (d) is incorrect because it is an entry to record cash received on account.

13. In a job order cost system using predetermined factory overhead rates, indirect materials usually are recorded initially as an increase in

   a. Work-in-process control.
   b. Factory overhead applied.
   c. Factory overhead control.
   d. Stores control.

The correct answer is (d). *(CPA 1187 T-41)*
REQUIRED: The initial recording of indirect materials under a job order cost system using predetermined factory overhead rates.
DISCUSSION: Initially, all indirect and direct materials are recorded as an increase to stores control. Stores control is an inventory account that keeps record of all materials that are purchased. Only when the materials are requested for specific jobs are they taken out of stores control.

14. What is the journal entry to record the issuance of materials and supplies to a production department?

a.	Supplies	XX	
	Stores control		XX
b.	Work-in-process	XX	
	Factory O/H control	XX	
	Stores control		XX
c.	Stores control	XX	
	Work-in-process		XX
d.	Accounts payable	XX	
	Stores control	XX	
	Supplies		XX

The correct answer is (b). *(Publisher)*
REQUIRED: The journal entry to record the issuance of materials and supplies.
DISCUSSION: The proper entry to record the issuance of materials to production is to increase the work-in-process account by the amount of the direct materials issued. The factory overhead control account should be increased by the amount of indirect materials (supplies) issued. The total amount of materials and supplies issued should be credited, i.e., an inventory account.
Answers (a) and (d) are incorrect because supplies and stores control are different titles for the same asset account. Answer (c) is incorrect because it is the entry to record the return of direct materials from the manufacturing department to inventory.

15. In a job order cost system, direct labor costs usually are recorded initially as an increase in

   a. Factory overhead applied.
   b. Factory overhead control.
   c. Finished goods control.
   d. Work-in-process control.

The correct answer is (d). *(CPA 587 T-42)*
REQUIRED: The account to which direct labor is first charged in a job order cost system.
DISCUSSION: Direct labor costs are inventoriable costs and thus are initially debited to the work-in-process control account.
Answers (a) and (b) are incorrect because direct labor costs are not overhead costs. Answer (c) is incorrect because when using a job order cost system, direct labor is initially charged to WIP control. When the goods are finished, then direct labor will be transferred from WIP control to finished goods control.

16. In a job order cost system, the application of factory overhead would usually be reflected in the general ledger as an increase in

a. Factory overhead control.
b. Finished goods control.
c. Work-in-process control.
d. Cost of goods sold.

The correct answer is (c). *(CPA 1185 T-38)*
REQUIRED: The account that is increased when overhead is applied in a job order cost system.
DISCUSSION: In a job order cost system, the correct entry to record the application of factory overhead to specific jobs is to charge WIP control and credit factory overhead applied using a predetermined overhead rate. The effect is to increase the WIP control account.
Answer (a) is incorrect because factory overhead control increases when actual factory overhead costs are incurred. Answer (b) is incorrect because finished goods control increases only when goods are completed. Answer (d) is incorrect because cost of goods sold is only increased when products are sold.

17. What is the entry to record completion of a particular product or group of products?

a. Finished goods XX
      Cost of goods sold   XX
b. Work-in-process XX
      Finished goods   XX
c. Finished goods XX
      Work-in-process   XX
d. Cost of goods sold XX
      Work-in-process   XX

The correct answer is (c). *(Publisher)*
REQUIRED: The journal entry to record completion of a job.
DISCUSSION: The correct entry to record completion of a job is to charge finished goods inventory and credit WIP for the amounts of actual direct materials, actual direct labor, and applied factory overhead used.
Answer (a) is incorrect because it is the reverse of the entry to expense inventory that is sold. Answer (b) is incorrect because it reverses the entry to transfer cost of goods finished from WIP to FG. Answer (d) is incorrect because all items sold are charged to FG inventory before being transferred to CGS; no entries should transfer costs directly from WIP to CGS.

18. In processing goods through a factory, materials are successively run through production departments A, B, and C. For product-costing purposes, when dealing with items received from A, department B should treat them as

a. Raw materials.
b. Work-in-process.
c. Finished goods.
d. Equivalent units.

The correct answer is (a). *(CPA 574 T-17)*
REQUIRED: The treatment of processed goods as they progress through a factory.
DISCUSSION: As materials are processed by various departments, each succeeding department treats the transfer from the preceding department as raw materials.
Answer (b) is incorrect because WIP consists of the incomplete units within a process at the end of a period. Answer (c) is incorrect because finished goods have been completed and sent to inventory or to the next processing department. Answer (d) is incorrect because equivalent units are the total equivalent whole units processed, including the partial units of production in both BWIP and EWIP.

19. In job order costing, payroll taxes paid by the employer for factory employees are preferably accounted for as

a. Direct labor.
b. Factory overhead.
c. Indirect labor.
d. Administrative costs.

The correct answer is (b). *(CPA 579 T-22)*
REQUIRED: The accounting treatment for the employer's share of payroll taxes.
DISCUSSION: The employer's share of factory employees' payroll taxes should be accounted for as factory overhead. Fringe benefits are also usually accounted for as factory overhead.
Answer (a) is incorrect because accounting for payroll taxes as direct labor will result in inconsistencies as the maximum payroll tax threshold is reached; e.g., there will be higher labor costs at the beginning than at the end of the year. Answer (c) is incorrect because indirect labor is the cost of labor not directly involved in the production process. It is also a component of factory overhead. Answer (d) is incorrect because administrative costs, which are period costs, not product costs, are expensed in the period incurred.

Module 5.3: Application of Overhead

20. Under a job order system of cost accounting, the dollar amount of the entry involved in the transfer of inventory from work-in-process to finished goods is the sum of the costs charged to all jobs

a. Started in process during the period.
b. In process during the period.
c. Completed and sold during the period.
d. Completed during the period.

The correct answer is (d). *(CPA 1172 T-31)*
REQUIRED: The costs included in the entry to transfer inventory to finished goods in a job order cost system.
DISCUSSION: In a job order cost system, the entry to transfer inventory from WIP to FG is

Finished goods	XX	
Work-in-process		XX

The amount of the entry is the sum of the costs (irrespective of the period in which they were incurred) charged to all jobs completed during the period.
Answer (a) is incorrect because it does not include the cost of goods started in a prior period and completed in this period. Answer (b) is incorrect because it includes the cost of any goods not completed at the end of the period. Answer (c) is incorrect because it excludes the cost of goods completed during the period but not yet sold.

5.3 Application of Overhead

21. Factory overhead is best described as

a. Manufacturing costs in excess of standard costs.
b. Indirect manufacturing costs.
c. Avoidable and discretionary factory costs.
d. Spoilage and other unproductive costs.

The correct answer is (b). *(Publisher)*
REQUIRED: The definition of factory overhead.
DISCUSSION: Factory overhead consists of indirect manufacturing costs that cannot be traced to specific units of production but are incurred as part of the production process; i.e., production could not occur without incurring these costs. Factory overhead is usually allocated to products based upon the level of activity incurred during a period of time, e.g., direct labor hours or machine hours.
Answer (a) is incorrect because it describes unfavorable variances. Answer (c) is incorrect because direct costs, i.e., direct labor and direct material, may be both avoidable and discretionary. Answer (d) is incorrect because spoilage can be a necessary outcome of the manufacturing process. To produce good units, some units may have to be spoiled.

22. The numerator in the overhead application rate is

a. Estimated overhead costs.
b. Actual overhead costs.
c. The activity level.
d. (a) minus (b).

The correct answer is (a). *(Publisher)*
REQUIRED: The numerator of the overhead application rate ratio.
DISCUSSION: The overhead application rate is established at the beginning of each year to determine how much overhead to accumulate throughout the period. The estimated overhead costs are divided by the activity level or capacity in terms of units to arrive at the desired rate.
Answer (b) is incorrect because actual overhead is not known at the beginning of the period; the overhead rate is predetermined. Answer (c) is incorrect because the activity level is the ratio's denominator.

23. There are several alternative activity bases for applying overhead. Which activity base is not commonly used?

a. Direct labor hours.
b. Direct labor cost.
c. Machine hours.
d. Sales value of product produced.

The correct answer is (d). *(Publisher)*
REQUIRED: The activity base not appropriate for applying overhead.
DISCUSSION: Overhead is normally applied to production according to an activity base such as direct labor hours, direct labor cost, or machine hours. An activity base should have a relatively close correlation to the incurrence of overhead; e.g., if overhead is largely maintenance and is based upon the frequency of equipment operation, the activity base may well be machine hours. The sales value of the product produced is not a variable with a causal relationship with the incurrence of overhead.

24. In a capital intensive industry, which activity base would be most appropriate for applying overhead?

a. Direct labor hours.
b. Direct labor cost.
c. Machine hours.
d. Sales value of product produced.

The correct answer is (c). *(Publisher)*
REQUIRED: The best activity base for applying overhead in a capital intensive industry.
DISCUSSION: In capital intensive industries, the amount of overhead would probably be related more to machine hours than to either direct labor hours or direct labor cost.
Answers (a) and (b) are incorrect because each is a more appropriate activity base for a labor intensive industry. Answer (d) is incorrect because the sales value of product produced is virtually never an appropriate activity base on which to allocate overhead.

25. Why are annual overhead application rates used?

a. To budget overhead.
b. Seasonal variability of overhead costs.
c. Seasonal variability of activity levels.
d. Both (b) and (c).

The correct answer is (d). *(Publisher)*
REQUIRED: The reason for annual overhead application rates.
DISCUSSION: Annual overhead application rates smooth seasonal variability of overhead costs and activity levels. If overhead were applied to the product as incurred, the overhead rate per unit in most cases would vary considerably from week to week or month to month. The purpose of an annual overhead application rate is to simulate constant overhead over the year.
Answer (a) is incorrect because one budgets overhead by estimating the total costs to be incurred. Answers (b) and (c) are incorrect because they are both reasons for the use of annual overhead application rates.

26. In a labor intensive industry in which more overhead (service, support, more expensive equipment, etc.) is incurred by the more highly skilled and paid employees, which activity base would be most appropriate for applying overhead?

a. Direct labor hours.
b. Direct labor cost.
c. Machine hours.
d. Sales value of product produced.

The correct answer is (b). *(Publisher)*
REQUIRED: The best activity base for applying overhead in a labor intensive industry.
DISCUSSION: In labor intensive industries, overhead is usually allocated on a labor activity base. If more overhead is incurred by the more highly skilled and paid employees, the overhead rate should be based upon direct labor costs rather than direct labor hours.
Answer (a) is incorrect because direct labor hours would be appropriate if overhead were incurred uniformly by all types of employees. Answer (c) is incorrect because machine hours is an appropriate activity base when overhead varies with machine time used. Answer (d) is incorrect because sales value is virtually never an appropriate activity base for allocating overhead.

Module 5.3: Application of Overhead

27. Application rates for factory overhead best reflect anticipated fluctuations in sales over a cycle of years when they are computed under the concept of

a. Maximum capacity.
b. Normal capacity.
c. Practical capacity.
d. Expected actual capacity.

The correct answer is (b). *(CPA 575 T-37)*
REQUIRED: The concept of capacity for best applying overhead over a cycle of years.
DISCUSSION: Normal capacity is the level of activity that will approximate demand over a period that includes seasonal, cyclical, and trend variations. Deviations in one year will be offset in subsequent years.
Answer (a) is incorrect because maximum capacity is the level at which output is maximized regardless of efficiency. This level is impossible to maintain and results in underapplied overhead. Answer (c) is incorrect because practical capacity is the maximum level at which output is produced efficiently. It usually also results in underapplied overhead. Answer (d) is incorrect because expected actual activity is a short-run activity level. It minimizes under- or overapplied overhead but does not provide a consistent basis for assigning overhead cost. Per unit overhead will fluctuate because of short-term savings in the expected production level.

28. Which of the following items is not included in (charged to) factory overhead?

a. Factory depreciation and supplies.
b. Costs of service departments.
c. Costs of marketing departments.
d. Costs of maintenance departments.

The correct answer is (c). *(Publisher)*
REQUIRED: The item not charged to factory overhead.
DISCUSSION: Marketing costs, e.g., salaries of sales personnel, sales commissions, and advertising, are expensed as incurred; i.e., they are period costs. They cannot be allocated to the product because these marketing costs are not associated with the manufacturing process.
Answer (a) is incorrect because factory depreciation and supplies are excellent examples of indirect costs that are considered overhead. Answers (b) and (d) are incorrect because service and maintenance departments are not directly related to the production of specific goods; i.e, their costs are indirect and are associated with the manufacturing process. Thus, they can be allocated to the final output.

29. The denominator of the overhead application rate can be based on one of several production capacities. Which would result in the lowest expected over- or underapplied overhead?

a. Theoretical capacity.
b. Expected volume.
c. Normal volume.
d. Practical capacity.

The correct answer is (b). *(Publisher)*
REQUIRED: The production capacity used in the application of overhead that results in the lowest expected over- or underapplied overhead.
DISCUSSION: Overhead is applied according to a rate found by dividing budgeted overhead for a period by an activity level. If actual activity differs from the denominator of the overhead application rate (which is the predetermined activity level), a volume variance, i.e., too much or too little overhead, will be applied to product. The expected volume is that predicted for the period. Thus, expected volume as a denominator should result in the lowest expected over- or underapplied overhead.
Answer (a) is incorrect because theoretical capacity is the absolute capacity assuming continuous operations, i.e., even on Sundays, holidays, etc., and can never be attained. Answer (c) is incorrect because normal volume is an average expected volume over a series of years. It will vary from the expected volume on a year-by-year basis. Answer (d) is incorrect because practical capacity is theoretical capacity adjusted for holidays, maintenance time, etc. It is very difficult to attain.

Module 5.3: Application of Overhead

30. Which concept of capacity applies the least amount of overhead to units of production?

   a. Theoretical capacity. — THE LARGEST POSSIBLE
   b. Expected volume.
   c. Normal volume.
   d. Practical capacity.

The correct answer is (a). *(Publisher)*
REQUIRED: The concept of capacity that applies the least overhead to production.
DISCUSSION: The larger the denominator in the overhead application rate, the smaller the rate and the less cost assigned to product. Theoretical capacity, which is the absolute capacity during continuous operations, ignoring holidays, maintenance time, etc., provides the largest denominator in the ratio.

31. Many firms use two overhead accounts: factory overhead control and factory overhead applied. During the period, which account receives numerous debits and credits?

   a. Factory overhead applied.
   b. Factory overhead control.
   c. Both.
   d. Neither.

The correct answer is (d). *(Publisher)*
REQUIRED: The overhead account(s) with numerous debits and credits during the period.
DISCUSSION: When both factory overhead control and factory overhead applied are used, all overhead incurred is debited to factory overhead control. All overhead applied is credited to factory overhead applied. The only credits to factory overhead control are to close the account at the end of the period and to correct errors. The only debits to factory overhead applied are to close the account at the end of the period and to correct errors.

32. When the amount of overapplied factory overhead is significant, the entry to close overapplied factory overhead will most likely require

   a. A debit to cost of goods sold.
   b. Debits to cost of goods sold, finished goods inventory, and work-in-process inventory.
   c. A credit to cost of goods sold.
   d. Credits to cost of goods sold, finished goods inventory, and work-in-process inventory.

The correct answer is (d). *(CIA 1185 IV-10)*
REQUIRED: The most likely entry to close overapplied factory overhead.
DISCUSSION: Under a normal costing system, overhead is applied to all jobs worked on during the period at a predetermined rate. Therefore, since cost of goods sold, finished goods inventory, and work-in-process inventory all relate to jobs worked on during the period, they should each be adjusted by their proportionate share of over- or underapplied overhead. The entry to close overapplied overhead would require credits to these three accounts.
Answer (a) is incorrect because cost of goods sold should be credited (not debited) for its share of overapplied overhead. Answer (b) is incorrect because cost of goods sold, finished goods inventory, and work-in-process inventory should be credited (not debited) for their share of overapplied overhead. Answer (c) is incorrect because, although it is commonly used, it is not as conceptually sound as answer (d).

33. Underapplied factory overhead related to a decrease in production should be charged to

   a. WIP inventory.
   b. FG inventory.
   c. Cost of goods sold.
   d. WIP inventory and FG inventory.
   e. WIP inventory, FG inventory, and cost of goods sold.

The correct answer is (e). *(CIA 582 IV-26)*
REQUIRED: The account(s) to which underapplied factory overhead resulting from a decrease in production should be charged.
DISCUSSION: Underapplied factory overhead should be allocated to work-in-process, finished goods, and cost of goods sold on a pro rata basis. This apportionment may be based on either the percent of total overhead or the percent of total cost. Under- or overapplied factory overhead may also be charged (credited) to cost of goods sold. This latter method is theoretically less accurate.

Module 5.3: Application of Overhead

34. Worley Company has underapplied overhead of $45,000 for the year. Before disposition of the underapplied overhead, selected year-end balances from Worley's accounting records were

Sales	$1,200,000
Cost of goods sold	720,000
Direct materials inventory	36,000
Work-in-process inventory	54,000
Finished goods inventory	90,000

Under Worley's cost accounting system, over- or underapplied overhead is allocated to appropriate inventories and CGS based on year-end balances. In its year-end income statement, Worley should report CGS of

a. $682,500.
b. $684,000.
c. $756,000.
d. $757,500.

The correct answer is (d). *(CPA 1183 P-44)*
REQUIRED: The amount of cost of goods sold after allocation of underapplied overhead.
DISCUSSION: The allocation of underapplied overhead increases CGS. The underapplied overhead of $45,000 for the year should be allocated on a pro rata basis to work-in-process ($54,000), finished goods ($90,000), and CGS ($720,000). The sum of these three items is $864,000. Thus, $37,500 should be allocated to CGS [($720,000 ÷ $864,000) x $45,000]. CGS after allocation is $757,500 ($37,500 + $720,000). The remaining $7,500 should be allocated proportionately between work-in-process and finished goods.

35. Woodman Company applies factory overhead on the basis of direct labor hours. Budget and actual data for direct labor and overhead for the year are as follows:

	Budget	Actual
Direct labor hours	600,000	550,000
Factory overhead costs	$720,000	$680,000

The factory overhead for Woodman for the year is

a. Overapplied by $20,000.
b. Overapplied by $40,000.
c. Underapplied by $20,000.
d. Underapplied by $40,000.
e. Neither underapplied nor overapplied.

The correct answer is (c). *(CMA 1283 4-5)*
REQUIRED: The amount of underapplied factory overhead.
DISCUSSION: At the beginning of the year, the budgeted factory overhead costs of $720,000 must be divided by the 600,000 estimated direct labor hours to produce an overhead application rate of $1.20 per direct labor hour. During the year, 550,000 direct labor hours were actually worked, resulting in the application of $660,000 of overhead (550,000 x $1.20). Since $680,000 of overhead costs were actually incurred, overhead was underapplied by $20,000 ($680,000 - $660,000).

36. Property taxes on a manufacturing plant are an element of

	Conversion Cost	Period Cost
a.	Yes	No
b.	Yes	Yes
c.	No	Yes
d.	No	No

The correct answer is (a). *(CPA 1183 T-37)*
REQUIRED: The method(s) of accounting for property taxes on a manufacturing plant.
DISCUSSION: Property taxes on a manufacturing plant are a component of overhead and therefore a product rather than a period cost. Moreover, overhead and direct labor are conversion costs, thus, property taxes are a part of conversion costs. It is not possible for a cost to be both a period cost and a conversion cost.

37. Accounting for factory overhead costs involves averaging in

	Job Order Costing	Process Costing
a.	Yes	No
b.	Yes	Yes
c.	No	Yes
d.	No	No

The correct answer is (b). *(CPA 1183 T-39)*
REQUIRED: The accounting system(s) using average factory overhead costs.
DISCUSSION: Overhead consists of indirect costs that are averaged over the entire period, usually a year, based upon an activity base. The total of the estimated indirect costs is divided by the activity base, e.g., estimated direct labor hours, and allocated to the product based upon actual activity level. Consequently, factory overhead costs are averaged in both job order and process costing systems.

38. If predetermined overhead is greater than the incurred overhead by $4,850,

    a. Overhead is overapplied; one should credit overhead for $4,850.

    b. Overhead is underapplied; one should debit overhead for $4,850.

    c. Overhead is overapplied; one should debit overhead for $4,850.

    d. Overhead is underapplied; one should credit overhead for $4,850.

The correct answer is (c). *(Publisher)*
REQUIRED: The effect of an excess of predetermined overhead over incurred overhead.
DISCUSSION: If predetermined overhead exceeds actual (incurred) overhead, more overhead has been applied than incurred (other things constant). The theoretically proper correction for overapplied overhead at the end of the year is to debit overhead for $4,850 and credit CGS, finished goods, and work-in-process, proportionately.

39. At the beginning of the year, Smith Inc. budgeted the following:

Units	10,000
Sales	$100,000
Less:	
Total variable expenses	60,000
Total fixed expenses	20,000
Net income	$ 20,000
Factory overhead:	
Variable	$ 30,000
Fixed	10,000

There were no beginning inventories. At the end of the year, there was no work-in-process; total factory overhead incurred in the year was $39,500; and underapplied factory overhead was $1,500. Factory overhead was applied on the basis of budgeted unit production. How many units were produced this year?

    a. 10,250.

    b. 9,500.

    c. 10,000.

    d. 9,250.

The correct answer is (b). *(Publisher)*
REQUIRED: The number of units produced given various overhead data.
DISCUSSION: Given actual overhead of $39,500 and underapplied overhead of $1,500, overhead applied was $38,000 ($39,500 - $1,500). Overhead is applied at the rate of $4 per unit ($40,000 budgeted overhead ÷ 10,000 budgeted units). Accordingly, 9,500 units were produced ($38,000 applied overhead ÷ $4 per unit application rate).

40. A company manufactures plastic products for the home and restaurant market. The company also does contract work for other customers and utilizes a job order costing system. The flexible budget covering next year's expected range of activity is

Direct labor hours	50,000	80,000	110,000
Machine hours	40,000	64,000	88,000
Variable O/H costs	$100,000	$160,000	$220,000
Fixed O/H costs	150,000	150,000	150,000
Total O/H costs	$250,000	$310,000	$370,000

A predetermined overhead rate based on direct labor hours is used to apply total overhead. Management has estimated that 100,000 direct labor hours will be used next year. The predetermined overhead rate per direct labor hour to be used to apply total overhead to the individual jobs next year is

    a. $3.36.

    b. $3.50.

    c. $3.70.

    d. $3.88.

The correct answer is (b). *(CIA 1184 IV-21)*
REQUIRED: The predetermined overhead rate per direct labor hour.
DISCUSSION: The predetermined overhead rate is calculated by dividing the total fixed overhead by the activity level to arrive at a unit fixed overhead cost that is added to the unit variable overhead cost. The unit variable overhead rate is the same at each activity level.

$$\text{Unit Fixed O/H Rate} = \frac{\text{Total Fixed O/H}}{\text{Activity Level}} = \frac{\$150,000}{100,000} = \$1.50$$

$$\frac{\text{Total variable O/H}}{110,000 \text{ DLH}} = \frac{\$220,000}{110,000} = \$2$$

Predetermined O/H rate = $1.50 + $2.00 = $3.50

Module 5.3: Application of Overhead

41. Schneider, Inc. had the following information relating to Year 1.

Budgeted factory overhead	$74,800
Actual factory overhead (INCURRED)	$78,300
Applied factory overhead	$76,500
Estimated labor hours	44,000

If Schneider decides to use the actual results from Year 1 to determine the Year 2 overhead rate, what will the Year 2 overhead rate be?

a. $1.650.
b. $1.700.
c. $1.738.
d. $1.740.
e. $1.780.

The correct answer is (d). *(R. Gruber)*
REQUIRED: The overhead rate for Year 2 using Year 1 data.
DISCUSSION: The Year 1 overhead rate is calculated as $1.70 ÷ DLH ($74,800 ÷ 44,000 DLH). Since applied factory overhead is a result of actual DLH times the overhead rate, the actual direct labor hours for Year 1 are 45,000 ($76,500 ÷ $1.70). Next, the overhead rate for Year 2 is $1.74 ÷ DLH ($78,300 ÷ 45,000 DLH).

42. The XYZ Company uses a predetermined overhead rate. XYZ prepared the following budget at the beginning of the year:

Direct labor cost	$12,000
Factory overhead	$25,000
Direct labor hours	9,000
Machine hours	1,500

During the month of January, the cost sheet for order number 100 indicates $20 of raw materials, $50 of direct labor, 10 hours of direct labor, and 5 machine hours. Order number 100 consists of 49 units of product. XYZ applies overhead based on direct labor cost. What amount of overhead should be applied to order number 100?

a. $50.00.
b. $104.17.
c. $20.00.
d. $87.62.
e. $100.00.

The correct answer is (b). *(Publisher)*
REQUIRED: The amount of overhead applied given budgeted and actual cost data and the activity base.
DISCUSSION: XYZ Company applies overhead based on direct labor cost. Since overhead was budgeted at $25,000 and direct labor cost at $12,000, the overhead application rate is $2.083 ($25,000 ÷ $12,000). Since $50 of direct labor was incurred, $104.17 of overhead should be applied ($50 x $2.083). Alternatively, factory overhead cost is slightly more than twice the direct labor cost ($25,000 ÷ $12,000) and the overhead on a job with $50 of direct labor cost would be slightly more than $100, i.e., $104.17.

43. At the end of the last fiscal year, Baehr Company had the following account balances:

Overapplied overhead	$ 1,000
Cost of goods sold	980,000
Work-in-process inventory	38,000
Finished goods inventory	82,000

The most common treatment of the overapplied overhead would be to

a. Prorate it between work-in-process inventory and finished goods inventory.
b. Prorate it among work-in-process inventory, finished goods inventory and cost of goods sold.
c. Carry it as a deferred credit on the balance sheet.
d. Report it as miscellaneous operating revenue on the income statement.
e. Credit it to cost of goods sold.

The correct answer is (e). *(CMA 1277 4-21)*
REQUIRED: The most common treatment of overapplied overhead.
DISCUSSION: While the theoretically preferable treatment is to allocate overapplied overhead among cost of goods sold, work-in-process, and finished goods inventory, the common practice is to credit cost of goods sold, thereby fully recognizing the overapplied amount in the current period. Here, the amount involved is not significant and only cost of goods sold would normally be adjusted.
Answers (a) and (b) are incorrect because proration among work-in-process, finished goods, and cost of goods sold is not commonly done when the amount is insignificant. Answer (c) is incorrect because overapplied overhead is never carried as a deferred credit. Answer (d) is incorrect because the overapplication does not arise from operations but is a result of the difference between the actual and estimated overhead rates.

Module 5.3: Application of Overhead

44. Carley Products has no work-in-process or finished goods inventories at the close of business on December 31, 1989. The balances of Carley's accounts as of December 31, 1989 are as follows:

Cost of goods sold	$2,040,000
General selling and administrative expenses	900,000
Sales	3,600,000
Factory overhead control	700,000
Factory overhead applied	648,000

Carley Products' income before income taxes 1989 is

- a. $660,000.
- b. $608,000.
- c. $712,000.
- d. $1,508,000.
- e. None of the above.

The correct answer is (b). *(CMA 1283 4-12)*
REQUIRED: The pretax income assuming an overhead application difference.
DISCUSSION: The pretax income is equal to sales less cost of goods sold, general selling and administrative expenses, and underapplied factory overhead.

Sales	$3,600,000
CGS	(2,040,000)
Underapplied overhead	(52,000)
Gross margin	$1,508,000
GS&A expenses	(900,000)
Income before income taxes	$ 608,000

---

45. What is the entry to close overhead accounts and to charge underapplied overhead to cost of goods sold?

- a. Cost of goods sold   XX
       Finished goods   XX
- b. Factory O/H control   XX
       Factory O/H applied   XX
       Cost of goods sold   XX
- c. Cost of goods sold   XX
       Factory O/H applied   XX
- d. Cost of goods sold   XX
       Factory O/H applied   XX
       Factory O/H control   XX

The correct answer is (d). *(Publisher)*
REQUIRED: The journal entry to close the overhead accounts and to charge underapplied overhead to cost of goods sold.
DISCUSSION: The correct entry to close the overhead accounts and to charge underapplied overhead to CGS is to debit the factory overhead applied account for the amount of overhead applied for the period and to credit factory overhead control for the amount of overhead actually incurred for the period. The amount actually incurred exceeds the amount of overhead applied because overhead is underapplied. The difference is the amount charged to CGS.
Answer (a) is incorrect because it is the entry to transfer the CGS from inventory to CGS. Answer (b) is incorrect because it reflects overapplied overhead. Answer (c) is incorrect because it does not close the overhead accounts.

---

46. What entry would close the overhead accounts and prorate underapplied overhead among the relevant accounts?

- a. Cost of goods sold   XX
       Finished goods control   XX
       Work-in-process control   XX
       Factory O/H applied   XX
           Factory O/H control   XX
- b. Cost of goods sold   XX
       Finished goods control   XX
       Work-in-process control   XX
       Factory O/H control   XX
           Factory O/H applied   XX
- c. Cost of goods sold   XX
       Factory O/H control   XX
           Work-in-process control   XX
           Factory O/H applied   XX
           Finished goods control   XX
- d. Cost of goods sold   XX
       Finished goods control   XX
       Work-in-process control   XX
       Factory O/H applied   XX
           O/H summary   XX

The correct answer is (a). *(Publisher)*
REQUIRED: The journal entry to close the overhead accounts and to prorate underapplied overhead among the relevant accounts.
DISCUSSION: To determine the correct entry to close the overhead accounts and to prorate underapplied overhead, one must first calculate the relative percentages of overhead in the jobs that were (1) sold, (2) finished, and (3) in the work-in-process stage. The percentage for each category is then multiplied times the total underapplied overhead to arrive at the dollar amounts charged to the corresponding accounts. The factory overhead applied account will be debited and factory overhead control will be credited to close the overhead accounts. The proration to the relevant accounts will be a debit because of the underapplication (when overhead applied was closed to the control account, a debit balance remained).
Answers (b) and (d) are incorrect because they do not close the overhead accounts. Answer (c) is incorrect because the factory overhead control and applied accounts are reversed as to debits and credits, and WIP and FG should be debited, not credited.

Module 5.3: Application of Overhead

47. Overapplied factory overhead would result if

a. The plant were operated at less than normal capacity.
b. Factory overhead costs incurred were less than costs charged to production.
c. Factory overhead costs incurred were unreasonably large in relation to units produced.
d. Factory overhead costs incurred were greater than costs charged to production.

The correct answer is (b). *(CPA 573 T-32)*
REQUIRED: The situation that would result in overapplied overhead.
DISCUSSION: Overapplied overhead is the result of charging more factory overhead costs to production than were actually incurred. Applied overhead rates are based on estimates and thus will rarely equal the actual rates.
Answer (a) is incorrect because operating at less than normal capacity usually results in underapplied overhead. Answer (c) is incorrect because unreasonably large overhead costs result in underapplied overhead since only a reasonable amount would be expected and applied. Answer (d) is incorrect because, if factory overhead costs incurred are greater than those charged to production, overhead will be underapplied.

48. Cox Company found that the differences in product costs resulting from the application of predetermined overhead rates rather than actual overhead rates were immaterial even though actual production was substantially less than planned production. The most likely explanation is that

a. Overhead was composed chiefly of variable costs.
b. Several products were produced simultaneously.
c. Fixed factory overhead was a significant cost.
d. Costs of overhead items were substantially higher than anticipated.

The correct answer is (a). *(CPA 573 T-27)*
REQUIRED: A likely explanation for a small difference between applied and actual overhead.
DISCUSSION: Total variable overhead costs change in proportion to changes in the activity level. Total fixed costs do not. For the difference between applied and actual overhead to be immaterial when actual production is substantially less than planned production, overhead costs must be composed chiefly of variable costs.
Answer (b) is incorrect because, for overhead application purposes, the simultaneous production of several products is similar to producing one product. Answer (c) is incorrect because, if fixed factory overhead had been significant, a material difference would have arisen. Answer (d) is incorrect because, if actual costs are substantially higher than anticipated, overhead will be underapplied by a substantial amount.

49. Avery Co. uses a predetermined factory overhead rate based on direct labor hours. For the month of October, Avery's budgeted overhead was $300,000 based on a budgeted volume of 100,000 direct labor hours. Actual overhead amounted to $325,000 with actual direct labor hours totaling 110,000. How much was the overapplied or underapplied overhead?

a. $30,000 overapplied.
b. $30,000 underapplied.
c. $5,000 overapplied.
d. $5,000 underapplied.

The correct answer is (c). *(CPA 1184 Q-13)*
REQUIRED: The over- or underapplied overhead.
DISCUSSION: Over- or underapplied overhead is determined by comparing actual overhead incurred with overhead applied based upon the predetermined overhead rate. The predetermined overhead rate was $3.00 per DLH ($300,000 ÷ 100,000). Actual overhead was $325,000, and overhead applied was $330,000 ($3 x 110,000). Since $330,000 (applied) exceeds $325,000 (actual), Avery had $5,000 of overapplied overhead.

50. Cannon Cannery, Inc. estimated its factory overhead at $510,000 for the year, based on a normal capacity of 100,000 direct labor hours. Standard direct labor hours for the year totaled 105,000, while the factory overhead control account at the end of the year showed a balance of $540,000. How much was the underapplied factory overhead for the year?

a. $0.
b. $4,500.
c. $27,000.
d. $30,000.

The correct answer is (b). *(CPA 1182 Q-36)*
REQUIRED: The amount of underapplied overhead.
DISCUSSION: Underapplied overhead is the difference between the actual overhead and the applied overhead. The overhead rate per hour is $5.10 ($510,000 budgeted costs ÷ 100,000 budgeted hours). The applied overhead was $535,500 ($5.10 x 105,000 actual hours). The actual overhead incurred of $540,000 less the applied overhead of $535,500 results in $4,500 of underapplied overhead.

Questions 51 through 55 are based on Baehr Company, which is a manufacturing company with a fiscal year which runs from July 1 to June 30. The company uses a job order accounting system for its production costs. A predetermined overhead rate based upon direct labor hours is used to apply overhead to individual jobs. A flexible budget of overhead costs was prepared for the fiscal year as shown below.

Direct labor hours	100,000	120,000	140,000
Variable overhead costs	$325,000	$390,000	$455,000
Fixed overhead costs	216,000	216,000	216,000
Total overhead	$541,000	$606,000	$671,000

Although the annual ideal capacity is 150,000 direct labor hours, company officials have determined 120,000 direct labor hours to be normal capacity for the year.

The information presented below and in the opposite column is for November. Jobs 83-50 and 83-51 were completed during November.

Inventories November 1
- Raw materials and supplies: $10,500
- Work-in-process (Job 83-50): 54,000
- Finished goods: 112,500

Purchases of raw materials and supplies
- Raw materials: $135,000
- Supplies: 15,000
- Total: $150,000

Materials and supplies requisitioned for production
- Job 83-50: $45,000
- Job 83-51: 37,500
- Job 83-52: 25,500
- Supplies: 12,000
- Total: $120,000

Factory direct labor hours
- Job 83-50: 3,500
- Job 83-51: 3,000
- Job 83-52: 2,000
- Total: 8,500

Labor costs
- Direct labor wages: $51,000
- Indirect labor wages (4,000 hours): 15,000
- Supervisory salaries: 6,000
- Total: $72,000

Building occupancy costs (heat, light, depreciation, etc.)
- Factory facilities: $6,500
- Sales offices: 1,500
- Administrative offices: 1,000
- Total: $9,000

Factory equipment costs
- Power: $4,000
- Repairs and maintenance: 1,500
- Depreciation: 1,500
- Other: 1,000
- Total: $8,000

51. The predetermined overhead rate to be used to apply overhead to individual jobs during the fiscal year is

a. $3.25 per DLH.
b. $4.69 per DLH.
c. $5.05 per DLH.
d. $5.41 per DLH.
e. None of the above.

The correct answer is (c). (CMA 1277 4-16)
REQUIRED: The predetermined rate to apply overhead to individual jobs.
DISCUSSION: The predetermined overhead rate is the estimated total overhead divided by the direct labor hours at normal capacity. The normal capacity for the year is 120,000 hours and related overhead costs are $606,000. The overhead rate is therefore $5.05 ($606,000 ÷ 120,000 hours).

Note: Without prejudice to your answer to Question 51, assume the predetermined overhead rate is $4.50 per direct labor hour. Use this amount in answering Questions 52 through 55.

52. The total cost of Job 83-50 is

a. $81,750.
b. $135,750.
c. $142,750.
d. $146,750.
e. None of the above.

The correct answer is (b). (CMA 1277 4-17)
REQUIRED: The total cost for a job begun in a prior period and completed currently.
DISCUSSION: Job 83-50 was completed during November after having been started in a previous period (BWIP was $54,000). During the period, $45,000 in material costs were added. Additionally, direct labor was incurred at the rate of $6.00 per hour ($51,000 ÷ 8,500 total DLH). Direct labor cost for November for Job 83-50 was thus $21,000 ($6.00 x 3,500 DLH). Overhead applied was $15,750 (given overhead rate of $4.50 x 3,500 DLH). Total cost was $135,750 ($54,000 + $45,000 + $21,000 + $15,750).

Module 5.3: Application of Overhead   87

53. The factory overhead costs applied to job 83-52 during November were

   a. $9,000.
   b. $47,500.
   c. $46,500.
   d. $8,000.
   e. None of the above.

The correct answer is (a). *(CMA 1277 4-18)*
   REQUIRED: The factory overhead costs applied to an incomplete job at the end of the period.
   DISCUSSION: The overhead rate is given as $4.50 per hour. Job 83-52 incurred 2,000 direct labor hours resulting in $9,000 ($4.50 x 2,000 DLH) of overhead applied to that job in November.

54. The total amount of overhead applied to jobs during November was

   a. $29,250.
   b. $38,250.
   c. $47,250.
   d. $56,250.
   e. None of the above.

The correct answer is (b). *(CMA 1277 4-19)*
   REQUIRED: The total overhead applied to jobs during the current period.
   DISCUSSION: During November, 8,500 direct labor hours were incurred. The overhead application rate is given as $4.50 per hour. Thus, the total overhead applied was $38,250 ($4.50 x 8,500 DLH).

55. Actual factory overhead incurred during November was

   a. $38,000.
   b. $41,500.
   c. $47,500.
   d. $50,500.
   e. None of the above.

The correct answer is (c). *(CMA 1277 4-20)*
   REQUIRED: The actual factory overhead incurred during the period.
   DISCUSSION: Actual factory overhead incurred during November consisted of factory equipment costs, factory occupancy costs (heat, light, depreciation, etc.), indirect labor wages and supervisory salaries ($15,000 + $6,000), and supplies requisitioned for production.

Factory equipment costs	$ 8,000
Factory occupancy costs	6,500
Indirect labor wages and supervisory salaries	21,000
Supplies	12,000
Actual overhead	$47,500

56. Regan Company operates its factory on a two-shift basis and pays a late-shift differential of 15%. Regan also pays a premium of 50% for overtime work. Since Regan manufactures only for stock, the cost system provides for uniform direct-labor hourly charges for production done without regard to shift worked or work done on an overtime basis. Overtime and late-shift differentials are included in Regan's factory overhead application rate. The May payroll for production workers is as follows:

Wages at base direct-labor rates	$325,000
Shift differentials	25,000
Overtime premiums	10,000

For the month of May, what amount of direct labor should Regan charge to work-in-process?

   a. $325,000.
   b. $335,000.
   c. $350,000.
   d. $360,000.

The correct answer is (a). *(CPA 1183 P-43)*
   REQUIRED: The amount of direct labor given shift pay differentials and overtime premiums.
   DISCUSSION: As the question indicates, the cost system provides for uniform direct hourly charges for production done without regard to shift work or work done on an overtime basis. These are both included in factory overhead. Accordingly, both the $25,000 and $10,000 should be charged to the overhead account, and only $325,000 should be charged to the WIP account as direct labor.

Module 5.3: Application of Overhead

Questions 57 through 60 are based on the Summit Company, which provided the inventory balances and manufacturing cost data shown in the opposite column for the month of January.

Under Summit's cost system, any over- or underapplied overhead is closed to the cost of goods sold account at the end of the calendar year.

Inventories:	January 1	January 31
Direct materials	$30,000	$40,000
Work-in-process	15,000	20,000
Finished goods	65,000	50,000

	Month of January
Factory overhead applied	$150,000
Cost of goods manufactured	515,000
Direct materials used	190,000
Actual factory overhead	144,000

57. What was the total amount of direct materials purchases during January?

a. $180,000.
b. $190,000.
c. $195,000.
d. $200,000.

The correct answer is (d). *(CPA 583 P-22)*
REQUIRED: The total amount of direct materials purchases during the period.
DISCUSSION: The direct materials inventory increased by $10,000 during the month, and $190,000 worth of material was used. Accordingly, $200,000 of materials must have been purchased during January.

58. How much direct labor cost was incurred during January?

a. $170,000.
b. $175,000.
c. $180,000.
d. $186,000.

The correct answer is (c). *(CPA 583 P-23)*
REQUIRED: The direct labor cost incurred during the period.
DISCUSSION: The direct labor cost incurred during the period is the amount charged to the WIP (manufacturing) account. Debits to that account are the BWIP of $15,000, the direct materials used of $190,000, factory overhead applied of $150,000, and the direct labor, which is the unknown. The sum of these debits must equal $515,000 (CGM) plus the EWIP of $20,000.

CGM		$515,000
EWIP		20,000
		$535,000
Less:		
BWIP	$ 15,000	
Direct materials	190,000	
Fac. O/H applied	150,000	
	$355,000	(355,000)
Direct labor cost		$180,000

59. What would cost of goods sold be if under- or overapplied overhead were closed to cost of goods sold?

a. $509,000.
b. $524,000.
c. $530,000.
d. $536,000.

The correct answer is (b). *(Publisher)*
REQUIRED: CGS if under- or overapplied overhead is closed to CGS.
DISCUSSION: CGS before the allocation of under- or overapplied overhead is the CGM of $515,000 adjusted by the decrease in finished goods of $15,000 ($65,000 - $50,000), which is $530,000 ($515,000 + $15,000). Since $6,000 more overhead was applied than actually incurred ($150,000 - $144,000), the $6,000 overapplied overhead would reduce CGS from $530,000 to $524,000.

Module 5.4: Work-in-Process Account Calculations

60. What would cost of goods sold be if under- or overapplied overhead were allocated to inventories and cost of goods sold?

a. $509,700.
b. $524,700.
c. $526,300.
d. $530,300.

The correct answer is (b). *(Publisher)*
REQUIRED: CGS if under- or overapplied overhead is allocated to inventories and CGS.
DISCUSSION: The allocation of overapplied overhead reduces CGS (see Q. 59). The CGS before allocation of under- or overapplied overhead is $530,000. The $6,000 of overapplied overhead is to be allocated to WIP inventory, FG inventory, and CGS in the ratios of 20/600, 50/600, and 530/600, because the ending balances of WIP, FG, and CGS are $20,000, $50,000, and $530,000. Thus, of the $6,000 overapplied overhead, $5,300 ($6,000 x 53/60) would be credited to the $530,000 of unadjusted CGS, bringing the adjusted CGS to $524,700 ($530,000 - $5,300).

5.4 Work-In-Process Account Calculations

61. A company had the following total usage of direct labor and direct materials:

	Hours	Pounds
Direct Labor ($8 per hour)	400	
Direct Materials ($10 per pound)		300

Incomplete job #101 has used 20 hours of direct labor and 8 pounds of direct materials. Factory overhead is applied at the rate of $2 per direct labor dollar. What is the balance in work-in-process relating to job #101?

a. $560 debit.
b. $560 credit.
c. $12,600 debit.
d. $12,600 credit.

The correct answer is (a). *(CIA 587 IV-3)*
REQUIRED: The balance in work-in-process relating to the job.
DISCUSSION: The direct labor attributable to the job is $160 (20 hrs. x $8/hr.). Direct materials cost is $80 ($10/lb x 8 lbs.). Factory overhead is $320 ($2 x $160 direct labor dollars). Accordingly, the total work-in-process is $560. This amount is the debit balance in the account. When the job is complete, the transfer to finished goods will require a credit to work-in-process and a debit to finished goods.

62. Tillman Corporation uses a job order cost system and has two production departments, M and A. Budgeted manufacturing costs for the year are:

	Dept. M	Dept. A
Direct materials	$700,000	$100,000
Direct labor	200,000	800,000
Manufacturing overhead	600,000	400,000

The actual material and labor costs charged to Job No. 432 during the year were as follows:

Direct material		$25,000
Direct labor:		
Dept. M	$ 8,000	
Dept. A	12,000	20,000

Tillman applies manufacturing overhead to production orders on the basis of direct labor cost using departmental rates predetermined at the beginning of the year based on the annual budget. The total annual manufacturing costs associated with Job No. 432 should be

a. $50,000.
b. $55,000.
c. $65,000.
d. $75,000.

The correct answer is (d). *(CPA 581 P-38)*
REQUIRED: The total manufacturing costs associated with a job if overhead is based on direct labor cost applied using departmental rates.
DISCUSSION: Total manufacturing costs consist of materials, labor, and overhead. Materials and labor are given; overhead rates are to be determined for each department. Departmental rates are calculated by dividing departmental manufacturing overhead by direct labor costs.

Dept. M = $\frac{\$600,000}{\$200,000}$ = $3 per $1 of DLC

Dept. A = $\frac{\$400,000}{\$800,000}$ = $.50 per $1 of DLC

For Job No. 432:
Dept. M overhead = $3 x $8,000 = $24,000
Dept. A overhead = $.50 x $12,000 = $6,000

Total manufacturing costs for Job No. 432 = $25,000 material + $20,000 labor + $24,000 M overhead + $6,000 A overhead = $75,000.

Module 5.4: Work-in-Process Account Calculations

63. Lucas Co. has a job order cost system. For the month of April, the following debits (credits) appeared in the general ledger account, work-in-process:

April
1	Balance	$ 24,000
30	Direct materials	80,000
30	Direct labor	60,000
30	Factory overhead	54,000
30	To finished goods	(200,000)

Lucas applies overhead to production at a predetermined rate of 90% based on direct labor cost. Job No. 100, the only job still in process at the end of April, has been charged with factory overhead of $4,500. The amount of direct materials charged to Job No. 100 was

a. $18,000.

b. $8,500.

c. $5,000.

d. $4,500.

The correct answer is (b). *(CPA 586 Q-22)*
REQUIRED: The amount of direct materials charged to the only job in process at the end of the period.
DISCUSSION: The ending balance in the WIP account is $18,000 ($24,000 + $80,000 + $60,000 + $54,000 - $200,000), the sum of all debits, $218,000, to the account less the $200,000 credit. The $18,000 balance consists of materials, labor, and overhead for Job No. 100. Overhead is given as $4,500 (90% of direct labor cost). Direct labor is thus $5,000 ($4,500 ÷ .90) and the amount of direct materials is $8,500.

$$DM + DL + OH = \$18,000$$
$$DM + DL + .9\,DL = \$18,000$$
$$DM + \$5,000 + \$4,500 = \$18,000$$
$$DM = \$8,500$$

64. The Childers Company manufactures widgets. During the fiscal year just ended, the company incurred prime costs of $1,500,000 and conversion costs of $1,800,000. Overhead is applied at the rate of 200% of direct labor cost. How much of the above costs represent material cost?

a. $1,500,000.

b. $300,000.

c. $900,000.

d. $600,000.

The correct answer is (c). *(A. Wilson)*
REQUIRED: The calculation of material costs for the fiscal year just ended.
DISCUSSION: Prime cost is the sum of direct material and labor costs. Conversion cost is the sum of labor and overhead costs.

$$OH = 200\% \times DL$$
$$DL + OH = \$1,800,000$$
$$DL + 2DL = \$1,800,000$$
$$3DL = \$1,800,000$$
$$DL = \$600,000$$

$$DM + DL = \$1,500,000$$
$$DM + \$600,000 = \$1,500,000$$
$$DM = \$900,000$$

65. Ajax Corporation transferred $72,000 of raw materials to its production department in February and incurred $37,000 of conversion costs ($22,000 of direct labor and $15,000 of overhead). At the beginning of the period, $14,000 of inventory (material and conversion costs) was in process. At the end of the period, $18,000 of inventory was in process. What was the cost of goods manufactured?

a. $105,000.

b. $109,000.

c. $123,000.

d. $141,000.

The correct answer is (a). *(Publisher)*
REQUIRED: The cost of goods manufactured for the period.
DISCUSSION: The total cost incurred in the production process, (the sum of BWIP, direct materials, direct labor, and overhead, less the cost of goods not completed during the period (EWIP)), is the cost of goods manufactured.

BWIP	$ 14,000
Materials	72,000
Conversion costs	37,000
Total	$123,000
Less EWIP	(18,000)
CGM	$105,000

Module 5.4: Work-in-Process Account Calculations

Questions 66 and 67 are based on Kaden Corp., which has two divisions -- Ace and Bow. Ace has a job order cost system and manufactures machinery on special order for unrelated customers. Bow has a process cost system and manufactures Product Zee, which is sold to Ace as well as to unrelated companies. Ace's work-in-process account at April 30 comprised the following:

Ace applies factory overhead at 90% of direct labor cost. Job No. 125, which was the only job in process at April 30, has been charged with factory overhead of $4,500. Bow's cost to manufacture Product Zee is $3.00 per unit, which is sold to Ace for $5.00 per unit and to unrelated customers for $6.00 per unit.

Balance, April 1	$ 24,000
Direct materials (including transferred-in cost)	80,000
Direct labor	60,000
Factory overhead	54,000
Transferred to finished goods	(200,000)

66. Direct materials (including transferred-in cost) charged to Job No. 125 amounted to

   a. $5,000.
   b. $8,500.
   c. $13,500.
   d. $18,000.

The correct answer is (b). *(CPA 585 Q-15)*
REQUIRED: The amount of direct materials in EWIP.
DISCUSSION: The EWIP consists of material, labor, and overhead. EWIP is

BWIP	$ 24,000
DM	80,000
DL	60,000
FOH	54,000
CGM	(200,000)
EWIP	$ 18,000

FOH is applied at 90% of DL, and FOH was $4,500 on Job 125. Thus, direct labor is $5,000 ($4,500 ÷ .9). Direct materials charged therefore amounted to $8,500 ($18,000 EWIP - $4,500 FOH - $5,000 DL).

67. How much is the transfer price for Product Zee?

   a. $2.00.
   b. $3.00.
   c. $5.00.
   d. $6.00.

The correct answer is (c). *(CPA 585 Q-16)*
REQUIRED: The transfer price.
DISCUSSION: The transfer price is the price at which an item is "sold" in intracompany transactions. This price is usually less than the market price, but it may, at times, be set at a price equal to or greater than market to achieve overall corporate objectives. Here, the transfer price is given as $5.00.

68. The work-in-process of Parrott Corporation increased $11,500 from the beginning to the end of November. Costs incurred during November were material $12,000, labor $63,000, and overhead $21,000. What was the cost of goods manufactured during November?

   a. $93,500.
   b. $84,500.
   c. $126,000.
   d. $132,500.

The correct answer is (b). *(Publisher)*
REQUIRED: The cost of goods manufactured for the period.
DISCUSSION: Since the work-in-process inventory increased by $11,500 from the beginning to the end of November, not all of the $96,000 in costs incurred during the period was transferred out. Deducting the $11,500 increase in work-in-process inventory from the $96,000 of actual costs incurred during the month ($12,000 + $63,000 + $21,000) gives $84,500, the cost of goods manufactured.

Module 5.4: Work-in-Process Account Calculations

69. If the CGS for the Cole Manufacturing Co. is $105,000 and FG inventory decreased by $9,000 during the year, what was the year-end CGM?

a. $96,000.
b. $105,000.
c. $114,000.
d. $124,000.

The correct answer is (a). *(Publisher)*
REQUIRED: The cost of goods manufactured given a decline in the finished goods inventory.
DISCUSSION: The cost of goods manufactured is the cost of goods sold less the inventory decrease during the year. Since inventory decreased by $9,000, that much of the $105,000 cost of goods sold came from beginning inventory. Hence, $96,000 of the cost related to goods manufactured during the period.

70. Luna Co.'s year-end manufacturing costs were as follows:

Direct materials and direct labor	$500,000
Depreciation of manufacturing equipment	70,000
Depreciation of factory building	40,000
Janitor's wages for cleaning factory premises	15,000

How much of these costs should be inventoried for external reporting purposes?

a. $625,000.
b. $610,000.
c. $585,000.
d. $500,000.

The correct answer is (a). *(CPA 586 Q-26)*
REQUIRED: The computation of inventory costs for external reporting purposes.
DISCUSSION: Inventoriable costs are those costs directly related to the product including direct material, direct labor, overhead and any other expenses necessary to produce the product. All the costs listed are inventoriable:

DM and DL	$500,000
Depreciation of equipment	70,000
Depreciation of building	40,000
Janitor's wages	15,000
Total inventoriable costs	$625,000

Questions 71 and 72 are based on Blum Corp., which manufactures plastic coated metal clips. The information in the next column was among Blum's year-end manufacturing costs.

Wages
Machine operators	$200,000
Maintenance workers	30,000
Factory foremen	90,000

Materials Used
Metal wire	$500,000
Lubricant for oiling machinery	10,000
Plastic coating	380,000

---

71. Blum's year-end direct labor amounted to

a. $200,000.
b. $230,000.
c. $290,000.
d. $320,000.

The correct answer is (a). *(CPA 1185 Q-2)*
REQUIRED: The amount of direct labor costs for the accounting period.
DISCUSSION: Direct labor consists of the labor costs incurred for those employees who work on the actual production of the product. In this problem, only the machine operators' wages ($200,000) are considered direct labor. The wages of the factory foremen and maintenance workers are indirect labor and therefore part of factory overhead.

72. Blum's year-end direct materials amounted to

a. $890,000.
b. $880,000.
c. $510,000.
d. $500,000.

The correct answer is (b). *(CPA 1185 Q-3)*
REQUIRED: The amount of direct material costs for the accounting period.
DISCUSSION: Direct materials are those which are part of the product. Since plastic coated metal clips are being made, only the plastic coating and metal wire ($880,000) used to make the clips are considered direct material. All other supplies, including lubricant for oiling the machinery, are part of manufacturing overhead.

Module 5.4: Work-in-Process Account Calculations

Questions 73 through 77 are based on selected cost data (in thousands) concerning the past fiscal year's operations of the Televans Manufacturing Company, which are presented below and in the opposite column.		
	Inventories	
	Beginning	Ending
Raw materials	$75	$ 85
Work-in-process	80	30
Finished goods	90	110

Raw materials used	$326
Total manufacturing costs charged to production during the year (including raw materials, direct labor, and factory overhead applied at a rate of 60% of direct labor cost)	686
Cost of goods available for sale	826
Selling and general expenses	25

73. The cost of raw materials purchased during the year amounted to

a. $411.
b. $360.
c. $316.
d. $336.
e. None of the above.

The correct answer is (d). *(CMA 1277 4-12)*
REQUIRED: The cost of raw materials purchased during the year.
DISCUSSION: A T-account analysis of raw materials provides an easy solution. If the inventory increased by $10 even though raw materials worth $326 were used, purchases must have been $336.

Raw Materials			
BI	$ 75	$326	Transferred
Purchases	336		
EI	$ 85		

74. Direct labor costs charged to production during the year amounted to

a. $135.
b. $225.
c. $360.
d. $216.
e. None of the above.

The correct answer is (b). *(CMA 1277 4-13)*
REQUIRED: The direct labor costs charged to production during the year.
DISCUSSION: The total manufacturing costs charged to production were $686. Materials used cost $326. Thus, $360 ($686 - $326) is attributable to labor and overhead. Overhead is given as 60% of direct labor.

$$\text{Labor} + .6 \text{ Labor} = \$360$$
$$\text{Labor} = \$225$$

75. The cost of goods manufactured during the year was

a. $636.
b. $766.
c. $736.
d. $716.
e. None of the above.

The correct answer is (c). *(CMA 1277 4-14)*
REQUIRED: The cost of goods manufactured (CGM) during the year.
DISCUSSION: The CGM is the amount credited to WIP and debited to FG inventory. It represents the cost of goods completed during the period and is similar to "purchases." CGM may be determined using the FG inventory data. The cost of goods available for sale, which is BI + CGM, equals CGS + EI.

$$BI + CGM = CGS + EI$$
$$\$90 + CGM = \$826$$
$$CGM = \$736$$

CGM can also be computed as the sum of all debits to work-in-process minus EWIP.

Work-in-Process			
BWIP	$ 80		
DL, DM, O/H	686	$736	Transferred
EWIP	$ 30		

Questions 76 and 77 are based on the information preceding Q. 73.

76. The cost of goods sold during the year was

a. $736.
b. $716.
c. $691.
d. $801.
e. None of the above.

The correct answer is (b). *(CMA 1277 4-15)*
REQUIRED: The cost of goods sold during the year.
DISCUSSION: The cost of goods sold equals goods available for sale ($826) less the ending FG inventory ($110).

$$\$826 - \$110 = \$716$$

77. The selling and general expenses of $25,000 are

a. Considered period costs since they are expensed as incurred.
b. Incorporated into overhead and charged to production.
c. Charged directly to finished goods upon completion of products. They are not included as labor, material, or overhead.
d. Not relevant to the past fiscal year's operations.

The correct answer is (a). *(Publisher)*
REQUIRED: The proper treatment of the selling and general expenses.
DISCUSSION: Selling and general expenses are expensed as incurred and are not considered product costs. They are deemed to be period costs because they are not identifiable with particular products and inventoried. Also, they are charged to expense immediately since they are not considered to provide benefits in future periods.
Answers (b) and (c) are incorrect because selling and general expenses are expensed and not considered product costs. Answer (d) is incorrect because expenses are relevant; they reduce the income for the just-completed fiscal year.

Questions 78 and 79 are based on the Hamilton Company, which uses job order costing. Factory overhead is applied to production at a predetermined rate of 150% of direct labor cost. Any over- or underapplied factory overhead is closed to the cost of goods sold account at the end of each month. Additional information is available as follows:

Job 101 was the only job in process at January 31, with accumulated costs as follows:

Direct materials	$4,000
Direct labor	2,000
Applied factory overhead	3,000
	$9,000

Jobs 102, 103, and 104 were started during February.

Direct materials requisitions for February totaled $26,000.

Direct labor cost of $20,000 was incurred for February.

Actual factory overhead was $32,000 for February.

The only job still in process on February 28 was Job 104, with costs of $2,800 for direct materials and $1,800 for direct labor.

78. The cost of goods manufactured for February was

a. $77,700.
b. $78,000.
c. $79,700.
d. $85,000.

The correct answer is (a). *(CPA 1182 P-22)*
REQUIRED: The cost of goods manufactured (CGM) for the period.
DISCUSSION: CGM is the sum of the costs in BWIP and all the costs incurred during the period minus the costs in EWIP. In computing CGM, applied overhead is used ($30,000 = 150% x $20,000 DL cost). The $7,300 in EWIP includes $2,800 for direct materials, $1,800 for direct labor, and $2,700 for applied overhead (at 150% of DL cost).

BWIP	$ 9,000
Direct labor	20,000
Applied O/H (150% of DL cost)	30,000
Direct materials	26,000
EWIP	(7,300)
CGM	$77,700

Module 5.4: Work-in-Process Account Calculations

79. Over- or underapplied factory overhead should be closed to the cost of goods sold account at February 28 in the amount of

a. $700 overapplied.
b. $1,000 overapplied.
c. $1,700 underapplied.
d. $2,000 underapplied.

The correct answer is (d). *(CPA 1182 P-23)*
REQUIRED: The amount of over- or underapplied factory overhead closed to CGS.
DISCUSSION: The amount of over- or underapplied overhead is the difference between the actual overhead incurred and the overhead applied. The amount of overhead applied was $30,000 (150% x $20,000 DL cost). The amount of overhead incurred was $32,000. Therefore, underapplied overhead of $2,000 ($32,000 actual - $30,000 applied) should be closed to CGS.

Questions 80 and 81 are based on the following data. Pardise Company budgets on an annual basis for its fiscal year. The following beginning and ending inventory levels (in units) are planned for the fiscal year of July 1 through June 30.

	July 1	June 30
Raw material*	40,000	50,000
Work-in-process	10,000	10,000
Finished goods	80,000	50,000

*Two (2) units of raw material are needed to produce each unit of finished product.

---

80. If Pardise Company plans to sell 480,000 units during the fiscal year, the number of units it would have to manufacture during the year would be

a. 440,000 units.
b. 480,000 units.
c. 510,000 units.
d. 450,000 units.
e. Some amount other than those given above.

The correct answer is (d). *(CMA 686 4-26)*
REQUIRED: The number of units that would be manufactured for a given sales level.
DISCUSSION: The company needs 480,000 units of finished goods to sell plus 50,000 for the ending inventory, or a total of 530,000 units. Beginning inventory is 80,000 units. Therefore, only 450,000 units (530,000 - 80,000) need to be manufactured this year.

81. If 500,000 finished units were to be manufactured during the fiscal year by Pardise Company, the units of raw material needed to be purchased would be

a. 1,000,000 units.
b. 1,020,000 units.
c. 1,010,000 units.
d. 990,000 units.
e. Some amount other than those given above.

The correct answer is (c). *(CMA 686 4-27)*
REQUIRED: The number of units of raw material needed to be purchased during the year for a given production volume.
DISCUSSION: Since each unit of finished goods requires two units of raw materials, 1,000,000 units (500,000 x 2) of raw materials are needed for production. Since 50,000 are required for the ending inventory, the total needed is 1,050,000 units. Given that 40,000 are in beginning inventory, only 1,010,000 will have to be purchased.

5.5 Journal Entries

82. ABC Company estimates its total vacation costs for the year to be $360,000. Direct labor costs are $180,000 monthly and indirect labor costs are $45,000. ABC has chosen to accrue vacation costs monthly instead of recognizing them as incurred. Select the journal entry to record payroll and accrue the estimated vacation costs for the month of January.

a.	Work-in-process	$180,000	
	Factory O/H control	75,000	
	Est. liability for vacation pay		$ 30,000
	Accrued payroll		225,000
b.	Wage expense	$225,000	
	Accrued payroll		$225,000
c.	Vacation expense	$300,000	
	Accrued payroll		$300,000
d.	Work-in-process	$225,000	
	Accrued payroll		$225,000

The correct answer is (a). *(Publisher)*
REQUIRED: The journal entry to accrue estimated vacation costs for the month of January.
DISCUSSION: (1) Debit work-in-process for direct labor incurred. (2) Debit factory overhead control for indirect labor and estimated vacation costs [$45,000 + 1/12($360,000)]. (3) Credit estimated liability for vacation pay for 1/12 of the annual expected cost of $360,000. (4) Credit accrued payroll for the gross payroll (total due to employees including their deductions). Note that the liability for vacation pay should be debited for any vacation pay taken.
Total vacation costs for the year are estimated to be $360,000. The explanation assumes that the annual cost is divided by 12 to arrive at a monthly cost of $30,000. More sophisticated approaches are available, e.g., accruing vacation costs in proportion to total labor expense.

83. What is the journal entry to record Legal Corporation's payment of state unemployment taxes for $600? Assume the tax has been accrued.

a.	State unemployment taxes payable	$600	
	Cash		$600
b.	State unemployment taxes payable	$600	
	Accrued payroll		$600
c.	Factory overhead	$600	
	State unemployment taxes payable		$600
d.	Accrued payroll	$600	
	Cash		$600

The correct answer is (a). *(Publisher)*
REQUIRED: The journal entry to record payment of state unemployment taxes.
DISCUSSION: The correct journal entry to record the payment of accrued state unemployment taxes is to debit state unemployment taxes payable and credit cash for the amount of state unemployment taxes due.
Answers (b) and (c) are incorrect because cash is credited when a liability is paid. Answer (d) is incorrect because the question indicates that a tax liability, not accrued payroll, had been credited.

84. Ajax Candy Company has a gross payroll of $75,000 per month consisting of $65,000 of direct labor and $10,000 of indirect factory labor. Assume that the tax rate on employers is .7% for federal unemployment, 1.6% for state unemployment, and 6.7% for Social Security benefits, a total payroll tax rate of 9%. Select the journal entry to accrue the monthly payroll and payroll taxes.

a.	Salary expense	$75,000	
	Accrued wages		$75,000
b.	Salary expense	$81,750	
	Accrued wages		$75,000
	Accrued payroll tax		6,750
c.	Work-in-process	$65,000	
	Factory O/H control	16,750	
	Accrued payroll		$75,000
	Employer payroll taxes payable		6,750
d.	Work-in-process	$6,750	
	Accrued payroll taxes payable		$6,750

The correct answer is (c). *(Publisher)*
REQUIRED: The journal entry to accrue company payroll taxes.
DISCUSSION: (1) Debit work-in-process for the amount of direct labor costs. (2) Debit factory overhead for the amount of indirect labor costs plus the employer payroll tax ($10,000 + $6,750). (3) Credit accrued payroll for the amount of total direct and indirect labor costs. (4) Credit employer's payroll taxes payable for the amount of the payroll tax (.09 x $75,000 = $6,750).

Module 5.5: Journal Entries

85. The Herron Company has a gross payroll of $2,000 per day based on a normal 40-hour workweek. Withholdings for income taxes amount to $200 per day. Gross payroll consists of $1,200 direct labor, $400 indirect labor, $280 selling expenses, and $120 administrative expenses each day. Select the journal entry to record the payment of the weekly payroll. Assume that the journal entry (ignore the differing amounts) in answer (c) in Question 84 on the previous page was used to record the payroll.

a.	Accrued payroll	$5,000	
	Cash		$5,000
b.	Accrued payroll	$10,000	
	Cash		$8,330
	Employees' income taxes payable		1,000
	Employees' FICA taxes payable		670
c.	Accrued payroll	$10,000	
	Cash		$8,330
	Work-in-process		1,670
d.	Work-in-process	$6,000	
	Factory overhead	2,900	
	Selling and administrative expense	2,000	
	Accrued payroll		$10,000
	Employer payroll taxes payable		900

The correct answer is (b). *(Publisher)*
REQUIRED: The journal entry to record the payment of the weekly payroll.
DISCUSSION: (1) Debit accrued payroll for the balance in the account. (2) Credit cash for the actual amount of cash disbursed. (3) Credit employees' income taxes payable for the amount of taxes withheld from the employees' paychecks. (4) Credit employees' FICA taxes payable and other liabilities for the amount of FICA taxes and other items withheld from the employees' paychecks.
Income taxes of $200 per day ($1,000 per week) should be withheld from the employees for income taxes payable. An amount should also be withheld for the employees' portion of FICA taxes. In this instance, the amount is $670, although no percentage is given. Employees' FICA taxes payable should be recognized and no other entry given will satisfy the requirement.
Alternatively, if the employee withholdings were recognized as liabilities when the payroll was accrued, the entry would be to debit the payroll liability and credit cash for $8,330.
Answer (a) is incorrect because the amount is $8,330, not $5,000. Answer (c) is incorrect because employee withholding liabilities are credited, not WIP. Answer (d) is incorrect because it records the payroll rather than its payment.

86. What would the journal entry be for the purchase of $500 of materials and $250 of supplies for cash?

a.	Supplies and materials	$750	
	Accounts payable		$750
b.	Work-in-process	$500	
	Factory overhead	250	
	Accounts payable		$750
c.	Stores control	$750	
	Cash		$750
d.	Work-in-process	$750	
	Cash		$750

The correct answer is (c). *(Publisher)*
REQUIRED: The journal entry for the cash purchase of materials and supplies.
DISCUSSION: The correct entry to record the purchase of materials and supplies in a cost center would be to debit the stores control account for the combined cost of the materials and supplies ($750) and to credit cash.
Answers (a) and (b) are incorrect because the supplies and materials were purchased with cash. Answer (b) is also incorrect because the materials and supplies are not debited to WIP and factory overhead, respectively, until they are used or transferred out of storage. Answer (d) is incorrect because raw material is charged to WIP only when put into production. Supplies are charged to overhead when used.

87. If $200 of materials and $125 of supplies were issued to work-in-process, which of the following entries would be correct?

a.	Work-in-process	$325	
	Materials		$200
	Supplies		125
b.	Work-in-process	$125	
	Overhead control	200	
	Materials		$200
	Supplies		125
c.	Work-in-process	$200	
	Overhead control	125	
	Stores control		$325
d.	Materials and supplies	$325	
	Stores control		$325

The correct answer is (c). *(Publisher)*
REQUIRED: The entry to record the issuance of materials and supplies.
DISCUSSION: The cost of materials should be debited to the WIP account as they are used in the production of goods. The cost of supplies should be debited to factory overhead control as they are used because their use cannot be identified with particular products. The credit should be to stores control or, if used, separate materials and supplies accounts.
Answer (a) is incorrect because supplies are charged to overhead as they are used. Answer (b) is incorrect because the overhead and WIP figures are reversed. Answer (d) is incorrect because it transfers the $325 from one inventory account to another.

Module 5.5: Journal Entries

88. What would be the correct journal entry if $5,000 of direct labor and $1,250 of indirect labor were incurred?

a.	Work-in-process	$6,250	
	Accrued payroll		$6,250
b.	Work-in-process	$5,000	
	Overhead control	1,250	
	Accrued payroll		$6,250
c.	Work-in-process	$6,250	
	Overhead control	1,250	
	Accrued payroll		$6,250
	Applied overhead		1,250
d.	Payroll expense	$6,250	
	Accrued payable		$6,250

The correct answer is (b). *(Publisher)*
REQUIRED: The journal entry to record the incurrence of direct and indirect labor.
DISCUSSION: The WIP account is charged with the $5,000 direct labor cost. The $1,250 of indirect labor is debited to factory overhead control because the labor cannot be identified with a particular product; e.g., general maintenance is a cost of production that cannot be allocated to specific products. The liability of $6,250 must also be recognized. Accounting for payroll taxes is assumed to be done when the payroll is paid by debiting accrued payroll and crediting cash and the employee withholding liabilities.
Answer (a) is incorrect because the indirect labor should be charged to overhead. Answer (c) is incorrect because only $5,000 goes to WIP. The remaining $1,250 is charged to overhead. Answer (d) is incorrect because factory labor costs must be inventoried rather than expensed.

89. The completion of Job #21, with total costs of $4,900, would result in which of the following entries?

a.	Finished goods	$4,900	
	Work-in-process		$4,900
b.	Finished goods	$4,900	
	Job #21		$4,900
c.	Cost of goods available	$4,900	
	Work-in-process		$4,900
d.	Work-in-process	$4,900	
	Finished goods		$4,900

The correct answer is (a). *(Publisher)*
REQUIRED: The entry to record the completion of a job.
DISCUSSION: During production, all the labor, material, and overhead are charged to WIP. Upon completion, the account must be credited for the total cost of the job. Thus, WIP will be credited and finished goods will be debited for $4,900. Upon sale, the cost will be transferred from finished goods to CGS.
Answer (b) is incorrect because, in the general ledger, the credit is to WIP rather than a specific subsidiary account, although there are subsidiary ledgers or job cost cards for both the WIP and the FG accounts. Answer (c) is incorrect because the cost of goods available account does not exist. Cost of goods available for sale is the sum of beginning inventories plus purchases or CGM. Answer (d) is incorrect because it is the reverse of the correct entry.

90. If the year's overhead costs incurred are $29,000, and $25,000 in costs have been applied to the product, what would be the appropriate entry to close these accounts (assuming no proration)?

a.	Cost of goods sold	$ 4,000	
	Overhead applied	25,000	
	Overhead control		$29,000
b.	Overhead control	$25,000	
	Cost of goods sold	4,000	
	Overhead applied		$29,000
c.	Cost of goods sold	$29,000	
	Overhead applied		$29,000
d.	Work-in-process	$29,000	
	Overhead control		$29,000

The correct answer is (a). *(Publisher)*
REQUIRED: The journal entry to close actual overhead and applied overhead without proration.
DISCUSSION: When separate overhead control and overhead applied accounts are used, all overhead incurred is charged to the overhead control account. As overhead is applied, it is credited to overhead applied. Accordingly, the entry to close these accounts is to debit the applied account and credit the control account. Given no proration, the difference is taken directly to CGS. Material differences should be prorated among the WIP, FG, and CGS accounts. The proration should be in proportion to the amount of the current period's overhead already applied to the accounts.
Answer (b) is incorrect because overhead control should be credited. Answer (c) is incorrect because overhead applied should not be closed in entirety to CGS. Answer (d) is incorrect because it would be the correct entry to apply overhead for the entire period if overhead applied had been credited.

Module 5.5: Journal Entries

91. Based on the facts in the previous question, which of the following entries would close the overhead accounts and prorate the underapplied overhead among these relevant accounts? (Of the $25,000 applied, $2,500 is still in EWIP and $5,000 is still in finished goods as part of unsold inventory.)

a.
Cost of goods sold	$1,333	
Finished goods	1,333	
Work-in-process	1,334	
Overhead control	25,000	
Overhead applied		$29,000

b.
Cost of goods sold	$2,800	
Finished goods	800	
Work-in-process	400	
Overhead applied	25,000	
Overhead control		$29,000

c.
Cost of goods sold	$2,000	
Finished goods	1,500	
Work-in-process	500	
Factory overhead applied	25,000	
Overhead summary		$29,000

d.
Overhead applied	$29,000	
Overhead control		$25,000
Cost of goods sold		2,000
Finished goods		1,500
Work-in-process		500

The correct answer is (b). *(Publisher)*
REQUIRED: The entry that will close the overhead accounts and prorate the underapplied overhead.
DISCUSSION: Overhead applied has a credit balance. Hence, the closing entry must include a debit to the account. The reverse is true of the control account. In this case, only 10% of the $25,000 overhead applied remains in the WIP account ($2,500 ÷ $25,000). Accordingly, 10% of the $4,000 of underapplied overhead should be charged to work-in-process (10% x $4,000). Finished goods contains 20% ($5,000 ÷ $25,000) of the already applied overhead. Accordingly, $800 (20% x $4,000) should be charged to finished goods. The remaining 70% of applied overhead has been charged to cost of goods sold. Thus, 70% of the underapplied overhead ($2,800) should be charged to cost of goods sold.
Answers (a) and (c) are incorrect because the proration should be 70%, 20%, and 10%, respectively, not 33%, 33%, and 34%, or 50%, 37.5%, and 12.5%. Also, the credit should be to overhead control. Answer (d) is incorrect because the amounts are wrong and the entry is reversed.

92. Select the journal entry to record the application of $500 of indirect labor.

a.
Job #21	$500	
Overhead control		$500

b.
Work-in-process	$500	
Overhead control		$500

c.
Payroll payable	$500	
Overhead control (Job #21)		$500

d.
Work-in-process	$500	
Overhead applied		$500

The correct answer is (d). *(Publisher)*
REQUIRED: The journal entry to record the application of indirect labor.
DISCUSSION: The application of indirect overhead requires a debit to WIP and a credit to overhead applied. Two accounts, overhead control and overhead applied, are used in the questions in this module. They are used to accumulate the indirect costs (debits) that arise during the period (factory overhead control) and to allocate the budgeted indirect costs on some reasonable basis to the cost of production (factory overhead applied). Thus, as costs are incurred, they are debited to overhead control. When they are applied or transferred, they are credited to overhead applied. Only one account could be used. All debits and credits would go to one account, but no cumulative totals would be available.
Answer (a) is incorrect because it represents the entry to the subsidiary job card. When the $500 is transferred to WIP in a job order cost system, the cost has to be allocated or charged to specific jobs so the subsidiary ledger of job cost cards will equal the total amount in the WIP account in the general ledger. Answers (a), (b), and (c) are incorrect because, assuming two separate overhead accounts are used, entries to transfer cost to the WIP account are made to overhead applied. Answer (c) is also incorrect because the overhead control account does not have a subsidiary ledger.

Module 5.6: Comprehensive

93. A company manufactures pipes and uses a job order costing system. During May, the following jobs were started (no other jobs were in process) and the following costs were incurred:

	Job X	Job Y	Job Z	Total
Materials requisitioned	$10,000	$20,000	$15,000	$45,000
Direct labor	5,000	4,000	2,500	11,500
	$15,000	$24,000	$17,500	$56,500

In addition, estimated overhead of $300,000 and direct labor costs of $150,000 were estimated to be incurred during the year. Actual overhead of $24,000 was incurred in May; overhead is applied on the basis of direct labor dollars. If only Job X and Job Z were completed during the month, the appropriate entry to record the initiation of all jobs would be

a. Work-in-process $79,500
   Direct material $45,000
   Direct labor   11,500
   Applied factory overhead 23,000

b. Work-in-process $80,500
   Direct material $45,000
   Direct labor   11,500
   Factory overhead   24,000

c. Work-in-process $80,500
   Direct material $45,000
   Direct labor   11,500
   Applied factory overhead 24,000

d. Direct labor $11,500
   Direct material   45,000
   Work-in-process $56,500

The correct answer is (a). *(CIA 1184 IV-4)*
REQUIRED: The entry to record work-in-process for the month.
DISCUSSION: Work-in-process is debited for the direct material, direct labor, and overhead charged to jobs initiated during the month. Materials and labor are given as $45,000 and $11,500, respectively. Overhead applied is calculated by multiplying the predetermined rate by the activity base. The $2 rate ($300,000 ÷ $150,000) times the $11,500 activity base equals overhead applied (charged to WIP), or $23,000.

Answer (b) is incorrect because the incurrence of overhead is reflected by a debit to factory overhead and credits to various accounts. Answer (c) is incorrect because it reflects the amount of overhead incurred ($24,000), not applied ($23,000). Answer (d) is incorrect because direct material, direct labor, and applied overhead should be credited and WIP debited.

5.6 Comprehensive

Questions 94 through 96 are based on the following information, which was presented as part of Question 3 on Part 3 of the December 1980 CMA examination.

Tastee-Treat Company prepares, packages, and distributes six frozen vegetables in two different sized containers. The different vegetables and different sizes are prepared in large batches. The company employs a normal cost job order costing system. Manufacturing overhead is assigned to batches by a predetermined rate on the basis of direct labor hours. The manufacturing overhead costs incurred by the company during two recent years (adjusted for changes using current prices and wage rates) are presented in the opposite column.

	1989	1990
Direct labor hours worked	2,760,000	2,160,000
Manufacturing overhead costs incurred (adjusted for changes in current prices and wage rates):		
Indirect labor	$11,040,000	$ 8,640,000
Employee benefits	4,140,000	3,240,000
Supplies	2,760,000	2,160,000
Power	2,208,000	1,728,000
Heat and light	552,000	552,000
Supervision	2,865,000	2,625,000
Depreciation	7,930,000	7,930,000
Property taxes and insurance	3,005,000	3,005,000
Total overhead costs	$34,500,000	$29,880,000

Module 5.6: Comprehensive

94. What is the variable overhead rate?

a. $7.20.
b. $5.40.
c. $6.30.
d. $7.70.

The correct answer is (d). *(Publisher)*
REQUIRED: The variable overhead rate given total overhead costs and hours worked for two prior periods.
DISCUSSION: The variable overhead rate is calculated using the high/low method, which assumes a linear relationship between the two flexible budgets given. The variable overhead rate is equal to the difference in total overhead cost divided by the difference in total labor hours worked.

$$\frac{\$34,500,000 - \$29,880,000}{2,760,000 - 2,160,000} = \frac{\$4,620,000}{600,000}$$

$$= \$7.70/DLH$$

95. What will the total overhead rate be for a 2,300,000 direct labor hour level of activity in 1990?

a. $7.70.
b. $13.46.
c. $5.76.
d. $12.52.

The correct answer is (b). *(Publisher)*
REQUIRED: The projected total overhead rate given cost data and hours worked for two prior periods.
DISCUSSION: The total overhead rate equals the variable overhead rate plus the quotient of fixed overhead divided by the activity level. Fixed overhead is equal to total overhead less the total variable overhead (calculated using the variable overhead rate of $7.70) at either of the activity levels. Thus, total fixed overhead is $13,248,000. Total fixed overhead plus total variable overhead at the budgeted activity level equals the total overhead. The total overhead rate is $13.46 ($30,958,000 ÷ 2,300,000 DLH).

Total overhead--1989	$34,500,000
Total variable overhead	
(2,760,000 DLH x $7.70)	(21,252,000)
Total fixed overhead	$13,248,000

Total overhead costs at 2,300,000 DLH:	
Total variable overhead	
(2,300,000 DLH x $7.70)	$17,710,000
Total fixed overhead	13,248,000
Total overhead	$30,958,000

$$\text{Total overhead rate} = \frac{\$30,958,000}{2,300,000} = \$13.46$$

96. Which of the following is a false statement about evaluating product pricing decisions?

a. Prices are based on a company's cost rather than market factors.
b. There is little product differentiation possible because of the highly competitive market.
c. Short-term prices should cover at least variable costs.
d. Long-term prices are designed to cover total overhead costs taking into consideration container sizes.

The correct answer is (a). *(Publisher)*
REQUIRED: The false statement concerning product pricing decisions.
DISCUSSION: Product pricing decisions should consider market factors such as the potential volume of sales, the degree of product differentiation possible, and short-term and long-term pricing goals. Such goals might include a projected profit or return on investment, a given market share, or the need to meet competition. Although cost is a necessary factor in the pricing decision, to base a company's prices only on cost usually results in incorrect product pricing decisions.
Answers (b), (c), and (d) are incorrect because each is a true statement about product pricing since they deal with market factors (b) as well as, long- and short-term pricing goals (c and d).

Module 5.6: Comprehensive

Questions 97 through 99 are based on the following information. Farber Company employs a normal (nonstandard) absorption cost system. The information in the next column is from the financial records of the company for December 31 of the year just ended.

- Total manufacturing costs were $2,500,000.
- Cost of goods manufactured was $2,425,000.
- Applied factory overhead was 30% of total manufacturing costs.
- Factory overhead was applied to production at a rate of 80% of direct labor cost.
- Work-in-process inventory at January 1 was 75% of work-in-process inventory at December 31.

---

97. Farber Company's total direct labor cost for the year was

a. $750,000.
b. $600,000.
c. $900,000.
d. $937,500.
e. Some amount other than those given above.

The correct answer is (d). *(CMA 1285 4-25)*
REQUIRED: The total direct labor cost for the year.
DISCUSSION: Total manufacturing cost of $2,500,000 is composed of raw materials, direct labor, and factory overhead. Factory overhead is 30% of total manufacturing costs, or $750,000. If factory overhead is 80% of direct labor cost, direct labor cost is $937,500 ($750,000 ÷ 80%).

98. Total cost of direct material used by Farber Company for the year was

a. $750,000.
b. $812,500.
c. $850,000.
d. $1,150,000.
e. Some amount other than those given above.

The correct answer is (b). *(CMA 1285 4-26)*
REQUIRED: The total cost of direct material used during the year.
DISCUSSION: Factory overhead is 30% of total manufacturing costs, or $750,000. In the preceding question, direct labor was found to be $937,500. Thus, raw materials must account for the remaining $812,500 ($2,500,000 - $750,000 - $937,500).

99. The carrying value of Farber Company's work-in-process inventory at December 31 is

a. $300,000.
b. $225,000.
c. $100,000.
d. $75,000.
e. Some amount other than those given above.

The correct answer is (a). *(CMA 1285 4-27)*
REQUIRED: The carrying value of the work-in-process inventory.
DISCUSSION: Cost of goods manufactured ($2,425,000) equals total manufacturing costs ($2,500,000) plus beginning work-in-process (75% of EWIP) minus ending work-in-process. The ending work-in-process is $300,000.

$2,500,000 + .75 EWIP - EWIP = $2,425,000
$2,500,000 - .25 EWIP = $2,425,000
EWIP = $75,000/.25
EWIP = $300,000

Questions 100 through 104 are based on the following information, which was presented as part of Question 4 on the Practice I section of the November 1974 CPA Examination.

Helper Corporation, manufactures one product and accounts for costs by a job order cost system. You have obtained the following information for the year ended December 31 from the Corporation's books and records:

- Total manufacturing cost added during the year was $1,000,000 based on actual direct material, actual direct labor, and factory overhead applied based on actual direct labor dollars.
- Cost of goods manufactured was $970,000 also based on actual direct material, actual direct labor, and applied factory overhead.
- Factory overhead was applied to work-in-process at 75% of direct labor dollars. Applied factory overhead for the year was 27% of the total manufacturing cost.
- Beginning work-in-process inventory, January 1, was 80% of ending work-in-process inventory, December 31.

Module 5.6: Comprehensive

100. How is the amount of overhead applied determined by cost personnel at Helper Corporation given no direct labor cost figure?

a. Multiply 27% by total manufacturing cost.
b. Multiply 27% by cost of goods manufactured.
c. Multiply 75% by direct labor cost.
d. Multiply 75% by total labor cost.

The correct answer is (a). *(Publisher)*
REQUIRED: How to calculate applied overhead given no direct labor cost figure.
DISCUSSION: In this instance, factory overhead applied can be determined by its proportion of total manufacturing cost. Total manufacturing cost is equal to $1,000,000. Factory overhead is $270,000, which is 27% of the total.

101. If factory overhead applied is $270,000, how much direct labor was incurred?

a. $360,000.
b. $385,700.
c. $346,150.
d. $350,000.

The correct answer is (a). *(Publisher)*
REQUIRED: The amount of direct labor given factory overhead applied.
DISCUSSION: The factory overhead is applied at 75% of direct labor cost. Given that $270,000 is the amount of factory overhead applied, direct labor cost is equal to $360,000 ($270,000 ÷ 75%).

102. Total manufacturing costs for the year plus beginning work-in-process inventory equals

a. Cost of goods manufactured.
b. Ending work-in-process.
c. Manufacturing costs to account for.
d. Goods available for sale.

The correct answer is (c). *(Publisher)*
REQUIRED: The definition of manufacturing cost to account for.
DISCUSSION: Manufacturing costs to account for include the BWIP plus manufacturing costs incurred during the period. Manufacturing costs incurred during the period include direct material used, direct labor, and factory overhead applied.
Answer (a) is incorrect because CGM equals total manufacturing cost plus BWIP minus EWIP. Answer (b) is incorrect because the bulk of manufacturing costs incurred for the year have been transferred first to finished goods and then to CGS. Answer (d) is incorrect because goods available for sale is the sum of beginning finished goods plus CGM.

103. What is the ending work-in-process inventory?

a. $120,000.
b. $150,000.
c. $30,000.
d. $140,000.

The correct answer is (b). *(Publisher)*
REQUIRED: The ending work-in-process inventory (EWIP).
DISCUSSION: EWIP plus the CGM is equal to the sum of BWIP plus total manufacturing cost added. BWIP is 80% of EWIP.

EWIP + $970,000 = BWIP + $1,000,000
.8 EWIP = BWIP
EWIP + $970,000 = .8 EWIP + $1,000,000
.2 EWIP = $30,000
EWIP = $150,000

104. What are the total manufacturing costs to account for?

a. $1,150,000.
b. $1,140,000.
c. $1,120,000.
d. $1,130,000.

The correct answer is (c). *(Publisher)*
REQUIRED: The total manufacturing costs to account for.
DISCUSSION: Total manufacturing costs to account for equal BWIP plus total manufacturing cost added. BWIP inventory is $120,000 (.8 x $150,000). This plus $1,000,000 of total manufacturing cost added equals $1,120,000.

Module 5.6: Comprehensive

Questions 105 through 120 are based on the following information, which was presented as part of Question 5 on the Practice II section of the May 1973 CPA examination.

Custer Manufacturing Corp., a calendar-year corporation, uses a job order cost system for its production of various plastic parts for the aircraft industry. On October 9, production was started on Job No. 487 for 100 front bubbles (windshields) for commercial helicopters.

Production of the bubbles begins in the Fabricating Department where sheets of plastic (purchased as raw material) are melted down and poured into molds. The molds are then placed in a special temperature and humidity room to harden the plastic. The hardened plastic bubbles are then removed from the molds and hand-worked to remove imperfections.

After fabrication the bubbles are transferred to the Testing Department where each bubble must meet rigid specifications. Bubbles that fail the tests are scrapped and there is no salvage value.

Bubbles passing the tests are transferred to the Assembly Department where they are inserted into metal frames. The frames, purchased from vendors, require no work prior to installing the bubbles.

The assembled unit is then transferred to the Shipping Department for crating and shipment. Crating material is relatively expensive and most of the work is done by hand.

The following information concerning Job No. 487 is available as of December 31:

1. Direct materials charged to the job:

    a. 1,000 sq. ft. of plastic at $12.75 per sq. ft. was charged to the Fabricating Department. This amount was to meet all plastic material requirements of the job assuming no spoilage.

    b. 74 metal frames at $408.52 each were charged to the Assembly Department.

    c. Packing material for 40 units at $75 per unit was charged to the Shipping Department.

2. Direct labor charges through December 31 were as follows:

	Total	Per Unit
Fabricating Department	$1,424	$16
Testing Department	444	6
Assembly Department	612	12
Shipping Department	256	8
	$2,736	

3. Differences between actual and applied manufacturing overhead for the year ended December 31 were immaterial. Manufacturing overhead is charged to the four production departments by various allocation methods, all of which you approve. Manufacturing overhead charged to the Fabricating Department is allocated to jobs based on heat-room hours; the other production departments allocate manufacturing overhead to jobs on the basis of direct labor dollars charged to each job within the department. The following reflects the manufacturing overhead rates for the year ended December 31:

	Rate Per Unit
Fabricating Department	$.45/hour
Testing Department	$.68/direct labor dollar
Assembly Department	$.38/direct labor dollar
Shipping Department	$.25/direct labor dollar

4. Job No. 487 used 855 heat-room hours during the year ended December 31.

5. Following is the physical inventory for Job No. 487 as of December 31:

Fabricating Department:

1) 50 sq. ft. of plastic sheet.
2) 8 hardened bubbles, 1/4 complete as to direct labor.
3) 4 complete bubbles.

Testing Department:

1) 15 bubbles which failed testing when 2/5 of testing was complete. No others failed.
2) 7 bubbles complete as to testing.

Assembly Department:

1) 13 frames with no direct labor.
2) 15 bubbles and frames, 1/3 complete as to direct labor.
3) 3 complete bubbles and frames.

Shipping Department:

1) 9 complete units, 2/3 complete as to packing material and 1/3 complete as to direct labor.
2) 10 complete units, 100% complete as to packing material and 50% complete as to direct labor.
3) 1 unit complete for shipping was dropped off the loading docks. There is no salvage.
4) 23 units have been shipped prior to December 31.
5) There was no inventory of packing materials in the shipping department at December 31.

Module 5.6: Comprehensive

105. What is the amount of plastic transferred in from raw materials?

a. $12,750
b. $21,750.
c. $10,750.
d. $11,750.

The correct answer is (a). *(Publisher)*
REQUIRED: The amount of plastic transferred in from raw materials.
DISCUSSION: The first few paragraphs describe a job order process. The numbered paragraphs 1 through 4 describe the inputs to each of the WIP accounts. Paragraph 5 provides the EWIP for each WIP account.
The amount transferred from raw materials is equal to the price per unit times the quantity transferred in. A thousand square feet of plastic at $12.75 per sq. ft. was transferred to the Fabricating Department. Hence, $12,750 worth of plastic was transferred in.

106. What is the amount of plastic used in the Fabricating Department?

a. $637.50.
b. $12,112.50.
c. $15,300.00.
d. $12,750.00.

The correct answer is (b). *(Publisher)*
REQUIRED: The amount of materials used in the Fabricating Department.
DISCUSSION: The plastic used in Fabricating was 950 sq. ft. (1,000 sq. ft. - 50 sq. ft. in EI). At $12.75 per sq. ft., $12,112.50 worth of plastic was used.
The ending inventory was worth $637.50 (50 sq. ft. x $12.75). Thus, the $12,750 transferred in was either used ($12,112.50) or in EI ($637.50). See the previous question.

107. What is the amount of materials transferred out from the Fabricating Department to other departments?

a. $12,246.65.
b. $9,615.43.
c. $10,582.50.
d. $17,566.36.

The correct answer is (c). *(Publisher)*
REQUIRED: The amount of materials transferred out of the Fabricating Department.
DISCUSSION: The amount of materials transferred out is equal to the number of units transferred out times the price per unit. Given that 1,000 sq. ft. of plastic was charged to the job, 10 sq. ft. (1,000 sq. ft. ÷ 100 bubbles) of material is needed to make one bubble. Given that 50 sq. ft. (5 units) of plastic remain in the Fabricating Department, and 12 bubbles are in various stages of completion, 83 bubbles (100 - 5 - 12) must have been transferred out. The 83 units transferred out represent 830 sq. ft. of plastic, worth $10,582.50 (830 sq. ft. x $12.75).
The 12 bubbles remaining in the Fabricating Department are worth $1,530 (120 sq. ft. x $12.75). Hence, EWIP ($1,530) plus the amount transferred out ($10,582.50) equals the amount used of $12,112.50 (see the previous question).

108. What is the amount of labor charged to the Fabricating Department?

a. $1,328.00.
b. $2,273.73.
c. $1,808.75.
d. $1,424.00.

The correct answer is (d). *(Publisher)*
REQUIRED: The amount of labor charged to the Fabricating Department.
DISCUSSION: The amount of labor charged to the Fabricating Department is given as $1,424. To check, this amount is equal to 89 units complete as to labor times the $16 per unit charge. The 89 units consist of 83 transferred out plus 4 complete bubbles and 8 bubbles 1/4 complete (which is equivalent to complete).

109. What is the amount of overhead charged to the Fabricating Department?

a. $336.15.
b. $384.75.
c. $446.80.
d. $960.00.

The correct answer is (b). *(Publisher)*
REQUIRED: The amount of overhead charged to the Fabricating Department.
DISCUSSION: The amount of overhead charged to the Fabricating Department for Job No. 487 is $384.75 ($.45/hour overhead rate x 855 heat-room hours).

Module 5.6: Comprehensive

> Questions 110 through 112 are based on the information presented on page 104.

110. What is the amount of labor and overhead transferred from Fabricating to Testing?

  a. $1,328.00 and $336.15.
  b. $1,460.00 and $437.25.
  c. $1,268.00 and $436.15.
  d. $1,458.00 and $361.15.

The correct answer is (a). *(Publisher)*
REQUIRED: The amount of labor and overhead transferred from Fabricating to Testing.
DISCUSSION: The total amount of labor transferred out is equal to labor per unit times the number of units transferred out. The total overhead transferred out is equal to the overhead per unit times the number of units transferred out.
 Labor transferred out equals $1,328 (83 units x $16/unit). The melting, etc. takes place at the beginning of the process, and the 8 units 1/4 finished are already "hardened." Accordingly, 95 units have gone through the heat room: 83 transferred out, 4 finished but not transferred, and 8 in process. Overhead per unit equals $.45 per hour for 9 heat-room hours per unit (855 hours ÷ 95 units). The amount of overhead transferred was $336.15 (83 units x 9 hours/unit x $.45/hour).

111. What is the total balance of work-in-process inventory in the Fabricating Department as of December 31?

  a. $1,465.30.
  b. $1,674.60.
  c. $637.50.
  d. $1,808.75.

The correct answer is (b). *(Publisher)*
REQUIRED: The balance of WIP inventory in the Fabricating Department at year-end.
DISCUSSION: WIP inventory is equal to the raw materials, direct labor, and factory overhead remaining in inventory. Caution must be exercised in this calculation because the question specifically refers to the balance of WIP inventory and not to the raw materials still in the Fabricating Department that have not yet been worked on.

1. Material cost is $127.50 per unit (10 sq. ft. x $12.75), and 12 units are in process for a total of $1,530.
2. Labor cost is $16 for each of the 4 complete units and $4 for each of the 8 units 1/4 complete, a total of $96.
3. Overhead is $48.60 (12 bubbles x 9 hours x $.45).
4. The total is $1,674.60 ($1,530 + $96 + $48.60).

Authors' Note: The following analysis of the Fabricating Department WIP account is presented as a summary of the previous 7 questions. Parentheses indicate a credit.

Fabricating Department

	Plastic	Materials	Labor	Overhead	Totals
Transferred in from raw materials	$12,750.00	-0-	-0-	-0-	$12,750.00
Production to date	(12,112.50)	$12,112.50	$1,424.00	$384.75	1,808.75
Transferred out to other departments	-0-	(10,582.50)	(1,328.00)	(336.15)	(12,246.65)
Balance at December 31:					
Raw materials	$ 637.50	-0-	-0-	-0-	$ 637.50
Work-in-process	-0-	$ 1,530.00	$ 96.00	$ 48.60	$ 1,674.60

112. What is the amount of overhead charged to the Testing Department?

  a. $248.88.
  b. $301.92.
  c. $269.88.
  d. $238.18.

The correct answer is (b). *(Publisher)*
REQUIRED: The amount of overhead charged to the Testing Department.
DISCUSSION: Testing Department overhead is applied based on direct labor dollars at a rate of 68% of direct labor. Given that $444 in direct labor was incurred, overhead applied was $301.92 (68% x $444).

Module 5.6: Comprehensive

Questions 113 through 115 are based on the information presented on page 104.

113. What is the amount of spoilage in the Testing Department?

a. $2,273.73.
b. $4,135.00.
c. $2,636.15.
d. $3,217.73.

The correct answer is (a). *(Publisher)*
REQUIRED: The amount of spoilage in the Testing Department.
DISCUSSION: The amount of spoilage in the Testing Department is equal to the transferred in materials, labor, and overhead charges accumulated for the units spoiled plus labor and overhead applied for those in the Testing Department. The costs transferred in equal $12,246.65 (see the preceding Qs. 107 and 110).

Material	$10,582.50
Labor	1,328.00
Overhead	336.15
Total	$12,246.65

Dividing this amount by the 83 units transferred in gives a $147.55 unit cost. The 15 spoiled units cost $2,213.25 (15 x $147.55) when transferred in. The units were 2/5 complete at the time of failure. The labor cost applied to the 15 spoiled units in the Testing Department was $36.00 (15 units x $6.00/unit x 2/5). Overhead applied at .68/labor dollar was $24.48 (.68/dollar x $36). The total amount of spoilage is equal to transferred in cost plus labor and overhead applied in the Testing Department, or $2,273.73 ($2,213.25 + $36 + $24.48).

114. What is the balance of work-in-process inventory in the Testing Department as of year-end?

a. $1,103.41.
b. $1,032.85.
c. $1,674.60.
d. $2,173.73.

The correct answer is (a). *(Publisher)*
REQUIRED: The balance of work-in-process inventory in the Testing Department.
DISCUSSION: The balance of WIP inventory in the Testing Department is equal to the amount of transferred-in costs plus the labor and overhead incurred in the Testing Department. There are 7 units remaining in the Testing Department, each complete with respect to transferred-in costs, labor, and overhead. The unit cost transferred in is $147.55 (see previous question). Labor cost per unit is $6, and overhead per unit is $4.08 ($.68/labor dollar x $6). The cost of each unit is thus $157.63 ($147.55 + $6 + $4.08), and EWIP is $1,103.41 (7 units x $157.63/unit).

Authors' Note: The following analysis of the Testing Department WIP account is presented as a summary of the previous 3 questions. Parentheses indicate a credit.

	Testing Department			
	Transferred In	Labor	Overhead	Totals
Transferred in from other departments	$12,246.65	-0-	-0-	$12,246.65
Production to date	-0-	$444.00	$301.92	745.92
Transferred out to other departments	(9,000.55)	(366.00)	(248.88)	(9,615.43)
Spoilage	(2,213.25)	(36.00)	(24.48)	(2,273.73)
Balance of work-in-process at year-end	$1,032.85	$42.00	$28.56	$1,103.41

115. What are the amounts transferred into the Assembly Department from raw materials and from the Testing Department?

a. $30,230.48 and $9,615.43.
b. $26,115.24 and $4,307.21.
c. $25,056.53 and $8,743.15.
d. $30,230.48 and $4,307.21.

The correct answer is (a). *(Publisher)*
REQUIRED: The amounts transferred into the Assembly Department.
DISCUSSION: The amount of raw materials transferred into the department is $30,230.48 (74 frames x $408.52). The Testing Department received 83 bubbles from the Fabricating Department. Of these, 15 were defective and 7 were in EWIP. Thus, the Testing Department transferred 61 bubbles (83 - 15 - 7) to the Assembly Department. At a unit cost of $157.63 (see Q. 114), they were worth $9,615.43 ($157.63 x 61).

Questions 116 through 120 are based on the information presented on page 104.

116. What is the balance of raw materials in the Assembly Department as of year-end?

a. $7,353.36.
b. $5,615.36.
c. $5,310.76.
d. $9,614.00.

The correct answer is (c). *(Publisher)*
REQUIRED: The balance of raw materials in the Assembly Department at year-end.
DISCUSSION: The balance of raw materials in the Assembly Department is $5,310.76 (13 unprocessed frames x $408.52).

117. What is the amount of the work-in-process balance as of year-end in the Assembly Department?

a. $10,323.18.
b. $9,615.43.
c. $8,621.15.
d. $9,000.55.

The correct answer is (a). *(Publisher)*
REQUIRED: The Assembly Department EWIP.
DISCUSSION: EWIP in the Assembly Department consists of DM, DL, and O/H attached to the EWIP. The 13 metal frames are considered raw materials, not EWIP. The EWIP consists of 15 bubbles and frames 1/3 complete as to labor, and 3 complete units. The transferred-in cost per unit is $157.63, and the metal frame cost per unit is $408.52. Thus, material costs are $10,190.70 [($157.63 + $408.52) x 18]. Labor at $12 per EUP (given) times the 8 EUP [(15 x 1/3)+ 3 complete] is $96. O/H is 38% of labor, or $36.48 (38% of $96). Total cost is thus $10,323.18 ($10,190.70 + $96 + $36.48).

118. What is the amount transferred from the Shipping Department to cost of goods sold?

a. $13,402.33.
b. $15,311.33.
c. $25,066.13.
d. $15,357.33.

The correct answer is (d). *(Publisher)*
REQUIRED: The amount transferred from the Shipping Department.
DISCUSSION: CGS consists of cost transferred in plus DM, DL, and O/H for units completed. Transferred-in costs were $25,056.53 for 43 units ($582.71 per unit). Packing materials were $75 per unit. Labor was $8 per unit. O/H was $2 per unit (.25 x $8). Of the 43 units transferred in, 19 are in EWIP, 1 unit was completely destroyed in an accident after it was packed, and 23 units were shipped. The amount transferred out was $15,357.33 [23 x ($582.71 + $75 + $8 + $2)].

119. What is the amount of spoilage in packing material?

a. $1,200.
b. $75.
c. $86.
d. $921.

The correct answer is (b). *(Publisher)*
REQUIRED: The amount of spoilage in packing material.
DISCUSSION: Spoilage is the production that is damaged or otherwise fails to meet the criteria for sale in the ordinary course of business. Spoiled units are sold for salvage value or junked. The amount of spoilage in packing material equals the number of units in packing material spoiled times the price per unit ($75). In this instance, only one unit was spoiled.

120. What is the balance of work-in-process inventory in the Shipping Department as of year-end?

a. $12,335.49.
b. $12,287.49.
c. $12,351.49.
d. $11,151.49.

The correct answer is (c). *(Publisher)*
REQUIRED: The Shipping Department EWIP.
DISCUSSION: The transferred in costs are $11,071.49 (19 units x $582.71). Material costs are $1,200, which is $75 per unit times 16 EUP [(9 units x 2/3) + 10 complete]. Labor costs are $64, which is $8 per unit times 8 EUP [(9 x 1/3) + (10 x 1/2)]. Overhead cost is $16.00 ($.25 x $64 direct labor dollars).

Transferred in	$11,071.49
Material	1,200.00
Labor	64.00
Overhead	16.00
EWIP	$12,351.49

CHAPTER SIX
PROCESS COSTING

6.1 Basic Process Costing . . . . (10 questions)	109
6.2 Operation Costing . . . . (4 questions)	112
6.3 Transferred-In Costs . . . . (6 questions)	113
6.4 Equivalent Units of Production (EUP) . . . . (9 questions)	115
6.5 FIFO vs. Weighted Average Assumption for EUP . . . . (16 questions)	118
6.6 FIFO EUP Calculation . . . . (10 questions)	123
6.7 Weighted Average EUP Calculation . . . . (17 questions)	126
6.8 Comprehensive . . . . (25 questions)	132

This chapter focuses on process costing. Process costing is the costing approach used to determine unit cost for continuous process manufacturing. The units of production are usually perceived to be relatively homogeneous. The primary difference between job order costing and process costing is in the area of subsidiary ledgers. Special attention is paid in this chapter to the difference between the FIFO assumption and the weighted average assumption regarding the cost flows. In addition, several questions are provided that give the opportunity to work through the entire set of calculations regarding process costing.

6.1 Basic Process Costing

1. When should process costing techniques be used in assigning costs to products?

a. If the product is manufactured on the basis of each order received.
b. When production is only partially completed during the accounting period.
c. If the product is composed of mass-produced homogeneous units.
d. Whenever standard costing techniques should not be used.

The correct answer is (c). *(CPA 575 T-27)*
REQUIRED: When process costing techniques should be used.
DISCUSSION: Like products that are mass produced should be accounted for using process costing techniques to assign costs to products. Costs are accumulated by departments or cost centers rather than by jobs, WIP is stated in terms of EUP, and unit costs are established on a departmental basis. Process costing is an averaging process which calculates the average cost of all units.
Answer (a) is incorrect because a job order cost system accounts for products manufactured on the basis of each order received. Answer (b) is incorrect because both job order and process costing methods assign costs to partially completed units. Answer (d) is incorrect because standard costing techniques can be used in conjunction with either process costing or job order costing.

2. Which of the following is a characteristic of a process costing system?

a. Work-in-process inventory is restated in terms of completed units.
b. Costs are accumulated by order.
c. It is used by a company manufacturing custom machinery.
d. Standard costs are not applicable.

The correct answer is (a). *(CPA 1176 T-23)*
REQUIRED: The characteristic of a process costing system.
DISCUSSION: One characteristic of a process costing system is that WIP inventory is restated in terms of completed units. All units are stated in terms of EUP so that average unit costs may be calculated. For example, 100 units 50% complete equal 50 EUP.
Answers (b) and (c) are incorrect because each is characteristic of a job order system, which accumulates costs by individual jobs. Answer (d) is incorrect because standard costs can be used in conjunction with either job order or process costing systems.

Module 6.1: Basic Process Costing

3. A true process costing system could make use of each of the following except

a. Standards.
b. Individual lots.
c. Variable costing.
d. Responsibility accounting.

The correct answer is (b). *(CPA 579 T-29)*
REQUIRED: The element not found in a process costing system.
DISCUSSION: A process costing system is used for mass and continuous production processes. It assigns unit costs on the basis of the average costs of all units. A job order costing system is appropriate when producing individual, differentiable jobs, batches, or units (lots).
Answers (a), (c), and (d) are incorrect because each can be used in a process costing system. Standards are predetermined rates used in the valuation of inventory. Variable costing overhead attaches variable overhead to the goods produced and expenses fixed overhead in the period incurred. Responsibility accounting accumulates and reports costs by levels of responsibility.

4. From the industries listed below, which one is most likely to use process costing in accounting for production costs?

a. Road builder.
b. Electrical contractor.
c. Newspaper publisher.
d. Automobile repair shop.

The correct answer is (c). *(CIA 1187 IV-5)*
REQUIRED: The industry most likely to use process costing.
DISCUSSION: Process costing is used for continuous process manufacturing of relatively homogeneous units. Newspapers are published in long runs of identical items, hence process costing is indicated.
Answers (a), (b), and (d) are incorrect because each requires a job order system since the particular projects are unique.

5. Which of the following characteristics applies to process costing but not to job order costing?

a. Identifiable batches of production.
b. Equivalent units of production.
c. Averaging process.
d. Use of standard costs.

The correct answer is (b). *(CPA 577 T-39)*
REQUIRED: The item that applies to process costing but not to job order costing.
DISCUSSION: EUP are calculated in a process costing system. EUP allow WIP to be stated in terms of completed units, a step not necessary in a job order system where costs are individually assigned to each job. Stating WIP in terms of EUP permits calculation of average unit costs for mass-produced homogeneous goods.
Answer (a) is incorrect because job order costing is used for identifiable batches of production. Answer (c) is incorrect because both costing techniques use an averaging process. Answer (d) is incorrect because standard costs can be used with either process or job order costing.

6. An equivalent unit of material or conversion cost is equal to

a. The amount of material or conversion cost necessary to complete one unit of production.
b. A unit of work-in-process inventory.
c. The amount of material or conversion cost necessary to start a unit of production in work-in-process.
d. Fifty percent of the material or conversion cost of a unit of finished goods inventory (assuming a linear production pattern).

The correct answer is (a). *(CPA 578 T-37)*
REQUIRED: The definition of equivalent units.
DISCUSSION: Equivalent units measure the amount of work performed in each production phase in terms of fully processed units during a given period. Incomplete units are restated as the equivalent amount of completed units. The calculation is made separately for material and conversion cost (direct labor and overhead).
Answer (b) is incorrect because a unit of WIP inventory is not completed; an EUP is equal to one completed unit. Answer (c) is incorrect because an EUP is the amount of material and conversion cost to complete, not start, a unit. Answer (d) is incorrect because an EUP is the amount of material and conversion cost to complete 100%, not 50%, of a unit.

Module 6.1: Basic Process Costing

7. In the computation of manufacturing cost per equivalent unit, the weighted average method of process costing considers

   a. Current costs only.
   b. Current costs plus cost of beginning work-in-process inventory.
   c. Current costs plus cost of ending work-in-process inventory.
   d. Current costs less cost of beginning work-in-process inventory.

The correct answer is (b). *(CPA 581 T-45)*
   REQUIRED: The costs used in the weighted average method.
   DISCUSSION: The weighted average method of process costing combines the costs of work done in the previous period and the current period. Thus, the cost of the equivalent units is equal to the current cost (current period) plus the cost of BWIP (previous period).
   Answer (a) is incorrect because the FIFO method considers only current costs. Answer (c) is incorrect because the costs are being counted twice. The costs in EWIP are already included in current costs. Answer (d) is incorrect because BWIP costs are added to the current costs in the weighted average method.

8. An error was made in the computation of the percentage of completion of the current year's ending work-in-process (EWIP) inventory. The error resulted in assigning a lower percentage of completion to each component of the inventory than actually was the case. What is the effect of this error upon

1. The computation of total equivalent units.
2. The computation of costs per equivalent unit.
3. Costs assigned to cost of goods completed for the period.

	1	2	3
a.	Understate	Overstate	Overstate
b.	Understate	Understate	Overstate
c.	Overstate	Understate	Understate
d.	Overstate	Overstate	Understate

The correct answer is (a). *(CPA 1177 T-34)*
   REQUIRED: The effects of understating the percentage of completion of EWIP.
   DISCUSSION: If the percentage of completion assigned is lower than actually attained, equivalent units (EUP) will be understated. For example, if the actual percentage is 75%, but 50% is assigned and 100 units are in process, EUP will be 50 instead of 75. This error results in higher (overstated) costs per equivalent unit and higher (overstated) costs assigned to finished goods for the period (assuming costs are constant).
   Answer (b) is incorrect because the costs per equivalent unit will be overstated if fewer equivalent units are used in the computation and costs remain constant. Answers (c) and (d) are incorrect because the equivalent units would be understated if an error resulted in assigning a lower than actual percentage of completion.

9. A valid reason for using predetermined overhead rates for process costing purposes is

   a. The unrepresentative unit cost that would otherwise result when total factory overhead fluctuates significantly from period to period.
   b. The non-comparability of the degree of completion of units in work-in-process from 1 month to the next when predetermined rates are not used.
   c. The noncomparability of FIFO and weighted average equivalent units of production for overhead when predetermined rates are not used.
   d. The difference in transfer prices that will occur between two different plants of a company making the same product when predetermined rates are not used.

The correct answer is (a). *(CIA 585 IV-10)*
   REQUIRED: The reason for using predetermined overhead rates.
   DISCUSSION: Predetermined overhead rates are used for costing purposes to minimize the effect of fluctuating overhead from period to period. These fluctuations may be caused by seasonal factors and/or other causes of variability. If not annualized or normalized, these fluctuations would result in significantly different unit costs of the same products in different periods.
   Answers (b) and (c) are incorrect because predetermined overhead rates do not enter the calculations for degree of completion and for equivalent units of production. Answer (d) is incorrect because use of predetermined overhead rates may result in transfer prices that less accurately measure the costs of products internally produced in comparison with those externally purchased.

10. In developing a factory overhead application rate for use in a process costing system, which of the following could be used in the denominator?

a. Estimated direct labor hours.
b. Actual direct labor hours.
c. Estimated factory overhead.
d. Actual factory overhead.

The correct answer is (a). *(CPA 587 T-41)*
REQUIRED: The possible denominator in a predetermined overhead rate.
DISCUSSION: The predetermined overhead rate is calculated by dividing the estimated overhead by the activity base. An activity base may be direct labor hours, direct labor dollars, machine hours, or some other reasonable base.
Answers (b) and (d) are incorrect because actual amounts are not known. Answer (c) is incorrect because estimated factory overhead is the numerator.

6.2 Operation Costing

11. Operation costing is appropriate for products that are

a. Unique.
b. Produced in batches or production runs.
c. Homogeneous.
d. Related to food and beverage industries.

The correct answer is (b). *(Publisher)*
REQUIRED: The kind of product appropriate for operation costing.
DISCUSSION: Operation costing is used when goods are produced in batches or production runs. While the production procedures or operations are similar, the types of items processed are different, e.g., different models of furniture, etc.
Answer (a) is incorrect because, when the products are unique, job order costing is appropriate. Answer (c) is incorrect because, when the product is homogeneous, process costing is appropriate. Answer (d) is incorrect because the products of the food and beverage industry may be either unique or homogeneous, and produced in jobs, lots, or batches.

12. Which component of the product usually varies by product type in operation costing systems?

a. Material.
b. Direct labor.
c. Overhead.
d. All of the above.

The correct answer is (a). *(Publisher)*
REQUIRED: The variable component(s) under operation costing systems.
DISCUSSION: When operation costing is employed, the basic materials usually vary by production run, but the processes used are similar (e.g., milling, grinding, finishing, painting, polishing, etc.).
Answers (b), (c), and (d) are incorrect because the materials rather than the conversion procedures vary by production run.

13. Operation costing is a product costing system best described as

a. Job order costing.
b. The cost accounting system designed for hospitals.
c. Process costing.
d. A blend of job order and process costing.

The correct answer is (d). *(Publisher)*
REQUIRED: The best description of operation costing.
DISCUSSION: Operation costing is a hybrid of job order costing and process costing. As in process costing, a single average unit conversion cost is applied based on operations. Material costs are applied to the individual batches in the same manner as in job order costing. It is used to account for the costs of batch processing of relatively large numbers of similar units in individual production runs.
Operation costing is appropriate for the processing of different types of material through the same basic operations, such as woodworking, finishing, and polishing for different product lines of furniture. It generally has many more WIP accounts since there is one for each process or operation.
Answers (a) and (c) are incorrect because operation costing is a hybrid form of each method. Answer (b) is incorrect because operation costing was developed for batch processing operations.

14. Which manufacturing operation would not be suited to use operation costing?

a. Shoes.
b. Clothing.
c. Furniture manufactured with production runs of each style, type, etc.
d. Oil refining.

The correct answer is (d). *(Publisher)*
REQUIRED: The manufacturing operation not suited to operation costing.
DISCUSSION: The products of the oil refining industry are homogeneous and are not produced in batches. While refineries can vary the nature of their output slightly, they essentially produce a continuous flow of products.
Answers (a), (b), and (c) are incorrect because each produces in production runs or batches the same kind of product, but with different styles and materials.

6.3 Transferred-In Costs

15. In a production cost report using process costing, transferred-in costs are similar to

a. Material added at a point during the process.
b. Conversion costs added during the process.
c. Costs transferred to the next process.
d. Costs included in beginning inventory.

The correct answer is (a). *(CPA 1176 T-24)*
REQUIRED: The type of cost most similar to transferred-in costs.
DISCUSSION: Transferred-in costs are similar to material added at a point during the process because both attach to (become part of) the product at that point, which is usually the beginning of the process. Computations for transferred-in costs are usually separate from those for other material costs and conversion costs.
Answer (b) is incorrect because conversion costs (direct labor and overhead) are usually continuously added throughout the process. Answer (c) is incorrect because transferred-out costs are those attached to completed units. Answer (d) is incorrect because the beginning inventory of a period (the ending inventory of the prior period) usually includes material costs and conversion costs.

16. What are transferred-in costs as used in a process cost accounting system?

a. Labor that is transferred from another department within the same plant instead of hiring temporary workers from the outside.
b. Costs of the product of a previous internal process that is subsequently used in a succeeding internal process.
c. Supervisory salaries that are transferred from an overhead cost center to a production cost center.
d. Ending work-in-process inventory of a previous process that will be used in a succeeding process.

The correct answer is (b). *(CPA 1177 T-33)*
REQUIRED: The definition of transferred-in costs.
DISCUSSION: Transferred-in costs are the costs of the product of a previous internal process that is subsequently used in a succeeding internal process. Transferred-in costs are similar to material costs added at the beginning of the process.
Answers (a) and (c) are incorrect because transferred-in costs are the costs (material costs and conversion costs) of the units transferred. Labor transferred from another department and supervisory salaries are part of conversion costs, not transferred-in costs. Answer (d) is incorrect because another department's EWIP is still in that department awaiting further processing and has not yet been transferred.

17. In a process costing system, how is the unit cost affected in a production cost report when materials are added in a department subsequent to the first department and the added materials result in additional units?

   a. The first department's unit cost is increased, which necessitates an adjustment of the transferred-in unit cost.
   b. The first department's unit cost is decreased, which necessitates an adjustment of the transferred-in unit cost.
   c. The first department's unit cost is increased, but it does not necessitate an adjustment of the transferred-in unit cost.
   d. The first department's unit cost is decreased, but it does not necessitate an adjustment of the transferred-in unit cost.

The correct answer is (b). *(CPA 575 T-25)*
REQUIRED: The effect of adding materials in a subsequent department, thereby creating additional units.
DISCUSSION: If additional units are created in a process (e.g., by adding material in a subsequent department), the number of equivalent units increases and the unit cost decreases since the total transferred-in cost remains constant. Thus, an adjustment to the transferred-in unit cost is necessary.
Answers (a) and (c) are incorrect because, as additional units are created, the number of equivalent units increases and the unit cost decreases. Answer (d) is incorrect because a retroactive adjustment to the transferred-in unit cost is necessary since more units were subsequently created.

18. Purchased materials are added in the second department of a three-department process. This addition increases the number of units produced in the second department and will

   a. Always change the direct labor cost percentage in the ending work-in-process inventory.
   b. Never cause an adjustment to the unit cost transferred in from the first department.
   c. Always increase total unit costs.
   d. Always decrease total ending work-in-process inventory.

The correct answer is (a). *(CPA 1181 T-43)*
REQUIRED: The effect of adding materials in a subsequent department, thus creating more units.
DISCUSSION: When direct materials, direct labor, and/or overhead are applied to units, production costs increase. When materials are added to the production process in the second department, thus increasing the number of units produced, more units are available to absorb the direct labor and overhead costs, and the labor and overhead cost percentages are reduced (relative to material cost).
Answer (b) is incorrect because, if work done in a subsequent department increases the units produced in a previous department, an adjustment to the transferred-in unit cost is necessary. Answer (c) is incorrect because, as the number of units produced increases, the unit cost of production usually decreases. Answer (d) is incorrect because the increase is in units with a corresponding decrease in unit costs, but total inventory value is not affected.

19. Purchased materials are added in the second department of a three-department process. This addition does not increase the number of units produced in the second department and will

   a. Not change the dollar amount transferred to the next department.
   b. Decrease total ending work-in-process inventory.
   c. Increase the factory overhead portion of the ending work-in-process inventory.
   d. Increase total unit cost.

The correct answer is (d). *(CPA 1181 T-45)*
REQUIRED: The effect of adding materials in a subsequent department when units produced remain constant.
DISCUSSION: Adding materials to a production process without changing the number of units produced increases the unit cost. The numerator (total cost) increases while the denominator (total units) remains the same.
Answer (a) is incorrect because, if purchased materials are added to the process, the cost will be added to the total cost transferred to the next department. Answer (b) is incorrect because the unit cost, and therefore the cost of EWIP, increases when materials are added. Answer (c) is incorrect because materials cost is separate from overhead.

20. Why are transferred-in costs differentiated from other types of direct material?

    a. They usually consist of the basic units being produced.
    b. They are of greater value than most other materials added.
    c. They are greater in value than the value of all other material added.
    d. They are added at the beginning of the process, unlike other direct material.

The correct answer is (a). *(Publisher)*
REQUIRED: Why transferred-in costs are distinguished from other types of direct material.
DISCUSSION: Usually, transferred-in costs pertain to the units of production that move from one process to another. Thus, they are the basic units being produced. Direct materials are added to the basic units during processing.
Answers (b) and (c) are incorrect because value is not an issue in differentiating between transferred-in costs and other direct material. Answer (d) is incorrect because direct material may be added at the beginning of a process and, conceivably, the transferred-in material (i.e., basic units) could be added to the process after the direct materials were processed.

6.4 Equivalent Units of Production (EUP)

21. Why are equivalent units of production used in process accounting?

    a. To measure the efficiency of the production process.
    b. To establish standard costs.
    c. To provide a means of allocating cost to partially completed units.
    d. To allocate overhead to production.

The correct answer is (c). *(Publisher)*
REQUIRED: The purpose of calculating equivalent units of production (EUP).
DISCUSSION: EUP are used to allocate cost to incomplete goods. Thus, if 50% of the material has been added to 100 units in process, there are 50 EUP for materials. Similarly, if 30% of the conversion costs have been incurred for 1,000 units, 300 EUP have been produced.
Answers (a) and (b) are incorrect because EUP are calculated only to allocate production costs. Answer (d) is incorrect because overhead is generally allocated based on a measure of activity, e.g., percent of material added, labor cost, or machine hours.

22. If 100 units are 70% complete, 30 units 60% complete, 200 units 40% complete, and 60 units 5% complete, how many EUP have been produced?

    a. 70.
    b. 171.
    c. 175.
    d. 390.

The correct answer is (b). *(Publisher)*
REQUIRED: The amount of EUP if goods are in various stages of completion.
DISCUSSION: EUP are calculated by multiplying the number of units times the completion percentage. As the table below indicates, 171 EUP were produced, but the total number of units in EWIP is 390 (100 + 30 + 200 + 60).

```
100 units x 70% =  70
 30 units x 60% =  18
200 units x 40% =  80
 60 units x  5% =   3
390 units         171 EUP
```

23. EUP analysis is usually applied to

    a. Materials and conversion costs.
    b. Materials costs only.
    c. Conversion costs only.
    d. Overhead costs.

The correct answer is (a). *(Publisher)*
REQUIRED: The type(s) of costs relevant to EUP analysis.
DISCUSSION: EUP analysis is usually done separately for materials and conversion costs. A production process may use several types of materials, e.g., transferred-in cost plus additional raw materials. There may be several conversion activities as well. Hence, the percentage of completion is rarely the same for both costs.
Answers (b) and (c) are incorrect because EUP analysis is usually applied to both materials and conversion costs. Answer (d) is incorrect because overhead is part of conversion costs.

24. Glo Co., a manufacturer of combs, budgeted sales of 125,000 units for the month of April. The following additional information is provided:

	Number of units
Actual inventory at April 1	
Work-in-process	None
Finished goods	37,500
Budgeted inventory at April 30	
Work-in-process (75% processed)	8,000
Finished goods	30,000

How many equivalent units of production did Glo budget for April?

  a. 126,500.
  b. 125,500.
  c. 123,500.
  d. 117,500.

The correct answer is (c). *(CPA 587 Q-39)*
REQUIRED: The equivalent units of production budgeted for April.
DISCUSSION: Given that there is no BWIP, it makes no difference whether FIFO or weighted average is used. The total amount of goods to be completed during the month is 117,500 units [125,000 units of budgeted sales less the budgeted decrease in inventory of 7,500 (37,500 - 30,000)]. Since there will be 8,000 units 75% complete in ending inventory (remember, no beginning inventory), the total expected EUP is 123,500 (117,500 + 6,000).

Questions 25 through 27 are based on the Jorcano Manufacturing Company, which uses a process cost system to account for the costs of its only product, Product D. Production begins in the fabrication department where units of raw material are molded into various connecting parts. After fabrication is complete, the units are transferred to the assembly department. There is no material added in the assembly department. After assembly is complete, the units are transferred to a packaging department where packing material is placed around the units. After the units are ready for shipping, they are sent to a shipping area.

At year-end, June 30, the following inventory of Product D is on hand:

No unused raw material or packing material.
Fabrication department: 300 units, 1/3 complete as to raw material and 1/2 complete as to direct labor.
Assembly department: 1,000 units 2/5 complete as to direct labor.
Packaging department: 100 units 3/4 complete as to packing material and 1/4 complete as to direct labor.
Shipping area: 400 units.

---

25. The number of equivalent units of raw material in all inventories at June 30 is

  a. 300.
  b. 100.
  c. 1,600.
  d. 925.

The correct answer is (c). *(CPA 1173 P-28)*
REQUIRED: The equivalent units of raw material in all inventories.
DISCUSSION: Raw material is added only in the first department (fabrication). Therefore, all units in subsequent departments are 100% complete in terms of raw materials. In the fabrication department, however, 300 units are 1/3 complete with respect to raw materials. Thus, the number of EUP of raw material in all inventories is 1,600.

Fabrication (1/3 x 300 units)	100
Assembly	1,000
Packaging	100
Shipping	400
Total EUP	1,600

26. The number of equivalent units of fabrication department direct labor in all inventories at June 30 is

 a. 1,650.
 b. 150.
 c. 300.
 d. 975.

The correct answer is (a). *(CPA 1173 P-29)*
 REQUIRED: The EUP of fabrication department direct labor in all inventories.
 DISCUSSION: All units beyond the fabrication department are complete in terms of fabrication direct labor. In the fabrication department, 50% of the 300 units are complete as to labor. Therefore, total EUP is 1,650.

Fabrication (1/2 x 300 units)	150
Assembly	1,000
Packaging	100
Shipping	400
Total EUP	1,650

27. The number of equivalent units of packing material in all inventories at June 30 is

 a. 75.
 b. 475.
 c. 100.
 d. 425.

The correct answer is (b). *(CPA 1173 P-30)*
 REQUIRED: The number of equivalent units of packing material in all inventories.
 DISCUSSION: Units prior to the packaging department have no packing material. All units beyond the packaging department are complete in terms of packing material. The 100 units in the packaging department are 3/4 complete as to packing material. Therefore, the number of EUP of packing material in all inventories is 475.

Packaging (3/4 x 100 units)	75
Shipping	400
Total EUP	475

28. Separate EUP calculations are usually not made for

 a. Conversion costs.
 b. Transferred-in costs.
 c. Other material costs.
 d. Direct labor costs.

The correct answer is (d). *(Publisher)*
 REQUIRED: The cost for which a separate EUP calculation is usually not made.
 DISCUSSION: Overhead is usually applied on the basis of a direct labor activity base such as hours or cost. Thus, a single EUP calculation is made for conversion costs (direct labor and overhead). There is no basis for separating these costs because they are incurred uniformly.
 Answer (a) is incorrect because EUP can be calculated as to conversion costs. Answers (b) and (c) are incorrect because transferred-in costs are usually included at the beginning of the process, whereas other materials may be added at various points in the operation.

29. Kew Co. had 3,000 units in work-in-process at April 1 which were 60% complete as to conversion cost. During April, 10,000 units were completed. At April 30, 4,000 units remained in work-in-process which were 40% complete as to conversion cost. Direct materials are added at the beginning of the process. How many units were started during April?

 a. 9,000.
 b. 9,800.
 c. 10,000.
 d. 11,000.

The correct answer is (d). *(CPA 586 Q-25)*
 REQUIRED: The number of units started in April.
 DISCUSSION: Set up a physical flow formula and calculate the unknown.

 BWIP + Started = Completed + EWIP
 3,000 + x = 10,000 + 4,000
 Units Started = 11,000

6.5 FIFO vs. Weighted Average Assumption for EUP

30. When using the first-in, first-out method of process costing, total equivalent units of production for a given period of time is equal to the number of units

a. In work-in-process at the beginning of the period times the percent of work necessary to complete the items, plus the number of units started during the period, less the number of units remaining in work-in-process at the end of the period times the percent of work necessary to complete the items.

b. In work-in-process at the beginning of the period, plus the number of units started during the period, plus the number of units remaining in work-in-process at the end of the period times the percent of work necessary to complete the items.

c. Started into process during the period, plus the number of units in work-in-process at the beginning of the period.

d. Transferred out during the period, plus the number of units remaining in work-in-process at the end of the period times the percent of work necessary to complete the items.

The correct answer is (a). *(CPA 583 T-41)*
REQUIRED: The method to determine total equivalent units when using the FIFO method.
DISCUSSION: The computation of EUP for a period using the FIFO method of process costing includes only the conversion costs and material added to the product in that period and excludes any work done in previous periods. Accordingly, FIFO EUP include work and material to complete BWIP, plus work and material to complete units started this period, minus work and material needed to complete EWIP.
Answers (b) and (c) are incorrect because the work needed to complete BWIP, not the total WIP, is included in the computation. In addition, answer (b) adds, instead of subtracts, the work needed to complete EWIP, and answer (c) ignores the work needed to complete EWIP. Answer (d) is incorrect because it defines weighted average EUP, which includes the material and conversion costs in BWIP. It also incorrectly includes the percent of work necessary to complete EWIP. Only the costs and EUP already accumulated in EWIP should be part of the EUP calculation.

31. To compute equivalent units of production (EUP) using the FIFO method of process costing, work for the period must be stated in units

a. Completed during the period and units in ending inventory.

b. Completed from beginning inventory, started and completed during the period, and units completed in ending inventory.

c. Started during the period and units transferred out during the period.

d. Processed during the period and units completed during the period.

The correct answer is (b). *(CPA 579 T-39)*
REQUIRED: The units included in EUP when using FIFO process costing.
DISCUSSION: FIFO process costing treats BWIP as though it were a batch of goods distinct from the goods started during the current period. Hence, beginning inventory costs are not averaged or mingled with current costs, and the EUP calculation excludes conversion and material costs incurred in prior periods.
Answer (a) is incorrect because the work and materials in BWIP must be excluded when using FIFO. Answer (c) is incorrect because the EUP must reflect the work to complete BWIP and the work done on EWIP. Answer (d) is incorrect because the FIFO method accounts for prior and current costs separately, so EUP in BWIP must be excluded from the current period's EUP.

32. The units transferred in from the first department to the second department should be included in the computation of the equivalent units for the second department under which of the following methods of process costing?

	FIFO	Weighted Average
a.	Yes	Yes
b.	Yes	No
c.	No	Yes
d.	No	No

The correct answer is (a). *(CPA 581 T-46)*
REQUIRED: The cost flow method(s) which include(s) transferred-in costs in EUP calculations.
DISCUSSION: The units transferred from the first to the second department should be included in the computation of equivalent units for the second department regardless of the cost flow assumption used. The transferred-in units are considered raw material added at the beginning of the period.

33. The percentage of completion of the beginning work-in-process inventory should be considered in the computation of the equivalent units of production for which of the following methods of process costing?

	FIFO	Weighted Average
a.	Yes	No
b.	Yes	Yes
c.	No	Yes
d.	No	No

The correct answer is (a). *(CPA 1182 T-43)*
REQUIRED: The process costing method(s) using BWIP in the computation of EUP.
DISCUSSION: The FIFO method computes equivalent units by adding the number of units completed and the EUP in EWIP, and then subtracting the EUP in BWIP. Note that weighted average makes no distinction between work done on BWIP last period and work done this period.

  Units completed and transferred out
+ EUP in EWIP
  Weighted average EUP
- EUP in BWIP (for last period)
  FIFO EUP

34. In a given process costing system, the equivalent units of production are computed using the weighted-average method. With respect to conversion costs, the percentage of completion for the current period only is included in the calculation of the

	Beginning Work-In-Process Inventory	Ending Work-In-Process Inventory
a.	No	No
b.	No	Yes
c.	Yes	No
d.	Yes	Yes

The correct answer is (b). *(CPA 1184 T-49)*
REQUIRED: The in-process inventories in which conversion costs are calculated.
DISCUSSION: The weighted-average process costing method considers only the degree of completion of EWIP in the calculation of EUP. Since this method includes the costs incurred in the prior period for units in BWIP, EUP are equal to units completed and transferred out plus the EUP completed in EWIP.

35. Assuming that there was no beginning work-in-process (BWIP) inventory, and the ending work-in-process (EWIP) inventory is 50% complete as to conversion costs, the number of equivalent units as to conversion costs would be

a. The same as the units completed.
b. The same as the units placed in process.
c. Less than the units completed.
d. Less than the units placed in process.

The correct answer is (d). *(CPA 1185 T-39)*
REQUIRED: The number of EUP as to conversion costs.
DISCUSSION: Conversion cost EUP equals the units that were started and completed this period, plus the EUP in EWIP. Since the units in EWIP are 50% complete as to conversion costs, they will not be fully counted for purposes of determining EUP.
Answers (a) and (b) are incorrect because conversion cost EUP would equal units started and completed if there was no EWIP. Answer (c) is incorrect because conversion cost EUP would be less than units completed if EUP in BWIP exceed that in EWIP.

36. There are two approaches to calculating EUP. One is to begin with the total work that could be done, i.e., the units in BWIP and those transferred in. The other approach is to

a. Begin with the total work that could not be done, e.g., work already completed in BWIP.
b. Begin with the total work that has been done (units transferred out and the completed EUP in EWIP).
c. Begin with the total work that has been done (units transferred out and the EUP required to complete EWIP).
d. There is only one method to calculate EUP.

The correct answer is (b). *(Publisher)*
REQUIRED: The alternate approach to computing EUP.
DISCUSSION: Total work that can be done is one starting point for computing EUP. Total work that can be done is the sum of the units in BWIP and those transferred in. In FIFO, only EUP to complete BWIP are added. Under the weighted average method, the work done to date is included rather than just work in the current period. The EUP required to complete EWIP is deducted from the total work that can be done. The other approach is to consider all the work done, i.e., to add the units transferred out to the units already completed in EWIP.
Answer (a) is incorrect because EUP calculations concern work that was done. Answer (c) is incorrect because, to compute the work that was done, one must add the completed EUP in EWIP. Answer (d) is incorrect because there are at least two methods to calculate EUP.

Questions 37 through 40 are related to the following list of nine concepts.

1. EUP to complete BWIP.
2. EUP from last period in BWIP.
3. Units transferred in.
4. Total units transferred out.
5. Units transferred out that were started and completed this period.
6. Units transferred out that were started last period and completed this period.
7. EUP to complete EWIP.
8. EUP completed in EWIP.
9. Total units in BWIP.

37. What is a correct formula for weighted average EUP?

a. 1 + 2 + 3 + 7.
b. 2 + 4 - 8.
c. 1 + 2 + 3 - 7.
d. 4 + 5 + 6 + 8.

The correct answer is (c). *(Publisher)*
REQUIRED: The formula for weighted average EUP.
DISCUSSION: Weighted average EUP is computed as all the work that could have been done (the total EUP transferred in), less work that was not done (the EUP required to complete EWIP). The formula is 1 + 2 + 3 - 7.
Answer (a) is incorrect because one subtracts the work to complete EWIP. Answer (b) is incorrect because it results in double counting: the work done last period in BWIP is also included in the total units transferred out. Answer (d) is incorrect because units started and completed this period plus the units started last period and completed this period equal the total units transferred out.

38. What is another correct formula for weighted average EUP?

a. 8 + 6 + 5.
b. 8 + 4 + 2 + 1.
c. 8 + 7 + 4 + 2.
d. 8 + 6 + 5 - 2.

The correct answer is (a). *(Publisher)*
REQUIRED: Another correct formula for weighted average EUP.
DISCUSSION: Another approach is to consider the total work that has been done. The sum of the units started and completed this period and those started last period and completed this period (total units transferred out) plus the EUP completed in EWIP is the total work done (8 + 6 + 5).
Answer (b) is incorrect because the units in BWIP are included in the units transferred out. Answer (c) is incorrect because the EUP to complete WIP has not been done and should not be part of this period's EUP. Answer (d) is incorrect because it is the formula for FIFO EUP.

39. What is the correct formula for FIFO EUP?

a. 1 + 3 - 7.
b. 1 + 2 + 3 - 8.
c. 1 + 4 - 7.
d. 9 - 5 - 6.

The correct answer is (a). *(Publisher)*
REQUIRED: A correct formula for determining FIFO EUP.
DISCUSSION: One FIFO approach is to determine the EUP that could be produced in this period. The total work that can be done is that needed to finish BWIP and complete all the goods transferred in. The EUP needed to finish any EWIP should then be deducted (1 + 3 - 7).
Answer (b) is incorrect because the work done last period in BWIP is not part of FIFO EUP, nor is the work completed this period subtracted. Answer (c) is incorrect because the EUP to complete BWIP are included in the total units transferred out. Answer (d) is incorrect because it is the number of physical units (not EUP) in EWIP.

40. What is another correct formula for FIFO EUP?
    a. 8 + 4.
    b. 8 + 4 - 2.
    c. 8 + 7 + 6 + 5.
    d. 7 + 4 + 2 + 1.

The correct answer is (b). *(Publisher)*
REQUIRED: Another correct formula for FIFO EUP.
DISCUSSION: Another approach to computing FIFO EUP is to begin with the work that was done, which is the EUP completed in EWIP plus the units transferred out. Subtracting the work that had been done in the prior period gives the FIFO EUP (8 + 4 - 2).
   Answer (a) is incorrect because it is the weighted average EUP. Answer (c) is incorrect because it includes the work needed to complete EWIP. Answer (d) is incorrect because BWIP is included in units transferred out.

41. Assuming that there was no beginning work-in-process inventory, and the ending work-in-process inventory is 100% complete as to material costs, the number of equivalent units as to material costs would be
    a. The same as the units placed in process.
    b. The same as the units completed.
    c. Less than the units placed in process.
    d. Less than the units completed.

The correct answer is (a). *(CPA 584 T-42)*
REQUIRED: The number of EUP as to material costs.
DISCUSSION: Since there is no BWIP, it is immaterial whether FIFO or weighted average is used. Since EWIP is 100% complete, the EUP for material costs would be equal to the number of units placed in process.
   Answer (b) is incorrect because this would be true only if there were no EWIP. Answer (c) is incorrect because this would be true only if EWIP were less than 100% complete as to material costs. Answer (d) is incorrect because the EUP must at least equal the number of units completed.

42. FIFO requires separate costing of goods started last period and finished this period and goods started and completed this period. Weighted average does not. Which is the true statement about the cost of completed goods transferred under FIFO to the next production department or to finished goods inventory?
    a. The two amounts are kept separate.
    b. The two amounts are kept separate but are combined by the next department.
    c. The two amounts are considered combined as the goods are transferred.
    d. The goods started and completed this period are transferred prior to those started last period and completed this period.

The correct answer is (c). *(Publisher)*
REQUIRED: The correct statement about the cost of completed goods transferred under FIFO.
DISCUSSION: Under FIFO, goods started last period and completed this period are differentiated from goods started and completed this period. The goods started last period but completed this period include the costs from last period as well as this period's costs to complete, whereas goods started and completed this period include only current costs. In the weighted average method, the costs of the prior and current periods are averaged.
   When the goods are transferred to the next department or to finished goods under FIFO, however, they are considered transferred out at one average cost so that a multitude of layers of inventory is not created. This is consistent with the basic concept of process costing.
   Answer (a) is incorrect because, if the two amounts are kept separate, separate layers would continue to multiply as the units of product are passed through additional WIP accounts. Answer (b) is incorrect because the two amounts are combined before transfer to the next department. Answer (d) is incorrect because, under FIFO, the goods that were started last period and completed this period are deemed to be completed first and transferred first.

43. Walden Company has a process cost system using the FIFO cost method. All materials are introduced at the beginning of the process in Department One. The following information is available for the month of January:

	Units
WIP, January 1 (40% complete as to conversion costs)	500
Started	2,000
Transferred to Department Two	2,100
WIP, January 31 (25% complete as to conversion costs)	400

What are the EUP for the month of January?

	Materials	Conversion
a.	2,500	2,200
b.	2,500	1,900
c.	2,000	2,200
d.	2,000	2,000

The correct answer is (d). *(CPA 583 P-21)*
REQUIRED: The FIFO EUP for materials and conversion costs.
DISCUSSION: Under FIFO, only the current period's EUP are considered. Accordingly, EUP for materials would be 2,000 units since that many were started in January. The EUP for conversion costs are the 300 EUP to complete the BWIP (500 x 60%) plus the 2,000 units started in January minus the 300 units (75% x 400) to complete EWIP, a total of 2,000 (300 + 2,000 - 300).
An alternative calculation is to add the 100 units completed (400 x 25%) in EWIP plus the 2,100 units completed during the period and to subtract the 200 units (40% x 500) work done as of the beginning of January (100 + 2,100 - 200).

44. Using the facts from the previous question concerning Walden Company, what are the EUP under the weighted average method?

	Materials	Conversion
a.	2,500	2,200
b.	2,500	1,900
c.	2,000	2,200
d.	2,000	2,000

The correct answer is (a). *(Publisher)*
REQUIRED: The weighted average EUP for materials and conversion costs.
DISCUSSION: Under weighted average, all the costs of materials, i.e., those started last period and those started this period, are averaged. Thus, the EUP for materials is 2,500 (500 started last period and 2,000 started this period). The EUP for conversion would have been 2,500 if all the ending inventory had been completed. Since 400 units were only 25% complete, 300 EUP were not complete. Therefore, the EUP for conversion is 2,200 (2,500 - 300).
Also, the EUP of weighted average can be reconciled to FIFO EUP. The difference is that weighted average includes the material and work in BWIP that was completed last period. Accordingly, 2,000 material EUP per FIFO was increased to 2,500 because of the 500 units from BWIP. The 2,000 conversion EUP under FIFO is increased to 2,200 under weighted average because 500 units in BWIP were 40% complete.

45. Lawton Company produces canned tomato soup and is budgeting sales of 250,000 units for the month of January. Actual inventory units at January 1 and budgeted inventory units at January 31 are as follows:

	Units
Actual inventory at January 1:	
Work-in-process	None
Finished goods	75,000
Budgeted inventory at January 31:	
Work-in-process (75% processed)	16,000
Finished goods	60,000

How many equivalent units of production is Lawton budgeting for January?

a. 235,000.

b. 247,000.

c. 251,000.

d. 253,000.

The correct answer is (b). *(CPA 583 P-31)*
REQUIRED: The equivalent units of production budgeted for January.
DISCUSSION: Given that there is no BWIP, it makes no difference whether FIFO or weighted average is used. The total amount of goods to be completed during the month is 235,000 units [250,000 units of budgeted sales less the budgeted decrease in inventory of 15,000 (75,000 - 60,000)]. Since there will be 16,000 units 75% complete in ending inventory (remember, no beginning inventory), the total expected EUP is 247,000 (235,000 + 12,000).

6.6 FIFO EUP Calculation

46. Material is added at the beginning of a process in a process costing system. The BWIP for the process this period was 30% complete as to conversion costs. Using the FIFO method of costing, the number of equivalent units of material for the process during this period is equal to the

a. BI this period for the process.
b. Units started this period in the process.
c. Units started this period in the process plus the BI.
d. Units started this period in the process plus 70% of the BI this period.

The correct answer is (b). *(CPA 576 T-31)*
REQUIRED: The equivalent units of material using the FIFO method of costing.
DISCUSSION: The number of EUP using the FIFO method of process costing is determined by the work done in the current period. No work, material, or costs accumulated in the previous period are included in the equivalent units calculations. If material is added at the beginning of the process, only the units started during the period would be included in the equivalent unit calculation for material.
Answers (a), (c), and (d) are incorrect because each includes beginning inventory. Work done or material added in a previous period is not included in the FIFO calculation of EUP. Answer (d) is the number of equivalent units of conversion costs if there is no EWIP.

47. With the following data for a company using the FIFO process cost system, calculate the equivalent units for materials and conversion costs.

	Whole Units	Percent Complete Materials	Conversion Costs
Beginning inventory	10	100%	30%
Transferred in	100		
Transferred out	80		
Ending inventory	30	100%	40%

a. 89 materials, 100 conversion costs.
b. 100 materials, 89 conversion costs.
c. 110 materials, 99 conversion costs.
d. 130 materials, 119 conversion costs.

The correct answer is (b). *(CIA 587 IV-4)*
REQUIRED: The equivalent units for materials and conversion costs based on FIFO.
DISCUSSION: Because the number of EUP under a FIFO assumption is determined solely on the basis of work done in the current period, the EUP in BWIP are ignored. Of the 100 units transferred in, 70 (80 - 10 units in BWIP) were transferred out (100% complete) and 30 (100% complete as to materials) were in EWIP. Thus, 100 (70 + 30) equivalent units of materials must have been produced. The equivalent units for conversion cost equaled 89 [(.7 x 10 units in BWIP) + 70 units begun and completed + (.4 x 30 units in EWIP)].

48. The Wilson Company manufactures the famous "Ticktock" watch on an assembly-line basis. January 1 work-in-process consisted of 5,000 units partially completed. During the month an additional 110,000 units were started and 105,000 units were completed. The ending work-in-process was 3/5 complete as to conversion costs. Conversion costs are added evenly throughout the process. The following conversion costs were incurred:

Beginning costs for work-in-process	$ 1,500
Total current conversion costs	273,920

The conversion costs assigned to ending work-in-process totaled $15,360 using the FIFO method of process costing. What was the percentage of completion, as to conversion costs on the 5,000 units in BWIP?

a. 20%.
b. 40%.
c. 60%.
d. 80%.

The correct answer is (d). *(A. Wilson)*
REQUIRED: The percent completion as to conversion costs of BWIP.
DISCUSSION: Ending work-in-process is 10,000 (5,000 + 110,000 - 105,000) units which are 3/5 complete representing 6,000 equivalent units of conversion (10,000 x 3/5). Conversion cost per unit is $15,360 ÷ 6,000 units which is $2.56 per unit. Total equivalent conversion units for the month is $273,920 ÷ $2.56/unit = 107,000 units. Total equivalent units are the sum of equivalent units to finish beginning units, units started and completed, and ending equivalent units. Assuming that 100,000 units were started this period and completed, the amount of conversion added to BWIP this period is determined below:

107,000 units = BWIP + units started & completed + EQIP
107,000 units = BWIP + 100,000 units + 6,000 units
BWIP = 1,000 units this period

That means BWIP was equal to 4,000 EUP with respect to conversion, or 80% complete (4,000 ÷ 5,000).

Module 6.6: FIFO EUP Calculation

49. Assuming FIFO, use the following data to compute the EUP for conversion costs:

	Units	% Complete (Conversion)
BWIP	100	75%
Units started	10,000	
EWIP	150	40%

- a. 10,250.
- b. 10,040.
- c. 9,935.
- d. 9,910.

The correct answer is (c). *(K. Boze)*
REQUIRED: The EUP for conversion costs, assuming FIFO.
DISCUSSION: The FIFO method for EUP assumes the units in beginning inventory are finished first, and then those units started this period are finished second. In this period, BWIP required only 25% conversion to be complete, 9,850 units (10,000 started - 150 EWIP) were started and completed, and EWIP is only 40% complete as to conversion costs.

Finished BWIP	100 x .25 =	25
Units started and completed		9,850 = 9,850
Conversion applied to EWIP	150 x .40 =	60
Equivalent units		9,935

50. The following data refer to the units processed by the grinding department for a recent month.

Beginning work-in-process	12,000
Units started	200,000
Units completed	192,000
Ending work-in-process	20,000

The beginning work-in-process was 60% complete, and the ending work-in-process is 70% complete. What are the equivalent units of production for the month using the FIFO method?

- a. 210,800.
- b. 198,800.
- c. 185,200.
- d. 184,000.

The correct answer is (b). *(CIA 586 IV-10)*
REQUIRED: Equivalent units of production for the month using the FIFO method.
DISCUSSION: EUP under the FIFO method is computed by adding work done during the period on ending work-in-process inventory (EWIP) to units completed during the period and subtracting any work done in prior periods (BWIP). EUP for the month is

Units completed	192,000
EWIP (20,000 x .7)	14,000
BWIP (12,000 x .6)	(7,200)
	198,800

51. A company produces plastic drinking cups and uses a process cost system. Cups go through three departments -- mixing, molding, and packaging. During the month of June the following information is known about the mixing department

Work-in-process at June 1	10,000 units
	An average 3/4 complete
Units complete during June	140,000 units
Work-in-process at June 30	20,000 units
	An average 1/4 complete

Materials are added at two points in the process; Material A is added at the beginning of the process and Material B at the midpoint of the mixing process. Conversion costs are incurred uniformly throughout the mixing process. Under a FIFO costing flow, the equivalent units for Material A, Material B, and conversion costs respectively for the month of June (assuming no spoilage) would be

- a. 150,000; 130,000; and 137,500.
- b. 150,000; 140,000; and 135,000.
- c. 160,000; 130,000; and 135,000.
- d. 160,000; 140,000; and 137,500.

The correct answer is (a). *(CIA 1186 IV-5)*
REQUIRED: The equivalent units for Material A, Material B, and conversion costs.
DISCUSSION: The FIFO calculation considers only the work done in the current period. Since A is added at the beginning of the process, the BWIP was complete with regard to A. Thus, assuming no spoilage, the equivalent units of production (EUP) for A equaled 150,000 (140,000 units completed + 20,000 EWIP - 10,000 BWIP). Since B is added at the midpoint, the units in BWIP, but not those in EWIP, had received B. The EUP for B were therefore 130,000 (140,000 units completed - 10,000 BWIP). The FIFO EUP for conversion costs were 137,500 (130,000 units started and completed + 2,500 EUP to complete BWIP + 5,000 EUP (20,000 x 1/4) in EWIP).

Module 6.6: FIFO EUP Calculation 125

Questions 52 through 55 are based on the Cutting Department, which is the first stage of Mark Company's production cycle. Conversion costs for this department were 80% complete as to BWIP and 50% complete as to EWIP. Information as to conversion costs in the Cutting Department for January is as follows:

	Units	CC
WIP at January 1	25,000	$22,000
Units started and costs incurred during January	135,000	$143,000
Units completed and transferred to next department during January	100,000	

---

52. Using the FIFO method, what was the conversion cost of WIP in the Cutting Department at January 31?

a. $33,000.
b. $38,100.
c. $39,000.
d. $45,000.

The correct answer is (c). *(CPA 1180 P-33)*
REQUIRED: The conversion cost of EWIP using the FIFO method.
DISCUSSION: When using the FIFO method of process costing, EUP for a period include only the work done that period and exclude any work done in a prior period. The total of conversion cost EUP for the period is calculated below.

	Units	Work Done in Current Period	CC (EUP)
BWIP	25,000	20%	5,000
Started & completed	75,000	100%	75,000
EWIP	60,000	50%	30,000
Total EUP			110,000

The total of the conversion costs for the period is given as $143,000. Dividing by total EUP of 110,000 gives a unit cost of $1.30. The conversion cost of the EWIP inventory is equal to the EUP in EWIP (30,000) times the unit cost ($1.30) for the current period, or $39,000.

53. What were the conversion costs per EUP last period and this period, respectively?

a. $1.10 and $1.30.
b. $1.10 and $1.43 ÷ $1.35.
c. $1.30 and $1.30.
d. $1.30 and $1.43.

The correct answer is (a). *(Publisher)*
REQUIRED: The conversion costs per EUP for this period and last period.
DISCUSSION: This period's conversion cost per EUP is computed as $1.30 in the previous question. Last period's conversion cost per EUP is $1.10, which is conversion costs of $22,000 divided by 20,000 EUP (25,000 units, 80% complete).

54. What is the per unit conversion cost of goods started last period and completed this period?

a. $22,000 ÷ 25,000.
b. $1.10.
c. $28,500 ÷ 25,000.
d. $1.30.

The correct answer is (c). *(Publisher)*
REQUIRED: The unit conversion cost of goods started last period, completed this period.
DISCUSSION: The total of the units started last period and completed this period is 25,000. These units were 80% completed at the start of the period, at a cost of $22,000. The cost to complete was $6,500 (5,000 EUP x $1.30). The total cost of $28,500 is divided by 25,000 to obtain the unit cost ($1.14).

55. What is the per unit conversion cost of goods started this period and completed this period using the FIFO method?

a. $22,000 ÷ 25,000.
b. $1.10.
c. $28,500 ÷ 25,000.
d. $1.30.

The correct answer is (d). *(Publisher)*
REQUIRED: The unit conversion cost of goods started and completed this period.
DISCUSSION: The current unit cost of production is $1.30 as computed in Question 54 above. The conversion accomplished with respect to EWIP is also costed at $1.30 per FIFO.
The weighted average method would cost all of the units transferred out and the equivalent units completed in EWIP at an average cost of $165,000 ÷ 130,000 units, or $1.27.

6.7 Weighted Average EUP Calculation

56. In the computation of manufacturing cost per equivalent unit, the weighted average method of process costing considers

a. Current costs only.
b. Current costs plus cost of ending work-in-process inventory.
c. Current costs plus cost of beginning work-in-process inventory.
d. Current costs less cost of beginning work-in-process inventory.

The correct answer is (c). *(CPA 586 T-42)*
REQUIRED: The components of cost per equivalent unit when using the weighted average method of process costing.
DISCUSSION: When using the weighted average method of process costing, the costs from last period in beginning work-in-process are averaged with current costs in computing the manufacturing cost per equivalent unit.
Answer (a) is incorrect because only current costs are used when there is no BWIP. Answer (b) is incorrect because current costs include those costs in EWIP, not BWIP. Answer (d) is incorrect because BWIP is added to, not subtracted from, current costs when using the weighted average method.

57. BWIP was 60% complete as to conversion costs, and EWIP was 45% complete as to conversion costs. The dollar amount of the conversion cost included in EWIP (using the weighted average method) is determined by multiplying the average unit conversion costs by what percentage of the total units in EWIP?

a. 100%.
b. 60%.
c. 55%.
d. 45%.

The correct answer is (d). *(CPA 582 T-42)*
REQUIRED: The percentage of units in EWIP used to calculate conversion costs under the weighted average method.
DISCUSSION: Equivalent units of conversion costs in EWIP inventory using the weighted average method are computed as percentage completed in EWIP inventory times total number of units in EWIP inventory.
Answer (a) is incorrect because EWIP is by definition only partially completed. Answer (b) is incorrect because 60% was the percentage of work done on BWIP in the prior period. Answer (c) is incorrect because 55% is the percentage of work needed to finish EWIP.

58. Dex Co. had the following production for the month of June.

	Units
Work-in-process at June 1	10,000
Started during June	40,000
Completed and transferred to finished goods during June	33,000
Abnormal spoilage incurred	2,000
Work-in-process at June 30	15,000

Materials are added at the beginning of the process. As to conversion cost, the beginning work-in-process was 70% completed and the ending work-in-process was 60% completed. Spoilage is detected at the end of the process. Using the weighted average method, the equivalent units for June, with respect to conversion costs, were

a. 42,000.
b. 44,000.
c. 45,000.
d. 46,000.

The correct answer is (b). *(CPA 1186 Q-37)*
REQUIRED: The EUP for conversion costs using the weighted average method.
DISCUSSION: The weighted average method averages BWIP costs and current costs. Thus, all the work completed this period, including that started last period, is included in EUP. The costs assigned to abnormal spoilage would be recognized as a loss when realized. Thus, abnormal spoilage is included in the EUP calculation. Also, all the units are considered because inspection for spoilage is at the end of the process. The EUP calculation for conversion costs is:

Units completed	33,000
Abnormal spoilage	2,000
Work to date on EWIP (15,000 x 60%)	9,000
Equivalent units	44,000

Module 6.7: Weighted Average EUP Calculation

59. Materials are added at the start of the process in Cedar Company's blending department, the first stage of the production cycle. The following information is available for July:

	Units
Work-in-process, July 1 (60% complete as to conversion costs)	60,000
Started in July	150,000
Transferred to the next department	110,000
Lost in production	30,000
Work-in-process, July 31 (50% complete as to conversion costs)	70,000

Under Cedar's cost accounting system, the costs incurred on the lost units are absorbed by the remaining good units. Using the weighted average method, what are the equivalent units for the materials unit cost calculation?

a. 120,000.
b. 145,000.
c. 180,000.
d. 210,000.

The correct answer is (c). *(CPA 1181 P-21)*
REQUIRED: The materials EUP using the weighted average method.
DISCUSSION: Under the weighted average method of process costing, previous period and current costs are commingled. The spoilage is absorbed by the good units, so all material costs are allocated to units completed and EWIP. Since materials are added at the beginning of the process, all units completed and in EWIP are 100% complete with respect to materials. Thus, the EUP for materials equal 180,000.

Units completed	110,000
EWIP	70,000
Total EUP	180,000

Questions 60 and 61 are based on Bronson Company, which had 6,000 units in work-in-process at January 1 that were 60% complete as to conversion costs. During January 20,000 units were completed. At January 31, 8,000 units remained in WIP which were 40% complete as to conversion costs. Materials are added at the beginning of the process.

---

60. Using the weighted average method, the equivalent units for January for conversion costs were

a. 19,600.
b. 22,400.
c. 23,200.
d. 25,600.

The correct answer is (c). *(CPA 1182 P-32)*
REQUIRED: The EUP for conversion costs using the weighted average method.
DISCUSSION: The weighted average method does not consider the degree of completion of BWIP when computing EUP.

	Units	%	CC EUP
Completed	20,000	100	20,000
EWIP	8,000	40	3,200
Equivalent units			23,200

61. How many units were started during January?

a. 18,000.
b. 19,600.
c. 20,000.
d. 22,000.

The correct answer is (d). *(CPA 1182 P-33)*
REQUIRED: The number of units started during the period.
DISCUSSION: The number of units started can be determined using the following equation:

BWIP + Units started = EWIP + Units completed
6,000 + Units started = 8,000 + 20,000
Units started = 22,000

Module 6.7: Weighted Average EUP Calculation

62. Bart Co. adds materials at the beginning of the process in Department M. The following information pertains to Department M's work-in-process during April.

	Units
Work-in-process at April 1	
(60% complete as to conversion cost)	3,000
Started in April	25,000
Completed in April	20,000
Work-in-process at April 30	
(75% complete as to conversion cost)	8,000

Under the weighted average method, the equivalent units for conversion cost are

a. 26,000.
b. 25,000.
c. 24,200.
d. 21,800.

The correct answer is (a). *(CPA 587 Q-40)*
REQUIRED: The EUP for conversion costs using the weighted average method.
DISCUSSION: The 60% completion rate for BWIP is ignored because, when using the weighted average method, prior period costs of BWIP and current costs are combined. Therefore, the EUP for BWIP is equal to the actual physical units.

Units completed	20,000
Work done on EWIP (8,000 x 75%)	6,000
Equivalent units	26,000

---

63. Sussex Corporation's production cycle starts in the Mixing Department. The following information is available for April:

	Units
WIP, April 1 (50% complete)	40,000
Started in April	240,000
WIP, April 30 (60% complete)	25,000

Materials are added at the beginning of the process in the Mixing Department. Using the weighted average method, what are the equivalent units of production for the month of April?

	Materials	Conversion
a.	240,000	250,000
b.	255,000	255,000
c.	270,000	280,000
d.	280,000	270,000

The correct answer is (d). *(CPA 1180 P-28)*
REQUIRED: The EUP for materials and conversion costs using the weighted average method.
DISCUSSION: Materials are added at the beginning of the process, and conversion costs are assumed to be incurred uniformly. Units completed can be determined under the weighted average method using the following formula:

BWIP + Units started = EWIP + Units completed

	Units	%	Mat. EUP	%	CC EUP
Completed	255,000	100	255,000	100	255,000
EWIP	25,000	100	25,000	60	15,000
Equivalent units			280,000		270,000

---

64. The Wiring Department is the second stage of Flem Company's production cycle. On May 1, the BWIP contained 25,000 units which were 60% complete as to conversion costs. During May, 100,000 units were transferred in from the first stage of Flem's production cycle. On May 31, EWIP contained 20,000 units which were 80% complete as to conversion costs. Materials are added at the end of the process. Using the weighted average method, the EUP on May 31 were

	Trans-in Costs	Materials	Conversion Costs
a.	100,000	125,000	100,000
b.	125,000	105,000	105,000
c.	125,000	105,000	121,000
d.	125,000	125,000	121,000

The correct answer is (c). *(CPA 579 P-35)*
REQUIRED: The EUP for materials, conversion costs, and transferred-in costs using the weighted average method.
DISCUSSION: Materials are added at the end of the process, and conversion costs are assumed to be incurred uniformly. By definition, transferred-in costs are always 100% complete. The number of units completed equals 105,000 (25,000 BWIP + 100,000 transferred in - 20,000 EWIP).

	Units	T-I EUP	%	Mat. EUP	%	CC EUP
Completed	105	105	100	105	100	105
EWIP	20	20	0	-	80	16
EUP		125		105		121

Module 6.7: Weighted Average EUP Calculation

65. The following information pertains to Top Co.'s Division D for the month of May.

	Number of Units	Cost of Materials
BWIP at May 1	30,000	$11,000
Started in May	80,000	36,000
Completed in May	85,000	
EWIP at May 31	25,000	

All materials are added at the beginning of the process. Using the weighted average method, the cost per equivalent unit for materials is

a. $0.43.
b. $0.45.
c. $0.55.
d. $0.59.

The correct answer is (a). *(CPA 1186 Q-27)*
REQUIRED: The cost per equivalent unit for materials using the weighted average method.
DISCUSSION: Previous period's and current period's costs are combined when the weighted average method of process costing is used. Department A adds materials at the beginning of the process.

	Units	%	Materials EUP
Completed	85,000	100	85,000
EWIP	25,000	100	25,000
Equivalent units			110,000

The total materials cost incurred was $47,000 ($11,000 + $36,000). Therefore, the cost per equivalent unit is $0.43 ($47,000 ÷ 110,000).

66. Maurice Company adds materials at the beginning of the process in the Forming Department, which is the first of two stages of its production cycle. Information concerning the materials used in the Forming Department in April is as follows:

	Units	Materials Costs
WIP, April 1	12,000	$ 6,000
Units started	100,000	51,120
Units completed and transferred to next department	88,000	

Using the weighted average method, what was the materials cost of WIP at April 30?

a. $6,120.
b. $11,040.
c. $12,000.
d. $12,240.

The correct answer is (d). *(CPA 1179 P-33)*
REQUIRED: The materials cost of EWIP using the weighted average method.
DISCUSSION: Maurice Company uses the weighted average method of process costing, which combines the previous period's and current period's costs. Since materials are added at the beginning of the process, all units in beginning inventory, started, and transferred out during the period are complete as to materials.

	Units	%	Materials EUP
Completed	88,000	100	88,000
EWIP	24,000	100	24,000
Equivalent units			112,000

The total materials cost incurred is $57,120 ($6,000 + $51,120). The cost per equivalent unit is $0.51 ($57,120 ÷ 112,000). Given 24,000 equivalent units in EWIP (12,000 BWIP + 100,000 started - 88,000 transferred), the EWIP materials cost is $12,240 ($0.51 x 24,000).

67. During March, Bly Company's Department Y equivalent unit product costs, computed under the weighted average method, were as follows:

Materials	$1
Conversion	3
Transferred-in	5

Materials are introduced at the end of the process in Department Y. There were 4,000 units (40% complete as to conversion costs) in WIP at March 31. The total costs assigned to the March 31 WIP inventory should be

a. $36,000.
b. $28,800.
c. $27,200.
d. $24,800.

The correct answer is (d). *(CPA 585 Q-12)*
REQUIRED: The total costs of EWIP using weighted average.
DISCUSSION: The unit costs of EUP under weighted average are already computed. EWIP consists of 4,000 units 40% complete as to conversion costs (1,600 EUP). Since materials are added at the end of the process, there is no material cost, only transferred-in cost.

Transferred in (4,000 x $5)	$20,000
Conversion (1,600 x $3)	4,800
EWIP	$24,800

Module 6.7: Weighted Average EUP Calculation

68. Roy Company manufactures Product X in a two-stage production cycle in Departments A and B. Materials are added at the beginning of the process in Department B. Roy uses the weighted average method. Conversion costs for Department B were 50% complete as to the 6,000 units in BWIP and 75% complete as to the 8,000 units in EWIP. 12,000 units were completed and transferred out of Department B during February. An analysis of the costs relating to WIP and production activity in Department B for February follows:

	Transferred In Costs	Materials Costs	Conversion Costs
WIP, February 1:			
Costs attached	$12,000	$2,500	$1,000
Feb. activity:			
Costs added	$29,000	$5,500	$5,000

The total cost per equivalent unit transferred-out for February of Product X, rounded to the nearest penny, was

a. $2.75.
b. $2.78.
c. $2.82.
d. $2.85.

The correct answer is (b). *(CPA 580 P-33)*
REQUIRED: The total cost per equivalent unit transferred out using the weighted average method.
DISCUSSION: The total cost per equivalent unit transferred out is equal to the unit cost for transferred-in costs, material costs, and conversion costs. Transferred-in costs are by definition 100% complete. Given that materials are added at the beginning of the process in Department B, all units are complete as to materials. Conversion costs are assumed to be uniformly incurred.

	Units	T-I	%	Mat.	%	CC
Completed	12	12	100	12	100	12
EWIP	8	8	100	8	75	6
Equivalent units		20		20		18

Transferred-in $\dfrac{(\$12{,}000 + \$29{,}000)}{20{,}000 \text{ EUP}} = \$2.05$

Material cost $\dfrac{(\$2{,}500 + \$5{,}500)}{20{,}000 \text{ EUP}} = .40$

Conversion cost $\dfrac{(\$1{,}000 + \$5{,}000)}{18{,}000 \text{ EUP}} = .33$

Total unit cost $\underline{\$2.78}$

---

69. Information for the month of January concerning Department A, the first stage of Ogden Corporation's production cycle, is as follows:

	Materials	Conversion
BWIP	$8,000	$6,000
Current costs	40,000	32,000
Total costs	$48,000	$38,000
Equivalent units using weighted average method	100,000	95,000
Average unit costs	$0.48	$0.40
Goods completed		90,000 units
EWIP		10,000 units

Materials are added at the beginning of the process. The ending work-in-process is 50% complete as to conversion costs. How would the total costs accounted for be distributed, using the weighted average method?

	Goods Completed	Ending Work-In-Process
a.	$79,200	$6,800
b.	$79,200	$8,800
c.	$86,000	$0
d.	$88,000	$6,800

The correct answer is (a). *(CPA 582 P-26)*
REQUIRED: The distribution of total costs between goods completed and EWIP using the weighted average method.
DISCUSSION: The weighted average method combines the costs in BWIP with those for the current period. Materials are added at the beginning of the process and conversion costs are assumed to be incurred uniformly. Equivalent unit and average unit cost calculations were given.

Completed goods:
Materials ($.48 x 90,000) $43,200
Conversion costs ($.40 x 90,000) 36,000
Cost of completed goods $79,200

Given that conversion costs for EWIP are 50% complete, there are 5,000 (50% x 10,000) equivalent units of conversion cost in ending inventory.

EWIP:
Materials ($.48 x 10,000) $4,800
Conversion costs ($.40 x 5,000) 2,000
Cost of EWIP $6,800

Module 6.7: Weighted Average EUP Calculation

70. Barnett Company adds materials at the beginning of the process in Department M. Conversion costs were 75% complete as to the 8,000 units in WIP at May 1 and 50% complete as to the 6,000 units in WIP at May 31. During May, 12,000 units were completed and transferred to the next department. An analysis of the costs relating to WIP at May 1 and to production activity for May is as follows:

	Costs	
	Materials	Conversion
WIP, May 1	$9,600	$4,800
Costs added in May	15,600	14,400

Using the weighted average method, the total cost per equivalent unit for May was

a. $2.47.
b. $2.50.
c. $2.68.
d. $3.16.

The correct answer is (c). *(CPA 1183 P-46)*
REQUIRED: The total cost per equivalent unit for the month under the weighted average method.
DISCUSSION: Calculate materials first, noting that they were added at the beginning of the period. 8,000 units were in BWIP. 10,000 units were added during the period (6,000 units in EWIP + 12,000 units completed - 8,000 units BWIP). The total EUP material is thus 18,000 (8,000 + 10,000). Divide the 18,000 EUP into the total material costs of $25,200 ($9,600 + $15,600) to obtain a unit material cost of $1.40.
For conversion, the 8,000 EUP in BWIP plus the 10,000 units added during the month minus the 3,000 EUP (6,000 x 50%) of work not completed in EWIP totals 15,000 EUP. Divide 15,000 EUP into the costs of $19,200 ($4,800 + $14,400) to obtain conversion EUP costs of $1.28. Add the material EUP cost of $1.40 to the conversion EUP cost of $1.28 to obtain total EUP costs of $2.68.

Questions 71 and 72 are based on Department A. On September 30, work-in-process totaled 9,000 units 60% complete (based on conversion costs added uniformly throughout the department and material added at the start of the process). A total of 100,000 units were transferred to the next department during October. On October 31, a total of 8,000 units 40% complete (based on conversion costs) were still in process in Department A.

---

71. Using the weighted-average cost flow method, which of the following equivalent units should be used in the calculation of costs for October?

	Equivalent Units		
	Transfer Costs	Materials	Conversion
a.	108,000	100,000	103,200
b.	108,000	100,000	100,000
c.	108,000	108,000	103,200
d.	109,000	101,000	104,200

The correct answer is (c). *(CIA 1184 IV-6)*
REQUIRED: The EUP for transfer costs, materials, and conversion.
DISCUSSION: Materials are added at the beginning of the process, and conversion costs are incurred uniformly. In calculating weighted average EUP for October, the following assumptions apply: transferred-in costs are 100% complete by definition, materials are 100% complete, and EWIP is 40% complete as to conversion.

(000 omitted)

	Units	T-I EUP	%	Mat. EUP	%	CC EUP
Completed	100	100	100%	100	100%	100
EWIP	8	8	100%	8	40%	3.2
EUP		108		108		103.2

72. Assume transfers to the next department were 5,000 fewer because of normal spoilage. Total transfer costs for the new equivalent units, relative to those costs calculated in Q. 71 above, would be

a. The same.
b. Greater.
c. Less.
d. Cannot be determined from data given.

The correct answer is (a). *(CIA 1184 IV-7)*
REQUIRED: The effect of normal spoilage on transfer costs.
DISCUSSION: The costs related to normal spoilage are allocated to good units passing through the inspection point. Since the point of inspection is not mentioned, it is assumed to be at the end of the process. Thus, the cost of completing 5,000 spoiled units is included in the cost of the 95,000 good units.

6.8 Comprehensive

73. On November 1, Yankee Company had 20,000 units of WIP in Department No. 1 which were 100% complete as to material costs and 20% complete as to conversion costs. During November, 160,000 units were started in Department No. 1 and 170,000 units were completed and transferred to Department No. 2. WIP on November 30 was 100% complete as to material costs and 40% complete as to conversion costs. By what amount would the equivalent units for conversion costs for the month of November differ if the FIFO method were used instead of the weighted average method?

a. 20,000 decrease.
b. 16,000 decrease.
c. 8,000 decrease.
d. 4,000 decrease.

The correct answer is (d). *(CPA 1177 P-35)*
REQUIRED: The difference in EUP between the FIFO and the weighted average method.
DISCUSSION: The weighted average method combines previous and current period work while the FIFO method only includes the EUP for the work done in the current period. Thus, the difference will be the EUP for BWIP.

Units in Department No. 1

BWIP (20%)	20,000	170,000	Transferred
Started	160,000		
		10,000	EWIP (40%)

Conversion Costs
Wtd. Avg. EUP

Transferred	170,000
EWIP (40% x 10,000)	4,000
Wtd. Avg. EUP	174,000

FIFO EUP

Transferred:	
BWIP (80% x 20,000)	16,000
Started and completed	150,000
EWIP (40% x 10,000)	4,000
FIFO EUP	170,000

The difference is that weighted average includes the work done in the previous period (20% of BWIP was completed in the prior period). Accordingly, the difference is that weighted average EUP is greater than FIFO EUP by 20% of 20,000, or 4,000.

74. A company produces white paint in bulk. On May 1, the mixing department, which has used a weighted-average process costing system, had 12,000 unfinished gallons of paint in process approximately 50% complete with regard to conversion costs. Materials are added at the beginning of the process and yield a gallon of paint for each gallon of materials added to the process. During the month of May, 100,000 gallons of material were added and 10,000 gallons, 80% complete with regard to conversion, were in process at the end of May. What is the difference in material and conversion equivalent units, respectively, incurred during May if the first-in, first-out process costing method is employed, rather than the weighted average method?

	Difference in Material Equivalent Units	Difference in Conversion Equivalent Units
a.	No difference	6,000 increase
b.	6,000 decrease	6,000 increase
c.	6,000 increase	6,000 decrease
d.	12,000 decrease	6,000 decrease

The correct answer is (d). *(CIA 1184 IV-11)*
REQUIRED: The difference in EUP between the weighted average and FIFO methods.
DISCUSSION: The weighted average method combines the BWIP work and material of the previous and current periods, while the FIFO method only includes the EUP for the work done in the current period. The difference will be the EUP in BWIP. Here, the BWIP is 100% complete as to materials, so the decrease in material EUP under FIFO is 12,000 (1.0 x 12,000). BWIP is 50% complete as to conversion and therefore contains 6,000 EUP (.5 x 12,000). Use of FIFO will thus result in a 6,000 decrease in EUP.

Module 6.8: Comprehensive

75. Using the periodic inventory system, the BI is $22,000, EI is $18,000, and CGS for the period is $108,000. What was the cost of goods manufactured?

a. $112,000.
b. $104,000.
c. $96,000.
d. $122,000.
e. None of the above.

The correct answer is (b). *(Publisher)*
REQUIRED: The cost of goods manufactured, given inventories and CGS.
DISCUSSION: The cost of goods available for sale is beginning inventory plus the cost of goods manufactured. These goods available are either sold or not. In this period, the goods not sold (ending inventory) were $18,000, and the cost of goods sold was $108,000. Thus, goods available for sale equaled $126,000. Since the beginning inventory is given as $22,000, cost of goods manufactured is $104,000 ($126,000 - $22,000).

Questions 76 and 77 are based on the Collins Company, which, on April 1, had 6,000 units of WIP in Department B, the second and last stage of its production cycle. The costs attached to these 6,000 units were $12,000 of costs transferred in from Department A, $2,500 of material costs added in Department B, and $2,000 of conversion costs added in Department B. Materials are added at the beginning of the process in Department B. Conversion was 50% complete on April 1. During April, 14,000 units were transferred in from Department A at a cost of $27,000, and material costs of $3,500 and conversion costs of $3,000 were added in Department B. On April 30, Department B had 5,000 units of WIP, 60% complete as to conversion costs. The costs attached to these 5,000 units were $10,500 of costs transferred in from Department A, $1,800 of material costs added in Department B, and $800 of conversion costs added in Department B.

---

76. Using the weighted average method, what were the equivalent units for the month of April?

	Transferred-in Costs	Materials Costs	Conversion Costs
a.	15,000	15,000	15,000
b.	19,000	19,000	20,000
c.	20,000	20,000	18,000
d.	25,000	25,000	20,000

The correct answer is (c). *(CPA 577 P-36)*
REQUIRED: The EUP for transferred-in costs, materials, and conversion costs using the weighted average method.
DISCUSSION: In Department B, materials are added at the beginning of the production process, and conversion costs are assumed to be incurred uniformly. Transferred-in costs are also incurred at the beginning of the process and are by definition 100% complete. The number of units completed equals 15,000 (6,000 BWIP + 14,000 transferred in - 5,000 EWIP).

	Units	T-I EUP	%	Mat. EUP	%	CC EUP
Completed	15	15	100	15	100	15
EWIP	5	5	100	5	60	3
Equivalent units		20		20		18

77. Using the weighted average method, what was the cost per equivalent unit for conversion costs?

a. $4,200 ÷ 15,000.
b. $5,800 ÷ 18,000.
c. $5,800 ÷ 20,000.
d. $5,000 ÷ 18,000.

The correct answer is (d). *(CPA 577 P-37)*
REQUIRED: The cost per equivalent unit for conversion costs.
DISCUSSION: The weighted average method combines the previous period's and current period's costs. In this question, $2,000 of conversion cost was attached to the BWIP and $3,000 was spent in the current period. The total conversion cost incurred was $5,000. Since 18,000 equivalent units [15 units completed (100%) + 5 units in EWIP (60%)] were produced, the cost per equivalent unit was $5,000 ÷ 18,000.

Module 6.8: Comprehensive

Questions 78 and 79 are based on the information below and in the opposite column.

	Units	Costs
BWIP	5,000	$ 6,300
Units transferred in	35,000	58,000
Units completed	37,000	
EWIP	3,000	

	T-I Costs	Materials Costs	Conversion Costs	Total Costs
BWIP	$ 2,900	$ --	$ 3,400	$ 6,300
UTI	17,500	25,500	15,000	58,000
	$20,400	$25,500	$18,400	$64,300

Conversion costs were 20% complete as to BWIP and 40% complete as to EWIP. All materials are added at the end of the process. The weighted average method is used.

78. The cost per equivalent unit for conversion costs, rounded to the nearest penny, is

a. $0.44.
b. $0.46.
c. $0.48.
d. $0.50.

The correct answer is (c). *(CPA 578 P-25)*
REQUIRED: The conversion costs per EUP using the weighted average method.
DISCUSSION: The weighted average method of process costing commingles previous and current costs. Conversion costs are assumed to be incurred uniformly throughout the process.

	Units	% of Completion	CC EUP
Completed	37,000	100	37,000
EWIP	3,000	40	1,200
Equivalent units			38,200

The total conversion costs incurred are $18,400 ($3,400 + $15,000). Therefore, the conversion cost per EUP is $0.48 ($18,400 ÷ 38,200).

79. The portion of the total cost of ending work-in-process attributable to transferred-in cost is

a. $0.
b. $1,500.
c. $1,530.
d. $1,650.

The correct answer is (c). *(CPA 578 P-26)*
REQUIRED: The transferred-in costs in the EWIP using the weighted average method.
DISCUSSION: Transferred-in costs are similar to material added at the beginning of the process. The total transferred-in costs are $20,400. The number of EUP for transferred-in costs is 40,000 (37,000 completed + 3,000 EWIP), since transferred-in costs are always 100% complete. The transferred-in cost per EUP is thus $0.51 ($20,400 ÷ 40,000), and the transferred-in cost of EWIP is $1,530 ($.51 x 3,000).

Questions 80 through 90 are based on the following information, which was presented as part of Question 4 on the Practice II section of the May 1979 CPA examination.

You are engaged in the audit of the December 31 financial statements of Spirit Corporation, a manufacturer of digital watches. You are attempting to verify the costing of the EWIP and finished goods which were recorded on Spirit's books as follows:

	Units	Cost
WIP (50% complete as to labor and overhead)	300,000	$ 660,960
Finished goods	200,000	1,009,800

Materials are added to production at the beginning of the manufacturing process, and overhead is applied to each product at the rate of 60% of direct labor costs. There was no finished goods inventory on January 1. A review of Spirit's inventory cost records disclosed the following information:

		Costs (in thousands)	
	Units	Materials	Labor
WIP, 1/1 (80% complete as to labor and overhead)	200	$ 200	$ 315
Units started in production	1,000		
Material costs		$1,300	
Labor costs			$1,995
Units completed	900		

Module 6.8: Comprehensive

80. What are the EUP for labor under the weighted average method?
    a. 1,200,000 units.
    b. 1,050,000 units.
    c. 900,000 units.
    d. 1,140,000 units.

The correct answer is (b). *(Publisher)*
REQUIRED: The equivalent units of labor produced under the weighted average method.
DISCUSSION: The number of equivalent units of labor is equal to the units completed during the period plus the equivalent units in EWIP. EWIP is 50% complete as to labor. Hence, the number of equivalent units of labor is 1,050,000 EUP (the 900,000 units completed during the year plus 50% of the 300,000 units in EWIP).

81. What are the equivalent units of labor produced under the FIFO method?
    a. 890,000 units.
    b. 900,000 units.
    c. 1,140,000 units.
    d. 1,210,000 units.

The correct answer is (a). *(Publisher)*
REQUIRED: EUP for labor under the FIFO method.
DISCUSSION: In the previous question, the weighted average EUP for labor was determined to be 1,050,000 EUP. The difference between weighted average and FIFO is that FIFO does not include the EUP or costs in BWIP. There were 200,000 units as of January 1 that were 80% complete. Hence, 160,000 EUP were in BI and must be subtracted from the weighted average EUP of 1,050,000 to obtain the FIFO EUP for labor of 890,000.

82. What is the total cost for overhead using the weighted average method?
    a. $2,310,000.
    b. $1,162,000.
    c. $1,562,000.
    d. $1,386,000.

The correct answer is (d). *(Publisher)*
REQUIRED: The total cost for overhead using the weighted average method.
DISCUSSION: The total cost for overhead is equal to 60% of the labor cost. The labor cost in BWIP is given as $315,000, and the labor cost added during the current period is $1,995,000. Overhead costs are therefore $1,386,000 (60% x $2,310,000).

83. What is the total cost of overhead using the FIFO method?
    a. $1,386,000.
    b. $1,680,000.
    c. $2,310,000.
    d. $1,197,000.

The correct answer is (d). *(Publisher)*
REQUIRED: The total cost of overhead using the FIFO method.
DISCUSSION: The total labor cost under FIFO is that incurred in the current period ($1,995,000). This does not include the labor costs in BWIP. The $315,000 of BWIP labor costs are not included in the FIFO calculation. Since overhead is applied at 60% of the labor cost, total FIFO overhead costs are $1,197,000 (.6 x $1,995,000).

84. What is the cost per EUP for labor using the weighted average method?
    a. $2.00.
    b. $2.15.
    c. $2.20.
    d. $1.90.

The correct answer is (c). *(Publisher)*
REQUIRED: The cost per EUP for labor using the weighted average method.
DISCUSSION: The cost per EUP for labor under the weighted average method is equal to the labor cost in BWIP plus the current cost, all divided by EUP. EUP is 1,050,000. Total labor cost is $315,000 plus $1,995,000, or a total of $2,310,000. The unit cost of labor is thus $2.20 ($2,310,000 ÷ 1,050,000).

85. Using the FIFO method for EUP, what is the cost per EUP of labor?
    a. $315,000 ÷ 160,000.
    b. $1,995,000 ÷ 890,000.
    c. $2,310,000 ÷ 1,050,000.
    d. $1,995,000 ÷ 900,000.

The correct answer is (b). *(Publisher)*
REQUIRED: The FIFO cost per equivalent unit of production.
DISCUSSION: The FIFO cost of labor per EUP is the current period's labor costs of $1,995,000 divided by the 890,000 EUP for the period.

Module 6.8: Comprehensive

> Questions 86 and 87 are based on the information provided on page 134.

86. What is the total cost for the ending inventory of finished goods using the weighted average method?

a. $869,000.
b. $954,000.
c. $900,000.
d. $786,000.

The correct answer is (b). *(CPA 579 Q-C4)*
REQUIRED: The total cost of finished goods ending inventory using the weighted average method.
DISCUSSION: The calculation of the total cost of finished goods requires calculation of the equivalent units of production and the unit cost per EUP, and multiplication of the finished goods quantity by the cost per equivalent unit. (The calculation is presented below).

Equivalent Units of Production (Weighted Average Method)

	Materials	Labor	Overhead
Units completed during year	900,000	900,000	900,000
EWIP, December 31 (50% complete as to labor and overhead)	300,000	150,000	150,000
Equivalent units of production	1,200,000	1,050,000	1,050,000

Unit Costs of Production

	Materials	Labor	Overhead	Total
BWIP costs	$ 200,000	$ 315,000	$ 189,000	$ 704,000
Current costs	1,300,000	1,995,000	1,197,000	4,492,000
Total costs	$1,500,000	$2,310,000	$1,386,000	$5,196,000
Equivalent units of production	1,200,000	1,050,000	1,050,000	--
Cost per EUP	$ 1.25	$ 2.20	$ 1.32	$ 4.77

Finished goods = 200,000 units x $4.77 = $954,000

87. If the FIFO method were being used, how would the table of data above differ?

a. Work to be completed in BWIP would be added to the EUP data, and BWIP costs would be deleted from the cost data.

b. They would be the same because the difference between FIFO and weighted average is how the "cost per EUP" is used, not how it is calculated.

c. There would be no EUP related to BWIP, nor would there be any costs associated with BWIP included in the data.

d. Work that was completed last period in BWIP would be deleted from the EUP data, and costs incurred last period in BWIP would be deleted from the cost data.

The correct answer is (d). *(Publisher)*
REQUIRED: The difference between the FIFO method and the weighted average method.
DISCUSSION: In comparison with weighted average, the FIFO method only considers work done and costs incurred this period. The weighted average method averages the costs incurred last period that remain in BWIP with the costs incurred this period. Accordingly, the table of data computing EUP under the weighted average method would be modified by eliminating EUP completed last period and also last period's costs in BWIP.

Answer (a) is incorrect because the work that has been done, not the work to be completed, would be deleted from the FIFO data. Answer (b) is incorrect because the work completed as of the beginning of the period and related costs in BWIP are not included in FIFO calculations. Answer (c) is incorrect because the EUP and related costs required to complete BWIP are included in FIFO calculations.

Module 6.8: Comprehensive

> Questions 88 through 90 are based on the information provided on page 134.

88. The cost that should be assigned to the 300,000 units in EWIP using the weighted average method is

a. $900,000.
b. $875,000.
c. $918,000.
d. $903,000.

The correct answer is (d). *(Publisher)*
REQUIRED: The cost assigned to EWIP under the weighted average method.
DISCUSSION: The 300,000 units in EWIP are 100% complete with respect to materials and 50% complete as to labor and overhead. Remember, EWIP is equal to the equivalent units in ending inventory times the respective cost per EUP.

Materials ($1.25 x 300,000)	$375,000
Labor ($2.20 x 150,000)	330,000
Overhead ($1.32 x 150,000)	198,000
Total cost	$903,000

89. The cost per books of finished goods in ending inventory is

a. $1,009,800.
b. $954,000.
c. $869,000.
d. $1,012,200.

The correct answer is (a). *(Publisher)*
REQUIRED: The cost per books of finished goods in ending inventory.
DISCUSSION: The cost per books of finished goods is given as $1,009,800. Evidently, some cost allocations during 1984 were improperly estimated.

90. The amount debited to work-in-process inventory for the correcting entry is

a. $242,040.
b. $231,650.
c. $186,240.
d. $217,323.

The correct answer is (a). *(Publisher)*
REQUIRED: The amount debited to WIP as a correcting entry.
DISCUSSION: The correcting entry should debit the WIP account $242,040 ($903,000 cost of EWIP as calculated minus $660,960 cost per books given). The credits would be to finished goods for $55,800 ($1,009,800 - $954,000) and to CGS for $186,240 (the amount necessary to balance the entry).

91. Paulson Company had inventories at the beginning and end of the year as follows:

	1/1	12/31
Raw materials	$55,000	$65,000
Work-in-process	96,000	80,000
Finished goods	50,000	85,000

During the year, the following costs were incurred:

Raw materials purchased	$400,000
Direct labor payroll	220,000
Factory overhead	330,000

Paulson's cost of goods sold for the year was

a. $921,000.
b. $956,000.
c. $966,000.
d. $979,000.

The correct answer is (a). *(CPA 583 P-18)*
REQUIRED: The cost of goods sold given inventory and current period cost data.
DISCUSSION: To compute CGS, one must know the cost of goods manufactured. Note that there is an increase in finished goods inventory of $35,000 ($85,000 - $50,000). CGS will thus be CGM minus $35,000.

CGM is $16,000 more than all of the manufacturing costs incurred in the year because WIP inventory decreased by $16,000 ($96,000 - $80,000). Total costs of manufacturing are $550,000 ($220,000 labor + $330,000 overhead) plus the raw materials used. Since the raw materials inventory increased by $10,000 ($65,000 - $55,000), the raw materials used totaled $390,000. Thus, the total manufacturing costs incurred are $940,000 ($390,000 material, $220,000 labor, and $330,000 overhead).

Increasing this amount by the $16,000 increase in WIP inventories gives a cost of goods manufactured of $956,000. CGM must be decreased by the $35,000 increase in FG inventory to determine CGS of $921,000.

92. For many years a company has manufactured three different models of fiberglass boats: X, Y, and Z. All boats start in the molding department, are transferred to the trimming and sanding department, and then are transferred to the finishing department where they are painted and have accessories added. Model X is a basic 14' model which the company uses to promote a full range of products. Model Y is the company's best selling boat, a 16' model with options available. Model Z is a top-of-the-line 20' boat with all the accessories that the company has to offer. Since all boats go through each department, the company uses a process costing system. Listed below are the recent average direct costs per unit by department:

Month 1	Materials	Conversion	Total
Molding	$321	$ 27	$348
Trimming & Sanding	13	45	58
Finishing	45	35	80
Total per unit	$379	$107	$486

Month 2	Materials	Conversion	Total
Molding	$393	$ 36	$429
Trimming & Sanding	23	61	84
Finishing	55	40	95
Total per unit	$471	$137	$608

Because of the large increase in per unit equivalent costs, the controller wants to investigate this change. The most likely reason for the change is

a. An increase in the spoilage factor for material and downtime for labor in the second month.

b. A different mix of products X, Y, and Z being produced in the second month.

c. A change to higher costing materials in the second month.

d. The common costs of the fiberglass have been incorrectly allocated in Month 2.

The correct answer is (b). *(CIA 585 IV-9)*
REQUIRED: The reason for the change in average direct costs.
DISCUSSION: Unit average direct costs are the sum of materials and conversion costs directly attributable to specific products. The controller is investigating a significant change in these costs from one period to another. Because of the product quality and size variations, it is likely that a different mix of products will cause a significant change in average direct costs. The increases probably resulted from greater production of the larger and more expensive boats.

Answer (a) is incorrect because only a change in production mix is likely to have caused increased costs of both materials and conversion in all departments. Answer (c) is incorrect because better materials may result in lower conversion costs. Answer (d) is incorrect because misallocation of common costs does not account for total direct cost differences.

Module 6.8: Comprehensive

> Questions 93 through 97 are based on the processing operations of HDG Enterprises. Assume that process conversion costs are uniform but a number of materials are added at different points in the process. Material 1 is added at the beginning of the process. The transferred-in costs are added at the 20% point in the process. Material 2 is added uniformly from the 50% to the 70% points in the process. Material 3 is added at the 75% point in the process, and Material 4 is added uniformly at the 90% to the 100% points in the process. The January BWIP was 10,000 units 60% complete, 60,000 units were added, and EWIP was 20,000 units 95% complete.

93. What was the Material 3 EUP for the month?

	FIFO	Weighted Average
a.	50,000	60,000
b.	60,000	60,000
c.	60,000	70,000
d.	70,000	70,000

The correct answer is (d). *(Publisher)*
REQUIRED: EUP for Material 3 for the month.
DISCUSSION: Material 3 is added at the 75% point in the process. None of Material 3 was in BWIP. Accordingly, it had to be added to the 10,000 units in BWIP and all the 60,000 units started this period since the EWIP was 95% complete. Accordingly, the month's Material 3 EUP are 70,000 units for both FIFO and weighted average.

94. What was the Material 1 EUP for the month?

	FIFO	Weighted Average
a.	50,000	60,000
b.	60,000	60,000
c.	60,000	70,000
d.	70,000	70,000

The correct answer is (c). *(Publisher)*
REQUIRED: EUP for Material 1 for the month.
DISCUSSION: Material 1 is added at the very beginning of the process. Accordingly, BWIP had 10,000 units of material 1 in it. During the period, 60,000 units were added. Thus, for FIFO the EWIP is 60,000 units (current work done); for weighted average it is 70,000 units (60,000 units added this period plus the 10,000 units in BWIP).

95. What was the conversion EUP for the month?

	FIFO	Weighted Average
a.	50,000	60,000
b.	63,000	69,000
c.	60,000	70,000
d.	53,000	59,000

The correct answer is (b). *(Publisher)*
REQUIRED: EUP for conversion for the month.
DISCUSSION: Under weighted average, the conversion EUP include the 50,000 units complete (10,000 BWIP plus 60,000 started less 20,000 EWIP) plus the 19,000 EUP in EWIP (20,000 x 95%), or 69,000 EUP.
For FIFO, the 69,000 EUP for weighted average is reduced by the 6,000 (10,000 units x 60%) of work completed in BWIP.

96. What was the Material 2 EUP for the month?

	FIFO	Weighted Average
a.	50,000	60,000
b.	60,000	70,000
c.	65,000	70,000
d.	63,000	67,000

The correct answer is (c). *(Publisher)*
REQUIRED: EUP for Material 2 for the month.
DISCUSSION: Material 2 is added uniformly from the 50% to the 70% portion of the process. Accordingly, of the 10,000 BWIP at the 60% completion point, only 5,000 EUP would be in BWIP. Thus, an additional 5,000 units would be added to BWIP. Also, Material 2 had been added to all 60,000 units started during the period because EWIP is at the 95% point. Accordingly, EWIP would be 65,000 for FIFO and 70,000 for weighted average.

97. What was the Material 4 EUP for the month?

	FIFO	Weighted Average
a.	50,000	60,000
b.	60,000	60,000
c.	65,000	70,000
d.	70,000	70,000

The correct answer is (b). *(Publisher)*
REQUIRED: EUP for Material 4 for the month.
DISCUSSION: Material 4 is added uniformly between the 90% and the 100% point in the process. Accordingly, BWIP which was 60% complete would have no Material 4. Thus, weighted average and FIFO EUP are the same. All 50,000 units completed would contain Material 4, plus there would be 10,000 EUP in EWIP, half of the 20,000 EWIP because Material 4 is added uniformly between the 90% and 100% points.

CHAPTER SEVEN
SPOILAGE, WASTE, AND SCRAP

> 7.1 Definitions .... (20 questions) 141
> 7.2 Applications .... (13 questions) 146
> 7.3 Journal Entries .... (6 questions) 150
> 7.4 Comprehensive .... (29 questions) 152

Spoilage, waste, and scrap are common occurrences in both job order and process costing. However, the primary emphasis in these materials is on the issues regarding process costing for two reasons: (1) the professional examinations stress spoilage, waste, and scrap in reference to process costing, and (2) the production processes for homogeneous products seem to lend themselves conceptually to an analysis of spoilage, waste, and scrap. Keep in mind that the issues regarding spoilage, waste, and scrap could easily be adapted to, and in fact are built into, job order systems.

7.1 Definitions

1. Which of the following is an inventoriable cost?

	Abnormal Spoilage	Normal Spoilage
a.	No	No
b.	No	Yes
c.	Yes	No
d.	Yes	Yes

The correct answer is (b). *(CPA 1181 T-57)*
REQUIRED: The proper classification of normal and abnormal spoilage in terms of inventoriable costs.
DISCUSSION: Inventoriable costs are all costs that are expected to occur. Normal spoilage is the level of spoilage that usually occurs (i.e., the expected amount of spoilage), and thus these costs are inventoriable. Abnormal spoilage is the amount that occurs beyond the normal (expected) level. Abnormal spoilage costs are not inventoriable since they were not expected (i.e., they are losses).

2. Normal spoilage is defined as
   a. Spoilage that results from normal operations.
   b. Uncontrollable waste as a result of a special production run.
   c. Spoilage that arises under inefficient operations.
   d. Controllable spoilage.

The correct answer is (a). *(CPA 1175 T-C6)*
REQUIRED: The definition of normal spoilage in the production process.
DISCUSSION: Normal spoilage is the spoilage that occurs under normal operating conditions. It is essentially uncontrollable in the short run. Normal spoilage arises under efficient operations and is treated as a product cost.
Answers (b) and (c) are incorrect because, if spoilage occurs from a special production run or from inefficient operations, it is abnormal. Answer (d) is incorrect because, if spoilage is controllable, it should be controlled under normal circumstances.

3. If inspection is at the 60% point of the process and defective units are removed upon inspection, how many EUP would be assigned to normal and abnormal spoilage, respectively, if 700 units of each were found during the period?
   a. 420, 420.
   b. 420, 700.
   c. 700, 420.
   d. 700, 700.

The correct answer is (a). *(Publisher)*
REQUIRED: The computation of EUP assigned to normal and abnormal spoilage.
DISCUSSION: EUP assigned to spoilage are based upon the actual processing costs incurred. If 700 spoiled units are 60% complete, 420 EUP have been produced. Accordingly, 420 EUP should be assigned to both normal and abnormal spoilage.

Module 7.1: Definitions

4. In contrast to normal spoilage, abnormal spoilage
   a. Is considered part of good production.
   b. Arises under efficient operating conditions.
   c. Is controllable in the short run.
   d. Is not an inherent result of the particular manufacturing process.

The correct answer is (d). *(CIA 1186 IV-6)*
REQUIRED: The true statement about abnormal spoilage.
DISCUSSION: Abnormal spoilage is spoilage that is not expected to occur under normal, efficient operating conditions. The cost of abnormal spoilage should be separately identified and reported to management. Abnormal spoilage is typically treated as a period cost (a loss) because of its unusual nature.
Answers (a) and (b) are incorrect because each applies only to normal spoilage, which is the spoilage that occurs under normal operating conditions. Normal spoilage is essentially uncontrollable in the short run. Normal spoilage arises under efficient operations and is treated as a product cost. Answer (c) is incorrect because abnormal spoilage is not controllable in the short run.

5. Generally, costs of normal spoilage are charged to goods manufactured during the period. When should they also be allocated to EWIP?
   a. When the inspection point is at the end of the process.
   b. When there is no BWIP.
   c. When there is no EWIP.
   d. When the inspection point is prior to the end of the process and goods in EWIP have passed the inspection point.

The correct answer is (d). *(Publisher)*
REQUIRED: When normal spoilage costs should be allocated to EWIP.
DISCUSSION: Normal spoilage costs should be allocated to all good units, i.e., all units that have passed the inspection point. In typical accounting problems, the inspection point is at the end of the process. Therefore, goods in EWIP have not passed the inspection point. If the inspection point is prior to the end of the process, however, and goods in EWIP have passed the inspection point, a portion of the normal spoilage costs should be allocated to EWIP.
Answer (a) is incorrect because, when the inspection point is at the end of the process, goods in EWIP have not yet passed the inspection point. Answer (b) is incorrect because the allocation question only arises at the inspection point, which is not related to the existence of BWIP. Answer (c) is incorrect because costs cannot be allocated to EWIP if there is no EWIP.

6. In a process costing system, the cost of abnormal spoilage should be
   a. Prorated between units transferred out and ending inventory.
   b. Included in the cost of units transferred out.
   c. Treated as a loss in the period incurred.
   d. Ignored.

The correct answer is (c). *(CIA 1185 IV-6)*
REQUIRED: The best accounting treatment for abnormal spoilage.
DISCUSSION: Abnormal spoilage is spoilage that is not expected to occur under normal, efficient operating conditions. Because of its unusual nature, abnormal spoilage is typically treated as a loss in the period in which it is incurred.
Answers (a) and (b) are incorrect because abnormal spoilage costs are not considered a component of the cost of good units produced. Answer (d) is incorrect because abnormal spoilage costs must be taken out of the manufacturing account.

7. Normal spoilage and abnormal spoilage should be classified as

	Normal	Abnormal
a.	Period cost	Period cost
b.	Product cost	Period cost
c.	Period cost	Product cost
d.	Product cost	Product cost

The correct answer is (b). *(CPA 1180 T-46)*
REQUIRED: The correct classification of normal and abnormal spoilage.
DISCUSSION: Normal spoilage is the level of spoilage that is expected, while abnormal spoilage is all spoilage beyond the normal level. Since normal spoilage is expected, it is a cost of producing the goods, i.e., a product cost. Abnormal spoilage is not expected, so it is expensed in the period incurred, i.e., a period cost.

Module 7.1: Definitions

8. If an overhead account is not charged for inconsistent normal spoilage, what account may be used?

a. Spoilage loss.
b. Spoilage random fluctuations.
c. Cost of sales.
d. Materials usage variance.

The correct answer is (b). *(Publisher)*
REQUIRED: The alternative method of accounting for inconsistent normal spoilage.
DISCUSSION: If it is desirable to account for inconsistent normal spoilage costs separately from the overhead account, a spoilage random fluctuations account might be used. Just as the overhead account averages indirect manufacturing costs for a year, so would the spoilage random fluctuations account average inconsistent normal spoilage over a year.
Answers (a) and (c) are incorrect because inconsistent normal spoilage is not abnormal spoilage. Answer (d) is incorrect because the materials usage variance is concerned with quantities of direct material that vary from standard quantities used in production.

9. If a process has several inspection points, how should the costs of normal spoilage be accounted for?

a. Charged to the cost of goods completed during the period.
b. Allocated to EWIP and goods completed during the period based on their relative values.
c. Allocated to the good units passing through each inspection point.
d. Allocated to EWIP and goods completed during the period based on units.

The correct answer is (c). *(Publisher)*
REQUIRED: How to allocate normal spoilage costs along several inspection points.
DISCUSSION: At each inspection point, the costs of normal spoilage should be allocated to the good units passing through the inspection point. Consequently, the cost of moving the good units to the inspection point includes the material and conversion costs of the normally spoiled units as well as those of the good units.

10. A product that does not meet quality control standards and needs to be reworked to be salable as either an irregular or a good product is classified as

a. Spoiled goods.
b. Defective goods.
c. Scrap material.
d. Waste material.

The correct answer is (b). *(Publisher)*
REQUIRED: The classification of a product requiring rework to be salable.
DISCUSSION: Defective goods are products that have not met the quality control standards at the completion of the production process. Defective goods require rework to be salable as either an irregular item or a good product.
Answer (a) is incorrect because spoiled goods are sold for salvage value or destroyed. Answer (c) is incorrect because scrap material is raw material that may be put back into a different production process or sold to outsiders. Answer (d) is incorrect because waste material has no further use.

11. In a job order accounting situation, assume that there are $45,000 of charges to a given job consisting of $25,000 material, $10,000 direct labor, and $10,000 applied overhead. The job yields 500 units of a product of which 100 are rejected as spoiled with no salvage value. The cost of the spoilage is determined to be $9,000. If the firm wishes to use this job as the basis for setting a spoilage standard for comparison to future work, the conceptually superior way to express the spoilage rate would be

a. 20% of total inputs.
b. 25% of good outputs.
c. 90% of labor inputs.
d. 36% of material inputs.

The correct answer is (b). *(F. Mayne)*
REQUIRED: The calculation of a normal spoilage rate to be used for future comparison.
DISCUSSION: Normal spoilage is spoilage which occurs under efficient operating conditions. It is spoilage that is uncontrollable in the short run, and therefore should be expressed as a function of good output (treated as a product cost). The rate can be determined using the ratio of cost of spoiled units/cost of good units less cost of spoiled units or spoiled units/good units. Thus, the rate would be 25% [$9,000 ÷ ($45,000 - $9,000) or 100 units ÷ (500 - 100) units].

Module 7.1: Definitions

12. Scrap material consists of
   a. Defective units that may be used or sold.
   b. Raw materials remaining from the production cycle but usable for purposes other than the original purpose.
   c. Raw materials remaining from the production cycle but not usable for any purpose.
   d. Finished goods that do not meet quality control standards and cannot be reworked.

The correct answer is (b). *(Publisher)*
REQUIRED: The cost accounting definition of scrap material.
DISCUSSION: Scrap material consists of raw materials left over from the production cycle but still usable for purposes other than those for which it was originally intended. Scrap material may be sold to outside customers, usually for a nominal amount, or may be used for a different production process.
   Answer (a) is incorrect because scrap is raw material which may not necessarily be defective. Answer (c) is incorrect because it defines waste material. Answer (d) is incorrect because scrap is raw material, not finished goods.

13. Waste material consists of
   a. Raw materials remaining from the production cycle but not usable for any purpose.
   b. Finished goods that do not meet quality control standards and cannot be reworked.
   c. Defective units that may be used or sold.
   d. Raw materials remaining from the production cycle but usable for purposes other than the original purpose.

The correct answer is (a). *(Publisher)*
REQUIRED: The cost accounting definition of waste material.
DISCUSSION: Waste material is the amount of raw materials left over from a production process or production cycle for which there is no further use. Waste material usually is not salable at any price and must be discarded.
   Answers (b) and (c) are incorrect because waste describes unusable raw materials, not some form of finished goods. Answer (d) is incorrect because waste material is not usable for any purpose.

14. Spoiled goods are
   a. Raw materials remaining from the production cycle but usable for purposes other than the original purpose.
   b. Defective units that may be used or sold.
   c. Finished goods that do not meet quality control standards and cannot be reworked.
   d. Raw materials remaining from the production cycle but not usable for any purpose.

The correct answer is (c). *(Publisher)*
REQUIRED: The cost accounting definition of spoiled goods.
DISCUSSION: Spoiled goods are finished units that do not meet quality control standards. These finished goods usually cannot be reworked. Spoiled goods are usually sold for scrap value or discarded.
   Answers (a) and (d) are incorrect because spoiled goods describe finished goods, not raw materials. Answer (b) is incorrect because spoiled goods usually cannot be used or sold, except at scrap value, whereas, defective units can be reworked and sold.

15. Which of the following is the preferable accounting treatment of spoilage in an actual or normal cost system?
   a. Disregard spoilage; the average unit cost of the good units will include all costs.
   b. Treat all spoilage as a loss or as a component of overhead.
   c. Separate spoilage into normal and abnormal spoilage; normal spoilage costs are allocated to good units and abnormal spoilage to a loss account.
   d. Separate spoilage into fixed and variable costs; fixed costs are allocated to good units and variable costs are a component of overhead.

The correct answer is (c). *(Publisher)*
REQUIRED: The appropriate accounting treatment of spoilage.
DISCUSSION: By separating spoilage into normal and abnormal spoilage and allocating the normal spoilage costs to good units and abnormal spoilage to a loss account, the spoilage costs are accounted for as they occur.
   Answer (a) is incorrect because, by disregarding spoilage, all costs are lumped in the average unit cost of the good units produced, providing management with erroneous information regarding the amount of spoilage and unit costs. Answer (b) is incorrect because, if all spoilage is treated as a loss or as a component of factory overhead, the breakdown between normal and abnormal spoilage will not be known. Answer (d) is incorrect because the fixed versus variable cost distinction is not made for the allocation of spoilage.

Module 7.1: Definitions

16. In a process costing system which assumes that normal spoilage occurs at the end of a process, the cost attributable to normal spoilage should be assigned to

a. Ending work-in-process inventory.

b. Cost of goods manufactured and ending work-in-process inventory in the ratio of units worked on during the period to units remaining in work-in-process inventory.

c. Cost of goods manufactured (transferred out).

d. A separate loss account in order to highlight production inefficiencies.

The correct answer is (c). *(CPA 1178 T-36)*
REQUIRED: The inventory to which to assign normal spoilage costs when it occurs at the end of the process.
DISCUSSION: Normal spoilage is an example of a product cost in that it attaches to a product and is expensed when sold. When normal spoilage occurs at the end of the process, the product must be complete before the spoilage can be detected. Therefore, all normal spoilage costs should be assigned to finished goods inventory.
Answers (a) and (b) are incorrect because the EWIP contains no spoiled units since spoilage does not occur until processing is complete. Answer (d) is incorrect because normal spoilage costs attach to the product since they are expected. Abnormal spoilage costs are charged to a separate loss account.

17. Assuming the value of scrap sales is material, when is it not necessary to record the value of scrap in inventory as it is produced?

a. When it is sold regularly, e.g., daily, weekly, etc.

b. When the unit value fluctuates.

c. If it is recognized as miscellaneous revenue.

d. If it is recognized as an offset to overhead.

The correct answer is (a). *(Publisher)*
REQUIRED: When a company need not record a significant inventory value of scrap.
DISCUSSION: If scrap material is sold on a regular basis, e.g., daily, its value should be recorded either as a contra cost or as a revenue on a regular basis, and income will be accounted for properly. If it is not sold regularly and not recorded in inventory, income may be misstated.
Answer (b) is incorrect because failure to record significant scrap value can misstate income. Answers (c) and (d) are incorrect because the issue is timing the recognition of scrap value, not the account used.

18. Shrinkage should be accounted for as

a. Miscellaneous revenue.

b. An offset to overhead.

c. Reworked units.

d. Spoilage.

The correct answer is (d). *(Publisher)*
REQUIRED: The proper accounting treatment of shrinkage.
DISCUSSION: Shrinkage is material lost through the manufacturing process (e.g., heat, compression, etc.). It is accounted for in the same manner as spoilage. If shrinkage is normal, it is charged to the product. If it is abnormal, it is charged as a loss.
Answers (a) and (b) are incorrect because shrinkage usually does not result in scrap or waste products that can be sold and accounted for as a revenue or contra cost. Answer (c) is incorrect because reworked units are those reprocessed to produce good units.

19. Seconds or slightly defective units should be accounted for as

a. Miscellaneous revenue.

b. An offset to overhead.

c. Reworked units.

d. Spoilage.

The correct answer is (d). *(Publisher)*
REQUIRED: How seconds or slightly defective units should be accounted for.
DISCUSSION: Seconds are spoiled goods in that they do not have the value of normal good output. Accordingly, the difference between their net realizable value and the NRV of normal units is usually accounted for as spoilage, i.e., charged to product if normal and charged as a loss if abnormal.
Answers (a) and (b) are incorrect because seconds or slightly defective units usually have enough value not to be considered scrap or a contra cost. Answer (c) is incorrect because seconds may or may not be reworked.

20. A manufacturer of electric motors expects 4% of output to be rejected at the final inspection point. These rejected units are sold through special channels at less than 10% of normal selling price. The proper assignment of the costs associated with these defective units is to

a. Charge to the cost of inspection.
b. Charge to general factory overhead.
c. Charge as an unfavorable material usage variance.
d. Accumulate and add to the cost of good units completed during the period.

The correct answer is (d). *(CIA 1187 IV-6)*
REQUIRED: The proper assignment of the costs associated with defective units.
DISCUSSION: Normal spoilage is expected to occur under normal operating conditions. It is included in the cost of the good units produced (treated as a product cost).
Answer (a) is incorrect because inspection cost is an overhead item. Answer (b) is incorrect because normal spoilage is a cost directly identifiable with the good units. Answer (c) is incorrect because the spoilage may not be attributable to defective materials. Also, the costs associated with spoilage include labor and overhead as well as materials.

7.2 Applications

21. Under Heller Company's job order cost system, estimated costs of defective work (considered normal in the manufacturing process) are included in the predetermined factory overhead rate. During March, Job No. 210 for 2,000 hand saws was completed at the following costs per unit:

Direct materials	$ 5
Direct labor	4
Factory overhead (applied at 150% of direct labor cost)	6
	$15

Final inspection disclosed 100 defective saws, which were reworked at a cost of $2 per unit for direct labor, plus overhead at the predetermined rate. The defective units fall within the normal range. What is the total rework cost and to what account should it be charged?

a. $200 to work-in-process.
b. $200 to factory overhead control.
c. $500 to work-in-process.
d. $500 to factory overhead control.

The correct answer is (d). *(CPA 582 P-27)*
REQUIRED: The rework cost for defective units and the account to which it should be charged.
DISCUSSION: The rework cost includes the direct labor costs ($2/unit) and the factory overhead costs incurred ($2 x 150% per unit) to rework the 100 defective units.

$$[\$2 + (\$2 \times 1.50)] \; 100 \text{ units} = \$500.$$

The rework cost should be allocated among all units by charging it to the factory overhead control.

22. In manufacturing its products for the month of March, Kane Co. incurred normal spoilage of $10,000 and abnormal spoilage of $12,000. How much spoilage cost should Kane charge as a period cost for the month of March?

a. $22,000.
b. $12,000.
c. $10,000.
d. $0.

The correct answer is (b). *(CPA 586 Q-21)*
REQUIRED: The amount of spoilage charged as a period cost.
DISCUSSION: Normal spoilage arises under efficient operating conditions and is, therefore, a product cost. On the other hand, abnormal spoilage is not expected to occur under efficient operating conditions, and therefore is a period cost. Thus, the amount of spoilage charged as a period cost is the $12,000 related to abnormal spoilage.

23. In its July production, Gage Corp., which does not use a standard cost system, incurred total production costs of $800,000, of which Gage attributed $30,000 to normal spoilage and $20,000 to abnormal spoilage. Gage should account for this spoilage as

a. Inventoriable cost of $30,000 and period cost of $20,000.
b. Period cost of $30,000 and inventoriable cost of $20,000.
c. Inventoriable cost of $50,000.
d. Period cost of $50,000.

The correct answer is (a). *(CPA 1185 Q-5)*
REQUIRED: The treatment of normal and abnormal spoilage.
DISCUSSION: Abnormal spoilage is not expected to occur under efficient operating conditions and is a loss, i.e., a period cost. Normal spoilage arises under efficient operating conditions and is an inventoriable (product) cost. Thus, the $30,000 associated with normal spoilage is an inventoriable cost and the $20,000 related with abnormal spoilage is a period cost.

Questions 24 and 25 are based on Harper Co.'s Job 501 for the manufacture of 2,200 coats, which was completed during August at the unit costs presented below. Final inspection of Job 501 disclosed 200 spoiled coats which were sold to a jobber for $6,000.

Direct materials	$20
Direct labor	18
Factory overhead (includes an allowance of $1 for spoiled work)	18
	$56

---

24. Assume that spoilage loss is charged to all production during August. What would be the unit cost of the good coats produced on Job 501?

a. $53.00.
b. $55.00.
c. $56.00.
d. $58.60.

The correct answer is (c). *(CPA 1182 P-28)*
REQUIRED: The unit cost of goods produced when spoilage is charged to all production.
DISCUSSION: The unit cost of goods produced includes direct materials, direct labor, and factory overhead. Since the spoilage is included in the calculation of overhead, it must be considered normal and a product cost. Thus, the unit cost remains $56.

25. Assume instead that the spoilage loss is attributable to the exacting specifications of Job 501 and is charged to this specific job. What would be the unit cost of the good coats produced on Job 501?

a. $55.00.
b. $57.50.
c. $58.60.
d. $61.60.

The correct answer is (b). *(CPA 1182 P-29)*
REQUIRED: The unit cost of goods produced if the actual spoilage loss is charged to this job.
DISCUSSION: If the spoilage is charged to this specific job (rather than to factory overhead), the spoilage allowance should be removed from the factory overhead rate. The overhead application rate thus drops to $17 because this job's spoilage is not typical and will not be averaged with other "typical" jobs. The costs of producing the 2,000 good coats include the costs incurred in the production of the 2,200 coats, less the $6,000 received for the spoiled coats. The unit cost is net cost of production divided by the number of good coats produced (2,000).

$$\frac{2,200(\$20 + \$18 + \$17) - \$6,000}{2,000} = \$57.50$$

Module 7.2: Applications

26. Read, Inc. instituted a new process in October. During October, 10,000 units were started in Department A. Of the units started, 1,000 were lost in the process, 7,000 were transferred to Department B, and 2,000 remained in work-in-process at October 31. The work-in-process at October 31 was 100% complete as to material costs and 50% complete as to conversion costs. Material costs of $27,000 and conversion costs of $40,000 were charged to Department A in October. What were the total costs transferred to Department B?

a. $46,900.
b. $53,600.
c. $56,000.
d. $57,120.

The correct answer is (c). *(CPA 1177 P-34)*
REQUIRED: The total costs transferred to Department B.
DISCUSSION: Since there is no BWIP, it does not matter whether a FIFO or weighted average costing method is used. Since the problem does not state whether the 1,000 lost units are considered normal or abnormal spoilage, one must assume normal spoilage (i.e., the costs are absorbed only by the good units). The material cost of $27,000 is to be allocated to 9,000 units ($3.00/unit), of which 7,000 have been completed and transferred and 2,000 are in EWIP. The conversion costs of $40,000 are to be allocated to 8,000 EUP (7,000 complete units and 2,000 units in EWIP, 50% complete), or $5/unit. Thus, the 7,000 units completed cost $8/unit ($5 + $3), and total costs are $56,000.

27. During March, Hart Company incurred the following costs on Job 109 for the manufacture of 200 motors:

Original cost accumulation:
Direct materials	$ 660
Direct labor	800
Factory overhead (150% of DL)	1,200
	$2,660

Direct costs of reworking 10 units:
Direct materials	$ 100
Direct labor	160
	$ 260

The rework costs were attributable to the exacting specifications of Job 109, and the full rework costs were charged to this specific job. What is the cost per finished unit of Job 109?

a. $15.80.
b. $14.60.
c. $14.00.
d. $13.30.

The correct answer is (a). *(CPA 1183 P-54)*
REQUIRED: The cost per finished unit of a job, given rework costs.
DISCUSSION: Since the rework costs are attributable to the exacting specifications of Job 109, the full rework costs should be charged to this specific job. Accordingly, the cost of reworking the 10 units must include $260 of direct costs and an additional charge for overhead.

Original cost	$2,660.00
Rework direct costs	260.00
Rework O/H (150% x $160 DL)	240.00
Job 109 total costs	$3,160.00
Divided by 200 motors	÷ 200.00
Job 109 unit cost	$ 15.80

28. Refer to the previous question. If the rework had been normal spoilage, i.e., not related to a specific job, the rework costs would have been charged to

a. Job 109, as in the previous question.
b. Factory overhead.
c. Finished goods.
d. Cost of goods sold.

The correct answer is (b). *(Publisher)*
REQUIRED: The normal treatment of rework costs in a job order system.
DISCUSSION: To allocate rework costs to all jobs throughout the period, they should be passed through the overhead account. An alternative is to use a specific account to achieve this averaging effect, e.g., the spoilage random fluctuation account.
Answers (a) and (c) are incorrect because only costs attributable to a specific job are charged to that job. Answer (d) is incorrect because spoilage costs are never taken directly to cost of goods sold.

29. Barkley Company adds materials at the beginning of the process in Department M. Data concerning the materials used in March production are as follows:

	Units
Work-in-process at March 1	16,000
Started during March	34,000
Completed and transferred to next department during March	36,000
Normal spoilage incurred	4,000
Work-in-process at March 31	10,000

Using the weighted average method, the equivalent units for the materials unit cost calculations are

 a. 30,000.
 b. 34,000.
 c. 40,000.
 d. 46,000.

The correct answer is (d). *(CPA 583 P-30)*
REQUIRED: The equivalent units of material using the weighted average method.
DISCUSSION: During March, the cost of 50,000 units of material was incurred (16,000 in WIP plus 34,000 started), resulting in 36,000 completed units and 10,000 units in EWIP. The cost of the 4,000 spoiled units should be spread to the 46,000 good units because the spoilage was normal. In the materials unit cost calculation, the total March material costs to be accounted for are divided by EUP assumed to have passed inspection. These EUP consist of 36,000 transferred plus 10,000 in EWIP, or 46,000 EUP.

30. Refer to the previous question. If the units of EWIP had not passed the inspection point, what percentage of material costs would have been charged to goods completed and transferred during the period?

 a. 40/50.
 b. 30/50.
 c. 36/46.
 d. 30/46.

The correct answer is (a). *(Publisher)*
REQUIRED: The percentage of total material costs charged to goods transferred if EWIP had not been inspected.
DISCUSSION: If the 10,000 units in EWIP had not yet passed the inspection point, they can be presumed to contain additional spoilage. Also, the given 4,000 units of spoiled goods relate only to the 40,000 units that had passed the inspection point (36,000 were good and 4,000 were bad). Accordingly, the material cost of the 36,000 units transferred out was the cost of material for 40,000 units divided by 50,000 units of material costs incurred (16,000 units in WIP + 34,000 started during the period), or 40/50 of the total material cost.

31. A company that manufactures baseballs begins operations on January 1. Each baseball requires three elements: a hard plastic core, several yards of twine that are wrapped around the plastic core, and a piece of leather to cover the baseball. The plastic core is started down a conveyor belt and is automatically wrapped with twine to the approximate size of a baseball at which time the leather cover is sewn to the wrapped twine. Finished baseballs are inspected and defective ones are pulled out. Defective baseballs cannot be economically salvaged and are destroyed. Normal spoilage is 3% of the number of baseballs that pass inspection. Cost and production reports for the first week of operations are:

Raw material cost	$ 840
Conversion cost	315
	$1,155

During the week 2,100 baseballs were completed and 2,000 passed inspection. There was no ending work-in-process. Calculate abnormal spoilage.

 a. $33.
 b. $22.
 c. $1,100.
 d. $55.

The correct answer is (b). *(CIA 586 IV-6)*
REQUIRED: Abnormal spoilage for the week.
DISCUSSION: Abnormal spoilage is calculated as the total unit cost times the amount of spoilage in excess of expected normal spoilage. Total unit cost is of

Material cost ($840 ÷ 2,100 EUP)	$0.40
Conversion cost ($315 ÷ 2,100 EUP)	0.15
	$0.55

Spoilage in excess of normal spoilage is 40 units [100 spoiled units - (.03 x 2,000 good units)]. Abnormal spoilage is thus $22 ($.55 x 40).

Module 7.3: Journal Entries

32. Assume 550 units were worked on during a period in which a total of 500 good units were completed. Normal spoilage consisted of 30 units; abnormal spoilage, 20 units. Total production costs were $2,200. The company accounts for abnormal spoilage separately on the income statement as loss due to abnormal spoilage. Normal spoilage is not accounted for separately. What is the cost of the good units produced?

   a. $2,000.
   b. $2,080.
   c. $2,120.
   d. $2,200.

The correct answer is (c). *(CIA 587 IV-5)*
REQUIRED: The cost of the good units produced given normal and abnormal spoilage.
DISCUSSION: Abnormal spoilage is not expected to occur under efficient operating conditions. Thus, abnormal spoilage is excluded from the cost of the good units. Hence, the total production cost of $2,200 is reduced by $80 [20 units × ($2,200 ÷ 550 total units)] to arrive at the $2,120 cost of good units.

33. A company produces small pencil erasers. Two percent of normal input is expected to be spoiled in the process. Inspection occurs at the end of the process and rejected units are disposed of as scrap with no cost recovery. In a recent period, the following data were obtained:

	Units
Total units started	750,000
Defective units rejected (including normal and abnormal spoilage)	20,000

	Costs
Materials	$14,750
Conversion	7,750
Total	$22,500

The cost for the units transferred to finished goods during this 24-hour period, assuming no ending work-in-progress, is

   a. $21,900.
   b. $22,050.
   c. $22,350.
   d. $22,500.

The correct answer is (c). *(CIA 584 IV-8)*
REQUIRED: The cost of units transferred given normal and abnormal spoilage.
DISCUSSION: The normal spoilage is included in cost estimates and has no effect on transferred costs. Abnormal spoilage should be charged to expense. The total cost of $22,500 divided by 750,000 units gives the unit cost of $.03. Abnormal spoilage equals total spoilage less normal spoilage.

20,000 − (.02 × 750,000) = 5,000
5,000 × $.03 = $150 charged to expense
$22,500 − $150 = $22,350

7.3 Journal Entries

34. Ten items out of a lot of 60 were spoiled, which was considered normal. Costs accumulated to the point at which spoilage can be detected amounted to $50 per unit. The salvage value is estimated at $15 per unit. Normal spoilage is included in the predetermined overhead rate. What entry would record this?

   a. Stores control $150
      Dept. O/H control   350
         Work-in-process $500

   b. O/H control $500
         Work-in-process $500

   c. Stores control $500
         Work-in-process $500

   d. Work-in-process $500
         Stores control $150
         O/H control   350

The correct answer is (a). *(Publisher)*
REQUIRED: The journal entry to record the spoilage costs attributed to work done on all jobs.
DISCUSSION: The correct journal entry to record the spoilage costs of $500 and spread this cost over all the jobs is to debit stores control for the salvage value, $150 (10 units × $15); debit department overhead control for the balance of the spoilage cost $350 (10 units × $35); and credit work-in-process for the total spoilage costs of $500 (10 units × $50). In this way normal spoilage is spread over all production rather than being charged to a specific job.

35. Refer to the previous question. If all 200 units were considered abnormal spoilage, what would be the entry to record the completion of the 2,000 good units and the abnormal spoilage?

a.	Finished goods	$11,000	
	Work-in-process		$11,000
b.	Cost of goods sold	$11,000	
	Finished goods		$11,000
c.	Finished goods	$10,300	
	Loss from abnormal spoilage	700	
	Work-in-process		$11,000
d.	Finished goods	$10,000	
	Loss from abnormal spoilage	1,000	
	Work-in-process		$11,000

The correct answer is (d). *(Publisher)*
REQUIRED: The journal entry to record completion of good units and abnormal spoilage.
DISCUSSION: Given that all 200 spoiled units are abnormal spoilage, $1,000 (200 units x $5) must be treated as a period cost and debited to an account such as loss from abnormal spoilage. Finished goods will be debited for only $10,000 (2,000 units x $5) because no normal spoilage costs exist to be allocated to good units. The cost of all units (2,200 units x $5) is credited to (transferred from) WIP.
Answer (a) is incorrect because it is the entry to transfer the 2,200 units to finished goods if there had been no spoilage. Answer (b) is incorrect because it records the sale of goods. Answer (c) is incorrect because it is the appropriate entry in the preceding question to record the cost of good units and the abnormal spoilage (60 units).

36. Assume that a firm produced 2,000 good units with 60 units of normal spoilage and 140 units of abnormal spoilage. Total costs incurred are $11,000, resulting in a unit cost of $5. The journal entry to record the completion of 2,000 good units and 60 units of normal spoilage at $5 per unit is

a.	Finished goods	$10,000	
	Work-in-process		$10,000
b.	Cost of goods sold	$10,000	
	Finished goods		$10,000
c.	Finished goods	$10,300	
	Work-in-process		$10,300
d.	Finished goods	$10,000	
	Cost of spoiled goods	300	
	Work-in-process		$10,300

The correct answer is (c). *(Publisher)*
REQUIRED: The journal entry to record the completion of good units and defective units.
DISCUSSION: The journal entry to record the completion of 2,000 units at a cost of $5 per unit, including normal spoilage, is to debit both the finished goods account and the work-in-process account for $10,300, which is the cost of goods manufactured (2,000 units x $5) plus normal spoilage costs (60 units x $5). The abnormal spoilage (140 x $5 = $700) would be debited to an expense account. Note that normal spoilage costs are spread over the good units while abnormal spoilage costs are written off as period costs.

37. Campbell Co. incurred $200 of rework costs on 20 defective units. Rework costs consisted of $40 of materials, $100 of labor, and $60 of overhead. What entry would record the normal incurrence of these defective work (rework) costs assuming spoilage costs are included in the predetermined overhead rate?

a.	Stores control	$40	
	O/H control	60	
	Work-in-process		$100
b.	O/H control	$200	
	Stores control		$ 40
	Accrued payroll		100
	O/H applied		60
c.	Stores control	$200	
	O/H control		$200
d.	O/H applied	$60	
	Stores control		$40
	O/H control		20

The correct answer is (b). *(Publisher)*
REQUIRED: The journal entry to record the normal incurrence of defective work costs.
DISCUSSION: The correct journal entry to record the normal incurrence of $200 of defective work costs is to debit overhead control for the full amount of the defective work costs of $200; credit the stores control account for the amount of parts directly used in the reworking process ($40); credit the accrued payroll account for the amount of labor costs incurred to rework the defective items ($100); and credit the overhead applied account for the amount of overhead applied to the particular job ($60).

38.
Acme sold $6,090 of scrap on account. Acme accounts for scrap as an offset to factory overhead. What entry would record the sale of scrap?

a. Accounts receivable $6,090
       Finished goods $6,090

b. Accounts receivable $6,090
       Work-in-process $6,090

c. Accounts receivable $6,090
       Revenue (from
       sale of scrap) $6,090

d. Accounts receivable $6,090
       O/H control $6,090

The correct answer is (d). (Publisher)
REQUIRED: The correct journal entry to record a credit sale of scrap.
DISCUSSION: The correct journal entry to record the sale of $6,090 worth of scrap is to debit the A/R account and credit the department overhead control account for $6,090. All products bear the cost of scrap under this method. If the overhead budget was developed with an estimate for scrap sales, the overhead rate would be lower than if no allowance for the sale of scrap were included.

39.
Most firms account for normal spoilage differently from abnormal spoilage. What journal entry is appropriate to record abnormal spoilage?

a. Loss from abnormal spoilage   XX
      Work-in-process   XX

b. Extraordinary loss   XX
      Work-in-process   XX

c. Cost of goods spoiled   XX
      Finished goods   XX

d. Finished goods   XX
      Work-in-process   XX

The correct answer is (a). (Publisher)
REQUIRED: The journal entry to record abnormal spoilage.
DISCUSSION: The correct journal entry to record abnormal spoilage is to debit a loss account and credit the work-in-process account for the amount of abnormal spoilage.
Answer (b) is incorrect because abnormal spoilage is not extraordinary since it is neither infrequent nor unusual. Answer (c) is incorrect because the amount is expensed as a loss, and the credit is to work-in-process. Answer (d) is incorrect because it is the entry to record completion of good units.

7.4 Comprehensive

Questions 40 through 44 are based on JC Company, which employs a process cost system. A unit of product passes through three departments -- molding, assembly, and finishing -- before it is complete. Finishing Department information for May follows:

	Units
Work-in-process inventory--May 1	1,400
Units transferred in from the Assembly Department	14,000
Units spoiled	700
Units transferred out to finished goods inventory	11,200

Raw material is added at the beginning of the processing in the Finishing Department without changing the number of units being processed.

WIP was 70% complete as to conversion on May 1 and 40% complete as to conversion on May 31. All spoilage was discovered at final inspection before the units were transferred to finished goods; 560 of the units spoiled were within the limit considered normal.

The JC Company employs the weighted average costing method. The equivalent units and the current costs per equivalent unit of production for each cost factor are as follows:

	EUP	Current Costs per EUP
Transferred-in	15,400	$5.00
Raw materials	15,400	1.00
Conversion cost	13,300	3.00
Total cost per EUP		$9.00

40.
The cost of production transferred to the finished goods inventory is

a. $100,800.
b. $105,840.
c. $107,100.
d. $102,060.
e. None of the above.

The correct answer is (b). (CMA 680 4-1)
REQUIRED: The weighted average cost of production transferred to finished goods.
DISCUSSION: The costs assigned to finished goods inventory consist of the costs attached to the units transferred out plus the costs of normal spoilage (so the good units absorb the cost of normal spoilage). Since spoilage is detected at the end of the process, its unit cost ($9) is the same as the unit cost for good units. The cost of production transferred to finished goods is $105,840 [(11,200 good units + 560 spoiled units) x $9]. The remaining 140 units are abnormal spoilage and are written off as a period cost.

Module 7.4: Comprehensive   153

41. The cost assigned to WIP on May 31 is

   a. $28,000.
   b. $31,000.
   c. $25,200.
   d. $30,240.
   e. None of the above.

The correct answer is (c). *(CMA 680 4-2)*
   REQUIRED: The cost of EWIP using the weighted average method.
   DISCUSSION: To determine the cost assigned to EWIP, one must first determine the EUP in EI. BI plus units transferred in, minus the units completed and transferred, minus the spoilage, equals EWIP of 3,500 units (1,400 + 14,000 - 11,200 - 700). Material is added at the beginning of the process and transferred-in costs are treated as if they were materials added at the beginning of the process. Since conversion is 40% complete, the EUP for conversion costs are 1,400 (3,500 x 40%).

Transferred-in (3,500 x $5)	$17,500
Materials (3,500 x $1)	3,500
Conversion cost (1,400 x $3)	4,200
EWIP costs	$25,200

42. If the total costs of prior departments included in the WIP of the Finishing Department on May 1 amounted to $6,300, the total cost transferred in from the Assembly Department to the Finishing Department during May is

   a. $70,000.
   b. $62,300.
   c. $70,700.
   d. $63,700.
   e. None of the above.

The correct answer is (c). *(CMA 680 4-3)*
   REQUIRED: The total costs transferred in during the period using the weighted average method.
   DISCUSSION: The total transferred-in cost is calculated by multiplying the transferred-in equivalent units by the cost per equivalent unit (15,400 x $5 = $77,000). Since $6,300 was included in the BWIP, the remainder ($77,000 - $6,300 = $70,700) must have been transferred in during the month.

43. The cost associated with the abnormal spoilage is

   a. $6,300.
   b. $1,260.
   c. $560.
   d. $840.
   e. None of the above.

The correct answer is (b). *(CMA 680 4-4)*
   REQUIRED: The cost associated with abnormal spoilage.
   DISCUSSION: The cost of abnormal spoilage is calculated by multiplying the total unit cost (since spoilage is detected at final inspection after all costs have been incurred) by the amount of abnormal spoilage. There are 140 units of abnormal spoilage (700 spoiled - 560 considered normal spoilage). The cost of abnormal spoilage is $1,260 (140 units x $9).

44. The costs associated with abnormal spoilage ordinarily would be

   a. Charged to inventory.
   b. Charged to a material variance account.
   c. Charged to retained earnings.
   d. Charged to manufacturing overhead.
   e. Charged to a special loss account.

The correct answer is (e). *(CMA 680 4-5)*
   REQUIRED: The proper handling of abnormal spoilage costs.
   DISCUSSION: Abnormal spoilage costs are usually charged to a loss account (treated as a period cost), while normal spoilage costs are usually attached to the good units produced (treated as a product cost).
   Answer (a) is incorrect because normal spoilage is absorbed by the good units produced. Answer (b) is incorrect because variances of material prices and/or usage are charged to the material variance account. Answer (c) is incorrect because abnormal spoilage does not meet the criteria for a prior period adjustment. Answer (d) is incorrect because charging abnormal spoilage to manufacturing overhead is possible, but it is not the ordinary method. If charged to overhead, it is subsequently treated as a product rather than period cost.

Module 7.4: Comprehensive

Questions 45 through 52 are based on the following information, which was presented as part of Question 8 on Part 4 of the December 1977 CMA examination.

Ranka Company manufactures high quality leather products. The company's profits have declined during the past 9 months. Ranka has used unit cost data (which were developed 18 months ago) in planning and controlling its operations. In an attempt to isolate the causes of poor profit performance, management is investigating the manufacturing operations of each of its products.

One of Ranka's main products is fine leather belts. The belts are produced in a single, continuous process in the Bluett Plant. During the process, leather strips are sewn, punched, and dyed. Buckles are attached by rivets when the belts are 70% complete as to direct labor and overhead (conversion costs). The belts then enter a final finishing stage to conclude the process. Labor and overhead are applied continuously during the process.

The leather belts are inspected twice during the process: (1) right before the buckles are attached (70% point in the process) and (2) at the conclusion of the finishing stage (100% point in the process). Ranka uses the weighted average method to calculate its unit costs.

The leather belts produced at the Bluett Plant sell wholesale for $9.95 each. Management wants to compare the current manufacturing costs per unit with the prices on the market for leather belts. Top management has asked the Bluett Plant to submit data on the cost of manufacturing the leather belts for the month of October. These data will be used to evaluate whether modifications in the production process should be initiated or whether an increase in the selling price of the belts is justified. The cost per equivalent unit being used for planning and control purposes is $5.35 per unit.

The work-in-process inventory consisted of 400 partially completed units on October 1. The belts were 25% complete as to conversion costs. The costs included in the inventory on October 1 were:

Leather strips	$1,000
Conversion costs	300
	$1,300

During October, 7,600 leather strips were placed in production. A total of 6,800 good leather belts were completed. A total of 300 belts were identified as defective at the two inspection points - 100 at the first inspection point (before buckle is attached) and 200 at the final inspection point (after finishing). This quantity of defective belts was considered normal. In addition, 200 belts were removed from the production line when the process was 40% complete as to conversion costs because they had been damaged as a result of a malfunction during the sewing operation. This malfunction was considered an unusual occurrence, so the spoilage was classified as abnormal. Defective (spoiled) units are not reprocessed and have zero salvage value. The work-in-process inventory on October 31 consisted of 700 belts which were 50% complete as to conversion costs.

The costs charged to production for October were:

Leather strips	$20,600
Buckles	4,550
Conversion costs	20,700
Total	$45,850

---

45. What are the total equivalent units for the leather strips for the month?

a. 7,000.
b. 8,000.
c. 7,500.
d. 8,600.

The correct answer is (b). *(Publisher)*
REQUIRED: The total equivalent units for the product.
DISCUSSION: Leather strip equivalent units are the total completed during the month plus normal spoilage plus abnormal spoilage plus any work-in-process at month-end.

Completed during the month	6,800
Normal spoilage:	
1st inspection	100
2nd inspection	200
Abnormal spoilage	200
Work-in-process at 10/31	700
Total equivalent units	8,000

46. What is the cost per equivalent unit for the buckles?

a. $.65.
b. $1.25.
c. $.66.
d. $.84.

The correct answer is (a). *(Publisher)*
REQUIRED: The cost per equivalent unit for the added part.
DISCUSSION: The buckles are attached when the belts are 70% complete. The cost per EUP for the buckles is the cost assigned to the buckles divided by the EUP. 6,800 buckles added to belts completed during the month plus 200 units of normal spoilage equal 7,000 EUP (there are no buckles in EWIP as it is only 50% complete). $4,550 in costs is attributable to the 7,000 buckles. $4,550 ÷ 7,000 = $.65 per EUP.

47. What is the total production cost to account for in October?

a. $45,850.
b. $47,150.
c. $52,150.
d. $43,516.

The correct answer is (b). *(Publisher)*
REQUIRED: The total cost of production to account for.
DISCUSSION: Total BWIP cost is $1,300, and costs charged to production during the month are $45,850. Thus, the total cost to account for is $47,150. Alternatively, the cost can be calculated by adding each component.

Material ($1,000 + $20,600)	$21,600
Buckles	4,550
Conversion ($300 + $20,700)	21,000
Total costs	$47,150

48. What is the total cost per equivalent unit?

a. $5.50.
b. $6.00.
c. $6.56.
d. $6.15.

The correct answer is (d). *(Publisher)*
REQUIRED: The total cost per equivalent unit.
DISCUSSION: The total cost per EUP is the sum of EUP costs for strips, buckles, and conversion. Note that the 100 units of normal spoilage at the first inspection were 70% complete (70 EUP), and the 200 units of abnormal spoilage were 40% complete (80 EUP). EWIP was 50% complete.

	Leather Strips	Buckles	Conversion Cost
Completed during the month	6,800	6,800	6,800
Normal spoilage			
1st inspection	100	--	70
2nd inspection	200	200	200
Abnormal spoilage	200	--	80
WIP at 10/31	700	--	350
Equivalent units	8,000	7,000	7,500

Cost per EUP:	
Strips [($1,000 + $20,600) ÷ 8,000]	$2.70
Buckles ($4,550 ÷ 7,000)	.65
Conversion [($300 + $20,700) ÷ 7,500]	2.80
Total cost per EUP	$6.15

49. What is the total cost of normal spoilage?

a. $2,323.
b. $1,754.
c. $1,696.
d. $1,264.

The correct answer is (c). *(Publisher)*
REQUIRED: The total cost of normal spoilage for the products.
DISCUSSION: The cost of normal spoilage is equal to the EUP attributable to normal spoilage times the EUP cost for each component (computed in the preceding question).

Leather (300 x $2.70)	$ 810
Buckles (200 x $.65)	130
Conversion (270* x $2.80)	756
Total	$1,696

*Consists of 200 units 100% complete and 100 units 70% complete.

50. What is the total work-in-process as of October 31?

a. $1,890.
b. $3,160.
c. $2,320.
d. $2,870.

The correct answer is (d). *(Publisher)*
REQUIRED: The total ending work-in-process inventory.
DISCUSSION: The cost of EWIP is equal to the EUP in each category times the appropriate unit cost. Leather strips, the only item in EI as of October 31, are 100% complete as to leather and 50% complete as to conversion.

Leather strips (700 x $2.70)	$1,890
Conversion (700 x .5 x $2.80)	980
Total	$2,870

> Questions 51 and 52 are based on the information provided on page 154.

51. What is the average cost per unit for finished goods?

a. $6.93.
b. $6.40.
c. $6.16.
d. $6.74.

The correct answer is (b). *(Publisher)*
REQUIRED: The average cost per unit for finished goods.
DISCUSSION: The average cost for finished goods is the total cost of the good units completed plus the cost of normal spoilage, divided by the number of good units completed. The cost of good units completed is $41,820 (6,800 x $6.15). The cost of normal spoilage is $1,696. Thus, $43,516 ($41,820 + $1,696) is the total cost transferred. $43,516 ÷ 6,800 = $6.40 per unit.

52. If the 300 defective belts (normal spoilage) were repaired and management wanted to be sure the incremental costs did not exceed the cost of producing new units, how would the rework costs be accounted for?

a. As normal materials, labor, and overhead.
b. Charged only to those belts repaired.
c. Expensed as extraordinary.
d. Charged to overhead and spread over the cost of all products.

The correct answer is (b). *(Publisher)*
REQUIRED: The appropriate accounting treatment to maximize control over rework costs.
DISCUSSION: To maximize control, the costs relating to the repair of the 300 defective belts should be separated from other costs. The costs might flow through the WIP accounts but should be kept separate (like a specific job in job order costing). Alternatively, another WIP type account for rework might be established on a job lot basis, which would prevent spending more for the rework than manufacturing a new product. Generally, manufacturers prefer to rework items rather than throw them away.
Answer (a) is incorrect because, if the rework costs are accounted for as normal materials, labor, and overhead, the costs of reworking are averaged in with the costs of production, which would bury rework costs exceeding the costs of normal production. Answer (c) is incorrect because extraordinary items must be both unusual and infrequent; normal spoilage is neither. Answer (d) is incorrect because charging the costs to overhead would give no effective control over the cost to rework.

Questions 53 through 66 are based on the following information, which was presented as part of Question 3 on the Practice I section of the November 1971 CPA examination.

Ballinger Paper Products manufactures a high quality paper box. The box department applies two separate operations -- cutting and folding. The paper is first cut and trimmed to the dimensions of a box form by one machine group. One square foot of paper is equivalent to four box forms. The trimmings from this process have no scrap value. Box forms are then creased and folded (i.e., completed) by a second machine group. Any partially processed boxes in the department are cut box forms that are ready for creasing and folding. These partially processed boxes are considered 50% complete as to labor and overhead. The materials department maintains an inventory of paper in sufficient quantities to permit continuous processing, and transfers to the box department are made as needed. Immediately after folding, all good boxes are transferred to the finished goods department.

During June, the materials department purchased 1,210,000 square feet of unprocessed paper for $244,000. Conversion costs for the month were $226,000. A quantity equal to 30,000 boxes was spoiled during paper cutting, and 70,000 boxes were spoiled during folding. All spoilage has a zero salvage value, is considered normal, and cannot be reprocessed. All spoilage loss is allocated between the completed units and partially processed boxes. Ballinger applies the weighted average cost method to all inventories. Inventory data for June are given below.

		June 1		June 30
Inventory	Physical Unit	Units on Hand	Cost	Units on Hand
Materials Dept.: paper	square feet	390,000	$76,000	200,000
Box Dept.: boxes cut, not folded	number	800,000	55,000*	300,000
Fin. Goods Dept.: completed boxes on hand	number	250,000	18,000	50,000

* $35,000 materials + $20,000 conversion cost

53. What is the cost of paper available in June?
   a. $244,000.
   b. $280,000.
   c. $312,000.
   d. $320,000.

The correct answer is (d). *(Publisher)*
REQUIRED: The cost of materials available in the period.
DISCUSSION: The cost of paper available in June is equal to the inventory at the beginning of the month ($76,000) plus the purchases ($244,000). Total cost of paper available is $320,000.

54. What is the number of units transferred out of the materials department?
   a. 5,600,000.
   b. 1,400,000.
   c. 6,200,000.
   d. 200,000.

The correct answer is (b). *(Publisher)*
REQUIRED: The units transferred out of the materials department.
DISCUSSION: The number of units (square feet) transferred out of the materials department equals the units available minus the EI. The number of units available of 1,600,000 (390,000 BI + 1,210,000 purchases) minus the EI of 200,000 gives 1,400,000 units transferred out of the materials department.

55. What is the cost of units transferred out of the materials department?
   a. $140,000.
   b. $280,000.
   c. $320,000.
   d. $244,000.

The correct answer is (b). *(Publisher)*
REQUIRED: The cost of units transferred out of the materials department.
DISCUSSION: The units measured in the materials department are square feet. The cost of the units transferred out is the number of units multiplied by their unit cost. The cost of units available (see Q. 53) is $320,000. The number of units available is 390,000 BI plus 1,210,000 purchased, or 1,600,000. Thus, each unit costs $.20 ($320,000 ÷ 1,600,000). The units transferred out equal units available (1,600,000) minus EI (200,000). The cost of the units transferred out is $280,000 (1,400,000 × $.20).

56. What is the number of units transferred out of the box department?
   a. 5,600,000.
   b. 200,000.
   c. 6,000,000.
   d. 6,400,000.

The correct answer is (c). *(Publisher)*
REQUIRED: The units transferred out of the box department.
DISCUSSION: The units (number of boxes) transferred out of the box department equal the BI plus the units transferred in from the materials department minus the initial spoilage, terminal spoilage, and any EI. The units transferred in from materials are reclassified on a 4-to-1 basis. Each square foot of paper is equivalent to four box forms. The boxes cut but not folded (BWIP = 800,000) plus the materials transferred in of 1,400,000 (equivalent to 5,600,000 new units) equals 6,400,000 units available. After deducting initial spoilage of 30,000, terminal spoilage of 70,000, and EI of 300,000, 6,000,000 units were transferred out (6,400,000 - 100,000 - 300,000).

57. What is the total number of units transferred from finished goods to cost of goods sold?
   a. 1,400,000.
   b. 6,000,000.
   c. 5,600,000.
   d. 6,200,000.

The correct answer is (d). *(Publisher)*
REQUIRED: The units transferred from finished goods to cost of goods sold.
DISCUSSION: The units transferred from FG to CGS include BI plus the units transferred to the FG department, minus any EI and spoilage. Beginning FG inventory consisted of 250,000 completed boxes; 6,000,000 new units were transferred in; and the EI was 50,000. Spoilage occurred only in the previous department. Consequently, 6,200,000 units were transferred out (250,000 + 6,000,000 - 50,000).

Questions 58 through 61 are based on information provided on page 156.

58. What is the number of equivalent units of production for material and conversion costs, respectively, for the box department under the weighted average method of process costing?

a. 6,000,000; 6,150,000.
b. 5,500,000; 5,750,000.
c. 5,700,000; 5,850,000.
d. 6,300,000; 6,150,000.

The correct answer is (d). *(Publisher)*
REQUIRED: The EUP for material and conversion costs under the weighted average method.
DISCUSSION: The EUP for June equal the number of good units transferred out plus the work completed in EWIP for the beginning and ending inventories in the box department. EWIP is 100% complete with respect to materials and 50% complete with respect to conversion costs.

	Materials	Conversion Costs
Transferred out - good	6,000,000	6,000,000
Inventory, June 30	300,000	150,000
EUP	6,300,000	6,150,000

59. What is the number of EUP for material and conversion costs, respectively, for the box department under the FIFO method of process costing?

a. 6,000,000; 6,150,000.
b. 5,500,000; 5,750,000.
c. 5,700,000; 5,850,000.
d. 6,300,000; 6,150,000.

The correct answer is (b). *(Publisher)*
REQUIRED: The EUP for material and conversion costs under the FIFO method.
DISCUSSION: The EUP under FIFO are the EUP for weighted average less the EUP that were completed as of June 1. Note that under FIFO, costs of prior periods are not averaged with costs of the current period. The June 1 BWIP in the box department was 800,000 units which are 100% complete as to material and 50% complete as to conversion. Accordingly, the weighted average EUP of 6,300,000 and 6,150,000 (see Q. 58) should be reduced by the EUP in BWIP of 800,000 and 400,000, respectively.

60. What are the unit material and conversion costs, respectively assuming weight average, for June for the box department?

a. $.05; $.04.
b. $.09; $.04.
c. $.06; $.04.
d. $.05; $.09.

The correct answer is (a). *(Publisher)*
REQUIRED: The unit material and conversion costs for the box department.
DISCUSSION: The unit costs are equal to the weighted average EUP divided into the total costs for materials and conversion costs. Material cost is $315,000. BWIP contained $35,000 of material cost and $280,000 of material was transferred to manufacturing (Q. 55). Divide $315,000 material cost by 6,300,000 EUP to determine per unit material cost of $.05. Conversion costs are given as $226,000 in June and $20,000 in BWIP. Divide $246,000 ($226,000 + $20,000) by the 6,150,000 EUP to determine per unit conversion cost of $.04.

61. What is the total unit cost for June for the box department?

a. $.09.
b. $.13.
c. $.10.
d. $.14.

The correct answer is (a). *(Publisher)*
REQUIRED: The total unit cost for June.
DISCUSSION: The total unit cost for the box department for the month is $.09, which is the sum of the material unit cost of $.05 and the conversion unit cost of $.04, as calculated in Q. 60.

Module 7.4: Comprehensive

> Questions 62 through 66 are based on information provided on page 156.

62. What is the number of total completed units and their material costs, respectively, for the box department?

a. 6,000,000; $540,000.
b. 5,400,000; $300,000.
c. 6,000,000; $300,000.
d. 2,900,000; $190,000.

The correct answer is (c). *(Publisher)*
REQUIRED: The total completed units and their material costs for the box department.
DISCUSSION: The total completed units equal the total units available, minus EI and spoilage. Their material costs equal the completed units times $.05 (unit cost for materials).

	Materials		
	Units	Unit Cost	Amount
Total units	6,300,000	$.05	$315,000
Inventory, 6/30	(300,000)	.05	(15,000)
Completed units	6,000,000	.05	$300,000

63. What are the total completed units and their conversion costs, respectively, in the box department?

a. 6,150,000; $561,000.
b. 6,000,000; $240,000.
c. 6,000,000; $540,000.
d. 6,150,000; $540,000.

The correct answer is (b). *(Publisher)*
REQUIRED: The total completed units and their conversion costs for the box department.
DISCUSSION: The conversion costs for the completed units equal the conversion costs available minus the conversion costs in EI.

	Conversion Costs		
	Units	Unit Cost	Amount
EUP	6,150,000	$.04	$246,000
Inventory, 6/30	(150,000)	.04	(6,000)
Total	6,000,000	.04	$240,000

64. How many units are available in finished goods and what is their cost?

a. 6,000,000; $558,000.
b. 250,000; $18,000.
c. 6,250,000; $620,625.
d. 6,250,000; $558,000.

The correct answer is (d). *(Publisher)*
REQUIRED: The available units in the finished goods department and their cost.
DISCUSSION: The number of units available is equal to the BI (250,000) plus the units accepted from the previous department (6,000,000), or 6,250,000. The cost of the initial inventory was $18,000, and the cost attributable to the 6,000,000 units accepted is $540,000 ($300,000 materials + $240,000 conversion costs). A total cost of $558,000 should be assigned to the 6,250,000 available units.

65. What is the unit cost for finished goods?

a. $.0893.
b. $.09.
c. $.0718.
d. $.0910.

The correct answer is (a). *(Publisher)*
REQUIRED: The total unit cost for finished goods.
DISCUSSION: The unit cost for finished goods equals the cost of inventory on June 1 ($18,000) plus the cost of units transferred in ($540,000), for a total of $558,000, which is then divided by the 6,250,000 available units. The unit cost is thus $.0893.

66. What is the cost of units sold for June?

a. $553,535.
b. $540,000.
c. $558,000.
d. $600,000.

The correct answer is (a). *(Publisher)*
REQUIRED: The cost of units sold for June.
DISCUSSION: The cost of units sold for June is the cost of total available units ($558,000) minus the cost of EI. The unit cost is the cost of total available units divided by the number of units (6,250,000), or $.0893 per unit, as calculated in Q. 65. EI consisted of 50,000 units at a unit cost of $.0893, or $4,465, resulting in a cost of units sold of $553,535 ($558,000 − $4,465).

Module 7.4: Comprehensive

67. What is a "Quantity of Production Report"?

   a. A report of the units completed this period in comparison with the immediately preceding period, and a moving average of the number completed during the twelve preceding periods.
   b. A report that details the units transferred into one or more manufacturing accounts during a period and the disposition of these units, i.e., the units completed, spoiled, and in EWIP.
   c. A cost of goods manufactured statement.
   d. A report that lists and accounts for all debits to the manufacturing account during the period and the disposition of these costs, i.e., the costs of units completed, spoiled, and in EWIP.

The correct answer is (b). *(Publisher)*
REQUIRED: The description of a quantity of production report.
DISCUSSION: A quantity of production report adds the units in BWIP and those entering the process during the period, and indicates the disposition of those units, i.e., the units completed, spoiled, and in EWIP, respectively.
Answer (a) is incorrect because the quantity of production report is only concerned with the units put into and transferred out of the process in the current period. Answer (c) is incorrect because the cost of goods manufactured statement gives the cost of goods completed rather than an accounting for all of the units that went into the process. Answer (d) is incorrect because it describes a cost of production report.

68. What is a "Cost of Production Report"?

   a. A report that lists and accounts for all debits to the manufacturing account during the period and the disposition of these costs, i.e., the costs of units completed, spoiled, and in EWIP.
   b. A report that details the units transferred into one or more manufacturing accounts during a period and the disposition of these units, i.e., the units completed, spoiled, and in EWIP.
   c. A cost of goods manufactured statement.
   d. A report that analyzes all of the variances from standard costs and the disposition of these variances by allocation among inventory accounts and CGS or by a charge only to CGS.

The correct answer is (a). *(Publisher)*
REQUIRED: The description of a cost of production report.
DISCUSSION: A cost of production report is a formalized statement of the data in a manufacturing or work-in-process account or accounts. All the debits in the account are added to determine the total cost for which the process is accountable. A listing gives the disposition of those costs to cost of goods completed, spoilage, EWIP, etc.
Answer (b) is incorrect because it describes a quantity of production report. Answer (c) is incorrect because the cost of goods manufactured account states the cost of goods completed, not the disposition of the costs incurred during the period. Answer (d) is incorrect because it describes an analysis of standard cost variances.

CHAPTER EIGHT
JOINT PRODUCTS AND BY-PRODUCTS

8.1 Definition of Joint/By-Products	(7 questions)	161
8.2 Allocation of Joint Costs	(8 questions)	163
8.3 Relative Sales Value	(14 questions)	165
8.4 Joint Costs/Relative Sales Value	(20 questions)	168
8.5 Sell/Process Decisions	(9 questions)	176
8.6 Journal Entries	(15 questions)	179
8.7 Comprehensive	(15 questions)	184

This chapter is concerned with the allocation methods for inventory purposes, the role of joint costs in decision making, and the accounting for by-products. The differentiation between the accounting treatment for inventory purposes and the accounting treatment for decision purposes is important. Remember, all joint cost allocations are arbitrary.

8.1 Definition of Joint/By-Products

1. If a company obtains two salable products from the refining of one ore, the refining process should be accounted for as a(n)

a. Mixed cost process.
b. Joint process.
c. Extractive process.
d. Reduction process.

The correct answer is (b). *(CPA 1177 T-39)*
REQUIRED: The type of costing process when two products are refined from one raw material.
DISCUSSION: When two or more separate products are produced by a common manufacturing process from a common input, the outputs from the process are called joint products. The common costs of two or more joint products with significant values are generally allocated to the joint products based upon the products' net realizable values at the point they became separate products.
Answer (a) is incorrect because mixed costs are costs that have both fixed and variable components. Answers (c) and (d) are incorrect because extractive and reduction processes are technical manufacturing terms and have no special meaning in cost accounting.

2. Joint costs are useful for

a. Setting the selling price of a product.
b. Determining whether to continue producing an item.
c. Controlling costs.
d. Evaluating management by means of a responsibility reporting system.
e. Determining inventory cost for accounting purposes.

The correct answer is (e). *(CIA 577 IV-3)*
REQUIRED: How joint costs are useful in cost accounting.
DISCUSSION: Joint costs are useful for inventory costing when a product is divided into two or more identifiable products through the production process. The joint costs of production must be allocated on some basis, such as relative sales value.
Answers (a) and (b) are incorrect because items such as additional processing costs, competitive conditions in sales markets, and the relative contribution margin of all products coming from the original product must be considered in setting selling prices and deciding whether to continue producing the common products. Joint costs are useful only for inventory costing of unsold units. Answer (c) is incorrect because joint costs for an individual product cannot be controlled; i.e., they are either incurred to produce all the joint products or not. Answer (d) is incorrect because management of one department may have no control over joint costs.

Module 8.1: Definition of Joint/By-Products

3. Which of the following components of production are allocable as joint costs when a single manufacturing process produces several salable products?

a. Materials, labor, and overhead.
b. Materials and labor only.
c. Labor and overhead only.
d. Overhead and materials only.

The correct answer is (a). *(CPA 579 T-31)*
REQUIRED: The components allocable as joint costs.
DISCUSSION: Joint costs are those costs incurred prior to the split-off point to produce two or more goods manufactured simultaneously by a single process or series of processes. Joint costs, which include materials, labor, and overhead, are not separately identifiable and must be allocated to the individual joint products.

4. Which of the following statements best describes a by-product?

a. A product that is produced from material that would otherwise be scrap.
b. A product that has a lower unit selling price than the main product.
c. A product created along with the main product whose sales value does not cover its cost of production.
d. A product that usually produces a small amount of revenue when compared to the main product's revenue.

The correct answer is (d). *(CPA 575 T-36)*
REQUIRED: The best description of a by-product.
DISCUSSION: By-product denotes one or more products of relatively small total value that are produced simultaneously with a product of greater value and quantity, generally called the "main product."
Answer (a) is incorrect because a by-product is produced with other products simultaneously from a common raw material or other input. Answer (b) is incorrect because a by-product has an insignificant, not just lower, selling price. Answer (c) is incorrect because the costs of producing joint products, including by-products, are not individually identifiable; they must be allocated by some means such as relative sales value.

5. By-products could have which of the following characteristics?

	Zero Costs Beyond Split-off	Additional Costs Beyond Split-off
a.	No	No
b.	No	Yes
c.	Yes	Yes
d.	Yes	No

The correct answer is (c). *(CPA 1186 T-44)*
REQUIRED: The characteristics of by-products.
DISCUSSION: By-products are joint products that have minor sales value as compared to the sales value of the major product(s). To be salable, the by-product may, or may not, require additional processing beyond the split-off point. Thus, the existence of costs beyond the split-off point are not required (but can exist).

6. The characteristic which is most often used to distinguish a product as either a joint product or a by-product is the

a. Amount of labor used in processing the product.
b. Amount of separable product costs that are incurred in processing.
c. Amount (i.e., weight, inches, etc.) of the product produced in the manufacturing process.
d. Relative sales value of the products produced in the process.

The correct answer is (d). *(CIA 1186 IV-7)*
REQUIRED: The trait that most often distinguishes a joint product from a by-product.
DISCUSSION: The difference between joint products and by-products lies in their relative sales values. Joint products have relative sales values that are significant in relation to each other. By-products have minor sales values compared with the major product(s).
Answers (a) and (b) are incorrect because neither provides a basis for defining joint/by-products or states a customary basis for allocating joint costs. Answer (c) is incorrect because while it gives a possible allocation base for joint costs, it does not define the joint/by-product distinction.

7. For the purposes of cost accumulation, which of the following are identifiable as different individual products before the split-off point?

	By-products	Joint Products
a.	Yes	Yes
b.	Yes	No
c.	No	No
d.	No	Yes

The correct answer is (c). *(CPA 587 T-44)*
REQUIRED: The type of product that is identifiable before the split-off point, for purposes of cost allocation.
DISCUSSION: In a joint production process, neither by-products nor joint products are separately identifiable as individual products until the split-off point. This is the definition of the split-off point. Common costs up to the split-off point are usually related to both joint products and by-products. After split-off, additional costs can be traced, and charged to, the individual products. These additional costs are called separable costs.

8.2 Allocation of Joint Costs

8. Each of the following is a method to allocate joint costs except

   a. Relative sales value.
   b. Relative profitability.
   c. Relative weight, volume, or linear measure.
   d. Average unit cost.

The correct answer is (b). *(CPA 1178 T-48)*
REQUIRED: The method not used to allocate joint costs.
DISCUSSION: There are several methods of allocating joint production costs, including the quantitative (physical unit) method, based on some physical measure such as volume, weight, or a linear measure; the market or sales value method, based on the relative market values of the separate products; the weighted average method, based on a predetermined standard or index of production; and the average unit cost method. Relative profitability is not possible to allocate joint costs because the method of joint cost allocation determines profitability.

9. If two or more products share a common process before they are separated, the joint costs should be allocated in a manner that

   a. Assigns a proportionate amount of the total cost to each product by means of a quantitative basis.
   b. Maximizes total earnings.
   c. Minimizes variations in unit of production costs.
   d. Does not introduce an element of estimation into the process of accumulating costs for each product.

The correct answer is (a). *(CPA 578 T-38)*
REQUIRED: The manner in which joint costs should be allocated.
DISCUSSION: There are several methods of allocating joint production costs, including the quantitative (physical unit) method, based on some physical measure such as volume, weight, or a linear measure; the market or sales value method, based on the relative market values of the separate products; the weighted average method, based on a predetermined standard or index of production; and the average unit cost method. Each of these methods assigns a proportionate amount of the total cost to each product on a quantitative basis.
Answers (b) and (c) are incorrect because the objective of joint cost allocation is inventory costing of unsold units. Answer (d) is incorrect because most accounting techniques introduce an element of estimation into the process of accumulating costs, e.g., depreciation.

10. At the split-off point, products may be immediately salable or may require further processing. Which of the following products have both of these characteristics?

	By-products	Joint Products
a.	No	No
b.	No	Yes
c.	Yes	No
d.	Yes	Yes

The correct answer is (d). *(CPA 1181 T-49)*
REQUIRED: Product(s) that can be sold or processed further at the split-off point.
DISCUSSION: The difference between joint products and by-products lies in their relative sales value compared to other products being produced. The term joint products is used when the relative sales values of the individual products are significant in relation to each other. The term by-products is used when the products have a minor sales value as compared with the major product(s).

11. Under an acceptable method of costing by-products, inventory costs of the by-product are based on the portion of the joint production cost allocated to the by-product

a. But any subsequent processing cost is debited to the cost of the main product.
b. But any subsequent processing cost is debited to revenue of the main product.
c. Plus any subsequent processing cost.
d. Less any subsequent processing cost.

The correct answer is (c). *(CPA 581 T-49)*
REQUIRED: The correct statement about inventory costs for by-product(s).
DISCUSSION: By-product is a term used to denote one or more products of relatively small total value that are produced simultaneously with a product of greater value and quantity, generally called the "main product." One method of accounting for by-products is to recognize the value as it is produced. Inventory costs of the by-products would be based on an allocation of some portion of joint costs plus any subsequent processing costs.
Answers (a), (b), and (d) are incorrect because, under this method, separable processing costs must be assigned to by-products.

12. One of the accepted methods of accounting for a by-product is to recognize the value of the by-product as it is produced. Under this method, inventory costs for the by-product would be based on

a. An allocation of some portion of joint costs but not any subsequent processing costs.
b. Neither an allocation of some portion of joint costs nor any subsequent processing costs.
c. Subsequent processing costs less an allocation of some portion of joint costs.
d. An allocation of some portion of joint costs plus any subsequent processing costs.

The correct answer is (d). *(CPA 1179 T-33)*
REQUIRED: Basis for costing when assigning value as the by-products are produced.
DISCUSSION: By-product is a term used to denote one or more products of relatively small total value that are produced simultaneously with a product of greater value and quantity, generally called the "main product." Inventory costs of the by-products when using the method that recognizes a product's value as it is produced would be based on an allocation of some portion of joint costs plus any subsequent processing costs.
Answer (a) is incorrect because, after split-off, any cost separately attributed to the by-product should be added to the cost of that product. Answer (b) is incorrect because, under the specified accounting method, joint costs and subsequent processing costs must both be charged to the by-product. Answer (c) is incorrect because the allocation of joint costs is added to, not subtracted from, the subsequent processing costs after split-off.

13. In the two immediately preceding questions, why was joint cost allocated to by-products?

a. They were treated as joint products even though they presumably met the definition of by-products by having small relative sales values.
b. All by-products must be allocated some portion of joint costs.
c. By requirement of the Cost Accounting Standards Board (CASB).
d. Because the by-products produced a loss.

The correct answer is (a). *(Publisher)*
REQUIRED: An explanation of the allocation of joint cost to by-products.
DISCUSSION: The preferred treatment of by-products is to account for their revenues or net realizable values as a reduction in the joint cost prior to allocation of joint cost to joint products. It is acceptable, however, to allocate joint cost to by-products as well as to joint products. In that case, they are treated like joint products even though they could be called by-products due to their small relative value.
Answers (b) and (c) are incorrect because allocation of joint cost to by-products is required by neither GAAP nor the CASB. Answer (d) is incorrect because if joint cost is allocated to the by-products based on relative sales value, the by-products will produce an income if joint products produce income. The gross profit (loss) percentage is the same on all joint products, which include by-products under this allocation treatment.

Module 8.3: Relative Sales Value

14. The issue concerning recognition of by-product revenue and/or sales is similar to the same issues involving

  a. Joint products.
  b. Scrap.
  c. Product costs.
  d. Period costs.

The correct answer is (b). *(Publisher)*
REQUIRED: The item that involves issues similar to those dealing with by-products.
DISCUSSION: Scrap and by-products are usually similar in nature, both physically and from an accounting point of view. Scrap might even be considered a by-product of a manufacturing process. While joint cost is almost never allocated to scrap, joint cost may be allocated to by-products. The main issue, however, is when to recognize revenue from the sale of the scrap or by-product: at the time of production or at the time of sale. Generally, the revenue or sales value is considered a reduction of the cost of the joint products or material costs.
Answer (a) is incorrect because the timing of revenue recognition is usually not an issue for joint products. Answers (c) and (d) are incorrect because product and period costs are not related to revenue recognition.

15. It is theoretically preferable to account for by-products by

  a. Attaching the further processing costs and matching this with revenue at point of sale.
  b. Attaching the further processing costs and an appropriate share of joint costs and matching this with revenue at point of sale.
  c. Attaching no cost and considering revenue from sale as other income.
  d. Attaching no cost and reducing the cost of the main product by the net realizable value of the by-product.

The correct answer is (d). *(Publisher)*
REQUIRED: The theoretically preferable method of accounting for by-products.
DISCUSSION: Because of the minor sales value of by-products, more expedient cost accounting procedures are used. Instead of attaching costs to the by-products, their net realizable value is considered a reduction of the cost of the main products.
Answers (a) and (b) are incorrect because each attaches cost to the by-products, which is a procedure reserved for main products. Although used in practice, answer (c) is less preferable because it overstates the cost of the main products.

8.3 Relative Sales Value

16. Joint costs are most frequently allocated based upon relative

  a. Profitability.
  b. Conversion costs.
  c. Prime costs.
  d. Sales value.

The correct answer is (d). *(CPA 581 T-48)*
REQUIRED: The basis upon which joint costs are most frequently allocated.
DISCUSSION: In the relative sales value method (a frequently used way to allocate joint costs to joint products), joint costs are allocated based upon the products' proportion of total sales revenue. For joint products salable at the split-off point, the relative sales value is the selling price at split-off. If further processing is needed, the relative sales value is approximated by subtracting the additional processing costs from the final sales value.
Answer (a) is incorrect because profitability cannot be determined until joint costs have been allocated. Answer (b) is incorrect because conversion costs include only direct labor and factory overhead. Answer (c) is incorrect because prime costs include only direct labor and direct materials.

17. Relative sales value at split-off is used to allocate

	Cost Beyond Split-off	Joint Costs
a.	Yes	Yes
b.	Yes	No
c.	No	Yes
d.	No	No

The correct answer is (c). *(CPA 1182 T-44)*
REQUIRED: The use for relative sales value at the split-off point.
DISCUSSION: The relative sales value for each product is used to allocate joint costs. The costs beyond the split-off point can be identified to and thus assigned to each product. Therefore, no allocation is needed.

Module 8.3: Relative Sales Value

18. For purposes of allocating joint costs to joint products using the relative sales value at split-off method, the costs beyond split-off

    a. Are allocated in the same manner as the joint costs.
    b. Are deducted from the relative sales value at split-off.
    c. Are deducted from the sales value at point of sale.
    d. Do not affect the allocation of the joint costs.

The correct answer is (c). (CPA 1184 T-52)
REQUIRED: The effect of costs beyond split-off on cost allocation.
DISCUSSION: Relative sales value at split-off is used to allocate joint costs to joint products based upon their relative proportions of total sales revenue. For joint products requiring no additional processing, the relative sales value is the price at split-off. For joint products requiring additional processing, the relative sales value is estimated by subtracting the additional processing costs from the terminal sales value.
    Answer (a) is incorrect because the costs beyond split-off can be attributed to a specific product. Answer (b) is incorrect because costs beyond split-off are deducted from the final sales value, not from sales value at split-off. Answer (d) is incorrect because the costs beyond split-off are deducted from the final sales value to arrive at relative sales value at split-off.

19. For purposes of allocating joint costs to joint products, the relative sales value at split-off method could be used in which of the following situations?

	No Costs Beyond Split-off	Costs Beyond Split-off
a.	Yes	Yes
b.	Yes	No
c.	No	Yes
d.	No	No

The correct answer is (a). (CPA 582 T-44)
REQUIRED: The situation(s) in which the relative sales value at split-off method could be used to allocate joint costs.
DISCUSSION: The relative sales value at split-off method is used to allocate joint costs to the separate products at the split-off point. Joint costs are allocated based upon each product's proportion of total sales revenue. For joint products salable at the split-off point, the relative sales value is the selling price at split-off. If further processing is needed, the relative sales value is approximated by subtracting additional processing costs from the final sales value.

20. The method of accounting for joint product costs that will produce the same gross profit rate for all products is the

    a. Relative sales value method.
    b. Physical measure method.
    c. Actual costing method.
    d. Services received method.

The correct answer is (a). (CPA 1172 T-29)
REQUIRED: The method of accounting for joint product costs that produces the same gross profit rate for all products.
DISCUSSION: The relative sales value method produces the same gross profit rate because it requires a weighted market value for each unit.
    Answer (b) is incorrect because physical measure may not be related to the market value of separate products. Answer (c) is incorrect because cost allocation is used since the actual cost of the products cannot be determined. Answer (d) is incorrect because services received has no meaning in joint product costing.

21. A company produces three main joint products and one by-product. The by-product's relative sales value is quite low compared to that of the main products. The preferable accounting for the by-product's net realizable value is as

    a. An addition to the revenues of the other products allocated on their respective net realizable values.
    b. Revenue in the period it is sold.
    c. A reduction in the common cost to be allocated to the three main products.
    d. A separate net realizable value upon which to allocate some of the common costs.

The correct answer is (c). (CIA 585 IV-11)
REQUIRED: The preferable accounting method for by-products.
DISCUSSION: Because of the relatively small sales value, a cost-effective allocation method is used for by-products. The net realizable value of by-products is usually deducted from the cost of the main products.
    Answers (a) and (d) are incorrect because each attributes the allocation characteristics of main products to by-products. Answer (b) is incorrect because the NRV is recognized as a contra cost in the period the by-product is produced.

Module 8.3: Relative Sales Value

22. Actual sales values at the split-off point for joint products Y and Z are not known. For purposes of allocating joint costs to products Y and Z, the relative sales value at split-off method is used. An increase in the costs beyond split-off occurs for product Z, while those of product Y remain constant. If the selling prices of finished products Y and Z remain constant, the percentage of the total joint costs allocated to product Y and product Z would

   a. Decrease for product Y and product Z.
   b. Decrease for product Y and increase for product Z.
   c. Increase for product Y and product Z.
   d. Increase for product Y and decrease for product Z.

The correct answer is (d). *(CPA 1187 T-43)*
REQUIRED: The effect on the allocation of joint costs, given an increase in separable costs beyond split-off for one product.
DISCUSSION: Since the actual sales values of products Y and Z are not known, an approximate sales value is determined by subtracting any estimated costs after split-off from the estimated sales value. Assuming constant selling prices, and increasing costs for product Z, the sales value at split-off for Z must necessarily be decreasing. The relative sales value method allocates joint costs on the ratio of each products relative sales value at split-off to the total sales value at split-off for all products. Therefore, the costs allocated to Z must be decreasing while the costs allocated to Y are increasing.

Questions 23 through 29 are based on Earl Corporation, which manufactures a product that gives rise to a by-product called "Zafa". The only costs associated with Zafa are selling costs of $1 for each unit sold. Earl accounts for Zafa sales first by deducting its separable costs from such sales, and then by deducting this net amount from cost of sales of the major product. This year, 1,000 units of Zafa were sold at $4 each.

---

23. If Earl changes its method of accounting for Zafa sales by showing the net amount as additional sales revenue, Earl's gross margin would

   a. Be unaffected.
   b. Increase by $3,000.
   c. Decrease by $3,000.
   d. Increase by $4,000.

The correct answer is (a). *(CPA 1182 Q-39)*
REQUIRED: The effect on gross margin of changing the treatment of by-product sales.
DISCUSSION: The gross margin is computed by subtracting cost of goods sold from sales revenue. Before the change, the net amount was deducted from cost of sales (i.e., it increased the gross margin). Since after the change the net amount is added to regular sales with no additional increase in cost of goods sold, the gross margin will not change.

24. If Earl changes its method of accounting for Zafa sales by showing the net amount as "Other Income," Earl's gross margin would

   a. Be unaffected.
   b. Increase by $3,000.
   c. Decrease by $3,000.
   d. Decrease by $4,000.

The correct answer is (c). *(CPA 1182 Q-40)*
REQUIRED: The effect on gross margin of accounting for by-product sales as other income.
DISCUSSION: Sales revenue minus cost of goods sold is gross margin. If the net revenue from the by-product is recorded as other income rather than being deducted from cost of goods sold, the gross margin will decrease by $3,000 [1,000 x ($4 sales - $1 CGS)].

25. If Earl recorded the net realizable value of Zafa as inventory as it was produced, what would the per unit value be?

   a. $1.
   b. $2.
   c. $3.
   d. $4.

The correct answer is (c). *(Publisher)*
REQUIRED: The unit net realizable value of the by-product.
DISCUSSION: The net realizable value is selling price less cost to complete and cost to dispose. The selling price of Zafa was $4, and the selling costs are $1. There are no completion or additional processing costs. Accordingly, unit net realizable value is $3.

Module 8.4: Joint Costs/Relative Sales Value

Questions 26 through 29 are based on the information on page 167.

26. If the net realizable value were recorded as inventory, what account would be credited?

a. Finished goods inventory.
b. Cost of sales.
c. Work-in-process.
d. Other income.

The correct answer is (c). *(Publisher)*
REQUIRED: The account credited if the by-product is recorded as inventory as it is produced.
DISCUSSION: As a by-product is produced, by-product inventory is debited and production costs are credited; i.e., the net realizable value of the by-product is considered a reduction in the costs of production. Thus the work-in-process account would be credited.

27. If Earl's production of Zafa were 1,500 units for the year and net realizable value were recorded as inventory, Earl's net income would increase by

a. $6,000.
b. $4,500.
c. $3,000.
d. $1,500.

The correct answer is (b). *(Publisher)*
REQUIRED: The change in net income if 1,500 units were produced and inventory were valued at net realizable value.
DISCUSSION: If inventory is valued at net realizable value, and if production exceeds sales by 500 units (1,500 produced - 1,000 sold), inventory will increase by $4,500 (1,500 units x $3 per unit net realizable value). This increase in inventory decreases production costs by $4,500, which in turn increases profits by $4,500.

28. If Earl recorded Zafa inventory at net realizable value as it was produced this year, what would be the profit recognized next year on a sale of 500 units?

a. $0.
b. $500.
c. $1,000.
d. $1,500.

The correct answer is (a). *(Publisher)*
REQUIRED: The profit from the sale of inventory valued at net realizable value.
DISCUSSION: Since net realizable value is selling price minus completion and disposal cost, there is no profit upon sale. The sale of 500 units of Zafa with an inventory value of $3 per unit would produce no profit because they would be sold for $4 per unit, and have a $1 per unit selling cost ($4 revenue - $3 inventory cost - $1 selling cost = $0). Earl must mark the cost up to realize any profit.

29. If the values of by-products are recorded as produced, why should they be recorded at net realizable value less normal profit?

a. To permit a sales profit to be recognized upon sale.
b. To be valued at the lower of cost or market.
c. To control the loss upon sale.
d. To recognize a profit when the inventory value is recorded.

The correct answer is (a). *(Publisher)*
REQUIRED: Why by-products should be valued at net realizable value less normal profit.
DISCUSSION: If inventory is valued at NRV minus normal profit, normal profit is recognized upon sale of the product. This treatment provides incentive to sell the by-product.
Answer (b) is incorrect because valuing at NRV less normal profit ignores the literal concept of cost. Answer (c) is incorrect because valuation at NRV less normal profit implies that some profit is to be recognized upon sale. Answer (d) is incorrect because if a cost is credited for the value of the inventory, no profit is recorded when inventory is recorded, i.e., debit inventory and credit WIP.

8.4 Joint Costs/Relative Sales Value

30. Lowe Co. manufactures products A and B from a joint process. Sales value at split-off was $700,000 for 10,000 units of A, and $300,000 for 15,000 units of B. Using the sales value at split-off approach, joint costs properly allocated to A were $140,000. Total joint costs were

a. $98,000.
b. $200,000.
c. $233,333.
d. $350,000.

The correct answer is (b). *(CPA 586 Q-39)*
REQUIRED: The total joint costs given the joint costs properly allocated to one product.
DISCUSSION: The relative sales value is a cost allocation method that allocates joint costs in proportion to the relative sales value of the individual products. Total sales value is $1,000,000 ($700,000 for A + $300,000 for B). The $140,000 of joint costs allocated to product A were 7/10 of total joint costs. The calculation for total joint costs (Y) is

$$(7/10)Y = \$140,000$$
$$Y = \$140,000 \div (7/10)$$
$$Y = \$200,000$$

Module 8.4: Joint Costs/Relative Sales Value

31. A company processes raw material into products F1, F2, and F3. Each ton of raw material produces five units of F1, two units of F2, and three units of F3. Joint-processing costs to the split-off point are $15/ton. Further processing results in the following per unit figures:

	F1	F2	F3
Additional processing costs per unit	$28	$30	$25
Selling price per unit	30	35	35

If joint costs are allocated by the net realizable value of finished product, what proportion of joint costs should be allocated to F1?

a. 20%.
b. 30%.
c. 33-1/3%.
d. 50%.

The correct answer is (a). *(CIA 586 IV-11)*
REQUIRED: The proportion of joint costs that should be allocated to product F1.
DISCUSSION: To determine the proportion of joint costs to be allocated to F1, the net realizable values of the three products must be calculated. Net realizable value per unit is selling price minus additional processing costs.

F1: 5(30 - 28) = 10
F2: 2(35 - 30) = 10
F3: 3(35 - 25) = 30
                   50

The amount of joint costs to be allocated to F1 is 10/50 or 20%.

32. A company manufactures products X and Y using a joint process. The joint processing costs are $10,000. Products X and Y can be sold at split-off for $12,000 and $8,000 respectively. After split-off, product X is processed further at a cost of $5,000 and sold for $21,000 whereas product Y is sold without further processing. If the company uses the net realizable value method for allocating joint costs, the joint cost allocated to X is

a. $4,000.
b. $5,000.
c. $6,000.
d. $6,667.

The correct answer is (c). *(CIA 1185 IV-11)*
REQUIRED: The joint costs allocated to Product X.
DISCUSSION: Under the net realizable value method, joint costs are allocated based on their relative net realizable value unless sales price quotations are available at split-off. Since split-off sales price quotations are available, the amount of joint costs allocated to product X can be computed as follows:

$$\frac{\text{Sales value of Product X}}{\text{Total sales value}} \times \text{Joint costs}$$

$$= \frac{\$12,000}{\$20,000} \times \$10,000$$

$$= \$6,000$$

33. Ohio Corporation manufactures liquid chemicals A and B from a joint process. Joint costs are allocated on the basis of relative sales value at split-off. It costs $4,560 to process 500 gallons of product A and 1,000 gallons of product B to the split-off point. The sales value at split-off is $10 per gallon for product A and $14 for product B. Product B requires an additional process beyond split-off at a cost of $1 per gallon before it can be sold. What is Ohio's cost to produce 1,000 gallons of product B?

a. $3,360.
b. $3,660.
c. $4,040.
d. $4,360.

The correct answer is (d). *(CPA 1180 P-32)*
REQUIRED: The cost to produce 1,000 gallons of a joint product.
DISCUSSION: The total cost to produce 1,000 gallons of product B is the joint costs allocated to the product at split-off plus any subsequent processing costs. The calculation is

	Net Realizable Value	Weighting Factor	Joint Costs Allocated
A	$ 5,000		
B	14,000	(14/19) x $4,560	$3,360
	$19,000		

The $1,000 additional processing costs after split-off plus the $3,360 joint cost allocated gives $4,360, the cost to produce 1,000 gallons of product B.

Module 8.4: Joint Costs/Relative Sales Value

34. Helen Corp. manufactures products W, X, Y, and Z from a joint process. Additional information is as follows:

Product	Units Produced	Sales Value at Split-off	If Processed Further Additional Costs	Sales Value
W	6,000	$ 80,000	$ 7,500	$ 90,000
X	5,000	60,000	6,000	70,000
Y	4,000	40,000	4,000	50,000
Z	3,000	20,000	2,500	30,000
	18,000	$200,000	$20,000	$240,000

Assuming that total joint costs of $160,000 were allocated using the relative sales value at split-off approach, what joint costs were allocated to each product?

	W	X	Y	Z
a.	$40,000	$40,000	$40,000	$40,000
b.	$53,333	$44,444	$35,556	$26,667
c.	$60,000	$46,667	$33,333	$20,000
d.	$64,000	$48,000	$32,000	$16,000

The correct answer is (d). *(CPA 1178 P-21)*
REQUIRED: The joint costs allocated to each product using the relative sales value at split-off approach.
DISCUSSION: The relative sales value is a cost allocation method that allocates joint costs in proportion to the relative sales of the individual products. The calculation is

	Sales Value at Split-Off	Weighting Factor	Joint Costs Allocated
W	$ 80,000	8/20 x $160,000	$ 64,000
X	60,000	6/20 x 160,000	48,000
Y	40,000	4/20 x 160,000	32,000
Z	20,000	2/20 x 160,000	16,000
	$200,000		$160,000

Note that the costs incurred after split-off are not joint costs and are therefore not included.

35. A cheese company produces natural cheese from cow's milk. As a result of the process, a secondary product, whey, is produced in a proportion of one pound for each pound of cheese. The data give the standards set for 1,000 pounds of cow's milk:

Input: 1,000 pounds of cow's milk at $.20/pound
40 hours of labor at $10/hour
Overhead is applied at a basis of 100% of direct labor cost

Output: 450 pounds of cheese
450 pounds of whey

The following prices and demand are expected:

	Price per Pound	Demand in Pounds
Cheese	$2.00	450
Whey	.80	375

Given that the cheese company allocates common costs on the basis of net realizable values, the allocated common costs per 1,000 pounds of cow's milk for cheese and whey would be (rounded to nearest dollar), respectively,

	Common Cost Allocation to Cheese	to Whey
a.	$450	$150
b.	$500	$500
c.	$714	$286
d.	$750	$250

The correct answer is (d). *(CIA 1184 IV-23)*
REQUIRED: The common cost allocation to the joint products.
DISCUSSION: The relative sales value method allocates costs in proportion to the relative sales value of the individual products. The total common costs are

Milk (1,000 lbs. x $.20)		$ 200
Labor (40 hrs. x $10)		400
O/H (1.0 x $400 DL cost)		400
Common costs		$1,000

Sales Value:
Cheese ($2 x 450)	$ 900	75%
Whey ($.80 x 375)	300	25%
Total	$1,200	
Cost to cheese (75% x 1,000)	$ 750	
Cost to whey (25% x 1,000)	250	
	$1,000	

Note that if only 375 pounds of whey can be sold, the other 75 pounds are worthless and are not allocated any common cost.

Module 8.4: Joint Costs/Relative Sales Value

36. A lumber company produces two-by-fours and four-by-eights as joint products and sawdust as a by-product. The packaged sawdust can be sold for $2 per pound. Packaging costs for the sawdust are $.10 per pound and sales commissions are 10% of sales price. The by-product net revenue serves to reduce joint processing costs for joint products. Joint products are assigned joint costs based on board feet. Data follows:

Joint processing costs	$ 50,000
Two-by-fours produced (board feet)	200,000
Four-by-eights produced (board feet)	100,000
Sawdust produced (pounds)	1,000

What is the cost assigned to two-by-fours?

a. $32,000.
b. $32,133.
c. $32,200.
d. $33,333.

The correct answer is (c). *(CIA 587 IV-6)*
REQUIRED: The cost assigned to a joint product when joint products and a by-product are produced.
DISCUSSION: The net revenue from sale of the by-product is $1,700 [($2 price x 1,000 lbs.) - ($.10 x 1,000 lbs.) - (.1 x $2 x 1,000 lbs.)]. Joint processing costs to be allocated to joint products are therefore $48,300 ($50,000 - $1,700 net by-product revenue). Of this amount, $32,200 should be assigned to the two-by-fours [$48,300 x (200,000 board feet of two-by-fours ÷ 300,000 total board feet)].

37. Lite Co. manufactures products X and Y from a joint process that also yields a by-product, Z. Revenue from sales of Z is treated as a reduction of joint costs. Additional information is as follows:

	Products			
	X	Y	Z	Total
Units produced	20,000	20,000	10,000	50,000
Joint costs	?	?	?	$262,000
Sales value at split-off	$300,000	$150,000	$10,000	$460,000

Joint costs were allocated using the sales value at split-off approach. The joint costs allocated to product X were

a. $75,000.
b. $100,800.
c. $150,000.
d. $168,000.

The correct answer is (d). *(CPA 1186 Q-39)*
REQUIRED: The joint cost allocated using relative sales value.
DISCUSSION: The relative sales value method allocates joint costs in proportion to the relative sales value of the individual products. The relative minor value of the by-product is not allocated to any joint products (sales proceeds are contra CGS). Given total joint costs to allocate of $252,000 ($262,000 - $10,000) and the total sales value at split-off for main products of $450,000 ($300,000 product X + $150,000 product Y), the calculation for joint costs allocated to product X is

$$300/450 \times \$252,000 = \$168,000$$

38. Gilbert Manufacturing Company manufactures two products, Alt and Bat. They are initially processed from the same raw material and then, after split-off, further processed separately. Additional information is as follows:

	Alt	Bat	Total
Final sales price	$9,000	$6,000	$15,000
Joint costs prior to split-off point	?	?	6,600
Costs beyond split-off point	3,000	3,000	6,000

Using the relative sales value approach, what are the assigned joint costs of Alt and Bat, respectively?

a. $3,300 and $3,300.
b. $3,960 and $2,640.
c. $4,400 and $2,200.
d. $4,560 and $2,040.

The correct answer is (c). *(CPA 1176 P-24)*
REQUIRED: The allocated joint costs using the relative sales value approach.
DISCUSSION: Joint costs are those incurred up to the split-off point. The relative sales value method allocates joint costs in proportion to the relative sales value of the individual products. In this question, because no sales value is given at split-off, an approximate sales value at split-off is determined by working backwards from the final sales value.

	Final Sales Value	Less Costs Beyond Split-Off	Approximate NRV After Split-Off
Alt	$9,000	$(3,000)	$6,000
Bat	6,000	(3,000)	3,000
			$9,000

Given total joint costs of $6,600, the allocation is:

Alt: 6/9 x $6,600 = $4,400
Bat: 3/9 x $6,600 = $2,200

Module 8.4: Joint Costs/Relative Sales Value

Questions 39 and 40 are based on Vreeland, Inc., which manufactures products X, Y, and Z from a joint process. Joint product costs were $60,000. Additional information is provided below.

Product	Units Produced	Sales Value at Split-Off	If Processed Further Sales Values	Additional Costs
X	6,000	$40,000	$55,000	$9,000
Y	4,000	$35,000	$45,000	$7,000
Z	2,000	$25,000	$30,000	$5,000

---

39. Assuming that joint product costs are allocated using the physical measures (units produced) approach, what were the total costs allocated to product X?

a. $27,000.
b. $29,000.
c. $33,000.
d. $39,000.

The correct answer is (d). *(CPA 1177 P-27)*
REQUIRED: The total costs allocated to a joint product using the physical units produced method.
DISCUSSION: When using the physical measures approach, joint costs are allocated on the basis of each product's relative portion of the total number of physical units produced. The total costs allocated to product X are equal to the cost allocated at split-off plus the additional costs to complete. The weighting factor is 6,000 units of X divided by 12,000 total units produced.

	Weighting Factor	Joint Cost Allocated
	6/12 x $60,000	$30,000
Cost allocated at split-off		$30,000
Additional costs		9,000
Total costs allocated		$39,000

---

40. Assuming that joint product costs are allocated using the relative sales value at split-off approach, what were the total costs allocated to product Y?

a. $27,000.
b. $28,000.
c. $28,350.
d. $32,200.

The correct answer is (b). *(CPA 1177 P-28)*
REQUIRED: The total costs allocated to product Y using relative sales value.
DISCUSSION: The total costs allocated to product Y are equal to the cost allocated at split-off plus the additional costs to complete. The relative sales value method allocates joint costs in proportion to the relative sales value of the individual products. Since the split-off sale value is known ($35,000) and the total sales value is $100,000 ($40,000 + $35,000 + $25,000), the calculation is

	Weighting Factor	Joint Cost Allocated
	35/100 x $60,000	$21,000
Cost allocated at split-off		$21,000
Additional processing cost		7,000
Total costs allocated		$28,000

Questions 41 and 42 are based on Forward, Inc., which manufactures products P, Q, and R from a joint process.
Additional information:

	P	Q	R	Total
Units produced	4,000	2,000	1,000	7,000
Joint costs	$36,000	?	?	$60,000
Sales value at split-off	?	?	$15,000	$100,000
Additional costs if processed further	$7,000	$5,000	$3,000	$15,000
Sales value if processed further	$70,000	$30,000	$20,000	$120,000

Module 8.4: Joint Costs/Relative Sales Value

41. Assuming that joint product costs are allocated using the relative sales value at split-off approach, what joint costs were allocated to products Q and R?

a. $12,000 for Q and $12,000 for R.
b. $14,400 for Q and $9,600 for R.
c. $15,000 for Q and $9,000 for R.
d. $16,000 for Q and $8,000 for R.

The correct answer is (c). *(CPA 578 P-22)*
REQUIRED: The joint costs allocated using the relative sales value method.
DISCUSSION: The $36,000 of joint costs allocated to P are 60% of the $60,000 in total joint costs. The sales value of R is $15,000, and the total sales value is $100,000. To determine the joint costs allocated to Q and R, solve for the allocation to R and then subtract the joint costs for P and R from the total joint costs to get the allocation for Q.

	Sales Value	Weighting Factor	Joint Cost Allocated
P		given	$36,000
Q		forced	15,000
R	$ 15,000	15/100 x $60,000	9,000
	$100,000	given	$60,000

42. Assuming that joint costs are allocated using the relative sales value at split-off approach, what was the sales value at split-off for product P?

a. $58,333.
b. $59,500.
c. $60,000.
d. $63,000.

The correct answer is (c). *(CPA 578 P-23)*
REQUIRED: The sales value at split-off using relative sales value.
DISCUSSION: The $36,000 of joint costs allocated to P is 60% of the $60,000 in total joint costs ($36,000 ÷ $60,000 = 60%). Let Y = relative sales value of P.

$$(Y \div \$100,000) \times \$60,000 = \$36,000$$
$$Y \div \$100,000 = \$36,000 \div \$60,000$$
$$Y = .6 \times \$100,000$$
$$Y = \$60,000$$

43. Andy Company manufactures products N, P, and R from a joint process. The following information is available:

	N	P	R	Total
Units produced	12,000	?	?	24,000
Joint costs	$ 48,000	?	?	$120,000
Sales value at split-off	?	?	$50,000	$200,000
Additional costs if processed further	$ 18,000	$14,000	$10,000	$ 42,000
Sales value if processed further	$110,000	$90,000	$60,000	$260,000

Assuming that joint product costs are allocated using the relative sales value at split-off approach, what was the sales value at split-off for products N and P?

	Product N	Product P
a.	$ 66,000	$84,000
b.	$ 80,000	$70,000
c.	$ 98,000	$84,000
d.	$100,000	$50,000

The correct answer is (b). *(CPA 579 P-32)*
REQUIRED: The relative sales value at split-off for two joint products.
DISCUSSION: The relative sales value method allocates joint costs in proportion to the relative sales value of the individual products.

	Sales Value	Weighting Factor	Joint Cost Allocated
N	X	(X ÷ 200) 120,000	$ 48,000
P	Y		
R	$ 50,000	(50 ÷ 200) 120,000	
	$200,000		$120,000

X is calculated below from the information given. Note that 40% of the cost is allocated to product N, which means the sales value of N is 40% of the total sales value. Y is equal to the difference between total sales value at split-off ($200,000) and the sales value for products N and P ($80,000 + $50,000), or $70,000.

$$(X \div \$200,000) \times \$120,000 = \$48,000$$
$$X \div \$200,000 = .4$$
$$X = \$80,000$$

Module 8.4: Joint Costs/Relative Sales Value

44. Ashwood Company manufactures three main products, F, G, and W, from a joint process. Joint costs are allocated on the basis of relative sales value at split-off. Additional information for June production activity follows:

	F	G	W	Total
Units produced	50,000	40,000	10,000	100,000
Joint costs	?	?	?	$450,000
Sales value at split-off	$420,000	$270,000	$60,000	$750,000
Additional costs if processed further	$ 88,000	$ 30,000	$12,000	$130,000
Sales value if processed further	$538,000	$320,000	$78,000	$936,000

Assuming that the 10,000 units of W were processed further and sold for $78,000, what was Ashwood's gross profit on this sale?

a. $21,000.
b. $28,500.
c. $30,000.
d. $66,000.

The correct answer is (c). (CPA 1181 P-22)
REQUIRED: The gross profit on the sale of a joint product that is processed beyond split-off.
DISCUSSION: The relative sales value method allocates joint costs in proportion to the relative sales value of the individual products. Since the split-off sales value of $60,000 is known, this value should be used to determine the joint cost allocation to the products. The total sales value at split-off is $750,000.

	Sales Value	Weighting Factor	Joint Cost Allocated
W	$ 60,000	60/750 x $450,000	$ 36,000

The joint cost allocated at split-off is thus $36,000. The units are processed further at a cost of $12,000 and sold for $78,000. The gross profit is thus $30,000 ($78,000 - $36,000 - $12,000).

Questions 45 and 46 are based on Warfield Corporation, which manufactures products C, D, and E from a joint process. Joint costs are allocated on the basis of relative sales value at split-off. Additional information is presented below.

	C	D	E	Total
Units produced	6,000	4,000	2,000	12,000
Joint costs	$ 72,000	?	?	$120,000
Sales value at split-off	?	?	$30,000	$200,000
Additional costs if processed further	$ 14,000	$10,000	$ 6,000	$ 30,000
Sales value if processed further	$140,000	$60,000	$40,000	$240,000

---

45. How much of the joint costs should Warfield allocate to product D?

a. $24,000.
b. $28,800.
c. $30,000.
d. $32,000.

The correct answer is (c). (CPA 583 P-35)
REQUIRED: The joint costs allocated to product D.
DISCUSSION: Since total joint costs are $120,000 and total sales value at split-off is $200,000, the ratio of joint costs to sales value is 60% ($120,000/$200,000). Since the joint costs of product C are $72,000, C's sales value at split-off is $120,000 ($72,000 ÷ 60%). Given product C's sales value of $120,000, D's sales value is $50,000 ($200,000 - $30,000E - $120,000C). Thus, the joint costs of product D are $30,000, which is 60% of D's $50,000 sales value at split-off.

46. Assuming that the 2,000 units of product E were processed further and sold for $40,000, what was Warfield's gross profit on the sale?

a. $4,000.
b. $14,000.
c. $16,000.
d. $22,000.

The correct answer is (c). (CPA 583 P-36)
REQUIRED: The profit on sale of product E that was processed further.
DISCUSSION: Since 2,000 of product E were allocated joint costs of $18,000 (60% of $30,000) (see Q. 45 for the computation of 60%), the profit on the sale of 2,000 units would be $16,000 ($40,000 sales value - $6,000 additional costs - $18,000 joint costs).

Module 8.4: Joint Costs/Relative Sales Value

47. Crowley Company produces joint products A and B from a process that also yields a by-product, Y. The by-product requires additional processing before it can be sold. The cost assigned to the by-product is its market value less additional costs incurred after split-off (NRV method). Information concerning a batch produced in January at a joint cost of $40,000 is as follows:

Product	Units Produced	Market Value	Costs After Split-off
A	800	$44,000	$4,500
B	700	32,000	3,500
Y	500	4,000	1,000

How much of the joint cost should be allocated to the joint products?

a. $35,000.
b. $36,000.
c. $37,000.
d. $39,000.

The correct answer is (c). *(CPA 583 P-38)*
REQUIRED: The amount of joint cost allocated to the joint products.
DISCUSSION: The joint costs to be allocated are the total joint costs less the NRV allocated to the by-product, which is $3,000 ($4,000 market value - $1,000 costs after split-off). Accordingly, $37,000 of joint cost ($40,000 - $3,000) should be allocated to the joint products.

Questions 48 and 49 are based on Grafton Company, which produces joint products A and B in Department One from a process which also yields by-product W. Product A and by-product W are sold after separation, but product B must be further processed in Department Two before it can be sold. The cost assigned to the by-product is its market value less $.40 per pound for delivery expense (NRV method). Information relating to a batch produced in July is presented in the opposite column.

Product	Production (in pounds)	Sales Price per Pound
A	2,000	$4.50
B	4,000	9.00
W	500	1.50

Joint cost in Department One $18,000
Product B additional process cost in Department Two $10,000

---

48. For joint cost allocation purposes, what is the NRV at the split-off point of product B?

a. $46,000.
b. $45,000.
c. $36,000.
d. $26,000.

The correct answer is (d). *(CPA 1183 P-51)*
REQUIRED: The net realizable value of product B at the split-off point.
DISCUSSION: Product B's NRV at split-off is $36,000 selling price ($9 x 4,000 lbs. produced) minus the additional processing cost in Department Two of $10,000. Thus, the NRV of product B at the split-off point is $26,000.

49. How much of the joint cost incurred in Department One should be allocated to the joint products?

a. $17,250.
b. $17,450.
c. $17,800.
d. $18,550.

The correct answer is (b). *(CPA 1183 P-52)*
REQUIRED: The joint cost to be allocated to joint products.
DISCUSSION: The joint cost of $18,000 less the NRV of the by-product is the amount of joint cost to be allocated to products A and B. The NRV of by-product W is the $750 selling price ($1.50 x 500 lbs.) less $200 ($.40 x 500 lbs.) of delivery expense, or $550. The joint cost allocable to joint products is $17,450 ($18,000 initial joint cost - $550 by-product NRV).

8.5 Sell/Process Decisions

50. Which of the following is often subject to further processing in order to be salable?

	By-products	Scrap
a.	No	No
b.	No	Yes
c.	Yes	Yes
d.	Yes	No

The correct answer is (d). *(CPA 586 T-44)*
REQUIRED: Whether scrap and/or by-products incur further processing in order to be salable.
DISCUSSION: Scrap and by-products are usually similar in nature, both physically and from an accounting point of view. Scrap might even be considered a by-product of a manufacturing process. However, by-products generally have a greater sales value than scrap. And also, scrap rarely receives any additional processing in order to be salable.

51. Yardley Corporation uses a joint process to produce products A, B, and C. Each product may be sold at its split-off point or processed further. Additional processing costs are entirely variable and are traceable to the respective products. Joint production costs were $50,000 and are allocated by Yardley using the relative sales value at split-off approach.

			If Processed Further	
Product	Units Produced	Sales Value at Split-off	Sales Value	Additional Costs
A	20,000	$ 45,000	$60,000	$20,000
B	15,000	75,000	98,000	20,000
C	15,000	30,000	62,000	18,000
		$150,000		

To maximize profits, which products should Yardley process further?

a. A only.
b. C only.
c. B and C only.
d. None, because of the joint costs.

The correct answer is (c). *(CPA 576 P-35)*
REQUIRED: The product(s) that should be processed further to maximize profits.
DISCUSSION: It is profitable to process the units further as long as the incremental revenue exceeds the incremental costs. Joint costs are irrelevant because they are sunk costs.

		(000 omited)	
	A	B	C
Sales value if processed further	$60	$98	$62
Less sales value at split-off	(45)	(75)	(30)
Incremental revenue	$15	$23	$32
Less incremental costs	(20)	(20)	(18)
Excess revenue over cost	$(5)	$ 3	$14

Thus, processing B and C further will maximize profits.

52. A company manufactures two joint products at a joint cost of $1,000. These products can be sold at split-off or, when further processed at an additional cost, sold as higher quality items. The decision to sell at split-off or further process should be based on the

a. Assumption that the $1,000 joint cost is irrelevant.
b. Allocation of the $1,000 joint cost using the relative sales value approach.
c. Assumption that the $1,000 joint cost must be allocated using a physical-measure approach.
d. Allocation of the $1,000 joint cost using any equitable and rational allocation basis.

The correct answer is (a). *(CPA 577 T-34)*
REQUIRED: The basis for deciding whether to sell at split-off or process further.
DISCUSSION: In determining whether to sell a product at the split-off point or process the item further at additional cost, the joint cost of the products is irrelevant because it is a sunk (already expended) cost. The cost of additional processing (incremental costs) should be weighed against the benefits received (incremental revenues). The sell/process further decision should be based on that relationship.
Answers (b), (c), and (d) are incorrect because the $1,000 is a sunk cost regardless of how it is allocated and thus is irrelevant in deciding whether to process further.

Module 8.5: Sell/Process Decisions

53. The Pendall Company manufactures products Dee and Eff from a joint process. Product Dee has been allocated $2,500 of total joint costs of $20,000 for the 1,000 units produced. Dee can be sold at the split-off point for $3 per unit, or it can be processed further with additional costs of $1,000 and sold for $5 per unit. If Dee is processed further and sold, the result would be

a. A breakeven situation.
b. An additional gain of $1,000 from further processing.
c. An overall loss of $1,000.
d. An additional gain of $2,000 from further processing.

The correct answer is (b). *(CPA 1182 Q-26)*
REQUIRED: The effect of further processing the product.
DISCUSSION: If 1,000 units of Dee are sold at the split-off point, sales revenue of $3,000 ($3 x 1,000) will be received. If the units are processed further, sales revenue will be $5,000 ($5 x 1,000), but an additional cost of $1,000 will be incurred. Incremental revenue is $2,000 ($5,000 - $3,000) and incremental cost is $1,000, making the net effect on income from further processing a $1,000 increase.

Questions 54 and 55 are based on Watkins Co., which produces three products, X, Y, and Z, from a particular joint process. Each product may be sold at the point of split-off or processed further. Additional processing requires no special facilities, and production costs of further processing are entirely variable and traceable to the products involved. Last year all three products were processed beyond split-off. Joint production costs for the year were $60,000. Sales values and costs needed to evaluate Watkins' production policy follow.

			If Processed Further	
Product	Units Produced	Sales Value at Split-off	Sales Value	Additional Costs
X	6,000	$25,000	$42,000	$9,000
Y	4,000	41,000	45,000	7,000
Z	2,000	24,000	32,000	8,000

Joint costs are allocated to the products in proportion to the relative physical volume of output.

---

54. For units of Z, the unit production cost most relevant to the sell or process further decision is

a. $5.
b. $12.
c. $4.
d. $9.

The correct answer is (c). *(CPA 574 P-11)*
REQUIRED: The relevant unit production cost in a sell or process further decision.
DISCUSSION: The most relevant unit cost in a sell or process further decision is the incremental cost of additional processing. The joint costs are irrelevant because they are sunk costs. For the product Z decision,

$$\frac{\text{Incremental Costs}}{\text{Units}} = \frac{\$8,000}{2,000} = \$4$$

55. To maximize profits, Watkins should subject which products to additional processing?

a. X only.
b. X, Y, and Z.
c. Y and Z only.
d. Z only.

The correct answer is (a). *(CPA 574 P-12)*
REQUIRED: The product(s) that should be processed further to maximize profits.
DISCUSSION: As long as the incremental revenue exceeds the incremental cost, it is profitable to process the units further. Joint costs are irrelevant to this decision because they are sunk costs.

(000 omitted)

	Sales Value	Sales Value at Split-off	Increm. Revenue	Increm. Costs	Increase (Decrease)
X	$42 -	$25 =	$17 -	$9 =	$8
Y	45 -	41 =	4 -	7 =	(3)
Z	32 -	24 =	8 -	8 =	0

Since product X is the only one with a net increase, only it should be processed further.

Questions 56 and 57 are based on N-Air Corporation, which uses a joint process to produce three products: A, B, and C, all derived from one input. The company can sell these products at the point of split-off (end of the joint process) or process them further. The joint production costs during October were $10,000. N-Air allocates joint costs to the products in proportion to the relative physical volume of output. Other information follows.

Product	Units Produced	Unit Sales Price at Split-off	If Processed Further Unit Sales Price	If Processed Further Unit Additional Cost
A	1,000	$4.00	$5.00	$ .75
B	2,000	2.25	4.00	1.20
C	1,500	3.00	3.75	.90

56. Assuming that all products were sold at the split-off point during October, the gross profit from the production process would be

a. $13,000.
b. $10,000.
c. $8,625.
d. $3,000.
e. Negative.

The correct answer is (d). *(CIA 1182 IV-9)*
REQUIRED: The gross profit from the production process if all products are sold at the split-off point.
DISCUSSION: If all products are sold at split-off, the gross profit is computed as

Product A ($4.00 x 1,000)	$ 4,000
Product B ($2.25 x 2,000)	4,500
Product C ($3.00 x 1,500)	4,500
Total sales	$13,000
Joint costs	(10,000)
Gross profit	$ 3,000

57. Assuming sufficient demand exists, N-Air could sell all the products at the prices above at either the split-off point or after further processing. In order to maximize its profits, N-Air Corporation should

a. Sell product A at split-off and perform additional processing on products B and C.
b. Sell product B at split-off and perform additional processing on products C and A.
c. Sell product C at split-off and perform additional processing on products A and B.
d. Sell products A, B, and C at split-off.
e. Perform additional processing on products A, B, and C.

The correct answer is (c). *(CIA 1182 IV-10)*
REQUIRED: The product(s) that should be processed further to maximize profits.
DISCUSSION: To maximize profits, it must be determined whether each product's incremental revenues will exceed its incremental costs. Remember, joint costs are irrelevant because they are sunk costs.

	A	B	C
Units sales price if processed further	$5.00	$4.00	$3.75
Less unit sales price at split-off	(4.00)	(2.25)	(3.00)
Incremental revenue per unit	$1.00	$1.75	$ .75
Less incremental unit cost	(.75)	(1.20)	(.90)
Excess unit revenue over unit cost	$ .25	$ .55	$ (.15)

It is most profitable for N-Air to process products A and B further and to sell product C at the split-off point.

58. How should one make a decision with respect to the profitability of an individual joint product?

a. Based on total profitability of all joint products.
b. Attempt to maximize the profitability of each joint product after including individual joint costs.
c. Ignore all joint costs with respect to both decisions concerning individual products and decisions concerning the joint products as a whole.
d. Ignore joint costs when attempting to maximize the profitability of a single joint product.

The correct answer is (d). *(Publisher)*
REQUIRED: How to make decisions with respect to profitability of individual joint products.
DISCUSSION: When dealing with an individual joint product, decisions with respect to the profitability of that individual joint product should be made without considering any joint costs allocated to that product. With respect to an individual joint product, joint costs are sunk costs (i.e., already spent) and are irrelevant to decisions concerning the profitability of the individual joint product. Joint costs should only be considered when making decisions concerning the profitability of the joint products as a whole.
Answer (a) is incorrect because the total profitability of all joint products does not affect the profitability of an individual joint product. Answer (b) is incorrect because joint costs should be excluded. Answer (c) is incorrect because joint costs cannot be ignored when making decisions concerning the joint products as a whole.

8.6 Journal Entries

59. The journal entry to record separable manufacturing outlays of a by-product is

a.	By-product inventory	XX	
	Cash		XX
b.	Work-in-process	XX	
	Cash		XX
c.	Finished goods	XX	
	Work-in-process		XX
d.	By-product inventory	XX	
	Work-in-process		XX

The correct answer is (a). *(Publisher)*
REQUIRED: The journal entry to record separable manufacturing outlays for a by-product.
DISCUSSION: By-products are usually accounted for within separate inventory accounts. Therefore, the separable manufacturing outlays would be debited to by-product inventory with a corresponding credit to cash. Separate accounting for by-products is recommended because they are treated differently from common or joint products.

60. The journal entry to record net realizable value per unit for a by-product is

a.	By-product inventory	XX	
	Cash		XX
b.	By-product inventory	XX	
	Work-in-process		XX
c.	Finished goods	XX	
	Work-in-process		XX
d.	Work-in-process	XX	
	By-product inventory		XX

The correct answer is (b). *(Publisher)*
REQUIRED: The journal entry to record net realizable value per unit for a by-product.
DISCUSSION: Net realizable value per unit for by-products is debited to the by-product inventory account and credited to work-in-process.

61. The journal entry to record disposal costs for a by-product sold is

a.	Disposal costs	XX	
	Cash		XX
b.	Work-in-process	XX	
	Cash		XX
c.	Finished goods	XX	
	Cash		XX
d.	Cost of goods sold	XX	
	Cash		XX

The correct answer is (a). *(Publisher)*
REQUIRED: The journal entry to record disposal costs for a by-product sold.
DISCUSSION: Disposal costs for a by-product are accounted for as a period cost. Therefore, disposal costs must be debited, with a credit to cash and/or accounts payable, as appropriate.

62. The journal entry to record sale of a by-product is

a.	By-product revenue	XX	
	By-product inventory		XX
b.	Cash	XX	
	By-product inventory		XX
c.	Cash	XX	
	Cost of goods sold		XX
d.	Cash	XX	
	By-product revenue		XX

The correct answer is (d). *(Publisher)*
REQUIRED: The journal entry to record the sale of a by-product.
DISCUSSION: Sale of a by-product results in a debit to cash and a credit to by-product revenue. Having a separate account for by-product revenue allows by-product revenue to be analyzed in relation to total sales. Note that if the by-product were sold on account, the debit would be to accounts receivable.

Module 8.6: Journal Entries

63. The journal entry to record cost of a by-product sold is as follows

   a. Finished goods   XX
          By-product inventory   XX
   b. Cash   XX
          By-product inventory   XX
   c. By-product revenue   XX
          By-product inventory   XX
   d. Cost of by-product sold   XX
          By-product inventory   XX

The correct answer is (d). *(Publisher)*
REQUIRED: The journal entry to record the cost of a by-product sold.
DISCUSSION: Cost of by-product sold is debited for the cost of the inventory, which should be equal to the total realizable value carried in the by-product inventory account. By-product inventory is credited for this same amount.

Questions 64 through 67 are based on the following information, which was presented as part of Question 5 on the Practice II section of the May 1982 CPA examination.

Lares Confectioners, Inc. makes a candy bar called Rey that sells for $.50 per pound. The manufacturing process also yields a product known as Nagu. Without further processing, Nagu sells for $.10 per pound. With further processing, Nagu sells for $.30 per pound. During the month of April, total joint manufacturing costs up to the point of separation consisted of the charges to work-in-process presented in the opposite column.

Raw materials	$150,000
Direct labor	120,000
Factory overhead	30,000

Production for the month aggregated 394,000 pounds of Rey and 30,000 pounds of Nagu. To complete Nagu during the month of April and obtain a selling price of $.30 per pound, further processing of Nagu during April would entail the following additional costs:

Raw materials	$2,000
Direct labor	1,500
Factory overhead	500

---

64. What would be the journal entries for Nagu if it is processed further and transferred to finished goods, with joint costs being allocated between Rey and Nagu based on relative sales value at the split-off point?

   a. Work-in-process (Nagu) $4,500
         Work-in-process (Rey) $4,500
      Work-in-process (Nagu) $4,000
         Raw materials $2,000
         Direct labor   1,500
         Factory overhead   500
      Finished goods (Nagu) $8,500
         Work-in-process (Nagu) $8,500

   b. Work-in-process (Nagu) $8,500
         Work-in-process (Rey) $8,500
      Finished goods (Nagu) $8,500
         Work-in-process (Nagu) $8,500

   c. Finished goods (Nagu) $8,500
         Work-in-process (Nagu) $8,500

   d. Work-in-process (Rey) $4,500
         Work-in-process (Nagu) $4,500
      Work-in-process (Rey) $4,000
         Raw materials $2,000
         Direct labor   1,500
         Factory overhead   500
      Finished goods (Rey) $8,500
         Work-in-process (Rey) $8,500

The correct answer is (a). *(Publisher)*
REQUIRED: The journal entries for joint products and further processing.
DISCUSSION: The initial journal entry requires the joint costs to be allocated between Rey and Nagu based on relative sales value at split-off. Total joint costs are $300,000 ($150,000 raw materials + $120,000 direct labor + $30,000 factory overhead). The ratio to calculate Nagu's joint costs is

$$\frac{\text{Sales value of Nagu}}{\text{Total sales value of Rey and Nagu}}$$

$$\frac{30,000 \text{ lbs.} \times \$.10}{(394,000 \text{ lbs.} \times \$.50) + (30,000 \text{ lbs.} \times \$.10)}$$

$$= \frac{\$3,000}{\$200,000} = .015 \text{ joint cost ratio}$$

Nagu's joint costs are $4,500 ($300,000 × .015), and the journal entry is a debit to WIP (Nagu) and a credit to WIP (Rey) for this amount. The next journal entry to reflect the cost of further processing Nagu, would be to debit WIP (Nagu) and credit raw materials, direct labor, and factory overhead for the additional costs incurred. The final journal entry would be to transfer the WIP costs of $8,500 to finished goods.

Module 8.6: Journal Entries

65. What would be the journal entry for Nagu if it is further processed as a by-product and transferred to the warehouse at net realizable value, which reduces Rey's manufacturing costs?

a. By-product inventory (Nagu) $3,000
    Work-in-process (Rey) $3,000

b. By-product inventory (Nagu) $4,000
    Raw materials $2,000
    Direct labor   1,500
    Factory overhead   500

c. Work-in-process (Rey) $5,000
    Raw materials   2,000
    Direct labor   1,500
    Factory overhead   500
    By-product inventory
      (Nagu) $9,000

d. By-product inventory (Nagu) $9,000
    Raw materials $2,000
    Direct labor   1,500
    Factory overhead   500
    Work-in-process (Rey)   5,000

The correct answer is (d). *(Publisher)*
REQUIRED: The journal entry to transfer a by-product at net realizable value.
DISCUSSION: Net realizable value is the selling price less the cost necessary to process further. After further processing, the net realizable value of Nagu is $5,000 ($9,000 selling price of 30,000 lbs. @ $.30/lb. - $2,000 materials - $1,500 DL - $500 O/H). Thus, the journal entry is a debit to by-product inventory of Nagu for the selling price and corresponding credits to raw materials, direct labor, and factory overhead. The final credit of $5,000 is to work-in-process (Rey).

By-product inventory (Nagu)
  (30,000 lbs. @ $.30/lb.) $9,000
Raw materials $2,000
Direct labor   1,500
Factory overhead   500
Work-in-process (Rey)   5,000

66. If the joint costs of $300,000 were allocated based on relative net realizable values and Nagu was considered a joint product rather than a by-product, what would be the journal entries for Nagu and Rey to record the cost allocation and subsequent processing to the point at which both are in finished goods inventory?

a. Finished goods (Rey) $292,574
    Work-in-process (Nagu)   7,426
      Work-in-process (joint) $300,000
    Work-in-process (Nagu) $4,000
      Raw materials $2,000
      Direct labor   1,500
      Factory overhead   500
    Finished goods (Nagu) $11,426
      Work-in-process (Nagu) $11,426

b. Work-in-process (Nagu) $4,000
    Raw materials $2,000
    Direct labor   1,500
    Factory overhead   500

c. Work-in-process (Nagu) $4,967
    Work-in-process (joint) $4,967
    Work-in-process (Nagu) $4,000
      Raw materials $2,000
      Direct labor   1,500
      Factory overhead   500

d. Finished goods (Rey) $295,033
    Work-in-process (Nagu)   4,967
      Work-in-process (joint) $300,000
    Work-in-process (Nagu) $4,000
      Raw materials $2,000
      Direct labor   1,500
      Factory overhead   500
    Finished goods (Nagu) $8,967
      Work-in-process (Nagu) $8,967

The correct answer is (a). *(Publisher)*
REQUIRED: The journal entries to reflect transfer of joint products to finished goods after joint cost allocation based on relative net realizable value.
DISCUSSION: The final sales value of Nagu is $9,000 (30,000 pounds x $.30). The cost of additional processing is $4,000 ($2,000 + $1,500 + $500). Its net realizable value is thus $5,000. The sales value of Rey continues to be $197,000 (394,000 x $.50). Thus, the allocation of the $300,000 of common costs is $292,574 to Rey {[($197,000 ÷ $5,000) + $197,000] x $300,000} and $7,426 to Nagu {[($5,000 ÷ $5,000) + $197,000] x $300,000}. The amount transferred to finished goods (Nagu) is thus the sum of the joint cost allocation and the additional processing costs ($7,426 + $4,000 = $11,426).

Module 8.6: Journal Entries

67. Refer to the information presented on page 180. Select the proper journal entry for Nagu if it is transferred as a by-product at sales value to the warehouse without further processing, with a corresponding reduction of Rey's manufacturing costs.

a.	By-product inventory		$3,000
	Finished goods	$3,000	
b.	By-product inventory		$3,000
	Work-in-process	$3,000	
c.	Work-in-process		$3,000
	By-product inventory	$3,000	
d.	Cost of goods sold		$3,000
	By-product inventory	$3,000	

The correct answer is (b). *(Publisher)*
REQUIRED: The appropriate journal entry to record a by-product transfer.
DISCUSSION: To transfer a by-product at sales value with a corresponding reduction of manufacturing costs requires estimation of the sales value of the transferred item. The selling price of Nagu is $3,000 (30,000 lbs. produced x $.10/lb. incremental cost) without further processing. The sales value is to be accounted for as a reduction in manufacturing costs. Therefore, the debit and credit are to by-product inventory and work-in-process, respectively.

By-product inventory (Nagu)	$3,000	
Work-in-process (Rey)		$3,000

Questions 68 through 73 are based on Company Z, which manufactures Product X. Coincidental with production of X, by-product Y is produced. Company Z uses the net realizable value method of accounting for the by-product. This amount is deducted from the cost of production of Product X. Any separable manufacturing costs are charged to an inventory account. Company Z produced 21,000 units of X this week. The company also produced 2,100 units of Y at a separable manufacturing cost of $1.25 per unit.

---

68. The journal entry to record the cost of producing by-product Y is

a.	Work-in-process - Y	$2,625	
	Work-in-process - X		$2,625
b.	Work-in-process	$2,100	
	By-product inventory		$2,100
c.	By-product inventory	$2,625	
	Cash		$2,625
d.	Cost of goods manufactured	$2,625	
	By-product inventory		$2,625

The correct answer is (c). *(Publisher)*
REQUIRED: The journal entry to charge by-product inventory for separable manufacturing costs.
DISCUSSION: Separable manufacturing costs are inventoried in a separate inventory account. In this case, the designated account is by-product inventory.

2,100 units Y x $1.25 = $2,625

69. The journal entry to record the disposal of 1,100 units of Y at a cost of $.12/unit is

a.	Work-in-process	$120	
	Cash		$120
b.	Cost of goods sold	$132	
	Cash		$132
c.	Disposal costs	$132	
	Cash		$132
d.	Disposal costs	$132	
	By-product inventory		$132

The correct answer is (c). *(Publisher)*
REQUIRED: The journal entry to record the disposal cost of a by-product.
DISCUSSION: Disposal costs are charged to an expense account at the time of sale. Thus, the 1,100 units of Y with a disposal cost of $.12 per unit cost $132. The separable disposal cost on marketing cost are later charged to expense in the same time period that the units are sold.

Module 8.6: Journal Entries

70. The journal entry to record net realizable value of by-product Y if it sells for $5 each is

    a. By-product inventory $7,623
           Cash $7,623

    b. By-product inventory $7,623
           Work-in-process $7,623

    c. Cash $10,500
           By-product revenues $10,500

    d. Work-in-process $7,623
           By-product inventory $7,623

The correct answer is (b). *(Publisher)*
REQUIRED: The journal entry to record the net realizable value of the by-product.
DISCUSSION: The net realizable value of unit Y is the selling price less any separable manufacturing cost less any disposal cost. Unit net realizable value is thus $3.63 ($5 sales price - $1.25 separable manufacturing costs - $.12 disposal costs). The by-product inventory account is increased by $7,623 ($3.63 x 2,100 units), and the work-in-process account is decreased by this amount. Thus, present production has been reduced by the net realizable value of the by-product produced.

71. The journal entry to record the cost if 1,100 units of by-product Y are sold is

    a. Cost of by-products sold $5,368
           By-product inventory $5,368

    b. Cost of goods sold $5,368
           By-product inventory $5,368

    c. Cost of by-products sold $5,500
           Finished goods $5,500

    d. Cash $5,500
           By-product inventory $5,500

The correct answer is (a). *(Publisher)*
REQUIRED: The journal entry to record the cost of units of by-product sold.
DISCUSSION: The cost of by-products sold has two components: the net realizable value removed from work-in-process and the separable manufacturing costs. The cost of units sold is the sum of the NRV ($3.63 per unit calculated in Q. 75) plus the separable unit manufacturing cost ($1.25) times the number of units sold, or $5,368 ($4.88 x 1,100 units sold). The cost of by-products sold account is then debited at the time of sale, and the by-product inventory account is credited by the same amount.

72. The amount in the by-product inventory account is

    a. $3,630.
    b. $3,750.
    c. $5,000.
    d. $4,880.

The correct answer is (d). *(Publisher)*
REQUIRED: The amount remaining in the by-product inventory account.
DISCUSSION: The by-product inventory balance is the number of units in inventory times the unit cost of the by-product ($3.63 NRV + $1.25 separable cost = $4.88). The number of units in inventory is 1,000 (2,100 units produced - 1,100 units sold). The remaining by-product inventory is $4,880 ($4.88 x 1,000 units).

73. The journal entry to record the sale (at $5.00/unit) of the remaining 1,000 units of by-product Y is

    a. Cash $5,000
           By-product inventory $5,000

    b. By-product costs $3,750
           By-product revenue $3,750

    c. Cash $5,000
           General revenue $5,000

    d. Cash $5,000
           By-product revenue $5,000

The correct answer is (d). *(Publisher)*
REQUIRED: The journal entry to record the sale of the remaining units of by-product.
DISCUSSION: The sale of the remaining units is similar to the initial sale: cash is debited and by-product revenue is credited. This method of recording by-product revenue maintains appropriate recognition of the by-product revenue. A company's entry regarding separate manufacturing costs and other costs thus provides information to management regarding the effect of the by-product on the revenues and expenses of the firm.

8.7 Comprehensive

Questions 74 through 79 are based on the following information, which was presented as part of Question 7 on Part 4 of the June 1981 CMA examination.

Doe Corporation grows, processes, cans, and sells three main pineapple products - sliced pineapple, crushed pineapple, and pineapple juice. The outside skin is cut off in the Cutting Department and processed as animal feed. The skin is treated as a by-product. Doe's production process is as follows:

Pineapples first are processed in the Cutting Department. The pineapples are washed and the outside skin is cut away. Then the pineapples are cored and trimmed for slicing. The three main products (sliced, crushed, juice) and the by-product (animal feed) are recognizable after processing in the Cutting Department. Each product is then transferred to a separate department for final processing.

The trimmed pineapples are forwarded to the Slicing Department where they are sliced and canned. Any juice generated during the slicing operation is packed in the cans with the slices.

The pieces of pineapple trimmed from the fruit are diced and canned in the Crushing Department. Again, the juice generated during this operation is packed in the can with the crushed pineapple.

The core and surplus pineapple generated from the Cutting Department are pulverized into a liquid in the Juicing Department. An evaporation loss equal to 8% of the weight of the good output produced in this department occurs as the juices are heated.

The outside skin is chopped into animal feed in the Feed Department.

The Doe Corporation uses the net realizable value (relative sales value) method to assign costs of the joint process to its main products. The by-product is inventoried at its market value.

A total of 270,000 pounds entered the Cutting Department during May. The schedule below shows the costs incurred in each department, the proportion by weight transferred to the four final processing departments, and the selling price of each product.

Doe uses the net realizable value method of determining inventory values for all products and by-products.

May Processing Data and Costs

Department	Costs Incurred	Proportion of Product by Weight Transferred to Departments	Selling Price per Pound of Final Product
Cutting	$60,000	--	None
Slicing	4,700	35%	$.60
Crushing	10,580	28	.55
Juicing	3,250	27	.30
Animal Feed	700	10	.10
Total	$79,230	100%	

74. How many net pounds of pineapple juice were produced in May?

a. 72,900.
b. 79,200.
c. 64,525.
d. 67,500.

The correct answer is (d). *(Publisher)*
REQUIRED: The net pounds of pineapple juice produced during the period.
DISCUSSION: The gross pounds of pineapple juice is 27% of the 270,000 total pounds entered into the various production units, or 72,900 pounds. We are also told that 8% is lost to evaporation. The net amount of pineapple juice is thus

$$X = 72,900 - .08X$$
$$1.08X = 72,900$$
$$X = 67,500 \text{ lbs.}$$

75. What is the net realizable value at the split-off point of pineapple slices?

a. $52,000.
b. $56,700.
c. $49,800.
d. $39,200.

The correct answer is (a). *(Publisher)*
REQUIRED: The net realizable value at split-off of pineapple slices.
DISCUSSION: The net realizable value at the split-off point can be estimated as the final sales revenue minus separable costs for further processing. Sales value equals the pounds of slices (270,000 x 35% = 94,500) times the selling price ($.60 per pound), or $56,700. The separable costs are given as $4,700. Therefore, the net realizable value at split-off is $52,000 ($56,700 - $4,700).

Module 8.7: Comprehensive

76. What is the total amount of separable costs for the three main products?

   a. $15,280.
   b. $18,530.
   c. $16,750.
   d. $12,280.

The correct answer is (b). *(Publisher)*
REQUIRED: The total amount of separable costs for the three main products.
DISCUSSION: Separable costs for the three main products is the cost to further process the items to a salable state. The incremental costs incurred in slicing, crushing, and juicing are given. They total to $18,530 ($4,700 + $10,580 + $3,250). The incremental costs incurred for animal feed are not included because they are the separable costs for the by-product.

77. What is the total amount of joint costs for the Cutting Department to be assigned to each of the three main products in accordance with Doe's policy?

   a. $60,000.
   b. $57,300.
   c. $58,000.
   d. $62,300.

The correct answer is (c). *(Publisher)*
REQUIRED: The total joint costs to be allocated to the main products.
DISCUSSION: The joint costs to be allocated to main products are the Cutting Department costs less any net revenue from the by-product. The animal feed's net revenue is $2,000 [sales value of $2,700 (270,000 lbs. x 10% x $.10/lb.) less separable costs of $700]. The balance of joint costs of $58,000 ($60,000 total joint costs - $2,000 net by-product revenue) must be allocated to the main products in proportion to their net realizable values.

78. How much of the joint costs is allocated to crushed pineapple?

   a. $13,020.
   b. $18,320.
   c. $9,860.
   d. $17,980.

The correct answer is (d). *(Publisher)*
REQUIRED: The joint costs allocated to crushed pineapple.
DISCUSSION: The weights are found as percentages of total pounds. Remember the 8% shrinkage (evaporation) for the juice. Slices = 270,000 x 35%; Crushed = 270,000 x 28%.

Product	Pounds Produced	Selling Price	Sales Revenue	Separable Costs
Slices	94,500	$.60	$ 56,700	$ 4,700
Crushed	75,600	.55	41,580	10,580
Juice	67,500*	.30	20,250	3,250
			$118,530	$18,530

* amount computed in Q. 74

	Net Realizable Value Amount	Percent
Slices	$ 52,000	52%
Crushed	31,000	31
Juice	17,000	17
	$100,000	100%

The joint costs to be allocated are $60,000 less $2,000 net by-product revenue, or $58,000 (as computed in Q. 77). The joint costs allocated to crushed pineapple are $17,980 (31% x $58,000).

79. What is the gross margin for the pineapple juice?

   a. $9,860.
   b. $7,140.
   c. $3,250.
   d. $20,250.

The correct answer is (b). *(Publisher)*
REQUIRED: The gross margin for pineapple juice.
DISCUSSION: Gross margin for pineapple juice equals the sales revenue less the separable costs and the juice's allotted proportion of joint costs.

Sales revenue (67,500 lbs. x $.30)	$20,250
Separable cost	(3,250)
Proportionate joint costs*	(9,860)
Gross margin	$ 7,140

* $58,000 x 17% (as set up in Q. 78)

Module 8.7: Comprehensive

Questions 80 through 84 are based on the following information, which was presented as part of Question 5 on the Practice II section of the May 1980 CPA examination.

Adept Company is a manufacturer of two products known as "Prep" and "Pride." Incidental to the production of these two products, Adept produces a by-product known as "Wilton." The manufacturing process covers two departments, Grading and Saturating.

The manufacturing process begins in the Grading department when raw materials are started in process. Upon completion of processing in the Grading department, the by-product "Wilton" is produced, which accounts for 20% of the material processed. This by-product needs no further processing and is transferred to finished goods.

The net realizable value of the by-product "Wilton" is accounted for as a reduction of the cost of materials in the Grading department. The current selling price of "Wilton" is $1 per pound and the estimated selling and delivery costs total $.10 per pound.

The remaining output is transferred to the Saturating department for the final phase of production. In the Saturating department, water is added at the beginning of the production process, which results in a 50% gain in weight of the materials in production.

Adept uses the FIFO method of process costing. The information presented below is available for the month of November.

Inventories	November 1 Quantity (pounds)	Value	November 30 Quantity (pounds)
Work-in-process:			
Grading dept.	None	--	None
Saturating dept.	1,600	$17,600	2,000
Finished goods:			
Prep	600	14,520	1,600
Pride	2,400	37,110	800
Wilton	None	--	None

The work-in-process inventory (labor and overhead) in the Saturating department is estimated to be 50% complete both at the beginning and end of November.

Costs of production for November are as follows:

Costs of Production	Materials Used	Labor and Overhead
Grading department	$265,680	$86,400
Saturating department	--	86,000

The material used in the Grading department weighed 36,000 pounds.

80. How much by-product is accounted for, in pounds, during the month?

   a. 7,200.
   b. 3,600.
   c. 7,000.
   d. 6,500.

The correct answer is (a). *(Publisher)*
REQUIRED: The by-product accounted for in pounds.
DISCUSSION: The pounds of by-product accounted for is equal to 20% of the material processed, which is given for the Grading department in November as 36,000 pounds. Therefore, 7,200 pounds of by-product were produced (20% of 36,000).

Module 8.7: Comprehensive

81. What is the total equivalent unit cost in the Grading department?

a. $12.22.
b. $12.00.
c. $9.00.
d. $15.00.

The correct answer is (b). *(Publisher)*
REQUIRED: The total equivalent unit costs for the Grading department.
DISCUSSION: The total equivalent unit cost is the equivalent unit cost of materials plus conversion cost. Note that there is no BWIP or EWIP. Also, the EUP are 28,800 (36,000 units started times 80%, because 20% becomes the by-product Wilton). The NRV of Wilton is $6,480 [7,200 units produced, as calculated in the previous question, x ($1.00 - $.10 selling costs)], which reduces the cost of material in the Grading department.

Description	Material	Labor/Overhead	Total
Manufacturing costs:			
November	$265,680	$86,400	$352,080
Less:			
NRV of by-product	(6,480)	-0-	(6,480)
Total costs	$259,200	$86,400	$345,600
Divided by 28,800 EUP = EUP cost	$ 9.00	$ 3.00	$ 12.00

82. What is the total amount of ending work-in-process for the Grading department?

a. $345,600.
b. $86,400.
c. $0.
d. $259,200.

The correct answer is (c). *(Publisher)*
REQUIRED: The total amount of ending work-in-process.
DISCUSSION: The question states that there is no ending work-in-process in the Grading department.

83. What is the total cost transferred out of the Grading department?

a. $345,600.
b. $259,200.
c. $265,680.
d. $279,300.

The correct answer is (a). *(Publisher)*
REQUIRED: The total cost transferred out of the Grading department.
DISCUSSION: Total cost transferred out is current cost less any net realizable value (NRV) of the by-product. Total current costs were $352,080 ($265,680 material + $86,400 labor and overhead). NRV of the by-product was $6,480 (see the calculation in Q. 81). Therefore, total cost transferred out of the Grading department was $345,600 ($352,080 - $6,480).

84. What are the equivalent units in pounds to account for in the Saturating department?

a. 42,800.
b. 43,200.
c. 43,000.
d. 44,800.

The correct answer is (d). *(Publisher)*
REQUIRED: The equivalent units in pounds to account for in the Saturating department.
DISCUSSION: The pounds to be accounted for in the Saturating department equal the beginning inventory plus the amount transferred in plus the water added. The amount transferred in is the 36,000 lbs. used in Grading minus 20% used for Wilton, or 28,800 lbs. The water added is 50% of the amount transferred in. The pounds to be accounted for are

Beginning inventory	1,600
Transferred in (from Grading)	28,800
Water added (28,800 x 50%)	14,400
Pounds to be accounted for	44,800

Module 8.7: Comprehensive

Questions 85 through 88 are based on Hovart Corporation, which manufactures two products out of a joint process -- Compod and Ultrasene. The joint (common) costs incurred are $250,000 for a standard production run that generates 120,000 gallons of Compod and 80,000 gallons of Ultrasene. Compod sells for $2.00 per gallon while Ultrasene sells for $3.25 per gallon.

85. If there are no additional processing costs incurred after the split-off point, the amount of joint cost of each production run allocated to Compod on a physical-quantity basis is

  a. $100,000.
  b. $120,000.
  c. $130,000.
  d. $150,000.
  e. Some amount other than those given above.

86. If there are no additional processing costs incurred after the split-off point, the amount of joint cost of each production run allocated to Ultrasene on a net realizable value (gross market value) basis is

  a. $100,000.
  b. $120,000.
  c. $130,000.
  d. $150,000.
  e. Some amount other than those given above.

87. If additional processing costs beyond the split-off point are $.10 per gallon for Compod and $1.10 per gallon for Ultrasene, the amount of joint cost of each production run allocated to Ultrasene on a physical quantity basis is

  a. $100,000.
  b. $148,000.
  c. $142,500.
  d. $150,000.
  e. Some amount other than those given above.

88. If additional processing costs beyond the split-off point are $.10 per gallon for Compod and $1.10 per gallon for Ultrasene, the amount of joint cost of each production run allocated to Compod on a net realizable value (net market value) basis is

  a. $100,000.
  b. $107,500.
  c. $142,500.
  d. $150,000.
  e. Some amount other than those given above.

The correct answer is (d). (CMA 1285 4-8)
REQUIRED: The amount of joint cost to be allocated using the physical quantity basis.
DISCUSSION: Since Compod is 60% of the total quantity (120,000 gal./200,000 gal.), $150,000 (60% x $250,000) of the joint cost should be allocated to Compod.

The correct answer is (c). (CMA 1285 4-9)
REQUIRED: The joint cost allocation using relative sales value.
DISCUSSION: The market value is $240,000 (120,000 gal. x $2 per gal.) for Compod and $260,000 (80,000 gal. x $3.25 per gal.) for Ultrasene. The total sales value is $500,000. Since Ultrasene accounts for 52% ($260,000/$500,000) of the total value, $130,000 (52% x $250,000) of the joint cost is allocated to Ultrasene.

The correct answer is (a). (CMA 1285 4-10)
REQUIRED: The joint cost allocation if additional costs are incurred after split-off and the physical quantity basis is used.
DISCUSSION: The additional processing costs are irrelevant if the allocation is based on physical quantities. Since Ultrasene makes up 40% (80,000 gal./200,000 gal.) of the total quantity, it will be allocated 40% of the $250,000 joint costs or $100,000.

The correct answer is (c). (CMA 1285 4-11)
REQUIRED: The joint cost allocation based on relative sales value if additional costs are incurred beyond split-off.
DISCUSSION: When using the relative sales value method, processing costs incurred beyond the point of separation are deducted from the ultimate market values in determining the market values at split-off. For Compod, the value at the split-off point is computed by deducting $12,000 ($.10 x 120,000 gal.) from the fair market value of $240,000 ($2 x 120,000 gal.). The value at split-off is thus $228,000. The value at split-off for Ultrasene is found by deducting $88,000 ($.10 x 80,000 gal.) from the ultimate market value of $260,000 ($3.25 x 80,000 gal.). The value at split-off for Ultrasene is thus $172,000. The total value at split-off is $400,000 ($228,000 + $172,000). Since Compod accounts for 57% ($228,000/$400,000) of the total, it should be allocated 57% of the $250,000 in joint costs, or $142,500.

CHAPTER NINE
SERVICE COST ALLOCATIONS

9.1 Cost Allocation .... (20 questions)	189
9.2 Calculations .... (23 questions)	195

Service department allocations, which are a part of overhead, are allocated to production (user) departments. Service cost allocations could indeed be made in service industries as well as manufacturing organizations. Thus, the concept of cost allocations permeates our society regardless of the type of industry. Allocations considered in this chapter include the direct method, the step method, and the reciprocal services method (which uses simultaneous equations).

9.1 Cost Allocation

1. Which of the following statements best describes cost allocation?

   a. A company can maximize or minimize total company income by selecting different bases on which to allocate indirect costs.
   b. A company should select an allocation base to raise or lower reported income on given products.
   c. A company's total income will remain unchanged no matter how indirect costs are allocated.
   d. A company, as a general rule, should allocate indirect costs randomly or based on an "ability-to-bear" criterion.

The correct answer is (c). *(CPA 1175 P-31)*
   REQUIRED: The best statement about cost allocation.
   DISCUSSION: Indirect costs are not identifiable with any particular segment/division/product; they are incurred by the enterprise as a whole. Accordingly, how they are allocated has no effect on net income of the overall entity.
   Answer (a) is incorrect because the method of allocation of indirect costs affects net income figures of individual segments of the enterprise but not net income of the overall entity. Answers (b) and (d) are incorrect because the allocation base should be the most representative of the usage of services by divisions or segments.

2. Cost allocation concepts are appropriate

   a. Only as management deems appropriate.
   b. In manufacturing, nonmanufacturing, and service organizations.
   c. In allocating costs to production departments, but not from one service department to another.
   d. None of the above.

The correct answer is (b). *(Publisher)*
   REQUIRED: The appropriate statement about cost allocation concepts.
   DISCUSSION: Cost allocation concepts and the various approaches used in cost allocation may be applied to nonmanufacturing and service organizations as well as to manufacturing entities.
   Answer (a) is incorrect because cost allocation concepts must be used consistently, not at management's discretion. Answer (c) is incorrect because costs are allocated from one service department to another in the step and reciprocal allocation methods.

Module 9.1: Cost Allocation

3. In order to identify costs that relate to a specific product, an allocation base should be chosen that
    a. Does not have a cause and effect relationship.
    b. Has a cause and effect relationship.
    c. Considers variable costs but not fixed costs.
    d. Considers direct materials and direct labor but not factory overhead.

The correct answer is (b). *(CPA 581 T-43)*
REQUIRED: The allocation base that best identifies costs related to a specific product.
DISCUSSION: A cause and effect relationship should be used as an allocation basis when identifying costs that relate to a specific product. The purpose is to determine the product's actual cost, including such indirect overhead as costs of using other departments' services.
Answer (a) is incorrect because random allocation will not lead to useful or relevant total cost analysis. Answers (c) and (d) are incorrect because fixed costs and factory overhead are each product costs.

4. One management purpose for allocating joint costs of a processing center to the various products produced is
    a. To develop accurate processing cost variances by product.
    b. To report more correct standard product costs for comparative analysis.
    c. To establish inventory values for unsold units.
    d. To record accurate cost of sales by product line.
    e. None of the above.

The correct answer is (c). *(CMA 1273 4-11)*
REQUIRED: The management purpose for allocating joint costs.
DISCUSSION: The primary management purpose for allocating joint costs of a processing center to the various items produced is to establish inventory values for unsold units. Although the allocation of joint costs is by its very nature arbitrary, absorption costing methods require them to be allocated to the products produced.
Answer (a) is incorrect because an arbitrary allocation of joint costs does not provide an accurate variance per product. The more useful variance is for the joint process. Answer (b) is incorrect because standard costs are not reported externally, and an arbitrary allocation may diminish their accuracy. Answer (d) is incorrect because allocation is required by GAAP for reporting cost of sales as well as inventory, but the result is not necessarily more accurate.

5. Cost pools are
    a. Limited to five from one independent business organization.
    b. Accounts which are used for only production departments.
    c. Accounts in which a variety of costs are accumulated prior to allocation to cost objectives.
    d. None of the above.

The correct answer is (c). *(Publisher)*
REQUIRED: The definition of a cost pool.
DISCUSSION: Cost pools are accounts in which a variety of similar costs are accumulated prior to allocation to cost objectives. The O/H account is a cost pool into which various types of O/H are accumulated prior to their allocation.
Answer (a) is incorrect because the number of accounts is not limited. Answer (b) is incorrect because cost pools can be used for other departments besides production.

6. Cost objectives
    a. May be intermediate cost objectives, if the costs charged to the intermediate cost objective are later reallocated to another cost objective.
    b. May be final cost objectives if the cost objective is the job, product, or process itself.
    c. Should be logically linked with the cost pool.
    d. All of the above.

The correct answer is (d). *(Publisher)*
REQUIRED: The true statement(s) about cost objectives.
DISCUSSION: Cost objectives are the intermediate and final disposition of cost pools. Cost objectives first may be intermediate as cost pools move from their originating point to the final cost objective. Cost objectives may be final cost objectives such as a job, product, or process itself, and should be logically linked with the cost pool based on a cause and effect relationship.

Module 9.1: Cost Allocation

7. What is the function of a cost allocation base?

   a. To accumulate costs.
   b. To allocate costs.
   c. To establish a cost objective.
   d. To disaggregate costs.

The correct answer is (b). *(Publisher)*
REQUIRED: The function of a cost allocation base.
DISCUSSION: A cost allocation base is the means by which costs are allocated. The cost allocation base is some variable (activity) that has a strong correlation with the incurrence of cost by the cost objective. For example, direct labor hours is frequently used as a cost allocation base because indirect costs are frequently incurred as a result of activity.
  Answer (a) is incorrect because cost pools accumulate costs. Answer (c) is incorrect because establishing a cost objective involves selecting the products, service, contracts, geographical areas, etc., to which costs will be allocated. Answer (d) is incorrect because cost allocation is a basis of aggregating (not separating) costs by cost objective.

8. Which of the following is true in respect to plant-wide and departmental overhead rates?

   a. Only one overhead control account is necessary for a plant-wide overhead rate.
   b. Each production department requires a separate overhead cost pool for a departmental overhead rate.
   c. The departmental overhead rate concept is relatively more complex than the plant-wide overhead rate concept.
   d. All of the above.

The correct answer is (d). *(Publisher)*
REQUIRED: The true statement(s) about plant-wide O/H and departmental O/H rates.
DISCUSSION: A firm with a relatively simple production and accounting system would use only one O/H control account with one plant-wide O/H rate. In a more complex environment, the firm would need a separate O/H cost pool for each department. The departmental O/H rate is relatively more complex than the plant-wide because of the number of accounts as well as the number of O/H rates that must be established prior to implementation. A departmental O/H rate allows for a more accurate application of O/H to a specific job when products require different methods of production; e.g., product A requires more machine hours but fewer labor hours than product B. If a plant-wide rate were used based on labor hours, product A would not be allocated its fair share of O/H.

9. The allocation of general overhead costs to operating departments can be least justified in determining

   a. Income of a product or functional unit.
   b. Costs for making management's decisions.
   c. Costs of products sold.
   d. Costs for government's "cost-plus" contracts.
   e. Costs of products remaining in inventory.

The correct answer is (b). *(CIA 581 IV-17)*
REQUIRED: Inappropriate use of allocating cost data to operating departments.
DISCUSSION: In the short run, management decisions are made in reference to incremental costs without regard to O/H (fixed) costs because fixed O/H cannot be changed in the short run. Thus, the emphasis in the short run should be on controllable costs. Relatedly, service department costs, allocated as a part of O/H, may not be controllable in the short run.
  Answers (a), (c), (d), and (e) are incorrect because each is a decision requiring full cost data.

10. The overhead allocation method that allocates service department costs without consideration of services rendered to other service departments is the

   a. Step-down method.
   b. Direct method.
   c. Reciprocal method.
   d. None of the above.

The correct answer is (b). *(Publisher)*
REQUIRED: The method that allocates service department costs only to the production departments.
DISCUSSION: The direct method of overhead allocation apportions service department costs directly to production departments. It makes no allocation of services rendered to other service departments.
  Answer (a) is incorrect because the step-down method allocates costs of service departments to production and other service departments. Answer (c) is incorrect because the reciprocal method recognizes services interchanged among service departments.

11. The controller and the vice president of production of Terry Co. are discussing the predetermined O/H rates to be established for the upcoming year. The controller takes the position that predetermined rates can be set individually for fixed and variable elements of O/H costs. The product VP asserts that individual unit rates may be set for the production departments to the final units of goods and services, but that it seems impossible to set unit rates for fixed and variable O/H elements of service to production. As their accountant, you advise that it is proper to allocate fixed and variable elements of O/H costs by individual predetermined O/H rates for

   a. Service departments to production departments.
   b. Production departments to the final output units of goods and services.
   c. Both (a) and (b) above.
   d. None of the above.

The correct answer is (c). *(Publisher)*
REQUIRED: The propriety of developing predetermined O/H rates for fixed and variable costs.
DISCUSSION: Determining predetermined O/H rates is appropriate for both fixed and variable elements of O/H costs. Known as establishing dual rates, it permits the capacity costs to be assessed, an appropriate rate to be charged to the using department, and appropriate deviations from the utilization of capacity to be noted. Setting a variable O/H rate permits analysis of the utilization of variable overhead as well as of any spending variances. Thus, it is proper to use individual predetermined O/H rates for allocating O/H costs from service to production departments and from production departments to the final output.

12. The most accurate method for allocating service department costs is the

   a. Step-down method.
   b. Direct method.
   c. Reciprocal method.
   d. None of the above.

The correct answer is (c). *(Publisher)*
REQUIRED: The most accurate method of allocating service department costs.
DISCUSSION: The reciprocal allocation method allocates O/H costs of service departments among other service departments providing reciprocal services, thus acknowledging all possible sources of cost. The step-down method (also called the step or sequential method) ignores the reciprocity that may occur between service departments. The direct method ignores any services rendered to other service departments.

13. In which of the following overhead allocation methods may no other service department costs be charged back to a particular service department after the first service department's cost has been allocated?

   a. The reciprocal method and the direct method.
   b. The step-down method and the reciprocal method.
   c. The direct method and the step-down method.
   d. None of the above.

The correct answer is (c). *(Publisher)*
REQUIRED: The cost allocation methods in which no costs can be charged back to a service department after its own costs have been allocated.
DISCUSSION: In the direct method, service department costs are not allocated to other service departments. In the step-down method, service department costs are acknowledged and allocated to other service departments but no reallocation (charge back) takes place.
Answers (a) and (b) are incorrect because, in the reciprocal method, service department costs are allocated among other service departments providing reciprocal services. This requires reallocation and simultaneous equations to solve for several variables.

14. The method of overhead allocation that usually starts with the service department rendering the greatest amount of service to the greatest number of other service departments and progresses in descending order to the service department rendering service to the least number of other service departments is the

   a. Step-down method.
   b. Direct method.
   c. Step-down and direct methods.
   d. None of the above.

The correct answer is (a). *(Publisher)*
REQUIRED: The term for the described sequence of overhead allocation.
DISCUSSION: In the step-down method of overhead allocation, the allocation process starts with the department that renders service to the greatest number of other service departments and progresses in descending order to the service department rendering the least service to the other service departments.
Answers (b) and (c) are incorrect because, under the direct method, service department costs are not allocated to other service departments, so no step-downs would be necessary.

Module 9.1: Cost Allocation

15. If two service departments service the same number of other service departments when using the step-down method, which service department's costs are allocated first?

   a. The service department with the most direct cost.
   b. The service department with the most employees.
   c. The service department most crucial to the operation of the production department.
   d. None of the above; the reciprocal method must be used.

The correct answer is (a). *(Publisher)*
REQUIRED: Given two departments servicing an equal number of other service departments, the service department whose costs are allocated first using the step-down method.
DISCUSSION: Normally, the cost of the service department that services the greatest number of other service departments is allocated first. In the event that two or more service departments service an equal number of other service departments, the service department with the greatest costs allocates its costs first.

16. The variable costs of service departments should be allocated to production departments by using

   a. Actual short-run output based on predetermined rates.
   b. Actual short-run output based on actual rates.
   c. The service department's expected costs of long-run capacity.
   d. The service department's actual costs based on actual utilization of services.

The correct answer is (a). *(Publisher)*
REQUIRED: The allocation basis of service departments' variable costs to production departments.
DISCUSSION: The most appropriate method of O/H allocation of variable service department costs to production departments is to take the actual usage by the production department times the predetermined rate. This basis gives the user department responsibility for the actual usage at the predetermined rate.
   Answer (b) is incorrect because the actual rate may differ substantially from the estimated rate, and the production department would usually have had no control over the actual rate. Answer (c) is incorrect because the capacity costs of the service department should be allocated by a fixed O/H rate or lump-sum charge based upon the capacity needs of the production department. Answer (d) is incorrect because neither party would have an understanding about the estimated rate.

17. The fixed costs of service departments should be allocated to production departments based on

   a. Actual short-run utilization based on predetermined rates.
   b. Actual short-run units based on actual rates.
   c. The service department's expected costs of long-run capacity.
   d. The service department's actual costs based on actual utilization of services.

The correct answer is (c). *(Publisher)*
REQUIRED: The appropriate basis for allocating fixed costs of service departments to production departments.
DISCUSSION: The fixed costs of service departments should be allocated to production departments in lump-sum amounts on the basis of the service department's budgeted costs of long-term capacity to serve. This basis allows the production department to develop (budget) a certain capacity needed from the service departments and to agree on the assessment of costs. Analysis of actual results permits evaluation of the service departments' ability to provide the estimated volume of service.
   Answers (a), (b), and (d) are incorrect because each contains elements of actual units, use, and/or costs which transfers any efficiencies or inefficiencies of the service department to the production department.

18. An automotive company has three divisions. One division manufactures new replacement parts for automobiles; another rebuilds engines; and the third does repair and overhaul work on a line of trucks. All three divisions use the services of a central payroll department. The best method of allocating the cost of the payroll department to the various operating divisions is

   a. Total labor hours incurred in the divisions.
   b. Value of production in the divisions.
   c. Direct labor costs incurred in the divisions.
   d. Machine hours used in the divisions.

The correct answer is (a). *(CIA 1187 IV-3)*
REQUIRED: The best method of allocating payroll department costs.
DISCUSSION: The costs incurred by the payroll department are indirect. They cannot feasibly be directly identified with particular cost objectives. Accordingly, an allocation base must be chosen that systematically and rationally apportions the costs to the cost objectives. This base should reflect a relationship with the incurrence of the cost. The best method listed is total labor hours since payroll preparation cost varies directly with labor effort.
Answer (b) is incorrect because production value may be lower in a department that generates higher payroll costs. Answer (c) is incorrect because it does not consider indirect labor. Also, payroll costs tend to vary more with total hours and employees than with labor rates. Answer (d) is incorrect because machine hours do not necessarily correlate with costs incurred for payroll preparation.

19. The janitorial department provides cleaning services to all departments of a large store. Management wishes to allocate the janitorial costs to the various departments that benefit from the service. Which would be the most reasonable allocation base for janitorial costs?

   a. Sales of each department.
   b. Square footage of each department.
   c. Number of employees in each department.
   d. Total direct costs of each department before any allocations.

The correct answer is (b). *(CIA 1187 IV-8)*
REQUIRED: The most reasonable allocation base for janitorial costs.
DISCUSSION: The allocation of service department cost should be based upon a measure (the allocation base) that rationally relates the independent variable (a cost objective, such as a production department) to the dependent variable (the costs, such as those incurred by a service department). Since janitorial costs should vary directly with the area serviced, square footage is an appropriate allocation base.
Answers (a), (c), and (d) are incorrect because none has a necessary cause-effect relationship with janitorial cost.

20. The county hospital maintains a 24-hour X-ray department which performs X-ray and sonogram services. The county reimburses the hospital for the services performed on indigent patients, while paying patients are charged directly for the services. The costs of the X-ray department would best be allocated to indigent care based on

   a. The number of total X-rays taken over a given period of time.
   b. The percentage of indigent to total cases handled over a given period of time.
   c. The number of hours the department is open.
   d. The average number of minutes spent on each patient.

The correct answer is (b). *(CIA 1186 IV-3)*
REQUIRED: The best cost allocation base.
DISCUSSION: Allocation of service department cost should be based on some variable (activity) that has a strong correlation with the incurrence of cost by the cost objective. Assuming indigents are not more or less likely than paying patients to require such procedures, the cost of X-ray and sonograms could reasonably be allocated on the basis of relative patient volume.
Answer (a) is incorrect because it does not take into account the sonogram services. Answer (c) is incorrect because it would be impossible to determine what percentage of total hours was devoted to indigent care. Answer (d) is incorrect because it does not necessarily correlate with costs incurred.

9.2 Calculations

21. A hospital has a $100,000 expected utility bill this year. The janitorial, accounting, and orderlies departments are service functions to the operating, hospital rooms, and laboratories departments. Floor space assigned to each department is

Department	Square Footage
Janitorial	1,000
Accounting	2,000
Orderlies	7,000
Operating	4,000
Hospital Rooms	30,000
Laboratories	6,000
	50,000

How much of the $100,000 will eventually become the hospital rooms department total costs, assuming a direct allocation based on square footage is used?

a. $60,000.

b. $72,000.

c. $75,000.

d. $80,000.

The correct answer is (c). *(CIA 587 IV-7)*
REQUIRED: The hospital rooms department total costs assuming a direct allocation based on square footage.
DISCUSSION: The direct method allocates service department costs without regard to service provided to other service departments. Consequently, the $100,000 utility expense will be apportioned among the three production departments on the basis of square footage. The hospital rooms department's share will be $75,000 {$100,000 x [30,000 square feet ÷ (4,000 + 30,000 + 6,000) total square feet]}.

22. Boa Corp. distributes service department overhead costs directly to producing departments without allocation to the other service department. Information for the month of June is as follows.

	Service Departments	
	Maintenance	Utilities
Overhead costs incurred	$20,000	$10,000

Service provided to departments:

Maintenance	--	10%
Utilities	20%	--
Producing - A	40%	30%
Producing - B	40%	60%
Totals	100%	100%

The amount of maintenance department costs distributed to Producing - A department for June was

a. $8,000.

b. $8,800.

c. $10,000.

d. $11,000.

The correct answer is (c). *(CPA 1185 Q-1)*
REQUIRED: The service department cost allocation using the direct method.
DISCUSSION: The direct method of overhead allocation apportions service department costs directly to production departments. It makes no allocation of services rendered to other service departments. Therefore, the 20% of maintenance costs attributable to utilities is ignored. Since a total of 80% (40% + 40%) is directly attributable to producing departments A and B, 1/2 of the total maintenance cost or $10,000 [(40 ÷ 80) x $20,000] is to be allocated to a single department.

Questions 23 and 24 are based on Computer Complex, which offers two main services: (1) time on a time-shared computer system and (2) proprietary computer programs. Computer time is provided by the operation department (Op) and programs are written by the programming department (P). The percentage of each service used by each department for a typical period is presented below.

User	Op	P
Op	--	40%
P	30%	--
Sold to customers	70%	60%
Total	100%	100%

In a typical period, the operation department spends $4,500 and the programming department spends $2,500.

23. Under the step-down method, what is the cost of the computer time and the computer programs for sale?

	Time	Programs
a.	$4,500	$2,500
b.	$3,150	$3,850
c.	$1,350	$5,650
d.	$2,700	$4,300
e.	$3,000	$4,000

The correct answer is (b). (R. Gruber)
REQUIRED: The allocation of service department costs under the step-down method.
DISCUSSION: In the step-down method of overhead allocation, the allocation process starts with the department that renders service to the greatest number of other service departments and progresses in descending order to the service department rendering the least service to the other service departments. Since the operation department renders the greatest amount of service to any one user (40% of $4,500 vs. 30% of $2,500), allocation of its costs is made first. Thus, $3,150 (70% x $4,500) is allocated to the operation department which is the cost of computer time. The remaining operation cost of $1,350 ($4,500 - $3,150) is allocated to the programming department along with programming costs of $2,500 to give a total of $3,850 ($1,350 + $2,500) allocated to the programming department which is the cost of programs.

24. Under the reciprocal method what is the solution to the service cost allocation problem?

a. Op = 4,500 + .40 P; P = 2,500 + .30 Op.
b. Op = 4,500 + .70 P; P = 2,500 + .60 Op.
c. Op = 2,500 + .40 P; P = 4,500 + .30 Op.
d. Op = 2,500 + .70 P; P = 4,500 + .60 Op.

The correct answer is (a). (R. Gruber)
REQUIRED: The allocation of service department costs under the reciprocal method.
DISCUSSION: The reciprocal method takes into account services provided by each service department to each other. The first step is to set up equations representing the complete reciprocated cost of each service department. The Op department's complete cost is its own cost of $4,500 plus 40% of P department's cost. The P department's complete cost is its own cost of $2,500 plus 30% of Op department's cost.

$$Op = \$4,500 + .40\ P$$
$$P = \$2,500 + .30\ Op$$

Questions 25 through 29 are based on the following information. Hartwell Company distributes the service department overhead costs directly to producing departments without allocation to the other service departments. Information for the month of January is presented in the next column.

	Maintenance	Utilities
Overhead costs incurred	$18,700	$9,000
Service provided to:		
Maintenance department	--	10%
Utilities department	20%	--
Producing department A	40%	30%
Producing department B	40%	60%

Module 9.2: Calculations

> Questions 25 through 29 are based on the information presented at the bottom of page 196.

25. The amount of utilities department costs distributed to producing department B for January should be

   a. $3,600.
   b. $4,500.
   c. $5,400.
   d. $6,000.

The correct answer is (d). *(CPA 582 P-21)*
REQUIRED: The amount of service department costs distributed to a producing department under the direct method.
DISCUSSION: Direct allocation ignores services rendered by one service department to other service departments. Here, the $9,000 utilities department cost will be allocated 30/90 (90% = the sum of the producing departments' percentage usages) to department A and 60/90 to department B.

26. Assume instead that Hartwell Company distributes the service departments' overhead costs based on the step-down method. Which of the following methods is true?

   a. Allocate maintenance expense to departments A and B.
   b. Allocate maintenance expense to departments A and B and the utilities department.
   c. Allocate utilities expense to the maintenance department and departments A and B.
   d. None of the above.

The correct answer is (b). *(Publisher)*
REQUIRED: Method of allocating service department costs under the step-down method.
DISCUSSION: Under the step-down method, the maintenance department would allocate its $18,700 of cost first because it has the greatest total cost. Note that both the maintenance and utilities departments provide service to one other service department. Thus, the criterion for first allocation is greatest cost, not greatest number of service departments.

27. Under the step-down method, how much of Hartwell's utilities department cost is allocated between departments A and B?

   a. $9,900.
   b. $10,800.
   c. $12,740.
   d. $27,700.

The correct answer is (c). *(Publisher)*
REQUIRED: The total utility cost to be allocated to the two producing departments under the step-down method.
DISCUSSION: As determined in Q. 26, the maintenance department budget is allocated first under the step-down method. Thus, $3,740 (20% of the $18,700) is allocated to the utilities department. Now the utilities department has $12,740 ($9,000 + $3,740) to allocate between departments A and B.

28. Assume that Hartwell Company distributes service department overhead costs based on the reciprocal method, what would be the formula to determine the total maintenance costs?

   a. M = $18,700 + .10U.
   b. M = $9,000 + .20U.
   c. M = $18,700 + .30U + .40A + .40B.
   d. M = $27,700 + .40A + .40B.

The correct answer is (a). *(Publisher)*
REQUIRED: The formula to determine the maintenance costs under the reciprocal method.
DISCUSSION: Under the reciprocal method, simultaneous equations are developed to determine the gross costs of each service department, taking into account the interactive effect of other service departments providing interservice department service. For maintenance, the cost is $18,700 plus 10% of the utilities cost. 40% of this amount will be applied to A and 40% to B. The 20% that has already been assigned to the utilities department is reflected in the set of simultaneous equations.

29. Assume that Hartwell Company distributes utilities department overhead costs based on the reciprocal method, what would be the formula to determine the total utilities costs?

   a. U = $18,700 + .10M.
   b. U = $9,000 + .20M.
   c. U = $18,700 + .30M + .40H + .40B.
   d. U = $27,700 + .40A + .40B.

The correct answer is (b). *(Publisher)*
REQUIRED: The formula to determine the utilities costs under the reciprocal method.
DISCUSSION: Under the reciprocal method, simultaneous equations are developed to determine the gross costs of each service department, taking into account the interactive effect of other service departments providing interservice department service. For utilities, the cost is $9,000 plus 20% of the maintenance cost. 30% of it will be applied to A and 60% to B. The 10% that has already been assigned to the maintenance department is reflected in the set of simultaneous equations.

Questions 30 through 41 are based on the following information, which was presented as Question 40 on Part IV of the May 1980 CIA examination.

Barnes Company has two service departments and three production departments, each producing a separate product. For a number of years, Barnes has allocated the costs of the service departments to the production departments on the basis of the annual sales revenue dollars. In a recent audit report, the internal auditor stated that the distribution of service department costs on the basis of annual sales dollars would lead to serious inequities. It was recommended that maintenance and engineering service hours be used as a better service cost allocation basis. For illustrative purposes, the following information was appended to the audit report.

	Service Departments		Production Departments		
	Maintenance	Engineering	Product A	Product B	Product C
Maintenance hours used		400	800	200	200
Engineering hours used	400		800	400	400
Department direct costs	$12,000	$54,000	$80,000	$90,000	$50,000

30. Using simultaneous equations, what would be the total Engineering Department cost after allocation of interservice department costs but before allocation to the Maintenance and Production departments?

   a. $12,000.
   b. $54,000.
   c. $60,000.
   d. $57,000.

The correct answer is (c). *(CIA 580 IV-40)*
REQUIRED: The Engineering Department's total cost before further allocation.
DISCUSSION: Simultaneous equations are developed to solve cost allocations involving interdepartmental service costs when using the reciprocal allocation method. Here, Maintenance and Engineering provide services to each other. Engineering has $54,000 of direct costs, which does not include the cost of some Maintenance services. The Maintenance Department's $12,000 of direct costs does not include its share of the Engineering costs. Solving the following simultaneous equations indicates that Engineering's cost after allocation back and forth with Maintenance is $60,000. Note that the total hours of maintenance is 1,600, of which 400 is used by Engineering, i.e., 25%. Similarly, out of 2,000 total hours of Engineering, 400 are used by Maintenance, i.e., 20%.

$$M = \text{Maintenance Department's total cost}$$
$$E = \text{Engineering Department's total cost}$$
$$M = \$12{,}000 + .2E$$
$$E = \$54{,}000 + .25M$$
$$E = \$54{,}000 + .25(\$12{,}000 + .2E)$$
$$E = \$54{,}000 + \$3{,}000 + .05E$$
$$.95E = \$57{,}000$$
$$E = \$60{,}000$$

31. How much Engineering Department cost was allocated to Departments A, B, and C under the reciprocal method?

   a. $48,000.
   b. $54,000.
   c. $60,000.
   d. None of the above.

The correct answer is (a). *(Publisher)*
REQUIRED: Total Engineering costs allocated to the production departments.
DISCUSSION: The Engineering Department's $60,000 in costs (Q. 30) is allocated based on the denominator of 2,000 total hours.

A (800 ÷ 2,000) x $60,000 = $24,000
B (400 ÷ 2,000) x $60,000 = $12,000
C (400 ÷ 2,000) x $60,000 = $12,000
                              $48,000

Module 9.2: Calculations

32. Using simultaneous equations (i.e., the reciprocal method), what would be the total Maintenance Department cost prior to allocation to the Engineering and Production departments?

a. $24,000.
b. $12,000.
c. $20,800.
d. $15,600.

33. Under the reciprocal method, what portion of Maintenance Department cost is allocated to Department A?

a. 800/1,600.
b. 800/1,200.
c. 200/1,200.
d. 200/1,600.

34. Using the direct method of cost allocation, how much maintenance cost would be allocated to the Engineering Department?

a. $3,000.
b. $0.
c. $1,500.
d. $6,000.

35. Using the direct method of cost allocation, what amount of maintenance cost would be allocated to Department C?

a. $3,000.
b. $0.
c. $2,000.
d. $8,000.

The correct answer is (a). *(Publisher)*
REQUIRED: The Maintenance Department total cost before further allocation.
DISCUSSION: Substituting the Engineering Department's $60,000 (from Q. 30) into the equation for maintenance costs,

$$E = \$60,000$$
$$M = \$12,000 + .2E$$
$$M = \$12,000 + \$12,000 = \$24,000$$

The correct answer is (a). *(Publisher)*
REQUIRED: The portion of maintenance expense allocated to Department A under the reciprocal method.
DISCUSSION: The Maintenance Department expense is $24,000 (per the reciprocal method), as calculated in Q. 32. It is allocated

800/1,600 to A
200/1,600 to B
200/1,600 to C

Note that $18,000 of maintenance cost is allocated to Departments A, B, and C, but only $12,000 was actually incurred. This is because the Engineering Department's actual expense was $54,000, but only $48,000 was allocated.

The correct answer is (b). *(Publisher)*
REQUIRED: The amount of maintenance cost allocated to the Engineering Department using the direct method.
DISCUSSION: Under the direct method of cost allocation, no service department costs are allocated to another service department. Thus, there would be no maintenance cost allocated to the Engineering Department.

The correct answer is (c). *(Publisher)*
REQUIRED: The amount of maintenance cost allocated to Dept. C using the direct method.
DISCUSSION: Using the direct method of cost allocation, the amount of maintenance cost allocated to Dept. C would be based on the hours utilized in proportion to the hours utilized by all the production departments. No proportion of the maintenance cost would be allocated to another service department. The Production Departments used a total of 1,200 maintenance hours, of which Department C used 200.

$$200/1,200 \times \$12,000 = \$2,000$$

36. Refer to the information presented on page 198. Using the direct method of cost allocation, what amount of engineering cost would be allocated to Department A?

a. $20,800.
b. $27,000.
c. $0.
d. $54,000.

The correct answer is (b). *(Publisher)*
REQUIRED: The amount of engineering cost allocated to Dept. A using the direct method.
DISCUSSION: The use of the direct method of cost allocation precludes any interdepartmental cost allocation from one service department to another. Thus, the $54,000 of engineering costs are to be allocated only to Production Departments. Based on engineering hours used, Dept. A uses 50% (800/1,600) of the total hours. Thus, Dept. A would be allocated $27,000 (50% x $54,000).

For Questions 37 through 41, refer to the information on page 198 and assume that maintenance costs are allocated first (although, normally, engineering costs would be allocated first because they are greater than maintenance costs).

---

37. Using the step-down method of cost allocation, how much maintenance cost would be allocated to the Engineering Department?

a. $1,500.
b. $6,000.
c. $0.
d. $3,000.

The correct answer is (d). *(Publisher)*
REQUIRED: The maintenance cost allocated to Engineering using the step-down method.
DISCUSSION: In the step-down or sequential method of overhead allocation, and assuming that maintenance costs are allocated first, they would be allocated to the Engineering Dept. proportional to the maintenance hours used, in this case, 400 hours. The total number of maintenance hours used was 1,600; the proportion of maintenance hours used by the Engineering Dept. is thus 25%.

$$1/4 \times \$12,000 = \$3,000$$

38. Using the step-down method of cost allocation, and allocating maintenance first, what amount of maintenance cost would be allocated to Department B?

a. $6,000.
b. $1,500.
c. $11,000.
d. $9,500.

The correct answer is (b). *(Publisher)*
REQUIRED: The maintenance cost allocated to Dept. B using the step-down method.
DISCUSSION: The step-down method of cost allocation uses the proportion of hours of maintenance utilized in Dept. B (200) compared to the total used in Engineering and all the Production Departments (1,600). Dept. B's share of the maintenance cost would be

$$200/1,600 \times \$12,000 = \$1,500$$

39. Using the step-down method of cost allocation, and allocating maintenance first, what amount of engineering costs would be allocated to the Maintenance Department?

a. $10,800.
b. $9,500.
c. $3,000.
d. $0.

The correct answer is (d). *(Publisher)*
REQUIRED: The engineering costs allocated to Maintenance under the step-down method.
DISCUSSION: Under the step-down method, once a department's costs have been allocated to subsequent departments, no reallocation back to that department takes place. Thus, there would be no engineering costs reallocated to the Maintenance Dept.

40. Using the step-down method of cost allocation, and allocating maintenance first, what amount of engineering costs would be allocated to Department C?

a. $9,000.
b. $14,250.
c. $9,500.
d. $6,000.

The correct answer is (b). *(Publisher)*
REQUIRED: The engineering costs allocated to Dept. C using the step-down method.
DISCUSSION: Using the step-down method, the total engineering costs allocated to Dept. C equal the actual engineering costs ($54,000) plus the engineering allocation from the Maintenance Dept. ($3,000) times the proportion of Dept. C hours used compared to the total (400/1,600).

($54,000 + $3,000) x (400/1,600) = $14,250

41. Using the step-down method of cost allocation, what is the total amount of service department costs allocated to Department A?

a. $38,000.
b. $37,500.
c. $40,000.
d. $34,500.

The correct answer is (d). *(Publisher)*
REQUIRED: The total service department costs allocated to Dept. A using the step-down method.
DISCUSSION: Using the step-down method, the service department costs allocated to Dept. A include maintenance costs of 800/1,600 x $12,000 = $6,000, plus the amount of engineering costs allocated to Dept. A. Engineering costs are $54,000 plus $3,000 of the maintenance cost allocated to engineering under the step-down method. $57,000 x 800/1,600 = $28,500. Thus, $34,500 ($6,000 + $28,500) of service department costs are allocated to Dept. A.

Questions 42 and 43 are based on the following information. Hermo Company has just completed a hydroelectric plant at a cost of $21,000,000. The plant will provide the company's power needs for the next 20 years. Hermo will use only 60% of the power output annually. At this level of capacity, Hermo's annual operating costs will amount to $1,800,000, of which 80% are fixed.

Quigley Company currently purchases its power from MF Electric at an annual cost of $1,200,000. Hermo could supply this power thus increasing output of the plant to 90% of capacity. This would reduce the estimated life of the plant to 14 years.

---

42. If Hermo decides to supply power to Quigley, it wants to be compensated for the decrease in the life of the plant and the appropriate variable costs. Hermo has decided that the charge for the decreased life should be based on the original cost of the plant calculated on a straight-line basis. The minimum annual amount that Hermo would charge Quigley would be

a. $450,000.
b. $630,000.
c. $990,000.
d. $1,050,000.
e. Some amount other than those given above.

The correct answer is (b). *(CMA 1286 5-17)*
REQUIRED: The minimum amount that can be charged for electricity.
DISCUSSION: The minimum charge would include any variable costs incurred plus depreciation on a straight-line basis. Currently, variable costs are $360,000 at 60% of capacity ($1,800,000 x 20%). If Quigley purchases energy equal to an additional 30% of capacity, it can be assumed that the increase in total variable costs will be half of the variable costs for 60% of capacity, or $180,000. Also, allocating $21,000,000 over 14 years results in an annual depreciation of $1,500,000. Of this amount, 30% will relate to the capacity sold. Thus, the depreciation charge to Quigley is $450,000 (30% x $1,500,000). The total charge is $630,000 ($450,000 depreciation + $180,000 VC).

43. The maximum amount Quigley would be willing to pay Hermo annually for the power is

a. $600,000.
b. $1,050,000.
c. $1,200,000.
d. $450,000.
e. Some amount other than those given above.

The correct answer is (c). *(CMA 1286 5-18)*
REQUIRED: The maximum amount the buyer would be willing to pay.
DISCUSSION: Since Quigley is currently paying $1,200,000, it would not want to pay any more for the same service.

CHAPTER TEN
ABSORPTION AND VARIABLE COSTING

> 10.1 Variable Costing .... (14 questions) 203
> 10.2 Absorption Costing vs. Variable Costing .... (17 questions) 207
> 10.3 Calculations .... (40 questions) 212

Absorption costing versus variable (direct) costing is a topic of special concern in textbooks and on the professional examinations. Absorption costing is primarily used for inventory valuation purposes and external reporting. Variable costing is used solely for internal decision making. Some firms use variable costing throughout the year and, at year-end, make an adjustment to their inventory to convert it to absorption costing. Allocation of fixed overhead to inventory is the difference between variable costing and absorption costing. The difference in income between the two methods is the change in units of inventory times the unit fixed cost (assuming, as usual in accounting problems, that fixed cost per unit is constant).

10.1 Variable Costing

1. In the application of "direct costing" as a cost-allocation process in manufacturing,

  a. Variable direct costs are treated as period costs.
  b. Nonvariable indirect costs are treated as product costs.
  c. Variable indirect costs are treated as product costs.
  d. Nonvariable direct costs are treated as product costs.
  e. None of the above.

The correct answer is (c). *(CIA 577 IV-18)*
REQUIRED: The correct statement about direct costing.
DISCUSSION: Direct costing considers only variable manufacturing costs to be product costs, i.e., inventoriable. Fixed manufacturing costs are considered period costs and are expensed as incurred.
Answer (a) is incorrect because variable (i.e., direct) manufacturing costs are accounted for as product costs, not period costs. Answers (b) and (d) are incorrect because, in direct costing, all nonvariable (fixed) manufacturing costs are treated as period costs, not product costs.

2. A basic tenet of direct costing is that period costs should be currently expensed. What is the rationale behind this procedure?

  a. Period costs are uncontrollable and should not be charged to a specific product.
  b. Period costs are generally immaterial in amount and the cost of assigning the amounts to specific products would outweigh the benefits.
  c. Allocation of period costs is arbitrary at best and could lead to erroneous decisions by management.
  d. Because period costs will occur whether or not production occurs, it is improper to allocate these costs to production and defer a current cost of doing business.

The correct answer is (d). *(CPA 1178 T-39)*
REQUIRED: The rationale behind the direct costing method.
DISCUSSION: Fixed costs are a basic expense of being in business; i.e., they are incurred to continue operating the business regardless of production levels. Accordingly, they are not controllable in the short run and should not be deferred.
Answer (a) is incorrect because period costs are controllable at higher levels of management in the long run. Answer (b) is incorrect because period costs are generally material in amount. Answer (c) is incorrect because while the allocation of period costs may be arbitrary, the more basic rationale behind direct costing is the lack of controllability in the short run.

Module 10.1: Variable Costing

3. Under variable or direct costing, fixed manufacturing overhead costs would be classified as

   a. Period costs.
   b. Product costs.
   c. Selling costs.
   d. Inventoriable costs.

The correct answer is (a). *(CIA 1186 IV-8)*
REQUIRED: The classification of fixed manufacturing overhead under direct costing.
DISCUSSION: The distinction between absorption costing and direct costing is in the treatment of fixed manufacturing costs. Absorption costing treats them as product costs by allocating them to inventory and cost of goods sold. Direct costing treats all fixed manufacturing costs as period costs by expensing them as incurred.
Answers (b) and (d) are incorrect because absorption, not direct, costing treats such costs as product (inventoriable) costs. Answer (c) is incorrect because selling and fixed manufacturing overhead costs are treated separately although both are period costs in a direct costing system.

4. Which of the following is a term more descriptive of the type of cost accounting often called "direct costing"?

   a. Out-of-pocket costing.
   b. Variable costing.
   c. Relevant costing.
   d. Prime costing.

The correct answer is (b). *(CPA 575 T-40)*
REQUIRED: The term that best describes direct costing.
DISCUSSION: Direct costing considers only variable manufacturing costs to be product costs, i.e., inventoriable. Fixed manufacturing costs are considered period costs.
Answer (a) is incorrect because out-of-pocket costs refer to those requiring immediate expenditure. Answer (c) is incorrect because relevant costs are those that vary with alternative decisions. Answer (d) is incorrect because prime costing includes only direct labor and direct material costs (i.e., no variable overhead).

5. What costs are treated as product costs under variable (direct) costing?

   a. Only direct costs.
   b. Only variable production costs.
   c. All variable costs.
   d. All variable and fixed manufacturing costs.

The correct answer is (b). *(CPA 576 T-23)*
REQUIRED: The costs allocated to product under direct costing.
DISCUSSION: Product costs under direct costing include DM, DL, and variable O/H. Each is a variable production cost.
Answer (a) is incorrect because variable overhead must also be included. Answer (c) is incorrect because only variable production costs, not variable general costs, are product costs in direct costing. Answer (d) is incorrect because absorption costing, not variable costing, includes all variable and fixed production costs.

6. Inventory under the direct costing method includes

   a. Direct materials cost, direct labor cost, but no factory overhead cost.
   b. Direct materials cost, direct labor cost, and variable factory overhead cost.
   c. Prime cost but not conversion cost.
   d. Prime cost and all conversion cost.

The correct answer is (b). *(CPA 1181 T-47)*
REQUIRED: The elements included in direct costing inventory.
DISCUSSION: Direct costing inventory includes only variable manufacturing costs: DM, DL, and variable O/H. Fixed factory O/H is treated as a period cost.
Answer (a) is incorrect because variable O/H should be included. Answer (c) is incorrect because prime cost consists only of DM and DL. Answer (d) is incorrect because conversion cost includes fixed O/H, which is not a component of inventory under direct costing.

Module 10.1: Variable Costing

7. Which of the following must be known about a production process in order to institute a direct costing system?

   a. The variable and fixed components of all costs related to production.
   b. The controllable and noncontrollable components of all costs related to production.
   c. Standard production rates and times for all elements of production.
   d. Contribution margin and breakeven point for all goods in production.

The correct answer is (a). *(CPA 1180 T-31)*
REQUIRED: The elements needed to institute a direct costing system.
DISCUSSION: Direct costing "inventories" only variable manufacturing costs. Fixed manufacturing costs are treated as period costs. Thus, one need only be able to determine the variable and fixed manufacturing costs to institute a direct costing system.
Answer (b) is incorrect because even fixed costs are controllable in the long run. Answer (c) is incorrect because standard costing is not necessary to institute direct costing, i.e., actual costs may be used. Answer (d) is incorrect because CM and BEP require knowing selling prices as well as variable and fixed costs.

8. Under the direct costing concept, unit product cost would most likely be increased by

   a. A decrease in the remaining useful life of factory machinery depreciated on the units-of-production method.
   b. A decrease in the number of units produced.
   c. An increase in the remaining useful life of factory machinery depreciated on the sum-of-the-years'-digits method.
   d. An increase in the commission paid to salesmen for each unit sold.

The correct answer is (a). *(CPA 573 T-34)*
REQUIRED: The change most likely to increase unit product cost under direct costing.
DISCUSSION: Direct costing considers only variable manufacturing costs to be product costs. Fixed manufacturing costs are period costs. The units-of-production depreciation method would be included in variable overhead. Thus, a decrease in the remaining useful life of machinery would probably increase the unit product cost.
Answer (b) is incorrect because variable costs per unit remain constant. Answer (c) is incorrect because SYD depreciation would affect fixed manufacturing overhead not variable overhead. Answer (d) is incorrect because commissions are a selling expense, i.e., a period cost, not a product cost.

9. Why is direct costing not in accordance with generally accepted accounting principles?

   a. Fixed manufacturing costs are assumed to be period costs.
   b. Direct costing procedures are not well known in industry.
   c. Net earnings are always overstated when using direct costing procedures.
   d. Direct costing ignores the concept of lower of cost or market when valuing inventory.

The correct answer is (a). *(CPA 578 T-50)*
REQUIRED: Why direct costing is not acceptable per GAAP.
DISCUSSION: Direct costing considers only variable manufacturing costs as product costs. Fixed manufacturing costs are considered period costs. Proponents of absorption costing argue that inventories must carry their fair share of fixed costs. The accounting profession has not accepted direct costing for external reporting.
Answer (b) is incorrect because direct costing is a heavily emphasized concept both in education and in industry. Answer (c) is incorrect because the relationship of direct costing earnings relative to absorption costing earnings varies with the relationship of production levels to sales levels. Answer (d) is incorrect because the lower of cost or market concept is compatible with direct costing, i.e., one can compare market with direct rather than absorption costs.

10. When using a direct costing system, the contribution margin discloses the excess of

    a. Revenues over fixed costs.
    b. Projected revenues over the break-even point.
    c. Revenues over variable costs.
    d. Variable costs over fixed costs.

The correct answer is (c). *(CPA 1177 T-30)*
REQUIRED: The definition of contribution margin (CM) in a direct costing system.
DISCUSSION: Contribution margin is the difference between revenues and variable costs. No distinction is made between variable product costs and variable selling costs; both are deducted from revenue to arrive at CM.
Answer (a) is incorrect because CM is the excess of total revenue over total variable costs, not over fixed costs. Answer (b) is incorrect because it is projected net income. Answer (d) is incorrect because it is a nonsense concept.

Module 10.1: Variable Costing

11. Which of the following is an argument against the use of direct (variable) costing?

a. Absorption costing overstates the balance sheet value of inventories.
b. Variable factory overhead is a period cost.
c. Fixed factory overhead is difficult to allocate properly.
d. Fixed factory overhead is necessary for the production of a product.

The correct answer is (d). *(CIA 1187 IV-9)*
REQUIRED: The argument against the use of direct (variable) costing.
DISCUSSION: Direct costing treats fixed manufacturing costs as period costs, while absorption costing accumulates them as product costs. If product costs are viewed as all manufacturing costs incurred to produce output, fixed factory overhead should be inventoried since it is necessary for production. The counter argument in favor of direct costing is that fixed factory overhead is more closely related to capacity to produce than to the production of individual units. Internal reporting for cost behavior analysis is more useful if it concentrates on the latter.
Answer (a) is incorrect because direct costing arguably understates inventory. Answer (b) is incorrect because variable overhead is a product cost under any cost system. Answer (c) is incorrect because it is an argument against absorption costing.

12. Which of the following statements is true for a firm that uses "direct" (variable) costing?

a. The cost of a unit of product changes because of changes in number of units manufactured.
b. Profits fluctuate with sales.
c. An idle facility variation is calculated.
d. Product costs include "direct" (variable) administrative costs.
e. None of the above.

The correct answer is (b). *(CMA 1273 4-1)*
REQUIRED: The correct statement about direct costing.
DISCUSSION: In a direct (variable) costing system, only the variable costs are recorded as product costs. All fixed costs are expensed in the period incurred. Because changes in the relationship between production levels and sales levels do not cause changes in the amount of fixed manufacturing cost that is expensed, profits more directly follow the trends in sales.
Answers (a) and (c) are incorrect because they are characteristics of absorption costing systems. Answer (d) is incorrect because neither direct nor absorption costing includes administrative costs in inventory.

13. In an income statement prepared as an internal report using the variable costing method, which of the following terms should appear?

	Gross profit (margin)	Operating income
a.	Yes	Yes
b.	Yes	No
c.	No	No
d.	No	Yes

The correct answer is (d). *(CPA 1187 T-46)*
REQUIRED: The income classification for a variable costing income statement.
DISCUSSION: Gross profit (margin) is selling price less CGS. The computation of CGS takes into account fixed manufacturing overhead in inventory. Absorption costing calculates gross profit. Variable costing treats fixed manufacturing overhead as an expense in the period of occurrence. In variable costing, the contribution margin (sales less variable costs) is calculated, not a gross profit (margin). Both methods, however, compute operating income on their income statements.

14. Other things being equal, income computed by the direct costing method will exceed that computed by an absorption costing method if

a. Units produced exceed units sold.
b. Units sold exceed units produced.
c. Fixed manufacturing costs increase.
d. Variable manufacturing costs increase.

The correct answer is (b). *(CPA 1171 T-20)*
REQUIRED: When net income under direct costing will exceed absorption costing income.
DISCUSSION: When units sold exceed the units produced, the absorption costing method expenses more than a single period's amount of fixed O/H. The direct costing method expenses a single period's O/H every period. When sales levels exceed production levels, absorption costing expenses more fixed O/H than direct costing and results in lower income, assuming a constant per unit fixed O/H.

10.2 Absorption Costing vs. Variable Costing

15. The absorption costing method includes in inventory

	Fixed Factory Overhead	Variable Factory Overhead
a.	No	No
b.	No	Yes
c.	Yes	Yes
d.	Yes	No

The correct answer is (c). *(CPA 1185 T-43)*
REQUIRED: The overhead that is included in inventory under absorption (full) costing.
DISCUSSION: In absorption (or full) costing, materials, labor, and variable and fixed overhead are included in inventory and the cost of inventory sold. This differs from direct costing in which only variable manufacturing costs are added to inventory.

16. Assuming absorption costing, which of the following columns includes only product costs?

	A	B	C	D
Direct labor	X		X	X
Direct materials	X	X		X
Sales materials		X		
Advertising costs			X	
Indirect factory materials	X	X		X
Indirect labor		X	X	X
Sales commissions		X		
Factory utilities	X		X	X
Administrative supplies expense		X		
Administrative labor			X	
Depreciation on administration building			X	
Cost of research on customer demographics				X

a. A.
b. B.
c. C.
d. D.

The correct answer is (d). *(CIA 1187 IV-51)*
REQUIRED: The column that includes only product costs.
DISCUSSION: Product costs are the costs of producing the product and are usually directly identifiable with it. Thus, product costs include the costs of the factors of production identifiable with the product, which usually include direct materials, direct labor, and factory (not general) overhead. Factory overhead includes both fixed and variable elements, e.g., factory utilities, indirect labor, and indirect materials. Product costs are inventoried until the product is sold, at which time they are expensed.
Answers (a), (b), and (c) are incorrect because sales commissions, depreciation on the administration building, sales materials, administrative supplies, advertising costs, administrative labor, and demographic research are not directly identifiable with the product or factory overhead items. Each is a period cost.

17. When using full absorption costing, what costs attendant to an element of production (material, labor, or overhead) are used in order to compute variances from standard amounts?

a. Total costs.
b. Variable costs.
c. Fixed costs.
d. Controllable costs.

The correct answer is (a). *(CPA 1178 T-42)*
REQUIRED: Costs used to compute variances from standard amounts under absorption costing.
DISCUSSION: Variances from standards are calculated as the difference between total actual costs and total standard costs. This is because absorption costing charges total costs to inventory.
Answers (b), (c), and (d) are incorrect because each is only one element of total costs. Variances may be computed for each of these elements.

18. Gross margin is equal to sales minus

a. Variable expenses.
b. Variable selling and administrative expenses.
c. Variable manufacturing expenses.
d. Cost of goods sold.

The correct answer is (d). *(Publisher)*
REQUIRED: The missing variable in the cost accounting definition of gross margin.
DISCUSSION: Gross margin is equal to sales less CGS. CGS is BI + CGM − EI, wherein each is presented at full cost, i.e., including applicable fixed manufacturing cost.
Answers (a), (b), and (c) are incorrect because none includes CGS in the calculation. Each lists expenses that may or may not be part of CGS.

19. The Blue Company has failed to reach its planned activity level during its first 2 years of operation. The following table shows the relationship between units produced, sales, and normal activity for these years and the projected relationship for Year 3. All prices and costs have remained the same for the last 2 years and are expected to do so in Year 3. Income has been positive in both Year 1 and Year 2.

	Units Produced	Sales	Planned Activity
Year 1	90,000	90,000	100,000
Year 2	95,000	95,000	100,000
Year 3	90,000	90,000	100,000

Because Blue Company uses an absorption costing system, one would predict gross margin for Year 3 to be

a. Greater than Year 1.
b. Greater than Year 2.
c. Equal to Year 1.
d. Equal to Year 2.

The correct answer is (c). *(CIA 585 IV-5)*
REQUIRED: The true interperiod gross margin relationship.
DISCUSSION: Gross margin equals sales minus CGS (BI + CGM - EI). An absorption costing system applies fixed as well as variable overhead to products. Since Blue's production each year was less than planned activity, each year overhead was underapplied. Hence, Blue must have debited underapplied overhead each year to CGS, WIP, and FG. Because production always equaled sales, however, no inventories existed at any year-end, and thus each annual underapplication should have been debited entirely to CGS. Consequently, gross margin for Years 1 and 3 must be the same since the gross revenue and CGS were identical for the two periods.

Answer (a) is incorrect because the gross margins for Years 1 and 3 are equal. Answers (b) and (d) are incorrect because, with other factors held constant, the greater sales volume in Year 2 should have produced a greater gross margin than in Years 1 or 3.

20. A company manufactures a single product for its customers by contracting in advance of production. Therefore, the company only produces units that will be sold by the end of each period. During the last period, the following sales were made and costs incurred:

Sales	$40,000
Direct materials	9,050
Direct labor	6,050
Rent (9/10 factory, 1/10 office)	3,000
Depreciation on factory equipment	2,000
Supervision (2/3 factory, 1/3 office)	1,500
Salespeople's salaries	1,300
Insurance (2/3 factory, 1/3 office)	1,200
Office supplies	750
Advertising	700
Depreciation on office equipment	500
Interest on loan	300

Based on the above data, the gross margin percentage for the last period (rounded to nearest percent) was

a. 41%.
b. 44%.
c. 46%.
d. 49%.

The correct answer is (c). *(CIA 584 IV-1)*
REQUIRED: The gross margin percentage given sales and cost data.
DISCUSSION: The gross margin percentage is gross profit (sales minus CGS) divided by sales. Sales are given as $40,000, and expenses included in cost of goods sold are listed below.

Sales		$40,000
Cost of goods sold		
Direct materials	$9,050	
Direct labor	6,050	
Rent (9/10 x $3,000)	2,700	
Depreciation	2,000	
Supervision (2/3 x $1,500)	1,000	
Insurance (2/3 x $1,200)	800	(21,600)
		$18,400

$18,400 is 46% of $40,000.

Note that office expenses are usually general and administrative expenses, which are period rather than product costs.

Module 10.2: Absorption Costing vs. Variable Costing

21. An income statement is prepared as an internal report. Under which of the following methods would the term contribution margin appear?

	Absorption Costing	Direct Costing
a.	No	No
b.	No	Yes
c.	Yes	No
d.	Yes	Yes

The correct answer is (b). *(CPA 582 T-45)*
REQUIRED: The costing method under which the term contribution margin appears in an income statement.
DISCUSSION: Contribution margin is sales minus variable costs. Direct costing considers only variable costs as product costs, so contribution margin appears in a direct costing income statement. Absorption costing treats both variable and fixed costs as product costs. Thus, variable costs are not stated separately and contribution margin would not appear in the income statement.

22. In an income statement prepared as an internal report using the variable costing method, fixed factory overhead would

a. Not be used.
b. Be used in the computation of operating income but not in the computation of the contribution margin.
c. Be used in the computation of the contribution margin.
d. Be treated the same as variable factory overhead.

The correct answer is (b). *(CPA 1186 T-45)*
REQUIRED: The treatment of fixed factory overhead in an income statement under variable costing.
DISCUSSION: Under the variable costing method, sales less variable expenses equal the contribution margin. Fixed selling and administrative costs, along with fixed factory overhead, are deducted from the contribution margin to arrive at operating income. Thus, fixed costs are used only in the computation of operating income.
Answer (a) is incorrect because fixed factory overhead is deducted from contribution margin to determine operating income. Answer (c) is incorrect because fixed factory overhead is not used in the computation of the contribution margin, only variable expenses are used. Answer (d) is incorrect because variable factory overhead is used in the computation of contribution margin and fixed factory overhead is not.

23. A company had income of $50,000 using direct costing for a given period. Beginning and ending inventories for that period were 13,000 units and 18,000 units, respectively. Ignoring income taxes, if the fixed overhead application rate were $2.00 per unit, what would the income have been using absorption costing?

a. $40,000.
b. $50,000.
c. $60,000.
d. Cannot be determined from the information given.

The correct answer is (c). *(CPA 1175 P-18)*
REQUIRED: The calculation of income using absorption costing.
DISCUSSION: The difference in net income between direct costing and absorption costing is the change in fixed manufacturing overhead in inventory. Fixed manufacturing overhead is expensed in direct costing and included in inventory in absorption costing.
The EI had 5,000 units more than BI. Thus, inventory value would increase by $10,000 (5,000 @ $2) in absorption costing due to fixed manufacturing overhead. The $10,000 increase in inventory value increases the $50,000 net income per direct costing to $60,000 for absorption costing.

24. Unabsorbed fixed overhead costs in an absorption costing system are

a. Fixed factory costs not allocated to units produced.
b. Variable overhead costs not allocated to units produced.
c. Excess variable overhead costs.
d. Costs that should be controlled.
e. None of the above.

The correct answer is (a). *(CMA 1273 4-12)*
REQUIRED: The cause of underapplied or unabsorbed overhead costs.
DISCUSSION: In absorption costing, fixed O/H costs are usually added to product cost based on a predetermined unit basis, which is usually total expected fixed manufacturing costs divided by the number of units expected to be produced. This rate hypothetically distributes all fixed factory O/H to the units produced. Unabsorbed fixed O/H results when all O/H costs are not absorbed, i.e., not applied to the product. This could happen if there are variances in the fixed costs or the number of units produced.
Answers (b) and (c) are incorrect because the question specifies fixed O/H costs, not variable costs. Answer (d) is incorrect because fixed costs cannot be controlled in the short run.

Module 10.2: Absorption Costing vs. Variable Costing

Questions 25 through 31 are based on the assumption that total fixed costs and other elements in the overhead rate calculation do not change. This should be your assumption unless specified otherwise.

25. What factor, related to manufacturing costs, causes the difference in net earnings computed using absorption costing and net earnings computed using direct costing?

a. Absorption costing considers all costs in the determination of net earnings, whereas direct costing considers fixed costs to be period costs.

b. Absorption costing allocates fixed costs between cost of goods sold and inventories, and direct costing considers all fixed costs to be period costs.

c. Absorption costing "inventories" all direct costs, but direct costing considers direct costs to be period costs.

d. Absorption costing "inventories" all fixed costs for the period in ending finished goods inventory, but direct costing expenses all fixed costs.

The correct answer is (b). *(CPA 581 T-47)*
REQUIRED: The cause of the difference in net earnings under direct versus absorption costing.
DISCUSSION: Absorption costing allocates fixed manufacturing costs between inventory and CGS, thus charging to the period only those fixed manufacturing costs allocated to CGS. Direct costing expenses fixed manufacturing costs in the period incurred.
Answer (a) is incorrect because both absorption costing and direct costing consider all costs in determining net earnings; but they recognize fixed costs as expenses at different points in the accounting process. Answer (c) is incorrect because both absorption costing and direct costing "inventory" direct (variable) costs; but absorption costing also inventories fixed manufacturing costs. Answer (d) is incorrect because absorption costing "inventories" only a portion of fixed manufacturing overhead, i.e., that relating to work-in-process and finished goods inventory. The fixed manufacturing costs associated with goods sold are expensed as part of CGS.

26. Net earnings determined using full absorption costing can be reconciled to net earnings determined using direct costing by computing the difference between

a. Inventoried fixed costs in the beginning and ending inventories and any deferred over- or underapplied fixed factory overhead.

b. Inventoried discretionary costs in the beginning and ending inventories.

c. Gross margin (absorption costing method) and contribution margin (direct costing method).

d. Sales as recorded under the direct costing method and sales as recorded under the absorption costing method.

The correct answer is (a). *(CPA 1177 T-31)*
REQUIRED: The reconciliation of net earnings using absorption costing and direct costing.
DISCUSSION: Net earnings under direct costing and absorption costing differ due to the difference in treatment of fixed manufacturing costs. Direct costing treats all fixed manufacturing costs as period costs; absorption costing treats fixed manufacturing costs as product costs. When production and sales are equal, net income is equal under both methods. When production and sales differ, however, the net income differs and is reconciled by determining the changes in fixed costs inventoried.
Answer (b) is incorrect because inventoried discretionary costs, which is not a normal accounting term, may include both fixed and variable elements. Answer (c) is incorrect because the difference between gross margin and contribution margin does not determine the change in the fixed costs inventoried. Answer (d) is incorrect because sales are recorded the same way under both costing methods.

27. Net profit under absorption costing may differ from net profit determined under direct costing. How is this difference calculated?

a. Change in the quantity of all units in inventory times the relevant fixed costs per unit.

b. Change in the quantity of all units produced times the relevant fixed costs per unit.

c. Change in the quantity of all units in inventory times the relevant variable cost per unit.

d. Change in the quantity of all units produced times the relevant variable cost per unit.

The correct answer is (a). *(CPA 575 P-22)*
REQUIRED: The calculation for the difference in net profit between absorption costing and direct costing.
DISCUSSION: Direct costing treats all fixed costs as period costs; absorption costing treats fixed costs as product costs. The difference between net profit under the two methods can be determined by multiplying the fixed manufacturing cost per unit by the change in the number of units in inventory (assuming a constant per unit fixed manufacturing cost).
Answer (b) is incorrect because it ignores the effect of units sold. Answer (c) is incorrect because the difference is caused by fixed, not variable, costs. Answer (d) is incorrect because it ignores the effect of units sold and uses variable, not fixed, costs.

Module 10.2: Absorption Costing vs. Variable Costing 211

28. Net income reported under absorption costing will exceed net income reported under direct costing for a given period if

   a. Production equals sales for that period.
   b. Production exceeds sales for that period.
   c. Sales exceed production for that period.
   d. The variable overhead exceeds the fixed overhead.

The correct answer is (b). *(CPA 1176 P-26)*
REQUIRED: The condition under which net income computed using absorption costing would exceed net income computed using direct costing.
DISCUSSION: Producing more than is sold in a period results in more fixed manufacturing costs being expensed under direct costing than under absorption costing. Therefore, less net income is reported under direct costing.
   Answer (a) is incorrect because it causes the same amount of fixed costs to be expensed and the income to be equal. Answer (c) is incorrect because it results in more direct costing earnings than absorption costing earnings. Answer (d) is incorrect because it has no effect on net income under the two costing methods.

29. A company's net income recently increased by 30% while its inventory increased to equal a full year's sales requirements. Which of the following accounting methods would be most likely to produce the favorable income results?

   a. Absorption costing.
   b. Direct costing.
   c. Variable costing.
   d. Standard direct costing.

The correct answer is (a). *(CIA 584 IV-5)*
REQUIRED: The method likely to produce favorable income when inventory increases.
DISCUSSION: Inventory increases when production exceeds sales. In absorption costing, fixed costs that would be expensed under direct costing are deferred to future periods. If a company has very high fixed costs and a relatively low contribution margin, income may be increased by producing in excess of sales.
   Answers (b), (c), and (d) are incorrect because direct costing net income is less than that under absorption costing when production exceeds sales. Direct and variable costing are synonymous.

30. Fleet, Inc. manufactured 700 units of Product A, a new product, during the year. Product A's variable and fixed manufacturing costs per unit were $6.00 and $2.00, respectively. The inventory of Product A on December 31 consisted of 100 units. There was no inventory of Product A on January 1. What would be the change in the dollar amount of inventory on December 31 if direct costing were used instead of absorption costing?

   a. $800 decrease.
   b. $200 decrease.
   c. $0.
   d. $200 increase.

The correct answer is (b). *(CPA 1176 P-25)*
REQUIRED: The difference in inventory using direct rather than absorption costing.
DISCUSSION: Given an inventory increase of 100 units during the year and the fixed manufacturing cost per unit of $2.00, $200 (100 units x $2.00) of overhead would be deferred using absorption costing but expensed immediately using direct costing. Thus, direct costing inventory would be $200 less than absorption costing.

31. Direct costing has an advantage over absorption costing for which of the following purposes?

   a. Analysis of profitability of products, territories, and other segments of a business.
   b. Determining the CVP relationship among the major factors of selling price, sales mix, and sales volume.
   c. Minimizing the effects of inventory changes on net income.
   d. Minimizing the effects of the arbitrary allocation of fixed costs.
   e. All of the above.

The correct answer is (e). *(Publisher)*
REQUIRED: The advantage(s) of direct or variable costing over absorption costing.
DISCUSSION: Variable costing is preferred by management over absorption costing for analysis of profitability of products, territories, and other segments of a business since it excludes fixed costs that are difficult to allocate accurately. Variable costing provides a method of analyzing profit based on the major factors of price, sales mix, volume, and variable manufacturing and nonmanufacturing costs. Variable costing is not affected by inventory changes in which fixed manufacturing costs are held back from the income statement or expensed in greater amounts than incurred in the accounting period. Variable costing minimizes the effects that the arbitrary allocation of fixed costs has on financial statements.

10.3 Calculations

32. During January, Gable, Inc. produced 10,000 units of product F with costs as follows:

Direct materials	$40,000
Direct labor	22,000
Variable overhead	13,000
Fixed overhead	10,000
	$85,000

What is Gable's unit cost of product F for January, calculated on the direct costing basis?

a. $6.20.
b. $7.20.
c. $7.50.
d. $8.50.

The correct answer is (c). *(CPA 581 P-23)*
REQUIRED: The unit cost of a product under direct costing.
DISCUSSION: Direct costing inventory includes only variable manufacturing costs: direct materials, direct labor, and variable overhead. Fixed overhead is treated as a period cost. The calculation for per unit inventory cost is

$$\frac{\$40,000 + \$22,000 + \$13,000}{10,000 \text{ units}} = \$7.50/\text{unit}$$

Questions 33 and 34 are based on Kirklin Co., a manufacturer operating at 95% of capacity. Kirklin has been offered a new order at $7.25 per unit requiring 15% of capacity. No other use of the 5% current idle capacity can be found. However, if the order were accepted, the subcontracting for the required 10% additional capacity would cost $7.50 per unit. The variable cost of production for Kirklin on a per-unit basis follows:

Materials	$3.50
Labor	1.50
Variable overhead	1.50
	$6.50

---

33. In applying the contribution margin approach to evaluating whether to accept the new order, assuming subcontracting, what value would be computed for average variable cost per unit?

a. $6.83.
b. $7.17.
c. $7.25.
d. $7.50.

The correct answer is (b). *(CIA 584 IV-6)*
REQUIRED: The average variable cost per unit of the new order.
DISCUSSION: Variable cost is equal to the direct costs associated with a product, an order, or other decision. In this case, one-third of the order has a variable cost of $6.50, and two-thirds of the order has a variable cost of $7.50. Thus, the average variable cost is $7.17 {($6.50 ÷ 3) + [(2 x $7.50) ÷ 3]}.

34. The expected contribution margin per unit on the new order would be

a. $.08.
b. $.25.
c. $.33.
d. $.42.

The correct answer is (a). *(CIA 584 IV-7)*
REQUIRED: The unit contribution margin on the new order.
DISCUSSION: The unit contribution margin on the new order is the selling price of $7.25 less the average variable cost. The average variable cost is $7.17, as calculated in the preceding question. Accordingly, the unit contribution margin on the order would be $.08.

35. A company manufactures 50,000 units of a product and sells 40,000 units. Total manufacturing cost per unit is $50 (variable manufacturing cost $10, fixed manufacturing cost $40). Assuming no beginning inventory, what is the effect on net income if absorption costing is used instead of variable costing?

a. Net income is $400,000 lower.
b. Net income is $400,000 higher.
c. Net income is the same.
d. Net income is $200,000 higher.

The correct answer is (b). *(CIA 586 IV-5)*
REQUIRED: The effect on net income under absorption costing rather than variable costing.
DISCUSSION: Net income under absorption costing is calculated by first deducting CGS from sales to obtain gross margin. Then, deduct selling and administrative expenses to obtain net income. Net income under variable costing is calculated by deducting variable cost of units sold to determine contribution margin, from which all fixed costs are deducted to determine net income. No fixed costs are inventoriable. Unit costs under absorption and variable costing are given as $50 and $10, respectively. Net income under absorption costing is $400,000 higher (10,000 in inventory x $40 difference in unit inventoriable cost).

Module 10.3: Calculations

Questions 36 through 38 are based on Lina Co., which produced 100,000 units of Product Zee during the month of June. Costs incurred during June were as follows:	Direct materials used	$100,000
	Direct labor used	80,000
	Variable manufacturing overhead	40,000
	Fixed manufacturing overhead	50,000
	Variable selling and general expenses	12,000
	Fixed selling and general expenses	45,000
		$327,000

36. What was Product Zee's unit cost under absorption costing?

a. $3.27.
b. $2.70.
c. $2.20.
d. $1.80.

The correct answer is (b). *(CPA 1184 Q-19)*
REQUIRED: The product's unit cost under absorption costing.
DISCUSSION: Unit cost under absorption costing is equal to the sum of manufacturing costs divided by the production units.

$$\frac{\$100,000 + \$80,000 + \$40,000 + \$50,000}{100,000} = \$2.70$$

37. What was Product Zee's unit cost under variable (direct) costing?

a. $2.82.
b. $2.70.
c. $2.32.
d. $2.20.

The correct answer is (d). *(CPA 1184 Q-20)*
REQUIRED: The product's unit cost under variable (direct) costing.
DISCUSSION: Unit cost under variable (direct) costing is equal to the sum of variable manufacturing costs divided by the production units.

$$\frac{\$100,000 + \$80,000 + \$40,000}{100,000} = \$2.20$$

38. What is the difference between absorption costing and direct costing net income assuming sales of 90,000 units at $6 per unit and no beginning inventories?

a. $5,000.
b. $(5,000).
c. $10,000.
d. $45,000.

The correct answer is (a). *(Publisher)*
REQUIRED: The difference between absorption and direct costing net income.
DISCUSSION: Net income under absorption costing is calculated by first deducting CGS from selling price to arrive at the gross margin. Then, selling and administrative expenses are deducted from gross margin to arrive at net income. Net income under direct costing is calculated by deducting variable costs of units sold and all fixed costs. No fixed costs are inventoriable. Unit costs under absorption and direct costing are $2.70 and $2.20, respectively. The difference between absorption and direct costing net income amounts is $5,000 (10,000 units in inventory x $.50 difference in unit inventoriable cost).

39. During May, Roy Co. produced 10,000 units of Product X. Costs incurred by Roy during May:

Direct materials	$10,000
Direct labor	20,000
Variable manufacturing overhead	5,000
Variable selling and general	3,000
Fixed manufacturing overhead	9,000
Fixed selling and general	4,000
Total	$51,000

Under absorption costing, Product X's unit cost was

a. $5.10.
b. $4.40.
c. $3.80.
d. $3.50.

The correct answer is (b). *(CPA 587 Q-29)*
REQUIRED: The product's unit cost under absorption costing.
DISCUSSION: Unit cost under absorption costing is equal to the sum of manufacturing costs divided by the production units. Selling and general expenses are not considered a product cost.

$$\frac{\$10,000 + \$20,000 + \$5,000 + \$9,000}{10,000} = \$4.40$$

Questions 40 through 43 are based on JV Co., which produces a single product that sells for $7.00 per unit. Standard capacity is 100,000 units per year. 100,000 units were produced and 80,000 units were sold during the year. Manufacturing costs and selling and administrative expenses are presented in the next column.

There were no variances from the standard variable costs. Any under- or overapplied overhead is written off directly at year-end as an adjustment to cost of goods sold.

	Fixed Costs	Variable Costs
Raw materials	$ -0-	$1.50 per unit produced
Direct labor	-0-	1.00 per unit produced
Factory overhead	150,000	.50 per unit produced
Selling and administrative	80,000	.50 per unit sold

JV had no inventory at the beginning of the year.

40. In presenting inventory on the balance sheet at December 31, the unit cost under absorption costing is

a. $2.50.
b. $3.00.
c. $3.50.
d. $4.50.

The correct answer is (d). *(CPA 578 P-33)*
REQUIRED: The unit inventory cost based on absorption costing.
DISCUSSION: Absorption costing for inventory includes a prorated share of fixed manufacturing overhead. The proration is based on the number of units produced in a given time period.

$$\frac{\$150,000 \text{ fixed O/H}}{100,000 \text{ units}} = \$1.50/\text{unit}$$

Raw materials	$1.50
Direct labor	1.00
Variable overhead	.50
Fixed overhead	1.50
Unit cost	$4.50

41. What is the net income under direct costing?

a. $50,000.
b. $80,000.
c. $90,000.
d. $120,000.

The correct answer is (a). *(CPA 578 P-34)*
REQUIRED: The net income under direct costing.
DISCUSSION: Net income under direct costing is calculated by deducting variable costs of units sold and all fixed costs. No fixed costs are inventoriable.

Revenue (80,000 x $7.00)		$560,000
Variable CGS (80,000 x $3.00)		(240,000)
Variable S&A (80,000 x $.50)		(40,000)
Contribution margin		$280,000
Fixed:		
Manufacturing	$150,000	
S&A	80,000	(230,000)
Net income		$ 50,000

42. What is the net income under absorption costing?

a. $50,000.
b. $80,000.
c. $90,000.
d. $120,000.

The correct answer is (b). *(Publisher)*
REQUIRED: The net income under absorption costing.
DISCUSSION: Net income under absorption costing is calculated by first deducting CGS (based on the unit cost calculated in Q. 41) from sales to arrive at the gross margin. Then, selling and administrative expenses are deducted from gross margin to arrive at net income.

Revenue (80,000 units x $7.00)		$560,000
CGS (80,000 units x $4.50)		(360,000)
Gross margin		$200,000
S&A expenses:		
Variable	$40,000	
Fixed	80,000	(120,000)
Net income		$ 80,000

43. If there were a difference between absorption costing net income and variable (direct) costing net income in the calculations in Qs. 41 and 42, what might be the explanation for this difference?

   a. Shrinkage, theft, and miscellaneous losses.
   b. Miscalculations by management.
   c. The change in fixed manufacturing overhead included in inventory.
   d. The change in fixed selling and administrative expenses included in inventory.

44. A company has the following cost data:

Fixed manufacturing costs	$2,000
Fixed selling, general, and administrative costs	1,000
Variable selling costs per unit sold	1
Variable manufacturing costs per unit	2
Beginning inventory	0 units
Production	100 units
Sales	90 units at $40 per unit

Variable and absorption cost net incomes are

   a. $320 variable, $520 absorption.
   b. $330 variable, $530 absorption.
   c. $520 variable, $320 absorption.
   d. $530 variable, $330 absorption.

45. Keller Company, a manufacturer of rivets, uses absorption costing. Keller's manufacturing costs were as follows:

Direct materials and direct labor	$800,000
Depreciation of machines	100,000
Rent for factory building	60,000
Electricity to run machines	35,000

How much of these costs should be inventoried?

   a. $800,000.
   b. $835,000.
   c. $935,000.
   d. $995,000.

The correct answer is (c). *(Publisher)*
REQUIRED: Why net income might vary between absorption costing and variable costing.
DISCUSSION: The only difference between the two costing methods is in the amount of fixed manufacturing O/H in inventory during a given accounting period. JV Company had no BI in which fixed manufacturing overhead could be accumulated. Also, JV Company did not sell all the product produced. Consequently, units held in EI would have included fixed manufacturing O/H under absorption costing, but not under direct costing. Had they sold all 100,000 units produced, absorption costing and variable costing would have yielded the same net income.

The correct answer is (b). *(CIA 587 IV-8)*
REQUIRED: The variable and absorption cost net incomes.
DISCUSSION: The only difference between variable (direct) cost and absorption cost net incomes is that the latter treats fixed manufacturing cost as inventoriable. Thus, the ending absorption cost inventory includes $200 [10 units x ($2,000 ÷ 100 units)] of fixed costs that would be expensed in a variable cost income statement. Since absorption cost net income is $530 (see below), variable cost net income is $330 ($530 - $200).

Sales (90 x $40)	$3,600
Variable costs [($1 + $2) x 90]	(270)
Fixed mfg. costs ($2,000 x 90/100)	(1,800)
Fixed S,G,&A costs	(1,000)
Absorption cost NI	$ 530

The correct answer is (d). *(CPA 1182 Q-30)*
REQUIRED: The amount of costs that are inventoried under absorption costing.
DISCUSSION: Under absorption costing, the inventoried costs consist of all direct materials, direct labor, and manufacturing overhead. Manufacturing overhead includes depreciation, factory rent, and power for the machines. Therefore, the total cost to be inventoried is $995,000 ($800,000 + $100,000 + $60,000 + $35,000).

Module 10.3: Calculations

Questions 46 through 49 are based on the following information from Peterson Company's records for the year ended December 31. There was no finished goods inventory at January 1, and there were no work-in-process inventories at the beginning and end of the year.	Net sales	$1,400,000
	Cost of goods manufactured: Variable	$ 630,000
	Fixed	$ 315,000
	Operating expenses: Variable	$ 98,000
	Fixed	$ 140,000
	Units manufactured	70,000
	Units sold	60,000

46. What would be Peterson's finished goods inventory cost at December 31 under the variable (direct) costing method?

a. $90,000.
b. $104,000.
c. $105,000.
d. $135,000.

The correct answer is (a). *(CPA 582 P-39)*
REQUIRED: The finished goods inventory cost under the direct costing method.
DISCUSSION: Direct costing considers only variable manufacturing costs as product costs. Fixed manufacturing costs are considered period costs. The total variable manufacturing cost is given as $630,000. Given 70,000 units produced, unit cost was $9.00 ($630,000 ÷ 70,000 units). Given EI of 10,000 units, total cost of FG inventory is $90,000 ($9 x 10,000).

47. What would be Peterson's finished goods inventory cost at December 31 under the absorption costing method?

a. $90,000.
b. $104,000.
c. $105,000.
d. $135,000.

The correct answer is (d). *(Publisher)*
REQUIRED: The finished goods inventory cost under the absorption costing method.
DISCUSSION: Absorption costing considers both variable and fixed manufacturing costs as product costs. Unit CGM is equal to the sum of the variable ($630,000) plus fixed ($315,000) costs divided by the number of units manufactured (70,000), or $13.50 per unit. Given that 10,000 units remain in inventory, EI is $135,000.

48. Under the absorption costing method, Peterson's operating income for the year would be

a. $217,000.
b. $307,000.
c. $352,000.
d. $374,500.

The correct answer is (c). *(CPA 582 P-40)*
REQUIRED: The operating income under the absorption costing method.
DISCUSSION: In absorption costing, the unit costs include both fixed and variable manufacturing costs. Fixed manufacturing costs are given as $315,000.

Sales	$1,400,000
CGS (60,000 x $13.50)	(810,000)
Gross margin	$ 590,000
Operating expenses	
Variable	(98,000)
Fixed	(140,000)
Operating income	$ 352,000

49. Under the variable costing method, Peterson's operating income for the year would be

a. $217,000.
b. $307,000.
c. $352,000.
d. $135,000.

The correct answer is (b). *(Publisher)*
REQUIRED: The operating income under the variable costing method.
DISCUSSION: In variable costing, the unit CGS includes only the variable manufacturing costs, which were $9.00 per unit ($630,000 ÷ 70,000). The income statement would appear as follows:

Sales	$1,400,000
CGS (60,000 x $9)	(540,000)
Variable operating expenses	(98,000)
Contribution margin	$ 762,000
Fixed costs:	
CGM	(315,000)
Operating	(140,000)
Operating income	$ 307,000

Module 10.3: Calculations

> Questions 50 through 53 are based on the Gordon Company, which began its operations on January 1, and produces a single product that sells for $10 per unit. Gordon uses an actual (historical) cost system. During the year, 100,000 units were produced and 80,000 units were sold. There was no work-in-process inventory at December 31.
>
> Manufacturing costs and selling and administrative expenses for the year were as follows:
>
> | | Fixed Costs | Variable Costs |
> |---|---|---|
> | Raw materials | $ -0- | $2.00 per unit produced |
> | Direct labor | -0- | 1.25 per unit produced |
> | Factory O/H | 120,000 | .75 per unit produced |
> | Selling and administrative | 70,000 | 1.00 per unit sold |

50. What would be Gordon's operating income for the year under the variable (direct) costing method?

a. $114,000.
b. $210,000.
c. $234,000.
d. $330,000.

The correct answer is (b). *(CPA 583 P-33)*
REQUIRED: Operating income under the direct costing method.
DISCUSSION: The direct costing income statement begins with sales of 80,000 units at $10 less CGS at $4 and other variable costs at $1. Then $190,000 of fixed costs ($120,000 + $70,000) are deducted.

Sales			$800,000
CGS			
RM	$200,000		
DL	125,000		
Var. O/H	75,000		
CGM	400,000		
Less EI	(80,000)		
CGS		$320,000	
Var. S&A		80,000	(400,000)
Contribution margin			$400,000
Fixed costs:			
Manufacturing		$120,000	
Selling		70,000	
			(190,000)
Operating Income			$210,000

51. What would be Gordon's finished goods inventory at December 31 under the variable costing method?

a. $80,000.
b. $104,000.
c. $110,000.
d. $124,000.

The correct answer is (a). *(Publisher)*
REQUIRED: The ending finished goods inventory under the variable costing method.
DISCUSSION: Under variable costing, fixed manufacturing overhead is not included in inventory. Inventoriable costs are raw materials, direct labor, and variable factory overhead ($2.00 + $1.25 + $.75 = $4.00).

20,000 EI units x $4 unit CGS = $80,000 EI

52. What would be Gordon's operating income for the year under the absorption costing method?

a. $304,000.
b. $384,000.
c. $234,000.
d. $210,000.

The correct answer is (c). *(Publisher)*
REQUIRED: The operating income under the absorption costing method.
DISCUSSION: The absorption costing income statement begins with sales at $10 per unit less CGS of $5.20 per unit ($2 materials + $1.25 labor + $.75 variable manufacturing O/H + $1.20 fixed manufacturing O/H).

Sales			$800,000
CGS		80,000	
		x $5.20	(416,000)
Gross margin			384,000
S&A expenses:			
Variable		80,000	
Fixed		70,000	(150,000)
Operating income			$234,000

Module 10.3: Calculations

53. Refer to the information presented on page 217. What would be Gordon's finished goods inventory at December 31 under the absorption costing method?

a. $80,000.
b. $104,000.
c. $110,000.
d. $124,000.

The correct answer is (b). *(CPA 583 P-34)*
REQUIRED: The ending finished goods inventory under the absorption costing method.
DISCUSSION: Under absorption costing, fixed manufacturing overhead is included in inventory. Fixed manufacturing overhead was $120,000 and 100,000 units were produced, so fixed manufacturing cost per unit is $1.20 ($120,000 ÷ 100,000 units). Inventoriable costs are $5.20 per unit ($4.00 variable manufacturing costs + $1.20 fixed manufacturing costs). Since there are 20,000 units in inventory, EI is $104,000.

Questions 54 through 57 are based on the following annual flexible budget which has been prepared for use in making decisions relating to Product X.

	100,000 Units	150,000 Units	200,000 Units
Sales volume	$800,000	$1,200,000	$1,600,000
Manufacturing costs:			
Variable	$300,000	$450,000	$600,000
Fixed	200,000	200,000	200,000
	$500,000	$650,000	$800,000
Selling and other expenses:			
Variable	$200,000	$300,000	$400,000
Fixed	160,000	160,000	160,000
	$360,000	$460,000	$560,000
Income (or loss)	$(60,000)	$90,000	$240,000

The 200,000 unit budget has been adopted and will be used for allocating fixed manufacturing costs to units of Product X. At the end of the first six months the following information is available:

	Units
Production completed	120,000
Sales	60,000

All fixed costs are budgeted and incurred uniformly throughout the year and all costs incurred coincide with the budget. Over- and underapplied fixed manufacturing costs are deferred until year-end. Annual sales have the following seasonal pattern:

	Portion of Annual Sales
First quarter	10%
Second quarter	20%
Third quarter	30%
Fourth quarter	40%

---

54. The amount of fixed factory costs applied to product during the first 6 months under absorption costing would be

a. Overapplied by $20,000.
b. Equal to the fixed costs incurred.
c. Underapplied by $40,000.
d. Underapplied by $80,000.
e. None of the above.

The correct answer is (a). *(CPA 571 Q-18)*
REQUIRED: The correct statement about the amount of applied factory overhead.
DISCUSSION: Under absorption costing, fixed O/H is applied based on the number of units produced. Fixed O/H equals $200,000. Since production is budgeted at 200,000 units, the fixed O/H rate is $1 per unit. Production completed in the first 6 months equals 120,000 units, so $120,000 of overhead was applied. Since all costs incurred coincide with the budget, only half of the $200,000 budgeted fixed O/H was incurred, or $100,000. Therefore, O/H is overapplied by $20,000 ($120,000 - $100,000).

---

55. Reported net income (or loss) for the first 6 months under absorption costing would be

a. $160,000.
b. $80,000.
c. $40,000.
d. $(40,000).
e. None of the above.

The correct answer is (c). *(CPA 571 Q-19)*
REQUIRED: Net income (loss) under the absorption costing method.
DISCUSSION: Variable manufacturing cost is $3 per unit and fixed manufacturing cost equals $1 per unit. Selling price is $8 per unit ($1,600,000 ÷ 200,000 units). The variable selling expenses are $2 per unit ($400,000 ÷ 200,000 units). The fixed selling expenses equal $80,000 for the 6-month period, 1/2 of the $160,000 annual selling expense.

Revenue	$480,000
CGS	(240,000)
Gross margin	$240,000
Variable selling expense	(120,000)
Fixed selling expense	(80,000)
Net income	$40,000

Module 10.3: Calculations

56. Reported net income (or loss) for the first 6 months under direct costing would be

a. $144,000.
b. $72,000.
c. $0.
d. $(36,000).
e. None of the above.

The correct answer is (c). *(CPA 571 Q-20)*
REQUIRED: Net income (loss) under the direct costing method.
DISCUSSION: Sales were 60,000 units at $8, variable manufacturing cost at $3, variable selling cost at $2, and fixed costs were 50% of the annual amounts.

Revenue	$480,000
CGS	(180,000)
Variable selling expense	(120,000)
Fixed manufacturing expense	(100,000)
Fixed selling expense	(80,000)
Net income	$ -0-

57. Assuming that 90,000 units of Product X were sold during the first 6 months and that this is to be used as a basis, the revised budget estimate for the total number of units to be sold during this year would be

a. 360,000.
b. 240,000.
c. 200,000.
d. 120,000.
e. None of the above.

The correct answer is (e). *(CPA 571 Q-21)*
REQUIRED: Annual sales budget based on the first 6 months of the year.
DISCUSSION: To calculate the annual sales budget based on the first 6 months of the year, the number of units sold during the first 6 months and the appropriate portion of the annual sales that the 90,000 units represent must be examined. The 90,000 units of Product X sold during the first 6 months represent 30% of the annual sales (10% 1st qtr. + 20% 2nd qtr.), so annual sales would be projected at 300,000 units (90,000 ÷ .30).

Questions 58 and 59 are based on information presented in the next column, which was taken from Valenz Company's records for the fiscal year ended November 30.

Direct materials used	$300,000
Direct labor	100,000
Variable factory overhead	50,000
Fixed factory overhead	80,000
Sell. & admin. costs - variable	40,000
Sell. & admin. costs - fixed	20,000

---

58. If Valenz Company uses variable (direct) costing, the inventoriable costs for the current fiscal year are

a. $400,000.
b. $450,000.
c. $490,000.
d. $530,000.
e. Some amount other than those given above.

The correct answer is (b). *(CMA 1286 4-18)*
REQUIRED: The inventoriable costs using the direct costing method.
DISCUSSION: Under direct costing, the only costs that are capitalized are the variable costs of manufacturing. These include

Direct materials used	$300,000
Direct labor	100,000
Variable factory overhead	50,000
Total inventoriable costs	$450,000

59. Using absorption (full) costing, inventoriable costs are

a. $400,000.
b. $450,000.
c. $530,000.
d. $590,000.
e. Some amount other than those given above.

The correct answer is (c). *(CMA 1286 4-19)*
REQUIRED: The inventoriable costs using the absorption costing method.
DISCUSSION: The absorption method is required for financial statements prepared according to GAAP. It charges all costs of production to inventories. The variable cost of materials ($300,000), direct labor ($100,000), variable factory overhead ($50,000), and the fixed factory overhead ($80,000) are included. They total $530,000.

Questions 60 through 69 are based on the following information, which was presented as part of Question 4 on Part 4 of the December 1979 CMA examination.

The vice president for sales of Huber Corporation has received the income statement for November. The statement has been prepared on the direct cost basis and is reproduced in the opposite column. The firm has just adopted a direct costing system for internal reporting purposes.

The controller attached the following notes to the statements:

The unit sales price for November averaged $24.

The standard unit manufacturing costs for the month were

Variable cost	$12
Fixed cost	4
Total cost	$16

The unit rate for fixed manufacturing costs is a predetermined rate based upon a normal monthly production of 150,000 units.

Production for November was 45,000 units in excess of sales.

The inventory at November 30 consisted of 80,000 units.

Huber Corporation
Income Statement
For the Month of November
($000 omitted)

Sales		$2,400
Less:		
Variable standard CGS		(1,200)
Manufacturing margin		$1,200
Less:		
Fixed manufacturing costs at budget	$600	
Fixed manufacturing cost spending variance	-0-	(600)
Gross margin		$ 600
Less:		
Fixed selling and administrative costs		(400)
Net income before taxes		$ 200

---

60. The net income before taxes under absorption costing is

  a. $400.
  b. $380.
  c. $780.
  d. $280.

The correct answer is (b). *(Publisher)*
REQUIRED: Net income before taxes using absorption costing.
DISCUSSION: Under absorption costing, CGS includes a fixed manufacturing cost per unit. Note that production for November was 45,000 units above sales; sales were 100,000 units ($2,400,000 ÷ $24), so 145,000 units were produced. O/H was underapplied by 5,000 units since normal volume is 150,000 units. Underapplied fixed O/H is $20,000 (5,000 units x $4/unit fixed cost) and is charged to CGS.

Sales (100,000 units x $24)		$2,400
Less cost of goods sold:		
Variable cost per unit	$ 12.00	
Fixed cost per unit	4.00	
Total unit cost	$ 16.00	
Volume in units	x 100,000	
CGS at standard	$ 1,600	
Production volume variance (5,000 units at $4)	20	(1,620)
Gross margin		$ 780
Less: Fixed S&A costs		(400)
Net income before taxes		$ 380

61. What is the value of ending inventory on November 30 under absorption costing?

  a. $1,280,000.
  b. $960,000.
  c. $880,000.
  d. $1,040,000.

The correct answer is (a). *(Publisher)*
REQUIRED: The value of ending inventory under absorption costing.
DISCUSSION: Under absorption costing, both variable and fixed manufacturing costs are included in inventory.

Variable cost	$12.00
Fixed cost	4.00
Total manufacturing cost	$16.00

November 30 inventory was 80,000 units x $16 = $1,280,000. The $20,000 volume variance could not have been prorated because $1,280,000 is the largest alternative answer.

Module 10.3: Calculations

62. What is the value of ending inventory on November 30 under variable costing?

a. $960,000.
b. $1,280,000.
c. $800,000.
d. $945,000.

The correct answer is (a). *(Publisher)*
REQUIRED: The value of ending inventory under variable costing.
DISCUSSION: Only variable manufacturing costs are included in inventory under variable costing. Given variable cost per unit of $12.00: 80,000 units in EI x $12.00 = $960,000.

63. The difference in ending inventory under variable costing and absorption costing is represented by

a. FOH of $4 unit.
b. VOH of $13 unit.
c. FOH of $13 unit.
d. VOH of $4 unit.

The correct answer is (a). *(Publisher)*
REQUIRED: The difference in the value of EI under variable and absorption costing.
DISCUSSION: Ending inventory under variable costing and under absorption costing differs by the fixed manufacturing overhead, which, in this case, is $4 per unit.
The change in inventory was 45,000 units, which at $4/unit equals $180,000 (the difference between direct and absorption costing).

64. Direct manufacturing cost per unit is

a. $12.
b. $16.
c. $14.
d. $13.

The correct answer is (a). *(Publisher)*
REQUIRED: The direct manufacturing cost per unit.
DISCUSSION: Direct cost per unit includes only variable manufacturing costs, which is given as $12.

65. The absorption manufacturing cost per unit is

a. $12.
b. $16.
c. $14.
d. $13.

The correct answer is (b). *(Publisher)*
REQUIRED: The absorption manufacturing cost per unit.
DISCUSSION: The absorption cost per unit includes both variable and fixed manufacturing cost, which is given as $12 + $4 = $16.

Questions 66 through 69 are based on the assumption that Huber Corporation uses actual costing for fixed overhead, and that, in all prior months, the plant operated at capacity.

---

66. How many units were produced during November?

a. 100,000.
b. 145,000.
c. 150,000.
d. 155,000.

The correct answer is (b). *(Publisher)*
REQUIRED: Production level at capacity for the period.
DISCUSSION: Since direct costing CGS was 1,200,000 and the unit variable cost was $12, 100,000 units were sold. Production is given as 45,000 units in excess of sales, i.e., 145,000 units.

67. Under FIFO, what is Huber's November income using absorption costing?

a. $200,000.
b. $212,400.
c. $380,000.
d. $391,200.

The correct answer is (d). *(Publisher)*
REQUIRED: Absorption income for the period using FIFO.
DISCUSSION: BI contained 35,000 units (80,000 EI less production excess over sales of 45,000). EI contained 80,000 units. Under FIFO, all 80,000 would be valued at $4.14 or $331,200. Thus, net income would be $391,200, which is $11,200 more than net income reported in Q. 60, where all inventory was valued at $4/unit. Note that as long as fixed cost/unit remains constant, the difference in absorption and direct costing income is the change in inventory units times the unit fixed cost. Here, however, unit fixed costs changed and the standard reconciliation of absorption and variable costing does not work.

Questions 68 and 69 are based on the information presented on page 220 and the assumption that precedes question 66 on page 221.

68. What is the actual unit fixed cost for units produced in November?

a. $4.00.
b. $4.10.
c. $4.14.
d. $4.46.

The correct answer is (c). *(Publisher)*
REQUIRED: Fixed cost per unit produced in the period.
DISCUSSION: Standard fixed O/H cost was given as $4/unit, and 150,000 units was the budgeted monthly activity. Therefore, actual fixed O/H is $600,000 per month. As computed in Q. 66, 145,000 units were produced in November. Actual unit fixed cost is thus $600,000 ÷ 145,000, or $4.14.

69. Under LIFO, what is Huber's November income using absorption costing?

a. $386,300.
b. $331,200.
c. $391,200.
d. $326,300.

The correct answer is (a). *(Publisher)*
REQUIRED: Absorption income for the period using LIFO.
DISCUSSION: Under LIFO, EI of 80,000 units consists of 35,000 at $4 and 45,000 at $4.14, because inventory increased 45,000 units during November. This totals $326,300. Thus, income would be $4,900 less than for FIFO (because EI was $4,900 less--the only variable that changed). For FIFO, income was $391,200 and for LIFO it is $386,300 (see Q. 67).

Note that if unit fixed costs differ from period to period, the formula -- change in inventory x unit fixed costs -- does not reconcile absorption and variable costing income.

Questions 70 and 71 are based on the following information. Osawa Inc. planned and actually manufactured 200,000 units of its single product in its first year of operations. Variable manufacturing costs were $30 per unit of product. Planned and actual fixed manufacturing costs were $600,000 and selling and administrative costs totaled $400,000. Osawa sold 120,000 units of product during the year at a selling price of $40 per unit.

70. Osawa's operating income using absorption (full) costing is

a. $200,000.
b. $440,000.
c. $600,000.
d. $840,000.
e. Some amount other than those given above.

The correct answer is (b). *(CMA 1285 4-14)*
REQUIRED: The operating income under absorption costing.
DISCUSSION: Absorption costing net income is computed as follows:

Sales (120,000 x $40)	$4,800,000
Variable production costs ($30 x 200,000 units)	$6,000,000
Fixed production costs	600,000
Total production costs (200,000 units)	$6,600,000
Ending inventory (80,000 x $35)	(2,640,000)
Cost of goods sold	$3,960,000
Gross profit	$ 840,000
Selling and administrative expense	(400,000)
Net income	$ 440,000

71. Osawa's operating income using variable (direct) costing is

a. $200,000.
b. $440,000.
c. $800,000.
d. $600,000.
e. Some amount other than those given above.

The correct answer is (a). *(CMA 1285 4-15)*
REQUIRED: The operating income under direct costing.
DISCUSSION: The contribution margin from manufacturing (sales - variable costs) is $10 ($40 - $30) per unit sold, or $1,200,000 (120,000 units x $10). The fixed costs of manufacturing ($600,000) and selling and administrative costs ($400,000) are deducted from the contribution margin to arrive at an operating income of $200,000. The difference between the absorption income of $440,000 (see preceding question) and the $200,000 of direct costing income is attributable to capitalization of the fixed manufacturing costs under the absorption method. Since 40% of the goods produced are still in inventory (80,000 ÷ 200,000), 40% of the $600,000 in fixed costs, or $240,000, was capitalized under the absorption method. That amount was expensed under the direct costing method.

CHAPTER ELEVEN
COST/VOLUME/PROFIT ANALYSIS

11.1 Concepts	(18 questions)	223
11.2 Assumptions	(6 questions)	228
11.3 High-Low Calculations	(5 questions)	230
11.4 Basic Breakeven Problems	(17 questions)	231
11.5 Changes in CVP Variables	(20 questions)	236
11.6 Targeted Profit	(25 questions)	242
11.7 Multiproduct Breakeven	(23 questions)	250
11.8 Working Backwards	(27 questions)	257
11.9 Comprehensive	(74 questions)	265

This chapter begins the planning and control section of this book (Chapters 11 through 14), which is intended to link the traditional cost accounting area (Chapters 4 through 10) to nonroutine decisions (Chapters 15 through 21). Cost/volume/profit (CVP) analysis is based on the concept that fixed costs in the short run are not relevant for decision making. A variety of problems is provided in this chapter to show the pervasive nature of CVP issues. In fact, all the chapters on planning and control are, in essence, built upon the issue of CVP analysis. You should be well versed in CVP analysis before continuing with the remainder of the planning and control chapters.

11.1 Concepts

1. Cost/volume/earnings (profit) analysis allows management to determine the relative profitability of a product by

a. Highlighting potential bottlenecks in the production process.

b. Keeping fixed costs to an absolute minimum.

c. Determining the contribution margin per unit and projected profits at various levels of production.

d. Assigning costs to a product in a manner that maximizes the contribution margin.

The correct answer is (c). *(CPA 577 T-40)*
REQUIRED: The purpose of cost/volume/profit analysis.
DISCUSSION: CVP analysis studies the relationships among sales volume, sales price, fixed costs, variable costs, and profit. It allows management to determine the UCM, i.e., the difference between unit sales price and unit variable cost. The CM is used to project the BEP as well as profits at various levels of production.
Answers (a) and (b) are incorrect because CVP analysis controls neither physical production nor production costs. Answer (d) is incorrect because CVP is a means of estimating profitability at various sales levels rather than a technique of accounting for costs.

2. The most useful information derived from a breakeven chart is the

a. Amount of sales revenue needed to cover enterprise variable costs.

b. Amount of sales revenue needed to cover enterprise fixed costs.

c. Relationship among revenues, variable costs, and fixed costs at various levels of activity.

d. Volume or output level at which the enterprise breaks even.

The correct answer is (c). *(CPA 573 T-29)*
REQUIRED: The most useful information derived from a breakeven chart.
DISCUSSION: Breakeven analysis is a means of predicting the relationships among revenues, variable costs, and fixed costs at various production levels. It allows management to discern the probable effects of changes in sales volume, sales price, costs, product mix, etc.
Answers (a), (b), and (d) are incorrect because each is only one aspect of the relationship among revenues, variable costs, and fixed costs.

3. Cost-volume-profit (CVP) analysis is a key factor in many decisions, including choice of product lines, pricing of products, marketing strategy, and utilization of productive facilities. A calculation used in a CVP analysis is the breakeven point. Once the breakeven point has been reached, operating income will increase by the

   a. Gross margin per unit for each additional unit sold.
   b. Contribution margin per unit for each additional unit sold.
   c. Fixed costs per unit for each additional unit sold.
   d. Variable costs per unit for each additional unit sold.
   e. Sales price per unit for each additional unit sold.

The correct answer is (b). *(CMA 1286 5-12)*
   REQUIRED: The amount by which operating income will increase once the breakeven point has been reached.
   DISCUSSION: At the breakeven point, total revenue equals the fixed cost plus the variable cost. Beyond the BEP, each unit sale will increase operating income by the unit contribution margin (unit sales price - unit variable cost) because fixed cost will already have been recovered.
   Answer (a) is incorrect because the gross margin equals sales price minus cost of goods sold, including fixed cost. Answers (c), (d), and (e) are incorrect because operating income will increase by the UCM.

4. Cost/volume/profit relationships that are curvilinear may be analyzed linearly by considering only

   a. Fixed and semi-variable costs.
   b. Relevant fixed costs.
   c. Relevant variable costs.
   d. A relevant range of volume.

The correct answer is (d). *(CPA 573 T-26)*
   REQUIRED: When curvilinear cost/volume/profit relationships may be analyzed linearly.
   DISCUSSION: CVP analysis is assumed to be linear over a relevant range of activity (volume). Over the "relevant" range of activity, total fixed costs and unit variable costs are assumed to be constant.
   Answers (a), (b), and (c) are incorrect because the linear approximation of a curvilinear CVP relationship is achieved not by limiting the costs considered but by restricting analysis to a given range of activity.

5. Which of the following factors is involved in studying cost/volume/profit relationships?

   a. Levels of production.
   b. Variable costs.
   c. Fixed costs.
   d. Product mix.
   e. All of the above.

The correct answer is (e). *(CIA 578 IV-7)*
   REQUIRED: The characteristic(s) of CVP relationships.
   DISCUSSION: CVP analysis considers such variables as sales price, variable costs, fixed costs, levels of production, and product mix. It permits management to estimate the effects on profitability of changes in these factors and is thus a significant planning tool.

6. In cost/volume/profit analysis, the greatest profit will be earned at

   a. 100% of normal productive capacity.
   b. The production point with the lowest marginal cost.
   c. The production point at which average total revenue exceeds average marginal cost.
   d. The production point with lowest average cost.
   e. The point at which marginal cost and marginal revenue are equal.

The correct answer is (e). *(CIA 976 IV-15)*
   REQUIRED: The point of greatest profit according to CVP analysis.
   DISCUSSION: The greatest profit will be earned when marginal revenue is equal to marginal cost. At that point, incremental revenues no longer exceed incremental costs, so selling an additional unit would not increase profit.
   Answers (a), (b), and (d) are incorrect because each ignores the revenue element and considers only production capacity and cost. Answer (c) is incorrect because profit is maximized when marginal rather than average revenue equals marginal (not average marginal) cost.

7. A travel agency needs to set a price for a package tour for one of the post-season football bowl games. The price must cover the chartered cost of the plane, in-flight meals, motel accommodations, continental breakfasts, and game tickets. The technique that would be most helpful in the agency's planning is

   a. A transportation algorithm.
   b. Discounted cash flow.
   c. Linear programming.
   d. Payback analysis.
   e. Cost/volume/profit analysis.

The correct answer is (e). *(CMA 1280 5-1)*
REQUIRED: The most relevant analytical technique for making a short-run decision.
DISCUSSION: CVP analysis is used to estimate the revenue needed to cover total costs plus the targeted profit by computing the UCM. The UCM is divided into the sum of fixed costs plus targeted profit to arrive at the BEP in units.
Answer (a) is incorrect because transportation algorithms are specialized applications of linear programming to schedule efficient delivery of items from sources (e.g., factories, warehouses, etc.) to destinations (e.g., stores). Answers (b) and (d) are incorrect because they are capital budgeting techniques. Answer (c) is incorrect because linear programming is a means of finding the most economical way to allocate scarce resources.

8. The margin of safety is a key concept of CVP analysis. The margin of safety is

   a. The contribution margin rate.
   b. The difference between budgeted contribution margin and actual contribution margin.
   c. The difference between budgeted contribution margin and breakeven contribution margin.
   d. The difference between budgeted sales and breakeven sales.
   e. The difference between the breakeven point in sales and cash flow breakeven.

The correct answer is (d). *(CMA 1286 5-13)*
REQUIRED: The definition of the margin of safety.
DISCUSSION: The margin of safety measures the amount by which sales may decline before losses occur. It is the excess of budgeted or actual sales over sales at the BEP. It may be stated in either units sold or sales revenue.
Answer (a) is incorrect because the contribution margin rate is computed by dividing contribution margin by sales. Answers (b) and (c) are incorrect because the margin of safety is expressed in revenue or units, not contribution margin. Answer (e) is incorrect because cash flow breakeven is not relevant.

9. The method of cost accounting that lends itself to breakeven analysis is

   a. Variable.
   b. Standard.
   c. Absolute.
   d. Absorption.

The correct answer is (a). *(CPA 579 T-37)*
REQUIRED: The method of cost accounting used in breakeven analysis.
DISCUSSION: Variable costs are emphasized in breakeven analysis. Total revenue less the total variable costs equals the CM, which is a major tool in breakeven analysis.
Answer (b) is incorrect because, since standard costs are not necessarily variable, standard cost is not associated with variable costs unless so stated. Answer (c) is incorrect because the term absolute cost accounting is nonsensical in this context. Answer (d) is incorrect because absorption costs also include fixed costs. BE analysis emphasizes variable costs.

10. At the breakeven point, fixed cost is always

    a. Less than the contribution margin.
    b. Equal to the contribution margin.
    c. More than the contribution margin.
    d. More than the variable cost.

The correct answer is (b). *(CPA 1181 T-50)*
REQUIRED: The relationship of fixed cost to CM at the breakeven point.
DISCUSSION: At the BEP, the point at which no profit or loss occurs, fixed cost must equal the CM (total revenue - total variable cost).
Answer (a) is incorrect because, at the BEP, fixed cost will never be less than the CM. If fixed costs are less, operations are profitable. Answer (c) is incorrect because if fixed costs are more than CM, the company is operating at a loss, i.e., not at the BEP. Answer (d) is incorrect because, at the BEP, fixed cost may be less than, more than, or equal to total variable cost.

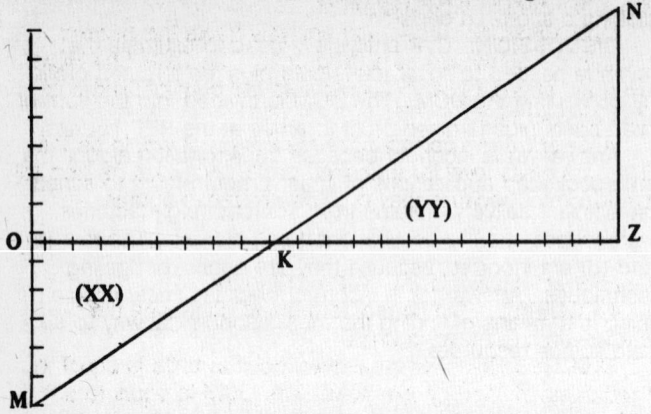

Questions 11 and 12 are based on the following chart.

11. On the profit/volume chart above,
    a. Areas XX and YY and point K represent profit, loss, and volume of sales at the breakeven point, respectively.
    b. Line OZ represents the volume of sales.
    c. Lines OM and NZ represent fixed costs.
    d. Line MN represents total costs.
    e. None of the above.

The correct answer is (b). *(CMA 1273 4-6)*
REQUIRED: The correct statement concerning the given profit/volume chart.
DISCUSSION: In the P/V graph shown, the vertical axis represents profit and the horizontal axis (OZ) represents sales volume.
Answer (a) is incorrect because XX, YY, and point K are loss, profit, and the breakeven point, in that order. Answer (c) is incorrect because OM is fixed cost and NZ is the profit at volume Z. Answer (d) is incorrect because MN is the contribution margin.

12. The vertical scale represents
    a. Volume of sales.
    b. Units produced.
    c. Profit above O and loss below O.
    d. Contribution margin.
    e. None of the above.

The correct answer is (c). *(CMA 1273 4-7)*
REQUIRED: The variable represented on the vertical scale of the P/V chart.
DISCUSSION: On a P/V graph, the horizontal axis represents the level of production and the vertical axis the profit or loss. Profit is above the horizontal axis and loss is below.
Answers (a) and (b) are incorrect because volume of sales or production is represented by the horizontal axis. Answer (d) is incorrect because the contribution margin is represented by line MN.

13. The figure below is a cost/volume/profit chart for a manufacturing company. Which of the answer choices correctly describes a labeled item in the chart?

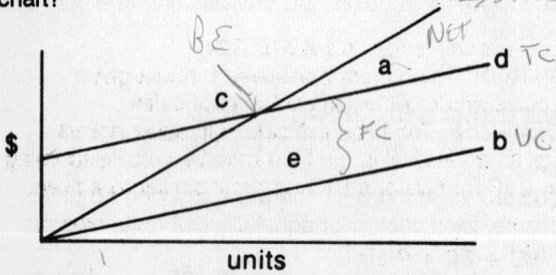

    a. Area a represents the area of net loss.
    b. Line b graphs total fixed costs.
    c. Point c represents the point at which the marginal contribution per unit increases.
    d. Line d graphs total costs.
    e. Area e (between lines b and d) represents the contribution margin.

The correct answer is (d). *(CIA 581 IV-21)*
REQUIRED: The correct statement concerning the CVP chart.
DISCUSSION: The CVP chart shows variable costs (line b), fixed cost (area e), breakeven point (intersection point c), total revenue (45° line from the origin), fixed costs plus variable costs (line d), profit (vertical axis), and volume in units (horizontal axis).
Answer (a) is incorrect because area a represents net profit. Answer (b) is incorrect because line b graphs variable costs. Answer (c) is incorrect because point c is the breakeven point. Answer (e) is incorrect because area e represents fixed costs.

Module 11.1: Concepts

14. The dollar amount of sales needed to attain a desired profit is calculated by dividing the contribution margin ratio (CMR) into

  a. Fixed cost.
  b. Desired profit.
  c. Desired profit plus fixed cost.
  d. Desired profit less fixed cost.

The correct answer is (c). *(CPA 1181 T-56)*
REQUIRED: The formula to calculate the amount of sales resulting in a desired profit.
DISCUSSION: Breakeven analysis treats the desired profit in the same way as a fixed cost. The CMR (the UCM over unit selling price) is divided into the sum of fixed cost plus desired profit.
Answer (a) is incorrect because the result would be the BEP, not sales level for a desired profit. Answers (b) and (d) are incorrect because they provide nonsense figures.

15. Given the following notations, what is the breakeven sales level in units?

SP = selling price per unit
FC = total fixed cost
VC = variable cost per unit

  a. SP ÷ (FC ÷ VC)
  b. FC ÷ (VC ÷ SP)
  c. VC ÷ (SP - FC)
  d. FC ÷ (SP - VC)

The correct answer is (d). *(CPA 575 T-26)*
REQUIRED: The correct formula to determine the breakeven sales level in units.
DISCUSSION: The breakeven point in units is equal to fixed costs divided by the UCM. The UCM is equal to unit selling price minus unit variable costs.
Answers (a), (b), and (c) are incorrect because they provide nonsense results. Answer (b) is close because FC ÷ [1 - (VC ÷ SP)] defines breakeven in sales dollars.

16. A company's breakeven point in sales dollars may be affected by equal percentage increases in both selling price and variable cost per unit (assume all other factors are equal within the relevant range). The equal percentage changes in selling price and variable cost per unit will cause the breakeven point in sales dollars to

  a. Decrease by less than the percentage increase in selling price.
  b. Decrease by more than the percentage increase in the selling price.
  c. Increase by less than the percentage increase in selling price.
  d. Increase by more than the percentage increase in selling price.
  e. Remain unchanged.

The correct answer is (e). *(CIA 582 IV-23)*
REQUIRED: The effect of equal percentage changes in selling price and variable cost on the breakeven point in sales dollars.
DISCUSSION: The BEP in sales dollars is equal to the fixed cost divided by the CMR. Accordingly, equal percentage changes in selling price and variable cost per unit will not affect the BEP in sales dollars. For example,

Sales price	$1.00
Variable cost	$ .60
Unit contribution margin	$ .40

CMR = UCM ÷ Unit selling price = .40 ÷ 1.00 = 40%. Given a fixed cost of $100, the BEP in sales dollars is $100 ÷ 40% = $250. Raising the selling price and variable cost both by 20% to $1.20 and $.72, respectively, leaves the CMR at 40% (.48 ÷ 1.20). Similarly, lowering the selling price and variable cost to $.80 and $.48, respectively, leaves the CMR at 40% (.32 ÷ .80).

17. If a company's variable costs are 70% of sales, which formula represents the computation of dollar sales that will yield a profit equal to 10% of the contribution margin when S equals sales in dollars for the period and FC equals total fixed costs for the period?

  a. S = .2 ÷ FC
  b. S = FC ÷ .2
  c. S = .27 ÷ FC
  d. S = FC ÷ .27

The correct answer is (d). *(CPA 576 T-24)*
REQUIRED: The correct breakeven formula given variable costs and profit as percentages of sales.
DISCUSSION: The breakeven point in sales dollars when a given profit level is required may be calculated using the basic CVP formula and treating profit similar to a fixed cost.

S = VC + FC + Profit
S = .70S + FC + (.10)(.30)S
S = .70S + FC + (.03)S
.27S = FC
S = FC ÷ .27

18. Advocates of CVP analysis argue that
a. Fixed costs are irrelevant for decision making.
b. Fixed costs are mandatory for CVP decision making.
c. Differentiation between the patterns of variable costs and fixed costs is critical.
d. Fixed costs are necessary to calculate inventory valuations.

The correct answer is (c). *(Publisher)*
REQUIRED: An assumption made in CVP analysis.
DISCUSSION: In CVP analysis, fixed costs are included in the analysis but the primary question involves the relationships that fixed costs have within the relevant range as well as the pattern of fixed costs. Thus, the key concept is that both fixed and variable costs are used in CVP and the two types of cost must be differentiated.
Answer (a) is incorrect because CVP analysis does use fixed costs. Answer (b) is incorrect because CVP analysis is also applicable to organizations with only variable costs. Answer (d) is incorrect because CVP is not usually concerned with inventory valuation.

11.2 Assumptions

19. Breakeven analysis assumes over the relevant range that
a. Total costs are linear.
b. Fixed costs are nonlinear.
c. Variable costs are nonlinear.
d. Selling prices are nonlinear.

The correct answer is (a). *(CPA 587 T-47)*
REQUIRED: An assumption underlying breakeven analysis.
DISCUSSION: Breakeven analysis assumes that the cost and revenue factors used in the formula are linear and do not fluctuate with volume. Therefore, it is assumed that fixed costs are fixed over the relevant range of volume, and that variable cost per unit remains constant as volume changes within the relevant range.

20. Cost/volume/profit analysis is a technique available to management to understand better the interrelationships of several factors which affect a firm's profit. As with many such techniques, the accountant oversimplifies the real world by making assumptions. Which of the following is not a major assumption underlying CVP analysis?
a. All costs incurred by a firm can be separated into their fixed and variable components.
b. The product selling price per unit is constant at all volume levels.
c. Operating efficiency and employee productivity are constant at all volume levels.
d. For multiproduct situations, the sales mix can vary at all volume levels.
e. Costs vary only with changes in volume.

The correct answer is (d). *(CMA 1277 4-1)*
REQUIRED: The assumption that does not underlie CVP analysis.
DISCUSSION: The inherent simplifying assumptions used in CVP analysis are the following: costs and revenues are predictable and are linear over the relevant range; variable costs change proportionally with activity level; changes in inventory are insignificant in amount; fixed costs remain constant over the relevant range of volume; prices remain fixed; production equals sales; there is a relevant range in which the various relationships are true; all costs are either fixed or variable; efficiency is constant; costs vary only with changes in volume; and there is a constant mix of products (or only one product). That is, the sales mix of multiproduct situations cannot vary with volume.

21. Which of the following is not an assumption of cost/volume/profit analysis?
a. The variable cost per unit varies over the relevant range of activity.
b. The sales mix is unchanged over the relevant range of activity.
c. The total fixed cost is constant over the relevant range of activity.
d. The total variable cost changes in direct proportion to changes in the level of activity over the relevant range of activity.

The correct answer is (a). *(CIA 583 IV-29)*
REQUIRED: The incorrect assumption for CVP analysis.
DISCUSSION: The inherent simplifying assumptions used in CVP analysis are the following: costs and revenues are predictable and are linear over the relevant range; total variable costs change proportionally with activity level; changes in inventory are insignificant in amount; fixed costs remain constant over the relevant range of volume; prices remain fixed; production equals sales; there is a constant mix of products (or only one product); there is a relevant range in which the various relationships are true; all costs are either fixed or variable; efficiency is constant; and costs vary only with changes in volume. Thus, variable costs per unit are assumed constant over the relevant range.

Module 11.2: Assumptions

22. In preparing a cost-volume-profit analysis for his candle manufacturing business, Joe Stark is considering raising his prices $1.00 per candle. Stark is concerned about the impact this will have on his volume of sales at craft fairs. Stark is concerned about

a. The equilibrium point.
b. The elasticity of demand.
c. The substitution effect.
d. The nature of supply.
e. The maximization of utility.

The correct answer is (b). *(CMA 1285 I-18)*
REQUIRED: The concept related to a concern about the effect of a price increase on sales.
DISCUSSION: As prices are increased, total revenue may increase or decrease depending on the elasticity of demand. If demand is elastic, a price increase will tend to reduce revenues. If demand is inelastic, a price increase will tend to raise revenues. Thus, when Joe is concerned with the effect the dollar increase will have on revenues, he is concerned with the elasticity of demand for his candles.
Answer (a) is incorrect because the increase will do nothing to affect the equilibrium point since it will not shift the supply or the demand curve. Answer (c) is incorrect because the substitution effect is implicit in the concept of elasticity. The fewer substitutes, the less elastic will be the demand for a good. Answer (d) is incorrect because, in Joe's cost-volume-profit analysis, the nature of the supply curve does not come into consideration. Answer (e) is incorrect because utility theory is also implicit in the concept of elasticity. If demand is elastic, consumers derive less utility from paying a higher price. Thus, elasticity is Joe's dominant concern.

23. An activity for which CVP analysis would not provide useful data is

a. Product pricing.
b. Selection of channels for product distribution.
c. Reporting on income tax returns.
d. Level of manpower employed.
e. Special sales promotions.

The correct answer is (c). *(CIA 976 IV-3)*
REQUIRED: When CVP analysis does not provide useful data.
DISCUSSION: Reporting on income tax returns is based on events that have already occurred. CVP analysis is a budgeting or planning tool used to estimate the effects of future events.
Answer (a) is incorrect because CVP analysis may be used to determine the price needed to earn a desired profit. Answer (b) is incorrect because the channel of distribution is selected based upon potential sales volume, marketing costs, the appropriate sales price, etc. which can be analyzed via CVP relationships. Answer (d) is incorrect because the level of manpower employed affects direct labor costs. Variable cost based on projected demand can be a significant element of CVP analysis. Answer (e) is incorrect because special sales promotions may be accepted or rejected based on CVP analysis.

24. In working on a CVP analysis, the accountant is unsure of the exact results and/or assumptions under which to operate. What can the accountant do to help management in this CVP decision?

a. Nothing. It is not the responsibility of the accountant to be concerned with the ambiguity of the results and/or assumptions.
b. Ascertain the probabilities of various outcomes and work with management on understanding those probabilities in reference to the CVP decision.
c. Calculate the probabilities of various outcomes and make the decision for management.
d. Use a random number table to generate a decision model and make the decision for management.

The correct answer is (b). *(Publisher)*
REQUIRED: The approach to take in a probabilistic CVP decision.
DISCUSSION: The assumptions under which CVP analysis operates primarily hinge on certainty. Once uncertainty enters the situation, the results are not nearly so clear. Thus, the accountant should make an appropriate effort to ascertain the probabilities of various outcomes. The accountant can then work with management to help make the appropriate decision.
Answer (a) is incorrect because it is the responsibility of the accountant to be involved with management and aid in their decision making. Answer (c) is incorrect because it is not appropriate for the accountant to make the decision. Management should make the decision with the accountant's advice and help. Answer (d) is incorrect because, although using a random number table may be part of the decision process, the decision should not rest with the accountant alone.

11.3 High-Low Calculations

25. When trying to separate fixed costs and variable costs, the accountant may use a crude technique known as
 a. The least squares method.
 b. Computer simulation.
 c. The high-low method.
 d. Matrix algebra.

The correct answer is (c). *(Publisher)*
REQUIRED: The rough method of estimating fixed and variable costs proportions in a mixed cost situation.
DISCUSSION: Fixed and variable portions of mixed costs may be roughly estimated by identifying the highest cost and the lowest cost within the relevant range. The difference between these two points in dollars and activity levels is the variable rate. Once the variable rate is found, the fixed portion is determinable. The high-low method is easy to do and gives an approximation of the mixed cost formula enabling management to progress in their decision making. The costs of using more sophisticated methods sometimes outweigh the incremental accuracy benefits they achieve. In these cases, the high-low method is "close enough."
Answers (a), (b), and (d) are incorrect because they are more sophisticated methods of identifying the fixed and variable costs.

Questions 26 and 27 are based on the maintenance expenses of a company, which are to be analyzed for purposes of constructing a flexible budget. Examination of past records disclosed the following costs and volume measures:

	Highest	Lowest
Cost per month	$39,200	$32,000
Machine hours	24,000	15,000

---

26. Using the high-low-point method of analysis, the estimated variable cost per machine hour is
 a. $1.25.
 b. $12.50.
 c. $0.80.
 d. $0.08.

The correct answer is (c). *(CPA 574 P-6)*
REQUIRED: Variable cost per machine hour using the high-low-point method.
DISCUSSION: The unit variable cost is found by dividing the change in total costs by the change in machine hours, the given measure of activity.

$$\frac{\text{Change in TC}}{\text{Change in MH}} = \frac{\$7,200}{9,000} = \$.80 \text{ VC/unit}$$

27. Using the high-low technique, estimate the annual fixed cost for maintenance expenditures.
 a. $447,360.
 b. $240,000.
 c. $230,400.
 d. $384,000.

The correct answer is (b). *(CPA 574 P-7)*
REQUIRED: The estimated annual fixed cost for maintenance expenditures.
DISCUSSION: The first step in finding the fixed cost using the high-low method is to determine the variable cost per unit by dividing the change in total cost by the change in activity (stated in machine hours). This was computed as $.80/hour in Q. 26. The fixed cost is found by substituting the variable cost into either of the activity/cost functions.

Monthly FC = TC - VC
Monthly FC = $32,000 - (15,000)(.80) = $20,000
Monthly FC = $39,200 - (24,000)(.80) = $20,000

Estimated annual fixed cost expenditures are 12 months x $20,000 = $240,000

28. Jackson, Inc. is preparing a flexible budget for next year and requires a breakdown of the cost of steam used in its factory into the fixed and variable elements. The following data on the cost of steam used and direct labor hours worked are available for the last 6 months of this year:

Month	Cost of Steam	Direct Labor Hours
July	$ 15,850	3,000
August	13,400	2,050
September	16,370	2,900
October	19,800	3,650
November	17,600	2,670
December	18,500	2,650
Total	$101,520	16,920

Assuming that Jackson uses the high-low method of analysis, the estimated variable cost of steam per direct labor hour is

a. $4.00.
b. $5.42.
c. $5.82.
d. $6.00.

The correct answer is (a). *(CPA 1181 P-25)*
REQUIRED: The variable cost per direct labor hour using the high-low method.
DISCUSSION: The high-low method estimates variable cost by dividing the difference in costs incurred at the highest and lowest observed levels of activity by the difference in activity. Here, the highest level of activity is 3,650 in October, and the lowest is 2,050 in August. The variable cost is found by dividing the change in cost by the change in activity (direct labor hours).

$$\frac{\$19,800 - \$13,400}{3,650 - 2,050} = \frac{\$6,400 \text{ cost}}{1,600 \text{ DLH}} = \$4.00/\text{DLH}$$

29. A company allocates its variable factory overhead based on direct labor hours. During the past three months, the actual direct labor hours and the total factory overhead allocated were as follows:

	January	February	March
Direct labor hours	1,000	3,000	5,000
Total factory overhead allocated	$80,000	$140,000	$200,000

Based upon this information, monthly fixed factory overhead was

a. $30,000.
b. $50,000.
c. $46,667.
d. $33,333.

The correct answer is (b). *(CIA 583 IV-5)*
REQUIRED: The monthly fixed overhead given direct labor hours and the total overhead allocation.
DISCUSSION: This question requires solving simultaneous equations because both the variable overhead per direct labor hour (Y) and fixed overhead (X) are unknown.

$$\$80,000 = X + 1,000Y$$
$$\$140,000 = X + 3,000Y$$
$$\$60,000 = 2,000Y$$
$$Y = \$30 \text{ per direct labor hour}$$

Substituting,
$$\$80,000 = X + 1,000(\$30)$$
$$X = \$50,000$$

11.4 Basic Breakeven Problems

30. Kauffman Company is considering building a new plant to produce Product A. The expected unit selling price of Product A is $100 per unit. The contribution margin ratio of Product A is 40%. Expected annual fixed costs are $600,000. What is the breakeven point in terms of units of Product A?

a. 10,000.
b. 15,000.
c. 1,000,000.
d. 1,500,000.

The correct answer is (b). *(H. Collier)*
REQUIRED: The breakeven point in units.
DISCUSSION: The BEP in units is equal to fixed cost divided by the difference between unit selling price and unit variable cost (UCM). The contribution margin ratio for Product A is 40%: variable costs are 60% of the selling price (SP) or $60 ($100 x .60).

$$\text{BEP} = \frac{\$600,000 \text{ FC}}{\$100 \text{ SP} - \$60 \text{ VC}} = 15,000 \text{ units}$$

Module 11.4: Basic Breakeven Problems

31. A company manufactures a single product which sells for $30. If the company has fixed costs of $150,000 and a contribution margin of 40%, what is the breakeven point in sales dollars?

  a. $250,000.
  b. $275,000.
  c. $375,000.
  d. $525,000.

The correct answer is (c). *(CIA 1187 IV-12)*
  REQUIRED: The breakeven point (BEP) in sales dollars.
  DISCUSSION: The unit contribution margin is $12 (40% x $30 unit price). The BEP in units is thus 12,500 ($150,000 FC ÷ $12), and the BEP in sales dollars is $375,000 (12,500 x $30). An alternative is to divide fixed costs by the contribution margin percentage.

32. BE&H Manufacturing is considering dropping a product line. It currently produces a multi-purpose woodworking clamp in a simple manufacturing process which utilizes special equipment. Variable costs amount to $6.00 per unit. Fixed overhead costs, exclusive of depreciation, have been allocated to this product at a rate of $3.50 a unit and will continue whether or not production ceases. Depreciation on the special equipment amounts to $20,000 a year. If production of the clamp is stopped, the special equipment can be sold for $18,000; if production continues, however, the equipment will be useless for further production at the end of 1 year and will have no salvage value. The clamp has a selling price of $10 a unit. Ignoring tax effects, the minimum number of units that would have to be sold in the current year to break even on a cash flow basis is

  a. 4,500 units.
  b. 36,000 units.
  c. 20,000 units.
  d. 5,000 units.

The correct answer is (a). *(CMA 679 5-13)*
  REQUIRED: The breakeven point in units on a cash flow basis.
  DISCUSSION: The BEP in units is equal to fixed cost divided by the difference between unit selling price and unit variable cost (UCM). The $18,000 salvage value, the cash flow to be received if production is discontinued, is treated here as a fixed cost. Hence, continuation of the product line will permit the firm to break even or make a profit only if the total CM is $18,000 or more.

$$BEP = \frac{\$18,000}{\$10 - \$6} = 4,500 \text{ units}$$

Fixed overhead allocated is not considered in this calculation because it is not a cash flow and will continue regardless of the decision.

33. Doe Co. wants to sell a product at a gross margin of 20%. The cost of the product is $2.00. The selling price should be

  a. $1.60.
  b. $2.10.
  c. $2.40.
  d. $2.50.

The correct answer is (d). *(CPA 1186 Q-40)*
  REQUIRED: The selling price, given the gross margin and the cost of the product.
  DISCUSSION: The gross margin is equal to the selling price less the cost of the product.
  Selling price (SP) - Cost = Gross margin
  SP - $2.00 = 20% x SP
  .8SP = $2.00
  SP = $2.50

34. A company producing widgets expects to incur fixed costs during the next year of $3 million. It also expects to incur handling costs of $1 per widget, labor costs of $3 per widget, and materials costs of $2 per widget. The company only produces widgets when ordered and, therefore, does not incur any carrying costs. It sells widgets for $10 each. The number of widgets that must be sold next year in order to break even is

  a. 500,000 units.
  b. 600,000 units.
  c. 750,000 units.
  d. 1,000,000 units.

The correct answer is (c). *(CIA 1186 IV-40)*
  REQUIRED: The unit sales breakeven point.
  DISCUSSION: Since the variable unit cost is $6 ($1 + $3 + $2), the unit contribution margin is $4 ($10 - $6). Dividing the UCM into the fixed costs gives a breakeven point in unit sales of 750,000 ($3,000,000 ÷ $4 per unit).

Module 11.4: Basic Breakeven Problems

Questions 35 and 36 are based on the following data available for the current year.

	Whole Company	Division 1	Division 2
Variable manufacturing cost of goods sold	$ 400,000	$220,000	$ 80,000
Unallocated costs (e.g., president's salary)	100,000		
Fixed costs controllable by division managers (e.g., advertising, engineering supervision costs)	90,000	50,000	40,000
Net revenues	1,000,000	600,000	400,000
Variable selling and administrative costs	130,000	70,000	60,000
Fixed costs controllable by others (e.g., depreciation, insurance)	120,000	70,000	50,000

35. Based upon the information presented above, the contribution margin for the company was

a. $400,000.
b. $470,000.
c. $530,000.
d. $600,000.

The correct answer is (b). *(CIA 1186 IV-16)*
REQUIRED: The contribution margin for the company.
DISCUSSION: Contribution margin is sales minus variable costs. Direct costing considers only variable costs as product costs, so contribution margin appears in a direct costing income statement. Absorption costing treats both variable and fixed costs as product costs. Thus, variable costs are not stated separately and contribution margin would not appear in the income statement. Accordingly, the CM is $470,000 ($1,000,000 net revenues − $400,000 variable CGS − $130,000 variable S&A costs).

36. Using the information presented above, the contribution by Division 1 was

a. $190,000.
b. $260,000.
c. $310,000.
d. $380,000.

The correct answer is (a). *(CIA 1186 IV-17)*
REQUIRED: The contribution by Division 1.
DISCUSSION: The contribution by Division 1 equals its net revenue minus all costs traceable to it. The contribution is $190,000 ($600,000 net revenue − $220,000 − $50,000 − $70,000 − $70,000).

37. Kent Co.'s operating percentages were as follows:

Sales		100%
Cost of sales		
Variable	50%	
Fixed	10	60
Gross profit		40
Other operating expenses		
Variable	20	
Fixed	15	35
Operating income		5%

Kent's sales totaled $2,000,000. At what sales level would Kent break even?

a. $1,900,000.
b. $1,666,667.
c. $1,250,000.
d. $833,333.

The correct answer is (b). *(CPA 1186 Q-34)*
REQUIRED: The breakeven point in sales dollars.
DISCUSSION: The BEP in sales dollars is fixed costs divided by the CMR. The CMR is the CM divided by sales. The CM equals the sales price less variable costs. The contribution margin ratio is:

Sales		100%
Less variable expenses:		
Cost of sales	50%	
Other operating expenses	20	70
Contribution margin ratio		30%

Total fixed costs are $500,000 [(10% × $2,000,000) + (15% × $2,000,000)]. The breakeven point in sales dollars is equal to $1,666,667 ($500,000 ÷ 30%).

Module 11.4: Basic Breakeven Problems

38. In planning its operations for next year based on a sales forecast of $6,000,000, Wallace, Inc. prepared the following estimated costs and expenses:

	Variable	Fixed
Direct materials	$1,600,000	
Direct labor	1,400,000	
Factory overhead	600,000	$900,000
Selling expenses	240,000	360,000
Administrative expenses	60,000	140,000
	$3,900,000	$1,400,000

What would be the amount of sales dollars at the breakeven point?

a. $2,250,000.
b. $3,500,000.
c. $4,000,000.
d. $5,300,000.

The correct answer is (c). *(CPA 1181 P-35)*
REQUIRED: The breakeven point in sales dollars.
DISCUSSION: The BEP in sales dollars is equal to fixed cost divided by the contribution margin ratio. The CMR is equal to the CM divided by sales.

$$CM = Sales - Variable\ Costs$$
$$CM = \$6,000,000 - \$3,900,000 = \$2,100,000$$
$$CMR = CM \div Sales = \frac{\$2,100,000}{\$6,000,000} = .35$$
$$BEP\ \$ = \frac{FC}{CM \div Sales}$$
$$BEP\ \$ = \frac{\$1,400,000}{.35} = \$4,000,000$$

39. The following information pertains to Nova Co.'s cost-volume-profit relationships:

Breakeven point in units sold	1,000
Variable costs per unit	$500
Total fixed costs	150,000

How much will be contributed to profit before income taxes by the 1,001st unit sold?

a. $650.
b. $500.
c. $150.
d. $0.

The correct answer is (c). *(CPA 586 Q-27)*
REQUIRED: The contribution to profit by the first unit sold after the breakeven point.
DISCUSSION: The BEP in units equals fixed cost divided by the UCM. Thus, a firm operating above the BEP will increase profit by the amount of the CM for each unit sold. Since only one unit will be sold above the BEP, the contribution to profit will be the unit contribution margin. The unit contribution margin is:

$$BEP\ in\ units = \frac{Total\ Fixed\ Costs}{Unit\ Contribution\ Margin}$$
$$1,000 = \frac{\$150,000}{UCM}$$
$$1,000\ UCM = \$150,000$$
$$UCM = \$150$$

40. Two companies are expected to have annual sales of 1,000,000 decks of playing cards next year. Estimates for next year are presented below:

	Company 1	Company 2
Selling price per deck	$3.00	$3.00
Cost of paper per deck	.62	.65
Printing ink per deck	.13	.15
Labor per deck	.75	1.25
Variable overhead per deck	.30	.35
Fixed costs	$960,000	$252,000

Given these data, which of the following responses is correct?

	Breakeven Point in Units for Company 1	Breakeven Point in Units for Company 2	Volume in Units at Which Profits of Company 1 and Company 2 Are Equal
a.	800,000	420,000	1,180,000
b.	800,000	420,000	1,000,000
c.	533,334	105,000	1,000,000
d.	533,334	105,000	1,180,000

The correct answer is (a). *(CIA 1184 IV-3)*
REQUIRED: The breakeven points and the indifference point for the companies.
DISCUSSION: Breakeven in units is found by dividing the fixed costs by the UCM.

$$Company\ 1 = \frac{\$960,000}{\$3 - .62 - .13 - .75 - .30} = 800,000$$

$$Company\ 2 = \frac{\$252,000}{\$3 - .65 - .15 - 1.25 - .35} = 420,000$$

The indifference point of unit volume and profit is the point at which total revenue minus total cost equals profit is the same for both companies. Given that unit price is the same and unit volume (U) is unknown, total costs should be equal.

$$U(\$.62 + .13 + .75 + .30) + \$960,000 =$$
$$U(\$.65 + .15 + 1.25 + .35) + \$252,000$$
$$\$1.80U + \$960,000 = \$2.40U + \$252,000$$
$$\$.60U = \$708,000$$
$$U = 1,180,000$$

Module 11.4: Basic Breakeven Problems

41. Thomas Company sells products X, Y, and Z. Thomas sells three units of X for each unit of Z, and two units of Y for each unit of X. The contribution margins are $1.00 per unit of X, $1.50 per unit of Y, and $3.00 per unit of Z. Fixed costs are $600,000. How many units of X would Thomas sell at the breakeven point?

a. 40,000.
b. 120,000.
c. 360,000.
d. 400,000.

The correct answer is (b). *(CPA 1180 P-29)*
REQUIRED: The breakeven point in units of a specific product in a sales mix.
DISCUSSION: The BEP in units equals fixed cost divided by the UCM. With the given sales mix (3 units of X to each unit of Z and 2 units of Y to each unit of X), a composite UCM must be calculated. The composite UCM of $15 is the denominator for computing the BEP in composite units.

$$\underset{X}{3(\$1.00)} + \underset{Y}{(2 \times 3)(\$1.50)} + \underset{Z}{1(\$3.00)} = \$15$$

$$BEP = \frac{\$600,000}{\$15} = 40,000 \text{ composite units}$$

Each composite unit has 3 units of X; therefore, 120,000 units of X will be sold at the BEP (40,000 composite units times 3X).

42. Marling Company is contemplating an expansion program based on the following budget data:

Expected sales $600,000
Variable costs $420,000
Fixed expenses $120,000

What is the amount of breakeven sales?

a. $400,000.
b. $420,000.
c. $540,000.
d. $660,000.

The correct answer is (a). *(CPA 1182 Q-27)*
REQUIRED: The breakeven point in sales dollars.
DISCUSSION: The BEP in sales dollars is fixed costs divided by the CMR. The CMR is the CM divided by sales price. The CM equals the sales price less variable costs per unit.

CM = Sales - Variable Costs
CM = $600,000 - $420,000 = $180,000
CMR = $180,000 ÷ $600,000 = .30

$$BEP \$ = \frac{\$120,000}{.30} = \$400,000$$

43. Lyman Company has the opportunity to increase annual sales $100,000 by selling to a new, riskier group of customers. The uncollectible expense is expected to be 15%, and collection costs will be 5%. The company's manufacturing and selling expenses are 70% of sales, and its effective tax rate is 40%. If Lyman should accept this opportunity, the company's after tax profits would increase by

a. $6,000.
b. $10,000.
c. $10,200.
d. $14,400.
e. Some amount other than those given above.

The correct answer is (a). *(CMA 687 I-27)*
REQUIRED: The after tax increase in profit.
DISCUSSION: Sales increase by $100,000. Collection and bad debt expense is 20% of sales (15% + 5%). Total variable expenses for the new sales will be 90% (20% + 70%) of each sales dollar.

Sales	$100,000	
Less costs	90,000	(90% x $100,000)
Additional profit	10,000	
Less taxes	4,000	(40% x $10,000)
After tax profit	$ 6,000	

44. Gata Co. plans to discontinue a department with a $48,000 contribution to overhead, and allocated overhead of $96,000, of which $42,000 cannot be eliminated. What would be the effect of this discontinuance on Gata's pretax profit?

a. Increase of $48,000.
b. Decrease of $48,000.
c. Increase of $6,000.
d. Decrease of $6,000.

The correct answer is (c). *(CPA 586 Q-40)*
REQUIRED: The effect of discontinuing a department on pretax profit.
DISCUSSION: Consider only the revenue and cost elements that will differ if the department is terminated. The department has $42,000 of allocated overhead which will not be eliminated if the department is terminated. Thus, $54,000 ($96,000 - $42,000) of overhead will be eliminated. However, $48,000 of contribution to overhead will also be eliminated. The net pretax effect on income would be a $6,000 increase to income (eliminating $54,000 of costs - $48,000 of income).

Module 11.5: Changes in CVP Variables

Questions 45 and 46 are based on Rica Company, to which the information presented in the opposite column pertains.

Sales (50,000 units)	$1,000,000
Direct materials and direct labor	300,000
Factory overhead:	
Variable	40,000
Fixed	70,000
Selling and general expenses:	
Variable	10,000
Fixed	60,000

45. How much was Rica's breakeven point in number of units?

a. 9,848.
b. 10,000.
c. 18,571.
d. 26,000.

The correct answer is (b). *(CPA 1184 Q-14)*
REQUIRED: The BEP in units given fixed and variable costs, unit sales, and sales revenue.
DISCUSSION: The BEP in units is calculated by dividing the fixed costs by the UCM.

CM = $1,000,000 - $300,000 - $40,000 - $10,000
CM = $650,000
UCM = $650,000 ÷ 50,000
UCM = $13
BEP = ($70,000 + $60,000) ÷ $13 = 10,000

46. What was Rica's contribution margin ratio?

a. 66%.
b. 65%.
c. 59%.
d. 35%.

The correct answer is (b). *(CPA 1184 Q-15)*
REQUIRED: The contribution margin ratio.
DISCUSSION: The CMR is calculated by dividing the UCM by the sales price. Sales price is $20 ($1,000,000 sales ÷ 50,000 units).

CMR = $13 ÷ $20 = 65%

11.5 Changes in CVP Variables

47. Tonykinn Company is contemplating marketing a new product. Fixed costs to be incurred are $800,000 for production of 75,000 units or less and $1,200,000 for more than 75,000 units. The variable cost ratio is 60% for the first 75,000 units, though it drops to 50% for units in excess of 75,000. If the product is expected to sell for $25 per unit, how many units must Tonykinn sell to break even?

a. 120,000.
b. 111,000.
c. 96,000.
d. 80,000.
e. 53,333.

The correct answer is (b). *(C.J. Skender)*
REQUIRED: The breakeven point in units with changing fixed and variable cost behavior patterns.
DISCUSSION: The BEP in units is equal to fixed cost divided by the difference between unit selling price and unit variable cost, or the unit contribution margin (UCM). At less than 75,000 units, fixed costs are $800,000 and UCM is $10 [$25 - (60% x $25)]. 80,000 units ($800,000 ÷ $10) must be sold, but this is not within the relevant range. At a production level greater than 75,000 units, fixed costs are $1,200,000 but there are two UCM layers. The first 75,000 units will produce a contribution margin of $750,000 (75,000 x $10). Therefore, another $450,000 ($1,200,000 - $750,000) must be covered. Relevant UCM is $12.50 [$25 - (50% x $25)] for units in excess of 75,000. Additional units needed are 36,000 ($450,000 ÷ $12.50). Total units to sell to break even are 111,000 (75,000 + 36,000).

48. During June, a company expects sales revenue from its only product to be $300,000 fixed costs to be $90,000, and variable costs to be $120,000. If the company's actual sales revenue during June is $350,000, its profit would be

a. $90,000.
b. $105,000.
c. $120,000.
d. $140,000.

The correct answer is (c). *(CIA 1186 IV-11)*
REQUIRED: The profit given actual revenue and cost behavior data.
DISCUSSION: Profit at the expected sales level is $90,000 ($300,000 - $90,000 FC - $120,000 VC), and the contribution margin ratio is 60% [($300,000 - $120,000 VC) ÷ $300,000]. Since the company is beyond the breakeven point, the entire contribution margin from the additional sales revenue is profit. Thus, total profit is $120,000 [$90,000 + (60% x $50,000)].

Module 11.5: Changes in CVP Variables

49. The Childers Company sells widgets. At an annual sales volume of 75,000 units the company breaks even. At an annual sales volume of 100,000 units the company reports a profit of $200,000. The annual fixed costs for the Childers Company are

   a. $600,000.
   b. $800,000.
   c. $75,000.
   d. Insufficient information to determine amount of fixed costs.

The correct answer is (a). *(A. Wilson)*
REQUIRED: The annual fixed costs.
DISCUSSION: The profit increased by $200,000 while the sales volume increased by 25,000 units. This increase in profit is a result of an increase in contribution margin. Contribution margin is

$$\$200,000 \div 25,000 \text{ units} = \$8/\text{unit}$$

The BEP in units is equal to fixed costs divided by the unit contribution margin (UCM).

$$\text{BEP} = \frac{\text{Fixed costs}}{\$8/\text{unit}} = 75,000 \text{ units}$$

$$\text{Fixed costs} = \$600,000$$

50. An organization's sales revenue is expected to be $72,600, a 10% increase over last year. For the same period, total fixed costs of $22,000 are expected to be the same as last year. If the number of units sold is expected to increase by 1,100, the marginal revenue per unit will be

   a. $4.
   b. $6.
   c. $20.
   d. $46.
   e. None of the above.

The correct answer is (b). *(CIA 578 IV-18)*
REQUIRED: The marginal revenue per unit given the increase in sales.
DISCUSSION: Marginal revenue (MR) is the incremental revenue for each additional unit sold (increase in revenue ÷ increase in units sold). If expected revenue of $72,600 is a 10% increase over that for the prior year, the prior year's revenue must have been $66,000 ($72,600 ÷ 110%).

$$\text{MR} = \frac{\$72,600 - \$66,000}{1,100} = \frac{\$6,600}{1,100} = \$6$$

51. A manufacturer produces a product that sells for $10 per unit. Variable costs per unit are $6 and total fixed costs are $12,000. At this selling price, the company earns a profit equal to 10% of total dollar sales. By reducing its selling price to $9 per unit, the manufacturer can increase its unit sales volume by 25%. Assume that there are no taxes and that total fixed costs and variable costs per unit remain unchanged. If the selling price were reduced to $9 per unit, the profit would be

   a. $3,000.
   b. $4,000.
   c. $5,000.
   d. $6,000.

The correct answer is (a). *(CIA 1185 IV-9)*
REQUIRED: The expected profit given the change in selling price.
DISCUSSION: In order to determine the profit under the new pricing policy, first compute the sales volume under the old policy by solving for X.

$$\$10X - \$6X - \$12,000 = 0.1(\$10X)$$
$$X = 4,000 \text{ units}$$

Profit at the new price ($9) is

Expected volume at $9 = 125% x 4,000 = 5,000
Profit = ($9 x 5,000) - ($6 x 5,000) - $12,000 = $3,000

52. The contribution margin ratio always increases when the

   a. Variable costs as a percentage of net sales increase.
   b. Variable costs as a percentage of net sales decrease.
   c. Breakeven point increases.
   d. Breakeven point decreases.

The correct answer is (b). *(CPA 1186 T-48)*
REQUIRED: The relationship of contribution margin ratio to sales and variable costs.
DISCUSSION: The CM is variable costs subtracted from sales. The CMR equals CM divided by sales. Therefore, an increase in the CMR will occur when variable costs as a percentage of net sales decrease (i.e., when the numerator of the ratio increases).

Answer (a) is incorrect because, if variable costs as a percentage of net sales increase, the CMR will decrease (the numerator of the ratio decreases). Answers (c) and (d) are incorrect because the BEP changes with changes in fixed costs as well as changes in the CM; i.e., increased fixed costs can change BEP without a change in CMR.

Module 11.5: Changes in CVP Variables

53. Which of the following would decrease contribution margin per unit the most?

a. A 15% decrease in selling price.
b. A 15% increase in variable expenses.
c. A 15% increase in selling price.
d. A 15% decrease in variable expenses.
e. A 15% decrease in fixed expenses.

The correct answer is (a). *(CMA 1273 4-4)*
REQUIRED: The change in a CVP variable causing the greatest decrease in UCM.
DISCUSSION: UCM equals sales price minus variable costs per unit.
Only answers (a) and (b) are possibilities. Answer (a) is correct and answer (b) is incorrect as shown in this example:

```
Original:    SP = $100
             VC =   50
             CM = $ 50
SP - 15%:    SP = $ 85
             VC =   50
             CM = $ 35      ($15 decrease)
VC + 15%:    SP = $100.00
             VC =   57.50
             CM = $ 42.50   ($7.50 decrease)
```

Answers (c) and (d) are incorrect because an increase in selling price or a decrease in variable expenses would increase UCM. Answer (e) is incorrect because a decrease in fixed expenses has no effect on the UCM.

54. The contribution margin increases when sales volume remains the same and

a. Variable cost per unit decreases.
b. Variable cost per unit increases.
c. Fixed costs decrease.
d. Fixed costs increase.

The correct answer is (a). *(CPA 582 T-50)*
REQUIRED: The cause of an increased CM when sales volume remains constant.
DISCUSSION: CM equals sales minus variable costs. With constant sales volume, an increase in the CM may occur only if either the sales price increases or the variable costs decrease.
Answer (b) is incorrect because, when variable cost per unit increases, CM decreases if sales volume remains the same. Answers (c) and (d) are incorrect because the CM does not vary with fixed costs.

55. If the fixed costs attendant to a product increase while variable costs and sales price remain constant, what will happen to contribution margin (CM) and breakeven point (BEP)?

	CM	BEP
a.	Increase	Decrease
b.	Decrease	Increase
c.	Unchanged	Increase
d.	Unchanged	Unchanged

The correct answer is (c). *(CPA 580 T-47)*
REQUIRED: The effect of an increase in fixed costs on the CM and the BEP.
DISCUSSION: The BEP in units is equal to the fixed costs divided by the UCM (sales price - variable cost per unit). Therefore, an increase in the fixed costs would have no effect on the CM, but would cause the BEP to increase, i.e., more units would have to be sold to cover the increased fixed costs.

56. A company increased the selling price for its product from $1.00 to $1.10 a unit when total fixed costs increased from $400,000 to $480,000 and variable cost per unit remained unchanged. How would these changes affect the breakeven point?

a. The breakeven point in units would be increased.
b. The breakeven point in units would be decreased.
c. The breakeven point in units would remain unchanged.
d. The effect cannot be determined from the information given.

The correct answer is (d). *(CPA 575 T-28)*
REQUIRED: The effect on the BEP of an increase in both selling price and fixed costs.
DISCUSSION: The breakeven point in units equals fixed costs divided by the UCM (selling price - variable costs). Therefore, to determine the new breakeven point, the variable cost per unit must be known as well as the total fixed costs and the new selling price per unit. Because the increase in selling price lowers the breakeven point while the increase in fixed costs raises it, the net effect of these changes cannot be determined when variable costs are not known.

Module 11.5: Changes in CVP Variables

57. To obtain the breakeven point stated in terms of dollars of sales, total fixed costs are divided by which of the following?

a. Variable cost per unit.

b. Variable cost per unit ÷ sales price per unit.

c. Fixed cost per unit.

d. (Sales price per unit - variable cost per unit) ÷ sales price per unit.

The correct answer is (d). *(CPA 1184 T-55)*
REQUIRED: The formula to calculate the breakeven point in sales dollars.
DISCUSSION: The BEP in sales dollars is calculated by dividing fixed costs by the CMR. The CMR is the UCM (sales price - variable cost per unit) divided by the sales price. The formulas are

$$CMR = \frac{SP - VC}{SP}$$

$$BEP \, \$ = \frac{FC}{CMR}$$

58. The contribution margin per unit is the difference between the selling price and the variable cost per unit, and the contribution margin ratio is the ratio of the unit contribution margin to the selling price per unit. If the selling price and the variable cost per unit both increase 10% and fixed costs do not change, what is the effect on the contribution margin per unit and the contribution margin ratio?

a. Both remain unchanged.

b. Both increase.

c. Contribution margin per unit increases and the contribution margin ratio remains unchanged.

d. Contribution margin per unit increases and the contribution margin ratio decreases.

The correct answer is (c). *(CPA 575 T-31)*
REQUIRED: The effect on the contribution margin per unit and contribution margin ratio of a 10% increase in both the selling price and the variable costs.
DISCUSSION: Unit contribution margin equals selling price minus variable costs. Therefore, equal percentage increases in the selling price and the variable cost per unit will cause a proportionate increase in the unit contribution margin.

The CMR equals the unit contribution margin divided by selling price. Since the selling price and variable cost per unit both increase in the same proportion, the CMR would be unchanged. For example, if SP is $20 and variable cost is $10, the CMR is 50%. If the selling price and variable cost are increased by 10% to $22 and $11, respectively, the CMR remains 50%.

59. Green Company produces Product A and sells it for $18.00. The following cost data apply:

Type of Cost	Per Unit
Direct materials (3 lbs x $1.50)	$ 4.50
Direct labor	6.45
Variable overhead	1.35
Fixed overhead	1.50
Variable selling expense	1.10
Fixed selling expense	2.20
	$17.10

Green has thought of marketing a new Product B with the same cost structure as Product A except that the price will be $15.60. Green Company currently has the plant capacity necessary for this expansion. Because of the cost structure, Green Company will find the production and sale of Product B in the short run to be

a. Not profitable unless the price can be raised to $17.10.

b. Not profitable at any price.

c. Not profitable at $15.60 because the fixed selling expense and fixed manufacturing overhead will not be covered by the price.

d. Profitable to produce and sell Product B in the short run at the price of $15.60.

The correct answer is (d). *(CIA 585 IV-6)*
REQUIRED: The short-run profitability of a product given cost data and excess capacity.
DISCUSSION: With excess capacity, production is profitable if the incremental revenues are greater than the incremental costs. Here, the incremental costs equal total costs less any fixed costs ($17.10 - $1.50 - $2.20 = $13.40). If Product B can be sold for a price greater than $13.40, short-run production will be profitable. Long-run profitability, however, will depend on fixed costs as well as variable costs and sales price.

Module 11.5: Changes in CVP Variables

Questions 60 through 64 are based on the SAB Company, which uses a profit-volume graph similar to the one shown below to represent the cost/volume/profit relationships of its operations. The vertical (y-axis) is the profit in dollars and the horizontal (x-axis) is the volume in units. The diagonal line is the contribution margin line.

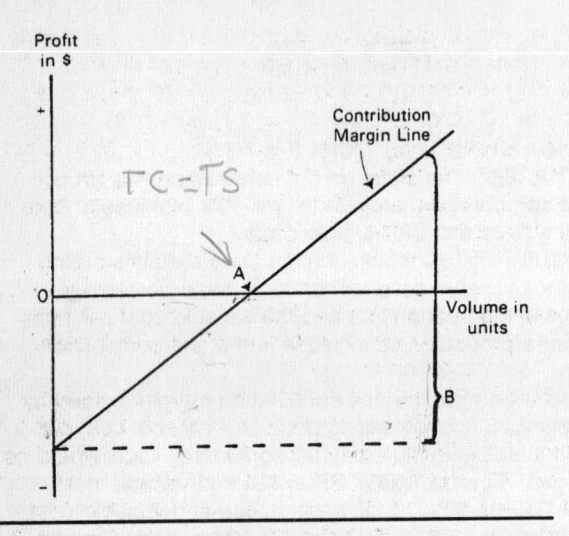

60. Point A on the profit-volume graph represents

    a. The point at which fixed costs equal sales.
    b. The point at which fixed costs equal variable costs.
    c. A volume level of zero units.
    d. The point at which total costs equal total sales.
    e. The point at which the rate of contribution margin increases.

The correct answer is (d). *(CMA 679 4-20)*
  REQUIRED: What is represented by point A on the P-V graph.
  DISCUSSION: Point A is the intersection of the contribution margin line and the zero profit (zero loss) line; i.e., total costs equal total sales at point A.
  Answers (a) and (b) are incorrect because the graph does not provide information about sales or variable costs. Answer (c) is incorrect because a volume level of zero units lies at point O, the intersection of the x and y axes. Answer (e) is incorrect because the contribution rate does not increase in cost/volume/profit analysis, which assumes linearity.

61. The vertical distance from the dotted line to the contribution margin line denoted as B on the profit-volume graph represents

    a. The total contribution margin.
    b. The contribution margin per unit.
    c. The contribution margin rate.
    d. Total sales.
    e. The sum of the variable and fixed costs.

The correct answer is (a). *(CMA 679 4-21)*
  REQUIRED: What is represented by the vertical distance labeled B.
  DISCUSSION: The vertical distance denoted by B is the total contribution margin.
  Answer (b) is incorrect because the UCM is the slope of the CM line, i.e., the vertical increase per one unit increase in volume. Answer (c) is incorrect because the CMR is the same as the UCM. Answer (d) is incorrect because sales information is not provided in the graph except for net sales minus the variable costs, which is the CM. Answer (e) is incorrect because the graph only provides information about fixed costs, which are equal to the difference between the origin (O) and the intersection of the broken line with the vertical axis.

Module 11.5: Changes in CVP Variables

62. If SAB Company's fixed costs were to increase,
   a. The contribution margin line would shift upward parallel to the present line.
   b. The contribution margin line would shift downward parallel to the present line.
   c. The slope of the contribution margin line would be more pronounced (steeper).
   d. The slope of the contribution margin line would be less pronounced (flatter).
   e. The contribution margin line would coincide with the present contribution margin line.

The correct answer is (b). *(CMA 679 4-22)*
REQUIRED: The effects of increased fixed costs on the contribution margin (CM) line.
DISCUSSION: If fixed costs increase, the fixed cost line (the broken line) would shift downward. This shift will result in a higher BEP (currently point A, which would move to the right as the CM line moves down) and a CM line parallel to but below and to the right of the present line. The new CM line would therefore begin at a lower point on the vertical axis.
Answer (a) is incorrect because the CM line would shift upward if fixed costs were decreased, not increased. Answers (c) and (d) are incorrect because the slope of the CM line cannot change if the CM itself (sales price - variable cost per unit) does not change. Fixed cost changes do not affect the CM itself. Answer (e) is incorrect because, when fixed costs increase, the CM line will shift downward, not remain in the same place.

63. If SAB Company's variable costs per unit were to increase but its unit selling price stays constant,
   a. The contribution margin line would shift upward parallel to the present line.
   b. The contribution margin line would shift downward parallel to the present line.
   c. The slope of the contribution margin line would be more pronounced (steeper).
   d. The slope of the contribution margin line would be less pronounced (flatter).
   e. The slope of the contribution margin line probably would change but how it would change is not determinable.

The correct answer is (d). *(CMA 679 4-23)*
REQUIRED: The effects of changes in variable costs per unit on the contribution margin line.
DISCUSSION: If the variable costs per unit increase, while selling price is constant, the CM itself will decrease and the slope of the CM line will also be less.
Answer (a) is incorrect because a decrease in fixed costs shifts the CM line upward. Answer (b) is incorrect because an increase in fixed costs shifts the contribution line downward. Answer (c) is incorrect because a decrease in variable costs, assuming a constant selling price, increases the slope of the CM line. Answer (e) is incorrect because, if the CM increases, the slope will increase; if the CM decreases, the slope will decrease.

64. If SAB Company decided to increase its unit selling price to offset exactly the increase in the variable cost per unit, the
   a. Contribution margin line would shift upward parallel to the present line.
   b. Contribution margin line would shift downward parallel to the present line.
   c. Slope of the contribution margin line would be pronounced (steeper).
   d. Slope of the contribution margin line would be less pronounced (flatter).
   e. Contribution margin line would coincide with the present contribution margin line.

The correct answer is (e). *(CMA 679 4-24)*
REQUIRED: The effect on the contribution margin line of an equal increase in both selling price and unit variable cost.
DISCUSSION: If the selling price is increased by an amount exactly equal to the increase in variable costs per unit, the new CM (Sales - VC) would still be equal to the old CM. Therefore, the new CM line will coincide with the present CM line. The only effect is that the sales price and variable costs per unit are greater. Neither of these is shown on the breakeven chart, however.
Answers (a) and (b) are incorrect because the CM line will not shift since fixed costs were not changed. Answers (c) and (d) are incorrect because the UCM remains constant, and no change in the slope will occur.

65. Which of the following will result in raising the breakeven point?

a. An increase in the sales price per unit.
b. An increase in the semivariable cost per unit.
c. A decrease in the variable cost per unit.
d. An increase in the contribution margin per unit.
e. A decrease in income tax rates.

The correct answer is (b). *(CIA 577 IV-11)*
REQUIRED: The change in a CVP factor that will raise the breakeven point.
DISCUSSION: The BEP equals fixed cost divided by the UCM (selling price - unit variable cost). An increase in semivariable costs increases fixed costs and/or variable costs. An increase in either will raise the BEP. If fixed costs increase, more units must be sold, assuming the same UCM, to cover the greater fixed costs. If variable costs increase, the UCM will decrease and again more units must be sold to cover the fixed costs.
Answers (a) and (c) are incorrect because, if other factors are constant, an increase in sales price or a decrease in unit variable cost increases the CM and lowers the BEP. Answer (d) is incorrect because an increase in the CM decreases the BEP. Answer (e) is incorrect because, if income taxes are taken into account, they are treated as variable costs. A decrease in variable costs lowers the BEP.

66. Each of the following would affect the breakeven point except a change in the

a. Number of units sold.
b. Variable cost per unit.
c. Total fixed costs.
d. Sales price per unit.

The correct answer is (a). *(CPA 579 T-32)*
REQUIRED: The change that would not affect the breakeven point.
DISCUSSION: The three components of the breakeven formula are fixed cost, selling price, and variable cost per unit (BEP = FC ÷ UCM). UCM equals selling price less unit variable costs. A change in any of these will affect the BEP. Hence, variations in production/sales levels theoretically have no effect on the BEP (even though they affect the level of profitability).
Answers (b), (c), and (d) are incorrect because each is a variable in the BE formula.

11.6 Targeted Profit

67. In using cost-volume-profit analysis to calculate expected unit sales, which of the following should be added to fixed costs in the numerator?

a. Predicted operating loss.
b. Predicted operating profit.
c. Unit contribution margin.
d. Variable costs.

The correct answer is (b). *(CPA 1187 T-48)*
REQUIRED: The addition to fixed costs when calculating expected unit sales.
DISCUSSION: When a targeted profit (T) is desired, the profit is treated as a fixed cost (FC). Consequently, the calculation of expected unit sales is

(FC + T) ÷ UCM = Units

Since a net gain is profit, it would be added to fixed costs in the CVP calculation.

68. Last year, the marginal contribution rate of Lamesa Company was 30%. This year, fixed costs are expected to be $120,000, the same as last year, and sales are forecasted at $550,000, a 10% increase over last year. For the company to increase income by $15,000 in the coming year, the marginal contribution rate must be

a. 20%.
b. 30%.
c. 40%.
d. 70%.

The correct answer is (b). *(CPA 569 T-10)*
REQUIRED: The marginal contribution rate to increase annual income by a targeted amount.
DISCUSSION: Determining the marginal CMR to increase income by $15,000 in the coming year requires the calculation of last year's net income. Last year's sales must have been $500,000 ($550,000 ÷ 110%). The CMR for last year is given as 30%, resulting in a $150,000 CM ($500,000 x .3). Fixed costs equaled $120,000 last year. Thus, last year's net income was $30,000 ($150,000 CM - $120,000 FC).
The targeted income in the coming year is thus $45,000 ($30,000 + $15,000 increase). Fixed costs remain at $120,000. Accordingly, a $165,000 CM is necessary. Next year's sales are forecasted at $550,000. Dividing $165,000 by $550,000 gives a CMR next year of 30%.

Module 11.6: Targeted Profit

69. In using cost-volume-profit analysis to calculate an expected sales level expressed in units, which of the following should be subtracted from fixed costs in the numerator?

a. Predicted operating loss.
b. Predicted operating profit.
c. Unit contribution margin.
d. Variable costs.

The correct answer is (a). *(CPA 586 T-47)*
REQUIRED: The subtraction from fixed costs when calculating expected unit sales.
DISCUSSION: When a targeted profit (T) is desired, the profit is treated as a fixed cost (FC). Consequently, the calculation of expected unit sales is

$$(FC + T) \div UCM = Units$$

Since a net loss is negative profit, it would be subtracted from fixed costs in the CVP calculation.

70. Eriksen Company has budgeted its activity for October based on the following information:

Sales are budgeted at $300,000. All sales are credit sales and a provision for doubtful accounts is made monthly at the rate of 3% of sales.
Merchandise inventory was $70,000 at September 30, and a $10,000 increase is planned for the month.
All merchandise is marked up to sell at invoice cost plus 50%.
Estimated cash disbursements for selling and administrative expenses for the month are $40,000.
Depreciation for the month is projected at $5,000.

Eriksen is projecting operating income for October in the amount of

a. $96,000.
b. $56,000.
c. $55,000.
d. $46,000.

The correct answer is (d). *(CPA 1182 P-30)*
REQUIRED: Operating income given sales, inventory, the markup on merchandise, and expenses.
DISCUSSION: The operating income is found by subtracting all associated expenses from sales revenue. The key calculation is the cost of goods sold. Merchandise is marked up to sell at the invoice cost plus 50%. Consequently, $300,000 in sales equals 150% of cost of sales.

Sales revenue	$300,000
Cost of goods sold ($300,000 ÷ 150%)	(200,000)
Gross profit	$100,000
Selling & administrative expenses	(40,000)
Depreciation expense	(5,000)
Bad debt expense ($300,000 x 3%)	(9,000)
Net income	$ 46,000

Questions 71 and 72 are based on a company that produced the following data (rounded) on its product.

Number of Units Produced	Unit Cost Fixed	Unit Cost Variable	Total	Marginal Cost	Marginal Revenue
1	100	85	185	85	90
2	50	70	120	55	90
3	33	65	98	55	90
4	25	67	92	73	90
5	20	75	95	107	90

71. How many units should be produced?

a. 2.
b. 3.
c. 4.
d. 5.

The correct answer is (c). *(CIA 1183 IV-23)*
REQUIRED: The number of units to be produced given marginal cost and marginal revenue.
DISCUSSION: Marginal revenue exceeds marginal cost for the fourth but not the fifth unit. Production should continue until marginal cost equals marginal revenue. Accordingly, four units should be produced.

72. If two units of product were produced and sold, the total contribution margin would be

a. $25.
b. $40.
c. $50.
d. $70.

The correct answer is (b). *(CIA 1183 IV-24)*
REQUIRED: The total contribution margin if two units are produced and sold.
DISCUSSION: Contribution margin is defined as total revenue less variable costs. Total revenue for two units is $180 (2 x $90 marginal revenue), and total variable costs are $140 (2 x $70 unit cost). The contribution margin is $40 ($180 - $140).

Module 11.6: Targeted Profit

73. Wilson Company prepared the following preliminary forecast concerning product G for next year assuming no expenditure for advertising:

Selling price per unit	$10
Unit sales	100,000
Variable costs	$600,000
Fixed costs	$300,000

Based on a market study in December of this year, Wilson estimated that it could increase the unit selling price by 15% and increase the unit sales volume by 10% if $100,000 were spent on advertising. Assuming that Wilson incorporates these changes in its forecast, what should be the operating income from product G?

a. $175,000.
b. $190,000.
c. $205,000.
d. $365,000.

The correct answer is (c). *(CPA 1182 P-39)*
REQUIRED: The operating income assuming increases in advertising expense, selling price, and volume of sales.
DISCUSSION: Spending $100,000 for advertising is projected to increase unit sales by 10% to 110,000 even when unit selling price is increased by 15% to $11.50. Assuming variable cost per unit ($600,000 ÷ 100,000 = $6) and fixed costs ($300,000) remain constant, net operating income will be $205,000 after deducting the $100,000 in advertising expenses.

Sales (110,000 x $11.50)	$1,265,000
Variable costs (110,000 units x $6)	(660,000)
Fixed costs	(300,000)
Advertising expense	(100,000)
Net operating income	$ 205,000

---

74. Pitt Company is considering a proposal to replace existing machinery used for the manufacture of product A. The new machines are expected to create increased annual fixed costs of $120,000. Variable costs should decrease by 20%, however, because of a reduction in direct labor hours and more efficient usage of direct materials. Before this change was under consideration, Pitt had budgeted product A sales and costs for the year as follows:

Sales	$2,000,000
Variable costs	70% of sales
Fixed costs	$400,000

Assuming that Pitt implemented the above proposal by January 1, what would be the increase in budgeted operating profit for product A for the year?

a. $160,000.
b. $280,000.
c. $360,000.
d. $480,000.

The correct answer is (a). *(CPA 1181 P-30)*
REQUIRED: The increase in budgeted operating profit given a purchase of new machines with attendant changes in costs.
DISCUSSION: Variable costs were originally estimated at 70% of sales (70% x $2,000,000 = $1,400,000), and fixed costs were budgeted at $400,000. Hence, the operating profit was originally projected at $200,000 (given sales of $2,000,000). The new machines are expected to increase fixed costs to $520,000 ($400,000 + $120,000) but to reduce variable costs by 20% (20% x 70% of sales = 14% of sales saving). Therefore, income should increase by $160,000.

Sales revenue	$2,000,000
Variable costs (56% of sales)	(1,120,000)
Contribution margin	$ 880,000
Fixed costs estimated	(520,000)
Revised estimated income	$ 360,000
Original estimated income	(200,000)
Increase in estimated income	$ 160,000

---

75. Information concerning Label Corporation's product A follows:

Sales	$300,000
Variable costs	$240,000
Fixed costs	$ 40,000

Assuming that Label increased sales of product A by 20%, what should the net income from product A be?

a. $20,000.
b. $24,000.
c. $32,000.
d. $80,000.

The correct answer is (c). *(CPA 577 P-24)*
REQUIRED: The net income assuming the given percentage increase in sales.
DISCUSSION: Additional sales of 20% results in sales revenue of $360,000, up from $300,000. Variable costs are 80% of sales ($240,000 ÷ $300,000). Thus, variable costs will be $288,000 (80% x $360,000) at the new level of sales, and the net income from product A will be $32,000.

Sales revenue (120% x $300,000)	$360,000
Variable costs (80% of sales)	(288,000)
Contribution margin	$ 72,000
Fixed costs	(40,000)
Operating income	$ 32,000

Module 11.6: Targeted Profit

76. Lindsay Company reported the following results from sales of 5,000 units of product A for the month of June:

Sales	$200,000
Variable costs	(120,000)
Fixed costs	(60,000)
Operating income	$ 20,000

Assume that Lindsay increases the selling price of product A by 10% on July 1. How many units of product A would have to be sold in July to generate an operating income of $20,000?

a. 4,000.
b. 4,300.
c. 4,500.
d. 5,000.

77. Sun Company's tentative budget for product H for the year is as follows:

Sales	$600,000
Variable manufacturing costs	360,000
Fixed costs:	
Manufacturing	90,000
Selling and administrative	110,000

Ms. Johnston, the marketing manager, proposes an aggressive advertising campaign costing an additional $50,000 and resulting in a 30% unit sales increase for product H. Assuming that Johnston's proposal is incorporated into the budget for product H, what should be the increase in the budgeted operating profit for the year?

a. $12,000.
b. $22,000.
c. $72,000.
d. $130,000.

78. Adly Corp. wishes to earn a 30% return on its $100,000 investment in equipment used to produce product X. Based on estimated sales of 10,000 units of product X next year, the costs per unit would be as follows:

Variable manufacturing costs	$5
Fixed selling and administrative costs	2
Fixed manufacturing costs	1

At how much per unit should product X be priced for sale?

a. $5.
b. $8.
c. $10.
d. $11.

The correct answer is (a). *(CPA 1181 P-32)*
REQUIRED: The sales in units to generate a certain profit given an increase in selling price.
DISCUSSION: To determine how many units must be sold to achieve a desired profit, the unit contribution margin must first be calculated. The original sales price was $40 ($200,000 sales ÷ 5,000 units). Accordingly, the new price is $44 (110% x $40). Variable cost is $24 ($120,000 ÷ 5,000 units).

UCM = Sales price - unit variable cost
UCM = $44 - $24 = $20

$$\text{BEP Units} = \frac{\text{Fixed Costs} + \text{Desired Profit}}{\text{Unit Contribution Margin}}$$

$$\frac{\$60,000 + \$20,000}{\$20} = 4,000 \text{ units}$$

The correct answer is (b). *(CPA 581 P-36)*
REQUIRED: The increase in budgeted operating profit assuming an additional advertising expenditure increases volume by a given amount.
DISCUSSION: Sales is projected to increase by 30% to $780,000. Variable costs are 60% of sales ($360,000 ÷ $600,000). Accordingly, variable costs will increase to $468,000 (60% x $780,000), and the new contribution margin will be $312,000. Since fixed costs will be $250,000 ($90,000 mfg. + $110,000 S&A + $50,000 advert.), the revised income estimate is $22,000 greater than the original.

Sales revenue (130% x $600,000)	$780,000
Variable costs (60% of sales)	(468,000)
Contribution margin	$312,000
Fixed costs	(250,000)
Revised estimated income	$ 62,000
Original estimated income	(40,000)
Increase in operating income	$ 22,000

The correct answer is (d). *(CPA 586 Q-31)*
REQUIRED: The sales price per unit to earn a desired return on investment.
DISCUSSION: Product X costs $8 ($5 + $2 + $1) to manufacture and sell. Next year, product X's total costs will be $80,000 ($8 x 10,000 units). Adly wants to recognize a 30% return on a $100,000 investment, or $30,000 profit (.30 x $100,000) on product X. Cost of $80,000 plus profit of $30,000 equals $110,000 of total revenue generated from sales of product X. Since 10,000 units will be produced, the price per unit will be $11.00 ($110,000 ÷ 10,000 units).

Module 11.6: Targeted Profit

79. Orange Company's controller developed the following direct costing income statement for 1989:

			Per Unit
Sales (150,000 units at $30)		$4,500,000	$30
Variable costs:			
Direct materials	$1,050,000		7
Direct labor	1,500,000		10
Mfg. overhead	300,000		2
Selling & mkg.	300,000		2
		3,150,000	$21
Contribution margin		$1,350,000	$ 9
Fixed costs:			
Mfg. overhead	$ 600,000		4
Selling & mkg.	300,000		$ 2
		900,000	6
Net income		$ 450,000	$ 3

Orange Co. based its 1990 budget on the assumption that fixed costs, unit sales, and the sales price would remain as they were in 1989, but with net income being reduced to $300,000. By July of 1990, the controller was able to predict that unit sales would increase over 1989 levels by 10%. Based on the 1990 budget and the new information, the predicted 1990 net income would be

  a. $300,000.
  b. $330,000.
  c. $420,000.
  d. $585,000.

The correct answer is (c). *(CIA 585 IV-8)*
  REQUIRED: The projected net income given constant FC and sales price and different estimates of unit sales.
  DISCUSSION: Projected net income is estimated total revenue less estimated total costs. Given the original assumption that FC, unit sales, and sales price remain the same, and that net income will be reduced, the variable costs must increase. If the July 1990 prediction that unit sales will increase by 10% from 150,000 to 165,000 is based on the budgeted FC, sales price, and VC, then predicted net income will increase from $300,000 to $420,000.

$$TR - FC - VC = \$300,000$$
$$TR - \$900,000 - VC = \$300,000$$
$$TR - VC = \$1,200,000$$
$$CM = \$1,200,000$$

Budgeted UCM = $1,200,000 ÷ 150,000 units = $8

Total CM = 165,000 units x $8 =	$1,320,000
FC =	(900,000)
Net income	$ 420,000

80. A company has just completed the final development of its only product, general recombinant bacteria, that can be programmed to kill most insects before dying themselves. The product has taken 3 years and $6,000,000 to develop. The following costs are expected to be incurred on a monthly basis for the normal production level of 1,000,000 pounds of the new product.

	1,000,000 pounds
Direct materials	$ 300,000
Direct labor	1,250,000
Variable overhead	450,000
Fixed overhead	2,000,000
Variable selling, general and administrative expenses	900,000
Fixed selling, general, and administrative expenses	1,500,000
Total	$6,400,000

At a sales price of $5.90 per pound, the sales in pounds necessary to ensure a $3,000,000 profit the first year would be (to the nearest thousand pounds)

  a. 13,017,000 pounds.
  b. 14,000,000 pounds.
  c. 15,000,000 pounds.
  d. 25,600,000 pounds.

The correct answer is (c). *(CIA 1186 IV-10)*
  REQUIRED: The sales in pounds necessary to ensure a specified profit in year one.
  DISCUSSION: In breakeven analysis, total revenue equals fixed costs plus variable costs. If a given profit is desired, it is treated as a fixed cost. Exclusive of profit, the annual fixed cost is $42,000,000 (12 months x $3,500,000 per month of overhead and SG&A expense). The variable cost per pound is $2.90 [($300,000 + $1,250,000 + $450,000 + $900,000) ÷ 1,000,000 lbs.]. If X equals sales in pounds, the level of sales needed to earn a $3,000,000 profit is

$$\$5.90X = \$3,000,000 + \$42,000,000 + \$2.90X$$
$$\$3X = \$45,000,000$$
$$X = 15,000,000 \text{ pounds}$$

Note this analysis assumes there are no additional costs when production exceeds the normal level of 1,000,000 pounds per month.

Module 11.6: Targeted Profit

Questions 81 and 82 are based on the information presented in the opposite column.	Fixed manufacturing cost	$15,000
	Fixed selling and administrative costs	10,000
	Variable selling costs per unit sold	15
	Variable manufacturing costs per unit	25
	Sales price per unit	100
	Desired net income	30,000
	Average income tax rate	40%

81. What is the total amount of revenue that would result in the desired net income?

 a. $41,667.
 b. $91,667.
 c. $100,000.
 d. $125,000.

The correct answer is (d). *(CIA 587 IV-9)*
REQUIRED: The total amount of revenue that would result in the desired net income.
DISCUSSION: The desired net income should be treated as a fixed cost for breakeven purposes. The desired pre-tax income is $50,000 [$30,000 after-tax net income ÷ (1 − .4 tax rate)], and the total of fixed costs is $25,000 ($15,000 + $10,000). The contribution percentage is 60% [($100 price − $40 VC) ÷ $100]. Accordingly, the total revenue needed to produce the desired net income is $125,000 [($50,000 + $25,000) ÷ .6].

82. What is the breakeven point in units sold?

 a. 333.
 b. 417.
 c. 917.
 d. 1,250.

The correct answer is (b). *(CIA 587 IV-10)*
REQUIRED: The breakeven point in units sold.
DISCUSSION: The breakeven point in units sold equals total fixed costs ($25,000) divided by the unit contribution margin ($100 price − $40 VC = $60), or 417 units.

83. Dallas Corporation wishes to market a new product for $1.50 a unit. Fixed costs to manufacture this product are $100,000 for less than 500,000 units and $150,000 for 500,000 or more units. The contribution margin is 20%. How many units must be sold to realize net income from this product of $100,000?

 a. 333,333.
 b. 500,000.
 c. 666,667.
 d. 833,333.

The correct answer is (d). *(CPA 577 P-25)*
REQUIRED: The sales in units to realize a targeted profit.
DISCUSSION: The calculation to find the number of units to be sold to generate a targeted profit is to divide the sum of total fixed costs plus targeted profit by the $.30 UCM (20% x $1.50). Since the fixed costs will vary with production, a trial and error process must be used to find the correct relevant range. At less than 500,000 units, the sum of fixed costs ($100,000) and targeted profit ($100,000) is $200,000. Consequently, 666,667 units ($200,000 ÷ $.30) must be sold to cover this amount. Since 666,667 units is above the relevant range for fixed costs of $100,000, fixed costs at the next level of production must be used. At a production level of greater than 500,000 units, fixed costs will be $150,000, and 833,333 units ($250,000 ÷ $.30) must be sold to generate $100,000 of income.

84. During March, Adams Company had sales of $5,000,000, variable costs of $3,000,000, and fixed costs of $1,500,000 for product M. Assume that cost behavior and unit selling price remain unchanged during April. In order for Adams to realize operating income of $300,000 from product M for April, sales would have to be

 a. $3,750,000.
 b. $4,050,000.
 c. $4,500,000.
 d. $4,800,000.

The correct answer is (c). *(CPA 1182 P-31)*
REQUIRED: The sales level necessary to earn a targeted income.
DISCUSSION: To determine the amount of sales needed to realize a profit of $300,000, the sum of fixed costs and desired profit is divided by the contribution margin ratio. The contribution margin is $2,000,000 ($5,000,000 sales − $3,000,000 variable costs), and the ratio is therefore 40% ($2,000,000 CM ÷ $5,000,000 sales). The sum of fixed costs ($1,500,000) and desired profit ($300,000) divided by 40% is $4,500,000.

Module 11.6: Targeted Profit

> Questions 85 through 88 are based on Donnelly Corporation, which manufactures and sells T-shirts imprinted with college names and slogans. Last year, the shirts sold for $7.50 each, and the variable cost to manufacture them was $2.25 per unit. The company needed to sell 20,000 shirts to break even. The net income last year was $5,040. Donnelly's expectations for the coming year include the following:
>
> - The sales price of the T-shirts will be $9.
> - Variable cost to manufacture will increase by one-third.
> - Fixed costs will increase by 10%.
> - The income tax of 40% will be unchanged.

85. The selling price that would maintain the same contribution margin rate as last year is

a. $9.00.
b. $8.25.
c. $10.00.
d. $9.75.

The correct answer is (c). *(CMA 687 4-10)*
REQUIRED: The selling price to maintain the same contribution margin rate.
DISCUSSION: Last year, unit variable cost was $2.25, so the unit contribution margin (UCM) was $5.25 ($7.50 price - $2.25), and the contribution margin rate (CMR) was 70% ($5.25 ÷ $7.50). If variable costs increase by one-third, the new variable cost will be $3 ($2.25 x 4/3). If a 70% CMR is desired, the $3 variable cost will be 30% of sales, and the unit sales price will be $10 ($3 ÷ 30%).

86. The number of T-shirts Donnelly must sell to break even in the coming year is

a. 17,500.
b. 19,250.
c. 20,000.
d. 22,000.

The correct answer is (b). *(CMA 687 4-11)*
REQUIRED: The breakeven point in units sold.
DISCUSSION: The breakeven point (BEP) in units equals fixed cost divided by UCM. Fixed cost for the previous year was $105,000 (20,000 units at breakeven x $5.25 UCM). Fixed cost for the current year is $115,500 (110% x $105,000). The new UCM is $6 ($9 selling price - $3 variable cost). Accordingly, the BEP is 19,250 units ($115,500 ÷ $6).

87. Sales for the coming year are expected to exceed last year's by 1,000 units. If this occurs, Donnelly's sales volume in the coming year will be

a. 22,600 units.
b. 21,960 units.
c. 23,400 units.
d. 21,000 units.

The correct answer is (a). *(CMA 687 4-12)*
REQUIRED: The unit sales in the coming year if it exceeds last year's volume by a given number of units.
DISCUSSION: Since last year's after-tax profit was $5,040, pre-tax net income must have been $8,400 [$5,040 ÷ (1 - 40% tax rate)]. Because fixed cost has been fully recovered at the BEP, all of the UCM beyond that sales level is included in pre-tax net income. The UCM was $5.25, so the units sold in excess of the 20,000-unit BEP equaled 1,600 ($8,400 ÷ $5.25). If 21,600 total units were sold last year, an increase of 1,000 units results in sales of 22,600 units.

88. If Donnelly Corporation wishes to earn $22,500 in net income for the coming year, the company's sales volume in dollars must be

a. $213,750.
b. $257,625.
c. $207,000.
d. $229,500.

The correct answer is (d). *(CMA 687 4-13)*
REQUIRED: The sales in dollars necessary to earn a specified net income.
DISCUSSION: An after-tax net income of $22,500 equals a pre-tax income of $37,500 [$22,500 ÷ (1 - 40% tax rate)]. With a UCM of $6 contributing toward the $153,000 total of fixed cost ($115,500) and desired profit ($37,500), 25,500 units ($153,000 ÷ $6) must be sold. At $9 per unit, sales revenue is $229,500.

Module 11.6: Targeted Profit

> Questions 89 through 91 are based on the following information. Madden Company has projected its income before taxes for next year as shown below. Madden is subject to a 40% income tax rate.
>
> | | | |
> |---|---|---|
> | Sales (160,000 units) | | $8,000,000 |
> | Cost of sales | | |
> | Variable costs | $2,000,000 | |
> | Fixed costs | 3,000,000 | |
> | Total costs | | 5,000,000 |
> | Income before taxes | | $3,000,000 |

89. Madden's breakeven point in units sold for the next year would be

  a. 100,000 units.
  b. 96,000 units.
  c. 80,000 units.
  d. 60,000 units.
  e. Some amount other than those given above.

The correct answer is (c). *(CMA 1286 5-14)*
  REQUIRED: The breakeven point in units for the next year.
  DISCUSSION: The BEP in units is determined by dividing the fixed costs by contribution margin (in dollars) per unit. Unit selling price is $50 ($8,000,000 ÷ 160,000 units). Unit variable cost is $12.50 ($2,000,000 ÷ 160,000 units). Hence, the unit contribution margin is $37.50 ($50 - $12.50), and the BEP is 80,000 units ($3,000,000 FC ÷ $37.50).

90. If Madden wants $4,500,000 of income before taxes, the required sales in dollars would be

  a. $6,000,000.
  b. $7,600,000.
  c. $5,000,000.
  d. $10,000,000.
  e. Some amount other than those given above.

The correct answer is (d). *(CMA 1286 5-15)*
  REQUIRED: The required sales to achieve a specified before-tax income.
  DISCUSSION: The desired profit should be treated as a fixed cost, and summed with the given fixed cost. This should be divided by the contribution margin ratio to determine the desired level of sales. The contribution margin ratio is 75% ($37.50 UCM ÷ $50 unit selling price). The required sales are therefore $10,000,000 [($3,000,000 FC + $4,500,000 profit) ÷ 75%].

91. Madden's net assets are $36,000,000. The dollar sales that must be achieved for Madden to earn a 10% after tax return on assets would be

  a. $8,800,000.
  b. $16,000,000.
  c. $12,000,000.
  d. $6,880,000.
  e. Some amount other than those given above.

The correct answer is (c). *(CMA 1286 5-16)*
  REQUIRED: The dollar sales needed to achieve a given after-tax income.
  DISCUSSION: The sum of the fixed costs and the desired before-tax income should be divided by the contribution margin ratio. Since the tax rate is 40%, the income remaining after taxes is 60% of before-tax income. Thus, after-tax income of $3,600,000 (10% x 36,000,000 net assets) equals before-tax income of $6,000,000 ($3,600,000 ÷ 60%), and the desired sales level is $12,000,000 [($3,000,000 FC + $6,000,000 profit) ÷ 75%].

11.7 Multiproduct Breakeven

92. The following table represents payoffs for farm products for three different sales levels. Which one of the products would be illogical if only three products can be produced?

Demand	Product A	Product B	Product C	Product D
Sales 1	(10,000)	6,000	8,000	(12,000)
Sales 2	26,000	19,000	22,000	17,000
Sales 3	31,000	38,000	33,000	37,000

a. Product A.
b. Product B.
c. Product C.
d. Product D.

The correct answer is (d). *(CIA 1187 III-44)*
REQUIRED: The illogical product if only three products can be produced.
DISCUSSION: Product D is illogical if exactly three of the products are to be produced. Regardless of the probabilities of reaching the various sales levels, Product B is always preferable to D because it has a higher payoff at each level. Hence, B is said to dominate D. However, A, B, and C are not dominated by another product.
Production of D can also be seen to be illogical under most of the theoretical criteria used in decision making under uncertainty (absence of any probabilistic information about outcomes). The maximin criterion (maximize the minimum payoff) favors the product mix ABC (payoff of + $4,000 at the lowest sales level). The minimax regret criterion (minimize the maximum opportunity loss or regret) also favors ABC (a regret of $6,000 at sales level three). The insufficient reason criterion (treat all sales levels as equally probable) likewise favors ABC (it has the highest expected value). Only the maximax criterion (maximize the maximum payoff) results in the choice of another mix (BCD has a payoff of $108,000 at sales level three). However, this decision rule would customarily be used only by risk-seeking, not risk-averse or risk-neutral, decision makers.

93. Von Stutgatt International's breakeven point is 8,000 racing bicycles and 12,000 5-speed bicycles. If the selling price and variable costs are $570 and $200 for a racer, and $180 and $90 for a 5-speed respectively, what is the weighted average contribution margin?

a. $100.
b. $202.
c. $145.
d. $179.

The correct answer is (b). *(J.B. Romal)*
REQUIRED: The weighted average contribution margin.
DISCUSSION: The contribution margin is selling price less variable costs.

Racer: $570 - $200 = $370
5-Speed: $180 - $90 = $ 90

The sales mix is:

$\frac{8,000}{8,000 + 12,000}$ = 40% racers

$\frac{12,000}{8,000 + 12,000}$ = 60% 5-speeds

Multiply the CM by the sales mix for each product, and add the results.

($370 x 40%) + ($90 x 60%) = CM
$148 + $54 = $202

94. Bjax Corporation has a separate production line for each of two products: A and B. Product A has a contribution margin of $4 per unit; Product B has a contribution margin of $5 per unit; and the corporation's nonvariable expenses of $200,000 are unchanged regardless of volume. Under these conditions, which of the following statements will always be applicable?

a. At a sales volume in excess of 25,000 units of A and 25,000 units of B, operations will be profitable.
b. The ratio of net profit to total sales for B will be larger than A.
c. The contribution margin per unit of direct material is lower for A than for B.
d. Income will be maximized if only B is sold.
e. None of the above.

The correct answer is (a). *(CIA 577 IV-2)*
REQUIRED: The statement that is always true given contribution margins and fixed costs for two products.
DISCUSSION: If Bjax Corporation has a sales volume in excess of 25,000 units of A and 25,000 units of B, operations will always be profitable. Given Product A's contribution margin of $4 per unit, 25,000 units would yield a contribution margin of $100,000. The contribution margin per unit for Product B is given as $5; therefore, 25,000 units would yield a contribution margin of $125,000. The total contribution margin for the two products is $225,000 ($100,000 + $125,000). Since fixed costs are $200,000, there is a net profit of $25,000.
Answers (b) and (c) are incorrect because no information is given about sales or direct materials. Answer (d) is incorrect because, if only B is sold, the income made from A would be lost. Each product can be produced without affecting the other.

Module 11.7: Multiproduct Breakeven

> Questions 95 and 96 are based on the following data pertaining to two types of products manufactured by Korn Corp.:
>
> | | Per Unit | |
> |---|---|---|
> | | Sales Price | Variable Costs |
> | Product Y | $120 | $ 70 |
> | Product Z | 500 | 200 |
>
> Fixed costs total $300,000 annually. The expected mix in units is 60% for product Y and 40% for product Z.

95. How much is Korn's breakeven sales in units?

a. 857.
b. 1,111.
c. 2,000.
d. 2,459.

The correct answer is (c). *(CPA 586 Q-29)*
REQUIRED: The breakeven point in units for a two-product firm.
DISCUSSION: The BEP in units is equal to fixed cost divided by the difference between unit selling price and unit variable cost, or the unit contribution margin (UCM). The UCM for product Y equals $50 ($120 - $70), and the UCM for product Z equals $300 ($500 - $200). For multiproduct breakeven, weighted average UCM is used.

$$BEP = \frac{\text{Fixed costs}}{\text{Weighted average UCM}}$$

$$= \frac{\$300,000}{(60\% \times \$50) + (40\% \times \$300)}$$

$$= \frac{\$300,000}{\$30 + \$120} = 2,000 \text{ units}$$

96. How much is Korn's breakeven sales in dollars?

a. $300,000.
b. $420,000.
c. $475,000.
d. $544,000.

The correct answer is (d). *(CPA 586 Q-30)*
REQUIRED: The breakeven point in sales dollars, for a two-product firm.
DISCUSSION: The BEP in sales dollars is equal to the fixed costs divided by the contribution margin ratio. The CMR is the CM divided by sales. The CM equals the sales price less variable costs. For a multiproduct firm, the weighted average CM and sales must be found.

Weighted average CM = (Sales - VC) x mix %

WACM = [($120 - $70) x 60%] + [($500 - $200) x 40%]
     = $150

Weighted average sales = unit price x mix %

WAS = ($120 x 60%) + ($500 x 40%)
    = $272
CMR = $150 ÷ $272 = .551

BEP in sales dollars = $\frac{\$300,000}{.551}$ = $544,464

Module 11.7: Multiproduct Breakeven

Questions 97 through 102 are based on the officers of Bradshaw Company, who are reviewing the profitability of the company's four products and the potential effects of several proposals for varying the product mix. An excerpt from the income statement and other data follow:

	Totals	Product P	Product Q	Product R	Product S
Sales	$62,600	$10,000	$18,000	$12,600	$22,000
Cost of goods sold	44,274	4,750	7,056	13,968	18,500
Gross profit	$18,326	$ 5,250	$10,944	$ (1,368)	$ 3,500
Operating expenses	12,012	1,990	2,976	2,826	4,220
Income before income taxes	$ 6,314	$ 3,260	$ 7,968	$ (4,194)	$ (720)
Units sold		1,000	1,200	1,800	2,000
Sales price per unit		$ 10.00	$ 15.00	$ 7.00	$ 11.00
Variable cost of goods sold per unit		$ 2.50	$ 3.00	$ 6.50	$ 6.00
Variable operating expenses per unit		$ 1.17	$ 1.25	$ 1.00	$ 1.20

Each of the following proposals is to be considered independently of the other proposals. Consider only the product changes stated in each proposal; the activity of other products remains stable. Ignore income taxes.

97. If product R is discontinued, the effect on income will be

a. $900 increase.
b. $4,194 increase.
c. $12,600 decrease.
d. $1,368 increase.
e. None of the above.

The correct answer is (a). *(CPA 1172 Q-20)*
REQUIRED: The effect on income if one product in a mix is discontinued.
DISCUSSION: If product R is discontinued, the effect would be a $900 increase in income. Fixed costs are assumed to remain the same. The variable costs per unit of R are $7.50 ($6.50 + $1.00). Since the sales price per unit is $7.00, there is a negative UCM of $.50 ($7.00 - $7.50). Given 1,800 units sold, the loss is $900. Discontinuing the R product line would thus increase income by $900.

98. If product R is discontinued and a consequent loss of customers causes a decrease of 200 units in sales of Q, the total effect on income will be

a. $15,600 decrease.
b. $2,866 increase.
c. $2,044 increase.
d. $1,250 decrease.
e. None of the above.

The correct answer is (d). *(CPA 1172 Q-21)*
REQUIRED: The effect on income if discontinuing one product also decreases sales of another product.
DISCUSSION: If R is discontinued, the effect on income is a $900 increase, as computed in the previous question. Q's contribution is computed as follows:

Sales price - unit variable costs = UCM
$15.00 - $3.00 - $1.25 = $10.75

Q's CM per unit of $10.75 times the 200-unit decrease equals a $2,150 reduction in income. The net effect is a decrease in income of $1,250 ($2,150 loss - $900 gain).

99. If the sales price of R is increased to $8 with a decrease in the number of units sold to 1,500, the effect on income will be

a. $2,199 decrease.
b. $600 decrease.
c. $750 increase.
d. $2,199 increase.
e. None of the above.

The correct answer is (e). *(CPA 1172 Q-22)*
REQUIRED: The effect on income if the sales price of a product increases and sales volume declines.
DISCUSSION: If 1,500 units of R are sold at $8, the unit contribution margin is $.50 ($8.00 - $6.50 - $1.00 = $.50), and the total contribution margin is $750. As computed in Q. 97, R presently has a negative CM of $900. The net effect is an increase in income of $1,650 ($750 CM + recovery of the $900 negative CM).

Module 11.7: Multiproduct Breakeven

100. The plant in which R is produced can be used to produce a new product, T. Total variable costs and expenses per unit of T are $8.05, and 1,600 units can be sold at $9.50 each. If T is introduced and R is discontinued, the total effect on income will be

   a. $2,600 increase.
   b. $2,320 increase.
   c. $3,220 increase.
   d. $1,420 increase.
   e. None of the above.

The correct answer is (c). *(CPA 1172 Q-23)*
REQUIRED: The effect on income when a new product is introduced and an old one discontinued.
DISCUSSION: If 1,600 units of T can be sold at $9.50 each, the unit contribution margin (UCM) is $1.45 ($9.50 - $8.05), and the total CM is $2,320 (1,600 x $1.45). Product R currently contributes a negative CM of $900. Hence, the net effect of discontinuing R and introducing T is a $3,220 increase in income ($2,320 + $900).

101. Part of the plant in which P is produced can easily be adapted to the production of S, but changes in quantities may make changes in sales prices advisable. If production of P is reduced to 500 units (to be sold at $12 each), and production of S is increased to 2,500 units (to be sold at $10.50 each), the total effect on income will be

   a. $1,765 decrease.
   b. $250 increase.
   c. $2,060 decrease.
   d. $1,515 decrease.
   e. None of the above.

The correct answer is (d). *(CPA 1172 Q-24)*
REQUIRED: The effect on income if the production and prices of two products change.
DISCUSSION:

New CM
P 500($12 - $3.67)   = $ 4,165
S 2,500($10.50 - $7.20) = 8,250
                         $12,415

Old CM
P 1,000($10 - $3.67) = $ 6,330
S 2,000($11 - $7.20) =   7,600
                         $13,930

New CM - Old CM   = Loss in income
$12,415 - $13,930   = $(1,515)

102. Production of P can be doubled by adding a second shift, but higher wages must be paid, increasing the variable cost of goods sold to $3.50 for each additional unit. If the 1,000 additional units of P can be sold at $10 each, the total effect on income will be

   a. $10,000 increase.
   b. $5,330 increase.
   c. $6,500 increase.
   d. $2,260 increase.
   e. None of the above.

The correct answer is (b). *(CPA 1172 Q-25)*
REQUIRED: The effect on income if additional units can be produced and variable manufacturing costs increase.
DISCUSSION: The sale of the 1,000 additional units at a price of $10 and a variable cost of $3.50 produce a UCM of $5.33 ($10 - $3.50 - $1.17). If 1,000 additional units are sold, the effect on net income will be a $5,330 increase (1,000 x $5.33).

103. A company must decide which one of the following four products to manufacture.

Product	Sales Price	Variable Cost	Direct Labor Hours Per Unit
M	$10	$ 7	1.5
N	20	12	2.0
O	5	2	0.5
P	8	4	1.0

Which product will result in the highest contribution margin per hour?

   a. M.
   b. N.
   c. O.
   d. P.

The correct answer is (c). *(CIA 587 IV-20)*
REQUIRED: The product that will result in the highest contribution margin per hour.
DISCUSSION: Contribution margin equals price minus variable cost. The contribution margins of M, N, O, and P are $3 ($10 - $7), $8 ($20 - $12), $3 ($5 - $2), and $4 ($8 - $4), respectively. However, the contribution margins per hour are $2 ($3 ÷ 1.5), $4 ($8 ÷ 2.0), $6 ($3 ÷ 0.5), and $4 ($4 ÷ 1.0), respectively. Therefore, O has the highest contribution margin per hour.

Module 11.7: Multiproduct Breakeven

> Questions 104 and 105 are based on the following information. A company sells two products, X and Y. The sales mix consists of a composite unit of 2 units of X for every 5 units of Y (2:5). Fixed costs are $49,500. The unit contribution margins for X and Y are $2.50 and $1.20, respectively.

104. Considering the company as a whole, the number of composite units to break even would be

    a. 1,650.
    b. 4,500.
    c. 8,250.
    d. 9,900.

The correct answer is (b). *(CIA 586 IV-8)*
REQUIRED: The composite breakeven point.
DISCUSSION: The composite breakeven point for a multiproduct firm is computed by dividing total fixed costs by a composite contribution margin.

Composite contribution margin = 2($2.50) + 5($1.20) = $11

Breakeven point = $49,500 ÷ $11 = 4,500 composite units

105. If the company had a profit of $22,000, the unit sales must have been

	Product X	Product Y
a.	5,000	12,500
b.	13,000	32,500
c.	23,800	59,500
d.	28,600	71,500

The correct answer is (b). *(CIA 586 IV-9)*
REQUIRED: The computation of unit sales given profit.
DISCUSSION: Unit sales can be computed by adding profit to fixed costs and dividing by the composite contribution margin.

$$\frac{FC + Profit}{Composite\ CM} = \frac{\$49,500 + \$22,000}{\$11}$$

$$= 6,500\ composite\ units$$

This translates to 13,000 units of Product X and 32,500 units of Product Y.

> Questions 106 through 111 are based on the Dooley Co., which manufactures two products, baubles and trinkets. The following are projections for the coming year.
>
> | | Baubles Units | Amount | Trinkets Units | Amount | Totals |
> |---|---|---|---|---|---|
> | Sales | 10,000 | $10,000 | 7,500 | $10,000 | $20,000 |
> | Costs | | | | | |
> | Fixed | | $ 2,000 | | $ 5,600 | $ 7,600 |
> | Variable | | 6,000 | | 3,000 | 9,000 |
> | | | $ 8,000 | | $ 8,600 | $16,600 |
> | Income before taxes | | $ 2,000 | | $ 1,400 | $ 3,400 |

106. Assuming that the facilities are not jointly used, the breakeven output (in units) for baubles would be

    a. 8,000.
    b. 7,000.
    c. 6,000.
    d. 5,000.

The correct answer is (d). *(CPA 1170 Q-35)*
REQUIRED: The BEP in units for one product in a product mix.
DISCUSSION: The breakeven point in units is equal to the selling price minus the variable cost (UCM) divided into fixed cost. The CM equals $.40 per unit ($1.00 SP - $.60 VC). Dividing the $2,000 fixed cost by the CM results in a BEP of 5,000 units.

Module 11.7: Multiproduct Breakeven

107. Assuming that the facilities are not jointly used, the breakeven volume (dollars) for trinkets would be

a. $8,000.
b. $7,000.
c. $6,000.
d. $5,000.

The correct answer is (a). *(CPA 1170 Q-36)*
REQUIRED: The breakeven volume in dollars for one product in a product mix.
DISCUSSION: The breakeven volume in dollars is calculated by dividing the CMR into the fixed cost. Fixed costs are given as $5,600. The CMR is 70% (sales of $10,000 less variable costs of $3,000 divided by the $10,000 sales). The BEP in dollars is $8,000 ($5,600 ÷ .7).

108. Assuming that consumers purchase composite units of four baubles and three trinkets, the composite unit contribution margin would be

a. $4.40.
b. $4.00.
c. $1.33.
d. $1.10.

The correct answer is (a). *(CPA 1170 Q-37)*
REQUIRED: The composite unit contribution margin.
DISCUSSION: The composite UCM is the sum of the UCM the two products weighted according to their proportions in the composite unit. There are four baubles and three trinkets in each composite unit. Each bauble has a UCM of $.40 (Q. 106); each trinket has a UCM of $.933 [($10,000 sales - $3,000 VC) ÷ 7,500 units]. The composite UCM is $4.40 [(4 x $.40) + (3 x $.933)].

109. If consumers purchase composite units of four baubles and three trinkets, the breakeven output for the two products would be

a. 6,909 baubles; 6,909 trinkets.
b. 6,909 baubles; 5,182 trinkets.
c. 5,000 baubles; 8,000 trinkets.
d. 5,000 baubles; 6,000 trinkets.

The correct answer is (b). *(CPA 1170 Q-38)*
REQUIRED: The breakeven output in units for two products.
DISCUSSION: The BE output for two products is calculated by dividing their composite UCM into the fixed cost to arrive at the number of composite units necessary to break even. Then the unit composite output is multiplied by the number of composite units in each grouping. The composite UCM is $4.40 and total fixed cost is $7,600, which results in a BEP of slightly more than 1,727 composite units ($7,600 ÷ $4.40). Because there are four baubles and three trinkets in each composite unit, the BE output consists of approximately 6,909 baubles (1,727 x 4) and 5,182 trinkets (1,727 x 3).

110. If baubles and trinkets become one-to-one complements and there is no change in the Dooley Co.'s cost function, the breakeven volume would be

a. $22,500.
b. $15,750.
c. $13,300.
d. $10,858.

The correct answer is (c). *(CPA 1170 Q-39)*
REQUIRED: The breakeven volume for two products that are one-to-one complements.
DISCUSSION: The BE volume for one-to-one complements would be equal to the fixed cost divided by the composite UCM. Fixed costs are $7,600; the composite UCM in this case would be $1.33 ($.40 + $.933). The number of units sold at the BEP is 5,715 ($7,600 ÷ $1.33). Multiplying units sold by the composite unit selling price of $2.33 ($1 per bauble, $1.33 per trinket) gives BE sales volume of approximately $13,300. Alternatively, dividing the $7,600 fixed costs by the unit CMR of .57, gives a BE sales dollar volume of $13,300. The unit CMR is found by dividing $1.33 (composite UCM) by $2.33 (composite unit sales price).

111. If a composite unit is defined as one bauble and one trinket, the composite contribution margin ratio would be

a. 7/10.
b. 4/7.
c. 2/5.
d. 19/50.

The correct answer is (b). *(CPA 1170 Q-40)*
REQUIRED: The composite contribution margin ratio.
DISCUSSION: The CMR is equal to the UCM divided by the selling price. The composite UCM is $1.33. The composite selling price is $2.33. The ratio is 4/7 ($1.33 ÷ $2.33).

Module 11.7: Multiproduct Breakeven

Questions 112 through 114 are based on the Moorehead Manufacturing Company, which produces two products for which the following data have been tabulated. Fixed manufacturing cost is applied at a rate of $1.00 per machine hour.

Per Unit	XY-7	BD-4
Selling price	$4.00	$3.00
Variable manufacturing cost	$2.00	$1.50
Fixed manufacturing cost	$ .75	$ .20
Variable selling cost	$1.00	$1.00

The sales manager has had a $160,000 increase in the budget allotment for advertising and wants to apply the money to the most profitable product. The products are not substitutes for one another in the eyes of the company's customers.

112. Suppose the sales manager chooses to devote the entire $160,000 to increased advertising for XY-7. The minimum increase in sales units of XY-7 required to offset the increased advertising would be

a. 640,000 units.
b. 160,000 units.
c. 80,000 units.
d. 128,000 units.
e. None of the above.

The correct answer is (b). *(CMA 679 5-25)*
REQUIRED: The minimum increase in sales units to offset increased advertising costs.
DISCUSSION: The contribution margin for XY-7 is $1 per unit ($4 sales price - $3 variable costs). Thus, 160,000 units of XY-7 would generate an additional $160,000 of CM, sufficient to cover the increase in advertising costs.

113. Suppose the sales manager chooses to devote the entire $160,000 to increased advertising for BD-4. The minimum increase in sales dollars of BD-4 required to offset the increased advertising would be

a. $160,000.
b. $320,000.
c. $960,000.
d. $1,600,000.

The correct answer is (c). *(CMA 679 5-26)*
REQUIRED: The minimum increase in sales dollars to offset increased advertising costs.
DISCUSSION: Sales dollars must increase sufficiently to cover the $160,000 increase in advertising. The unit contribution margin for BD-4 is $.50 ($3 - $2.50 variable costs), and the CM ratio is approximately 16.7% (UCM ÷ sales price). Dividing the $160,000 by 16.7% gives the sales dollars necessary to generate a CM of $960,000 ($160,000 ÷ .167 = $958,084).

114. Suppose Moorehead has only 100,000 machine hours that can be made available to produce XY-7 and BD-4. If the potential increase in sales units for either product resulting from advertising is far in excess of these production capabilities, which product should be advertised and what is the estimated increase in contribution margin earned?

a. Product XY-7 should be produced, yielding a contribution margin of $75,000.
b. Product XY-7 should be produced, yielding a contribution margin of $133,333.
c. Product BD-4 should be produced, yielding a contribution margin of $250,000.
d. Product BD-4 should be produced, yielding a contribution margin of $187,500.

The correct answer is (c). *(CMA 679 5-27)*
REQUIRED: The more profitable product and the estimated increase in contribution margin.
DISCUSSION: The machine hours are a scarce resource that must be allocated to the product(s) in such a proportion as to maximize the total contribution margin. Given that potential sales of either product are in excess of production capacity, only the product with the greater contribution margin per unit of scarce resource should be produced. XY-7 requires .75 hours; BD-4 requires .2 hours of machine time (given fixed manufacturing cost applied at $1 per machine hour of $.75 for XY-7 and $.20 for BD-4).
XY-7 has a CM of $1.33 per machine hour ($1 UCM ÷ .75 hours) and BD-4 has a CM of $2.50 per machine hour ($.50 ÷ .2 hours). Therefore, only BD-4 should be produced, yielding a CM of $250,000 (100,000 x $2.50). The key to the analysis is CM per unit of scarce resource.

11.8 Working Backwards

115. Birney Company is planning its advertising campaign for next year and has prepared a budget based on a zero advertising expenditure:

Normal plant capacity	200,000 units
Sales	150,000 units
Selling price	$25 per unit
Variable manufacturing costs	$15 per unit
Fixed manufacturing costs	$800,000
Fixed selling and adm. costs	$700,000

An advertising agency claims that an aggressive advertising campaign would enable Birney to increase its unit sales by 20%. What is the maximum amount that Birney can pay for advertising and obtain an operating profit of $200,000?

a. $100,000.
b. $200,000.
c. $300,000.
d. $550,000.

The correct answer is (a). *(CPA 1181 P-34)*
REQUIRED: The maximum advertising expenses allowable given an increase in sales and a targeted profit.
DISCUSSION: Given that advertising will increase sales by 20%, sales will increase to 180,000 units (150,000 x 120%). Since the unit contribution margin is $10 ($25 sales price - $15 unit variable cost), the total CM for 180,000 units is $1,800,000. Total fixed costs equal $1,500,000 ($800,000 manufacturing + $700,000 selling and administrative). Deducting the targeted profit of $200,000 and the fixed costs from the total CM gives the maximum amount that may be expended for advertising ($100,000).

Contribution margin	$1,800,000
Fixed costs	1,500,000
Income before advertising	300,000
Targeted net income	200,000
Available for advertising	$ 100,000

116. The Seahawk Company is planning to sell 200,000 units of Product B. The fixed costs are $400,000, and the variable costs are 60% of the selling price. To realize a profit of $100,000, the selling price per unit would have to be

a. $3.75.
b. $4.17.
c. $5.00.
d. $6.25.

The correct answer is (d). *(CPA 579 P-26)*
REQUIRED: The selling price per unit to realize a targeted profit.
DISCUSSION: To find the selling price per unit, the equation for breakeven sales dollars with an expected profit must be used. The CMR is 40% (1 - 60% variable costs).

BEP $ = (FC + expected profit) ÷ CMR
BEP $ = ($400,000 + $100,000) ÷ 40% = $1,250,000

The unit price is therefore $6.25 ($1,250,000 ÷ 200,000 units).

117. A company prices its most expensive wheelbarrow at 150% of the previous month's per-unit costs. The following costs are expected to be incurred in March based on a normal activity level of 3,000 of the expensive wheelbarrows:

Variable costs:		
Sheet metal and tubing	$30,500	
Wood handles	7,500	
Wheels	13,750	
Bolts	1,250	
Direct labor	22,000	
Total variable cost		$ 75,000
Fixed costs		42,000
Total cost		$117,000

If the costs behave exactly as predicted in March, but only 2,000 units are produced, the price per unit in April will be

a. $29.25 less than if 3,000 units were produced.
b. $10.50 less than if 3,000 units were produced.
c. $29.25 more than if 3,000 units were produced.
d. $10.50 more than if 3,000 units were produced.

The correct answer is (d). *(CIA 585 IV-2)*
REQUIRED: The difference in price per unit given a change in activity level.
DISCUSSION: The difference in price per unit is calculated by subtracting the price at 2,000 units from the price at 3,000 units. The price at 3,000 units is 150% of the unit total cost. Unit total cost is $39.00 ($117,000 ÷ 3,000). Thus, selling price at 3,000 units is $58.50 (1.5 x $39). The unit sales price at a production level of 2,000 units is 150% of the sum of last month's unit VC ($75,000 ÷ 3,000 = $25) and this month's unit FC ($42,000 ÷ 2,000 = $21), or $69 [1.5 x ($25 + $21)]. The difference is $10.50 ($69 - $58.50). This calculation assumes that unit VC and total fixed costs do not change in the relevant range.

118. Purvis Company manufactures a product that has a variable cost of $50 per unit. Fixed costs total $1,000,000 and are allocated on the basis of the number of units produced. Selling price is computed by adding a 10% markup to full cost. How much should the selling price be per unit for 100,000 units?

a. $55.
b. $60.
c. $61.
d. $66.

The correct answer is (d). *(CPA 1182 Q-33)*
REQUIRED: The selling price based on absorption costing and a cost markup.
DISCUSSION: Full cost, including both variable and fixed costs, must be determined. The fixed cost per unit equals $10 ($1,000,000 ÷ 100,000). The variable costs per unit are given as $50. Full cost is thus $60 per unit, and the selling price is $66 (110% x $60).

119. Anthony Company has projected cost of goods sold of $4,000,000, including fixed costs of $800,000. Variable costs are expected to be 75% of net sales. What will be the projected net sales?

a. $4,266,667.
b. $4,800,000.
c. $5,333,333.
d. $6,400,000.

The correct answer is (a). *(CPA 1180 P-25)*
REQUIRED: The projected net sales given the BEP, fixed costs, and the ratio of variable costs to sales.
DISCUSSION: Cost of goods sold equals the sum of fixed and variable costs. Given variable costs of 75% of net sales,

$4,000,000 = .75 (net sales) + $800,000
.75 (net sales) = $3,200,000
Net sales = $4,266,667

120. Gerber Company is planning to sell 200,000 units of product O for $2.00 a unit. The contribution margin ratio is 25%. Gerber will break even at this level of sales. What would be the fixed costs?

a. $100,000.
b. $160,000.
c. $200,000.
d. $300,000.

The correct answer is (a). *(CPA 581 P-40)*
REQUIRED: The fixed costs given unit sales price, CMR, and breakeven volume.
DISCUSSION: At the breakeven point, the contribution margin is equal to fixed costs. Given the contribution margin ratio as 25% of sales, and sales equal to $400,000 (200,000 units x $2.00 per unit), the contribution margin is $100,000 ($400,000 x 25%). Since fixed costs equal the contribution margin at the breakeven point, fixed costs are also $100,000.

121. Warfield Company is planning to sell 100,000 units of Product T for $12.00 a unit. The fixed costs are $280,000. In order to realize a profit of $200,000, what would the variable costs be?

a. $480,000.
b. $720,000.
c. $900,000.
d. $920,000.

The correct answer is (b). *(CPA 581 P-35)*
REQUIRED: The variable costs given sales price, volume, profit, and fixed costs.
DISCUSSION: Profit equals sales minus the sum of fixed and variable costs. Accordingly,

VC = sales - fixed costs - profit
VC = $1,200,000 - $280,000 - $200,000
VC = $720,000

122. Day Company is a medium-sized manufacturer of lamps. During the year a new line called "Twilight" was made available to Day's customers. The breakeven point for sales of Twilight is $400,000 with a contribution margin of 40%. Assuming that the operating profit for the Twilight line for the year amounted to $200,000, total sales for the year amounted to

a. $600,000.
b. $840,000.
c. $900,000.
d. $950,000.

The correct answer is (c). *(CPA 580 P-26)*
REQUIRED: The total sales given profit, BEP, and CMR.
DISCUSSION: The contribution margin ratio is 40% of sales. Therefore, the contribution margin at the breakeven point is $160,000 ($400,000 x 40%). Because the contribution margin is equal to fixed costs at the breakeven point, fixed costs are also $160,000. The sum of the operating profit of $200,000 and fixed costs of $160,000 may be treated as the contribution margin at the desired profit level. Dividing $360,000 by 40% gives total sales of $900,000.

Module 11.8: Working Backwards

123. The Ernie Company has provided information concerning its projections for the coming year as follows:

Net sales	$10,000,000
Fixed manufacturing costs	$ 1,000,000

Ernie projects variable manufacturing costs of 60% of net sales. Assuming no change in inventory, what will the projected cost of goods sold be?

a. $5,000,000.
b. $6,000,000.
c. $7,000,000.
d. $8,000,000.

The correct answer is (c). *(CPA 1179 P-40)*
REQUIRED: The cost of goods sold given sales, fixed costs, variable costs as a percentage of sales, and no change in inventory.
DISCUSSION: In this case, cost of goods sold is synonymous with cost of goods manufactured because the prior period costs in the beginning inventory that are included in cost of sales equal the current manufacturing costs accumulated in the ending inventory. Cost of goods manufactured is the sum of the variable and fixed manufacturing costs necessary to produce the product. The variable costs are given as 60% of net sales (60% x $10,000,000 = $6,000,000). Variable costs plus fixed costs equal cost of goods manufactured ($6,000,000 + $1,000,000 = $7,000,000).

124. The Cum-Clean Corporation produces a variety of cleaning compounds and solutions for both industrial and household use. While most of its products are processed independently, a few are related.

"Grit 337" is a coarse cleaning powder with many industrial uses. It costs $1.60 a pound to make and has a selling price of $2 a pound.

A small portion of the annual production of this product is retained for further processing in the Mixing Department where it is combined with several other ingredients to form a paste which is marketed as a silver polish selling for $4 per jar. This further processing requires 1/4 pound of Grit 337 per jar. Other ingredients, labor, and variable overhead associated with this further processing cost $2.50 per jar. Variable selling costs amount to $.30 per jar. If the decision were made to cease production of the silver polish, $5,600 of fixed Mixing Department costs could be avoided.

The minimum number of jars of silver polish that would have to be sold to justify further processing of Grit 337 is

a. 5,600 jars.
b. 4,667 jars.
c. 7,000 jars.
d. 8,000 jars.
e. None of the above.

The correct answer is (c) or (d). *(CMA 679 5-24)*
REQUIRED: The unit sales needed to justify further processing of a product.
DISCUSSION: Further processing requires 1/4 pound of Grit 337 per unit, which results in a unit material cost of either $.40 or $.50, depending on whether all the Grit 337 produced can be sold. If all the Grit 337 can be used, the material cost should be $.50 ($2 ÷ 4) since that is the sales price foregone by processing the product further. Additional variable costs are $2.80 ($2.50 processing and $.30 selling costs). Moreover, $5,600 of fixed costs are associated with the silver polish. Thus, the contribution margin is either $.70 or $.80, depending on whether the material is priced at $.40 or $.50.

	$ .40	material
	2.50	variable costs
	.30	selling cost
VC =	$3.20	($3.30 if material is $.50)

If total variable costs are $3.20, the unit contribution margin is $.80 ($4.00 - $3.20), and 7,000 jars ($5,600 fixed costs ÷ $.80 unit contribution margin) must be sold to break even. If the contribution margin is $.70 because the material cost is considered to be $.50, 8,000 jars ($5,600 fixed costs ÷ $.70 unit contribution margin) are required to break even. This is one of the few problems for which the ICMA has publicly permitted more than one answer.

125. Singer, Inc. sells product R for $5 per unit. The fixed costs are $210,000 and the variable costs are 60% of the selling price. What would be the amount of sales if Singer is to realize a profit of 10% of sales?

a. $700,000.
b. $525,000.
c. $472,500.
d. $420,000.

The correct answer is (a). *(CPA 582 P-34)*
REQUIRED: The sales to obtain a given profit on sales given selling price, FC, and VC.
DISCUSSION: To determine the sales volume needed to realize a profit of 10% of sales, the CM must be recalculated to include the targeted 10% profit. The original UCM was $2 ($5 - $3), because VC are 60% of selling price. When the "variable costs" are increased to $3.50/unit to include a $.50 profit (10% of sales price), the CM is $1.50 ($5 selling price - $3.50 VC and profit). Dividing the $210,000 of fixed costs by the $1.50 UCM gives 140,000 sales units. Multiplying by the selling price results in the $700,000 ($5 x 140,000) in sales revenue needed to produce a 10% profit on sales.

Module 11.8: Working Backwards

126. The Ship Company is planning to produce two products, Alt and Tude. Ship is planning to sell 100,000 units of Alt at $4 a unit and 200,000 units of Tude at $3 a unit. Variable costs are 70% of sales for Alt and 80% of sales for Tude. In order to realize a total profit of $160,000, what must the total fixed costs be?

a. $80,000.
b. $90,000.
c. $240,000.
d. $600,000.

The correct answer is (a). *(CPA 1179 P-27)*
REQUIRED: The total fixed costs given sales levels, sales prices, CMRs, and total profit for sales of two products.
DISCUSSION: Profit equals sales minus the sum of fixed and variable costs. Therefore,

Sales:	
Alt (100,000 x $4)	$ 400,000
Tude (200,000 x $3)	600,000
Total sales	$1,000,000
Variable costs:	
Alt ($400,000 x 70%)	$ 280,000
Tude ($600,000 x 80%)	480,000
Total variable costs	$ 760,000

Fixed costs = sales - variable costs - profit
Fixed costs = $1,000,000 - $760,000 - $160,000
Fixed costs = $80,000

127. The following data apply to Frelm Corporation for a given period:

Total variable cost per unit	$3.50
Contribution margin/sales	30%
Breakeven sales (present volume)	$1,000,000

Frelm wants to sell an additional 50,000 units at the same selling price and contribution margin. By how much can fixed costs increase to generate a gross margin equal to 10% of the sales value of the additional 50,000 units to be sold?

a. $50,000.
b. $57,500.
c. $67,500.
d. $125,000.

The correct answer is (a). *(CPA 1175 P-19)*
REQUIRED: The maximum increase in fixed costs permitting a given percentage of profit on sale of additional units.
DISCUSSION: Unit selling price equals unit variable cost plus the unit contribution margin. Given that the contribution margin ratio is 30%, the unit variable cost ($3.50) must equal 70% of the unit selling price, which must therefore be $5 ($3.50 ÷ 70%). If fixed costs remained constant, the incremental contribution margin from the sale of 50,000 additional units would be $75,000 ($250,000 sales revenue x 30%). Since the targeted profit is only 10% of the incremental revenue (10% x $250,000 = $25,000), fixed costs may increase by $50,000 ($75,000 - $25,000).

Questions 128 through 131 are based on Xerbert Co., for which the following data are available.

Xerbert Co.
Budget and Actual Income Statements
For the Year Ended December 31
(000s omitted)

	Budget			Actual		
	Xenox	Xeon	Total	Xenox	Xeon	Total
Unit sales	150	100	250	130	130	260
Net dollar sales	$900	$1,000	$1,900	$780	$1,235	$2,015
Variable expenses	450	750	1,200	390	975	1,365
	$450	$ 250	$ 700	$390	$ 260	$ 650
Fixed expenses			$ 200			$ 190
Manufacturing			153			140
Marketing			95			90
Total fixed expenses			$ 448			$ 420
Income before taxes			$ 252			$ 230

Module 11.8: Working Backwards

128. The percentage difference between actual and budgeted breakeven in units was that actual was

a. 5% above budget.
b. 6.67% below budget.
c. 6.67% above budget.
d. 5% below budget.
e. 12% above budget.

The correct answer is (a). *(CMA 683 4-7)*
REQUIRED: The percentage difference between actual and budgeted breakeven in units.
DISCUSSION: According to the budget (000 omitted), sales of 250 units would produce a contribution margin of $700, or $2.80 per unit. Dividing the $448 of budgeted fixed costs by $2.80 gives a breakeven point of 160 units. The 260 actual units sold produced a contribution margin of $650, or $2.50 per unit. Dividing the $420 of fixed costs by $2.50 gives a breakeven point of 168 units. Consequently, the actual breakeven point is 5% (8 ÷ 160) above the budget.

129. The budgeted total volume of 250,000 units was based upon Xerbert's achieving a market share of 10%. Actual industry volume reached 2,580,000 units. The portion of Xerbert's increased volume attributable to improved market share is

a. 100%.
b. 80%.
c. 20%.
d. 4%.
e. None of the above.

The correct answer is (c). *(CMA 683 4-8)*
REQUIRED: The percentage of the increased volume attributable to increased market share.
DISCUSSION: Based on the revised industry volume, Xerbert should have sold 258,000 units (10% x 2,580,000). Since 260,000 were actually sold, the company increased its market share by 2,000, which is 20% of the 10,000-unit (260,000 - 250,000) increase.

130. The variance of actual contribution margin from budgeted contribution margin attributable to sales price is

a. $50,000 unfavorable.
b. $115,000 unfavorable.
c. $115,000 favorable.
d. $65,000 favorable.
e. $65,000 unfavorable.

The correct answer is (e). *(CMA 683 4-9)*
REQUIRED: The variance of actual from budgeted contribution margin attributable to sales price.
DISCUSSION: First, compute what sales would have been if all sales had been made at budgeted prices. The budgeted prices of each product were $6 and $10 per unit, respectively. Actual sales in units multiplied by the budgeted prices equals total sales of $2,080,000. Since actual sales were only $2,015,000, the variance of $65,000 is unfavorable (less than budgeted).

131. The variance of actual contribution margin from budgeted contribution attributable to unit variable cost changes is

a. $165,000 unfavorable.
b. $165,000 favorable.
c. $137,000 favorable.
d. $137,000 unfavorable.
e. Zero because actual unit variable costs were the same as budgeted unit variable costs.

The correct answer is (e). *(CMA 683 4-10)*
REQUIRED: The variance of actual from budgeted contribution margin attributable to variable cost changes.
DISCUSSION: Calculate variable costs by multiplying actual units sold by the budgeted variable costs per unit. The budgeted unit costs were $3 and $7.50, respectively (000 omitted). Since actual variable costs ($3 x 130 = $390 and $7.50 x 130 = $975) were identical to budgeted costs at the actual volume, the variance was zero.

Questions 132 through 137 are based on the Statement of Income for Davann Co., presented in the opposite column, which represents the operating results for the current fiscal year ending December 31. Davann had sales of 1,800 tons of product during the current year. The manufacturing capacity of Davann's facilities is 3,000 tons of product. Consider each question's situation separately.	Sales	$900,000
	Variable costs	
	Manufacturing	$315,000
	Selling costs	180,000
	Total variable costs	$495,000
	Contribution margin	$405,000
	Fixed costs	
	Manufacturing	$ 90,000
	Selling	112,500
	Administration	45,000
	Total fixed costs	$247,500
	Net income before income taxes	$157,500
	Income taxes (40%)	(63,000)
	Net income after income taxes	$ 94,500

132. The breakeven volume in tons of product for the year is

  a. 420.
  b. 1,100.
  c. 495.
  d. 550.
  e. None of the above.

The correct answer is (b). *(CMA 1280 4-8)*
REQUIRED: The breakeven point in units.
DISCUSSION:

$$\text{BEP units} = \frac{\text{fixed costs}}{\text{unit contribution margin}}$$

The selling price per unit is $500/ton ($900,000 sales ÷ 1,800 tons). The variable cost per unit is $275/ton ($495,000 total variable costs ÷ 1,800 tons). The UCM is $225 ($500 sales price − $275 unit variable cost). The unit BEP is thus 1,100 tons ($247,500 FC ÷ $225 UCM).

133. If the sales volume is estimated to be 2,100 tons in the next year, and if the prices and costs stay at the same levels and amounts next year, the after-tax net income that Davann can expect for next year is

  a. $135,000.
  b. $110,250.
  c. $283,500.
  d. $184,500.
  e. None of the above.

The correct answer is (a). *(CMA 1280 4-9)*
REQUIRED: The after-tax net income if sales volume increases and prices and costs remain constant.
DISCUSSION: Since selling price and variable costs per unit, as calculated in the previous question, are $500 and $275, respectively, next year's after-tax income can be computed as follows:

Sales ($500 x 2,100 tons)	$1,050,000
Variable costs ($275 x 2,100 tons)	(577,500)
Fixed costs	(247,500)
Income before taxes	$ 225,000
Taxes at 40%	(90,000)
Net income	$ 135,000

134. Davann has a potential foreign customer that has offered to buy 1,500 tons at $450 per ton. Assume that all of Davann's costs would be at the same levels and rates as last year. What net income after taxes would Davann make if it took this order and rejected some business from regular customers so as not to exceed capacity?

  a. $297,500.
  b. $252,000.
  c. $211,500.
  d. $256,500.
  e. None of the above.

The correct answer is (c). *(CMA 1280 4-10)*
REQUIRED: The after-tax net income resulting from a special order.
DISCUSSION: Total foreign sales would be $675,000 (1,500 tons x $450), and sales to regular customers will account for the other 1,500 tons of capacity (1,500 x $500 = $750,000). Total sales would thus be $1,425,000. Variable costs would be $825,000 (3,000 tons x $275).

Sales	$1,425,000
Less:	
Variable costs	(825,000)
Fixed costs	(247,500)
Income before taxes	$ 352,500
Taxes at 40%	(141,000)
Net income	$ 211,500

135. Ignore the facts presented in the previous questions, and assume that Davann plans to market its product in a new territory. Davann estimates that an advertising and promotion program costing $61,500 annually would need to be undertaken for the next two or three years. In addition, a $25 per ton sales commission over and above the current commission to the sales force in the new territory would be required. How many tons would have to be sold in the new territory to maintain Davann's current after-tax income of $94,500?

a. 307.5.
b. 1,095.
c. 273.333.
d. 1,545.

The correct answer is (a). *(CMA 1280 4-11)*
REQUIRED: The incremental sales in units to cover additional fixed costs and an incremental variable cost.
DISCUSSION:

$$\text{BEP units} = \frac{\text{fixed costs}}{\text{unit contribution margin}}$$

The $25 per ton sales commission is added to the unit variable cost, which increases to $300. The unit contribution margin is reduced to $200 ($500 selling price - $300 unit VC). The incremental fixed costs are $61,500. The additional units to be sold to maintain current income are 307.5 tons ($61,500 additional fixed costs ÷ $200 unit contribution margin).

136. Davann is considering replacing a highly labor-intensive process with an automatic machine. This change would result in an increase of $58,500 annually in manufacturing fixed costs. The variable manufacturing costs would decrease $25 per ton. The new breakeven volume in tons would be

a. 990.
b. 1,224.
c. 1,854.
d. 612.
e. None of the above.

The correct answer is (b). *(CMA 1280 4-12)*
REQUIRED: The new breakeven point in units if fixed costs increase and variable costs decrease.
DISCUSSION:

$$\text{BEP units} = \frac{\text{fixed costs}}{\text{unit contribution margin}}$$

The new fixed costs are $306,000 (original FC of $247,500 + $58,500 increase). The new variable cost is $250 (old unit VC of $275 - $25 decrease). The new UCM is $250 (selling price of $500 - $250 unit VC). The breakeven point in units is thus 1,224 tons ($306,000 ÷ $250).

137. Ignore the facts presented in Q. 136, and assume that Davann estimates that the per ton selling price will decline 10% next year. Variable costs will increase $40 per ton and the fixed costs will not change. What sales volume in dollars will be required to earn an after-tax net income of $94,500 next year?

a. $1,140,000.
b. $825,000.
c. $1,500,000.
d. $1,350,000.
e. None of the above.

The correct answer is (d). *(CMA 1280 4-13)*
REQUIRED: The sales volume in dollars to attain a targeted net income if sales price declines and variable costs increase.
DISCUSSION: Given a 10% decrease, the new selling price will be $450 ($500 x 90% = $450). The new unit variable cost will be $315 (original unit VC of $275 + $40). The new UCM is $135 ($450 - $315), and the CMR is 30% ($135 ÷ $450). The after-tax net income of $94,500 is equivalent to $157,500 before taxes given a tax rate of 40% ($94,500 ÷ 60%).

$$\text{BEP in \$} = \frac{\text{fixed costs + desired income}}{\text{contribution margin ratio}}$$

$$= \frac{\$247,500 + \$157,500}{30\%}$$

$$= \$1,350,000$$

Questions 138 through 141 are based on DisKing Company, which is a retailer of video disks. The projected after-tax net income for the current year is $120,000 based on a sales volume of 200,000 video disks. DisKing has been selling the disks at $16 each. The variable costs consist of the $10 unit purchase price of the disks and a handling cost of $2 per disk. DisKing's annual fixed costs are $600,000, and DisKing is subject to a 40% income tax rate. Management is planning for the coming year when it expects that the unit purchase price of the video disks will increase 30%.

138. DisKing Company's breakeven point for the current year in number of video disks is

a. 100,000 units.
b. 150,000 units.
c. 50,000 units.
d. 60,000 units.

The correct answer is (b). *(CMA 684 4-11)*
REQUIRED: The breakeven point for the current year.
DISCUSSION: The BEP in units is equal to FC divided by UCM.

$$\frac{FC}{UCM} = \frac{\$600,000}{\$16 - \$10 - \$2} = 150,000 \text{ units}$$

139. An increase of 10% in projected unit sales volume for the current year would result in an increased after-tax income of

a. $80,000.
b. $32,000.
c. $48,000.
d. $12,000.

The correct answer is (c). *(CMA 684 4-12)*
REQUIRED: The after-tax net income given a volume increase.
DISCUSSION: The increase in net income will equal the UCM ($4) times the increased quantity. A 10% increase equals 20,000 units.

Increase in pre-tax income (20,000 x $4)	$80,000
Less taxes (40%)	(32,000)
After-tax net income	$48,000

140. The volume of sales in dollars that DisKing Company must achieve in the coming year to maintain the same after-tax net income as projected for the current year if unit selling price remains at $16 is

a. $12,800,000.
b. $14,400,000.
c. $11,520,000.
d. $32,000,000.

The correct answer is (a). *(CMA 684 4-13)*
REQUIRED: The targeted sales dollars to achieve the same after-tax net income.
DISCUSSION: Current projected net income is

Sales (200,000 x $16)	$3,200,000
Less VC ($12 x 200,000)	(2,400,000)
CM	$ 800,000
FC	(600,000)
Net income	$ 200,000
Taxes (40%)	(80,000)
Net income	$ 120,000

To achieve $120,000 of after-tax net income ($200,000 pre-tax), given a projected purchase price of $13 ($10 x 130%), will require coverage of FC ($600,000) and pre-tax income ($200,000). Since UCM will equal $1 ($16 - $13 - $2), unit sales must be 800,000 ($800,000 ÷ $1), and sales revenue must be $12,800,000 ($16 x 800,000).

141. In order to cover a 30% increase in the disk's purchase price for the coming year and still maintain the current contribution margin ratio, DisKing Company must establish a selling price per disk for the coming year of

a. $19.60.
b. $19.00.
c. $20.80.
d. $20.00.

The correct answer is (d). *(CMA 684 4-14)*
REQUIRED: The selling price necessary to maintain the current CMR.
DISCUSSION: The current CMR is 25% ($4 UCM ÷ $16), and the expected unit VC is $15 ($13 + $2); the new sales price must be $20 ($15 ÷ .75).

11.9 Comprehensive

Questions 142 through 144 are based on the following information, which was presented as part of Question 5 on the Practice II section of the May 1976 CPA examination.

The management of Freedom, Inc. has performed cost studies and projected the following annual costs based on 40,000 units of production and sales:

	Total Annual Costs	Percent of Variable Portion of Total Annual Costs
Direct material	$400,000	100%
Direct labor	360,000	75
Mfg. overhead	300,000	40
Selling, general, and adm.	200,000	25

142. What unit selling price will yield a 10% profit from sales of 40,000 units?

a. $33.50/unit.
b. $35/unit.
c. $40/unit.
d. $30/unit.

The correct answer is (b). *(Publisher)*
REQUIRED: The unit selling price to generate a targeted profit on a given volume of sales.
DISCUSSION: Total revenue minus total cost equals the targeted profit. In this case, a 10% profit on sales is desired at the 40,000 unit level. Costs total $1,260,000. Thus, solve the following calculation:

Let X = unit selling price to yield a 10% profit on sales

Total sales - total costs = projected profit

$$40,000X - \$1,260,000 = .1(40,000X)$$
$$36,000X = \$1,260,000$$
$$X = \$35 \text{ per unit}$$

143. What is the total variable cost for Freedom, Inc.?

a. $1,260,000.
b. $840,000.
c. $420,000.
d. $960,000.

The correct answer is (b). *(Publisher)*
REQUIRED: The total variable costs.
DISCUSSION: The total variable costs are the total of variable costs in each category.

	Total Annual Costs	% of Total Annual Costs That is Variable	Variable Costs
Direct material	$ 400,000	x 100% =	$400,000
Direct labor	360,000	x 75 =	270,000
Mfg. overhead	300,000	x 40 =	120,000
Selling, general & adm.	200,000	x 25 =	50,000
Totals	$1,260,000		$840,000

144. What is the total fixed cost for Freedom, Inc.?

a. $400,000.
b. $330,000.
c. $800,000.
d. $420,000.

The correct answer is (d). *(Publisher)*
REQUIRED: The total fixed costs.
DISCUSSION: The total fixed costs may be calculated by the reciprocals of the proportion of total annual costs that are variable or by subtracting total variable cost from total cost ($1,260,000 - $840,000 = $420,000).

	Total Annual Costs	% of Total Annual Costs That is Fixed	Fixed Costs
Direct material	$ 400,000	0%	$ ---
Direct labor	360,000	25	90,000
Mfg. overhead	300,000	60	180,000
Selling, general & adm.	200,000	75	150,000
Totals	$1,260,000		$420,000

Questions 145 through 152 are based on the following information, which was presented as part of Question 2 on the Practice II section of the May 1970 CPA examination.

Metal Industries, Inc. operates its production department only when orders are received for one or both of its two products, two sizes of metal discs. The manufacturing process begins with the cutting of doughnut-shaped rings from rectangular strips of sheet metal; these rings are then pressed into discs. The sheets of metal, each 4 feet long and weighing 32 ounces, are purchased at $1.36 per running foot. The department has been operating at a loss for the past year as shown below.

Sales for the year	$172,000
Less: expenses	177,200
Net loss for the department	$ 5,200

The following information is available.

1. Ten thousand 4-foot pieces of metal yielded 40,000 large discs, each weighing 4 ounces and selling for $2.90, and 40,000 small discs, each weighing 2.4 ounces and selling for $1.40.

2. The corporation has been producing at less than "normal capacity" and has had no spoilage in the cutting step of the process. The skeletons remaining after the rings have been cut are sold for scrap at $.80 per pound.

3. The variable conversion cost of each large disc is 80% of the disc's direct material cost, and variable conversion cost of each small disc is 75% of the disc's direct material cost. Variable conversion costs are the sum of direct labor and variable overhead.

4. Fixed costs were $86,000.

145. The material net cost per ounce is

a. $.20.
b. $.16.
c. $.17.
d. $.18.

The correct answer is (a). *(Publisher)*
REQUIRED: The material net cost per ounce.
DISCUSSION: The cost per ounce is the net cost of good material divided by the ounces of good material.

	Parts Per Strip	Weight Per Unit	Total
Yield from each 4-foot length strip of metal:			
Large discs	4	4.0 oz.	16.0
Small discs	4	2.4 oz.	9.6
Balance = scrap			6.4
Cost per piece (4 ft. @ $1.36)			$5.44
Less scrap value @ $.80/lb.:			
6.4 oz. x $.05/oz. =			.32
Net cost of good material			$5.12
Divided by oz. of good material			25.6
Material cost per oz.			$ .20

146. The prorated material costs per unit for the large and small discs, respectively, are

a. $.64 and $.38.
b. $.80 and $.48.
c. $.68 and $.40.
d. $.72 and $.43.

The correct answer is (b). *(Publisher)*
REQUIRED: The prorated material cost per unit for the two products.
DISCUSSION: The prorated material cost per unit is the weight of good material per unit times the unit cost of good material for each size of disc.

Prorated material cost per unit:
Large discs (4 oz. @ $.20) $ .80
Small discs (2.4 oz. @ $.20) $ .48

147. The net cost of good material per metal strip is

a. $5.76.
b. $6.40.
c. $5.12.
d. $5.44.

The correct answer is (c). *(Publisher)*
REQUIRED: The net cost of good material per metal strip.
DISCUSSION: The net cost of good material per metal strip is the number of discs times the material cost per unit of each kind of disc.

Large discs (4 x $.80) $3.20
Small discs (4 x $.48)   1.92
Net cost of good material per metal strip $5.12

Module 11.9: Comprehensive

148. The amounts allocated for conversion cost for the large and small discs, respectively, are

a. $.38 and $.36.
b. $.64 and $.36.
c. $.23 and $.13.
d. $.46 and $.23.

The correct answer is (b). *(Publisher)*
REQUIRED: The amounts allocated to each product for conversion cost.
DISCUSSION: The amounts allocated for conversion cost are 80% and 75% times the direct material cost of the large disc and the small disc, respectively.

	Large Disc	Small Disc
Material cost	$ .80	$ .48
Variable conversion cost as a percentage of direct material cost	x 80%	x 75%
Amount allocated for conversion cost	$ .64	$ .36

149. Total variable costs per unit for the large and small discs, respectively, are

a. $1.02 and $.86.
b. $1.44 and $.84.
c. $.91 and $.53.
d. $1.18 and $.66.

The correct answer is (b). *(Publisher)*
REQUIRED: The total variable costs per unit for the two products.
DISCUSSION: The total variable costs per unit for the large and small discs are the sum of the materials and conversion costs for each.

	Large Disc	Small Disc
Material cost	$ .80	$ .48
Conversion cost	.64	.36
Total variable cost/unit	$1.44	$ .84

150. Contribution margins per unit for the large and small discs, respectively, are

a. $1.88 and $.54.
b. $1.46 and $.56.
c. $1.99 and $.87.
d. $1.72 and $.74.

The correct answer is (b). *(Publisher)*
REQUIRED: The contribution margin per unit for each of the two products.
DISCUSSION: The UCM is the selling price (given) less total variable cost for each unit.

	Large Disc	Small Disc
Selling price per unit	$2.90	$1.40
Less unit variable cost	1.44	.84
UCM	$1.46	$ .56

151. If the material cost for large and small discs is $.85 and $.51, respectively, and the normal production capacity is 50,000 units, what is the breakeven point?

a. 45,806.
b. 43,608.
c. 39,908.
d. 41,206.

The correct answer is (a). *(Publisher)*
REQUIRED: The breakeven point (BEP) for this product mix given new material costs.
DISCUSSION: The BEP is the fixed costs (given as $86,000) divided by the composite UCM. Each composite unit contains 1 small disc and 1 large disc with respective selling prices given as $1.40 and $2.90, or a composite sales price of $4.30. The respective material cost is changed for this question to $.51 and $.85, and respective conversion cost is assumed to remain 75% and 80% of direct material cost. 75% of $.51 is $.3825 and 80% of $.85 is $.68.

BEP (units) = FC ÷ UCM

Product	Sales Price	Material Cost	Conversion Cost	Total VC
Small discs	$1.40	$.51	$.3825	$0.8925
Large discs	$2.90	$.85	$.68	$1.53
Totals	$4.30			$2.4225
Less VC	($2.4225)			
UCM	$1.8775			

Breakeven output = $\dfrac{\$86,000}{\$1.8775}$ = 45,806 units

Module 11.9: Comprehensive

152. Refer to the data preceding Q. 145. The total contribution margins for the large and small discs, respectively, are

a. $68,800 and $29,600.
b. $79,600 and $34,800.
c. $58,400 and $22,400.
d. $75,200 and $21,600.

The correct answer is (c). *(Publisher)*
REQUIRED: The total contribution margins for each of the two products.
DISCUSSION: The CM in total is equal to the UCM times the number of units sold.

	Large Disc	Small Disc
UCM	$1.46	$.56
Number of units sold	x 40,000	x 40,000
Total CM	$58,400	$22,400

Questions 153 through 160 are based on the following information, which was presented as part of Question 3 on Part 4 of the June 1976 CMA examination.

All-Day Candy Company is a wholesale distributor of candy. The company services grocery, convenience, and drug stores in a large metropolitan area.

Small but steady growth in sales has been achieved by the company over the past few years while candy prices have been increasing. The company is formulating its plans for the coming fiscal year. Presented adjacent are the data used to project the current year's after-tax net income of $110,400.

Manufacturers of candy have announced that they will increase prices of their products an average of 15% in the coming year due to increases in raw material (sugar, cocoa, peanuts, etc.) and labor costs. All-Day Candy Company expects that all other costs will remain at the same rates or levels as the current year.

Average selling price	$4.00 per box
Average variable costs	
Cost of candy	$2.00 per box
Selling expenses	.40 per box
Total	$2.40 per box
Annual fixed costs	
Selling	$ 160,000
Administrative	280,000
Total	$ 440,000
Expected annual sales volume (390,000 boxes)	$1,560,000

The tax rate is 40%.

---

153. What is the current contribution margin per box?

a. $2.00.
b. $2.40.
c. $1.60.
d. $4.00.

The correct answer is (c). *(Publisher)*
REQUIRED: The current contribution margin per box.
DISCUSSION: The unit contribution margin is equal to the sales price minus the unit variable costs. Sales price equals $4 and unit variable costs equal $2.40. The contribution margin is thus $1.60 per box.

154. What is the breakeven point in units before a 15% increase in prices?

a. 200,000.
b. 275,000.
c. 175,000.
d. 100,000.

The correct answer is (b). *(Publisher)*
REQUIRED: The breakeven point in units prior to the price increase.
DISCUSSION: The breakeven point in units is found by dividing annual fixed cost by the contribution margin per box. Annual fixed costs total $440,000. As computed in Q. 153, the contribution margin is $1.60 per box. The BEP is thus 275,000 boxes ($440,000 ÷ $1.60).

155. If fixed costs double, what happens to the breakeven point?

a. Increases but by less than a factor of two.
b. Decreases by less than a factor of two.
c. Increases by a factor of two.
d. Decreases by a factor of two.

The correct answer is (c). *(Publisher)*
REQUIRED: The effect of fixed costs doubling.
DISCUSSION: Doubling the fixed costs doubles the breakeven point in both sales and units of sales. It takes twice as much contribution margin (which is constant as a percent of sales and as a unit amount) to cover the fixed costs.

Module 11.9: Comprehensive

156. If the current contribution margin ratio is maintained, what would be the selling price of the candy to cover the 15% increase?

   a. $4.00.
   b. $4.15.
   c. $4.60.
   d. $4.50.

The correct answer is (d). *(Publisher)*
REQUIRED: The adjusted selling price to maintain the contribution margin ratio given a cost increase.
DISCUSSION: The current CMR is UCM ÷ sales price, or 40% ($1.60 ÷ $4.00), and the variable cost ratio, VC ÷ sales price, is 60%. The variable cost of candy is expected to increase by 15% to $2.30 ($2 x 115%), and variable selling expenses are expected to remain at $.40 per box, for total variable costs of $2.70.

$$\$2.70 \div 60\% = \$4.50$$

157. If candy costs increase 15% but the selling price remains at $4.00 per box, what will be the breakeven point in units?

   a. 338,462.
   b. 346,457.
   c. 285,715.
   d. 305,556.

The correct answer is (a). *(Publisher)*
REQUIRED: The BEP in units if the sales price remains the same but costs increase.
DISCUSSION: Candy costs are expected to increase 15% to $2.30 per box while the selling price per box ($4) and selling expenses ($.40 per box) are expected to remain the same. Thus, the new UCM will be $1.30 ($4.00 - $2.70). Fixed costs of $440,000 divided by the $1.30 UCM equal 338,462 boxes to break even.

158. If the candy costs remain constant but the selling price increases 15%, what will be the breakeven point in sales dollars?

   a. $648,000.
   b. $838,462.
   c. $920,000.
   d. $1,556,953.

The correct answer is (c). *(Publisher)*
REQUIRED: The BEP in dollars if costs remain constant but sales price increases 15%.
DISCUSSION: The new selling price would be $4.60 (4.00 x 1.15). The UCM becomes $2.20 ($4.60 sales price - $2.40 unit variable costs). Dividing the $440,000 fixed costs by the $2.20 UCM results in BEP of 200,000 units. Multiplying by the $4.60 sales price results in BE sales of $920,000.

159. Why was the tax rate at 40% not a factor in the previous two questions?

   a. At the breakeven point there is zero profit.
   b. Income taxes are normally ignored in CVP analysis.
   c. The problem ignores income taxes.
   d. Income tax is a variable cost that is incorporated into CVP analysis.

The correct answer is (a). *(Publisher)*
REQUIRED: Why the 40% tax rate is not relevant to breakeven problems.
DISCUSSION: At breakeven, there is no income and thus no income tax.

160. If net income after taxes is to remain the same after the cost of candy increases but no increase in the sales price is made, how many boxes of candy must All-Day sell?

   a. 480,000.
   b. 400,000.
   c. 27,600.
   d. 29,300.

The correct answer is (a). *(Publisher)*
REQUIRED: The number of units to be sold to earn the same net income after taxes given a cost increase.
DISCUSSION: One approach is to reconstruct the present income statement to determine net income after taxes and then work backward to determine the level of sales (and the number of boxes to be sold) to maintain the same level of profitability.
Alternatively, only the current CM need be calculated because all costs other than CM remain the same. Present sales of $1,560,000 times the present CMR of 40% (both given in the problem) is $624,000, the total CM. To maintain total CM with a $1.30 UCM ($4.00 - $2.70), 480,000 boxes ($624,000 ÷ $1.30) will have to be sold.

Module 11.9: Comprehensive

Questions 161 through 168 are based on the following information, which was presented as part of Question 4 on the Practice I section of the November 1973 CPA examination.

Columbus Hospital operates a general hospital but rents space and beds to separate entities for specialized treatment such as pediatrics, maternity, psychiatric, etc. Columbus charges each separate entity for common services to its patients like meals and laundry and for all administrative services such as billings, collections, etc. All uncollectible accounts are charged directly to the entity. Space and bed rentals are fixed for the year.

For the entire year ended June 30, the Pediatrics Department at Columbus Hospital charged each patient an average of $65 per day, had a capacity of 60 beds, operated 24 hours per day for 365 days, and had revenue of $1,138,800.

Expenses charged by the hospital to the Pediatrics Department for the year ended June 30 were

	Basis of Allocation	
	Patient Days	Bed Capacity
Dietary	$ 42,952	
Janitorial		$ 12,800
Laundry	28,000	
Lab, other than direct charges to patients	47,800	
Pharmacy	33,800	
Repairs and maint.	5,200	7,140
General adm. services		131,760
Rent		275,320
Billings and collections	40,000	
Bad debt expense	47,000	
Other	18,048	25,980
	$262,800	$453,000

The only personnel directly employed by the Pediatrics Department are supervising nurses, nurses, and aides. The hospital has minimum personnel requirements based on total annual patient days. Hospital requirements beginning at the minimum, expected level of operation follow:

Annual Patient Days	Aides	Nurses	Supervising Nurses
10,000 - 14,000	21	11	4
14,001 - 17,000	22	12	4
17,001 - 23,725	22	13	4
23,726 - 25,550	25	14	5
25,551 - 27,375	26	14	5
27,376 - 29,200	29	16	6

The staffing levels above represent full-time equivalents, and it should be assumed that the Pediatrics Department always employs only the minimum number of required full-time equivalent personnel.

Annual salaries for each class of employee follow: supervising nurses, $18,000; nurses, $13,000; and aides, $5,000. Salary expense for the year ended June 30 for supervising nurses, nurses, and aides was $72,000, $169,000, and $110,000, respectively.

The Pediatrics Department operated at 100% capacity during 111 days of the past year. It is estimated that during 90 of these capacity days, the demand averaged 17 patients more than capacity and even went as high as 20 patients more on some days. The hospital has an additional 20 beds available for rent for the coming fiscal year.

---

161. The variable expense per patient day is

a. $15.08.
b. $12.50.
c. $15.00.
d. $50.00.

The correct answer is (c). *(Publisher)*
REQUIRED: The variable expense per patient day.
DISCUSSION: Total variable expenses divided by total patient days equals the expense per patient day. The number of patient days is 17,520 ($1,138,800 revenue ÷ $65 average day charge). Note that variable costs totalling $262,800 are allocated on the basis of patient days versus fixed costs, which are allocated on the basis of bed capacity. Thus, variable expense per patient day is $15 ($262,800 variable costs ÷ 17,520 patient days).

162. The contribution margin per patient day is

a. $49.92.
b. $52.50.
c. $50.00.
d. $52.00.

The correct answer is (c). *(Publisher)*
REQUIRED: The contribution margin per patient day.
DISCUSSION: The CM per patient day is revenue per patient day less variable expense per patient day. Average revenue per patient day is given as $65. Variable expenses, as computed in Q. 161, are $15. The CM per patient day is thus $50 ($65 - $15).

163.
How many patient days are necessary to cover fixed costs for bed capacity and for supervisory nurses?

a. 9,500.
b. 11,500.
c. 12,500.
d. 10,500.

The correct answer is (d). *(Publisher)*
REQUIRED: The number of patient days to cover certain fixed costs.
DISCUSSION: Fixed costs, including rent, allocated by the hospital total $453,000. The salaries of supervisory nurses are given as $72,000, which is the required minimum, i.e., four nurses at $18,000. Thus, fixed costs plus supervisory nurse salaries at breakeven equal total fixed costs of $525,000. Total fixed costs divided by the $50 UCM calculated in Q. 162 equals the number of patient days necessary to cover fixed costs: 10,500 days.

164.
The number of patient days needed to cover total costs is

a. 14,200.
b. 15,200.
c. 15,820.
d. 14,220.

The correct answer is (c). *(Publisher)*
REQUIRED: The number of patient days needed to cover total costs.
DISCUSSION: The number of patient days needed to cover total costs is calculated by dividing total costs by the CM per patient day. Total costs include the total fixed expenses of $525,000 (see Q. 163), plus salary expense for aides and nurses. Salaries can be estimated first by determining the number of dollars used at the 10,500 patient days level, which is the number of patient days necessary to cover fixed costs. Twenty-one aides (at $5,000) and 11 nurses (at $13,000) are necessary at that level of activity for a salary total of $248,000. Thus, the total costs to be covered equal $773,000 ($525,000 FC + $248,000 salaries), or 15,460 patient days ($773,000 ÷ $50). The salary expense of aides and nurses of 15,460 patient days requires one additional aide and one additional nurse, thus increasing the total salary expense by $18,000 to total $266,000. Thus, the total expenses to be covered equal $791,000 ($525,000 + $266,000) divided by $50 UCM equals 15,820 patient days. Salaries at 15,820 patient days is the same as for 15,460 patient days.

165.
If the Pediatrics Department rented an additional 20 beds and all other factors remain the same as in the past year, what would be the increase in revenue?

a. $99,450.
b. $87,750.
c. $105,450.
d. $89,750.

The correct answer is (a). *(Publisher)*
REQUIRED: The incremental revenue if capacity increases.
DISCUSSION: Incremental revenue is equal to the additional patient days multiplied by the revenue per patient day. The number of additional patients per day is given in the last paragraph of the facts as 17 patients for 90 days. 17 x 90 = additional 1,530 patient days. 1,530 x $65 = $99,450 incremental revenue.

166.
Continuing to consider the 20 additional rented beds, the increase in total variable cost applied per patient day is

a. $22,935.
b. $22,950.
c. $22,965.
d. $23,935.

The correct answer is (b). *(Publisher)*
REQUIRED: The increase in total variable cost if capacity increases.
DISCUSSION: Increased total variable cost is equal to the additional patient days times the variable cost per patient day. Additional patient days = 1,530. Variable cost per patient day = $15. 1,530 x $15 = $22,950.

Module 11.9: Comprehensive

167. Refer to the information given on page 270. What is the increased fixed cost applied for bed capacity, given the increased number of beds?

a. $151,000.
b. $173,950.
c. $147,000.
d. $152,000.

The correct answer is (a). *(Publisher)*
REQUIRED: The increased fixed cost based on the increased bed capacity.
DISCUSSION: Incremental cost based on bed capacity is the cost per bed times the additional number of beds. The average cost per bed is $7,550 ($453,000 total cost ÷ 60 bed present capacity). The 20 additional beds at $7,550 equals increased cost of $151,000. Note that this reallocation of cost currently being incurred by another department appropriately uses average cost per unit.

168. Refer to the information given on page 270. Total annual gain (loss) from renting the additional 20 beds is

a. $69,400.
b. $79,500.
c. $(74,500).
d. $(72,500).

The correct answer is (c). *(Publisher)*
REQUIRED: The total annual gain or loss from increasing capacity.
DISCUSSION: The total annual gain or loss from renting an additional 20 beds is the difference between the incremental revenue and the incremental cost. Incremental revenue was calculated in Q. 165 as $99,450. Incremental cost (Qs. 166 and 167) equals $173,950 ($22,950 variable cost + $151,000 fixed cost). The difference is a $74,500 loss.

Questions 169 through 173 are based on the following information, which was presented as part of Question 4 on Part 4 of the December 1973 CMA examination.

Mr. Calderone started a pizza restaurant in 1986. For this purpose a building was rented for $400 per month. Two women were hired to work full time at the restaurant and six college students were hired to work 30 hours per week delivering pizza. This level of employment has been consistent. An outside accountant was hired for tax and bookkeeping purposes, for which Mr. Calderone pays $300 per month. The necessary restaurant equipment and delivery cars were purchased with cash. Mr. Calderone has noticed that expenses for utilities and supplies have been rather constant. Mr. Calderone increased his business between 1986 and 1989. Profits have more than doubled since 1986. Mr. Calderone does not understand why profits have increased faster than volume.

A projected income statement for the year ended December 31, 1990, prepared by the accountant, is shown below.

Sales		$95,000
Cost of food sold	$28,500	
Wages & fringe benefits:		
Restaurant help	8,150	
Delivery help	17,300	
Rent	4,800	
Accounting services	3,600	
Depreciation:		
Delivery equipment	5,000	
Restaurant equipment	3,000	
Utilities	2,325	
Supplies	1,200	(73,875)
Net income before taxes		$21,125
Income taxes (30%)		(6,338)
Net income		$14,787

Note: The average pizza sells for $2.50.

---

169. What is the tax shield on the noncash fixed costs?

a. $2,400.
b. $11,212.
c. $3,400.
d. $5,400.

The correct answer is (a). *(Publisher)*
REQUIRED: The tax shield on the noncash fixed cost.
DISCUSSION: When noncash expenses, e.g., depreciation, are charged as an expense, in effect they protect that amount of revenue from taxation. In this instance, $8,000 of depreciation x 30% tax rate = $2,400, the tax shield.

Module 11.9: Comprehensive

170. What is the breakeven point in number of pizzas that must be sold?

a. 25,929.
b. 23,569.
c. 18,150.
d. 42,114.

The correct answer is (a). *(Publisher)*
REQUIRED: The breakeven point in units to be sold.
DISCUSSION: The BEP in units is fixed costs divided by the UCM. Fixed costs include, in this instance, all costs other than cost of food sold, which is the only variable cost. Thus, fixed costs equal $45,375 ($73,875 total costs minus $28,500 variable costs). If variable costs equal 30% of sales ($28,500 ÷ $95,000), then the average pizza has a variable cost of $.75 (30% of $2.50). The UCM per unit is thus equal to $2.50 - $.75 = $1.75. The BEP is 25,929 units ($45,375 of fixed costs ÷ $1.75 UCM).

171. What is the net cash flow from the projected 1990 income statement?

a. $17,987.
b. $22,787.
c. $14,787.
d. $19,787.

The correct answer is (b). *(Publisher)*
REQUIRED: The net cash flow from the projected (pro forma) income statement.
DISCUSSION: The net cash flow from the pro forma income statement is the net income ($14,787) plus any noncash expenses ($8,000 depreciation). Net cash flow thus equals $22,787.

172. What is the cash flow breakeven point in number of pizzas that must be sold?

a. 19,986.
b. 21,284.
c. 13,990.
d. 10,273.

The correct answer is (a). *(Publisher)*
REQUIRED: The cash flow breakeven point in units.
DISCUSSION: The cash flow BEP in units is equal to the cash flow effect of fixed costs divided by the UCM. Cash flow fixed costs equal all fixed costs less the noncash fixed costs of depreciation ($5,000 + $3,000) adjusted for the tax shield of noncash fixed costs. The tax shield as calculated in Q. 169 is 30% (the effective tax rate) times the annual depreciation of $8,000.

Cash flow fixed costs	
Wages	$25,450
Rent	4,800
Accounting services	3,600
Utilities and supplies	3,525
	$37,375
Less: Tax shield on noncash fixed costs	(2,400)
	$34,975

$$\text{BEP} = \frac{\$34,975}{\$1.75 \text{ UCM}} = 19,986$$

173. What is the breakeven point in units if a $20,000 after tax net income is desired?

a. 30,826.
b. 29,578.
c. 37,357.
d. 42,255.

The correct answer is (d). *(Publisher)*
REQUIRED: The breakeven point in units given a targeted net income.
DISCUSSION: The BEP in units given a targeted net income is found by adding the fixed costs to the desired after-tax profit adjusted by (1 minus the tax rate), and then dividing by the UCM.

$$\frac{\$45,375 + [\$20,000 \div (1 - .3)]}{\$1.75 \text{ UCM}} =$$

$$\frac{\$45,375 + \$28,571}{\$1.75 \text{ UCM}} = 42,255 \text{ pizzas}$$

Module 11.9: Comprehensive

Questions 174 through 179 are based on the following information, which was presented as part of Question 9 on Part 5 of the June 1976 CMA examination.

Aplet Inc. purchased Avcont Company in 1978 during Aplet's expansion period. The subsidiary has been quite profitable until recently. Beginning in 1987 the market share dropped, costs increased (primarily due to increased prices of inputs), and the profits turned into losses. The income statements for 1987 and 1988 are presented along with an estimate of the 1989 income (made in October 1989).

Avcont Company
Income Statement for Years Ending December 31
(000 omitted)

	1987	1988	1989 (Est.)
Industry unit sales	1,300	1,200	1,200
Avcont unit sales	120	110	110
Sales	$1,200	$1,100	$1,100
Less: Variable costs			
Raw materials	$ 175	$ 170	$ 175
Labor	210	215	225
Mfg. overhead	100	99	100
Selling	125	115	120
Administrative	50	50	60
	$ 660	$ 649	$ 680
Variable contribution margin	$ 540	$ 451	$ 420
Less: Fixed costs			
Manufacturing[1]	$ 200	$ 210	$ 230
Selling[1]	125	140	145
Administration[1]	135	145	145
	$ 460	$ 495	$ 520
Net income (loss)	$ 80	$ (44)	$ (100)

[1] Depreciation and amortization included in fixed costs:

Manufacturing	$ 60	$ 70	$ 70
Selling	5	6	6
Administration	8	8	9
	$ 73	$ 84	$ 85

The subsidiary management is optimistic about the volume of sales for 1990. Recent sales promotion efforts seem to be beneficial, and Avcont expects to increase unit sales 10% during 1990 even though industry volume is expected to decline to 1,100,000 units. However, Avcont management also knows its variable cost rates will increase 10% in 1990 over 1989 levels.

Avcont management wants to take action to reverse the unsatisfactory results the company has been experiencing. One proposal under consideration is to increase the price of Avcont's product. Some members of management believe that the market might accept an 8% increase in prices at this time without affecting the expected 10% increase in unit sales volume because there have been no price increases in this market since 1986. Several other companies are also considering price increases for 1990.

Members of Aplet management question the feasibility of a price increase because Avcont is operating in an industry that is experiencing declining sales. In addition, the marketing department believes a price increase will have an impact on the expected increase in unit sales volume during 1990. Its estimate of the possible outcomes on unit sales and the related probabilities for the 8% price increase is as follows:

Increase (Decrease) in 1990 Unit Sales Volume	Probability
10%	.4
5	.3
0	.2
(5)	.1
	1.0

---

174. Assuming that the 8% price increase and the 10% sales volume increase for 1990 occur, what will the contribution margin be?

  a. $400,000.
  b. $420,000.
  c. $277,200.
  d. $484,000.

The correct answer is (d). *(Publisher)*
REQUIRED: The contribution margin after a sales volume and price increase.
DISCUSSION: The contribution margin is equal to sales less variable costs. Sales are expected to increase by a unit sales volume of 10% and a price increase of 8%. Variable costs are expected to increase by 10%.

Sales ($1,100,000 x 1.10 x 1.08)	$1,306,800
Less variable costs ($680,000 x 1.10 x 1.10)	822,800
Contribution margin	$ 484,000

175. What will 1990 profits be given a 10% sales volume and 8% price increase?

  a. $(58,000).
  b. $58,000.
  c. $36,000.
  d. $(36,000).

The correct answer is (d). *(Publisher)*
REQUIRED: Estimated income for the next year.
DISCUSSION: Net income in 1990 will equal sales less variable costs less fixed expenses. Thus, expected loss for 1990 equals $36,000.

Sales ($1,100,000 x 1.10 x 1.08)	$1,306,800
Less variable costs ($680,000 x 1.10 x 1.10)	(822,800)
Contribution margin (Q. 174)	$ 484,000
Less fixed expenses	(520,000)
Expected loss for 1990	$ (36,000)

176. If Avcont must borrow all funds it spends above cash intake, what amounts will it borrow for 1989 and 1990?

a. $15,000, $0.
b. $15,000, $49,000.
c. $0, $49,000.
d. $100,000, $36,000.

The correct answer is (a). *(Publisher)*
REQUIRED: The funds that must be borrowed for the current year and the next.
DISCUSSION: The funds needed to borrow are net loss or net income adjusted by the fixed expenses not requiring cash outlays from funds from operations. The combination of the price and volume increase will reduce Avcont's need for funds from the corporate treasury during 1990. In addition, the depreciation and amortization included in fixed costs do not require an outlay of cash. Consequently, Avcont can expect a positive cash flow during 1990 rather than the negative flow experienced in 1989. The company's cash position still is not strong, however.

	1989	1990
Net loss	$(100,000)	$(36,000)
Fixed costs not requiring cash outlays	85,000	85,000
Funds from operations	$ (15,000)	$ 49,000

177. The expected increase or decrease in 1990 unit sales volume based upon the accounting departments probabilistic assessments is

a. 0%.
b. 7.5%.
c. 5%.
d. 10%.

The correct answer is (c). *(Publisher)*
REQUIRED: The percentage increase or decrease in unit sales volume based upon probabilistic assessments.
DISCUSSION: The effective value of a probability function is the probability times the payoff.

Expected change in	Probability	Payoff
10%	.4	.040
5%	.3	.015
0%	.2	0
-5%	.1	-.005
		.050

178. If the increase in volume is 5% rather than 10% given the price increase of 8%, what will be the 1990 unit contribution margin?

a. $3.925.
b. $3.80.
c. $3.82.
d. $4.00.

The correct answer is (d). *(Publisher)*
REQUIRED: The unit contribution margin given a 5% volume increase.
DISCUSSION: In Q. 174, a contribution margin of $484,000 for 121,000 units (110,000 x 110%) was calculated. Unit contribution margin does not change due to changes in volume but remains at $4.00 ($484,000 ÷ 121,000). Alternatively, in 1989 the sales price was $10.00 ($1,100 ÷ 110) and the unit variable cost was $6.18 ($680 ÷ 110). The sales price increased 8% to $10.80 and the UVC increased 10% to $6.80 ($6.18 x 1.10).

179. What will 1990 profits be given 5% rather than 10% increase in sales volume assuming the 8% price increase?

a. $(36,000).
b. $(58,000).
c. $36,000.
d. $58,000.

The correct answer is (b). *(Publisher)*
REQUIRED: The profits for 1990 given sales volume and price increases.
DISCUSSION: Net income in 1990 will equal sales less variable costs less fixed expenses.

Sales ($1,100,000 x 1.05 x 1.08)	$1,247,400
Less variable costs ($68,000 x 1.10 x 1.05)	785,400
Contribution margin	$ 462,000
Less fixed costs	(520,000)
Expected loss	$ (58,000)

Questions 180 through 186 are based on the Siberian Ski Company, which recently expanded its manufacturing capacity to allow it to produce up to 15,000 pairs of cross-country skis of either the mountaineering model or the touring model. The sales department assures management that it can sell between 9,000 and 13,000 pairs (units) of either product this year. Because the models are very similar, Siberian Ski will produce only one of the two models. The information in the opposite column was compiled by the accounting department.

	Model Mountaineering	Touring
Selling price per unit	$88.00	$80.00
Variable costs per unit	52.80	52.80

Fixed costs will total $369,600 if the mountaineering model is produced but will be only $316,800 if the touring model is produced. Siberian Ski Company is subject to a 40% income tax rate.

180. The contribution margin ratio of the touring model is

a. 40%.
b. 66%.
c. 51.5%.
d. 34%.
e. None of the above.

The correct answer is (d). *(CMA 681 5-1)*
REQUIRED: The contribution margin ratio of one model.
DISCUSSION: The contribution margin ratio is equal to the unit contribution margin (sales price minus unit variable costs) divided by the selling price. Since the touring model has a selling price of $80.00 and variable costs of $52.80, the unit contribution margin is $27.20. The contribution margin ratio is thus 34% ($27.20 ÷ $80.00).

181. If Siberian Ski Company desires an after-tax net income of $24,000, how many pairs of touring model skis will the company have to sell?

a. 13,118.
b. 12,529.
c. 13,853.
d. 4,460.
e. None of the above.

The correct answer is (a). *(CMA 681 5-2)*
REQUIRED: The sales volume in units to earn a targeted after-tax net income.
DISCUSSION: The sales volume (U) necessary to earn a targeted after-tax net income of $24,000 requires calculation of the pretax income. Pretax income is after-tax income divided by 1 minus the tax rate, $24,000 ÷ (1 - .4) = $40,000. Add this amount to fixed costs and divide by the UCM to give the sales in units necessary to reach the desired profit.

$$\frac{\$316,800 + \$40,000}{\$80.00 - \$52.80} = \frac{\$356,800}{\$27.20}$$

$$= 13,118 \text{ units}$$

182. The total sales revenue at which Siberian Ski Company would make the same profit or loss regardless of the ski model it decided to produce is

a. $880,000.
b. $422,400.
c. $924,000.
d. $686,400.
e. None of the above.

The correct answer is (a). *(CMA 681 5-3)*
REQUIRED: The dollar volume sales to produce the same profit (loss) regardless of model.
DISCUSSION: The sales revenue that will generate the same profit or loss regardless of the ski model selected must have the same CM. Accordingly, set the CM equations (S - VC - FC) for each model equal to each other. The VC for the touring model is 66% ($52.80 ÷ $80.00) of sales and FC is $316,800. The VC for the mountaineering model is 60% ($52.80 ÷ $88.00) of sales and FC is $369,600.

$$S - .66S - \$316,800 = S - .60S - \$369,600$$
$$.34S - \$316,800 = .40S - \$369,600$$
$$.06S = \$52,800$$
$$S = \$880,000$$

Module 11.9: Comprehensive

183. If the Siberian Ski Company sales department could guarantee the annual sale of 12,000 skis of either model, Siberian would

a. Produce touring skis because they have a lower fixed cost.

b. Be indifferent as to which model is sold because each model has the same variable cost per unit.

c. Produce only mountaineering skis because they have a lower breakeven point.

d. Be indifferent as to which model is sold because both are profitable.

e. Produce mountaineering skis because they are more profitable.

The correct answer is (e). *(CMA 681 5-4)*
REQUIRED: The most profitable model at a guaranteed sales level.
DISCUSSION: The most profitable model is the one that generates the greatest CM less fixed costs. The company should choose to manufacture the item that is most profitable in total, i.e., the mountaineering model.

	Mountaineering	Touring
Contribution margin:		
12,000 x (88 - 52.80)	$422,400	
12,000 x (80 - 52.80)		$326,400
Fixed costs	369,600	316,800
Net income	$ 52,800	$ 9,600

184. How much would the variable cost per unit of the touring model have to change before it had the same breakeven point in units as the mountaineering model?

a. $2.68/unit increase.

b. $4.53/unit increase.

c. $5.03/unit decrease.

d. $2.97/unit decrease.

e. None of the above.

The correct answer is (d). *(CMA 681 5-5)*
REQUIRED: The required change in one model's VC to match the other model's BEP.
DISCUSSION: First, calculate the BEP (FC ÷ UCM) in units of the mountaineering models:

$369,600 ÷ $35.20 = 10,500 units.

Second, using the same number of units, determine the required UCM for the model:

$316,800 ÷ UCM = 10,500 units
Touring UCM = $30.17

Third, calculate the touring model's variable costs at the new CM:

$80.00 - X = $30.17
X = $49.83
$52.80 - $49.83 = $2.97 decrease

185. If the variable cost per unit of touring skis decreases by 10%, and the total fixed cost of touring skis increases by 10%, the new breakeven point will be

a. Unchanged from 11,648 pairs because the cost changes are equal and offsetting.

b. 10,730 pairs.

c. 13,007 pairs.

d. 12,812 pairs.

e. None of the above.

The correct answer is (b). *(CMA 681 5-6)*
REQUIRED: The revised BEP for one model given a decrease in variable cost and an increase in fixed cost.
DISCUSSION: The revised variable costs will be $52.80 x 90% = $47.52. The new fixed costs will be $316,800 x 110% = $348,480. The revised breakeven point is equal to the new fixed costs divided by the new UCM of $32.48 ($80.00 - $47.52).

$348,480 ÷ $32.48 = 10,730 units

186. Which of the following statements is not an assumption made when employing a cost/volume/profit study for decision analysis?

a. Volume is the only relevant factor affecting costs.

b. Changes in beginning and ending inventory levels are insignificant in amount.

c. Sales mix is variable as total volume changes.

d. Fixed costs are constant over the relevant volume range.

e. Efficiency and productivity are unchanged.

The correct answer is (c). *(CMA 681 5-7)*
REQUIRED: The assumption not made in a cost/volume/profit study.
DISCUSSION: In order to solve CVP problems, items (a), (b), (d), and (e) are assumed to be patterns over which the linear relationship of cost and revenues hold. Sales mix is assumed to be constant, not variable.

Questions 187 through 192 are based on the following information which was presented as part of Question 5 on Part 4 of the June 1978 CMA examination.

Pralina Products Company is a regional firm with three major product lines--cereals, breakfast bars, and dog food. The income statement for the year ended April 30, 1989, is shown below; the statement was prepared by product line using absorption (full) costing. Explanatory data related to the items presented in the income statement appear in the adjoining column.

(000 omitted)

	Cereals	Breakfast Bars	Dog Food	Total
Sales in pounds	2,000	500	500	3,000
Revenue from sales	$1,000	$400	$200	$1,600
Cost of sales				
Raw materials	$ 330	$160	$100	$ 590
Direct labor	90	40	20	150
Factory overhead	108	48	24	180
Total cost of sales	$ 528	$248	$144	$ 920
Gross margin	$ 472	$152	$ 56	$ 680
Operating expenses				
Selling expenses				
Advertising	$ 50	$ 30	$ 20	$ 100
Commissions	50	40	20	110
Salaries and benefits	30	20	10	60
Total selling expenses	$ 130	$ 90	$ 50	$ 270
General and adm. expenses:				
Licenses	$ 50	$ 20	$ 15	$ 85
Salaries and benefits	60	25	15	100
Total general and adm. expenses	$ 110	$ 45	$ 30	$ 185
Total operating expenses	$ 240	$135	$ 80	$ 455
Operating income before taxes	$ 232	$ 17	$(24)	$ 225

1. Cost of sales. The company's inventories of raw materials and finished products do not vary significantly from year to year. The inventories at April 30, 1989, were essentially identical to those at April 30, 1988.

Factory overhead was applied to products at 120% of direct labor dollars. The factory overhead for the 1988-89 fiscal year were as follows:

Variable indirect labor and supplies	$ 15,000
Variable employee benefits on factory labor	30,000
Supervisory salaries and related benefits	35,000
Plant occupancy costs	100,000
Total factory overhead	$180,000

Pralina had no over- or underapplied overhead at year-end.

2. Advertising. The company has been unable to determine any direct causal relationship between the level of sales volume and the level of advertising expenditures. Because management believes advertising is necessary, however, an annual advertising program is implemented for each product line. Each product line is advertised independently of the others.

3. Commissions. Sales commissions are paid at the rates of 5% on the cereals and 10% on the breakfast bars and dog food.

4. Licenses. The various licenses required for each product line are renewed annually.

5. Salaries and related benefits. Sales and general and administrative personnel devote time and effort to all product lines. Salaries and wages are allocated on the basis of management's estimates of time spent on each product line.

187. What is the total variable factory overhead used by all three products?

 a. $45,000.
 b. $180,000.
 c. $90,000.
 d. $52,000.

The correct answer is (a). *(Publisher)*
REQUIRED: The total variable factory overhead.
DISCUSSION: The total variable factory overhead is $45,000, which is the sum of variable indirect labor and supplies ($15,000) plus the variable employee benefits on factory labor ($30,000). Plant occupancy costs are clearly fixed. Supervisory salaries and benefits are also fixed, because presumably they do not vary with activity level.

Module 11.9: Comprehensive

188. What is the manufacturing contribution margin for dog food?

a. $148,000.
b. $74,000.
c. $56,000.
d. $112,000.

The correct answer is (b). *(Publisher)*
REQUIRED: The manufacturing contribution margin for one product.
DISCUSSION: The manufacturing CM is equal to the revenue from sales less variable manufacturing costs. Sales of dog food are given as $200,000. Variable manufacturing costs include raw materials ($100,000), direct labor ($20,000), and variable factory O/H ($24,000 x 25% = $6,000), for total variable manufacturing costs of $126,000. Note that $45,000 ($15,000 + $30,000) or 25% ($45,000 ÷ $180,000) of factory O/H is variable. The manufacturing CM thus equals $74,000 ($200,000 - $126,000).

189. What is the cereal's contribution margin to operating income? Assume both advertising and licensing are variable costs.

a. $503,000.
b. $403,000.
c. $447,000.
d. $520,000.

The correct answer is (b). *(Publisher)*
REQUIRED: The contribution margin of one product to operating income.
DISCUSSION: The product contribution margin is equal to the revenue from the product less variable manufacturing costs, other variable costs, and any direct operating expenses.

Revenue from sales	$1,000,000
Variable manufacturing costs:	
Raw materials	330,000
Direct labor	90,000
Variable O/H ($108,000 x 25%)	27,000
Total variable mfg. costs	$ 447,000
Manufacturing CM	$ 553,000
Other variable costs:	
Commissions	(50,000)
Contribution margin	$ 503,000
Direct operating expenses:	
Advertising	$ 50,000
Licenses	50,000
Total direct operating expenses	$ 100,000
Product contribution	$ 403,000

190. What is the total manufacturing contribution margin?

a. $553,000.
b. $225,000.
c. $815,000.
d. $705,000.

The correct answer is (c). *(Publisher)*
REQUIRED: The total manufacturing contribution margin for three products.
DISCUSSION: The total manufacturing contribution margin is equal to total sales less total variable manufacturing costs.

Revenue from sales	$1,600,000
Variable manufacturing costs	
Raw materials	590,000
Direct labor	150,000
Variable O/H ($180,000 x 25%)	45,000
Total variable manufacturing costs	$ 785,000
Manufacturing CM	$ 815,000

> Questions 191 and 192 are based on the information presented on page 278.

191. The advantages of cost/volume/profit analysis include

a. Assisting management in planning sales volume and profitability.
b. Identifying products that can easily support an increase in sales promotion expense.
c. Assisting in the decision process to eliminate a product line.
d. Accepting or rejecting a special order at a special price.
e. All of the above.

The correct answer is (e). *(Publisher)*
REQUIRED: The advantage(s) of CVP analysis.
DISCUSSION: The advantages of CVP analysis for Pralina include each of the items. The determination of the contribution margin of each product as well as the total CM for all products will assist management in planning sales volume and profitability. This includes the calculation of a BEP. The identification of products that can support heavy sales promotion expenditures or assist in the process of targeting advertising. CVP analysis will assist Pralina in decisions relating to adding or eliminating a product or a product line. Finally, CVP analysis will help determine whether to accept special orders and at what price.

192. What are the difficulties Pralina could expect to have when using CVP analysis?

a. The separation of mixed costs into the fixed and variable components.
b. The decision on how to treat joint and/or common costs.
c. The estimation of efficiency and productivity within the relevant range as well as setting the relevant range itself.
d. The probabilities that a constant sales mix will occur within the relevant range and what that constant sales mix is.
e. All of the above.

The correct answer is (e). *(Publisher)*
REQUIRED: The difficulties in using CVP analysis.
DISCUSSION: All of the items suggest difficulties in applying CVP analysis. CVP analysis is based on a series of assumptions, including the ability to estimate the relevant range, to keep the sales mix constant, and to separate mixed costs into fixed and variable components. Each of these assumptions requires a substantial amount of judgment on the part of management.

> Questions 193 through 198 are based on the Able Company, which has one department that produces three replacement parts for the company. However, only one part can be produced in any month because of the adjustments that must be made to the equipment. The department can produce up to 15,000 units of any one of the three parts in each month. The company expresses the monthly after tax cost/volume/profit relationships for each part using an equation method. The format of the equations and the equation for each replacement part are given in the opposite column.

$$(ATR) \times [(SP - VC) \times (U) - FC]$$

ATR = after-tax rate
SP = selling price
VC = variable cost
U = units
FC = fixed costs

Part	Part Equations
AL45	.6 [($4.00 - $1.25)(U) - $33,400]
BT62	.6 [($4.05 - $2.55)(U) - $15,000]
GM17	.6 [($4.10 - $2.00)(U) - $22,365]

193. The contribution margin per unit for Part BT62 is

a. $4.05.
b. $2.55.
c. $0.50.
d. $1.50.
e. Not determinable from these facts.

The correct answer is (d). *(CMA 682 4-10)*
REQUIRED: The unit contribution margin for one of three products.
DISCUSSION: The UCM is equal to the selling price less the variable costs per unit. Given the selling price of $4.05 and variable costs of $2.55, Part BT62's unit contribution margin is $1.50 ($4.05 - $2.55).

Module 11.9: Comprehensive

194. The breakeven volume in units for Part GM17 is

a. 10,650 units.
b. 6,390 units.
c. 17,750 units.
d. 13,419 units.
e. None of the above.

The correct answer is (a). *(CMA 682 4-11)*
REQUIRED: The breakeven volume in units for one of the products.
DISCUSSION: The breakeven volume in units is found by dividing the fixed costs by the UCM. Fixed costs for Part GM17 equal $22,365. The UCM is $2.10 ($4.10 - $2.00).

$$\frac{\$22,365}{\$2.10} = 10,650 \text{ BEP units}$$

195. If Able Company produces and sells 13,000 units of Part AL45, the amount of Able's after-tax net income attributable to this product would be

a. $8,090.
b. $2,350.
c. $1,410.
d. $940.
e. None of the above.

The correct answer is (c). *(CMA 682 4-12)*
REQUIRED: The after-tax net income for sale of a given volume of the third product.
DISCUSSION: The after-tax net income attributable to 13,000 units of Part AL45 is calculated first by finding the revenue less variable costs less fixed costs, and then adjusting for taxes. Given that the tax rate is 40%, the after-tax rate is 60%, or .60.

$$13,000(\$4 - \$1.25) - \$33,400 = \$2,350$$
$$.6(\$2,350) = \$1,410$$

196. The number of units of Part BT62 required to be produced and sold to contribute $4,140 to Able's net income after-tax is

a. 14,600 units.
b. 12,800 units.
c. 5,400 units.
d. 9,000 units.
e. None of the above.

The correct answer is (a). *(CMA 682 4-13)*
REQUIRED: The number of units of one product to be sold to generate a targeted after-tax income.
DISCUSSION: The desired after-tax net income divided by (1 - tax rate) gives the necessary pre-tax income ($6,900). Then add fixed cost ($15,000) and divide by the UCM to obtain the BEP in units.

$$\frac{\$21,900}{\$4.05 - \$2.55} = 14,600 \text{ units of BT62}$$

197. The production and unit sales volume level at which Able Company will be indifferent as to whether Part BT62 or GM17 is produced is

a. 7,365 units.
b. 4,092 units.
c. 10,380 units.
d. 12,275 units.
e. None of the above.

The correct answer is (d). *(CMA 682 4-14)*
REQUIRED: The unit sales volume at which two parts are equally profitable.
DISCUSSION: The company does not care which product it produces if they are equally profitable. Therefore, set the CM equations of the parts equal to each other.

$$\text{CM for BT62} = \text{CM for GM17}$$
$$(\$4.05 - \$2.55)U - \$15,000 = (\$4.10 - \$2.00)U - \$22,365$$
$$\$1.50U - \$15,000 = \$2.10U - \$22,365$$
$$\$7,365 = \$.60U$$
$$12,275 = U$$

198. The maximum monthly contribution to Able's after-tax net income that can be realized when production in this department is at capacity is

a. $4,710.
b. $4,500.
c. $5,481.
d. $9,135.
e. None of the above.

The correct answer is (c). *(CMA 682 4-15)*
REQUIRED: The maximum effect on after-tax net income.
DISCUSSION: The department can produce up to 15,000 units of any one of the parts each month. The maximum effect on Able's after-tax net income is thus determined by taking each part and computing the after-tax income at 15,000 units for each.

AL45: .6 [($4.00 - $1.25)(15,000) - $33,400] = $4,710
BT62: .6 [($4.05 - $2.55)(15,000) - $15,000] = $4,500
GM17: .6 [($4.10 - $2.00)(15,000) - $22,365] = $5,481

Questions 199 through 207 are based on the following information, which was presented as part of Question 4 on Part 5 of the December 1977 CMA examination.

The Keylo Co. manufactures a line of plastic products that are sold through hardware stores. The company sales have declined slightly for the past 2 years leaving them with idle plants and equipment.

A Keylo engineer met a former college classmate while attending a recent convention of machinery builders. The classmate is employed by the Paddington Co., which is also in the plastic products business. During the course of their conversation it became evident that Keylo might be able to make a particular product for Paddington with the currently unused equipment and space.

The following requirements were specified by Paddington for the new product:

1. Paddington needs 80,000 units per year for the next 3 years.
2. The product is to be built to Paddington specifications.
3. Keylo is not to enter into the independent production of the product during the 3-year contract.
4. Paddington would provide Keylo, without charge, a special machine to finish the product. The machine becomes the property of Keylo at the end of the 3-year period.

Although Keylo is not operating at capacity, the company generated a profit last year as shown in the income statement presented in the opposite column.

The Keylo engineering, production, and accounting departments agreed upon the following facts if the contracts were accepted:

1. Manufacturing
   a. The present idle capacity would be fully used.
   b. One additional supervisor would be required; the annual salary would be $15,000 at the present rates.
   c. The annual requirements for material and labor would increase by 10% at current prices.
   d. The power and supply requirements would increase 10% at current prices due to the reactivation of idle machines.
   e. The machine provided by Paddington would increase the annual power and supply costs by $10,000 and $4,000, respectively, at current prices.
   f. The Paddington machine would have no value to Keylo at the end of the contract.

2. General administration: No additional general administrative costs would be incurred.

3. Sales: Other than a sales commission of $10,000 paid to the salespersons arranging the contract, no additional sales administrative costs would be incurred.

4. Other information:
   a. Estimated cost increases due to inflation for the entire 3-year period are

   - Material   5%
   - Labor   10%
   - Power   20%
   - Depreciation   0
   - Sales commissions 0
   - Income taxes   0
   - All other items 10%

   b. Inventory balances which have remained stable for the past 3 years will not be increased or decreased by the production of the new product.

Keylo Co.
Income Statement
For the Fiscal Year Ended October 31
(000 omitted)

	$ Amount	Percent
Sales	$1,500	100%
Cost of goods sold		
Material	$ 200	13%
Direct labor	400	27
Overhead (1)	390	26
Cost of goods sold	$ 990	66%
Manufacturing margin		
before unapplied overhead	$ 510	34%
Unapplied manufacturing		
overhead (2)	(10)	(1)
Manufacturing margin	$ 500	33%
Operating expenses		
Sales commissions	$ 60	4%
Sales administration	30	2
General administration	110	7
Total operating expenses	$ 200	13%
Net income before		
income taxes	$ 300	20%
Income taxes (40%)	(120)	(8)
Net income	$ 180	12%

(1) Schedule of Manufacturing Overhead
   Variable
   Indirect labor $100
   Supplies   40
   Power   120
   Fixed costs applied
   Administration   60
   Depreciation   70
                          $390

(2) Schedule of Unapplied Manufacturing Overhead (due to idle capacity)
   Depreciation $10

Module 11.9: Comprehensive

199. What would be the incremental cost for material?

a. $63,000.
b. $53,000.
c. $132,000.
d. $73,000.

The correct answer is (a). *(Publisher)*
REQUIRED: The incremental cost for material of producing a special order.
DISCUSSION: The incremental costs are the cost changes due to the contract increase and to the inflation rate.

(000 omitted)	Material
Current amounts	$ 200
Contract increase	x 10%
Inflation factor	x 1.05
Years	x 3
Incremental cost	$63.0

200. What is the incremental cost for direct labor?

a. $132,000.
b. $120,000.
c. $63,000.
d. $53,000.

The correct answer is (a). *(Publisher)*
REQUIRED: The incremental cost for direct labor of producing a special order.
DISCUSSION: The incremental costs are the cost changes due to the contract increase and to the inflation rate.

(000 omitted)	Direct Labor
Current amounts	$ 400
Contract increase	x 10%
Inflation factor	x 1.10
Years	x 3
Incremental cost	$132.0

201. What would be the incremental cost for supplies?

a. $56,400.
b. $26,400.
c. $49,200.
d. $36,400.

The correct answer is (b). *(Publisher)*
REQUIRED: The incremental cost for supplies.
DISCUSSION: The incremental costs are the cost changes due to the contract increase and to the inflation rate. Note that Keylo's own increased requirement levels of power must be added to the increases needed for Paddington's machine.

(000 omitted)	Supplies	Additional Supplies
Current amounts	$ 40	$ -0-
Contract increase	x 10%	$ 4
Inflation factor	x 1.10	x 1.10
Years	x 3	x 3
Incremental costs	$ 13.2 +	$ 13.2 = $26.4

202. What would be the incremental cost for power?

a. $79,200.
b. $14,400.
c. $81,000.
d. $85,500.

The correct answer is (a). *(Publisher)*
REQUIRED: The incremental cost for power.
DISCUSSION: The incremental costs are the cost changes due to the contract increase and to the inflation rate. Note that Keylo's own increased requirement levels of power must be added to the increases needed for Paddington's machine.

(000 omitted)	Power	Additional Power
Current amounts	$ 120	$ -0-
Contract increase	x 10%	$ 10
Inflation factor	x 1.20	x 1.20
Years	x 3	x 3
Incremental costs	$ 43.2 +	$ 36.0 = $79.2

Questions 203 through 205 are based on the information presented on page 282.

203. What would be the incremental cost for supervision?

a. $56,400.
b. $26,400.
c. $49,500.
d. $36,500.

The correct answer is (c). *(Publisher)*
REQUIRED: The incremental cost for supervision.
DISCUSSION: The incremental costs are the cost changes due to the contract increase and to the inflation rate. The additional supervisor's salary of $15,000 constitutes an increase in administrative costs under the new contract.

(000 omitted)	Administration
Contract increase	$ 15
Inflation factor	x 1.10
Years	x 3
Amount	$ 49.5

204. What would be the incremental cost for sales commission?

a. $2,400.
b. $3,600.
c. $6,000.
d. $10,000.

The correct answer is (d). *(Publisher)*
REQUIRED: The incremental cost for sales commission.
DISCUSSION: The sales commission cost is $10,000 for arranging the contract as specified in the problem.

205. If the order did not contribute to net income after taxes, what would be the total price?

a. $432,120.
b. $360,100.
c. $144,000.
d. $430,100.

The correct answer is (b). *(Publisher)*
REQUIRED: The breakeven point from the 3-year order.
DISCUSSION: The BEP from the 3-year order is the selling price equal to the incremental costs. Since, in effect, Keylo would be trading dollars, the BEP sales price would be $360,100, the amount of the incremental costs.

Material	$ 63,000
Direct labor	132,000
Indirect labor	--
Supplies	13,200
Additional supplies	13,200
Power	43,200
Additional power	36,000
Administration	49,500
Depreciation (applied & unapplied)	--
Sales commission	10,000
	$360,100

Module 11.9: Comprehensive

> Questions 206 and 207 are based on the information presented on page 282.

206. What price should Keylo set for the 3-year order (240,000 units) if the company wants to make 10% after taxes?

a. $216,060.

b. $432,120.

c. $430,100.

d. $144,000.

The correct answer is (b). *(Publisher)*
REQUIRED: The sales price necessary to earn a targeted after-tax income.
DISCUSSION: The total sales price(s) is the sum of the incremental costs plus 10% of sales plus taxes. Taxes equal .40 (sales - incremental costs).

$$S = \$360{,}100 + .1S + .4(S - \$360{,}100)$$
$$S = \$360{,}100 + .1S + .4S - \$144{,}040$$
$$.5S = \$216{,}060$$
$$S = \$432{,}120$$

207. What variable does the incremental cost analysis discussion on page 282 ignore?

a. Indirect labor.

b. Depreciation.

c. Administration expense.

d. Time value of money.

The correct answer is (d). *(Publisher)*
REQUIRED: The variable that the incremental cost analysis ignores.
DISCUSSION: The incremental cost analysis assumes that the monies received that are for sales of new products are paid continuously as there is no discounting or adjusting for timing of incremental payments out and incremental receipts in.
Answer (a) is incorrect because there is no indirect labor involved with this project. Answers (b) and (c) are incorrect because each is included in the analysis.

Questions 208 through 215 are based on the following information, which was presented as part of Question 3 on Part 5 of the June 1980 CMA examination.

Stac Industries is a multi-product company with several manufacturing plants. The Clinton Plant manufactures and distributes two household cleaning and polishing compounds--regular and heavy duty--under the Cleen-Brite label. The forecasted operating results for the first 6 months of the year when 100,000 cases of each compound are expected to be manufactured and sold are presented in the following statement.

Cleen-Brite Compounds - Clinton Plant
Forecasted Results of Operations
For the 6-Month Period Ending June 30
(000 omitted)

	Regular	Heavy Duty	Total
Sales	$2,000	$3,000	$5,000
Cost of sales	1,600	1,900	3,500
Gross profit	$ 400	$1,100	$1,500
Selling and adm. expenses			
Variable	$ 400	$ 700	$1,100
Fixed*	240	360	600
Total S&A expenses	$ 640	$1,060	$1,700
Income (loss) before taxes	$ (240)	$ 40	$ (200)

* The fixed selling and administrative expenses are allocated between the two products on the basis of dollar sales volume on the internal reports.

The regular compound sold for $20 a case and the heavy duty sold for $30 a case during the first 6 months. The manufacturing costs by case of product are presented in the schedule at the top of the next column. Each product is manufactured on a separate production line. Annual normal manufacturing capacity is 200,000 cases of each product. However, the plant is capable of producing 250,000 cases of regular compound and 350,000 cases of heavy duty compound annually.

	Cost per Case	
	Regular	Heavy Duty
Raw materials	$ 7	$ 8
Direct labor	4	4
Variable manufacturing overhead	1	2
Fixed manufacturing overhead*	4	5
Total manufacturing cost	$16	$19
Variable selling and administrative costs	$ 4	$ 7

* Depreciation charges are 50% of the fixed manufacturing overhead of each line.

The schedule below reflects the consensus of top management regarding the price/volume alternatives for the Cleen-Brite products for the last 6 months of the year. They are essentially the same alternatives management had during the first 6 months of the year.

Regular Compound		Heavy Duty Compound	
Alternative Prices (per case)	Sales Volume (in cases)	Alternative Prices (per case)	Sales Volume (in cases)
$18	120,000	$25	175,000
20	100,000	27	140,000
21	90,000	30	100,000
22	80,000	32	55,000
23	50,000	35	35,000

Top management believes the loss for the first 6 months reflects a tight profit margin caused by intense competition. Management also believes that many companies will be forced out of this market by next year and profits should improve.

---

208. What is the variable cost per case for the regular compound?

a. $11.
b. $12.
c. $14.
d. $16.
e. $20.

The correct answer is (d). *(Publisher)*
REQUIRED: The variable cost per case of regular compound.
DISCUSSION: The variable cost is $16 which consists of

Raw materials	$ 7
Direct labor	4
Variable O/H	1
Variable S&A	4
	$16

Module 11.9: Comprehensive

209. What price should Stac select to maximize sales revenues from the regular compound?

a. $18.
b. $20.
c. $21.
d. $22.
e. $23.

The correct answer is (a). *(Publisher)*
REQUIRED: Selling price per regular case to maximize sales.
DISCUSSION: Compute the expected sales of each of the five possible sales prices given.

Selling price per case	$18	$20	$21	$22	$23
	120	100	90	80	50
	$2,160	$2,000	$1,890	$1,760	$1,150

A sales price of $18 results in the greatest sales revenue.

210. What price should Stac select for the regular compound?

a. $18.
b. $20.
c. $21.
d. $22.
e. $23.

The correct answer is (d). *(Publisher)*
REQUIRED: The price to generate the maximum CM for one product.
DISCUSSION: The appropriate calculation involves comparing the CM per case times the volume in cases at each alternative and choosing the selling price with the highest CM. Variable costs per case of regular compound are $16 ($7 raw materials + $4 direct labor + $1 variable O/H + $4 variable S&A).

Selling price per case	$18	$20	$21	$22	$23
Variable cost per case	16	16	16	16	16
CM per case	$2	$4	$5	$6	$7
Volume in cases (000 omitted)	120	100	90	80	50
Total CM (000 omitted)	$240	$400	$450	$480	$350

211. What is the contribution margin per case for the heavy duty compound at a $27 selling price?

a. $4.
b. $6.
c. $11.
d. $21.
e. $22.

The correct answer is (b). *(Publisher)*
REQUIRED: The contribution margin per case of heavy duty compound when sold for $27.
DISCUSSION: The variable cost is $21 ($8 material, $4 labor, $2 variable O/H, and $7 variable S&A). Subtract the $21 VC from the $27 selling price to determine UCM of $6.

212. At the sales price of $25, what is the expected net income (loss) before taxes from sales of the heavy duty compound assuming the dollar sales of regular compound equaled the sales of heavy duty compound?

a. $(100,000).
b. $400,000.
c. $660,000.
d. $900,000.

The correct answer is (a). *(Publisher)*
REQUIRED: The net income (loss) before taxes from the sale of heavy duty compound.
DISCUSSION: Assuming the sales of regular compound are equal to the sales of heavy duty compound allows for a 50-50 allocation of the $600,000 of fixed S&A cost. Fixed manufacturing cost for the year is $1,000,000 ($5/unit x 200,000 normal capacity). For the second 6 months, the amount is therefore $500,000.

Sales ($25 x 175,000)	$4,375,000
Variable costs ($21 x 175,000)	3,675,000
CM	$ 700,000
Fixed S&A overhead	(300,000)
Fixed manufacturing overhead	(500,000)
Expected loss	$ (100,000)

Questions 213 through 215 are based on the information presented on page 286.

213. What price should Stac select for the heavy duty compound?

a. $25.
b. $27.
c. $30.
d. $32.
e. $35.

The correct answer is (c). *(Publisher)*
REQUIRED: The price to generate the maximum CM for the other product.
DISCUSSION: The appropriate calculation involves comparing the CM per case times the volume in cases at each alternative and choosing the selling price with the highest CM. Variable costs per case of heavy duty compounds are $21 ($8 raw materials + $4 direct labor + $2 variable O/H + $7 variable S&A).

Selling price per case	$25	$27	$30	$32	$35
Variable cost per case	21	21	21	21	21
CM per case	$4	$6	$9	$11	$14
Volume in cases (000 omitted)	175	140	100	55	35
Total CM (000 omitted)	$700	$840	$900	$605	$490

214. What is the total contribution margin for the regular compound if Stac sells 50,000 units at $23 per unit?

a. $350,000.
b. $550,000.
c. $800,000.
d. $420,000.

The correct answer is (a). *(Publisher)*
REQUIRED: The total contribution margin generated by one product at a given sales volume and price.
DISCUSSION: The total CM for the regular compound generated by selling 50,000 units at a price of $23 per unit is equal to the total selling price less all variable costs.

	(000 omitted)
Sales	$1,150
Variable costs	
S&A (50,000 x $4)	$200
Manufacturing [50,000 x ($7 + $4 + $1)]	600
Total variable costs	$800
Contribution margin	$350

215. What is the total variable cost for the heavy duty compound if Stac sells 35,000 units at $35 per unit?

a. $800,000.
b. $735,000.
c. $1,225,000.
d. $490,000.

The correct answer is (b). *(Publisher)*
REQUIRED: The total variable cost for the other product at a given sales volume and price.
DISCUSSION: The variable costs for the heavy duty compound total $21 per case, as computed in Q. 213. The total variable cost at a sales volume of 35,000 is thus $735,000 (35,000 x $21 VC/unit).

CHAPTER TWELVE
BUDGETING

| 12.1 Budget Definitions .... (33 questions) | 289 |
| 12.2 Budgeting Computations .... (45 questions) | 297 |

Budgeting is an outgrowth of cost/volume/profit analysis. The static budget is a base budget from which to generate flexible budgets. In addition, master budgets encompassing the entire firm are covered, with special emphasis on cash budgets.

12.1 Budget Definitions

1. A budget is
   a. A quantitative expression of a plan.
   b. An aid to planning.
   c. An aid to coordination.
   d. An aid to control.
   e. All of the above.

The correct answer is (e). *(Publisher)*
REQUIRED: The true statement(s) about a budget.
DISCUSSION: A budget contains all the elements listed. A budget is a quantitative model of a plan of action as conceptualized by management. A budget functions as an aid to planning, coordination, and control, and will help the organization operate effectively.

2. A master budget contains all of the following budgets except
   a. Sales budget.
   b. Production budget.
   c. Distribution budget.
   d. Estimation of competitor activity.
   e. Finance budget.

The correct answer is (d). *(Publisher)*
REQUIRED: The type of budget(s) not included in a master budget.
DISCUSSION: A master budget has all other budgets as subsets. Thus, the quantification of estimates and forecasts by management from all functional areas are contained in the master budget. These results are then put together into a formal quantitative model recognizing the organization's objectives, inputs, and outputs. Note that other organizations' activities are not reflected in an organization's budget.

3. Budgets in not-for-profit organizations serve as
   a. Authorization for management behavior and constraints upon that behavior.
   b. Planning documents.
   c. Tools to motivate management.
   d. The planning and control function.
   e. All of the above.

The correct answer is (e). *(Publisher)*
REQUIRED: The use(s) of budgets in not-for-profit organizations.
DISCUSSION: Not-for-profit organizations use budgets in a similar manner as for-profit organizations, and also use them as authorization and constraint devices for management behavior.

4. Which of the following is usually perceived as being budget's greatest advantage to management?
   a. Performance analysis.
   b. Increased communication.
   c. Increased coordination.
   d. Required planning.

The correct answer is (d). *(Publisher)*
REQUIRED: The major contribution of budgeting to management.
DISCUSSION: Managers in a formal budget setting are forced to examine the future and be prepared to respond to future conditions. Without budgets, many operations would fail because of inadequate planning.

290   Module 12.1: Budget Definitions

5. A planning calendar in budgeting is the

   a. Calendar period covered by the budget.
   b. Schedule of activities for the development and adoption of the budget.
   c. Calendar period covered by the annual budget and the long-range plan.
   d. Sales forecast by months in the annual budget period.
   e. Schedule of dates at which goals are to be met.

The correct answer is (b). *(CMA 683 4-4)*
REQUIRED: The definition of a planning calendar in budgeting.
DISCUSSION: According to MAP Statement on Management Accounting No. 2, a planning calendar is a list of dates indicating when specific information useful in the preparation of a budget is to be presented by one information source to others. The calendar is so structured that information accumulates until the complete budget is issued at a specified date.
Answers (a), (c), (d), and (e) are incorrect because each concerns the period covered by the budget itself rather than the period during which the budget is prepared.

6. The primary variable affecting active participation and commitment to the budget and the control system is

   a. Management efforts to achieve the budget rather than optimize results.
   b. The rigid adherence to the budget without recognizing changing conditions.
   c. Top management involvement in support of the budget.
   d. The opportunity budgeting gives to ambitious managers for department growth.

The correct answer is (c). *(Publisher)*
REQUIRED: The primary variable affecting budget participation and commitment.
DISCUSSION: Top management involvement in support of the budget/control system is absolutely vital for the continued success of the operation. The attitude of top management will affect the implementation of the budget and control system because lower level management will recognize and reflect top management's attitude.
Answer (a) is incorrect because "managing to a budget" can result in suboptimal achievement. Answer (b) is incorrect because rigid adherence to the budget could prevent a manager from taking an appropriate action and thus miss a profitable opportunity. Answer (d) is incorrect because budgets should not help individuals build empires.

7. The goals and objectives upon which an annual profit plan is based should be limited to

   a. Financial measures such as net income, return on investment, earnings per share, etc.
   b. Quantitative measures such as growth in unit sales, number of employees, manufacturing capacity, etc.
   c. Qualitative measures of organizational activity such as product innovation leadership, product quality levels, product safety, etc.
   d. The financial and quantitative measures.
   e. A combination of financial, quantitative, and qualitative measures.

The correct answer is (e). *(CMA 683 4-6)*
REQUIRED: The goals and objectives upon which an annual profit plan should be based.
DISCUSSION: A profit plan should be based on financial, quantitative, and qualitative measures such as all of those listed. The profit plan is merely a tool for achieving the organization's goals as established by top management. Accordingly, the goals and objectives of the profit plan are only as limited as those of the organization.

8. Organizations have various names for budgets that have been estimated into the future. Profit planning is one of those terms. Another term for budgeted financial statements is

   a. Inflation-adjusted budgets.
   b. Pro forma budgets.
   c. Sample budgets.
   d. Historical budgets.

The correct answer is (b). *(Publisher)*
REQUIRED: An alternate term for budgeted financial statements.
DISCUSSION: Budgeted financial statements are sometimes referred to as pro forma budgets as well as profit plans. These are probably the most frequently used terms.

Module 12.1: Budget Definitions

9. Which of the following would not normally be included in the operating budget of a firm?

   a. Direct materials budget.
   b. Selling expense budget.
   c. Budgeted balance sheet.
   d. Sales budget.

The correct answer is (c). *(Publisher)*
REQUIRED: The item not normally included in an operating budget.
DISCUSSION: An operating budget normally includes the sales, production, selling and administrative, and budgeted income statement components. The budgeted balance sheet is not normally part of the operating budget.

10. Which of the following is not normally included in the financial budget?

   a. Capital budget.
   b. Cash budget.
   c. Selling expense budget.
   d. Budgeted statement of changes in financial position.
   e. Budgeted balance sheet.

The correct answer is (c). *(Publisher)*
REQUIRED: The item not normally included in a financial budget.
DISCUSSION: The financial budget normally includes the capital budget, the cash budget, the budgeted balance sheet, and the budgeted statement of changes in financial position. The selling expense budget would normally be included in an operating budget, not a financial budget.

11. The usual starting point for a master budget is

   a. The production budget.
   b. The selling expense budget.
   c. The sales forecast.
   d. The direct materials budget.

The correct answer is (c). *(Publisher)*
REQUIRED: The beginning point in a master budget.
DISCUSSION: Normally, the master budget is geared to estimated sales. Management must thus begin the budgeting process by determining the estimated activity level. The other budgets will flow from the estimated sales budget; i.e., the production, the resulting inventory levels, and other activities will all have budgets geared to what must be generated for estimated sales.

12. In preparing a cash budget, which of the following is normally the starting point for projecting cash requirements?

   a. Fixed assets.
   b. Sales.
   c. Accounts receivable.
   d. Inventories.

The correct answer is (b). *(CIA 587 IV-39)*
REQUIRED: The starting point for projecting cash requirements.
DISCUSSION: The cash budget details projected receipts and disbursements. It is based on the projected sales level because cash flows are budgeted based on sales. The timing and amounts of receipts from credit as well as cash sales must be determined. Cash disbursements are a function of the production and other activities needed to support expected sales.
Answers (a), (c), and (d) are incorrect because each is estimated after sales are predicted; e.g., fixed assets should be acquired that are necessary to meet expected demand.

13. In estimating the sales volume for a master budget, which of the following techniques may be used to improve the estimate?

   a. Group discussions among management.
   b. Statistical analyses, including regression analysis.
   c. Econometric studies.
   d. Estimating from previous sales volume.
   e. All of the above.

The correct answer is (e). *(Publisher)*
REQUIRED: Technique(s) used to improve the sales volume estimate.
DISCUSSION: The many elements of forecasting sales volume include management analysis and opinions, statistical analyses (including regression analysis), econometric studies, and previous sales volume and market history. Other economic indicators, including general economic indications and industry economic indicators, may also be used. Market research studies may be employed. The firm may have an unfilled order book from which it can estimate the amount of work necessary to complete the orders on hand. Regardless of the methods used, the key is that a great deal of subjectivity enters into the budget process.

Module 12.1: Budget Definitions

14. The primary role of the budget director and the budgeting department is to

a. Settle disputes among operating executives during the development of the annual operating plan.
b. Develop the annual profit plan by selecting the alternatives to be adopted from the suggestions submitted by the various operating segments.
c. Justify the budget to the executive committee of the board of directors.
d. Compile the budget and manage the budget process.
e. Force the final profit plan to conform to top management goals.

The correct answer is (d). *(CMA 683 4-2)*
REQUIRED: The primary role of the budget director and the budgeting department.
DISCUSSION: The budgeting department is responsible for compiling the budget and managing the budget process. The budget director and the department are not responsible for actually developing the estimates on which the budget is based. This role is performed by those to whom the resulting budget will be applicable.
Answers (a), (b), and (c) are incorrect because the budget director has staff, not line, authority. (S)he has a technical and advisory role. The final decision-making responsibility rests with line management. Answer (e) is incorrect because the budgeting department must work with estimates provided by line managers and is in no position to affect projected profitability.

15. Rough Rapids Manufacturing currently uses the company budget only as a planning tool. Management has decided that it would be beneficial to also use budgets for control purposes. In order to implement this change, the management accountant must

a. Organize a budget committee.
b. Appoint a budget director.
c. Report daily to operating management all deviations from plan.
d. Synchronize the budgeting and accounting system with the organizational structure.
e. Develop forecasting procedures.

The correct answer is (d). *(CMA 686 4-17)*
REQUIRED: The action required to use a planning budget for control purposes.
DISCUSSION: A budget is a means of control because it sets cost guidelines with which actual performance can be compared. The feedback provided by comparison of actual and budgeted performance reveals whether a manager has used company assets efficiently. If a budget is to be used for control purposes, however, the accounting system must be designed to produce information required for the control process. Moreover, the budgeting and accounting system must be related to the organizational structure so that variances will be assigned to the proper individuals.
Answers (a) and (b) are incorrect because a budget director and committee are needed even if a budget is to be used only for planning. Answer (c) is incorrect because daily reporting is usually not necessary. Also, reporting all deviations would not be cost beneficial. Answer (e) is incorrect because the company should already be using forecasting procedures if the budget is being used as a planning tool.

16. When an organization prepares a forecast, it

a. Presents a statement of expectations for a period of time but does not present a firm commitment.
b. Consolidates the plans of the separate requests into one overall plan.
c. Presents the plan for a range of activity so that the plan can be adjusted for changes in activity levels.
d. Classifies budget requests by activity and estimates the benefits arising from each activity.
e. Divides the activities of individual responsibility centers into a series of packages which are ranked ordinally.

The correct answer is (a). *(CMA 679 4-10)*
REQUIRED: The function performed by a forecast.
DISCUSSION: A forecast is a statement of expectations for a period of time. It is the best estimate at a point in time, given a set of assumptions, but makes no firm commitment.
Answer (b) is incorrect because it describes an overall budget. Answer (c) is incorrect because it describes a flexible budget. Answer (d) is incorrect because it describes a program planning and budgeting system (PPBS). Answer (e) is incorrect because it describes one aspect of a zero-based budget (ZBB).

Module 12.1: Budget Definitions

17. A distinction between forecasting and planning

a. Is not valid because they are synonyms.
b. Arises because they are based upon different assumptions about economic events.
c. Results from the use of forecasts in planning.
d. Is that forecasting is a management activity while planning is a technical activity.
e. Is that forecasting relies exclusively on statistical techniques while planning does not.

The correct answer is (c). *(CMA 683 4-1)*
REQUIRED: The distinction between forecasting and planning.
DISCUSSION: Planning is defined (according to MAP Statement on Management Accounting No. 2) as the process of seeking out alternative courses of action, evaluating them by various techniques, including forecasting, and deciding which actions to take to attain goals. Forecasting is defined as a process of predicting or projecting a future event or condition.
Answer (a) is incorrect because the terms are not synonyms. Answer (b) is incorrect because planning and forecasting are based on the same underlying assumptions. Answers (d) and (e) are incorrect because planning and forecasting are both management activities that may be based on statistical techniques.

18. The concept of "management by exception" refers to management's

a. Consideration of only those items that vary materially from plans.
b. Consideration of only rare events.
c. Consideration of items selected at random.
d. Lack of a predetermined plan.

The correct answer is (a). *(CPA 1172 T-30)*
REQUIRED: The item exemplifying the concept of "management by exception."
DISCUSSION: Under management by exception, primary emphasis is placed upon those results differing from plans. Management does not have time to examine every deviation, so material items become the focal point.
Answer (b) is incorrect because management by exception examines all events which differ significantly from plans whether rare or frequent. Answer (c) is incorrect because selection of random items may permit management to overlook important items. Answer (d) is incorrect because management must have a plan, i.e., standards, expected results, etc., to use management by exception.

19. Zero-base budgeting

a. Involves the review of changes made to an organization's original budget.
b. Does not provide a projection of annual expenditures.
c. Is a method peculiar to budgeting by program.
d. Involves the review of each cost component from a cost/benefit perspective.
e. Emphasizes the relationship of effort to projected annual revenues.

The correct answer is (d). *(CIA 578 IV-9)*
REQUIRED: The description of zero-base budgeting (ZBB).
DISCUSSION: ZBB divides the activities of individual responsibility centers into a series of packages ranked ordinally. ZBB requires managers to start over each budget period and justify each expenditure. Thus, ZBB involves a review of each cost component from a cost/benefit perspective.
Answer (a) is incorrect because ZBB involves more than a review of the changes made to an organization's original budget. The entire budget process is repeated from point zero in each period. Answer (b) is incorrect because ZBB is an expense budget which requires a projection of annual expenditures. Answer (c) is incorrect because ZBB is not limited to a specific program and can be used by a whole organization. Answer (e) is incorrect because ZBB is usually used in situations with no annual projected revenues. In the public sector, a market revenue function generally does not exist.

294 Module 12.1: Budget Definitions

20. A budget system referred to as the "program planning and budgeting system (PPBS)"

a. Drops the current month or quarter and adds a future month or a future quarter as the current month or quarter is completed.

b. Consolidates the plans of the separate requests into one overall plan.

c. Divides the activities of individual responsibility centers into a series of packages which are ranked ordinally.

d. Classifies budget requests by activity and estimates the benefits arising from each activity.

e. Presents the plan for a range of activity so the plan can be adjusted for changes in activity levels.

The correct answer is (d). *(CMA 679 4-5)*
REQUIRED: The description of a program planning and budgeting system (PPBS).
DISCUSSION: A program planning and budgeting system (PPBS) classifies budget requests by activity and estimates the benefits arising from each activity. PPBS also incorporates long-range planning in its analysis.
Answer (a) is incorrect because it describes a continuous budget. Answer (b) is incorrect because it describes an overall budget. Answer (c) is incorrect because it describes a zero-base budget. Answer (e) is incorrect because it describes a flexible budget.

21. Ineffective budgets and/or control systems are characterized by

a. The use of budgets as a planning tool only and disregarding them for control purposes.

b. The use of budgets for harassment of individuals as opposed to motivation.

c. The ignoring of budgets once prepared.

d. The lack of timely feedback in the use of the budget.

e. All of the above.

The correct answer is (e). *(Publisher)*
REQUIRED: The characteristic(s) of ineffective budget control systems.
DISCUSSION: Ineffective budget control systems are characterized by each of the items noted. The use of budgets for planning only is a problem that must be resolved through the education process. Management must be educated to use the budget documents for control, not just planning. Management must learn that budgets can motivate and help individuals achieve professional growth as well as the goals of the firm. Ignoring budgets obviously contributes to the ineffectiveness of the budget system. Finally, feedback must be timely or lower management and employees will soon recognize that budget feedback is so late it provides no information, making the budget a worthless device.

22. The primary difference between a fixed (static) budget and a variable (flexible) budget is that a fixed budget

a. Includes only fixed costs, while a variable budget includes only variable costs.

b. Is concerned only with future acquisitions of fixed assets, while a variable budget is concerned with expenses which vary with sales.

c. Cannot be changed after the period begins, while a variable budget can be changed after the period begins.

d. Is a plan for a single level of sales (or other measure of activity), while a variable budget consists of several plans, one for each of several levels of sales (or other measure of activity).

The correct answer is (d). *(CPA 1172 T-27)*
REQUIRED: The primary difference between fixed and variable budgets.
DISCUSSION: A fixed (static) budget presents a plan for only one volume of activity and does not adjust the forecasts for changes in the level of activity. The flexible (variable) budget eliminates this deficiency in the static budget by adjusting the budget for the actual level of activity, i.e., by presenting a separate plan for various levels of activity.
Answer (a) is incorrect because it describes a fixed cost budget. Answer (b) is incorrect because it describes a capital budget. Answer (c) is incorrect because it describes an unadjustable (unchangeable) budget.

Module 12.1: Budget Definitions

23. The basic difference between a master budget and a flexible budget is that a

a. Flexible budget considers only variable costs but a master budget considers all costs.
b. Flexible budget allows management latitude in meeting goals whereas a master budget is based on a fixed standard.
c. Master budget is for an entire production facility but a flexible budget is applicable to single departments only.
d. Master budget is based on one specific level of production and a flexible budget can be prepared for any production level within a relevant range.

The correct answer is (d). *(CPA 579 T-38)*
REQUIRED: The basic difference between a master budget and a flexible budget.
DISCUSSION: The master budget forecasts at only one volume of activity and does not adjust for changes in the activity level; i.e., it is static. The flexible budget provides plans for a range of activity so that the budget can be adapted to the actual level.
Answer (a) is incorrect because it describes the difference between a variable and a direct costing budget. Answer (b) is incorrect because a flexible budget does not allow management latitude in meeting goals, although it does better define the goals and sets a greater responsibility upon management to meet them. Answer (c) is incorrect because budgets for a single department are called departmental budgets.

24. When production levels are expected to decline within a relevant range, and a flexible budget is used, what effects would be anticipated with respect to each of the following?

	Fixed Costs Per Unit	Variable Costs Per Unit
a.	Increase	Increase
b.	Increase	No change
c.	No change	No change
d.	No change	Increase

The correct answer is (b). *(CPA 1184 T-54)*
REQUIRED: The effect on unit costs when production declines.
DISCUSSION: Fixed costs per unit increase within the relevant range of activity as production decreases because there are fewer units absorbing the unchanged total fixed costs. Unit variable costs are assumed to remain the same per unit over the relevant range.

25. A flexible budget is appropriate for a

	Direct-Labor Budget	Marketing Budget
a.	No	No
b.	No	Yes
c.	Yes	No
d.	Yes	Yes

The correct answer is (d). *(CPA 584 T-40)*
REQUIRED: The situation in which a flexible budget is appropriate.
DISCUSSION: A flexible budget is a budget adjusted for the actual level of activity. Therefore, it is appropriate for any level of activity. A flexible budget approach is appropriate for both a direct labor budget and a marketing budget since each contains some elements that vary with the activity level and some that do not.

26. A flexible budget is

a. Not appropriate when costs and expenses are affected by fluctuations in volume limits.
b. Appropriate for any relevant level of activity.
c. Appropriate for control of factory overhead but not for control of direct materials and direct labor.
d. Appropriate for control of direct materials and direct labor but not for control of factory overhead.

The correct answer is (b). *(CPA 585 T-43)*
REQUIRED: The situation in which a flexible budget is appropriate.
DISCUSSION: A flexible budget is a budget adjusted for the actual level of activity. Therefore, it is appropriate for any level of activity.
Answer (a) is incorrect because the volume limits refer to the relevant range that is generally applicable. Answers (c) and (d) are incorrect because flexible budgets generally include both fixed and variable costs and, accordingly, are appropriate for controlling material, labor, and overhead costs.

Module 12.1: Budget Definitions

27. The flexible budget for a producing department may include

	Direct Labor	Factory Overhead
a.	No	Yes
b.	No	No
c.	Yes	No
d.	Yes	Yes

The correct answer is (d). *(CPA 587 T-46)*
REQUIRED: Elements for a flexible budget of a producing department.
DISCUSSION: A flexible budget is a budget adjusted for the actual level of activity. Therefore, it is appropriate for any level of activity. The flexible budget for a producing department would include inventoriable costs, such as direct material, direct labor, and variable factory overhead.

28. If a company wishes to establish a factory overhead budget system in which estimated costs can be derived directly from estimates of activity levels, it should prepare a

a. Capital budget.
b. Cash budget.
c. Discretionary budget.
d. Fixed budget.
e. Flexible budget.

The correct answer is (e). *(CPA 572 T-19)*
REQUIRED: The budget from which estimated costs can be derived from estimates of activity.
DISCUSSION: A flexible budget is based on several forecasts of activity levels and thus can be adjusted to the actual activity level. The estimated costs of factory overhead can therefore be derived directly from estimates of activity levels in a flexible budget.
Answer (a) is incorrect because a capital budget focuses on the acquisitions of fixed assets. Answer (b) is incorrect because a cash budget is concerned with the company's cash inflows, outflows, and balances. Answer (c) is incorrect because a discretionary budget plans for annual fixed costs that arise from top management decisions directly reflecting corporate policy. Answer (d) is incorrect because a fixed budget does not change with the volume of activity.

29. In flexible budgeting, if the index of activity were based on units of output, the index would

a. Fluctuate with efficiency.
b. Lead to a favorable variance.
c. Hide the inefficient use of inputs.
d. Lead to an unfavorable variance.

The correct answer is (a). *(CIA 583 IV-1)*
REQUIRED: The effect of basing the index of activity on output in flexible budgeting.
DISCUSSION: The index of activity is the basis on which costs are spread, e.g., number of units, machine hours, etc. Using units of output, the index fluctuates with the level of efficiency and production. If production is inefficient, the units of output will decline.
Answers (b), (c), and (d) are incorrect because variances occur as a result of manufacturing efficiency and effectiveness, not the index of activity used to budget and measure performance. Input is compared to output regardless of the activity base.

30. A continuous profit plan

a. Is a plan that is revised monthly or quarterly.
b. Is an annual plan that is part of a 5-year plan.
c. Is a plan devised by a full-time planning staff.
d. Is used only in process manufacturing companies.
e. Works best for a company that can reliably forecast events a year or more into the future.

The correct answer is (a). *(CMA 683 4-3)*
REQUIRED: The definition of a continuous profit plan.
DISCUSSION: According to MAP Statement on Management Accounting No. 2, a continuous profit plan is one that adds a period in the future as each current period ends. For example, at the end of each month, the plan may be extended to embrace the succeeding 12-month period. The effect is to maintain a stable planning horizon instead of one that is reduced as the fiscal year progresses.
Answer (b) is incorrect because a continuous plan covers a stable planning horizon defined according to the needs of the particular company. Answers (c), (d), and (e) are incorrect because a continuous plan may be used in any kind of business and may be developed by part-time planners.

Module 12.2: Budgeting Computations

31. Flexible budgeting is a reporting system wherein the

a. Budget standards may be adjusted at will.
b. Planned level of activity is adjusted to the actual level of activity before the budget comparison report is prepared.
c. Reporting dates vary according to the levels of activity reported upon.
d. Statements included in the budget report vary from period to period.

The correct answer is (b). *(CPA 573 T-22)*
REQUIRED: The description of flexible budgeting.
DISCUSSION: A flexible budget provides plans for a range of activity so that the budget can be adapted to the actual level of activity.
Answer (a) is incorrect because, if budget standards could be adjusted at will, performance could not be measured. Answer (c) is incorrect because a budget is made for a specified time period, provides information for that time period, and may be compared to other time periods. Answer (d) is incorrect because whether the statements in the budget report vary has no bearing on the type of budget used.

32. When sales volume is seasonal in nature, certain items in the budget must be coordinated. The three most significant items to coordinate in budgeting seasonal sales volume are

a. Production volume, finished goods inventory, and sales volume.
b. Raw material, work-in-process, and finished goods inventories.
c. Raw material inventory, work-in-process inventory, and production volume.
d. Direct labor hours, work-in-process inventory, and sales volume.
e. Raw material inventory, direct labor hours, and manufacturing overhead costs.

The correct answer is (a). *(CMA 686 4-18)*
REQUIRED: The three most significant items to coordinate when budgeting seasonal sales volume.
DISCUSSION: In a seasonal business, demand for the company's goods exhibits sharp fluctuations. Coordinating sales volume with earlier production volume and accumulation of finished goods inventories therefore becomes especially important.
Answers (b), (c), and (e) are incorrect because these inventories must be coordinated in all businesses, whether seasonal or not. Also, the seasonal nature of sales is ignored in these answers. Answer (d) is incorrect because work-in-process is not as important to a seasonal business as finished goods inventories.

33. Which one of the following is the best objective performance criterion for an electrical engineer?

a. Exhibition of creative talents on company projects.
b. Project completion within budget constraints.
c. Ability to work well with fellow engineers on projects.
d. Cooperativeness with superiors and upper-level management.

The correct answer is (b). *(CIA 1185 III-13)*
REQUIRED: The best objective performance criterion for an electrical engineer.
DISCUSSION: Quantifiable standards are the most objective since measurement of performance is readily accomplished. A budget is a quantitative standard for controlling cost, output, or time spent on a project.
Answer (a) is incorrect because creativity is difficult if not impossible to measure. Answers (c) and (d) are incorrect because each requires subjective judgment.

12.2 Budgeting Computations

34. Management has prepared a graph showing the total costs of operating branch warehouses throughout the country. The cost line crosses the vertical axis at $200,000. The total cost of operating one branch is $350,000. The total cost of operating ten branches is $1,700,000. For purposes of preparing a flexible budget based on the number of branch warehouses in operation, what formula would be used to determine budgeted costs at various levels of activity?

a. Y = $200,000 + $150,000X.
b. Y = $200,000 + $170,000X.
c. Y = $350,000 + $200,000X.
d. Y = $350,000 + $150,000X.

The correct answer is (a). *(CIA 1187 IV-10)*
REQUIRED: The formula for preparing a flexible budget.
DISCUSSION: Fixed cost (FC) is $200,000, the amount at which the total cost (TC) line crosses the y-axis (when no warehouses are in operation). The total variable cost (VC) of operating 10 warehouses is $1,500,000 ($1,700,000 TC - $200,000 FC), so the variable cost per warehouse is $150,000 ($1,500,000 ÷ 10). Y(TC) is therefore equal to $200,000 (FC) plus $150,000X (VC).

35. Dean Company is preparing a flexible budget for the coming year and the following maximum capacity estimates for Department M are available:

Direct labor hours	60,000
Variable factory overhead	$150,000
Fixed factory overhead	$240,000

Assume that Dean's normal capacity is 80% of maximum capacity. What would be the total factory overhead rate, based on direct labor hours, in a flexible budget at normal capacity?

a. $6.00.
b. $6.50.
c. $7.50.
d. $8.13.

The correct answer is (c). *(CPA 1182 P-21)*
REQUIRED: The total factory overhead rate at normal capacity.
DISCUSSION: The total factory overhead rate includes both fixed and variable overhead. The variable overhead rate per direct labor hour is $2.50 ($150,000 ÷ 60,000 hours). The fixed overhead is allocated based on expected hours. The normal capacity is 80% of maximum, which is 48,000 hours (80% x 60,000). Thus, the fixed overhead rate is $5.00 per direct labor hour ($240,000 ÷ 48,000 hours). The total factory overhead rate is $7.50 per direct labor hour ($2.50 variable + $5.00 fixed).

36. Reid Company is budgeting sales of 100,000 units of product R for the month of September. Production of one unit of product R requires two units of material A and three units of material B. Actual inventory units at September 1 and budgeted inventory units at September 30 are as follows:

	Actual	Budgeted
Product R	20,000	10,000
Material A	25,000	18,000
Material B	22,000	24,000

How many units of material B is Reid planning to purchase during September?

a. 328,000.
b. 302,000.
c. 298,000.
d. 272,000.

The correct answer is (d). *(CPA 1182 P-27)*
REQUIRED: The number of units of material B to be purchased during September.
DISCUSSION: The total units of product R required for the month must be computed. Then the total number of units of material B can be computed.

Budgeted sales of product R	100,000
Less: Beginning inventory (actual)	(20,000)
Add: Ending inventory (budgeted)	10,000
Units of R to be produced	90,000
Units of B required for each R	x 3
Units of B required for production	270,000
Less: Beginning inventory (actual)	(22,000)
Add: Ending inventory (budgeted)	24,000
Units of material B to be purchased	272,000

37. Betz Company's sales budget shows the following projections for the year ending December 31:

Quarter	Units
First	60,000
Second	80,000
Third	45,000
Fourth	55,000
Total	240,000

Inventory at December 31 of the prior year was budgeted at 18,000 units. The quantity of finished goods inventory at the end of each quarter is to equal 30% of the next quarter's budgeted sales of units. How much should the production budget show for units to be produced during the first quarter?

a. 24,000.
b. 48,000.
c. 66,000.
d. 72,000.

The correct answer is (c). *(CPA 1182 Q-28)*
REQUIRED: The units to be produced during the first quarter.
DISCUSSION: The units needed for the first quarter include the 60,000 units to be sold in the first quarter and 30% of the second quarter's sales (80,000 x .3 = 24,000). Therefore, 84,000 units (24,000 + 60,000) are needed in the first quarter. Given 18,000 units in beginning inventory, 66,000 units must be produced during the first quarter (84,000 - 18,000).

Module 12.2: Budgeting Computations

38. RedRock Company uses flexible budgeting for cost control. RedRock produced 10,800 units of product during March, incurring an indirect materials cost of $13,000. Its master budget for the year reflected an indirect materials cost of $180,000 at a production volume of 144,000 units. A flexible budget for March production would reflect indirect material costs of

- a. $13,000.
- b. $13,500.
- c. $13,975.
- d. $11,700.
- e. Some amount other than those given above.

The correct answer is (b). *(CMA 686 4-22)*
REQUIRED: The indirect material costs shown on a flexible budget prepared for a given volume.
DISCUSSION: If annual costs are $180,000 for 144,000 units, the unit cost is $1.25 ($180,000 ÷ 144,000 units). Thus, at a production volume of 10,800, the total costs budgeted are $13,500 ($1.25 x 10,800 units).

39. The Shocker Company's sales budget shows quarterly sales for the next year as follows:

Quarter 1	10,000 units
Quarter 2	8,000 units
Quarter 3	12,000 units
Quarter 4	14,000 units

Company policy is to have a finished goods inventory at the end of each quarter equal to 20% of the next quarter's sales. Budgeted production for the second quarter of the next year would be

- a. 7,200 units.
- b. 8,000 units.
- c. 8,800 units.
- d. 8,400 units.
- e. Some amount other than those given above.

The correct answer is (c). *(CMA 1287 4-28)*
REQUIRED: The budgeted production for the second quarter.
DISCUSSION: The beginning inventory for Quarter 2 should be 1,600 units (20% x 8,000 units of budgeted sales). The ending inventory should be 2,400 units (20% x 12,000 units of sales budgeted for Quarter 3). Since BI plus production minus EI equals Quarter 2 sales, production must be 8,800 units.

$$1,600 + X - 2,400 = 8,000$$
$$X = 8,800$$

40. The Jung Corporation's budget calls for the following production:

Quarter 1	45,000 units
Quarter 2	38,000 units
Quarter 3	34,000 units
Quarter 4	48,000 units

Each unit of product requires 3 pounds of direct material. The company's policy is to begin each quarter with an inventory of direct materials equal to 30% of that quarter's direct material requirements. Budgeted direct materials purchases for the third quarter would be

- a. 114,600 pounds.
- b. 89,400 pounds.
- c. 38,200 pounds.
- d. 29,800 pounds.
- e. Some amount other than those given above.

The correct answer is (a). *(CMA 1287 4-29)*
REQUIRED: The budgeted direct materials purchases for the third quarter.
DISCUSSION: Beginning inventory should be 30,600 pounds (30% x 3 pounds x 34,000 units of budgeted sales). Ending inventory should be 43,200 pounds (30% x 3 pounds x 48,000 units of budgeted sales for Quarter 4). Since BI plus purchases minus EI equals Quarter 3 budgeted sales, purchases must be 114,600.

$$30,600 + X - 43,200 = 3 \times 34,000 = 102,000$$
$$X = 114,600$$

41. Total production costs for Gallop, Inc. are budgeted at $230,000 for 50,000 units of budgeted output and $280,000 for 60,000 units of budgeted output. Because of the need for additional facilities, budgeted fixed costs for 60,000 units are 25% more than budgeted fixed costs for 50,000 units. How much is Gallop's budgeted variable cost per unit of output?

 a. $1.60.
 b. $1.67.
 c. $3.00.
 d. $5.00.

The correct answer is (c). *(CPA 1175 P-20)*
REQUIRED: The budgeted variable cost per unit given total budgeted costs.
DISCUSSION: Total budgeted costs equals fixed costs plus variable costs. Given that fixed costs (FC) increase 25% from one output level to another, simultaneous equations are required to determine variable costs per unit (VC).

$$50{,}000VC + FC = \$230{,}000$$
$$60{,}000VC + 1.25FC = \$280{,}000$$

$$FC = \$230{,}000 - 50{,}000VC$$

Substituting for FC in the second equation,

$$60{,}000VC + 1.25(\$230{,}000 - 50{,}000VC) = \$280{,}000$$
$$60{,}000VC + \$287{,}500 - 62{,}500VC = \$280{,}000$$
$$2{,}500VC = \$7{,}500$$
$$VC = \$3.00$$

42. Brooks Company uses the following flexible budget formula for annual maintenance cost:

Total cost = $7,200 + $0.60 per machine hour

The current month's budget is based upon 20,000 hours of planned machine time. Maintenance cost included in this flexible budget is

 a. $11,400.
 b. $12,000.
 c. $12,600.
 d. $19,200.

The correct answer is (c). *(CPA 1182 P-34)*
REQUIRED: The monthly budget for maintenance costs.
DISCUSSION: The annual maintenance cost is a mixed cost containing both fixed and variable elements. To calculate the monthly total fixed costs, divide the annual amount by 12.

Fixed maintenance costs: $7,200 ÷ 12 = $600 per month

Variable maintenance costs: 20,000 x $.60/hour = $12,000

Total maintenance costs = $12,600

43. A company prepares a flexible budget each month for manufacturing costs. Formulas have been developed for all costs within a relevant range of 5,000 to 15,000 units per month. It is known that the budget for electricity (a semivariable cost) is $19,800 at 9,000 units per month, and $21,000 at 10,000 units per month. How much should be budgeted for electricity for the coming month if 12,000 units are to be produced?

 a. $26,400.
 b. $25,200.
 c. $23,400.
 d. $22,200.

The correct answer is (c). *(CIA 586 IV-12)*
REQUIRED: The amount that should be budgeted for electricity given desired units of production.
DISCUSSION: A flexible budget consists of a fixed cost component and a variable cost component. The fixed cost component can be expected to remain constant throughout the budget's relevant range. The variable cost component, however, will change at a constant rate within the budget's range. Here, the increase in budgeted cost of $1,200 ($21,000 - $19,800) per 1,000 units of production can therefore be attributed to the variable cost component. The flexible budget for 12,000 units of production will be $23,400 [the cost for 10,000 ($21,000) plus $2,400 (2 x $1,200)].

Module 12.2: Budgeting Computations

Questions 44 through 46 are based on the following information, which was presented as part of Question 5 on the Practice II section of the May 1982 CPA examination.

	Purchases	Sales
January	$42,000	$72,000
February	48,000	66,000
March	36,000	60,000
April	54,000	78,000

Collections from Montero Corp.'s customers are normally 70% in the month of sale, and 20% and 9%, respectively, the 2 months following the sale. The balance is uncollectible. Montero takes full advantage of the 2% discount allowed on purchases paid for by the 10th of the following month. Purchases for May are budgeted at $60,000, while sales for May are forecasted at $66,000. Cash disbursements for expenses are expected to be $14,400 for the month of May. Montero's cash balance at May 1 was $22,000.

44. What are the expected cash collections during May?

a. $46,200.
b. $67,200.
c. $66,000.
d. $61,800.

The correct answer is (b). *(Publisher)*
REQUIRED: The expected cash collections during May.
DISCUSSION: The expected cash collections during any month equal 9% of the sales of two months before, 20% of the sales of one month before, and 70% of the current month's sales.

Month	Sales	%	Expected Collections
March	$60,000	9	$ 5,400
April	78,000	20	15,600
May	66,000	70	46,200
Total collections (May)			$67,200

45. What are the expected cash disbursements for May?

a. $68,400.
b. $67,320.
c. $52,920.
d. $69,450.

The correct answer is (b). *(Publisher)*
REQUIRED: The expected cash disbursements for May.
DISCUSSION: The expected cash disbursements for any month equal the previous month's purchases less the 2% discount, plus any cash disbursements for expenses in the current period.

April purchases	$54,000
Less: 2% cash discount	(1,080)
Net purchases	$52,920
Cash expenses	14,400
Total cash disbursements for May	$67,320

46. What was the cash balance on April 1, assuming cash disbursements for expenses increased 20% from April to May?

a. $72,540.
b. $(3,260).
c. $22,000.
d. $21,880.

The correct answer is (b). *(Publisher)*
REQUIRED: The cash balance on April 1.
DISCUSSION: The solutions approach is to back up from the $22,000 cash balance on May 1 by adding collections and subtracting disbursements for April. Expected collections for April:

Month	Sales	%	Expected Collections
April	$78,000	70	$54,600
March	60,000	20	12,000
February	66,000	9	5,940
Total			$72,540

Expected disbursements for April:

March purchases	$36,000
Less: 2% cash discount	720
Net purchases	$35,280
Cash expenses ($14,400 ÷ 120%)	12,000
Total disbursements for April	$47,280
Expected collections	$72,540
Expected disbursements	(47,280)
Balance, April 30	$22,000
Balance, April 1 is thus	$ (3,260)

Module 12.2: Budgeting Computations

Questions 47 through 50 are based on the following information. D. Tomlinson Retail seeks your assistance to develop cash and other budget information for May, June, and July. At April 30, the Company had cash of $5,500, accounts receivable of $437,000, inventories of $309,400, and accounts payable of $133,055. The budget is to be based on the following assumptions:

Sales
Each month's sales are billed on the last day of the month.
Customers are allowed a 3% discount if payment is made within 10 days after the billing date. Receivables are booked gross.
60% of the billings are collected within the discount period, 25% are collected by the end of the month, 9% are collected by the end of the second month, and 6% prove uncollectible.

Purchases
54% of all purchases of material and selling, general, and administrative expenses are paid in the month purchased and the remainder in the following month.
Each month's units of ending inventory is equal to 130% of the next month's units of sales.
The cost of each unit of inventory is $20.
Selling, general, and administrative expenses, of which $2,000 is depreciation, are equal to 15% of the current month's sales.

Actual and projected sales are as follows:

	Dollars	Units
March	$354,000	11,800
April	363,000	12,100
May	357,000	11,900
June	342,000	11,400
July	360,000	12,000
August	366,000	12,200

---

47. Budgeted purchases for May and June are

a. $241,800 and $236,000.
b. $238,000 and $228,000.
c. $225,000 and $243,600.
d. $357,000 and $342,000.

The correct answer is (c). *(Publisher)*
REQUIRED: The budgeted purchases in dollars for two periods.
DISCUSSION: Each month's units of EI equal 130% of the next month's units of sales. Thus, the purchases each month are equal to the EI plus the sales of the current month less the BI.

	May	June
Sales	11,900	11,400
EI	14,820	15,600
	26,720	27,000
Less BI	(15,470)	(14,820)
Purchases	11,250	12,180
Unit price	x $20	x $20
Purchase cost	$225,000	$243,600

---

48. Budgeted cash disbursements during the month of June are

a. $292,900.
b. $287,379.
c. $294,900.
d. $285,379.

The correct answer is (d). *(CPA 573 P-43)*
REQUIRED: The budgeted cash disbursements during the month of June.
DISCUSSION: Budgeted cash disbursements during June are affected by the A/P remaining at May 31 and by the cash disbursements made in June. 46% of May purchases and expenses are paid in June. 54% of June purchases and expenses are paid in June. Depreciation expense of $2,000 is a noncash expenditure and should be deducted from the selling, general, and administrative expenses for each month. SG&A expenses equal 15% of the current month's sales. Cash disbursements in June for purchases are $235,044 [($225,000 x 46%) + ($243,600 x 54%)]. Cash disbursements for other expenses are $50,335, which is the total of

June: 54% x [($342,000 x 15%) - $2,000] plus
May: 46% x [($357,000 x 15%) - $2,000]

Therefore, total cash disbursements during June are $285,379 ($235,044 + $50,335).

49. Budgeted cash collections during the month of May are

a. $333,876.
b. $355,116.
c. $340,410.
d. $355,656.

The correct answer is (a). *(CPA 573 P-44)*
REQUIRED: The budgeted cash collections during the month of May.
DISCUSSION: Each month's cash collections contain three elements: (1) 60% of the billings are collected with a 3% discount, (2) 25% are collected at the end of the month, (3) 9% are collected by the end of the month.

For the month of May, items 1 and 2 are sales from April. Item 3 is sales from March.

.97 x .60 x $363,000 (April)	$211,266
.25 x $363,000 (April)	90,750
.09 x $354,000 (March)	31,860
Cash collections for May	$333,876

50. The budgeted number of units of inventory to be purchased during July is

a. 15,860.
b. 12,260.
c. 12,000.
d. 15,600.

The correct answer is (b). *(CPA 573 P-45)*
REQUIRED: The budgeted units of inventory to be purchased during July.
DISCUSSION: The budgeted units of inventory to be purchased during July equal the EI of July (130% of the unit sales in August) plus the sales units in July, less the BI of July. BI of July is equal to 130% of July sales.

EI - (130% x 12,200)	15,860
July sales	12,000
	27,860
BI - (130% x 12,000)	(15,600)
Units to be purchased (July)	12,260

51. The Fresh Company is preparing its cash budget for the month of May. The following information is available concerning its accounts receivable:

Estimated credit sales for May	$200,000
Actual credit sales for April	$150,000
Estimated collections in May for credit sales in May	20%
Estimated collections in May for credit sales in April	70%
Estimated collections in May for credit sales prior to April	$ 12,000
Estimated write-offs in May for uncollectible credit sales	$ 8,000
Estimated provision for bad debts in May for credit sales in May	$ 7,000

What are the estimated cash receipts from accounts receivable collections in May?

a. $142,000.
b. $149,000.
c. $150,000.
d. $157,000.

The correct answer is (d). *(CPA 1179 P-22)*
REQUIRED: The estimated cash receipts from accounts receivable collections in May.
DISCUSSION: The estimated cash receipts from accounts receivable collections in May are equal to the estimated amount to be collected on credit sales in May plus the estimated amount to be collected in May on credit sales in previous months.

Estimated credit receipts in May for May ($200,000 x 20%)	$ 40,000
Estimated credit receipts in May for April ($150,000 x 70%)	105,000
Estimated collections for credit sales prior to April	12,000
Estimated cash to be collected in May	$157,000

The estimated write-offs in May for uncollectible credit sales and the estimated provision for bad debts in May for credit sales in May are not used in the calculation because the percent of estimated collections are assumed to be based on the gross credit sales amounts.

Module 12.2: Budgeting Computations

Questions 52 through 55 are based on the following information, which was presented as part of Question 4 on the Practice II section of the November 1978 CPA examination.

Scarborough Corporation manufactures and sells two products, Thingone and Thingtwo. In July 1989, Scarborough's budget department gathered the following data to project sales and budget requirements for 1990:

1990 Projected Sales

Product	Units	Price
Thingone	60,000	$ 70
Thingtwo	40,000	100

1990 Inventories - in units

Product	Expected January 1, 1990	Desired December 31, 1990
Thingone	20,000	25,000
Thingtwo	8,000	9,000

To produce one unit of Thingone and Thingtwo, the following raw materials are used:

Raw Material	Unit	Thingone	Thingtwo
A	lbs.	4	5
B	lbs.	2	3
C	each	—	1

Projected data for 1990 with respect to raw materials are as follows:

Raw Material	Anticipated Purchase Price	Expected Inventories 1/1/90	Desired Inventories 12/31/90
A	$8	32,000 lbs.	36,000 lbs.
B	5	29,000 lbs.	32,000 lbs.
C	3	6,000 each	7,000 each

Projected direct labor requirements for 1990 and rates are as follows:

Thingone - 2 hours per unit at $3 per hour
Thingtwo - 3 hours per unit at $4 per hour

Overhead is applied at the rate of $2 per direct labor hour.

52. What is the production budget in units for each product for 1990?

	Thingone	Thingtwo
a.	65,000	41,000
b.	85,000	49,000
c.	60,000	40,000
d.	80,000	48,000

The correct answer is (a). *(Publisher)*
REQUIRED: The production budget in units for each product.
DISCUSSION: To calculate the production required in units, determine the projected sales, desired inventories, and expected inventories at the beginning of the cycle.

	Thingone	Thingtwo
Projected sales	60,000	40,000
Desired inventories, December 31, 1990	25,000	9,000
	85,000	49,000
Less expected inventories, January 1, 1990	(20,000)	(8,000)
Production required (units)	65,000	41,000

Module 12.2: Budgeting Computations

53. What is the raw materials budget in quantities for 1990?

	A	B	C
a.	533,000	314,000	54,000
b.	469,000	256,000	42,000
c.	465,000	253,000	41,000
d.	501,000	285,000	48,000

The correct answer is (b). *(Publisher)*
REQUIRED: The raw materials budget in quantities for 1990.
DISCUSSION: The raw materials budget consists of raw materials A, B, and C. Thingone and Thingtwo require different proportions of each item. Once production requirements are established, add desired EI and subtract the BI of each raw material to arrive at purchases required.

	A	B	C
Thingone (65,000 units projected to be produced)	260,000	130,000	-0-
Thingtwo (41,000 units projected to be produced)	205,000	123,000	41,000
Production requirements	465,000	253,000	41,000
Add desired inventories, 12/31/90	36,000	32,000	7,000
Total requirements	501,000	285,000	48,000
Less expected inventories, 1/1/90	(32,000)	(29,000)	(6,000)
Purchase requirements (units)	469,000	256,000	42,000

54. What is the direct labor budget in dollars for 1990?

	Thingone	Thingtwo
a.	$390,000	$369,000
b.	$520,000	$492,000
c.	$390,000	$492,000
d.	$492,000	$390,000

The correct answer is (c). *(Publisher)*
REQUIRED: The direct labor budget in dollars.
DISCUSSION: The direct labor budget in dollars is the estimated unit production times the hours per unit times the expected rate, which gives the direct labor dollars for each product.

	Projected Production (units)	Hours Per Unit	Total Hours	Rate	Total
Thingone	65,000	2	130,000	$3	$390,000
Thingtwo	41,000	3	123,000	4	492,000

55. What is the budgeted finished goods inventory for Thingtwo for 1990 in dollars?

a. $522,000
b. $108,000
c. $630,000
d. $684,000

The correct answer is (d). *(Publisher)*
REQUIRED: The budgeted finished goods inventory in dollars for Thingtwo.
DISCUSSION: The budgeted FG inventory includes DM, DL, and O/H associated with Thingtwo times the desired inventory.

Raw materials
  A (5 pounds @ $8) $40
  B (3 pounds @ $5)   15
  C (1 each @ $3)   3 $ 58
Direct labor (3 hours @ $4)   12
Overhead (3 hours @ $2)   6
Per unit cost $ 76
Units in EI   x 9,000
EI value $684,000

Questions 56 and 57 are based on Berol Company, which plans to sell 200,000 units of finished product in July and anticipates a growth rate in sales of 5% per month. The desired monthly ending inventory in units of finished product is 80% of the next month's estimated sales. There are 150,000 finished units in the inventory on June 30. Each unit of finished product requires 4 pounds of direct material at a cost of $1.20 per pound. There are 800,000 pounds of direct material in the inventory on June 30.

56. Berol's production requirement in units of finished product for the 3-month period ending September 30 is

   a. 712,025 units.
   b. 630,000 units.
   c. 664,000 units.
   d. 665,720 units.
   e. None of the above.

The correct answer is (d). *(CMA 684 4-23)*
REQUIRED: The production requirement for finished goods.
DISCUSSION: The production requirement for FG for the 3 months is calculated using the following equation:

   Sales (105% of previous month's)
   - BI
   + Desired EI (80% of next month's sales)
   Production

	July	August	September	October
Sales	200,000	210,000	220,500	231,525
- BFG	(150,000)	(168,000)	(176,400)	(185,220)
+ EFG	168,000	176,400	185,220	
Production	218,000	218,400	229,320	

218,000 + 218,400 + 229,320 = 665,720

57. Without prejudice to the answer to the preceding question, assume Berol plans to produce 600,000 units of finished product in the 3-month period ending September 30, and to have direct materials inventory on hand at the end of the 3-month period equal to 25% of the use in that period. The estimated cost of direct materials purchases for the 3-month period ending September 30 is

   a. $2,200,000.
   b. $2,400,000.
   c. $2,640,000.
   d. $2,880,000.
   e. None of the above.

The correct answer is (c). *(CMA 684 4-24)*
REQUIRED: The estimated cost of direct materials purchases.
DISCUSSION: Each finished unit requires 4 pounds of direct materials. If production is 600,000 units, 2,400,000 pounds are required for finished goods. Given 800,000 pounds in beginning inventory and 600,000 [25% x (600,000 x 4)] required for ending inventory, 2,200,000 pounds must be purchased at a cost of $2,640,000 ($2,200,000 x $1.20).

Direct Materials (pounds)

800,000	2,400,000
2,200,000	
600,000	

58. Using the following data, compute the cash financing needs or excess cash to invest.

Cash balance, beginning	$ 20,000
Collections from customers	150,000
Disbursements:	
For direct materials	25,000
For other costs and expenses	30,000
For payroll	75,000
For income taxes	6,000
For machinery purchase	30,000
Minimum cash balance desired	20,000

   a. Excess cash -- $4,000.
   b. Excess cash -- $14,000.
   c. Financing need -- $10,000.
   d. Financing need -- $16,000.

The correct answer is (d). *(CIA 1187 IV-13)*
REQUIRED: The cash financing needs or excess cash to invest.
DISCUSSION: Total cash available is $170,000 ($20,000 + $150,000). Total cash to be disbursed is $166,000 ($25,000 + $30,000 + $75,000 + $6,000 + $30,000). Excess cash available is $4,000. Since the minimum cash balance desired is $20,000, the financing need is $16,000.

Module 12.2: Budgeting Computations

59. CMR is a retail mail order firm that currently uses a central collection system that requires all checks to be sent to its Boston headquarters. An average of 5 days is required for mailed checks to be received, 4 days for CMR to process them and 1½ days for the checks to clear through the bank. A proposed lockbox system would reduce the mail and process time to 3 days and the check clearing time to 1 day. CMR has an average daily collection of $100,000. If CMR should adopt the lockbox system, its average cash balance would increase by

- a. $650,000.
- b. $250,000.
- c. $800,000.
- d. $400,000.
- e. Some amount other than those given above.

The correct answer is (a). *(CMA 1286 1-30)*
REQUIRED: The amount of the increase in the average cash balance if a lockbox system is adopted.
DISCUSSION: Checks are currently tied up for 10½ days (5 for mailing, 4 for processing, and 1½ for clearing). If that were reduced to 4 days, CMR's cash balance would increase by $650,000 (6½ days x $100,000 per day).

60. Terry Company is preparing its cash budget for the month of April. The following information is available concerning its inventories:

Inventories at beginning of April	$ 90,000
Estimated purchases for April	440,000
Estimated CGS for April	450,000
Estimated payments in April for purchases in March	75,000
Estimated payments in April for purchases prior to March	20,000
Estimated payments in April for purchases in April	75%

What are the estimated cash disbursements for inventories in April?

- a. $401,250.
- b. $405,000.
- c. $425,000.
- d. $432,500.

The correct answer is (c). *(CPA 1179 P-21)*
REQUIRED: The estimated cash disbursements for inventory in April.
DISCUSSION: The estimated cash disbursements for inventory in April are equal to the cash expected to be used for inventories. The inventory amount and CGS data for April are not relevant.

Estimated purchases for April	$440,000
Estimated payments in April for purchases in April	x 75%
Estimated payments for April purchases	$330,000
Estimated payments for March purchases	75,000
Estimated payments for purchases prior to March	20,000
Estimated cash disbursements for inventories in April	$425,000

61. Walsh, Inc. is preparing its cash budget for the month of November. The following information is available concerning its inventories:

Inventories at beginning of November	$180,000
Estimated CGS for November	900,000
Estimated inventories at end of November	160,000
Estimated payments in November for purchases prior to November	210,000
Estimated payments in November for purchases in November	80%

What are the estimated cash disbursements for inventories in November?

- a. $720,000.
- b. $914,000.
- c. $930,000.
- d. $1,042,000.

The correct answer is (b). *(CPA 1178 P-22)*
REQUIRED: The estimated cash disbursements for inventory in November.
DISCUSSION: Purchases for November equal CGS minus BI plus EI.

Cost of goods sold	$900,000
Beginning inventories	(180,000)
Ending inventories	160,000
Purchases	$880,000
Estimated payments for November purchases	x 80%
Estimated payments for November purchases	$704,000
Estimated payments for purchases prior to November	210,000
Estimated cash disbursements for inventory in November	$914,000

Questions 62 through 64 are based on Patsy Corp., which has estimated its activity for December.

Variable selling, general, and administrative expense (SG&A) includes a charge for uncollectible accounts of 1% of sales. Total SG&A is $35,500 per month plus 15% of sales. Depreciation expense of $20,000 per month is included in fixed SG&A.

Selected data from these estimated amounts are as follows:

Sales	$350,000
Gross profit (based on sales)	30%
Increase in trade accounts receivable during month	$ 10,000
Change in accounts payable during month	$ -0-
Increase in inventory during month	$ 5,000

62. On the basis of the above data, what are the estimated cash receipts from operations for December?

a. $336,500.
b. $340,000.
c. $346,500.
d. $350,000.

The correct answer is (a). *(CPA 1176 P-35)*
REQUIRED: The estimated cash receipts from operations for December.
DISCUSSION: The estimated cash receipts for December are equal to all the cash expected to be received in December. The increase in accounts receivable reduces the amount of cash inflow. No cash was collected for the 1% of sales expected to be uncollectible. Thus,

Sales	$350,000
Uncollectible accounts (1% sales)	(3,500)
Increase in accounts receivable	(10,000)
Estimated Dec. cash receipts	$336,500

63. What are Patsy's estimated cash disbursements from operations for December?

a. $309,500.
b. $313,000.
c. $314,500.
d. $318,000.

The correct answer is (c). *(CPA 1176 P-36)*
REQUIRED: The estimated cash disbursements for December.
DISCUSSION: Uncollectible accounts and depreciation charges do not affect cash flow, nor does the increase in the balance of A/R. Since depreciation and the uncollectible accounts charges are not disbursements, they must be subtracted from the SG&A expenses. The estimated cash disbursements are as follows:

Sales		$350,000
Cost of goods sold		x 70%
Disbursements for CGS		$245,000
Increase in inventory		5,000
SG&A expenses:		
Fixed SG&A	$35,500	
Variable SG&A*	52,500	
Depreciation	(20,000)	
Uncollectible accounts	(3,500)	64,500
Estimated Dec. cash disbursements		$314,500

*Variable SG&A: $350,000 x 15% = $52,500

64. What is the estimated net income for December?

a. $11,000.
b. $17,000.
c. $35,500.
d. $52,500.

The correct answer is (b). *(Publisher)*
REQUIRED: The estimated net income for December.
DISCUSSION: Variable expenses total 85% of sales (70% CGS + 15% SG&A), leaving a 15% contribution margin. The contribution margin is thus $52,500 ($350,000 x 15%). Subtract the $35,500 of fixed costs to find estimated net income of $17,000.

Module 12.2: Budgeting Computations

65. Reid Company is developing a forecast of March cash receipts from credit sales. Credit sales for March are estimated to be $320,000. The accounts receivable balance at February 29, is $300,000; one-quarter of the balance represents January credit sales and the remainder is from February sales. All accounts receivable from months prior to January have been collected or written off. Reid's history of accounts receivable collections is as follows:

In the month of sale	20%
In the first month after month of sale	50%
In the second month after month of sale	25%
Written off as uncollectible at the end of the second month after month of sale	5%

Based on the above information, what is Reid's forecast of March cash receipts from credit sales?

a. $176,500.
b. $195,250.
c. $253,769.
d. $267,125.

The correct answer is (d). *(CPA 1180 P-23)*
REQUIRED: The estimated cash receipts in March from credit sales.
DISCUSSION: The January and February sales must be calculated to determine March cash receipts. The balance of accounts receivable is $300,000, of which one-fourth is the January balance ($75,000) and three-fourths is the February balance ($225,000). Since 70% of January sales have been collected (20% in the month of sale and 50% in the first month after the month of sale), sales remaining to be collected represent 30% of January sales. Thus, $75,000 ÷ .30 = $250,000 January sales. Since 20% of February sales have been collected, February sales not yet collected represent 80% of February sales. Thus, $225,000 ÷ .80 = $281,250 February sales.

Collections in March:
March sales ($320,000 x 20%)	$ 64,000
February sales ($281,250 x 50%)	140,625
January sales ($250,000 x 25%)	62,500
Estimated March cash receipts	$267,125

66. Sussex Company has budgeted its operations for February. No change in inventory level during the month is planned. Selected data from estimated amounts are as follows:

Net loss	$100,000
Increase in accounts payable	40,000
Depreciation expense	35,000
Decrease in gross amount of trade accounts receivable	60,000
Purchase of office equipment on 45-day credit terms	15,000
Provision for estimated warranty liability	10,000

What change in cash position is expected for February?

a. $15,000 decrease.
b. $25,000 decrease.
c. $30,000 increase.
d. $45,000 increase.

The correct answer is (d). *(CPA 1181 P-28)*
REQUIRED: The expected change in cash position for February.
DISCUSSION: The expected change in cash position is the net increase or decrease in expected cash receipts and disbursements. The purchase of office equipment on credit does not affect cash. Depreciation expense and provision for estimated warranty liabilities are expenses not affecting the cash position of the firm and must be added back to net income. When A/P increases, less cash has left the firm to pay expenses. Therefore, the increase in A/P must be added back to net income. When A/R decreases, the company has collected more cash than it has advanced credit. Therefore, cash must be increased by the decrease in A/R.

Net loss	$(100,000)
Depreciation expense	35,000
Provision for warranty liability	10,000
Adjusted net loss	$ (55,000)
Increase in A/P	40,000
Decrease in A/R	60,000
Expected increase in cash position	$ 45,000

Module 12.2: Budgeting Computations

Questions 67 through 70 are based on Kelly Company, which is a retail sporting goods store that uses accrual accounting for its records. Facts regarding Kelly's operations are as follows:

- Sales are budgeted at $220,000 for December and $200,000 for January.
- Collections are expected to be 60% in the month of sale and 38% in the month following the sale. 2% of sales are expected to be uncollectible.
- Gross margin is 25% of sales.
- A total of 80% of the merchandise held for resale is purchased in the month prior to the month of sale and 20% is purchased in the month of sale. Payment for merchandise is made in the month following the purchase.
- Other expected monthly expenses to be paid in cash are $22,600.
- Annual depreciation is $216,000.

Kelly Company's statement of financial position at the close of business on November 30 is reproduced in the next column.

Kelly Company
Statement of Financial Position
November 30

Assets
Cash	$ 22,000
Accounts receivable (net of $4,000 allowance for uncollectible accounts)	76,000
Inventory	132,000
PP&E (net of $680,000 accumulated depreciation)	870,000
Total assets	$1,100,000

Liabilities and Stockholders' Equity
Accounts payable	$ 162,000
Common stock	800,000
Retained earnings	138,000
Total liabilities and stockholders' equity	$1,100,000

---

67. The budgeted cash collections for December are

a. $208,000.
b. $132,000.
c. $203,600.
d. $212,000.
e. None of the above.

The correct answer is (a). *(CMA 1283 4-22)*
REQUIRED: The amount of budgeted cash collections for the month.
DISCUSSION: Since collections are 60% of the current month's sales and 38% of the previous month's sales, total collections should be

Accounts receivable	$ 76,000
60% x December sales of $220,000	132,000
Budgeted cash collections	$208,000

68. The pro forma income (loss) before income taxes for December is

a. $32,400.
b. $28,000.
c. $14,400.
d. $10,000.
e. None of the above.

The correct answer is (d). *(CMA 1283 4-23)*
REQUIRED: The pro forma income (loss) before taxes for the month.
DISCUSSION: Sales are budgeted at $220,000. Given that cost of goods sold is 75% of sales, or $165,000, gross profit is $55,000. Deduct cash expenses of $22,600, depreciation of $18,000 ($216,000 ÷ 12), and bad debt expense of $4,400 ($220,000 x 2%). This leaves an income of $10,000.

69. The projected balance in accounts payable on December 31 is

a. $162,000.
b. $204,000.
c. $153,000.
d. $160,000.
e. None of the above.

The correct answer is (c). *(CMA 1283 4-24)*
REQUIRED: The projected balance in accounts payable at the end of the month.
DISCUSSION: The balance is equal to the purchases made during December since all purchases are paid for in the month following purchase. The amount purchased in December is given as 20% of December's sales and 80% of January's sales. Thus, of the $220,000 of merchandise sold during December, 20%, or $44,000, would have been purchased during the month. January's sales are expected to be $200,000, so 80% of that amount, or $160,000, would have been purchased during December. December purchases are thus estimated as $204,000 at the company's selling prices. Since the merchandise costs only 75% of the retail value, the balance in the purchases account at month-end is projected to be $153,000 (75% x $204,000).

Module 12.2: Budgeting Computations

70. The projected balance in inventory on December 31 is

   a. $160,000.
   b. $120,000.
   c. $153,000.
   d. $150,000.
   e. None of the above.

The correct answer is (b). *(CMA 1283 4-25)*
REQUIRED: The expected inventory balance at the end of the month.
DISCUSSION: The inventory is expected to be 80% of January's needs ($200,000 projected January sales x 80% = $160,000). Therefore, the ending inventory will consist of goods that the company could sell for $160,000. Given a gross margin of 25%, cost will be 75% of sales, or $120,000 (75% x $160,000).

71. In preparing its budget for July, Robinson Company has the following information:

Accounts receivable at June 30	$350,000
Estimated credit sales for July	400,000
Estimated collections in July for credit sales in July and prior months	320,000
Estimated write-offs in July for uncollectible credit sales	16,000
Estimated provision for doubtful accounts for credit sales in July	12,000

What is the projected balance of accounts receivable at July 31?

   a. $402,000.
   b. $414,000.
   c. $426,000.
   d. $430,000.

The correct answer is (b). *(CPA 1182 P-38)*
REQUIRED: The projected balance in accounts receivable at July 31.
DISCUSSION: The provision for doubtful accounts for credit sales in July does not affect the accounts receivable balance until it is written off as uncollectible. The projected balance of accounts receivable at July 31 is computed below.

Beginning balance	$350,000
Credit sales for July	400,000
Collections in July	(320,000)
Write-offs in July	(16,000)
Balance at July 31	$414,000

72. Pratt Company is preparing its cash budget for the month ending November 30. The following information pertains to Pratt's past collection experience from its credit sales:

Current month's sales	12%
Prior month's sales	75%
Sales 2 months prior to current month	6%
Sales 3 months prior to current month	4%
Cash discounts (2/30, net/90)	2%
Doubtful accounts	1%

Credit sales:

November - estimated	$200,000
October	180,000
September	160,000
August	190,000

How much is the estimated credit to A/R as a result of collections expected during November?

   a. $170,200.
   b. $174,200.
   c. $176,200.
   d. $180,200.

The correct answer is (c). *(CPA 1182 Q-23)*
REQUIRED: The amount of collections credited to accounts receivable in November.
DISCUSSION: The total estimated credit to accounts receivable is found by computing each credit to the accounts receivable account. Note that the cash discount will have no effect on the credit to accounts receivable arising from collections.

November ($200,000 x .12)	$ 24,000
October ($180,000 x .75)	135,000
September ($160,000 x .06)	9,600
August ($190,000 x .04)	7,600
Total credit to A/R	$176,200

Questions 73 through 78 are based on the Russon Corporation, a retailer whose sales are all made on credit. Sales are billed twice monthly, on the 10th of the month for the last half of the prior month's sales, and on the 20th of the month for the first half of the current month's sales. The terms of all sales are 2/10, net/30. Based upon past experience, the collection of accounts receivable is as follows:

Within the discount period	80%
On the 30th day	18%
Uncollectible	2%

Russon's average markup on its products is 20% of the sales price. All sales and purchases occur uniformly throughout the month.

The sales value of shipments for May and the forecasts for the next 4 months follow:

May (actual)	$500,000
June	600,000
July	700,000
August	700,000
September	400,000

Russon purchases merchandise for resale to meet the current month's sales demand and to maintain a desired monthly ending inventory of 25% of the next month's sales. All purchases are on credit with terms of net/30. Russon pays for 50% of a month's purchases in the month of purchase and 50% in the month following the purchase.

73. How much cash can Russon plan to collect in September from sales made in August?

a. $337,400.
b. $343,000.
c. $400,400.
d. $280,000.
e. None of the above.

The correct answer is (a). *(CMA 680 4-7)*
REQUIRED: Expected cash collections in September from August sales.
DISCUSSION: Cash collections in September from August sales include the billings made on August 20 and September 10.

August 20 (.18 x $350,000)	$ 63,000
September 10 (.80 x .98 x $350,000)	274,400
September collections on August sales	$337,400

74. The budgeted dollar value of Russon's inventory on August 31 will be

a. $110,000.
b. $80,000.
c. $112,000.
d. $100,000.
e. None of the above.

The correct answer is (b). *(CMA 680 4-8)*
REQUIRED: The budgeted dollar value of inventory on August 31.
DISCUSSION: The ending inventory balance is 25% of next month's sales. Therefore, the sales value of August ending inventory should be 25% of September sales of $400,000. Since the average markup is 20% of the sales price, sales = CGS + .2 sales (CGS = .8 sales). Cost of goods sold for September equals $320,000 ($400,000 x .80). August desired ending inventory is $80,000 (25% x $320,000).

Module 12.2: Budgeting Computations

75. How much cash can Russon Corporation plan to collect from accounts receivable collections during July?

a. $574,000.
b. $662,600.
c. $619,000.
d. $608,600.
e. None of the above.

The correct answer is (d). *(CMA 680 4-6)*
REQUIRED: Expected July cash collections from accounts receivable.
DISCUSSION: All Russon's sales are on account with billing twice monthly. Remember that on the 10th of the month, billings are sent for the last half of the prior month's sales and on the 20th for the first half of the current month's sales. Since all sales and purchases occur uniformly throughout the month, the calculation is as follows:

Billing date for collections received in July:

June 10 (.18 x $250,000)	$ 45,000
June 20 (.18 x $300,000)	54,000
July 10 (.80 x .98 x $300,000)	235,200
July 20 (.80 x .98 x $350,000)	274,400
July collections	$608,600

76. How much merchandise should Russon plan to purchase during June?

a. $520,000.
b. $460,000.
c. $500,000.
d. $580,000.
e. None of the above.

The correct answer is (c). *(CMA 680 4-9)*
REQUIRED: Planned merchandise purchases for June.
DISCUSSION: Desired EI plus CGS for the month less BI equals purchases.

EI [(.80 x $700,000) x .25]	$ 140,000
CGS (.80 x $600,000)	480,000
Required goods for June	$ 620,000
BI (.25 x $480,000)	$(120,000)
Purchases	$ 500,000

77. The amount Russon should budget in August for the payment of merchandise is

a. $560,000.
b. $500,000.
c. $667,000.
d. $600,000.
e. None of the above.

The correct answer is (e). *(CMA 680 4-10)*
REQUIRED: Planned payments for merchandise in August.
DISCUSSION: Payments for merchandise in August include half the August purchases and half the July purchases. Desired EI plus CGS less BI is equal to purchases.

	July	August
EI	$140,000	$ 80,000
CGS	560,000	560,000
Required goods	$700,000	$640,000
BI	(140,000)	(140,000)
Purchases	$560,000	$500,000
Divided by	÷ 2	÷ 2
Payments	$280,000	$250,000

78. Russon has found that most retailers in the area use markup percentages based upon cost rather than sales. Assuming MS equals the markup percentage based upon sales price and MC equals the markup percentage based upon cost, what formula would Russon use to convert its markup on sales to one based upon cost?

a. MC = MS ÷ (1 + MS).
b. MC = MS ÷ (1 - MS).
c. MC = (1 - MS) ÷ MS.
d. MC = (1 + MS) ÷ MS.
e. The markup on cost cannot be derived from the markup on sales.

The correct answer is (b). *(CMA 680 4-11)*
REQUIRED: The formula to convert markup on sales to markup based on cost.
DISCUSSION: The markup on sales (MS) is margin divided by sales. The markup on cost (MC) is margin divided by sales less margin. Sales less margin equals cost. For example, if the markup on sales is 20% (i.e., $20 of $100), the cost is $80. Thus, the markup on cost is $20 ÷ $80, or 25%. Substituting into each of the formulas in the answer choices, only MC = MS ÷ (1 - MS) is correct.

$$20 \div 80 = \frac{20 \div 100}{1 - 20 \div 100}$$

$$25\% = .2 \div .8$$

CHAPTER THIRTEEN
STANDARD COSTS

13.1 Standard Cost Concepts	(27 questions)	315
13.2 Materials	(29 questions)	322
13.3 Labor	(33 questions)	330
13.4 Overhead	(65 questions)	339
13.5 Sales Volume	(21 questions)	359
13.6 Combination	(24 questions)	365
13.7 Journal Entries	(20 questions)	372
13.8 Comprehensive	(65 questions)	379

Standard costing is a key concept given as much or more coverage than cost/volume/profit on the professional examinations. Thus, the student who is going to do well on professional examinations regarding management accounting issues must be well versed in both cost/volume/profit and standard costs. In this chapter, coverage is emphasized on the manufacturing variances, to match the emphasis given on the professional examinations. Most of these concepts are also applicable to service industries and not-for-profit industries. As such, they are of increasing importance to practitioners.

13.1 Standard Cost Concepts

1. A standard cost system may be used in

a. Job order costing but not process costing.
b. Either job order costing or process costing.
c. Process costing but not job order costing.
d. Neither process costing nor job order costing.

The correct answer is (b). *(CPA 584 T-43)*
REQUIRED: The cost accumulation system(s) that may use a standard cost system.
DISCUSSION: A standard cost system "costs" the product at standard (predetermined) costs and compares expected with actual cost. This comparison allows deviations (i.e., variances) from expected results to be identified and investigated. A standard cost system can be used in both job order and process costing systems to isolate variances.

2. A difference between standard costs used for cost control and the budgeted costs representing the same manufacturing effort

a. Can exist because standard costs must be determined after the budget is completed.
b. Can exist because standard costs represent what costs should be while budgeted costs represent expected actual costs.
c. Can exist because budgeted costs are historical costs while standard costs are based on engineering studies.
d. Can exist because budgeted costs include some "slack" or "padding" while standard costs do not.
e. Cannot exist because the amounts should be the same.

The correct answer is (b). *(CMA 683 4-5)*
REQUIRED: The difference between standard costs and budgeted costs.
DISCUSSION: In the long run, they should be the same. In the short run, however, they may differ because standard costs represent what costs should be, while budgeted costs represent expected actual costs. Budgeted costs may vary widely from standard costs in certain months, but, for an annual budget period, the amounts should be similar.
Answer (a) is incorrect because standard unit costs are considered during the budgetary process. Answer (c) is incorrect because standard costs are not necessarily determined by engineering studies. Answers (d) and (e) are incorrect because standard costs are usually based on currently attainable standards when a process is under control without regard to variances. Budgeted costs include expected deviations from the standards.

Module 13.1: Standard Cost Concepts

3. Standard costing is an important part of which of the following budgeting techniques?

a. Standing budgets.
b. Flexible budgets.
c. Financial budgets.
d. Operating budgets.

The correct answer is (b). *(Publisher)*
REQUIRED: The budgeting technique using standard costs.
DISCUSSION: The main budgeting technique involved with standard cost is the flexible budget. Flexible budgets are those budgets that can measure actual performance by adjusting for changes in volume. The flexible budget is the one that would have been created if management had known the actual activity level. By isolating the components of the budget into its variable and fixed components, management is able to set appropriate standards for each category, which is standard cost.

4. Which of the following is a purpose of standard costing?

a. Determine "breakeven" production level.
b. Control costs.
c. Eliminate the need for subjective decisions by management.
d. Allocate cost with more accuracy.

The correct answer is (b). *(CPA 577 T-36)*
REQUIRED: The purpose of a standard cost accumulation system.
DISCUSSION: Standard costing is used to isolate the variances between expected costs and actual costs. It allows management to measure performance and to correct inefficiencies, which help to control costs.
Answer (a) is incorrect because a standard costing system is not needed to perform breakeven CVP analysis. Answer (c) is incorrect because standard costs are used by management as an aid in decision making. Answer (d) is incorrect because standard costing does not allocate costs more accurately, especially when there are variances.

5. Which one of the following is true concerning standard costs?

a. Standard costs are estimates of costs attainable only under the most ideal conditions, but rarely practicable.
b. Standard costs are difficult to use with a process-costing system.
c. If properly used, standards can help motivate employees.
d. Unfavorable variances, material in amount, should be investigated, but large favorable variances need not be investigated.

The correct answer is (c). *(CPA 575 P-33)*
REQUIRED: The true statement about standard costs.
DISCUSSION: Standards are used as a norm against which actual results may be compared. One of the benefits of a standard cost system is that it can be used to motivate employees in that it gives them a goal to work toward.
Answer (a) is incorrect because standard costs should be attainable under efficient conditions. Answer (b) is incorrect because a standard cost system is ideally suited to a process-costing system. Answer (d) is incorrect because all material variances should be investigated, whether favorable or unfavorable.

6. When standard costs are used in a process-costing system, how, if at all, are equivalent units involved or used in the cost report at standard?

a. Equivalent units are not used.
b. Equivalent units are computed using a "special" approach.
c. The actual equivalent units are multiplied by the standard cost per unit.
d. The standard equivalent units are multiplied by the actual cost per unit.

The correct answer is (c). *(CPA 576 T-30)*
REQUIRED: The way equivalent units are used in a standard cost report.
DISCUSSION: A process-costing system is used to account for continuous production of homogeneous goods. EUP are calculated to determine how many complete units could have been produced, if there had been no BWIP and no EWIP. For example, if there are 100 units in EWIP 40% complete, the same amount of work could have produced 40 complete units. To determine the cost of the units produced, these EUP are multiplied by the standard cost per unit.
Answers (a) and (b) are incorrect because EUP are calculated in the regular manner. Answer (d) is incorrect because standard EUP is a nonsense term.

7. Sales volume variance is
   a. Flexible budget amounts - static budgeted amounts.
   b. Actual operating income - flexible budget operating income.
   c. Actual unit price - budget unit price x the actual units.
   d. Budgeted unit price x the difference between actual inputs and budgeted inputs for the actual activity level achieved.

The correct answer is (a). *(Publisher)*
   REQUIRED: The definition of sales volume variance.
   DISCUSSION: Sales volume variance assumes that, unit prices remaining constant, the only variable change is the sales volume activity level. Thus, the difference between the flexible budget amounts and the static budgeted amounts is the sales volume variance. The resulting variance is based on the change in sales volume exclusively.
   Answer (b) is incorrect because it is the definition of the flexible budget variance in operating income. Answer (c) is incorrect because it defines the price variance. Answer (d) is incorrect because it defines an efficiency variance.

8. An efficiency variance is
   a. Flexible budget amounts - static budgeted amounts.
   b. Actual operating income - flexible budget operating income.
   c. Actual unit price - budget unit price x the actual units.
   d. Budgeted unit price x the difference between actual inputs and budgeted inputs for the actual activity level achieved.

The correct answer is (d). *(Publisher)*
   REQUIRED: The definition of an efficiency variance.
   DISCUSSION: An efficiency variance compares the actual use of inputs with the budgeted quantity of inputs allowed for the activity level achieved. When multiplied by the budgeted unit price, it isolates the cost effect of using more or fewer units of input than budgeted.

9. The flexible budget variance in operating income is
   a. Actual operating income - flexible budget operating income.
   b. Budgeted unit price x the difference between actual inputs and budgeted inputs for the actual activity level achieved.
   c. Flexible budget amounts - static budgeted amounts.
   d. Actual unit price - budget unit price x the actual units.

The correct answer is (a). *(Publisher)*
   REQUIRED: The definition of the flexible budget variance in operating income.
   DISCUSSION: This analysis permits an examination of the difference in operating income between the actual and the flexible budget. The flexible budget is the budget that would have been created had management known the actual activity level. Any deviations from that budget should be explained by changes in any of the items shown on the flexible budget except the activity level.

10. When computing variances from standard costs, the difference between actual and standard price multiplied by actual quantity yields a
    a. Combined price-quantity variance.
    b. Price variance.
    c. Volume variance.
    d. Mix variance.

The correct answer is (b). *(CPA 577 T-37)*
   REQUIRED: The variance determined by multiplying the difference between actual and standard price by actual quantity.
   DISCUSSION: Letting A = actual, S = standard, P = price, and Q = quantity, the price variance can be denoted by (AP - SP) x AQ, which gives the deviation between the expected outlay and actual outlay due to the price difference.
   Answer (a) is incorrect because the combined price-quantity variance is denoted by (AP x AQ) - (SP x SQ). Answer (c) is incorrect because volume variance, a fixed overhead variance, is the difference between budgeted fixed costs and output at standard fixed costs. Answer (d) is incorrect because mix variance is the deviation resulting from changing proportions in the original sales or production mix.

Module 13.1: Standard Cost Concepts

11. A company controls its production costs by comparing its actual monthly production costs with the expected levels. Any significant deviations from expected levels are investigated and evaluated as a basis for corrective actions. The quantitative technique that is most probably being used is

a. Correlation analysis.
b. Differential calculus.
c. Risk analysis.
d. Standard cost variance analysis.
e. Time series or trend regression analysis.

The correct answer is (d). *(CPA 572 T-31)*
REQUIRED: The quantitative technique described in the situation.
DISCUSSION: Standard cost variance analysis is a technique that compares the forecasted costs with actual costs. The standard cost system differentiates the expected cost from the actual cost, which allows routine identification of deviations from expected results.
Answer (a) is incorrect because correlation analysis measures the strength of the linear relationship between two variables. Answer (b) is incorrect because differential calculus is used to measure the slope of curved lines, i.e., nonlinear functions. Answer (c) is incorrect because risk analysis is used to evaluate the risk between items. Answer (e) is incorrect because time series or trend regression analysis is regression with time as an independent variable.

12. The best basis upon which cost standards should be set to measure controllable production inefficiencies is

a. Engineering standards based on ideal performance.
b. Normal capacity.
c. Recent average historical performance.
d. Engineering standards based on attainable performance.
e. Practical capacity.

The correct answer is (d). *(CMA 1279 4-11)*
REQUIRED: The best basis upon which cost standards should be set to measure controllable production inefficiencies.
DISCUSSION: A standard cost system separates the expected cost from the actual cost. Thus, deviations from expected results are identified on a routine basis. The best standards are based on attainable performance so that any deviation will denote inefficiencies that deserve review and have a reasonable probability of responding to management attention.
Answer (a) is incorrect because ideal standards are a result of the most efficient operations, which usually cannot be met or maintained. Answer (b) is incorrect because normal capacity is the level of production that will satisfy average consumer demand over a span of time which includes seasonal, cyclical, and trend factors. Answer (c) is incorrect because historical performance may be a bad indicator of future performance. Answer (e) is incorrect because practical capacity is the maximum level at which the plant or department can possibly operate most efficiently, i.e., ideal capacity less allowances for external contingencies such as supply shortages.

13. The standards used by shoe manufacturers to determine size categories are best classified as

a. Ideal standards.
b. External standards.
c. Engineered standards.
d. Productivity standards.

The correct answer is (b). *(CIA 1185 III-11)*
REQUIRED: The kind of standard used by manufacturers to determine size categories.
DISCUSSION: External standards are established outside the entity. Government regulations and trade association standards are examples. Standardization of shoe sizes is derived from external factors and is of obvious benefit to consumers.
Answer (a) is incorrect because ideal standards are seldom attainable. Answer (c) is incorrect because engineered standards relate to machine capacities under perfect conditions, e.g., no downtime, etc. Answer (d) is incorrect because productivity standards concern output per unit of time and are based on an analysis of the task and the skills of the worker(s).

Module 13.1: Standard Cost Concepts

14. When performing input/output variance analysis in standard costing, "standard hours allowed" is a means of measuring

a. Standard output at standard hours.
b. Actual output at standard hours.
c. Standard output at actual hours.
d. Actual output at actual hours.

The correct answer is (b). *(CPA 577 T-38)*
REQUIRED: The use of "standard hours allowed" in input/output variance analysis.
DISCUSSION: The standard hours allowed is the standard hours for the actual output. This permits generation of a flexible budget for management review.
Answer (a) is incorrect because the standard hours allowed is for actual output, not standard output. Answer (c) is incorrect because actual output at the standard hours allowed is used in input/output analysis. Answer (d) is incorrect because standard hours allowed is in terms of standard, not actual, hours.

15. The absolute minimum cost possible under the best conceivable operating conditions is a description of which type of standard cost?

a. Currently attainable (expected).
b. Theoretical.
c. Normal.
d. Practical.

The correct answer is (b). *(CPA 1180 T-48)*
REQUIRED: The standard cost that describes the absolute minimum cost under the best operating conditions.
DISCUSSION: A theoretical (or ideal) cost standard is the most efficient use of all resources to produce at the absolute minimum cost. It is probably never attainable.
Answer (a) is incorrect because currently attainable standards are based on the capacity for the next period. Answer (c) is incorrect because normal costs are based on a constant, average utilization level of plant and workers over a multi-period time. Answer (d) is incorrect because practical costs are the theoretical costs less an allowance for internal or external contingencies (which is still very difficult to attain).

16. A company employing very tight (high) standards in a standard cost system should expect that

a. No incentive bonus will be paid.
b. Most variances will be unfavorable.
c. Employees will be strongly motivated to attain the standards.
d. Costs will be controlled better than if lower standards were used.

The correct answer is (b). *(CPA 1172 T-23)*
REQUIRED: The effect of tight standards in a standard cost system.
DISCUSSION: Tight standards are hard to meet and usually result in unfavorable variances, since little slack is permitted.
Answer (a) is incorrect because the tightness of the standards have no prescribed relationship to paying incentive bonuses. Answer (c) is incorrect because tight standards that are difficult to meet will probably result in less motivation. Answer (d) is incorrect because tight standards may point out too many inefficiencies to work on than would reasonable standards.

17. Which of the following factors should not be considered when deciding whether to investigate a variance?

a. Magnitude of the variance.
b. Trend of the variances over time.
c. Likelihood that an investigation will eliminate future occurrences of the variance.
d. Cost of investigating the variance.
e. Whether the variance is favorable or unfavorable.

The correct answer is (e). *(CIA 579 IV-2)*
REQUIRED: The factor not relevant in deciding whether to investigate a variance.
DISCUSSION: A variance shows a deviation of actual results from the expected or budgeted results. All material variances should be investigated, whether favorable or unfavorable.
Answer (a) is incorrect because only material variances should be investigated. Answer (b) is incorrect because the trend of variances over time should be considered. A negative variance that has been getting progressively smaller might not need investigating, whereas a variance that is progressively growing should be investigated promptly. Answer (c) is incorrect because the objective of variance investigation is pinpointing responsibility and taking corrective action toward eliminating variances. Answer (d) is incorrect because the benefits of each step in the entire standard cost process must be cost effective. Benefits should exceed costs.

18. Standard costing will produce the same income before extraordinary items as actual costing when standard cost variances are assigned to

a. Work-in-process and finished goods inventories.
b. An income or expense account.
c. Cost of goods sold and inventories.
d. Cost of goods sold.

The correct answer is (c). *(CPA 573 T-23)*
REQUIRED: The account(s) to allocate the standard cost variances so that standard costing income equals actual costing income.
DISCUSSION: Assigning variances to cost of goods sold and inventories, based on production and sales for the period will allocate the variance the same as actual costing; i.e., standard costing is converted to actual costing.
Answer (a) is incorrect because a good portion of the variance usually needs to be allocated to CGS. Answers (b) and (d) are incorrect because the variance also needs to be allocated to the inventory accounts.

19. If the total materials variance (actual cost of materials used compared with the standard cost of the standard amount of materials required) for a given operation is favorable, why must this variance be further evaluated as to price and usage?

a. There is no need to further evaluate the total materials variance if it is favorable.
b. Generally accepted accounting principles require that all variances be analyzed in three stages.
c. All variances must appear in the annual report to equity owners for proper disclosure.
d. To allow management to evaluate the efficiency of the purchasing and production functions.

The correct answer is (d). *(CPA 578 T-44)*
REQUIRED: The reason for evaluating a favorable variance as to price and usage.
DISCUSSION: A standard cost system differentiates the expected cost from the actual cost, which allows deviations from expected results to be identified on a timely basis. An overall variance may include both unfavorable and favorable variances. By separating the overall variance, the price variance is used to evaluate the purchasing department, and the usage variance pinpoints any production inefficiencies.
Answer (a) is incorrect because all significant variances should be investigated, regardless of the direction of the variance. Answer (b) is incorrect because GAAP require neither standard costs in general nor any means of implementing standard costs in particular. Answer (c) is incorrect because variances usually are not reported to third parties and do not appear in the annual report.

20. When items are transferred from stores to production, an accountant debits work-in-process and credits materials accounts. During production, a materials quantity variance may occur. The materials quantity variance is debited for an unfavorable variance and credited for a favorable variance. The intent of variance entries is to provide

a. Accountability for materials lost during production.
b. A means of safeguarding assets in the custody of the system.
c. Compliance with GAAP.
d. Information for use in controlling the cost of production.

The correct answer is (d). *(CIA 1187 II-10)*
REQUIRED: The intent of variance entries.
DISCUSSION: One step in the control process is measurement of actual results against standards. For example, the standard quantity of materials for a given output is established prior to production. If the actual material usage exceeds the standard, the variance is unfavorable and corrective action may be needed. Corrective action is another step in the control process.
Answers (a) and (b) are incorrect because accountability is adequately established by the inventory entries. Thus, safeguarding assets is not a necessary function of variance accounts. Answer (c) is incorrect because internal cost accounting information need not comply with GAAP.

21. Which department is customarily held responsible for an unfavorable materials usage variance?

a. Quality control.
b. Purchasing.
c. Engineering.
d. Production.

The correct answer is (d). *(CPA 581 T-50)*
REQUIRED: The department usually responsible for an unfavorable materials usage variance.
DISCUSSION: Responsibility for variances should bear some relationship to the decision and control processes used. Materials usage should be the primary responsibility of the production management personnel.
Answers (a) and (c) are incorrect because quality control and engineering are responsible for design, engineering, and quality standards. Answer (b) is incorrect because purchasing usually is responsible for materials price variance.

Module 13.1: Standard Cost Concepts

22. At the end of its fiscal year, Graham Co. had several substantial variances from standard variable manufacturing costs. The one which should be allocated between inventories and cost of sales is the one attributable to

a. Additional cost of raw material acquired under a speculative purchase contract.

b. A breakdown of equipment.

c. Overestimates of production volume for the period resulting from failure to predict an unusual decline in the market for the company's product.

d. Increased labor rates won by the union as a result of a strike.

23. The standard unit cost is used in the calculation of which of the following variances?

	Materials Price Variance	Materials Usage Variance
a.	No	No
b.	No	Yes
c.	Yes	No
d.	Yes	Yes

24. How should a usage variance that is significant in amount be treated at the end of an accounting period?

a. Reported as a deferred charge or credit.

b. Allocated among work-in-process inventory, finished goods inventory, and cost of goods sold.

c. Charged or credited to cost of goods manufactured.

d. Allocated among cost of goods manufactured, finished goods inventory, and cost of goods sold.

25. What is the normal year-end treatment of immaterial variances recognized in a cost accounting system utilizing standards?

a. Reclassified to deferred charges until all related production is sold.

b. Allocated among cost of goods manufactured and ending work-in-process inventory.

c. Closed to cost of goods sold in the period in which they arose.

d. Capitalized as a cost of ending finished goods inventory.

The correct answer is (d). *(CPA 573 T-36)*
REQUIRED: The standard variable manufacturing cost variance to allocate to inventory and CGS.
DISCUSSION: A standard cost system differentiates the expected cost from the actual cost. Thus, deviations from expected results are identified on a routine basis. Increased wages are a part of doing business and usually increase the cost of the items made and sold.
Answer (a) is incorrect because gains and losses on speculation are not product costs. Answer (b) is incorrect because, during a breakdown, variable manufacturing costs should not be incurred. Answer (c) is incorrect because it would result in a volume variance which concerns fixed not variable manufacturing costs.

The correct answer is (d). *(CPA 1182 T-50)*
REQUIRED: The variance(s) using standard unit costs.
DISCUSSION: The materials price variance is calculated by multiplying the difference between actual price and standard price by the actual units purchased [(AP - SP)AQ]. The materials usage variance is calculated by multiplying the difference between the actual usage and the standard usage by the standard price [(AQ - SQ)SP]. Therefore, the standard unit cost is used to compute both the materials price variance and the materials usage variance.

The correct answer is (b). *(CPA 579 T-25)*
REQUIRED: The treatment of a usage variance at the end of a period.
DISCUSSION: Allocating a variance among work-in-process, finished goods, and cost of goods sold will properly match the variance to the items produced. This procedure adjusts the respective accounts, which are expressed in terms of standard costs, to actual costs.
Answer (a) is incorrect because some of the variance should be allocated to cost of goods sold. Answers (c) and (d) are incorrect because cost of goods manufactured refers to a flow of goods (i.e., the goods transferred from WIP to finished goods), rather than a balance at year-end.

The correct answer is (c). *(CPA 579 T-33)*
REQUIRED: The normal year-end treatment of immaterial variances accumulated in a standard cost accounting system.
DISCUSSION: Normally, all immaterial variances are closed to CGS in the period in which they arose. It is done this way for simplicity, rather than allocating the variance between the inventories and CGS.
Answer (a) is incorrect because immaterial variances cannot be said to provide future benefit. Answers (b) and (d) are incorrect because, if allocated, the allocation should be to EWIP, FG inventory, and CGS in proportion to the relative flow of goods. However, due to cost/benefit analysis, only material variances are usually allocated in this manner.

26. Which of the following is not an acceptable treatment of factory overhead variances at an interim reporting date?

   a. Apportion the total only between work-in-process and finished goods inventories on hand at the end of the interim reporting period.
   b. Apportion the total only between that part of the current period's production remaining in inventories at the end of the period and that part sold during the period.
   c. Carry forward the total to be offset by opposite balances in later periods.
   d. Charge or credit the total to the cost of goods sold during the period.

The correct answer is (a). *(CPA 574 T-18)*
REQUIRED: The unacceptable treatment of factory overhead variances at an interim reporting date.
DISCUSSION: Factory overhead variances may be carried to future interim periods as deferred charges or credits, charged or credited to CGS, or apportioned between inventories and CGS. To apportion the total only between WIP and FG would not allocate a proper proportion to CGS.
Answers (b), (c), and (d) are incorrect because each is an acceptable accounting treatment for factory overhead variances under appropriate circumstances. Allocating the variance between CGS and inventories is the usual process for material variances. Carrying the balance forward is appropriate when a future benefit from the variance exists. Charging the variance against CGS is appropriate when the variance is immaterial.

27. The budget for a given cost during a given period was $80,000. The actual cost for the period was $72,000. Considering these facts, it can be said that the plant manager has done a better than expected job in controlling the cost if

   a. The cost is variable and actual production was 90% of budgeted production
   b. The cost is variable and actual production equaled budgeted production.
   c. The cost is variable and actual production was 80% of budgeted production.
   d. The cost is a discretionary fixed cost and actual production equaled budgeted production.

The correct answer is (b). *(CPA 1172 T-35)*
REQUIRED: The evaluation of job performance compared to budget.
DISCUSSION: When comparing the actual job performance to budget, the deviations must be noted and compared to the appropriate budget that would have been in effect had perfect information been available. In this case, if this cost was a variable cost and actual production matched the budgeted production, $80,000 is the expected actual cost. Since the actual cost was $72,000, the plant manager has done a good job in controlling the cost.
Answer (a) is incorrect because, if the cost were variable and actual production were 90% of budgeted production, the plant manager would merely have met the standard (90% x $80,000 = $72,000). Answer (c) is incorrect because, if the cost were variable and actual production were 80% of budgeted production, the plant manager did a less-than-adequate job in controlling the cost. The standard would then be $64,000 (80% of $80,000). Answer (d) is incorrect because it is impossible to determine if the discretionary fixed cost has been changed by the plant manager or someone else.

13.2 Materials

28. In a standard cost system, the materials price variance is obtained by multiplying the

   a. Actual price by the difference between actual quantity purchased and standard quantity used.
   b. Actual quantity purchased by the difference between actual price and standard price.
   c. Standard price by the difference between standard quantity purchased and standard quantity used.
   d. Standard quantity purchased by the difference between actual price and standard price.

The correct answer is (b). *(CPA 1173 T-34)*
REQUIRED: The method used to compute the materials price variance.
DISCUSSION: The materials price variance measures the difference between what was actually paid for the goods purchased and the standard amount allowed for the goods purchased. Therefore, it is computed by multiplying the difference between actual price and standard price by the actual quantity purchased:

$$(AP - SP)AQ$$

This assumes price variances are isolated at the time of purchase. If they are isolated when the materials are used, the variance is the difference between standard and actual price times the amount used (not amount purchased).

Module 13.2: Materials

29. An unfavorable price variance occurs because of

a. Price increases on raw materials.
b. Price decreases on raw materials.
c. Less than anticipated levels of waste in the manufacturing process.
d. More than anticipated levels of waste in the manufacturing process.

The correct answer is (a). *(CPA 1180 T-50)*
REQUIRED: Why an unfavorable price variance occurs.
DISCUSSION: A standard cost system differentiates the expected cost from the actual cost. Thus, deviations from expected results are identified on a routine basis. An increase in the actual price of raw material over the standard price will result in an unfavorable price variance.
Answer (b) is incorrect because a decrease in price would result in a favorable price variance. Answer (c) is incorrect because less waste would result in a favorable materials usage variance. Answer (d) is incorrect because more waste would result in an unfavorable materials usage variance.

30. What type of direct material variances for price and usage will arise if the actual number of pounds of materials used exceeds standard pounds allowed but actual cost was less than standard cost?

	Usage	Price
a.	Unfavorable	Favorable
b.	Favorable	Favorable
c.	Favorable	Unfavorable
d.	Unfavorable	Unfavorable

The correct answer is (a). *(CPA 579 T-20)*
REQUIRED: Whether material price and usage variances are favorable or unfavorable.
DISCUSSION: A favorable price variance arises when the actual costs are less than standard costs. An unfavorable usage variance results when actual units used exceeds standard units allowed.
Answer (b) is incorrect because the actual usage would have to be less than standard usage for a favorable usage variance. Answer (c) is incorrect because actual usage would have to be less than standard usage for a favorable usage variance, and actual costs would have to be greater than standard costs for an unfavorable price variance. Answer (d) is incorrect because the actual costs would have to be greater than the standard costs for an unfavorable price variance.

31. If a company follows a practice of isolating variances at the earliest time, what would be the appropriate time to isolate and recognize a direct material price variance?

a. When material is issued.
b. When material is purchased.
c. When material is used in production.
d. When the purchase order is originated.

The correct answer is (b). *(CPA 1184 T-50)*
REQUIRED: The best time to isolate a direct materials price variance.
DISCUSSION: The time of purchase is the most appropriate point to isolate and recognize a price variance. Analysis here permits an earlier examination of variances.
Answers (a) and (c) are incorrect because time elapses between when the materials are purchased and issued or used. Answer (d) is incorrect because the transaction has not yet been consummated.

32. Materials usage variances are normally chargeable to which department?

a. Production.
b. Purchasing.
c. Finished goods.
d. Materials storage.

The correct answer is (a). *(CIA 586 IV-3)*
REQUIRED: The department to which materials usage variances are normally chargeable.
DISCUSSION: Variances are chargeable to the department with control over the differences that occur. Since the production department usually controls how much materials are used, materials usage variances are normally chargeable to that department.
Answers (b), (c), and (d) are incorrect because the purchasing, finished goods, and materials storage departments do not have control over materials usage.

33. Which of the following would least likely cause an unfavorable materials quantity (usage) variance?

a. Materials that do not meet specifications.
b. Machinery that has not been maintained properly.
c. Labor that possesses skills equal to those required by the standards.
d. Scheduling of substantial overtime.
e. A mix of raw material that does not conform to plan.

The correct answer is (c). *(CIA 582 IV-22)*
REQUIRED: The item least likely to cause an unfavorable materials quantity variance.
DISCUSSION: An efficiency, or usage, variance for materials occurs when more or less material than the standard is used. Unfavorable variances are when actual is more than standard. Labor that is skilled commensurate with materials usage standards should achieve standard materials usage; i.e., little or no variance should arise.
Answers (a), (b), (d), and (e) are incorrect because each is a possible cause of an unfavorable materials quantity usage variance.

34. Todco planned to produce 3,000 units of its single product, Teragram, during November. The standard specifications for one unit of Teragram include six pounds of material at $.30 per pound. Actual production in November was 3,100 units of Teragram. The accountant computed a favorable materials purchase price variance of $380 and an unfavorable materials quantity variance of $120. Based on these variances, one could conclude that

a. More materials were purchased than were used.
b. More materials were used than were purchased.
c. The actual cost of materials was less than the standard cost.
d. The actual usage of materials was less than the standard allowed.
e. That actual cost and usage of materials were both less than standard.

The correct answer is (c). *(CMA 1287 4-30)*
REQUIRED: The implication of favorable price variance or an unfavorable quantity variance.
DISCUSSION: A favorable price variance indicates that the materials were purchased at a price less than standard. The unfavorable quantity variance indicates that the quantity of materials used for actual production exceeded the standard quantity for the good units produced.
Answers (a) and (b) are incorrect because the quantity of materials purchased cannot be determined from the information given. Answers (d) and (e) are incorrect because the actual usage was greater than standard.

35. Information on Kennedy Company's direct material costs is as follows:

Standard unit price	$3.60
Actual quantity purchased	1,600
Standard quantity allowed for actual production	1,450
Materials purchase price variance - favorable	$240

What was the actual purchase price per unit, rounded to the nearest penny?

a. $3.06.
b. $3.11.
c. $3.45.
d. $3.75.

The correct answer is (c). *(CPA 1179 P-38)*
REQUIRED: The actual purchase price per unit.
DISCUSSION: The actual price per unit can be found by subtracting the favorable price variance ($240) from the standard cost ($5,760) and dividing by the number of units purchased.

Total standard cost (1,600 units at $3.60)	$5,760
Less: Materials price variance	(240)
Total actual cost	$5,520
Divided by actual quantity	÷1,600
Actual cost per unit	$ 3.45

Module 13.2: Materials

36. Information on Rex Co.'s direct material costs for May is as follows:

Actual quantity of direct materials purchased and used	30,000 lbs.
Actual cost of direct materials	$84,000
Unfavorable direct materials usage variance	3,000
Standard quantity of direct materials allowed for May production	29,000 lbs.

For the month of May, what was Rex's direct materials price variance?

a. $2,800 favorable.
b. $2,800 unfavorable.
c. $6,000 unfavorable.
d. $6,000 favorable.

The correct answer is (d). *(CPA 1185 Q-9)*
REQUIRED: The direct material price variance.
DISCUSSION: The direct material price variance is the difference between the actual price (AP) of direct materials and the standard price (SP) per unit times the actual quantity (AQ). The actual price is $2.80/lb. ($84,000/30,000 lbs.). The standard price is $3 per lb. based on the unfavorable usage variance of $3,000 resulting from 1,000 lbs. of excess usage (30,000 - 29,000). The actual quantity is 30,000 lbs. Therefore, the direct material price variance is AQ (AP - SP) or 30,000 ($2.80 - $3) = ($6,000). The $6,000 is favorable because the AP is less than the SP.

37. Perkins Company, which has a standard cost system, had 500 units of raw material X in its inventory at June 1, purchased in May for $1.20 per unit and carried at a standard cost of $1.00. The following information pertains to raw material X for the month of June:

Actual number of units purchased	1,400
Actual number of units used	1,500
Standard number of units allowed for actual production	1,300
Standard cost per unit	$1.00
Actual cost per unit	$1.10

The unfavorable materials purchase price variance for raw material X for June was

a. $0.
b. $130.
c. $140.
d. $150.

The correct answer is (c). *(CPA 1182 Q-24)*
REQUIRED: The direct materials purchase price (MPV) variance.
DISCUSSION: The materials purchase price variance is found by multiplying the difference between the standard cost per unit and actual cost per unit by the actual number of units purchased. An unfavorable variance results when the actual cost exceeds the standard cost. Note that the 500 units previously purchased for $1.20/unit are carried at $1.00/unit. This means material price variances are identified and recognized at the point of purchase.

AQ(AP - SP) = MPV
1,400($1.10 - $1.00) = $140 unfavorable

38. During March, Younger Company's direct material costs for the manufacture of product T were as follows:

Actual unit purchase price	$6.50
Standard quantity allowed for actual production	2,100
Quantity purchased and used for actual production	2,300
Standard unit price	$6.25

Younger's material usage variance for March

a. $1,250 unfavorable.
b. $1,250 favorable.
c. $1,300 unfavorable.
d. $1,300 favorable.

The correct answer is (a). *(CPA 581 P-28)*
REQUIRED: The material usage variance (MUV) for the month.
DISCUSSION: The material usage variance is found by multiplying the difference between actual and standard usage by the standard price. An unfavorable variance results when actual usage is greater than standard.

SP(AQ - SQ) = MUV
$6.25(2,300 - 2,100) = $1,250 unfavorable

Module 13.2: Materials

39. Information on Material Company's direct material costs is as follows:

Actual units of direct materials used	20,000
Actual direct material costs	$40,000
Standard price per unit of direct materials	$ 2.10
Direct material efficiency variance - favorable	$ 3,000

What was Material's direct material price variance?

a. $1,000 favorable.
b. $1,000 unfavorable.
c. $2,000 favorable.
d. $2,000 unfavorable.

The correct answer is (c). *(CPA 579 P-37)*
REQUIRED: The direct material price variance (MPV).
DISCUSSION: The direct material price variance is found by finding the difference between the actual price (AP) of direct materials and the standard price (SP) per unit times the actual quantity (AQ).

$$AQ(AP - SP) = MPV$$
$$20,000(\$2.00 - \$2.10) = \$2,000 \text{ favorable}$$

40. A company uses a standard cost system to account for its only product. The materials standard per unit was 4 lbs. at $5.10 per lb. Operating data for April were as follows:

Material used	7,800 lbs.
Cost of material used	$40,950
Number of finished units produced	2,000

The material usage variance for April was

a. $1,020 favorable.
b. $1,050 favorable.
c. $1,170 unfavorable.
d. $1,200 unfavorable.

The correct answer is (a). *(CIA 1185 IV-3)*
REQUIRED: The material usage variance for the month.
DISCUSSION: The material usage variance is the difference between actual and standard usage times the standard price. Actual usage was 7,800 lbs. Standard usage was 8,000 lbs. (2,000 units x 4 lbs.). Standard price was $5.10/lb. Thus, the material usage variance was $1,020 [(7,800 - 8,000) x $5.10]. The variance is favorable because actual materials used was less than the standard quantity.

41. Each finished unit of Product DX-25 contains 60 pounds of raw material. The manufacturing process must provide for a 20% waste allowance. The raw material can be purchased for $2.50 a pound under terms of 2/10, n/30. The company takes all cash discounts. The standard direct material cost for each unit of DX-25 is

a. $180.00.
b. $187.50.
c. $183.75.
d. $176.40.
e. None of the above.

The correct answer is (c). *(CMA 684 4-25)*
REQUIRED: The standard direct material cost for each unit.
DISCUSSION: The net standard direct material cost is equal to the cost per pound times the quantity required, including waste allowance, less the cash discount. If a finished unit contains 60 pounds after a 20% waste allowance, 75 pounds (60 ÷ .8) are required.

75 x $2.50 =	$187.50
Less 2% =	(3.75)
Standard unit cost	$183.75

42. Durable Company installs shingle roofs on houses. The standard material cost for a Type R house is $1,250, based on 1,000 units at a cost of $1.25 each. During April, Durable installed roofs on 20 Type R houses, using 22,000 units of material at a cost of $1.20 per unit, and a total cost of $26,400. Durable's material price variance for April is

a. $1,000 favorable.
b. $1,100 favorable.
c. $1,400 unfavorable.
d. $2,500 unfavorable.

The correct answer is (b). *(CPA 1180 P-38)*
REQUIRED: The material price variance (MPV) for the month.
DISCUSSION: The MPV is determined by multiplying the difference between actual price (AP) and standard price (SP) by the actual units (AQ) of materials. A favorable variance results when actual price is less than standard price.

$$AQ(AP - SP) = MPV$$
$$22,000(\$1.20 - \$1.25) = \$1,100 \text{ favorable}$$

Module 13.2: Materials

43. Buckler Company manufactures desks with vinyl tops. The standard material cost for the vinyl used per Model S desk is $27.00, based on 12 square feet of vinyl at a cost of $2.25 per square foot. A production run of 1,000 desks in March resulted in usage of 12,600 square feet of vinyl at a cost of $2.00 per square foot, a total cost of $25,200. The usage variance resulting from the above production run was

a. $1,200 unfavorable.
b. $1,350 unfavorable.
c. $1,800 favorable.
d. $3,150 favorable.

The correct answer is (b). *(CPA 582 P-31)*
REQUIRED: The material usage variance (MUV) for the month.
DISCUSSION: The usage variance is found by multiplying the difference between the actual usage and the standard usage by the standard price. An unfavorable variance results when actual usage is greater than standard.

$$SP(AQ - SQ) = MUV$$
$$\$2.25(12,600 - 12,000) = \$1,350 \text{ unfavorable}$$

44. Throop Company had budgeted 50,000 units of output using 50,000 units of raw materials at a total material cost of $100,000. Actual output was 50,000 units of product, requiring 45,000 units of raw materials at a cost of $2.10 per unit. The direct material price variance and usage variance were

	Price	Usage
a.	$4,500 unfavorable	$10,000 favorable
b.	$5,000 favorable	$10,500 unfavorable
c.	$5,000 unfavorable	$10,500 favorable
d.	$10,000 favorable	$4,500 unfavorable

The correct answer is (a). *(CPA 1181 P-26)*
REQUIRED: The materials price and usage variance.
DISCUSSION: The material price variance (MPV) is determined by multiplying the difference between actual and standard price by the actual quantity. The material usage variance (MUV) is found by multiplying the difference between the actual and standard usage by the standard price. A favorable variance results when the actual is less than the standard.

$$AQ(AP - SP) = MPV$$
$$45,000(\$2.10 - \$2.00) = \$4,500 \text{ unfavorable}$$
$$SP(AQ - SQ) = MUV$$
$$\$2.00(45,000 - 50,000) = \$10,000 \text{ favorable}$$

45. Materials mix variance is

a. (Inputs allowed - inputs used) x (budgeted average materials price).
b. (Inputs allowed - inputs used) x (budgeted specific labor rate - budgeted average labor rate).
c. (Inputs allowed - inputs used) x (budgeted average labor rate).
d. (Inputs allowed - inputs used) x (budgeted specific material prices - budgeted average material price).

The correct answer is (d). *(Publisher)*
REQUIRED: The definition of materials mix variance.
DISCUSSION: Material yield and material mix variances further break down the material usage variance. They are appropriate only if certain classes or types of materials can be substituted for each other.

Material mix variance is calculated to determine the effects upon the material cost attributable to the change in the mix of materials used. Thus, it is the amount of each class of material actually used times the difference between the budgeted price for each class of material and the budgeted average material cost for all materials in the mix. Because this substitutability of materials may not be present in every situation, the material mix variance is only suitable for analysis when the manager has some control over the composition of the mix.

46. Materials yield variance is

a. (Inputs allowed - inputs used) x (budgeted average materials price).
b. (Inputs allowed - inputs used) x (budgeted specific labor rate - budgeted average labor rate).
c. (Inputs allowed - inputs used) x (budgeted average labor rate).
d. (Inputs allowed - inputs used) x (budgeted specific material prices - budgeted average material price).

The correct answer is (a). *(Publisher)*
REQUIRED: The definition of materials yield variance.
DISCUSSION: The yield variance is the difference in total units used times the average price. Material yield variance is a calculation based on the assumed components of materials in producing a given output.

Answer (b) is incorrect because it is the definition of labor mix variance. Answer (c) is incorrect because it is the definition of the labor yield variance. Answer (d) is incorrect because it is the definition of material mix variance.

Questions 47 through 56 are based on the following information, which was presented as part of Question 5 on Part 4 of the June 1982 CMA examination.

Energy Modification Company produces a gasoline additive, Gas Gain. This product increases engine efficiency and improves gasoline mileage by creating a more complete burn in the combustion process. Careful controls are required during the production process to ensure that the proper mix of input chemicals is achieved and that evaporation is controlled. Loss of output and efficiency may result if the controls are not effective. The standard cost of producing a 500-liter batch of Gas Gain is $135. The standard materials mix and related standard cost of each chemical used in a 500-liter batch are presented in the opposite column.

Chemical	Standard Input Quantity in Liters	Standard Cost per Liter	Total Cost
Echol	200	$.200	$ 40.00
Protex	100	.425	42.50
Benz	250	.150	37.50
CT-40	50	.300	15.00
	600		$135.00

The quantities of chemicals purchased and used during the current production period are shown in the schedule below. A total of 140 batches of Gas Gain were manufactured during the current production period. Silly Willy, the controller of Energy Modification Company, determines its costs and chemical usage variations at the end of each production period.

Chemical	Quantity Purchased (Liters)	Total Purchase Price	Quantity Used (Liters)
Echol	25,000	$ 5,365	26,600
Protex	13,000	6,240	12,880
Benz	40,000	5,840	37,800
CT-40	7,500	2,220	7,140
Total	85,500	$19,665	84,420

47. What is the purchase price variance for Echol?

a. $365 unfavorable.
b. $715 unfavorable.
c. $160 favorable.
d. $30 favorable.

The correct answer is (a). *(Publisher)*
REQUIRED: The purchase price variance for Echol.
DISCUSSION: The purchase price variance is equal to the actual cost less the standard price times the actual quantity purchased. The variance is unfavorable if actual price paid is greater than standard.

Actual	SP x AQ Purchased	Price Variance
$5,365 -	($.20 x 25,000) =	$365 U

An alternate formula for this and the next three questions is that the variance equals the actual units purchased (AQ) times the actual price (AP) less standard price (SP), i.e., AQ(AP - SP).

48. What is the purchase price variance for Protex?

a. $365 unfavorable.
b. $715 unfavorable.
c. $160 favorable.
d. $30 favorable.

The correct answer is (b). *(Publisher)*
REQUIRED: The purchase price variance for Protex.
DISCUSSION: The purchase price variance is equal to the actual cost less the standard price times the actual quantity purchased.

Actual	SP x AQ Purchased	Price Variance
$6,240 -	($.425 x 13,000) =	$715 U

49. What is the purchase price variance for Benz?

a. $365 unfavorable.
b. $715 unfavorable.
c. $160 favorable.
d. $30 favorable.

The correct answer is (c). *(Publisher)*
REQUIRED: The purchase price variance for Benz.
DISCUSSION: The purchase price variance is equal to the actual cost less the standard price times the actual quantity purchased.

Actual	SP x AQ Purchased	Price Variance
$5,840 -	($.15 x 40,000) =	$160 F

Module 13.2: Materials

50. What is the purchase price variance for CT-40?

a. $365 unfavorable.
b. $715 unfavorable.
c. $160 favorable.
d. $30 favorable.

The correct answer is (d). *(Publisher)*
REQUIRED: The purchase price variance for CT-40.
DISCUSSION: The purchase price variance is equal to the actual cost less the standard price times the actual quantity purchased.

Actual	SP x AQ Purchased	Price Variance
$2,220 -	($.30 x 7,500) =	$30 F

51. What is the material usage variance for Echol?

a. $420 unfavorable.
b. $476 favorable.
c. $280 favorable.
d. $42 unfavorable.

The correct answer is (c). *(Publisher)*
REQUIRED: The material usage variance (MUV) for Echol.
DISCUSSION: The material usage variance is equal to the standard cost times the difference between the actual quantity used and the standard quantity allowed for the output achieved. The material usage variance is favorable if actual quantity used is less than standard. SQ allowed for actual output is 28,000 liters (200 liters standard input per batch x 140 batches).

SP(AQ - SQ) = MUV
$.20 x (26,600 - 28,000) = $280 favorable

52. What is the material usage variance for Protex?

a. $42 unfavorable.
b. $280 favorable.
c. $420 unfavorable.
d. $476 favorable.

The correct answer is (d). *(Publisher)*
REQUIRED: The material usage variance (MUV) for Protex.
DISCUSSION: The material usage variance is equal to the standard cost times the difference between the actual quantity used and the standard quantity allowed for the output achieved. SQ allowed for actual output is 14,000 liters (100 liters standard input per batch x 140 batches).

SP(AQ - SQ) = MUV
$.425 x (12,880 - 14,000) = $476 favorable

53. What is the material usage variance for Benz?

a. $280 favorable.
b. $476 favorable.
c. $420 unfavorable.
d. $42 unfavorable.

The correct answer is (c). *(Publisher)*
REQUIRED: The material usage variance (MUV) for Benz.
DISCUSSION: The material usage variance is equal to the standard cost times the difference in the actual quantity used and the standard quantity allowed for the output achieved. SQ allowed for actual output is 35,000 liters (250 liters standard input per batch x 140 batches).

SP(AQ - SQ) = MUV
$.15 x (37,800 - 35,000) = $420 unfavorable

54. What is the material usage variance for CT-40?

a. $280 favorable.
b. $476 favorable.
c. $420 unfavorable.
d. $42 unfavorable.

The correct answer is (d). *(Publisher)*
REQUIRED: The material usage variance (MUV) for CT-40.
DISCUSSION: The material usage variance is equal to the standard cost times the difference in the actual quantity used and the standard quantity allowed for the output achieved. SQ allowed for actual output is 7,000 liters (50 liters standard input per batch x 140 batches).

SP(AQ - SQ) = MUV
$.30 x (7,140 - 7,000) = $42 unfavorable

Module 13.3: Labor

> Questions 55 and 56 are based on the information preceding Q. 47.

55. What is the materials mix variance for this operation?

a. $294 favorable.
b. $388.50 favorable.
c. $94.50 unfavorable.
d. $890 unfavorable.

The correct answer is (b). *(Publisher)*
REQUIRED: The materials mix variance.
DISCUSSION: The materials mix variance is equal to the difference between the actual quantity times the standard cost per input and the actual input times the standard cost. In effect, the calculation is to determine the cost differential attributable to the components' being in different proportions than expected. The materials mix variance is favorable if the standard cost is less than the standard weighted average cost. Also see question 45.

Standard weighted average cost =

$$\frac{(200 \times \$.20) + (100 \times \$.425) + (250 \times \$.15) + (50 \times \$.30)}{600}$$

= $135 ÷ 600
= $.225/liter

Standard cost of actual quantity used (140 batches x $135) less $294 net F usage variance	$18,606.00
Standard weighted average cost of actual quantity used ($.225/liter x 84,420)	18,994.50
Materials mix variance	$ 388.50 F

56. What is the materials yield variance for this operation?

a. $294.50 favorable.
b. $388.50 favorable.
c. $94.50 unfavorable.
d. $890 unfavorable.

The correct answer is (c). *(Publisher)*
REQUIRED: The materials yield variance.
DISCUSSION: The materials yield variance is computed by first finding the difference between the actual input and the standard expected input for the actual production. The deviation in input is then multiplied by the standard weighted average cost per input unit to obtain the yield difference. Also see question 46.

Actual production	140 batches
Actual quantity used	84,420
Standard input for actual production (140 batches x 600 standard input)	84,000
Unfavorable input variance	420
Standard weighted average cost per liter (Q. 55)	x $ .225
Materials yield variance	$94.50 U

Note that the sum of the mix ($388.50 F) and yield ($94.50 U) variances equals the sum of the usage variances, or $294 F ($280 F + $476 F + $420 U + $42 U).

13.3 Labor

57. An unfavorable labor efficiency variance means that

a. The actual labor rate was higher than the standard labor rate.
b. The total labor variance must also be unfavorable.
c. Actual labor hours worked exceeded standard labor hours for the production level achieved.
d. Overtime labor was used during the period.

The correct answer is (c). *(CPA 1181 T-52)*
REQUIRED: The cause of an unfavorable labor efficiency variance.
DISCUSSION: An unfavorable labor efficiency variance results from actual hours worked exceeding standard hours.
Answer (a) is incorrect because it describes an unfavorable rate variance. Answer (b) is incorrect because the overall variance can still be favorable even if a single variance is unfavorable. Answer (d) is incorrect because overtime labor usually leads to unfavorable rate, not efficiency, variances due to the overtime premium paid.

Module 13.3: Labor

58. Given that

AH = Actual hours,
SH = Standard hours allowed for actual production,
AR = Actual rate, and
SR = Standard rate,

which formula represents the calculation of the labor efficiency variance?

  a. SR(AH - SH).
  b. AR(AH - SH).
  c. AH(AR - SR).
  d. SH(AR - SR).

The correct answer is (a). *(CPA 1175 T-17)*
REQUIRED: The formula for calculating the labor efficiency variance.
DISCUSSION: A standard cost system differentiates the expected cost from the actual cost. Thus, deviations from expected results can be identified on a routine basis. The labor efficiency variance is found by the formula SR(AH - SH). This formula permits a comparison of the actual hours versus the standard hours to determine the extent of efficient labor use.
Answers (b) and (d) are incorrect because neither is a formula used in variance analysis. Answer (c) is incorrect because AH(AR - SR) gives the labor rate variance.

59. A debit balance in the labor efficiency variance indicates that

  a. Standard hours exceed actual hours.
  b. Actual hours exceed standard hours.
  c. Standard rate and standard hours exceed actual rate and actual hours.
  d. Actual rate and actual hours exceed standard rate and standard hours.

The correct answer is (b). *(CPA 1176 T-31)*
REQUIRED: The cause of a debit balance in the labor efficiency variance.
DISCUSSION: A debit balance denotes an unfavorable labor efficiency situation in which actual hours exceed standard hours.
Answer (a) is incorrect because SH greater than AH would result in a credit balance. Answer (c) is incorrect because it would result in a credit balance in both the labor efficiency and the labor rate accounts. Answer (d) is incorrect because it would result in a debit balance in both the labor efficiency and the labor rate accounts.

60. During the last 3 months, a manufacturer incurred an unfavorable labor efficiency variance. Which of the following is the least likely cause of this variance?

  a. Substandard materials were purchased at a discount at a supplier's liquidation.
  b. For one week only half of the work force, those with the highest seniority, were called in to work.
  c. A second production line with all new personnel was started.
  d. The cost-of-living adjustment for the 3-month period was $.10 more per hour than expected.

The correct answer is (d). *(CIA 1183 IV-1)*
REQUIRED: The least likely cause of an unfavorable labor efficiency variance.
DISCUSSION: The labor efficiency variance is the difference between actual and standard hours required to perform a function times the standard labor rate. Cost-of-living adjustments affect the labor rate variance, not the labor efficiency variance.
Answers (a), (b), and (c) are incorrect because each is a likely cause of the variance. Substandard materials probably take longer to process than standard materials; reducing the work force by half may introduce inefficiencies caused by lack of specialization; and new personnel will require more time to complete a function than those with experience.

61. When a change in the manufacturing process reduces the number of direct labor hours and standards are unchanged, the resulting variance will be

  a. A favorable labor usage variance.
  b. An unfavorable labor usage variance.
  c. An unfavorable labor rate variance.
  d. A favorable labor rate variance.
  e. Both (a) and (d) above.

The correct answer is (a). *(CIA 976 IV-17)*
REQUIRED: The effect of decreasing direct labor hours without changing the standards.
DISCUSSION: When the number of direct labor hours are reduced, without changing the standard number of hours, a favorable labor usage variance results because actual hours will be less than standard hours.
Answer (b) is incorrect because it would result from the direct labor hours increasing, with the standards held constant. Answers (c) and (d) are incorrect because they concern labor rate, not labor efficiency, variances.

Module 13.3: Labor

62. Which of the following unfavorable variances would be directly affected by the relative position of a production process on a learning curve?

a. Materials mix.
b. Materials price.
c. Labor rate.
d. Labor efficiency.

The correct answer is (d). *(CPA 1181 T-53)*
REQUIRED: The variance affected by the learning curve.
DISCUSSION: The efficiency of the employees varies with how long they have been performing the particular task. Thus, more experienced employees are expected to be more efficient, which affects the labor efficiency variance.
Answers (a), (b), and (c) are incorrect because the learning curve depicts the efficiency of the employees in performing a certain task. It has little correlation with materials price or mix, or the labor rate variances.

63. Excess direct labor wages resulting from overtime premium will be disclosed in which type of variance?

a. Yield.
b. Quantity.
c. Labor efficiency.
d. Labor rate.

The correct answer is (d). *(CPA 578 T-43)*
REQUIRED: The variance that will reflect overtime premiums.
DISCUSSION: A standard cost system differentiates the expected cost from the actual cost. Thus, deviations from expected results can be identified on a routine basis. The premium paid for overtime hours increases the labor rate, which would be reflected in the labor rate variance.
Answers (a), (b), and (c) are incorrect because overtime wages do not affect the yield, quantity, or efficiency of labor.

64. Which of the following is the most probable reason a company would experience an unfavorable labor rate variance and a favorable labor efficiency variance?

a. The mix of workers assigned to the particular job was heavily weighted toward the use of higher paid, experienced individuals.
b. The mix of workers assigned to the particular job was heavily weighted toward the use of new, relatively low paid unskilled workers.
c. Because of the production schedule, workers from other production areas were assigned to assist in this particular process.
d. Defective materials caused more labor to be used in order to produce a standard unit.

The correct answer is (a). *(CPA 1178 T-43)*
REQUIRED: Probable reason for an unfavorable labor rate variance and a favorable labor efficiency variance.
DISCUSSION: More experienced people may perform more efficiently, but they usually cost more to use.
Answer (b) is incorrect because unskilled workers may result in an unfavorable labor efficiency variance. Also, the labor rate variance would be favorable since they are paid less. Answer (c) is incorrect because untrained labor who are paid at unbudgeted amounts may result in both an unfavorable labor efficiency variance and an unfavorable labor rate variance. Answer (d) is incorrect because defective materials usually cause an unfavorable materials efficiency variance.

65. How is a labor rate variance computed?

a. The difference between standard and actual rate times standard hours.
b. The difference between standard and actual hours times actual rate.
c. The difference between standard and actual rate times actual hours.
d. The difference between standard and actual hours times the difference between standard and actual rate.

The correct answer is (c). *(CPA 578 T-45)*
REQUIRED: The formula for computing the labor rate variance.
DISCUSSION: The labor rate variance is computed by finding the difference between standard and actual rate and then multiplying by actual hours: AH(AR - SR).
Answers (a) and (b) are incorrect because they give no useful variances. Answer (d) is incorrect because it is the rate/usage variance in three-way analysis of labor variances (not widely used).

66. The difference between the actual labor rate multiplied by the actual hours worked and the standard labor rate multiplied by the standard labor hours is the

a. Total labor variance.
b. Labor rate variance.
c. Labor usage variance.
d. Labor efficiency variance.

The correct answer is (a). *(CPA 1182 T-48)*
REQUIRED: The variance defined by the difference between total actual labor costs and total standard costs allowed.
DISCUSSION: The actual labor cost is found by multiplying the actual labor rate times the actual labor hours. The standard cost for good output is found by multiplying the standard rate times the standard hours. The total labor rate variance is the difference between the actual labor costs and the standard labor cost.
Answer (b) is incorrect because the labor rate variance is AH(AR - SR). Answer (c) is incorrect because the labor usage variance is SR(AH - SH). Answer (d) is incorrect because the labor efficiency variance is the same as the labor usage variance.

67. Listed below are four names for different kinds of standards associated with a standard cost system. Which one describes the labor costs that should be incurred under efficient operating conditions?

a. Ideal.
b. Basic.
c. Maximum-efficiency.
d. Currently attainable.

The correct answer is (d). *(CPA 1176 T-30)*
REQUIRED: The type of cost incurred under efficient operations.
DISCUSSION: Currently attainable standards refers to the efficient operation of labor and resources. They are difficult, but possible to achieve.
Answer (a) is incorrect because ideal standards are impossible to reach; i.e., they include no waste at all. Answer (b) is incorrect because basic standards is a nonsense concept in this context. Answer (c) is incorrect because maximum-efficiency standards are like the ideal and are not readily achievable.

68. Information on Barber Company's direct labor costs for the month of January is as follows:

Actual direct labor hours	34,500
Standard direct labor hours	35,000
Total direct labor payroll	$241,500
Direct labor efficiency variance - favorable	$3,200

What is Barber's direct labor rate variance?

a. $17,250 unfavorable.
b. $20,700 unfavorable.
c. $21,000 unfavorable.
d. $21,000 favorable.

The correct answer is (b). *(CPA 581 P-27)*
REQUIRED: The direct labor rate variance for the month.
DISCUSSION: The direct labor rate variance is determined by multiplying the difference between actual and standard rate times the actual hours: AH(AR - SR). To determine the standard rate, divide the direct labor efficiency variance by the difference between the actual and standard hours. To determine the actual rate, divide the total direct labor payroll by the actual hours.

$3,200 ÷ (34,500 - 35,000) = $ 6.40 SR
$241,500 ÷ 34,500 = 7.00 AR
.60 diff.
x34,500 AH
DL rate variance $20,700 U

69. Information on Hanley's direct labor costs for the month of January is as follows:

Actual direct labor rate	$7.50
Standard direct labor hours allowed	11,000
Actual direct labor hours	10,000
Direct labor rate variance - favorable	$5,500

The standard direct labor rate in January was

a. $6.95.
b. $7.00.
c. $8.00.
d. $8.05.

The correct answer is (d). *(CPA 582 P-25)*
REQUIRED: The standard direct labor rate for the month.
DISCUSSION: Rely on the basic equation for labor rate variance as shown below.

AH(AR - SR) = rate variance
10,000($7.50 - SR) = $5,500 F
$7.50 - SR = $5,500 ÷ 10,000 or $.55

When the rate variance is favorable, the SR is greater than the AR. In this case, the SR is greater by $.55. Thus SR = $8.05 ($7.50 + $.55).

Module 13.3: Labor

70. Thorp Co.'s records for April disclosed the following data relating to direct labor:

Actual cost	$10,000
Rate variance	1,000 favorable
Efficiency variance	1,500 unfavorable
Standard cost	$9,500

Actual direct labor hours for April amounted to 2,000. Thorp's standard direct labor rate per hour in April was

a. $5.50.
b. $5.00.
c. $4.75.
d. $4.50.

The correct answer is (a). *(CPA 586 Q-28)*
REQUIRED: The standard direct labor rate per hour for the month.
DISCUSSION: There were 2,000 actual direct labor hours (AH); therefore the actual direct labor rate (AR) is $5 ($10,000 ÷ 2,000 hrs.). Rely on the basic equation for labor rate variance as shown below.

$$AH(AR - SR) = \text{rate variance}$$
$$2{,}000 \text{ hrs.} (\$5 - SR) = (\$1{,}000)$$
$$\$5 - SR = (\$1{,}000) \div 2{,}000 \text{ hrs.}$$
$$\$5 - SR = (\$.50)$$
$$SR = \$5.50$$

71. Lion Company's direct labor costs for the month of January were as follows:

Actual direct labor hours	20,000
Standard direct labor hours	21,000
Direct labor rate variance - (unfav.)	$3,000
Total payroll	$126,000

What was Lion's direct labor efficiency variance?

a. $6,000 favorable.
b. $6,150 favorable.
c. $6,300 favorable.
d. $6,450 favorable.

The correct answer is (b). *(CPA 580 P-39)*
REQUIRED: The direct labor efficiency variance (DLEV) for the month.
DISCUSSION: The formula for direct labor efficiency variance is the standard rate times the difference between the actual hours and the standard hours: SR(AH - SH). The standard rate is the actual payroll minus the rate variance, all divided by actual hours.

$$SR = (\$126{,}000 - \$3{,}000) \div 20{,}000$$
$$= \$123{,}000 \div 20{,}000$$
$$= \$6.15$$

$$SR(AH - SH) = DLEV$$
$$\$6.15(20{,}000 - 21{,}000) = \$6{,}150 \text{ F}$$

72. The direct labor standards for producing a unit of a product are two hours at $10 per hour. Budgeted production was 1,000 units. Actual production was 900 units and direct labor cost was $19,000 for 2,000 direct labor hours. The direct labor efficiency variance was

a. $1,000 favorable.
b. $1,000 unfavorable.
c. $2,000 favorable.
d. $2,000 unfavorable.

The correct answer is (d). *(CIA 1186 IV-13)*
REQUIRED: The direct labor efficiency variance for the month.
DISCUSSION: The labor efficiency variance equals the standard labor rate times the difference between the actual hours and the standard hours allowed for the actual output. Since 1,800 (2 hrs. x 900 units) standard hours are allowed for the actual production, the variance is $2,000 U [(2,000 actual - 1,800 standard hours) x $10 standard rate].

73. A company's direct labor costs for manufacturing its only product were as follows for October:

Standard direct labor hours per unit of product	1
Number of finished units produced	10,000
Standard rate per direct labor hour	$ 10
Actual direct labor costs incurred	$103,500
Actual rate per direct labor hour	$ 9

The direct labor efficiency variance for October was

a. $2,500 favorable.
b. $11,500 favorable.
c. $3,500 unfavorable.
d. $15,000 unfavorable.

The correct answer is (d). *(CIA 1185 IV-2)*
REQUIRED: The direct labor efficiency variance for the month.
DISCUSSION: The direct labor efficiency variance is the difference between actual and standard hours times the standard labor rate. Actual hours were 11,500 ($103,500 ÷ $9). Given standard hours of 10,000 and the standard labor rate of $10 per hour, the direct labor efficiency variance was $15,000 [(11,500 - 10,000) x $10]. Since the number of actual hours used was greater than standard hours budgeted, the variance is unfavorable.

74. Using the information given below, determine the labor efficiency variance:

Labor price per hour	$ 20
Standard labor price per gallon of output at 20 gal./hr.	$ 1
Standard labor cost of 8,440 gallons of actual output	$8,440
Actual total inputs (410 hours at $21.00/hr.)	$8,610

a. $410 unfavorable.

b. $240 favorable.

c. $170 unfavorable.

d. $410 favorable.

The correct answer is (b). *(CIA 586 IV-2)*
REQUIRED: The labor efficiency variance.
DISCUSSION: The labor efficiency variance is the difference between the actual and standard hours required to perform a task times the standard labor rate. Actual hours used was 410. Standard hours was 422 ($8,440 ÷ $20). The standard rate was $20. Thus, the labor efficiency variance is $20 x (410 - 422) or $(240). This variance is favorable because actual hours used was less than standard hours.

75. Information on Westcott Company's direct labor costs is as follows:

Standard direct labor hours	10,000
Standard direct labor rate	$ 3.75
Actual direct labor rate	$ 3.50
Direct labor usage (efficiency) variance - unfavorable	$4,200

What were the actual hours worked, rounded the nearest hour?

a. 10,714.

b. 11,120.

c. 11,200.

d. 11,914.

The correct answer is (b). *(CPA 1179 P-37)*
REQUIRED: The actual hours worked given various direct labor variables.
DISCUSSION: Using the given variables and the formula for the standard rate, the actual hours worked is found as follows:

$$SR(AH - SH) = \$4,200 \text{ DLEV}$$
$$\$3.75(AH - 10,000) = \$4,200$$
$$AH - 10,000 = 1,120$$
$$AH = 11,120$$

76. Tub Co. uses a standard cost system. The following information pertains to direct labor for product B for the month of October:

Standard hours allowed for actual production	2,000
Actual rate paid per hour	$ 8.40
Standard rate per hour	$ 8.00
Labor efficiency variance	$1,600 U

What were the actual hours worked?

a. 1,800.

b. 1,810.

c. 2,190.

d. 2,200.

The correct answer is (d). *(CPA 1186 Q-21)*
REQUIRED: The actual hours worked.
DISCUSSION: The standard hours allowed were 2,000 and there is a $1,600 unfavorable labor efficiency variance, i.e., actual hours exceeded standard hours. The labor efficiency variance is the standard rate ($8/hour) times the excess hours. Since the variance is $1,600, the excess hours were 200 ($1,600 ÷ $8). Thus actual hours were 2,200 (2,000 standard + 200 excess).

77. Information on Townsend Company's direct labor costs for May is as follows:

Standard direct labor rate	$6.00
Actual direct labor rate	$5.80
Standard direct labor hours	20,000
Actual direct labor hours	21,000
Direct labor rate variance - favorable	$4,200

What is Townsend's total direct labor payroll for May?

a. $116,000.
b. $117,600.
c. $120,000.
d. $121,800.

The correct answer is (d). *(CPA 1181 P-24)*
REQUIRED: The direct labor payroll for the month of May.
DISCUSSION: The direct labor payroll is found simply by multiplying the actual rate by the actual hours.

$$21,000 \times \$5.80 = \$121,800$$

78. Sullivan Corporation's direct labor costs for the month of March is as follows:

Standard direct labor hours	42,000
Actual direct labor hours	40,000
Direct labor rate variance - favorable	$8,400
Standard direct labor rate per hour	$6.30

What was Sullivan's total direct labor payroll for the month of March?

a. $243,600.
b. $244,000.
c. $260,000.
d. $260,400.

The correct answer is (a). *(CPA 1180 P-35)*
REQUIRED: The direct labor payroll for March.
DISCUSSION: When the actual direct labor rate is unknown, the total direct labor payroll is found by multiplying the actual hours by the standard rate, then subtracting the favorable labor variance.

$$(40,000 \times \$6.30) - \$8,400 = \$243,600$$

Alternatively, the rate variance is $.21 F ($8,400 ÷ 40,000), which makes the actual rate $6.09.

$$\$6.09 \times 40,000 \text{ actual hours} = \$243,600$$

79. Each unit of Product XK-46 requires 3 direct labor hours. Employee benefit costs are treated as direct labor costs. Data on direct labor are as follows:

Number of direct employees	25
Weekly productive hours per employee	35
Estimated weekly wages per employee	$245
Employee benefits (related to weekly wages)	25%

The standard direct labor cost per unit of Product XK-46 is

a. $21.00.
b. $26.25.
c. $29.40.
d. $36.75.
e. None of the above.

The correct answer is (b). *(CMA 684 4-26)*
REQUIRED: The standard direct labor cost per unit.
DISCUSSION: The standard direct labor unit cost equals three hours times the cost per DLH. This amount is determined by adding employee benefits to weekly wages and dividing by hours per week.

Weekly wages	$245.00
Plus benefits (.25 x $245)	61.25
	$306.25
Divided by hours/week	÷ 35
Cost/DLH	$ 8.75
DLH/unit	x 3
Unit DL cost	$ 26.25

Module 13.3: Labor

80. Labor yield variance is
   a. (Inputs allowed - inputs used) x (budgeted average materials price).
   b. (Inputs allowed - inputs used) x (budgeted specific labor rate - budgeted average labor rate).
   c. (Inputs allowed - inputs used) x (budgeted average labor rate).
   d. (Inputs allowed - inputs used) x (budgeted specific material prices - budgeted average material price).

The correct answer is (c). *(Publisher)*
REQUIRED: The definition of labor yield variance.
DISCUSSION: Labor yield and labor mix variances are further breakdowns of labor efficiency variance (all price variances are excluded). Labor yield identifies the effect of more or less total units (of labor) being used. The average labor rate is used. Labor yield variances assume that various types (classes) of labor are used which have different labor rates. The key to analyzing labor yield variance is to recognize that the labor rate is held constant. You must ask, if the mix of labor inputs were held constant, what would be the effect of using fewer or more numbers of hours. This analysis assumes that more than one type of labor is both available and partially substitutable.

81. Labor mix variance is
   a. (Inputs allowed - inputs used) x (budgeted average materials price).
   b. (Inputs allowed - inputs used) x (budgeted specific labor rate - budgeted average labor rate).
   c. (Inputs allowed - inputs used) x (budgeted average labor rate).
   d. (Inputs allowed - inputs used) x (budgeted specific material prices - budgeted average material price).

The correct answer is (b). *(Publisher)*
REQUIRED: The definition of labor mix variance.
DISCUSSION: Labor mix variance is a measure of the extent to which management substituted more expensive or less expensive labor in differing proportions than estimated and used hours differently than estimated.

Questions 82 and 83 are based on Goodman Company's direct labor costs:

Standard direct labor hours	30,000
Actual direct labor hours	29,000
Direct labor usage (efficiency) variance - favorable	$ 4,000
Direct labor rate variance - favorable	$ 5,800
Total payroll	$110,200

---

82. What was Goodman's standard direct labor rate?
   a. $3.54.
   b. $3.80.
   c. $4.00.
   d. $5.80.

The correct answer is (c). *(CPA 577 P-33)*
REQUIRED: The standard direct labor rate for the period.
DISCUSSION: Actual payroll is found by first multiplying the actual hours times the actual rate. Adding the rate variance converts actual payroll to actual hours at standard rate. To get the standard rate, divide the standard payroll by the actual hours.

Actual payroll	$110,200
Favorable variance	5,800
Actual hours at standard rate	$116,000

$116,000 standard payroll ÷ 29,000 actual hours
= $4.00 standard rate

83. What was Goodman's actual direct labor rate?
   a. $3.60.
   b. $3.80.
   c. $4.00.
   d. $5.80.

The correct answer is (b). *(CPA 577 P-32)*
REQUIRED: The actual direct labor rate for the period.
DISCUSSION: The direct labor rate is the actual payroll divided by the actual direct labor hours.

$$\frac{\$110,200}{29,000} = \$3.80$$

Questions 84 through 89 are based on the following information, which was presented as part of Question 4 on Part 4 of the June 1978 CMA exam.

Landeau Manufacturing Company has a process cost accounting system. A monthly analysis compares actual results with both a monthly plan and a flexible budget. Standard direct labor rates used in the flexible budget are established at the time the annual plan is formulated and held constant for the entire year. Standard direct labor rates in effect for the fiscal year ending June 30 and standard hours allowed for the output in April are:

	Standard DL Rate per Hour	Standard DLH Allowed for Output
Labor class III	$8.00	500
Labor class II	$7.00	500
Labor class I	$5.00	500

The wage rates for each labor class increased on January 1 under the terms of a new union contract negotiated in December of the previous fiscal year. The standard wage rates were not revised to reflect the new contract.

The actual direct labor hours (DLH) worked and the actual direct labor rates per hour experienced for the month of April were as follows:

	Actual Direct Labor Rate per Hour	Actual Direct Labor Hours
Labor class III	$8.50	550
Labor class II	$7.50	650
Labor class I	$5.40	375

84. What is the total direct labor variance?

a. $1,575 unfavorable.
b. $750 unfavorable.
c. $325 unfavorable.
d. $500 unfavorable.

The correct answer is (a). *(Publisher)*
REQUIRED: The total direct labor variance.
DISCUSSION: Total labor variance is equal to the actual labor cost less the standard labor cost expected at that activity level.

Class III $8.00 x 500 = $ 4,000
Class II $7.00 x 500 =   3,500
Class I $5.00 x 500 =   2,500
                        $10,000 standard labor

Class III $8.50 x 550 = $ 4,675
Class II $7.50 x 650 =   4,875
Class I $5.40 x 375 =   2,025
                        $11,575 actual labor

The $1,575 variance ($11,575 - $10,000) is unfavorable because actual exceeded standard.

85. The direct labor rate variance is

a. $750 U.
b. $825 U.
c. $750 F.
d. $825 F.

The correct answer is (a). *(Publisher)*
REQUIRED: The direct labor rate variance for the month.
DISCUSSION: The direct labor rate variance is equal to the difference between the standard and actual labor rate times the actual hours.

	Rates Per Hour			Actual	Variance
	Standard	Actual	Difference	Hours	in Dollars
LCIII	$8.00 - $8.50	=	$.50U	x 550	= $275 U
LCII	$7.00 - $7.50	=	$.50U	x 650	= $325 U
LCI	$5.00 - $5.40	=	$.40U	x 375	= $150 U
					$750 U

86. The direct labor efficiency variance is

a. $750 U.
b. $625 F.
c. $600 U.
d. $825 U.

The correct answer is (d). *(Publisher)*
REQUIRED: The direct labor efficiency variance for the month.
DISCUSSION: The labor efficiency variance is equal to the actual hours less the standard hours allowed multiplied by the standard rate.

	Actual Hours	Standard Hours	Hourly Variance	Rate	Variance
LCIII	550 - 500	=	50U	x $8.00	= $ 400 U
LCII	650 - 500	=	150U	x $7.00	= $1,050 U
LCI	375 - 500	=	125F	x $5.00	= $ 625 F
					$ 825 U

87. What is the labor yield variance for Landeau in April?

a. $500.
b. $750.
c. $825.50.
d. $1,500.

The correct answer is (a). *(Publisher)*
REQUIRED: The labor yield variance for April.
DISCUSSION: The labor yield variance is the total efficiency variance based on an average wage rate. Here, total hours worked were 1,575 (550 + 650 + 375) and standard was 1,500 (500 + 500 + 500). The difference of 75 hours is multiplied by the weighted average standard rate of $6.67 ($10,000 ÷ 1,500 standard DLH), which equals a $500 unfavorable variance. Also see question 80.

88. What is the labor mix variance for Landeau in April?

a. $50.00.
b. $325.00.
c. $66.67.
d. $180.00.

The correct answer is (b). *(Publisher)*
REQUIRED: The labor mix variance for April.
DISCUSSION: The labor mix variance is the difference between actual and standard hours for each class of labor times the difference between budgeted standard and weighted average standard labor rate (which was calculated in Q. 87) for that class of labor. Also see question 81.

Class	Standard Hours	Actual Hours	Variance	Bud. Std. - W.A. Std.	Product
III	500	550	- 50	+$1.33	$ 66.67 U
II	500	650	- 150	+ .33	50.00 U
I	500	375	+125	- 1.67	208.33 U
					$325.00 U

89. The labor mix and labor yield variances together equal

a. Total labor variance.
b. Labor rate variance.
c. Labor efficiency variance.
d. Both labor efficiency and overhead efficiency variances.
e. None of the above.

The correct answer is (c). *(Publisher)*
REQUIRED: The variance composed of labor mix and labor yield variances.
DISCUSSION: Labor mix and labor yield variances are a further breakdown of total labor efficiency variance. For example, in Qs. 87 and 88, labor yield variance was $500 U and labor mix variance was $325 U, which sums to the total labor efficiency variance of $825 U, as computed in Q. 86.

13.4 Overhead

90. Differences in product costs resulting from the application of actual overhead rates rather than predetermined overhead rates could be immaterial if

a. Production is not stable.
b. Fixed factory overhead is a significant cost.
c. Several products are produced simultaneously.
d. Overhead is composed only of variable costs.

The correct answer is (d). *(CPA 1169 T-13)*
REQUIRED: When using actual overhead rather than predetermined overhead rates is immaterial.
DISCUSSION: Actual overhead and predetermined amounts of overhead would be most similar if overhead is composed primarily of variable costs. Variable overhead costs fluctuate most directly with activity level.
Answers (a), (b), and (c) are incorrect because fluctuating production levels, significant fixed factory overhead, or a product mix may cause significant differences between the predetermined and actual overhead rates.

91. The budget variance for fixed factory overhead for the normal-volume, practical-capacity, and expected-activity levels would be the same

a. Except for normal volume.
b. Except for practical capacity.
c. Except for expected activity.
d. For all three activity levels.

The correct answer is (d). *(CPA 1172 T-33)*
REQUIRED: The true statement about budget variance for fixed factory overhead for varying capacity levels.
DISCUSSION: The budget variance is the difference between actual and budgeted fixed factory overhead. The type of application rate used on the products would have no effect on the fixed overhead budget variance.

Module 13.4: Overhead

92. In a standard cost system, an unfavorable overhead volume variance would result if

a. There is an unfavorable labor efficiency variance.
b. There is a favorable labor rate variance.
c. Production is less than planned.
d. All of the above.
e. None of the above.

The correct answer is (c). *(CIA 975 IV-19)*
REQUIRED: The situation(s) resulting in an unfavorable overhead volume variance.
DISCUSSION: An unfavorable volume variance results when actual production is less than the expected production level. Fixed overhead is applied at the predetermined rate but, since production is less than estimated, less overhead is charged to production than anticipated, leaving some overhead unallocated. This can be viewed as the cost of idle capacity.
Answers (a) and (b) are incorrect because no direct correlation exists between the labor variances and the overhead volume variance.

93. When the firm prepares its budget in terms of the expected activity level of operation, the volume variance theoretically should be disposed of as a

a. Loss due to idle capacity.
b. Revision of the overhead rate based on actual activity.
c. Deferred charge to future periods.
d. Charge to cost of goods sold.

The correct answer is (b). *(CPA 1172 T-34)*
REQUIRED: Disposal of volume variance when overhead is applied based on the expected level of operations.
DISCUSSION: The volume variance deals with fixed overhead and should be adjusted to match actual activity.
Answer (a) is incorrect because fixed O/H is a product cost that should be allocated to the product when produced, and recognized as cost of sales when sold. Answer (c) is incorrect because volume variances can provide no future benefits; i.e., they should not be deferred. Answer (d) is incorrect because some of the variance should be allocated to FG and WIP (if they exist).

94. In a standard cost system, when production is greater than the estimated unit or denominator level, there will be

a. An unfavorable capacity variance.
b. A favorable materials and labor usage variance.
c. A favorable volume variance.
d. An unfavorable manufacturing overhead variance.
e. A favorable fixed overhead budget variance.

The correct answer is (c). *(CIA 976 IV-18)*
REQUIRED: The type of variance when production exceeds the denominator level.
DISCUSSION: A favorable volume variance results when actual production exceeds the expected production level. Fixed O/H is applied at the predetermined (budgeted) rate but, since production is greater than estimated, more O/H is charged to production than anticipated. The estimated unit or denominator level is the activity base on which fixed O/H is allocated.
Answer (a) is incorrect because capacity variance is a nonsense term. Answer (b) is incorrect because a favorable materials and labor usage variance results when less materials are used and fewer direct labor hours are incurred than expected. Answer (d) is incorrect because more O/H, not less, is applied than incurred when actual production exceeds expected production. Answer (e) is incorrect because the fixed factory overhead budget variance is independent of activity level.

95. The fixed overhead application rate is a function of a predetermined "normal" activity level. If standard hours allowed for good output equal this predetermined activity level for a given period, the volume variance will be

   a. Zero.
   b. Favorable.
   c. Unfavorable.
   d. Either favorable or unfavorable, depending on the budgeted overhead.

The correct answer is (a). *(CPA 576 T-34)*
REQUIRED: The volume variance when standard hours allowed for good output equal the predetermined activity level.
DISCUSSION: The volume variance is the difference between the budgeted fixed overhead and the overhead applied based upon standard hours allowed for good output. Thus, if no difference occurs between the predetermined activity level and the standard hours allowed, no deviation should occur.
Answer (b) is incorrect because a favorable volume variance means standard hours allowed exceed the predetermined (budgeted) output. Answer (c) is incorrect because an unfavorable volume variance means standard hours allowed are less than budgeted standard hours. Answer (d) is incorrect because there is no variance.

96. A company uses an absorption-costing system with standard costs. For last year it showed a $24,875 unfavorable production volume variance. The unfavorable production volume variance occurred because the

   a. Estimated fixed overhead used in determining the fixed overhead rate was less than actual fixed overhead.
   b. Estimated fixed overhead used in determining the fixed overhead rate was more than actual fixed overhead.
   c. Actual activity level for output was greater than the denominator volume (prechosen activity level).
   d. Actual activity level for output was less than the denominator volume (prechosen activity level).

The correct answer is (d). *(CIA 585 IV-13)*
REQUIRED: The cause of an unfavorable production volume variance.
DISCUSSION: An unfavorable production volume variance occurs when the budgeted input is greater than the standard input for the actual output. The result is that overhead is not applied to the extent originally estimated.

97. A company uses a two-way analysis for overhead variances: budget (controllable) and volume. The volume variance is based on the

   a. Total overhead application rate.
   b. Volume of total expenses at various activity levels.
   c. Variable overhead application rate.
   d. Fixed overhead application rate.

The correct answer is (d). *(CPA 1176 T-29)*
REQUIRED: The variable on which volume variance is based.
DISCUSSION: The volume variance arises from over- or underapplication of budgeted fixed O/H. A predetermined (budgeted) activity level is normally used to calculate the fixed O/H rate per unit. A volume variance occurs when there is a difference between this budgeted capacity and standard hours allowed for good output.
Answers (a) and (b) are incorrect because the total O/H application rate and total expenses contain both variable and fixed rates. Volume variance only contains fixed O/H. Answer (c) is incorrect because the volume variance is only applicable to fixed, not variable, O/H.

98. Under the two-variance method for analyzing factory overhead, the factory overhead applied to production is used in the computation of the

	Controllable (Budget) Variance	Volume Variance
a.	Yes	No
b.	Yes	Yes
c.	No	Yes
d.	No	No

The correct answer is (c). *(CPA 587 T-43)*
REQUIRED: The variance that uses factory overhead applied in its computation.
DISCUSSION: The controllable (budget) variance is the difference between actual overhead incurred and budgeted overhead at standard input allowed for actual output [lump sum budgeted fixed overhead + (the variable overhead rate x standard input)]. The volume variance is the difference between budgeted fixed overhead and fixed overhead absorbed (applied).

99. Under the two-variance method for analyzing factory overhead, the difference between the actual factory overhead and the factory overhead applied to production is the

a. Controllable variance.
b. Net overhead variance.
c. Efficiency variance.
d. Volume variance.

The correct answer is (b). *(CPA 1185 T-41)*
REQUIRED: The variance which equals the difference between the actual factory overhead and factory overhead applied.
DISCUSSION: Net overhead variance is the difference between actual and applied overhead.
Answer (a) is incorrect because the controllable (budget) variance is the difference between actual overhead incurred and budgeted overhead at standard hours allowed. Answer (c) is incorrect because the efficiency variance is the difference between the quantity of actual inputs and the quantity of inputs that should have been used, multiplied by the budgeted rate. It is wholly attributable to variable overhead. Answer (d) is incorrect because the volume variance is the difference between overhead at standard hours allowed for actual output and overhead absorbed (applied).

100. When using the two-variance method for analyzing factory overhead, the difference between the budget allowance based on standard hours allowed and the factory overhead applied to production is the

a. Net overhead variance.
b. Controllable variance.
c. Volume variance.
d. Efficiency variance.

The correct answer is (c). *(CPA 586 T-43)*
REQUIRED: The variance that equals the difference between the budget allowance based on standard hours allowed and the factory overhead applied.
DISCUSSION: The volume variance is the difference between budgeted overhead at the standard input allowed for actual output and overhead absorbed (applied). The difference is attributable solely to the difference between budgeted fixed overhead and the fixed overhead applied.
Answer (a) is incorrect because net overhead variance is the difference between actual overhead and applied overhead. Answer (b) is incorrect because the controllable (budget) variance is the difference between actual overhead incurred and budgeted overhead at standard hours allowed. Answer (d) is incorrect because the efficiency variance is the difference between the quantity of actual inputs and the quantity of inputs that should have been used, multiplied by the budgeted price.

Module 13.4: Overhead

101. Fixed overhead volume variance is

   a. The measure of the lost profits resulting from the lack of sales volume.
   b. The measure of lost contribution margin from the lack of sales volume.
   c. The amount of the underapplied or overapplied budgeted fixed overhead costs.
   d. The potential cost reduction that can be achieved from better cost control.
   e. The measure of production inefficiency.

The correct answer is (c). *(CMA 1279 4-10)*
REQUIRED: The correct statement about fixed overhead volume variance.
DISCUSSION: The volume variance is based on the fixed O/H application rate. A predetermined (budgeted) activity level is used to calculate the fixed O/H rate. The difference between this budgeted capacity and standard hours allowed for good output, times the predetermined rate, is the volume variance. It is by definition the amount of under- or overapplied budgeted fixed O/H.
   Answers (a) and (b) are incorrect because fixed O/H allocation is completely independent of revenue. Answer (d) is incorrect because application of fixed O/H is a cost allocation, not a cost control technique. Answer (e) is incorrect because production inefficiency is measured by labor efficiency and material usage variances.

102. The planned activity level for the assembly department of the Shields Company during the month of December was 10,000 direct labor hours. The actual number of direct labor hours worked during December was 9,000. Overhead is allocated on the basis of actual direct labor hours. What kind of variance occurred?

   a. A favorable labor rate variance.
   b. An unfavorable labor rate variance.
   c. A favorable overhead volume variance
   d. An unfavorable labor efficiency variance.
   e. An unfavorable overhead volume variance.

The correct answer is (e). *(CIA 1182 IV-11)*
REQUIRED: The variance when budgeted DLH exceeds actual, and overhead is allocated based on actual DLH.
DISCUSSION: When the budgeted capacity is greater than actual production, an unfavorable fixed O/H volume variance results. A predetermined (planned) activity level is used to calculate the fixed O/H rate. An unfavorable volume variance occurs when actual activity (here, DLH since that is the basis for O/H application) is less than budgeted. Unfavorable means some budgeted fixed O/H has not been applied.
   Answer (a) is incorrect because a favorable labor rate variance means the actual labor rate is less than standard. Answer (b) is incorrect because an unfavorable labor rate variance means the actual labor rate exceeds standard. Answer (c) is incorrect because a favorable overhead volume variance means actual production levels exceed budgeted production levels. Answer (d) is incorrect because an unfavorable labor efficiency variance means actual hours worked exceed standard hours allowed for good output.

103. Which of these variances is least significant for cost control?

   a. Labor price variance.
   b. Material quantity variance.
   c. Overhead budget variance.
   d. Overhead volume variance.
   e. Labor quantity variance.

The correct answer is (d). *(CMA 1273 4-13)*
REQUIRED: The variance least significant for cost control.
DISCUSSION: The overhead volume variance occurs when actual activity levels differ from anticipated levels. It is an excellent example of cost allocation as opposed to cost control.

104. Margolos, Inc. ends the month with a volume variance of $6,360 unfavorable. If budgeted fixed overhead of $480,000 was applied on the basis of 32,000 budgeted machine hours and budgeted variable overhead was $170,000, what were the actual number of machine hours (AH) for the month?

   a. 32,425.
   b. 32,318.
   c. 31,682.
   d. 31,576.

The correct answer is (d). *(J.B. Romal)*
REQUIRED: The actual number of machine hours for the period.
DISCUSSION: The volume variance (VV) arises from the difference between budgeted fixed overhead and the fixed overhead applied at the standard rate based on the standard input allowed for good output. The overhead rate is $480,000 ÷ 32,000 = $15/machine hour.

$$VV = \text{Budgeted Fixed O/H} - \text{Applied Fixed O/H}$$
$$6,360 = \$480,000 - (\$15 \times AH)$$
$$15 \times AH = \$480,000 - 6,360$$
$$AH = \$473,640 \div \$15$$
$$AH = 31,576.$$

> Questions 105 through 107 are based on Dori Castings, a job order shop that uses a full absorption, standard cost system to account for its production costs. The overhead costs are applied on a direct labor hour basis.

105. Dori's choice of production volume as a denominator for calculating its factory overhead rate

    a. Has no effect on the fixed factory overhead rate for applying costs to production.

    b. Has an effect on the variable factory overhead rate for applying costs to production.

    c. Has no effect on the fixed factory overhead budget variance.

    d. Has no effect on the fixed factory overhead production volume variance.

    e. Has no effect on the overall (net) fixed factory overhead variance.

The correct answer is (c). *(CMA 1284 4-1)*
REQUIRED: The effect of using production volume as the denominator in calculating the overhead rates.
DISCUSSION: The use of a production volume as the denominator in calculating overhead rates has no effect on the fixed factory overhead budget variance. This variance is the difference between actual fixed costs and budgeted (lump sum) fixed costs.
    Answer (a) is incorrect because as the denominator changes, the rate changes. Answer (b) is incorrect because by definition, the total variable factory overhead varies with the activity level, but total fixed overhead and unit variable overhead do not. Answer (d) is incorrect because this variance is the difference between budgeted fixed overhead and fixed overhead applied based on the predetermined rate. Answer (e) is incorrect because this variance is the difference between the actual fixed overhead and the fixed overhead applied based on the predetermined rate.

106. A production volume variance will exist for Dori in a month when

    a. Production volume differs from sales volume.

    b. Actual direct labor hours differ from standard allowed direct labor hours.

    c. There is a budget variance in fixed factory overhead costs.

    d. The fixed factory overhead applied on the basis of standard allowed direct labor hours differs from actual fixed factory overhead.

    e. The fixed factory overhead applied on the basis of standard allowed direct labor hours differs from the budgeted fixed factory overhead.

The correct answer is (e). *(CMA 1284 4-2)*
REQUIRED: The definition of a production volume variance.
DISCUSSION: A fixed overhead production volume variance is the difference between the budgeted fixed factory overhead and the overhead applied based on a predetermined rate and standard direct labor hours allowed for the actual output.
    Answer (a) is incorrect because sales volume is irrelevant. Answer (b) is incorrect because it describes the difference that is the basis of the variable overhead efficiency variance. Answer (c) is incorrect because the budget variance is the difference between actual and budgeted fixed overhead costs. Answer (d) is incorrect because it describes the overall fixed overhead budget variance.

107. The amount of fixed factory overhead that Dori would apply to finished production is

    a. The actual direct labor hours times the standard fixed factory overhead rate per direct labor hour.

    b. The standard allowed direct labor hours for the actual units of finished output times the standard fixed factory overhead rate per direct labor hour.

    c. The standard units of output for the actual direct labor hours worked times the standard fixed factory overhead rate per unit of output.

    d. The actual fixed factory overhead cost per direct labor hour times the standard allowed direct labor hours.

    e. The actual fixed factory overhead cost per direct labor hour times the actual direct labor hours worked on finished production.

The correct answer is (b). *(CMA 1284 4-4)*
REQUIRED: The fixed factory overhead application basis.
DISCUSSION: Fixed factory overhead in a standard costing system is applied to the product based on the predetermined overhead rate multiplied by the standard hours allowed for the actual output. Thus, the applied fixed factory overhead is limited to the standard amount.

Module 13.4: Overhead

108. The following information is available from the Tyro Company:

Actual factory overhead	$15,000
Fixed overhead expenses, actual	$7,200
Fixed overhead expenses, budgeted	$7,000
Actual hours	3,500
Standard hours	3,800
Variable overhead rate per DLH (STD rate)	$2.50

Assuming that Tyro uses a three-way analysis of overhead variances, what is the spending variance?

a. $750 favorable.
b. $750 unfavorable.
c. $950 favorable.
d. $1,500 unfavorable.

109. A spending variance for variable overhead based on direct labor hours is the difference between actual variable overhead cost and variable overhead cost that should have been incurred for the actual hours worked. This variance results from

a. Price and quantity differences for overhead costs.
b. Price differences for overhead costs.
c. Quantity differences for overhead costs.
d. Differences caused by variations in production volume.

110. Under the three-variance method for analyzing factory overhead, the difference between the actual factory overhead and the factory overhead applied to production is the

a. Net overhead variance.
b. Controllable variance.
c. Efficiency variance.
d. Spending variance.

The correct answer is (a). *(CPA 578 P-32)*
REQUIRED: The spending variance, assuming a three-way variance analysis.
DISCUSSION: The spending variance is the difference between the actual O/H incurred and the budgeted overhead at actual hours. In essence, this is the O/H "rate" variance. The spending variance is found by adding the budgeted fixed O/H to the result of the actual hours times the variable O/H rate. The result is compared to actual O/H.

Budgeted O/H $7,000 + (3,500 x $2.50)	$15,750
Actual O/H	(15,000)
	$ 750 F

Three-way analysis of variance combines the budget and spending variances of four-way analysis of variance. It consists of spending, efficiency, and volume variances.

The correct answer is (a). *(CPA 1172 T-25)*
REQUIRED: The source of a spending variance for variable overhead.
DISCUSSION: Variable overhead includes numerous items, and an overall rate is required. The spending variance is made up of many price and quantity differences, some favorable, some unfavorable. The spending variance is the difference between actual factory overhead incurred and budgeted factory overhead based on actual hours worked.
Answers (b) and (c) are incorrect because the spending variance is concerned with both price and quantity differences. Answer (d) is incorrect because a change in production volume will not affect the spending variance, although it would affect the efficiency variance.

The correct answer is (a). *(CPA 585 T-39)*
REQUIRED: The definition of net overhead variance.
DISCUSSION: The three-way analysis of overhead variances consists of spending, efficiency, and production volume variances, but regardless of whether two-, three-, or four-way analysis is used, the net overhead variance is the difference between actual total overhead and the total overhead applied to the product.
Answer (b) is incorrect because, in two-way analysis, the controllable (budget) variance is the difference between total actual overhead and the sum of budgeted fixed costs and variable overhead based on standard input allowed for the actual output. Answer (c) is incorrect because the efficiency variance in three- or four-way analysis is the difference between variable overhead at the standard rate for actual input and at the standard rate for standard input. Answer (d) is incorrect because, in three-way analysis, the spending variance is the difference between actual total overhead and the sum of budgeted fixed costs and the variable overhead based on the actual input at the standard rate. It combines the variable overhead spending and the fixed overhead budget variances used in four-way analysis.

Module 13.4: Overhead

111. Under the three-variance method for analyzing factory overhead, the difference between the actual factory overhead and the budget allowance based on actual hours is the

  a. Efficiency variance.
  b. Spending variance.
  c. Volume variance.
  d. Idle capacity variance.

The correct answer is (b). *(CPA 1184 T-51)*
REQUIRED: The definition of spending variance in a three-way analysis.
DISCUSSION: In three-way analysis, the spending variance is the difference between actual total overhead and the sum of budgeted fixed costs and the variable overhead based on the actual input at the standard rate. It combines the variable overhead spending and the fixed overhead budget variances used in four-way analysis.
 Answer (a) is incorrect because the efficiency variance in three- or four-way analysis is the difference between variable overhead at the standard rate for actual input and at the standard rate for standard input. Answers (c) and (d) are incorrect because the production volume (idle capacity) variance is the difference between budgeted lump-sum fixed overhead and fixed overhead applied based on the predetermined rate and the standard input allowed for the actual output.

112. Under the three-variance method for analyzing factory overhead, which of the following is used in the computation of the spending variance?

	Actual Factory Overhead	Budget Allowance Based on Actual Hours
a.	No	Yes
b.	No	No
c.	Yes	No
d.	Yes	Yes

The correct answer is (d). *(CPA 1187 T-42)*
REQUIRED: The components of spending variance.
DISCUSSION: In three-way analysis, the spending variance is the difference between actual total overhead and the sum of budgeted fixed costs and the variable overhead based on the actual input at the standard rate. It combines the variable overhead spending and the fixed overhead budget variances used in four-way analysis.

113. Overhead spending variance is the difference between the

  a. Actual overhead cost and budgeted overhead cost for actual hours worked.
  b. Standard overhead cost and budgeted overhead cost for actual hours worked.
  c. Actual overhead cost and standard overhead cost for standard hours.
  d. Standard overhead cost and budgeted overhead cost for standard hours.

The correct answer is (a). *(CIA 586 IV-4)*
REQUIRED: The formula for overhead spending variance.
DISCUSSION: Overhead spending variance is the difference between actual O/H incurred and the budgeted O/H at actual hours. In essence, this is the overhead "rate" variance.
 Answer (b) is incorrect because actual O/H rather than standard O/H should be used. Answer (c) is incorrect because actual rather than standard hours should be used. Answer (d) is incorrect because actual cost and hours should be used rather than standard cost and hours.

114. Selo Imports utilizes flexible budgeting for the control of costs. The company's annual master budget includes $324,000 for fixed production supervisory salaries at a volume of 180,000 units. Supervisory salaries are expected to be incurred uniformly through the year. During September, 15,750 units were produced and production supervisory salaries incurred were $28,000. A performance report for September would reflect a budget variance of

  a. $350F.
  b. $350U.
  c. $1,000U.
  d. $1,000F.
  e. Some amount other than those given above.

The correct answer is (c). *(CMA 687 4-17)*
REQUIRED: The budget variance given budgeted and actual fixed costs and sales.
DISCUSSION: The $324,000 for supervisory salaries is a fixed cost, at a rate of $27,000 per month. Since these costs are fixed, volume is irrelevant. Thus, the variance is the difference between actual costs of $28,000 and the budgeted costs of $27,000, or 1,000 unfavorable.

Module 13.4: Overhead

115. Air, Inc. uses a standard cost system. Overhead cost information for Product CO for the month of October is as follows:

Total actual overhead incurred	$12,600
Fixed overhead budgeted	$3,300
Total standard overhead rate per DLH	$4
Variable overhead rate per DLH	$3
Standard hours allowed for actual production	3,500

What is the overall or net overhead variance?

a. $1,200 favorable.
b. $1,200 unfavorable.
c. $1,400 favorable.
d. $1,400 unfavorable.

116. Information on Overhead Company's overhead costs is as follows:

Standard applied overhead	$80,000
Budgeted O/H based on std. DLH allowed	84,000
Budgeted O/H based on actual DLH	83,000
Actual overhead	86,000

What is the total overhead variance?

a. $2,000 unfavorable.
b. $3,000 favorable.
c. $4,000 favorable.
d. $6,000 unfavorable.

117. Peters Company uses a flexible budget system and prepared the following information for the year:

Percent of capacity	80%	90%
Direct labor hours	24,000	27,000
Variable factory overhead	$48,000	$54,000
Fixed factory overhead	$108,000	$108,000
Total factory overhead rate per DLH	$6.50	$6.00

Peters operated at 80% of capacity during the year, but applied factory overhead based on the 90% capacity level. Assuming that actual factory overhead was equal to the budgeted amount for the attained capacity, what is the amount of overhead variance for the year?

a. $6,000 overabsorbed.
b. $6,000 underabsorbed.
c. $12,000 overabsorbed.
d. $12,000 underabsorbed.

The correct answer is (c). *(CPA 1178 P-37)*
REQUIRED: The overall overhead variance for the month.
DISCUSSION: The overall overhead variance can be found by finding the difference between actual overhead incurred and the overhead applied at the standard hours allowed. The standard overhead allowed is found by multiplying the standard hours allowed by the total overhead rate per hour.

$$(3,500 \times \$4) - \$12,600 = \$1,400 \text{ F}$$

The variance is favorable because actual overhead incurred was less than standard.

The correct answer is (d). *(CPA 579 P-39)*
REQUIRED: The total overhead variance for the period.
DISCUSSION: The total overhead variance is the difference between the actual overhead incurred and the standard overhead applied. An unfavorable variance results when actual overhead is greater than standard overhead applied.

$$\$86,000 \text{ act. O/H} - \$80,000 \text{ std. O/H} = \$6,000 \text{ U}$$

The correct answer is (d). *(CPA 581 P-25)*
REQUIRED: The amount of overhead variance for the year.
DISCUSSION: Total overhead variance is computed by determining the difference between the actual overhead and applied overhead. Given that no variation occurred for variable overhead, you need only fixed overhead. The fixed overhead rate at the 90% activity level is

$$\frac{\$108,000 \text{ fixed O/H}}{27,000 \text{ DLH}} = \$4$$

Given that the actual activity level achieved was 80%, and that standard hours allowed was 24,000, $96,000 (24,000 x $4.00) of fixed overhead was applied.

$108,000 fixed O/H - $96,000 applied O/H
= $12,000 underapplied

118. Dickey Company had total underapplied overhead of $15,000. Additional data:

Variable Overhead:
Applied based on standard DLH allowed $42,000
Budgeted based on standard DLH   38,000

Fixed Overhead:
Applied based on standard DLH allowed   30,000
Budgeted based on standard DLH   27,000

What is the actual total overhead?

a. $50,000.
b. $57,000.
c. $80,000.
d. $87,000.

The correct answer is (d). *(CPA 581 P-26)*
REQUIRED: The actual total overhead for the period.
DISCUSSION: The total actual overhead is the sum of the total applied overhead ($42,000 variable + $30,000 fixed) and the $15,000 underapplied overhead.

$42,000 + $30,000 + $15,000 = $87,000

119. Compute the variable overhead efficiency variance, using the following data:

Standard labor hours per good unit produced   2
Good units produced   1,000
Actual labor hours used   2,100
Standard variable overhead per standard labor hour $ 3
Actual variable overhead   6,500

a. $200 favorable.
b. $200 unfavorable.
c. $300 favorable.
d. $300 unfavorable.

The correct answer is (d). *(CIA 587 IV-14)*
REQUIRED: The variable overhead efficiency variance.
DISCUSSION: The variable overhead variance is similar to the labor and material variances. It consists of the spending variance (price or rate) and efficiency variance (time or quantity). Variable overhead is usually assigned to the product, and its variances are analyzed in terms of an activity base, usually direct labor hours. The efficiency variance is thus the standard variable overhead rate ($3) times the difference (100 hours) between the actual (2,100) and standard hours (1,000 x 2 = 2,000), or $300. The variance is unfavorable because actual hours exceeded standard hours allowed for the actual output.

120. Using the information presented below, calculate the total overhead spending variance.

Budgeted fixed overhead $10,000
Standard variable overhead (2 DLH at $2 per DLH) $4 per unit
Actual fixed overhead $10,300
Actual variable overhead $19,500
Budgeted volume (5,000 units x 2 DLH)   10,000 DLH
Actual direct labor hours (DLH)   9,500
Units produced   4,500

a. $500 unfavorable.
b. $800 unfavorable.
c. $1,000 unfavorable.
d. $1,300 unfavorable.

The correct answer is (b). *(CIA 1185 IV-4)*
REQUIRED: The total overhead (O/H) spending variance.
DISCUSSION: Total O/H spending variance is the difference between total actual O/H and total budgeted O/H for actual activity. Total actual O/H was $29,800 ($19,500 + $10,300). Budgeted O/H for actual activity was $29,000 [$10,000 + (9,500 x 2)]. Therefore, total O/H spending variance was $800 ($29,800 - $29,000). Since actual O/H was greater than budgeted O/H, the variance is unfavorable.

Module 13.4: Overhead

121. Union Company uses a standard cost accounting system. The following overhead costs and production data are available for August:

Standard fixed overhead rate per DLH	$1
Standard variable overhead rate per DLH	$4
Budgeted monthly DLH	40,000
Actual DLH worked	39,500
Standard DLH allowed for actual production	39,000
Overall overhead variance - favorable	$2,000

The applied factory overhead for August should be

a. $195,000.
b. $197,000.
c. $197,500.
d. $199,500.

The correct answer is (a). *(CPA 1181 P-24)*
REQUIRED: The applied factory overhead for the month.
DISCUSSION: The applied factory overhead is the standard direct hours allowed for actual production multiplied by the total standard overhead rate per hour.

$$39,000(\$4 \text{ VOH} + \$1 \text{ FOH}) = \$195,000$$

122. Nil Co. uses a predetermined factory overhead application rate based on direct labor cost. For the year ended December 31, Nil's budgeted factory overhead was $600,000, based on a budgeted volume of 50,000 direct labor hours, at a standard direct labor rate of $6 per hour. Actual factory overhead amounted to $620,000, with actual direct labor cost of $325,000. For the year, overapplied factory overhead was

a. $20,000.
b. $25,000.
c. $30,000.
d. $50,000.

The correct answer is (c). *(CPA 1186 Q-29)*
REQUIRED: The overapplied factory overhead (O/H) for the period.
DISCUSSION: Nil Co. applies factory O/H using a predetermined O/H rate, based on direct labor cost. O/H was budgeted for $600,000 based on a budgeted labor cost of $300,000 ($6 x 50,000 hrs.), or $2 of O/H will be applied for each dollar of labor. Since actual labor cost is $325,000, $650,000 ($2 x $325,000) of O/H was applied during the period. Actual O/H was $620,000, thus $30,000 ($650,000 - $620,000) was overapplied.

123. Information on Ripley Company's overhead costs for the January production activity is as follows:

Budgeted fixed overhead	$ 75,000
Standard fixed overhead rate per DLH	$ 3
Standard variable overhead rate per DLH	$ 6
Standard DLH allowed for actual production	24,000
Actual total overhead incurred	$220,000

Ripley has a standard absorption and flexible budgeting system, and uses the two-variance method (two-way analysis) for overhead variances. The volume (denominator) variance for January is

a. $3,000 unfavorable.
b. $3,000 favorable.
c. $4,000 unfavorable.
d. $4,000 favorable.

The correct answer is (a). *(CPA 1180 P-39)*
REQUIRED: The volume variance for the month using two-way variance analysis.
DISCUSSION: The volume variance is the difference between the budgeted fixed overhead and the overhead applied based on the standard hours allowed times the standard fixed overhead rate and the standard input allowed for actual output. An unfavorable variance results when budgeted overhead is greater than applied overhead.

$$\$75,000 - (24,000 \times \$3) = \$3,000 \text{ U}$$

349

Module 13.4: Overhead

124. Alden Company has a standard absorption and flexible budgeting system and uses a two-way analysis of overhead variances. Selected data for the February production activity are:

Budgeted fixed factory overhead costs	$64,000
Actual factory overhead incurred	$230,000
Variable factory overhead rate per DLH	$5
Standard DLH	32,000
Actual DLH	32,000

The budget (controllable) variance for February is

a. $1,000 favorable.
b. $1,000 unfavorable.
c. $6,000 favorable.
d. $6,000 unfavorable.

The correct answer is (d). *(CPA 580 P-35)*
REQUIRED: The budget (controllable) variance for the month in a two-way analysis of variance.
DISCUSSION: Two-way analysis computes only two overhead variances: the budget (controllable) variance and the volume variance. The budget variance is the difference between actual overhead incurred and standard allowed for output. The budget variance is computed by first multiplying the variable overhead rate by the standard direct labor hours, giving the budgeted variable overhead. The fixed overhead is added to the variable overhead for the total standard overhead. The difference between the actual and standard total overhead is the budget variance. An unfavorable variance results when actual is greater than standard.

$230,000 - [$64,000 + (32,000 × $5)] = $6,000 U

125. Baxter Corporation's master budget calls for the production of 5,000 units of product monthly. The master budget includes indirect labor of $144,000 annually; Baxter considers indirect labor to be a variable cost. During the month of April, 4,500 units of product were produced, and indirect labor costs of $10,100 were incurred. A performance report utilizing flexible budgeting would report a budget variance for indirect labor of

a. $1,900 unfavorable.
b. $700 favorable.
c. $1,900 favorable.
d. $700 unfavorable.
e. Some amount other than those given above.

The correct answer is (b). *(CMA 687 4-18)*
REQUIRED: The budget variance for indirect labor.
DISCUSSION: The $144,000 annual amount equals $12,000 per month. Since volume is expected to be 5,000 units per month, and the $12,000 is considered a variable cost, budgeted cost per unit is $2.40 ($12,000 ÷ 5,000 units). If 4,500 units are produced, the total variable costs should be $10,800 (4,500 units × $2.40). Subtracting the $10,100 of actual costs from the budgeted figure results in a favorable variance of $700.

126. Universal Company uses a standard cost system and prepared the following budget at normal capacity for the month of January:

Direct labor hours	24,000
Variable factory overhead	$48,000
Fixed factory overhead	$108,000
Total factory overhead per DLH	$6.50

Actual data for January were as follows:

Direct labor hours worked	22,000
Total factory overhead	$147,000
Standard DLH allowed for capacity attained	21,000

Using the two-way analysis of overhead variances, what is the budget (controllable) variance for January?

a. $3,000 favorable.
b. $5,000 favorable.
c. $9,000 favorable.
d. $10,500 unfavorable.

The correct answer is (a). *(CPA 583 P-39)*
REQUIRED: The controllable (budget) variance for the month.
DISCUSSION: Two-way analysis computes only two overhead variances: the budget (controllable) variance and the volume variance. The budget variance is computed by multiplying the variable O/H rate times the standard direct labor hours allowed for capacity attained, resulting in the budgeted variable O/H. The fixed O/H is then added to the budgeted variable O/H, giving the total budgeted O/H. The difference between the actual O/H and standard total O/H is the budget (controllable) variance. Actual O/H equals $147,000. Budgeted variable O/H equals $2 per hour ($48,000 ÷ 24,000 DLH). The variance is favorable because budgeted exceeds actual.

DLH allowed	21,000
Budgeted variable rate	× $2
Variable O/H	$42,000
Fixed O/H	108,000
Total budgeted O/H	$150,000

$147,000 actual O/H - $150,000 total budgeted O/H = $3,000 F

Module 13.4: Overhead

127. Simson Company's master budget shows straight-line depreciation on factory equipment of $258,000. The master budget was prepared at an annual production volume of 103,200 units of product. This production volume is expected to occur uniformly throughout the year. During September, Simson produced 8,170 units of product, and the accounts reflected actual depreciation on factory machinery of $20,500. Simson controls manufacturing costs with a flexible budget. The flexible budget amount for depreciation on factory machinery for September would be

   a. $19,475.
   b. $20,425.
   c. $20,500.
   d. $21,500.
   e. Some amount other than those given above.

The correct answer is (d). *(CMA 686 4-23)*
   REQUIRED: The amount of depreciation expense shown on the flexible budget for the month.
   DISCUSSION: Since depreciation is a fixed cost, that cost will be the same each month regardless of production. Therefore, the budget for September would show depreciation of $21,500 ($258,000 annual depreciation x 1/12).

128. Martin Company uses a two-way analysis of overhead variances. Selected data for the April production activity are as follows:

Actual variable factory O/H incurred	$196,000
Variable factory O/H rate per DLH	$6
Standard DLH allowed	33,000
Actual DLH	32,000

Assuming that budgeted fixed overhead costs are equal to actual fixed costs, the budget (controllable) variance for April is

   a. $2,000 favorable.
   b. $4,000 unfavorable.
   c. $4,000 favorable.
   d. $6,000 favorable.

The correct answer is (a). *(CPA 582 P-22)*
   REQUIRED: The budget variance if budgeted fixed costs equal actual fixed costs under two-way analysis of variance.
   DISCUSSION: Two-way or two-variance analysis looks only at budget (controllable) and volume variances. When actual fixed equals budgeted fixed, the budget variance equals the variable budget variance. It is the difference between actual variable overhead and standard hours allowed time the variable overhead rate per hour. A favorable variance results when actual is less than standard.

   $196,000 - (33,000 x $6) = $2,000 F

129. Using the following information, calculate the variable overhead efficiency variance.

Actual direct labor hours used	4,700
Units produced	1,500
Standard labor hours per unit produced	3
Budgeted variable overhead per standard direct labor hour	$ 2
Actual variable overhead incurred	$9,500

   a. $100 favorable.
   b. $100 unfavorable.
   c. $400 favorable.
   d. $400 unfavorable.

The correct answer is (d). *(CIA 1187 IV-14)*
   REQUIRED: The variable overhead efficiency variance.
   DISCUSSION: This variance equals the standard rate per unit of the activity measure (direct labor hours) times the difference between the actual activity and the standard activity for the actual output. The variance is $400 U {$2/hr. x [4,700 actual hrs. - (3 std. hrs./unit x 1,500 units)]}. This variance is unfavorable because actual hours exceeded the standard hours allowed for actual output.

130. Using the data from the previous question, compute the variable overhead spending variance.

   a. $100 favorable.
   b. $100 unfavorable.
   c. $400 favorable.
   d. $400 unfavorable.

The correct answer is (b). *(CIA 1187 IV-15)*
   REQUIRED: The variable overhead spending variance.
   DISCUSSION: This variance equals the difference between the actual variable overhead incurred and the standard cost based on the actual activity level. The variance is $100 U [$9,500 - ($2/hr. x 4,700 actual hrs.)]. The variance is unfavorable because the actual cost exceeded the standard cost.

Questions 131 through 135 are based on Edney Company, which employs a standard absorption system for product costing. The standard cost of its product is as follows:

Raw materials	$14.50
Direct labor (2 DLH x $8)	16.00
Manufacturing overhead (2 DLH x $11)	22.00
Total standard cost	$52.50

The manufacturing overhead rate is based upon a normal activity level of 600,000 direct labor hours.

Edney planned to produce 25,000 units each month during the year. The budgeted annual manufacturing overhead is

Variable	$3,600,000
Fixed	3,000,000
	$6,600,000

During November, Edney produced 26,000 units. Edney used 53,500 direct labor hours in November at a cost of $433,350. Actual manufacturing overhead for the month was $260,000 fixed and $315,000 variable. The total manufacturing overhead applied during November was $572,000.

131. The variable manufacturing overhead spending variance for November is

a. $9,000 unfavorable.
b. $4,000 unfavorable.
c. $11,350 unfavorable.
d. $9,000 favorable.
e. $6,000 favorable.

The correct answer is (e). *(CMA 1283 4-17)*
REQUIRED: The variable manufacturing overhead spending variance for the month.
DISCUSSION: The variable overhead spending variance is the difference between actual variable costs and actual hours times the standard variable cost rate. The overhead rate is given as $11 per direct labor hour, of which 6/11 ($3,600,000/$6,600,000) represents variable costs. The $11 overhead application rate thus consists of $6 variable and $5 fixed costs. The spending variance is

VOH rate x actual DLH ($6 x 53,500)	$321,000
Actual variable costs	(315,000)
Favorable VOH spending variance	$ 6,000

132. The variable manufacturing overhead efficiency variance for November is

a. $3,000 unfavorable.
b. $9,000 unfavorable.
c. $1,000 favorable.
d. $12,000 unfavorable.
e. $0.

The correct answer is (b). *(CMA 1283 4-18)*
REQUIRED: The variable overhead efficiency variance.
DISCUSSION: The variable overhead efficiency variance is the difference between the actual hours at standard cost and the standard hours at standard cost. Actual output was 26,000 units. Standard input for this output at 2 DLH per unit was 52,000 hours. Thus, $312,000 (52,000 x $6) minus $321,000 (53,500 x $6) equals $9,000 unfavorable. The company used 1,500 hours too many to produce 26,000 units. Each of these excessive hours cost $6, and $6 times 1,500 hours equals a $9,000 unfavorable variance.

133. The fixed manufacturing overhead spending (budget) variance for November is

a. $10,000 favorable.
b. $10,000 unfavorable.
c. $6,000 favorable.
d. $4,000 unfavorable.
e. $0.

The correct answer is (b). *(CMA 1283 4-19)*
REQUIRED: The fixed overhead spending (budget) variance for the month.
DISCUSSION: This variance is calculated by subtracting budgeted costs from actual fixed costs incurred. The monthly budgeted costs for fixed overhead are $250,000 ($3,000,000 ÷ 12 months). Actual costs are given as $260,000. The variance is thus $10,000 ($260,000 - $250,000) unfavorable.

Module 13.4: Overhead

134. The fixed manufacturing overhead volume variance for November is

a. $10,000 favorable.
b. $10,000 unfavorable.
c. $3,000 unfavorable.
d. $22,000 favorable.
e. $0.

The correct answer is (a). *(CMA 1283 4-20)*
REQUIRED: The fixed overhead volume variance for the month.
DISCUSSION: The overhead volume variance is the difference between the budgeted amount and the fixed costs applied based on the standard rate and standard hours allowed for actual output. Thus, $250,000 budgeted minus $260,000 (52,000 hours x $5 standard cost) equals a $10,000 favorable variance. The company planned to produce 25,000 units per month. Actual production was 26,000 units, or 1,000 extra units, each requiring two hours of labor time. Therefore, fixed overhead was applied for 2,000 more hours (at standard) than had been planned. Since each hour absorbed $5 of the fixed overhead, there is a favorable variance of 2,000 hours times $5 per hour, or $10,000. The variance is favorable because it indicates full utilization of capacity.

135. The total variance related to efficiency of the manufacturing operation for November is

a. $9,000 unfavorable.
b. $12,000 unfavorable.
c. $21,000 unfavorable.
d. $11,000 unfavorable.
e. $25,000 unfavorable.

The correct answer is (c). *(CMA 1283 4-21)*
REQUIRED: The total variance related to efficiency of the manufacturing operation.
DISCUSSION: The total efficiency variance concerns both overhead and direct labor. It was determined in Q. 132 above that the overhead efficiency variance was $9,000 unfavorable. In addition, the labor efficiency variance of 1,500 DLH (53,500 - 52,000) times $8 standard cost per hour, or $12,000, is unfavorable. The total efficiency variance is thus $21,000 unfavorable ($9,000 overhead + $12,000 labor).

Questions 136 and 137 are based on Beth Company, which has budgeted fixed factory overhead costs of $50,000 per month and a variable factory overhead rate of $4 per direct labor hour. The standard direct labor hours allowed for October production were 18,000. An analysis of the factory overhead indicates that, in October, Beth had an unfavorable budget (controllable) variance of $1,000 and a favorable volume variance of $500. Beth uses a two-way analysis of overhead variances.

---

136. The actual factory overhead incurred in October is

a. $121,000.
b. $122,000.
c. $122,500.
d. $123,000.

The correct answer is (d). *(CPA 578 P-30)*
REQUIRED: The actual factory overhead in a two-way analysis of variance.
DISCUSSION: The actual O/H is the unfavorable budget variance plus the budgeted O/H. Budgeted O/H is the sum of fixed plus variable O/H.

$50,000 + (18,000 x $4) = $122,000 budget
            1,000 budget variance
           $123,000 actual

137. Beth's applied factory overhead in October is

a. $121,000.
b. $122,000.
c. $122,500.
d. $123,000.

The correct answer is (c). *(CPA 578 P-31)*
REQUIRED: The applied factory overhead in a two-way analysis of variance.
DISCUSSION: The applied factory overhead is the sum of the budgeted overhead (Q. 136) and the favorable volume variance.

$122,000 + $500 = $122,500

Module 13.4: Overhead

> Questions 138 through 141 are based on Derf Company, which applies overhead on the basis of direct labor hours. Two direct labor hours are required for each product unit. Planned production for the period was set at 9,000 units. Manufacturing overhead is budgeted at $135,000 for the period, of which 20% of this cost is fixed. The 17,200 hours worked during the period resulted in production of 8,500 units. Variable manufacturing overhead cost incurred was $108,500 and fixed manufacturing overhead cost was $28,000. Derf Company uses a four variance method for analyzing manufacturing overhead.

138. The variable overhead spending variance for the period is

a. $5,300 unfavorable.
b. $1,200 unfavorable.
c. $6,300 unfavorable.
d. $6,500 unfavorable.
e. $7,500 unfavorable.

The correct answer is (a). *(CMA 1287 4-24)*
REQUIRED: The variable overhead spending variance.
DISCUSSION: The variable overhead spending variance is a price variance. It is the difference between actual variable overhead costs (actual activity times the actual rate) and actual activity times the standard rate. Overhead costs were budgeted at $135,000, of which 80%, or $108,000, was variable. Since 18,000 hours were expected to be worked (9,000 units x 2 hours), the variable overhead rate was $6 per hour ($108,000 ÷ 18,000 hours). The variable overhead applied was $103,200 ($6 x 17,200 actual hours). The variance was $5,300 unfavorable ($108,500 actual VOH - $103,200 standard).

139. The variable overhead efficiency (quantity) variance for the period is

a. $5,300 unfavorable.
b. $1,200 unfavorable.
c. $1,500 unfavorable.
d. $6,500 unfavorable.
e. $6,300 unfavorable.

The correct answer is (b). *(CMA 1287 4-25)*
REQUIRED: The variable overhead efficiency variance.
DISCUSSION: The variable overhead efficiency (quantity) variance is the standard variable overhead rate times the difference between the actual activity and the standard activity allowed for the actual output. The production of 8,500 units required 17,000 standard hours. Since 17,200 hours were worked at a rate of $6 per hour (see Q. 138), the variance is $1,200 unfavorable (200 hours x $6).

140. The fixed overhead budget (spending) variance for the period is

a. $6,300 unfavorable.
b. $2,500 unfavorable.
c. $1,500 unfavorable.
d. $1,000 unfavorable.
e. $1,200 unfavorable.

The correct answer is (d). *(CMA 1287 4-26)*
REQUIRED: The fixed overhead budget variance.
DISCUSSION: The fixed overhead budget variance is the difference between actual fixed costs and budgeted fixed costs. Budgeted fixed costs were $27,000 (20% x $135,000), and actual fixed costs were $28,000, a variance of $1,000 unfavorable.

141. The fixed overhead volume (denominator) variance for the period is

a. $750 unfavorable.
b. $2,500 unfavorable.
c. $1,500 unfavorable.
d. $1,000 unfavorable.
e. $2,700 unfavorable.

The correct answer is (c). *(CMA 1287 4-27)*
REQUIRED: The fixed overhead volume variance.
DISCUSSION: The fixed overhead volume variance is the difference between budgeted fixed costs and the product of the standard fixed overhead rate times the standard activity allowed for the actual output. At a production level of 18,000 hours (9,000 units x 2 hours), fixed costs were budgeted at $27,000 (20% x $135,000), or $1.50 per hour. Since 17,000 standard hours were allowed for the actual output of 8,500 units, fixed overhead applied was $25,500 (17,000 x $1.50), a variance of $1,500 unfavorable ($27,000 - $25,500). This underapplication of fixed overhead is unfavorable because it indicates an underuse of facilities; that is, activity was less than budgeted. Unlike other variances, this variance does not measure deviations from expected costs but rather departure from the expected use of productive capacity.

Module 13.4: Overhead

> Questions 142 through 144 are based upon the following information supplied by Patie Company which uses a standard FIFO, process cost system to account for its only product, Mituea. Patie has found that direct machine hours (DMH) provide the best estimate of the application of overhead. The standard direct machine hours allowed for each unit is four (4) hours.
>
> Using simple linear regression analysis in the form y = a + b(DMH), where "a" are fixed costs and "b" are variable, Patie has developed the following overhead budget for a normal activity level of 100,000 direct machine hours.
>
> | ITEM (y) | a | b |
> |---|---|---|
> | Supplies | | $ 0.50 |
> | Indirect Labor | $ 54,750 | 6.50 |
> | Depreciation--Plant and Equipment | 27,000 | |
> | Property Taxes and Insurance | 32,300 | |
> | Repairs and Maintenance | 14,550 | 1.25 |
> | Utilities | 3,400 | 4.75 |
> | Total Overhead | $132,000 | $13.00 |

142. What is the standard overhead rate?

a. $13.00 per DMH.
b. $132,000.
c. $1.32 per DMH
d. $14.32 per DMH.

The correct answer is (d). *(L.J. McCarthy)*
REQUIRED: The standard overhead rate.
DISCUSSION: The total overhead equation is y = 132,000 + 13(DMH). This is derived by summing individual overhead items. The fixed portion needs to be converted to a rate by dividing it by normal capacity. Thus, the fixed overhead rate is 132,000 ÷ 100,000 = 1.32. To calculate the total overhead rate, add the fixed rate to the variable rate. Therefore, the total overhead rate per DMH is $1.32 + $13.00 = $14.32.

143. If 23,500 equivalent units were produced during the year, using 98,700 direct machine hours, how much overhead should be applied to production?

a. $1,413,384.
b. $1,432,000.
c. $1,346,080.
d. $1,222,000.

The correct answer is (c). *(L.J. McCarthy)*
REQUIRED: The amount of standard O/H applied to production.
DISCUSSION: In a standard cost system, overhead is applied using the standard activity allowed for production. The standard activity allowed is the standard activity per equivalent unit times the actual production or 4 DMH x 23,500 = 94,000. The overhead applied then is 94,000 x $14.32 = $1,346,080.

144. Assuming actual fixed overhead incurred was $133,250 and actual variable overhead incurred was $1,225,000, what is the total overhead variance?

a. $12,170 unfavorable.
b. $12,170 favorable.
c. $55,134 unfavorable.
d. $55,134 favorable.

The correct answer is (a). *(L.J. McCarthy)*
REQUIRED: The total overhead variance for the year.
DISCUSSION: The total overhead variance is the over- or underapplied overhead. This is the applied overhead minus the actual overhead. From the previous question, the applied overhead was $1,346,080 and the actual overhead is $1,358,250 ($133,250 + $1,225,000). Thus the amount of underapplied overhead is $1,346,080 - $1,358,000 = $12,170 unfavorable.

Module 13.4: Overhead

Questions 145 through 152 are based on the following information.

Dept. 203--Work-in-Process--Beginning of Period

Job No.	Material	Labor	Overhead	Total
1376	$17,500	$22,000	$33,000	$72,500

Department 203 overhead rate for the period:

Budgeted overhead
Variable--Indirect materials		$ 16,000
Indirect labor		56,000
Employee benefits		24,000
Fixed--Supervision		20,000
Depreciation		12,000
Total		$128,000
Budgeted direct labor dollars		$ 80,000
Rate per direct labor dollar ($128,000/$80,000)		160%

Department 203 costs for the period:

Incurred by Jobs

Job	Material	Labor	Other	Total
1376	$ 1,000	$ 7,000	--	$ 8,000
1377	26,000	53,000	--	79,000
1378	12,000	9,000	--	21,000
1379	4,000	1,000	--	5,000

Not Incurred by Jobs

	Material	Labor	Other	Total
Indirect materials & supplies	15,000	--	--	15,000
Indirect labor	--	53,000	--	53,000
Employee benefits	--	--	$23,000	23,000
Depreciation	--	--	12,000	12,000
Supervision	--	20,000	--	20,000
Total	$58,000	$143,000	$35,000	$236,000

---

145. The actual overhead for Department 203 for the period was

a. $156,000.
b. $123,000.
c. $70,000.
d. $112,000.
e. Not shown above.

The correct answer is (b). *(CMA 678 4-13)*
REQUIRED: The actual overhead for the department.
DISCUSSION: Actual overhead is determined by adding all the items incurred.

	Actual
Indirect materials	$ 15,000
Indirect labor	53,000
Employee benefits	23,000
Supervision	20,000
Depreciation	12,000
	$123,000

146. Department 203 overhead for the period was

a. $11,000 underapplied.
b. $11,000 overapplied.
c. $44,000 underapplied.
d. $44,000 overapplied.
e. Not shown above.

The correct answer is (a). *(CMA 678 4-14)*
REQUIRED: The under- or overapplied overhead for the period.
DISCUSSION: The amount of overhead incurred is $123,000. The amount applied is 160% of the direct labor incurred. Assume Dept. 203 uses the FIFO method. The direct labor is $70,000 ($7,000 + $53,000 + $9,000 + $1,000). Do not include labor in BWIP, i.e., the $22,000 on job 1376, or supervisory costs.

(160% x $70,000) - $123,000 = $11,000 U

147. The volume variance for Department 203 for the period was

a. $16,000 unfavorable.
b. $12,000 unfavorable.
c. $0.
d. $15,000 unfavorable.
e. Not shown above.

The correct answer is (e). *(CMA 678 4-15)*
REQUIRED: The volume variance for the period.
DISCUSSION: The volume variance is the difference between budgeted fixed costs ($32,000) and applied fixed O/H at standard hours allowed. The application rate for fixed O/H is 40% of direct labor ($32,000 ÷ $80,000 = 40%). $70,000 of direct labor was incurred on jobs 1376-1379; thus, $28,000 (40% x $70,000) of fixed O/H was applied.

$32,000 - $28,000 = $4,000 U

148. The overhead spending variance for Department 203 for the period was

a. $5,000 unfavorable.
b. $7,000 unfavorable.
c. $16,000 unfavorable.
d. $12,000 unfavorable.
e. Not shown above.

The correct answer is (b). *(CMA 678 4-16)*
REQUIRED: The overhead spending variance for Department 203.
DISCUSSION: The overhead spending variance is made up of both variable and fixed O/H. The variance is the difference between the actual costs incurred and the results of the actual input at the standard price plus budgeted fixed O/H. Note that the variable O/H application rate is 120% of direct labor and the fixed O/H application rate is 40%. The variance is unfavorable because the company spent more than it had budgeted.

Actual overhead:	
Variable ($15,000 + $53,000 + $23,000)	$ 91,000
Fixed ($20,000 + $12,000)	32,000
	$123,000

Budgeted overhead:	
Variable ($70,000 x 120%)	$ 84,000
Fixed ($20,000 + $12,000)	32,000
	$116,000

Spending variance = $123,000 - $116,000 = $7,000 U

149. The overhead efficiency variance for Department 203 for the period was

a. $0.
b. $4,000.
c. $7,000.
d. $11,000.
e. None of the above.

The correct answer is (a). *(Publisher)*
REQUIRED: The overhead efficiency variance for the period.
DISCUSSION: Variable overhead is charged to product based on actual labor cost incurred. Thus, there is no difference between actual hours and standard hours, and therefore no efficiency variance. Note that the total O/H variance of $11,000 U (Q. 146) consists of $4,000 U volume variance (Q. 147) plus $7,000 U spending variance (Q. 148).

150. Job number 1376 was the only job completed and sold in the period. What amount was included in cost of goods sold for this job?

a. $72,500.
b. $91,700.
c. $80,500.
d. $19,200.
e. The amount is not shown above.

The correct answer is (b). *(CMA 678 4-17)*
REQUIRED: The cost of the job completed when sold.
DISCUSSION: Cost of goods sold is the sum of direct materials, direct labor, and factory overhead. Job 1376 had $72,500 of costs at the beginning of the period. To bring it to completion required $1,000 of material, $7,000 of labor, and $11,200 (160% x $7,000) of overhead. Total costs thus equal $72,500 + $1,000 + $7,000 + $11,200 = $91,700.

151. The value of work-in-process inventory at the end of the period was

a. $105,000.
b. $180,600.
c. $228,000.
d. $205,800.
e. Not shown above.

The correct answer is (d). *(CMA 678 4-18)*
REQUIRED: The value of work-in-process inventory at the end of the period.
DISCUSSION: WIP inventory consists of materials, labor, and overhead (160% x direct labor). Jobs 1377, 1378, and 1379 remain in process since only 1376 was completed.

	Material	Labor	Overhead	Total
1377	$26,000	$53,000	$ 84,800	$163,800
1378	12,000	9,000	14,400	35,400
1379	4,000	1,000	1,600	6,600
	$42,000	$63,000	$100,800	$205,800

Module 13.4: Overhead

152. Refer to the data preceding Q. 145. Assume that overhead was underapplied in the amount of $14,000 for Department 203. If underapplied overhead was distributed between cost of goods sold and inventory, how much of the underapplied overhead was charged to the year-end work-in-process inventory?

a. $9,685.
b. $4,315.
c. $12,600.
d. $1,400.
e. The amount is not shown above.

The correct answer is (c). *(CMA 678 4-19)*
REQUIRED: The amount of underapplied overhead charged to year-end WIP.
DISCUSSION: Under/overapplied O/H should be allocated proportionately to the inventory in WIP, finished goods, and CGS. Underapplied overhead of $14,000 for Department 203 should thus be allocated between work-in-process and the finished goods. Overhead in EWIP in Department 203 is $100,800 (see Q. 151), and O/H of $11,200 was in Job 1376, which was finished.

$$\frac{\$100,800}{\$100,800 + \$11,200} \times \$14,000 = \$12,600$$

Questions 153 and 154 are based on a monthly normal volume of 50,000 units (100,000 direct labor hours). Raff Co.'s standard cost system contains the following overhead costs:

Variable	$6 per unit
Fixed	8 per unit

The following information pertains to the month of March

Units actually produced	38,000
Actual direct labor hours worked	80,000

Actual overhead incurred:

Variable	$250,000
Fixed	384,000

---

153. For March, the unfavorable variable overhead spending variance was

a. $6,000.
b. $10,000.
c. $12,000.
d. $22,000.

The correct answer is (b). *(CPA 586 Q-23)*
REQUIRED: The unfavorable variable overhead (O/H) spending variance.
DISCUSSION: The variable overhead spending variance is the difference between actual variable costs and actual hours times the standard variable cost rate per hour. Since the standard output is 50,000 units in 100,000 hours, it takes 2 hours per unit. The standard variable costs are $6/unit or $3 per hour ($6 ÷ 2 hrs.). Actual variable cost is given as $250,000. Actual hours times the standard variable cost per hour equals $240,000 ($3 x 80,000 hrs.). Thus, the unfavorable O/H spending variance is $10,000 ($240,000 - $250,000).

154. For March, the fixed overhead volume variance was

a. $96,000 unfavorable.
b. $96,000 favorable.
c. $80,000 unfavorable.
d. $80,000 favorable.

The correct answer is (a). *(CPA 586 Q-24)*
REQUIRED: The fixed overhead volume variance for the month.
DISCUSSION: The overhead volume variance is the difference between the budgeted amount and the fixed costs applied based on the standard rate and standard hours allowed for actual output. Since the standard output is 50,000 units in 100,000 hours, it takes 2 hours per unit. The standard hours allowed for the number of actual units produced is 76,000 hrs. (2 x 38,000 units). The standard rate per hour is $4 ($8 ÷ 2 hrs.). Budgeted fixed overhead equals $400,000 ($8 x 50,000 units). Therefore the O/H volume variance is

$$\$400,000 - (76,000 \text{ hrs.} \times \$4) = \text{OH VV}$$
$$\$400,000 - \$304,000 = \$96,000 \text{ U}$$

The variance is unfavorable because budgeted costs are greater than the costs applied.

13.5 Sales Volume

155. The sales quantity variance is

a. (Actual units - master budget units) x (budgeted UCM - average UCM).

b. (Actual units - master budget units) x (budgeted average UCM).

c. (Budgeted market share percent) x (actual market size - budgeted market size) x (budgeted UCM).

d. (Actual market share percent - budgeted market share percent) x (actual market size) x (budgeted UCM).

The correct answer is (b). *(Publisher)*
REQUIRED: The definition of sales quantity variance.
DISCUSSION: The sales quantity (volume) variance focuses on the firm's aggregate results. It assumes a constant product mix and an average contribution margin for the composite unit. It is the difference between actual and budgeted units times the budgeted average UCM.
Answer (a) is incorrect because it defines the sales mix variance. Answer (c) is incorrect because it defines the market size variance. Answer (d) is incorrect because it defines the market mix variance.

156. The sales mix variance is

a. (Actual units - master budget units) x (budgeted UCM - budgeted average UCM).

b. (Actual units - master budget units) x (budgeted average UCM).

c. (Budgeted market share percent) x (actual market size - budgeted market size) x (budgeted UCM).

d. (Actual market share percent - budgeted market share percent) x (actual market size) x (budgeted UCM).

The correct answer is (a). *(Publisher)*
REQUIRED: The definition of sales mix variance.
DISCUSSION: The sales mix variance is a sum of variances: for each product in the mix, the difference between units old and expected to be sold is multiplied by the difference between the budgeted UCM for the product and the budgeted average UCM for all products; the results of this computation for each product are then added to determine the mix variance. The sales mix variance measures the effect of the change in the budgeted average UCM associated with the changes in the quantities of items in the mix. The sales mix variance is favorable when more units with a higher than average UCM are sold or when fewer units with a lower than average UCM are sold.

157. The sales mix variance

a. Would be an unfavorable five percent whenever a five percent decrease occurs in a company's overall sales volume.

b. Would be favorable when a company sells less of the products bearing unit contribution margins higher than average.

c. Measures the effect of the deviation from the budgeted average contribution margin per unit associated with a change in the quality of a particular product.

d. Would be unfavorable when a company sells less of the products bearing unit contribution margins lower than average.

The correct answer is (c). *(CIA 1186 IV-12)*
REQUIRED: The true statement about the sales mix variance.
DISCUSSION: The sales mix variance is a sum of variances: for each product in the mix, the difference between units sold and expected to be sold is multiplied by the difference between the budgeted unit contribution margin (UCM) for the product and the budgeted average UCM for all products. The results of these computations are then added to determine the mix variance. This variance measures the effect of the change in the budgeted average UCM associated with the changes in the quantities of items in the mix. The sales mix variance is favorable when more units with a higher than average UCM are sold or when fewer units with a lower than average UCM are sold.
Answer (a) is incorrect because the sales mix variance is unaffected by a change in overall sales volume, assuming the proportions of products sold remain constant. However, an unfavorable sales quantity variance would arise given a 5% decrease in overall sales volume since a 5% decrease in contribution margin would occur. This variance is computed by holding the sales mix, budgeted prices, and budgeted costs constant. It measures the change in contribution margin caused by a change in overall volume. Answer (b) is incorrect because the variance would be unfavorable. Answer (d) is incorrect because the variance would be favorable.

Module 13.5: Sales Volume

158. The market size variance is

a. (Actual units - master budget units) x (budgeted UCM - average UCM).

b. (Actual units - master budget units) x (budgeted average UCM).

c. (Budgeted market share percent) x (actual market size - budgeted market size) x (budgeted UCM).

d. (Actual market share percent - budgeted market share percent) x (actual market size) x (budgeted UCM).

The correct answer is (c). *(Publisher)*
REQUIRED: The definition of market size variance.
DISCUSSION: Market size variance gives an indication of the change in contribution margin caused by a change in the market size. The market size and market share variances are relevant to industries in which total level of sales and market share are known, e.g., the automobile industry. The market size variance measures the effect of changes in an industry's sales on an individual company, and the market share variance analyzes the impact of a change in market share.

159. The market share variance is

a. (Actual units - master budget units) x (budgeted UCM - average UCM).

b. (Actual units - master budget units) x (budgeted average UCM).

c. (Budgeted market share percent) x (actual market size - budgeted market size) x (budgeted UCM).

d. (Actual market share percent - budgeted market share percent) x (actual market size) x (budgeted UCM).

The correct answer is (d). *(Publisher)*
REQUIRED: The definition of market share variance.
DISCUSSION: The market share variance gives an indication of the amount of contribution margin gained (forgone) because of a change in the market share.

160. The gross profit of Reade Company for each of the years ended December 31, 1989 and 1988 was as follows:

	1989	1988
Sales	$792,000	$800,000
Cost of goods sold	464,000	480,000
Gross profit	$328,000	$320,000

Assuming that 1989 selling prices were 10% lower, what would be the decrease in gross profit due to the change in selling prices?

a. $8,000.

b. $72,000.

c. $79,200.

d. $88,000.

The correct answer is (d). *(CPA 582 P-32)*
REQUIRED: The change in gross profit given a reduction in selling price.
DISCUSSION: With a 10% decrease in prices in 1989, that year's sales are 90% of what would have been if 1988 prices had been in effect. Dividing 1989 sales of $792,000 by 90% gives the $880,000 of sales there would have been at 1988 prices. Therefore, sales and gross profit are $88,000 ($880,000 - $792,000) less because of the 10% decrease in selling price.

161. Actual and budgeted information about the sales of a product are presented below for June:

	Actual	Budget
Units	8,000	10,000
Sales Revenue	$92,000	$105,000

The sales price variance for June was

a. $8,000 favorable.

b. $10,000 favorable.

c. $10,000 unfavorable.

d. $10,500 unfavorable.

e. $8,500 unfavorable.

The correct answer is (a). *(CIA 1185 IV-12)*
REQUIRED: The sales price variance for the month.
DISCUSSION: Sales price variance is the difference between actual price and budgeted price times actual units. Actual price was $11.50 ($92,000 ÷ 8,000). Budgeted price was $10.50 ($105,000 ÷ 10,000). Sales price variance is thus $8,000 [($11.50 - $10.50) x 8,000 actual units]. The variance is favorable because actual sales price was greater than budgeted sales price.

Module 13.5: Sales Volume

162. The following information is available for the Mitchelville Products Company for the month of July.

	Master Budget	Actual
Units	4,000	3,800
Sales revenue	$60,000	$53,200
Variable manufacturing costs	16,000	19,000
Fixed manufacturing costs	15,000	16,000
Variable selling and administrative expense	8,000	7,600
Fixed selling and administrative expense	9,000	10,000

The contribution margin volume variance for the month of July would be

a. $400 unfavorable.

b. $1,800 unfavorable.

c. $200 favorable.

d. $6,800 unfavorable.

e. $7,600 unfavorable.

The correct answer is (b). *(CMA 687 4-16)*
REQUIRED: The contribution margin volume variance.
DISCUSSION: The volume variance isolates the effect of selling more or less units than budgeted. It equals budgeted unit contribution margin (UCM) times the difference between budgeted and actual units sold. Given expected sales of 4,000 units and revenue of $60,000, unit price is $15. Variable costs are $16,000 for manufacturing and $8,000 for selling, and unit variable cost is $6 ($24,000 ÷ 4,000 units). The UCM is $9 ($15 - $6). Since actual sales were 200 units less than budgeted (4,000 - 3,800), the lost contribution margin was $1,800 ($9 x 200). This variance is unfavorable because actual sales were less than budgeted.

163. Garfield Company, which sells a single product, provided the following data from its income statements for the calendar years 1989 and 1988.

	1989
Sales (150,000 units)	750,000 $175,000
Costs of goods sold	525,000
Gross profit	$225,000

	1988 (Base Year)
Sales (180,000 units)	$720,000
Costs of goods sold	575,000
Gross profit	$145,000

In an analysis of variation in gross profit between the two years, what would be the effects of changes in sales price and sales volume?

	Sales Price	Sales Volume
a.	$150,000 F	$120,000 U
b.	$150,000 U	$120,000 F
c.	$180,000 F	$150,000 U
d.	$180,000 U	$150,000 F

The correct answer is (a). *(CPA 1181 P-31)*
REQUIRED: The effects of changes in sales price and sales volume
DISCUSSION: The 1989 sales price must have been $5 ($750,000 ÷ 150,000 units); the 1988 sales price was $4 ($720,000 ÷ 180,000 units). The sales price effect is computed by multiplying the 1989 units sold by the change in price per unit from 1989 to 1988. The increase in unit price created a favorable gross sales effect.

[150,000 units x ($5 - $4)] = $150,000 F

The sales volume effect is computed by multiplying the change in units from 1988 to 1989 by the unit price 1988. Note that the 1988 price is used so that only the change in volume will be reflected.

(150,000 - 180,000) x $4 = $120,000 U

The decrease in number of units sold created an unfavorable sales volume effect.

164. Kane Corporation has a practical production capacity of one million units. The current year's master budget was based on the production and sales of 700,000 units during the current year. Actual production for the current year was 720,000 units while actual sales amounted to only 600,000 units. The units are sold for $20 each and the contribution margin ratio is 30%. The dollar amount which best quantifies the marketing department's failure to achieve budgeted performance for the current year is

a. $2,400,000 unfavorable.

b. $2,000,000 unfavorable.

c. $720,000 unfavorable.

d. $600,000 unfavorable.

e. Some other amount.

The correct answer is (d). *(CMA 1279 4-1)*
REQUIRED: The sales volume effect on budgeted performance.
DISCUSSION: The marketing department's 100,000-unit shortfall in sales affected the company's gross profit unfavorably. The dollar amount which best quantifies the failure can be computed by multiplying the difference between the budgeted sales and actual sales by the selling price per unit, and then multiplying by the contribution margin ratio.

(700,000 - 600,000)$20 = $2,000,000
x   .30
$ 600,000 U

The increase in units produced is not needed in the calculation.

Questions 165 through 169 are based on Folsom Fashions, which sells a line of women's dresses. Folsom's performance report for November is shown in the opposite column.

The company uses a flexible budget to analyze its performance and to measure the effect on operating income of the various factors affecting the difference between budgeted and actual operating income.

	Actual	Budget
Dresses sold	5,000	6,000
Sales	$235,000	$300,000
Variable costs	145,000	180,000
Contribution margin	$ 90,000	$120,000
Fixed costs	84,000	80,000
Operating income	$ 6,000	$ 40,000

165. The effect of the sales volume variance on the contribution margin for November is

   a. $30,000 unfavorable.
   b. $18,000 unfavorable.
   c. $20,000 unfavorable.
   d. $15,000 unfavorable.
   e. $65,000 unfavorable.

The correct answer is (c). (CMA 1284 4-17)
REQUIRED: The effect of the sales volume variance on CM.
DISCUSSION: The sales volume variance is the difference between the actual volume and budgeted volume times the budgeted UCM.

$$(5,000 - 6,000) \times \frac{\$120,000}{6,000} = \$20,000 \text{ U}$$

166. The sales price variance for November is

   a. $30,000 unfavorable.
   b. $18,000 unfavorable.
   c. $20,000 unfavorable.
   d. $15,000 unfavorable.
   e. $65,000 unfavorable.

The correct answer is (d). (CMA 1284 4-18)
REQUIRED: The amount of the sales price variance for the month.
DISCUSSION: The sales price variance is the actual number of units sold (5,000) times the difference between budgeted selling price ($300,000 ÷ 6,000) and actual selling price ($235,000 ÷ 5,000).

$$(\$50 - \$47) \times 5,000 = \$15,000 \text{ U}$$

167. The variable cost flexible budget variance for November is

   a. $5,000 favorable.
   b. $5,000 unfavorable.
   c. $4,000 favorable.
   d. $4,000 unfavorable.
   e. $6,000 favorable.

The correct answer is (a). (CMA 1284 4-19)
REQUIRED: The variable cost flexible budget variance.
DISCUSSION: The variable cost flexible budget variance is equal to the difference between actual variable costs and actual quantity sold times the budgeted unit variable cost ($180,000 ÷ 6,000 = $30).

$$(\$30 \times 5,000) - \$145,000 = \$5,000 \text{ F}$$

168. The fixed cost variance for November is

   a. $5,000 favorable.
   b. $5,000 unfavorable.
   c. $4,000 favorable.
   d. $4,000 unfavorable.
   e. $1,000 favorable.

The correct answer is (d). (CMA 1284 4-20)
REQUIRED: The fixed cost variance for the month.
DISCUSSION: The fixed cost variance equals the difference between actual fixed costs and budgeted fixed costs.

$$\$84,000 - \$80,000 = \$4,000 \text{ U}$$

Module 13.5: Sales Volume   363

169. What additional information would be needed for Folsom to calculate the dollar impact of a market unit share change on operating income for November?

a. Folsom's budgeted market share and the budgeted total market size.
b. Folsom's budgeted market share, the budgeted total market size, and average market selling price.
c. Folsom's budgeted market share and the actual total market size.
d. Folsom's actual market share and the actual total market size.
e. There is no information that would make such a calculation possible.

The correct answer is (c). *(CMA 1284 4-21)*
REQUIRED: The information necessary for a market unit share calculation.
DISCUSSION: Market unit share calculations are made to determine the effects that actual market size, budgeted market share, and actual market share have on contribution margin and on operating income. Thus, analysis of the effects of market penetration is possible, given sufficient data.
Answers (a) and (b) are incorrect because the actual market size must be known to determine the effects of changes in market share. Also, the market selling price is not needed. Answer (d) is incorrect because the budgeted market share must be known. The actual market share can be derived given sales data and actual market size.

Questions 170 through 175 are based on the year-end income statement of DUO, Inc. presented below (000 omitted) and relate to the calculation of variances that explain the difference between the actual profit and budgeted profit in terms of sales price, cost, sales mix, and sales volume.

	Product AR-10		Product ZR-7		Total	
	Budget	Actual	Budget	Actual	Budget	Actual
Unit sales	2,000	2,800	6,000	5,600	8,000	8,400
Sales	$6,000	$7,560	$12,000	$11,760	$18,000	$19,320
CGS	$2,400	$2,800	$ 6,000	$ 5,880	$ 8,400	$ 8,680
Fixed costs	1,800	1,900	2,400	2,400	4,200	4,300
Total costs	$4,200	$4,700	$ 8,400	$ 8,280	$12,600	$12,980
Net profit	$1,800	$2,860	$ 3,600	$ 3,480	$ 5,400	$ 6,340

---

170. The net effect on profit of the unit sales volume variance of product AR-10 is

a. $1,060 unfavorable.
b. $1,560 favorable.
c. $1,440 favorable.
d. Some amount other than those given above which can be calculated from the information given.
e. Some amount other than those given above which cannot be calculated from the information given.

The correct answer is (c). *(CMA 678 4-1)*
REQUIRED: The net effect on profit of the unit sales volume variance of product AR-10.
DISCUSSION: The net effect on profit from the unit sales volume is computed by first finding the budgeted unit CM of AR-10. The UCM is then multiplied by the change in unit sales from budget to actual.

Sales	$6,000
Variable costs	2,400
Contribution margin	$3,600

$3,600 ÷ 2,000 = $1.80 UCM
$1.80 x (2,800 - 2,000) = $1,440 F

The sales volume variance is favorable because actual sales exceed budget sales.

---

171. The net effect on profit from the change in the unit cost of goods sold of product ZR-7 is?

a. $280 unfavorable.
b. $300 favorable.
c. $120 favorable.
d. Some amount other than those given above which can be calculated from the information given.
e. Some amount other than those given above which cannot be calculated from the information given.

The correct answer is (a). *(CMA 678 4-3)*
REQUIRED: The net effect on profit from the change in the unit CGS for product ZR-7.
DISCUSSION: The net effect of the change in the unit CGS is computed by first finding the budgeted and actual per unit CGS. The difference between the two unit CGS amounts is then multiplied by actual unit sales.

Budgeted CGS = $6,000 ÷ 6,000 units = $1
Actual CGS = $5,880 ÷ 5,600 units = $1.05

$1 - $1.05 = $(.05)
$(.05) x 5,600 = $280 U

The effect on profit is unfavorable because actual unit CGS exceeds budgeted.

Module 13.5: Sales Volume

> Questions 172 through 175 are based on the information presented on page 363.

172. The net effect on profit of the sales price variance for product ZR-7 is
a. $400 unfavorable.
b. $560 favorable.
c. $240 favorable.
d. Some amount other than those given above which can be calculated from the information given.
e. Some amount other than those given above which cannot be calculated from the information given.

The correct answer is (b). *(CMA 678 4-2)*
REQUIRED: The net effect on profit of the sales price variance for product ZR-7.
DISCUSSION: The net effect on profit from the sales price variance is computed by first finding the budgeted per unit sales price. Then the per unit actual sales price is computed. Multiply the difference in price between budgeted sales price and actual sales price by the actual number of units to get the effect on profit.

Budgeted sales price per unit: $12,000 ÷ 6,000 = $2
Actual sales price per unit: $11,760 ÷ 5,600 = $2.10
$2.10 - $2 = $.10 sales price variance
$.10 x 5,600 = $560 F

The sales price variance is favorable because actual sales price exceeds budget sales price.

173. If products AR-10 and ZR-7 are substitutes for each other, a sales mix and sales volume variation for the combined products can be calculated. If this combination is calculated, the net effect on profit of the change in the unit sales mix is
a. $480 favorable.
b. $506 favorable.
c. $560 favorable.
d. $940 favorable.
e. $1,040 favorable.

The correct answer is (c). *(CMA 678 4-4)*
REQUIRED: The net effect on profit of the change in the unit sales mix.
DISCUSSION: The sales mix variance is the difference between budgeted individual UCM and the budgeted average UCM. Budgeted average CM is the $9,600 CM ($18,000 sales - $8,400 CGS) divided by the 8,000 total units budgeted.

	Actual-Budgeted		Bud. Ind. UCM		Bud. Avg. UCM	
AR-10	(2,800 - 2,000)	x	(1.80	-	1.20)	= $480
ZR-7*	(5,600 - 6,000)	x	(1.00	-	1.20)	= 80
						$560

*The negative 400 units times the negative $.20 equals a positive $80.

174. The sales volume variance calculation that would complement the variance calculated in the previous question is
a. $480 favorable.
b. $506 favorable.
c. $560 favorable.
d. $940 favorable.
e. $1,040 favorable.

The correct answer is (a). *(CMA 678 4-5)*
REQUIRED: The sales volume variance given the previous question's calculations.
DISCUSSION: The sales volume (quantity) variance is the difference between the actual volume and the budgeted volume in units for each product times the budgeted average CM for all units.

	Actual Volume		Budgeted Volume		Budgeted Avg. Margin	
AR-10	(2,800	-	2,000)	x	$ 1.20	= $960 F
ZR-7	(5,600	-	6,000)	x	$ 1.20	= (480) U
Favorable sales volume variance						$480 F

175. The sales mix and sales volume variances account for the variance in which income statement item?
a. Sales.
b. Cost of sales.
c. Gross profit.
d. Contribution margin.

The correct answer is (d). *(Publisher)*
REQUIRED: The variation explained by sales volume and sales mix variances.
DISCUSSION: The sales volume and sales mix variances explain the change in CM because they incorporate the CM and number of units sold. The budgeted CM is $9,600 ($18,000 - $8,400), and the actual CM is $10,640 ($19,320 - $8,680). The difference is $1,040 F, which is the sum of the sales volume and sales mix variances computed in Qs. 173 and 174 ($560 F + $480 F).

13.6 Combination

Questions 176 through 179 are based on Denham Company, which began operations on January 3. Standard costs were established in early January assuming a normal production volume of 160,000 units. However, Denham produced only 140,000 units of product and sold 100,000 units at a selling price of $180 per unit during the year. Variable costs totaled $7,000,000, of which 60% were manufacturing and 40% were selling. Fixed costs totaled $11,200,000, of which 50% were manufacturing and 50% were selling. Denham had no raw materials or work-in-process inventories at December 31. Actual input prices and quantities per unit of product were equal to standard.

176. Denham's cost of goods sold at standard cost using full absorption costing is

a. $8,200,000.
b. $7,200,000.
c. $6,500,000.
d. $7,000,000.
e. None of the above.

The correct answer is (c). *(CMA 1283 4-13)*
REQUIRED: The cost of goods sold at standard cost for the year.
DISCUSSION: Since total variable costs for manufacturing were $4,200,000 ($7,000,000 total VC x 60%) for 140,000 units, and there were no variances (actual input prices and quantities equaled standard), standard cost must be $30 per unit ($4,200,000 ÷ 140,000 units). Fixed costs for manufacturing were $5,600,000 ($11,200,000 total FC x 50%) for an expected 160,000 units, giving a standard cost for fixed manufacturing overhead of $35 per unit ($5,600,000 ÷ 160,000). The expected unit cost of goods sold would thus have been $65 ($30 + $35). Given 100,000 units sold, the cost of goods sold is $6,500,000 (100,000 x $65).

177. The value assigned to Denham's December 31 inventory using variable (direct) costing is

a. $2,800,000.
b. $1,200,000.
c. $2,000,000.
d. $3,000,000.
e. None of the above.

The correct answer is (b). *(CMA 1283 4-14)*
REQUIRED: The value of ending inventory under direct costing.
DISCUSSION: If direct costing is used, inventories include only the variable costs of manufacturing; fixed costs are not inventoriable because they are treated as period costs. Since variable manufacturing costs were $30 per unit (see Q. 176), the total value of the 40,000 units in ending inventory (140,000 produced - 100,000 sold) is $1,200,000 (40,000 x $30).

178. Denham's manufacturing overhead volume variance using full absorption costing is

a. $800,000 unfavorable.
b. $800,000 favorable.
c. $700,000 unfavorable.
d. $700,000 favorable.
e. None of the above.

The correct answer is (c). *(CMA 1283 4-15)*
REQUIRED: The manufacturing overhead volume variance using full absorption costing.
DISCUSSION: Fixed costs amounted to $35 per unit given a volume of 160,000 units (see Q. 176). The volume variance can be determined by multiplying the cost per unit times the difference between actual and standard volumes. Since the company applied no overhead to 20,000 planned units, the underapplication of overhead, or unfavorable volume variance, is $700,000 ($35 x 20,000 units).

179. Denham's income from operations using variable (direct) costing is

a. $3,400,000.
b. $1,800,000.
c. $2,600,000.
d. $1,000,000.
e. None of the above.

The correct answer is (d). *(CMA 1283 4-16)*
REQUIRED: The income from operations using direct costing.
DISCUSSION: The direct costing income statement recognizes all fixed costs as period costs.

Sales ($180 x 100,000 units)	$18,000,000
Variable mfg. cost ($30 x 100,000 units)	(3,000,000)
Fixed cost	(11,200,000)
Variable selling cost ($28 x 100,000 units)	(2,800,000)
Income from operations	$ 1,000,000

Module 13.6: Combination

Questions 180 through 184 are based on Butrico Manufacturing Corporation, which uses a standard cost system that records raw materials at actual cost, records materials price variance at the time that raw materials are issued to work-in-process, and prorates all variances at year-end. Variances associated with direct materials are prorated based on the direct material balances in the appropriate accounts, and variances associated with direct labor and manufacturing overhead are prorated based on the direct labor balances in the appropriate accounts.

The following information is available for Butrico for the year ended December 31:

Finished goods inventory at 12/31:	
Direct material	$ 87,000
Direct labor	130,500
Applied manufacturing overhead	104,400
Raw materials inventory at 12/31	$ 65,000
Cost of goods sold for the year ended 12/31:	
Direct material	$348,000
Direct labor	739,500
Applied manufacturing overhead	591,600
Direct material price variance (unfavorable)	10,000
Direct material usage variance (favorable)	15,000
Direct labor rate variance (unfavorable)	20,000
Direct labor efficiency variance (favorable)	5,000
Manufacturing overhead incurred	690,000

There were no beginning inventories and no ending work-in-process inventory. Manufacturing overhead is applied at 80% of standard direct labor.

180. The amount of direct material price variance to be prorated to finished goods inventory at December 31 is a

   a. $1,740 debit.
   b. $2,000 debit.
   c. $2,610 credit.
   d. $3,000 credit.

The correct answer is (b). *(CPA 573 P-39)*
REQUIRED: The materials price variance to be allocated to finished goods inventory.
DISCUSSION: The material price variance is prorated between FG and CGS (so that EWIP and raw materials inventory are carried at actual cost). The materials in FG are divided by the sum of the materials in FG and CGS to give the portion of the direct material price variance to be allocated to FG. This ratio is multiplied by the $10,000 direct material price variance.

$$\frac{\$87,000}{\$348,000 + \$87,000} \times \$10,000 = \$2,000 \text{ U}$$

Remember that materials in the raw materials inventory are not added to the denominator because the variances are not recognized until issued. Since the variance is unfavorable, the FG account must be debited for $2,000.

Module 13.6: Combination

181. The total amount of direct material in finished goods inventory at December 31, after all material variances have been prorated, is

 a. $86,130.
 b. $87,870.
 c. $88,000.
 d. $86,000.

The correct answer is (d). *(CPA 573 P-40)*
REQUIRED: The amount of direct material in FG inventory after all variance allocation.
DISCUSSION: The amount allocated to FG is the $2,000 debit for the price variance (Q. 180) and a credit for the material usage variance:

$$\frac{\$87,000}{\$348,000 + \$87,000} \times \$15,000 = \$3,000 \text{ F}$$

Total direct material in FG inventory is thus $87,000 + $2,000 - $3,000 = $86,000.

182. The total amount of direct labor in finished goods inventory at December 31, after all variances have been prorated, is

 a. $134,250.
 b. $131,850.
 c. $132,750.
 d. $126,750.

The correct answer is (c). *(CPA 573 P-41)*
REQUIRED: The amount of direct labor in FG inventory after all variance proration.
DISCUSSION: The direct labor rate variance is prorated between FG and CGS by dividing the DL amount in FG by the sum of the DL amounts in FG and CGS. This ratio is then multiplied by the $20,000 DL rate variance, resulting in a debit.

$$\frac{\$130,500}{\$130,500 + \$739,500} \times \$20,000 = \$3,000 \text{ U}$$

The amount of the efficiency variance is found in the same manner, resulting in a credit:

$$\frac{\$130,500}{\$130,500 + \$739,500} \times \$5,000 = \$750 \text{ F}$$

Total direct labor in FG inventory is thus $130,500 + $3,000 - $750 = $132,750.

183. What amount of manufacturing overhead variance should be allocated to cost of sales?

 a. $5,100 credit.
 b. $2,000 debit.
 c. $900 credit.
 d. $5,144 credit.

The correct answer is (a). *(Publisher)*
REQUIRED: The amount of manufacturing overhead variance allocated to cost of sales.
DISCUSSION: To prorate the manufacturing O/H variance between FG and CGS, divide CGS applied O/H by the sum of FG and CGS applied O/H. This ratio is then multiplied by the O/H variance ($690,000 O/H incurred - $696,000 O/H applied = $6,000 F), resulting in a credit to CGS.

$$\frac{\$591,600}{\$104,400 + \$591,600} \times \$6,000 = \$5,100 \text{ F}$$

184. The total cost of goods sold for the year ended December 31, after all variances have been prorated, is

 a. $1,682,750.
 b. $1,691,250.
 c. $1,683,270.
 d. $1,693,850.

The correct answer is (a). *(CPA 573 P-42)*
REQUIRED: The total cost of goods sold after all variances have been allocated.
DISCUSSION: The direct labor rate variance allocated to CGS is a $17,000 debit since $3,000 of the overall $20,000 was allocated to FG (Q. 182). The amount of direct labor efficiency variance allocated to CGS is a $4,250 credit (after the $750 credit to FG in Q. 182). The debit to CGS for the materials price variance is $8,000 (after the $2,000 FG allocation in Q. 180). The credit to CGS for the materials usage variance is $12,000 (after the $3,000 credit in Q. 181). Finally, the manufacturing O/H prorated amount is a $5,100 credit (Q. 183).

Unadjusted CGS	$1,679,100
	17,000
	8,000
	(4,250)
	(12,000)
	(5,100)
	$1,682,750

Questions 185 through 187 are based on the following information relating to the month of April for Marilyn, Inc., which uses a standard cost system.

Marilyn uses a two-way analysis of overhead variances: budget (controllable) and volume.

Actual total direct labor	$43,400
Actual hours used	14,000
Standard hours allowed for good output	15,000
Direct labor rate variance-debit	$ 1,400
Actual total overhead	$32,000
Budgeted fixed costs	$ 9,000
"Normal" activity in hours	12,000
Total overhead application rate per standard direct labor hour	$ 2.25

185. What was Marilyn's direct labor usage (efficiency) variance for April?

a. $3,000 favorable.
b. $3,000 unfavorable.
c. $3,200 favorable.
d. $3,200 unfavorable.

The correct answer is (a). *(CPA 576 P-19)*
REQUIRED: The direct labor usage variance for the month.
DISCUSSION: The labor usage variance is the difference between actual hours and standard hours times the standard direct labor rate. The standard labor rate is the actual total labor minus the labor rate variance, all divided by the actual hours. A favorable (debit) usage variance results when actual hours are less than standard hours.

$$\frac{\$43,400 - \$1,400}{14,000 \text{ act. hrs.}} = \$3 \text{ standard rate}$$

$$(14,000 - 15,000) \times \$3 = \$3,000 \text{ F}$$

186. What was Marilyn's budget (controllable) variance for April?

a. $500 favorable.
b. $500 unfavorable.
c. $2,250 favorable.
d. $2,250 unfavorable.

The correct answer is (b). *(CPA 576 P-20)*
REQUIRED: The budget (controllable) variance.
DISCUSSION: The budget (controllable) variance is the difference between the actual O/H incurred and that budgeted based on standard hours allowed for the good output. The fixed O/H rate was $9,000 ÷ 12,000 "normal" hrs., or $.75. The variable rate is $1.50 (the total rate of $2.25 less $.75 fixed). At 15,000 hours, $22,500 variable O/H applied plus $9,000 budgeted fixed costs (which do not change with volume) is $500 less than the total O/H incurred of $32,000, i.e., $500 U.

187. What was Marilyn's volume variance for April?

a. $500 favorable.
b. $500 unfavorable.
c. $2,250 favorable.
d. $2,250 unfavorable.

The correct answer is (c). *(CPA 576 P-21)*
REQUIRED: The volume variance for the month.
DISCUSSION: The volume variance is the difference between budgeted hours and standard hours allowed times the fixed overhead rate per hour. A favorable variance results when actual hours are less than standard hours.

$$(12,000 - 15,000) \times \$.75 \text{ (Q. 186)} = \$2,250 \text{ F}$$

Questions 188 through 192 are based on Tolbert Manufacturing Company, which uses a standard cost system in accounting for the costs of production of its only product, product A. The standards for the production of one unit of product A are as follows:

Direct materials: 10 feet of item 1 at $.75 per foot and 3 feet of item 2 at $1 per foot.
Direct labor: 4 hours at $3.50 per hour.
Manufacturing overhead: applied at 150% of standard direct labor costs.

There was no inventory on hand at the end of the year. Material price variances are isolated at purchase. Following is a summary of costs and related data for the production of product A during the year:

100,000 feet of item 1 were purchased at $.78 per foot.
30,000 feet of item 2 were purchased at $.90 per foot.
8,000 units of product A were produced which required 78,000 feet of item 1; 26,000 feet of item 2; and 31,000 hours of direct labor at $3.60 per hour.
6,000 units of product A were sold.

Module 13.6: Combination

188. The total debits to the raw materials account for the purchase of item 1 should be

a. $75,000.
b. $78,000.
c. $58,500.
d. $60,000.

The correct answer is (a). *(CPA 1173 P-23)*
REQUIRED: The amount debited to raw materials for purchases.
DISCUSSION: In a standard costing system, when price variances are isolated at purchase, all items purchased are charged in at standard. Given 100,000 feet of item 1 at a standard price of $.75, the debit is $75,000.

189. The total debits to the work-in-process account for direct labor should be

a. $111,600.
b. $108,500.
c. $112,000.
d. $115,100.

The correct answer is (c). *(CPA 1173 P-24)*
REQUIRED: The total debits to work-in-process for direct labor.
DISCUSSION: All labor is charged at standard. There were 32,000 hours allowed for good output of 8,000 units charged in.

32,000 std. DLH x $3.50 std. rate/hr.
= $112,000 debited to the WIP account.

190. Before allocation of standard variances, the balance in the material usage variance account for item 2 was

a. $1,000 credit.
b. $2,600 debit.
c. $600 debit.
d. $2,000 debit.

The correct answer is (d). *(CPA 1173 P-25)*
REQUIRED: The balance of the material usage variance account for item 2 before allocation.
DISCUSSION: The material usage variance is the difference between actual usage and standard usage multiplied by the standard price. An unfavorable variance (debit) results when the actual usage (26,000 feet) is greater than standard allowed (24,000 feet).

(26,000 - 24,000) x $1 = $2,000 U.

191. If all standard variances are prorated to inventories and cost of goods sold, the amount of material usage variance for item 2 to be prorated to raw materials inventory would be

a. $0.
b. $333 credit.
c. $333 debit.
d. $500 debit.

The correct answer is (a). *(CPA 1173 P-26)*
REQUIRED: The material usage variance for item 2 to prorate to raw materials inventory.
DISCUSSION: The material usage variance is not prorated to the raw materials inventory. The purpose of prorating variances is to match the variance to the accounts that contain the variance. Raw materials inventory does not contain a usage variance. This variance should be prorated among WIP inventory, FG inventory, and CGS.

192. If all standard variances are prorated to inventories and cost of goods sold, the amount of material price variance for item 1 to be prorated to raw materials inventory would be

a. $0.
b. $647 debit.
c. $600 debit.
d. $660 debit.

The correct answer is (d). *(CPA 1173 P-27)*
REQUIRED: The item 1 materials price variance to be prorated to raw materials inventory.
DISCUSSION: The material price variance contained in raw materials inventory is the EI of item 1 divided by the total amount purchased times the material price variance. Item 1 EI is 22,000 (zero BI + 100,000 purchased - 78,000 needed to produce).

$$\frac{22,000}{100,000} \times [(\$.75 - \$.78) \times 100,000] = \$660 \text{ U}$$

> Questions 193 through 199 are based on Eastern Company, which manufactures special electrical equipment and parts. Eastern employs a standard cost accounting system with separate standards established for each product.
>
> A special transformer is manufactured in the Transformer Department. Production volume is measured by direct labor hours in this department and a flexible budget system is used to plan and control department overhead.
>
> Standard costs for the special transformer are determined annually in September for the coming year. The standard cost of a transformer for the year was computed at $67, as shown below.
>
> Direct materials
>   Iron   5 sheets x $2 $10
>   Copper   3 spools x $3   9
> Direct labor   4 hours x $7   28
> Variable overhead   4 hours x $3   12
> Fixed overhead   4 hours x $2   8
> Total $67
>
> Overhead rates were based upon normal and expected monthly capacity for the year, both of which were 4,000 direct labor hours. Practical capacity for this department is 5,000 direct labor hours per month. Variable overhead costs are expected to vary with the number of direct labor hours actually used.
>
> During October, 800 transformers were produced. This was below expectations because a work stoppage occurred during contract negotiations with the labor force. Once the contract was settled, the department scheduled overtime in an attempt to catch up to expected production levels.
>
> The following costs were incurred in October:
>
> | Direct Material | Direct Materials Purchased | Materials Used |
> |---|---|---|
> | Iron | 5,000 sheets @ $2.00/sheet | 3,900 sheets |
> | Copper | 2,200 spools @ $3.10/spool | 2,600 spools |
>
> Direct labor
>   Regular time: 2,000 hours @ $7.00
>   1,400 hours @ $7.20
>
> Overtime: 600 of the 1,400 hours were subject to overtime premium. The total overtime premium of $2,160 is included in variable overhead in accordance with company accounting practices.
>
> Variable overhead: $10,000
> Fixed overhead: $ 8,800

193. The most appropriate time to record any variance of actual material prices from standard is

  a. At year-end, when all variances will be known.
  b. At the time of purchase.
  c. At the time of material usage.
  d. As needed to evaluate the performance of the purchasing manager.
  e. None of the above.

The correct answer is (b). *(CMA 1277 4-22)*
REQUIRED: The best time to record material price variance.
DISCUSSION: The most appropriate time to record price variances is at the time of purchase. The variances then can be identified with each group of items purchased and in the period purchased.
    Answer (a) is incorrect because year-end will be too late to take any corrective action. Answer (c) is incorrect because recording variances at purchase rather than at usage identifies differences sooner. Answer (d) is incorrect because monitoring variances should be a continuous process.

194. The labor rate (price) variance is

  a. $280 unfavorable.
  b. $340 unfavorable.
  c. $1,680 unfavorable.
  d. $2,440 unfavorable.
  e. None of the above.

The correct answer is (a). *(CMA 1277 4-24)*
REQUIRED: The labor rate variance for the period.
DISCUSSION: The labor rate variance is the difference between the actual rate and the standard rate times the actual hours. The standard rate is $7, but 1,400 hours were worked at $7.20, resulting in a $280 unfavorable labor rate variance ($.20 x 1,400). The overtime premium is not considered part of direct labor. Rather, it is a part of variable overhead.

Module 13.6: Combination

195. The total material quantity variance is
 a. $200 favorable.
 b. $400 favorable.
 c. $600 favorable.
 d. $400 unfavorable.
 e. None of the above.

The correct answer is (d). *(CMA 1277 4-23)*
REQUIRED: The total material quantity variance.
DISCUSSION: The material quantity variance is the difference between the actual usage and the standard usage times the standard price for the quantity produced.

Standard materials for 800 transformers:
Iron sheets (800 x 5) = 4,000
Copper spools (800 x 3) = 2,400

	Actual	-	Standard	=	Variance
Iron sheets	3,900	-	4,000	=	100 F
Copper spools	2,600	-	2,400	=	200 U

Iron sheets   100 F x $2/sheet = $200 F
Copper spools   200 U x $3/spool = $600 U
Total material quantity variance   = $400 U

196. The variable overhead spending variance is
 a. $200 favorable.
 b. $400 unfavorable.
 c. $600 unfavorable.
 d. $1,600 unfavorable.
 e. None of the above.

The correct answer is (a). *(CMA 1277 4-25)*
REQUIRED: The variable overhead spending variance for the period.
DISCUSSION: The variable overhead spending variance is the difference between the actual variable overhead and the actual hours times the standard rate:

$10,000 - (3,400 x $3) = $200 F

197. The efficiency variance in variable overhead is the standard variable overhead rate times the difference between standard labor hours of output and
 a. 2,000 hours.
 b. 2,600 hours.
 c. 2,800 hours.
 d. 3,400 hours.
 e. None of the above.

The correct answer is (d). *(CMA 1277 4-26)*
REQUIRED: The missing variable in the variable overhead efficiency variance formula.
DISCUSSION: The efficiency variance is the standard variable overhead rate times the difference between the standard labor hours and the actual labor hours. Actual DLH = 2,000 + 1,400 = 3,400.

198. The budget (spending) variance for fixed overhead is
 a. $2,400 unfavorable.
 b. $0.
 c. $800 unfavorable.
 d. Not calculable from the problem.
 e. None of the above.

The correct answer is (c). *(CMA 1277 4-27)*
REQUIRED: The budget variance for fixed overhead.
DISCUSSION: The budget variance for fixed overhead is the difference between actual fixed overhead and budgeted fixed overhead. The actual fixed overhead is given as $8,800. Budgeted fixed costs were $8,000 (4,000 DLH of normal and expected monthly capacity for the year x $2 fixed O/H rate).

$8,800 actual - $8,000 = $800 U

199. The fixed overhead volume variance is
 a. $400 unfavorable.
 b. $2,200 unfavorable.
 c. $2,400 unfavorable.
 d. $1,600 unfavorable.
 e. None of the above.

The correct answer is (d). *(CMA 1277 4-28)*
REQUIRED: The fixed overhead volume variance.
DISCUSSION: The fixed overhead volume variance is the difference between the budgeted fixed overhead (4,000 DLH normal capacity x $2/hr.) and what was applied. The 800 units produced times the standard rate (4 hrs./unit x $2/hr. = $8/unit) equals $6,400.

$8,000 - $6,400 = $1,600 U

13.7 Journal Entries

200. Which entry is an example of recording direct materials used and material price and quantity variances? (Assume that materials price variances are recorded at time of transfer to WIP, not at time of purchase.)

a.	Work-in-process	XX	
	Finished goods	XX	
	DM price variance	XX	
	Inventory		XX
b.	Finished goods	XX	
	DM price variance	XX	
	DM quantity variance	XX	
	Inventory		XX
c.	Inventory	XX	
	Work-in-process	XX	
	DM price variance		XX
d.	Work-in-process	XX	
	DM price variance	XX	
	DM quantity variance	XX	
	Inventory		XX

The correct answer is (d). *(Publisher)*
REQUIRED: The journal entry to record direct materials used and quantity and price variances.
DISCUSSION: The entry to record direct materials used is to debit WIP at standard prices and standard quantities. In this problem, all direct material variances are recorded at the time the WIP account is charged. Both direct material price and quantity variances are unfavorable, since they are debits (the actual costs accumulated in the inventory account exceed standard costs).
Answers (a) and (b) are incorrect because direct materials variances are recorded when direct materials costs are transferred to WIP, not finished goods. Answer (c) is incorrect because the question indicates price variances are recorded when direct materials are transferred to WIP, not when the materials are purchased.

201. What is the journal entry to record accrued payroll and the proper allocation of direct labor costs when actual hours exceed standard hours but the actual wage rate was less than the standard wage rate?

a.	Wage expense	XX	
	DL efficiency variance	XX	
	Accrued payroll		XX
b.	Work-in-process	XX	
	DL efficiency variance	XX	
	DL price variance		XX
	Accrued payroll		XX
c.	Accrued payroll	XX	
	DL price variance	XX	
	Work-in-process		XX
	DL efficiency variance		XX
d.	Work-in-process	XX	
	DL price variance	XX	
	DL efficiency variance		XX
	Accrued payroll		XX

The correct answer is (b). *(Publisher)*
REQUIRED: The journal entry to record accrued payroll and the proper allocation of direct labor costs.
DISCUSSION: To record accrued payroll, charge the WIP account at the standard wage rate times the standard number of hours. One should credit the accrued payroll account for the actual payroll dollar amount. Because actual hours used exceeded standard, there is an unfavorable direct labor efficiency variance (a debit). The favorable direct labor price variance (a credit) is a result of the actual labor rate's being lower than the standard wage rate.
Answer (a) is incorrect because it fails to record the price variance or to debit WIP for labor costs. Answers (c) and (d) are incorrect because the price variance is favorable (a credit), the efficiency variance is unfavorable (a debit), and the accrual of payroll requires a credit.

202. What is the journal entry to record an unfavorable direct material price variance when material is purchased?

a.	Work-in-process	XX	
	DM price variance	XX	
	Accounts payable		XX
b.	Inventory	XX	
	DM quantity variance	XX	
	Accounts payable		XX
c.	Stores	XX	
	DM price variance	XX	
	Accounts payable		XX
d.	Finished goods	XX	
	DM price variance	XX	
	Accounts payable		XX

The correct answer is (c). *(Publisher)*
REQUIRED: The journal entry to record a direct materials price variance.
DISCUSSION: To record a direct materials price variance at the time of purchase, charge inventory for the actual quantity purchased times the standard unit price. Credit accounts payable for the actual quantity times the actual price. The difference between the actual price paid and the standard price allowed should be recorded as the price variance. Note the actual price paid was greater than the standard price (i.e., unfavorable).
  Answer (a) is incorrect because the purchase of materials should be debited to inventory. Answer (b) is incorrect because the price, not quantity, variances account should be debited. Answer (d) is incorrect because materials are debited to inventory when purchased.

203. Company Z uses a standard cost system wherein materials are carried at actual price until transferred to the WIP account. In project A, 500 units of X were used at a cost of $10 per unit. Standards require 450 units to complete this project. The standard price is established at $9 per unit. Select the proper journal entry.

a.	Work-in-process	$4,950	
	DM price variance	500	
	DM quantity variance		$ 450
	Inventory		5,000
b.	Work-in-process	$5,950	
	DM price variance		$ 500
	DM quantity variance		450
	Inventory		5,000
c.	Work-in-process	$4,050	
	DM price variance	500	
	DM quantity variance	450	
	Inventory		$5,000
d.	Work-in-process	$5,000	
	Inventory		$5,000

The correct answer is (c). *(Publisher)*
REQUIRED: The journal entry to record direct materials issued and related variances.
DISCUSSION: The entry to record direct materials used is to debit WIP at standard prices and standard quantities (450 units x $9 = $4,050). In this question, all direct material variances are recorded at the time WIP is charged.
  Both the materials price variance and the materials quantity variance must be calculated. The project used more units at a higher price than estimated, so both variances will be unfavorable (debits).

Material quantity variance
  (500 - 450) x $9 = $450 U
Material price variance
  500 units x ($10 - $9) = $500 U

Inventory is credited for the actual prices and actual quantities (500 x $10 = $5,000).
  Answers (a) and (b) are incorrect because both variances should be unfavorable (debits). Answer (d) is incorrect because it fails to record the variances (materials are carried at actual prices until transferred to WIP).

204. If a project required 50 hours to complete at a cost of $10 per hour, when it should have taken only 45 hours at a cost of $12 per hour, what would be the proper entry?

a.	Work-in-process	$540	
	DL efficiency variance	60	
	DL price variance		$100
	Accrued payroll		500
b.	Wage expense	$440	
	DL efficiency variance	60	
	Accrued payroll		$500
c.	Work-in-process	$460	
	DL price variance	100	
	DL efficiency variance		$ 60
	Accrued payroll		500
d.	Work-in-process	$500	
	Accrued payroll		$500

The correct answer is (a). *(Publisher)*
REQUIRED: The journal entry to record accrued payroll and labor cost variances.
DISCUSSION: The entry to record accrued payroll is to charge WIP at the standard wage rate times the standard number of hours and to credit accrued payroll for the actual payroll dollar amount. The project required more hours but a lower wage rate than estimated. Hence, the labor efficiency variance will be unfavorable (a debit). The labor price variance will be favorable (a credit).

  Labor eff. var. (50 - 45) x $12 = $60 U
  Labor price var. ($12 - $10) x 50 = $100 F

  Answer (b) is incorrect because it omits the price variance and fails to inventory the labor costs. Answer (c) is incorrect because it is the proper entry if the hourly rate were greater than estimated but hours worked were less. Answer (d) is incorrect because it is the entry when no labor variances have occurred.

205. Assume price variances are recorded at the time of purchase of goods. What is the journal entry to record a direct material price variance if materials are purchased at $5 per unit for $650 and their standard price is $4 per unit?

a.	Inventory	$650	
	Accounts payable		$650
b.	Inventory	$520	
	DM price variance	130	
	Accounts payable		$650
c.	Inventory	$520	
	Work-in-process	130	
	Cash		$650
d.	Finished goods	$520	
	DM price variance	130	
	Cash		$650

The correct answer is (b). *(Publisher)*
REQUIRED: The journal entry to record a direct materials price variance.
DISCUSSION: The entry to record a direct material price variance at the time of purchase is to charge inventory for the $520, which is the actual quantity purchased ($650 ÷ $5 per unit = 130 units) times the standard unit price ($4). Accounts payable is credited for AQ x AP = $650. The difference between the AP paid and SP allowed should be recorded in the price variance account. Since AP was greater than SP, the price variance account should be debited for the difference. Since 130 units were purchased ($650 ÷ $5 per unit), the price variance is $130 [130 x ($5 - $4)] unfavorable.

Answer (a) is incorrect because it assumes the price variance is not recorded at time of purchase. Answer (c) is incorrect because the variance should be charged to a separate account, not WIP. Answer (d) is incorrect because the materials should be debited to an inventory account.

206. What is the journal entry if all materials purchased in the previous question were used to complete a project which should normally require 100 units?

a.	Work-in-process	$650	
	DM price variance		$130
	Inventory		520
b.	Work-in-process	$520	
	DM price variance	130	
	Inventory		$650
c.	DM quantity variance	$130	
	Work-in-process	520	
	Inventory		$650
d.	Work-in-process	$400	
	DM quantity variance	120	
	Inventory		$520

The correct answer is (d). *(Publisher)*
REQUIRED: The journal entry to record the direct materials used.
DISCUSSION: The entry to record direct materials used is to charge WIP for the standard quantity requisitioned times the standard unit price (100 units x $4/unit = $400). Inventory will be credited for the actual quantity requisitioned times the standard unit price, or $520 (130 x $4). When actual quantity used exceeds standard quantity allowed, an unfavorable direct material quantity variance results. The variance account should be charged (debited) for the difference of $120 (30 extra units x $4 standard unit cost).

Answer (a) is incorrect because a quantity (not price) variance should be debited (not credited). Answer (b) is incorrect because it records an unfavorable price, not quantity, variance. Answer (c) is incorrect because it confuses the amounts of the price and quantity variances.

207. What entry would record actual variable factory overhead incurred?

a.	Variable O/H control	XX	
	Accounts payable		XX
b.	Variable O/H applied	XX	
	Accounts payable		XX
c.	Variable O/H control	XX	
	Work-in-process		XX
d.	Variable O/H control	XX	
	Variable O/H applied		XX

The correct answer is (a). *(Publisher)*
REQUIRED: The journal entry to record the actual variable factory overhead incurred.
DISCUSSION: The entry to record actual variable O/H incurred is to charge the variable O/H control account for the actual amount of O/H incurred. A corresponding credit is made to accounts payable or any other appropriate account. Subsequently, O/H will be transferred from O/H applied to WIP at the standard rate.

Answers (b), (c), and (d) are incorrect because they are nonsense entries. Actual O/H costs are debited to the O/H control account. O/H applied to products at a predetermined rate is credited to the applied account and debited to WIP.

Module 13.7: Journal Entries

208. What entry would record the application of variable overhead at a predetermined rate?

a. O/H control XX
    Cash XX
b. O/H control XX
    Variable O/H applied XX
c. Work-in-process XX
    Variable O/H applied XX
d. Work-in-process XX
    Fixed O/H control XX

The correct answer is (c). *(Publisher)*
REQUIRED: The journal entry to record the application of variable factory overhead.
DISCUSSION: The entry to record the application of variable O/H to production is to charge the WIP account and enter a corresponding credit to variable O/H applied for the amount of O/H computed using a predetermined O/H rate and an appropriate allocation base (e.g., DLH). Alternatively, debit WIP and credit the O/H control account directly.
Answer (a) is incorrect because it records an actual O/H expenditure. Answer (b) is incorrect because O/H control should be debited only for actual costs. Answer (d) is incorrect because the question calls for variable O/H.

209. To isolate a favorable variable overhead efficiency variance and an unfavorable variable overhead spending variance, which of the following entries would be made?

a. Variable O/H applied XX
    Variable O/H spending
      variance XX
    Variable O/H efficiency
      variance XX
    Cost of goods sold XX
b. Fixed O/H budget variance XX
    Fixed O/H control XX
    Fixed O/H applied XX
c. Variable O/H applied XX
    Fixed overhead applied XX
    Variable and fixed
      O/H control summary XX
d. Variable O/H spending
    variance XX
    Variable O/H applied XX
    Variable O/H efficiency
      variance XX
    Variable O/H control XX

The correct answer is (d). *(Publisher)*
REQUIRED: The journal entry to isolate variable overhead variances.
DISCUSSION: Given an unfavorable variable O/H spending variance (actual variable O/H rate exceeded standard) and a favorable variable O/H efficiency variance (actual input was less than standard allowed), the entry to record their isolation for the year is to debit variable O/H spending variance and credit variable O/H efficiency variance. The variable O/H applied account should be charged for the balance in its account. Variable O/H control is credited for its balance. These entries will result in a zero balance in both the applied and the control accounts. The variance between applied and incurred O/H is thus recognized in the accounts.
Answer (a) is incorrect because the efficiency variance is favorable (a credit). Furthermore, if the net variance is not to be closed to income summary, it should be allocated between CGS and the inventories. For external reporting purposes, the net variance must be treated as a product cost and allocated between CGS and the inventories so that inventories maintained at standard cost may be adjusted to actual cost. Answers (b) and (c) are incorrect because the question concerns variable O/H.

210. Which entry will close the variance accounts in Q. 209?

a. Variable and fixed
    O/H control summary XX
    Cost of goods sold XX
    Variable O/H
      spending variance XX
b. Income summary XX
    Cost of goods sold XX
c. Fixed O/H budget variance XX
    Fixed O/H volume variance XX
    Fixed O/H control XX
d. Income summary XX
    Variable O/H efficiency
      variance XX
    Variable O/H spending
      variance XX

The correct answer is (d). *(Publisher)*
REQUIRED: The journal entry to close the given variance accounts.
DISCUSSION: The entry to record the closing of an unfavorable variable O/H spending variance and a favorable variable O/H efficiency variance is to charge the latter for the balance in the account and credit the former for its balance. The difference between the two accounts can be charged or credited to CGS or to income summary. For external reporting purposes, the net variance must be treated as a product cost and allocated between CGS and the inventories so that inventories maintained at standard cost may be adjusted to actual cost. But if inventory is to be shown at standard, the net variance is treated as a period cost and closed to income summary.
Answer (a) is incorrect because O/H control would have been closed when the variances were recorded (Q. 209). Also, if the variances are treated as product costs they would be allocated between CGS and the inventories. Answer (b) is incorrect because it does not close the variance accounts. Answer (c) is incorrect because the question concerns variable overhead variances.

Module 13.7: Journal Entries

211. Alpha Company paid janitors $5 per hour to clean the production area. What would the proper journal entry be to account for this expense for the month of June if a total of 530 hours were worked by the janitors this month?

a.	Salaries expense	$2,650	
	Payroll		$2,650
b.	Variable O/H control	$2,650	
	Variable O/H applied		$2,650
c.	Variable O/H control	$2,650	
	Payroll payable		$2,650
d.	Variable O/H applied	$2,650	
	Payroll payable		$2,650

The correct answer is (c). *(Publisher)*
REQUIRED: The journal entry to record the actual variable overhead incurred.
DISCUSSION: The entry to record actual variable O/H incurred ($5 x 530 hours = $2,650) is to charge the variable O/H control account. A corresponding credit is made to accounts payable or any other appropriate account.
Answer (a) is incorrect because accumulation of actual indirect costs related to production is done in the O/H control account. Answers (b) and (d) are incorrect because O/H application is usually based on standard rates and a given activity base, not amounts actually incurred. O/H is applied by crediting O/H control (or a separate applied O/H account) and debiting WIP.

212. Alpha Company (see Q. 211) had initially set its standard cost of janitorial work at $4.50 per hour. Select the appropriate entry that will record the application of the 530 hours worked by the janitors.

a.	Work-in-process	$2,385	
	Variable O/H applied		$2,385
b.	Work-in-process	$2,385	
	Variable O/H control		$2,385
c.	Variable O/H control	$ 265	
	Work-in-process	2,385	
	Variable O/H applied		$2,650
d.	Cost of goods sold	$2,385	
	Variable O/H applied		$2,385

The correct answer is (a). *(Publisher)*
REQUIRED: The journal entry to record the application of variable overhead.
DISCUSSION: The entry to record the application of variable overhead is to charge the WIP account and enter a corresponding credit to the variable factory overhead applied account for the amount of overhead computed using the predetermined overhead rate (530 x $4.50 = $2,385).
Answer (b) is incorrect because O/H control is debited for O/H incurred. Answer (c) is incorrect because the O/H application is at $4.50, not $5.00, per hour. Answer (d) is incorrect because the goods are not currently sold; they are being manufactured.

213. Using the information in Qs. 211 and 212, and what entry would account for the isolation of the variance that occurred?

a.	Factory O/H applied	$2,650	
	Variance summary		$ 265
	Factory O/H control		2,385
b.	Factory O/H applied	$2,385	
	Variable O/H spending variance	265	
	Factory O/H control		$2,650
c.	Factory O/H applied	$2,385	
	Variable O/H efficiency variance	265	
	Variable O/H control		$2,650
d.	Factory O/H control	$2,385	
	Variable spending variance	265	
	Factory O/H applied		$2,650

The correct answer is (b). *(Publisher)*
REQUIRED: The journal entry to record the isolation of variances for the year.
DISCUSSION: Using information in Q. 212, account for the spending variance by recognizing it as a debit, given that more was spent for that activity than was estimated, i.e., an unfavorable variable O/H spending variance. The entry to record the isolation of this variance for the year is to charge the variable O/H spending variance account for the appropriate amounts. The variable O/H applied account should be charged for the balance in its account. The variable O/H control account is credited for the balance in its account. These entries will result in a zero balance in both the applied and the control accounts.
Answer (a) is incorrect because the variance is a debit to a spending variance account, not a credit to a variance summary. Answer (c) is incorrect because the variance is a spending variance resulting from an actual cost greater than the standard cost, not an efficiency variance. Answer (d) is incorrect because the factory O/H applied is debited and factory O/H control is credited to close out the accounts.

214. Alpha Company had a favorable variable overhead efficiency variance of $1,600 and an unfavorable spending variance of $265. What entry would close these accounts?

a.
Income summary	$1,335	
Variable O/H spending variance	265	
Variable O/H efficiency variance		$1,600

b.
Variance summary	$1,865	
Cost of goods sold		$1,865

c.
Variable O/H efficiency variance	$1,600	
Variable O/H spending variance		$265
Income summary		1,335

d.
Variable O/H efficiency variance	$1,600	
Variable O/H spending variance	265	
Income summary		$1,865

The correct answer is (c). *(Publisher)*
REQUIRED: The journal entry to close an unfavorable spending variance and a favorable variable overhead efficiency variance.
DISCUSSION: The entry to record the closing of an unfavorable variable overhead spending variance and a favorable variable overhead efficiency variance is to charge the latter and credit the former. The difference between the two accounts can be charged or credited to CGS or to income summary. A favorable net variance of $1,335 is the result ($1,600 F − $265 U = $1,335 F). The net favorable variance is credited to income summary (or allocated between CGS and the inventories).
Answer (a) is incorrect because the net variance is favorable and should be credited to income summary. Answer (b) is incorrect because it does not close the variance accounts. Moreover, the net variance is $1,335. Answer (d) is incorrect because the spending variance is unfavorable and was initially debited. Closing the account thus requires a credit.

215. What is the year-end journal entry to close the fixed factory overhead account (assuming underutilization of capacity)?

a.
Fixed O/H applied	XX	
Production volume variance	XX	
Fixed O/H control		XX

b.
Fixed O/H applied	XX	
Fixed O/H control		XX

c.
Fixed O/H control	XX	
Fixed O/H applied		XX

d.
Fixed O/H applied	XX	
Production volume variance		XX
Fixed O/H control		XX

The correct answer is (a). *(Publisher)*
REQUIRED: The year-end journal entry to close the fixed overhead, assuming underutilization of capacity.
DISCUSSION: The journal entry to record the closing of the fixed O/H account is to charge fixed O/H applied and credit fixed O/H control for their respective balances. The difference between the two variance accounts should be debited to the production volume variance account assuming underutilization of capacity. This variance (the idle capacity variance) is the difference between budgeted fixed cost and that which is applied. Underutilization of capacity means that O/H will be underapplied (i.e., the predetermined O/H application rate was based on a greater than actual volume), thus producing an unfavorable variance (a debit).
Answer (b) is incorrect because it does not recognize the unfavorable volume variance. Answer (c) is incorrect because the control account was initially debited and the application account credited and must be reversed to close. Also, the entry does not recognize the volume variance. Answer (d) is incorrect because the variance is unfavorable (a debit).

216. To adjust finished goods inventory for external reporting, which of the following journal entries may be made?

a.
Finished goods inventory adjustment account	XX	
Fixed O/H		XX

b.
Work-in-process	XX	
Fixed O/H		XX

c.
Fixed O/H	XX	
Work-in-process		XX

d.
Finished goods	XX	
Work-in-process		XX

The correct answer is (a). *(Publisher)*
REQUIRED: The entry to adjust FG inventory for external reporting purposes.
DISCUSSION: The journal entry to record the adjustment of FG inventory for external reporting purposes is to charge the FG inventory adjustment account for the desired amount and make a corresponding credit to fixed O/H. The entry reflects proration of an unfavorable O/H variance so as to adjust the inventory to approximate actual cost. To avoid alteration of the inventory accounts, the proration is taken to an adjustment account.
Answer (b) is incorrect because it is an adjustment to WIP. Answer (c) is incorrect because costs are not transferred from WIP to O/H. Answer (d) is incorrect because it represents the transfer of completed units to FG.

Module 13.7: Journal Entries

217. Omega Company would have applied $32,500 of fixed factory overhead if output equalled the master budget. On a normal volume basis, the standard hours allowed are 2,000, and overhead is applied at a rate of $15 per hour. Select the entry to close the fixed factory overhead accounts.

a.	Fixed O/H control	$30,000	
	Production volume variance	2,500	
	Fixed O/H applied		$32,500
b.	Cost of goods sold	$32,500	
	Fixed O/H control		$32,500
c.	Work-in-process	$30,000	
	O/H price variance	2,500	
	Fixed O/H applied		$32,500
d.	Fixed O/H applied	$30,000	
	Production volume variance	2,500	
	Fixed O/H control		$32,500

The correct answer is (d). *(Publisher)*
REQUIRED: The year-end journal entry to close the fixed O/H accounts.
DISCUSSION: The journal entry to record the closing of the fixed O/H accounts is to charge fixed O/H applied and credit the fixed O/H control account for their respective balances. The difference between the two accounts should be charged to the production volume variance account. Here, that variance is unfavorable since O/H is underapplied. Volume was evidently less than anticipated, and the predetermined rate based on normal volume was therefore inadequate. A rate based on a master budget accurately reflecting the period's actual volume would have been adjusted upward to compensate for the decline below normal volume. Note that normal volume is an average volume over a period of years, while the master budget volume is that expected for only the current period.

Standard hours	2,000
Predetermined overhead rate	$15/hour
Applied using standard volume	$30,000
Applied using master volume	$32,500

Answer (a) is incorrect because the normal balances in the applied O/H and O/H control accounts are a credit and a debit, respectively. Hence, the closing entries must be the reverse. Answers (b) and (c) are incorrect because neither closes both O/H accounts.

218. How would Omega Company (see Q. 217) adjust its finished goods inventory of $20,000 upward if goods manufactured and sold were $80,000 to satisfy external reporting requirements?

a.	Fixed O/H	$500	
	FG inventory adjustment		$500
b.	FG inventory adjustment	$500	
	Production volume variance		$500
c.	Fixed O/H	$2,000	
	Work-in-process		$2,000
d.	Finished goods	$2,000	
	Work-in-process		$2,000

The correct answer is (b). *(Publisher)*
REQUIRED: The journal entry to adjust FG inventory for external reporting purposes.
DISCUSSION: The journal entry to record the adjustment of FG inventory for external reporting purposes is to charge the FG inventory adjustment account for the desired amount and make a corresponding credit to the production volume variance. The entry reflects the proration of an unfavorable O/H variance so as to adjust the inventory to approximate actual cost. To avoid alteration of the inventory accounts, the proration is taken to an adjustment account. Note that $20,000 is 20% of the total goods produced ($20,000 in inventory plus $80,000 sold). Thus, only $500 ($2,500 x .20) would be prorated to inventory ($2,000 would go to CGS).

219. Assume the same information as in Q. 218. What would be the entry under the FIFO method if Omega's finished goods inventory were sold in the following period?

a.	Cost of goods sold	$2,000	
	Finished goods		$2,000
b.	Cost of goods sold	$2,000	
	Inventory		$2,000
c.	Cost of goods sold	$500	
	FG inventory adjustment		$500
d.	Finished goods	$500	
	External inventory		$500

The correct answer is (c). *(Publisher)*
REQUIRED: The journal entry under FIFO when adjusted inventory is sold in the following period.
DISCUSSION: The journal entry to record the sale of inventory that was adjusted in the previous period is to charge the cost of goods sold account and credit the finished goods inventory adjustment account for the balance in the latter account.

13.8 Comprehensive

Questions 220 through 229 are based on the following information, which was presented as part of Question 1 on Part 4 of the December 1972 CMA examination.

The Carberg Corporation manufactures and sells a single product. The cost system used by the company is a standard cost system. The standard cost per unit of product is shown below:

Material (1 lb. plastic x $2.00)	$ 2.00
Direct labor (1.6 hrs. x $4.00)	6.40
Variable overhead cost	3.00
Fixed overhead cost	1.45
	$12.85

The overhead cost per unit was calculated from the following annual overhead cost budget for a 60,000-unit volume:

Variable overhead cost		
Indirect labor (30,000 hrs. x $4)	$120,000	
Supplies-oil (60,000 gals. x $.50)	30,000	
Allocated variable service department costs	30,000	
Total variable overhead cost	$180,000	

Fixed overhead cost	
Supervision	$ 27,000
Depreciation	45,000
Other fixed costs	15,000
Total fixed overhead cost	$ 87,000
Total budgeted annual overhead cost at 60,000	$267,000

The charges to the manufacturing department for November, when 5,000 units were produced, are given below:

Material (5,300 lbs. x $2.00)	$10,600
Direct labor (8,200 hrs. x $4.10)	33,620
Indirect labor (2,400 hrs. x $4.10)	9,840
Supplies - oil (6,000 gals. x $.55)	3,300
Allocated variable service dept. costs	3,200
Supervision	2,475
Depreciation	3,750
Other fixed costs	1,250
Total	$68,035

The purchasing department normally buys about the same quantity as is used in production during a month. In November, 5,200 lbs. were purchased at a price of $2.10 per pound.

220. For the month of November, Carberg Corporation's materials purchase price (isolated at point of purchase) and materials quantity variances are

a. $530 U; $600 U.
b. $520 U; $600 U.
c. $500 F; $300 F.
d. $520 U; $300 U.

The correct answer is (b). *(Publisher)*
REQUIRED: The materials purchase price and materials quantity variances.
DISCUSSION: The materials price variance is the difference between the standard price and the actual price times the quantity purchased. 5,200 lbs. were purchased. The standard price of $2 per unit less the actual price paid of $2.10 results in an unfavorable price variance of $.10 per unit. $.10 x 5,200 = $520 unfavorable materials price variance.
The materials quantity variance is the difference between the actual materials quantity and the standard materials quantity times the standard price per pound. 5,300 lbs. were actually used. The quantity allowed at the standard level was 5,000 lbs. (5,000 units x 1 lb./unit), resulting in an unfavorable quantity variance of 300 lbs. $2 standard price/lb. x 300 lbs. = $600 unfavorable materials quantity variance.

221. For the month of November, Carberg Corporation's direct labor wage rate and direct labor usage variances are

a. $820 U; $800 F.
b. $800 U; $800 U.
c. $600 U; $800 U.
d. $820 U; $800 U.

The correct answer is (d). *(Publisher)*
REQUIRED: The direct labor rate and direct labor usage variances.
DISCUSSION: The direct labor rate variance is the difference between the standard rate and the actual rate times the actual number of hours used. The standard rate is $4, and the actual hourly rate is $4.10. $4 - $4.10 = $.10/hr. unfavorable variance. 8,200 actual hours used x $.10 = $820 unfavorable labor rate variance.
The direct labor usage variance is the difference between the actual labor hours (8,200) and the 8,000 standard labor hours allowed for output (5,000 x 1.6 hours/unit), times the standard labor rate. The standard rate is $4 per hour. The 200 unfavorable DLH (8,200 - 8,000) results in an unfavorable DL usage variance of $800 (200 x $4).

Module 13.8: Comprehensive

> Questions 222 through 226 are based on the information presented on page 379.

222. The total variable overhead incurred during November is

a. $12,140.
b. $13,140.
c. $16,340.
d. $13,040.

The correct answer is (c). *(Publisher)*
REQUIRED: The total variable overhead incurred during November.
DISCUSSION: The total variable overhead applied to the units includes the indirect labor, supplies, and allocated variable service department costs. In this case, these items were $9,840, $3,300, and $3,200, respectively, totaling $16,340.

223. Total fixed overhead incurred during November is

a. $7,475.
b. $6,125.
c. $4,900.
d. $5,000.

The correct answer is (a). *(Publisher)*
REQUIRED: The total fixed overhead incurred during November.
DISCUSSION: Total fixed overhead is equal to supervision, depreciation, and other fixed costs. Supervision was $2,475; depreciation was $3,750; other fixed costs were $1,250. The total is $7,475.

224. Total budgeted variable overhead for 5,000 units is

a. $7,250.
b. $12,500.
c. $15,000.
d. $5,000.

The correct answer is (c). *(Publisher)*
REQUIRED: The total budgeted variable overhead for the units produced.
DISCUSSION: First, take the total variable overhead cost of $180,000 a year for 60,000 units a year and divide by 12 months to get $15,000. Or divide by 60,000 units to get $3.00 per unit and then multiply by 5,000 units to get $15,000. Note that this is the amount of variable overhead applied to the finished goods.

225. Total fixed overhead to be applied to 5,000 units is

a. $22,250.
b. $7,250.
c. $5,250.
d. $7,000.

The correct answer is (b). *(Publisher)*
REQUIRED: Total budgeted fixed overhead for the units produced.
DISCUSSION: The standard fixed O/H cost of $1.45/unit multiplied by 5,000 units is $7,250. Note that this is the amount of fixed O/H applied to FG.

226. What is total budgeted fixed overhead for November?

a. $7,250.
b. $7,425.
c. $7,500.
d. $15,000.

The correct answer is (a). *(Publisher)*
REQUIRED: Total budgeted fixed overhead for November.
DISCUSSION: Budgeted fixed O/H is $7,250, which is $87,000 ÷ 12 months. Note that budgeted fixed O/H usually varies from applied fixed O/H. In this problem, they are the same because budgeted activity of 5,000 units (60,000 annually ÷ 12) equals actual production.

Module 13.8: Comprehensive

> Questions 227 through 229 are based on the information presented on page 379.

227. The variable overhead variance is

a. $1,430 unfavorable.
b. $1,340 unfavorable.
c. $1,200 unfavorable.
d. $1,600 favorable.

The correct answer is (b). *(Publisher)*
REQUIRED: The variable overhead variance (controllable or budget variance).
DISCUSSION: The difference between the variable O/H incurred and applied variable O/H is the variable O/H variance. $16,340 of variable overhead was incurred during November (Q. 222). The budgeted (applied) variable overhead was $15,000 (Q. 224).

$$\$16,340 - \$15,000 = \$1,340 \text{ U.}$$

228. The fixed overhead variance is

a. $225 unfavorable.
b. $225 favorable.
c. $236 favorable.
d. $200 unfavorable.

The correct answer is (a). *(Publisher)*
REQUIRED: The fixed overhead variance for the month.
DISCUSSION: The fixed O/H variance is the difference between the fixed O/H incurred and the applied fixed O/H. The fixed O/H incurred this month was $7,475 (Q. 223). The applied overhead was $7,250 (Q. 225).

$$\$7,475 - \$7,250 = \$225 \text{ U.}$$

229. If the materials quantity variance is unfavorable, which department should be charged?

a. Purchasing department.
b. Manufacturing department.
c. Both departments share the variance if it can be shown to be a result of inefficiency in both departments.
d. None of the above.

The correct answer is (c). *(Publisher)*
REQUIRED: The department responsible for the materials quantity variance.
DISCUSSION: Both the purchasing and the manufacturing departments may share the variance if it can be shown that it is a result of decisions made in both departments. For example, the materials quantity variance may be partially the result of incorrect materials purchased by the purchasing department and/or incorrect usage by the manufacturing department. Normally, price variances are charged to the purchasing department, and quantity variances to the production department.

Module 13.8: Comprehensive

Questions 230 through 238 are based on Organet Stamping Company, which manufactures a variety of products made of plastic and aluminum components. During the winter months, substantially all of the production capacity is devoted to the production of lawn sprinklers for the following spring and summer season. Other products are manufactured during the remainder of the year. Because a variety of products are manufactured throughout the year, factory volume is measured by production labor hours rather than units of production.

Production and sales volume have grown steadily for the past several years, as can be seen from the following schedule of standard production labor content of annual output:

This year	32,000 hours
1 year ago	30,000 hours
2 years ago	27,000 hours
3 years ago	28,000 hours
4 years ago	26,000 hours

The company has developed standard costs for its several products. Standard costs for each year are set in the preceding October. The standard cost of a sprinkler this year was $2.50, computed as follows:

Direct materials		
Aluminum	0.2 lbs. x $0.40 per lb.	$0.08
Plastic	1.0 lbs. x $0.38 per lb.	0.38
Production		
Labor	0.3 hrs. x $4.00 per hr.	1.20
Overhead (calculated using 30,000 production labor hours as normal capacity)		
Variable	0.3 hrs. x $1.60 per hr.	0.48
Fixed	0.3 hrs. x $1.20 per hr.	0.36
Total		$2.50

During February of this year, 8,500 good sprinklers were manufactured. The following costs were incurred and charged to production:

Materials requisitioned for production	
Aluminum (1,900 lbs. x $0.40 per lb.)	$ 760
Plastic	
Regular grade (6,000 lbs. x $0.38 per lb.)	2,280
Low grade* (3,500 lbs. x $0.38 per lb.)	1,330
Production labor	
Straight time (2,300 hrs. x $4.00 per hr.)	9,200
Overtime (400 hrs. x $6.00 per hr.)	2,400
Overhead	
Variable	5,200
Fixed	3,100
Costs charged to production	$24,270

Material price variations are not charged to production but to a material price variation account at the time the invoice is entered. All materials are carried in inventory at standard prices. Material purchases for February were:

Aluminum (1,800 lbs. x $0.48 per lb.)	$ 864
Plastic	
Regular grade (3,000 lbs. x $0.50)	1,500
Low grade* (6,000 lbs. x $0.29)	1,740

* Due to plastic shortages, the company was forced to purchase lower grade plastic than called for in the standards, which increased the number of sprinklers rejected on inspection.

---

230. The total variance from standard cost of the costs charged to production for February is

a. $3,080 unfavorable.
b. $3,020 unfavorable.
c. $3,140 favorable.
d. $3,020 favorable.
e. None of the above.

The correct answer is (b). *(CMA 1274 4-1)*
REQUIRED: The total variance from standard cost.
DISCUSSION: The total variance from standard cost of the costs charged to production is the difference between the actual costs charged to production ($24,270) and the standard cost per sprinkler times the number of sprinklers manufactured in February. 8,500 units were produced, and $2.50 was the standard cost per unit. $2.50 x 8,500 = $21,250. The variance is thus $3,020 ($24,270 - $21,250) unfavorable.

231. The standard material quantities already include an allowance for acceptable material scrap loss. In this situation, the material use variance would most likely be caused by

a. Defective aluminum.
b. Improper processing by labor.
c. Inadequate allowance for scrap loss.
d. Substitute plastic.
e. None of the above.

The correct answer is (d). *(CMA 1274 4-2)*
REQUIRED: The cause of material usage variance.
DISCUSSION: The question clearly indicates that the substitute plastic is a lower grade and that inspection rejects more units. Accordingly, the most likely cause of unacceptable material usage variance is the substitute plastic.

Module 13.8: Comprehensive

232. The spending or budget variance for the fixed portion of the overhead costs for February is

a. $100 unfavorable.
b. $60 favorable.
c. Zero.
d. Not calculable from the problem.
e. None of the above.

The correct answer is (a). *(CMA 1274 4-3)*
REQUIRED: The spending or budget variance for the fixed overhead for the month.
DISCUSSION: The spending or overhead variance is the difference between actual fixed overhead and budgeted fixed overhead. Actual fixed overhead is given as $3,100. The monthly budgeted fixed overhead is one-twelfth of the annual fixed overhead. The annual overhead is $36,000 (30,000 hours expected capacity x the $1.20/hr. fixed O/H rate). Budgeted fixed O/H is thus $3,000 ($36,000 ÷ 12). The budget variance for fixed overhead is $100 unfavorable ($3,100 actual - $3,000 standard).

233. The labor efficiency (quantity) variance is standard price times the difference between standard labor hours of output and

a. 2,300 hours.
b. 2,700 hours.
c. 2,900 hours.
d. 2,500 hours.
e. None of the above.

The correct answer is (b). *(CMA 1274 4-4)*
REQUIRED: The missing variable in the formula for labor efficiency variance.
DISCUSSION: The labor efficiency variance is equal to the standard price times the difference between the standard quantity and the actual quantity. Thus, the question requires calculation of the actual quantity of hours used. 2,300 hours of straight time plus 400 hours of overtime totals 2,700 total hours.

234. The labor rate (price) variance (assume overtime premium is not charged to overhead) is

a. $0.
b. $600 unfavorable.
c. $800 unfavorable.
d. $1,400 unfavorable.
e. $2,400 unfavorable.

The correct answer is (c). *(CMA 1274 4-5)*
REQUIRED: The labor rate variance for the month.
DISCUSSION: If the $2.00 overtime premium is not charged to overhead, it is considered a rate variance. All wages were at the standard $4/hr. except the 400 hours of overtime at $6/hr. Thus, the labor rate variance is $800 unfavorable (400 hrs. of overtime at a $2/hr. premium). The $2/hr. premium represents the amount over the standard rate. Note that it is possible to plan (budget) and account for overtime cost as overhead.

235. The manufacturing overhead volume variance is the result of

a. Inadequate cost control effort.
b. Sales volume exceeding production volume.
c. Actual production hours exceeding standard production hours of output.
d. The overapplication of fixed cost to output.
e. None of the above.

The correct answer is (d). *(CMA 1274 4-6)*
REQUIRED: The cause of the manufacturing overhead volume variance.
DISCUSSION: The manufacturing overhead volume variance arises from more (less) fixed overhead being applied in a period than is budgeted. Budgeted fixed overhead was calculated in Q. 232 as $3,000. Fixed overhead applied is standard hours allowed for output multiplied by the standard rate. 8,500 units of output x .3 hours per unit equals 2,550 hours allowed, times $1.20/hour (given) equals $3,060 applied overhead. Thus, $60 of overhead was overapplied ($3,060 - $3,000).

236. The total variance from standard cost of the costs charged to production for February if variable standard costing had been used rather than absorption costing is

a. $3,160 unfavorable.
b. $2,980 unfavorable.
c. $6,080 unfavorable.
d. $1,860 unfavorable.
e. None of the above.

The correct answer is (b). *(CMA 1274 4-7)*
REQUIRED: The total variance from standard cost based on variable costing.
DISCUSSION: Variable standard costing would include all variable costs, but not fixed overhead. Thus, the actual variable overhead production cost is $24,270 total cost - $3,100 FC = $21,170. Compared to the standard variable cost of 8,500 units at $2.14 per unit ($2.50 absorption less $.36 fixed overhead), or $18,190, the variance would be $2,980 unfavorable ($21,170 - $18,190).

> Questions 237 and 238 are based on the information presented on page 382.

237. If a variable standard costing system had been used, the variable overhead budget variance would have been

   a. $1,120 unfavorable.
   b. $1,220 unfavorable.
   c. $1,160 unfavorable.
   d. $1,280 unfavorable.
   e. None of the above.

The correct answer is (a). *(CMA 1274 4-8)*
REQUIRED: The variable overhead budget variance under variable costing.
DISCUSSION: The variable overhead budget variance is the difference between the actual variable O/H cost and the budgeted O/H cost for the actual volume (standard quantity allowed for output). Actual variable overhead of $5,200 minus the budgeted variable overhead of $4,080 (8,500 x $.48) equals an unfavorable variance of $1,120.

238. The variations of material prices from standard would best be reported as

   a. Materials price variance - $36 favorable.
   b. Materials price variance - aluminum, $144 unfavorable; plastic, $180 favorable.
   c. Materials price variance - aluminum, $144 unfavorable; plastic, $360 unfavorable; material substitution, $540 favorable.
   d. Materials price variance - aluminum, $144 unfavorable; plastic, $360 unfavorable; price difference due to plastic substitution not reported.
   e. None of the above. It should not be reported because material prices are uncontrollable.

The correct answer is (c). *(CMA 1274 4-9)*
REQUIRED: The materials price variance for the three materials.
DISCUSSION: The materials price variance is the actual quantity purchased times the difference between actual price and standard price.

Aluminum: (1,800 lbs.) x ($.48 - $.40) = $144 U
Plastic: (3,000 lbs.) x ($.50 - $.38) = $360 U
Substitute: (6,000 lbs.) x ($.29 - $.38) = $540 F

Module 13.8: Comprehensive

> Questions 239 and 240 are based on the following processing standards which have been set for Duo Co.'s clerical workers:
>
> | | |
> |---|---:|
> | Number of hours per 1,000 papers processed | 150 |
> | Normal number of papers processed per year | 1,500,000 |
> | Wage rate per 1,000 papers | $ 600 |
> | Standard variable cost of processing 1,500,000 papers | $900,000 |
> | Fixed costs per year | $150,000 |
>
> The following information pertains to the 1,200,000 papers that were processed during year:
>
> | | |
> |---|---:|
> | Total cost | $915,000 |
> | Labor cost | $760,000 |
> | Labor hours | 190,000 |

239. For the year, Duo's expected total cost to process the 1,200,000 papers, assuming standard performance, should be

   a. $910,000.
   b. $900,000.
   c. $870,000.
   d. $840,000.

The correct answer is (c). *(CPA 587 Q-32)*
REQUIRED: The expected total cost assuming standard performance.
DISCUSSION: The variable cost is $720,000 [(1,200,000 papers ÷ 1,000) x $600]. The fixed costs are $150,000. Thus, expected total cost is $870,000 ($720,000 + $150,000).

240. For the year, Duo's labor rate variance would be

   a. $40,000 unfavorable.
   b. $32,000 favorable.
   c. $10,000 unfavorable.
   d. $0.

The correct answer is (d). *(CPA 587 Q-33)*
REQUIRED: The labor rate variance (LRV).
DISCUSSION: The labor rate variance is computed by finding the difference between standard and actual rate and then multiplying by actual hours: AH(AR - SR). Actual labor cost was $760,000 for 190,000 hours. The standard rate is $600 ÷ 150 hours.

$$AH(AR - SR) = LRV$$
$$190,000\ [(\$760,000 ÷ 190,000) - (\$600 ÷ 150)] = 0$$

Questions 241 through 246 are based on the following information, which was presented as part of Question 2 on Part 4 of the June 1976 CMA examination.

The Felton Company manufactures a complete line of radios. Because a large number of models have plastic cases, the company has its own molding department for producing the cases. The month of April was devoted to the production of plastic cases for one of the portable radios, Model SX76.

The Molding Department has two operations: molding and trimming. There is no interaction of labor in these two operations. The standard labor cost for producing 10 plastic cases for Model SX76 is as follows:

Molders (.50 hrs. x $6.00/hr.) $3.00
Trimmers (.25 hrs. x $4.00/hr.)   1.00
                                        $4.00

During April, 70,000 plastic cases were produced in the Molding Department. However, 10% of these cases (7,000) had to be discarded because they were found to be defective at final inspection. The Purchasing Department had changed to a new plastic supplier to take advantage of a lower price for comparable plastic. The new plastic turned out to be of a lower quality and resulted in the rejection of completed cases.

Direct labor hours worked and direct labor costs charged to the Molding Department are:

Molders (3,800 hrs. x $6.25) $23,750
Trimmers (1,600 hrs. x $4.15)   6,640
Total labor charges $30,390

As a result of poor scheduling by the Production Scheduling Department, the foreman of the Molding Department had to shift molders to the trimming operation for 200 hours during April. The company paid the molding workers their regular hourly rate even though they were performing a lower rated task. There was no significant loss of efficiency caused by the shift. In addition, the foreman of the department indicated that 75 hours and 35 hours of idle time occurred in the molding and trimming operations respectively as a result of unexpected machinery repairs required during the month.

The monthly report which compares actual costs with standard cost of output for the month of April shows the following standard labor cost for the Molding Department:

Standard labor cost of output
[63,000 x ($4.00 ÷ 10)] $25,200

241. The labor rate variance for the molders and trimmers is

    a. $360 favorable; $875 favorable.
    b. $950 unfavorable; $240 unfavorable.
    c. $950 favorable; $420 unfavorable.
    d. $840 unfavorable; $175 favorable.

The correct answer is (b). *(Publisher)*
REQUIRED: The labor rate variance.
DISCUSSION: The molders incurred 3,800 hrs. The standard rate was $6. The actual rate was $6.25. 3,800 x $.25 = $950 unfavorable.
The trimmers incurred 1,600 hours. The standard rate was $4. The actual rate was $4.15. The difference is $.15 per hour. 1,600 x $.15 = $240 unfavorable.

242. The labor substitution (shifting of molders to trimming operations) variance is

    a. $200 favorable.
    b. $360 favorable.
    c. $400 unfavorable.
    d. $200 unfavorable.

The correct answer is (c). *(Publisher)*
REQUIRED: The labor substitution variance from shifting one labor type to another.
DISCUSSION: Calculation of the labor substitution variance requires the identification of the 200 hours from the shift from molders, whose standard rate is $6 per hour, to the trimming operation, where the standard rate is $4 per hour. 200 x ($4 - $6) = $400 unfavorable substitution variance.

243. The material substitution (additional labor due to inferior plastic) variance for molders and trimmers is

    a. $900 unfavorable; $700 favorable.
    b. $3,600 favorable; $800 unfavorable.
    c. $1,800 unfavorable; $900 favorable.
    d. $2,100 unfavorable; $700 unfavorable

The correct answer is (d). *(Publisher)*
REQUIRED: The material substitution variance for molders and trimmers.
DISCUSSION: The new plastic wasted molder and trimmer labor to produce 7,000 cases that were discarded because of defects at final inspection. The standard labor cost for producing 10 plastic cases is $3 for molders and $1 for trimmers. Thus, the molders material substitution variance in labor is (7,000 ÷ 10) x $3 = $2,100 unfavorable. The trimmers material substitution variance in labor is (7,000 ÷ 10) x $1 = $700 unfavorable.

Module 13.8: Comprehensive

244. The idle time variance for molders and trimmers is

a. $430 unfavorable; $150 favorable.
b. $385 unfavorable; $160 unfavorable.
c. $540 favorable; $210 unfavorable.
d. $450 unfavorable; $140 unfavorable.

The correct answer is (d). *(Publisher)*
REQUIRED: The idle time variance.
DISCUSSION: The idle time variance for molders and trimmers is equal to the idle time hours times the standard rate. 75 hours of idle time were recorded by molders, whose standard rate was $6. 75 x $6 = $450 U. 35 hours of idle time were recorded by trimmers, at $4 standard rate. 35 x $4 = $140 U.

245. The efficiency variances for molders and trimmers, respectively, are

a. $0; $210 F.
b. $60 U; $150 U.
c. $150 U; $60 U.
d. $2,100 U; $0.

The correct answer is (c). *(Publisher)*
REQUIRED: The labor efficiency variance for molders and trimmers.
DISCUSSION: Molders incurred 3,800 hours, of which 300 hours were over the standard of 3,500 hours (70,000 ÷ 10 x .5 hr.). Of these 300 hours, 200 were transferred to trimming and 75 were idle time. Thus, only 25 hours resulted from less than standard efficiency. 25 hours x $6 = $150 U for molders.

Trimmers incurred 1,600 hours, which was 150 under standard of 1,750 hours (70,000 ÷ 10 x .25 hr.). Recall that 200 hours were transferred from molding, which changes the 150 hr. F to 50 hr. U, of which 35 hours were idle time, which leaves an efficiency variance of 15 hours at $4, or $60 U.

246. The total labor variance for molders and trimmers is

a. $4,620 favorable.
b. $5,190 unfavorable.
c. $5,010 favorable.
d. $5,320 unfavorable.

The correct answer is (b). *(Publisher)*
REQUIRED: The total labor variance for molders and trimmers.
DISCUSSION: Calculation of the total labor variance requires the determination of the standard labor cost of the output achieved compared to the actual labor cost. The actual labor cost was given as $30,390. The standard labor cost is equal to $25,200, which is the 63,000 good units produced x ($4 ÷ 10). $25,200 - $30,390 = $5,190 U.

This total variance is the sum of the variances calculated in Qs. 241, 242, 243, and 244.

Rate ($950 U + $240 U)	$1,190 U
Labor substitution	400 U
Material substitution ($2,100 U + $700 U)	2,800 U
Idle time ($450 U + $140 U)	590 U
	$4,980 U
Plus an operating efficiency variance of molders ($150 U) and trimmers ($60 U)	210 U
	$5,190 U

This last variance is based on the actual hours spent producing good cases less the standard hours allowed for production of good cases times the standard rate.

Questions 247 through 251 are based on the following information, which was presented as part of Question 3 on Part 4 of the June 1979 CMA examination.

The Lonn Manufacturing Co. produces two primary chemical products to be used as base ingredients for a variety of products. This year's budget for the two products was

(000 omitted)

	X-4	Z-8	Total
Production output in gallons	600	600	1,200
Direct material	$1,500	$1,875	$3,375
Direct labor	900	900	1,800
Total prime manufacturing cost	$2,400	$2,775	$5,175

The following planning assumptions were used for the budget for both products:

- Direct material yield at 96%.
- Direct labor rate of $6 per hour.

The year's actual direct production cost (000 omitted) was

	X-4	Z-8	Total
Production output in gallons	570.0	658.0	1,228.0
Direct material	$1,368.0	$2,138.5	$3,506.5
Direct labor	936.0	1,092.0	2,028.0
Total prime manufacturing cost	$2,304.0	$3,230.5	$5,534.5

The actual production yield was 95% for X-4 and 94% for Z-8. The direct labor cost per hour for both products was $6.50.

---

247. What is the budgeted direct material cost for product X-4?

a. $2.50/gallon.
b. $2.40/gallon.
c. $2.28/gallon.
d. $2.00/gallon.

The correct answer is (b). *(Publisher)*
REQUIRED: The direct material cost for product X-4.
DISCUSSION: The direct material cost for product X-4 is calculated as follows:

Budgeted input quantity required for 600,000 gal. of output
= 600,000 ÷ .96 = 625,000 gals.

Budgeted direct material cost = $1,500,000 ÷ 625,000 gals.
= $2.40/gal.

Module 13.8: Comprehensive

248. The direct material price variance of product X-4 is

   a. $36,000 favorable.
   b. $36,000 unfavorable.
   c. $22,800 favorable.
   d. $72,000 favorable.

The correct answer is (d). *(Publisher)*
   REQUIRED: The direct material price variance of product X-4.
   DISCUSSION: The direct material price variance is the difference between the actual price per gallon and the budgeted price per gallon times the actual quantity purchased.

   600,000 gal.* x ($2.28/gal.** - $2.40/gal.***)
   600,000 gal. x $.12/gal. = $72,000 favorable

   *95% yield = 570,000 gallons. Gallons of input required for 95% yield = 570,000 ÷ .95 = 600,000 gallons.
   **Total actual material cost/actual quantity
      $1,368,000 ÷ 600,000 gal. = $2.28/gal.
   ***Budgeted price per gallon, per Q. 247.

249. The direct material efficiency variance for product X-4 is

   a. $15,000 unfavorable.
   b. $15,000 favorable.
   c. $14,400 favorable.
   d. $24,000 favorable.

The correct answer is (a). *(Publisher)*
   REQUIRED: The direct material efficiency variance for product X-4.
   DISCUSSION: The direct material efficiency variance for a product is the difference between the actual input quantity and the budgeted input quantity for the production level achieved times the budgeted price per input gallon (per Q. 247).

   $2.40/input gal. x (600,000 gal.* - 593,750 gal.**)
   $2.40/input gal. x 6,250 input gal. = $15,000 U

   *95% yield = 570,000 gallons. Gallons of input required for 95% yield = 570,000 ÷ .95 = 600,000 gallons.
   **Budgeted input usage for production achieved
      = outputs achieved/standard yield
      = 570,000 ÷ .96
      = 593,750 gallons

250. What is the direct labor rate variance for product Z-8?

   a. $84,000 unfavorable.
   b. $42,000 unfavorable.
   c. $84,000 favorable.
   d. $16,000 unfavorable.

The correct answer is (a). *(Publisher)*
   REQUIRED: The direct labor rate variance for product Z-8.
   DISCUSSION: The direct labor rate variance is the difference between the actual rate and budgeted rate per hour times the actual hours used.

   168,000* x ($6.50 - $6)
   168,000 hrs. x $0.50 = $84,000 unfavorable

   *Actual direct labor hours = actual total DL cost/actual DL rate
      = $1,092,000 ÷ $6.50 per DLH
      = 168,000 actual DLH

251. What is the direct labor efficiency variance for product Z-8?

   a. $21,000 unfavorable.
   b. $21,000 favorable.
   c. $96,222 favorable.
   d. $96,222 unfavorable.

The correct answer is (a). *(Publisher)*
   REQUIRED: The direct labor efficiency variance for product Z-8.
   DISCUSSION: The direct labor efficiency variance is the actual DLH (168,000 hours, per Q. 250) minus the budgeted DLH for production achieved times the budgeted rate per hour ($6).
   At 600,000 gallons, there are 150,000 DLH budgeted ($900,000 ÷ $6). Thus, for 658,000 gallons, DLH is 164,500 [(658,000 ÷ 600,000) x 150,000].

   $6 x (168,000 - 164,500)
   $6 x 3,500 hrs. = $21,000 unfavorable

Module 13.8: Comprehensive

Questions 252 through 256 are based on the following information, which was presented as part of Question 7 on Part 4 of the December 1979 CMA examination.

The Lenco Co. employs a standard cost system as part of its cost control program. The standard cost per unit is established at the beginning of each year. Standards are not revised during the year for any changes in material or labor inputs or in the manufacturing processes. Any revisions in standards are deferred until the beginning of the next fiscal year. However, in order to recognize such changes in the current year, the company includes planned variances in the monthly budgets prepared after such changes have been introduced.

The following labor standard was set for one of Lenco's products effective July 1, the beginning of the fiscal year.

Class I labor (4 hrs. x $6.00)	$24.00
Class II labor (3 hrs. x $7.50)	22.50
Class V labor (1 hr. x $11.50)	11.50
Standard labor cost per 100 units	$58.00

The standard was based upon the quality of material that had been used in prior years and what was expected to be available for the fiscal year. The labor activity is performed by a team consisting of four persons with Class I skills, three persons with Class II skills, and one person with Class V skills. This is the most economical combination for the company's processing system.

The manufacturing operations occurred as expected during the first five months of the year. The standard costs contributed to effective cost control during this period. However, there were indications that changes in the operations would be required in the last half of the year. The company had received a significant increase in orders for delivery in the spring. There were an inadequate number of skilled workers available to meet the increased production. As a result, the production teams, beginning in January, would be made up of more Class I labor and less Class II labor than the standard required. The teams would consist of six Class I persons, two Class II persons, and one Class V person. This labor team would be less efficient than the normal team. The reorganized teams work more slowly so that only 90 units are produced in the same time period that 100 units would normally be produced. No raw materials will be lost as a result of the change in the labor mix. Completed units have never been rejected in the final inspection process as a consequence of faulty work; this is expected to continue.

In addition, Lenco was notified by its material supplier that a lower quality material would be supplied after January 1. One unit of raw material normally is required for each good unit produced. Lenco and its supplier estimated that 5% of the units manufactured would be rejected upon final inspection due to defective material. Normally, no units are lost due to defective material.

---

252. Using lower quality material and the new labor teams, what will be the quantity of direct materials that must be entered into production in order to produce 42,750 units of good production in January?

a. 46,500.
b. 45,000.
c. 44,887.
d. 42,750.

The correct answer is (b). *(Publisher)*
REQUIRED: The quantity of direct materials to enter into production under new labor and material conditions.
DISCUSSION: Lenco wishes to produce 42,750 units of good production, given that there is 5% spoilage. Conversely, 95% are good, and 42,750 equals 95% of units required to be started.

42,750 ÷ .95 = 45,000 units started

253. The equivalent material units of labor needed to produce 42,750 units are

a. 52,500.
b. 50,000.
c. 45,000.
d. 47,500.

The correct answer is (b). *(Publisher)*
REQUIRED: The equivalent material units of labor needed for a given level of production.
DISCUSSION: An equivalent material unit of labor is the amount of labor needed to complete a good unit of output, i.e., assuming no spoilage or inefficiency. Material EUP is the number of direct material units divided by the labor efficiency. For 42,750 good units, 45,000 direct material units are required, which, when divided by a 90% labor efficiency, equals 50,000 equivalent material units of labor.

Module 13.8: Comprehensive

254. The hours of Class I, II, and V labor that will be needed to produce 42,750 good units from the material input are

	Class I	Class II	Class V
a.	2,850	950	450
b.	3,000	1,000	500
c.	2,700	1,050	400
d.	2,565	1,000	500

The correct answer is (b). *(Publisher)*
REQUIRED: The hours of Classes I, II, and V labor needed for a given level of production.
DISCUSSION: Calculation of the hours of appropriate classes of labor that would be needed to produce 42,750 good units requires the proportional amount of labor originally budgeted to produce 50,000 units. For 100 units, 6, 2, and 1 hours of Class I, II, and V, respectively, are required (note the revised mix of workers which resulted in the 10% loss in efficiency). To produce 50,000 units, multiply these proportions by 500 (50,000 ÷ 100), resulting in

Class I: 6 x 500 = 3,000 hours
Class II: 2 x 500 = 1,000 hours
Class V: 1 x 500 = 500 hours

255. The expected labor cost at production of 42,750 units for Class I, Class II, and Class V labor is

a. $15,390; $7,125; $6,038.
b. $17,100; $7,875; $5,175.
c. $16,200; $6,750; $5,463.
d. $18,000; $7,500; $5,750.

The correct answer is (d). *(Publisher)*
REQUIRED: The budgeted labor cost at the given level of production.
DISCUSSION: Using the budgeted hours calculated in Q. 254, the expected labor cost at production of 42,750 units for Class I, Class II, and Class V labor is

Class I labor (3,000 DLH x $6.00)	$18,000
Class II labor (1,000 DLH x $7.50)	7,500
Class V labor (500 DLH x $11.50)	5,750

256. The planned labor variance for January is

a. $6,455 unfavorable.
b. $3,618 unfavorable.
c. $5,355 favorable.
d. $3,758 unfavorable.

The correct answer is (a). *(Publisher)*
REQUIRED: The planned labor variance for January.
DISCUSSION: The planned labor variance is the difference between the normal labor cost and the expected labor cost.

Normal labor cost [42,750 x ($58 ÷ 100)]		$24,795
Expected labor cost		
Class I labor (3,000 DLH x $6.00)	$18,000	
Class II labor (1,000 DLH x $7.50)	7,500	
Class V labor (500 DLH x $11.50)	5,750	31,250
Total planned labor variance		$ 6,455 U

Module 13.8: Comprehensive

Questions 257 through 268 are based on the following information, which was presented as part of Question 4 on the Practice II section of the November 1981 CPA examination.

Armando Corporation manufactures a product with the following standard costs:

Direct materials (20 yards x $1.35 per yard)	$27
Direct labor (4 hours x $9.00 per hour)	36
Factory overhead (applied at 5/6 of direct labor. Ratio of variable costs to fixed costs: 2 to 1)	30
Total standard cost per unit of output	$93

Standards are based on normal monthly production involving 2,400 DLH (600 units of output).

The following information pertains to the month of July:

Direct materials purchased (18,000 yards x $1.38 per yard)	$24,840
Direct materials used	9,500 yards
Direct labor (2,100 hours x $9.15 per hour)	$19,215
Actual factory overhead	$16,650

500 units of the product were actually produced in July.

257. The variable factory overhead rate per direct labor hour is

a. $10.
b. $5.
c. $20.
d. $8.

The correct answer is (b). *(Publisher)*
REQUIRED: The variable factory overhead rate per direct labor hour.
DISCUSSION: Remembering that the ratio of variable to fixed factory O/H is 2 to 1, then variable factory O/H must be $20. DLH/unit = 2,400 DLH ÷ 600 units of output = 4 DLH/unit. Thus, $20 ÷ 4 = $5/DLH variable factory O/H rate.

258. The total fixed factory overhead based on normal activity is

a. $4,970.
b. $6,400.
c. $5,600.
d. $6,000.

The correct answer is (d). *(Publisher)*
REQUIRED: The total fixed factory overhead based on normal activity.
DISCUSSION: Normal activity is scheduled to be 2,400 direct labor hours. Fixed factory overhead per direct labor hour is 1/3 of the total factory overhead rate (1/3 x $30 = $10) divided by 4 hours, or $2.50 per direct labor hour. $2.50 x 2,400 = $6,000.

259. The materials price variance (isolated at time of purchase) for the month ended July 31 is

a. $560 favorable.
b. $540 unfavorable.
c. $450 favorable.
d. $490 unfavorable.

The correct answer is (b). *(Publisher)*
REQUIRED: The materials price variance for the month of July.
DISCUSSION: The materials price variance is the difference between the standard cost of the materials purchased per unit and actual cost of the materials purchased per unit times the quantity actually purchased ($1.35/yard - $1.38/yard) x 18,000 yards = $540 U.

260. The materials usage variance for the month ended July 31 is

a. $695 favorable.
b. $650 unfavorable.
c. $675 favorable.
d. $756 favorable.

The correct answer is (c). *(Publisher)*
REQUIRED: The materials usage variance for the month of July.
DISCUSSION: The materials usage variance is the difference between the actual quantity used and the standard quantity allowed for the achieved production times the standard cost per unit.

(9,500 - $10,000*) x $1.35 = $675 F.

*Std. qty. allowed = 500 units x 20 yds. = 10,000 yds.

261. The labor rate variance for the month ended July 31 is

a. $315 unfavorable.
b. $426 favorable.
c. $384 unfavorable.
d. $351 favorable.

The correct answer is (a). *(Publisher)*
REQUIRED: The labor rate variance for the month of July.
DISCUSSION: The labor rate variance is the difference between the standard rate and the actual labor rate times the actual hours:

($9/hr. - $9.15/hr.) x 2,100 hrs. = $315 U.

Module 13.8: Comprehensive

262. The labor efficiency variance for the month ended July 31 is

a. $930 unfavorable.
b. $890 unfavorable.
c. $857 favorable.
d. $900 unfavorable.

The correct answer is (d). *(Publisher)*
REQUIRED: The labor efficiency variance for July.
DISCUSSION: The labor efficiency variance is the difference between the standard hours allowed and the actual hours used times the standard labor rate.

$$(2,000^* - 2,100) \times \$9 = \$900 \text{ U}$$

*Std. hrs. allowed = 500 units x 4 hrs./unit = 2,000 hrs.

263. Budgeted factory overhead at standard hours is

a. $16,000.
b. $10,000.
c. $14,000.
d. $18,000.

The correct answer is (a). *(Publisher)*
REQUIRED: The budgeted factory overhead at standard hours.
DISCUSSION: Budgeted factory overhead at standard hours is the fixed overhead budget plus the variable overhead budget at the normal activity level.

Fixed overhead (see Q. 258)	$ 6,000
Variable overhead (500 units x 4 hours x $5.00)	10,000
Budgeted factory overhead at standard hours	$16,000

264. The controllable factory overhead variance for the month ended July 31 is

a. $1,350 favorable.
b. $6,650 unfavorable.
c. $650 unfavorable.
d. $2,650 unfavorable.

The correct answer is (c). *(Publisher)*
REQUIRED: The controllable factory overhead variance.
DISCUSSION: The controllable factory overhead variance is the difference between the actual factory overhead and the budgeted factory overhead at the level achieved.

Actual total factory overhead	$16,650
Budgeted factory overhead at standard hours (see Q. 263)	16,000
Controllable factory overhead variance	$ 650 U

265. The total applied factory overhead is

a. $16,000.
b. $15,000.
c. $11,880.
d. $18,000.

The correct answer is (b). *(Publisher)*
REQUIRED: The total applied factory overhead.
DISCUSSION: Total applied factory overhead is the standard hours allowed for actual production achieved (500 units x 4 hrs./unit = 2,000) times the predetermined overhead rate (5/6 of direct labor x $9/hr. = $7.50):

$$2,000 \times \$7.50 = \$15,000$$

266. The factory overhead volume variance for the month ended July 31 is

a. $2,000 favorable.
b. $0.
c. $1,000 unfavorable.
d. $4,120 unfavorable.

The correct answer is (c). *(Publisher)*
REQUIRED: The production volume variance.
DISCUSSION: The production volume variance is the difference between budgeted factory overhead at standard hours and the applied factory overhead.

Budgeted factory overhead at standard hours (Q. 263)	$16,000
Applied total factory O/H (Q. 265)	15,000
Capacity factory O/H variance	$ 1,000 U

267. What are the standard costs of production?

a. $31,500.
b. $33,000.
c. $46,500.
d. $55,800.

The correct answer is (c). *(Publisher)*
REQUIRED: Standard cost of producing 500 units.
DISCUSSION: Standard unit cost of $93 times the 500 units is $46,500, which is the amount transferred from WIP to FG inventory.

Module 13.8: Comprehensive

268. Refer to the information at the top of page 392. What are the total actual costs of production?

a. $32,325.
b. $48,975.
c. $60,705.
d. $54,600.

The correct answer is (b). *(Publisher)*
REQUIRED: Actual cost of the 500 units.
DISCUSSION: The actual costs of direct labor and overhead are given. Material cost is that used (9,500 units x $1.38).

Material	$13,110
Labor	19,215
Overhead	16,650
Actual cost	$48,975

The difference between actual and standard cost of $2,475 ($48,975 - $46,500) is explained by the variances in Qs. 259, 260, 261, 262, 264, and 265, except that the material price variance (Q. 259) is recomputed for only the 9,500 yards actually used ($.03 price difference x 9,500).

Questions 269 through 274 are based on Dash Company, which adopted a standard cost system several years ago. The standard costs for the prime costs of its single product are as follows:

Material (8 kilograms x $5.00/kg.)	$40.00
Labor (6 hours x $8.20/hr.)	$49.20

The operating data in the opposite column were taken from the records for November:

- In-process beginning inventory - none.
- In-process ending inventory - 800 units, 75% complete as to labor; material is issued at the beginning of processing.
- Units completed - 5,600 units.
- Budgeted output - 6,000 units.
- Purchases of materials - 50,000 kilograms.
- Total actual labor costs - $300,760.
- Actual hours of labor - 36,500 hour.
- Material usage variance - $1,500 unfavorable.
- Total material variance - $750 unfavorable.

---

269. The labor efficiency variance for November is

a. $4,100 unfavorable.
b. $5,740 favorable.
c. $15,580 favorable.
d. $23,780 unfavorable.
e. None of the above.

The correct answer is (b). *(CMA 1281 4-2)*
REQUIRED: The labor efficiency variance.
DISCUSSION: The labor efficiency variance is the difference between the standard hours allowed times the standard rate and the actual hours used times the standard rate. Keep in mind that the EWIP is 75% complete as to labor, which is the equivalent of 600 units.

5,600 units + 800(.75) EWIP = 6,200 labor EUP

(SQ x SP) = 6,200 EUP x 6 hrs./unit x $8.20/hr. = $305,040
(AQ x SP) = 36,500 hrs. x $8.20/hr. = $299,300

$305,040 - $299,300 = $5,740 F

---

270. The labor rate variance for November is

a. $1,460 unfavorable.
b. $1,460 favorable.
c. $4,120 unfavorable.
d. $4,120 favorable.
e. None of the above.

The correct answer is (a). *(CMA 1281 4-1)*
REQUIRED: The labor rate variance for the month.
DISCUSSION: The labor rate variance is the difference between the actual cost of labor and actual hours at the standard price. The actual cost is given as $300,760. The actual hours are given as 36,500. The standard rate of $8.20 times 36,500 is $299,300.

$300,760 - $299,300 = $1,460 U

Module 13.8: Comprehensive

271. The actual kilograms of material used in the production process during November is

a. 45,100 kg.
b. 49,900 kg.
c. 50,000 kg.
d. 51,500 kg.
e. None of the above.

The correct answer is (d). *(CMA 1281 4-3)*
REQUIRED: The actual kilograms of material used in the production process.
DISCUSSION: Calculation of the actual kilograms of material requires working backward from the $1,500 unfavorable materials usage variance. First, calculate the number of kilograms at standard for the 5,600 units completed plus the 800 units in EWIP: 8 kg. x 6,400 units = 51,200 kg. The standard cost of material is 51,200 kg. x $5 = $256,000. Adding back the $1,500 unfavorable usage variance, actual cost at standard price must have been $257,500. Dividing by $5 per unit = 51,500 kgs. used in November.

272. The actual price paid per kilogram of material during November is

a. $4.495.
b. $4.985.
c. $5.015.
d. $5.135.
e. None of the above.

The correct answer is (b). *(CMA 1281 4-4)*
REQUIRED: The actual price paid per kilogram of material.
DISCUSSION: The materials usage variance was $1,500 unfavorable and the total material variance was $750 unfavorable, so the materials price variance must have been $750 favorable. The standard price ($5) times the actual quantity indicates that Dash should have paid $250,000, but the $750 favorable materials price variance indicates that $249,250 actually was paid for the 50,000 units. $249,250 ÷ 50,000 = $4.985 per unit.

273. The total amounts of material and labor cost transferred to the finished goods account for November is

a. $499,520.
b. $535,200.
c. $550,010.
d. $561,040.
e. None of the above.

The correct answer is (a). *(CMA 1281 4-5)*
REQUIRED: The total amounts of material and labor cost transferred to finished goods.
DISCUSSION: The total amounts of material and labor transferred to finished goods is the number of units transferred times the standard cost per unit: 5,600 units x $89.20 = $499,520.

274. The total amount of material and labor cost in the ending balance of work-in-process inventory at the end of November is

a. $0.
b. $9,840.
c. $61,520.
d. $71,360.
e. None of the above.

The correct answer is (c). *(CMA 1281 4-6)*
REQUIRED: The total amount of material and labor in EWIP.
DISCUSSION: Ending work-in-process consists of the materials and labor left in the account after transfer. There are 800 units that are 100% complete as to materials and are 75% complete as to labor.

Materials: 800 units x $40/unit	$32,000
Labor: 800 units x .75 x $49.20/unit	29,520
	$61,520

Questions 275 through 284 are based on Cain Company, which has an automated production process, and consequently, machine hours are used to describe production activity. A full absorption costing system is employed by the company. The annual profit plan for the coming fiscal year is finalized in April of each year. The profit plan for the fiscal year ending May 31 called for 6,000 units to be produced, requiring 30,000 machine hours. The full absorption costing rate for the fiscal year was determined using 6,000 units of planned production.

Cain develops flexible budgets for different levels of activity for use in evaluating performance. A total of 6,200 units were actually produced during the fiscal year requiring 32,000 machine hours. The schedule presented below compares Cain Company's actual costs for the fiscal year with the profit plan and the budgeted costs for two different activity levels.

Cain Company
Manufacturing Cost Report
For the Fiscal Year Ended May 31
(in thousands of dollars)

Item	Profit Plan (6,000 units)	Flexible Budgets for 31,000 Machine Hours	Flexible Budgets for 32,000 Machine Hours	Actual Costs
Direct material				
G27 aluminum	$252.0	$260.4	$268.8	$270.0
M14 steel alloy	78.0	80.6	83.2	83.0
Direct labor				
Assembler	273.0	282.1	291.2	287.0
Grinder	234.0	241.8	249.6	250.0
Manufacturing overhead				
Maintenance	24.0	24.8	25.6	25.0
Supplies	129.0	133.3	137.6	130.0
Supervision	80.0	82.0	84.0	81.0
Inspector	144.0	147.0	150.0	147.0
Insurance	50.0	50.0	50.0	50.0
Depreciation	200.0	200.0	200.0	200.0
Total cost	$1,464.0	$1,502.0	$1,540.0	$1,523.0

275. The actual cost of material used in one unit of product is

a. $55.00.
b. $56.77.
c. $58.83.
d. $56.94.
e. None of the above.

The correct answer is (d). *(CMA 682 4-2)*
REQUIRED: The actual cost of material used in one unit of product.
DISCUSSION: The actual (not budgeted) cost of material used in one unit of product is the sum of the actual costs of each of the materials used divided by the number of units produced.

Actual costs: $270,000 (G27) + $83,000 (M14) = $353,000
$353,000 ÷ 6,200 units = $56.94 per unit

276. The cost of material that should be processed per machine hour is

a. $11.00.
b. $11.03.
c. $10.66.
d. $10.31.
e. None of the above.

The correct answer is (a). *(CMA 682 4-3)*
REQUIRED: The cost of material that should be processed per machine hour.
DISCUSSION: The cost of both materials divided by the budgeted machine hours equals the cost of material per machine hour. For example, at 32,000 hours:

$352,000 ÷ 32,000 machine hours = $11/machine hour

Or, at 31,000 hours:

$341,000 ÷ 31,000 machine hours = $11/machine hour

Module 13.8: Comprehensive

277. The budgeted direct labor cost for each unit produced is

a. $81.77/unit.
b. $86.61/unit.
c. $87.23/unit.
d. $84.50/unit.
e. None of the above.

The correct answer is (d). *(CMA 682 4-4)*
REQUIRED: The budgeted direct labor cost for each unit produced.
DISCUSSION: The budgeted direct labor cost for each unit produced is equal to the total labor cost divided by the budgeted number of units. At 30,000 hours (6,000 units), total budgeted direct labor cost was $273,000 + $234,000 = $507,000. $507,000 ÷ 6,000 units = $84.50 per unit.

278. The variable manufacturing overhead rate per machine hour in a flexible budget formula would be

a. $12.41.
b. $10.10.
c. $48.13.
d. $48.80.
e. None of the above.

The correct answer is (b). *(CMA 682 4-5)*
REQUIRED: The variable manufacturing O/H rate per machine hour in a flexible budget.
DISCUSSION: Variable manufacturing O/H consists of maintenance, supplies, supervision, and inspection. Note that insurance and depreciation do not change with the activity level. Comparing these totals for the profit plan and the two budgeted activity levels (increment of $20,200 lowest to highest) with the 2,000-hour increment in activity level gives the variable manufacturing O/H rate.

30,000 hr.	31,000 hr.	32,000 hr.
$ 24.0	$ 24.8	$ 25.6
129.0	133.3	137.6
80.0	82.0	84.0
144.0	147.0	150.0
$377.0	$387.1	$397.2

$20,200 ÷ 2,000 = $10.10/machine hr.

279. The manufacturing overhead volume variance for the current year is

a. $14,900 unfavorable.
b. $21,600 favorable.
c. $10,800 favorable.
d. $0.
e. None of the above.

The correct answer is (c). *(CMA 682 4-7)*
REQUIRED: The manufacturing overhead volume variance for the current year.
DISCUSSION: First, compute the variable cost of each component of manufacturing overhead, i.e., the change in estimated cost per 1,000 hours of activity. Then, fixed O/H = total O/H - variable O/H. For maintenance, the O/H change is $.8 x 30,000 machine hours = $24,000, which is the full maintenance budget; i.e., there is no fixed component. The same is true of supplies of $4.3/1,000 hours. Supervision, however, at $2.0 times 30,000 hours equals $60,000, not $80,000; i.e., there is $20,000 of fixed costs. Inspection at $3.0 per 1,000 results in $90,000, not $144,000, for $54,000 of fixed costs. Insurance and depreciation are completely fixed costs. Total fixed manufacturing overhead is $324,000, as computed below.

Supervision	$ 20,000
Inspector	54,000
Insurance	50,000
Depreciation	200,000
Total fixed cost	$324,000

The predetermined overhead rate was set at the 30,000-hour level. The total fixed manufacturing overhead divided by the activity level gives a predetermined overhead rate of $10.80. 6,200 units were produced this year, giving standard hours allowed of 31,000 hours (6,200 units x 5 DLH/unit). Thus, 1,000 hours of fixed overhead in excess of that estimated (30,000) resulted in a $10,800 favorable volume variance.

$10.80 x 1,000 hours = $10,800 F

Module 13.8: Comprehensive

> Questions 280 through 284 are based on the information preceding Q. 275.

280. Cain Company calculates spending, efficiency, and volume variances when analyzing manufacturing overhead costs. The manufacturing overhead spending variance for the year is

a. $4,100 favorable.
b. $14,200 favorable.
c. $6,000 unfavorable.
d. $10,100 unfavorable.
e. None of the above.

The correct answer is (b). *(CMA 682 4-6)*
REQUIRED: The manufacturing overhead spending variance for the year.
DISCUSSION: The manufacturing overhead spending variance is the difference between actual overhead cost and budgeted overhead cost in the flexible budget.

Actual	Budget	
25.0	25.6	-0.6
130.0	137.6	-7.6
81.0	84.0	-3.0
147.0	150.0	-3.0
50.0	50.0	0
200.0	200.0	0
633.0	647.2	14.2 F

281. The manufacturing overhead efficiency variance is

a. $10,800 favorable.
b. $14,900 unfavorable.
c. $21,600 unfavorable.
d. $10,100 unfavorable.
e. $0.

The correct answer is (d). *(Publisher)*
REQUIRED: The overhead efficiency variance.
DISCUSSION: The efficiency variance is actual hours less standard hours times the standard rate. It is also the difference between actual hours x standard rate minus variable O/H applied (the latter being standard hours times standard rate for the actual units produced). The standard hours for 6,200 units are 31,000 (6,200 x 5). The actual hours are 32,000. The efficiency variance is $10.10/hr. x 1,000 hours, or $10,100.

282. How much overhead was applied to finished goods?

a. $633,000.
b. $647,900.
c. $668,800.
d. $653,900.

The correct answer is (b). *(Publisher)*
REQUIRED: The amount of overhead applied to finished goods.
DISCUSSION: Overhead is applied on the basis of $20.90 per standard hour ($10.10 variable from Q. 278 and $10.80 fixed from Q. 279). 6,200 units were produced at 5 standard hours, which total 31,000 hours.

31,000 hours x $20.90 = $647,900

283. What is the total overhead variance?

a. $0.
b. $14,900 favorable.
c. $35,800 unfavorable.
d. $20,900 favorable.

The correct answer is (b). *(Publisher)*
REQUIRED: The amount of the total overhead variance.
DISCUSSION: The actual overhead is $633,000 (Q. 280), and standard applied overhead is $647,900 (Q. 282). The difference is $14,900.

Spending	$14,200 F
Volume	10,800 F
Efficiency	10,100 U
Total O/H variance	$14,900 F

284. Using the flexible budget formula, the total budgeted manufacturing cost (in thousands of dollars) for an output of 6,050 units would be

a. $1,486.15.
b. $1,476.20.
c. $1,465.66.
d. $1,473.50.
e. None of the above.

The correct answer is (d). *(CMA 682 4-9)*
REQUIRED: The total budgeted manufacturing cost for a given output.
DISCUSSION: The total budgeted manufacturing cost for an output of 6,050 units is the sum of the fixed costs plus the variable cost times the level of activity. Variable cost equals $190 per unit (the change in total cost per 1,000 units (38) times 5 machine hours per unit). Fixed costs are computed in Q. 279. Total manufacturing cost equals

$324,000 + ($190 x 6,050 units) = $1,473,500

CHAPTER FOURTEEN
RESPONSIBILITY ACCOUNTING

> 14.1 Basic Concepts .... (38 questions) 399
> 14.2 Decentralization and Transfer Pricing .... (21 questions) 409
> 14.3 Comprehensive .... (43 questions) 416

This chapter takes the idea of standard costs and flexible budgets one step further by addressing responsibility accounting and divisional performance in decentralized operations. Transfer pricing among divisions of the same organization is covered, with emphasis on the concept that no single correct transfer price can be found for the firm because of the many subjective issues involved.

14.1 Basic Concepts

1. What term identifies an accounting system in which the operations of the business are broken down into cost centers and the control function of a foreperson, sales manager, or supervisor is emphasized?

   a. Responsibility accounting.
   b. Operations-research accounting.
   c. Control accounting.
   d. Budgetary accounting.

The correct answer is (a). *(CPA 575 T-21)*
REQUIRED: The accounting system in which operations are broken into cost centers.
DISCUSSION: Responsibility accounting stresses that managers should only be held responsible for factors under their control. To achieve this, the operations of the business are broken down into responsibility centers.
   Answer (b) is incorrect because operations-research accounting deals with quantitative optimization methods such as linear programming and inventory models. Answer (c) is incorrect because control accounting accounts for all costs allocated to a cost center as opposed to those for which the cost center is responsible. Answer (d) is incorrect because budgetary accounting uses budgets and compares actual results to the budgeted goals.

2. The Atwood Company uses a performance reporting system that reflects the company's decentralization of decision making. The departmental performance report shows one line of data for each subordinate who reports to the group vice president. The data presented shows the actual costs incurred during the period, the budgeted costs, and all variances from budget for that subordinate's department. The Atwood Company is using a type of system called

   a. Flexible budgeting.
   b. Responsibility accounting.
   c. Contribution accounting.
   d. Cost-benefit accounting.
   e. Program budgeting.

The correct answer is (b). *(CMA 686 4-15)*
REQUIRED: The system used in a company with decentralized decision making.
DISCUSSION: Responsibility accounting stresses that managers should only be held responsible for factors under their control. To achieve this, the operations of the business are broken down into responsibility centers. Costs are classified as controllable and noncontrollable to assign responsibility. The assignment of responsibility implies that some revenues and costs can be changed through effective management. A responsibility accounting system should have certain controls which provide for feedback reports indicating deviations from expectations. Management may then focus on those deviations for either reinforcement or correction.
   Answer (a) is incorrect because nothing indicates whether a flexible budget is used. Answer (c) is incorrect because contribution reporting emphasizes the contribution margin provided by department or product. Answer (d) is incorrect because nothing indicates whether the system is cost beneficial. Answer (e) is incorrect because program budgeting is a system in which budgets are prepared by program rather than by line item costs (such as salaries or supplies).

Module 14.1: Basic Concepts

3. In a responsibility accounting system, costs are classified into categories on the basis of

a. Fixed and variable costs.
b. Prime and overhead costs.
c. Administrative and nonadministrative costs.
d. Controllable and noncontrollable costs.
e. Direct and indirect costs.

The correct answer is (d). *(CIA 582 IV-24)*
REQUIRED: The cost classification used in a responsibility accounting system.
DISCUSSION: In a responsibility accounting system, costs are classified as controllable and noncontrollable to assign responsibility. The assignment of responsibility implies that some revenues and costs can be changed through effective management.
Answers (a), (b), (c), and (e) are incorrect because each may be controllable or noncontrollable costs in a responsibility accounting system.

4. Segmented income statements are most meaningful to managers when they are prepared

a. On an absorption cost basis.
b. On a cost behavior basis.
c. On a cash basis.
d. In a single-step format.
e. In a multiple-step format.

The correct answer is (b). *(CMA 686 4-13)*
REQUIRED: The most meaningful way of preparing segmented statements.
DISCUSSION: Statements that categorize costs by behavior are most meaningful since they permit analysis of the effects of certain changes in production and volume. The behavior of costs may be fixed, variable, mixed, or semifixed.
Answer (a) is incorrect because the allocation of fixed costs to segments may be too arbitrary to make absorption statements useful. Answer (c) is incorrect because accrual basis statements are more useful than cash basis statements. Answers (d) and (e) are incorrect because the possible advantages of the multiple-step format are more significant for outsiders than for insiders who have the additional information available.

5. A segment of an organization is referred to as a profit center if it has

a. Authority to make decisions affecting the major determinants of profit, including the power to choose its markets and sources of supply.
b. Authority to make decisions affecting the major determinants of profit, including the power to choose its markets and sources of supply and significant control over the amount of invested capital.
c. Authority to make decisions over the most significant costs of operations, including the power to choose the sources of supply.
d. Authority to provide specialized support to other units within the organization.
e. Responsibility for combining material, labor, and other factors of production into a final output.

The correct answer is (a). *(CMA 679 4-1)*
REQUIRED: The authority required for a segment of an organization to be a profit center.
DISCUSSION: A profit center is a segment of a company responsible for both revenues and expenses. A profit center has the authority to make decisions concerning markets (revenues) and sources of supply (costs).
Answer (b) is incorrect because it describes an investment center, which is responsible for revenues, expenses, and the amount of invested capital. Answer (c) is incorrect because it describes a cost center. Answer (d) is incorrect because it describes a service center, which provides specialized support to other units of the organization. Answer (e) is incorrect because it describes a production center, which combines labor, material, and other factors of production into a final output.

Module 14.1: Basic Concepts

6. A segment of an organization is referred to as an investment center if it has

a. Authority to make decisions affecting the major determinants of profit, including the power to choose its markets and sources of supply.

b. Authority to make decisions affecting the major determinants of profit, including the power to choose its markets and sources of supply and significant control over the amount of invested capital.

c. Authority to make decisions over the most significant costs of operations, including the power to choose the sources of supply.

d. Authority to provide specialized support to other units within the organization.

e. Responsibility for developing markets for and selling the output of the organization.

The correct answer is (b). *(CMA 679 4-2)*
REQUIRED: The authority required for a segment to be an investment center.
DISCUSSION: In investment centers, managers are responsible for all activities, including costs, revenues, and investments. An investment center is a profit center with significant control over the amount of capital invested. This includes control over making investments such as receivables and property, plant, and equipment, as well as entry into new markets.
Answer (a) is incorrect because it describes a profit center, which is responsible for controlling expenses and generating revenues. Answer (c) is incorrect because it describes a cost center, which has authority only over the sources of supply. Answer (d) is incorrect because it describes a service center, which provides specialized support to other units of the organization. Answer (e) is incorrect because it describes a revenue center, which is responsible for developing markets and selling the firm's products.

7. The segment margin of the Wire Division of Lerner Corporation would not include

a. Net sales of the Wire Division.

b. Fixed selling expenses of the Wire Division.

c. Variable selling expenses of the Wire Division.

d. The Wire Division's fair share of the salary of Lerner Corporation's president.

e. Variable manufacturing costs of the Wire Division.

The correct answer is (d). *(CMA 686 4-14)*
REQUIRED: The item not included in a statement showing segment margin.
DISCUSSION: As defined in Statement on Management Accounting 2, "Management Accounting Terminology," segment margin is the contribution margin for each segment of a business less all separable fixed costs, both discretionary and committed. It is a measure of long-run profitability. Thus, an allocation of the corporate president's salary would not be included in segment margin because it is neither a variable cost nor a separable fixed cost.
Answer (a) is incorrect because sales of the division would appear on the statement. Answer (b) is incorrect because the division's fixed selling expenses are separable fixed costs. Answers (c) and (e) are incorrect because variable costs of the division are included.

8. In a responsibility accounting system, a feedback report that focuses on the difference between budgeted amounts and actual amounts is an example of

a. Management by exception.

b. Assessing blame.

c. Granting rewards to successful managers.

d. Ignoring other variables for which the budgeted goals were met.

The correct answer is (a). *(Publisher)*
REQUIRED: The term for feedback reports that focus on changes between budgeted and actual amounts.
DISCUSSION: A responsibility accounting system should have certain controls which provide for feedback reports indicating deviations from expectations. Management may then focus on those deviations for either reinforcement or correction.
Answers (b) and (c) are incorrect because the responsibility accounting system should not be used exclusively to assess blame or to give rewards. Answer (d) is incorrect because feedback reports concentrate on deviations, but not to the total exclusion of other budgeted variables.

Module 14.1: Basic Concepts

9. When used for performance evaluation, periodic internal reports based on a responsibility accounting system should not

a. Be related to the organization chart.
b. Include allocated fixed overhead.
c. Include variances between actual and budgeted controllable costs.
d. Distinguish between controllable and noncontrollable costs.

The correct answer is (b). *(CPA 1173 T-33)*
REQUIRED: The item not a feature of internal reports based on responsibility accounting.
DISCUSSION: Allocated fixed overhead should not be included in internal reports based on a responsibility accounting system because it cannot be controlled by a manager of a cost or profit center.
Answer (a) is incorrect because the organizational chart, which outlines the authority/responsibility chain of a company, is an integral part of the responsibility accounting system. Answer (c) is incorrect because a main purpose of internal reports is to show the variances between actual and budgeted controllable costs so corrective action can be taken when and where needed. Answer (d) is incorrect because, in responsibility accounting, managers are only held responsible for costs they have the authority to control.

10. Costs are accumulated by a responsibility center for control purposes when using

	Job Order Costing	Process Costing
a.	Yes	Yes
b.	Yes	No
c.	No	No
d.	No	Yes

The correct answer is (a). *(CPA 1186 T-42)*
REQUIRED: The product costing method that uses responsibility centers to accumulate costs.
DISCUSSION: A responsibility center is a subunit (part or segment) of an organization whose manager is accountable for a specified set of activities. Job order and process costing may both accumulate their costs by responsibility centers.

11. The format for internal reports in a responsibility accounting system is prescribed by

a. Generally accepted accounting principles.
b. The Financial Accounting Standards Board.
c. The American Institute of Certified Public Accountants.
d. Management.

The correct answer is (d). *(Publisher)*
REQUIRED: The source of authority for the format of internal reports.
DISCUSSION: The responsibility for internal reports is management's. Management may direct the accountant to provide a report in any format deemed suitable for the decision process. The accountant should work closely with management to make these reports an effective communication device regarding the firm and its decisions.
Answers (a), (b), and (c) are incorrect because each concerns external financial reporting, not internal reporting.

12. The report to a territorial sales manager which shows the contribution to profit by each salesperson in the territory is called

a. A profit report.
b. An absorption profit report.
c. A gross profit report.
d. A distribution report.
e. A responsibility report.

The correct answer is (e). *(CMA 1279 4-5)*
REQUIRED: The report that shows the contribution to profit by each salesperson.
DISCUSSION: In a responsibility accounting system, the responsibility report attributes revenues and expenses to the persons responsible for them. Thus, a report showing the profit contribution by each salesperson in a territory is a responsibility report.
Answer (a) is incorrect because a profit report is a more general report. Answer (b) is incorrect because reports based on absorption accounting allocate fixed overhead which cannot be controlled. Answer (c) is incorrect because all controllable costs are allocated to profit centers or individuals in a responsibility report, while the gross profit report allocates only the product costs. Answer (d) is incorrect because a distribution report shows the movement of product units rather than product revenues and expenses.

Module 14.1: Basic Concepts

13. Overtime conditions and pay were recently set by the personnel department. The production department has just received a request for a rush order from the sales department. The production department protests that additional overtime costs would be incurred as a result of the order. The sales department argues the order is from an important customer. The production department processes the order. In order to control costs, which department should be charged with the overtime costs generated as a result of the rush order?

   a. Personnel department.
   b. Production department.
   c. Sales department.
   d. Shared by production department and sales department.

The correct answer is (c). *(CIA 587 IV-15)*
REQUIRED: The department charged with overtime generated by a rush order.
DISCUSSION: Managerial performance should be evaluated only on the basis of those factors controllable by the manager. Managers may control revenues, costs, and/or investment in resources. A well-designed responsibility accounting system establishes responsibility centers within the organization. The sales department should therefore be responsible for the overtime costs because it can best judge whether the additional cost of the rush order is justified. The IIA also gave credit for answers (b) and (d) since charging the full overtime cost to the sales department would give the production department no incentive to control those costs.

Answer (a) is incorrect because the personnel department has no effect on the incurrence of production overtime.

14. A production manager would normally be responsible for which of the following?

	A	B	C	D
Direct labor	X	X		
Direct materials	X	X	X	
Sales materials				X
Advertising costs				X
Indirect factory materials	X	X		X
Indirect labor	X	X	X	X
Sales commissions				X
Factory utilities	X	X		X
Administrative supplies expense	X			
Administrative labor	X			
Depreciation on administration building			X	
Cost of research on customer demographics			X	

   a. A.
   b. B.
   c. C.
   d. D.

The correct answer is (b). *(CIA 1187 IV-53)*
REQUIRED: The items for which a production manager would normally be responsible.
DISCUSSION: A production manager would normally be responsible for the costs of producing the product (product costs). These include direct labor, direct materials, and factory overhead (such as indirect labor, indirect materials, and factory utilities). The other items listed are period costs.

Answers (a), (c), and (d) are incorrect because a production manager is not customarily responsible for period costs.

15. Micro Manufacturers uses an accounting system that charges costs to the manager who has been delegated the authority to make the decisions incurring the costs. For example, if the sales manager accepts a rush order that requires the incurrence of additional manufacturing costs, these additional costs are charged to the sales manager because the authority to accept or decline the rush order was given to the sales manager. This type of accounting system is known as

   a. Functional accounting.
   b. Contribution accounting.
   c. Reciprocal allocation.
   d. Transfer price accounting.
   e. Profitability accounting.

The correct answer is (e). *(CMA 686 4-16)*
REQUIRED: The accounting system in which costs are charged to managers with authority to incur the costs.
DISCUSSION: Profitability accounting is accounting for profit centers. When sales managers have the authority and responsibility to control costs, they are a profit center.

Answer (a) is incorrect because a functional accounting system is one in which costs are accumulated by the nature of the function performed. Answer (b) is incorrect because contribution accounting is a system in which costs are divided according to whether they are fixed or variable. Answer (c) is incorrect because reciprocal allocation is a method of allocating service department costs to producing departments. Answer (d) is incorrect because transfer price accounting is the process of charging other departments for transfers between departments.

Module 14.1: Basic Concepts

16. A management decision may be beneficial for a given profit center, but not for the entire company. From the overall company viewpoint, this decision would lead to

  a. Suboptimization.
  b. Centralization.
  c. Goal congruence.
  d. Maximization.

The correct answer is (a). *(CPA 576 T-40)*
REQUIRED: The effect when a decision benefits a profit center but not the company.
DISCUSSION: Suboptimization occurs when one segment of a company takes an action which benefits itself but not the firm as a whole.
Answer (b) is incorrect because centralization describes the extent to which decision-making authority is centered in a few individuals. Answer (c) is incorrect because goal congruence occurs when the goals of subordinates and top managers are shared. Answer (d) is incorrect because maximization is the quantitative or qualitative achievement of the best results by choosing an action.

17. In a responsibility accounting system, the process in which a supervisor and a subordinate jointly determine the subordinate's goals and plans for achieving these goals is

  a. Top-down budgeting.
  b. Bottom-up budgeting.
  c. Imposed budgeting.
  d. Management by objectives.

The correct answer is (d). *(Publisher)*
REQUIRED: The process of joint determination of a subordinate's goals.
DISCUSSION: The management by objectives (MBO) approach is a procedure in which a subordinate and a supervisor agree on goals and the methods of achieving them and develop a plan in accordance with that agreement. The subordinate is then evaluated with reference to the plan at the end of the plan period.
Answers (a) and (c) are incorrect because a top-down budget is generated by top management and distributed to (imposed on) lower-level managers. Answer (b) is incorrect because a bottom-up budget is generated by lower-level management and aggregated as it moves through the chain of command.

18. A company built a plant to produce a new product. Which of the decisions below is now probably the most important that management will have to make?

  a. What profit to make.
  b. What costs to incur.
  c. What customers to accept.
  d. What price to charge.
  e. What return on capital to receive.

The correct answer is (d). *(CIA 581 IV-19)*
REQUIRED: The most important decision after building a plant to produce a new product.
DISCUSSION: Determining what price to charge is the most important decision because the price affects the number of units produced, the profit made, and the return on capital.
Answers (a) and (e) are incorrect because each will be determined by the price charged. Answer (b) is incorrect because the major costs have already been incurred in readying the plant for production. Answer (c) is incorrect because choosing customers is not as important as determining price.

19. The most desirable measure of departmental performance for evaluating the departmental manager is departmental

  a. Revenue less controllable departmental expenses.
  b. Net income.
  c. Contribution to indirect expenses.
  d. Revenue less departmental variable expenses.

The correct answer is (a). *(CPA 573 T-24)*
REQUIRED: The most desirable measure of departmental performance.
DISCUSSION: The most desirable measure for evaluating a departmental manager is one that holds the manager responsible for the revenues and expenses (s)he can control. This is the basic concept of responsibility accounting.
Answer (b) is incorrect because net income includes fixed and general administrative expenses over which the manager has no control. Answer (c) is incorrect because some indirect expenses may not be controllable by the manager, (e.g., general administration). Answer (d) is incorrect because some variable expenses may not be controllable by the manager, while some nonvariable expenses may be.

Module 14.1: Basic Concepts

20. Of little or no relevance in evaluating the performance of an activity would be

   a. Flexible budgets for mixed costs.
   b. Fixed budgets for mixed costs.
   c. The difference between planned and actual results.
   d. The planning and control of future activities.

The correct answer is (b). *(CPA 571 T-38)*
REQUIRED: The item of little or no relevance in evaluating performance of an activity.
DISCUSSION: Evaluating performance would be difficult if fixed budgets were used for mixed costs because the respective amounts of fixed and variable costs could not be determined. When evaluating the performance of an activity, only variable costs are relevant, i.e., those that fluctuate with production. The fixed costs are irrelevant because they will not vary regardless of the quality of performance.
Answer (a) is incorrect because flexible budgets of mixed costs permit separation of fixed and variable costs. Answer (c) is incorrect because analyzing variances is one of the primary means of evaluating performance. Answer (d) is incorrect because planning and control are the purposes of the budgeting process, which requires evaluation of performance.

21. Internal reports prepared under the responsibility accounting approach should be limited to which of the following costs?

   a. Only variable costs of production.
   b. Only conversion costs.
   c. Only controllable costs.
   d. Only costs properly allocable to the cost center under generally accepted accounting principles.

The correct answer is (c). *(CPA 1178 T-47)*
REQUIRED: The costs included in internal reports prepared under the responsibility accounting approach.
DISCUSSION: Internal reports prepared under the responsibility accounting approach should be based on controllable costs. In responsibility accounting, managers are only responsible for revenues and expenses that they can control.
Answer (a) is incorrect because all such variable costs may not be controlled by the manager, who may also control costs which are not variable. Answer (b) is incorrect because conversion costs include factory overhead, which is not a controllable cost. Answer (d) is incorrect because noncontrollable costs may be allocated under GAAP.

22. Of most relevance in deciding how or which costs should be assigned to a responsibility center is the degree of

   a. Avoidability.
   b. Causality.
   c. Controllability.
   d. Variability.

The correct answer is (c). *(CPA 571 T-35)*
REQUIRED: The most relevant variable in assigning costs to a responsibility center.
DISCUSSION: Costs should be assigned to a responsibility center based on controllability by the individual manager. The allocation should recognize that certain costs are controllable at one level but become noncontrollable at others.
Answer (a) is incorrect because avoidable costs are those saved by not choosing a given alternative. A manager will control costs other than those (s)he can avoid. Answer (b) is incorrect because, while a cause and effect relationship may exist between the activity managed and a given cost, the cost may not be controllable. Answer (d) is incorrect because a manager may control costs that are not variable.

23. The measure of employee attitude toward objectives which is most relevant in participative budgeting is the level of

   a. Absorption.
   b. Appreciation.
   c. Arbitrariness.
   d. Aspiration.

The correct answer is (d). *(CPA 571 T-37)*
REQUIRED: The attitude toward objectives most relevant to participative budgeting.
DISCUSSION: The participative budgeting process should link employee attitudes toward company objectives to the aspirations of the individuals. The greater the degree of congruence between the individuals' aspirations and company objectives, the greater the motivation toward successful completion of these objectives.

24. Which of the following items of cost would be least likely to appear in a performance report based on responsibility accounting techniques for the supervisor of an assembly line in a large manufacturing situation?

    a. Supervisor's salary.
    b. Materials.
    c. Repairs and maintenance.
    d. Direct labor.

The correct answer is (a). *(CPA 579 T-34)*
REQUIRED: The cost least likely to appear in a performance report based on responsibility accounting techniques.
DISCUSSION: Responsibility accounting holds managers responsible only for costs or revenues they can control. A supervisor's own salary is usually not considered a controllable cost in the short run.
Answers (b), (c), and (d) are incorrect because a line supervisor can exert at least some control over each of these elements of cost.

25. Which of the following would least likely be included in a marketing department's performance report?

    a. Budgeted sales revenue.
    b. Standard variable cost of goods sold.
    c. Actual sales revenue.
    d. Actual absorption cost of goods sold.

The correct answer is (d). *(CIA 583 IV-2)*
REQUIRED: The data least likely to appear in a marketing department's performance report.
DISCUSSION: The report should include standard variable rather than actual absorption cost of goods sold. In performance reports, only controllable costs are charged to profit or activity centers. The marketing department has no control over the cost of production.
Answers (a) and (c) are incorrect because the comparison of budgeted with actual sales revenue is an index of the marketing department's performance. Answer (b) is incorrect because the contribution margin included in the report is the difference between the standard variable cost of goods sold and the selling price.

26. Manor Company plans to discontinue a department with a contribution to overhead of $24,000 and allocated overhead of $48,000, of which $21,000 cannot be eliminated. The effect of this discontinuance on Manor's pretax profit would be a(n)

    a. Decrease of $3,000.
    b. Increase of $3,000.
    c. Decrease of $24,000.
    d. Increase of $24,000.

The correct answer is (b). *(CPA 1182 Q-21)*
REQUIRED: The effect on pretax profit of discontinuing a department given its overhead cost and contribution to overhead.
DISCUSSION: The departmental report indicates a $24,000 operating loss ($24,000 contribution to earnings minus $48,000 overhead). If the department were eliminated, the net loss would be $21,000 ($0 contribution - $21,000 overhead). Thus, net income would be increased by $3,000.

27. In evaluating a profit center or an investment center, top management should concentrate on

    a. Dollar sales.
    b. Net income.
    c. Profit percentages.
    d. Return on investment.

The correct answer is (d). *(Publisher)*
REQUIRED: The area on which management should concentrate in evaluating a segment.
DISCUSSION: Each segment of a business should be evaluated based upon return on investment to judge operating performance. ROI is comparable to calculations made both within and without a particular organization. Management may review the investment opportunities available within or without the firm. In essence, net income is stated as a proportion of investment capital.
Answers (a), (b), and (c) are incorrect because none gives a measure of operating performance based on resources required.

Module 14.1: Basic Concepts

28. A major problem in comparing profitability measures among companies is the

a. Lack of general agreement over which profitability measure is best.
b. Differences in the size of the companies.
c. Differences in the accounting methods used by the companies.
d. Differences in the dividend policies of the companies.
e. Effect of interest rates on net income.

The correct answer is (c). *(CMA 685 4-11)*
REQUIRED: A major problem in profitability comparisons.
DISCUSSION: The use of different accounting methods impairs comparability. Consequently, financial statements must be adjusted to permit intercompany comparisons.
Answer (a) is incorrect because, even if a general agreement were reached, different accounting methods would still impair comparability. Answers (b), (d), and (e) are incorrect because none directly affects the measure of a company's profitability to the same extent as the choice of accounting principles.

29. The return on investment calculation only considers the following components:

S = Sales
I = Investment
NI = Net income

Which of the following formulas best describes the return on investment calculation?

a. $(I \div S) \times (S \div NI) = I \div NI$.
b. $(S \div I) \times (NI \div S) = NI \div I$.
c. $(I \div S) \times (NI \div S) = (I \times NI) \times (S \times S)$.
d. $(S \div I) \times (S \div NI) = (S \times S) \div (I \times NI)$.

The correct answer is (b). *(Publisher)*
REQUIRED: The formula for return on investment.
DISCUSSION: The first term in the formula for return on investment is sales divided by the investment (the number of times the investment capital has turned over through the sales mechanism). This amount is multiplied by the net income expressed as a percentage of sales (NI ÷ S) to give the return on investment (net income divided by investment). The basic formula for return on investment is thus $(S \div I) \times (NI \div S) = NI \div I$.

30. A company's return on investment is affected by a change in

	Capital Turnover	Profit Margin on Sales
a.	Yes	Yes
b.	Yes	No
c.	No	No
d.	No	Yes

The correct answer is (a). *(CPA 1185 T-49)*
REQUIRED: The item(s) that affect return on investment (ROI).
DISCUSSION: The basic formula for ROI is $(S \div I) \times (NI \div S) = NI \div I$. See Q. 29 for definition of S, I, and NI. The first term in the equation represents the number of times the invested capital has turned over through the sales mechanism. The second term in the equation represents the profit margin on sales. Thus, ROI is affected by both capital turnover and profit margin on sales.

31. The return on investment (ROI) ratio measures

a. Only asset turnover.
b. Only earnings as a percent of sales.
c. Both asset turnover and earnings as a percent of sales.
d. Asset turnover and earnings as a percent of sales, correcting for the effects of differing depreciation methods.

The correct answer is (c). *(CIA 584 IV-24)*
REQUIRED: The definition of what is measured by the ROI ratio.
DISCUSSION: If one knows earnings (profit margin) as a percent of sales (net income/sales) and asset turnover (sales/average total assets), one can compute the rate of return on total assets (net income/average total assets).
Answers (a) and (b) are incorrect because, individually, each is incomplete. Answer (d) is incorrect because no adjustment is indicated for differing depreciation methods. ROI is more accurate, however, if a correction is made for the effects of using different depreciation methods. Depreciation affects both the numerator and the denominator of the ratio.

Module 14.1: Basic Concepts

32. Which of the following will not improve return on investment if other factors are constant?

   a. Decreasing expenses.
   b. Decreasing assets.
   c. Increasing selling prices.
   d. Increasing sales volume while holding fixed expenses constant.
   e. None of the above.

The correct answer is (e). *(Publisher)*
REQUIRED: The decision that does not improve return on investment.
DISCUSSION: Any of the actions listed would increase the return on investment. Management and the accounting profession are much concerned with classification of expenses and assets and other decisions involving the accounting for these items to achieve a proper calculation of return on investment.

33. Assuming that sales and net income remain the same, a company's return on investment will

   a. Increase if invested capital increases.
   b. Decrease if invested capital decreases.
   c. Decrease if the invested capital-employed turnover rate decreases.
   d. Decrease if the invested capital-employed turnover rate increases.

The correct answer is (c). *(CPA 586 T-49)*
REQUIRED: The effect on ROI of a decrease in investment turnover.
DISCUSSION: The basic formula for return on investment is $(S \div I) \times (NI \div S) = NI \div I$. See Q. 29 on page 407 for definition of S, I, and NI. Holding sales and NI constant while decreasing the turnover rate $(S \div I)$ would decrease the ROI because of increased investment (the profit margin and numerator of the turnover ratio are constant, so the denominator of the ratio must increase).
Answer (a) is incorrect because if invested capital increases while sales and net income remain constant, ROI will decrease. Answer (b) is incorrect because if invested capital decreases while sales and net income remain constant, ROI will increase. Answer (d) is incorrect because if the invested capital-employed turnover rate increases, ROI will increase.

34. Return on investment (ROI) is a term often used to express income earned on capital invested in a business unit. A company's ROI would be increased if

   a. Sales increased by the same dollar amount as expenses and total assets increased.
   b. Sales remained the same and expenses were reduced by the same dollar amount that total assets increased.
   c. Sales decreased by the same dollar amount that expenses increased.
   d. Sales and expenses increased by the same percentage that total assets increased.
   e. Net profit margin on sales increased by the same percentage that total assets increased.

The correct answer is (b). *(CMA 684 4-9)*
REQUIRED: The instance in which ROI will increase.
DISCUSSION: The basic formula for return on investment is $(S \div I) \times (NI \div S) = NI \div I$. If NI increases (because expenses have decreased) by the same amount that I increases (because total assets have increased), ROI will increase. For example, if NI equals 100 and I equals 1,000, the ROI is 10%. An increase of 20 in each term raises the ROI to 11.8%.
Answer (a) is incorrect because ROI $(NI \div I)$ will decrease if investment (total assets) increases while NI remains the same. Answer (c) is incorrect because a reduction in NI causes a decrease in ROI if investment is constant. Answers (d) and (e) are incorrect because ROI would not change if net profit were originally positive.

35. To properly motivate divisional management, the divisional ROIs should be

   a. Equal.
   b. Greater in the less profitable divisions to motivate those divisions to achieve higher ROIs.
   c. Lower in more profitable divisions in which motivation is unnecessary.
   d. Different based upon strategic goals of the firm.

The correct answer is (d). *(Publisher)*
REQUIRED: The best motivational philosophy regarding the ROIs of different divisions.
DISCUSSION: Each division within a firm should have an ROI based on the strategic goals of the firm consistent with its competitive environment.
Answer (a) is incorrect because equal goals should not be set owing to differences in competitive environment, the strategic goals of the firm, and risk. Answers (b) and (c) are incorrect because neither of these options would encourage a positive ROI.

36. Residual income is the
   a. Contribution margin of an investment center, less the imputed interest on the invested capital used by the center.
   b. Contribution margin of an investment center, plus the imputed interest on the invested capital used by the center.
   c. Income of an investment center, less the imputed interest on the invested capital used by the center.
   d. Income of an investment center, plus the imputed interest on the invested capital used by the center.

The correct answer is (c). *(CPA 1187 T-44)*
   REQUIRED: The definition of residual income.
   DISCUSSION: Residual income is income of an investment center minus an imputed interest charge for invested capital.
   Answers (a) and (b) are incorrect because contribution margin does not reflect all expenses of an investment center. Answer (d) is incorrect because imputed interest is subtracted from income, not added.

37. The appropriate measurement device for the assets included in an investment should be
   a. Replacement cost.
   b. Net realizable value.
   c. Net book value.
   d. Liquidation value.
   e. Any of the above.

The correct answer is (e). *(Publisher)*
   REQUIRED: The appropriate measurement(s) for assets included in an investment.
   DISCUSSION: The appropriate valuation process for the assets included in an investment is dependent upon the action undertaken. Any of the measurement devices given may be useful for acquisition, disposal, and/or evaluation. To evaluate each of these decisions, however, the total present value should always be compared with the appropriate measurement alternative.

38. ROI, residual income, and present value techniques are sophisticated budgeting and accounting methods, yet relatively few organizations adopt these concepts in their entirety for internal purposes. What is a possible reason for this reluctance?
   a. Behavioral implications of changing the system.
   b. External influences from the larger environment.
   c. The cost of developing the systems exceeds the perceived benefits.
   d. Misunderstanding the importance of budgeting in responsibility accounting.
   e. All of the above.

The correct answer is (e). *(Publisher)*
   REQUIRED: The reason(s) for not using better accounting systems.
   DISCUSSION: Each of the alternatives given provides a partial explanation for management's failure to use more sophisticated techniques. The motivational benefits of a new system may not materialize because managers believe their self-interests were better served by the old system. The external environment (e.g., financial institutions, customers, vendors) may be reluctant to change. The costs of developing a sophisticated system may be greater than the benefits. For these and other reasons, the costs of education must be included in the budgeting process. Furthermore, management may be overlooking the importance of the budgeting process and its close relation to the more sophisticated techniques. A relatively modest incremental commitment might create a significantly more sophisticated system.

14.2 Decentralization and Transfer Pricing

39. The primary difference between centralization and decentralization is
   a. Separate offices for all managers.
   b. Geographical separation of divisional headquarters and central headquarters.
   c. The extent of freedom of decision making by many levels of management.
   d. The relative size of the firm.

The correct answer is (c). *(Publisher)*
   REQUIRED: The primary difference between centralization and decentralization.
   DISCUSSION: The primary distinction between centralization and decentralization is in the degree of freedom of decision making by managers at many levels. In decentralization, decision making is at as low a level as possible. The premise is that the local manager can make better (more informed) decisions than a centralized manager. Centralization is based on the theory that decision making must be consolidated so that activities throughout the organization may be more effectively coordinated. In most organizations, a mixture of these approaches is found to be best.

40. Which of the following is most liable to be a disadvantage of decentralization?

a. Lower-level employees will develop less rapidly than in a centralized organization.
b. Lower-level employees will complain of not having enough to do.
c. Top management will have less time available to devote to unique problems.
d. Lower-level managers may make conflicting decisions.

The correct answer is (d). *(CIA 1185 III-5)*
REQUIRED: The item most liable to be a disadvantage of decentralization.
DISCUSSION: The disadvantages of decentralization include a tendency to focus on short-run results to the detriment of the long-term health of the entity, an increased risk of loss of control by top management, the increased difficulty of coordinating interdependent units, and less cooperation and communication among competing decentralized unit managers.
Answer (a) is incorrect because decentralization encourages development of lower-level managers since they will have greater authority. Answer (b) is incorrect because more tasks will be delegated to lower-level employees. Answer (c) is incorrect because top managers will be freed from operating problems.

41. Which of the following is not a cost of decentralization?

a. Dysfunctional decision making owing to disagreements of managers regarding overall goals and subgoals of the individual decision makers.
b. A decreased understanding of the overall goals of the organization.
c. Increased costs for developing the information system.
d. Decreased costs of corporate-level staff services and management talent.

The correct answer is (d). *(Publisher)*
REQUIRED: The item not a cost of decentralization.
DISCUSSION: The costs of centralized staff may actually decrease under decentralization. On the other hand, the corporate staff and the various services they provide may have to be duplicated in various divisions, thus increasing overall costs.
Suboptimal decisions may result from disharmony between organizational goals, subgoals of the division, and the individual goals of managers. The overall goals of the firm may more easily be misunderstood because individual managers may not see the larger picture. Moreover, the information system necessary for adequate reporting in a decentralized mode will tend toward redundancy, which increases costs.

42. The CEO of a rapidly growing high-technology firm has exercised centralized authority over all corporate functions. Because the company now operates in four geographically dispersed locations, the CEO is considering the advisability of decentralizing operational control over production and sales. Which of the following conditions probably would result from and be a valid reason for decentralizing?

a. Greater local control over compliance with government regulations.
b. More efficient use of headquarters staff officials and specialists.
c. Quicker and better operating decisions.
d. Greater economies in purchasing.

The correct answer is (c). *(CIA 586 III-5)*
REQUIRED: The condition that would be a valid reason for decentralizing.
DISCUSSION: Decentralization results in greater speed in making operating decisions since they are made by lower level managers instead of being referred to top management. The quality of operating decisions should also be enhanced, assuming proper training of managers, because those closest to the problems should be the most knowledgeable about them.
Answer (a) is incorrect because compliance with governmental regulations is probably more easily achieved by centralization. A disadvantage of decentralization is the difficulty of assuring uniform action by units of the entity that have substantial autonomy. Answers (b) and (d) are incorrect because decentralization usually results in duplication of staff efforts, including purchasing.

43. Managerial effort is

a. The desire and the commitment to achieve a specific goal.
b. The sharing of goals by supervisors and subordinates.
c. The extent to which individuals have the authority to make decisions.
d. The extent of the attempt to accomplish a specific goal.

The correct answer is (d). *(Publisher)*
REQUIRED: The definition of managerial effort.
DISCUSSION: Managerial effort is the extent a manager attempts to accomplish a goal. Managerial effort may include psychological as well as physical commitment to a goal.
Answers (a), (b), and (c) are incorrect because they are the definitions of motivation, goal congruence, and autonomy, respectively.

Module 14.2: Decentralization and Transfer Pricing

44. Goal congruence is
  a. The desire and the commitment to achieve a specific goal.
  b. The sharing of goals by supervisors and subordinates.
  c. The extent to which individuals have the authority to make decisions.
  d. The extent of the attempt to accomplish a specific goal.

The correct answer is (b). *(Publisher)*
REQUIRED: The definition of goal congruence.
DISCUSSION: Goal congruence is agreement on the goals of the organization and/or the division by both supervisors and subordinates. Performance is assumed to be optimized when there is an understanding that personal and segmental goals mesh with those of the organization.
Answers (a), (c), and (d) are incorrect because they are the definitions of motivation, autonomy, and managerial effort, respectively.

45. Motivation is
  a. The desire and the commitment to achieve a specific goal.
  b. The sharing of goals by supervisors and subordinates.
  c. The extent to which individuals have the authority to make decisions.
  d. The extent of the attempt to accomplish a specific goal.

The correct answer is (a). *(Publisher)*
REQUIRED: The definition of motivation.
DISCUSSION: Motivation is the desire for a specific goal (goal congruence) and the commitment to accomplish the goal (managerial effort). Managerial motivation is thus a combination of managerial effort and goal congruence.
Answer (b) is incorrect because it is the definition of goal congruence. Answer (c) is incorrect because it is the definition of autonomy. Answer (d) is incorrect because it is the definition of managerial effort.

46. Which of the following is the most valid reason for using other than a full-cost based transfer price between decentralized units of a company? A full-cost price
  a. Is typically more costly to implement.
  b. Does not ensure the control of costs of a supplying unit.
  c. Is not available unless market based prices are available.
  d. Does not reflect the excess capacity of the supplying unit.

The correct answer is (b). *(CIA 584 IV-9)*
REQUIRED: The best reason why a full-cost transfer price should not be used.
DISCUSSION: Full cost includes both variable and fixed costs, including some costs that are not controllable by the supplying unit. The full-cost price therefore may not facilitate evaluation and control of the supplying unit's performance in reducing costs.
Answer (a) is incorrect because the costs of implementing the various transfer cost systems usually do not vary materially. Answer (c) is incorrect because full cost prices are based on historical cost, not market prices. Answer (d) is incorrect because another price may be justified even when the supplier has no excess capacity. Moreover, cost control is a more fundamental concern than reflecting excess capacity.

47. In a decentralized company in which divisions may buy goods from one another, the transfer pricing system should be designed primarily to
  a. Increase the consolidated value of inventory.
  b. Allow division managers to buy from outsiders.
  c. Minimize the degree of autonomy of division managers.
  d. Aid in the appraisal and motivation of managerial performance.

The correct answer is (d). *(CPA 1173 T-40)*
REQUIRED: The purpose that should be accomplished by a transfer pricing system.
DISCUSSION: The three basic criteria that the transfer pricing system in a decentralized company should satisfy are to 1) provide information allowing central management to evaluate divisions with respect to total company profit and each division's contribution to profit, 2) stimulate each manager's efficiency without losing each division's autonomy, and 3) motivate each divisional manager to achieve his/her own profit goal in a manner contributing to the company's success.
Answer (a) is incorrect because increasing inventory value is seldom a goal of the company. Answer (b) is incorrect because suboptimization results when goods are purchased from outsiders at prices in excess of the variable costs of goods transferred. Answer (c) is incorrect because decentralization enhances autonomy.

412 Module 14.2: Decentralization and Transfer Pricing

> Questions 48 through 50 deal with the setting of transfer prices within an organization.

48. The proposed transfer price is based upon the outlay cost. Outlay cost plus opportunity cost is

a. The retail price.
b. The price representing the cash outflows of the supplying division plus the contribution to the supplying division from an outside sale.
c. The price usually set by an absorption costing calculation.
d. The price set by charging for variable costs plus a lump-sum or an additional markup, but less than full markup.

49. The proposed transfer price is based upon cost plus price. Variable cost plus price is

a. The price on the open market.
b. The price representing the cash outflows of the supplying division plus the contribution to the supplying division from an outside sale.
c. The price usually set by an absorption costing calculation.
d. The price set by charging for variable costs plus a lump-sum or an additional markup, but less than full markup.

50. The proposed transfer price is based upon the full cost price. Full cost price is

a. The price on the open market.
b. The price representing the cash outflows of the supplying division plus the contribution to the supplying division from an outside sale.
c. The price usually set by an absorption costing calculation.
d. The price set by charging for variable costs plus a lump-sum or an additional markup, but less than full markup.

The correct answer is (b). *(Publisher)*
REQUIRED: The definition of outlay cost plus opportunity cost.
DISCUSSION: This cost is the price representing the cash outflows of the supplying division (outlay cost) plus the contribution from an outside sale (opportunity cost). Thus, it is essentially the price that would leave the supplying division indifferent as to whether it sold internally or externally.
Answer (a) is incorrect because it is the definition of the market price, assuming an arm's-length transaction. Answer (c) is incorrect because it is the definition of full cost. Answer (d) is incorrect because it is the definition of the variable cost plus price.

The correct answer is (d). *(Publisher)*
REQUIRED: The definition of variable cost plus price.
DISCUSSION: The variable cost plus price is the price set by charging for variable cost plus either a lump-sum or an additional markup but less than full markup price. This permits top management to enter the decision process and dictate that a division transfer at variable cost plus some appropriate amount.
Answer (a) is incorrect because it is the definition of the market price. Answer (b) is incorrect because it is the definition of outlay cost plus opportunity cost. Answer (c) is incorrect because it is the full cost price.

The correct answer is (c). *(Publisher)*
REQUIRED: The definition of full cost price.
DISCUSSION: Full cost price is the price usually set by an absorption costing calculation and includes materials, labor, and a full allocation of manufacturing O/H. This full cost price may lead to dysfunctional behavior by the supplying and receiving divisions, e.g., purchasing from outside sources at a slightly lower price that is substantially above the variable costs of internal production.
Answer (a) is incorrect because it is the definition of market price. Answer (b) is incorrect because it is the definition of the outlay cost plus opportunity cost. Answer (d) is incorrect because it is the variable cost plus price.

Module 14.2: Decentralization and Transfer Pricing

51. An internal report for a decentralized organization reports transfers between segments. For this internal report, transfer prices charged for a product with a determinable market price would usually be based on

  a. Cost or market, whichever is lower.
  b. Market price.
  c. Historical cost.
  d. Variable cost.

The correct answer is (b). *(CPA 1185 T-44)*
  REQUIRED: The preferable transfer price.
  DISCUSSION: The market price should be used as the transfer price to avoid waste and maximize efficiency in a competitive economy. This price also measures the product's profitability and the division managers' performance in a competitive environment.

52. Given a competitive outside market for identical intermediate goods, what is the best transfer price, assuming all relevant information is readily available?

  a. Average cost of production.
  b. Average cost of production, plus average production department allocated profit.
  c. Market price of the intermediate goods.
  d. Market price of the intermediate goods, less average production department allocated profit.

The correct answer is (c). *(CIA 1187 IV-16)*
  REQUIRED: The best transfer price for intermediate goods in a competitive market.
  DISCUSSION: The market price should be used as the transfer price to avoid waste and maximize efficiency in a competitive economy. This price also measures the product's profitability and the division managers' performance in a competitive environment.

53. Transfer prices based on actual costs of the selling division as opposed to standard costs

  a. Are preferred by the purchasing division.
  b. Often fail to provide the selling division with incentives to control costs.
  c. Often encourage the selling division to control costs.
  d. Often encourage the purchasing division to control costs.

The correct answer is (b). *(CIA 1185 IV-7)*
  REQUIRED: The consequences of basing transfer prices on actual costs of the selling division.
  DISCUSSION: The optimal transfer price of a selling division should be set at a point that will have the most desirable economic effect on the firm as a whole while at the same time continuing to motivate the management of every division to perform efficiently. Setting the transfer price based on actual costs rather than standard costs would give the selling division little incentive to control costs.
  Answer (a) is incorrect because actual costs to the selling division may be greater than the prevailing market price. Answer (c) is incorrect because basing transfer prices on actual costs provides no incentive to the selling division. Answer (d) is incorrect because the purchasing division is not motivated by the selling division's pricing policy.

54. A limitation of a full-cost based transfer pricing system is that

  a. There may be little incentive on the part of the supplying division to operate efficiently.
  b. There will be little incentive on the part of the supplying manager to supply goods and services.
  c. Managers may find the cost transfer system inconvenient.
  d. Managers may find that the transfer price is difficult to compute.

The correct answer is (a). *(CIA 587 IV-16)*
  REQUIRED: The limitation of a full-cost based transfer pricing system.
  DISCUSSION: If the full cost transfer price is charged, inefficiency may result because the vendor will recover its costs from a "captive" purchaser. If the purchasing division is free to buy at the market price from an outside supplier, however, the vendor will have a motive to practice cost conscious management.
  Answer (b) is incorrect because the supplier has an incentive to supply goods and services when its full costs are recoverable. Answers (c) and (d) are incorrect because a full cost system is more convenient than, for example, reconciling the conflicting records needed in a dual pricing system.

55. A company has two divisions, A and B, each operated as a profit center. A charges B $35 per unit for each unit transferred to B. Other data follow:

A's variable cost per unit	$30
A's fixed costs	$10,000
A's annual sales to B	5,000 units
A's sales to outsiders	50,000 units

A is planning to raise its transfer price to $50 per unit. Division B can purchase units at $40 each from outsiders, but doing so would idle A's facilities now committed to producing units for B. Division A cannot increase its sales to outsiders. From the perspective of the company as a whole, from whom should Division B acquire the units, assuming B's market is unaffected?

a. Outside vendors.

b. Division A, but only at the variable cost per unit.

c. Division A, but only until fixed costs are covered, then should purchase from outside vendors.

d. Division A, in spite of the increased transfer price.

The correct answer is (d). *(CIA 1183 IV-5)*
REQUIRED: The correct decision to purchase internally or from an outside supplier.
DISCUSSION: Opportunity costs are $0 because A's facilities would be idle if B did not purchase from A. Assuming fixed costs are not affected by the decision, the intracompany sale is preferable from the company's perspective since A's $30 variable unit cost is less than the outside vendor's cost of $40.
Answer (a) is incorrect because outside purchase will increase the company's cost of sales by $10 per unit. Answer (b) is incorrect because the transfer price is irrelevant to the decision since it does not affect overall profits. Answer (c) is incorrect because the company is initially concerned with covering variable rather than fixed costs.

56. A company is highly decentralized. Division X, which is operating at capacity, produces a component that it currently sells in a perfectly competitive market for $13 per unit. At the current level of production, the fixed cost of producing this component is $4 per unit and the variable cost is $7 per unit. Division Y would like to purchase this component from Division X. The price that Division X should charge Division Y for this component is

a. $7 per unit.

b. $11 per unit.

c. $13 per unit.

d. $15 per unit.

The correct answer is (c). *(CIA 1186 IV-15)*
REQUIRED: The transfer price of a product.
DISCUSSION: Since Division X is operating at capacity, any sales to Division Y would have an opportunity cost of $13 per unit, the revenue forgone by not selling to outsiders. Since Y would have to purchase the component from an outside supplier for $13 per unit, the company as a whole does not gain if X charges a price other than the market price. Moreover, in a decentralized system, each division is supposed to be a completely separate entity. Thus, X should charge the same price to Y as would be charged to an outside buyer.

57. A large, diversified energy corporation has a production division that drills for oil, and a supply division that sells oil-field equipment. The production division purchases valves from the supply division. The supply division incurs $150 variable cost and allocates $75 of fixed cost to each valve sold. The valves are also sold to nonaffiliated customers of the supply division for $260 each. What transfer price should the supply division charge the production division for each valve in order to achieve maximum efficiency?

a. $75.

b. $150.

c. $225.

d. $260.

The correct answer is (d). *(CIA 586 IV-7)*
REQUIRED: The most efficient transfer price to be charged by the supply division.
DISCUSSION: Because it is objective, the market price should be used by the supply division. Market price would allow the supply division to recover its full cost plus the opportunity cost of the transfer.
Answer (a) is incorrect because charging only fixed cost does not allow the supply division to recover variable and opportunity costs. Answer (b) is incorrect because charging only variable cost does not allow the supply division to recover fixed and opportunity costs. Answer (c) is incorrect because charging only actual (fixed plus variable) cost does not allow the supply division to recover the opportunity cost of the transfer.

58. Cohasset Company currently manufactures all component parts used in the manufacture of various hand tools. A steel handle is used in three different tools. The budget for these handles is 20,000 units with the following unit cost.

Direct material	$ .60
Direct labor	.40
Variable overhead	.10
Fixed overhead	.20
Total unit cost	$1.30

R&M Steel has offered to supply 20,000 units of the handle to Cohasset Company for $1.25 each, delivered. If Cohasset currently has idle capacity that cannot be used, accepting the offer will

a. Decrease the handle unit cost by $.05.
b. Increase the handle unit cost by $.15.
c. Decrease the handle unit cost by $.15.
d. Decrease the handle unit cost by $.25.
e. Increase the handle unit cost by $.05.

The correct answer is (b). *(CMA 687 5-20)*
REQUIRED: The effect on unit cost of buying rather than making when the firm has idle capacity.
DISCUSSION: Since the fixed cost will be incurred whether the company makes or buys the part, the relevant unit cost of making the part is the $1.10 variable cost ($1.30 - $.20 fixed overhead). The existence of idle capacity indicates that the firm has no opportunity cost to be considered in the calculation. Thus, accepting the offer would increase costs by $.15 per unit.

59. A company recently established a branch to sell its most popular fan. The company purchases these fans and stores them in a warehouse. The fans are then shipped from the warehouse to both the home office and the new branch F.O.B. destination. Home office management is responsible for setting the transfer price of the fans charged to the branch in a manner that will measure the long-run incremental cost of supplying the fans to the branch on a continuing basis. Per unit costs for the fans are

$50.00 purchase price
$ 2.50 shipping cost to warehouse
$ 3.00 handling cost including $1.00 of allocated administrative overhead
$ 3.50 shipping cost to branch paid by home office
$ 1.25 shipping cost to home office

The minimum transfer price that home office should charge the branch to meet its measurement objective is

a. $53.50.
b. $54.50.
c. $58.00.
d. $59.00.

The correct answer is (d). *(CIA 1184 IV-9)*
REQUIRED: The long-run incremental cost per unit.
DISCUSSION: The long-run incremental cost of supplying fans to the branch on a continuing basis includes all costs necessary to purchase, receive, and ship the fans to the branch.

$50 + $2.50 + $3.00* + $3.50 = $59.00

* The $1 of overhead presents some measurement difficulties, but in the long run some amount of overhead should be allocated.

14.3 Comprehensive

Questions 60 through 64 are based on Oslo Co.'s industrial photo-finishing division, Rho, which incurred the following costs and expenses in 1989.

	Variable	Fixed
Direct materials	$200,000	
Direct labor	150,000	
Factory overhead	70,000	$42,000
General, selling, and administrative	30,000	48,000
Totals	$450,000	$90,000

During 1989, Rho produced 300,000 units of industrial photo-prints, which were sold for $2.00 each. Oslo's investment in Rho was $500,000 and $700,000 at January 1, 1989 and December 31, 1989, respectively. Oslo normally imputes interest on investments at 15% of average invested capital.

60. For the year ended December 31, 1989, Rho's return on average investment was

a. 15.0%.
b. 10.0%.
c. 8.6%.
d. (5.0%).

The correct answer is (b). *(CPA 1186 Q-22)*
REQUIRED: The return on average investment.
DISCUSSION: The return on average investment equals net income from operations divided by average invested capital. Average invested capital is $600,000 [($500,000 + $700,000) ÷ 2].

Sales (300,000 units x $2)	$600,000
Less:	
Variable costs	450,000
Contribution margin	150,000
Less:	
Fixed costs	90,000
Net operating income	$ 60,000

61. For the year ended December 31, 1989, Rho's residual income (loss) was

a. $150,000.
b. $60,000.
c. $(45,000).
d. $(30,000).

The correct answer is (d). *(CPA 1186 Q-23)*
REQUIRED: The residual income (loss).
DISCUSSION: Residual income is equal to net operating income less imputed interest on invested capital. Net operating income and average investment were determined to be $60,000 and $600,000, respectively, in Q. 60. The imputed interest rate is 15%. Thus,

Net operating income	$ 60,000
Less:	
Imputed interest (15% x $600,000)	(90,000)
Residual income	$(30,000)

62. How many industrial photo-print units did Rho have to sell in 1989 to break even?

a. 180,000.
b. 120,000.
c. 90,000.
d. 60,000.

The correct answer is (a). *(CPA 1186 Q-24)*
REQUIRED: The breakeven point in units.
DISCUSSION: The breakeven point in units is total fixed costs divided by the unit contribution margin (UCM). The UCM is the selling price less variable costs per unit. Variable costs per unit equal $1.50 ($450,000 ÷ 300,000 units). Thus, the UCM equals $.50 ($2 - $1.50). Divide the $90,000 of fixed costs by the $.50 UCM to find the breakeven point of 180,000 units.

Module 14.3: Comprehensive

63. For the year ended December 31, 1989, Rho's contribution margin was

a. $250,000.
b. $180,000.
c. $150,000.
d. $60,000.

The correct answer is (c). *(CPA 1186 Q-25)*
REQUIRED: The contribution margin.
DISCUSSION: The contribution margin is sales of $600,000 (300,000 units at $2) less variable costs of $450,000 which is $150,000.

64. Based on Rho's 1989 financial data, and an estimated 1990 production of 350,000 units of industrial photo-prints, Rho's estimated 1990 total costs and expenses would be

a. $525,000.
b. $540,000.
c. $615,000.
d. $630,000.

The correct answer is (c). *(CPA 1186 Q-26)*
REQUIRED: The estimated total costs and expenses given an increase in production.
DISCUSSION: Over the relevant range, fixed costs will not fluctuate. In Q. 62 the variable cost per unit was computed to be $1.50. Thus, total costs and expenses would be

Variable ($1.50 x 350,000 units)	$525,000
Fixed	90,000
Total costs and expenses	$615,000

Questions 65 and 66 are based on the following selected data, which pertain to the Maple Division of Beyer Corp.:

Sales	$300,000
Average invested capital	100,000
Operating income	20,000
Capital turnover	3.0
Imputed interest rate	12%

---

65. The return on investment was

a. 6.67%.
b. 8.00%.
c. 20.00%.
d. 33.33%.

The correct answer is (c). *(CPA 586 Q-37)*
REQUIRED: The return on investment.
DISCUSSION: ROI is computed as follows.

$$ROI = \frac{S}{I} \times \frac{NI}{S}$$

$$ROI = \frac{\$300{,}000}{\$100{,}000} \times \frac{\$20{,}000}{\$300{,}000}$$

$$ROI = \frac{\$20{,}000}{\$100{,}000} = 20\%$$

66. The residual income was

a. $2,400.
b. $5,600.
c. $6,667.
d. $8,000.

The correct answer is (d). *(CPA 586 Q-38)*
REQUIRED: The residual income.
DISCUSSION: Residual income is the excess of the minimum rate of return times the investment. It is income of $20,000 less imputed interest of $12,000 ($100,000 x 12%), or $8,000.

Module 14.3: Comprehensive

Questions 67 through 74 are based on the following information, which was presented as part of Question 6 on Part 4 of the December 1981 CMA examination.

PortCo Products is a divisionalized furniture manufacturer. The divisions are autonomous segments, with each division being responsible for its own sales, costs of operations, working capital management, and equipment acquisition. Each division serves a different market in the furniture industry. Because the markets and products of the divisions are so different, there have never been any transfers between divisions.

The Commercial Division manufactures equipment and furniture that is purchased by the restaurant industry. The division plans to introduce a new line of counter and chair units which feature a cushioned seat for the counter chairs. John Kline, the division manager, has discussed the manufacturing of the cushioned seat with Russ Fiegel of the Office Division. They both believe a cushioned seat currently made by the Office Division for use on its deluxe office stool could be modified for use on the new counter chair. Consequently, Kline has asked Russ Fiegel for a price for 100-unit lots of the cushioned seat. The following conversation took place about the price to be charged for the cushioned seats:

Fiegel: "John, we can make the necessary modifications to the cushioned seat easily. The raw materials used in your seat are slightly different and should cost about 10% more than those used in our deluxe office stool. However, the labor time should be the same because the seat fabrication operation basically is the same. I would price the seat at our regular rate--full cost plus 30% markup."

Kline: "That's higher than I expected, Russ. I was thinking that a good price would be your variable manufacturing costs. After all, your capacity costs will be incurred regardless of this job."

Fiegel: "John, I'm at capacity. By making the cushion seats for you, I'll have to cut my production of deluxe office stools. Of course, I can increase my production of economy office stools. The labor time freed by not having to fabricate the frame or assemble the deluxe stool can be shifted to the frame fabrication and assembly of the economy office stool. Fortunately, I can switch my labor force between these two models of stools without any loss of efficiency. As you know, overtime is not a feasible alternative in our community. I'd like to sell it to you at variable cost, but I have excess demand for both products. I don't mind changing my product mix to the economy model if I get a good return on the seats I make for you. Here are my standard costs for the two stools and a schedule of my manufacturing overhead."

Kline: "I guess I see your point, Russ, but I don't want to price myself out of the market. Maybe we should talk to Corporate to see if they can give us any guidance."

Office Division
Standard Costs and Prices

	Deluxe Office stool	Economy Office stool
Raw materials		
Framing	$ 8.15	$ 9.76
Cushioned seat		
Padding	2.40	—
Vinyl	4.00	—
Molded seat		
(purchased)	—	6.00
Direct labor		
Frame fabrication (.5 × $7.50/DLH)	3.75	(.5 × $7.50/DLH) 3.75
Cushion fabrication (.5 × $7.50/DLH)	3.75	—
Assembly* (.5 × $7.50/DLH)	3.75	(.3 × $7.50/DLH) 2.25
Manufacturing		
Overhead (1.5DLH × $12.80/DLH)	19.20	(.8DLH × $12.80/DLH) 10.24
Total standard cost	$45.00	$32.00
Selling price (30% markup)	$58.50	$41.60

*Attaching seats to frames and attaching rubber feet.

Office Division
Manufacturing Overhead Budget

Overhead Item	Nature	Amount
Supplies	Variable—at current market prices	$ 420,000
Indirect labor	Variable	375,000
Supervision	Nonvariable	250,000
Power	Use varies with activity; rates are fixed	180,000
Heat and light	Nonvariable—light is fixed regardless of production while heat/air conditioning varies with fuel charges	140,000
Property taxes and insurance taxes	Nonvariable—any change in amounts/rates is independent of production	200,000
Depreciation	Fixed dollar total	1,700,000
Employee benefits	20% of supervision, direct and indirect labor	575,000
Total overhead		$3,840,000
Capacity in DLH		300,000
Overhead rate/DLH		$12.80

Module 14.3: Comprehensive

67. What amount of employee benefits is associated with direct labor costs?

a. $675,000.
b. $75,000.
c. $450,000.
d. $500,000.

The correct answer is (c). *(Publisher)*
REQUIRED: The amount of employee benefits that is associated with direct labor costs.
DISCUSSION: The total employee benefits include 20% of supervision and direct and indirect labor costs. To find the amount associated with direct labor, 20% of supervision and indirect labor costs are subtracted from total employee benefits [$575,000 - 20% x ($250,000 + $375,000)], or $450,000.

68. What is the variable manufacturing overhead rate?

a. $7.80/hr.
b. $11.25/hr.
c. $5.17/hr.
d. $5.00/hr.

The correct answer is (d). *(Publisher)*
REQUIRED: The variable manufacturing overhead rate.
DISCUSSION: To determine the variable manufacturing O/H rate, all variable amounts must be totaled ($1,500,000) and divided by the capacity in DLH (300,000).

	Total	Per DLH
Supplies	$ 420,000	$1.40
Indirect labor	375,000	1.25
Power	180,000	.60
Employee benefits:		
20% direct labor	450,000	1.50
20% indirect labor	75,000	.25
Total	$1,500,000	$5.00

69. What is the fixed manufacturing overhead rate?

a. $7.80/hr.
b. $11.25/hr.
c. $5.17/hr.
d. $5.00/hr.

The correct answer is (a). *(Publisher)*
REQUIRED: The fixed manufacturing O/H rate.
DISCUSSION: The fixed O/H rate is computed by using the same approach as in Q. 68. All fixed O/H is totaled ($2,340,000; see below) and divided by the 300,000 hour level of activity to determine the $7.80 hourly rate.

Supervision	$ 250,000
Heat and light	140,000
Property taxes and insurance	200,000
Depreciation	1,700,000
Benefits/Supervision	50,000
	$2,340,000

70. What is the transfer price per 100-unit lot based on variable manufacturing costs to produce the modified cushioned seat?

a. $1,329.
b. $1,869.
c. $789.
d. $1,986.

The correct answer is (a). *(Publisher)*
REQUIRED: The transfer price based on the variable manufacturing cost.
DISCUSSION: The variable manufacturing cost to produce a 100-unit lot is 100 times the sum of DM, DL, and variable O/H per seat.

Cushioned material		
Padding	$ 2.40	
Vinyl	4.00	
Total cushion material	$ 6.40	
Cost increase 10% (given)	x 1.10	
Cost of cushioned seat		$ 7.04
Cushion fabrication labor ($7.50/DLH x .5 DLH)		3.75
Variable overhead ($5.00/DLH x .5 DLH)		2.50
Total variable cost per cushioned seat		$13.29
Total variable cost per 100-unit lot		$1,329

Questions 71 through 74 are based on the information presented on page 418.

71. How many economy office stools can be produced with the labor hours currently used to make 100 deluxe stools?

a. 80.
b. 125.
c. 100.
d. 150.

The correct answer is (b). *(Publisher)*
REQUIRED: The economy stools that can be produced in the time spent to make 100 deluxe stools.
DISCUSSION: If labor hours used in cushion fabrication are used to make the modified cushioned seat, the number of economy office stools that can be produced is 125.

Labor hours to make 100 deluxe stools (1.5 x 100)	150 hrs.
Less: Labor hours to make 100 cushioned seats (cushion fabrication .5 x 100)	(50) hrs.
Labor hours available for economy stool	100 hrs.
Labor hours to make one economy stool	.8 hrs.
Stools produced by extra labor in economy stool production (100/.8 hrs.)	125 stools

72. When computing the opportunity cost for the deluxe office stool, what is the contribution margin per unit produced?

a. $25.20.
b. $15.84.
c. $13.56.
d. $33.30.

The correct answer is (a). *(Publisher)*
REQUIRED: The contribution margin per unit of the deluxe office stool.
DISCUSSION: The contribution margin per unit is equal to the selling price less the variable costs. Variable costs per unit for the deluxe office stool equal $33.30 and the selling price is $58.50. Therefore, the contribution margin is $25.20 per unit ($58.50 - $33.30). Note that the total standard cost is $45.00 which includes $11.70 of fixed O/H (1.5 hr. x $7.80), and that the variable costs are $33.30 ($45.00 - $11.70).

73. What is the opportunity cost of the Office Division?

a. $789.
b. $1,869.
c. $1,329.
d. $540.

The correct answer is (d). *(Publisher)*
REQUIRED: The opportunity cost of the Office Division.
DISCUSSION: Opportunity cost is the cost of the opportunity forgone. The opportunity cost here is the contribution margin forgone by shifting production to the economy office stool ($2,520 - $1,980 = $540).

	Deluxe		Economy
Selling price	$58.50		$41.60
Costs			
Material	$14.55		$15.76
Labor ($7.50 x 1.5)	11.25	($7.50 x .8)	6.00
Variable O/H ($5 x 1.5)	7.50	($5.00 x .8)	4.00
Fixed O/H	--		--
Total costs	$33.30		$25.76
Unit CM	$25.20		$15.84
Units produced	x 100		x 125
Total CM	$2,520		$1,980

74. Which of the following alternative transfer price systems would be the best policy for PortCo Products?

a. Full cost.
b. Variable manufacturing cost.
c. Variable manufacturing cost and opportunity cost.
d. Any of the above.

The correct answer is (c). *(Publisher)*
REQUIRED: The best intracompany transfer price policy for the firm.
DISCUSSION: The best policy for the firm would be to use the sum of the variable manufacturing cost and the opportunity cost as the transfer price. This is the appropriate transfer price system because the production division is indifferent between selling externally or internally. It ensures that the production division's contribution profit is the same under each alternative.

Module 14.3: Comprehensive

Questions 75 through 79 are based on the following information.

	Division X	Division Y	Division Z
Net income	$ 240,000	$ 100,000	$ --
Sales	1,200,000	1,500,000	--
Investment	800,000	--	15,000,000
Net income as % of sales	--	--	1%
Turnover of investment	--	--	2
Return on investment	--	1%	--

75. For Division Y, the net income as a percentage of sales is

a. 6.7%.
b. 1%.
c. 20%.
d. 2%.

The correct answer is (a). *(Publisher)*
REQUIRED: The calculation for net income as a percentage of sales for Division Y.
DISCUSSION: Net income as a percentage of sales is equal to net income divided by sales. Division Y net income equals $100,000. Sales equal $1,500,000. Thus, net income as a percentage of sales equals 6.7% for Division Y.

76. For Division Y, the turnover of investment is

a. 2.
b. .15.
c. .5.
d. 10.

The correct answer is (b). *(Publisher)*
REQUIRED: The turnover of investment for Division Y.
DISCUSSION: The turnover of investment is equal to the sales divided by the investment. Sales are $1,500,000. The investment is unknown, but it can be computed from the ROI. The 1% of ROI on net income of $100,000 means that the investment is $10,000,000 ($100,000 ÷ .01). The turnover of investment for Division Y is therefore .15 ($1,500,000 ÷ $10,000,000).

77. For Division Z, the return on investment is

a. 10%.
b. 1%.
c. 2%.
d. 20%.

The correct answer is (c). *(Publisher)*
REQUIRED: The return on investment for Division Z.
DISCUSSION: The ROI is equal to net income divided by the investment or the net income as a percentage of sales times the turnover of the investment. Here, net income as a percentage of sales equals 1%. The turnover of investment is 2. Hence, ROI must be 2%.

78. For Division Z, sales are

a. $300,000.
b. $30,000,000.
c. $3,000,000.
d. $3,300,000.

The correct answer is (b). *(Publisher)*
REQUIRED: The sales for Division Z.
DISCUSSION: Calculating sales for Division Z necessitates using the relationship between investment and turnover of investment. Given that investment was $15,000,000 and turnover of investment was 2, sales must have been $30,000,000.

79. What is the net income for Division Z?

a. $300,000.
b. $30,000,000.
c. $3,000,000.
d. $3,300,000.

The correct answer is (a). *(Publisher)*
REQUIRED: The net income for Division Z.
DISCUSSION: Net income for Division Z is equal to 2% of the investment (ROI was calculated in Q. 77). Given an investment of $15,000,000, Division Z's net income must be $300,000.
An alternative calculation is that since investment is equal to $15,000,000 and turnover of investment is equal to 2, sales must have been $30,000,000. Net income as a percentage of sales equals 1%, or $300,000 net income.

> Questions 80 through 87 are based on International Company, which has a division that produces components for its main product -- widgets. This division operates as a profit center and sells its components to other widget manufacturers. The present price of $50 per component is the basis for a negotiation with the manufacturing division, which has been purchasing 500,000 units per year from other sources. The external price is $48 per component due to the large number purchased. The component division has adequate capacity to provide the needs of the manufacturing division. However, the manufacturing division does not want to pay the full price of $50. The components' unit cost is presented below.
>
> | | |
> |---|---|
> | Direct materials | $18.00 |
> | Direct labor | 14.00 |
> | Variable overhead | 6.00 |
> | Fixed overhead (per unit based on a capacity of 4,000,000 units) | 4.00 |
> | Total cost | $42.00 |

80. The list price is
   a. $42.
   b. $38.
   c. $43.
   d. $48.
   e. $50.

The correct answer is (e). *(Publisher)*
  REQUIRED: The list price of the components.
  DISCUSSION: The list price is $50. That price is probably charged for the item for regular purchases. Only for large orders would the component division be able to give a quantity discount.

81. The market price is
   a. $42.
   b. $38.
   c. $43.
   d. $48.
   e. $50.

The correct answer is (d). *(Publisher)*
  REQUIRED: The market price of the components.
  DISCUSSION: The market price is at least the price for which the manufacturing division has been able to purchase the components externally. Although the $48 may be a discounted price for a quantity purchaser, it is the most relevant choice of those offered.

82. The full cost price is
   a. $42.
   b. $38.
   c. $43.
   d. $48.
   e. $50.

The correct answer is (a). *(Publisher)*
  REQUIRED: The full cost of the components.
  DISCUSSION: The full cost pricing approach uses absorption costing; i.e., all manufacturing costs, including fixed overhead, are counted. Thus, $42 is the full cost price.

Module 14.3: Comprehensive

83. The minimum price is
   a. $42.
   b. $38.
   c. $43.
   d. $48.
   e. $50.

The correct answer is (b). *(Publisher)*
   REQUIRED: The minimum price of the components.
   DISCUSSION: The minimum price at which the components can be expected to transfer is $38, the sum of the variable costs, including variable overhead.

84. The full cost plus price is
   a. $42.
   b. $38.
   c. $43.
   d. $48.
   e. $50.

The correct answer is (c). *(Publisher)*
   REQUIRED: The full cost plus price of the components.
   DISCUSSION: The full cost plus price is a full cost price ($42) plus some markup but less than the normal markup which might be charged. Thus, $42 plus an additional $1.00 results in a $43 price, the best choice offered.

85. Which range is appropriate for the intercompany transfer?
   a. $38-$42.
   b. $38-$43.
   c. $38-$48.
   d. $38-$50.
   e. $38-$52.

The correct answer is (c). *(Publisher)*
   REQUIRED: The price range within which the component division will sell components to the manufacturing division.
   DISCUSSION: The component division will not sell for less than its variable costs of $38. The manufacturing division will not buy for more than the lowest price available from other sources of $48.

86. Under what circumstances should the manufacturing division purchase components from other sources?
   a. If the full cost concept is followed.
   b. If the component division's costs increase 10%.
   c. Never under the present circumstances.
   d. Never.

The correct answer is (c). *(Publisher)*
   REQUIRED: When the manufacturing division should purchase components from external sources.
   DISCUSSION: Under current circumstances, there is no reason to purchase from external sources. The full cost ($42) of manufacture is less than the market price ($48) and there is slack capacity in the component division; i.e., no opportunity costs exist.

87. Which price concept is appropriate to this situation and benefits both divisions?
   a. Full cost price.
   b. Minimum price.
   c. Market price.
   d. Full cost plus price.

The correct answer is (d). *(Publisher)*
   REQUIRED: The interdivisional price concept appropriate for this company.
   DISCUSSION: "Full cost plus price" is the appropriate concept because the full cost is below the market price. Thus, the manufacturing division can pay less than market, and the component division can recover full cost and make a profit.
   Answer (a) is incorrect because the full cost price would not allow a profit for the component division. Answer (b) is incorrect because the minimum price would result in a loss for the component division. Answer (c) is incorrect because the market price would not permit any savings for the manufacturing division.

Module 14.3: Comprehensive

Questions 88 through 100 are based on the following information.

	Segment A	Segment B	Segment C	Segment D
Net income	$5,000	--	--	$90,000
Sales	$60,000	$750,000	$135,000	$1,800,000
Investment	$24,000	$500,000	$45,000	--
Net income as % of sales	--	--	--	--
Turnover of investment	--	--	--	--
ROI	--	--	20%	7.5%
Minimum ROI--dollars	--	--	--	$120,000
Minimum ROI--%	20%	6%	--	--
Residual income	--	-0-	$2,250	--

88. For Segment B, net income as a percentage of sales is

   a. 8%.
   b. 6.67%.
   c. 4%.
   d. 10%.

The correct answer is (c). *(Publisher)*
REQUIRED: The net income as a percentage of sales for Segment B.
DISCUSSION: You must derive the answer from interrelationships of data in the schedule. Residual income was zero, indicating that net income was equal to the minimum ROI. Given a 6% minimum ROI as a percentage of investment, 6% of the $500,000 investment is $30,000. Sales were $750,000, so net income ($30,000) is 4% of sales.

89. For Segment C, net income as a percentage of sales is

   a. 5%.
   b. 6.67%.
   c. 4%.
   d. 20%.

The correct answer is (b). *(Publisher)*
REQUIRED: The net income as a percentage of sales for Segment C.
DISCUSSION: Net income as a percentage of sales is the ROI divided by turnover of investment. The turnover of the investment is sales ($135,000) divided by the investment ($45,000), or 3. 20% ÷ 3 equals 6.67% net income as a percentage of sales for Segment C.

90. For Segment C, the turnover of investment is

   a. 3.
   b. 1.5.
   c. 2.5.
   d. 4.

The correct answer is (a). *(Publisher)*
REQUIRED: The turnover of investment for Segment C.
DISCUSSION: The turnover of investment for Segment C is calculated by dividing sales by investment. Given sales of $135,000 and investment of $45,000, Segment C's turnover of investment is 3.

91. For Segment D, the turnover of investment is

   a. 3.
   b. 1.5.
   c. 2.5.
   d. 4.

The correct answer is (b). *(Publisher)*
REQUIRED: The turnover of investment for Segment D.
DISCUSSION: The turnover of investment for Segment D is calculated by dividing sales by investment. For Segment D, net income ($90,000) as a percentage of sales ($1,800,000) equals 5%. ROI is given as 7.5%. Dividing net income as a percentage of sales (5%) into ROI (7.5%) gives a turnover of investment of 1.5.

92. For Segment A, ROI is

   a. 6%.
   b. 25%.
   c. 20.8%.
   d. 33%.

The correct answer is (c). *(Publisher)*
REQUIRED: The ROI for Segment A.
DISCUSSION: ROI is equal to net income divided by investment. Net income equals $5,000. Investment equals $24,000. ROI equals 20.8%.

Module 14.3: Comprehensive

93. For Segment B, ROI is
   a. 6%.
   b. 25%.
   c. 20%.
   d. 7.5%.

The correct answer is (a). *(Publisher)*
REQUIRED: The ROI for Segment B.
DISCUSSION: Note that residual income is given as zero. Thus, the actual ROI is the same as the minimum percentage ROI of 6%.

94. For Segment A, the minimum dollar ROI is
   a. $30,000.
   b. $6,750.
   c. $4,800.
   d. $120,000.

The correct answer is (c). *(Publisher)*
REQUIRED: The minimum rate of return in dollars.
DISCUSSION: The ROI in dollars is equal to the amount of the investment times the minimum rate of return percentage. The amount of the investment is $24,000. The minimum rate of return percentage is 20%. Therefore, the minimum ROI in dollars is $4,800.

95. For Segment B, the minimum dollar ROI is
   a. $30,000.
   b. $6,750.
   c. $4,800.
   d. $120,000.

The correct answer is (a). *(Publisher)*
REQUIRED: The minimum rate of return in dollars for Segment B.
DISCUSSION: The ROI in dollars is equal to the amount of the investment times the minimum rate of return percentage. The amount of the investment is $500,000. The minimum rate of return percentage is given as 6%. Thus, the minimum ROI in dollars equals $30,000.

96. For Segment C, the minimum dollar ROI is
   a. $30,000.
   b. $6,750.
   c. $4,800.
   d. $120,000.

The correct answer is (b). *(Publisher)*
REQUIRED: The minimum rate of return in dollars for Segment C.
DISCUSSION: The minimum ROI in dollars is equal to the minimum ROI percentage times the investment. The investment was $45,000. Neither the minimum percentage nor the minimum ROI is known. However, the ROI percentage (20%) and the investment ($45,000) are known. Hence, the net income is $9,000. Given residual income of $2,250, the minimum ROI in dollars must have been $6,750 ($9,000 - $2,250).

97. In Segment C, the minimum percentage of ROI is
   a. 20%.
   b. 6%.
   c. 15%.
   d. 10%.

The correct answer is (c). *(Publisher)*
REQUIRED: The minimum percentage of ROI for Segment C.
DISCUSSION: The minimum percentage of ROI in Segment C equals the minimum dollar ROI divided by the investment. The calculation in Q. 96 indicates that the minimum dollar ROI is $6,750. $6,750 ÷ 45,000 = 15%.

98. In Segment D, the minimum percentage of ROI is
   a. 20%.
   b. 6%.
   c. 15%.
   d. 10%.

The correct answer is (d). *(Publisher)*
REQUIRED: The minimum percentage of ROI for Segment D.
DISCUSSION: The minimum percentage of ROI for Segment D is the minimum ROI in dollars ($120,000) divided by the investment, which must be calculated. The ROI is given as 7.5%. The net income ($90,000) as a percentage of sales ($1,800,000) equals 5%. The turnover of investment (ROI ÷ net income as a percentage of sales) is 1.5, as calculated in Q. 91. Given turnover of 1.5 and sales of $1,800,000, investment must have been $1,200,000. The minimum percentage ROI is $120,000 divided by the $1,200,000 investment, or 10%.

> Questions 99 and 100 are based on the information presented on page 424.

99. In Segment A, the residual income is
a. $200.
b. $12,000.
c. $(30,000).
d. $(60,000).

The correct answer is (a). *(Publisher)*
REQUIRED: The residual income for Segment A.
DISCUSSION: Segment A's residual income is equal to the net income ($5,000) less the minimum ROI in dollars. Minimum ROI in dollars equals the minimum ROI percentage (20%) times the investment ($24,000), or $4,800. Residual income is therefore $200.

100. In Segment D, the residual income is
a. $1,200.
b. $12,000.
c. $(30,000).
d. $(60,000).

The correct answer is (c). *(Publisher)*
REQUIRED: The residual income for Segment D.
DISCUSSION: The minimum ROI in dollars is given as $120,000 and net income is given as $90,000. $90,000 - $120,000 = $(30,000) in residual income. Segment D did not achieve its minimum ROI and thus shows a negative residual income.

> Questions 101 and 102 are based on the following selected data for Beck Co.'s Beam Division:
>
> | | |
> |---|---:|
> | Sales | $1,000,000 |
> | Variable costs | 600,000 |
> | Traceable fixed costs | 100,000 |
> | Average invested capital | 200,000 |
> | Imputed interest rate | 15% |

101. How much is the residual income?
a. $100,000.
b. $270,000.
c. $300,000.
d. $330,000.

The correct answer is (b). *(CPA 585 Q-18)*
REQUIRED: The residual income for a division of a company.
DISCUSSION: Residual income is equal to the net income of an investment center less the minimum required return on invested capital.

$1,000,000 - $600,000 - $100,000 = $300,000 NI
$200,000 × 15% = (30,000) minimum ROI
$270,000 residual I

102. How much is the return on investment?
a. 75%.
b. 135%.
c. 150%.
d. 200%.

The correct answer is (c). *(CPA 585 Q-19)*
REQUIRED: The return on investment for a division of a company.
DISCUSSION: The return on investment is the net income divided by the average invested capital.

$$\frac{\$300,000}{\$200,000} = 150\%$$

CHAPTER FIFTEEN
NONROUTINE DECISIONS

15.1 Make or Buy . . . . (24 questions) 427
15.2 Special Order . . . . (14 questions) 435
15.3 Comprehensive . . . . (80 questions) 439

This chapter, the first in the section on nonroutine decisions, covers the basic nonroutine decisions as tested on most professional examinations as well as in most management accounting courses. The two classic issues are the make or buy decision and the special order decision. Note that relevant costs are the only costs that should be considered in nonroutine decisions; sunk costs must be ignored.

15.1 Make or Buy

1. In a make or buy decision,
   a. Only variable costs are relevant.
   b. Fixed costs that can be avoided in the future are relevant.
   c. Fixed costs that will continue regardless of the decision are relevant.
   d. Only conversion costs are relevant.

The correct answer is (b). *(CPA 580 T-44)*
REQUIRED: The relevant costs in a make or buy decision.
DISCUSSION: In make or buy decisions, both variable and fixed costs that can be avoided in the future are relevant quantitative factors. Qualitative factors may also be relevant to a decision. One must consider not only the costs of the respective options but also such other factors as whether a reliable source of supply is available if the decision is to buy the product and whether the purchased product is qualitatively superior to one made internally.
Answer (a) is incorrect because avoidable fixed costs and qualitative factors may also be relevant. Answer (c) is incorrect because fixed costs that will be incurred regardless of the decision are irrelevant. The relevant costs are the differential costs. Answer (d) is incorrect because conversion costs include factory overhead, part of which may be irrelevant. Moreover, they do not include material cost, which is relevant.

2. In a make or buy situation, which of the following qualitative factors is usually considered?
   a. Special technology.
   b. Skilled labor.
   c. Special materials requirements.
   d. Quality control.
   e. All of the above.

The correct answer is (e). *(Publisher)*
REQUIRED: The qualitative factor(s) affecting a make or buy decision.
DISCUSSION: Each of the items listed affects the make or buy decision. Special technology may be available either within or without the firm in reference to the particular product. The firm may possess necessary skilled labor or the supplier may. Special materials requirements may also affect the decision process since one supplier may have monopolized a key component. Assurance of quality control is often a reason for making rather than buying.

3. For the past 12 years, the Blue Company has produced the small electric motors that fit into its main product line of dental drilling equipment. As material costs have steadily increased, the controller of the Blue Company is reviewing the decision to continue to make the small motors and has identified the following facts:

1. The equipment used to manufacture the electric motors has a book value of $150,000.
2. The space now occupied by the electric motor manufacturing department could be used to eliminate the need for storage space now being rented.
3. Comparable units can be purchased from an outside supplier for $59.75.
4. Four of the persons who work in the electric motor manufacturing department would be terminated and given 8 weeks' severance pay.
5. A $10,000 unsecured note is still outstanding on the equipment used in the manufacturing process.

Which of the items above are relevant to the decision that the controller has to make?

 a. 1, 3, and 4.
 b. 2, 3, and 4.
 c. 2, 3, 4, and 5.
 d. 1, 2, 4, and 5.

The correct answer is (b). *(CIA 585 IV-12)*
REQUIRED: The relevant items for a make or buy decision.
DISCUSSION: In make or buy decisions, costs that can be avoided in the future are relevant. Here, the relevant costs are storage rental and personnel costs that will be avoided if the motors are purchased and the cost of purchase if the motors are not made.
Answers (a), (c), and (d) are incorrect because the book value of equipment already purchased and indebtedness already incurred are not costs that will vary with the decision made.

4. Which of the following qualitative factors favors the buy choice in a make or buy decision?

 a. Maintaining a long-run relationship with suppliers.
 b. Quality control is critical.
 c. The utilization of idle capacity.
 d. All of the above.

The correct answer is (a). *(Publisher)*
REQUIRED: The qualitative factor(s) favoring buying in a make or buy decision.
DISCUSSION: The maintenance of long-run relationships with suppliers may become paramount in a make or buy decision. Abandoning long-run supplier relationships may cause difficulty in obtaining needed parts when terminated suppliers find it advantageous not to supply parts in the future.
Answer (b) is incorrect because if quality is important, one can generally control it better in one's own plant. Answer (c) is incorrect because the utilization of idle capacity would more likely favor the decision to make.

5. In a make or buy decision, the decision process favors the use of total costs versus unit costs. The primary reason is that

 a. Unit cost may be calculated based on different volumes.
 b. Irrelevant costs may be included in the analysis.
 c. Allocated costs may be included in the analysis.
 d. All of the above.

The correct answer is (d). *(Publisher)*
REQUIRED: The advantage(s) of using total costs in a make or buy analysis.
DISCUSSION: Unit costs should be used with extreme care. In each situation, they may be calculated based on a different volume level from that anticipated, so comparability would be lost. Irrelevant costs included in the unit cost should be disregarded, and only relevant costs included in the analysis. Allocated costs should also be ignored and only the relevant costs that will change with the option chosen should be considered.

6. In deciding whether to manufacture a part or buy it from an outside vendor, a cost that is irrelevant to the short-run decision is

   a. Direct labor.
   b. Variable overhead.
   c. Fixed overhead that will be avoided if the part is bought from an outside vendor.
   d. Fixed overhead that will continue even if the part is bought from an outside vendor.

The correct answer is (d). *(CPA 1179 T-32)*
REQUIRED: The cost that is irrelevant to the short-run make or buy decision.
DISCUSSION: For short-run decisions, a company does not have to consider costs already incurred (sunk costs) and those future costs that will not vary with the course of action taken. Instead, a company must base its decision on the differential costs, those which vary with the option chosen and are therefore relevant to the decision.
Answers (a) and (b) are incorrect because each is a variable expense that is considered in short-run make or buy decisions. Answer (c) is incorrect because the fixed overhead that will be avoided if the part is bought from an outside vendor is a relevant differential cost.

Questions 7 and 8 are based on Kingston Company, which needs 10,000 units of a certain part to be used in its production cycle. If Kingston buys the part from Utica Company instead of making it, Kingston could not use the released facilities in another manufacturing activity. 60% of the fixed overhead applied will continue regardless of what decision is made.

The following information is available:

Cost to Kingston to make the part:
Direct materials	$ 6
Direct labor	24
Variable overhead	12
Fixed overhead applied	15
	$57
Cost to buy the part from Utica Company	$53

---

7. In deciding whether to make or buy the part, Kingston's total relevant costs to make the part are

   a. $342,000.
   b. $480,000.
   c. $530,000.
   d. $570,000.

The correct answer is (b). *(CPA 1181 P-40)*
REQUIRED: The total relevant costs in a make or buy decision if some of the fixed overhead applied to the manufacture of the item would be incurred even if it were purchased.
DISCUSSION: The relevant fixed overhead applied is $6 per unit ($15 x 40%) since that amount could be avoided by buying the product. All the variable costs are relevant since they are also avoidable costs. Thus, the relevant per unit cost in this make or buy decision is $48 ($6 + $24 + $12 + $6). The total relevant cost is $480,000 ($48 x 10,000 units).

8. Which alternative is more desirable for Kingston and by what amount?

   a. Buy, $50,000.
   b. Make, $50,000.
   c. Buy, $40,000.
   d. Make, $40,000.

The correct answer is (b). *(Publisher)*
REQUIRED: The more desirable alternative and the amount of the saving.
DISCUSSION: The make or buy decision compares the cost to buy the part from Utica Company ($53 per unit) with the relevant cost to produce the part internally ($48, as shown in Q. 7), resulting in a $5 per unit or $50,000 (10,000 x $5) total saving.

Module 15.1: Make or Buy

Questions 9 and 10 are based on the Blade Division of Dana Company, which produces hardened steel blades. One-third of the Blade Division's output is sold to the Lawn Products Division of Dana; the remainder is sold to outside customers. The Blade Division's estimated sales and standard cost data for the fiscal year ending June 30 are as follows:

	Lawn Products	Outsiders
Sales	$15,000	$40,000
Variable costs	(10,000)	(20,000)
Fixed costs	(3,000)	(6,000)
Gross margin	$ 2,000	$14,000
Unit sales	10,000	20,000

The Lawn Products Division has an opportunity to purchase 10,000 identical quality blades from an outside supplier at a cost of $1.25 per unit on a continuing basis. Assume that the Blade Division cannot sell any additional products to outside customers.

9. Should Dana allow its Lawn Products Division to purchase the blades from the outside supplier, and why?

   a. Yes, because buying the blades would save Dana Company $500.
   b. No, because making the blades would save Dana Company $1,500.
   c. Yes, because buying the blades would save Dana Company $2,500.
   d. No, because making the blades would save Dana Company $2,500.

The correct answer is (d). (CPA 1180 P-31)
REQUIRED: Whether a division of a company should purchase a product internally or externally.
DISCUSSION: In a make or buy decision, only relevant costs are considered. Relevant costs are those expected future costs that differ among options. Fixed costs generally are not considered in a make or buy decision unless it is known that a portion or all of them could be avoided by buying. Since the question gives no data on fixed overhead savings, we must assume the fixed costs will be incurred regardless of the decision made. Therefore, the cost to make is the $10,000 of variable costs. The Lawn Products Division can either buy identical blades outside the company for $12,500 ($1.25 x 10,000 units) or make them for $10,000. The company would save $2,500 by making the part itself.

10. Assume the Blade Division is now at capacity and sufficient demand exists to sell all production to outsiders at present prices. What is the differential cost (benefit) of producing the blade internally?

    a. $2,500 benefit.
    b. $0 differential cost.
    c. $7,500 cost.
    d. $10,000 cost.

The correct answer is (c). (Publisher)
REQUIRED: Differential cost (benefit) of producing the blade internally.
DISCUSSION: The opportunity cost of producing the blades internally is $10,000; the capacity can be used to produce 10,000 blades salable for $2 with a $1 variable cost. The 10,000 blades cost $12,500 if purchased on the outside. Thus, purchasing from the outside has a net cost of $2,500 ($12,500 cost less $10,000 CM from use of capacity now used for internal manufacture), resulting in a $7,500 cost to produce internally.

Questions 11 through 13 are based on Plainfield Company, which manufactures part G for use in its production cycle. The costs per unit for 10,000 units of part G are as follows:

Direct materials	$ 3
Direct labor	15
Variable overhead	6
Fixed overhead	8
	$32

Verona Company has offered to sell Plainfield 10,000 units of part G for $30 per unit. If Plainfield accepts Verona's offer, the released facilities could be used to save $45,000 in relevant costs in the manufacture of part H. In addition, $5 per unit of the fixed overhead applied to part G would be totally eliminated.

Module 15.1: Make or Buy

11. The total relevant costs to manufacture part G are

   a. $320,000.
   b. $300,000.
   c. $290,000.
   d. $250,000.

The correct answer is (c). *(Publisher)*
REQUIRED: The total relevant costs to manufacture part G.
DISCUSSION: The relevant costs to manufacture part G are DM, DL, variable O/H, and that portion of the fixed O/H that could be eliminated.

<u>Avoidable Costs</u>

Direct materials (10,000 x $3)	$ 30,000
Direct labor (10,000 x $15)	150,000
Variable O/H (10,000 x $6)	60,000
Fixed O/H applied (10,000 x $5)	50,000
Total cost to manufacture part G	<u>$290,000</u>

12. The total relevant costs to buy part G are

   a. $320,000.
   b. $300,000.
   c. $290,000.
   d. $255,000.

The correct answer is (d). *(Publisher)*
REQUIRED: The total relevant costs to buy part G.
DISCUSSION: The relevant costs to buy part G are the purchase price less any cost savings available. The purchase price is $300,000 ($30 x 10,000), less the cost savings on part H of $45,000, giving a total cost to buy of $255,000.

13. What alternative is more desirable and by what amount?

	Alternative	Amount
a.	Manufacture	$10,000
b.	Manufacture	$15,000
c.	Buy	$35,000
d.	Buy	$65,000

The correct answer is (c). *(CPA 581 P-29)*
REQUIRED: Whether to make or buy a product and the amount of the savings.
DISCUSSION: In a make or buy decision, only relevant costs are considered. Relevant costs are those expected future costs which will differ among options. Fixed costs generally are not considered in a make or buy decision unless it is known that a portion or all of fixed costs could be avoided by buying. In this situation, fixed costs do vary among the choices. Fixed overhead is applied at a rate of $5 per unit because that is the cost that would be avoided if the company decides to buy.
    Costs relevant to manufacturing part G are $290,000, as computed in Q. 11. Costs relevant to buying part G are $255,000, as computed in Q. 12. It is more desirable to buy at a savings of $35,000 ($290,000 - $255,000).

14. A company owns equipment that is used to manufacture important parts for its production process. The company plans to sell the equipment for $10,000 and to select one of the following alternatives: (1) acquire new equipment for $80,000, (2) purchase the important parts from an outside company at $4 per part. The company should quantitatively analyze the alternatives by comparing the cost of manufacturing the parts

   a. Plus $80,000 to the cost of buying the parts less $10,000.
   b. To the cost of buying the parts less $10,000.
   c. Less $10,000 to the cost of buying the parts.
   d. To the cost of buying the parts.

The correct answer is (d). *(CPA 577 T-35)*
REQUIRED: How a company should quantitatively analyze a make or buy decision.
DISCUSSION: In a make or buy decision, only relevant costs are considered. Relevant costs are those expected future costs that will differ among the options. Fixed costs generally are not considered in a make or buy decision unless it is known that a portion or all of fixed costs could be avoided by buying. The company should quantitatively analyze the alternatives by comparing the relevant cost of manufacturing the parts to the relevant cost of buying the parts.
    Answers (a), (b), and (c) are incorrect because the $10,000 is not a differential (relevant) cost since it will not change under either alternative.

Module 15.1: Make or Buy

15. The following standard costs pertain to a component part manufactured by Bor Co.:

Direct materials	$ 4
Direct labor	10
Factory overhead	40
Standard cost per unit	$54

Factory overhead is applied at $1 per standard machine hour. Fixed capacity cost is 60% of applied factory overhead, and is not affected by any "make or buy" decision. It would cost $49 per unit to buy the part from an outside supplier. In the decision to "make or buy," what is the total relevant unit manufacturing cost?

a. $54.
b. $38.
c. $30.
d. $5.

The correct answer is (c). *(CPA 587 Q-26)*
REQUIRED: The total relevant unit manufacturing cost considered in the make or buy decision.
DISCUSSION: In a make or buy decision, only relevant costs are considered. Relevant costs are those expected future costs that will differ among alternatives. Fixed costs generally are not considered in a make or buy decision unless it is known that a portion or all of fixed costs could be avoided by buying. The total relevant unit manufacturing cost for Bor's component part is $30.

Direct materials	$ 4
Direct labor	10
Factory overhead (40% of $40)	16
Relevant unit cost	$30

16. A company needs special gears for the coming year. The machinery to make the gears can be rented for $100,000 for one year. Alternatively, the company can buy the gears from another firm and avoid the rental cost. Since the demand for the gears may be high (0.6 probability) or low (0.4 probability) and contribution margins vary, the company prepared the following decision tree:

```
                                    Total
                                 Contribution
                                    Margin
                   High (0.6)    $200,000
     Make  Demand
                   Low (0.4)     $125,000

                   High (0.6)    $100,000
     Buy   Demand
                   Low (0.4)     $ 25,000
```

Which of the following statements is correct?

a. The expected value of making the gears is $20,000.
b. The expected value of buying the gears is $70,000.
c. Making the gears is the best choice.
d. Buying the gears is the best choice.

The correct answer is (b). *(CIA 584 IV-28)*
REQUIRED: The true statement about a decision tree.
DISCUSSION: The expected value of buying the gears is

$$.6 \times \$100,000 = \$60,000$$
$$.4 \times \$ 25,000 = \underline{10,000}$$
$$\$70,000$$

Answer (a) is incorrect because the expected value to make the gears is

$$.6 \times \$200,000 = \$120,000$$
$$.4 \times \$125,000 = \underline{50,000}$$
$$\$170,000$$
$$\text{Less machine rental } \underline{(100,000)}$$
$$\phantom{\text{Less machine rental }}\$ 70,000$$

Answers (c) and (d) are incorrect because making or buying the gears gives the same expected value from the data provided, although the projected CMs for the make decision are higher than those for the buy decision. This is because the annual machine rental is a fixed cost deducted from the CM, while the cost of buying the gears is a variable cost used to calculate the CM. The choice will have to be made based on available employees, plant capacity, working capital considerations, etc.

Module 15.1: Make or Buy

17. The Reno Company manufactures Part No. 498 for use in its production cycle. The cost per unit for 20,000 units of Part No. 498 are as follows:

Direct materials	$ 6
Direct labor	30
Variable overhead	12
Fixed overhead applied	16
	$64

The Tray Company has offered to sell 20,000 units of Part No. 498 to Reno for $60 per unit. Reno will make the decision to buy the part from Tray if there is a savings of $25,000 for Reno. If Reno accepts Tray's offer, $9 per unit of the fixed overhead applied would be totally eliminated. Furthermore, Reno has determined that the released facilities could be used to save relevant costs in the manufacture of Part No. 575. In order to have a savings of $25,000, the amount of relevant costs that would be saved by using the released facilities in the manufacture of Part No. 575 would have to be

a. $80,000.
b. $85,000.
c. $125,000.
d. $140,000.

The correct answer is (b). *(CPA 1179 P-36)*
REQUIRED: The relevant costs that must be saved by using the released facilities to achieve a targeted saving.
DISCUSSION: In a make or buy decision, only relevant costs are considered. In this problem, fixed overhead is applied at $9 per unit because that is the amount avoidable if the company decides to buy. The relevant unit costs to make:

Direct materials	$ 6
Direct labor	30
Variable overhead	12
Fixed overhead applied	9
Unit cost to make	$57

Since it costs $57 to make the part and $60 to buy, the cost saved by making is $60,000 ($3 saved per unit x 20,000 units). For the company to realize a savings of $25,000, the amount of relevant costs saved by using the released facilities would have to be $85,000.

18. The Lantern Corporation has 1,000 obsolete lanterns that are carried in inventory at a manufacturing cost of $20,000. If the lanterns are remachined for $5,000, they could be sold for $9,000. If the lanterns are scrapped, they could be sold for $1,000. What alternative is more desirable and what are the total relevant costs for that alternative?

a. Remachine and $5,000.
b. Remachine and $25,000.
c. Scrap and $20,000.
d. Neither, as there is an overall loss under either alternative.

The correct answer is (a). *(CPA 578 P-29)*
REQUIRED: Whether obsolete inventory should be scrapped or further processed and the relevant costs for the preferable alternative.
DISCUSSION: In a make or buy decision, only relevant costs are considered. The relevant cost is the $5,000 to remachine which will result in $9,000 revenue. The inventory costs of $20,000 are irrelevant since they are sunk (already incurred). Lantern should elect to remachine the obsolete inventory to realize $4,000 net revenue ($9,000 sales less $5,000 remachining cost) instead of the $1,000 from scrapping the goods.

19. Light Company has 2,000 obsolete light fixtures that are carried in inventory at a manufacturing cost of $30,000. If the fixtures are reworked for $10,000, they could be sold for $18,000. Alternatively, the light fixtures could be sold for $3,000 to a jobber located in a distant city. In a decision model analyzing these alternatives, the opportunity cost would be

a. $3,000.
b. $10,000.
c. $13,000.
d. $30,000.

The correct answer is (a). *(CPA 580 P-40)*
REQUIRED: The opportunity cost of reworking and selling obsolete inventory.
DISCUSSION: An opportunity cost is the maximum benefit that is forgone when a choice between alternatives has been made. The $3,000 for which the fixtures could be sold is the opportunity cost of reworking them. The $30,000 inventory cost is sunk (already incurred) and is not relevant to the decision whether to rework the fixtures. The decision to rework is preferable since it realizes an additional $5,000 ($18,000 sales - $3,000 opportunity cost - $10,000 cost of rework).

Questions 20 and 21 are based on the following information. Stewart Industries has been producing two bearings, components B12 and B18, for use in production.

	B12	B18
Machine hours required per unit	2.5	3.0
Standard cost per unit		
Direct material	$ 2.25	$ 3.75
Direct labor	4.00	4.50
Manufacturing overhead		
Variable*	2.00	2.25
Fixed**	3.75	4.50
	$12.00	$15.00

*Variable manufacturing overhead is applied on the basis of direct labor hours.
**Fixed manufacturing overhead is applied on the basis of machine hours.

Stewart's annual requirement for these components is 8,000 units of B12 and 11,000 units of B18. Recently, Stewart's management decided to devote additional machine time to other product lines resulting in only 41,000 machine hours per year that can be dedicated to the production of the bearings. An outside company has offered to sell Stewart the annual supply of the bearings at prices of $11.25 for B12 and $13.50 for B18. Stewart wants to schedule the otherwise idle 41,000 machine hours to produce bearings so that the company can minimize its costs (maximize its net benefits).

20. The net benefit (loss) per machine hour that would result if Stewart Industries accepts the supplier's offer of $13.50 per unit for component B18 is

   a. $.50.
   b. $(1.00).
   c. $1.50.
   d. $(1.75).
   e. Some amount other than those given above.

The correct answer is (b). (CMA 686 5-26)
REQUIRED: The net benefit (loss) per machine hour that would result from buying a component.
DISCUSSION: The variable costs of producing B18 total $10.50 ($3.75 + $4.50 + $2.25). Thus, purchasing at $13.50 would result in a loss of $3 per bearing. Since each bearing requires 3 hours of machine time, the loss is $1 per machine hour.

21. Stewart Industries will maximize its net benefits by

   a. Purchasing 4,800 units of B12 and manufacturing the remaining bearings.
   b. Purchasing 8,000 units of B12 and manufacturing 11,000 units of B18.
   c. Purchasing 11,000 units of B18 and manufacturing 8,000 units of B12.
   d. Purchasing 4,000 units of B18 and manufacturing the remaining bearings.
   e. Purchasing and manufacturing some amounts other than those given above.

The correct answer is (d). (CMA 686 5-27)
REQUIRED: The combination of purchasing and manufacturing that will maximize net benefits.
DISCUSSION: Purchasing will increase the company's costs by $3 ($11.25 - $2.25 - $4 - $2) for each B12 bearing, or $1.20 per hour ($3 ÷ 2.5 hrs). Buying B18 will only cost the company an additional $1 per machine hour (see preceding question). Thus, the company should make all the needed B12s and compensate for the machine hours constraint by purchasing B18s. Since each unit of B12 requires 2.5 hours of machine time, the company can produce the needed 8,000 units in 20,000 hours (2.5 x 8,000). The remaining 21,000 hours (41,000 - 20,000) can then be used for the production of 7,000 B18s (21,000 ÷ 3 hrs). Since the annual requirement of B18s is 11,000 units, the other 4,000 units will have to be purchased.

22. Gandy Company has 5,000 obsolete desk lamps that are carried in inventory at a manufacturing cost of $50,000. If the lamps are reworked for $20,000, they could be sold for $35,000. Alternatively, the lamps could be sold for $8,000 to a jobber located in a distant city. In a decision model analyzing these alternatives, the sunk cost would be

   a. $8,000.
   b. $15,000.
   c. $20,000.
   d. $50,000.

The correct answer is (d). (CPA 582 P-30)
REQUIRED: The sunk cost in a model analyzing a decision to sell or rework obsolete inventory.
DISCUSSION: A sunk cost is a past cost that is unavoidable and therefore irrelevant because it will not differ among alternatives. The cost of $50,000 at which the inventory is carried is sunk because it cannot be changed. Since selling the lamps immediately realizes only $8,000, while reworking them produces $15,000 in incremental revenue, the latter is the preferable option.

23. A company is deciding whether to exchange an old asset for a new asset. Within the context of the exchange decision, and ignoring income tax considerations, the undepreciated book balance of the old asset would be considered a(n)

	Sunk Cost	Irrelevant Cost
a.	No	No
b.	Yes	No
c.	No	Yes
d.	Yes	Yes

The correct answer is (d). *(CPA 584 T-49)*
REQUIRED: The classification of an old asset in an exchange decision.
DISCUSSION: A sunk cost is a past cost that is unavoidable; thus, it is irrelevant to future decisions because it will not differ among alternatives.

24. At December 31, Zar Co. had a machine with an original cost of $84,000, accumulated depreciation of $60,000, and an estimated salvage value of zero. On December 31, Zar was considering the purchase of a new machine having a 5-year life, costing $120,000, and having an estimated salvage value of $20,000 at the end of 5 years. In its decision concerning the possible purchase of the new machine, how much should Zar consider as sunk cost at December 31?

a. $120,000.
b. $100,000.
c. $24,000.
d. $4,000.

The correct answer is (c). *(CPA 585 Q-14)*
REQUIRED: The sunk costs in a decision to purchase a new machine.
DISCUSSION: A sunk cost is a past cost that is unavoidable and therefore irrelevant because it will not differ among alternatives. The remaining book value adjusted for salvage value is such a sunk cost.

$84,000 - $60,000 + $0 = $24,000

15.2 Special Order

25. Production of a special order will increase gross profit when the additional revenue from the special order is greater than

a. The nonvariable costs incurred in producing the order.
b. The direct material and labor costs in producing the order.
c. The fixed costs incurred in producing the order.
d. The indirect costs of producing the order.
e. The marginal cost of producing the order.

The correct answer is (e). *(CIA 577 IV-1)*
REQUIRED: When increased gross profit will result from a special order.
DISCUSSION: Gross profit will increase if the incremental or marginal cost of producing the order is less than the revenue from the special order. The revenue from the special order must only exceed the relevant variable costs since it is assumed that the fixed costs will not be affected.
Answers (a) and (c) are incorrect because nonvariable costs, another term for fixed costs, should not increase as a result of producing the special order. Answer (b) is incorrect because indirect variable costs of producing a special order, such as shipping expenses, should also be considered. Answer (d) is incorrect because direct labor and material costs associated with producing a special order must be considered.

26. In considering a special order that will enable a company to make use of presently idle capacity, which of the following costs would be irrelevant?

a. Materials.
b. Depreciation.
c. Direct labor.
d. Variable overhead.

The correct answer is (b). *(CPA 579 T-21)*
REQUIRED: The irrelevant cost when a special order permits use of idle capacity.
DISCUSSION: Since depreciation will be expensed whether the company takes the special order or not, it is irrelevant to the decision to accept the special order. Only the variable costs are relevant.
Answers (a), (c), and (d) are incorrect because the variable costs (materials, direct labor, and variable overhead) are relevant to a decision whether to take a special order.

Module 15.2: Special Order

27. Which of the following cost allocation methods would be used to determine the lowest price that could be quoted for a special order that would utilize idle capacity within a production area?

   a. Job order.
   b. Process.
   c. Variable.
   d. Standard.

The correct answer is (c). *(CPA 579 T-24)*
REQUIRED: The most appropriate cost allocation method for determining the lowest price quoted for a special order.
DISCUSSION: If idle capacity exists, the lowest price that could be quoted for a special order must cover the variable cost. Variable costing considers fixed cost to be a period cost, not a product cost. Fixed costs are not relevant to inventory costing with idle capacity because the fixed costs will be incurred whether or not any production occurs. Any additional revenue in excess of the variable costs will decrease losses or increase profits.
Answers (a) and (b) are incorrect because each is a cost accumulation procedure which considers fixed costs as product costs rather than period costs. Answer (d) is incorrect because standard costing attempts to measure deviations from expected costs.

Questions 28 and 29 are based on Wagner Company, which sells Product A at a price of $21 per unit. Wagner's cost per unit based on the full capacity of 200,000 units is as follows:

Direct materials	$ 4
Direct labor	5
Overhead (2/3 of which is fixed)	6
	$15

A special order offering to buy 20,000 units was received from a foreign distributor. The only selling costs that would be incurred on this order would be $3 per unit for shipping. Wagner has sufficient existing capacity to manufacture the additional units.

---

28. In negotiating a price for the special order, Wagner should set the minimum selling price per unit at

   a. $14.
   b. $15.
   c. $16.
   d. $18.

The correct answer is (a). *(CPA 582 P-24)*
REQUIRED: The minimum selling price per unit for a special order.
DISCUSSION: The minimum selling price should be equal to the incremental costs associated with the order. The total incremental cost is

Direct materials	$ 4
Direct labor	5
Variable overhead	2
Selling cost	3
Total incremental cost	$14

Only the variable overhead is considered an incremental cost because the fixed portion of $4 will be incurred regardless of whether the order is taken (given that Wagner has sufficient capacity).

29. To achieve an increase in operating income of $40,000, Wagner should charge a selling price of

   a. $14.
   b. $15.
   c. $16.
   d. $18.

The correct answer is (c). *(Publisher)*
REQUIRED: The price to achieve a targeted profit.
DISCUSSION: The minimum price is $14 per unit (as calculated in Q. 28), and 20,000 will be sold. With a targeted profit of $40,000, an increase in selling price of $2 per unit ($40,000 ÷ 20,000) is necessary ($14 + $2 = $16).

Module 15.2: Special Order

30. Spencer Company's regular selling price for its product is $10 per unit. Variable costs are $6 per unit. Fixed costs total $1 per unit based on 100,000 units, and remain unchanged within the relevant range of 50,000 units to total capacity of 200,000 units. After sales of 80,000 units were projected for the year, a special order was received for an additional 10,000 units. Spencer Company's minimum selling price for its product is

a. $6.
b. $7.
c. $8.
d. $9.

The correct answer is (a). *(Publisher)*
REQUIRED: The minimum selling price for a product.
DISCUSSION: The minimum selling price is the incremental cost incurred for the special order, or the $6 per unit variable cost.

31. Referring to Q. 30, to increase its operating income by $10,000, what price per unit should Spencer charge for this special order?

a. $7.
b. $8.
c. $10.
d. $11.

The correct answer is (a). *(CPA 1182 Q-29)*
REQUIRED: The minimum selling price per unit for a special order to reach a targeted income.
DISCUSSION: To increase the operating income, the special order must cover the incremental costs associated with the additional units plus the desired $10,000 increase in income. The variable cost is $6 per unit. An additional $1 per unit ($10,000 ÷ 10,000 units) must be charged to attain the desired income level of $10,000. The selling price per unit must therefore be $7. Because production is within the relevant range even after filling the special order, fixed costs are irrelevant to the pricing decision.

32. Woody Company, which manufactures sneakers, has enough idle capacity available to accept a special order of 20,000 pairs of sneakers at $6 a pair. The normal selling price is $10 a pair. Variable manufacturing costs are $4.50 a pair, and fixed manufacturing costs are $1.50 a pair. Woody will not incur any selling expenses as a result of the special order. Woody Company has a unit relevant cost of

a. $5.50.
b. $4.50.
c. $6.00.
d. $4.00.

The correct answer is (b). *(Publisher)*
REQUIRED: The unit relevant cost of a special order.
DISCUSSION: The unit relevant costs include only the variable manufacturing costs of $4.50. Fixed costs are irrelevant to this decision because they will be incurred whether the special order is taken or not (capacity is sufficient).

33. Referring to Q. 32, what would the effect on operating income be if the special order could be accepted without affecting normal sales?

a. $0.
b. $30,000 increase.
c. $90,000 increase.
d. $120,000 increase.

The correct answer is (b). *(CPA 1179 P-35)*
REQUIRED: The effect on operating income if the special order can be accepted without affecting normal sales.
DISCUSSION: The selling price for the special order of $6.00 less the relevant costs of $4.50 (Q. 32) provides a UCM of $1.50. The UCM of $1.50 multiplied by the 20,000 units increases operating income by $30,000.

Module 15.2: Special Order

34. Boyer Company manufactures basketballs. The forecasted income statement for the year before any special orders is as follows:

	Amount	Per Unit
Sales	$4,000,000	$10.00
Manufacturing CGS	3,200,000	8.00
Gross profit	$ 800,000	$ 2.00
Selling expenses	300,000	.75
Operating income	$ 500,000	$ 1.25

Fixed costs included in the above forecasted income statement are $1,200,000 in manufacturing CGS and $100,000 in selling expenses. Boyer received a special order offering to buy 50,000 basketballs for $7.50 each. There will be no additional selling expenses if Boyer accepts. Assume Boyer has sufficient capacity to manufacture 50,000 more basketballs. The unit relevant cost for Boyer's decision is

  a. $8.00.
  b. $5.00.
  c. $8.75.
  d. $5.75.

The correct answer is (b). *(Publisher)*
REQUIRED: The unit relevant cost of a special order.
DISCUSSION: The unit variable manufacturing CGS is the only cost relevant to this decision. Unit sales equal 400,000 ($4,000,000 ÷ $10 per unit). Total variable manufacturing CGS is $2,000,000 ($3,200,000 - $1,200,000 fixed costs). Thus, the unit variable manufacturing cost is $5 ($2,000,000 ÷ 400,000 units).

35. Referring to Q. 34, by what amount would operating income be increased or decreased as a result of accepting the special order?

  a. $25,000 decrease.
  b. $62,500 decrease.
  c. $100,000 increase.
  d. $125,000 increase.

The correct answer is (d). *(CPA 579 P-38)*
REQUIRED: The income effect of accepting the special order, assuming no additional selling expenses.
DISCUSSION: The relevant costs are those that will be affected by taking the special order. Only the unit variable manufacturing CGS of $5 is relevant (see Q. 34). The fixed costs are irrelevant because they will be incurred whether the special order is taken or not (plant capacity need not be expanded). The selling price of $7.50 less the unit variable manufacturing CGS of $5 provides a UCM of $2.50. The UCM of $2.50 multiplied by the 50,000 units results in an increase of $125,000 in operating income.

36. Argus Company, a manufacturer of lamps, budgeted sales of 400,000 lamps at $20 per unit for the year. Variable manufacturing costs were budgeted at $8 per unit, and fixed manufacturing costs at $5 per unit. A special order offering to buy 40,000 lamps for $11.50 each was received by Argus in April. Argus has sufficient plant capacity to manufacture the additional quantity of lamps; however, the production would have to be done by the present work force on an overtime basis at an estimated additional cost of $1.50 per lamp. Argus will not incur any selling expenses as a result of the special order. Argus Company would have a unit relevant cost of

  a. $8.00.
  b. $13.00.
  c. $9.50.
  d. $14.50.

The correct answer is (c). *(Publisher)*
REQUIRED: The unit relevant cost of a special order.
DISCUSSION: The unit relevant costs are those that would be affected by taking the special order. The variable manufacturing cost of $8 and the additional overtime wages are relevant costs. Overtime costs ($1.50 per unit) may be attributed to this specific job. Accordingly, the unit relevant cost is $9.50.

37. Referring to Q. 36, what would be the effect on operating income if the special order could be accepted without affecting normal sales?

   a. $60,000 decrease.
   b. $80,000 increase.
   c. $120,000 decrease.
   d. $140,000 increase.

The correct answer is (b). *(CPA 1180 P-34)*
REQUIRED: The effect on operating income if the special order can be accepted without affecting normal sales.
DISCUSSION: The relevant costs are those that will be affected by taking the special order. The fixed costs are irrelevant because they will be incurred whether the special order is taken or not (plant capacity need not be expanded). The selling price for the special order of $11.50 less the relevant costs of $9.50 (from Q. 36) provides a UCM of $2. The UCM of $2 times the 40,000 units increases operating income by $80,000.

38. Jordan Company budgeted sales of 400,000 calculators at $40 per unit for the year. Variable manufacturing costs were budgeted at $16 per unit, and fixed manufacturing costs at $10 per unit. A special order offering to buy 40,000 calculators for $18 each was received by Jordan in March. Jordan has sufficient plant capacity to manufacture the additional quantity; however, the production would have to be done on an overtime basis at an estimated additional cost of $3 per calculator. Acceptance of the special order would not affect Jordan's normal sales and no selling expenses would be incurred. What would be the effect on operating profit if the special order were accepted?

   a. $120,000 decrease.
   b. $40,000 decrease.
   c. $140,000 decrease.
   d. $80,000 increase.

The correct answer is (b). *(CPA 1182 P-35)*
REQUIRED: The effect on operating income if the special order is accepted.
DISCUSSION: The relevant costs of accepting the special order are the variable costs of $16 per unit and the additional labor cost necessary to fill the order. In this case, there is an overtime cost of $3 per unit. The fixed costs are constant and thus are not relevant (Jordan has sufficient capacity). The total cost per unit is $19 ($16 + $3). The sales price per unit is $18, so a negative contribution of $1 per unit would be realized. This gives a profit decrease of $40,000 ($1 x 40,000). The special order should not be accepted.

15.3 Comprehensive

39. The major pitfall in the contribution margin approach to pricing is

   a. Its failure to recognize fixed costs.
   b. Its failure to recognize depreciation expense.
   c. Its inability to control waste.
   d. Its inability to recognize financing costs of the production in question.

The correct answer is (a). *(Publisher)*
REQUIRED: The major pitfall in the contribution margin approach.
DISCUSSION: The major pitfall in the CM approach to pricing is its failure to incorporate fixed costs into the pricing decision. Although the fixed costs may be overlooked in the short run, they must be covered in the long run if the business is to survive.
Answer (b) is incorrect because depreciation is but one fixed cost not recognized in the CM approach. Answer (c) is incorrect because the CM approach and its alternatives are primarily concerned with managerial decision making rather than waste control. Answer (d) is incorrect because financing costs may be explicitly recognized as variable costs in this approach.

Questions 40 through 48 are based on the following information, which was presented as part of Question 3 on Part 5 of the June 1981 CMA examination.

The Ashley Co. manufactures and sells a household product marketed through direct mail and advertisements in home improvement and gardening magazines. Although similar products are available in hardware and department stores, none is as effective as Ashley's model.

The company uses a standard cost system in its manufacturing accounting. The standards have not undergone a thorough review in the past 18 months. The General Manager has seen no need for such a review because

- The material quality and unit costs were fixed by a 3-year purchase commitment signed in July 1987.
- A 3-year labor contract had been signed in July 1987.
- There have been no significant variations from standard costs for the past three quarters.

The standard cost for the product, as established in July 1987 is presented below:

Material (.75 lb. at $1 per lb.)	$0.75
Direct labor (.3 hrs. at $4 per hour)	1.20
Overhead (.3 hrs. at $7 per hour)	2.10
Standard manufacturing cost per unit	$4.05

The standard for overhead costs was developed from the following budgeted costs based upon an activity level of 1.0 million units (300,000 direct labor hours):

Variable manufacturing overhead	$ 600,000
Fixed manufacturing overhead	1,500,000
Total manufacturing overhead	$2,100,000

The earnings statement and the factory costs for the first quarter of 1989 are presented in the opposite column. The first quarter results indicate that Ashley probably will achieve its sales goal of 1.2 million units for the current year. A total of 320,000 units were manufactured during the first quarter in order to increase inventory levels needed to support the growing sales volume.

ACTION Hardware, a national chain, recently asked Ashley to manufacture and sell a slightly modified version of the product which ACTION would distribute through its stores.

ACTION has offered to buy a minimum quantity of 200,000 units each year over the next 3 years and has offered to pay $4.10 for each unit, F.O.B. shipping point.

The Ashley management is interested in the proposal because it represents a new market. The company has adequate capacity to meet the production requirements. However, in addition to the possible financial results of taking the order, Ashley must consider carefully the other consequences of this departure from its normal practices. The president asked an assistant to the general manager to make an estimate of the financial aspects of the proposal for the first 12 months.

The assistant recommended that the order not be accepted and presented the analysis shown below to support the recommendation.

Sales Proposal of ACTION Hardware
First Twelve Months Results

Proposed sales (200,000 at $4.10)	$820,000
Estimated costs and expenses	
Manufacturing (200,000 at $4.05)	$810,000
Sales salaries	10,000
Administrative salaries	20,000
Total estimated costs	$840,000
Net loss	$ (20,000)

Note: None of our regular selling costs are included because this is a new market. However, a 16.6% increase in sales and administrative salaries has been incorporated because sales volume will increase by that amount.

Ashley Co.
First Quarter Earnings
Period ended March 31, 1989

Sales (300,000 units)		$2,700,000
Cost of goods sold		
Standard cost of goods	$1,215,000	
Variation from standard costs	12,000	1,227,000
Gross profit		$1,473,000
Operating expenses		
Selling		
Advertising	$ 200,000	
Mailing list costs	175,000	
Postage	225,000	
Salaries	60,000	
Administrative		
Salaries	120,000	
Office rent	45,000	
Total operating expenses		825,000
Income before taxes		$ 648,000
Income taxes (45%)		291,600
Net income		$ 356,400

Ashley Co.
Factory Costs
For the Quarter Ended March 31, 1989

Materials	$ 266,000
Direct labor	452,000
Variable manufacturing overhead	211,000
Fixed manufacturing overhead	379,000
Total manufacturing costs	$1,308,000
Less: Standard cost of goods manufactured	$1,296,000
Unfavorable variation from standard cost	$ 12,000

40. One of the deficiencies in the financial analysis prepared by the general manager's assistant is that the

   a. Contribution margin is not calculated in the analysis.
   b. Sales projections are not realistic.
   c. Current changes in standard costs are recognized.
   d. Financial analysis is adequately prepared.

The correct answer is (a). *(Publisher)*
REQUIRED: The deficiency in the financial analysis.
DISCUSSION: A primary deficiency in the financial analysis is that no contribution margin analysis is calculated. The analysis uses a full standard cost approach to determine the profitability of a special project. Special projects should be evaluated based upon their incremental costs and benefits.
Answer (b) is incorrect because the sales projection is based on the buyer's minimum purchase quantity. Answer (c) is incorrect because a deficiency in the analysis is that current changes are not reflected. Answer (d) is incorrect because an adequate financial analysis should include CM data.

41. A determination should be made in regard to fixed manufacturing costs. This determination consists of

   a. Anticipating a decrease because of the allocation of fixed costs to include the special order.
   b. Anticipating an increase owing to the increased volume incurred as a result of the special order.
   c. No consideration should be made in regard to fixed manufacturing costs.
   d. Administrative and sales salaries.

The correct answer is (b). *(Publisher)*
REQUIRED: The necessary determination regarding fixed manufacturing costs.
DISCUSSION: The additional financial data needed for a more comprehensive analysis include an analysis of fixed manufacturing costs for any incremental increases as a result of increased volume. The special order may be such a significant proportion of the total manufacturing capacity that it will in effect increase fixed costs in a step pattern.
Answer (a) is incorrect because the special order will not decrease fixed costs. Only incremental increases in fixed costs would be allocated to the special order. Answer (c) is incorrect because one must consider a possible increase in fixed costs. Answer (d) is incorrect because administrative and sales salaries are not fixed manufacturing costs.

42. An important nonfinancial issue that Ashley Company should consider is

   a. Competition and new product inventions.
   b. Technological changes and depreciation.
   c. Charitable organizations.
   d. Morale of its employees.

The correct answer is (a). *(Publisher)*
REQUIRED: The greatest nonfinancial issue that should be considered.
DISCUSSION: Nonfinancial issues that Ashley should consider include competition and new product inventions. For example, the extent to which this modified version of the product competes with Ashley's own sales of the regular product is a crucial factor. The possibility that a competitor might accept the proposal may also enter into this decision. Another issue is Ashley's willingness to be locked into a long-term agreement, given the 3-year material and labor contracts that are due for renewal in about 1 year.
Answers (b), (c), and (d) are incorrect because each is a lesser issue in deciding whether to accept an order for a given quantity of a specifically described product.

43. Revisions of standards should be made for

   a. Variable overhead.
   b. Labor and material.
   c. Variable overhead and labor.
   d. Variable overhead, labor, and material.

The correct answer is (d). *(Publisher)*
REQUIRED: The item(s) needing revision of standards.
DISCUSSION: Revisions of standards are appropriate for variable overhead, direct labor, and raw materials. These three components have not been reviewed in the past 18 months. These items may have undergone significant change within this period, and additional change may be predicted in the immediate future.
Answers (a), (b), and (c) are incorrect because revision of the standards for all components of standard unit cost is needed.

Questions 44 through 47 are based on the information presented on page 440.

44. Assume that the factory costs incurred in the first quarter reflect the anticipated costs for the ACTION special purchase. What is the expected materials cost per unit?

a. $.75.
b. $1.00.
c. $.83.
d. $.80.

The correct answer is (c). *(Publisher)*
REQUIRED: The expected materials cost per unit for the special purchase.
DISCUSSION: The expected materials cost per unit based upon the factory costs incurred in the first quarter is equal to the materials cost in the first quarter divided by the number of units. The factory cost in the first quarter for materials was $266,000, and 320,000 units were manufactured. Thus, the unit materials cost equals $.83125.

45. Assume that the factory costs incurred in the first quarter reflect the anticipated costs for the ACTION special purchase. What is the total expected direct labor cost?

a. $240,000.
b. $452,000.
c. $282,500.
d. $200,000.

The correct answer is (c). *(Publisher)*
REQUIRED: The total expected direct labor cost for the special purchase.
DISCUSSION: The total expected direct labor cost is equal to the expected direct labor cost per unit multiplied by the anticipated number of units. Based on the incurred costs in the first quarter of $452,000 and the 320,000 units manufactured, the unit direct labor cost is equal to $1.4125. The sales proposal involves 200,000 units. Hence, the expected direct labor cost equals $282,500 ($1.4125 x 200,000).

46. Assume that the first quarter factory costs incurred reflect the anticipated costs for the ACTION special purchase. What is the expected variable overhead cost per unit?

a. $2.10.
b. $1.50.
c. $.60.
d. $.66.

The correct answer is (d). *(Publisher)*
REQUIRED: The expected variable overhead cost per unit for the special purchase.
DISCUSSION: The expected variable overhead cost per unit based on the first quarter production is equal to the variable manufacturing overhead cost incurred divided by the number of units manufactured. Accordingly, $211,000 divided by 320,000 equals $.659375.

47. Assume that the actual cost relationships in the quarter ended March 31, 1989 relevant to this decision about the sales proposal of ACTION Hardware are valid. What is the manufacturing contribution margin?

a. $580,625.
b. $239,375.
c. $820,000.
d. $10,000.

The correct answer is (b). *(Publisher)*
REQUIRED: The manufacturing contribution margin based on the cost data for the first quarter.
DISCUSSION: The manufacturing CM is calculated by deducting incremental manufacturing costs from the proposed sales. Assuming that the actual cost relationships for the quarter ended March 31 are valid, the per unit costs incurred during the quarter must be used to determine the CM. Using the unit costs for materials (Q. 44), labor (Q. 45), and variable manufacturing O/H (Q. 46), the manufacturing CM is calculated as below. Note that the decision to sell to ACTION will increase profits by $239,375 (not decrease them by $20,000).

Proposed sales (200,000 x $4.10)		$820,000
Incremental manufacturing costs:		
Material (200,000 x $.83125)	$166,250	
Labor (200,000 x $1.4125)	282,500	
Variable O/H (200,000 x $.659375)	131,875	580,625
Manufacturing CM		$239,375

Module 15.3: Comprehensive

48. Refer to the information presented on page 440. In the analysis provided by the assistant, the assumption regarding sales and administrative salaries may be deficient because of

   a. The inclusion of any sales and administrative expenses.
   b. The linear extrapolation of sales and administrative expenses.
   c. Both (a) and (b).
   d. Neither (a) nor (b); there is no deficiency regarding the inclusion of sales and administrative expenses.

The correct answer is (c). *(Publisher)*
REQUIRED: Whether and why the special order selling costs assumption is unsound.
DISCUSSION: The assistant included sales and administrative expenses as estimated costs of the special purchase. The assumption was also made that the increase in sales and administrative expenses would be linear. The inclusion of these expenses as variable costs in the contribution margin analysis is questionable. But even if these costs are not fixed, there is no basis for assuming that the increase is directly proportionate to sales.

Questions 49 through 52 are based on the following information, which was presented as part of Question 3 on Part 5 of the December 1977 CMA examination.

Bundt Foods Company produces and sells many products in each of its 35 different product lines. Occasionally a product or an entire product line is dropped because it ceases to be profitable. The company does not have a formalized program for reviewing its products on a regular basis to identify those products that should be eliminated.

At a recent meeting of Bundt Foods' top management, one person stated that there probably were several products or possibly a product line that were unprofitable or producing an unsatisfactory return on investment. After considerable discussion, management decided that Bundt Foods should establish a formalized product discontinuance program. The purpose of the program would be to review the company's individual products and product lines on a regular and ongoing basis to identify problem areas.

The vice president of finance has proposed that a person be assigned to the program on a full-time basis. This person would work closely with the marketing and accounting departments in determining (1) the factors that indicate when a product's importance is declining and (2) the underlying data that would be required in evaluating whether a product or product line should be discontinued.

---

49. Which of the following is not a benefit of Bundt's formalized product discontinuance program?

   a. Provides a structured planning mechanism.
   b. Helps identify problems in their initial stages.
   c. Allows less attention to be focused on the pricing of products.
   d. Helps establish a more profitable mix of products.

The correct answer is (c). *(Publisher)*
REQUIRED: The item not a benefit of a formalized product discontinuance program.
DISCUSSION: The benefits of a formalized product discontinuance program include (1) providing a structured planning mechanism; (2) identification of items or product lines with deteriorating profit margins, which assists in identifying areas that need improvement; (3) identifying problems in their initial stages, providing an opportunity for corrective action; and (4) establishment of a more profitable mix of products by providing a continuous review mechanism. This continuous review would permit an in-depth analysis of pricing and market conditions. Thus, the pricing of products would continue to be a prime concern.

50. Formalized procedures and better planning would enable executives to

   a. Spend more time on the golf course.
   b. Devote more time to profitable products.
   c. Decentralize the control process.
   d. Concentrate on the less important problems.

The correct answer is (b). *(Publisher)*
REQUIRED: The advantage of formalized procedures and better planning.
DISCUSSION: A product discontinuance program releases important and scarce resources, e.g., executives' time. Formalized procedures and better planning enable executives to devote their scarce resources to the more profitable and promising projects.
   Answer (a) is incorrect because it is a nonsense answer. Answer (c) is incorrect because formal procedures and better planning are useful in both centralized and decentralized organizations. This new program is actually centralizing the control process for Bundt. Answer (d) is incorrect because executives should concentrate on important issues.

444 Module 15.3: Comprehensive

51. Refer to the information preceding question 49 on page 443. Which of the following factors would not indicate the diminishing importance of a product or product line?

  a. Unfavorable future market potential.
  b. Increase in promotional budget.
  c. Declining market share.
  d. Increasing cost to sales ratio.

The correct answer is (b). *(Publisher)*
REQUIRED: The factor not indicating the declining importance of a product or product line.
DISCUSSION: The diminishing importance of a product or product line is indicated by unfavorable future market potential, declining sales volume and market share, and an increasing cost to sales ratio. Each of these indicators suggests that the product is a candidate for discontinuance. Increasing the promotional budget and sales effort merely to maintain sales at prior levels is also a negative indicator. However, an increase in the promotional budget per se does not mean that the product's importance has diminished.

52. Refer to the information preceding question 49 on page 443. All of the following accounting information would be helpful to management in making these decisions except

  a. Number of units previously sold.
  b. Comparison of past and present sales revenue totals.
  c. Inventory turnover for the time period.
  d. The market share for each product line.

The correct answer is (d). *(Publisher)*
REQUIRED: The accounting information not helpful in evaluating a product.
DISCUSSION: The accounting department normally provides management with information for making product evaluation decisions. Such accounting information includes the number of units previously sold, past and present sales revenue, inventory turnover, traceable fixed production and marketing costs, traceable variable production and marketing costs, and current and past pricing structure, including list price and discount policies. Market share information is useful in developing marketing strategies but not in determining the profitability of a product line.

Questions 53 through 57 are based on the following information, which was presented as part of Question 1 on Part 5 of the June 1976 CMA examination.

Anchor Company manufactures several different styles of jewelry cases. Management estimates that during the third quarter of this year the company will be operating at 80% of normal capacity. Because Anchor wants to increase utilization of plant capacity, the company will consider a special order.

Anchor has received special order inquiries from two companies. The first order is from JCP Inc., which would like to market a jewelry case similar to one of Anchor's cases. The JCP case would be marketed under JCP's own label. JCP has offered Anchor $5.75 per case for 20,000 cases to be shipped by October 1. The cost data for the Anchor jewelry case which is similar to the specifications of the JCP special order are as follows:

Regular selling price per unit	$9.00
Costs per unit	
Raw materials	$2.50
Direct labor (.5 hrs. x $6)	3.00
Overhead (.25 machine hrs. x $4)	1.00
Total costs	$6.50

According to the specifications provided by JCP Inc., the special order case requires less expensive raw materials. Consequently, the raw materials will only cost $2.25 per case. Management has estimated that the remaining costs, labor time, and machine time will be the same as for the Anchor case.

The second special order was submitted by the Krage Company for 7,500 jewelry cases at $7.50 per case. These jewelry cases, like JCP's, would be marketed under the Krage label and shipped by October 1. However, the Krage jewelry case is different from any jewelry case in the Anchor line. The estimated per unit costs of this case are as follows:

Raw materials	$3.25
Direct labor (.5 hrs. x $6)	3.00
Overhead (.5 machine hrs. x $4)	2.00
Total unit costs	$8.25

In addition, Anchor will incur $1,500 in additional set-up costs and will have to purchase a $2,500 special device to manufacture these cases; this device will be discarded once the special order is completed.

The Anchor manufacturing capabilities are limited to the total machine hours available. The plant capacity under normal operations is 90,000 machine hours per year or 7,500 machine hours per month. The budgeted fixed overhead for the year is $216,000. All manufacturing overhead costs are applied to production on the basis of machine hours at $4 per hour.

Anchor will have the entire third quarter to work on the special orders. Management does not expect any repeat sales to be generated from either special order. Company practice precludes Anchor from subcontracting any portion of an order when special orders are not expected to generate repeat sales.

Module 15.3: Comprehensive

53. What is the excess capacity of machine hours available in the third quarter?

a. 1,500 hours.
b. 4,500 hours.
c. 3,000 hours.
d. 18,000 hours.

The correct answer is (b). *(Publisher)*
REQUIRED: The excess capacity of machine hours available in the third quarter.
DISCUSSION: The excess capacity of machine hours available in the third quarter is equal to the proportionate capacity hours available in that quarter less any required regular production. The monthly plant capacity is 7,500 machine hours. The estimated monthly use is 80% of 7,500, or 6,000 machine hours, leaving excess capacity per month of 1,500 machine hours. Total excess capacity available is thus 4,500 machine hours (3 months x 1,500 hours).

54. What is the variable overhead rate per machine hour?

a. $.80.
b. $1.60.
c. $4.00.
d. $2.00.

The correct answer is (b). *(Publisher)*
REQUIRED: The variable overhead rate per machine hour.
DISCUSSION: Budgeted fixed O/H of $216,000 divided by 90,000 machine hours equals a fixed O/H rate of $2.40 per machine hour. Total O/H is charged at $4.00 per machine hour. Accordingly, the variable O/H rate is $1.60 per machine hour ($4.00 - $2.40).

55. Would you accept JCP's order?

a. Yes, it would be cost effective.
b. No, there are not enough hours in the quarter.
c. Yes, there are plenty of hours available.
d. No, it would cost too much.

The correct answer is (b). *(Publisher)*
REQUIRED: The feasibility of accepting the first special order.
DISCUSSION: JCP's order should be accepted only if sufficient capacity is available and the CM is positive. The unit material cost is $2.25 and unit direct labor cost is $3.00. The order requires .25 machine hours per case, and overhead should be charged at $1.60 per hour (see Q. 54). Hence, unit cost is $5.65 ($2.25 + $3.00 + $.40), and the UCM is positive (price = $5.75). But the plant capacity available is 4,500 hours (see Q. 53), and the required hours are 5,000 (.25 x 20,000 cases). Thus, insufficient machine hours are available for JCP's order.

56. What is the unit contribution margin per case for Krage's order?

a. $.25.
b. $(.75).
c. $1.25.
d. $.45.

The correct answer is (d). *(Publisher)*
REQUIRED: The unit contribution margin for the second special order.
DISCUSSION: The raw materials and direct labor costs for the Krage order are given. But since this is a special order not requiring excess capacity (.5 hours x 7,500 cases = 3,750 hours), the budgeted fixed costs are not relevant to the decision to accept the order. Fixed costs are budgeted at $2.40 per machine hour ($216,000 ÷ 90,000 hours capacity). Accordingly, overhead should be charged only for variable costs, at $1.60 per hour ($4 - $2.40).

Price offered per unit		$7.50
Production costs		
Raw materials	$3.25	
Direct labor (.5 x $6)	3.00	
Overhead (.5 x $1.60 VC)	.80	(7.05)
Unit contribution margin		$ .45

57. What is the actual gain (loss) incurred by accepting Krage's order?

a. $3,375.
b. $(625).
c. $1,520.
d. $(1,895).

The correct answer is (b). *(Publisher)*
REQUIRED: The gain or loss incurred by accepting the second special order.
DISCUSSION: The gain or loss incurred by accepting Krage's order requires calculation of all incremental costs and revenues. The CM as calculated in Q. 56 is $.45 per case. Total CM therefore equals $3,375 ($.45 x 7,500 cases). The fixed costs related to the order include set-up costs of $1,500 and the special device to be purchased for $2,500, a total of $4,000. $4,000 costs - $3,375 CM = $(625).

Questions 58 through 66 are based on the following information, which was presented as part of Question 3 on Part 4 of the December 1974 CMA examination.

The Scent Company sells men's toiletries to retail stores throughout the United States. For planning and control purposes, Scent is organized into 12 geographic regions with two to six territories within each region. One salesperson is assigned to each territory with exclusive rights to all sales made in that territory. Merchandise is shipped from the manufacturing plant to the 12 regional warehouses, and the sales in each territory are shipped from the regional warehouse. National headquarters allocates a specific amount at the beginning of the year for regional advertising.

The net sales for the Scent Company for the year ended September 30 totaled $10 million. Costs incurred by national headquarters for national administration, advertising, and warehousing are summarized as follows:

National administration	$250,000
National advertising	125,000
National warehousing	175,000
	$550,000

Each salesperson receives a base salary plus a 4% commission on all items sold in his/her territory. Bad debt expense has averaged 0.4% of net sales in the past. Travel and entertainment costs are incurred by the salespersons calling upon their customers. Freight-out is a function of the quantity of goods shipped and the distance shipped. Thirty percent of the insurance is expended for protection of the inventory while it is in the regional warehouse, and the remainder is incurred for the protection of the warehouse. Supplies are used in the warehouse for packing the merchandise that is shipped. Wages relate to the hourly paid employees who fill orders in the warehouse. The warehouse operating costs account contains such costs as heat, light, and maintenance.

The cost analyses and statistics by territory for the current year (presented below the income statement in the opposite column) are representative of both past experience and expected future operations.

Scent Company
Statement of Operations for
South Atlantic Region
For the Year Ended September 30

Net sales		$900,000
Costs and expenses:		
Advertising fees	$ 54,700	
Bad debt expense	3,600	
Cost of sales	460,000	
Freight-out	22,600	
Insurance	10,000	
Salaries and employee benefits	81,600	
Sales commissions	36,000	
Supplies	12,000	
Travel and entertainment	14,100	
Wages and employee benefits	36,000	
Warehouse depreciation	8,000	
Warehouse operating costs	15,000	
Total costs and expenses		753,600
Territory contribution		$146,400

The South Atlantic Region consists of two territories, Green and Purple. The salaries and employee benefits consist of the following data:

Regional vice president	$24,000
Regional marketing manager	15,000
Regional warehouse manager	13,400
Salespersons (one for each territory with all receiving the same salary base)	15,600
Employee benefits (20%)	13,600
	$81,600

	Green	Purple	Total
Sales	$300,000	$600,000	$900,000
Cost of sales	$184,000	$276,000	$460,000
Advertising fees	$ 21,800	$ 32,900	$ 54,700
Travel & entertainment	$ 6,300	$ 7,800	$ 14,100
Freight-out	$ 9,000	$ 13,600	$ 22,600
Units sold	150,000	350,000	500,000
Pounds shipped	210,000	390,000	600,000
Salesperson miles traveled	21,600	38,400	60,000

58. What are the total variable and fixed costs incurred in order-getting for the South Atlantic Region?

    a. $36,000 and $76,460.
    b. $27,000 and $18,000.
    c. $39,600 and $105,520.
    d. $26,400 and $76,660.

The correct answer is (c). *(Publisher)*
REQUIRED: The total variable and fixed costs incurred in order-getting.
DISCUSSION: Order-getting variable costs include the sales commissions of $36,000 (4% x $900,000 sales) and the bad debts of $3,600 (0.4% x $900,000 sales), a total of $39,600. Order-getting fixed costs include advertising fees ($54,700), travel and entertainment ($14,100), salaries for the salespersons and the regional marketing manager of $30,600 ($15,600 + $15,000), and employee benefits of $6,120 (20% of salaries). Total fixed order-getting costs are $105,520 ($54,700 + $14,100 + $30,600 + $6,120).

Module 15.3: Comprehensive

59. What are the total order-getting costs attributable to the Green Territory?

a. $50,660.
b. $76,460.
c. $50,060.
d. $105,520.

The correct answer is (a). *(Publisher)*
REQUIRED: The total order-getting costs attributable to the Green Territory.
DISCUSSION: The total order-getting costs attributable to the Green Territory include both variable and fixed costs directly related to the activities within the Green Territory. The variable costs are sales commissions and bad debts. Fixed costs are advertising fees, travel and entertainment, salaries, and employee benefits.

Variable costs:	
Sales commissions (.04 x $300,000)	$12,000
Bad debt (.004 x $300,000)	1,200
Total variable costs	$13,200
Fixed costs:	
Advertising fees	$21,800
Travel and entertainment	6,300
Salaries ($15,600 ÷ 2)	7,800
Employee benefits (.2 x $7,800)	1,560
Total fixed costs	$37,460
Total order-getting costs	$50,660

60. What are the total variable order-filling costs attributable to the Purple Territory? (Supplies and wages and employment benefits are allocated on the basis of pounds shipped; inventory insurance is allocated on the basis of cost of goods sold.)

a. $533,650.
b. $579,680.
c. $211,000.
d. $322,600.

The correct answer is (d). *(Publisher)*
REQUIRED: The total variable order-filling costs attributable to the Purple Territory.
DISCUSSION: The total variable order-filling costs attributable to the Purple Territory include the cost of sales, freight-out, supplies, wages and benefits, and insurance on inventory. The Purple Territory accounts for 65% (390,000 ÷ 600,000) of the pounds shipped by the Region and for 60% of CGS ($276,000 ÷ $460,000). Insurance on the inventory for the Region is $3,000 (.3 x $10,000). Purple's variable order-filling costs are:

Cost of sales	$276,000
Freight-out	13,600
Supplies (.65 x $12,000)	7,800
Wages and employment benefits (.65 x $36,000)	23,400
Insurance on inventory (.6 x $3,000)	1,800
Total variable order-filling costs	$322,600

61. What order-getting costs remain unallocated in the South Atlantic region?

a. $30,000.
b. $15,000.
c. $3,000.
d. $18,000.

The correct answer is (d). *(Publisher)*
REQUIRED: The unallocated order-getting costs in the South Atlantic region.
DISCUSSION: The unallocated order-getting costs in the South Atlantic region are those that cannot be attributed to either of the territories. These are the regional marketing manager's salary and associated employee benefits.

Salaries	$15,000
Employee benefits (.2 x $15,000)	3,000
Unallocated order-getting costs	$18,000

62. What administrative costs remain unallocated in the South Atlantic region?

a. $24,000.
b. $4,800.
c. $28,800.
d. $20,000.

The correct answer is (c). *(Publisher)*
REQUIRED: The unallocated administrative costs in the South Atlantic region.
DISCUSSION: The unallocated administrative costs in the South Atlantic region include only the regional vice president's salary and associated employee benefits.

Salary	$24,000
Employee benefits (.2 x $24,000)	4,800
Total administrative costs	$28,800

Module 15.3: Comprehensive

> Questions 63 through 66 are based on the information presented on page 446.

63. The total fixed and variable costs incurred in order-filling are

a. $46,080 and $533,600.
b. $322,600 and $533,600.
c. $324,800 and $753,600.
d. $269,000 and $453,000.

The correct answer is (a). *(Publisher)*
REQUIRED: The total fixed and variable costs incurred in order-filling.
DISCUSSION: Order-filling fixed costs include warehouse operating cost ($15,000), insurance on warehouse $7,000 ($10,000 - $3,000 insurance of inventory), depreciation ($8,000), salary of the warehouse manager ($13,400), and employee benefits of $2,680 (20% x $13,400), a total of $46,080.
Order-filling variable costs include cost of sales ($460,000), freight-out ($22,600), supplies ($12,000), wages and employee benefits ($36,000), and insurance on inventory of $3,000 (30% x $10,000 insurance expense), a total of $533,600.

64. What order-filling costs remain unallocated in the South Atlantic region?

a. $15,000.
b. $28,400.
c. $46,080.
d. $31,080.

The correct answer is (c). *(Publisher)*
REQUIRED: The unallocated order-filling costs in the South Atlantic region.
DISCUSSION: The unallocated order-filling costs in the South Atlantic region include the warehouse operating costs, insurance on the warehouse, depreciation, and the warehouse manager's salary and associated benefits.

Warehouse operating costs	$15,000
Warehouse insurance (.7 x $10,000)	7,000
Depreciation	8,000
Warehouse manager's salary	13,400
Employee benefits (.2 x $13,400)	2,680
Unallocated order-filling costs	$46,080

65. The total costs incurred for the South Atlantic Region are

a. $579,680.
b. $851,320.
c. $629,180.
d. $753,600.

The correct answer is (d). *(Publisher)*
REQUIRED: The total costs incurred for the South Atlantic Region.
DISCUSSION: The total costs incurred is the sum of total order-getting costs, total order-filling costs, and total administrative expenses. Total order-getting costs were calculated in Q. 58 as $145,120 ($39,600 VC + $105,520 FC) and total order-filling costs in Q. 63 as $579,680 ($533,600 VC + $46,080 FC). The fixed administrative expenses include the $24,000 salary of the regional vice president and employee benefits of $4,800 (20% x $24,000), for a grand total of $753,600 ($145,120 + $579,680 + $24,000 + $4,800). This total can be found in the statement of operations for the South Atlantic Region.

66. If Scent split the Purple Territory into two separate territories, what additional costs may be incurred?

a. Increase in salespersons' salaries.
b. Increase in salespersons' salaries and fringe benefits.
c. Increase in travel and entertainment expense.
d. No additional costs can be computed given the above information.

The correct answer is (b). *(Publisher)*
REQUIRED: The effect of splitting one territory into two separate territories.
DISCUSSION: The primary increase in cost incurred as a result of the territorial division would be to increase salespersons' salaries and fringe benefits since more sales staff would be needed.
Answer (a) is incorrect because, if salaries increase, so will fringe benefits (20% of salaries). Answer (c) is incorrect because travel and entertainment expense would not increase significantly. The two new territories would only cover the area of the original Purple Territory.

Module 15.3: Comprehensive

Questions 67 through 74 are based on the following information, which was presented as part of Question 2 on Part 5 of the December 1981 CMA examination.

Jenco Inc. manufactures a combination fertilizer/weedkiller under the name Fertikil. This is the only product Jenco produces. Fertikil is sold nationwide through normal marketing channels to retail nurseries and garden stores.

Taylor Nursery plans to sell a similar fertilizer/weedkiller compound through its regional nursery chain under its own private label. Taylor has asked Jenco to submit a bid for a 25,000-pound order of the private brand compound. While the chemical composition of the Taylor compound differs from Fertikil, the manufacturing process is very similar.

The Taylor compound would be produced in 1,000-pound lots. Each lot would require 60 direct labor hours and the following chemicals:

Chemicals	Quantity in Pounds
CW-3	400
JX-6	300
MZ-8	200
BE-7	100

The first three chemicals (CW-3, JX-6, MZ-8) are all used in the production of Fertikil. BE-7 was used in a compound that Jenco has discontinued. This chemical was not sold or discarded because it does not deteriorate and there have been adequate storage facilities. Jenco could sell BE-7 at the prevailing market price less $.10 per pound selling/handling expenses.

Jenco also has on hand a chemical called CN-5 which was manufactured for use in another product which is no longer produced. CN-5, which cannot be used in Fertikil, can be substituted for CW-3 on a one-for-one basis without affecting the quality of the Taylor compound. The quantity of CN-5 in inventory has a salvage value of $500.

Inventory and cost data for the chemicals that can be used to produce the Taylor compound are

Raw Material	Pounds in Inventory	Actual Price Per Pound When Purchased	Current Market Price Per Pound
CW-3	22,000	$ .80	$ .90
JX-6	5,000	$ .55	$ .60
MZ-8	8,000	$1.40	$1.60
BE-7	4,000	$ .60	$ .65
CN-5	5,500	$ .75	(salvage)

The current direct labor rate is $7 per hour. The manufacturing overhead rate is established at the beginning of the year and is applied consistently throughout the year using direct labor hours (DLH) as the base. The predetermined overhead rate for the current year, based on a two-shift capacity of 400,000 total DLH with no overtime, is as follows:

Variable manufacturing overhead	$2.25 per DLH
Fixed manufacturing overhead	3.75 per DLH
Combined rate	$6.00 per DLH

Jenco's production manager reports that the present equipment and facilities are adequate to manufacture the Taylor compound. However, Jenco is within 800 hours of its two-shift capacity this month before it must schedule overtime. If need be, the Taylor compound could be produced on regular time by shifting a portion of Fertikil production to overtime. Jenco's rate for overtime hours is one-and-one-half the regular pay rate, or $10.50 per hour. There is no allowance for any overtime premium in the manufacturing overhead rate.

Jenco's standard markup policy for new products is 25% of full manufacturing cost.

67. If Jenco bids this month for the special one-time order of 25,000 pounds, how much would be the total direct labor cost?

   a. $10,500.
   b. $12,950.
   c. $16,250.
   d. $2,450.

The correct answer is (b). *(Publisher)*

REQUIRED: The total direct labor cost for the one-time order.

DISCUSSION: Given that 25 lots are produced, each requiring 60 direct labor hours, 1,500 hours will be necessary. This one-time order requires 800 hours scheduled during regular time and 700 remaining hours of overtime. Thus, overtime is a relevant cost for this order. 1,500 DLH times $7.00 per DLH equals $10,500. 700 DLH times $3.50 per DLH (the overtime premium) equals $2,450. Total direct labor cost equals $12,950 ($10,500 + $2,450).

> Questions 68 through 70 are based on the information presented on page 449.

68. If Jenco bids this month for the special one-time order of 25,000 pounds, what would be the total overhead cost used for this decision?

   a. $5,625.
   b. $9,000.
   c. $3,375.
   d. $7,500.

The correct answer is (c). *(Publisher)*
REQUIRED: The total overhead cost for the one-time order.
DISCUSSION: The total O/H cost used for this decision would include only the variable O/H; the fixed O/H is not relevant for this one-time order. 1,500 direct labor hours would be used (see Q. 67). The variable O/H rate is $2.25 per hour. Thus, $3,375 of total O/H is relevant to this decision (1,500 DLH x $2.25).

69. If Jenco bids this month for the special one-time order of 25,000 pounds of the private brand, what would be the special order's total direct materials cost?

   a. $17,050.
   b. $18,425.
   c. $20,480.
   d. $19,625.

The correct answer is (b). *(Publisher)*
REQUIRED: The direct materials cost of the special order.
DISCUSSION: The special order of 25,000 pounds would require chemicals used in manufacturing the firm's main product (CW-3, JX-6, MZ-8). The relevant cost of these chemicals is the current market price per pound (the expected future cost). Chemicals not used in current production (BE-7 and CN-5) have a relevant cost equal to their value to the firm.

CW-3: 400 lbs. per lot x 25 lots = 10,000 lbs.

Substitute 5,500 lbs. of CN-5 on a one-for-one basis. The relevant cost is the salvage value.	$ 500
The remaining 4,500 lbs. of CW-3 have a relevant cost of $.90 per lb., the expected future cost.	4,050
JX-6: 300 lbs. per lot x 25 lots = 7,500 lbs. at $.60 per lb.	4,500
MZ-8: 200 lbs. per lot x 25 lots = 5,000 lbs. at $1.60 per lb.	8,000
BE-7: 100 lbs. per lot x 25 lots = 2,500 lbs. The relevant cost per lb. is $.55 ($.65 - $.10 handling charge), the amount Jenco could realize by selling BE-7.	1,375
Total direct materials cost	$18,425

70. What would the total variable cost of the special order be this month?

   a. $21,800.
   b. $36,350.
   c. $30,375.
   d. $34,750.

The correct answer is (d). *(Publisher)*
REQUIRED: The total variable cost of the special order.
DISCUSSION: The total cost of the special order is the sum of DM, DL, and O/H. The cost of materials was calculated at $18,425 (Q. 69). Overtime is a relevant cost of this order (see Q. 67). This special order will not increase fixed O/H costs and is not a continuing product that should contribute to fixed O/H. Therefore, fixed O/H is not relevant; the only relevant O/H charge is the variable O/H rate.

Total direct materials cost	$18,425
Direct labor (Q. 67)	12,950
Overhead (Q. 68)	3,375
Total cost of special order	$34,750

Module 15.3: Comprehensive

> Questions 71 through 74 are based on the information presented on page 449.

71. What is the full cost of the one-time special order of 25,000 pounds?

a. $18,425.
b. $12,950.
c. $55,906.
d. $40,375.

The correct answer is (d). *(Publisher)*
REQUIRED: The full cost of the one-time special order.
DISCUSSION: The full cost is the variable cost (as computed in Q. 70) plus fixed O/H. Fixed O/H is $3.75/DLH, and 1,500 hours are required.

Direct materials	$18,425
Direct labor	12,950
Variable overhead	3,375
Fixed overhead ($3.75 x 1,500)	5,625
Total cost of special order	$40,375

72. What would be the total direct labor cost for recurring 25-lot orders, assuming that 60% of each order can be completed during regular hours?

a. $12,600.
b. $10,500.
c. $16,500.
d. $18,225.

The correct answer is (a). *(Publisher)*
REQUIRED: The direct labor cost for recurring 25-lot orders given capacity overflow.
DISCUSSION: On recurring orders, the total direct labor cost equals direct labor hours times the standard rate, with adjustments for any overtime caused by the recurring orders. 60% of the production of a batch (1,500 x .6 = 900 DLH) can be done on regular time; the remaining 600 DLH directly incur overtime and are thus a relevant cost of this new product.

Regular time (1,500 DLH x $7.00 per DLH)	$10,500
Overtime premium (600 DLH x $3.50 per DLH)	2,100
Total direct labor cost	$12,600

73. What would be the total direct materials cost for recurring 25-lot orders?

a. $18,425.
b. $21,500.
c. $26,425.
d. $23,125.

The correct answer is (d). *(Publisher)*
REQUIRED: The total direct materials cost for the recurring 25-lot orders.
DISCUSSION: The total direct materials cost for recurring orders would include the regular price of each product times the number of pounds of each product. The substitution of CN-5 is no longer possible since Jenco's supply was exhausted in the first special batch.

CW-3: 10,000 lbs. x $.90/lb.	$ 9,000
JX-6: 7,500 lbs. x $.60/lb.	4,500
MZ-8: 5,000 lbs. x $1.60/lb.	8,000
BE-7: 2,500 lbs. x $.65/lb.	1,625
Total direct materials cost	$23,125

74. What would be the total overhead costs for recurring 25-lot orders?

a. $5,625.
b. $9,000.
c. $3,375.
d. $7,500.

The correct answer is (b). *(Publisher)*
REQUIRED: The total overhead costs for recurring orders.
DISCUSSION: The total O/H costs for recurring orders should include both variable and fixed O/H because a continuing product should contribute to fixed O/H as well as cover all variable costs. The O/H charge would be

1,500 DLH x $6/DLH = $9,000

Module 15.3: Comprehensive

> Questions 75 through 79 are based on the following information, which was presented as part of Question 8 on Part 5 of the June 1978 CMA examination.
>
> The Xyon Company has purchased 80,000 pumps annually from Kobec, Inc. The price has increased each year, reaching $68 per unit last year. Because the purchase price has increased significantly, Xyon management has asked that an estimate be made of the cost to manufacture it in its own facilities. Xyon's products consist of stampings and castings. The company has little experience with products requiring assembly.
>
> The engineering, manufacturing, and accounting departments have prepared a report for management which included the estimates shown below for an assembly run of 10,000 units. Additional production employees would be hired to manufacture the subassembly. However, no additional equipment, space, or supervision would be needed.
>
> The report states that total costs for 10,000 units are estimated at $957,000, or $95.70 a unit. The current purchase price is $68 a unit, so the report recommends a continued purchase of the product.
>
> | | |
> |---|---|
> | Components (outside purchases) | $120,000 |
> | Assembly labor(1) | 300,000 |
> | Factory overhead(2) | 450,000 |
> | General and administrative overhead(3) | 87,000 |
> | Total costs | $957,000 |
>
> (1) Assembly labor consists of hourly production workers.
> (2) Factory overhead is applied to products on a direct labor dollar basis. Variable overhead costs vary closely with direct labor dollars.
>
> | | | |
> |---|---|---|
> | Fixed O/H | 50% | of direct labor dollars |
> | Variable O/H | 100% | of direct labor dollars |
> | Factory O/H rate | 150% | of direct labor dollars |
>
> (3) General and administrative overhead is applied at 10% of the total cost of material (or components), assembly labor, and factory overhead.

75. What is the total incremental cost per unit to produce the 10,000 pumps?

a. $68.
b. $95.70.
c. $72.
d. $87.

The correct answer is (c). *(Publisher)*
REQUIRED: The total incremental cost per unit to produce the pumps.
DISCUSSION: The unit incremental cost to produce the pumps includes only those costs that vary. They are the costs of purchased components, assembly labor, and variable factory overhead (100% of direct labor).

Purchased components	$12.00
Assembly labor	30.00
Variable factory overhead	30.00
Total unit incremental cost	$72.00

Module 15.3: Comprehensive 453

76. The materials (purchased components) cost per unit for the first year would be

a. $12.00.
b. $9.60.
c. $11.20.
d. $10.80.

The correct answer is (a). *(Publisher)*
REQUIRED: The materials cost per unit for the first year.
DISCUSSION: The materials cost per unit for the first year would be expected to remain at $12 per unit ($120,000 ÷ 10,000 units). No volume discount is indicated, and the learning curve apparently would have no effect on materials.

77. What would the cumulative labor cost be for producing the pumps during the first year, assuming an 80% learning curve?

a. $1,228,800.
b. $3,417,600.
c. $2,400,000.
d. $7,656,000.

The correct answer is (a). *(Publisher)*
REQUIRED: The cumulative labor cost assuming an 80% learning curve.
DISCUSSION: With an 80% learning curve, the assembly labor should decrease by 20% each time there is a doubling of output. A learning curve is the result of an increase in efficiency from performing repetitive tasks.

Quantity		Cumulative	Total
Per Lot	Cumulative	Average Labor Cost per Unit	Cumulative Labor Cost
10,000	10,000	$30.00	$ 300,000
10,000	20,000	24.00 ($30 x .8)	480,000
20,000	40,000	19.20 ($24 x .8)	768,000
40,000	80,000	15.36 ($19.2 x .8)	1,228,800

The average cumulative cost of labor for the first 80,000 pumps is thus $15.36 per pump. Total labor cost is $1,228,800.

78. The total incremental cost for each pump produced with the 80% learning curve would be

a. $68.
b. $42.72.
c. $39.54.
d. $72.26.

The correct answer is (b). *(Publisher)*
REQUIRED: The total incremental cost for each pump produced with the 80% learning curve.
DISCUSSION: The 80% learning curve will provide operational savings in direct labor and variable factory overhead. The calculation in Q. 77 indicated that direct labor cost is $15.36 per unit with an 80% learning curve for the first 80,000 units produced. Variable factory overhead is applied at 100% of direct labor cost ($15.36 per unit). Purchased components are still $12 per unit. The total incremental cost is $42.72 per unit.

79. Should Xyon buy or make, and what is the relevant figure for the decision?

a. Make, with $2,022,400 savings.
b. Buy, with $3,160,000 savings.
c. Make, with $2,276,800 savings.
d. Xyon should be indifferent to make or buy.

The correct answer is (a). *(Publisher)*
REQUIRED: The savings by producing under the 80% learning curve assumption.
DISCUSSION: The savings owing to the 80% learning curve effect involved in the manufacture of the pumps is the difference between the total incremental cost and the cost of purchase. Total unit incremental cost of $42.72 (Q. 78) times production of 80,000 units would result in a total expenditure of $3,417,600. The cost of purchase is $5,440,000 ($68 x 80,000). The savings from manufacture is thus equal to $25.28 per unit, a total savings of $2,022,400.

Questions 80 through 86 are based on the following information, which was presented as part of Question 3 on Part 4 of the December 1973 CMA examination.

A.R. Oma, Inc. manufactures a line of men's perfumes and after-shaving lotions. The manufacturing process is basically a series of mixing operations with the addition of certain aromatic and coloring ingredients; the finished product is packaged in a company-produced glass bottle and packed in cases containing six bottles.

A.R. Oma feels that the sale of its product is heavily influenced by the appearance and appeal of the bottle and has therefore devoted considerable managerial effort to the bottle production process, resulting in the development of certain unique bottle-production processes in which management takes considerable pride.

The two areas (i.e., perfume production and bottle manufacture) have evolved in an almost independent manner; in fact, a rivalry has developed between management personnel as to which division is more important to A.R. Oma. This attitude is probably intensified because the bottle manufacturing plant was purchased intact 10 years ago and no real interchange of management personnel or ideas (except at the top corporate level) has taken place.

Since the acquisition, all bottle production has been absorbed by the perfume manufacturing plant. Each area is considered a separate profit center and evaluated as such. As the new corporate controller you are responsible for the definition of a proper transfer value to use in crediting the bottle production profit center and in debiting the packaging profit center.

At your request, the bottle division general manager has asked certain other bottle manufacturers to quote a price for the quantity and sizes demanded by the perfume division. These competitive prices are presented in the opposite column.

Volume	Total Price	Price Per Case
2,000,000 eq. cases*	$ 4,000,000	$2.00
4,000,000	$ 7,000,000	$1.75
6,000,000	$10,020,000	$1.67

A cost analysis of the internal bottle plant indicates that it can produce bottles at these costs:

Volume	Total Price	Cost Per Case
2,000,000 eq. cases*	$3,200,000	$1.60
4,000,000	$5,200,000	$1.30
6,000,000	$7,200,000	$1.20

*An "equivalent case" represents 6 bottles each.

Your cost analysts point out that these costs represent fixed costs of $1,200,000 and variable costs of $1 per equivalent case.

These figures have given rise to considerable corporate discussion as to the proper value to use in the transfer of bottles to the perfume division. This interest is heightened because a significant portion of a division manager's income is an incentive bonus based on profit center results.

The perfume production division has the following costs in addition to the bottle costs:

Volume	Total Cost	Cost Per Case
2,000,000 cases	$16,400,000	$8.20
4,000,000	$32,400,000	$8.10
6,000,000	$48,420,000	$8.07

After considerable analysis, the marketing research department has furnished you with the following price-demand relationship for the finished product:

Sales Volume	Total Sales Revenue	Sales Price Per Case
2,000,000 cases	$25,000,000	$12.50
4,000,000	$45,600,000	$11.40
6,000,000	$63,900,000	$10.65

For Questions 80 through 82, assume a volume level of 6,000,000 cases.

80. What is the net income for the bottle division at a volume of 6,000,000 cases using current prices?

- a. $10,000,000.
- b. $2,820,000.
- c. $1,600,000.
- d. $7,200,000.

The correct answer is (b). *(Publisher)*
REQUIRED: The net income for the bottle division at a volume of 6,000,000 cases.
DISCUSSION: The assumed total revenue for the bottle division is equal to $10,020,000 (6,000,000 x $1.67). The assumed total cost to produce is $7,200,000 (6,000,000 x $1.20). Divisional net income is therefore $2,820,000.

81. What is the total cost for the perfume division at a volume of 6,000,000 cases?

- a. $58,440,000.
- b. $48,420,000.
- c. $63,900,000.
- d. $18,300,000.

The correct answer is (a). *(Publisher)*
REQUIRED: The total cost for the perfume division.
DISCUSSION: The perfume division at a volume level of 6,000,000 cases would incur total costs of $58,440,000 ($48,420,000 perfume costs plus the bottle cost of $10,020,000). Note that the bottle cost is assumed to be the transfer price charged by the bottle division.

82. The total corporate profit would be

   a. $5,500,000.
   b. $11,100,000.
   c. $7,260,000.
   d. $8,280,000.

The correct answer is (d). *(Publisher)*
REQUIRED: The total corporate profit at the assumed volume.
DISCUSSION: The total corporate profit should exclude any intracompany intradivisional profits. Thus, the profits recognized by the bottle division are not recognized in the determination of total corporate profit. At a volume of 6,000 cases, gross revenue equals $63,900,000. Total cost equals $48,420,000 in perfume division costs plus $7,200,000 in bottle division costs (not the $10,020,000 market price used as the interdivisional transfer price), for a total cost of $55,620,000 and a net income of $8,280,000.

83. The most profitable volume for the perfume division (assuming bottles are priced at market prices set forth in the question) would be

   a. 2,000,000 cases.
   b. 4,000,000 cases.
   c. 6,000,000 cases.
   d. None of the above.

The correct answer is (b). *(Publisher)*
REQUIRED: The most profitable volume for the perfume division.
DISCUSSION: The most profitable volume for the perfume division is 4,000,000 cases. The total revenue is equal to $45,600,000 (4,000,000 x $11.40). The total cost equals $32,400,000 (4,000,000 x $8.10) in perfume division costs + $7,000,000 (4,000,000 x $1.75) market price of bottles, for a total cost of $39,400,000. The perfume division's net income is thus $6,200,000. This is greater than the net income at 6,000,000 cases of $5,460,000 and net income at 2,000,000 cases of $4,600,000.

84. Is the corporation maximizing profits at a volume of 6,000,000 cases?

   a. Yes, though it would be more profitable at a higher level.
   b. No, the most profit would be generated at a 4,000,000 case production level.
   c. Yes, 6,000,000 cases maximizes corporate earnings.
   d. No, the optimum production level is at 2,000,000 cases.

The correct answer is (c). *(Publisher)*
REQUIRED: The volume at which the corporation maximizes profits.
DISCUSSION: The corporation achieves maximum profit at the 6,000,000 case production level. This computation of corporate profit properly excludes the intracompany profit resulting from using the market price as the cost to the perfume division of the bottles transferred from the bottle division.

	Volume (000 omitted)		
Cases	2,000	4,000	6,000
Revenue	$25,000	$45,600	$63,900
Cost	19,600	37,600	55,620
Profit	$ 5,400	$ 8,000	$ 8,280

85. Which of the following conditions should exist for a profit center to be established?

   a. Proper organizational attitudes for decentralized operations.
   b. Freedom to sell to outside parties.
   c. Revenues and costs of each individual segment distinguishable from other segments.
   d. Other sources that are willing to quote a price for quantity and sizes demanded.
   e. All of the above.

The correct answer is (e). *(Publisher)*
REQUIRED: The condition(s) necessary for a profit center.
DISCUSSION: A profit center is a segment of a business that is responsible for both revenues and expenses and whose performance is measured by profits. All of the answer choices are conditions for the establishment of a profit center. Moreover, the segment must have the freedom to buy outside the company when it is advantageous to do so.

86. Refer to the information presented on page 454. Should the bottle division be organized as a profit center?

a. Yes.
b. No, because its sales are strictly internal to the corporation.
c. No, because the perfume division would not make a profit.
d. Undeterminable from the date given.

The correct answer is (b). *(Publisher)*
REQUIRED: The propriety of organizing the bottle division as a profit center.
DISCUSSION: The bottle division should not be organized as a profit center. It makes special bottles for the perfume division and therefore does not have an opportunity to sell to outside parties. The perfume division, however, could be treated as a profit center because there are other manufacturers willing to quote a price for their products. The perfume division also sells to outsiders.

Questions 87 through 91 are based on the following information, which was presented as part of Question 3 on Part 5 of the December 1980 CMA examination.

Helene's, a high-fashion women's dress manufacturer, is planning to market a new cocktail dress for the coming season. Helene's supplies retailers in the eastern and mid-Atlantic states.

Four yards of material are required to lay out the dress pattern. Some material remains after cutting which can be sold as remnants.

The leftover material could also be used to manufacture a matching cape and handbag. However, if the leftover material is to be used for the cape and handbag, more care will be required in the cutting, which will increase the cutting costs.

The company expects to sell 1,250 dresses if no matching cape and handbag are available. Helene's market research reveals that dress sales will be 20% higher if a matching cape and handbag are available. The market research indicates that the cape and/or handbag will not be sold individually but only as accessories with the dress. The various combinations of dresses, capes, and handbags that are expected to be sold by retailers are indicated in the opposite column.

	Percent of Total
Complete sets of dress, cape, and handbag	70%
Dress and cape	6%
Dress and handbag	15%
Dress only	9%
Total	100%

The material used in the dress costs $12.50 a yard or $50 for each dress. The cost of cutting the dress if the cape and handbag are not manufactured is estimated at $20 a dress, and the resulting remnants can be sold for $5 for each dress cut out. If the cape and handbag are to be manufactured, the cutting costs will be increased by $9 per dress. There will be no salable remnants if the capes and handbags are manufactured in the quantities estimated.

The selling prices and the costs to complete the three items once they are cut are

	Selling Price Per Unit	Unit Cost to Complete (Excludes Cost of Material and Cutting Operation)
Dress	$200.00	$80.00
Cape	27.50	19.50
Handbag	9.50	6.50

---

87. How many dresses will be produced if the accessories are produced as well?

a. 1,250.
b. 1,050.
c. 1,500.
d. 135.

The correct answer is (c). *(Publisher)*
REQUIRED: The total number of dresses produced if the accessories are made.
DISCUSSION: The total number of dresses sold is expected to increase by 20%. The base amount of dresses to be produced is 1,250. A 20% increase means that 1,500 dresses will be sold. It is assumed that Helene's will make enough dresses to fulfill estimated sales.

88. The unit incremental contribution margin for dresses is

a. $95.
b. $120.
c. $72.
d. $125.

The correct answer is (b). *(Publisher)*
REQUIRED: The incremental contribution margin per unit for dresses.
DISCUSSION: The unit incremental contribution margin for dresses is equal to the sales revenue less any variable costs to complete. Variable cost to complete is given as $80. The incremental contribution margin is thus $120 per unit ($200 price - $80).

Module 15.3: Comprehensive

89. What would be the total incremental contribution margin for the handbags?

a. $3,825.
b. $3,150.
c. $9,120.
d. $10,200.

The correct answer is (a). *(Publisher)*
REQUIRED: The total incremental contribution margin for the handbags.
DISCUSSION: The incremental CM is defined as the incremental sales units times the incremental UCM. Of the incremental sales, 70% are expected to be complete sets and 15% dress and handbag ensembles. Therefore, 1,275 handbags (85% x 1,500 incremental units) are expected to be sold. The incremental UCM of $3 ($9.50 price - $6.50 cost) results in a $3,825 incremental CM.

90. What will be the total additional costs of material and cutting if the accessories are produced?

a. $31,000.
b. $37,250.
c. $32,250.
d. $26,000.

The correct answer is (b). *(Publisher)*
REQUIRED: The total additional costs if the accessories are produced.
DISCUSSION: The total additional costs if the accessories are produced are:

Additional cutting costs ($9 x 1,500)	$13,500
Additional material costs ($50 x 250)	12,500
Lost remnant sales ($5 x 1,250)	6,250
Incremental cutting costs for the extra dresses ($20 x 250)	5,000
Total	$37,250

91. Assuming the accessories are produced, what will be the incremental profit?

a. $5,695.
b. $6,250.
c. $11,945.
d. $16,945.

The correct answer is (a). *(Publisher)*
REQUIRED: The incremental profit if the accessories are produced.
DISCUSSION: To calculate the incremental profit, one must first determine the incremental unit sales of the dresses, capes, and handbags. The next step is to compute the aggregate incremental contribution margin and deduct the additional costs.

	Percent of Total	Dresses	Capes	Handbags	Total
Complete sets	70%	1,050	1,050	1,050	
Dress and cape	6	90	90		
Dress and handbag	15	225		225	
Dress only	9	135			
Total units if accessories are introduced	100%	1,500	1,140	1,275	
Unit sales if accessories are not introduced		1,250	--	--	
Incremental sales		250	1,140	1,275	
Incremental UCM		x $120	x $8	x $3	
Total incremental CM		$30,000	$9,120	$3,825	$42,945
Additional costs (see Q. 90)					(37,250)
Incremental profit					$ 5,695

Questions 92 through 98 are based on the following information, which was presented as part of Question 5 on Part 5 of the June 1980 CMA examination.

Berco Company manufactures and wholesales hardware supplies. One of its product lines is composed of drill bit sets and router bit sets. The company employs a calendar year for reporting purposes.

The company is subject to voluntary wage and price guidelines. Berco's management is attempting to determine how much latitude it has for wage and price increases in the drill/router bit product-line and still be in compliance with the voluntary guidelines.

Certain key dates and time periods as specified in the guidelines are defined below.

Base Quarter - Last complete fiscal quarter prior to October 2, 1988. For Berco Company this quarter runs from July 1, 1988 through September 30, 1988.

Program Year - 12-month period immediately following the base quarter. The program year for Berco extends from October 1, 1988 through September 30, 1989.

Base Period - Two-year period measured from the end of the last calendar or complete fiscal quarter of 1985 through the corresponding quarter of 1987. The base period for Berco extends from December 31, 1985 through December 31, 1987.

Base Year - The 12-month period prior to the program year, or October 1, 1987 through September 30, 1988 for Berco Company.

The guidelines specify standards (with which Berco must comply) for wages and prices but the standards for each are not interrelated. The price standard is really a deceleration standard; i.e., the rate of the price increase allowed in the program year must be less than the price increase instituted in the base period.

Wage Standard - Increases in the hourly wage rate in the program year cannot be more than 7% of the average hourly pay rate in effect in the base quarter (July 1 - September 30, 1988).

Price Standard - The rate of price increase for a product line in the program year must be the lesser of (1) one-half of one percent (.5%) less than the average rate of price increase for a product line for the base period stated as an annual percentage, or (2) no more than 9.5% annually.

The regulations that accompany the standards define the average rate of price increase for a product line for the base period as the weighted average of the price increase rates of each individual product line during the base period (12/31/85-12/31/87), stated as an annual rate. The regulations specify that the average rate is to be calculated as follows: The price increase rate for the base period of each individual product in the line is to be weighted by the ratio of actual sales revenue of each individual product in the line to the actual total sales revenue of the product line as measured at the beginning of the base period. The weighted average price increase rates for the base period for all products in the product line are summed and then divided by two (base period is a two-year period) to get the average annual rate of price increase for a product line for the base period.

Once the allowable rate of price increase for a product line for the base period is determined (i.e., the amount calculated above less .5%, or the maximum of 9.5%), the rate of price increase is shared among all products in the line according to the ratio of actual sales revenue of each individual product in the line to the total sales revenue of the product line as measured at the end of the base quarter (September 30, 1988).

Historical data on wages and prices for the drill/router bit product line are given in the schedule presented in both columns below:

Quarter Ending	Drill Bits Unit Price	Units Sold in Millions	Revenue in Millions	Router Bits Unit Price	Units Sold in Millions	Revenue in Millions	Total Revenue in Millions	Labor Hours in Millions	Labor Costs in Millions
12/31/85	$3.00	5.00	$15.00	$12.00	3.75	$45.00	$60.0	2.20	$16.50
12/31/87	3.75	5.80	21.75	13.80	4.25	58.65	80.4	2.40	21.12
9/30/88	4.20	6.00	25.20	15.00	4.32	64.80	90.0	2.60	23.92

92. To what rate can the average hourly wage be increased if it cannot be raised by more than 7% above the rate in effect in the base quarter?

　a. $9.20.
　b. $10.24.
　c. $9.57.
　d. $9.84.

The correct answer is (d). *(Publisher)*
　REQUIRED: The maximum hourly wage rate consistent with the guidelines.
　DISCUSSION: The guidelines specify that the average hourly wage rate can be increased by not more than 7% of the average hourly pay rate in effect in a base quarter. Labor costs in millions in the base quarter were $23.92 and labor hours in millions were 2.6. The average hourly wage rate was therefore $9.20 per hour ($23.92 ÷ 2.6). The maximum hourly rate is $9.84 (107% x $9.20).

Module 15.3: Comprehensive   459

93. What are the unit rates of price increase for drill and router bits during the base period?

   a. 0% and 0%.

   b. 12.5% and 7.5%.

   c. 25% and 15%.

   d. 37.5% and 22.5%.

The correct answer is (b). *(Publisher)*
REQUIRED: The unit rate of price increase for drill and router bits during the base period.
DISCUSSION: The unit rate of price increase for drill and router bits during the base period must be calculated by subtracting the 1985 price from the 1987 price and dividing by the 1985 price, and then dividing that result by two to arrive at the annual rate for each item.

Drill bits: [($3.75 - $3) ÷ $3] x .5 = 12.5%
Router bits: [($13.80 - $12) ÷ $12] x .5 = 7.5%

94. What will be the weighted average price increase for the drill and router bits for the program year?

   a. 8.75%.

   b. 3.125%.

   c. 6%.

   d. 10%.

The correct answer is (a). *(Publisher)*
REQUIRED: The weighted average price for the product line increase during the program year.
DISCUSSION: The weighted average price increase for the drill and router bits for the program year would be the price increase per year times the ratio of sales at the beginning of the base period. The individual price increases for drill bits and router bits were calculated in Q. 93. Sales of drill bits were $15 million and sales of router bits were $45 million at the beginning of the base period, so the ratio is 1 to 3, or .25 to .75.

Drill bit (.125 x .25)   .03125
Router bit (.075 x .75)   .05625
Total   .08750

95. What is the maximum unit price increase during the program year for drill and router bits that would be allowed and still comply with the price guidelines?

   a. 7.5%.

   b. 15%.

   c. 8.75%.

   d. 8.25%.

The correct answer is (d). *(Publisher)*
REQUIRED: The maximum price increase permissible under the guidelines.
DISCUSSION: The maximum price increase must be the lesser of 1) .5% less than the average rate of price increase for a product line for the base period stated as an annual percentage, or 2) no more than 9.5% annually. As computed in Q. 94, the product line annual increase was 8.75%. Accordingly, the maximum price increase is 8.25% (8.75% - .5%).

96. How is the current rate of price increase shared between products?

	Drill Bit	Router Bit
a.	50%	50%
b.	25%	75%
c.	28%	72%
d.	33%	67%

The correct answer is (c). *(Publisher)*
REQUIRED: The pro rata share of the price increase between products.
DISCUSSION: The rate of price increase is shared among all products according to the proportion of actual sales revenue represented by each product at the end of the quarter, September 30, 1988. For this quarter, sales of drill bits was $25,200,000 and sales of router bits was $64,800,000 of the $90,000,000 total. Accordingly, drill bits represented 28% and router bits 72% of the total.

97. If Berco Company is allowed the maximum rate of price increase of 9.5% for its drill/router bit production, and if it increases the router bit price to $16.20 during the program year, what will be the weighted average price increase for routers?

   a. 5.623%.

   b. 13.35%.

   c. 5.76%.

   d. 3.74%.

The correct answer is (c). *(Publisher)*
REQUIRED: The weighted average price increase for router bits.
DISCUSSION: The rate of price increase is shared among all products in the line according to the ratio of actual sales revenue of each product to the total revenue of the line at the end of the base quarter. The question gives a router bit price increase of $1.20 ($16.20 - $15), which is 8% ($1.20 ÷ $15). The weighted average price increase of the router bits is thus 5.76% (72% x 8%).

98. Referring to the information presented on page 458, and specifically to Q. 97, what is the maximum price of drill bits for the program year that is within the price standards?

a. $4.20.
b. $4.76.
c. $13.35.
d. $3.74.

The correct answer is (b). *(Publisher)*
REQUIRED: Maximum price of drill bits for the program year that complies with the standards.
DISCUSSION: Router bits generate 72% of the revenue (Q. 96). The router bit price increase was 8%, and the weighted average price increase for the router bits is 5.76% (Q. 97). Given an allowable 9.5% overall increase for the product line, the weighted average price increase available for the drill bits is 3.74% (9.5% - 5.76%). The percentage price increase for the drill bits is 13.36%, as calculated below. The maximum drill bit price is thus $4.76 ($4.20 x 113.36%).

X = percent increase in drill bits
$28\%X$ = 3.74%
X = 13.36%

Questions 99 through 102 are based on the following information, which was presented as part of Question 7 on Part 5 of the December 1978 CMA examination.

Framar Inc. manufactures automation machinery according to customer specifications. The company is relatively new and has grown each year. Framar operated at about 75% of practical capacity during the year. The operating results for the most recent fiscal year are presented below.

Framar Inc.
Income Statement
For the Year Ended September 30
(000 omitted)

Sales		$25,000
Less: sales commissions		2,500
Net sales		$22,500
Expenses		
Direct material		$ 6,000
Direct labor		7,500
Manufacturing overhead-variable		
Supplies	$ 625	
Indirect labor	1,500	
Power	125	2,250
Manufacturing overhead-fixed		
Supervision	$ 500	
Depreciation	1,000	1,500
Corporate administration		750
Total Expenses		$18,000
Net income before taxes		$ 4,500
Income taxes (40%)		1,800
Net income		$ 2,700

Most of the management personnel had worked for firms in this type of business before joining Framar, but none of the top management had been responsible for overall corporate operations or for final decisions on prices. Nevertheless, the company has been successful.

The top management of Framar wants to have a more organized and formal pricing system to prepare quotes for potential customers. Therefore, it has developed the pricing formula presented below. The formula is based upon the company's operating results achieved during the most recent fiscal year. The relationships used in the formula are expected to continue during the next fiscal year. The company expects to operate at 75% of practical capacity during the next fiscal year.

APA Inc. has asked Framar to submit a bid on some custom-designed machinery. Framar used the new formula to develop a price and submitted a bid of $165,000 to APA Inc. The calculations to arrive at the bid price are given next to the pricing formula shown below.

Details of Formula		APA Bid Calculations
Estimated direct material cost	$XX	$ 29,200
Estimated direct labor cost	XX	56,000
Estimated manufacturing O/H calculated at 50% of DL	XX	28,000
Estimated corporate O/H calculated at 10% of DL	XX	5,600
Estimated total costs excluding sales commissions	$XX	$118,800
Add 25% for profits and taxes	XX	29,700
Suggested price (with profits) before sales commissions	$XX	$148,500
Suggested total price equal to suggested price divided by .9 to adjust for 10% sales commissions	$XX	$165,000

Module 15.3: Comprehensive

99. What would the contribution margin be if the bid is accepted?

a. $102,000.
b. $63,300.
c. $27,900.
d. $46,500.

The correct answer is (d). *(Publisher)*
REQUIRED: The contribution margin assuming the bid is accepted.
DISCUSSION: The CM is the gross revenue less any variable costs. Variable costs include the sales commission, DM, DL, and variable manufacturing O/H. Variable manufacturing O/H for the most recent fiscal year was 30% of direct labor ($2,250 ÷ $7,500). The cost relationships are expected to continue in the next fiscal year.

Submitted bid		$165,000
Less: Sales commission (10%)		16,500
Net sales		$148,500
Less variable costs:		
Direct material	$29,200	
Direct labor	56,000	
Variable mfg. O/H		
(30% of direct labor)	16,800	102,000
Contribution margin		$ 46,500

100. If the bid were accepted, what would be the increase in net income?

a. $27,900.
b. $46,500.
c. $63,300.
d. $148,500.

The correct answer is (a). *(Publisher)*
REQUIRED: The net increase in income if the bid is accepted.
DISCUSSION: The contribution margin for the APA job will increase net income assuming the fixed costs would be incurred even if the bid were rejected. The increase in net income is the contribution margin (calculated in Q. 99 as $46,500) less any income taxes at a rate of 40%. The increase in net income is thus $27,900 ($46,500 - $18,600).

101. Should Framar manufacture the machinery for a counteroffer of $127,000?

a. Yes, there is an increase in net income of $7,380.
b. Yes, there is an increase in net income of $12,300.
c. No, there is a net decrease in income of $12,700.
d. None of the above.

The correct answer is (a). *(Publisher)*
REQUIRED: Whether the job should be accepted at a lower price.
DISCUSSION: Acceptance of the counteroffer of $127,000 would result in a net increase in income. The incremental revenue exceeds the incremental costs, as computed below.

Counteroffer	$127,000
Sales commission (10%)	12,700
Net sales	$114,300
Variable manufacturing costs (Q. 111)	102,000
Contribution margin	$ 12,300
Income taxes (40%)	4,920
Increase in net income	$ 7,380

102. What is the lowest price Framar could quote on this machinery without reducing its net income after taxes?

a. $114,300.
b. $127,000.
c. $113,333.
d. $102,000.

The correct answer is (c). *(Publisher)*
REQUIRED: The lowest price that could be quoted without reducing net income after taxes.
DISCUSSION: The lowest price Framar could quote is the total incremental cost associated with the job. In this case, the bid should cover the variable manufacturing costs and the sales commission. Variable manufacturing cost is $102,000 and the sales commission is 10%. Dividing $102,000 by .9 gives a minimum sales price of $113,333.

Questions 103 through 109 are based on the following information, which was presented as part of Question 2 on Part 5 of the June 1979 CMA exam.

National Industries is a diversified corporation with separate and distinct operating divisions. Each division's performance is evaluated on the basis of total dollar profits and return on division investment.

The WindAir Division manufactures and sells air conditioner units. The coming year's budgeted income statement, based upon a sales volume of 15,000 units, appears below.

WindAir Division
Budgeted Income Statement
For the Next Fiscal Year

	Per Unit	Total (000 omitted)
Sales revenue	$400	$6,000
Manufacturing costs		
Compressor	$ 70	$1,050
Other raw materials	37	555
Direct labor	30	450
Variable overhead	45	675
Fixed overhead	32	480
Total manufacturing costs	$214	$3,210
Gross margin	$186	$2,790
Operating expenses		
Variable selling	$ 18	$ 270
Fixed selling	19	285
Fixed administrative	38	570
Total operating expenses	$ 75	$1,125
Net income before taxes	$111	$1,665

WindAir's division manager believes sales can be increased if the unit selling price of the air conditioners is reduced. A market research study conducted by an independent firm indicates that a 5% reduction in the selling price ($20) would increase sales volume 16% or 2,400 units. WindAir has sufficient production capacity to manage this increased volume with no increase in fixed costs.

At the present time WindAir uses a compressor in its units which it purchases from an outside supplier at a cost of $70 per compressor. The division manager of WindAir has approached the manager of the Compressor Division regarding the sale of a compressor unit to WindAir. The Compressor Division currently manufactures and sells a unit exclusively to outside firms which is similar to the unit used by WindAir. The specifications of the WindAir compressor are slightly different, which would reduce the Compressor Division's raw material cost by $1.50 per unit. In addition, the Compressor Division would not incur any variable selling costs on the units sold to WindAir. The manager of WindAir wants all of the compressors it uses to come from one supplier and has offered to pay $50 for each compressor unit.

The Compressor Division has the capacity to produce 75,000 units. The coming year's budgeted income statement for the Compressor Division is shown below and is based upon a sales volume of 64,000 units without considering WindAir's proposal.

Compressor Division
Budgeted Income Statement
For the Next Fiscal Year

	Per Unit	Total (000 omitted)
Sales revenue	$100	$6,400
Manufacturing costs		
Raw materials	$ 12	768
Direct labor	8	512
Variable overhead	10	640
Fixed overhead	11	704
Total manufacturing costs	$ 41	$2,624
Gross margin	$ 59	$3,776
Operating expenses		
Variable selling	$ 6	$ 384
Fixed selling	4	256
Fixed administrative	7	448
Total operating expenses	$ 17	$1,088
Net income before taxes	$ 42	$2,688

103. What is WindAir's current unit contribution margin on air conditioners?

a. $111.
b. $125.
c. $186.
d. $200.

The correct answer is (d). *(Publisher)*
REQUIRED: Unit contribution margin on air conditioning units.
DISCUSSION: Currently, the UCM is $200, because the unit selling price is $400 and the unit variable costs are $200. All the manufacturing costs are variable except fixed O/H of $32 per unit. There are also variable selling expenses of $18. Therefore, total variable costs are $200 ($214 - $32 + $18).

104. How much would WindAir's net income change if they acquired the compressors from an outside source and instituted the 5% price reduction?

a. $132,000.
b. $55,200.
c. $76,800.
d. $214,320.

The correct answer is (a). *(Publisher)*
REQUIRED: The change in net income given a price reduction and increased sales.
DISCUSSION: The CM before the price decrease is $200 per unit times the 15,000 units, or total CM of $3,000,000. Given the price decrease, the unit CM goes from $200 to $180 because the selling price decreases by $20 ($400 x 5%). The units sold increase by 2,400 to 17,400. Multiplying the new $180 UCM by 17,400 units results in a new CM of $3,132,000. CM thus increases $132,000 ($3,132,000 - $3,000,000).

Module 15.3: Comprehensive 463

105. Another approach to analyzing the change in contribution margin covered in the preceding question is to observe that as a result of decreasing selling price from $400 to $380 there will be a sales increase of 2,400 units at a contribution margin of $180. This increase in contribution margin of $432,000

a. Must be adjusted by the $480,000 of fixed costs.
b. Must be adjusted by the $20 loss of the contribution margin on 15,000 units previously budgeted.
c. Must be adjusted by the incremental fixed manufacturing O/H (2,400 units x $32).
d. Is the change in pretax income.

The correct answer is (b). *(Publisher)*
REQUIRED: An alternative approach to contribution margin analysis.
DISCUSSION: The increased volume of 2,400 units times the unit contribution margin is a volume variance ($432,000 favorable). The change in volume is brought about by a lower price which creates a sales price variance of $20/unit times the 15,000 units currently budgeted ($300,000 unfavorable). Thus, the decrease in price must be taken into account as well as the increase in volume.
Answers (a) and (c) are incorrect because fixed costs do not change with increase in volume. Answer (d) is incorrect because the $432,000 sales volume variance must be decreased by the $300,000 sales price variance.

106. How much would the Compressor Division make (lose) on the sale to WindAir of compressors (17,400 units) if it took the extra units out of external sales?

a. Decrease net income $35,500.
b. Decrease net income $129,800.
c. Decrease net income $59,000.
d. Increase net income $22,000.

The correct answer is (a). *(Publisher)*
REQUIRED: The gain (loss) on the sale of parts given a set price and reduction of external sales.
DISCUSSION: If the Compressor Division does sell all 17,400 units to WindAir, Compressor will only sell 57,600 units instead of 64,000 units to outside customers (75,000 maximum capacity - 17,400 sales to WindAir). To determine UCM, materials costs decrease by $1.50 for internal sales, and there are no variable selling expenses.

Unit Contribution Margin	Outside Sales	WindAir Sales
Selling price	$100	$50.00
Variable costs		
Raw materials	$ 12	$10.50
Direct labor	8	8.00
Overhead	10	10.00
Selling expenses	6	-0-
Total variable costs	$ 36	$28.50
Contribution margin	$ 64	$21.50

The loss in contribution from 6,400 sales lost to outsiders (64,000 - 57,600) is $409,600 ($64 x 6,400). Sale to WindAir would only contribute $374,100 ($21.50 x 17,400). The net result is a reduction in net income of $35,500 ($409,600 - $374,100).

107. If National Industries required the Compressor Division to sell 17,400 compressors to WindAir, how much would the corporation make (lose)?

a. $(409,600).
b. $722,100.
c. $312,500.
d. $(215,400).

The correct answer is (c). *(Publisher)*
REQUIRED: The net effect to the corporation of buying parts internally.
DISCUSSION: The total effect to the corporation will be the cost savings by using an internally manufactured part less the loss in contribution from sales to outsiders.

Outside purchase price	$ 70.00
Compressor Division's variable cost to produce	28.50
Savings per unit	$ 41.50
Number of units	x 17,400
Total cost savings	$722,100
Compressor Division's CM loss from sales to outsiders ($64 x 6,400; see Q. 106)	409,600
Increase in pre-tax net income	$312,500

Module 15.3: Comprehensive

Questions 108 and 109 are based on the information presented on page 462.

108. What would be the impact of decreasing the sales price 10% to obtain an increase in sales volume of 4,500 units?

	Contribution Margin	Net Income Before Taxes
a.	+$120,000	-$480,000
b.	+$120,000	+$120,000
c.	+$720,000	+$120,000
d.	+$720,000	+$720,000

The correct answer is (b). *(Publisher)*
REQUIRED: The effect of decreasing selling price further given a new increase in unit sales.
DISCUSSION: The 10% price decrease ($400 x 10%) would decrease the UCM from $200 to $160. The additional 4,500 units would increase the contribution margin $720,000 (4,500 x $160). The decrease in sales price would reduce the contribution margin $600,000 (15,000 x $40). The net effect is $120,000 favorable ($720,000 F - $600,000 U) for both the contribution margin and net income (the fixed costs do not change).

109. Regarding the Compressor Division, what is the unit contribution margin on compressors sold to a third party?

a. $36.
b. $42.
c. $59.
d. $64.

The correct answer is (d). *(Publisher)*
REQUIRED: The unit contribution margin on compressors sold to a third party.
DISCUSSION:

	Outside Sales
Selling price	$100
Variable costs	
Raw materials	$ 12
Direct labor	8
Overhead	10
Selling expenses	6
Total variable costs	$ 36
Contribution margin	$ 64

Questions 110 through 115 are based on the following information, which was presented as part of Question 7 on Part 5 of the December 1972 CMA examination.

George Jackson operates a small machine shop. He manufactures one standard product available from many other similar businesses and he also manufactures products to customer order. His accountant prepared the annual income statement shown below:

	Custom Sales	Standard Sales	Total
Sales	$50,000	$25,000	$75,000
Material	$10,000	$ 8,000	$18,000
Labor	20,000	9,000	29,000
Depreciation	6,300	3,600	9,900
Power	700	400	1,100
Rent	6,000	1,000	7,000
Heat and light	600	100	700
Other	400	900	1,300
	$44,000	$23,000	$67,000
	$ 6,000	$ 2,000	$ 8,000

The depreciation charges are for machines used in the respective product lines. The power charge is apportioned on the estimate of power consumed. The rent is for the building space which has been leased for 10 years at $7,000 per year. The rent and heat and light are apportioned to the product lines based on amount of floor space occupied. All other costs are current expenses identified with the product line incurring them.

A valued custom parts customer has asked Mr. Jackson to manufacture 5,000 special units for him. Mr. Jackson is working at capacity and would have to give up some other business to take this business. He cannot renege on custom orders already agreed to but he could reduce the output of his standard product by about one-half for one year while producing the specially requested custom part. The customer is willing to pay $7 for each part. The material cost will be about $2 per unit and the labor will be $3.60 per unit. Mr. Jackson will have to spend $2,000 for a special device which will be discarded when the job is done.

110. The opportunity cost of taking the order is

a. $9,150.
b. $3,550.
c. $12,500.
d. $6,230.

The correct answer is (b). *(Publisher)*
REQUIRED: The opportunity cost of taking the order.
DISCUSSION: The opportunity cost of taking the order is the incremental revenue forgone. The net cash flow given up by accepting the special order is 50% of standard sales less the variable costs associated with those sales.

Sales of standard product x 50%	$12,500
Less variable costs	$ 8,950
Opportunity cost of special order	$ 3,550

Module 15.3: Comprehensive

111. What is the incremental cost of the 5,000-unit order?

a. $30,000.
b. $21,050.
c. $38,950.
d. $18,550.

The correct answer is (b). *(Publisher)*
REQUIRED: The incremental cost of the special order.
DISCUSSION: The incremental cost of the order is equal to the cost incurred to fill the order less any cost reductions for standard products. Depreciation, rent, and heat and light are not affected by the order. Power might depend upon the particular requirements of the special units. Given no information, we must assume that the same amount of power will be used in each case.

Costs incurred to fill order:	
Material ($2 x 5,000 units)	$10,000
Labor ($3.60 x 5,000 units)	18,000
Special overhead	2,000
Costs incurred	$30,000
Costs reduced for standard products:	
Material (50% of standard)	$ 4,000
Labor (50% of standard)	4,500
Other (50% of standard)	450
Cost reductions	$ 8,950
Total incremental costs	$21,050

112. The total fixed costs of the order are

a. $2,550.
b. $1,450.
c. $3,300.
d. $21,050.

The correct answer is (a). *(Publisher)*
REQUIRED: The total fixed costs for the special order.
DISCUSSION: Fixed costs will be incurred whether or not the special order is accepted. The allocable fixed costs are 50% of those associated with standard production.

Depreciation	$1,800
Power	200
Rent	500
Heat and light	50
Fixed costs of the special order	$2,550

113. What is the full cost of the special order?

a. $38,950.
b. $24,620.
c. $21,050.
d. $32,550.

The correct answer is (d). *(Publisher)*
REQUIRED: The full cost of the special order.
DISCUSSION: The full cost of the order includes any allocated fixed costs. Since the special order displaces half of the standard production, 50% of the fixed costs allocable to that production should be assigned to it.

Costs incurred to fill order (Q. 111)	$30,000
Fixed costs (Q. 112)	2,550
Full cost	$32,550

114. What would be the cash advantage (disadvantage) if Jackson accepts the order?

a. $22,500.
b. $(4,250).
c. $(1,250).
d. $1,450.

The correct answer is (d). *(Publisher)*
REQUIRED: The cash advantage (disadvantage) of accepting the special order.
DISCUSSION: The net cash advantage of accepting the special order is calculated by comparing the net change in sales and the net change in cost.

New sales ($7 x 5,000 units)	$35,000	
Less: Standard sales	12,500	
Incremental sales		$22,500
Incremental costs (Q. 111)		21,050
Cash advantage		$ 1,450

Module 15.3: Comprehensive

115. Refer to the information presented on page 464. Which of the following is not a qualitative factor in making the decision?

a. The long-run consequences of failing to satisfy standard parts customers.
b. The reliability of the cost estimates.
c. The importance of this valued customer.
d. The income tax consequences of the proposed transaction.

The correct answer is (d). *(Publisher)*
REQUIRED: The factor not considered qualitative in making the decision.
DISCUSSION: Qualitative factors that are not reflected in the above numerical analyses are also important to the decision whether to accept this special order. Answers (a), (b), and (c) illustrate some of these qualitative factors. Others are employee morale (when workers are surprised by a special order), the possibility of receiving a more lucrative order, etc. The tax consequence is a quantitative factor.

Questions 116 through 118 are based on the following information. Leland Manufacturing uses 10 units of Part Number KJ37 each month in the production of radar equipment. The unit cost to manufacture one unit of KJ37 is presented below.

Direct materials	$ 1,000
Materials handling (20% of direct material cost)	200
Direct labor	8,000
Manufacturing overhead (150% of direct labor)	12,000
Total manufacturing cost	$21,200

Material handling represents the direct variable costs of the Receiving Department that are applied to direct materials and purchased components on the basis of their cost. This is a separate charge in addition to manufacturing overhead. Leland's annual manufacturing overhead budget is one-third variable and two-thirds fixed. Scott Supply, one of Leland's reliable vendors, has offered to supply Part Number KJ37 at a unit price of $15,000.

---

116. If Leland purchases the KJ37 units from Scott, the capacity Leland used to manufacture these parts would be idle. Should Leland decide to purchase the parts from Scott, the unit cost of KJ37 would

a. Increase by $4,800.
b. Decrease by $6,200.
c. Decrease by $3,200.
d. Increase by $1,800.

The correct answer is (a). *(CMA 1287 5-28)*
REQUIRED: The effect on unit cost if the part is purchased.
DISCUSSION: In addition to the $15,000 purchase price, the company would still incur $8,000 per unit of unavoidable (fixed) manufacturing overhead (2/3 of $12,000). The materials handling charge of 20% of the purchase price of components would add another $3,000 per unit (.2 x $15,000). Therefore, the unit cost of purchase would be $26,000 ($15,000 + $8,000 + $3,000), which is $4,800 more than the current cost of manufacturing.

117. Assume Leland Manufacturing is able to rent all idle capacity for $25,000 per month. If Leland decides to purchase the 10 units from Scott Supply, Leland's monthly cost for KJ37 would

a. Increase $48,000.
b. Increase $23,000.
c. Decrease $7,000.
d. Decrease $57,000.

The correct answer is (b). *(CMA 1287 5-29)*
REQUIRED: The effect on monthly cost of renting idle facilities.
DISCUSSION: Purchasing would increase unit cost by $4,800 (see preceding question), an increase of $48,000 per month (10 units x $4,800). However, the $25,000 of rental income would reduce the increase in net costs to $23,000 per month.

118. Assume that Leland Manufacturing does not wish to commit to a rental agreement but could use idle capacity to manufacture another product that would contribute $52,000 per month. If Leland elects to manufacture KJ37 in order to maintain quality control, Leland's opportunity cost is

a. $18,000.
b. $(20,000).
c. $4,000.
d. $(48,000).

The correct answer is (c). *(CMA 1287 5-30)*
REQUIRED: The opportunity cost of selecting the manufacturing option.
DISCUSSION: Opportunity cost is the maximum alternative earnings that might have been obtained if the productive good, service, or capacity had been applied to some alternative use. As computed in the two preceding questions, the additional total monthly cost of purchasing the component is $48,000. If the idle facilities could be used to produce a product contributing $52,000 per month, the net benefit opportunity cost of manufacture would be $4,000.

CHAPTER SIXTEEN
CAPITAL BUDGETING

16.1 General Concepts	(28 questions)	467
16.2 Payback	(16 questions)	474
16.3 Cost of Capital	(6 questions)	478
16.4 Net Present Value	(26 questions)	480
16.5 NPV, Original Investment	(7 questions)	488
16.6 Internal Rate of Return	(15 questions)	490
16.7 Cash Flow Calculations	(8 questions)	495
16.8 Comprehensive	(52 questions)	497

This chapter is an example of a large-scale nonroutine decision, evaluated over a longer period of time than the previous short-range decisions may have been. Thus, the capital budgeting chapter is analogous to the finance function of the firm as well as to the finance function of the professional examinations. A variety of techniques are discussed, with emphasis on the discounted cash flow approach, as reflected on the professional examinations.

16.1 General Concepts

1. Capital budgeting is concerned with

   a. Decisions affecting only capital intensive industries.
   b. Analysis of short-range decisions.
   c. Analysis of long-range decisions.
   d. Scheduling office personnel in office buildings.

The correct answer is (c). *(Publisher)*
REQUIRED: The definition of capital budgeting.
DISCUSSION: Capital budgeting is concerned with long-range decisions, such as whether to add a product line, to build new facilities, or to lease or buy equipment. Any decision regarding cash inflows and outflows over a period of more than 1 year probably needs capital budgeting analysis.
Answer (a) is incorrect because capital budgeting is useful for all long-range decision making. Answer (b) is incorrect because capital budgeting is not useful for short-range decisions. Answer (d) is incorrect because it is a nonsense answer.

2. Capital budgeting is used for the decision analysis of

   a. Adding or discontinuing new product lines.
   b. Adding or discontinuing facilities.
   c. Multiple profitable alternatives.
   d. Lease-or-buy decisions.
   e. All of the above.

The correct answer is (e). *(Publisher)*
REQUIRED: The usefulness of the capital budgeting process.
DISCUSSION: The capital budgeting process is a method of planning the efficient expenditure of the firm's resources on capital projects. Such planning is essential in view of the rising costs of scarce resources. Capital budgeting may be used for adding or discontinuing new product lines as well as for adding or discontinuing facilities, and for analyzing multiple profitable alternatives by permitting an examination of the NPV of each alternative. The lease-or-buy decision is a more specific example of an appropriate use of capital budgeting techniques.

Module 16.1: General Concepts

3. A company can replace the machinery currently used to manufacture its product with more efficient machinery. The new machinery will reduce labor costs and will also reduce the percentage of spoiled units. It is expected to have a useful life of 5 years. The most appropriate technique for determining whether or not the company should replace its machinery with the new, more efficient machinery is

   a. Cost-volume-profit analysis.
   b. Capital budgeting analysis.
   c. Regression analysis.
   d. Linear programming.

The correct answer is (b). *(CIA 1186 IV-21)*
REQUIRED: The best technique for determining whether machinery should be replaced.
DISCUSSION: Capital budgeting is concerned with long-range decisions, such as whether to add a product line, to build new facilities, or to lease or buy equipment. Any decision regarding cash inflows and outflows over a period of more than 1 year probably needs capital budgeting analysis.
Answer (a) is incorrect because CVP analysis studies the relationships among sales volume, sales price, fixed costs, variable costs, and profit. Answer (c) is incorrect because regression analysis attempts to find an equation for the relationship among variables. It assumes that a change in a dependent variable relates to a change in an independent variable. Answer (d) is incorrect because it is a means of optimizing a function subject to constraints.

4. The time value of money means that

   a. A dollar today is worth more than a dollar in the future.
   b. The longer one waits for a dollar, the more uncertain the receipt is.
   c. (a) and (b).
   d. None of the above.

The correct answer is (c). *(Publisher)*
REQUIRED: The true statement(s) about the time value of money.
DISCUSSION: The time value of money is concerned with two issues:

1) the investment value of money, and
2) the risk (uncertainty) inherent in any executory agreement.

5. Present value is

   a. The sum of dollars-in discounted to time zero.
   b. The sum of dollars-out discounted to time zero.
   c. (a) and (b).
   d. None of the above.

The correct answer is (c). *(Publisher)*
REQUIRED: The true statement(s) about present value.
DISCUSSION: The present value concept may be applied both to dollars-in (inflows) and to dollars-out (outflows). Thus, cash inflows and cash outflows may both be discounted to time zero (the present).

6. Risk can be controlled in capital budgeting situations by assuming a

   a. High accounting rate of return.
   b. Large net present value.
   c. High net income.
   d. Short payback period.

The correct answer is (d). *(CIA 1187 IV-22)*
REQUIRED: The assumption that controls risk in capital budgeting situations.
DISCUSSION: The payback period is the time needed for net cash inflows to cover the initial investment. The shorter the period, the sooner the investment will be recovered and the more accurate forecasts of results are likely to be. Hence, accepting only projects with short payback periods is a means of reducing risk.
Answers (a), (b), and (c) are incorrect because each states a measure of profitability, not a means of minimizing the riskiness of a project.

7. Future value is

   a. The sum of dollars-in discounted to time zero.
   b. The sum of dollars-out discounted to time zero.
   c. The value of a dollar-in or a dollar-out at a future time adjusted for any compounding effect.
   d. None of the above.

The correct answer is (c). *(Publisher)*
REQUIRED: The definition of future value.
DISCUSSION: The future value of a dollar is its value at a time in the future given its present value. The future value of a dollar is affected both by the discount rate and the time at which the dollar is received. Hence, both dollars-in and dollars-out in the future may be adjusted for the discount rate and any compounding that may occur.
Answers (a) and (b) are incorrect because each concerns present value.

Module 16.1: General Concepts 469

8. The discount rate ordinarily used in present value calculations is

   a. The Federal Reserve rate.
   b. The treasury bill rate.
   c. The minimum desired rate of return set by the firm.
   d. The prime rate.

The correct answer is (c). *(Publisher)*
REQUIRED: The discount rate customarily used in present value calculations.
DISCUSSION: The discount rate most often used in present value calculations is the minimum desired rate of return as set by management. The NPV arrived at in this calculation is a first step in the decision process. It indicates how the project's return compares with the minimum desired rate of return.
Answers (a), (b), and (d) are incorrect because, while each may be considered, the firm will set its minimum desired rate of return in view of its needs.

9. Net present value is

   a. The sum of discounted cash inflows.
   b. The sum of discounted cash outflows.
   c. The sum of discounted cash inflows less the sum of discounted cash outflows.
   d. The sum of discounted cash inflows plus discounted cash outflows.

The correct answer is (c). *(Publisher)*
REQUIRED: The definition of net present value.
DISCUSSION: Net present value is the sum of discounted cash inflows less any discounted cash outflows. Net present value may be either positive or negative.
Answers (a) and (b) are incorrect because each is a component of the net present value. Answer (d) is incorrect because NPV is the difference between cash inflows and outflows.

10. An assumption regarding net present value calculations is that

    a. All projects will be profitable.
    b. Reinvestment of the cash flows will be made at the discount rate.
    c. The life of all projects is greater than 7 years.
    d. None of the above.

The correct answer is (b). *(Publisher)*
REQUIRED: An assumption regarding net present value calculations.
DISCUSSION: An assumption regarding net present value calculations is that the cash inflow will be reinvested at the discount rate. If reinvestment is at other than the discount rate, the project should be reevaluated.
Answer (a) is incorrect because not all projects will be profitable. Answer (c) is incorrect because the project life may be greater or less than 7 years.

11. The method of project selection that considers the time value of money in a capital budgeting decision computes the

    a. Accounting rate of return on initial investment.
    b. Accounting rate of return on average investment.
    c. Discounted cash flow.
    d. Payback period.

The correct answer is (c). *(CPA 574 T-19)*
REQUIRED: The capital budgeting method that considers the time value of money.
DISCUSSION: The premise of the discounted cash flow technique is that the use of money has a cost (interest) as would the use of any other asset. Therefore, money to be received or spent in the future must be discounted at an appropriate interest rate to determine its present value. A comparison of present values allows potential projects to be ranked according to their profitability.
Answers (a), (b), and (d) are incorrect because none considers the time value of money. The accounting rate of return on initial investment equals projected net income divided by initial investment. If it is based on average investment, the denominator in the ratio equals one-half of the initial investment. The payback period (in years) is the annual net cash flow divided into the initial cash investment.

12. The capital budgeting technique known as accounting rate of return uses

	Depreciation Expense	Time Value of Money
a.	No	No
b.	No	Yes
c.	Yes	Yes
d.	Yes	No

The correct answer is (d). *(CPA 1187 T-49)*
REQUIRED: The component(s) of the accounting rate of return.
DISCUSSION: The accounting rate of return (ARR) is the expected net income divided by the initial investment or average investment (there is no basis for choice of one over the other). Depreciation expense is needed to compute the numerator component of the ARR. The time value of money is not needed for the ARR calculation.

13. The net present value and time adjusted rate of return methods of decision making in capital budgeting are superior to the payback method in that they

    a. Are easier to implement.

    b. Consider the time value of money.

    c. Require less input.

    d. Reflect the effects of depreciation and income taxes.

The correct answer is (b). *(CPA 1177 T-37)*
REQUIRED: Advantages of NPV and time adjusted rate of return methods over the payback method.
DISCUSSION: Both the time adjusted rate of return (integral rate of return) and the NPV methods of capital budgeting consider the time value of money. The NPV is the excess of the present values of future cash flows (discounted at a specified rate) over the net cost of the investment. The time adjusted rate of return is the maximum interest rate that a firm may pay such that the present value of future cash flows equals the cost of the investment. Each method ranks investment choices based on their profitability. The payback method only measures the time required for the investment dollars to be recaptured by the annual cash flows.

Answers (a) and (c) are incorrect because ease of calculation and less input are features of the payback method. Answer (d) is incorrect because all three methods ignore depreciation except for its effect on income taxes.

14. Which of the following capital expenditure planning and control techniques has been criticized because it might mistakenly imply that earnings are reinvested at the rate of return earned by the investment?

    a. Payback method.

    b. Average return on investment method.

    c. Present value method.

    d. Time adjusted rate of return method.

The correct answer is (d). *(CPA 575 T-23)*
REQUIRED: The technique that might imply that earnings are reinvested at the rate of return earned by the investment.
DISCUSSION: The time adjusted rate of return (internal rate of return) method determines the discount rate at which the NPV of the cash inflows or savings from the project will be equal to the initial cash outflows, i.e., the discount rate that equates the net present value with zero. This method assumes that reinvestment is at the internal rate of return, although its name might imply that earnings are reinvested at the rate of return earned by the investment.

Answers (a) and (b) are incorrect because neither is a discounted cash flow technique. Answer (c) is incorrect because the NPV method assumes reinvestment at the particular project's cost of capital.

15. A company is considering the purchase of a new conveyor belt system for carrying parts and subassemblies from building to building within its plant complex. It is expected that the system will have a useful life of at least 10 years and that it will substantially reduce labor and waiting-time costs. If the company's average cost of capital is about 15% and if some evaluation must be made of cost/benefit relationships, including the effects of interest, to determine the desirability of the purchase, the most relevant quantitative technique for evaluating the investment is

    a. Cost/volume/profit analysis.

    b. Payback analysis.

    c. Present value (or time adjusted rate of return) analysis.

    d. Program evaluation and review technique (PERT).

    e. Time series or trend regression analysis.

The correct answer is (c). *(CPA 572 T-22)*
REQUIRED: The investment evaluation technique that considers the cost/benefit relationship and the effects of interest.
DISCUSSION: A present value analysis compares the present value of the benefits of a given project to the present value of the project's costs. These two present values are determined by using the company's average cost of capital (interest rate). Similarly, a time adjusted rate of return (internal rate of return) analysis determines the discount rate at which the present value of the project's benefits equals the present value of the project's costs, i.e., the rate at which NPV equals zero.

Answer (a) is incorrect because CVP analysis identifies changes in income based on changes in cost and volume. Answer (b) is incorrect because a payback analysis does not consider the time value of money. It merely computes the number of periods required to return the original investment. Answer (d) is incorrect because PERT is a technique used to manage complex projects and identify critical processes. Answer (e) is incorrect because regression analysis is a statistical technique used to measure relationships of variables over time.

Module 16.1: General Concepts

16. Rao Manufacturing Co. is contemplating the replacement of its present cafeteria facilities with purchased automatic vending machines. Management is vitally concerned about the amounts and timing of the cash flows for each alternative. In evaluating the alternatives, Rao's management should employ

 a. Simulation techniques.
 b. Queuing theory.
 c. Linear algebra.
 d. Discounted cash flow techniques.
 e. Cost/volume/profit analysis.

The correct answer is (d). (CMA 1280 5-12)
REQUIRED: The appropriate technique for analyzing amounts and timing of cash flows.
DISCUSSION: Discounted cash flow techniques determine the present value of a stream of payments, which depends upon the amount and timing of each payment and the discount (interest) rate.
Answer (a) is incorrect because simulation techniques permit analysis of the effects of changing one or more variables in a mathematical model. Answer (b) is incorrect because queuing theory concerns waiting-line systems. Answer (c) is incorrect because linear algebra analyzes and manipulates a number of linearly-related variables. Answer (e) is incorrect because CVP analysis identifies changes in income based on changes in costs, revenues, and volume, not changes in cash flow amounts and timing.

17. When using one of the discounted cash flow methods to evaluate the desirability of a capital budgeting project, which of the following factors is generally not important?

 a. The method of financing the project under consideration.
 b. The timing of cash flows relating to the project.
 c. The impact of the project on income taxes to be paid.
 d. The amounts of cash flows relating to the project.

The correct answer is (a). (CPA 1174 T-29)
REQUIRED: The unimportant factor under the discounted cash flow methods.
DISCUSSION: The method of financing the project is not considered in a discounted cash flow analysis unless it affects the amounts and timing of cash flows and the discount rate.
Answers (b), (c), and (d) are incorrect because each is an important factor in evaluating the desirability of a capital budgeting project.

18. Which of the following best identifies the reason for using probabilities in capital budgeting decisions?

 a. Uncertainty.
 b. Cost of capital.
 c. Time value of money.
 d. Projects with unequal lives.

The correct answer is (a). (CPA 575 T-30)
REQUIRED: The reason for using probabilities in capital budgeting decisions.
DISCUSSION: Capital budgeting decisions are based upon an analysis of the future cash inflows and outflows related to an investment. Since these cash flows occur in the future and are thus uncertain, probabilities are assigned to each possible series of cash flows in order to make a single assumption about them for purposes of capital budgeting decisions.
Answers (b) and (c) are incorrect because the cost of capital and the time value of money are assumed to be known. Answer (d) is incorrect because probabilities are not required when the project's useful life is known (certain).

19. Risk to a company is affected by both project variability and how project returns correlate with those of the company's prevailing business. Overall company risk will be lowest when a project's returns exhibit

 a. Low variability and negative correlation.
 b. Low variability and positive correlation.
 c. High variability and positive correlation.
 d. High variability and no correlation.

The correct answer is (a). (CIA 1186 IV-39)
REQUIRED: The circumstance in which overall company risk will be lowest.
DISCUSSION: A common general definition is that risk is an investment with an unknown outcome, but a known probability distribution of returns (a known mean and standard deviation). An increase in the standard deviation (variability) of returns is synonymous with an increase in the riskiness of a project. Risk is also increased when the project's returns are positively (directly) correlated with other investments in the firm's portfolio; i.e., risk increases when returns on all projects rise or fall together. Consequently, the overall risk is decreased when projects have low variability and are negatively correlated (the diversification effect).

20. The effectiveness of the net present value method has been questioned as an evaluation technique for capital budgeting decisions on the basis that

   a. Predicting future cash flows is often difficult and clouded with uncertainties.
   b. The accounting rate of return method is usually more accurate and useful.
   c. The payback technique is theoretically more reliable.
   d. The computation involves some difficult mathematical applications that most accountants cannot perform.

The correct answer is (a). (CPA 1174 T-35)
   REQUIRED: The weakness of the net present value method for capital budgeting.
   DISCUSSION: Capital budgeting decisions are based upon an analysis of the cash inflows and outflows of projects over an extended time. Predicting future cash flows is often difficult and uncertain. The actual amounts and timing of future cash flows, discount rate, and reinvestment rate are all subject to uncertainty.
   Answers (b) and (c) are incorrect because the accounting rate of return and payback methods require prediction of the same future cash flows, yet are theoretically less preferred since the time value of money is not considered. Answer (d) is incorrect because all competent accountants can perform present value computations. The difficulty of the method is in predicting future events.

21. A measure which describes the risk of an investment project relative to other investments in general is called

   a. The coefficient of variation.
   b. The beta coefficient.
   c. The standard deviation.
   d. The expected return.

The correct answer is (b). (CIA 1187 IV-66)
   REQUIRED: The measure of the risk of an investment relative to investments in general.
   DISCUSSION: The required rate of return on equity capital in the capital asset pricing model is the risk-free rate (determined by government securities) plus the product of the market risk premium times the beta coefficient (beta measures the firm's risk). The market risk premium is the amount above the risk-free rate that will induce investment in the market. The beta coefficient of an individual stock is the correlation between the volatility (price variation) of the stock market and that of the price of the individual stock. For example, if an individual stock goes up 15% and the market only 10%, beta is 1.5.
   Answer (a) is incorrect because it compares risk to expected return (standard deviation/mean or expected return). Answer (c) is incorrect because it measures dispersion (risk) of project returns. Answer (d) is incorrect because it does not describe risk.

22. Consider a company whose beta value has decreased due to a change in its marketing strategy. Due to this change, the discount rate applied to expected cash flows of potential projects will be

   a. Reduced.
   b. Increased.
   c. Unchanged.
   d. Zero.

The correct answer is (a). (CIA 1185 IV-26)
   REQUIRED: The effect of a decrease in beta value on the discount rate applied to cash flows of potential projects.
   DISCUSSION: There is a positive relationship between a firm's beta value and the discount rate applied to cash flows. Thus, a decrease in beta value will reduce the discount rate.
   Answers (b) and (c) are incorrect because the discount rate will be decreased (not increased or unaffected). Answer (d) is incorrect because a zero discount rate incorrectly suggests that future cash flows do not need to be discounted for evaluation purposes.

23. Depreciation is incorporated explicitly in the discounted cash flow analysis of an investment proposal because it

   a. Is a cost of operations that cannot be avoided.
   b. Results in an annual cash outflow.
   c. Is a cash inflow.
   d. Reduces the cash outlay for income taxes.
   e. Represents the initial cash outflow spread over the life of the investment.

The correct answer is (d). (CMA 1277 5-14)
   REQUIRED: The purpose of incorporating depreciation into discounted cash flow analysis.
   DISCUSSION: Depreciation is a noncash expense and therefore is not incorporated into a cash flow analysis unless it affects a cash expense such as income taxes.
   Answers (a) and (b) are incorrect because depreciation is a noncash expense and therefore is not directly incorporated into the cash flow analysis. Answer (c) is incorrect because depreciation does not create a cash inflow, although it may reduce the cash outflow for taxes. Answer (e) is incorrect because, in a cash flow analysis, cash outflows are taken into account at the time they are made, not spread over the life of the investment.

Module 16.1: General Concepts

24. Carco Inc. wants to use discounted cash flow techniques when analyzing its capital investment projects. The company is aware of the uncertainty involved in estimating future cash flows. A simple method some companies employ to adjust for the uncertainty inherent in their estimates is to

a. Prepare a direct analysis of the probability of outcomes.
b. Use accelerated depreciation.
c. Adjust the minimum desired rate of return.
d. Increase the estimates of the cash flows.
e. Ignore salvage values.

The correct answer is (c). *(CMA 1278 5-8)*
REQUIRED: A simple method to adjust for the uncertainty of discounted cash flow techniques.
DISCUSSION: Uncertainty can be compensated for by adjusting the desired rate of return. The greater the amount of uncertainty in a given project, the higher the required rate of return will be. Thus, a project with a high degree of uncertainty will require a relatively high rate of return. The greater the risk, the greater the profit should be.
Answer (a) is incorrect because preparing an analysis of probability of outcomes is not a simple method of adjustment. Answer (b) is incorrect because depreciation should be considered in a capital project to accurately reflect cash flows, not to adjust for uncertainty. It is a noncash expense deductible for tax purposes and therefore affects the amounts of tax payments (cash outflows). Answers (d) and (e) are incorrect because increasing the estimated cash flows and/or ignoring salvage values introduces error into the capital budgeting analysis.

25. An optimal capital budget is determined by the point where the marginal cost of capital is

a. Minimized.
b. Equal to the average cost of capital.
c. Equal to the rate of return on total assets.
d. Equal to the marginal rate of return on investment.

The correct answer is (d). *(CIA 1187 IV-43)*
REQUIRED: The definition of an optimal capital budget.
DISCUSSION: According to microeconomic theory, a firm should produce until its marginal revenue equals its marginal cost. In capital budgeting terms, marginal revenue is the marginal rate of return on investment, and marginal cost is the company's marginal cost of capital (MCC). Hence, the firm should continue to invest until the cost of the last investment equals the return.
Answers (a) and (b) are incorrect because the firm must balance cost and return. Minimizing MCC or average cost of capital (ACC is minimized when it equals MCC) ignores possible returns. Answer (c) is incorrect because the rate of return on total assets is an average return. Setting MCC equal to this rate may result in acceptance of poor investments.

26. A company prefers to reinvest its earnings rather than pay them out in dividends when the expected rate of return on reinvested earnings exceeds the rate of return investors could obtain on other investments of comparable risk. Which of the following best reflects this preference?

a. A stable dividend per share policy.
b. A constant dividend payout ratio policy.
c. A regular dividend per share plus extras.
d. The residual theory of dividends.

The correct answer is (d). *(CIA 587 IV-41)*
REQUIRED: The item that best reflects the preference for reinvestment.
DISCUSSION: Under the residual theory of dividends, a rational investor should prefer reinvestment of retained earnings (internally generated equity) when the return exceeds what the investor could earn on investments of equal risk. The amount (the residual) of earnings paid as dividends is a function of investment opportunities and the ideal debt-equity ratio. At this ratio, the firm's marginal cost of capital is minimized. External equity is more costly than internal equity because of flotation costs. Thus, the marginal cost of capital is reduced by using retained earnings for equity financing rather than issuing new stock. However, if reinvestment of retained earnings would move the firm away from its ideal debt-equity ratio, internal equity should be paid out as dividends. Debt usually has a lower cost than equity, so most firms include debt in their capital structures.
Answers (a), (b), and (c) are incorrect because according to the residual theory, dividends should be adjusted depending on the desired capital structure and the investments available.

27. The Net Present Value (NPV) method and the Internal Rate of Return (IRR) model are used to analyze capital expenditures. The IRR model, as contrasted with the NPV model

  a. Is considered inferior because it fails to calculate compounded interest rate.
  b. Is a discounted cash flow model while the NPV model is not.
  c. Almost always gives a different decision than does the NPV method as to the acceptability of a given proposal.
  d. Assumes that the rate of return on the reinvestment of the cash proceeds is at the indicated rate of return of the project analyzed rather than at the discount rate used.
  e. Is preferred in practice because it is able to handle multiple desired hurdle rates which is impossible with the NPV model.

The correct answer is (d). *(CMA 1287 5-27)*
REQUIRED: The true statement about the difference between the IRR model and the NPV model.
DISCUSSION: One criticism of the IRR model is that it assumes that the rate of return on reinvestment of cash inflows is at the indicated rate of return of the project. The assumption is unrealistic since the IRR is merely the rate at which the NPV is zero, not a rate reflecting the expected interplay of market forces. The NPV method assumes reinvestment at the cost of capital, which is the discount rate used in the calculations.
  Answers (a) and (b) are incorrect because each is true of both models. Answer (c) is incorrect because the two methods almost always give the same answers as to acceptability. Answer (e) is incorrect because the NPV model is based on desired hurdle rates that must be met. The IRR model calculates the rate of return of a project without reference to the cost of capital.

28. A company uses discounted cash flow in deciding between investment alternatives and return on investment (as measured by quarterly net income to the division) in evaluating division management. Choose the item below which is a problem of such a system.

  a. Division management may be overly inclined to incur expenses with a longer term payoff such as advertising near the end of a period.
  b. There is wasted effort in that both discounted cash flow and net income to the division are calculated when only one is necessary.
  c. An overemphasis on long-term profit may occur.
  d. Product quality, employee relations, and development of subordinates may be underemphasized.

The correct answer is (d). *(CIA 587 IV-17)*
REQUIRED: The problem in using discounted cash flow and return on investment as evaluation methods.
DISCUSSION: Return on investment based on quarterly net income is a short-term measure of performance. Because improvements in product quality, etc. may not have an effect on ROI in the short-term, managers may be tempted to sacrifice long-term benefits for immediate profits.
  Answers (a) and (c) are incorrect because an overemphasis on short-term profit may occur that may lead to avoidance of expenses with a longer-term payoff. Answer (b) is incorrect because net income will be calculated whether or not discounted cash flow is needed for purposes of evaluation of investments.

16.2 Payback

29. The payback method measures

  a. How quickly investment dollars may be recovered.
  b. The cash flow from an investment.
  c. The economic life of an investment.
  d. The profitability of an investment.

The correct answer is (a). *(CPA 1172 T-21)*
REQUIRED: What the payback method measures in a capital budgeting analysis.
DISCUSSION: The payback method determines how long it takes for the investment dollars to be recovered by the annual net cash inflows. The time is computed by dividing the net investment by the average periodic net cash inflow.
  Answer (b) is incorrect because, although the payback method is computed by using the cash flows, it does not measure them. Answer (c) is incorrect because the asset's economic life has no relevance to the payback method. Answer (d) is incorrect because the payback method does not measure profitability.

Module 16.2: Payback

30. The payback capital budgeting technique considers

	Income Over Entire Life of Project	Time Value of Money
a.	No	No
b.	No	Yes
c.	Yes	Yes
d.	Yes	No

The correct answer is (a). *(CPA 1185 T-48)*
REQUIRED: Considerations of the payback capital budgeting technique.
DISCUSSION: The payback method computes the time needed to recapture an investment by dividing the cost of the initial investment by the periodic net cash flow. The strength of the method is its simplicity. Its basic disadvantage is that it provides no measure of profitability since it ignores the time value of money and the effects of cash flows after the payback period.

31. Which of the following is necessary to calculate the payback period for a project?

a. Useful life.
b. Minimum desired rate of return.
c. Net present value.
d. Annual cash flow.

The correct answer is (d). *(CPA 1180 T-33)*
REQUIRED: The variable necessary to calculate the payback period.
DISCUSSION: The payback period is computed by dividing the net investment dollars by the average periodic net cash inflow.
Answer (a) is incorrect because the useful life is irrelevant to the time needed to recover the investment. Answer (b) is incorrect because the minimum desired rate of return, which is the highest opportunity cost the company will forgo to invest in a particular project, is not relevant to the payback method. Answer (c) is incorrect because the payback period is not concerned with present value dollars but rather with the time it takes to recover the investment.

32. Which of the following capital expenditure planning and control techniques has been criticized because it fails to consider investment profitability?

a. Payback method.
b. Average return on investment method.
c. Present value method.
d. Time adjusted rate of return method.

The correct answer is (a). *(CPA 575 T-22)*
REQUIRED: The capital expenditure planning and control technique criticized because it disregards investment profitability.
DISCUSSION: The payback method uses the average periodic net cash inflows to determine the time it will take to recover the initial investment dollars. It does not consider the investment's profitability.
Answers (b), (c), and (d) are incorrect because each measures the profitability of an investment.

33. An advantage of using the payback method of evaluating capital budgeting alternatives is that payback is

a. Precise in estimates of profitability.
b. Easy to apply.
c. Not based on cash flow data.
d. Insensitive to the life of the project(s) considered.

The correct answer is (b). *(CPA 1175 T-20)*
REQUIRED: The advantage of using the payback method.
DISCUSSION: The payback method is simply the initial investment divided by the estimated periodic net cash inflows. Accordingly, rates of return and overall profitability need not be estimated.
Answer (a) is incorrect because the payback method does not estimate profitability. Answer (c) is incorrect because the payback method is based on cash flow data. Answer (d) is incorrect because, although the payback method does not take into account the life of the project, that is not considered a disadvantage.

34. The bailout payback period is

a. The payback method used by firms with federally insured loans.
b. The length of time for payback using cash flows plus the salvage value to recover the original investment.
c. (a) and (b).
d. None of the above.

The correct answer is (b). *(Publisher)*
REQUIRED: The definition of the bailout payback period.
DISCUSSION: The bailout payback period is the length of time required for the sum of the net cash flows from an investment plus its salvage value to equal the original investment. This period provides an opportunity for management to recognize when they must make a decision about recouping the project's original investment.

Module 16.2: Payback

35. Deficiencies associated with using the payback method to evaluate investment alternatives include

a. Cash flows after the payback period are ignored.

b. The present value of cash inflows is ignored.

c. Inflows of different time periods are treated equally.

d. Disproportionate weight is given to cash flows occurring in the future.

e. All of the above.

The correct answer is (e). *(CIA 581 IV-12)*
REQUIRED: The deficiencies associated with the payback method.
DISCUSSION: The payback method computes the time needed to recapture an investment by dividing the cost of the initial investment by the periodic net cash flow. The strength of the method is its simplicity. Its basic disadvantage is that it provides no measure of profitability since it ignores the time value of money and the effects of cash flows after the payback period. Consequently, each answer choice is a deficiency associated with the method.

36. A machine costing $1,000 produces total cash inflows of $1,400 over 4 years. Determine the payback period given the following cash flows:

Year	After-Tax Cash Flows	Cumulative Cash Flows
1	$400	$ 400
2	300	700
3	500	1,200
4	200	1,400

a. 2 years.

b. 2.60 years.

c. 2.86 years.

d. 3 years.

The correct answer is (b). *(CIA 1187 IV-19)*
REQUIRED: The payback period given the annual cash flows.
DISCUSSION: Since $700 will be received in the first 2 years, only $300 will remain to be recovered in year 3. The payback period is therefore 2.6 years [2 years + ($300 ÷ $500) of year 3].

37. Womark Company purchased a new machine on January 1 of this year for $90,000, with an estimated useful life of 5 years and a salvage value of $10,000. The machine will be depreciated using the straight-line method. The machine is expected to produce cash flow from operations, net of income taxes, of $36,000 a year in each of the next 5 years. The payback period will be

a. 2.2 years.

b. 2.5 years.

c. 4.0 years.

d. 4.5 years.

The correct answer is (b). *(CPA 582 P-36)*
REQUIRED: The payback period for a new machine given cost, salvage value, estimated useful life, and periodic cash flows.
DISCUSSION: The payback period is computed by dividing the initial investment by the annual expected net cash inflows.

$$\frac{\$90,000}{\$36,000} = 2.5 \text{ years}$$

The other information is irrelevant to the computation of the payback period.

38. Referring to Q. 37, assume the new machine's salvage value is $20,000 in years 1 and 2, and $15,000 in years 3 and 4. What will be the bailout period for the Womark Company on this new machine?

a. 1.4 years.

b. 2.2 years.

c. 1.9 years.

d. 3.4 years.

The correct answer is (c). *(Publisher)*
REQUIRED: The bailout period on an investment of a new machine.
DISCUSSION: The bailout period is the time period it takes to recover the original investment through cash flow plus the salvage value. During year 1, cost less salvage value is $70,000 and cash flow is $36,000. During year 2, the cost less salvage value remains $70,000 and the second cash flow of $36,000 recovers the $70,000 just before the end of the second year.

Module 16.2: Payback

39. A company is investigating the possibility of acquiring a machine that will cost $12,000 and will have annual depreciation for tax purposes of $2,400 for 5 years. The machine is expected to result in a cash saving from operations of $4,000 per year. If the tax rate is 50%, what is the payback period for the new machine?

a. 3 years.
b. 3.75 years.
c. 5 years.
d. 6 years.

The correct answer is (b). *(CIA 587 IV-22)*
REQUIRED: The payback period for the new machine.
DISCUSSION: The annual cash saving is $4,000, and annual depreciation is $2,400. The net $1,600 ($4,000 − $2,400) gain is subject to a 50% tax rate, so annual cash outflow for taxes is $800, and the net after-tax cash inflow is $3,200 ($4,000 − $800). The payback period equals 3.75 years ($12,000 investment ÷ $3,200 after-tax cash flow).

40. Energy Company is planning to spend $84,000 for a new machine, to be depreciated on the straight-line basis over 10 years with no salvage value. The related cash flow from operations, net of income taxes, is expected to be $10,000 a year for each of the first 6 years and $12,000 for each of the next 4 years. What is the payback period?

a. 4.4 years.
b. 7.6 years.
c. 7.8 years.
d. 8.0 years.

The correct answer is (d). *(CPA 1180 P-22)*
REQUIRED: The payback period given after-tax cash flows, depreciation, and salvage value.
DISCUSSION: The payback period is computed by dividing the initial investment by the annual net cash inflows. Since the cash flows are not uniform, the payback period must be calculated by subtracting each year's net after-tax cash inflow from the investment until zero is reached. Depreciation is ignored because the given cash flows are net of tax. After 6 years, $60,000 (6 × $10,000) will have been recovered. The remaining $24,000 will be recovered in 2 years ($12,000 × 2). The total payback period is thus 8 years.

41. Refer to Q. 40. Energy Company has also estimated the salvage value of the new machine at the end of year 1 to be $64,000. Salvage value will decline by $5,000 each year thereafter. What is the bailout payback period?

a. 2 years.
b. 3 years.
c. 4 years.
d. 5 years.

The correct answer is (b). *(Publisher)*
REQUIRED: The bailout payback period given estimates of salvage value.
DISCUSSION: The bailout period is the length of time required for the sum of the net cash flows plus salvage value to equal the original investment ($84,000). The cumulative cash flow (net of taxes) at the end of year 1 ($10,000) plus the year-1 salvage value of $64,000 equals a recovery of $74,000. The cumulative cash flow at the end of year 2 ($20,000) plus the year-2 salvage value of $59,000 ($64,000 − $5,000) equals a recoupment of $79,000. At the end of year 3 the cumulative cash flow of $30,000 plus the salvage value of $54,000 ($59,000 − $5,000) equals $84,000. The bailout period is thus 3 years.

42. An investment project is expected to yield $10,000 in annual revenues, has $2,000 in fixed costs per year, and requires an initial inventory of $5,000. Given a cost of goods sold of 60% of sales, what is the payback period in years?

a. 2.50.
b. 5.00.
c. 2.00.
d. 1.25.

The correct answer is (a). *(CIA 586 IV-25)*
REQUIRED: The payback period in years.
DISCUSSION: The payback period of an investment is computed by dividing the original investment by the net cash flow per year. Net cash flow per year is computed as follows:

Annual revenue	$10,000
CGS (60%)	6,000
Cash flow before fixed costs	$ 4,000
Fixed costs	2,000
Net cash flow	$ 2,000

$$\frac{\text{Original investment}}{\text{Net cash flow}} = \text{Payback period}$$

$$\frac{\$5,000}{\$2,000} = 2.5 \text{ years}$$

Module 16.3: Cost of Capital

43. The Polar Company is planning to purchase a new machine for $30,000. The payback period is expected to be 5 years. The new machine is expected to produce cash flow from operations, net of income taxes, of $7,000 a year in each of the next 3 years and $5,500 in the fourth year. Depreciation of $5,000 a year will be charged to income for each of the 5 years of the payback period. How much cash flow from operations, net of taxes, is the new machine expected to produce in the last (fifth) year of the payback period?

   a. $1,000.
   b. $3,500.
   c. $5,000.
   d. $8,500.

The correct answer is (b). (CPA 1179 P-23)
REQUIRED: The new machine's cash flow from operations, net of taxes, expected in the last year of the payback period.
DISCUSSION: The payback period is the time required to recover the initial investment cost. Three years of $7,000 net of tax cash inflow and $5,500 in the fourth year is a total of $26,500 that will have been recovered by the end of the fourth year. This leaves $3,500 ($30,000 - $26,500) to be recovered in the fifth year. Ignoring depreciation (because the cash flows are net of tax), the net cash inflow in year 5 is therefore expected to be $3,500.

44. Bernie Company purchased a new machine with an estimated useful life of 5 years with no salvage value for $45,000. The machine is expected to produce cash flow from operations, net of income taxes, as follows:

1st year	$ 9,000
2nd year	12,000
3rd year	15,000
4th year	9,000
5th year	8,000

Bernie will use the sum-of-the-years'-digits method to depreciate the new machine in its accounting records as follows:

1st year	$15,000
2nd year	12,000
3rd year	9,000
4th year	6,000
5th year	3,000

What is the payback period?

   a. 2 years.
   b. 3 years.
   c. 4 years.
   d. 5 years.

The correct answer is (c). (CPA 579 P-22)
REQUIRED: The payback period given after-tax cash flows, salvage value, cost, and SYD depreciation.
DISCUSSION: The payback period is computed by dividing the initial investment by the annual net cash inflows. Since the cash inflows are not uniform, the payback period must be calculated by subtracting each year's cash flow from the investment until zero is reached. The year in which the investment is fully recovered is the final year of the payback period. Bernie's payback period is 4 years, as calculated below. The SYD depreciation, a noncash expense, is ignored because the given cash inflows are net of tax.

$45,000	
(9,000)	Year 1
$36,000	
(12,000)	Year 2
$24,000	
(15,000)	Year 3
$ 9,000	
(9,000)	Year 4
$ -0-	

16.3 Cost of Capital

45. The minimum return a project must earn to leave the value of the company unchanged is the

   a. Current borrowing rate.
   b. Discount rate.
   c. Capitalization rate.
   d. Cost of capital.

The correct answer is (d). (CPA 1181 T-60)
REQUIRED: The minimum return a project must earn to leave the company's value unchanged.
DISCUSSION: Cost of capital may be defined as the rate of return a project must earn to leave the market value of the firm unchanged. It is typically a weighted average of the costs of all sources of funds (debt, common and preferred stock, and retained earnings).
Answer (a) is incorrect because the current borrowing rate may not be the same as the rate for the financing of the project. Answer (b) is incorrect because the discount rate is the interest rate charged by the Federal Reserve to its borrowers. "Discount rate" is also a generic term for any rate used to adjust future cash flows to determine their present value. Firms customarily use the cost of capital as the minimum discount rate (hurdle rate). Answer (c) is incorrect because it is the rate at which earnings are capitalized to value the firm.

Module 16.3: Cost of Capital

46. A company will receive cash from sales in 1 year that can be used to pay for materials. The supplier will allow payment in 1 year. If the company pays the supplier immediately, it will receive a 20% discount off the $100,000 purchase price, but it must borrow the full amount. A bank has offered the company three alternatives:

1) A 1-year loan at 18% with no other fees,
2) A 1-year loan at 15% with the provision that it maintains 20% of whatever amount it borrows as noninterest-bearing compensating balances over the life of the loan, or
3) A guaranteed $100,000 line of credit at 17% with the provision that the bank will collect a 1% fee on the average amount of unused funds. The company expects to borrow no other funds.

The company would achieve the lowest cost of financing by

a. Allowing the supplier to finance the materials and making payment at the end of 1 year.
b. Accepting the 1-year loan at 18% with no other provisions.
c. Accepting the 1-year loan at 15% with the compensating balance provisions.
d. Accepting the guaranteed line of credit at 17% with the fee required on the average amount of unused funds.

The correct answer is (d). *(CIA 1186 IV-43)*
REQUIRED: The means by which the company would achieve the lowest cost of financing.
DISCUSSION: If the company chooses the line of credit, it will pay 17% interest on $80,000 ($100,000 - $20,000 discount) and 1% on the $20,000 unused portion, a total of $13,800. The effective interest rate would thus be 17.25% ($13,800 ÷ $80,000).
Answer (a) is incorrect because if the company forgoes the cash discount, its effective rate is 25% ($20,000 ÷ $80,000 immediate cash price). Answer (b) is incorrect because an 18% effective rate exceeds that on the line of credit. Answer (c) is incorrect because the effective rate would be 18.75% [(15% x $100,000) ÷ $80,000 available funds].

47. The weighted average cost of capital approach to decision making is not directly affected by the

a. Value of the common stock.
b. Current budget for expansion.
c. Cost of debt outstanding.
d. Proposed mix of debt, equity, and existing funds used to implement the project.

The correct answer is (b). *(CPA 1177 T-44)*
REQUIRED: The item that does not affect the weighted average cost of capital approach.
DISCUSSION: The weighted average cost of capital approach to decision making determines the proportionate share of financing to be accomplished by different methods (debt, preferred stock, common stock, and retained earnings), and then weights the cost of each type of financing by the proportion to obtain a weighted average cost of capital. The current budget for expansion is presumably dependent on the firm's cost of capital. A decision to expand would not be economically rational if its rate of return did not at least equal the firm's cost of capital.
Answers (a), (c), and (d) are incorrect because each is a component of the weighted average cost of capital.

48. The basis for measuring the cost of capital derived from bonds and preferred stock, respectively, is the

a. Pre-tax rate of interest for bonds and stated annual dividend rate less the expected EPS for preferred stock.
b. Pre-tax rate of interest for bonds and stated annual dividend rate for preferred stock.
c. After-tax rate of interest for bonds and stated annual dividend rate less the expected EPS for preferred stock.
d. After-tax rate of interest for bonds and stated annual dividend rate for preferred stock.

The correct answer is (d). *(CPA 580 T-49)*
REQUIRED: The formulas for cost of capital derived from bonds and preferred stock.
DISCUSSION: The cost of capital is the weighted average cost to the firm of obtaining funds. The cost of issuing bonds is the after-tax interest rate, since actual interest payments are deductible for tax purposes. The cost of preferred stock is agreed to be the stock's annual dividend rate.
Answers (a) and (b) are incorrect because each refers to pre-tax rates of interest. Answer (c) is incorrect because it is a nonsense answer.

49. What capital budgeting method assumes that funds are reinvested at the company's cost of capital?

a. Payback.
b. Accounting rate of return.
c. Net present value.
d. Time adjusted rate of return.

The correct answer is (c). *(CPA 1176 T-32)*
REQUIRED: The capital budgeting method that assumes funds are reinvested at the company's cost of capital.
DISCUSSION: The NPV method determines the present value of an investment given a discount rate. Presumably, the project with the highest present value is the most favorable. This method assumes that reinvestment is at the company's cost of capital.
Answer (a) is incorrect because the payback period is the time required to recapture the initial investment cost. Answer (b) is incorrect because the accounting rate of return is the increase in dollars of accounting income attributable to the investment divided by the investment. Answer (d) is incorrect because the time adjusted rate of return method determines the discount rate by setting the present value of the future net cash flows from an investment equal to the amount of the investment, assuming that the cash flows can be reinvested at the rate obtained on the original investment, not at the company's cost of capital.

50. For a project to be acceptable to a company using the cost of capital method of analysis, the return on invested capital must

a. At least equal the amount of cash to cover interest and principal payments for any debt incurred to finance the project.
b. Generate sufficient capital to pay for itself within the economic life of the assets committed to the project.
c. At least equal the return on invested capital currently being generated by the company.
d. Generate sufficient capital resources to justify any additional capital expenditures and reduce idle capacity within the company.

The correct answer is (c). *(CPA 1177 T-43)*
REQUIRED: The acceptable return on invested capital to justify a project under the cost of capital method.
DISCUSSION: For the company's overall worth to remain constant, the return rate on an investment or project must be at least equal to the cost of capital, the weighted average of the costs of all the firm's sources of funds (bonds, common and preferred stock, and retained earnings).
Answers (a), (b), and (d) are incorrect because, in each case, the return might be less than the firm's cost of capital.

16.4 Net Present Value

51. The net present value (NPV) of a proposed project represents the

a. Cash flows less the present value of the cash flows.
b. Cash flows less the original investment.
c. Present value of the cash flows plus the present value of the original investment less the original investment.
d. Present value of the cash flows less the original investment.

The correct answer is (d). *(CPA 1180 T-32)*
REQUIRED: The definition of NPV.
DISCUSSION: The NPV is the difference between the present value of the future cash flows from the project discounted at an appropriate interest rate and the initial investment. If the NPV is zero or greater, the investment may be economically rational. The method is a technique for ranking investment proposals.
Answer (a) is incorrect because it is the amount of discount (interest) on the cash flows. Answer (b) is incorrect because the future cash flows must be discounted back to the present. Answer (c) is incorrect because it is nonsense.

52. The NPV capital budgeting technique can be used when cash flows from period to period are

	Uniform	Uneven
a.	No	Yes
b.	No	No
c.	Yes	No
d.	Yes	Yes

The correct answer is (d). *(CPA 586 T-48)*
REQUIRED: The cash flow(s) that can be used in NPV calculations.
DISCUSSION: The NPV is the difference between the present value of the future cash flows from the project discounted at an appropriate interest rate and the initial investment. The method is a technique for ranking investment proposals. The calculation can be performed on either uniform cash flows or uneven cash flows.

Module 16.4: Net Present Value

53. The discount rate (hurdle rate of return) must be determined in advance for the
   a. Internal rate of return method.
   b. NPV method.
   c. Payback period method.
   d. Time adjusted rate of return method.

54. Which of the following is always true with regard to the NPV approach?
   a. If a project is found to be acceptable under the NPV approach, it would also be acceptable under the internal rate of return (IRR) approach.
   b. The NPV and the IRR approaches will always rank projects in the same order.
   c. If a project is found to be acceptable under the NPV approach, it would also be acceptable under the payback approach.
   d. The NPV and payback approaches will always rank projects in the same order.

55. With the reduction in corporate income tax rates in 1987, the elimination of the Investment Tax Credit, and the elimination of the special capital gains tax rates, the present value of capital investment projects for a profitable company will
   a. Increase because of the elimination of the investment tax credit.
   b. Decrease because of the elimination of the investment tax credit and the reduction in the corporate income tax rates.
   c. Increase because of the elimination of the capital gains tax rate.
   d. Increase because of the reduction in the corporate income tax rate.

56. A proposed project has an expected economic life of 8 years. In the calculation of the NPV of the proposed project, salvage value would be
   a. Excluded from the calculation of the NPV.
   b. Included as a cash inflow at the estimated salvage value.
   c. Included as a cash inflow at the future amount of the estimated salvage value.
   d. Included as a cash inflow at the present value of the estimated salvage value.

The correct answer is (b). *(CPA 1185 T-47)*
REQUIRED: The capital budgeting technique that requires advance determination of the discount rate (hurdle rate of return).
DISCUSSION: The NPV is the difference between the present value of the future cash flows discounted at the cost of capital and the initial investment. The discount or hurdle rate is the rate used to determine the present value of cash flows and thus must be determined in advance.

The correct answer is (a). *(CIA 586 IV-29)*
REQUIRED: The statement that is always true regarding the net present value approach.
DISCUSSION: A project is acceptable under the NPV approach if the NPV is zero or greater. The IRR is the discount rate at which the NPV is zero. Thus, if the NPV is zero or greater, the IRR will at least equal the firm's hurdle rate (minimum required rate of return at which the NPV was calculated). The IRR method accepts a project if the IRR equals or exceeds the hurdle rate. Consequently, a project acceptable under the NPV method is also acceptable under the IRR method. However, the converse is not true. A project unacceptable because it has a negative NPV may have an IRR greater than the hurdle rate. The reason is that the IRR method makes the unreasonable assumption that future cash flows will be reinvested for the project's duration at the IRR rather than the hurdle rate.
Answer (b) is incorrect because the two approaches may rank projects differently (the IRR method assumes that reinvestment will be at the IRR, which is frequently not possible). Answers (c) and (d) are incorrect because the payback method provides no absolute indicator of acceptability. It simply ranks projects according to the time required to recover the investment. Because it does not adjust cash flows for the time value of money, the payback criterion may rank projects differently from the NPV method.

The correct answer is (d). *(CMA 687 5-17)*
REQUIRED: The effect of tax reform on the present value of capital investment.
DISCUSSION: Assuming a company is profitable, the decrease in tax rates will result in an increase in its after-tax income, thus increasing the present value of investment projects. Conversely, the elimination of the investment credit and special capital gains treatment would decrease present values. Thus, the only completely correct answer is (d).
Answer (a) is incorrect because the elimination of the investment credit would increase tax liabilities and reduce present values. Answer (b) is incorrect because the reduction in the tax rate would increase present values. Answer (c) is incorrect because the elimination of the favorable capital gains rate would reduce income and result in lower present values.

The correct answer is (d). *(CPA 587 T-48)*
REQUIRED: The treatment of salvage value in NPV calculations.
DISCUSSION: NPV is the difference between the required investment and the present value of the future cash flows. The estimated cash inflow from the salvage value at the end of the project should be included at its discounted (present value) amount.

57. If a company has a positive sum of the present values of all future cash flows related to a proposed capital expenditure discounted at the company's cost of capital, the

   a. Resultant amount is the maximum that should be paid for the asset.
   b. Return on the investment exceeds the company's cost of capital.
   c. Proposed investment is the best alternative.
   d. Discount rate used is not the proper cost of capital for this company.

The correct answer is (b). *(CPA 578 T-46)*
REQUIRED: The implications of a positive sum of present values of future cash flows discounted at the cost of capital.
DISCUSSION: The NPV is the difference between the present value of the future cash flows discounted at the cost of capital and the initial investment. If the NPV is greater than or equal to zero, the firm will earn a return greater than or equal to the company's cost of capital on the project.
Answer (a) is incorrect because the maximum that should be paid for the asset is the present value of the cash flows using the appropriate discount rate (usually the cost of capital). Answer (c) is incorrect because the investment, although sound, is only one possibility. It must be compared with other possible investments to make the best decision. Answer (d) is incorrect because a positive NPV suggests a sound investment, not an improper discount rate.

58. If income tax considerations are ignored, how is depreciation expense used in the following capital budgeting techniques?

	Internal Rate of Return	Net Present Value
a.	Excluded	Excluded
b.	Excluded	Included
c.	Included	Excluded
d.	Included	Included

The correct answer is (a). *(CPA 1186 T-49)*
REQUIRED: The effect of depreciation on capital budgeting techniques.
DISCUSSION: The IRR and NPV methods involve future cash flows. Depreciation is a noncash expense and is not part of either calculation except to the extent it affects income taxes.

59. Future, Inc. is in the enviable situation of having unlimited capital funds. The best decision rule, in an economic sense, for it to follow would be to invest in all projects in which

   a. The payback is less than 4 years.
   b. The accounting rate of return is greater than the earnings as a percent of sales.
   c. The payback reciprocal is greater than the internal rate of return.
   d. The internal rate of return is greater than zero.
   e. The NPV is greater than zero.

The correct answer is (e). *(CMA 1278 5-12)*
REQUIRED: The best investment decision rule given unlimited funds.
DISCUSSION: Given unlimited capital funds, Future should invest in all projects with a NPV greater than zero. It would be profitable to invest in any project for which the rate of return is greater than the cost of capital (i.e., when the NPV of the future cash flows discounted at the firm's cost of capital is positive).
Answers (a) and (c) are incorrect because the payback criterion for capital budgeting is neither efficient nor effective since it does not measure profitability. Answer (b) is incorrect because the accounting rate of return is accounting net income divided by the initial investment. Its major flaw is that it ignores the time value of money. Earnings as a percent of sales ignores the amount of required investment. Answer (d) is incorrect because the problem states that there are unlimited capital funds but does not specify the cost of capital. NPV analysis does take the cost of capital into account.

60. The profitability index is

   a. Another term for the excess present value index.
   b. The ratio of the present value to the original investment.
   c. (a) and (b).
   d. Neither of the above.

The correct answer is (c). *(Publisher)*
REQUIRED: The true statement(s) about the profitability index.
DISCUSSION: The profitability index is another term for the excess present value index. It measures the ratio of the present value of future cash flows to the original investment. In organizations with unlimited capital funds, this index will produce no conflicts in the decision process. If capital rationing is necessary, the index will be an insufficient determinant. The capital available as well as the dollar amount of the present value must both be considered.

Module 16.4: Net Present Value

61. A business has analyzed a proposed investment in depreciable assets using the NPV method. The analysis assumed the use of straight-line depreciation for tax purposes. If the assumption is changed to accelerated depreciation for tax purposes, the analysis will be redone. Which of the following best describes the effect of the change from straight-line to accelerated depreciation on the new analysis of the proposed investment?

a. The risk of the proposed investment will be larger than if straight-line depreciation is used.
b. The results will be invalid because accelerated depreciation cannot be used for tax purposes.
c. The cash flows in each period after income tax effects will be smaller than if straight-line depreciation is used.
d. The NPV of the proposed investment will be larger than if straight-line depreciation is used.

The correct answer is (d). *(CPA 575 P-21)*
REQUIRED: The effect of a change in depreciation on a NPV analysis.
DISCUSSION: The use of accelerated depreciation, with its higher depreciation charges in the early years, increases the initial cash flows (through lower tax payments) and decreases those later in the estimated useful life of the asset. The overall effect is to increase the NPV.
Answer (a) is incorrect because the risk would remain the same. Answer (b) is incorrect because accelerated depreciation may be used for tax purposes. Answer (c) is incorrect because the cash flows in the earlier periods would be larger since accelerated depreciation permits a greater depreciation rate during the early years of an asset's life.

62. When the profitability index or cost-benefit ratio for a project equals one

a. The net present value equals zero.
b. The present value of project returns is less than the present value of project cost.
c. The internal rate of return is less than the cost of capital.
d. The internal rate of return exceeds the cost of capital.

The correct answer is (a). *(CIA 1187 IV-65)*
REQUIRED: The true statement about the profitability index.
DISCUSSION: The profitability index is another term for the excess present value index. It measures the ratio of the present value of future cash flows to the original investment. The index will equal 1.0 when the present value of the future cash flows equals the investment.
Answer (b) is incorrect because when the net present value is less than zero, the ratio is less than 1.0. Answers (c) and (d) are incorrect because the IRR is a computed value that may or may not exceed the cost of capital. It is the discount rate at which the net present value is zero (profitability index = 1.0).

63. The following data relate to two capital-budgeting projects of equal risk:

Present Value of Cash Flows

Period	Project A	Project B
0	$(10,000)	$(30,000)
1	4,550	13,650
2	4,150	12,450
3	3,750	11,250

Which of the projects would be selected using the Profitability-Index (PI) approach and the NPV approach?

	PI	NPV
a.	B	A
b.	Either	B
c.	Either	A
d.	B	B

The correct answer is (b). *(CIA 586 IV-33)*
REQUIRED: The projects selected using the Profitability Index and the net present value approaches.
DISCUSSION: The Profitability Index (PI) is computed as the ratio of the present value of future cash flows to the net cash invested. In this case, the PI for both projects is identical.

$$\frac{\$4,550 + \$4,150 + \$3,750}{\$10,000} = 1.245$$

$$\frac{\$13,650 + \$12,450 + \$11,250}{\$30,000} = 1.245$$

The net present value of a project is the excess of the present values of future cash inflows over the net cost of the investment.

NPV_A = $12,450 - $10,000 = $2,450
NPV_B = $37,350 - $30,000 = $7,350

Project B is preferable under the net present value approach.

Module 16.4: Net Present Value

64. The accountant of Ronier, Inc. has prepared an analysis of a proposed capital project using discounted cash flow techniques. The manager has questioned the accuracy of the results because the discount factors employed in the analysis are based on the assumptions that the cash flows occurred at the end of the year when they actually occurred uniformly throughout each year. The net present value calculated by the accountant will

a. Not be in error.
b. Be slightly overstated.
c. Be unusable for actual decision making.
d. Be slightly understated but usable.
e. Produce an error the direction of which is undeterminable.

The correct answer is (d). *(CMA 1278 5-10)*
REQUIRED: The effect on NPV of assuming that uniformly incurred cash flows occurred at the end of the year.
DISCUSSION: The effect of assuming cash flows occur at the end of the year, when they actually occur uniformly, simply understates the present values of the future cash flows; they probably occur at midyear on the average.
Answers (a), (b), and (e) are incorrect because using year-end discount factors will understate the NPV, since cash flows in investment decisions do not all occur at the end of each year. Answer (c) is incorrect because the effect of using the year-end assumption produces a slight conservatism in the model, but it does not render unusable results.

65. The treasurer of a firm has an opportunity to purchase a secured 15% mortgage with 5 years remaining for $10,000. If the firm purchases the mortgage, they will receive five annual payments of $3,000 each. If the treasurer wants no less than a 12% return on long-term cash investments, the NPV of the mortgage would be:

Years:	1	2	3	4	5
Present value of $1 at 12%:	.89	.80	.71	.64	.57
Present value of $1 at 15%:	.87	.76	.66	.57	.50

a. $80.
b. $830.
c. $5,000.
d. Not enough information.

The correct answer is (b). *(CIA 1186 III-44)*
REQUIRED: The NPV of a mortgage.
DISCUSSION: The NPV is equal to the sum of the discounted future cash inflows minus the required investment. Since the firm will receive $3,000 annually over the next 5 years, the present value of cash inflows is the sum of the respective yearly discount rate times the $3,000. Note that the discount rate used is the firm's rate of return and not the mortgage's rate of return.

[$3,000 (.89 + .80 + .71 + .64 + .57)] = $10,830

$10,830 - initial investment = NPV
$10,830 - $10,000 = $830
NPV = $830

66. Maxwell Company has an opportunity to acquire a new machine to replace one of its present machines. The new machine would cost $90,000, have a 5-year life, and no estimated salvage value. Variable operating costs would be $100,000 per year. The present machine has a book value of $50,000 and a remaining life of 5 years. Its disposal value now is $5,000, but it would be zero after 5 years. Variable operating costs would be $125,000 per year. Ignore present value calculations and income taxes. Considering the 5 years in total, what would be the difference in profit before income taxes by acquiring the new machine as opposed to retaining the present one?

a. $10,000 decrease.
b. $15,000 decrease.
c. $35,000 increase.
d. $40,000 increase.

The correct answer is (d). *(CPA 1176 P-22)*
REQUIRED: The difference in pre-tax profit resulting from acquiring a new machine.
DISCUSSION: Ignoring both present value and tax considerations, the new machine's depreciation over its 5-year life will decrease income by $40,000 (the $90,000 additional cost of the new machine above the $50,000 book value of the old machine). The sale of the old machine also results in a $45,000 loss ($50,000 book value - $5,000 proceeds). Operating cost savings would be $25,000 per year and $125,000 (5 x $25,000) for the 5-year period. The net effect of the sale of the old machine is thus a $40,000 increase in income over the 5-year period.

Additional depreciation on the new machine	$(40,000)
Loss on sale of old machine	(45,000)
Operating cost savings	125,000
Increase in income	**$ 40,000**

Module 16.4: Net Present Value

67. Oran Co. has the opportunity to invest in a 2-year project that is expected to produce cash flows from operations, net of income taxes, of $100,000 in the first year and $200,000 in the second year. Oran requires an internal rate of return of 20%. The present value of $1 for one period at 20% is 0.833 and for two periods at 20% is 0.694. For this project, Oran should be willing to invest immediately a maximum of

a. $283,300.
b. $249,900.
c. $222,100.
d. $208,200.

The correct answer is (c). *(CPA 585 Q-13)*
REQUIRED: The NPV of a 2-year project.
DISCUSSION: The NPV is equal to the sum of the discounted future cash flows minus the required investment. An investment may be economically rational if the NPV is not less than zero. Oran's maximum investment should therefore be $222,100, an amount equal to the NPV of the future inflows from the project.

.833 x $100,000 = $ 83,300
.694 x $200,000 = $138,800
                  $222,100

68. An investment in a new piece of equipment costing $50,000 is expected to yield the following for each year of the equipment's 5-year useful life:

Revenues (all cash)	$40,000
Operating costs (all cash)	(18,000)
Depreciation	(10,000)
Contribution to net income	$12,000

The present value of $1 received annually for 5 years and discounted at the firm's cost of capital is 4.10, assuming that all cash flows occur at year-end. The benefit/cost ratio (profitability index) for this piece of equipment, ignoring tax effects, is

a. .984.
b. 1.200.
c. 1.804.
d. 3.280.
e. 2.200.

The correct answer is (c). *(CIA 581 IV-14)*
REQUIRED: The benefit/cost ratio for a new piece of equipment.
DISCUSSION: The benefit/cost ratio is determined by computing the present value of future cash flows and then dividing by the cost of the investment. The annual cash inflows are $22,000 ($40,000 cash revenues - $18,000 cash operating costs). The present value of $1 received annually for 5 years and discounted at the firm's cost of capital is given as 4.10. The benefit from this investment is thus $90,200 (4.1 x $22,000). The benefit/cost ratio is 1.804 ($90,200 ÷ $50,000 investment cost). The profitability index in capital budgeting is a variation of the NPV method that facilitates comparison of different sizes of investments.

69. Scott, Inc. is planning to invest $120,000 in a 10-year project. Scott estimates that the annual cash inflow, net of income taxes, from this project will be $20,000. Scott's desired rate of return on investments of this type is 10%. Information on present value factors is as follows:

	At 10%	At 12%
Present value of $1 for ten periods	0.386	0.322
Present value of an annuity of $1 for ten periods	6.145	5.650

Scott's expected rate of return on this investment is

a. Less than 10%, but more than 0%.
b. 10%.
c. Less than 12%, but more than 10%.
d. 12%.

The correct answer is (c). *(CPA 1180 P-26)*
REQUIRED: The approximate expected rate of return given the annual after-tax income, rate of return, and investment cost.
DISCUSSION: The initial investment of $120,000 will provide a 10-year, $20,000 annuity net of income taxes. First, solve for the implicit time value of money factor in the relationship between the $120,000 investment and the $20,000 net cash inflow from the investment: $120,000 ÷ $20,000 equals 6.00 time value of money factor. Since this figure falls between the annuity factors for 10% and 12%, the expected rate of return is greater than 10% but less than 12%.

70. Herman Company acquired an asset at a cost of $46,600 with an estimated life of 10 years. Annual after-tax net cash benefits are estimated to be $10,000 at the end of each year. The following amounts appear in the interest table for the present value of an annuity of $1 at year-end for 10 years:

16%	18%	20%
4.83	4.49	4.19

What is the maximum interest rate that could be paid for the capital employed over the life of this asset without loss on this project?

a. 16%.

b. 17%.

c. 18%.

d. 19%.

The correct answer is (b). *(CPA 1176 P-32)*
REQUIRED: The maximum interest rate for the capital without loss on the project.
DISCUSSION: The maximum interest rate to pay for the capital without loss is the one that would produce a NPV equal to zero, i.e., the rate at which the present value of the future cash flows equals the cost of the investment. Dividing the $46,600 cost of the investment by the annual annuity amount of $10,000 gives a time value of money factor of 4.66. Assuming linear interpolation in the given table, this factor corresponds to a discount rate of 17%.

$$\frac{(4.83 + 4.49)}{2} = 4.66 \text{ at } 17\%$$

71. Each of three mutually exclusive projects costs $200. Using the table provided, rank the projects in descending NPV order.

Year	Present Value Interest Factor (10%)	A	B	C
1	.91	$300	$200	$ 0
2	.83	200	100	100
3	.75	100	0	100
4	.68	0	100	200
5	.62	0	200	300

a. A, B, C.

b. B, A, C.

c. C, B, A.

d. A, C, B.

The correct answer is (d). *(CIA 585 IV-33)*
REQUIRED: The NPVs ranked in descending order.
DISCUSSION: The NPV is equal to the sum of the discounted future cash flows minus the required investment.

	A	B	C
	$273	$182	$ 0
	166	83	83
	75	0	75
	0	68	136
	0	124	186
PV	$514	$457	$480
	(200)	(200)	(200)
NPV	$314	$257	$280

72. Budcon Inc. has a small capital budget. When faced with indivisible projects each of which is estimated to generate a return which exceeds the company's cost of capital, the company should select the combination of projects that will fully utilize the budget and

a. Maximize the sum of the NPVs.

b. Maximize the sum of the IRRs.

c. Minimize the sum of the payback periods.

d. Have the highest present value indexes.

e. Rank the highest by their NPVs.

The correct answer is (a). *(CMA 1278 5-11)*
REQUIRED: The best combination of profitable projects given finite resources.
DISCUSSION: Given that the return on each project exceeds the firm's cost of capital, the firm's market value will increase regardless of which projects are chosen. Consequently, the projects should be evaluated according to their NPVs, the amounts by which the present values of future cash flows exceed the initial investments. The company should maximize this sum of NPVs to produce the greatest expected profit by choosing that combination of projects giving the highest aggregate NPV for the resources available.

Answers (b) and (e) are incorrect because neither maximizing the sum of the IRRs nor ranking by the projects' NPVs takes into account the sizes of the projects' investments. Answer (c) is incorrect because payback is neither an efficient nor an effective means of capital budgeting since it ignores the time value of money. Answer (d) is incorrect because the present value (profitability) index is the ratio of the present value of future cash flows to the investment outlay. Although it permits comparison of different-sized investment alternatives, the problem here is to select a mix of projects.

Module 16.4: Net Present Value

73. On January 1, Studley Company purchased a new machine for $100,000 to be depreciated over 5 years. It will have no salvage value at the end of 5 years. For book and tax purposes, depreciation will be $20,000 per year. It is expected to produce annual cash flow from operations, before income taxes, of $40,000. Assume that Studley uses a time adjusted rate of 12% and that its income tax rate will be 40% for all years. The present value of $1 at 12% for five periods is 0.57, and the present value of an ordinary annuity of $1 at 12% for five periods is 3.61. The NPV of the machine should be

a. $15,520 positive.
b. $15,520 negative.
c. $14,000 positive.
d. $13,680 negative.

The correct answer is (a). *(CPA 582 P-37)*
REQUIRED: The NPV of a machine given pre-tax cash flows, cost, depreciation, salvage, taxes, desired rate of return, and present value data.
DISCUSSION: The first step to compute the NPV is to calculate the after-tax cash flow. Depreciation is deductible for income tax purposes even though it is a noncash expense.

Cash inflow	$ 40,000
Depreciation	(20,000)
Taxable income	$ 20,000
Tax rate	x .40
Tax expense	$ 8,000

Therefore, the annual cash inflow net of taxes is $32,000 ($40,000 - $8,000). The present value of the five annual cash inflows is the present value of an ordinary annuity for 5 years at 12% (3.61) times $32,000, giving a present value of $115,520. Since the initial investment is $100,000, the NPV is $15,520.

74. On May 1, 1989, a company purchased a new machine that it does not have to pay for until May 1, 1991. The total payment on May 1, 1991 will include both principal and interest. Assuming interest at a 10% rate, the cost of the machine would be the total payment multiplied by what time value of money concept?

a. Future amount of annuity of 1.
b. Future amount of 1.
c. Present value of annuity of 1.
d. Present value of 1.

The correct answer is (d). *(CPA 585 T-45)*
REQUIRED: The factor to determine the value of a single future payment.
DISCUSSION: The cost of the machine is net of interest, which is imputed at 10%. The total payment (principal plus interest) must be multiplied by the present value of 1.
Answers (a) and (c) are incorrect because a single payment, not a series (an annuity), is involved. Answer (b) is incorrect because the value in the present (May 1, 1989), not the future (May 1, 1991), is required.

75. Axel Corp. is planning to buy a new machine with the expectation that this investment will earn a discounted rate of return of at least 15%. This machine, which costs $150,000, would yield an estimated net cash flow of $30,000 a year for 10 years, after income taxes. In order to determine the NPV of buying the new machine, Axel should first multiply the $30,000 by which of the following factors?

a. 20.304 (future amount of an ordinary annuity of $1).
b. 5.019 (present value of an ordinary annuity of $1).
c. 4.046 (future amount of $1).
d. 0.247 (present value of $1).

The correct answer is (b). *(CPA 1184 Q-18)*
REQUIRED: The factor used to determine the discounted value of a series of cash flows.
DISCUSSION: The series of equal annual estimated cash flows is considered to be an annuity. Discounting these future cash flows back to the present requires use of the present value factor for an ordinary annuity (an annuity in arrears, one in which the payments are received at the end of each period).
Answer (a) is incorrect because the present value, not the future amount, is required. Answers (c) and (d) are incorrect because the series of payments constitute an annuity.

76. Heller Company purchased a machine for $500,000 with a useful life of 5 years and no salvage value. The machine is being depreciated using the straight-line method. It is expected to produce annual cash flow from operations, net of income taxes, of $150,000. The present value of an ordinary annuity of $1 for five periods at 14% is 3.43. The present value of $1 for five periods at 14% is 0.52. Assuming that Heller uses a time adjusted rate of return of 14%, what is the machine's NPV?

a. $280,000.
b. $250,000.
c. $180,000.
d. $14,500.

The correct answer is (d). (CPA 1182 P-26)
REQUIRED: The NPV of a machine given after-tax cash flows, cost, depreciation, salvage, and present value data.
DISCUSSION: The NPV is the excess of the present value of the cash inflows above the net initial investment. The present value of the cash flows can be computed using the present value of an ordinary annuity for 7 years at the desired rate of return of 14%. The appropriate time value of money factor of 3.43 times the annual after-tax cash flow of $150,000 gives a present value of $514,500. The machine's NPV is thus a positive $14,500 ($514,500 - $500,000 initial investment). Depreciation is not used in the calculation since the given annual cash flows are net of taxes.

16.5 NPV, Original Investment

77. On January 1, a company invested in an asset with a useful life of 3 years. The company's expected rate of return is 10%. The cash flow and present and future value factors for the 3 years are as follows:

Year	Cash Inflow from the Asset	Present Value of $1 at 10%	Future Value of $1 at 10%
1	$ 8,000	.91	1.10
2	$ 9,000	.83	1.21
3	$10,000	.75	1.33

All cash inflows are assumed to occur at year-end. If the asset generates a positive net present value of $2,000, what was the amount of the original investment?

a. $20,250.
b. $22,250.
c. $30,991.
d. $33,991.

The correct answer is (a). (CIA 1185 IV-24)
REQUIRED: The original investment given NPV and PV and FV tables.
DISCUSSION: The net present value of a proposed investment is computed by subtracting the original investment from the present value of future cash flows. Therefore, the original investment is

$2,000 = ($8,000 x .91) + ($9,000 x .83) + ($10,000 x .75) - X
$2,000 = $7,280 + $7,470 + $7,500 - X
X + $2,000 = $22,250
X = $20,250

78. Garwood Company has purchased a machine which will be depreciated on the straight-line basis over an estimated useful life of 7 years with no salvage value. The machine is expected to generate cash flow from operations, net of income taxes, of $80,000 in each of the 7 years. Garwood's expected rate of return is 12%. Information on present value factors is as follows:

Present value of $1
  at 12% for seven periods   0.452
Present value of an ordinary annuity
  of $1 at 12% for seven periods   4.564

Assuming a positive net present value of $12,720, what was the cost of the machine?

a. $240,400.
b. $253,120.
c. $352,400.
d. $377,840.

The correct answer is (c). (CPA 1181 P-39)
REQUIRED: The cost of the machine given after-tax cash flows, present value data, and a positive NPV.
DISCUSSION: The net present value is defined as the excess of the present value of the future cash flows over the initial net investment. The after-tax annual cash flow is $80,000, and the time value of money factor of the present value of an ordinary annuity for 7 years at 12% is 4.564. The present value of the cash flows is thus $365,120. Given a positive NPV of $12,720, the cost of the machine must have been $352,400 ($365,120 - $12,720).

Module 16.5: NPV, Original Investment

79. Gene, Inc. invested in a machine with a useful life of 6 years and no salvage value. The machine was depreciated using the straight-line method. It was expected to produce annual cash inflow from operations, net of income taxes, of $2,000. The present value of an ordinary annuity of $1 for six periods at 10% is 4.355. The present value of $1 for six periods at 10% is 0.564. Assuming that Gene used a time adjusted rate of return of 10%, what was the amount of the original investment?

a. $5,640.
b. $8,710.
c. $9,000.
d. $11,280.

The correct answer is (b). *(CPA 579 P-27)*
REQUIRED: The original investment given after-tax future cash flows, present value data, and a time adjusted rate of return.
DISCUSSION: Under the internal rate of return (time adjusted rate of return) method, an interest rate is computed such that the present value of the expected future cash flows is equal to the cost of the investment (NPV = 0). Here, the interest rate is given and the initial investment must be calculated. The time value of money factor of the present value of an ordinary annuity for six periods at 10% is 4.355. Therefore, the present value of the cash flows and the cost of the investment are both $8,710 ($2,000 x 4.355).

80. Brunswick Company is planning to purchase a new machine. The payback period will be 6 years. The new machine is expected to produce cash flow from operations, net of income taxes, of $3,500 a year for each of the first 3 years of the payback period and $2,500 a year for each of the last 3 years. Depreciation of $2,000 a year will be charged to income for each of the 6 years. How much will the machine cost?

a. $6,000.
b. $12,000.
c. $18,000.
d. $21,000.

The correct answer is (c). *(CPA 581 P-30)*
REQUIRED: The cost of the machine given depreciation, the payback period, and nonuniform after-tax cash flows.
DISCUSSION: The payback period is the time required to recapture the initial investment. When the cash flows are not uniform, it is necessary to use a cumulative approach. The cost of the machine equals the total cash received over 6 years (the payback period). Depreciation is a noncash expense which is ignored in this case since the cash flow is given net of income taxes.

($3,500 x 3yrs) + ($2,500 x 3yrs) = $18,000 cost of the machine

81. Cause Company is planning to invest in a machine with a useful life of 5 years and no salvage value. The machine is expected to produce cash flow from operations, net of income taxes, of $20,000 in each of the 5 years. Cause's expected rate of return is 10%. Information on present value and future amount factors is as follows:

	Period				
	1	2	3	4	5
Present value of $1 at 10%	.909	.826	.751	.683	.621
Present value of an annuity of $1 at 10%	.909	1.736	2.487	3.170	3.791
Future amount of $1 at 10%	1.100	1.210	1.331	1.464	1.611
Future amount of an annuity of $1 at 10%	1.000	2.100	3.310	4.641	6.105

How much will the machine cost?

a. $32,220.
b. $62,100.
c. $75,820.
d. $122,100.

The correct answer is (c). *(CPA 1179 P-29)*
REQUIRED: The cost of the machine given present value and future value data and after-tax cash flows.
DISCUSSION: The receipt of an annual after-tax cash flow of $20,000 for 5 years is an annuity. Therefore, the present value of the investment can be determined. The present value of an ordinary annuity for five periods at 10% is 3.791. Hence, the present value of the expected cash flows is $75,820 ($20,000 x 3.791). Since no net present value is mentioned, one must assume that the present value of the cash flows is the cost of the machine.

82. The Fudge Company is planning to purchase a new machine which it will depreciate, for book purposes, on a straight-line basis over a 10-year period with no salvage value and a full year's depreciation taken in the year of acquisition. The new machine is expected to produce cash flow from operations, net of income taxes, of $66,000 a year in each of the next 10 years. A 12% accounting (book value) rate of return on the initial investment is expected. How much will the new machine cost?

a. $300,000.
b. $550,000.
c. $660,000.
d. $792,000.

The correct answer is (a). *(CPA 1179 P-24)*
REQUIRED: The cost of the new machine given the accounting (book value) rate of return.
DISCUSSION: The accounting rate of return equals net income divided by the initial investment. Net income is equal to the net cash flows (after taxes, operating expenses, etc.) minus depreciation. The approach to solve for the cost of the new machine is to set up an equation: the accounting rate of return times the cost of the machine is equal to net income (the cash flow from operations minus depreciation). In this problem, depreciation is calculated on a straight-line basis for 10 years with no salvage value (10% of cost/year).

$$.12 \text{ cost} = \$66,000 - .10 \text{ cost}$$
$$.22 \text{ cost} = \$66,000$$
$$\text{cost} = \$300,000$$

83. Hamilton Company invested in a 2-year project having an internal rate of return of 12% (IRR = 12%). The project is expected to produce cash flow from operations, net of income taxes, of $60,000 in the first year and $70,000 in the second year. The present value of $1 for one period at 12% is 0.893 and for two periods at 12% is 0.797. How much will the project cost?

a. $103,610.
b. $109,370.
c. $116,090.
d. $122,510.

The correct answer is (b). *(CPA 582 P-38)*
REQUIRED: The project's cost given the IRR, nonuniform cash flows, and present value data.
DISCUSSION: An IRR of 12% means that the cost of the project is equal to the present value of its cash inflows discounted at 12%. The IRR is the discount rate at which the NPV of a project is zero. As shown below, the present value of the discounted inflows, and thus the cost of the project, is $109,370, resulting in an NPV of zero.

Year 1 ($60,000 x .893) = $ 53,580
Year 2 ($70,000 x .797) = 55,790
Present value $109,370

16.6 Internal Rate of Return

84. The internal rate of return is

a. The discount rate at which the NPV of the cash flows is zero.
b. The breakeven borrowing rate for the project in question.
c. The yield rate/effective rate of interest quoted on long-term debt and other instruments.
d. All of the above.

The correct answer is (d). *(Publisher)*
REQUIRED: The true statement(s) about internal rate of return.
DISCUSSION: The internal rate of return (IRR) is the discount rate at which the present value of the cash flows equals the original investment. Thus, the NPV of the project is zero at the IRR. The IRR is also the maximum borrowing cost the firm could afford to pay for a specific project. The IRR is similar to the yield rate/effective rate quoted in the business media.

85. The three frequently used methods for ranking investment proposals are payback, net present value, and internal rate of return. One of the three is defined as the interest rate that equates the present value of expected cash flows and the cost of the project. A second method finds the present value of expected cash flows and subtracts the initial cost of the project. Which of the following terms match these respective definitions?

a. Net present value and payback.
b. Internal rate of return and net present value.
c. Internal rate of return and payback.
d. Net present value and internal rate of return.

The correct answer is (b). *(CIA 585 IV-32)*
REQUIRED: The terms for the defined investment ranking methods.
DISCUSSION: IRR is the method that equates the PV of cash flows with the cost of the project. The IRR is the rate at which NPV equals zero. NPV is the difference between the investment and the present value of the net future cash flows. The payback method calculates the time required to recapture the initial investment.

Module 16.6: Internal Rate of Return

86. The internal rate of return method and the net present value method normally yield identical rankings of possible investment decisions. However, under certain scenarios, dissimilar rankings are obtained. When such conflict occurs, the technique normally selected is

a. IRR because all reinvestment of funds occurs at the rate of the cost of capital and because it takes into consideration the relative size of the initial investment.

b. NPV because all reinvestment of funds occurs at the rate of the cost of capital and because it takes into consideration the relative size of the initial investment.

c. IRR because all reinvestment of funds occurs at the discount rate that will make the NPV of the project equal to zero.

d. NPV because all reinvestment of funds occurs at the discount rate that will make the NPV of the project equal to zero.

The correct answer is (b). *(CIA 1185 IV-32)*
REQUIRED: The technique normally selected when NPV and IRR yield dissimilar rankings.
DISCUSSION: When dissimilar results are obtained from the NPV and IRR ranking methods, the NPV method should be used because all reinvestment of funds occurs at the rate of the cost of capital. Also, NPV takes the relative size of the investment into consideration.
Answer (a) is incorrect because, under the IRR method, reinvestment does not take place at the cost of capital and investment size is ignored. Answer (c) is incorrect because reinvestment of funds cannot be guaranteed at the discount rate. Answer (d) is incorrect because the NPV method reinvests at the cost of capital, not the discount rate.

87. In capital budgeting analysis, the "payback reciprocal" may provide a quick and useful estimate of the internal rate of return only when

a. Cash inflows do not extend beyond the length of the payback period.

b. Cash inflow amounts vary erratically during the life of the investment.

c. Most of the cash inflows from an investment precede the investment outlay.

d. Cash inflows are uniform through the life of an investment which is long relative to its payback period.

e. The investment outlays are made uniformly throughout the life of the investment.

The correct answer is (d). *(CMA 1277 5-6)*
REQUIRED: When the "payback reciprocal" may provide a useful estimate of the IRR.
DISCUSSION: The payback period, the time required to recapture the initial investment, is the investment divided by the annual return. The payback reciprocal equals the annual return divided by the initial investment. This is the time adjusted rate of return if the investment has an infinite life. Therefore, if the annual cash flows are uniform and the life of an investment is long relative to the payback period, the payback reciprocal is a quick method of estimating the time adjusted rate of return.
Answer (a) is incorrect because the life of the investment must substantially exceed the payback period. Answer (b) is incorrect because annual cash flows must be uniform. Answer (c) is incorrect because cash inflows prior to the required investment outflow should be used to decrease the required investment. Answer (e) is incorrect because the investment outlay is assumed to be made at the inception of the project.

88. If the internal rate of return method is used in capital budgeting subject to capital rationing, a project would be accepted if the

a. Net present value is zero or positive.

b. Internal rate equals or exceeds the hurdle or cut-off rate.

c. Internal rate is less than the cost of capital.

d. Net present value calculated using the cost of capital is positive.

The correct answer is (b). *(CIA 1183 IV-6)*
REQUIRED: The appropriate decision rule under the internal rate of return method.
DISCUSSION: The IRR capital budgeting method computes the internal rate of return on each project by setting the initial investment cost equal to the present value of the net cash flows over the length of the project (zero net present value). The project should be considered if the internal rate equals or exceeds a prespecified hurdle or cut-off rate.
Answers (a) and (d) are incorrect because net present value is defined as zero to determine the internal rate of return. Answer (c) is incorrect because the cut-off rate will exceed the cost of capital, and thus no projects earning less should be undertaken.

Module 16.6: Internal Rate of Return

89. Your company is comparing the internal rate of return (IRR) to net present value (NPV) computations as alternative criteria for evaluating potential capital investments. Which of the following best describes IRR and/or NPV computations?

   a. The IRR assumes that the positive cash flows generated each year are reinvested at the computed rate of return.

   b. The IRR ignores the initial cost of the investment in its computations.

   c. The NPV ignores the company's cost of capital.

   d. The NPV method is more appropriate to use during periods of inflation.

   e. The two methods will give the same rankings because they both consider the time value of money.

The correct answer is (a). *(CIA 581 IV-16)*
REQUIRED: The best statement about IRR and/or NPV computations.
DISCUSSION: The internal rate of return method computes an interest rate (R) such that the present value of expected future cash flows is equal to the cost invested. Therefore, the earnings rate on an investment can be computed for any project. The best project is the one with the highest rate of return. This method assumes that all cash flows will be reinvested at the rate R. The NPV method assumes cash flows will be reinvested at the company's cost of capital.
Answer (b) is incorrect because both the IRR and the NPV methods consider the initial cost of the investment. Answer (c) is incorrect because the NPV method computes the NPV of an investment by discounting the future cash flows at the company's cost of capital. Answer (d) is incorrect because neither method adjusts for inflation. Answer (e) is incorrect because the methods assume different reinvestment rates. Projects may also be ranked differently if their costs are different.

90. Kipling Company invested in an 8-year project. It is expected that the annual cash flow from the project, net of income taxes, will be $20,000. Information on present values are:

Present value of $1 at 12% for eight periods	0.404
Present value of an ordinary annuity of $1 at 12% for eight periods	4.968

Assuming that Kipling based its investment decision on an internal rate of return of 12%, how much did the project cost?

   a. $160,000.
   b. $99,360.
   c. $80,800.
   d. $64,640.

The correct answer is (b). *(CPA 1182 P-40)*
REQUIRED: The cost of the project given present value data, annual after-tax cash flows, and an IRR.
DISCUSSION: When using the IRR method, an interest rate is computed such that the present value of the expected future cash flows is equal to the cost of the investment (NPV = 0). Here, the interest rate is given. The initial investment is the unknown. The cost of the project can be calculated by multiplying the annual cash flow net of income taxes ($20,000) by the present value of an ordinary annuity for eight periods at 12% (4.968), giving an initial investment of $99,360.

91. When computing the NPV of an investment, one uses the equation

$$PV = amount \times TVMF$$

where amount = the annual cash flow

    TVMF = the time value of money factor (usually of an annuity)
    PV = the present value

The TVMF incorporates time (number of periods) and interest rate (desired rate of return or cost of capital). In NPV capital budgeting problems, PV is the unknown. In the IRR formulation of the capital budgeting model, which variable is the unknown?

   a. Amount.
   b. PV.
   c. Interest rate.
   d. Time.

The correct answer is (c). *(Publisher)*
REQUIRED: The unknown variable in IRR capital budgeting formulations.
DISCUSSION: In internal rate of return (IRR), the discount rate which provides a NPV of zero is computed, i.e., the present value of the future cash inflows equals the cost of the investment. Thus the interest (discount) rate is the unknown.

Module 16.6: Internal Rate of Return

92. Assume a manager has the opportunity to make a net investment of $16,000 which will result in cost savings of $6,000 a year for 4 years. In applying the formula suggested in Q. 91, what would be the TVMF of the present value of an annuity used in the IRR capital budgeting model?

a. $6,000 ÷ $16,000.
b. $16,000 ÷ $6,000.
c. $3,000 ÷ $16,000.
d. $6,000 ÷ $8,000.

The correct answer is (b). *(Publisher)*
REQUIRED: The TVMF for an IRR capital budgeting structure.
DISCUSSION: The TVMF is a number found in a PV or FV table. It is based on the formula

PV = amount x TVMF.

In IRR problems the interest rate is unknown and the formula is restated as

TVMF = PV ÷ amount.

Here, the amount of the annual cash flow is $6,000 and the cost of the investment is $16,000; i.e., TVMF = $16,000 ÷ $6,000.

93. If the TVMF in Q. 92 were 2.5, what would be the IRR?

Present Value of an Annuity of $1.00 Received at the End of Each Period

Period	8%	10%	12%	14%	16%	18%	20%	22%	24%
1	.93	.91	.89	.88	.86	.85	.83	.82	.81
2	1.79	1.74	1.69	1.65	1.60	1.57	1.52	1.49	1.46
3	2.58	2.49	2.40	2.32	2.24	2.18	2.10	2.04	1.98
4	3.31	3.17	3.04	2.91	2.79	2.70	2.58	2.49	2.40
5	3.99	3.79	3.61	3.43	3.27	3.14	2.98	2.86	2.74

a. Just under 10%.
b. Just over 20%.
c. Just over 16.6%.
d. Just under 22%.

The correct answer is (d). *(Publisher)*
REQUIRED: The IRR when the TVMF, the number of periods, and a PV table are given.
DISCUSSION: Utilizing a PV of an annuity table for n=4 (there will be a $6,000 savings for 4 years), the nearest value to 2.5 for n=4 is 2.49 for 22%. Note that 20% was 2.58, which means 2.5 would be an interest rate just under 22%.

94. When do the TVMF tables for annuities assume payments are received?

a. Beginning of the year.
b. Uniformly during each year.
c. End of the year.
d. No assumption is made.

The correct answer is (c). *(Publisher)*
REQUIRED: The time when TVMF tables assume payments are to be made.
DISCUSSION: Payments are usually assumed to be made at the end of each period. This is called an annuity in arrears or ordinary annuity. Note that if payments were assumed to be made at the beginning of the period (annuity in advance or annuity due), the TVMFs for n=1 would all be 1.0, not values less than 1.0. Because the payment would be at the beginning of the period, there would be no discounting.

95. Assume that the IRR in Q. 93 was just under 22%. What is the effect of making the payments uniformly during each year instead of at year-end?

a. Increases the IRR by 3.141592%.
b. Decreases the IRR by 3.141592%.
c. Decreases the IRR to considerably less than 22%.
d. Increases the IRR to over 22%.

The correct answer is (d). *(Publisher)*
REQUIRED: The effect of making annuity payments uniformly during the period instead of at year-end.
DISCUSSION: Since the $6,000 annual payments would be received prior to year-end, the money is available sooner and thus the rate of return increases. Since the return in Q. 93 was very close to 22%, the actual IRR will exceed 22%.

96. Two projects have an initial outlay of $497 and each has an income stream lasting 3 years. Project A returns $200 per year for the 3 years. Project B returns $200 for the first 2 years and $248 for the third year.

Present Value - Amount

n	8%	10%	12%	14%
1	.9259	.9091	.8929	.8772
2	.8573	.8264	.7972	.7695
3	.7938	.7513	.7118	.6750

The appropriate internal rate of return valuation for Project B is

a. 200(.8772) + 200(.7695) + 248(.6750)
 = 496.74.

b. 200(.8929) + 200(.7972) + 248(.7118)
 = 514.41.

c. 200(.9091) + 200(.8264) + 248(.7513)
 = 533.42.

d. 200(.9259) + 200(.8573) + 248(.7938)
 = 553.50.

The correct answer is (a). *(CIA 1185 IV-31)*
REQUIRED: The appropriate internal rate of return for Project B.
DISCUSSION: The internal rate of return is the interest rate at which the present value of future cash flows is equal to the cost of the investment. Thus, the appropriate internal rate of return is 14%; i.e., the sum of the TVMF for 14% times each cash inflow should equal the initial outlay (here $497).

97. A project has a cost of $5,000 and is expected to produce a cash flow of $1,220 a year for 5 years. The anticipated rate of inflation is 10% per year. Using the table given, what is the internal rate of return? Note: Annuity factors are rounded to two places.

	Future Value of an Annuity of $1 Per Period for 5 Periods	Present Value of an Annuity of $1 Per Period for 5 Periods
7%	5.75	4.10
8%	5.87	3.99
9%	5.98	3.89
10%	6.11	3.79

a. 7%.
b. 8%.
c. 9%.
d. 10%.

The correct answer is (a). *(CIA 1184 IV-29)*
REQUIRED: The internal rate of return.
DISCUSSION: The internal rate of return is the discount rate that equates the present value of cash flows with the initial investment (NPV = 0).

	7%	8%	9%	10%
	$1,220	$1,220	$1,220	$1,220
	x 4.10	x 3.99	x 3.89	x 3.79
	$5,002	$4,868	$4,746	$4,624
	(5,000)	(5,000)	(5,000)	(5,000)
NPV	$ 2	$ (132)	$ (254)	$ (376)

98. At a company's cost of capital (hurdle rate) of 15%, a prospective investment has a positive net present value. Based on this information, it can be concluded that

a. The accounting rate of return is greater than 15%.
b. The internal rate of return is less than 15%.
c. The internal rate of return is greater than 15%.
d. The payback period is shorter than the life of the asset.

The correct answer is (c). *(CIA 1184 IV-10)*
REQUIRED: The correct inference given that NPV is positive at the cost of capital.
DISCUSSION: A positive NPV indicates that the PV of cash flows is greater than the initial investment. At the IRR, the PV of the cash flows equals the investment (NPV = 0). The IRR must therefore exceed the hurdle rate since the NPV is positive at the hurdle rate.
 Answers (a) and (d) are incorrect because neither the accounting rate of return nor the payback method uses present value. Answer (b) is incorrect because the IRR is greater than 15%.

16.7 Cash Flow Calculations

99. A company has analyzed four possible projects for a specific operation. The firm's cost of capital is 12%. Cash flow projections are provided below for the four possible projects:

Project	Initial Outflow	End of Year 1	End of Year 2	End of Year 3
Project A	$100,000	$90,000	$25,000	$20,000
Project B	100,000	30,000	85,000	20,000
Project C	100,000	40,000	95,000	0
Project D	100,000	90,000	45,000	0

All projects are assumed to have the same risk. Which project should the company select?

a. Project A.
b. Project B.
c. Project C.
d. Project D.

The correct answer is (d). *(CIA 1185 IV-27)*
REQUIRED: The project that should be selected.
DISCUSSION: Projects A, B, C, and D all return $135,000. Project D returns the $135,000 the quickest ($90,000 the first year and $45,000 the second year) and is thus the best investment.

100. Jarvis, Inc., a calendar year company, purchased a new machine for $28,000 on January 1. Depreciation for tax purposes will be $3,500 annually for 8 years. The accounting (book value) rate of return (ARR) is expected to be 15% on the initial increase in required investment. On the assumption of a uniform cash inflow, this investment is expected to provide annual cash flow from operations, net of income taxes, of

a. $3,500.
b. $4,025.
c. $4,200.
d. $7,700.

The correct answer is (d). *(CPA 1180 P-21)*
REQUIRED: Annual after-tax cash flow given uniform cash inflow and ARR.
DISCUSSION: Since only the initial investment ($28,000) and the accounting return on the investment (ARR = 15%) are given, the formula for the accounting rate of return must be used to compute the unknown net cash inflow.

$$\frac{\text{Net cash inflow - depreciation}}{\text{Initial investment}} = \text{ARR}$$

$$\frac{\text{Net cash inflow - \$3,500}}{\$28,000} = 15\%$$

Net cash inflow - $3,500 = $4,200.
Net cash inflow = $7,700

101. The Carter Company invested $67,000 in a 4-year machine. The machine's NPV was $8,000 using a 15% cost of capital. Information on cash flows and present value factors is as follows:

Year	Expected Cash Flow, Net of Taxes	Present Value of $1 @ 15%
1	$20,600	.87
2	24,000	.76
3	21,800	.66
4	?	.57

What is the expected cash flow, net of taxes, in year 4?

a. $8,600.
b. $16,450.
c. $24,450.
d. $28,860.
e. $42,895.

The correct answer is (e). *(C.J. Skender)*
REQUIRED: The after-tax cash flow.
DISCUSSION: The present value of cash inflows must equal $75,000 since there was a $67,000 cost and an $8,000 NPV. The net cash flow in year 4 is $42,895 as computed below.

PV of cash inflows	$75,000
PV Year 1 = (20,600)(.87)	(17,922)
PV Year 2 = (24,000)(.76)	(18,240)
PV Year 3 = (21,800)(.66)	(14,388)
PV Year 4	$24,450

The present value of cash flow in year 4 divided by the discount rate for year 4, equals the cash flow in year 4.

$24,450 ÷ .57 = $42,895

Module 16.7: Cash Flow Calculations

102. Hilltop Company invested $100,000 in a 2-year project. Hilltop's expected rate of return was 12%. The cash flow, net of income taxes, was $40,000 for the first year. Information on present value and future value factors is as follows:

Period	Present Value of $1 at 12%	Future Value of $1 at 12%
1	.8929	1.1200
2	.7972	1.2544

Assuming that the rate of return was exactly 12%, what was the cash flow, net of income taxes, for the second year of the project?

a. $51,247.
b. $60,000.
c. $64,284.
d. $80,638.

The correct answer is (d). *(CPA 1180 P-27)*
REQUIRED: The second-year after-tax cash flow given the rate of return, cash flow for the first year, and time value of money factors.
DISCUSSION: The unknown cash flow is the amount that, when discounted for two periods and added to the discounted cash flow for year 1, will result in a present value equal to the amount of the investment ($100,000). This calculation assumes that NPV is zero.

$100,000 = (.8929 \times \$40,000) + (.7972 \times \text{net cash flow})$

Cash flow (year 2) = $80,637.23

103. The following data are related to the cash flows of a risky capital-budgeting alternative:

Col. 1 Period	Col. 2 Expected Cash Flows	Col. 3 Certainty Equivalent Factors
1	1,000	.85
2	1,000	.75
3	1,000	.70

The discount rates available for this analysis are risk-free rate = 5%, cost of capital = 10%, and risk-adjusted discount rate = 15%. How would you discount these cash flows using the certainty-equivalent method (CE) and the risk-adjusted discount rate method (RADR).

	CE	RADR
a.	(Col.2xCol.3) at 10%	(Col.2xCol.3) at 5%
b.	(Col.2xCol.3) at 5%	(Col.2xCol.3) at 10%
c.	(Col.2xCol.3) at 10%	Col.2 at 15%
d.	(Col.2xCol.3) at 5%	Col.2 at 15%

The correct answer is (d). *(CIA 586 IV-32)*
REQUIRED: The discount cash flow formula using the certainty-equivalent method and the risk-adjusted discount rate method.
DISCUSSION: Under the certainty-equivalent method, expected cash flows are multiplied by a certainty equivalent factor and discounted at the risk-free rate. Under the risk-adjusted discount rate method, expected cash flows are discounted at the risk-adjusted discount rate.
Answers (a) and (c) are incorrect because the certainty-equivalent method uses the risk-free rate, not the cost of capital. Answer (b) is incorrect because the risk-adjusted discount rate discounts expected cash flows at the risk-adjusted rate.

104. Your firm has negotiated a contract with the federal government and has locked in the payment it will receive in each of the future years from this project. However, your company's costs for this project are uncertain. How should the certainty-equivalent (CE) approach be applied in this situation?

a. Discount cash inflows using cost of capital and CE values of cost using cost of capital.
b. Discount cash inflows using cost of capital and CE values of cost using risk-free rate.
c. Determine net cash inflows using CE values of cost and discount using cost of capital.
d. Determine net cash inflows using CE values of cost and discount using risk-free rate.

The correct answer is (d). *(CIA 586 IV-34)*
REQUIRED: The correct application of the certainty-equivalent approach.
DISCUSSION: Under the certainty-equivalent approach, expected cash flows should be multiplied by certainty-equivalent factors and discounted at the risk-free rate.
Answers (a), (b), and (c) are incorrect because the risk-free rate should be used rather than the cost of capital.

Module 16.8: Comprehensive

105. Tracy Corporation is planning to invest $80,000 in a 3-year project. Tracy's expected rate of return is 10%. The present value of $1 at 10% for 1 year is .909, for 2 years is .826, and for 3 years is .751. The cash flow, net of income taxes, will be $30,000 for the first year (present value of $27,270) and $36,000 for the second year (present value of $29,736). Assuming the rate of return is exactly 10%, what will the cash flow, net of income taxes, be for the third year?

   a. $17,268.
   b. $22,000.
   c. $22,994.
   d. $30,618.

The correct answer is (d). *(CPA 581 P-21)*
REQUIRED: The after-tax cash flow for year 3 given the rate of return, cash flows for 2 years, and present value data.
DISCUSSION: The $80,000 investment must be assumed to equal the present value of the three future cash inflows discounted at 10% (NPV = 0). The net cash flow in year 3 is $30,618, as computed below.

	$80,000
PV Year 1	(27,270)
PV Year 2	(29,736)
PV Year 3	$22,994

Year 3 cash flow = $22,994 ÷ .751 = $30,618

106. Saratoga Company is planning to purchase a new machine for $600,000. Depreciation for tax purposes will be $100,000 annually for 6 years. The new machine is expected to produce cash flow from operations, net of income taxes, of $150,000 a year in each of the next 6 years. The accounting (book value) rate of return on the initial investment is expected to be

   a. 8.3%.
   b. 12.0%.
   c. 16.7%.
   d. 25.0%.

The correct answer is (a). *(CPA 1181 P-38)*
REQUIRED: The book value rate of return on the initial investment.
DISCUSSION: The accounting rate of return is computed as the net cash flows minus depreciation (yielding net income), divided by the initial investment. Depreciation is $100,000 per year.

$$\text{ARR} = \frac{\$150,000 - \$100,000}{\$600,000} = 8.3\%$$

16.8 Comprehensive

107. A firm was evaluating a large project. It wants to develop not only the best guess of the outcome of the project, but also a list (or distribution) of outcomes that might occur. This firm would best achieve its objective by using

   a. The NPV approach for capital budgeting.
   b. The profitability-index approach for capital budgeting.
   c. Simulation as applied to capital budgeting.
   d. The IRR approach for capital budgeting.

The correct answer is (c). *(CIA 586 IV-30)*
REQUIRED: The best approach to use to develop a list of probable outcomes and a best guess as to the most likely outcome.
DISCUSSION: A firm wishing to generate more than one guess of possible outcomes would best achieve its objective through computer simulation. This approach allows for the exploration of several or many different alternatives or outcomes and the probability of achieving each.
Answers (a), (b), and (d) are incorrect because each only provides for or considers one possible outcome.

Module 16.8: Comprehensive

> Questions 108 through 110 are based on the following information. Logg Co. is planning to buy a coin-operated machine costing $40,000. For book and tax purposes, this machine will be depreciated $8,000 each year for 5 years. Logg estimates that this machine will yield an annual cash inflow, net of depreciation and income taxes, of $12,000. Logg's desired rate of return on its investments is 12%. At the following discount rates, the NPVs of the investment in this machine are:
>
> | Discount Rate | NPV |
> |---|---|
> | 12% | +$3,258 |
> | 14% | + 1,197 |
> | 16% | - 708 |
> | 18% | - 2,474 |

108. Logg's accounting rate of return on its initial investment in this machine is expected to be

a. 30%.
b. 15%.
c. 12%.
d. 10%.

The correct answer is (d). *(CPA 586 Q-33)*
REQUIRED: The accounting rate of return.
DISCUSSION: The accounting rate of return is equal to the expected increase in net income divided by the initial investment. The expected increase in net income is the cash flow of $12,000 less the depreciation expense of $8,000. The question states "net of depreciation"; this just means that the tax benefit due to depreciation is accounted for in the $12,000 cash flow. Thus, the ARR is equal to 10% [($12,000 - $8,000) ÷ $40,000]. Note that the ARR is sometimes based on the average rather than initial investment (the latter was specified in this question).

109. Logg's expected payback period for its investment in this machine is

a. 2.0 years.
b. 3.0 years.
c. 3.3 years.
d. 5.0 years.

The correct answer is (c). *(CPA 586 Q-34)*
REQUIRED: The payback period.
DISCUSSION: The payback period is computed by dividing the net investment dollars by the average periodic net cash inflow. The net investment is $40,000. The average periodic net cash inflow is $12,000, since the $12,000 is in equal annual amounts. Thus the payback period is 3.3 years ($40,000 ÷ $12,000).

110. Logg's expected IRR on its investment in this machine is

a. 3.3%.
b. 10.0%.
c. 12.0%.
d. 15.3%.

The correct answer is (d). *(CPA 586 Q-35)*
REQUIRED: The expected IRR.
DISCUSSION: The IRR is the rate necessary to equate the discounted after-tax cash flows with the initial investment. It is the rate of return where the NPV = 0. In the problem, we are given discount rates and NPVs. Some place between 14% and 16% the NPV = 0. Answer (d) is the only answer between 14% and 16%.

Module 16.8: Comprehensive

Questions 111 and 112 are based on the following information. Apex Corp. is planning to buy production machinery costing $100,000. This machinery's expected useful life is 5 years, with no residual value. Apex requires a rate of return of 20%, and has calculated the following data pertaining to the purchase and operation of this machinery:

Year	Estimated Annual Cash Inflow	Present Value of $1 at 20%
1	$ 60,000	.91
2	30,000	.76
3	20,000	.63
4	20,000	.53
5	20,000	.44
Totals	$150,000	3.27

111. Assuming that the cash inflow was received evenly during the year, the payback period is

   a. 2.50 years.
   b. 2.75 years.
   c. 3.00 years.
   d. 5.00 years.

The correct answer is (a). *(CPA 1185 Q-7)*
REQUIRED: The payback period.
DISCUSSION: The payback method determines how long it takes for the investment dollars to be recovered by the annual net cash inflows. After 2 years, $90,000 of the $100,000 initial investment has been recovered. Since the cash inflows occur evenly throughout the year, it will take only 50% of year 3's cash flow of $20,000 to collect the other $10,000. Thus, the payback period is 2.50 years.

112. Assuming that the cash inflow was received evenly during the year, the NPV is

   a. $9,400.
   b. $54,128.
   c. $80,000.
   d. $109,400.

The correct answer is (a). *(CPA 1185 Q-8)*
REQUIRED: The NPV.
DISCUSSION: The NPV is the difference between the present value of the future cash flows, discounted at an appropriate interest rate, and the initial investment.

NPV = $60,000(.91) + $30,000(.76) + $20,000(.63)
        + $20,000(.53) + $20,000(.44) - $100,000
NPV = $9,400

Module 16.8: Comprehensive

Questions 113 through 118 are based on the following information and require discounted cash flow calculations. Use the discount factors presented below for these items.

Discount Factors for 10% (Rounded)

Period	Present Value of $1.00	Present Value of an Annuity of $1.00 per Period
1	.91	.91
2	.83	1.74
3	.75	2.49
4	.68	3.17

Rockyford Co. must replace some machinery. This machinery has zero book value but its current market value is $1,800. One possibility is to invest in new machinery which has a cost of $40,000. This new machinery would produce estimated annual pre-tax operating cash savings of $12,500. Assume the new machinery will have a useful life of 4 years and have depreciation of $10,000 each year for book and tax purposes. It will have no salvage value at the end of 4 years. The investment in this new machinery would require an additional investment in working capital of $3,000.

If Rockyford accepts this investment proposal, the disposal of the old machinery and the investment in the new equipment will take place on December 31 of this year. The cash flows from the investment will occur during the next four calendar years.

Rockyford is subject to a 40% income tax rate for all ordinary income and capital gains and has a 10% after-tax cost of capital. All operating and tax cash flows are assumed to occur at year-end.

---

113. The present value of the after-tax cash flow arising from the disposal of the old machinery this year is

    a. $6,638.
    b. $720.
    c. $1,800.
    d. $1,080.
    e. None of the above.

The correct answer is (d). *(CMA 1278 5-1)*
REQUIRED: The present value of the after-tax cash flow arising from current disposal of old machinery.
DISCUSSION: The old machinery has a current market value of $1,800 but a zero book value. Thus, the gain on sale would be $1,800, resulting in $720 in taxes (40% x $1,800). Therefore, present value of the machine is $1,080 ($1,800 - $720) because the sale would take place currently.

114. The present value of the after-tax cash flows for the next 4 years attributable to the operating cash savings is

    a. $23,775.
    b. $39,625.
    c. $36,555.
    d. $15,850.
    e. None of the above.

The correct answer is (a). *(CMA 1278 5-2)*
REQUIRED: The after-tax future cash flows attributable to the operating cash savings.
DISCUSSION: Since the annual pre-tax operating savings is $12,500, the after-tax savings would be $7,500 ($12,500 x .60). The present value of an annuity of four payments of $7,500 is the present value factor of an ordinary annuity for four periods at 10% (3.17) times $7,500, or $23,775.

115. The present value of the tax shield effect of depreciation at the end of year 1 is

    a. $3,320.
    b. $10,920.
    c. $6,960.
    d. $3,640.
    e. None of the above.

The correct answer is (d). *(CMA 1278 5-3)*
REQUIRED: The present value of the tax shield effect of depreciation after year 1.
DISCUSSION: Annual depreciation is $10,000 per year for book and tax purposes. Thus, at the end of year 1, $10,000 of depreciation will have been taken, resulting in tax savings of $4,000 ($10,000 x .40). The present value of $4,000 1 year from now is $3,640 ($4,000 x .91).

Module 16.8: Comprehensive

116. The present value of the net effect on the income tax payments related to the project in year 2 is

   a. $3,320 inflow.
   b. $4,150 outflow.
   c. $830 outflow.
   d. $830 inflow.
   e. None of the above.

The correct answer is (c). *(CMA 1278 5-5)*
   REQUIRED: The present value of the net effect on the income tax payments related to the project in year 2.
   DISCUSSION: The depreciation in year 2 will be $10,000 under the DDB method. The net taxable income for year 2 from the operating savings is $2,500 ($12,500 annual savings - $10,000 depreciation). Since the tax rate is 40%, a tax liability of $1,000 ($2,500 x .4) will result. The present value of $1,000 discounted at 10% for two periods is $830 ($1,000 x .83).

117. Rockyford's additional investment in working capital of $3,000 required in the current year is

   a. A sunk cost that is not recovered.
   b. Considered part of the initial investment when determining the net present value.
   c. Spread over the 4-year life of the asset as a cash outflow.
   d. Is depreciated as if it were part of the cost of the new machinery.
   e. Ignored.

The correct answer is (b). *(CMA 1278 5-6)*
   REQUIRED: The correct treatment of the additional investment in working capital.
   DISCUSSION: The $3,000 additional investment in working capital is considered part of the initial investment when determining the net present value because it is a necessary expenditure to obtain the new machine.
   Answer (a) is incorrect because a sunk cost refers to a cost which has already been incurred. It is therefore irrelevant to the decision process. Here, the $3,000 will be recovered from the savings the new machine will produce. Answer (c) is incorrect because the $3,000 will be recouped in the first year. Answer (d) is incorrect because, under the historical cost principle, it is not acceptable to add the increase in working capital to the amount of the asset to be depreciated. Answer (e) is incorrect because the $3,000 is an additional cost to be included in the evaluation of the purchase.

118. Ander Co. can invest $4,980 in a piece of equipment with a 3-year life. If the minimum desired rate of return is 10% after taxes and the annual expected cash savings net of taxes is $2,500, what is the amount (rounded to the nearest dollar) by which the annual cash flows could change before the company would be indifferent to acquiring the equipment. Use the value data preceding Q. 113 on page 500.

   a. Decrease of $415.
   b. Decrease of $2,480.
   c. Decrease of $1,245.
   d. Decrease of $500.
   e. Decrease of $2,000.

The correct answer is (d). *(CMA 1278 5-7)*
   REQUIRED: The amount by which an expected annual savings can change before a company is indifferent to the investment.
   DISCUSSION: The present value of the equipment (amount needed to be spent today) is $4,980, and the present value of an annuity of $1 for three periods at 10% is 2.49. Therefore, the amount of the annual cash flow (savings) that equates the initial cash investment ($4,980) with the present value of the annuity is $2,000 ($4,980 ÷ 2.49). The company will invest in this machinery if the annual return is equal to or greater than $2,000. Since it presently returns $2,500, the annual savings may decrease by up to $500 ($2,500 - $2,000) before the company would become indifferent to the investment.

Module 16.8: Comprehensive

	At 12%	At 14%	At 16%
Present value of $1 for 5 periods	0.57	0.52	0.48
Present value of an annuity of $1 for 5 periods	3.6	3.4	3.3

Questions 119 through 121 are based on the following information. Allo Foundation, a tax-exempt organization, invested $200,000 in a 5-year project at the beginning of the year. Allo estimates that the annual cash savings from this project will amount to $65,000. Tax and book depreciation on the project will be $40,000 per year for 5 years. On investments of this type, Allo's desired rate of return is 12%. Information on present value factors is shown in the next column.

---

119. The NPV of the project is

a. $34,000.
b. $36,400.
c. $90,000.
d. $125,000.

The correct answer is (a). *(CPA 1186 Q-31)*
REQUIRED: The NPV of the project.
DISCUSSION: The NPV is the difference between the present value of the future cash flows from the project discounted at an appropriate interest rate and the initial investment. Since the cash savings from this investment are $65,000 a year for 5 years, the PV of an annuity for 5 periods is used to calculate the PV of the cash flows.

NPV = $65,000(3.6) - initial investment
    = $234,000 - $200,000
    = $34,000

Note that the 12% rate of return of the firm was used as the discount rate, and depreciation was not in the calculation because it is not a cash flow.

---

120. Allo's IRR on this project is

a. Less than 12%.
b. Less than 14%, but more than 12%.
c. Less than 16%, but more than 14%.
d. More than 16%.

The correct answer is (d). *(CPA 1186 Q-32)*
REQUIRED: The IRR.
DISCUSSION: The IRR is the discount rate necessary to equate the discounted after tax cash flows with the initial investment. In other words it is the rate where the NPV = 0.

NPV = $65,000(X) - $200,000
0 = $65,000(X) - $200,000
$200,000 = $65,000(X)
3.08 = X

X is equal to the TVMF. Comparing 3.08 to the annuity factors given in the problem shows that the IRR must be greater than 16%. Note that the TVMF is 3.6, 3.4, and 3.3 for 12%, 14%, and 16%. Thus 3.08 is a TVMF for an IRR greater than 16%.

---

121. For the project's first year, Allo's accounting rate of return, based on the project's average book value would be

a. 14.4%.
b. 13.9%.
c. 12.5%.
d. 12.0%.

The correct answer is (b). *(CPA 1186 Q-33)*
REQUIRED: The accounting rate of return.
DISCUSSION: The accounting rate of return is equal to the expected increase in net income divided by the average investment (note average investment is specified). The expected increase in net income is the $65,000 cash savings less depreciation on the investment of $40,000. The average investment is based on the average book value for the year. The average book value is $180,000; which is the average of the book value at the beginning of the year of $200,000 and the book value at the end of the year of $160,000 ($200,000 - $40,000). Thus, the ARR is equal to 13.9% ($25,000 ÷ $180,000).

Module 16.8: Comprehensive

Questions 122 through 126 are based on the following selected data pertaining to Mar Co.'s Alo Division for the current year:

Sales	$100,000
Variable costs	60,000
Traceable fixed costs	10,000
Average invested capital	20,000
Imputed interest rate on average invested capital	12%

In addition, consideration is being given to the possible purchase of a $30,000 machine for Alo, which is expected to result in a decrease of $12,000 per year in cash operating expenses. The new machine will have book and tax depreciation of $6,000 per year for 5 years. It will have no residual value at the end of 5 years.

122. Before the purchase of the $30,000 machine, Alo's breakeven point in sales dollars was

a. $16,667.
b. $25,000.
c. $30,000.
d. $70,000.

The correct answer is (b). *(CPA 587 Q-34)*
REQUIRED: The breakeven point in sales dollars.
DISCUSSION: The breakeven point in sales dollars is equal to fixed costs divided by the contribution margin ratio (CMR). The CMR is the contribution margin divided by sales. The contribution margin is sales less variable costs or $40,000 ($100,000 - $60,000). Thus, the CMR is 40% ($40,000 ÷ $100,000). Total fixed costs are $10,000. Thus, the breakeven point in sales dollars is equal to $25,000 ($10,000 ÷ 40%).

123. Before the purchase of the $30,000 machine, Alo's return on investment was

a. 60%.
b. 75%.
c. 138%.
d. 150%.

The correct answer is (d). *(CPA 587 Q-35)*
REQUIRED: The return on investment before the purchase of the machine.
DISCUSSION: The ROI is equal to net operating income divided by average invested capital. Net operating income is equal to $30,000 ($100,000 sales - $60,000 VC - $10,000 FC). Average invested capital is given as $20,000. ROI is $30,000 ÷ $20,000 = $150%.

124. Before the purchase of the $30,000 machine, Alo's residual income was

a. $27,600.
b. $30,000.
c. $32,400.
d. $40,000.

The correct answer is (a). *(CPA 587 Q-36)*
REQUIRED: The residual income before the purchase of the machine.
DISCUSSION: The residual income is equal to net operating income minus imputed interest on the average invested capital. The net operating income is $30,000 ($100,000 - $60,000 - $10,000). The imputed interest is $2,400 (12% x $20,000). Thus, the residual income is equal to $27,600 ($30,000 - $2,400).

125. For the new machine, the accounting rate of return based on initial investment would be

a. 12%.
b. 20%.
c. 30%.
d. 40%.

The correct answer is (b). *(CPA 587 Q-37)*
REQUIRED: The accounting rate of return.
DISCUSSION: The ARR is equal to the expected increase in net income divided by the initial investment (specified in the question). The expected increase in net income is equal to $6,000, computed as the $12,000 decrease in operating expenses less the $6,000 increase in depreciation. The initial investment is $30,000. Thus, the ARR is 20% ($6,000 ÷ $30,000).

126. If income taxes are ignored, the payback period for the new machine would be

a. 1.67 years.
b. 2.50 years.
c. 4.17 years.
d. 5.00 years.

The correct answer is (b). *(CPA 587 Q-38)*
REQUIRED: The payback period of the new machine.
DISCUSSION: The payback method determines how long it takes for the investment dollars to be recovered by the annual net cash inflows. It is determined by dividing the initial investment by the annual net cash flow. The initial investment is $30,000 and the annual cash inflows are $12,000. Note that depreciation is ignored because it is not a cash flow. Thus, the payback period is equal to 2.50 years ($30,000 ÷ $12,000).

Module 16.8: Comprehensive

Questions 127 through 130 are based on the Apex Company, which is evaluating a capital budgeting proposal for the current year. The initial investment would be $30,000. Assume depreciation expense on the investment (for book and tax purposes) would be $5,000 each year for 6 years; at the end of 6 years it would have no salvage value. The pre-tax annual cash inflow from this investment is $10,000, and the income tax rate is 40% paid the same year as incurred. The desired rate of return is 15%. All cash flows occur at year-end.

The relevant data follow:

Year	Present Value of an Annuity in Arrears of $1 at 15%
1	$ .870
2	1.626
3	2.284
4	2.856
5	3.353
6	3.785

127. What is the after-tax accounting rate of return on Apex's capital budgeting proposal?

a. 10%.
b. 16 2/3%.
c. 26 2/3%.
d. 33 1/3%.

The correct answer is (a). (CPA 575 P-25)
REQUIRED: The after-tax accounting rate of return.
DISCUSSION: The accounting rate of return (ARR) is computed by dividing the after-tax income (not cash flow) by the initial investment.

Pre-tax income	$10,000
Depreciation	(5,000)
Taxable income	$ 5,000
Income tax ($5,000 x .4)	(2,000)
After-tax income	$ 3,000

128. What is the after-tax payback reciprocal for Apex's capital budgeting proposal?

a. 20%.
b. 26 2/3%.
c. 33 1/3%.
d. 50%.

The correct answer is (b). (CPA 575 P-26)
REQUIRED: The after-tax payback reciprocal for the proposal.
DISCUSSION: The after-tax payback reciprocal is found by dividing net income plus depreciation by the amount of the initial investment. After-tax net income is $3,000 and depreciation is $5,000. The payback reciprocal is therefore 26 2/3% ($8,000 ÷ $30,000).

129. What is the net present value of Apex's capital budgeting proposal?

a. $(7,290).
b. $280.
c. $7,850.
d. $11,760.

The correct answer is (b). (CPA 575 P-27)
REQUIRED: The net present value of the capital budgeting proposal.
DISCUSSION: The NPV is the difference between the present value of the future cash flows discounted at the desired rate of return and the initial investment. Annual cash inflow is $8,000 ($3,000 after-tax income + $5,000 depreciation). The present value of an ordinary annuity of $1 for 6 years at 15% is 3.785. The present value of the cash flows is thus $30,280 (3.785 x $8,000), and the NPV is $280 ($30,280 - $30,000 investment).

130. How much would Apex have had to invest 5 years ago at 15% compounded annually to have $30,000 now?

a. $12,960.
b. $14,910.
c. $17,160.
d. Cannot be determined from the information given.

The correct answer is (b). (CPA 575 P-28)
REQUIRED: The amount invested 5 years ago given interest and targeted current amount.
DISCUSSION: To find the amount invested 5 years ago to have $30,000 today, compute the amount needed to be invested now to receive $30,000 in 5 years. To determine the amount needed to be invested, multiply the future sum desired ($30,000) by the present value of $1 for five periods at 15%. Since the factor is not given, it must be determined using the present value of an annuity table. The present value of $1 is the difference between the present value of an annuity for five periods (3.353) and the present value of an annuity for four periods (2.856), or .497. Accordingly, the present value of the future sum of $30,000 is $14,910 (.497 x $30,000).

Module 16.8: Comprehensive

> Questions 131 and 132 are based on Flemming, Inc., which is planning to acquire a new machine at a total cost of $36,000. The new machine would be depreciated for book and tax purposes by $6,000 per year for 6 years. It will have no salvage value at the end of 6 years. Flemming estimates that the annual cash flow from operations, before income taxes, from using this machine will be $9,000. Flemming's cost of capital is 8% and the income tax rate is 40%. The present value of $1 at 8% for 6 years is .630. The present value of an annuity of $1 in arrears at 8% for 6 years is 4.623.

131. What would the payback period be?

a. 4.0 years.
b. 4.6 years.
c. 5.7 years.
d. 6.7 years.

The correct answer is (b). *(CPA 578 P-19)*
REQUIRED: The payback period for a new machine.
DISCUSSION: The payback period is the time required to recapture the initial investment. The first step is to calculate the after-tax net cash inflow.

Pre-tax cash flow	$9,000
Depreciation	(6,000)
Taxable income	$3,000
After-tax income rate (1 - .4)	x .60
After-tax income	$1,800
Depreciation	6,000
Annual net cash inflow	$7,800

The initial investment ($36,000) divided by the annual after-tax cash flow ($7,800) gives the payback period (4.6 years).

132. What would the net present value be?

a. $59.
b. $5,607.
c. $10,800.
d. $13,140.

The correct answer is (a). *(CPA 578 P-20)*
REQUIRED: The net present value (NPV) of the new machine.
DISCUSSION: The NPV is the difference between the present value of the annual net cash inflows and the initial investment. Given an annual after-tax cash flow of $7,800 (Q. 131), the present value of the cash flows is $36,059 ($7,800 x 4.623), and the NPV is $59 ($36,059 - $36,000 investment).

> Questions 133 and 134 are based on Hanley Company, which purchased a machine for $125,000. The machine will have book and tax depreciation of $25,000 each year for 5 years. At the end of 5 years it will have no salvage value. The related cash flow from operations, net of income taxes, is expected to be $45,000 a year. Assume that Hanley's effective income tax rate is 40% for all years.

133. What is the payback period?

a. 2.1 years.
b. 2.3 years.
c. 2.8 years.
d. 4.2 years.

The correct answer is (c). *(CPA 1182 P-36)*
REQUIRED: The payback period for a new depreciable asset.
DISCUSSION: The payback period is the time required to recoup the initial investment. Since the investment is $125,000 and the net of tax annual cash flow is $45,000 (no salvage), the payback period is approximately 2.8 years ($125,000 ÷ $45,000).

134. What is the accounting (book value) rate of return on the initial increase in required investment?

a. 16%.
b. 24%.
c. 28%.
d. 36%.

The correct answer is (a). *(CPA 1182 P-37)*
REQUIRED: The accounting rate of return (ARR) on the investment in a new depreciable asset.
DISCUSSION: The ARR is computed by dividing the after-tax accounting income by the initial investment. The after-tax cash flow is $45,000, and annual depreciation is $25,000. The increase in accounting income attributable to the machine is thus $20,000, and the ARR is 16% ($20,000 ÷ $125,000). The ARR is conceptually weaker than the discounted cash flow models. Accordingly, one should be cautious in using this method for evaluating capital projects.

Questions 135 through 140 are based on Yipann Corporation, which is reviewing an investment proposal. The initial cost as well as the estimate of the book value of the investment at the end of each year, the net after-tax cash flows for each year, and the net income for each year are presented in the schedule below. All cash flows are assumed to take place at the end the year.

Year	Initial Cost and Book Value	Annual Net After-tax Cash Flows	Annual Net Income
0	$105,000		
1	70,000	$50,000	$15,000
2	42,000	45,000	17,000
3	21,000	40,000	19,000
4	7,000	35,000	21,000
5	0	30,000	23,000
			$95,000

The salvage value of the investment at the end of each year is equal to its book value. There would be no salvage value at the end of the investment's life.

Yipann uses a 24% after-tax target rate of return for new investment proposals. The discount figures for a 24% rate of return are given in the chart below.

Year	Present Value of $1.00 Received at the End of Period	Present Value of an Annuity of $1 Received at the End of Each Period
1	.81	.81
2	.65	1.46
3	.52	1.98
4	.42	2.40
5	.34	2.74
6	.28	3.02
7	.22	3.24

135. The traditional payback period for the investment proposal is

a. .875 years.
b. 1.933 years.
c. 2.250 years.
d. Over 5 years.
e. None of the above.

The correct answer is (c). (CMA 682 5-7)
REQUIRED: The traditional payback period for the investment proposal.
DISCUSSION: The traditional payback period is the time required to generate net after-tax cash flows equal to the initial investment. Since the cash flows generated by this investment will be uneven, they must be added each year until they equal the initial cost of $105,000. The sum of the first 2 years' net after-tax cash flows is $95,000 ($50,000 + $45,000). Hence, only $10,000 would remain to be recaptured in the third year. This amount is one fourth of the third year's net after-tax cash flow ($10,000 ÷ $40,000). Accordingly, the payback period is 2.25 years.

136. The bail-out payback period for the investment proposal is

a. .875 years.
b. .778 years.
c. 2.250 years.
d. 1.411 years.
e. None of the above.

The correct answer is (a). (CMA 682 5-8)
REQUIRED: The bail-out payback period for the investment proposal.
DISCUSSION: The bail-out payback period for an investment proposal is the time required for the sum of the net after-tax cash flow and the salvage value to equal the initial cost. The initial cost is $105,000 and the salvage value at the end of year 1 is equal to $70,000. Since the sum of the salvage value and after-tax cash flow for year 1 is $120,000 ($70,000 + $50,000), the recovery of the initial cost requires .875 years ($105,000 ÷ $120,000).

137. The accounting rate of return for the investment proposal over its life using the initial value of the investment is

a. 36.2%.
b. 18.1%.
c. 28.1%.
d. 38.1%.
e. None of the above.

The correct answer is (b). (CMA 682 5-9)
REQUIRED: The accounting rate of return for the investment proposal.
DISCUSSION: The accounting rate of return over the life of the investment using the initial value of the investment is the average annual net income generated divided by the initial value. Thus, the sum of the annual net incomes ($95,000) is divided by the number of years to arrive at the average net income of $19,000. The initial cost is $105,000, giving an 18.1% rate of return ($19,000 ÷ $105,000).

Module 16.8: Comprehensive

138. The net present value of the investment proposal is

a. $4,600.
b. $10,450.
c. $(55,280).
d. $115,450.
e. None of the above.

The correct answer is (b). *(CMA 682 5-10)*
REQUIRED: The NPV of the investment proposal.
DISCUSSION: The NPV is the difference between the sum of the present values of the annual after-tax cash flows and the initial investment. The initial cost is $105,000. The annual net after-tax cash flows are discounted based on the present value of $1 received at the end of the period at a 24% target rate of return.

Annual net after-tax cash flows

.81 x $50,000	=	$ 40,500
.65 x $45,000	=	$ 29,250
.52 x $40,000	=	$ 20,800
.42 x $35,000	=	$ 14,700
.34 x $30,000	=	$ 10,200
Total present value	=	$115,450

The net present value is thus $10,450 ($115,450 - $105,000).

139. The payback reciprocal, which is often used as an approximation of an investment proposal's internal rate of return, cannot be used for Yipann's investment proposal. Why not?

a. The life of an investment proposal must be at least twice the payback period.
b. The life of an investment proposal must be at least 10 years.
c. The net after-tax cash flows must be constant over the investment's life.
d. Only straight-line depreciation can be employed when determining the net after-tax cash flows.
e. The profitability index must be greater than one.

The correct answer is (c). *(CMA 682 5-11)*
REQUIRED: Why the payback reciprocal cannot be used to approximate the internal rate of return of this investment.
DISCUSSION: For the payback reciprocal to approximate the internal rate of return, the net after-tax cash flows must be constant over the life of the investment. Given uneven after-tax cash flows, the calculation of the payback period, the internal rate of return, and the net present value becomes a cumulative, year-by-year process.

140. When there are two mutually exclusive investments, management should select the project

a. That generates cash flows for the longer time.
b. Whose net after-tax flows exceed the initial investment.
c. That has the greater accounting rate of return.
d. Whose cash flows vary less.
e. That has the greater profitability index.

The correct answer is (e). *(CMA 682 5-12)*
REQUIRED: The criterion for choosing between mutually exclusive investments.
DISCUSSION: When management is confronted with two mutually exclusive investments, they should select the project that has the greater profitability index. The profitability index is the discounted future cash flows divided by the cost of the investment. For Yipann's proposal, for instance, the profitability index is 1.1 ($115,450 ÷ $105,000).
Answer (a) is incorrect because the generation of cash flows over a longer time may be insufficient to compensate for the difference in profitability. Answer (b) is incorrect because the net after-tax flows may exceed the initial investment in both proposals. Answer (c) is incorrect because the project with the greater accounting rate of return does not take into account the time value of money. Answer (d) is incorrect because cash flow stability may have nothing to do with relative profitability.

Questions 141 through 147 are based on the following information. Garrison Corporation is considering the replacement of an old machine that is currently being used. The old machine is fully depreciated but can be used by the corporation through 1993. If Garrison decides to replace the old machine, Picco Company has offered to purchase it for $60,000 on the replacement date. The old machine would have no salvage value in 1993.

If the replacement occurs, a new machine would be acquired from Hillcrest Industries on January 2, 1989. The purchase price of $1,000,000 for the new machine would be paid in cash at the time of replacement. Due to the increased efficiency of the new machine, estimated annual cash savings of $300,000 would be generated through 1993, the end of its expected useful life. The new machine is not expected to have any salvage value at the end of 1993.

All operating cash receipts, operating cash expenditures, and applicable tax payments and credits are assumed to occur at the end of the year. Garrison employs the calendar year for reporting purposes.

Discount tables for several different interest rates that are to be used in any discounting calculations are given below.

Present Value of $1.00 Received at End of Period

Period	9%	12%	15%	18%	21%
1	.92	.89	.87	.85	.83
2	.84	.80	.76	.72	.68
3	.77	.71	.65	.61	.56
4	.71	.64	.57	.51	.47
5	.65	.57	.50	.44	.39

Present Value of an Annuity of $1.00 Received at the End of Each Period

Period	9%	12%	15%	18%	21%
1	.92	.89	.87	.85	.83
2	1.76	1.69	1.63	1.57	1.51
3	2.53	2.40	2.28	2.18	2.07
4	3.24	3.04	2.85	2.69	2.54
5	3.89	3.61	3.35	3.13	2.93

For questions 141 through 143 only, assume that Garrison is not subject to income taxes.

141. If Garrison requires investments to earn a 12% return, the NPV for replacing the old machine with the new machine is

a. $171,000.
b. $136,400.
c. $143,000.
d. $83,000.
e. Some amount other than those given above.

The correct answer is (c). (CMA 1285 5-1)
REQUIRED: The NPV of the new machine.
DISCUSSION: The $300,000 of annual savings discounted at 12% has a present value of $1,083,000 ($300,000 x 3.61 PV of an ordinary annuity for five periods at 12%). The net cost of the new machine is the $1,000,000 purchase price minus the $60,000 cash inflow from the sale of the old machine, or $940,000. The resulting NPV is $143,000 ($1,083,000 present value of future savings - $940,000 cash outlay).

142. The IRR, to the nearest percent, to replace the old machine is

a. 9%.
b. 15%.
c. 17%.
d. 18%.
e. Over 21%.

The correct answer is (d). (CMA 1285 5-2)
REQUIRED: The IRR to the nearest percent for replacing the old machine.
DISCUSSION: The IRR is the discount rate at which the present value of the cash flows equals the original investment. Thus, the NPV of the project is zero at the IRR. The IRR is also the maximum borrowing cost the firm could afford to pay for a specific project. The IRR is similar to the yield rate/effective rate quoted in the business media. The formula for the IRR involving an annuity equates the annual cash flow, times an unknown annuity factor, with the initial net investment: $940,000 = $300,000 x Factor. The solution of the equation gives a factor of 3.133, which is found in the 18% column on the five-period line.

143. The payback period to replace the old machine with the new machine is

a. 1.14 years.
b. 2.78 years.
c. 3.13 years.
d. 3.33 years.
e. 5.00 years.

The correct answer is (c). (CMA 1285 5-3)
REQUIRED: The payback period for the new machine.
DISCUSSION: The payback method determines how long it takes for the investment dollars to be recovered by the annual net cash inflows. The time is computed by dividing the net investment by the average periodic net cash inflow. The initial net cash outlay divided by the annual cash savings equals 3.13 years ($940,000 ÷ $300,000).

Module 16.8: Comprehensive

> Questions 144 through 147 are based on the following additional assumptions.
>
> - Garrison requires all investments to earn a 12% after-tax rate of return to be accepted.
> - Garrison is subject to a marginal income tax rate of 40% on all income and gains (losses).
>
> - The new machine will have depreciation as follows:
>
> | Year | Depreciation |
> |---|---|
> | 1989 | $ 250,000 |
> | 1990 | 380,000 |
> | 1991 | 370,000 |
> | | $1,000,000 |

144. The present value of the after-tax cash flow associated with the salvage of the old machine is

a. $38,640.
b. $36,000.
c. $32,040.
d. $27,960.
e. Some amount other than those given above.

The correct answer is (a). *(CMA 1285 5-5)*
REQUIRED: The present value of the after-tax cash flow associated with the salvage of the old machine.
DISCUSSION: The old machine will be sold for $60,000, and the entire selling price represents a taxable gain because the book value is zero. At a 40% tax rate, the tax is $24,000. However, the tax will not be paid until the end of the year. Discounting the tax payment results in a present value of $21,360 ($24,000 x .89). This amount is subtracted from the $60,000 selling price (not discounted because received immediately) to yield an after-tax NPV of $38,640.

145. The present value of the annual after-tax cash savings that arise from the increased efficiency of the new machine throughout its life (calculated before consideration of any depreciation tax shield) is

a. $563,400.
b. $375,600.
c. $433,200.
d. $649,800.
e. Some amount other than those given above.

The correct answer is (d). *(CMA 1285 5-6)*
REQUIRED: The present value of the annual after-tax cash savings that arise from the new machine without consideration of the depreciation tax shield.
DISCUSSION: The annual savings of $300,000 must be reduced by the 40% tax, so the net effect of purchasing the new machine is an annual cash savings of $180,000 [(1 - .4) x $300,000]. The present value of the after-tax savings is thus $649,800 ($180,000 x 3.61 PV of an ordinary annuity for five periods at 12%).

146. The present value of the depreciation tax shield for 1990 is

a. $182,400.
b. $121,600.
c. $109,440.
d. $114,304.
e. Some amount other than those given above.

The correct answer is (b). *(CMA 1285 5-7)*
REQUIRED: The present value of the depreciation tax shield the second year of the machine's life.
DISCUSSION: The applicable depreciation for 1990 is $380,000. At a tax rate of 40%, the savings is $152,000 ($380,000 x 40%). Its present value is $121,600 ($152,000 x .80 PV of $1 for two periods at 12%).

147. If the new machine were sold for $80,000 on December 31, 1993, instead of the estimated salvage value of $0, the present value of the additional after-tax cash flow is

a. $18,240.
b. $27,360.
c. $45,600.
d. $48,000.
e. Some amount other than those given above.

The correct answer is (b). *(CMA 1285 5-8)*
REQUIRED: The present value of the additional after-tax cash flow resulting from a future sale of the new machine.
DISCUSSION: At the time of sale, the new machine would be fully depreciated, and any sale proceeds would be fully taxable as a gain. Hence, the $80,000 taxable gain would result in $32,000 of tax ($80,000 x .40), and the after-tax cash flow would be $48,000. Its present value would be $27,360 ($48,000 x .57 PV of $1 for five periods at 12%).

Questions 148 through 152 are based on the following information, which was presented as part of Question 3 on Part 5 of the June 1979 CMA examination.

Hazman Company plans to replace an old piece of equipment which is obsolete and expected to be unreliable under the stress of daily operations. The equipment is fully depreciated, and will have no salvage value.

One piece of equipment being considered would provide annual cash savings of $7,000 before income taxes. The equipment would cost $18,000 and have annual depreciation of $3,600 for 5 years, for both book and tax purposes. It would have no salvage value at the end of 5 years.

The company is subject to a 40% tax rate and has a 14% after-tax cost of capital.

Assume all operating revenues and expenses occur at the end of the year. Appropriate discount tables are presented in the opposite column.

Present Value of $1.00 Received at End of Period

Period	8%	10%	12%	14%	16%	18%	20%	22%	24%
1	.93	.91	.89	.88	.86	.85	.83	.82	.81
2	.86	.83	.80	.77	.74	.72	.69	.67	.65
3	.79	.75	.71	.67	.64	.61	.58	.55	.52
4	.73	.68	.64	.59	.55	.52	.48	.45	.42
5	.68	.62	.57	.52	.48	.44	.40	.37	.34

Present Value of an Annuity of $1.00 Received at the End of Each Period

Period	8%	10%	12%	14%	16%	18%	20%	22%	24%
1	.93	.91	.89	.88	.86	.85	.83	.82	.81
2	1.79	1.74	1.69	1.65	1.60	1.57	1.52	1.49	1.46
3	2.58	2.49	2.40	2.32	2.24	2.18	2.10	2.04	1.98
4	3.31	3.17	3.04	2.91	2.79	2.70	2.58	2.49	2.40
5	3.99	3.79	3.61	3.43	3.27	3.14	2.98	2.86	2.74

148. What is the after-tax payback period for Hazman Company's proposed investment in new equipment?

   a. 4.20 years.
   b. 3.19 years.
   c. 2.56 years.
   d. 8.80 years.

The correct answer is (b). *(Publisher)*
REQUIRED: The after-tax payback period for the investment in new equipment.
DISCUSSION: The payback period is the time required to recover the initial investment through after-tax cash flows. In this case, the initial investment is $18,000. The after-tax cash flow is $7,000 minus $2,800 taxes (40% x $7,000) plus the depreciation shield of $1,440 (40% x $3,600 annual depreciation), giving a net after-tax cash flow of $5,640. Alternatively, subtract depreciation per year from the pre-tax cash savings and multiply by (1 - tax rate) to yield net income after taxes. The depreciation is added back to net income after taxes to arrive at net after-tax cash flow: (7,000 - 3,600) x (1 - .40) + 3,600 = $5,640. The $18,000 investment divided by $5,640 equals 3.19 years.

149. What is the after-tax accounting rate of return for Hazman Company's proposed investment in new equipment?

   a. 16.9%.
   b. 33.9%.
   c. 22.7%.
   d. 11.3%.

The correct answer is (d). *(Publisher)*
REQUIRED: The after-tax accounting rate of return (ARR) for the initial investment.
DISCUSSION: The accounting rate of return is the annual average after-tax net income divided by the initial investment. The initial investment is $18,000. The after-tax net income is $2,040 [$7,000 savings minus $3,600 depreciation times (1 - tax rate)].

150. What is the after-tax net present value for Hazman Company's proposed investment in new equipment?

a. $5,640.00.
b. $1,440.00.
c. $1,345.20.
d. $2,300.00.

The correct answer is (c). *(Publisher)*
REQUIRED: The after-tax net present value (NPV) of the investment.
DISCUSSION: The NPV is the present value of the after-tax cash flows minus the initial investment. The annual after-tax cash flow is $5,640 (see Q. 148). The present value factor for an ordinary annuity is 3.43 at 14% (the cost of capital) for 5 years. The present value is thus $19,345.20 ($5,640 x $3.43), and the NPV is $1,345.20 ($19,345.20 - $18,000).

151. What is the after-tax profitability (present value) index for Hazman Company's proposed investment in new equipment?

a. 1.07.
b. 1.21.
c. 1.01.
d. .97.

The correct answer is (a). *(Publisher)*
REQUIRED: The after-tax profitability (present value) index.
DISCUSSION: The profitability index is the present value of the after-tax cash flows divided by the initial investment. The present value of after-tax cash flows is $19,345.20 (see Q. 150). Dividing by the $18,000 initial investment results in a 1.07 profitability index.

152. What is the after-tax internal rate of return for Hazman Company's proposed investment in new equipment?

a. 16.0%.
b. 17.2%.
c. 18.0%.
d. 20.0%.

The correct answer is (b). *(Publisher)*
REQUIRED: The after-tax internal rate of return (IRR).
DISCUSSION: The IRR is the rate necessary to equate the discounted after-tax cash flows with the initial investment. With the given present value data, the first step is to calculate the present values of the cash flows at 16% and 18%, respectively (the NPV was positive at 14%). The present value at 16% is $18,443. The present value at 18% is $17,710. The $18,000 investment lies between these two values, so answer (b), 17.2%, must be the best choice.

Module 16.8: Comprehensive

Questions 153 through 158 are based on the following information. Plasto Corporation is a manufacturer of plastic products. The company is embarking on a 5-year modernization and expansion plan. Thus, management is identifying all of the capital projects that it should consider. Financial analyses will be prepared for each identified project. Plasto will not select and implement all of the projects because some may not be financially attractive and some are mutually exclusive (i.e., choice of one project precludes the selection of any others); in addition, not all projects can be implemented due to a maximum dollar limit for capital projects.

The list of projects being considered is enumerated in the opposite column. All modernization and expansion projects would be completed in 3 years. The projects have varying lives, but none exceed 7 years. Plasto's criteria for evaluating and selecting projects is maximization of return and quickness of investment recovery.

Project Identification and Description	Investment	Estimated Life (in years)
Maintenance: Extensive maintenance of current manufacturing facilities including repairs and some replacement of equipment. This work must be done in order to keep existing facilities in operation until any retooling and/or expansion projects are completed.	$ 2,000,000	3
Retooling: Major retooling of current manufacturing facilities using general purpose equipment.	$ 6,000,000	5
Retooling: Major retooling of current manufacturing facilities using special purpose equipment (this project and the prior project are mutually exclusive projects).	$ 8,500,000	5
Make vs. Buy: Construction of new facilities to manufacture parts and supplies used in making products. Parts and supplies are currently being purchased.	$ 5,000,000	7
Expansion: Construction of new facilities to introduce new product NX-42.	$10,000,000	6
Expansion: Construction of new facilities to introduce new product LV-221.	$12,000,000	7

153. When attempting to determine if a project is profitable and should be pursued, Plasto should be sure that the project's

a. Payback is 3 years or less.
b. Return exceeds the company's historical return on stockholders' equity.
c. Return exceeds the company's historical return on net assets employed.
d. Return exceeds the interest rate that is charged on any debt that is incurred to finance the project.
e. Return exceeds a hurdle rate specified by Plasto's management.

The correct answer is (e). *(CMA 1286 5-19)*
REQUIRED: The true statement about the criteria for selecting projects.
DISCUSSION: An example of the application of the hurdle rate approach is the IRR method. The IRR capital budgeting method computes the IRR on each project by setting the initial investment cost equal to the present value of the net cash flows over the length of the project (zero net present value). The project should be considered if the internal rate equals or exceeds a prespecified hurdle or cut-off rate.

Answer (a) is incorrect because Plasto's management has not specified a 3-year payback period. Answers (b) and (c) are incorrect because historical returns are not relevant to making future investments. Answer (d) is incorrect because the interest rate on debt is not as important as the company's average cost of capital. Using debt, even at high interest, might lower the average cost of capital if some stockholders' equity is used to finance the investment.

Module 16.8: Comprehensive

154. The overriding concern for Plasto's maintenance project should be to

   a. Maximize salvage value.
   b. Minimize the present value of the cash outlays.
   c. Minimize the IRR.
   d. Maximize the payback period.
   e. Maximize the excess present value index.

The correct answer is (b). *(CMA 1286 5-20)*
REQUIRED: The overriding concern regarding the maintenance project.
DISCUSSION: The maintenance project must be undertaken to keep the existing facilities in operation. No cash inflows are expected from the maintenance project. Therefore, the primary consideration is to keep the cash outlays at a minimum, including those that can be avoided by timely maintenance.
Answer (a) is incorrect because salvage value is secondary compared to the goals of continuing operations and preventing future expenditures through timely maintenance. Answer (c) is incorrect because a company always wants to maximize its IRR. Answer (d) is incorrect because a company always wants to minimize its payback period. Answer (e) is incorrect because the excess present value (profitability) index (PV of future net cash flows/cost) cannot be computed since regular cash inflows cannot be calculated.

155. Which one of the following pairs of capital investment evaluation techniques would best satisfy Plasto's criteria for selecting capital projects?

   a. Accounting rate of return and present value payback.
   b. NPV and payback.
   c. Accounting rate of return and bailout payback.
   d. IRR and present value payback.
   e. Excess present value index and IRR.

The correct answer is (d). *(CMA 1286 5-21)*
REQUIRED: The pair of capital investment evaluation techniques that would best satisfy the criteria for selecting capital projects.
DISCUSSION: Plasto wants maximization of return and quickness of investment recovery. Thus, the IRR should be one of the evaluation techniques since this method measures return rates. The payback method would also be used, and present value payback is preferable to historical payback.
Answers (a) and (c) are incorrect because the ARR does not consider the time value of money. Answer (b) is incorrect because the NPV method does not provide a rate of return. Answer (e) is incorrect because the excess present value index does not measure time of recovery.

156. If Plasto is faced with capital rationing (i.e., maximum dollar amount allowed for capital projects is less than the outlays required for all projects), the best general method to employ to rank the projects would be the

   a. Present value payback.
   b. Excess present value index.
   c. NPV.
   d. IRR.
   e. Payback.

The correct answer is (c). *(CMA 1286 5-22)*
REQUIRED: The best method to rank projects when capital rationing exists.
DISCUSSION: The NPV is the difference between the present value of the future cash flows from the project discounted at an appropriate interest rate and the initial investment. If the NPV is zero or greater, the investment may be economically rational. Under a condition of capital rationing, the best evaluation method to use is the NPV method because the company will want to maximize the NPV of all projects that can be financed without exceeding the rationing limit.
Answers (a) and (e) are incorrect because payback is not a measure of profitability. Answer (b) is incorrect because the excess present value index will not necessarily maximize returns when capital is rationed since it does not consider investment size. Use of this method when capital is rationed may result in selection of smaller projects with high indexes and the rejection of other, larger projects with greater absolute returns. Answer (d) is incorrect because the IRR emphasizes the rate of return rather than the total present value of the dollar returns.

Questions 157 and 158 are based on the information presented on page 512.

157. If Plasto must decide between the two mutually exclusive retooling projects, the best general method to employ to decide between these projects would be the

a. Present value payback.
b. Excess present value index.
c. NPV.
d. IRR.
e. Payback.

The correct answer is (c). *(CMA 1286 5-23)*
REQUIRED: The best method to employ to decide between two mutually exclusive projects.
DISCUSSION: The NPV method would be preferable, especially when the lives of the two mutually exclusive projects are of different durations. The NPV method will insure that the company receives the greatest amount of dollars in return for its investment.
Answers (a) and (e) are incorrect because payback is not a measure of profitability but of how quickly the original investment is recovered. Answers (b) and (d) are incorrect because the excess present value index and the IRR do not consider the total present value of the dollar returns.

158. If Plasto employs discounted cash flow techniques in evaluating capital investment projects, this reflects that management recognizes

a. The importance of the time value of money.
b. That cash flow is important to maintaining operations and generating future acceptable profits.
c. The volatility of inflation and its effect on operations.
d. The importance of recovering the initial investment outlay as soon as possible.
e. The importance of incorporating risk in the evaluation process.

The correct answer is (a). *(CMA 1286 5-24)*
REQUIRED: The reason a company uses discounted cash flow techniques.
DISCUSSION: The premise of the discounted cash flow technique is that the use of money has a cost (interest) as would the use of any other asset. Therefore, money to be received or spent in the future must be discounted at an appropriate interest rate to determine its present value. A comparison of present values allows potential projects to be ranked according to their profitability.
Answer (b) is incorrect because the simple recognition of cash flows is not the same as using present value tables to measure the current worth of future flows. Answer (c) is incorrect because inflation is not a factor in present value analysis. The primary consideration is interest rates (which may include a factor for inflation that is difficult to measure accurately). Answer (d) is incorrect because it describes the payback method. Answer (e) is incorrect because interest, not risk, is the factor considered in the evaluation process. A risk factor is incorporated into the interest rate.

CHAPTER SEVENTEEN
INVENTORY PLANNING AND CONTROL

> 17.1 Order-Getting/Order-Filling Costs .... (13 questions) 515
> 17.2 Economic Order Quantity (EOQ) .... (21 questions) 518
> 17.3 Reorder Points, Safety Stock, Stockout Cost .... (5 questions) 524
> 17.4 Computations .... (31 questions) 526

Inventory planning and control has been an increasingly important function of the management accountant. The high inventory values necessary to maintain sales activity vis-à-vis the high carrying costs of that inventory have made this issue important in most firms. Regardless of just-in-time strategies and tactics, inventory planning and control remain a key issue to managers. In addition, the concept of inventory planning and control may even be applicable to nonmanufacturing environments. The economic utilization of staff accountants in service organizations seems especially applicable for this concept.

17.1 Order-Getting/Order-Filling Costs

1. Order-filling costs, as opposed to order-getting costs, include all but which of the following items?

a. Clerical processing of sales orders.
b. Credit check of new customers.
c. Packing and shipping of sales orders.
d. Collection of payments for sales orders.
e. Mailing catalogs to current customers.

The correct answer is (e). *(CMA 1279 4-2)*
REQUIRED: The variable not affecting order-filling costs.
DISCUSSION: Order-filling costs include the costs necessary to prepare and ship the order, including the resulting payment process. Thus, the clerical processing, credit check, packing, shipping, and collection of payments are part of the order-filling cycle. Mailing catalogs to current customers would not be a component of the order-filling costs. It is an order-getting cost.

2. In production management, product breakdown into component parts and lead times for procuring these parts is necessary for a(n)

a. Critical path method (CPM) system.
b. Material requirement planning (MRP) system.
c. Job balancing system.
d. Economic order quantity (EOQ) system.
e. ABC system.

The correct answer is (b). *(CMA 1286 5-10)*
REQUIRED: The production management system that requires breaking a product down into its components.
DISCUSSION: Materials requirement planning (MRP) is usually considered a computer-based information system designed to plan and control raw materials used in a production setting. It assumes that estimated demand for materials is reasonably accurate and that suppliers can deliver based upon this accurate schedule. It is crucial that delivery delays be avoided because, under MRP, production delays are almost unavoidable if the materials are not on hand. An MRP system uses a parts list, often called a bill of materials, and lead times for each type of material to obtain materials just as they are needed for planned production.
Answer (a) is incorrect because it is a project management and scheduling technique that determines the longest time path from the first to the last event for a project. Answer (c) is incorrect because it is not meaningful in this context. Answer (d) is incorrect because the EOQ model does not adjust for the dependent demand for the components of an inventory item. Answer (e) is incorrect because the main purpose of the ABC system is to increase control over items accounting for the most profit.

Module 17.1: Order-Getting/Order-Filling Costs

3. Which of the following costs is not included in inventory costing policy?

   a. Ordering costs.
   b. Marketing manager's salary.
   c. Carrying costs.
   d. Acquisition costs.

The correct answer is (b). *(Publisher)*
REQUIRED: The item not included in inventory policy.
DISCUSSION: Ordering costs are the costs of placing and processing the order. Carrying costs consist of the opportunity costs and the cash outflows of holding inventory. Acquisition costs are the costs of buying or manufacturing the inventory. The marketing manager's salary affects selling, not inventory, costs.

4. The inventory model that follows the concept that 80% of the value of an inventory is in 20% of the inventory items is the

   a. ABC system.
   b. Economic order quantity (EOQ) model.
   c. Just-in-time inventory system.
   d. Material requirement planning (MRP) system.
   e. Zero inventory model.

The correct answer is (a). *(CMA 1286 5-11)*
REQUIRED: The inventory system that follows the concept that 80% of the value of the inventory is in 20% of the items.
DISCUSSION: The ABC method of inventory control requires management to exert greatest control over the A classification items, which usually include a relatively small percentage of total items but a high percentage of the dollar volume. This method is analogous to the 80/20 rule, which says, for instance, that 20% of the customers account for 80% of the profit.
Answer (b) is incorrect because the EOQ model is intended to minimize the sum of holding and ordering costs. Answer (c) is incorrect because a just-in-time system attempts to reduce holding costs by scheduling deliveries of materials as closely as possible to when they are needed in production. Answer (d) is incorrect because an MRP system recognizes that the demand for one inventory item creates a dependent demand for the components of that item. Answer (e) is incorrect because it is not meaningful in this context.

5. A two-bin inventory order system is a

   a. Constant order-cycle system.
   b. EOQ reorder system.
   c. Constant order-quantity system.
   d. Inventory batching system.

The correct answer is (c). *(Publisher)*
REQUIRED: Another name for a two-bin inventory order system.
DISCUSSION: A two-bin inventory order system is a system in which two bins are used. Inventory is reordered when the first bin is used up. Essentially, the second bin provides for a safety stock plus the quantity used during the lead time in receiving the reorder. The amount of the inventory in the first bin is a constant quantity; thus, it is known as a constant order-quantity system; i.e., the same amount is ordered each time.
Answer (a) is incorrect because it describes the system in which an inventory is ordered on a uniform time cycle and the quantity varies. Answers (b) and (d) are incorrect because they are nonsense responses.

6. An inventory system in which fixed reorder dates are established and inventory is ordered based on usage up to that point is called

   a. Constant order-cycle system.
   b. Two-bin system.
   c. Constant order-quantity system.
   d. Inventory lead-time system.

The correct answer is (a). *(Publisher)*
REQUIRED: The inventory system establishing reorder points and ordering inventory based on past usage.
DISCUSSION: This question describes a constant order-cycle system, in which the order dates are fixed and the amount of inventory ordered is based upon usage to date and/or projected usage.
Answers (b) and (c) are incorrect because the two-bin or the constant order-quantity system orders a constant amount of inventory at each order rather than ordering at constant intervals of time. Answer (d) is incorrect because inventory lead-time system is a nonsense answer.

Module 17.1: Order-Getting/Order-Filling Costs

7. Which inventory costing system results in the best inventory turnover ratio in a period of rising prices?

a. LIFO.
b. FIFO.
c. Weighted average.
d. Perpetual.

The correct answer is (a). *(Publisher)*
REQUIRED: The inventory costing system resulting in the best inventory turnover ratio in a period of rising prices.
DISCUSSION: The inventory turnover ratio is cost of sales divided by average inventory. The best inventory turnover ratio is a high inventory turnover ratio because it indicates a better utilization of inventory. The ratio can be increased by increasing cost of sales or decreasing average inventory. In a period of rising prices, LIFO provides a lower inventory because cost of sales is made up of higher costs of more recently purchased goods, and inventory is made up of previously purchased, lower cost goods.
Answers (b) and (c) are incorrect because FIFO and weighted average costing result in higher inventory values during rising prices. Answer (d) is incorrect because it is an approach toward inventory record keeping, not an inventory costing system.

8. If one optimizes the inventory turnover ratio, which costs will not increase?

a. Total reorder costs.
b. Stockout costs.
c. Unit reorder costs.
d. Carrying costs.

The correct answer is (d). *(Publisher)*
REQUIRED: The cost that will not increase if the inventory turnover ratio is optimized.
DISCUSSION: Optimizing the inventory turnover ratio means increased cost of goods sold or decreased inventory. When one decreases the level of inventory, one decreases the carrying costs of inventory.
Answers (a) and (c) are incorrect because, with lower inventory levels, there would be more orders of fewer items. Thus total reorder costs will increase, and also unit reorder costs will increase. Answer (b) is incorrect because stockout costs increase as one maintains lower inventory levels.

9. Which condition would justify accepting a low inventory turnover ratio from the point of view of inventory management?

a. High carrying costs.
b. High stockout costs.
c. Short inventory order lead times.
d. Low inventory order costs.

The correct answer is (b). *(Publisher)*
REQUIRED: The condition that might justify acceptance of a low inventory turnover ratio.
DISCUSSION: High stockout costs justify maintaining relatively large inventory levels. If major customers would be lost because of stockouts, the higher costs of maintaining a large safety stock are acceptable.
Answers (a), (c), and (d) are incorrect because high inventory carrying costs, short inventory reorder lead time, and low inventory order costs all encourage more frequent orders of smaller quantities, which result in lower average inventory levels and higher inventory turnover ratio.

10. The control of order-filling costs

a. Can be accomplished through the use of flexible budget standards.
b. Requires a budget that shows budgeted expenses for the average level of activity.
c. Is related to pricing decisions, sales promotion, and customer reaction.
d. Is not crucial because they are typically fixed and not subject to frequent changes.
e. Is not crucial because the order-filling routine is entrenched and external influences are minimal.

The correct answer is (a). *(CMA 1279 4-3)*
REQUIRED: The correct statement about the control of order-filling costs.
DISCUSSION: Order-filling costs can be controlled by essentially the same techniques as those used in any other cost control structure. Thus, flexible budgeting techniques could be usefully applied to controlling order-filling costs.
Answer (b) is incorrect because the budget should be prepared for the appropriate, not the average, activity level. Answer (c) is incorrect because the control of order-filling costs may be only indirectly related to the variables noted. Answer (d) is incorrect because order-filling costs may frequently change. Answer (e) is incorrect because the order-filling routine should be dynamic, and flexible enough to adjust for changes in volume, etc.

11. Which of the following will not affect the budgeting of order-getting costs?

   a. Market research and tests.
   b. Location of distribution warehouses.
   c. Policies and actions of competitors.
   d. Sales promotion policies.
   e. General economic conditions.

The correct answer is (b). *(CMA 1279 4-4)*
REQUIRED: The variable not affecting order-getting costs.
DISCUSSION: Order-getting costs pertain to the variables necessary to obtain a particular order. Thus, budgeting and planning emphasis should be on market research, competitor analysis, promotion policies, general economic conditions, and all related policies and decisions affecting the organization up to the time of getting the order. The location of distribution warehouses is an order-filling cost consideration.

Questions 12 and 13 are based on the following information. Inventory management requires a firm to balance the quantity of inventory on hand for operations with the investment in inventory. Two categories of costs of concern in inventory management are carrying costs and ordering costs.

---

12. The carrying costs associated with inventory management include

   a. Insurance costs, shipping costs, storage costs, and obsolescence.
   b. Storage costs, handling costs, capital invested, and obsolescence.
   c. Purchasing costs, shipping costs, set-up costs, and quantity discounts lost.
   d. Obsolescence, set-up costs, capital invested, and purchasing costs.
   e. Insurance costs, obsolescence, shipping costs, and set-up costs.

The correct answer is (b). *(CMA 687 1-25)*
REQUIRED: The items included in carrying costs.
DISCUSSION: Carrying costs include storage costs, handling costs, insurance costs, interest on capital invested, and obsolescence.
Answer (a) is incorrect because shipping costs are an ordering cost, not a carrying cost. Answer (c) is incorrect because it states various ordering (or manufacturing) costs. Answers (d) and (e) are incorrect because the set-up costs for a production run are equivalent to ordering costs.

13. The ordering costs associated with inventory management include

   a. Insurance costs, purchasing costs, shipping costs, and obsolescence.
   b. Obsolescence, set-up costs, quantity discounts lost, and storage costs.
   c. Quantity discounts lost, storage costs, handling costs, and capital invested.
   d. Purchasing costs, shipping costs, set-up costs, and quantity discounts lost.
   e. Shipping costs, obsolescence, set-up costs, and capital invested.

The correct answer is (d). *(CMA 687 1-26)*
REQUIRED: The items included in ordering costs.
DISCUSSION: Ordering costs include purchasing costs, shipping costs, set-up costs for a production run, and quantity discounts lost.
Answer (a) is incorrect because insurance costs are a carrying cost. Answers (b) and (e) are incorrect because obsolescence, interest on invested capital, and storage costs are carrying costs. Answer (c) is incorrect because storage costs, handling costs, and capital invested are all carrying costs.

17.2 Economic Order Quantity (EOQ)

14. Which of the following could be determined by using the economic order quantity formula?

   a. Optimum size of production run.
   b. Safety stock.
   c. Stockout cost.
   d. Order point.

The correct answer is (a). *(CPA 1181 T-54)*
REQUIRED: The item calculated using the economic order quantity formula.
DISCUSSION: The EOQ is used to show the most economical quantity to purchase, resulting in the least carrying and ordering costs.
Answer (b) is incorrect because the amount of safety stock is determined by the number of stockouts a company will accept. Answer (c) is incorrect because the stockout cost is not affected by the EOQ. Answer (d) is incorrect because the order point is determined by daily usage and the lead time for an order.

15. The estimates necessary to compute the economic order quantity are

   a. Annual usage in units, cost per order, and annual cost of carrying one unit in stock.
   b. Annual usage in units, cost per unit of inventory, and annual cost of carrying one unit in stock.
   c. Annual cost of placing orders, and annual cost of carrying one unit in stock.
   d. Cost per unit of inventory, annual cost of placing orders, and annual carrying cost.

The correct answer is (a). *(CPA 1180 T-36)*
REQUIRED: The estimates necessary to compute the economic order quantity.
DISCUSSION: The estimates necessary to compute the EOQ are the annual usage in units, cost per order, and annual carrying cost per unit.
Answers (b) and (d) are incorrect because the actual cost per unit of inventory is not relevant to the EOQ. Answer (c) is incorrect because the annual estimated usage is needed.

16. The inability to accurately estimate demand is a problem. If demand is greater than the number of units available, sales will be lost. If demand is less than the number of units available, the carrying costs will increase. In order to minimize the costs associated with stocking more or less units than the actual demand, the company should use

   a. Queuing analysis.
   b. Inventory planning techniques.
   c. Linear programming.
   d. Program evaluation review techniques (PERT).

The correct answer is (b). *(CIA 1186 IV-19)*
REQUIRED: The method to minimize stocking more or less units than demanded.
DISCUSSION: Inventories provide a buffer to smooth out the differences in the time and location of demand and supply for a product. The purpose of inventory planning techniques is to determine the optimum level of inventory necessary to minimize costs, which include holding, ordering, and stockout (shortage) costs. Inventory models are quantitative models designed to control inventory costs by determining the optimum time to place an order and the optimum order quantity.
Answer (a) is incorrect because it is a method for minimizing the costs of waiting lines by balancing the cost of waiting against the cost of servicing the lines. Answer (c) is incorrect because it is a means of optimizing a function given specified constraints. Answer (d) is incorrect because PERT network diagrams are a method of controlling complex projects.

17. Some managers express the opinion that their "cash management problems are nothing more than inventory problems." They then proceed to use cash management models, such as the EOQ model, to determine the

   a. Credit and collection policies.
   b. Marketable securities level.
   c. Proper relationship between current assets and current liabilities.
   d. Proper blend of marketable securities and cash.
   e. Proper long-term capitalization.

The correct answer is (d). *(CMA 1286 1-33)*
REQUIRED: The true statement about cash management models.
DISCUSSION: Since cash and inventory are both nonearning assets, in principle they may be treated similarly. The alternative to holding cash, however, is to hold marketable securities that do earn interest or dividends. Thus, a cash management model would determine how much of a firm's liquidity should be held as cash and how much in the form of marketable securities.
Answer (a) is incorrect because credit and collection policies concern receivables and are not influenced by an EOQ model for inventory management. Answer (b) is incorrect because the level of marketable securities is in part determined by cash needs, so (d) is a better answer. Answer (c) is incorrect because the relationship between current assets and current liabilities concerns many factors other than cash management. Answer (e) is incorrect because the proper long-term capitalization is a subject of capital structure finance.

Module 17.2: Economic Order Quantity (EOQ)

18. Which of the following is a relevant factor in the determination of an economic order quantity?

  a. Physical plant insurance costs.
  b. Warehouse supervisory salaries.
  c. Variable costs of processing a purchase order.
  d. Physical plant depreciation charges.

The correct answer is (c). *(CPA 578 T-32)*
REQUIRED: The factor relevant to determining an economic order quantity.
DISCUSSION: To determine the EOQ, one must know reasonably accurate estimates of the carrying cost per unit, the annual usage, and the cost per order. The variable costs of processing a purchase order affect the cost of an order and thus the EOQ.
Answers (a), (b), and (d) are incorrect because physical plant insurance, warehouse supervisory salaries, and depreciation amounts will be incurred regardless of inventory size.

19. A parts supply firm has been having inventory management difficulties. Low inventory levels reduce carrying costs but stockouts tend to be more frequent. In addition, there tend to be more frequent orders of small quantities as a consequence of the stockouts. To improve its inventory management to minimize its carrying and order costs, the company would benefit most by using

  a. Integral calculus.
  b. Cost/volume/profit analysis.
  c. Learning curve techniques.
  d. EOQ modeling.
  e. Matrix algebra.

The correct answer is (d). *(CMA 1280 5-3)*
REQUIRED: The inventory method used to balance carrying and order costs.
DISCUSSION: The EOQ minimizes the cost of inventory, which includes the costs of ordering new inventory and the costs of holding inventory.
Answer (a) is incorrect because integral calculus is concerned with the amount of area under curves. Answer (b) is incorrect because CVP analysis predicts income at different volume levels based on established linear relationships among revenues, fixed costs, and variable costs. Answer (c) is incorrect because learning curve techniques estimate increases in efficiency that occur as time on the job increases. Answer (e) is incorrect because matrix algebra manipulates and solves a large system of linear equations. It is not appropriate for inventory management.

20. When calculating an inventory economic order quantity (EOQ), which of the following factors need not be considered?

  a. Safety stock level.
  b. Order-placing costs.
  c. Storage costs.
  d. Risk of inventory obsolescence and deterioration.
  e. Annual sales of a product.

The correct answer is (a). *(CIA 580 IV-13)*
REQUIRED: The factor that need not be considered in calculating EOQ.
DISCUSSION: The components needed to compute the EOQ are the annual demand (sales), cost of placing an order, and the annual carrying cost (including storage costs) per unit. The risk of obsolescence and deterioration is part of the inventory carrying cost. The safety stock level is not used in the EOQ calculation.

21. Which of the following is included in the economic order quantity formula?

	Inventory Carrying Cost	Stockout Cost
a.	Yes	No
b.	Yes	Yes
c.	No	Yes
d.	No	No

The correct answer is (a). *(CPA 585 T-49)*
REQUIRED: The variables in the economic order quantity formula.
DISCUSSION: The components needed to compute the EOQ are the annual demand (sales), cost of placing an order, and the annual carrying cost (including storage costs) per unit. The risk of obsolescence and deterioration is part of the inventory carrying cost. The stockout cost is not used in the EOQ calculation.

Module 17.2: Economic Order Quantity (EOQ)

22. How would the following be used in the economic order quantity formula?

	Inventory Carrying Cost	Cost per Purchase Order
a.	Numerator	Numerator
b.	Denominator	Numerator
c.	Denominator	Denominator
d.	Not used	Denominator

The correct answer is (b). *(CPA 587 T-50)*
REQUIRED: The economic order quantity formula.
DISCUSSION: The EOQ formula is

$$E = \sqrt{\frac{2AP}{S}}$$

A is the demand, or number of units used or sold per year; P is the cost of placing one order; S is the cost of carrying one unit for 1 year.
Thus, the inventory carrying cost is in the denominator and the cost per purchase order is in the numerator.

23. When economic order quantity (EOQ) models are used in inventory management, the models should be reviewed periodically for reasonableness. A change in which of the following items would cause a change in the quantity ordered, holding the frequency of orders constant and ignoring the cost of money?

a. Reorder point.
b. Unit demand.
c. Lead time.
d. Service level.

The correct answer is (b). *(CIA 586 III-16)*
REQUIRED: The change that would cause a change in quantity ordered, holding frequency of orders constant and ignoring the cost of money.
DISCUSSION: The EOQ formula is

$$X = \sqrt{\frac{2AD}{K}}$$

Where D is the demand, or number of units used per year; A is the cost of placing one order; K is the cost of carrying one unit for 1 year. A change in unit demand would cause a change in the economic order quantity, all other values held equal.
Answers (a), (c), and (d) are incorrect because changes in these factors do not affect the economic order quantity.

24. Siegal Company has correctly computed its economic order quantity as 500 units. However, management would rather order in quantities of 600 units. How will Siegal's total annual purchase order cost and total annual carrying cost for an order quantity of 600 units compare to the respective amounts for an order quantity of 500 units?

a. Higher purchase order cost and higher carrying cost.
b. Lower purchase order cost and lower carrying cost.
c. Higher purchase order cost and lower carrying cost.
d. Lower purchase order cost and higher carrying cost.

The correct answer is (d). *(CPA 1176 P-34)*
REQUIRED: The effect on purchase order and carrying costs of ordering quantities higher than the EOQ.
DISCUSSION: The EOQ model is used to minimize the total of ordering costs and carrying costs. Ordering costs are considered fixed per order, but carrying costs vary with the inventory level. Increasing the order quantity means there will be fewer orders per year, resulting in lower ordering costs per year. The carrying costs per year will increase, however, since units would remain in inventory longer.

25. Assuming that demand is deterministic, what is the essence of the economic order quantity (EOQ) model for inventory?

a. To minimize order costs or carrying costs and maximize the rate of inventory turnover.
b. To minimize order costs or carrying costs, whichever are higher.
c. To order sufficient quantity to meet the next period's demand.
d. To minimize the total of order costs and carrying costs.

The correct answer is (d). *(CPA 575 P-23)*
REQUIRED: The essence of the economic order quantity (EOQ) model for inventory.
DISCUSSION: The main purpose of the EOQ model is to find the number of units to order that will result in the least total of order costs and carrying costs.
Answer (a) is incorrect because the EOQ is not designed to affect inventory turnover. Answer (b) is incorrect because EOQ minimizes both order and carrying costs. Answer (c) is incorrect because the EOQ is the most economical amount to order, minimizing order and carrying costs.

Module 17.2: Economic Order Quantity (EOQ)

26. What effect, if any, will a last-in, first-out or first-in, first-out inventory method have on an economic order quantity?

a. No effect.
b. LIFO will increase the order quantity in times of rising prices.
c. LIFO will reduce the order quantity in times of rising prices.
d. FIFO will increase the order quantity in times of rising prices.

The correct answer is (a). *(CPA 577 T-41)*
REQUIRED: The effect of a LIFO or FIFO inventory method on an EOQ.
DISCUSSION: The EOQ is computed by using the annual quantity, cost per order, and the annual carrying cost per unit. The inventory method has no effect on these components of the EOQ, and therefore has no effect on the EOQ.

27. Given the following information, identify the correct calculation for the economic order quantity (EOQ).

Cost per purchase order	$20.00
Annual cost of carrying one unit in stock for 1 year	$.60
Annual quantity used in units	10,000

a. $\sqrt{\dfrac{2(10,000)(\$20)}{\$.60}}$

b. $\sqrt{\dfrac{10,000 \times \$20}{\$.60}}$

c. $\sqrt{\dfrac{2(10,000)(\$.60)}{\$20}}$

d. $\sqrt{\dfrac{10,000 \times \$.60}{\$20}}$

The correct answer is (a). *(CIA 1187 IV-20)*
REQUIRED: The correct calculation for the economic order quantity (EOQ).
DISCUSSION: The EOQ formula is

$$E = \sqrt{\dfrac{2AP}{S}} = \sqrt{\dfrac{2(10,000)(\$20)}{\$.60}}$$

A is the demand, or number of units used or sold per year; P is the cost of placing one order; S is the cost of carrying one unit for 1 year.

28. If a retail outlet has predictable order lead times and accurate consumer demand forecasts, the investment in merchandise inventory should be

a. A function of the economic order quantity and the optimum safety stock level.
b. A function of the expected average daily consumer demand.
c. At the point where the per-unit inventory carrying cost exceeds the stockout costs.
d. All of the above.
e. Answers (b) and (c) above.

The correct answer is (a). *(CIA 578 IV-5)*
REQUIRED: How the investment in inventory should be determined.
DISCUSSION: The economic order quantity is the increment of inventory ordered each time it is replenished. The optimum safety stock level determines the amount of inventory that should be kept on hand at all times. Both figures are necessary to determine investment in inventory.
Answer (b) is incorrect because the consumer demand forecasts are only one element in determining optimum inventory investment levels. The other EOQ elements and the safety stock level must also be considered. Answer (c) is incorrect because per unit inventory costs have no impact on stockout costs.

29. A ski manufacturing company dates invoices seasonally so that skis delivered in September will bear an invoice due date for the following February. Generally, by using this method, the manufacturer's inventory carrying costs are (lower; higher; constant) and the buyer is extended a (shorter; longer) credit period than would otherwise be the case.

a. Lower, longer.
b. Higher, longer.
c. Lower, shorter.
d. Higher, shorter.
e. Constant, longer.

The correct answer is (a). *(CIA 1182 IV-30)*
REQUIRED: The effect of a manufacturer's inventory practices on inventory carrying costs and the credit period.
DISCUSSION: By shipping the skis in September, the manufacturer transfers warehousing costs to the purchaser. Thus, the manufacturer's carrying costs are lower than would otherwise be the case. By invoicing for payment in February (5 months later), the credit terms extended to the customers are longer.
Answers (b), (d), and (e) are incorrect because carrying costs would be lower since items are not held in the ski manufacturer's inventory as long. Answer (c) is incorrect because 5 months is longer than the usual credit period of, say, 20 days.

Module 17.2: Economic Order Quantity (EOQ)

30. If Maxim's purchasing department orders raw materials in quantities larger than the optimum quantity recommended by the simple economic order quantity model to take advantage of a quantity discount, the company will experience

a. Carrying costs lower than if the optimum quantity were ordered.
b. Ordering costs higher than if the optimum quantity were ordered.
c. Ordering costs the same as if the optimum quantity were ordered.
d. Carrying costs higher than if the optimum were ordered, but lower ordering costs.
e. Ordering costs higher than if the optimum were ordered, but lower carrying costs.

The correct answer is (d). *(CMA 1278 5-24)*
REQUIRED: The effect on carrying and ordering costs of ordering quantities larger than EOQ.
DISCUSSION: If the company orders larger amounts to obtain the quantity discount, there will be greater quantities on hand. Therefore, carrying costs will be higher than the optimum, but ordering costs will be lower because they will order fewer times per year.
Answers (a) and (e) are incorrect because carrying costs would be higher since more units are on hand. Answers (b), (c), and (e) are incorrect because ordering costs would be lower, since the company is ordering fewer times per year.

31. For its economic order quantity model a company has a $10 cost of placing an order, and $2 annual cost of carrying one unit in stock. If the cost of placing an order increases by 20%, and the annual cost of carrying one unit in stock increases by 25%, and all other considerations remain constant, the economic order quantity will

a. Remain unchanged.
b. Decrease.
c. Increase.
d. Either increase or decrease depending on the reorder point.

The correct answer is (b). *(CPA 576 T-28)*
REQUIRED: The effect of equal increases in the cost of placing an order and the carrying cost on the EOQ.
DISCUSSION: The EOQ formula is

$$E = \sqrt{\frac{2AP}{S}}$$

where A = annual quantity used,
P = cost per order, and
S = annual carrying cost of one unit.

Plugging in the original ordering cost of $10 and the unit carrying cost of $2, the resulting EOQ is the square root of 10A. Simplify the calculations by removing A and the square root sign:

Original: $\frac{2 \times 10}{2} = 10$

20% changes: $\frac{2 \times 12}{2.5} = 9.6$

Answers (a) and (c) are incorrect because an increase in ordering and carrying costs will decrease the EOQ. Answer (d) is incorrect because the reorder point does not affect the EOQ.

32. The basic economic order quantity decision model can best be described as

a. Probabilistic, numerical, and descriptive.
b. Probabilistic, analytical, and optimizing.
c. Deterministic, numerical, and descriptive.
d. Deterministic, analytical, and optimizing.
e. Probabilistic, analytical, and descriptive.

The correct answer is (d). *(CMA 1277 5-9)*
REQUIRED: The best description of the basic EOQ decision model.
DISCUSSION: The EOQ is determinable because there are no probabilistic quantities. All elements of the EOQ formula are known (i.e., reasonably accurate estimates). The EOQ is analytical in that it analyzes the best order quantity in terms of several other factors. The EOQ is optimizing, since it balances optimal quantity to order with the least costs.
Answers (a), (b), and (e) are incorrect because the EOQ is not probabilistic. Answer (c) is incorrect because numerical is a meaningless quality in the context of optimization models; they are all quantitative. Answers (a), (c), and (e) are also incorrect because the EOQ is prescriptive (i.e., tells us what to do) rather than descriptive.

33. A company places orders for inventory with its suppliers for a certain item. The order size is determined in advance as

$$\text{Order Size} = \sqrt{\frac{2 \times \text{Cost to Place One Order} \times \text{Demand per Period}}{\text{Cost to Hold One Unit for One Period}}}$$

All orders are the same size. When the policy is implemented, demand per period is only half of what was expected when the order size was computed. Consequently, actual total inventory cost will be

a. Larger than if the expected demand per period had occurred and larger than if the actual demand per period had been used to calculate order size.

b. Larger than if the expected demand per period had occurred and smaller than if the actual demand per period had been used to calculate order size.

c. Smaller than if the expected demand per period had occurred and larger than if the actual demand per period had been used to calculate order size.

d. Smaller than if the expected demand per period had occurred and smaller than if the actual demand per period had been used to calculate order size.

The correct answer is (c). *(CPA 1175 P-26)*
REQUIRED: The effect on actual total inventory cost if demand per period is only half of what was expected when order size was computed.
DISCUSSION: Actual inventory costs will lie somewhere between the original EOQ formula's costs and the costs if the actually incurred demand had been used in the formula. The total inventory cost will be smaller than if the expected demand per period had occurred because the order costs will be lower. The total inventory cost will be larger than if the actual demand per period had been used to calculate the order size, however, because more carrying costs must be incurred to carry the larger-than-expected inventory.

34. Which of the following is not involved in the computation of the economic order quantity (EOQ)?

a. Lead time from order placement until order fulfillment.

b. Number of units expected to be sold or used during the year.

c. Cost of placing and receiving an order.

d. Cost of obtaining capital.

e. None of the above.

The correct answer is (a). *(CIA 577 IV-17)*
REQUIRED: The item not involved in computing the economic order quantity.
DISCUSSION: Lead time is used in weighing stockout costs and determining the order point, not quantity.
Answers (b), (c), and (d) are incorrect because each is used in computing the EOQ.

17.3 Reorder Points, Safety Stock, Stockout Cost

35. For inventory management, ignoring safety stocks, which of the following is a valid computation of the reorder point?

a. The economic order quantity.

b. The economic order quantity times the anticipated demand during lead time.

c. The anticipated demand per day during lead time times lead time in days.

d. The square root of the anticipated demand during the lead time.

The correct answer is (c). *(CPA 576 P-36)*
REQUIRED: The valid computation of the reorder point, ignoring safety stocks.
DISCUSSION: The order point (the quantity of remaining inventory signalling time to order) is found by multiplying the usage per day by the lead time in days.
Answer (a) is incorrect because the EOQ is used to determine the most efficient quantity to order. Answers (b) and (d) are incorrect because each is an irrelevant number.

36. The Polly Company wishes to determine the amount of safety stock that it should maintain for Product D that will result in the lowest cost. The following information is available:

Stockout cost	$80 per occurrence
Carrying cost of safety stock	$2 per unit
Number of purchase orders	5 per year

The options available to Polly are as follows:

Units of Safety Stock	Probability of Running Out of Safety Stock
10	50%
20	40%
30	30%
40	20%
50	10%
55	5%

The number of units of safety stock that will result in the lowest cost is

a. 20.
b. 40.
c. 50.
d. 55.

37. A business determines its inventory policy using the economic order quantity model that allows a finite stockout cost per period and backordering. Which of the following statements accurately describes that stockout cost?

a. The stockout cost will have to be accumulated in a special account for comparison with expected stockout cost.
b. The smaller the stockout cost, the more often stockout will occur.
c. The larger the stockout cost, the more often stockout will occur.
d. The smaller the stockout cost, the larger the average amount of inventory on hand will be.

38. The amount of inventory that a company would tend to hold in safety stock would increase as the

a. Sales level falls to a permanently lower level.
b. Cost of carrying inventory decreases.
c. Variability of sales decreases.
d. Cost of running out of stock decreases.
e. Length of time that goods are in transit decreases.

The correct answer is (d). *(CPA 579 P-28)*
REQUIRED: The number of units of safety stock resulting in the lowest cost.
DISCUSSION: Each alternative must be considered. The cost of safety stock is computed by multiplying the number of units of safety stock by the carrying cost per unit ($2). The estimated stockout cost is computed by multiplying the probability of a stockout by the stockout cost. The total stockout cost is the stockout cost per order times the number of orders per year (5). The total cost is determined by adding the carrying cost to the estimated stockout cost.

Safety Stock	Carrying Cost	Stockout Cost/order	Stockout Cost/5 orders	Total Cost
20	$ 40	$32	$160	$200
40	80	16	80	160
50	100	8	40	140
55	110	4	20	130

Therefore, the lowest costs will result if 55 units of safety stock are carried.

The correct answer is (b). *(CPA 1175 P-28)*
REQUIRED: The accurate statement describing stockout cost.
DISCUSSION: Stockout cost is an imputed cost established by management to represent the loss of customer goodwill and the loss of contribution margin because of inadequate inventory. If the stockout cost is small, the cost of inadequate inventory may be preferable to the costs of maintaining higher inventory levels.
Answer (a) is incorrect because stockout costs are primarily opportunity costs, which are not recorded in the accounting system. Answer (c) is incorrect because the larger the stockout costs, the more likely stockout will be avoided by carrying higher inventory levels. Answer (d) is incorrect because a smaller stockout cost would reduce the average inventory kept on hand.

The correct answer is (b). *(CMA 1285 1-5)*
REQUIRED: The factor that would cause the amount of inventory in safety stock to increase.
DISCUSSION: The optimum safety stock is that equating carrying cost with the opportunity cost of a stockout. The main disadvantage of holding a safety stock is the high carrying cost. If carrying costs were to decrease, it would be advantageous to increase safety stock and reduce further the risk of a costly stockout.
Answer (a) is incorrect because a reduction in sales levels would either decrease the need for a safety stock or result in no change. Answers (c), (d), and (e) are incorrect because each decreases the need for a safety stock.

39. A distribution company uses a reorder point inventory system. The company has just increased the service level objective on all of its items by placing orders more frequently. This action should lead to

a. Increased demand.
b. Increased cost per order.
c. Lower holding costs.
d. Lower shortage costs.

The correct answer is (d). *(CIA 1186 III-42)*
REQUIRED: The effect of increasing the service level.
DISCUSSION: Stockout (shortage) costs should decline because orders are placed more often. However, inventory carrying costs and total order costs will increase.
Answer (a) is incorrect because the frequency of orders does not affect customer demand. Answer (b) is incorrect because more frequent orders should not affect the cost per order. Answer (c) is incorrect because holding costs will increase when more inventory is maintained.

17.4 Computations

40. The following information pertains to material X used by Sage Co.:

Annual usage in units	20,000
Working days per year	250
Safety stock in units	800
Normal lead time in working days	30

Units of material X will be required evenly throughout the year. The order point is

a. 800.
b. 1,600.
c. 2,400.
d. 3,200.

The correct answer is (d). *(CPA 585 Q-11)*
REQUIRED: The order point given usage, work days, safety stock, and lead time.
DISCUSSION: The order point is determined by multiplying the units used per day by the normal lead time and adjusting for safety stock.

Daily usage (20,000 ÷ 250)	80
Days of lead time	x 30
	2,400
Safety stock	800
Order point	3,200

41. The following information relates to Eagle Company's material A:

Annual usage in units	7,200
Working days per year	240
Normal lead time in working days	20
Maximum lead time in working days	45

Assuming that the units of material A will be required evenly throughout the year, the safety stock and order point would be

	Safety Stock	Order Point
a.	600	750
b.	600	1,350
c.	750	600
d.	750	1,350

The correct answer is (d). *(CPA 580 P-38)*
REQUIRED: The safety stock and order point, assuming steady use throughout the year.
DISCUSSION: The order point is computed by multiplying the units used per day by the maximum lead time. The units used per day are the annual usage in units divided by the working days per year. Here, the order point is 1,350 [(7,200 ÷ 240) x 45]. The safety stock is computed by multiplying the difference between the normal lead time and the maximum lead time by the daily usage. Thus, Eagle's safety stock is

$$(45 - 20) \times (7,200 \div 240) = 750$$

42. Retif Company's budgeted sales and budgeted cost of sales for the coming year are $144,000,000 and $90,000,000, respectively. Short-term interest rates are expected to average 10%. If Retif can increase inventory turnover from its present level of 9 times per year to a level of 12 times per year, its cost savings in the coming year would be expected to be

a. $450,000.
b. $400,000.
c. $600,000.
d. $250,000.

The correct answer is (d). *(CMA 686 I-1)*
REQUIRED: The cost savings resulting from an increase in the inventory turnover rate.
DISCUSSION: The average inventory would decline from $10,000,000 ($90,000,000 ÷ 9) to $7,500,000 ($90,000,000 ÷ 12). At 10% interest, the savings in interest would amount to $250,000 annually ($2,500,000 inventory reduction x 10%).

43. The sales office of Helms, Inc. has developed the following probability distribution for daily sales of a perishable product:

X (Units Sold)	P (Sales = X)
100	.2
150	.5
200	.2
250	.1

The product is restocked at the start of each day. If the company desires a 90% service level in satisfying sales demand, the initial stock balance for each day should be

a. 250.
b. 160.
c. 200.
d. 150.

The correct answer is (c). *(CPA 574 P-13)*
REQUIRED: The initial stock balance for each day.
DISCUSSION: The initial daily stock level can be determined by adding the probabilities until .9 is reached. The corresponding unit sales at that point (200) equals the number of units needed in stock.

Questions 44 through 47 are based on the Gerald Company, whose management has targeted a desired 10% annual return on inventory investment. The data in the opposite column are available:

Optimal production run	500
Average inventory in units	250
Number of production runs	10
Cost per unit produced	$4
Set-up costs per production run	$10

---

44. What is the EOQ for Gerald Company?

a. 250.
b. 500.
c. 2,500.
d. 5,000.

The correct answer is (b). *(Publisher)*
REQUIRED: The economic order quantity for the company.
DISCUSSION: The economic order quantity is the order quantity that minimizes the sum of inventory ordering costs and inventory carrying costs. Since the optimal production run is given as 500 units, that is the EOQ.

45. Assuming that the units will be required evenly throughout the year, what are the total annual relevant costs using the EOQ approach?

a. $200.
b. $350.
c. $1,350.
d. $2,625.

The correct answer is (a). *(CPA 580 P-31)*
REQUIRED: The total annual relevant costs using the economic order quantity approach.
DISCUSSION: The EOQ approach can also be used for companies that produce their own inventory of parts or units for later processing. The two elements included in the annual costs under the EOQ model are total annual set-up costs (analogous to ordering costs) and the total annual costs to carry the average number of units in inventory for one year. Note that carrying costs include the desired rate of return on the investment in inventory.

Set-up costs ($10 x 10 runs)	$100
Carrying costs (10% x 250 units x $4)	100
Annual costs	$200

46. What is Gerald's cost of carrying one unit in inventory for 1 year?

a. $.10.
b. $.40.
c. $.50.
d. $1.00.

The correct answer is (b). *(Publisher)*
REQUIRED: The annual unit inventory carrying cost.
DISCUSSION: The cost per inventory unit is $4; the desired annual return on inventory investment is 10%, or $.40. Note that in Q. 45 the total inventory carrying cost for 250 units was $100. Thus, another way to compute annual unit carrying cost is $100 ÷ 250 units = $.40.

47. Refer to the data preceding Q. 44. What is the EOQ formula for Gerald?

a. $500 = \sqrt{\dfrac{2 \times 5{,}000 \times \$10}{S}}$

b. $250 = \sqrt{\dfrac{2AP}{S}}$

c. $250 = \sqrt{\dfrac{2 \times 5{,}000 \times \$10}{S}}$

d. $500 = \sqrt{\dfrac{2 \times 2{,}500 \times \$.40}{S}}$

The correct answer is (a). *(Publisher)*
REQUIRED: The EOQ formula for this company.
DISCUSSION: The EOQ, which considers the cost of setting up production runs (analogous to ordering costs) and carrying costs per unit of inventory, can be expressed by the formula

$$EOQ = \sqrt{\dfrac{2AP}{S}}$$

where A = Annual quantity used in units,
P = Set-up costs, and
S = Annual cost of carrying one unit in inventory ($.40, per Q. 46)

48. Garmar, Inc. has determined the following for a given year:

Economic order quantity
(standard order size) — 5,000 units
Total cost to place purchase orders
for the year — $10,000
Cost to place one purchase order — $50
Cost to carry one unit for 1 year — $4

What is Garmar's estimated annual usage in units?

a. 1,000,000.
b. 2,000,000.
c. 4,000,000.
d. Cannot be determined from the data.

The correct answer is (a). *(CPA 1176 P-33)*
REQUIRED: The estimated annual usage in units given EOQ and costs.
DISCUSSION: To find the number of orders placed in one year, the total cost to place purchase orders for the year should be divided by the cost to place one purchase order. Multiply the number of orders by the EOQ to find the estimated annual usage in units. Garmar's estimated annual usage in units is thus 1,000,000 [(10,000 ÷ 50) × 5,000].

49. Politan Company manufactures bookcases. Set-up costs are $2.00. Politan manufactures 4,000 bookcases evenly throughout the year. Using the economic order quantity approach, the optimal production run would be 200 when the cost of carrying one bookcase in inventory for one year is

a. $.05.
b. $.10.
c. $.20.
d. $.40.

The correct answer is (d). *(CPA 1179 P-31)*
REQUIRED: The cost of carrying one unit in inventory for one year, given the optimal production run.
DISCUSSION: The EOQ considers the cost of setting up production runs (analogous to ordering costs) and carrying costs per unit of inventory. The formula is

$$E = \sqrt{\dfrac{2AP}{S}}$$

where A = Annual quantity used in units,
P = Set-up costs, and
S = Annual cost of carrying one unit in inventory

The cost of carrying one bookcase is

$$200 = \sqrt{\dfrac{2 \times 4{,}000 \times \$2.00}{S}}$$

$$40{,}000 = \dfrac{2 \times 4{,}000 \times \$2.00}{S}$$

$$40{,}000S = \$16{,}000$$

$$S = \$.40$$

50. The following data refer to various annual costs relating to the inventory of a single-product company:

Unit Transportation-in on purchases	$.20
Storage per unit	.12
Insurance per unit	.10
Annual interest forgone from alternate investment of funds	$800
Annual number of units required	10,000

What is the annual carrying cost per unit?

a. $.22.
b. $.30.
c. $.42.
d. $.50.

The correct answer is (b). *(CPA 1175 P-29)*
REQUIRED: The annual carrying cost per unit of inventory.
DISCUSSION: The carrying costs include the costs of storage ($.12), insurance ($.10), and annual interest that could have been earned from an alternate investment of funds ($800 ÷ 10,000 units, or $.08 per unit). Therefore, total carrying cost per unit is $.30 ($.12 + $.10 + $.08).
Note that transportation-in costs are ignored because they are costs of obtaining, not carrying, the inventory.

51. Pierce, Inc. must manufacture 10,000 blades for its electric lawn mower division. The blades will be used evenly throughout the year. The set-up cost every time a production run is made is $80, and the cost to carry a blade in inventory for the year is $.40. Pierce's objective is to produce the blades at the lowest cost possible. Assuming that each production run will be for the same number of blades, how many production runs should Pierce make?

a. 3.
b. 4.
c. 5.
d. 6.

The correct answer is (c). *(CPA 1177 P-26)*
REQUIRED: The economic number of production runs.
DISCUSSION: To determine the optimal number of production runs, the economic order quantity must first be determined. The annual demand is divided by the EOQ to determine the optimal number of production runs. The EOQ is 2,000, as computed below.

$$E = \sqrt{\frac{2AP}{S}} = \sqrt{\frac{(2)(10,000)(\$80)}{\$.40}} = 2,000$$

where A = Annual demand,
P = Set-up costs, and
S = Cost to carry one unit.

Pierce should make 5 production runs (10,000 ÷ 2,000) during the year.

52. The Hancock Company wishes to determine the amount of safety stock they should maintain for Product No. 135 to result in the lowest cost. Each stockout costs $75 and the carrying costs of each unit of safety stock is $1. Product No. 135 will be ordered five times a year. Which of the following will produce the lowest cost?

a. A safety stock of 10 units which is associated with a 40% probability of running out of stock during an order period.
b. A safety stock of 20 units which is associated with a 20% probability of running out of stock during an order period.
c. A safety stock of 40 units which is associated with a 10% probability of running out of stock during an order period.
d. A safety stock of 80 units which is associated with a 5% probability of running out of stock during an order period.

The correct answer is (c). *(CPA 1177 P-32)*
REQUIRED: The level of safety stock and associated probability of running out that will produce the lowest cost.
DISCUSSION: To determine the number of units in safety stock that will result in the lowest cost, each alternative must be considered. The carrying cost of safety stock is the number of units of safety stock multiplied by the carrying costs per unit ($1). The estimated total stockout cost is the probability of a stockout times the stockout cost. The total stockout cost is the stockout cost per order times the number of orders per year. The total cost is the carrying cost plus the estimated total stockout cost. The lowest cost results when 40 units are carried in safety stock, as shown below.

Safety Stock	Carrying Cost	Stockout Cost/order	Stockout Cost/5 orders	Total Cost
10	$10	$30.00	$150.00	$160.00
20	20	15.00	75.00	95.00
40	40	7.50	37.50	77.50
80	80	3.75	18.75	98.75

Module 17.4: Computations

Questions 53 and 54 are based on the expected annual usage of a particular raw material of 2,000,000 units, and a standard order size of 10,000 units. The invoice cost of each unit is $500, and the cost to place one purchase order is $80.

53. The average inventory is

   a. 1,000,000 units.
   b. 5,000 units.
   c. 10,000 units.
   d. 7,500 units.

The correct answer is (b). *(CPA 574 P-4)*
REQUIRED: The average inventory given expected annual usage and standard order size.
DISCUSSION: The average inventory assuming no safety stock is computed by dividing the standard order size by two. Therefore, average inventory is 5,000 (10,000 ÷ 2).

54. The estimated annual order cost is

   a. $16,000.
   b. $100,000.
   c. $32,000.
   d. $50,000.

The correct answer is (a). *(CPA 574 P-5)*
REQUIRED: The estimated annual order cost given expected annual usage, standard order size, and the cost to place an order.
DISCUSSION: The annual order cost is computed by multiplying the cost per order by the number of orders per year. The number of orders per year is the annual usage divided by the standard order size. The estimated annual order cost is $16,000 [$80 x (2,000,000 ÷ 10,000)].

Questions 55 and 56 are based on the following information.
Assume an economic order quantity model with:

Annual Demand:	2,000 units	Price:	$7 per unit
Order Cost:	$30 per order	Lead Time:	5 working days
Holding Cost:	$12 per unit per year	EOQ:	100 units

EOQ formula = $\sqrt{2AD/k}$

Where:
A = cost per order
D = annual demand in units
k = annual carrying costs per unit

55. If the order cost ($30 per order) decreased by 10% the EOQ would be

   a. 90.
   b. 95.
   c. 105.
   d. 110.

The correct answer is (b). *(CIA 1187 III-37)*
REQUIRED: The EOQ given a decrease in order cost.
DISCUSSION: This problem simply requires substituting a changed value of A in the EOQ formula. A 10% reduction in the order cost gives a value of A equal to 27 (.9 x 30). Rounded to the nearest unit, the new EOQ is 95.

$$\sqrt{\frac{2 \times \$27 \times 2000}{\$12}} = 94.868$$

56. If backorders could be taken (at an added cost of $6 per item backordered), then

   a. EOQ would decrease.
   b. EOQ would increase.
   c. Lead time would decrease.
   d. There would be no change; backorders do not affect the EOQ model.

The correct answer is (b). *(CIA 1187 III-38)*
REQUIRED: The effect of providing for back orders in the EOQ model.
DISCUSSION: A back order is a sale made when the item is not in stock. If back orders are possible, inventory can be maintained at lower levels. Hence, the EOQ model is modified for the cost (b) of back orders. The new formula is

$$\sqrt{\frac{2AD}{k\left(\frac{b}{b+k}\right)}}$$

Substituting in the formula, and assuming the original $30 order cost, the new EOQ is 173.
Answer (a) is incorrect because EOQ increased from 100 to 173. Answer (c) is incorrect because lead time is not affected. Answer (d) is incorrect because the back order cost must be included in the model since the back order system replaces inventory.

Module 17.4: Computations

Questions 57 through 59 are based on Thoran Electronics, which began producing pacemakers last year. At that time the company forecasted the need for 10,000 integrated circuits annually. During the first year the company placed orders when the inventory dropped to 600 units so it would have enough to produce pacemakers continuously during a 3-week lead time. Unfortunately, the company ran out of this component on several occasions, causing costly production delays. Careful study of last year's experience resulted in the data in the opposite column.

Weekly Usage	Related Probability of Usage	Lead Time	Related Probability of Lead Time
280 units	.2	3 weeks	.1
180 units	.8	2 weeks	.9
	1.0		1.0

The study also suggested that usage during a given week was statistically independent of usage during any other week and that usage was also statistically independent of lead time.

57. Thoran's expected average usage during a regular production week is

a. 180 units.
b. 200 units.
c. 280 units.
d. 460 units.
e. None of the above.

The correct answer is (b). *(CMA 679 5-16)*
REQUIRED: The expected average usage during a regular production week.
DISCUSSION: The expected average usage is the weighted average weekly usage, which is computed by multiplying each estimated usage by the corresponding probability, and adding these products together. The expected average usage is thus

$$(280 \times .2) + (180 \times .8) = 200$$

58. The expected usage during lead time is

a. 840 units.
b. 400 units.
c. 360 units.
d. 420 units.
e. None of the above.

The correct answer is (d). *(CMA 679 5-17)*
REQUIRED: The expected usage during lead time.
DISCUSSION: The expected usage during lead time is the weighted average lead time times the average weekly usage (200; see Q. 57). The weighted average lead time is computed by multiplying each lead time by its corresponding probability:

$$(2 \text{ wks.} \times .9) + (3 \text{ wks.} \times .1) = 2.1$$

Expected usage during lead time is thus 420 (2.1 x 200).

59. If the company reorders integrated circuits when the inventory has dropped to a level of 700 units, the probability that it will run out of this component before the order is received is

a. .0008.
b. .0040.
c. .0104.
d. .0400.
e. None of the above.

The correct answer is (c). *(CMA 679 5-18)*
REQUIRED: The probability the company will run out of inventory.
DISCUSSION: Running out of components can only occur if there is a 3-week lead time because with a 2-week lead time, even if 280 units are sold each week, inventory of 140 units would remain [700 - (2 x 280)].
Considering the possibilities with a 3-week lead time, 700 units of sales can only be exceeded if 280 units are sold each week, or if 280 units are sold in 2 weeks and 180 units are sold in the third. The probability of 280 units being sold 3 weeks in a row is .008 (.2 x .2 x .2). The probability of 280 units demanded for 2 weeks and 180 units demanded for 1 week is .032 (.2 x .2 x .8). But there are three possible combinations of 2 weeks at 280 and 1 week at 180, so the .032 must be multiplied by 3, .096. The probability of stockout is summarized below.

Week 1	Week 2	Week 3	Probability
280(.2)	280(.2)	280(.2)	.008
280(.2)	280(.2)	180(.8)	.032
180(.8)	280(.2)	280(.2)	.032
280(.2)	180(.8)	280(.2)	.032
			.104

Probability of 3-week lead time   x .10
Probability of running out of stock given a 700-unit inventory   .0104

Questions 60 through 64 are based on Gerstein Company, which manufactures a line of deluxe office fixtures. The annual demand for its miniature oak file is estimated to be 5,000 units. The annual cost of carrying one unit in inventory is $10, and the cost to initiate a production run is $1,000. There are no miniature oak files on hand, and Gerstein has scheduled four equal production runs of the miniature oak file for the coming year, the first of which is to be run immediately. Gerstein has 250 business days per year. Assume that sales occur uniformly throughout the year and that production is instantaneous.

60. If Gerstein Company does not maintain a safety stock, the estimated total carrying costs for the miniature oak files for the coming year is

   a. $5,000.
   b. $6,250.
   c. $4,000.
   d. $10,250.

The correct answer is (b). *(CMA 1285 5-12)*
REQUIRED: The estimated carrying cost for the year assuming no safety stock.
DISCUSSION: With a demand of 5,000 units, no safety stock, and four runs, each run produces 1,250 units. The maximum inventory is 1,250, which would decline to zero by the time of the next run. Thus, the average inventory is 625 units (1,250 ÷ 2). The total annual carrying cost is $6,250 (625 x $10 per unit).

61. The estimated total set-up costs for the miniature oak files for the coming year is

   a. $5,000.
   b. $6,250.
   c. $4,000.
   d. $10,250.

The correct answer is (c). *(CMA 1285 5-13)*
REQUIRED: The estimated total set-up costs for the year.
DISCUSSION: Given four scheduled production runs and a set-up cost of $1,000 per run, the annual cost is $4,000.

62. If Gerstein were to schedule two equal production runs of the miniature oak files for the coming year, instead of four equal runs, the sum of carrying costs and set-up costs for the coming year would increase (decrease) by

   a. $4,250.
   b. $(2,000).
   c. $6,250.
   d. $(250).

The correct answer is (a). *(CMA 1285 5-14)*
REQUIRED: The change in the sum of annual carrying costs and set-up costs if the number of production runs is reduced.
DISCUSSION: As computed in the two preceding questions, the sum of the annual carrying and set-up costs is $10,250 for four production runs ($6,250 + $4,000). Set-up costs for two production runs are $2,000 per year. However, the carrying costs will increase because the average inventory will double to 1,250 units (2,500 ÷ 2). The carrying costs will be $12,500 (1,250 x $10). Thus, total costs will be $14,500 ($2,000 + $12,500), an increase of $4,250 ($14,500 - $10,250).

63. The number of production runs per year of the miniature oak files that would minimize the sum of carrying costs and set-up costs for the coming year is

   a. 7.
   b. 2.
   c. 4.
   d. 5.

The correct answer is (d). *(CMA 1285 5-15)*
REQUIRED: The annual number of production runs that would minimize the sum of carrying and set-up costs.
DISCUSSION: The EOQ is the square root of the following quantity: (twice annual demand x set-up cost) ÷ unit carrying cost. The EOQ is therefore the square root of 1,000,000 [(2 x 5,000 x $1,000) ÷ $10], or 1,000. Since annual demand is 5,000 units and the EOQ is 1,000, five production runs should be scheduled.

64. A safety stock of a 5-day supply of miniature oak files would increase Gerstein's planned average inventory in units by

   a. 0.
   b. 50.
   c. 100.
   d. 500.

The correct answer is (c). *(CMA 1285 5-16)*
REQUIRED: The increase in planned average inventory if a safety stock is maintained.
DISCUSSION: Given 250 business days to sell 5,000 units, average daily sales will be 20 units. A 5-day supply is thus 100 units.

Module 17.4: Computations

65. Ral Co. sells 20,000 radios evenly throughout the year. The cost of carrying one unit in inventory for 1 year is $8, and the purchase order cost per order is $32. What is the economic order quantity?

  a. 625.
  b. 400.
  c. 283.
  d. 200.

The correct answer is (b). *(CPA 587 Q-22)*
REQUIRED: The economic order quantity.
DISCUSSION: The EOQ is

$$EOQ = \sqrt{\frac{2AP}{S}}$$

A is the annual quantity used in units; P is the cost per order; S is the annual carrying cost per unit.

$$EOQ = \sqrt{\frac{2(20,000)(\$32)}{\$8}}$$

$$EOQ = \sqrt{160,000}$$

$$EOQ = 400 \text{ units}$$

> Questions 66 and 67 are based on H.P. Maxim Co., which uses a simple economic order quantity (EOQ) model that assumes instantaneous replenishment and known constant demand to minimize the sum of ordering costs and carrying costs for a raw material used in the manufacturing of toys.

66. An analytical technique useful in finding the order quantity that minimizes the sum of these costs is

  a. Line of balance.
  b. Integral calculus.
  c. Probability theory.
  d. Linear algebra.
  e. Differential calculus.

The correct answer is (e). *(CMA 1278 5-22)*
REQUIRED: The analytical technique useful in finding the order quantity that minimizes ordering and carrying costs.
DISCUSSION: Differential calculus can be used to find the point at which costs are at a minimum or maximum. The minimum/maximum point is where the slope of the total cost curve equals zero.
Answer (a) is incorrect because line of balance is not an analytical technique. Answer (b) is incorrect because integral calculus is used to find the area under a curve. Answer (c) is incorrect because probabilities are not involved in this problem. Answer (d) is incorrect because the total cost curve is not a linear equation.

67. If the annual total of ordering and carrying costs is given by the equation

$$y = (200,000 \div x) + .05x,$$

in which x is the number of units in each order, the quantity ordered that minimizes this total is

  a. 633 units.
  b. 2,000 units.
  c. 6,325 units.
  d. 4,000 units.
  e. None of the above.

The correct answer is (b). *(CMA 1278 5-23)*
REQUIRED: The order quantity to minimize total of ordering and carrying costs.
DISCUSSION: The order quantity to minimize total cost can be found using differential calculus by taking the first derivative of the given equation, setting the rate of change at zero, and solving for x, as shown below.

$$y = 200,000 \div x + .05x$$
$$y' = -200,000 \div x^2 + .05$$
$$\text{Let } \quad 0 = -200,000 \div x^2 + .05$$
$$0 = -200,000 + .05x^2$$
$$-.05x^2 = -200,000$$
$$x^2 = 4,000,000$$
$$x = 2,000$$

If you are not familiar with derivatives, the problem can be solved by trial and error. Plug each answer choice into the equation (i.e., let x = 633, 2,000, 6,325, and 4,000). The number resulting in the lowest cost is the answer; it is the minimum total cost.

Questions 68 through 70 are based on the following information. As the accounting consultant for Leslie Company you have compiled data on the day-to-day demand from Leslie's customers for Product A and the lead time to receive Product A from its supplier. The data are summarized in the probability tables presented in the opposite column. Leslie is able to deliver Product A to its customers the same day that Product A is received from its supplier. All units of Product A demanded but not available, due to a stockout, are back-ordered and are filled immediately when a new shipment arrives.

Unit Demand per Day	Probability of Occurrence
0	.45
1	.15
2	.30
3	.10
	1.00

Lead Time in Days	Probability of Occurrence
1	.40
2	.35
3	.25
	1.00

68. The probability of the demand for Product A being nine units during a 3-day lead time for delivery from the supplier is

a. .00025.

b. .10.

c. .025.

d. .25.

The correct answer is (a). *(CPA 573 P-16)*
REQUIRED: The probability of a given demand for Product A during a given lead time.
DISCUSSION: The probability that demand for Product A will be nine units during a 3-day lead time is the probability of selling nine units in 3 days times the probability of having the 3-day lead time. The probability of demand being nine units during a 3-day lead time is the cube of the probability of selling three units per day (.1 x .1 x .1, or .001). This probability is then multiplied by the probability of having a 3-day lead time: .25 x .001 = .00025.

69. If Leslie reorders 10 units of Product A when its inventory level is 10 units, the number of days during a 360-day year that Leslie will experience a stockout of Product A is

a. .75 days.

b. 36 days.

c. 10 days.

d. 0 days.

The correct answer is (d). *(CPA 573 P-17)*
REQUIRED: The number of days during a 360-day year that a stockout will occur.
DISCUSSION: The probability of stockout is determined by examining the probabilities of the unit demand and the lead time. Unit demand is a maximum of three per day; the maximum lead time is 3 days. Therefore, by the time the new stock has arrived, the maximum number of units that could be sold is nine, leaving one unit in inventory. At no time will the inventory be depleted if 10 units are reordered at the inventory level of 10 units.

70. Leslie has developed an inventory model based on the probability tables and desires a solution for minimizing total annual inventory costs. Included in inventory costs are the costs of holding Product A, ordering and receiving Product A, and incurring stockouts of Product A. The solution would state

a. At what inventory level to reorder and how many units to reorder.

b. Either at what inventory level to reorder or how many units to reorder.

c. How many units to reorder but not at what inventory level to reorder.

d. At what inventory level to reorder but not how many units to reorder.

The correct answer is (a). *(CPA 573 P-18)*
REQUIRED: The goal(s) in a model for minimizing total annual inventory costs.
DISCUSSION: Using the basic EOQ model in conjunction with a model for stockout costs results in a model describing both the reorder point and the economic order quantity. The reorder point is reached at an appropriate safety stock level that will minimize ordering costs, carrying costs, and stockout costs.

CHAPTER EIGHTEEN
PROBABILITY AND STATISTICS

18.1 Basic Definitions	(19 questions)	535
18.2 Appropriate Applications	(20 questions)	540
18.3 Probability Distributions	(18 questions)	546
18.4 Hypothesis Testing	(11 questions)	551
18.5 Expected Value	(35 questions)	555
18.6 Other Applications	(16 questions)	566

In this probability and statistics chapter, emphasis is also placed on recognizing the expected value calculations that may appear on professional examinations.

18.1 Basic Definitions

1. Probability theory is a technique

   a. For using mathematics to express a quantitative value for the likelihood of the occurrence of an event.
   b. That is the underlying assumption of modeling with uncertainty.
   c. Based upon objective and subjective estimates.
   d. All of the above.

The correct answer is (d). *(Publisher)*
REQUIRED: The true statement(s) about probability.
DISCUSSION: Probability theory is a mathematical technique used to express quantitatively the likelihood of the occurrence of an event. An event certain to occur has a probability of one; an event certain not to occur has a probability of zero. Probability is used as an underlying assumption for developing models regarding business plans in which uncertainty is a factor. Probability may be based upon objective estimates derived from experience or mathematical computations. It may also reflect subjective estimates such as the probability that a new product line will succeed.

2. What is the probability of the simultaneous occurrence of two mutually exclusive events?

   a. The probability that two or more events will all occur.
   b. The probability that one will occur given that the other has occurred.
   c. The occurrence of one event has no effect on the probability of another event.
   d. Two events cannot occur simultaneously.

The correct answer is (d). *(Publisher)*
REQUIRED: The definition of mutually exclusive events.
DISCUSSION: Mutually exclusive events cannot occur simultaneously. The usual example is that heads and tails cannot both occur on a single toss of a coin.
Answer (a) is incorrect because it is the definition of joint probability. Answer (b) is incorrect because it defines conditional probability. Answer (c) is incorrect because it describes independent events.

3. What is joint probability?

   a. The probability that two or more events will all occur.
   b. The probability that one event will occur given that another has occurred.
   c. The occurrence of one event has no effect on the probability of a second event.
   d. Two events cannot occur simultaneously.

The correct answer is (a). *(Publisher)*
REQUIRED: The definition of joint probability.
DISCUSSION: Joint probability is the probability that two or more events will occur. The joint probability for two events equals the probability of the first event times the conditional probability of the second event.
Answer (b) is incorrect because it defines conditional probability. Answer (c) is incorrect because it describes independent events. Answer (d) is incorrect because it describes mutually exclusive events.

4. What is conditional probability?
   a. The probability that two or more events will all occur.
   b. The probability that one event will occur given that the other has occurred.
   c. The occurrence of one event has no effect on the probability of a second event.
   d. Two events cannot occur simultaneously.

The correct answer is (b). *(Publisher)*
REQUIRED: The definition of conditional probability.
DISCUSSION: Conditional probability is the probability that one event will occur given that another has already occurred.
Answer (a) is incorrect because it is the definition of joint probability. Answer (c) is incorrect because it is the definition of independent events. Answer (d) is incorrect because it describes mutually exclusive events.

5. What is the probability of independent events?
   a. The probability that two or more events will all occur.
   b. The probability that one will occur given that the other has occurred.
   c. The occurrence of one event has no effect on the probability of the other event.
   d. The events cannot occur simultaneously.

The correct answer is (c). *(Publisher)*
REQUIRED: The definition of independent events.
DISCUSSION: Events are independent when the occurrence of one does not affect the probability of the other. For example, the tossing of two dice is usually viewed as the occurrence of two independent events.
Answer (a) is incorrect because it defines joint probability. Answer (b) is incorrect because it defines conditional probability. Answer (d) is incorrect because it defines mutually exclusive events.

6. In statistics, a parameter is never
   a. A characteristic of a population.
   b. A characteristic of a sample drawn from a population.
   c. The arithmetic average.
   d. The value at the 50th percentile.
   e. The most frequently occurring value.

The correct answer is (b). *(Publisher)*
REQUIRED: The item not part of the definition of a parameter in statistics.
DISCUSSION: A parameter is a characteristic of a population. Its value is computed using each element in the population. A statistic is a descriptive measure computed from sample data. A mean, a median, or a mode may be computed for population measurements and are parameters. If computed from samples, they are statistics.
Answer (a) is incorrect because it defines a parameter. Answers (c), (d), and (e) are incorrect because the mean, median, and mode can be either parameters or statistics.

7. In statistics, a statistic is never
   a. A characteristic of a population.
   b. A characteristic of a sample drawn from a population.
   c. The arithmetic average.
   d. The value at the 50th percentile.
   e. The most frequently occurring value.

The correct answer is (a). *(Publisher)*
REQUIRED: The item not part of the definition of a statistic in statistics.
DISCUSSION: A statistic is a characteristic of a sample drawn from a population. The statistic is a numerical value computed using only the elements of the sample drawn from the population. Thus it may or may not represent the population.
Answer (b) is incorrect because it defines a statistic. Answers (c), (d), and (e) are incorrect because the mean, median, and mode can be either parameters or statistics.

8. In statistics, the median is usually not
   a. A characteristic of a population.
   b. A characteristic of a sample drawn from a population.
   c. A measure of central tendency.
   d. The value at the 50th percentile.
   e. The most frequently occurring value.

The correct answer is (e). *(Publisher)*
REQUIRED: The true statement about the median in statistics.
DISCUSSION: When data are arranged in numerical order, one-half of the values are smaller than the median and one-half of the values are greater. Accordingly, this value occurs at the 50th percentile. It is not usually the most frequently occurring value, which is the mode.
Answers (a) and (b) are incorrect because a median may be either a parameter or a statistic. Answer (c) is incorrect because means, medians, and modes are all measures of central tendency. Answer (d) is incorrect because it defines the median.

Module 18.1: Basic Definitions   537

9. In statistics, the mode is usually not

   a. A characteristic of a population.
   b. A characteristic of a sample drawn from a population.
   c. A measure of central tendency.
   d. The value at the 50th percentile.
   e. The most frequently occurring value.

The correct answer is (d). *(Publisher)*
REQUIRED: The true statement about the mode in statistics.
DISCUSSION: The mode is the most frequently occurring value in a set of data. If all values are unique, there is no mode. In a symmetrical distribution, the mean, median, and mode would be the same. But it is not usually the value at the 50th percentile.
Answers (a) and (b) are incorrect because a mode may be either a parameter or a statistic. Answer (c) is incorrect because means, medians, and modes are all measures of central tendency. Answer (e) is incorrect because it defines the mode.

10. In probability analysis, the square root of the mean of the squared differences between the observed values and the expected value is the

    a. Objective function.
    b. Optimum corner point.
    c. EOQ.
    d. Standard deviation.

The correct answer is (d). *(CPA 1185 T-50)*
REQUIRED: The term for the square root of the mean of the squared differences between the observed values and the expected value.
DISCUSSION: The standard deviation (defined in question) measures the amount of variation within a set of numbers. If most numbers cluster around the mean, the standard deviation will be small.
Answer (a) is incorrect because the objective function is a mathematical statement used in linear programming to maximize or minimize a revenue or cost function. Answer (b) is incorrect because the optimum corner point is a term used in the graphical analysis of linear programming. Answer (c) is incorrect because the EOQ is an inventory model used to minimize inventory ordering and carrying costs.

11. Which of the following statements is correct concerning the appropriate measure of central tendency for the frequency distribution of loss experience shown below?

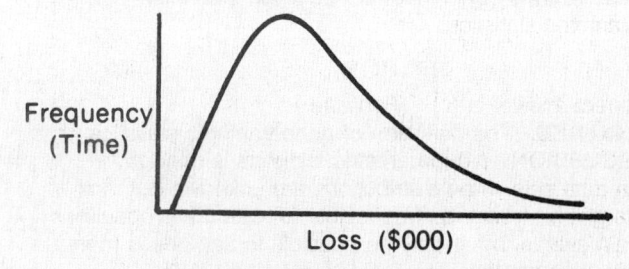

    Frequency (Time) vs. Loss ($000)

    a. The mean should be used since it represents the dollar loss which has occurred most frequently in the past.
    b. The mean, median, and mode are equally appropriate because the distribution is symmetrical.
    c. The mode is the most appropriate measure because it considers the dollar amount of the extreme losses.
    d. The median is the most appropriate measure because it is not affected by the extreme losses.
    e. The mean is the best measure of central tendency because it always lies between the median and mode.

The correct answer is (d). *(CIA 579 IV-1)*
REQUIRED: The appropriate measure of central tendency.
DISCUSSION: Measures of central tendency are the mode, the median, and the mean. The mode is the most frequently occurring value; the median is the value above and below which half of the events occur; and the mean is the average or the arithmetic mean. The median is the best estimate of the central tendency for this distribution because it is not biased by extremes. The given frequency distribution of loss is skewed by the extremely high losses. The median, which consists of absolute numbers of events, is unaffected by the magnitude of the greatest losses.
Answer (a) is incorrect because the mode, not the mean, is the most frequently occurring value. Answer (b) is incorrect because the example is an asymmetrical distribution. When the distribution is perfectly symmetrical, these three values are identical. Answer (c) is incorrect because the mode does not consider the extreme losses. It is simply the most frequently occurring value. Answer (e) is incorrect because, in this situation, the median lies between the mean and the mode. This distribution is skewed to the right because of the very high loss values. Consequently, the mean is to the right of both the mode and the median.

12. In statistics, the mean is usually not
    a. A characteristic of a population.
    b. A characteristic of a sample drawn from a population.
    c. The arithmetic average.
    d. A measure of central tendency.
    e. The most frequently occurring value.

The correct answer is (e). *(Publisher)*
REQUIRED: The true statement about the mean in statistics.
DISCUSSION: The mean, one of the measures of central tendency, is the arithmetic average of a set of numbers. Thus, it is not usually the most frequently occurring value.
  Answers (a) and (b) are incorrect because a mean may be either a parameter or a statistic. Answer (c) is incorrect because it defines the mean. Answer (d) is incorrect because means, medians, and modes are all measures of central tendency.

13. Descriptive statistics is
    a. A summary of large data sets.
    b. A method for drawing conclusions based upon sample data.
    c. Used to analyze data sets when the distributions are unknown but rank order is known.
    d. None of the above.

The correct answer is (a). *(Publisher)*
REQUIRED: The definition of descriptive statistics.
DISCUSSION: In descriptive statistics, measures of central tendency (mean, median, and mode) and measures of dispersion (e.g., standard deviation) are used to summarize large data sets.
  Answer (b) is incorrect because it describes inferential statistics. Answer (c) is incorrect because it describes nonparametric statistics. For example, the probabilities of a series of events are not known, but the most probable to the least probable can be ranked.

14. Inferential statistics is
    a. A summary of large data sets.
    b. A method for drawing conclusions about a population based upon sample data.
    c. Used to analyze data sets when the distributions are unknown but rank order is known.
    d. None of the above.

The correct answer is (b). *(Publisher)*
REQUIRED: The definition of inferential statistics.
DISCUSSION: Inferential statistics is a method for drawing conclusions about a population based upon sample data. It is an important technique in business because a complete survey of the entire population or universe is usually too costly and time consuming, if not impossible. Thus, cost/benefit analysis requires inferential statistics as a key component of the management accountant's statistical techniques.
  Answer (a) is incorrect because it defines descriptive statistics. Answer (c) is incorrect because it defines nonparametric statistics.

15. Nonparametric statistics is
    a. A summary of large data sets.
    b. A method for drawing conclusions based upon sample data.
    c. Used to analyze data sets when the distributions are unknown but rank order is known.
    d. None of the above.

The correct answer is (c). *(Publisher)*
REQUIRED: The definition of nonparametric statistics.
DISCUSSION: Nonparametric statistics is used to analyze data sets when distributions are unknown but rank order is given. It may be impossible to state the probabilities of certain events, but it may be possible to say one is more probable than another.
  Answer (a) is incorrect because it defines descriptive statistics. Answer (b) is incorrect because it defines inferential statistics.

16. Hypothesis testing includes all but which of the following steps?
    a. Sample data are generated.
    b. The hypothesis is formulated.
    c. The probability of the hypothesis given the sample data is computed.
    d. The hypothesis is rejected or not rejected based upon the sample measure.
    e. The standards are adjusted.

The correct answer is (e). *(Publisher)*
REQUIRED: The item not a part of hypothesis testing.
DISCUSSION: Hypothesis testing develops an assumption about the true state of nature. The first of the four steps is to formulate the hypothesis. Second, sample evidence is obtained. Third, the conditional probability that the hypothesis is true, given the observed evidence, and that the sample results observed have actually occurred, is computed. Fourth, the hypothesis is rejected if its probability is smaller than some subjective fixed level of probability chosen a priori. Adjusting standards is the final step in the control loop.

Module 18.1: Basic Definitions

17. Which of the following is not a measure of dispersion of a random variable?

  a. Range.
  b. Median.
  c. Standard deviation.
  d. Variance.
  e. Standard error of the mean.

The correct answer is (b). *(CIA 1182 IV-14)*
REQUIRED: The statistical concept that is not a measure of dispersion.
DISCUSSION: Measures of dispersion indicate the amount of variation within a set of numbers. Measures of central tendency, however, describe typical items in a population. The median, a measure of central tendency, is the halfway value when the raw data are arranged in numerical order from the highest to the lowest.
Answer (a) is incorrect because it is the difference between the largest and the smallest values. Answers (c) and (d) are incorrect because standard deviation is the square root of the variance. Answer (e) is incorrect because it is the standard deviation of sample means.

18. A t-test is a statistical test used to compare the

  a. Variances of two distributions.
  b. Independence of two variables.
  c. Correlation of two variables.
  d. Means of two distributions.
  e. Interaction between two variables.

The correct answer is (d). *(CMA 1286 5-7)*
REQUIRED: The use of a t-test.
DISCUSSION: The student's "t" distribution is a special distribution to be used when only small samples are available and the population variance is not given. It is mound-shaped and symmetric like a normal distribution, only typically flatter with more variation. A small sample is usually deemed to be less than 30. For samples larger than 30, the "t" distribution gives results similar to the standard normal distribution. It is used to compare the means of two distributions to determine whether there is any significant difference between the two groups from which the means were taken.
Answer (a) is incorrect because the "t" test compares means. Answers (b), (c), and (e) are incorrect because correlation analysis measures the relationship among variables.

19. A company can hire a consulting firm for $5,000 to estimate the demand for its product. The company believes that there is a 0.60 probability that the consulting firm will estimate that demand will be "high" (20,000 units) or a 0.40 probability that the demand will be "low" (10,000 units). In order to determine whether to hire the consulting firm, the company should

  a. Use sensitivity analysis to determine the effect of changes in demand.
  b. Use decision theory to compute the value of perfect information.
  c. Use linear programming to compute shadow prices.
  d. Use regression analysis to compute beta coefficients.

The correct answer is (b). *(CIA 1186 IV-20)*
REQUIRED: The method to determine whether greater forecast accuracy is cost effective.
DISCUSSION: Perfect information is the knowledge that a future state of nature (such as demand) will occur with certainty. The value of perfect information is the difference between the expected value without perfect information and the return if the best action is taken given perfect information. Thus, if the value of perfect information exceeds $5,000, the consultant should be hired.
Answer (a) is incorrect because sensitivity analysis is a technique to evaluate a model in terms of the effect of changing the values of the parameters. It answers "what if" questions. Answer (c) is incorrect because the shadow price of a constraint is the amount by which the contribution margin will increase as a result of relaxing that constraint in an LP model by one unit. The calculation of a shadow price is a simple example of sensitivity analysis. Answer (d) is incorrect because regression analysis attempts to find an equation for the relationship among variables. It assumes that a change in a dependent variable relates to a change in an independent variable. A beta coefficient is the slope of the regression line.

18.2 Appropriate Applications

20. Which of the following would be preferable in analyzing the statistical significance of cost variances incurred in a manufacturing process?

a. Linear programming.
b. Markov chains.
c. Monte Carlo simulation.
d. Probability theory.

The correct answer is (d). *(CIA 587 III-50)*
REQUIRED: The method for analyzing the statistical significance of cost variances.
DISCUSSION: An internal auditor may use statistical control charts based on probability theory to determine the significance of variances in a cost accounting system. Control limits are established using probability theory to determine the likelihood that an observed variance indicates the system is out of control. If an observation falls outside the limits, an investigation should be made to determine the cause of the deviation.
Answer (a) is incorrect because linear programming is used to make optimal use of limited resources. Answer (b) is incorrect because Markov chains relate to a decision process. Answer (c) is incorrect because the Monte Carlo method is used in simulation to generate values for a random variable.

21. What is the maximum amount that a manager should pay to obtain perfect information?

a. The expected value with perfect information.
b. The expected value with existing information.
c. The expected value with perfect information plus the expected value with existing information.
d. The expected value with perfect information less the expected value with existing information.

The correct answer is (d). *(Publisher)*
REQUIRED: The maximum amount that should be paid for perfect information.
DISCUSSION: Management should be willing to pay any amount up to the expected value of the perfect information (expected value with perfect information less expected value with existing information), thereby equating its incremental cost with the incremental benefits. If the additional cost of perfect information equals the expected value of perfect information, management will presumably be indifferent as to the action taken.

Questions 22 through 24 are based on the following decision rule. The Honorary Club plans to apply the expected value decision rule (criterion) to determine the number of cups of hot cider to stock.

---

22. The expected monetary value of an act is the

a. Sum of the conditional profit (loss) for each event.
b. Sum of the conditional profit (loss) of each event times the probability of each event occurring.
c. Conditional profit (loss) for the best event times the probability of each event occurring.
d. Sum of the conditional opportunity loss of each event times the probability of each event occurring.
e. Revenue less the costs for the act.

The correct answer is (b). *(CMA 686 5-23)*
REQUIRED: The definition of expected monetary value of an act.
DISCUSSION: Expected value analysis is an estimate of future monetary value based on forecasts and their related probabilities of occurrence. The expected value is found by multiplying the probability of each outcome by its payoff and summing the products. The payoff is the conditional profit (loss).
Answers (a) and (e) are incorrect because each omits adjustment for the probability of each event. Answer (c) is incorrect because all possibilities must be included. Answer (d) is incorrect because opportunity costs are not a part of the calculation.

23. The Honorary Club would select the demand level that
    a. Is closest to the expected demand.
    b. Has the greatest probability of occurring.
    c. Has the greatest expected opportunity loss.
    d. Has the greatest expected monetary value.
    e. Includes the event with the greatest conditional profit.

The correct answer is (d). *(CMA 686 5-24)*
REQUIRED: The demand level that should be selected.
DISCUSSION: The demand level selected should be the one that will generate the greatest return to the club. Answer (a) is incorrect because the weighting for probabilities and the monetary losses at lower demand levels may make the expected demand uneconomical. Answer (b) is incorrect because the probabilities must be multiplied by the dollar gain or loss from each level. Answer (c) is incorrect because the greatest loss should be avoided. Answer (e) is incorrect because the level that will produce the greatest conditional profit may not be the best when adjusted for probability of occurrence.

24. The expected value of perfect information is the
    a. Same as the expected profit under certainty.
    b. Sum of the conditional profit (loss) for the best event of each act times the probability of each event occurring.
    c. Difference between the expected profit under certainty and the expected opportunity loss.
    d. Difference between the expected profit under certainty and conditional profit for the best act under certainty.
    e. Difference between the expected profit under certainty and the expected monetary value of the best act under uncertainty.

The correct answer is (e). *(CMA 686 5-25)*
REQUIRED: The true statement about the expected value of perfect information.
DISCUSSION: The expected value of perfect information is the difference between the expected value given the probabilities of the possible actions and the return if the best action is taken given perfect information. In other words, it is the amount one would be willing to pay for perfect information, for example, the exact demand for cider at each game.
Answers (a) and (b) are incorrect because the expected value of perfect information is the difference between expected profit under certainty and expected profit under uncertainty. Answer (c) is incorrect because opportunity losses are not a consideration. Answer (d) is incorrect because perfect information would allow profit maximization for each possible act, not just the best act.

25. Which of the following is a characteristic of sensitivity analysis?
    a. Decision models may be developed with certainty equivalents.
    b. Decision models may be evaluated by changing data variables and observing the outcome.
    c. Emphasis may be placed on the effects of forecasting errors.
    d. All of the above.

The correct answer is (d). *(Publisher)*
REQUIRED: The characteristic(s) of sensitivity analysis.
DISCUSSION: Sensitivity analysis permits the decision maker to measure the effects of errors in certainty equivalents, which are estimated amounts developed by the best means available and assumed for purposes of a given decision model to be certain. The decision model then may be evaluated by changing certain data variables (certainty equivalents) critical to the success of the entity and observing the outcomes. This analysis allows the decision maker to quantify the effects of forecasting or prediction errors and to identify the most critical variables.

26. Managers have varying attitudes regarding risk. A manager who is risk neutral
    a. Neither seeks nor avoids risk.
    b. Has a linear utility function.
    c. Tends to choose options that involve large variations of actual monetary returns about expected monetary values.
    d. Tends to choose options that have very little variation about expected monetary returns.
    e. (a) and (b).

The correct answer is (e). *(Publisher)*
REQUIRED: The characteristic(s) of a risk-neutral manager.
DISCUSSION: A risk-neutral manager neither seeks nor avoids risk. (S)he will choose investments for which the expected monetary values are equal to the manager's subjectively perceived utility values (expressed in utils, an arbitrary measure). Thus, the decision maker has a linear utility function, one in which the monetary amounts and utils have a constant or directly proportional relationship. Thus, (s)he is indifferent to risk.
Answer (c) is incorrect because a risk seeker would tend to invest more than the expected monetary value. Answer (d) is incorrect because it describes the tendency of a risk-averse manager.

27. A car rental agency has a policy of replacing the tires on its car fleet as the tires wear out. Management wonders if there would be any cost savings if the tires are periodically replaced at one time on its fleet of 500 cars. The technique the car rental agency would find most useful is

   a. Gantt charting.
   b. Probability analysis.
   c. Linear programming.
   d. Learning curve techniques.
   e. Queuing theory.

The correct answer is (b). *(CMA 1280 5-15)*
REQUIRED: The technique most useful for determining future cost savings.
DISCUSSION: Probability theory provides a method for mathematically expressing the likelihood of a chance event's occurrence. Probabilities range from zero (the event cannot occur) to one (the event is certain to occur). Projecting cost savings in the future requires development of probabilities regarding alternative estimates of useful lives and costs.
   Answer (a) is incorrect because a Gantt chart (a bar chart on a horizontal time scale) is a managerial tool for project scheduling. Answer (c) is incorrect because it is a technique used to solve maximization/minimization problems through the solution of a system of linear equations. Answer (d) is incorrect because learning curve analysis evaluates productivity as a function of experience. Answer (e) is incorrect because it is a technique to minimize the sum of the cost of a waiting line and the cost of servicing it.

Questions 28 through 30 are based on the management of the Habre Manufacturing Company, which has been asked to make a report to the board of directors on credit and collection experience under the policies instituted last year. Because of the vast number of individual accounts receivable, management has decided to utilize statistical analysis techniques.

---

28. In addition to calculating the average collection period for Habre's accounts receivable for the presentation, a measure of dispersion also will be calculated. This measure is necessary to include statements concerning the

   a. Reliability of the average collection period.
   b. Type of probability distribution represented by the required time to collect the accounts.
   c. Kurtosis of the curve of the required times to collect the accounts.
   d. Skewness of the distribution of the required times to collect the accounts.
   e. None of the above.

The correct answer is (a). *(CMA 675 5-17)*
REQUIRED: The purpose of a measure of dispersion in a statistical analysis of accounts receivable.
DISCUSSION: Measures of dispersion indicate how much variation exists in a set of numbers. A low dispersion (variance) indicates that the average calculated is more likely to be a reliable estimate. A large dispersion suggests that the calculated statistic may be a less reliable estimate. Dispersion is measured by the range (largest value - smallest value), the variance (the average of the squared deviations from the mean), and the standard deviation (the square root of the variance).
   Answer (b) is incorrect because the dispersion does not completely describe a probability distribution. One must also know kurtosis and skewness. Answer (c) is incorrect because kurtosis refers to how sharply peaked the distribution is. Answer (d) is incorrect because skewness measures the asymmetry of a distribution (positive or right-skewed and negative or left-skewed).

---

29. The average collection period and the measure of dispersion can be used to calculate an expression of the margin of error or band around the estimate which, with specified probability, will include the true value. This expression is known as

   a. The standard deviation.
   b. The variance.
   c. The correlation interval.
   d. The confidence interval.
   e. None of the above.

The correct answer is (d). *(CMA 675 5-18)*
REQUIRED: The name for the margin of error within which the true value lies at a given probability.
DISCUSSION: The confidence interval is the range about the mean (plus or minus a certain value) within which the probability of an occurrence is known. For example, given a normal population, the probability of an occurrence within 1.96 standard deviations of the mean is 95%. In other words, approximately 95% of all items in a normal population fall within that range.
   Answer (a) is incorrect because it is a measure of dispersion used in the calculation of the confidence interval. Answer (b) is incorrect because it is the square of the standard deviation. Answer (c) is incorrect because it is a nonsense term.

30. Last year when the new credit policies were introduced, the vice-president of sales challenged them on the contention that collections are dependent upon the size of the buying firm. In order to support the policies in the face of this challenge, the decision has been made to include in the presentation a discussion of the statistical independence of a bad debt occurrence and size of the buying organization. These two events are said to be statistically independent if

   a. The probability of a bad debt is equal to the sum of the probability that the buyer is a small company plus the probability that the buyer is a large company.

   b. The probability of a bad debt plus the probability that the buyer is a small company equals the probability of a bad debt plus the probability that the buyer is a large company.

   c. The probability of a bad debt given that the buyer is a small company equals the probability of a bad debt divided by one minus the probability that the buyer is a large company.

   d. The probability of a bad debt given that the buyer is a small company equals the probability of a bad debt given that the buyer is a large company equals the probability of a bad debt.

The correct answer is (d). *(CMA 675 5-19)*
   REQUIRED: The definition of statistical independence.
   DISCUSSION: Events are statistically independent if and only if the probability of event A (a bad debt) does not change given that event B (e.g., the buyer is a large firm) occurs. Accordingly, the probability of event A is equal to the probability of event A given that event B occurs [P(A) = P(AB)]. Thus, the existence of B does not change the probability of A; i.e., A and B are totally unrelated.
   Answers (a), (b), and (c) are incorrect because each defines a conditional probability.

31. Solutions provided by quantitative techniques based on probabilities should be considered to be

   a. Numerically precise and correct.
   b. Approximations based solely on past experiences.
   c. The best estimate of expected results.
   d. Unaffected by environmental changes.
   e. None of the above.

The correct answer is (c). *(CIA 976 IV-11)*
   REQUIRED: The true statement about solutions provided by quantitative techniques based on probabilities.
   DISCUSSION: The use of probability theory provides an estimate of expected results. Deviation from the expected results is a normal result of a probabilistic or stochastic process.
   Answer (a) is incorrect because the solution may be correct but not precise since other results are possible (though less probable). Answer (b) is incorrect because past experience is not the only source of probability estimates. Answer (d) is incorrect because a change in the environment in which a process operates can affect the probable result of the process.

32. Management is concerned with the increasing customer returns of its new product. They are considering stopping production and shipment of the item until they can make an estimate of the number of defective products in their currently large inventory. An examination of every item on hand, however, would be too costly. Which of the following sampling plans would be most appropriate in this situation?

   a. Stop-or-go sampling.
   b. Discovery sampling.
   c. Ratio sampling.
   d. Attribute sampling.
   e. Acceptance sampling.

The correct answer is (d). *(CIA 581 IV-22)*
   REQUIRED: The appropriate sampling technique for estimating the number of defective products in the inventory.
   DISCUSSION: Attribute sampling, a means of estimating errors in a population, is appropriate when results are of the yes/no variety. For example, this method is useful for determining the number of defective items in an inventory.
   Answers (a), (b), and (e) are incorrect because each represents an application of attribute sampling. Answer (c) is incorrect because it is an application of variables sampling (sampling for amounts such as dollar values). Ratio sampling is used to estimate the ratio of the audited value of a population to its book value.

Module 18.2: Appropriate Applications

33. A manager who is risk averse
   a. Neither seeks nor avoids risk.
   b. Has a linear utility function.
   c. Tends to choose options that involve large variations of actual monetary returns about expected monetary values.
   d. Tends to choose options that have very little variation about expected monetary returns.
   e. (a) and (b).

The correct answer is (d). *(Publisher)*
REQUIRED: The definition of a risk-averse manager.
DISCUSSION: The risk-averse manager will avoid risk. (S)he prefers a certain return on investments over taking a chance on other investments that may involve high gains but also large losses. The utility function for the risk-averse manager increases at a decreasing rate.
Answers (a) and (b) are incorrect because each is typical of a risk-neutral manager. Answer (c) is incorrect because it describes a risk seeker.

34. A manager who is risk seeking
   a. Neither seeks nor avoids risk.
   b. Has a linear utility function.
   c. Tends to choose options that involve large variations of actual monetary returns about expected monetary values.
   d. Tends to choose options that have very little variation about expected monetary returns.
   e. (a) and (b).

The correct answer is (c). *(Publisher)*
REQUIRED: The definition of a risk-seeking manager.
DISCUSSION: A risk-seeking manager chooses risk. A risk seeker prefers investments that involve the potential for large gains, even though large losses may also be possible. The utility function for the risk seeker increases at an increasing rate; i.e., riskier investments are appealing. (S)he is a gambler and is willing to chance a big loss to get a big gain.
Answers (a) and (b) are incorrect because each is typical of a risk-neutral manager. Answer (d) is incorrect because it describes the risk-averse manager.

35. A company wishes to estimate the value of its inventory by dividing the inventory into several classes and then randomly selecting several items from each class. The relevant quantitative technique is
   a. Cross-sectional analysis.
   b. Monte Carlo simulation method.
   c. Random sampling.
   d. Risk analysis.
   e. Stratified random sampling.

The correct answer is (e). *(CPA 572 T-32)*
REQUIRED: The statistical method that divides inventory into classes and then randomly selects items from each class.
DISCUSSION: The purpose of stratification is to reduce the effect of high variability by dividing the population into subpopulations. Stratifying allows for greater emphasis on larger or more important items. In stratified random sampling, each item in a particular subpopulation has an equal chance of selection.
Answer (a) is incorrect because it is a technique in which inferences are drawn based on data from a variety of similar subjects. Answer (b) is incorrect because it is a technique used in simulations for generating values at random for selected variables. Answer (c) is incorrect because, in random sampling, each item in the entire population has an equal chance of selection. Answer (d) is incorrect because risk analysis measures the probable variability of returns from a particular project.

36. Statistical control charts would be appropriate to use in determining whether further investigation is needed of
   a. Variances in the quantity of raw materials used.
   b. The number of units produced by an individual worker.
   c. The number of sales calls made by an individual.
   d. All of the above.
   e. None of the above.

The correct answer is (d). *(CIA 976 IV-13)*
REQUIRED: The use(s) of statistical control charts.
DISCUSSION: Statistical control charts compare actual sample results against the expected results, an upper control limit, and a lower control limit. The band between the upper and lower control limits defines the scope allowed for chance variation. Observations outside of these limits should be investigated because they probably result from factors other than chance. Thus, all of these items would be proper applications of statistical control charts.

37. A dog food manufacturer is marketing a new type of dog food with a specified number of individual 8-ounce packages in a box. Automatic packaging equipment is used to fill the individual packages. The equipment is set for an 8-ounce fill. Each package was weighed during the first week of operation to determine the actual weight of the packages and to check on the functioning of the equipment. Management calculated the mean weight of the packages and the standard deviation. Management now wants to set the machine so that no more than 2% of the packages will have less than 8 ounces. The technique the company should employ is an application of

- a. Simulation techniques.
- b. Differential calculus.
- c. Time series analysis.
- d. Correlation and regression analysis.
- e. Statistical analysis.

The correct answer is (e). *(CMA 1280 5-9)*
REQUIRED: The technique to achieve the desired level of quality control.
DISCUSSION: Statistical analysis provides methods for drawing conclusions about a population based upon sample information. Statistical sampling permits a quantitative measurement of the precision of the sample (how closely it represents the population) and the risk that it will not be representative.
Answer (a) is incorrect because simulation uses mathematical models to predict future outcomes. Answer (b) is incorrect because it is a mathematical technique used to measure rates of change. Answer (c) is incorrect because time series analysis examines the relationship of two or more variables over time. Answer (d) is incorrect because they are techniques used to measure relationships between a dependent variable and one or more independent variables.

38. The statistical quality control department prepares a control chart showing the percentages of production that are defective. Simple statistical calculations provide control limits that tell whether assignable causes of variation are explainable on chance grounds. The chart is particularly valuable in determining whether the quality of material received from outside vendors is consistent from month to month. This chart is best known as a(n)

- a. C chart.
- b. P chart.
- c. R chart.
- d. X-bar chart.

The correct answer is (b). *(CIA 587 III-44)*
REQUIRED: The statistical quality control chart described.
DISCUSSION: Statistical control charts are graphic aids for monitoring the status of any process subject to random variations. They consist of three horizontal lines plotted on a horizontal time scale. The center line represents the average or mean value for the process being controlled. The other two lines are the upper control limit (UCL) and the lower control limit (LCL). The processes are measured periodically, and the values are plotted on the chart. If the value falls within the control limits, no action is taken. If the value falls outside the limits, the process is considered "out of control," and an investigation is made for possible corrective action. Another advantage of these charts is that they make trends visible. A P chart is one that is based on an attribute (acceptable/not acceptable) rather than a measure of a variable, specifically, the percentage of defects in a sample.
Answer (a) is incorrect because a C chart is also an attribute control chart. It shows defects per item. Answer (c) is incorrect because an R chart shows the range of dispersion of a variable, such as size or weight. Answer (d) is incorrect because an X-bar chart shows the sample mean for a variable.

39. Separate statistical samples of invoice payments in each of 15 branch offices of your company show a number of errors. In determining whether the quality of performance among the 15 offices is significantly different from overall quality, which of the following statistical distributions should you assume to be most applicable?

  a. Poisson.
  b. Chi-square.
  c. Student's t.
  d. Hypergeometric.
  e. Binomial.

The correct answer is (b). *(CIA 579 II-16)*
REQUIRED: The distribution used to ascertain whether the differences between samples are statistically significant.
DISCUSSION: The Chi-square distribution is used for tests of homogeneity. The Chi-square statistic (X^2) equals the sample variance (s^2) multiplied by its degree of freedom (n - 1) divided by the hypothesized population variance (σ^2). Here, quality may be viewed as involving little error or subsequently a small variance. Thus, the variance of the samples of each office could be tested.
Answer (a) is incorrect because it is a special case of the binomial distribution used especially in queuing analysis. Answer (c) is incorrect because the t-distribution is an adjusted normal distribution used when the sample size is small. Answer (d) is incorrect because it is similar to the binomial distribution. It involves sampling without replacement. Answer (e) is incorrect because it applies to binary situations, e.g., a yes/no, error/no error basis.

18.3 Probability Distributions

40. Decisions are frequently classified as those made under certainty and those made under uncertainty. Certainty exists when

  a. The probabilities for each outcome of an event can be assigned with a high degree of confidence.
  b. The probability of the event is less than 1.
  c. There is absolutely no doubt that an event will occur.
  d. There is more than one outcome for each possible action.
  e. The standard deviation of an event is greater than 0.

The correct answer is (c). *(CMA 1286 5-2)*
REQUIRED: The true statement about when certainty exists.
DISCUSSION: An event is certain if there is no doubt that it will occur. The probability is 1 if an event is certain to occur, and 0 if it is certain not to occur. Under conditions of certainty, consequences are therefore deterministic, not probabilistic or unknown.
Answer (a) is incorrect because it deals with risk, not certainty. Answer (b) is incorrect because a probability less than 1 would not be certainty. Answer (d) is incorrect because certainty implies a specific outcome. Answer (e) is incorrect because it is a nonsense answer.

41. A producer of salad dressing is using queuing analysis to determine how many mechanics should be available to adjust machinery in its large filling department. Similar high speed filling machinery is operated simultaneously on each of 13 separate production lines. Machine adjustment failures occur randomly through time such that the length of time between failures has an exponential distribution. The number of adjustment failures occurring during an 8-hour shift in the above situation would best be modeled by a

  a. Normal distribution.
  b. Binomial distribution.
  c. Poisson distribution.
  d. Continuous distribution.
  e. Uniform distribution.

The correct answer is (c). *(CMA 1278 5-29)*
REQUIRED: The type of distribution used in queuing analysis.
DISCUSSION: Queuing theory is a method used to examine the costs of waiting lines and of servicing them. The Poisson distribution is used for queuing theory because usually more than one event occurs in a given period of time. If n = number of items or samples, and p = the probability of an occurrence, then λ, where λ is both the value of the mean and variance in this distribution, is defined as np. The poisson distribution is defined as:

$$f(k) = \frac{\lambda^k e^{-\lambda}}{k!}$$

Where k is the number of occurrences and e is the natural logarithm (2.71828...).
Answer (a) is incorrect because it is a distribution which has a symmetrical, bell-shaped curve. Answer (b) is incorrect because it is a discrete distribution in which there are only two possible outcomes. Answer (d) is incorrect because it is a general term for distributions in which the outcomes may have any value, i.e., are not discrete. Answer (e) is incorrect because it describes a distribution in which all outcomes are equally likely.

Module 18.3: Probability Distributions

42. Which of the following is not an attribute of a probability distribution?

　a. The total probability associated with all possible occurrences equals 1.
　b. The possible probability of any event occurring is bounded by 0 and 1.
　c. It can be modeled by means of a formula or graph which provides the probabilities according to every possible outcome.
　d. There is only one possible outcome.
　e. They deal with random variables.

The correct answer is (d). *(Publisher)*
　REQUIRED: The item not an attribute of a probability distribution.
　DISCUSSION: A probability distribution is characterized by the following attributes: The probability of any event(s) is bounded by 0 (no chance) and 1 (certainty). The total probability of all possible outcomes must sum to 1. Also, a probability distribution models a random variable through the use of a formula or graph which provides the probability associated with the occurrence of certain values of the random variable. If there is only one possible outcome, the variable is not random, but constant and known with certainty.

43. A uniform distribution is best described as one in which

　a. The curve is symmetrical and bell-shaped.
　b. Sampling occurs without replacement.
　c. Each event has only two possible outcomes.
　d. Each outcome has the same probability.

The correct answer is (d). *(Publisher)*
　REQUIRED: The definition of a uniform distribution.
　DISCUSSION: A uniform distribution is one in which all outcomes are equally probable. Tossing one die is an example of an event with a uniform distribution.
　Answer (a) is incorrect because a normal distribution is symmetrically bell-shaped. Answer (b) is incorrect because it defines a hypergeometric distribution. Answer (c) is incorrect because an event has only two outcomes in a binomial distribution.

44. The binomial distribution is best described as one in which

　a. Each outcome has the same probability.
　b. Each event has only two possible outcomes.
　c. Sampling occurs without replacement.
　d. The curve is symmetrical and bell-shaped.

The correct answer is (b). *(Publisher)*
　REQUIRED: The definition of a binomial distribution.
　DISCUSSION: The binomial distribution, often used in quality control, gives the probability of each of the possible combinations of trial results when each trial has only two possible outcomes.
　Answer (a) is incorrect because it defines a uniform distribution. Answer (c) is incorrect because sampling without replacement occurs in a hypergeometric distribution. Answer (d) is incorrect because a normal distribution is symmetrically bell-shaped.

45. A hypergeometric distribution can best be described as one in which

　a. Each outcome has the same probability.
　b. Each event has only two possible outcomes.
　c. Sampling occurs without replacement.
　d. The curve is symmetrical and bell-shaped.

The correct answer is (c). *(Publisher)*
　REQUIRED: The best description of a hypergeometric distribution.
　DISCUSSION: The hypergeometric distribution is similar to the binomial distribution and is used for sampling without replacement. When the size of the population is not large, relative to the sample, the probability of a certain outcome is related to what occurred on preceding trials. The number of similar outcomes or "successes" follows a hypergeometric probability.
　Answer (a) is incorrect because it defines a uniform distribution. Answer (b) is incorrect because an event in a binomial distribution has but two possible outcomes. Answer (d) is incorrect because it describes a normal distribution.

Module 18.3: Probability Distributions

46. A normal distribution is best described as one in which

   a. Each outcome has the same probability.
   b. Each event has only two possible outcomes.
   c. Sampling occurs without replacement.
   d. The curve is symmetrical and bell-shaped.

The correct answer is (d). *(Publisher)*
REQUIRED: The definition of a normal distribution.
DISCUSSION: The normal distribution is the most significant probability distribution. It describes the distribution of the sample mean regardless of the distribution of the population, given the sample is large (typically greater than 30). It has a symmetrical bell-shaped curve centered around the sample mean.
   Answer (a) is incorrect because it defines a uniform distribution. Answer (b) is incorrect because it defines a binomial distribution. Answer (c) is incorrect because it defines a hypergeometric distribution.

47. The student's "t" distribution is best described as one in which

   a. The probability is assessed of the number of times a certain event occurs in a given interval of time or space.
   b. The probability of observing an occurrence at least as long (in time, e.g., life of a fuse, engine, etc.) as a specified time interval.
   c. Small samples of less than 30 are examined, when the underlying population is assumed to be normal.
   d. The fit between the actual data and the theoretical distribution is tested.

The correct answer is (c). *(Publisher)*
REQUIRED: The best description of the student's "t" distribution.
DISCUSSION: The student's "t" distribution is a special distribution to be used when only small samples are available and the population variance is not given. It is mound-shaped and symmetric like a normal distribution, only typically flatter with more variation. A small sample is usually deemed to be less than 30. For samples larger than 30, the "t" distribution gives results similar to the standard normal distribution.
   Answer (a) is incorrect because it defines a Poisson distribution. Answer (b) is incorrect because it defines an exponential distribution. Answer (d) is incorrect because it defines the Chi-square distribution.

48. A Poisson distribution is best described as one in which

   a. The probability is assessed of the number of times a certain event occurs in a given interval of time or space.
   b. The probability of observing an occurrence at least as long (in time, e.g., life of a fuse, engine, etc.) as a specified time interval.
   c. Small samples of less than 30 are examined, when the underlying population is assumed to be normal.
   d. The fit between the actual data and the theoretical distribution is tested.

The correct answer is (a). *(Publisher)*
REQUIRED: The best description of a Poisson distribution.
DISCUSSION: A Poisson distribution is used to model the number of times a specified event occurs over a period of time, or over a certain area or volume. It is similar to the binomial distribution when the sample is large and the probability of observing a desired event (p) times the sample size (n) is small, usually $np \leq 7$.
   Answer (b) is incorrect because it defines an exponential distribution. Answer (c) is incorrect because it defines the student's "t" distribution. Answer (d) is incorrect because it defines the Chi-square distribution.

49. The Chi-square distribution is best described as one in which

   a. The probability is assessed of the number of times a certain event occurs in a given interval of time or space.
   b. The probability of observing an occurrence at least as long (in time, e.g., life of a fuse, engine, etc.) as a specified time interval.
   c. Small samples of less than 30 are examined, when the underlying population is assumed to be normal.
   d. The fit between the actual data and the theoretical distribution is tested.

The correct answer is (d). *(Publisher)*
REQUIRED: The best description of the Chi-square distribution.
DISCUSSION: The Chi-square distribution is a special distribution used in examining the fit between actual data and the theoretical distribution. It tests the probability that a particular sample was drawn from a particular population.
   Answer (a) is incorrect because it defines a Poisson distribution. Answer (b) is incorrect because it defines an exponential distribution. Answer (c) is incorrect because it defines the student's "t" distribution.

Module 18.3: Probability Distributions

50. The exponential distribution is best described as one in which
    a. The probability is assessed of the number of times a certain event occurs in a given interval of time or space.
    b. The probability is assessed of observing an occurrence at least as long (in time, e.g., life of a fuse, engine, etc.) as a specified time interval.
    c. Small samples of less than 30 are examined, when the underlying population is assumed to be normal.
    d. The fit between the actual data and the theoretical distribution is tested.

The correct answer is (b). *(Publisher)*
REQUIRED: The best description of an exponential distribution.
DISCUSSION: An exponential distribution is one in which the probability is assessed of observing an occurrence with a length of time greater than a specified time interval. A common use of the exponential distribution is in modeling the length of life of electronic components, engines, etc. Thus, the probability that a time unit will exceed a prespecified time unit is calculated.
Answer (a) is incorrect because it defines a Poisson distribution. Answer (c) is incorrect because it defines the student's "t" distribution. Answer (d) is incorrect because it defines the Chi-square distribution.

51. The theorem that states that the distribution of the sample means from any underlying population is approximately normal when the sample size is large ($n \geq 30$) is
    a. Central limit theorem.
    b. Sample mean theorem.
    c. Maximum likelihood theorem.
    d. None. The above statement is not true.

The correct answer is (a). *(Publisher)*
REQUIRED: The theorem stating that the distribution of a sample mean is normal.
DISCUSSION: The central limit theorem states that the probability distribution of sample means generated from any underlying probability distribution is approximately normal. The mean of this distribution is the true population mean, and the variance is $\sigma^2 \div n$.
Answer (b) is incorrect because there is no such theorem. Answer (c) is incorrect because maximum likelihood is a form of estimation that finds the value that maximizes the joint probabilities of all random variables sampled.

52. The standard deviation of the sample mean in repeated sampling in comparison to the standard deviation of the population is always
    a. Larger.
    b. Smaller.
    c. The same.
    d. Cannot determine.

The correct answer is (b). *(Publisher)*
REQUIRED: The relationship between the standard deviation of the sample mean in repeated sampling and the standard deviation of the population.
DISCUSSION: The standard deviation of the sample mean ($\sigma \bar{y}$) is always smaller than the standard deviation of the population (σ). The standard deviation of the sample mean is equal to the standard deviation of the population divided by the square root of the sample size ($\sigma \div \sqrt{n}$). The lower number also makes intuitive sense because extreme values of a population are typically excluded due to the averaging process in calculating a sample mean. Thus, there is a smaller likelihood of dispersion around the true mean or a smaller standard deviation.

53. Given a normal distribution with unknown mean (μ), but known standard deviation of 10, the standard deviation of the mean of a sample size of 100 is
    a. 10.
    b. 100.
    c. 1.
    d. .1.

The correct answer is (c). *(Publisher)*
REQUIRED: The standard deviation of the mean of a given sample size.
DISCUSSION: The standard deviation of the mean is typically smaller than the population standard deviation. The formula for calculating the standard deviation of the mean is the standard deviation of the population divided by the square root of the sample size ($\sigma \div \sqrt{n}$). Since $\sigma = 10$ and $n = 100$, the standard deviation of the mean is $10 \div \sqrt{100} = 10 \div 10 = 1$.

54. What is the primary difference between a discrete and a continuous distribution?

   a. One is not a legitimate probability distribution.
   b. Continuous distributions are always symmetric, while discrete distributions are not.
   c. Continuous distributions deal with a range where any possible value in that interval has a probability of occurrence, while discrete distributions attribute probabilities only to a finite number of values over a range.
   d. Continuous distributions only model finite random variables, while discrete distributions may model any variable.

The correct answer is (c). *(Publisher)*
REQUIRED: The primary difference between a discrete and a continuous distribution.
DISCUSSION: A continuous distribution deals with random variables that may take an infinite number of values, while discrete distributions model only random variables that take on a finite number of values.
Answer (a) is incorrect because both are legitimate probability distributions. Answer (b) is incorrect because continuous probability distributions need not be symmetric. Answer (d) is incorrect because continuous probability distributions model random variables that may take on an infinite amount of values.

55. Which of the following is not a continuous probability distribution?

   a. Uniform.
   b. Normal.
   c. Poisson.
   d. Exponential.

The correct answer is (c). *(Publisher)*
REQUIRED: The item not a continuous probability distribution.
DISCUSSION: A continuous probability distribution deals with random variables that may assume an infinite number of values. For instance, if we possessed measuring equipment of infinite accuracy, we could continually divide an interval of time into smaller and smaller units. The normal, uniform, and exponential distribution are all examples of continuous probability distributions. The Poisson distribution, however, is a discrete (not continuous) distribution that measures finite events over a time interval or an area.

56. Which of the following is not a discrete distribution?

   a. Poisson.
   b. Exponential.
   c. Binomial.
   d. Hypergeometric.

The correct answer is (b). *(Publisher)*
REQUIRED: The item not a discrete distribution.
DISCUSSION: A discrete probability distribution is characterized by random variables involving all assumed finite values. An example is the number of times you get tails on 10 coin throws. The values may only be the integers (whole numbers) 1 through 10, not 1.1 or 5.6. The binomial, hypergeometric, and Poisson are all examples of discrete probability distributions. The exponential distribution, however, is continuous (not discrete).

57. Clay Co. operates three shipping terminals, referred to as X, Y, and Z. Of the total cargo shipped, terminals X, Y, and Z handle approximately 60%, 30%, and 10%, respectively, with error rates of 3%, 4%, and 6%, respectively. Clay's internal auditor randomly selects one shipping document, ascertaining that this document contains an error. The probability that the error occurred in terminal X is

   a. 60%.
   b. 50%.
   c. 23%.
   d. 3%.

The correct answer is (b). *(CPA 1186 Q-35)*
REQUIRED: The probability of an error occurring in one of three locations.
DISCUSSION: There is a 3.6% average error rate for the three terminals: [(60% x 3%) + (30% x 4%) + (10% x 6%)]. Since 1.8% (60% x 3%) of the average 3.6% error rate occurs in terminal X, there is a 50% (1.8% ÷ 3.6%) probability that a particular error occurred in terminal X.

18.4 Hypothesis Testing

> Questions 58 and 59 are based on J.R. Smythe, the manager for a company which manufactures custom desks, who is designing a series of statistical tools to be used in the measurement and control of costs. The desks are accounted for on a job order basis.

58. The production management has expressed the concern that there appears to be an increase in the average per unit cost to manufacture desks. In developing a statistical test to determine whether the average cost has increased, Smythe constructs a hypothesis of the difference in means which will imply

   a. A two-tailed test.
   b. A single-valued test.
   c. An operating characteristic test.
   d. A one-tailed test.
   e. None of the above.

The correct answer is (d). *(CMA 675 5-14)*
REQUIRED: The true statement about a test to determine average unit cost.
DISCUSSION: The hypothesis to be tested is whether the mean has increased, i.e., whether the mean is greater than a certain value. The null hypothesis might then be that there is no mean increase in the average per unit cost. Consequently, a one-tailed test is appropriate because it determines whether the new average is in the upper tail of the distribution.
Answer (a) is incorrect because it defines whether the average has risen or fallen (the null hypothesis is also rejected if the value falls in the lower tail of the distribution). Answer (b) is incorrect because it describes a single value, not a probability distribution. Answer (c) is incorrect because it is a nonsense term.

59. In developing the statistical test described in the previous question to determine whether manufacturing costs have increased, a null hypothesis would be formulated. In this case, the null hypothesis to be tested could be: Manufacturing costs have not increased. This testing procedure can lead to the wrong decision (e.g., Type I or alpha error, Type II or beta error). The wrong decision that can be made is

   a. To reject the null hypothesis that the cost has not increased when the cost in fact has increased.
   b. To reject the null hypothesis that the cost has not increased when the cost in fact has not increased.
   c. To accept the null hypothesis that the cost has not increased when the cost in fact has increased.
   d. Both (b) and (c) are wrong decisions.
   e. None of the above.

The correct answer is (d). *(CMA 675 5-15)*
REQUIRED: The incorrect decision(s) that may be made when testing a hypothesis.
DISCUSSION: Wrong decisions are of two types, Type I or alpha error and Type II or beta error. To reject the hypothesis that the costs have not increased when in fact they have not increased is a Type I or alpha error. It is also incorrect to accept the null hypothesis that costs have not increased when in fact they have increased (a Type II or beta error). Thus, both (b) and (c) are wrong decisions.
Answer (a) is incorrect because it is an appropriate decision. (The question calls for a wrong decision.)

Module 18.4: Hypothesis Testing

> Questions 60 through 66 are based on the ABC Company, which has made a claim that, on average, their diet soda has less than one calorie. A consumer testing service examined nine cans, and the amount of calories recorded were .9, .95, 1.0, 1.05, .85, 1.0, .95, .95, and .9. Assume the underlying population is approximately normal.

60. What are the sample mean and sample standard deviation, respectively?

	$\bar{x}$	s
a.	.95	.10
b.	.95	.0612
c.	1.00	1.00
d.	1.00	unknown
e.	.90	unknown

The correct answer is (b). *(Publisher)*
REQUIRED: The sample mean and sample standard deviation of a population.
DISCUSSION: The formula to calculate a sample mean is

$$\frac{\Sigma x_i}{n}$$

where Σ is a summation sign,
n is the sample size, and
x is the individual observation.

The sample mean is typically denoted as $\bar{x}$. The sample variance (s^2) is calculated as $\Sigma(x - \bar{x})^2 \div (n - 1)$. The sample standard deviation, s, is the square root of the variance.

x		$(x - \bar{x})$	$(x - \bar{x})^2$
.90		-.05	.0025
.95		0	0
1.00	$\bar{x} = (8.55) \div 9$	.05	.0025
1.05		.1	.01
.85	$= .95$	-.1	.01
1.0		.05	.0025
.95		0	0
.95		0	0
.90		-.05	.0025
8.55			.0300

Sample variance: $s^2 = (.03) \div 8 = .00375$

Sample standard deviation: $s = \sqrt{.00375} = .0612$

61. Let μ denote the true mean calories of all diet sodas produced by ABC Company. What hypothesis should be tested in order to show if ABC's claim is valid?

a. $H_o: \mu = 1$
   $H_a: \mu \neq 1$
b. $H_o: \mu \geq 1$
   $H_a: \mu < 1$
c. $H_o: \mu = 1$
   $H_a: \mu > 1$
d. $H_o: \mu = 0$
   $H_a: \mu < 1$

The correct answer is (b). *(Publisher)*
REQUIRED: The hypothesis to be tested to show if the advertising claim is valid.
DISCUSSION: When verifying a claim, a test of hypothesis is typically used. This involves setting up a null hypothesis (H_o) and an alternative hypothesis (H_a). The null hypothesis sets up a specific value (i.e., a point, not a range) that is hypothesized to be the true mean. The alternative hypothesis gives the other possible values of the true mean that are of interest in testing the claim. Since ABC claims their diet sodas have less than one calorie, and we are interested in seeing if this is true, we should test $H_o: \mu \geq 1$ (the mean calories of the diet sodas is one) against $H_a: \mu < 1$ (the number of mean calories of the diet sodas is less than one). Since we are only interested if the mean calories are less than one, we ignore testing possible values of the true mean greater than one. Looking at only one side of the value stated by the null hypothesis is called a one-tailed test.

Answer (a) is incorrect because it states a two-tailed test. Answer (c) is incorrect because we want to test that there is less than one calorie, not more. Answer (d) is incorrect because we are interested in possible values of the mean less than one, not less than zero.

Module 18.4: Hypothesis Testing   553

62. The appropriate means for testing this hypothesis is

   a. A Z-statistic.
   b. A t-statistic.
   c. An F-statistic.
   d. A Q-statistic.

The correct answer is (b). *(Publisher)*
REQUIRED: The appropriate statistic to test the hypothesis.
DISCUSSION: The t-statistic is appropriate to check small sample tests of hypotheses. It measures how the sample mean differs from the hypothesized true mean in standard deviations. The formula is

$$t = \frac{\bar{x} - \mu}{s \div \sqrt{n}}$$

if $\bar{x}$ = sample mean,
μ = hypothesized true mean
s = sample standard deviation
n = sample size.

The Z-statistic is appropriate when the standard deviation of the population is known or a large sample ($n > 30$) permits a reasonable approximation of the population standard deviation. The F-statistic tests differences in variances. Q-statistic is a nonsense term.

63. The value of the t-statistic is

   a. -2.45.
   b. -.817.
   c. 2.45.
   d. 4.65.

The correct answer is (a). *(Publisher)*
REQUIRED: The value of the test statistic.
DISCUSSION: Because $\bar{x}$ equals .95 (Q. 60), the hypothesized value of the true mean is 1, and the sample standard deviation equals .0612. The value of the t-statistic is

$$t = \frac{.95 - 1}{.0612 \div \sqrt{9}} = \frac{-.05}{.0612 \div 3} = \frac{-.05}{.0204} = -2.45$$

64. The appropriate number of degrees of freedom for this t-statistic is

   a. 8.
   b. 9.
   c. 7.
   d. 0.
   e. 1.

The correct answer is (a). *(Publisher)*
REQUIRED: The appropriate number of degrees of freedom for the t-statistic.
DISCUSSION: The degrees of freedom associated with the test statistic are the sample size minus the number of parameters being tested. Note here that there are measurements of calorie content for 9 cans of diet soda, i.e., 9 distinct observations. The only parameter tested is μ, the mean calorie content of the diet sodas, so the degrees of freedom are $(n - 1) = 9 - 1 = 8$.

65. The following data have been excerpted from a table of critical values of t:

d.f.	$t_{.10}$	$t_{.05}$	$t_{.025}$
5	1.476	2.015	2.571
6	1.440	1.943	2.447
7	1.415	1.895	2.365
8	1.397	1.860	2.306
9	1.383	1.833	2.262

The value of the "rejection region" for testing the hypothesis that ABC's soda has less than one calorie per can, if we desire 95% confidence, is

   a. 2.306.
   b. 1.86.
   c. 1.833.
   d. 2.262.
   e. 1.645.

The correct answer is (b). *(Publisher)*
REQUIRED: The value of the "rejection region" for testing the hypothesis for 95% confidence.
DISCUSSION: The "rejection region" is set by the value of the t-statistic at the appropriate degrees of freedom to allow a specific level of confidence. Choosing a 95% level of confidence means we must set up a value of t that will give us only a 5% probability of making a Type 1 error (i.e., rejecting the null hypothesis when the null hypothesis is true). The "rejection region" is bounded by this value. The problem is written

$$|t| > t_{.05}^{n-1}$$

meaning that the t-statistic calculated by the formula is greater than the t-value from a table of t-values, which correlates the appropriate degrees of freedom ($n - 1$) and the appropriate probability of making a Type 1 error (.05). In this case, with 8 degrees of freedom, the appropriate "rejection region" is $|t| > 1.86$. Thus, if we calculate a t-statistic greater than 1.86, we will reject the hypothesis that $\mu = 1$.

66. Refer to the information at the top of page 552. What conclusions can be made with 95% confidence?

   a. Reject the manufacturer's claim.
   b. Do not reject the manufacturer's claim.
   c. Cannot make a decision based on current information.
   d. Agree that all sodas have at most one calorie.

The correct answer is (b). *(Publisher)*
   REQUIRED: The conclusion with 95% confidence.
   DISCUSSION: Given a value of t that falls into a "rejection region" set up to insure at most a 5% probability of a Type 1 error, it can be concluded that the true mean is different than our hypothesized mean with 95% confidence. Since |-2.45| > 1.86, the proper conclusion is not to reject the manufacturer's claim since the true mean is believed to be less than 1 with 95% confidence.

67. A company is producing a machine part whose diameter must be 1.000 inches ± .010. Historical records show that the mean diameter of all parts produced since the project began has been 0.995 inches. A sample of five observations (0.985, 1.015, 1.012, 0.988, 0.980, with a mean of 0.996) would be

   a. Rejected by a quality control system that only used a mean chart ($\bar{x}$ chart).
   b. Accepted by a quality control system that only used a mean chart ($\bar{x}$ chart).
   c. Accepted by a quality control system that only used a range chart (R chart).
   d. Accepted by a quality control system that uses both mean and range charts.

The correct answer is (b). *(CIA 1185 III-12)*
   REQUIRED: The true statement about acceptance or rejection of a machine part using a range or mean chart.
   DISCUSSION: The sample has a mean of 0.996. Since the mean of the sample must lie between 0.990 and 1.01 (1.000 inches ± .010), the sample will be accepted if a mean ($\bar{x}$) chart is used. A mean chart displays central tendencies while a range chart shows acceptable high-low range.
   Answer (a) is incorrect because the sample will be accepted if a mean ($\bar{x}$) chart is used. Answers (c) and (d) are incorrect because each observation falls outside the required range, so the sample would be rejected if a range chart were used.

68. A consultant is reviewing the age composition of the employees of Giant National Bank as part of a study of the bank's hiring policies. A recent industry report shows that the percentage of workers over 50 years of age in individual banks is normally distributed and has an arithmetic mean of 10%. Using a t-test and a 95% confidence level, the consultant tested the hypothesis that there is no difference between the employees' age composition of Giant and that of other banks. A random sample of 100 Giant employees included four persons over 50 years of age. The calculated t-value was 4.0. How should the consultant interpret this t-value?

   a. Giant employs four times as many employees over age 50 as the average bank.
   b. Four percent of Giant's employees are over 50 years old.
   c. Since a t-value of 4.0 is considered small, there is no significant difference between the number of employees over 50 years of age in Giant and in other banks.
   d. Since a t-value of 4.0 is considered large, there is less than a 5% risk that the sample result would have occurred if the number of Giant's employees over age 50 were identical to that of other banks.
   e. Since a t-value of 4.0 is considered large, there is a 95% likelihood that the number of Giant's employees over age 50 does not differ from that of other banks.

The correct answer is (d). *(CIA 579 IV-3)*
   REQUIRED: How the t-value should be interpreted.
   DISCUSSION: The student or t-distribution should be useful whenever interval estimates of a population are required, the sample results are small, usually less than 30, and the underlying population is assumed to be approximately normal. For the two-tailed t-test, we accept the null hypothesis that there is no difference between a sample and a population when the calculated t-statistic is less than the t-value found in the table at that level of confidence. We reject the null hypothesis when the t-value calculated is greater than the value found in the table. A t-value of 4.0 is usually considered large, thus there is less than a 5% chance that we could have drawn the sample we did if, in fact, the sample mean is the same as the population mean.
   Answer (a) is incorrect because the t-value is not correlated with the ratio of the sizes of various groups in the population. Answer (b) is incorrect because the t-value is not a percent. It is a variable with a probability distribution (the student or t-distribution) which looks very much like the standard normal distribution except that its shape is dependent upon the number of degrees of freedom [the number of observations minus one, i.e., (n - 1)]. When the number of degrees of freedom is large (more than 30), the values associated with the standard normal and t-distributions are the same. Answer (c) is incorrect because a t-value of 4.0 is considered large, not small. Answer (e) is incorrect because a t-value of 4.0 means that there is a 95% likelihood that the null hypothesis is wrong or that there is a difference.

18.5 Expected Value

69. Jordan & Co. has been sued by a client for breach of warranty. Jordan's controller has accumulated data from the outcomes of similar cases. Jordan & Co. can best quantify its exposure to a loss in this situation by using

a. Regression analysis.
b. Markov analysis.
c. Expected value analysis.
d. Queuing theory.
e. Matrix algebra.

The correct answer is (c). *(CMA 1285 5-21)*
REQUIRED: The quantitative method that can be used to quantify expected losses.
DISCUSSION: Expected value analysis is an estimate of future monetary value based on forecasts and their related probabilities of occurrence. The expected value is found by multiplying the probability of each outcome by its payoff and summing the products. The probabilities used can be developed from experience, such as the results of past cases.
Answer (a) is incorrect because regression analysis is used to determine the effect on a dependent variable of changes in independent variables. Answer (b) is incorrect because Markov analysis involves a chain of analyses, with each link relying on the results of the preceding link. Answer (d) is incorrect because queuing theory is used to determine the optimum length of waiting lines. Answer (e) is incorrect because matrix algebra is a mathematical method that can be used to solve complex algebraic problems.

70. Arlington Inc. is attempting to predict the profitability of a new product line. The marketing department has developed three different forecasts of annual demand and their related probabilities of occurrence for the coming year--low (.2), medium (.5), and high (.3). To develop an estimate of the annual profit figure for the new product line, Arlington Inc. should employ

a. Queuing theory.
b. Expected value analysis.
c. Correlation and regression analysis.
d. Discounted cash flow techniques.
e. PERT/CPM analysis.

The correct answer is (b). *(CMA 1280 5-8)*
REQUIRED: The method to develop an estimate of annual profit for a new product line.
DISCUSSION: Expected value analysis is an estimate of future monetary value based on forecasts and their related probabilities of occurrence. The expected value is found by multiplying the probability of each outcome by its payoff and summing the products.
Answer (a) is incorrect because queuing theory is used in making decisions about the relative merits of permitting waiting lines or expending resources to reduce or eliminate them. Answer (c) is incorrect because correlation and regression analysis only measure the relationship of two or more variables, whether and how they move together. Answer (d) is incorrect because discounted cash flow techniques use time value of money concepts to evaluate investment opportunities. Answer (e) is incorrect because PERT/CPM analysis is a technique used to manage complex projects. It involves analyzing a network of tasks by estimating the time to complete each task.

71. A proprietor who just inherited a building is considering using it in a new business venture. Projections for the business are: revenue of $100,000; fixed cost of $30,000; and variable cost of $50,000. If the business is not started, the individual will work for a company for a wage of $23,000. Also, there are two offers to rent the building, one for $1,000 a month and one for $1,200 a month. What are the expected economic profits if the new business is started?

a. $20,000.
b. $(3,000).
c. $(15,000).
d. $(17,400).

The correct answer is (d). *(CIA 587 IV-44)*
REQUIRED: The expected economic profits if the new business is started.
DISCUSSION: If any input is paid a higher amount than it would receive from the next highest bidder for that input, then economic profit is said to be earned. When economic profit is earned, an input is being paid more for its services than is necessary to keep the input employed in production. If the new business is started, the proprietor will earn $20,000 ($100,000 - $30,000 FC - $50,000 VC). If it is not, the individual can earn $37,400 ($23,000 in wages + $14,400 in rent). The economic profit of starting the business is thus $(17,400).

Module 18.5: Expected Value

72. Expected value in decision analysis is

a. A standard deviation using the probabilities as weights.

b. An arithmetic mean using the probabilities as weights.

c. The square root of the squared deviations.

d. The standard deviation divided by the coefficient of variation.

e. A measure of the difference between the best possible outcome and the outcome of the original decision.

The correct answer is (b). *(CMA 1286 5-3)*
REQUIRED: The true statement about expected value.
DISCUSSION: Expected value analysis is an estimate of future monetary value based on forecasts and their related probabilities of occurrence. The expected value is found by multiplying the probability of each outcome by its payoff and summing the products. Expected value is thus an arithmetic mean using probabilities as weights.
Answer (a), (c), and (d) are incorrect because the standard deviation is a measure of dispersion of a population. Answer (e) is incorrect because expected value is a prospective measure.

73. Compute expected total stockout cost for the year based on the following: 12 orders per year, $.40 stockout cost per unit, and stockout probability estimates of:

Probability of Stockout	Stockout in Units
.20	50
.10	100

a. $8.

b. $48.

c. $96.

d. $480.

The correct answer is (c). *(CIA 1187 IV-21)*
REQUIRED: The expected total stockout cost for the year.
DISCUSSION: The cost of a 50-unit stockout is $20 (50 x $.40), and the cost of a 100-unit stockout is $40 (100 x $.40). The expected stockout cost is found by multiplying stockout cost times the associated probability times the annual number of orders and then adding the products.

Probability	Stockout Cost	Annual Orders	Expected Stockout Cost
.20	$20	12	$48
.10	$40	12	48
			$96

74. A firm has a choice of making Product A (fixed costs = $10,000 and variable costs = $5 per unit) or Product B (fixed costs = $20,000 and variable costs = $3 per unit). There are two possible projected sales levels for each product: sales of 10,000 units and sales of 20,000 units. The unit selling price of each product is $3.75. If the firm chooses to produce Product B and the 20,000 units are sold, then the resultant payoff would be

a. $(42,500).

b. $(12,500).

c. $(5,000).

d. $25,000.

The correct answer is (c). *(CIA 1187 III-47)*
REQUIRED: The resultant payoff from choosing a given option with the specified payoff.
DISCUSSION: Revenue for Product B will be $75,000 (20,000 units x $3.75). Total cost will be $80,000 [$20,000 FC + $60,000 VC ($3 x 20,000 units)]. Hence, the payoff is $(5,000).

75. A student organization wants to sell plants on campus to raise funds. They invest in a sales booth costing $50 which they can sell for $30 after the sales project. The plants can be purchased at $4 each and will be sold at $7 each. The cost of having plants delivered to the booth is $60. The unsold plants cannot be returned once delivered. The organization predicts sales to be 50 units. If actual sales are 40 units, what is the cost of the prediction error?

a. $0.

b. $20.

c. $30.

d. $40.

The correct answer is (d). *(CIA 1187 IV-18)*
REQUIRED: The cost of the prediction error.
DISCUSSION: The cost of the prediction error is found by comparing the outcome of the best possible action (buy 40 units) and the outcome of the planned action (buy 50 units) given the actual result. The predicted sales are 50 units. If 50 units are bought and actual sales are 40 units, the cost of the prediction error is the cost of the 10 units ($4 x 10 = $40) not sold. Since the costs of the sales booth and delivery of plants would not vary between the two actions, they are ignored for this purpose. Also, lost contribution margin is not part of the cost of the prediction error.

Module 18.5: Expected Value

76. Bye Co. is considering the sale of banners at the state university football championship game. Bye could purchase these banners for $.60 each. Unsold banners would be nonreturnable and worthless after the game. Bye would have to rent a booth at the stadium for $250. Bye estimates sales of 500 banners at $2.00 each. If Bye's prediction proves to be incorrect and only 300 banners were sold, the cost of this prediction error would be

a. $120.
b. $130.
c. $170.
d. $280.

The correct answer is (a). *(CPA 1185 Q-20)*
REQUIRED: The cost of the prediction error.
DISCUSSION: If 500 units are bought and actual sales are 300 units, the cost of the prediction error is the cost of the 200 units ($.60 x 200 = $120) not sold. The cost of the booth would not vary between the two actions and is ignored.

77. A construction contractor has been invited to submit a bid on a large and complicated construction project. The preparation of the bid proposal will cost about $20,000. Management feels that if the company bids low enough to result in a net profit of $50,000, there would be a 60% chance of getting the job. If the company bids high enough to result in a $100,000 net profit, the chance of getting the contract would be only 20%. What should the company do?

a. Bid only high enough to allow for a $50,000 profit because the expected value of the payoff is $22,000.

b. Bid high enough to allow for a $100,000 profit because the expected value of the payoff is $4,000.

c. Bid high enough to allow for a $100,000 profit because the expected value of the payoff is $20,000.

d. Make no bid.

The correct answer is (a). *(CIA 587 III-45)*
REQUIRED: The proper action given the cost of bidding and the probabilities of specified net profits.
DISCUSSION: For decisions involving risk, the concept of expected value provides a rational means for selecting the best action. The expected value of a choice is found by multiplying the probability of each outcome by its payoff, and summing the products. It represents the long-term average payoff for repeated trials. The best alternative is the one having the highest expected value. The expected value of bidding for a $50,000 net profit is $22,000 [(.6 x $50,000 - (.4 x $20,000)]. Bidding for a $100,000 net profit has an expected value of $4,000 [(.2 x $100,000) - (.8 x $20,000)]. Making no bid has an expected value of zero.

78. Olex Company is considering a proposal to introduce a new product, Vee. An outside marketing consultant prepared the following probability distribution describing the relative likelihood of monthly sales volume levels and related income (loss) for Vee:

Monthly Sales Volume	Probability	Income (Loss)
6,000	0.10	$(70,000)
12,000	0.20	10,000
18,000	0.40	60,000
24,000	0.20	100,000
30,000	0.10	140,000

If Olex decides to market Vee, the expected value of the added monthly income will be

a. $240,000.
b. $60,000.
c. $53,000.
d. $48,000.

The correct answer is (c). *(CPA 583 Q-17)*
REQUIRED: The expected value of added monthly income from marketing a new product.
DISCUSSION: The answer is found by weighting the income or (loss) value for each event in the table by the probability of its occurrence and adding the products.

Probability	Income (Loss)	Expected Value
0.10	$(70,000)	$ (7,000)
0.20	10,000	2,000
0.40	60,000	24,000
0.20	100,000	20,000
0.10	140,000	14,000
Total expected value		$53,000

79. A payoff table (matrix) for evaluating alternative courses of action attempts to deal with

a. Centralization.
b. Uncertainty.
c. Goal congruence.
d. Motivation.

The correct answer is (b). *(CPA 577 T-42)*
REQUIRED: The purpose of a payoff table for evaluating alternatives.
DISCUSSION: A payoff table is a summary of actions, events, probabilities, and outcomes. No outcome occurs with certainty. The problem lies in evaluating the probabilities of the possible events. Thus, the payoff table attempts to deal with uncertainties.
Answer (a) is incorrect because it is a term used to denote the degree of organizational control exercised by top management. Answer (c) is incorrect because it describes the degree of goal commonality of various groups. Answer (d) is incorrect because motivation is the manner in which people may be encouraged to sustain positive activity or discouraged from negative activity.

80. A company must produce one of four toys during its next production period. The appropriate payoff matrix is as follows:

		Products			
Demand	Probability	Toy A	Toy B	Toy C	Toy D
Poor	.3	(10,000)	6,000	8,000	(10,000)
Moderate	.5	26,000	19,000	22,000	36,000
Heavy	.2	31,000	38,000	32,000	23,000

The toy that should be produced based upon the highest expected payoff is

a. Toy A.
b. Toy B.
c. Toy C.
d. Toy D.

The correct answer is (c). *(CIA 1187 III-42)*
REQUIRED: The toy that should be produced based upon the highest expected payoff.
DISCUSSION: The expected value of the payoff for Toy C is $19,800 [(.3 x $8,000) + (.5 x $22,000) + (.2 x $32,000)]. Toy C has the highest payoff and should be produced.
Answer (a) is incorrect because the payoff is $16,200 [(.3 x $-10,000) + (.5 x $26,000) + (.2 x $31,000)]. Answer (b) is incorrect because the payoff is $18,900 [(.3 x $6,000) + (.5 x $19,000) + (.2 x $38,000)]. Answer (d) is incorrect because the payoff is $19,600 [(.3 x $-10,000) + (.5 x $36,000) + (.2 x $23,000)].

81. Joe Neil, CPA, has among his clientele a charitable organization that has a legal permit to conduct games of chance for fund-raising purposes. Neil's client derives its profit from admission fees and the sale of refreshments, and therefore wants to "break even" on the games of chance. In one of these games, the player draws one card from a standard deck of 52 cards. A player drawing any one of four "queens" wins $5, and a player drawing any one of 13 "hearts" wins $2. Neil is asked to compute the price that should be charged per draw, so that the total amount paid out for winning draws can be expected to equal the total amount received from all draws. Which one of the following equations should Neil use to compute the price (P)?

a. $5 - 2 = \frac{35}{52} P$

b. $\frac{4}{52}(5) + \frac{13}{52}(2) = \frac{35}{52} P$

c. $\frac{4}{52}(5 - P) + \frac{13}{52}(2 - P) = P$

d. $\frac{4}{52}(5) + \frac{13}{52}(2) = P$

The correct answer is (d). *(CPA 587 Q-21)*
REQUIRED: The expected payoff of an event.
DISCUSSION: Use expected value analysis to solve this problem. Given no profit, the price per ticket will be the expected payoff. One event is drawing a queen. This event has a probability of 4/52 and a payoff of $5. The other event is drawing a heart. This event has a probability of 13/52 and a payoff of $2. The expected payoff is:

$$\frac{4}{52}(\$5) + \frac{13}{52}(\$2)$$

Module 18.5: Expected Value

82. During 1989, Seco Corp. experienced the following power outages:

Number of Outages Per Month	Number of Months
0	3
1	2
2	4
3	3
	12

Each power outage results in out-of-pocket cost of $200. For $250 per month, Seco can lease an auxiliary generator to provide power during outages. If Seco leases an auxiliary generator in 1990, the estimated savings (or additional expenditures) for 1990 would be

a. $800.
b. $950.
c. $(600).
d. $(1,800).

The correct answer is (a). *(CPA 1186 Q-36)*
REQUIRED: The expected savings (or additional expenditures) of leasing an auxiliary generator.
DISCUSSION: The expected number of power outages is 19.

Number of Outages Per Month	×	Number of Months	=	Total Outages
0		3		0
1		2		2
2		4		8
3		3		9
				19

Total out-of-pocket costs for 19 outages is $3,800 ($200 x 19). Total lease costs would be $3,000 ($250 x 12). The estimated savings is $800 ($3,800 - $3,000).

Questions 83 and 84 are based on the following information. A wine maker must decide whether to harvest grapes now or in four weeks. Harvesting now will yield 100,000 bottles of wine netting $2 per bottle. If the wine maker waits and the weather turns cold (probability 0.2), the yield will be cut in half but net $3 per bottle. If the weather does not turn cold, the yield will depend on rain. With rain (probability 0.5), a full yield netting $4 per bottle will result. Without rain (probability 0.5), there will still be a full 100,000-bottle yield, but the net will be only $3 per bottle.

83. The optimal expected value is

a. $200,000.
b. $310,000.
c. $350,000.
d. $400,000.

The correct answer is (b). *(CIA 586 III-21)*
REQUIRED: The optimal expected value.
DISCUSSION: The expected value of harvesting now is

$$E(Now) = \$2(100,000) = \$200,000$$

The expected value of waiting is

$$E(Wait) = .2(\$3)(50,000) + .8[.5(\$4)(100,000)] + .5(\$3)(100,000)$$
$$= \$30,000 + \$280,000$$
$$= \$310,000 \text{ optimal expected value}$$

84. If the wine maker decides to wait, what is the probability that the yield would be less than harvesting now?

a. 0.0.
b. 0.2.
c. 0.4.
d. 0.5.

The correct answer is (b). *(CIA 586 III-22)*
REQUIRED: The probability of a lesser yield if the decision is to wait.
DISCUSSION: The only outcome that has a possibility lower than $200,000 for harvesting now would be if the wine maker waits and the weather turns cold. This would yield only $150,000 ($3 x 50,000 bottles). The probability of this occurrence is 0.2.

Module 18.5: Expected Value

Questions 85 through 87 are based on Bilco Oil Company, which currently sells three grades of gasoline: regular, premium, and "regular plus," which is a mixture of regular and premium. Regular plus is advertised as being "at least 50% premium." Although any mixture containing 50% or more premium gas could be sold as "regular plus," it is less costly to use exactly 50%. The percentage of premium gas in the mixture is determined by one small valve in the blending machine. If the valve is properly adjusted, the machine provides a mixture which is 50% premium and 50% regular. Assume that if the valve is out of adjustment the machine provides a mixture which is 60% premium and 40% regular.

Once the machine is started it must continue until 100,000 gallons of "regular plus" have been mixed. Cost data available:

Cost per gallon -- premium	$.32
-- regular	$.30
Cost of checking the valve	$80.00
Cost of adjusting the valve	$40.00

Subjective estimates of the probabilities of the valve's condition are estimated to be:

Event	Probability
Valve in adjustment	.7
Valve out of adjustment	.3

---

85. The expected cost of checking the valve and adjusting it if necessary would be

a. $80.
b. $120.
c. $92.
d. $100.
e. None of the above.

The correct answer is (c). *(CMA 1278 5-18)*
REQUIRED: The expected cost of checking and adjusting the valve.
DISCUSSION: To calculate the expected value of checking and adjusting the valve, one must add the cost of checking the valve to the cost of adjusting the valve weighted by the probability that the valve is out of adjustment. Thus, the cost is $92 [$80 + (.3 x $40)].

86. The conditional cost of not checking the valve when it is out of adjustment would be

a. $80.
b. $200.
c. $260.
d. $320.
e. None of the above.

The correct answer is (b). *(CMA 1278 5-19)*
REQUIRED: The conditional cost of not checking the valve.
DISCUSSION: The conditional cost is the difference between the cost of the fuel if the valve works properly ($31,000) and the cost if it does not ($31,200), a difference of $200.

100,000 x .5 x $.30 =	$15,000
100,000 x .5 x $.32 =	16,000
Cost when in adjustment	$31,000
100,000 x .4 x $.30 =	$12,000
100,000 x .6 x $.32 =	19,200
Cost out of adjustment	$31,200

87. Using the criterion of minimum expected cost, the valve would not be checked unless the probability that the valve is out of adjustment falls in the range of

a. 0 - .1299 inclusive.
b. .13 - .2499 inclusive.
c. .25 - .3799 inclusive.
d. .38 - .4999 inclusive.
e. .50 - 1.00 inclusive.

The correct answer is (e). *(CMA 1278 5-20)*
REQUIRED: The range of probability that would justify checking the valve.
DISCUSSION: The probability of maladjustment must be within a range in which checking the valve is economically valuable. Given that P is the probability of maladjustment, the expected cost of not checking is $200P (the conditional cost of not checking a maladjusted valve was determined in Q. 86). The cost of checking is $80, and the expected cost making a needed adjustment is $40P. If the expected cost of not checking is equated with the expected cost of checking and adjusting ($200P = $80 + $40P), P is bound to be .5. The cost of checking the valve when there is a 50% chance of adjusting it is $100 [$80 + ($40 x .5)]. The expected cost of not checking is $100 ($200 x .5). For any value of P greater than .5, the expected cost of not checking exceeds the expected cost of checking the valve, so P = .5 is the lowest bound wherein the valve should economically be tested.

Module 18.5: Expected Value

Questions 88 through 90 are based on the following decision tree.

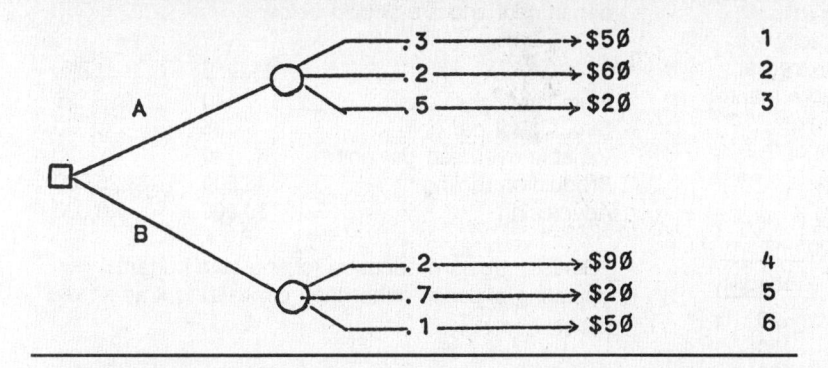

```
              .3 ──────→ $50    1
         ○    .2 ──────→ $60    2
      A /     .5 ──────→ $20    3
       /
   □
       \
      B \
          \   .2 ──────→ $90    4
           ○  .7 ──────→ $20    5
              .1 ──────→ $50    6
```

88. Which of the six branches provides the largest conditional dollar value?

   a. 1.
   b. 2.
   c. 6.
   d. 4.

The correct answer is (d). *(N. Ahadiat)*
REQUIRED: The largest conditional dollar value of a branch.
DISCUSSION: The conditional value is computed as the payoff times the probability of the payoff. The conditional values are:

Branches	Payoff	Probability	Conditional Value
1	$50	.3	15
2	60	.2	12
3	20	.5	10
4	90	.2	18
5	20	.7	14
6	50	.1	5

Thus, from the above table the largest conditional value is branch 4.

89. What is the expected value of alternative A?

   a. $37.00.
   b. $130.00.
   c. $43.33.
   d. $15.00

The correct answer is (a). *(N. Ahadiat)*
REQUIRED: The expected value of alternative A.
DISCUSSION: The expected value is the average value of all possible payoffs related to a plan of action. It is computed as the sum of a payoff of an event times the probability of the event. In this case:

$$E(A) = .3(\$50) + .2(\$60) + .5(\$20) = \$37$$

90. If the expected value is the only applicable criterion, which alternative is preferable?

   a. Both alternatives are equally acceptable.
   b. Alternative A.
   c. Alternative B.
   d. Cannot be determined.

The correct answer is (a). *(N. Ahadiat)*
REQUIRED: The expected value of both alternatives A and B.
DISCUSSION: The action with the largest expected value is the preferable action. Since both alternatives have an expected value of $37, both are equally attractive.

$$E(A) = .3(\$50) + .2(\$60) + .5(\$20) = \$37$$
$$E(B) = .2(\$90) + .7(\$20) + .1(\$50) = \$37$$

Module 18.5: Expected Value

Questions 91 through 97 are based on the following information. Gleason Company has two products, a frozen dessert and ready-to-bake breakfast rolls, ready for introduction. However, plant capacity is limited, and only one product can be introduced at present. Therefore, Gleason has conducted a market study, at a cost of $26,000, to determine which product will be more profitable. The results of the study show the following sales patterns.

Sales of Desserts at $1.80/unit		Sales of Rolls at $1.20/unit	
Volume	Probability	Volume	Probability
250,000	.30	200,000	.20
300,000	.40	250,000	.50
350,000	.20	300,000	.20
400,000	.10	350,000	.10

The costs associated with the two products have been estimated by Gleason's cost accounting department and are shown below.

	Dessert	Rolls
Ingredients per unit	$ .40	$ .25
Direct labor per unit	.35	.30
Variable overhead per unit	.40	.20
Production tooling*	48,000	25,000
Advertising	30,000	20,000

*Gleason treats production tooling as a current operating expense rather than capitalizing it as a fixed asset.

91. According to Gleason's market study, the expected value of the sales volume of the breakfast rolls is

a. 125,000 units.
b. 260,000 units.
c. 275,000 units.
d. 250,000 units.
e. Some amount other than those given above.

The correct answer is (b). (CMA 687 5-21)
REQUIRED: The expected value of the sales volume of breakfast rolls.
DISCUSSION: The expected value is found by multiplying the probability of each possibility times the potential volumes:

$$200,000 \times .20 = 40,000$$
$$250,000 \times .50 = 125,000$$
$$300,000 \times .20 = 60,000$$
$$350,000 \times .10 = \underline{35,000}$$
$$\text{Total} \quad \underline{260,000}$$

92. Applying a deterministic approach, Gleason's revenue from sales of frozen desserts would be

a. $549,000.
b. $195,000.
c. $540,000.
d. $216,000.
e. Some amount other than those given above.

The correct answer is (c). (CMA 687 5-22)
REQUIRED: The revenue from sales using a deterministic approach.
DISCUSSION: The word deterministic is used to characterize processes that are not probabilistic. Such an approach uses the most likely value. In this case, sales of desserts would most likely be 300,000 units. At $1.80 each, total revenue would be $540,000.

93. The expected value of Gleason's operating profit directly traceable to the sale of frozen desserts is

a. $198,250.
b. $150,250.
c. $471,000.
d. $120,250.
e. Some amount other than those given above.

The correct answer is (d). (CMA 687 5-23)
REQUIRED: The expected value of operating profit.
DISCUSSION: The expected value for sales of frozen desserts is

$$250,000 \times .30 = 75,000$$
$$300,000 \times .40 = 120,000$$
$$350,000 \times .20 = 70,000$$
$$400,000 \times .10 = \underline{40,000}$$
$$\underline{305,000}$$

At $1.80 each, the total revenue from 305,000 units would be $549,000. Variable costs would total $1.15 each ($.40 + $.35 + $.40), or $350,750 for 305,000 units. Fixed costs total $78,000 ($48,000 + $30,000). Thus, operating profit would be $120,250 ($549,000 - $350,750 - $78,000).

Module 18.5: Expected Value

94. The cost incurred by Gleason for the market study is

a. An incremental cost.
b. A prime cost.
c. An opportunity cost.
d. A sunk cost.
e. A conversion cost.

The correct answer is (d). *(CMA 687 5-25)*
REQUIRED: The term referring to the cost of the market study.
DISCUSSION: A sunk cost is a previously incurred cost that is the result of a past irrevocable management decision. Nothing can be done in the future about sunk costs. The market study cost is an example.
Answer (a) is incorrect because an incremental cost is the additional cost of a new strategy or increased production. It is also called a differential cost. Answer (b) is incorrect because prime costs are variable costs of direct material and direct labor. Answer (c) is incorrect because an opportunity cost is the revenue obtainable from an alternative use of a resource. Answer (e) is incorrect because conversion costs are those incurred to convert materials into a finished product. They include direct labor and factory overhead.

95. The advertising expense estimated by Gleason for the introduction of the new products is an example of

a. A conversion cost.
b. A discretionary cost.
c. A committed cost.
d. A sunk cost.
e. An opportunity cost.

The correct answer is (b). *(CMA 687 5-26)*
REQUIRED: The type of cost represented by advertising expense.
DISCUSSION: Discretionary costs refer to fixed costs that are not absolutely necessary to operate in the current period. The level of these costs is subject to a decision made by management each period. Advertising is a good example of a discretionary fixed cost.
Answer (a) is incorrect because conversion costs are incurred for labor and overhead. Answer (c) is incorrect because committed costs are those fixed costs arising from the possession of plant and equipment and a basic organization. These costs are affected primarily by long-run decisions as to a company's desired capacity. Answer (d) is incorrect because a sunk cost cannot be avoided. Answer (e) is incorrect because an opportunity cost represents the maximum revenue that could have been earned on the next best alternative use of a resource.

96. Assuming that Gleason elects to produce the frozen dessert, the profit that would have been earned on the breakfast rolls is

a. A deferrable cost.
b. A sunk cost.
c. An avoidable cost.
d. An opportunity cost.
e. An incremental cost.

The correct answer is (d). *(CMA 687 5-27)*
REQUIRED: The term referring to the profit lost by not choosing the alternative.
DISCUSSION: An opportunity cost is the maximum return that could have been earned on the next best alternative use of a resource. In this case, the lost profit on the rolls is an opportunity cost.
Answer (a) is incorrect because a deferrable cost is one that can be deferred to a future period. Answer (b) is incorrect because a sunk cost is one that cannot be reversed since it is the result of a past irrevocable decision. Answer (c) is incorrect because an avoidable cost is an ongoing cost that may be eliminated by ceasing to perform some economic activity or segment thereof or by improving the efficiency by which such activity is accomplished. Answer (e) is incorrect because an incremental cost is a change in costs resulting from variations in output or operations.

Module 18.5: Expected Value

97. Refer to the information at the top of page 562. In order to recover the costs of production tooling and advertising for the breakfast rolls, Gleason's sales of the breakfast rolls would have to be

   a. 37,500 units.
   b. 100,000 units.
   c. 60,000 units.
   d. 54,000 units.
   e. Some amount other than those given above.

The correct answer is (b). *(CMA 687 5-24)*
REQUIRED: The breakeven point in units for sales of the rolls.
DISCUSSION: In this CVP problem, fixed costs of $45,000 ($25,000 + $20,000) should be divided by the unit contribution margin $.45 ($1.20 selling price - $.25 - $.30 - $.20). The unit BEP is therefore 100,000.

Questions 98 through 102 are based on the following information. The Honorary Club sells fresh hot cider at Ivy University's home football games. The frequency distribution of the demand for cups of hot cider per game is presented below.

Unit Sales Volume	Probability
10,000 cups	.10
20,000 cups	.15
30,000 cups	.20
40,000 cups	.35
50,000 cups	.20
	1.00

The hot cider is sold for $1.00 a cup and the cost per cup is $.40. Any unsold hot cider is discarded because it will spoil before the next home game.

---

98. The estimated demand for hot cider at the next Ivy University home football game using an expected value approach is

   a. 30,000 cups.
   b. 34,000 cups.
   c. 40,000 cups.
   d. 50,000 cups.
   e. Some amount other than those given above.

The correct answer is (b). *(CMA 686 5-18)*
REQUIRED: The estimated demand using an expected value approach.
DISCUSSION: Expected value analysis is an estimate of future monetary value based on forecasts and their related probabilities of occurrence. The expected value is found by multiplying the probability of each outcome by its payoff and summing the products. For the hot cider problem, the estimated demand is calculated as follows:

```
10,000 x .10 =   1,000
20,000 x .15 =   3,000
30,000 x .20 =   6,000
40,000 x .35 =  14,000
50,000 x .20 =  10,000
Total   1.00 =  34,000
```

99. The estimated demand for hot cider at the next Ivy University home football game using a deterministic approach based on the most likely outcome is

   a. 30,000 cups.
   b. 34,000 cups.
   c. 40,000 cups.
   d. 50,000 cups.
   e. Some amount other than those given above.

The correct answer is (c). *(CMA 686 5-19)*
REQUIRED: The estimated demand using a deterministic approach based on the most likely outcome.
DISCUSSION: Since 40,000 cups are sold at more games than any other volume (albeit only 35% of the time), it is most likely that volume will be sold at the next game. A deterministic approach would thus treat the most likely outcome as certain.

100. The conditional profit (loss) per game of having 30,000 cups of hot cider available but only selling 20,000 cups of cider is

a. $8,000.
b. $12,000.
c. $18,000.
d. $3,000.
e. Some amount other than those given above.

The correct answer is (a). *(CMA 686 5-20)*
REQUIRED: The conditional profit (loss) of selling less than the supply on hand.
DISCUSSION: The 30,000 cups cost $.40 each, or $12,000. The 20,000 cups sold would generate $20,000 of revenue. Thus, the per game profit would be $8,000.

101. The conditional profit (loss) per game of having 30,000 cups of hot cider available and selling all 30,000 cups of hot cider is

a. $3,600.
b. $12,000.
c. $18,000.
d. $6,000.
e. Some amount other than those given above.

The correct answer is (c). *(CMA 686 5-21)*
REQUIRED: The conditional profit (loss) of selling the entire inventory.
DISCUSSION: The 30,000 cups cost $.40 each, or $12,000. The $30,000 of revenue ($1 x 30,000) would thus result in a profit of $18,000.

102. The conditional profit (loss) per game of having 30,000 cups of hot cider available but being able to sell 40,000 cups of hot cider if it had been available is

a. $18,000.
b. $6,300.
c. $28,000.
d. $24,000.
e. Some amount other than those given above.

The correct answer is (a). *(CMA 686 5-22)*
REQUIRED: The conditional profit (loss) of being able to sell more than the inventory.
DISCUSSION: The answer to this question is $18,000, the same as the preceding question, since sales would be $30,000 in any instance, and costs would be $12,000.

103. A firm obtained the following data based on the results shown below for 100 runs simulating the introduction of a new product.

Net Profit Before Tax:	$(5,000)	$0	$5,000	$10,000	$15,000
Frequency:	.30	.30	.20	.15	.05

The firm should

a. Expect to break even if the product is introduced.
b. Not introduce the product.
c. Expect to make a profit if the product is introduced.
d. Expect to lose money if the product is introduced.

The correct answer is (c). *(CIA 1185 III-25)*
REQUIRED: The conclusion to be drawn from simulation results.
DISCUSSION: To determine if the product should be introduced, an expected value calculation should be made.

EV = ($-5,000 x .3) + ($0 x .3) + ($5,000 x .2)
     + ($10,000 x .15) + ($15,000 x .05)
   = $1,750

Since the expected value is positive, the firm should expect to make a profit if the product is introduced.

18.6 Other Applications

104. For a repetitive production process, monthly quantity variances are normally distributed with a mean value of $800 and a standard deviation of $100. The firm wishes to investigate monthly quantity variances only when the likelihood that they were caused by random factors is less than 5%. In this situation the dollar range of acceptable quantity variances is between

- a. $600 - $1,000.
- b. $800 - $1,000.
- c. $0 - $200.
- d. $0 - $400.
- e. $700 - $900.

The correct answer is (a). *(CIA 580 IV-20)*
REQUIRED: The dollar range of acceptable quantity variances given a normal distribution and values for the mean and standard deviation.
DISCUSSION: To ascertain the range within which acceptable quantity variances may occur with 95% confidence that they are not caused by random factors, one must calculate a 95% confidence interval. This interval is equal to plus or minus 1.96 standard deviations from the mean. Given a standard deviation of $100 and a mean of $800, the interval ranges from $604 to $996. $800 ± 1.96 ($100).

105. The following contingency table was prepared from data developed during the audit of an inventory control system.

Age of Inventory in Units

Quality of Stock	6 Months or Less	6-12 Months	13 or More Months	Totals
High	18	20	17	55
Average	12	18	15	45
Low	15	7	8	30
Totals	45	45	40	130

Based on the above data, what is the number of low-quality items with age 6-12 months that one would expect to find in this sample of 130 items under the assumption that stock age does not affect stock quality?

- a. 7.0.
- b. 10.4.
- c. 14.4.
- d. 19.0.
- e. 43.3.

The correct answer is (b). *(CIA 583 II-9)*
REQUIRED: The expected number of low-quality items of a given age in a sample assuming stock age and stock quality are unrelated.
DISCUSSION: Given no relationship between stock age and stock quality, the numbers regarding the age of the inventory for specific qualities are irrelevant. Accordingly, one would expect that the proportion of low-quality items among those aged 6-12 months would be the same as the proportion for the entire sample (30 ÷ 130 = 23%). The expected number of low-quality items aged 6-12 months is thus 10.4 (23% x 45).

106. Clerks A, B, and C process 50%, 20%, and 30% of the sales orders, respectively. The percentage of errors made in processing a sales order by clerks A, B, and C are 2%, 5%, and 10%, respectively. A sales order is audited and found to be in error. What is the probability that this invoice was processed by clerk C?

- a. .30.
- b. .60.
- c. .10.
- d. .03.
- e. None of the above.

The correct answer is (b). *(CIA 582 II-19)*
REQUIRED: The probability that an error was committed by a specified person given the number of events and the error rate.
DISCUSSION: Given that an error has occurred, the question asks what was the likelihood that it was committed by C. The probability of an error was 5% [(50% x 2%) + (20% x 5%) + (30% x 10%)]. C therefore accounted for 60% of the total error [(30% x 10%) ÷ 5%].

Module 18.6: Other Applications

107. A plant has 6,000 male and 4,000 female employees. 20% of these employees work overtime. A random sample of 100 plant employees would be expected to contain about

  a. 60 males who worked overtime.
  b. 50 males.
  c. 8 females who worked overtime.
  d. 20 females.

The correct answer is (c). *(CIA 584 IV-29)*
REQUIRED: The correct statement about a random sample of a population of employees.
DISCUSSION: A sample of 100 randomly chosen employees would on average include 60 males and 40 females. If the probability of working overtime is independent of the sex of the employee, the probability of selecting a female who works overtime is .08 (.4 x .2). Since the sample size is 100, the expected value is 8 (.08 x 100).

Questions 108 and 109 are based on Brown Maintenance Services, which has been performing technical maintenance service on a wide variety of business machines for small businesses in a large metropolitan area for many years. Brown has been considering a change in its fee structure. The analysis requires a probability distribution for each week for the number of anticipated service calls related to each of several different types of equipment.

---

108. Phil Brown suggested establishing the distribution using the relative frequency of various numbers of weekly service calls over the last four years. The following tabulation was prepared:

Number of Calls	Number of Occurrences
801-850	4
851-900	10
901-950	80
951-1000	40
1001-1050	20
1051-1100	12
1101-1150	12
1151-1200	10
1201-1250	8
1251-1300	4
	200

The probability distribution established from this tabulation would lead to the conclusion that the probability of experiencing more than 1,150 calls for service during a given week would be

  a. .06.
  b. .89.
  c. .17.
  d. .11.

The correct answer is (d). *(CMA 679 5-14)*
REQUIRED: The probability according to the given distribution that a stated event will occur.
DISCUSSION: Based on past experience, the number of calls exceeded 1,150 during 22 (10 + 8 + 4) of the 200 weeks for which data are available. The probability of such an event is thus .11 (22 ÷ 200).

109. Bill Brown disagreed with his brother, arguing that the number and size of the companies with which they held maintenance contracts had changed recently. He concluded that this past experience was not relevant. Bill proposed the assumption of a uniform distribution with every possible number of calls from 801 to 1,300 being equally likely. Using this uniform distribution would lead to the conclusion that the probability of experiencing more than 1,150 calls during a week would be

  a. .40.
  b. .30.
  c. .70.
  d. .20.

The correct answer is (b). *(CMA 679 5-15)*
REQUIRED: The probability of a stated event given a uniform distribution.
DISCUSSION: There are ten 50-call intervals (see Q. 108) in this assumed uniform distribution of the number of calls. In a uniform distribution, each outcome has an equal probability of occurring (100% ÷ 10 = 10%). Three intervals (outcomes) are in the portion of the distribution representing calls in excess of 1,150. The probability that more than 1,150 calls will be made is thus .30 (3 x 10%).

Questions 110 through 112 are based on the Boston Company, which has pooled information from salesmen, customers, sales managers, and its economic research group to make a demand forecast for a new product line. From this information, annual demand in pounds (x) is forecast to be normally distributed with a mean (μ_x) of 500,000 pounds and standard deviation (σ_x) of 100,000 pounds.

110. This probability distribution for demand can be described as

a. Subjective, continuous, symmetric, and bimodal.
b. Objective, continuous, symmetric, and bimodal.
c. Subjective, discrete, symmetric, and unimodal.
d. Subjective, continuous, skewed right, and unimodal.
e. Subjective, continuous, symmetric, and unimodal.

The correct answer is (e). *(CMA 679 5-19)*
REQUIRED: The best description of the probability distribution for demand.
DISCUSSION: This probability distribution is stated to be normally distributed. It is therefore continuous, symmetrical, and unimodal. The information is subjective because it is based on a pool of estimates drawn from experts as well as an economic research group.
Answers (a) and (b) are incorrect because a normal distribution has only one mode (most frequent occurrence). A bimodal distribution has two peaks. Answer (c) is incorrect because the normal distribution is continuous, not discrete. The binomial distribution is an example of a discrete distribution. Answer (d) is incorrect because this distribution is symmetrical, not skewed. Skewed right means that the distribution has a larger tail to the right.

111. Letting x be the number of pounds demanded and $Z = (x - \mu_{x1}) \div \sigma_x$, the probability that more than 650,000 pounds will be demanded, P(x > 650,000) equals

a. $P(x \leq 650,000)$.
b. $P(Z \leq 1.5)$.
c. $P(Z > 1.5)$.
d. $1 - P(x < 350,000)$.
e. Some other value.

The correct answer is (c). *(CMA 679 5-20)*
REQUIRED: The probability that the demand will exceed a certain quantity.
DISCUSSION: $Z = (x - \mu_x) \div \sigma_x$ is a random variable formed from the underlying normal distribution of x (annual demand in pounds) that is also normally distributed but has a mean (μ_Z) of 0 and standard deviation (σ_Z) equal to 1. Thus, a Z value states how far a given value of x is away from its mean (μ_x) in terms of its standard deviation (σ_x).
Given that the mean is 500,000 pounds and the standard deviation is 100,000 pounds, the probability that more than 650,000 pounds will be demanded is equal to the probability of an occurrence greater than 1.5 standard deviations above the mean. Hence, the probability that the Z score is greater than 1.5 standard deviations is the correct answer. This may be determined simply by substituting the 1.5 standard deviation into the Z formula.

112. If Boston's new product line will have a selling price of $30 a pound, variable costs of $20 a pound, and attributable fixed costs of $3,500,000 per year, annual profit on the new product line will have a

a. Normal distribution with a mean of $5,000,000 and a standard deviation of $1,000,000.
b. Normal distribution with a mean of $1,500,000 and a standard deviation of $1,000,000.
c. Normal distribution with a mean of $1,500,000 and a standard deviation of $10,000,000.
d. Normal distribution with a mean of $5,000,000 and a standard deviation of $10,000,000.
e. Some other distribution and standard deviation.

The correct answer is (b). *(CMA 679 5-21)*
REQUIRED: The mean and standard deviation of the annual profit on a new product line.
DISCUSSION: The distribution of the expected profit is normal because it is based on the normally distributed estimation of sales. The unit contribution margin is $10 ($30 selling price − $20 variable cost). Consequently, the average CM is $5 million ($10 UCM × demand mean of 500,000 pounds). The $5 million CM less $3.5 million FC results in $1.5 million expected profit. The standard deviation of the profit is $1 million ($10 UCM × demand standard deviation of 100,000 pounds).

Sales (500,000 × $30)	$15,000,000
Variable costs (500,000 × $20)	(10,000,000)
Contribution margin	$ 5,000,000
Fixed costs	(3,500,000)
Profit	$ 1,500,000

Questions 113 through 115 are based on the ARC Radio Company, which is trying to decide whether to introduce as a new product a wrist "radio-watch" designed for shortwave reception of exact time as broadcast by the National Bureau of Standards. The "radio-watch" would be priced at $60, which is exactly twice the variable cost per unit to manufacture and sell it. The incremental fixed costs necessitated by introducing this new product would amount to $240,000 per year. Subjective estimates of the probable demand for the product are shown in the following probability distribution:

Annual Demand	Probability
6,000 units	.2
8,000 units	.2
10,000 units	.2
12,000 units	.2
14,000 units	.1
16,000 units	.1

113. The probability distribution is a

a. Normal distribution.
b. Symmetric distribution.
c. Continuous distribution.
d. Binomial distribution.
e. Discrete distribution.

The correct answer is (e). *(CMA 1277 5-11)*
REQUIRED: The kind of probability distribution given.
DISCUSSION: The given distribution is discrete because annual demand occurs at only six points and at even intervals. Demand is assumed not to occur at numbers other than these points (e.g., not at 6,943.4 units).
Answers (a), (b), and (c) are incorrect because the frequency distribution in the problem is neither continuous, symmetrical, nor unimodal (a normal distribution). In a continuous distribution, any level of demand might occur. In a symmetrical distribution, the left and right sides are the same. Here, the left side is higher than the right. Answer (d) is incorrect because a binomial distribution is discrete but involves only either/or outcomes.

114. The expected value of demand for the new product is

a. 11,000 units.
b. 10,200 units.
c. 9,000 units.
d. 10,600 units.
e. 9,800 units.

The correct answer is (b). *(CMA 1277 5-12)*
REQUIRED: The expected value of demand for the new product.
DISCUSSION: Expected value is a technique used to calculate results by weighting the conditional values by the probabilities of their occurrence. The expected value of demand for the product is the sum of the products of the possible payoffs multiplied by the probabilities of their occurrence.

6,000 × .2 =	1,200
8,000 × .2 =	1,600
10,000 × .2 =	2,000
12,000 × .2 =	2,400
14,000 × .1 =	1,400
16,000 × .1 =	1,600
Expected value	10,200

115. The probability that the introduction of this new product will not increase company's profit is

a. 0.00.
b. 0.04.
c. 0.40.
d. 0.50.
e. 0.60.

The correct answer is (c). *(CMA 1277 5-13)*
REQUIRED: The probability that the introduction of the new product will not increase profit.
DISCUSSION: With a gross margin of 50% (the price is twice the variable cost) and fixed costs of $240,000, the breakeven point in dollars is $480,000 ($240,000 ÷ .5). The selling price is $60 per unit, so the breakeven point in units is 8,000 ($480,000 ÷ $60). There is a 40% chance (.2 + .2) that demand will be 8,000 units or less.

116. Boyer Company is considering designing an educational computer software package. Boyer's management is aware that this project may not be feasible, that demand for the software may be low, and that competitors may offer a similar package before Boyer. Boyer can best evaluate the possible payoffs of the computer software project by using

   a. Differential calculus.
   b. Critical path analysis.
   c. Linear programming.
   d. Regression analysis.
   e. Decision tree analysis.

The correct answer is (e). *(CMA 1285 5-20)*
REQUIRED: The best method to evaluate the possible payoffs of a decision when there are known risks.
DISCUSSION: A decision tree diagram is used to determine the expected values of a variety of decisions given different levels of risk for each decision. A decision tree thus consists of the following: a set of choices for each decision; the events that might occur as a result of each choice; the probabilities of the various events; and the outcomes or payoffs of the events.
   Answer (a) is incorrect because differential calculus is a mathematical tool used to find minima and maxima. Answer (b) is incorrect because critical path analysis is used for project scheduling. Answer (c) is incorrect because linear programming is used to maximize returns or minimize costs given resource constraints. Answer (d) is incorrect because regression analysis is used to find relationships among a variety of variables.

117. A decision tree has been formulated for the possible outcomes of introducing a new product line.

```
         .7 ──── $100,000
  (#1) ──<
         .3 ──── $ 70,000
```

Branches related to Alternative #1 reflect the possible payoffs from introducing the product without an advertising campaign. The branches for Alternative #2 reflect the possible payoffs with an advertising campaign costing $40,000. The expected values of Alternatives #1 and #2, respectively, are

   a. #1: (.7 x $100,000) + (.3 x $70,000)
      #2: (.8 x $170,000) + (.2 x $80,000)

   b. #1: (.7 x $100,000) + (.3 x $70,000)
      #2: (.8 x $130,000) + (.2 x $40,000)

   c. #1: (.7 x $100,000) + (.3 x $70,000)
      #2: (.8 x $170,000) + (.2 x $80,000)
           - $40,000

   d. #1: (.7 x $100,000) + (.3 x $70,000)
           - $40,000
      #2: (.8 x $170,000) + (.2 x $80,000)
           - $40,000

The correct answer is (c). *(CIA 1183 IV-40)*
REQUIRED: The expected values of alternatives given a decision tree reflecting payoffs.
DISCUSSION: The expected value of an alternative is equal to the sum of the conditional values times the probabilities of their occurrence. For Alternative #2, the advertising expenditure is certain (probability = 1.0) and must be deducted in arriving at the expected value.

Alternative #1
   .7 x $100,000 = $70,000
   .3 x $ 70,000 =   21,000
                     $91,000

Alternative #2
   .8 x $170,000 = $136,000
   .2 x $ 80,000 =   16,000
   1.0 x $(40,000) = (40,000)
                     $112,000

118. The legal department of a firm prepared the decision tree below for a possible patent infringement suit.

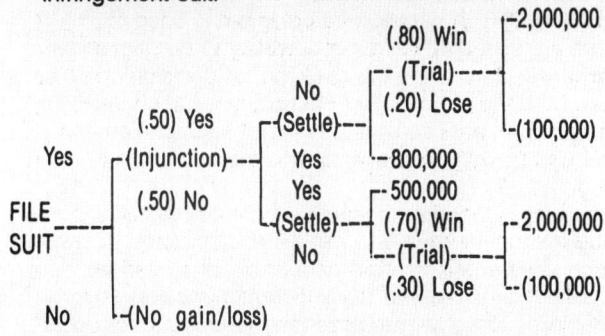

```
                              (.80) Win  ─ 2,000,000
                    No      ┌─(Trial)─
         (.50) Yes ─(Settle)─│ (.20) Lose
Yes     ─(Injunction)─       └─ 800,000         ─(100,000)
FILE     (.50) No            Yes
SUIT                         Yes    ─ 500,000
                            ─(Settle)─ (.70) Win  ─ 2,000,000
                                   No ─(Trial)─
                                      (.30) Lose ─(100,000)
No      ─(No gain/loss)
```

Based on the decision tree, the firm should

a. Not file the suit.
b. File suit; settle if injunction granted.
c. File suit; settle if injunction not granted.
d. Carry suit to trial.

The correct answer is (d). *(CIA 1185 III-28)*
REQUIRED: The action that should be taken based on the decision tree.
DISCUSSION: To solve this problem, expected outcomes for all possibilities must be computed. If the suit is filed and an injunction granted, the following expected outcomes exist:

E(Trial) = 0.5[0.8($2,000,000) + 0.2($-100,000)]
         = $790,000
E(Settle) = 0.5($800,000) = $400,000

If the suit is filed but the injunction not granted, the following expected outcomes exist:

E(Trial) = 0.5[0.7($2,000,000) + 0.3($-100,000)]
         = $685,000
E(Settle) = 0.5($500,000) = $250,000

Since all outcomes are positive, the suit should be filed. In addition, because the expected outcomes are greater, the suit should be taken to trial.

119. A battery manufacturer warrants its automobile batteries to perform satisfactorily for as long as the owner keeps the car. Auto industry data show that only 20% of car buyers retain their cars for 3 years or more. Historical data suggest

Number of Years Owned	Probability of Battery Failure	Battery Exchange Costs	Percentage of Failed Batteries Returned
Less than 3 years	0.2	$50	75%
3 years or more	0.6	$20	50%

If 50,000 batteries were sold this year, what is the estimated warranty cost?

a. $375,000.
b. $435,000.
c. $500,000.
d. $620,000.

The correct answer is (b). *(CIA 1183 IV-36)*
REQUIRED: The warranty cost for the year's battery sales.
DISCUSSION: The estimated number of battery failures in the first 3 years is 10,000 (.2 x 50,000). Only 75% are expected to be returned, however, so estimated warranty costs amount to only $375,000 (.75 x 10,000 x $50).

After 3 years, only 10,000 (.2 x 50,000) of the original buyers still own their cars from the year in question. Thus, 6,000 (.6 x 10,000) of these batteries remaining under warranty can potentially be returned. Since only 3,000 (.5 x 6,000) failed batteries are expected to be returned, warranty costs after 3 years are estimated to be $60,000 ($20 x 3,000). Total expected warranty costs are thus $435,000 ($375,000 + $60,000).

CHAPTER NINETEEN
REGRESSION ANALYSIS

19.1 Regression Definitions	(21 questions)	573
19.2 Regression Relationships	(32 questions)	578
19.3 Separating Fixed and Variable Costs	(6 questions)	588
19.4 Interpretation of Regression Results	(6 questions)	589
19.5 Multiple Calculations	(18 questions)	592

The emphasis on regression analysis on professional examinations has declined in recent years. Regression analysis is a sophisticated technique of separating mixed costs into fixed and variable costs, which is its primary application in cost accounting.

19.1 Regression Definitions

1. Simple regression analysis involves the use of

	Dependent Variables	Independent Variables
a.	One	None
b.	One	One
c.	One	Two
d.	None	Two

The correct answer is (b). *(CPA 1186 T-50)*
REQUIRED: The number of dependent and independent variables involved in simple regression analysis.
DISCUSSION: Regression analysis assumes that a change in the value of a dependent variable is related to the change in the value of an independent variable. Regression analysis attempts to find an equation for the linear relationship among variables. In simple regression analysis, one independent variable is used to predict one dependent variable. In multiple regression analysis, multiple independent variables are used to predict one dependent variable.

2. Simple linear regression is a method applied when it is believed the underlying relationship between two variables is linear. The least squares process estimates this hypothesized true relationship by minimizing the sum of squared errors of the observations in a sample about a fitted line. Which equation properly represents the underlying true relationship between variables?

a. $y = a + x$.
b. $y = a + bx$.
c. $y = a + bx + e$.
d. $y = a + bx^2 + e$.

The correct answer is (c). *(Publisher)*
REQUIRED: The equation representing the true relationship between variables.
DISCUSSION: The equation is based upon application of regression analysis to observations of the independent variable x and the dependent variable y. The result is an equation of y (the dependent variable) = a (which is the y-intercept) + bx (b being the slope, and x being the independent variable) + e (an error term). The error term indicates the degree of uncertainty.
Answers (a) and (b) are incorrect because they do not have an error term. Answer (d) is incorrect because it should be a linear, not curvilinear, function.

3. A nonlinear relationship between direct cost and production volume can cause a problem when using accounting data for

a. Simulation.
b. Regression analysis.
c. Capital budgeting.
d. Inventory control.

The correct answer is (b). *(CIA 1185 III-29)*
REQUIRED: When a nonlinear relationship between direct cost and production volume can cause a problem.
DISCUSSION: Linearity is a key assumption of regression analysis. A nonlinear relationship between direct cost and production would make regression an inappropriate analysis method.
Answers (a), (c), and (d) are incorrect because simulation, capital budgeting, and inventory control each utilize nonlinear models.

4. Which equation properly represents the least squares estimates of the relationship between variables? Let ^ denote least squares estimates of the values.

   a. $y = \hat{a} + \hat{b} + x$.
   b. $\hat{y} = \hat{a} + \hat{b}x + e$.
   c. $\hat{y} = \hat{a} + \hat{b}x$.
   d. $y = \hat{a} + \hat{b}x^2$.

The correct answer is (c). *(Publisher)*
REQUIRED: The equation representing a least squares estimate.
DISCUSSION: The least squares estimate is based upon the relationship that is found and described in the preceding question. The estimate has no provision for the error term, however. Rather, the error term is incorporated in the standard error of the estimate. The "hats" indicate an estimate. An estimate of y is based on estimates of both a and b. Least squares estimates represent a deterministic, not a probabilistic, estimate of the variable, so no error term should be included.
Answer (a) is incorrect because y is the actual value, and there is error according to actual value. Answer (b) is incorrect because it is an estimated value of the dependent variable, and there should be no error term. Answer (d) is incorrect because the estimated relationship should be linear, not curvilinear.

For Questions 5 through 9, use the usual formula for the regression equation: $y = a + bx + e$.

---

5. The dependent variable is

   a. a.
   b. y.
   c. b.
   d. x.
   e. e.

The correct answer is (b). *(Publisher)*.
REQUIRED: The symbol for the dependent variable.
DISCUSSION: The dependent variable in the regression equation is the item to be estimated (or calculated or predicted), i.e., y. In regression analysis, the objective is to predict a value of one variable (dependent) in terms of the values of one or more other variables (independent).
Answer (a) is incorrect because it is the y-axis intercept. Answer (c) is incorrect because it is the slope of the line. Answer (d) is incorrect because it is the independent variable. Answer (e) is incorrect because it is the error term.

6. The y-axis intercept is

   a. a.
   b. y.
   c. b.
   d. x.
   e. e.

The correct answer is (a). *(Publisher)*
REQUIRED: The symbol for the y-axis intercept in the regression equation.
DISCUSSION: The y-axis intercept is the a in the equation. The a is also the assumed fixed cost in most cost functions, even though it may lie outside the relevant range. It is the expected value of y when x is zero, and if it lies in the relevant range of the sample.
Answer (b) is incorrect because it is the dependent variable. Answer (c) is incorrect because it is the slope of the line. Answer (d) is incorrect because it is the independent variable. Answer (e) is incorrect because it is the error term.

7. The slope of the line is

   a. a.
   b. y.
   c. b.
   d. x.
   e. e.

The correct answer is (c). *(Publisher)*
REQUIRED: The symbol for the slope of the line.
DISCUSSION: The slope of a line is a constant that represents the proportionate change along the y axis for each change along the x axis. Thus, in a regression equation, slope represents the variable portion of the total cost in the cost function, i.e., the change in cost that occurs with a change in a unit of activity level.
Answer (a) is incorrect because it is the y-axis intercept. Answer (b) is incorrect because it is the dependent variable. Answer (d) is incorrect because it is the independent variable. Answer (e) is incorrect because it is the error term.

Module 19.1: Regression Definitions

8. The independent variable is
   a. a.
   b. y.
   c. b.
   d. x.
   e. e.

The correct answer is (d). *(Publisher)*
REQUIRED: The symbol for an independent variable.
DISCUSSION: The independent variable is the variable that is permitted to change and results in a change in the dependent variable.
Answer (a) is incorrect because it is the y-axis intercept. Answer (b) is incorrect because it is the dependent variable. Answer (c) is incorrect because it is the slope of the line. Answer (e) is incorrect because it is the error term.

9. The error term is
   a. a.
   b. y.
   c. b.
   d. x.
   e. e.

The correct answer is (e). *(Publisher)*
REQUIRED: The symbol for the error term in the regression equation.
DISCUSSION: The error term in the equation is e. The error term is usually assumed to have a mean of zero in linear regression, thus permitting calculations using the formula $y = a + bx$.
Answer (a) is incorrect because it is the y-axis intercept. Answer (b) is incorrect because it is the dependent variable. Answer (c) is incorrect because it is the slope of the line. Answer (d) is incorrect because it is the independent variable.

10. What is a dependent variable?
    a. Typically, the variable on the right-hand side of an equation.
    b. The variable that is to be predicted given another variable.
    c. The variable whose value is caused by another variable.
    d. The variable in a model thought to affect another variable.

The correct answer is (b). *(Publisher)*
REQUIRED: The definition of a dependent variable.
DISCUSSION: A dependent variable is usually the variable on the left-hand side of the equation that is felt to be affected by the independent variable. The dependent variable is typically the variable to be predicted.
Answer (a) is incorrect because a dependent variable is typically put on the left-hand side of the equation. Answer (c) is incorrect because regression analysis does not involve causality, only effect. Answer (d) is incorrect because it describes an independent variable.

11. Which variable in regression analysis is sometimes called the explanatory variable?
    a. Objective.
    b. Constant.
    c. Dependent.
    d. Independent.

The correct answer is (d). *(Publisher)*
REQUIRED: The synonym for an explanatory variable.
DISCUSSION: The explanatory variable is the independent variable that is thought to affect the dependent variable (regression measures effect, not causality).
Answer (a) is incorrect because the objective variable is a nonsense concept in this context. Answer (b) is incorrect because the constant is the y-intercept, or "a" in the regression equation $y = a + bx$. Answer (c) is incorrect because the dependent variable is the variable explained by the explanatory variable.

12. Simple regression analysis involves the use of how many variables?
    a. One.
    b. Two.
    c. Three.
    d. More than three.

The correct answer is (b). *(CPA 1179 T-37)*
REQUIRED: The number of variables used in simple regression analysis.
DISCUSSION: Regression analysis assumes a change in the value of a dependent variable is related to the change in value of an independent variable. Regression analysis attempts to find an equation for the linear relationship among variables. Since both an independent and a dependent variable are necessary to establish a linear relationship, two variables are involved in simple regression analysis.

576   Module 19.1: Regression Definitions

13. Which of the following techniques can be used to determine the variable and fixed portions of a company's costs?
    a. Game theory.
    b. Queuing theory.
    c. Regression analysis.
    d. Poisson analysis.

The correct answer is (c). *(CPA 576 P-33)*
REQUIRED: The technique to separate fixed and variable costs.
DISCUSSION: Regression analysis assumes a change in the value of a dependent variable is related to the change in the value of an independent variable. Regression analysis attempts to find an equation for the linear relationship among variables. Using this equation, a company's costs can be separated into variable and fixed portions.
Answer (a) is incorrect because it aids in decision making in competitive situations. Answer (b) is incorrect because it is a technique used to examine waiting lines. Answer (d) is incorrect because it is a statistical distribution technique.

14. Multiple regression analysis
    a. Establishes a cause and effect relationship.
    b. Does not produce measures of probable error.
    c. Measures the change in one variable associated with the change in one other variable only.
    d. Measures the change in one variable associated with the change in more than one other variable.

The correct answer is (d). *(CPA 1182 T-47)*
REQUIRED: The correct statement concerning multiple regression analysis.
DISCUSSION: Multiple regression analysis involves two or more independent variables in contrast to simple regression analysis, which includes only one independent variable.
Answer (a) is incorrect because regression analysis identifies only effect, not cause. Answer (b) is incorrect because it does produce a measure of probable error. The probable error indicates the goodness of the estimating model. Answer (c) is incorrect because it describes linear regression analysis.

15. Multiple regression analysis
    a. Establishes a cause and effect relationship.
    b. Is not a sampling technique.
    c. Involves the use of independent variables only.
    d. Produces measures of probable error.

The correct answer is (d). *(CPA 585 T-48)*
REQUIRED: The correct statement concerning multiple regression analysis.
DISCUSSION: Multiple regression analysis involves two or more independent variables in contrast to simple regression analysis, which includes only one independent variable. It includes computation of the standard error of the estimate, which indicates the goodness of fit of the estimation model. Goodness of fit is a measure of probable error.
Answer (a) is incorrect because regression analysis identifies only effect, not cause. Answer (b) is incorrect because regression analysis usually uses sampling techniques to estimate the relationship between variables. Answer (c) is incorrect because multiple regression analysis explains the behavior of a dependent variable in terms of the behavior of two or more independent variables.

16. To which of these independent variables would "set-up" expenses probably have the closest relationship?
    a. Machine hours.
    b. Direct labor hours.
    c. Number of shop orders.
    d. Direct labor cost.
    e. Number of employees.

The correct answer is (c). *(CMA 1273 5-9)*
REQUIRED: The independent variable most closely linked to set-up expense.
DISCUSSION: The dependent variable, set-up expenses, would be most closely related to the number of shop orders. The greater the number of orders, the greater the number of jobs to set up.
Answers (a), (b), (d), and (e) are incorrect because none is as related to set-up expenses as the number of shop orders.

Module 19.1: Regression Definitions

17. A company using regression analysis to correlate income to a variety of sales indicators found that the relationship between the number of sales managers in a territory and net income for the territory had a correlation coefficient of -1. Which is the best description of this situation?

    a. More sales managers should be hired.

    b. Imperfect negative correlation.

    c. Perfect inverse correlation.

    d. There is no correlation at all.

The correct answer is (c). *(CIA 587 III-41)*
REQUIRED: The significance of a correlation coefficient of -1.0.
DISCUSSION: A value of -1.0 indicates a perfectly inverse linear relationship between x and y. A value of zero indicates no linear relationship between x and y. A value of +1.0 indicates a perfectly direct relationship between x and y.
Answer (a) is incorrect because more sales managers should be terminated. Answer (b) is incorrect because an imperfect negative correlation would be a value between zero and -1.0. Answer (d) is incorrect because the correlation is -1.0, not zero.

18. Green Electronics repairs TV sets, radios, and phonographs. The company's service technicians are capable of repairing any of the three products, but the average time spent on each of the three types of products is quite different. The company has experienced above average sales growth during the past year and needs to estimate future repair hours to make staffing decisions. Which of the following procedures would be most appropriate for estimating future direct labor hours?

    a. Queuing theory.

    b. Linear programming.

    c. Regression analysis.

    d. Markov analysis.

    e. Monte Carlo simulation.

The correct answer is (c). *(CIA 581 IV-20)*
REQUIRED: The quantitative technique useful for estimating future labor hours.
DISCUSSION: Regression analysis can relate the change in the value of a dependent variable (direct labor hours) to the change in the value of an independent variable (sales). Then DLH can be estimated for future periods.
Answer (a) is incorrect because it is used to minimize the costs of waiting lines. Answer (b) is incorrect because it is a technique to optimize an objective function. Answer (d) is incorrect because it is used to predict a future state that is dependent upon the present state. Answer (e) is incorrect because it is used in simulation to generate random values for a given variable.

19. Which of the following quantitative techniques would be most useful to an internal auditor for the purpose of selecting particular accounts (e.g., monthly divisional revenues or expense accounts) for comprehensive review in the audit?

    a. Sensitivity analysis.

    b. Queuing theory.

    c. Regression analysis.

    d. Game theory.

    e. Gantt charting.

The correct answer is (c). *(CIA 581 II-3)*
REQUIRED: The quantitative method most useful in selecting items for an audit.
DISCUSSION: Regression analysis assumes that a change in the value of a dependent variable is related to the change in the value of an independent variable. Regression analysis attempts to find an equation for the linear relationship among variables.
Answer (a) is incorrect because it is used to examine changes in outcome when assumptions are changed. Answer (b) is incorrect because it is used to examine waiting lines. Answer (d) is incorrect because it aids in decision making when confronted with a competitor. Answer (e) is incorrect because it analyzes complex projects with many activities by using bar charts.

Questions 20 and 21 are based on Automite Company, which is an automobile replacement parts dealer in a large metropolitan community. Automite is preparing its sales forecast for the coming year. Data regarding both Automite's and industry sales of replacement parts in the community, and both the used and new automobile sales in the community for the last 10 years, have been accumulated.

20. If Automite wants to determine if there is a historical trend in the growth of its own sales of replacement parts and in the growth of industry sales of replacement parts, the company would employ

   a. Simulation techniques.
   b. Queuing theory.
   c. Linear programming.
   d. Time series analysis.
   e. Learning curve techniques.

The correct answer is (d). *(CMA 1280 5-16)*
REQUIRED: The quantitative method used to find trends over time.
DISCUSSION: Time series analysis can examine the company's and the industry's trends through time by using time as the independent variable in a simple regression equation. Thus, it is a special kind of regression analysis.
Answer (a) is incorrect because it is a technique for experimenting with logical/mathematical models, i.e., by varying values of variables in the model to determine the effects on the solution. Answer (b) is incorrect because it is used to examine waiting lines. Answer (c) is incorrect because it is a mathematical technique to optimize an objective function subject to constraints. Answer (e) is incorrect because it is used to examine costs and productivity as personnel become more experienced.

21. If Automite wants to determine if its sales of replacement parts are related to industry sales of replacement parts or to the sales of used and new automobiles, the company would employ

   a. Simulation techniques.
   b. Correlation and regression analysis.
   c. Queuing theory.
   d. Time series analysis.
   e. Dynamic programming.

The correct answer is (b). *(CMA 1280 5-17)*
REQUIRED: The quantitative method used to examine relationships between variables.
DISCUSSION: Regression analysis is called correlation analysis when it correlates the relationships among one set of variables with those among another set.
Answer (a) is incorrect because it is a technique for experimenting with logical/mathematical models. Answer (c) is incorrect because it is used to minimize the costs of waiting lines, e.g., for tellers in a bank. Answer (d) is incorrect because it is a technique to examine the change in variables over time. Answer (e) is incorrect because it is used to solve a series of independent but related problems.

19.2 Regression Relationships

22. For a simple regression analysis model that is used to allocate factory overhead, an internal auditor finds that the intersection of the line of best fit for the overhead allocation with the y-axis is $5,000. The slope of the trend line is .20. The independent variable, factory wages, amounts to $900,000 for the month. What is the estimated amount of factory overhead to be allocated for the month?

   a. $65,000.
   b. $180,000.
   c. $230,000.
   d. $92,500.
   e. $185,000.

The correct answer is (e). *(CIA 579 II-9)*
REQUIRED: The estimated factory overhead calculated using linear regression.
DISCUSSION: Since regression analysis assumes a change in the value of a dependent variable (factory O/H) is related to the change in the value of an independent variable (factory wages), the equation for the linear relationship can be expressed as the regression formula. Note that the y-intercept is given as $5,000.

$$y = a + bx$$
$$y = \$5,000 + .20x$$
$$x = \$900,000 \text{ (given)}$$
$$\text{Thus, } y = \$5,000 + .20(\$900,000)$$
$$y = \$185,000$$

Module 19.2: Regression Relationships

23. A retailer, in business for over 50 years, has developed the following regression model from the past 60 months of operating data:

Monthly sales dollars =
50,000 + 4.70A + 30B - 1,000X

Where A = number of customers
B = advertising dollars in month
X = 1 if a winter month
X = 0 if other months

An appropriate interpretation of this model is that

a. The business is seasonal, generating higher sales in winter months than other months.

b. Advertising is not cost effective.

c. Within the relevant range, each additional customer will make a purchase of $4.70 on average.

d. Sales are always expected to be at least $50,000.

The correct answer is (c). *(CIA 584 IV-30)*
REQUIRED: The valid interpretation of a regression equation.
DISCUSSION: The results of the equation change by the amount of the coefficient for each unit of the independent variables. Here, the regression equation forecasts the monthly sales dollars. Sales are estimated to be $50,000 plus $4.70 times the number of customers plus 30 times the advertising dollars spent in a month, less $1,000 for a winter month. Thus, within the relevant range, each additional customer is expected to increase monthly sales by $4.70.
Answer (a) is incorrect because, in winter months, sales are predicted to be $1,000 less. Answer (b) is incorrect because, for every dollar of advertising spent, $30 of revenue is generated. Answer (d) is incorrect because sales in winter months are expected to be at least $49,000, not $50,000.

24. You are attempting to express sales as a function of advertising expenditures (X_1), and per capita income (X_2) in your sales area. You have the following multiple linear regression equation:

$$Y = 10 + .51X_1 + .45X_2$$

Your coefficient of determination is .96. This coefficient of determination explains that

a. 96% of sales variations are due to an error term.

b. The dependent variable is not related to advertising expenditures and per capita income.

c. 96% of sales variations are explained by the equation.

d. Only 51% of the sales variations are explained by advertising expenditures.

The correct answer is (c). *(CIA 586 III-13)*
REQUIRED: An interpretation of the coefficient of determination.
DISCUSSION: The coefficient of determination can be interpreted as the proportion of the total variation in the dependent variable that is explained or accounted for by the independent variables. Thus, a coefficient of determination of .96 means that 96% of variations in sales is explained by the regression equation.
Answer (a) is incorrect because 4% of sales variations are explained by the error term. Answer (b) is incorrect because the regression equation provides a good prediction of the dependent variable in terms of advertising expenditures and per capita income. Answer (d) is incorrect because .51 is the coefficient of the independent variable advertising expenditures.

25. Based on the information given in Question 24, determine which of the following conclusions is valid regarding the coefficient of determination

a. More analysis is needed. The coefficient of determination leaves much unexplained.

b. The regression line fits that data used in the sample very well. You now have a strong indication of the possible relation involved with variations in sales.

c. The coefficient of determination is positive because the constant term is positive.

d. The coefficient of determination should always be greater than one.

The correct answer is (b). *(CIA 586 III-14)*
REQUIRED: The valid conclusion about the coefficient of determination.
DISCUSSION: The coefficient of determination of .96 signifies that 96% of variations in sales can be explained by the two independent variables. This leaves only 4% of variations explained by other factors. This equation thus permits accurate forecast of future sales levels.
Answer (a) is incorrect because no further analysis is needed when 96% of dependent variable variation is explained. Answer (c) is incorrect because there is no relationship between the intercept term (the constraint) and the coefficient of determination. Answer (d) is incorrect because a coefficient of determination can only vary in value from zero to one.

Module 19.2: Regression Relationships

> Questions 26 through 30 are based on analyzing the relationship of total factory overhead to changes in direct labor hours. The following relationship was found:
>
> $$y = \$1{,}000 + \$2x$$

26. The relationship as shown above is
a. Parabolic.
b. Curvilinear.
c. Linear.
d. Probabilistic.
e. None of the above.

The correct answer is (c). *(CMA 1273 4-15)*
REQUIRED: The type of relationship found in the given equation.
DISCUSSION: The relationship expressed by the equation would be linear if graphed.
Answers (a) and (b) are incorrect because each is curved; i.e., the equation expressing their relationships would have terms with exponents. Answer (d) is incorrect because it indicates a degree of uncertainty about the equation. No uncertainty is indicated in the overhead/DLH equation.

27. The above equation was probably found through the use of which of the following mathematical techniques?
a. Linear programming.
b. Multiple regression analysis.
c. Simple regression analysis.
d. Dynamic programming.
e. None of the above.

The correct answer is (c). *(CMA 1273 4-14)*
REQUIRED: The quantitative method probably used to find the equation.
DISCUSSION: Regression analysis assumes a change in the value of a dependent variable (here, factory O/H) is related to the change in the value of an independent variable (here, DLH). Management has found an equation that expresses that relationship.
Answer (a) is incorrect because it is a technique to optimize an objective function subject to constraints. Answer (b) is incorrect because it involves three or more variables, while the given equation involves two. Answer (d) is incorrect because it is used to solve a series of independent but related problems.

28. The y in the equation is an estimate of
a. Total variable costs.
b. Total factory overhead.
c. Total fixed costs.
d. Total direct labor hours.
e. None of the above.

The correct answer is (b). *(CMA 1273 4-16)*
REQUIRED: The variable represented by y in the regression equation.
DISCUSSION: Here, the dependent variable, y, is the amount of overhead predicted given the value of the independent variable x.

29. The $2 in the equation is an estimate of
a. Total fixed costs.
b. Variable costs per direct labor hour.
c. Total variable costs.
d. Fixed costs per direct labor hour.
e. None of the above.

The correct answer is (b). *(CMA 1273 4-17)*
REQUIRED: The item represented by the coefficient of the independent variable.
DISCUSSION: For each one-hour change in direct labor hours, certain variable costs change by $2. Note that total variable costs is not the correct answer because some portion of them may be related to an independent variable other than DLH. This equation is expressing only the relationship between total O/H and DLH.

Module 19.2: Regression Relationships

30. The use of such a relationship of total factory overhead to changes in direct labor hours is said to be valid only within the relevant range, which means

    a. Within a reasonable dollar amount for labor costs.
    b. Within the range of observations of the analysis.
    c. Within the range of reasonableness as judged by the department supervisor.
    d. Within the budget allowance for overhead.
    e. None of the above.

The correct answer is (b). *(CMA 1273 4-18)*
REQUIRED: The meaning of "relevant range" in regression analysis.
DISCUSSION: The relevant range indicates the range of values over which the cost/volume relationships are valid. Within the relevant range, the predicted values appear to be valid. The "relevant range" is determined by the range of the independent variable in the sample, and by the range of observations. The relevant range of the regression analysis is the portion of the least squares line between the minimum and maximum values of the independent variable. Predictive ability of regression should be limited to this region.
Answer (a) is incorrect because labor costs are not being predicted. Answer (c) is incorrect because it is not the qualitative judgment of the supervisor which is critical, but the quantitative analysis. Answer (d) is incorrect because budgeted O/H is affected by the relevant range, not vice versa.

Questions 31 through 34 are based on Quigley Co., which applies regression analysis toward the prediction of total revenues (y) (in dollars) by using advertising expenses (x) (in dollars) as the independent variable and obtains the following equation:

$$y = 1,000 + 10x$$

---

31. What is the interpretation of the value of 1,000?

    a. It is the predicted total revenue with no advertising expense.
    b. It is how much advertising will increase with 100 more dollars.
    c. It is the predicted total revenue with no advertising expense if the y-intercept is in the relevant range.
    d. It never has any interpretation.

The correct answer is (c). *(Publisher)*
REQUIRED: The interpretation of the constant in the regression equation predicting total revenues based on advertising expenses.
DISCUSSION: The 1,000 is the y-intercept of the relationship. It is the amount of revenue (y = 1,000) with no advertising, if and only if the y-intercept is in the relevant range of the data. The relevant range of the regression analysis is the portion of the least squares line between the minimum and maximum values of the independent variable. Predictive ability of regression should be limited to this region.
Answer (a) is incorrect because the y-intercept must lie in the relevant range. Answer (b) is incorrect because the 1,000 is the constant term, i.e., it is not affected by increasing advertising. Answer (d) is incorrect because it may be interpreted if it lies in the relevant range.

---

32. What is the interpretation of $\hat{y}$, the estimate of total revenues?

    a. Given an advertising expense, it is the true value of total revenues.
    b. Given an advertising expense, it is the true mean value of total revenue.
    c. Given an advertising expense, it is the estimated value of total revenue.
    d. It is the single observation of total revenues.

The correct answer is (c). *(Publisher)*
REQUIRED: The interpretation of the estimate of total revenues.
DISCUSSION: Given any advertising expense, $\hat{y}$ is only an estimated value of total revenues or mean total revenues. That is why regression analysis predictions should be used with caution, and only within the relevant range.
Answers (a) and (b) are incorrect because we do not know the true value or true mean value of y, only an estimate of the true value. Answer (d) is incorrect because it is an estimate rather than an observation.

Questions 33 and 34 are based on the information preceding Q. 31.

33. What is the interpretation of the value of 10?
   a. There is no interpretation.
   b. For each additional dollar placed into advertising expense, we would expect total revenues to rise by $10.
   c. It describes the predicted value of total estimates when advertising expense is zero.
   d. The variance of the coefficient b.

The correct answer is (b). *(Publisher)*
REQUIRED: The interpretation of the value of the slope in a regression equation.
DISCUSSION: The value of b indicates how much the estimate of total revenues changes with every change in $1 of advertising expenses.
Answer (a) is incorrect because 10 is the slope. Answer (c) is incorrect because it describes the y-intercept, or a in the formula. Answer (d) is incorrect because the variance is not given in the estimation equation.

34. Since the regression analysis implies a return of $10 to total revenues for every $1 of advertising, what conclusion can be reached?
   a. Increasing advertising continually.
   b. Decrease advertising.
   c. Advertising will always make more money than it costs.
   d. Advertising appears to contribute more than it costs to total revenue for the range of expenditures in the sample.

The correct answer is (d). *(Publisher)*
REQUIRED: The conclusion that can be reached from the model.
DISCUSSION: The relationship only holds for the relevant range, i.e., that contemplated by the sample.
Answers (a) and (c) are incorrect because they are only dealing with a fixed range of data and should not go beyond that range. Answer (b) is incorrect because they should increase advertising (but not continually and indefinitely).

35. In regression analysis, the coefficient of correlation is a measure of
   a. The amount of variation in the dependent variable explained by the independent variables.
   b. The amount of variation in the dependent variable unexplained by the independent variables.
   c. The slope of the regression line.
   d. The predicted value of the dependent variable.

The correct answer is (a). *(CIA 1185 III-18)*
REQUIRED: The definition of the coefficient of correlation.
DISCUSSION: The coefficient of correlation is a measure of the strength of the linear relationship between two or more variables. It is a measure of the amount of variation in a dependent variable that can be explained by independent variables.
Answer (b) is incorrect because it describes 1 minus the coefficient of correlation. Answer (c) is incorrect because the slope is the rate of change in the dependent variable in relation to the independent variable. Answer (d) is incorrect because the predicted value of the dependent variable is calculated by the regression formula (e.g., y = A + Bx for simple regression).

36. The correlation coefficient that indicates the weakest linear association between two variables is
   a. -0.73.
   b. -0.11.
   c. 0.12.
   d. 0.35.
   e. 0.72.

The correct answer is (b). *(CMA 1285 5-27)*
REQUIRED: The correlation coefficient that indicates the weakest linear association between two variables.
DISCUSSION: The correlation coefficient can vary from -1 to +1. A -1 indicates a perfect negative correlation and a +1 indicates a perfect positive correlation. A zero correlation coefficient would indicate no association between the variables. Therefore, the correlation coefficient that is nearest to zero would indicate the weakest linear association. Of the options given in the question, the correlation coefficient that is nearest to zero is -0.11.

37. Auto correlation or serial correlation means
   a. The proportion of the variance is explained by the independent variable.
   b. Observations are not independent.
   c. Independent variables are correlated with each other.
   d. Random sampling fails to represent the population.

The correct answer is (b). *(Publisher)*
REQUIRED: The true statement about auto or serial correlation.
DISCUSSION: Auto correlation and serial correlation are synonyms meaning the observations are not independent. An example would be when certain costs may rise with volume increase but not decline with volume decrease.
Answer (a) is incorrect because it is the definition of coefficient of determination. Answer (c) is incorrect because it is the definition of multicollinearity. Answer (d) is incorrect because it is the definition of bias.

38. As a preliminary step in the selection of variables to use in a statistical-forecasting model, the auditor has calculated the coefficient of correlation between the firm's sales and three economic indexes. The results were as follows:

Index	Coefficient of Correlation
A	.105
B	-.009
C	-.854

Which of the following statements indicates the best course of action for the auditor to take in the development of a forecasting model?

   a. Drop all three indexes from further consideration because a coefficient of correlation of ± 2.00 is necessary for a statistically significant relationship.
   b. Include only indexes B and C in the model because they have the only negative coefficients of correlation.
   c. Include only index C in the model because its coefficient of correlation is significant, while the coefficients of indexes A and B are likely to be insignificant.
   d. Include only index A in the model because it has the only positive coefficient of correlation.

The correct answer is (c). *(CIA 1184 IV-30)*
REQUIRED: The index(es) to use in a model based on the coefficient of correlation data.
DISCUSSION: The coefficient of correlation measures the degree and direction of the linear relationship between two or more variables. The relationship varies from perfectly inverse (-1) to perfectly direct (1). Index C has a high negative correlation and should be integrated into the auditor's forecasting model.
Answer (a) is incorrect because the maximum coefficient is ± 1. Answers (b) and (d) are incorrect because the model should include strongly correlated indicators, whether positive or negative.

39. Multicollinearity occurs when
   a. The proportion of the variance is explained by the independent variable.
   b. Observations are not independent.
   c. Independent variables are correlated with each other.
   d. Random sampling fails to represent the population.

The correct answer is (c). *(Publisher)*
REQUIRED: The definition of multicollinearity.
DISCUSSION: Multicollinearity means when two or more independent variables are correlated with each other. Thus multicollinearity occurs only in multiple regression equations.
Answer (a) is incorrect because it is the definition of coefficient of determination. Answer (b) is incorrect because it is the definition of auto correlation. Answer (d) is incorrect because it is the definition of bias.

40. Bias occurs when
  a. The proportion of the variance is explained by the independent variable.
  b. Observations are not independent.
  c. Independent variables are correlated with each other.
  d. The parameters obtained from random sampling fail to represent the population.

The correct answer is (d). *(Publisher)*
REQUIRED: The definition of bias.
DISCUSSION: Bias does not necessarily mean a psychological bias; it means that the random sample has failed to represent the population and thus does not estimate the true parameters of the underlying data. For example, if the mean of random samples does not on average represent the true population mean, we say the sample mean is biased.
  Answer (a) is incorrect because it is the definition of coefficient of determination. Answer (b) is incorrect because it is the definition of auto or serial correlation. Answer (c) is incorrect because it is the definition of multicollinearity.

41. What assumption need not be part of a regression model to assure unbiased estimates and minimum variance?
  a. Error term has constant variance.
  b. Expected value of the error term equals zero.
  c. The errors are independent.
  d. The distribution of the error term is normal.
  e. The error term and independent variable are uncorrelated.

The correct answer is (d). *(Publisher)*
REQUIRED: The assumption not needed to assure unbiased estimations and minimum variance.
DISCUSSION: Unbiased means that the estimates in the sample represent the true parameters in the population. Minimum variance means the model has the smallest possible variance of any other estimator. It is not necessary that the error terms be distributed normally. The only reason to require normality would be to be able to test the estimates using a t-test.
  Answers (a), (b), (c), and (e) are each required of models to assure unbiased estimates with minimum variance.

42. Coefficient of determination means
  a. The proportion of the variance is explained by the independent variable.
  b. Observations are not independent.
  c. Independent variables are correlated with each other.
  d. Random sampling fails to represent the population.

The correct answer is (a). *(Publisher)*
REQUIRED: The definition of coefficient of determination.
DISCUSSION: Coefficient of determination is the proportion of the variance of the dependent variable explained by the independent variable. It is also known as r squared or the coefficient of correlation squared.
  Answer (b) is incorrect because it is the definition of auto correlation. Answer (c) is incorrect because it is the definition of multicollinearity. Answer (d) is incorrect because it is the definition of bias.

43. The confidence interval represents
  a. A measure of variability of the actual observations from the least squares line.
  b. A range of values over which the probability may be estimated based upon the regression equation results.
  c. A variability about the least squares line that is uniform for all values of the independent variable in the sample.
  d. The proportion of the variance explained by the independent variable.

The correct answer is (b). *(Publisher)*
REQUIRED: The definition of confidence interval.
DISCUSSION: The confidence interval is the range of values over which probability may be estimated based upon the regression equation results. This involves taking the mean, adjusting for the standard deviation and the appropriate probability distribution, to arrive at the range.
  Answer (a) is incorrect because it describes the standard error of the estimate. Answer (c) is incorrect because it describes constant variance. Answer (d) is incorrect because it describes the coefficient of determination.

44. The standard error of the estimate represents
    a. A measure of variability of the actual observations from the least squares line.
    b. A range of values over which the probability may be estimated based upon the regression equation results.
    c. A variability about the least squares line that is uniform for all values of the independent variable in the sample.
    d. The proportion of the variance explained by the independent variable.

The correct answer is (a). *(Publisher)*
   REQUIRED: The definition of the standard error of estimates.
   DISCUSSION: The standard error of the estimate represents the deviation of the actual observations from the regression line. It is calculated based upon the sample drawn from the population.
   Answer (b) is incorrect because it describes a confidence interval. Answer (c) is incorrect because it describes constant variance. Answer (d) is incorrect because it describes the coefficient of determination.

45. Specification errors represent
    a. A measure of variability of the actual observations from the least squares line.
    b. A range of values over which the probability may be estimated based upon the regression equation results.
    c. A variability about the least squares line that is uniform for all values of the independent variable in the sample.
    d. The underlying assumptions of the regression equation that are not met.

The correct answer is (d). *(Publisher)*
   DISCUSSION: The definition of specification errors.
   REQUIRED: Specification errors represent the concept that the underlying assumptions of the regression equation are not met. The examples of these specification errors might be serial correlation, multicollinearity, nonlinearity, and abnormal distribution of the error term.
   Answer (a) is incorrect because it describes the standard error of estimates. Answer (b) is incorrect because it describes a confidence interval. Answer (c) is incorrect because it describes constant variance.

46. Constant variance represents
    a. A measure of variability of the actual observations from the least squares line.
    b. A range of values over which the probability may be estimated based upon the regression equation results.
    c. A variability about the least squares line that is uniform for all values of the independent variable in the sample.
    d. The underlying assumptions of the regression equation that are not met.

The correct answer is (c). *(Publisher)*
   REQUIRED: The definition of constant variance.
   DISCUSSION: Constant variance is the situation in which is found a uniform deviation of points from the regression line. This uniformity is based on the assumption that the distribution of the observations and errors is not affected by the size of the independent variables.
   Answer (a) is incorrect because it describes the standard error of estimates. Answer (b) is incorrect because it describes a confidence interval. Answer (d) is incorrect because constant variance is one of the basic assumptions underlying regression analysis.

47. Violation of which assumption underlying regression analysis is prevalent in time series analysis?
    a. Variance of error term is constant.
    b. Error terms are independent.
    c. Distribution of error terms is normal.
    d. Expected value of error term equals zero.

The correct answer is (b). *(Publisher)*
   REQUIRED: The assumption frequently violated in time series analysis.
   DISCUSSION: Time series analysis is a regression model in which the independent variable is time (e.g., years, 1984, 1985, 1986). In time series analysis, the value of the next time period is frequently dependent on the value of the time period before that. Hence, the error terms are usually correlated or dependent on the past period. The other three major requirements of regression analysis--constant variance of error term, normal distribution of error term, and an expected value of error term of zero--are usually met.

48. Regression analysis can be applied to cross-sectional data or to time-series data. For which of the following would a cross-sectional approach be most effective?

   a. Comparison of company performance relative to total industry performance.
   b. The selection of locations to visit for inspections of a multi-location operation.
   c. Comparison of current operations to historical performance.
   d. Selection of invoices for detailed testing.

The correct answer is (b). *(CIA 584 IV-31)*
REQUIRED: The situation appropriate for cross-sectional regression analysis.
DISCUSSION: Cross-sectional regression analysis examines relationships among many data items (e.g., many or different production methods or locations) at a particular time rather than across time. A broad variety of characteristics are identified throughout the data and selected items are identified for regression analysis. These selected items are categorized to provide an overview of the entity.

Answers (a) and (c) are incorrect because comparison of current company performance to past performance or to total industry performance implies a comparison across time, for which time-series or trend regression analysis is more appropriate. Answer (d) is incorrect because selection of invoices for detailed testing pertains to a sampling process and should probably be done by a random sample technique or a variation of it, like cluster, stratified, or dollar-unit sampling.

49. If the variance of the error term is not constant, the problem is called:

   a. Multicollinearity.
   b. Heteroscedasticity.
   c. Homoscedasticity.
   d. Exponential smoothing.

The correct answer is (b). *(Publisher)*
REQUIRED: The condition describing error terms that do not have constant variance.
DISCUSSION: When the variance of the error term is not constant, the condition is known as heteroscedasticity. It is caused by the fact that over the least squares line, the variances need not be uniform. For instance, we expect that the more output, the larger the variance (for large firms), and the smaller the output, the smaller the variance (for small firms). In other words, large observations have more variance than small observations.

Answer (a) is incorrect because multicollinearity describes the situation in which independent variables are not independent of each other. Answer (c) is incorrect because homoscedasticity is the condition in which the variance of the error term is constant. Answer (d) is incorrect because exponential smoothing is a forecasting technique which adjusts the previous period's forecast by the difference between the previous period's forecast and the actual occurrence.

50. If the error term is normally distributed about zero, then

   a. The parameter estimates of the y-intercept and slope also have a normal distribution.
   b. The estimate of the slope can be tested using a t-test.
   c. The probability that the error term is greater than zero is equal to the probability that it is less than zero for any observation.
   d. All of the above.

The correct answer is (d). *(Publisher)*
REQUIRED: The true statement(s) about an error term normally distributed about zero.
DISCUSSION: All three statements are true. This ideal situation permits t-tests (i.e., use of the normal distribution adjusted for degrees of freedom) to evaluate the significance of the estimates.

51. Omaha Sales Company asked a CPA's assistance in planning the use of multiple regression analysis to predict district sales. An equation has been estimated based upon historical data, and a standard error has been computed. When regression analysis based upon past periods is used to predict for a future period, the standard error associated with the predicted value, in relation to the standard error for the base equation, will be

   a. Smaller.
   b. Larger.
   c. The same.
   d. Larger or smaller, depending upon the circumstances.

The correct answer is (b). *(CPA 573 A-26)*
REQUIRED: The relationship of standard error associated with the predicted value to the standard error for the base equation.
DISCUSSION: The standard error associated with a predicted value is always larger because it takes into account two types of error. It contains the standard error of the estimate, which is the variability of the y values about the least squares line. It also contains a measure of the fact that the error associated with the least squares line only approximates the true relationship between x and y.

Questions 52 and 53 are based on the Mulvey Company, which derived the following cost relationship from a regression analysis of its monthly manufacturing overhead cost.

   C = $80,000 + $12M

where: C = monthly manufacturing overhead cost
       M = machine hours

The standard error of estimate of the regression is $6,000. The standard time required to manufacture one six-unit case of Mulvey's single product is 4 machine hours. Mulvey applies manufacturing overhead to production on the basis of machine hours, and its normal annual production is 50,000 cases.

---

52. Mulvey's estimated variable manufacturing overhead cost for a month in which scheduled production is 5,000 cases would be

   a. $80,000.
   b. $320,000.
   c. $240,000.
   d. $360,000.
   e. Some amount other than those given above.

The correct answer is (c). *(CMA 1285 5-17)*
REQUIRED: The estimated variable manufacturing overhead for a month given production volume.
DISCUSSION: Each case requires 4 hours of machine time. Thus, 5,000 cases would require 20,000 (5,000 cases x 4 hrs.) hours. At $12 per hour, the variable costs would total $240,000 ($12 x 20,000 hrs.).

53. Mulvey's predetermined fixed manufacturing overhead rate would be

   a. $1.60 per machine hour.
   b. $3.20 per machine hour.
   c. $4.00 per machine hour.
   d. $4.80 per machine hour.
   e. $.40 per machine hour.

The correct answer is (d). *(CMA 1285 5-18)*
REQUIRED: The predetermined fixed overhead application rate per machine hour.
DISCUSSION: According to the regression equation, the monthly fixed costs are $80,000. On an annual basis, the total is $960,000 (12 mon. x 80,000). For normal production of 50,000 cases, 200,000 hours (4 hrs. x 50,000) of machine time are required. Allocating the $960,000 of fixed costs over 200,000 hours of machine time results in a cost of $4.80 per machine hour ($960,000 ÷ 200,000).

19.3 Separating Fixed and Variable Costs

54. Which of the following methods can be used to determine the fixed and variable elements of a semivariable expense?

   a. Statistical scattergraph method.
   b. Linear programming.
   c. Input-output analysis.
   d. Program evaluation and review technique.

The correct answer is (a). *(CPA 1180 T-47)*
REQUIRED: An estimation method to separate fixed and variable costs.
DISCUSSION: Scatter diagrams may be used to estimate correlations. Each observation creates a point which represents the specific x and y values. The collinearity of these relationships and slope of the observations are visible, even if not explicitly calculated. Calculations (least squares) may be made to determine the equation of the line of best fit.

55. Which of the following is a useful technique in determining the fixed and variable elements of a semivariable expense?

   a. Linear programming.
   b. Queuing theory.
   c. Program evaluation and review technique.
   d. Simple regression analysis.

The correct answer is (d). *(CPA 578 T-33)*
REQUIRED: A quantitative method to determine fixed and variable cost elements.
DISCUSSION: Regression analysis assumes a change in the value of a dependent variable is related to the change in the value of an independent variable. Regression analysis can be used to find the slope of the variable cost line (the rate of change in variable costs per change in independent variable) and the fixed costs (the y-intercept).
Answer (a) is incorrect because it is used to optimize an objective function subject to constraints. Answer (b) is incorrect because it is used to examine waiting lines. Answer (c) is incorrect because it is used to examine complex projects for critical processes.

56. The effect of changes in semivariable costs in relation to another item, such as direct labor hours, can best be determined by which of the following mathematical techniques?

   a. Simplex method.
   b. Matrix algebra.
   c. Correlation analysis.
   d. Probability analysis.

The correct answer is (c). *(CPA 1175 T-18)*
REQUIRED: The quantitative method to determine the effect of changes in semivariable costs in relation to another item.
DISCUSSION: Regression analysis assumes a change in the value of a dependent variable is related to the change in the value of an independent variable. A regression equation can express the relationship between changes in semivariable costs and activity.
Answer (a) is incorrect because it is a general method of solving linear programming problems. Answer (b) is incorrect because it is used to manipulate linear equations. Answer (d) is incorrect because it is used to describe the degree of assurance that an event will occur.

57. Which of the following quantitative methods will separate a semivariable cost into its fixed and variable components with the highest degree of precision under all circumstances?

   a. High-low method.
   b. Simplex method.
   c. Least squares method.
   d. Scattergraph method.

The correct answer is (c). *(CPA 579 T-26)*
REQUIRED: The quantitative method that most precisely separates fixed and variable costs.
DISCUSSION: Least squares requires that the line which is fit to the data be such that the sum of the squares of the vertical deviations from the points to the line is a minimum.
Answer (a) is incorrect because it is less precise; it uses only a representative high and low point. Answer (b) is incorrect because it is a general method to solve linear programming problems. Answer (d) is incorrect because it uses a visual, fairly imprecise approach.

Module 19.4: Interpretation of Regression Results

58. Given actual amounts of a semivariable cost for various levels of output, which of the following will give the least precise mathematical measure of the fixed and variable components but be easiest to compute?

  a. Bayesian statistics.
  b. High-low method.
  c. Scattergram approach.
  d. Least squares method.

The correct answer is (b). *(Publisher)*
REQUIRED: The quantitative method which most easily but least precisely separates fixed and variable costs.
DISCUSSION: The high-low method utilizes only two observations, a representative high point and a representative low point, to determine the slope of the line defining the relationship between activity and the variable cost. Thus it is susceptible to error, but is easy to compute.
Answer (a) is incorrect because it is a technique in which future probabilities are based upon past probabilities and occurrences. Answer (c) is incorrect because it is not a mathematical or quantitative approach. Answer (d) is incorrect because least squares is a much more precise method than high-low.

59. Jacob Corp. wishes to determine the fixed portion of its maintenance expense (a semi-variable expense), as measured against direct labor hours, for the first three months of the year. The inspection costs are fixed; the adjustments necessitated by errors found during inspection account for the variable portion of the maintenance costs. Information for the first quarter is as follows:

	Direct Labor Hours	Maintenance Expense
January	34,000	$610
February	31,000	$585
March	34,000	$610

What is the fixed portion of Jacob's maintenance expense, rounded to the nearest dollar?

  a. $283.
  b. $327.
  c. $372.
  d. $408.

The correct answer is (b). *(Publisher)*
REQUIRED: The fixed portion of expense as measured against direct labor hours.
DISCUSSION: The high-low method can be used to determine the fixed and variable cost components of a mixed cost. The variable cost is found by dividing the change in total cost (TC) by the change in activity, e.g., DLH. The fixed cost is found by substituting the variable cost into either of the activity/cost functions. Alternatively, the fixed cost is the cost given a zero level of activity. Turn to Module 11.3 for additional questions on the high-low method.

$$\frac{\text{Change in TC}}{\text{Change in DLH}} = \frac{\$25}{3,000} = .00833$$

FC = TC - VC
FC = $585 - (31,000 × .00833) = $327
FC = $610 - (34,000 × .00833) = $327

19.4 Interpretation of Regression Results

60. The use of the least squares method to solve a multiple regression equation implies that

  a. The estimators will be upper limits that actual values will not exceed.
  b. The estimators will be unbiased and each will have a minimum variance.
  c. Nonlinear relationships cannot be fitted.
  d. The number of observations can be, at most, one less than the degrees of freedom.
  e. None of the above.

The correct answer is (b). *(CIA 578 IV-17)*
REQUIRED: The implication of using least squares to solve a multiple regression equation.
DISCUSSION: The least squares method squares the deviations between the regression line and the individual observations and chooses the regression line that has the lowest sum of the squared deviations, i.e., a minimum variance. It also assumes (and thus its use implies) that the estimators will be unbiased.
Answer (a) is incorrect because actual values may exceed estimators. Answer (c) is incorrect because the estimation of linear relationships implies nothing about nonlinear relationships. Answer (d) is incorrect because the number of observations must be greater than the degrees of freedom.

Module 19.4: Interpretation of Regression Results

61. If regression was applied to the data shown below, the coefficients of correlation and determination would indicate the existence of a

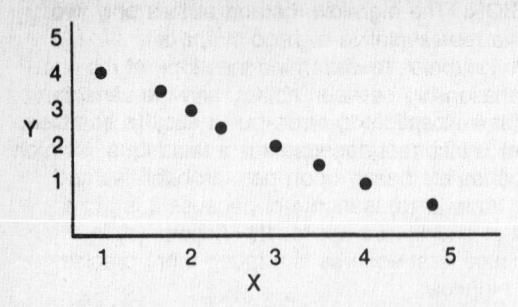

[Scatter plot showing points decreasing from upper-left (approximately (1,4)) to lower-right (approximately (5,0.5)) on X-Y axes with X from 1-5 and Y from 1-5]

a. Low linear relationship, high explained variation ratio.
b. High inverse linear relationship, high explained variation ratio.
c. High direct linear relationship, high explained variation ratio.
d. High inverse linear relationship, low explained variation ratio.

The correct answer is (b). *(CIA 1187 III-35)*
REQUIRED: The implications of the coefficients of correlation and determination for the given data.
DISCUSSION: The coefficient of correlation measures the degree and direction of the linear relationship between two or more variables. The relationship ranges from perfectly inverse (-1) to perfectly direct (1). If there is no relationship, the coefficient of correlation is 0. The coefficient of determination is the proportion of the variance of the dependent variable explained by the independent variable. It is the coefficient of correlation squared (R squared). Since the plotted points are almost in a straight line with a negative slope, the coefficient of correlation is almost -1, and the coefficient of determination is nearly +1. Thus, a high inverse linear relationship exists, and a high degree of variation is explained.

62. If the coefficient of correlation between two variables is zero, how might a scatter diagram of these variables appear?

a. Random points.
b. A least squares line that slopes up to the right.
c. A least squares line that slopes down to the right.
d. Under this condition, a scatter diagram could not be plotted on a graph.

The correct answer is (a). *(CPA 576 P-28)*
REQUIRED: The scatter diagram if the coefficient of correlation is zero.
DISCUSSION: Each observation creates a point which represents the x and y values. The collinearity of these relationships and slope of the observations is visible. If the coefficient of correlation is zero, there is no relationship between the variables, and the points would be randomly distributed.
Answer (b) is incorrect because it describes a direct (positive) relationship. Answer (c) is incorrect because it describes an inverse (negative) relationship. Answer (d) is incorrect because the points could be plotted on a scattergram, although it would have no meaning other than to confirm the lack of correlation between the variables.

63. A firm regressed overhead on units produced over the past year and found a coefficient of determination equal to 0.85 with a U-shaped residual error pattern. It is reasonable to conclude that the relationship between overhead and units produced is

a. Weak.
b. Causal.
c. Nonlinear.
d. Linear.

The correct answer is (c). *(CIA 1186 III-39)*
REQUIRED: The relationship between overhead and units produced.
DISCUSSION: A coefficient of determination measures the proportion of the total variation in y that is explained or accounted for by the regression equation. In this case the relationship is strong because 85% of that variation is explained. However, the relationship is curvilinear since the residual error pattern is U-shaped. The residual error pattern consists of the plots of the estimates of the error term in the linear regression equation.
Answer (a) is incorrect because the relationship is strong given a .85 coefficient of determination. Answer (b) is incorrect because regression analysis measures the strength of the relationship among variables, but it does not establish causation. Answer (d) is incorrect because the U-shaped residual error pattern reflects a nonlinear relationship.

Module 19.4: Interpretation of Regression Results

64. Assume that your company develops regression models for sales in its various lines of business. One of the models developed was

$$Y = 10,000 + 2,000X$$

where Y = sales
   X = number of customers making purchases

To which product lines is this model likely to relate?

   a. Used cars.
   b. Cosmetics.
   c. Shoes.
   d. Electrical appliances.

The correct answer is (a). *(CIA 1183 IV-35)*
REQUIRED: The independent variable in a regression equation.
DISCUSSION: The regression equation estimates the independent variable Y (sales) to be $10,000 plus $2,000 times the number of customers making purchases. A marginal purchase price of $2,000 means one would expect each additional customer to increase sales by $2,000. Thus, this regression model probably applies to used cars, which are much more costly than typical cosmetic, shoe, or electrical appliance purchases.

65. Meg Co. has developed a regression equation to analyze the behavior of its maintenance costs (Q) as a function of machine hours (Z). The following equation was developed by using 30 monthly observations with a related coefficient of determination of .90:

$$Q = \$6,000 + \$5.25Z$$

If 1,000 machine hours are worked in one month, the related point estimate of total maintenance costs would be

   a. $11,250.
   b. $10,125.
   c. $5,250.
   d. $4,725.

The correct answer is (a). *(CPA 587 Q-27)*
REQUIRED: The estimate of total maintenance costs given the regression equation and machine hours.
DISCUSSION: Using the given equation

$$\begin{aligned} Q &= \$6,000 + \$5.25Z \\ &= \$6,000 + \$5.25(1,000) \\ &= \$6,000 + \$5,250 \\ &= \$11,250 \end{aligned}$$

19.5 Multiple Calculations

Questions 66 through 69 are based on Martin Corporation, which operates 7 days a week and orders Product B from the Whiting Company each morning. Product B, which arrives soon after the order is placed, spoils if it is not sold at the end of the day.

The president of Martin has been using executive judgment to determine how much of Product B to order each morning. You, as Martin's controller, have noticed that a number of costly forecasting errors have been made by the president and wish to show that the use of a more sophisticated method of determining the order quantity of Product B would save money. As part of the preparation for your presentation of the use of various forecasting techniques, you have compiled the following data regarding the past 11 days of orders of and demand for Product B.

	X	Z	Y	Y-Z
		No. of Units Ordered	Demand in Units	No. of Units Spoiled (Short)
January 1		21	16	5
January 2		19	18	1
January 3		17	21	(4)
January 4		19	22	(3)
January 5		23	20	3
January 6		23	20	3
January 7		22	21	1
January 8		19	22	(3)
January 9		20	22	(2)
January 10		21	20	1
January 11		20	18	2
Total		224	220	4

In answering the following questions, round all calculations to the next highest whole number.

66. The formula for the least squares regression can be found with the following data.

Where

$$b = \frac{\Sigma xy - n\bar{x}\bar{y}}{\Sigma x^2 - n\bar{x}^2}$$

$$a = \bar{y} - b\bar{x}$$

and Σ = summation
n = number of observations
$\bar{x}$ = mean of the x values
$\bar{y}$ = mean of the y values

$$y = na + bx$$
$$xy = a(x) + b(x^2)$$

Using the least squares time regression technique for forecasting and based on the data for the first 11 days of January, the number of units that Martin's president should order on January 16 is

a. 23.
b. 20.
c. 21.
d. 22.

The correct answer is (d). *(CPA 573 P-19)*

REQUIRED: The number of units that should be ordered using the least squares method.

DISCUSSION: Least squares analysis requires that the line that is fit to the data be such that the sum of the squares of the vertical deviations from the points to the line be a minimum. To estimate the number of units Martin will order, use days as the independent variable (x) where 1 is January 1. The proper dependent variable (y) in this case is demand. The equation will give an estimate of the amount Martin should order to minimize the number of short or spoiled items if there are no expected changes in the future pattern of demand.

x	y	xy	x^2
1	16	16	1
2	18	36	4
3	21	63	9
4	22	88	16
5	20	100	25
6	20	120	36
7	21	147	49
8	22	176	64
9	22	198	81
10	20	200	100
11	18	198	121
66	220	1,342	506

$\bar{x} = 6;\ \bar{y} = 20$

$$b = \frac{1,342 - 11(6)(20)}{506 - 11(36)} = \frac{22}{110} = .2$$

$$a = 20 - .2(6) = 20 - 1.2 = 18.8$$

Substituting the desired day (16) into the equation,

$$18.8 + .2(16) = 18.8 + 3.2 = 22$$

the company should order 22 units of B for January 16.

Module 19.5: Multiple Calculations

67. Martin's president might also have based his January 2 order on the exponential smoothing technique of forecasting using an alpha of 0.2 and a base of 21 units. The equation is

Forecast = α (current observation) + (1 - α)(base)

The number of units ordered on January 2 would have been

- a. 20.
- b. 23.
- c. 19.
- d. 22.

68. After your presentation, the president favors the use of the exponential smoothing technique of forecasting, but he points out that during each month there is a single day in which demand will increase to 40 or 50 units and he desires to minimize the effect of this occurrence on the forecast. He should

- a. Use the exponential smoothing technique with a large alpha factor.
- b. Use the exponential smoothing technique with a small alpha factor.
- c. Use the least squares time regression technique rather than the exponential smoothing technique.
- d. Use a moving average technique rather than exponential smoothing.

69. The president mentions that he expects demand to jump to approximately 35 units per day and stay at that level. He wants to use the exponential smoothing technique of forecasting but wants it to respond as quickly as possible to this expected increase. He should

- a. Use a moving average technique rather than the exponential smoothing technique.
- b. Use the exponential smoothing technique with a large alpha factor.
- c. Use the exponential smoothing technique with a small alpha factor.
- d. Use the least squares time regression technique rather than exponential smoothing.

The correct answer is (a). *(CPA 573 P-20)*
REQUIRED: The number of units to be ordered using exponential smoothing.
DISCUSSION: Exponential smoothing is a technique used to minimize the effects of variations in time and random demand. Remember to round up the next highest whole number as required in the fact pattern. Note that on January 2, the current observation demanded the 16 units on January 1.

$$\begin{aligned} \text{Forecast} &= .2(16) + .8(21) \\ &= 3.2 + 16.8 \\ &= 20 \end{aligned}$$

The correct answer is (b). *(CPA 573 P-21)*
REQUIRED: The quantitative method that minimizes the effect of unusual demand.
DISCUSSION: Large fluctuations can be minimized by using a small alpha, which, in essence, reduces the effect of the current observation upon the forecast.
Answer (a) is incorrect because it would increase the weight of the current observation. Answer (c) is incorrect because it assumes a linear relationship. Answer (d) is incorrect because it has a bias toward the current observation.

The correct answer is (b). *(CPA 573 P-22)*
REQUIRED: The quantitative technique that responds most quickly to a change in demand.
DISCUSSION: Fluctuations in demand may be incorporated into the forecast most quickly by using a large alpha factor, which, in essence, increases the effect of the current observation upon the forecast.
Answer (a) is incorrect because it has a bias toward the current observation. Answer (c) is incorrect because it reduces the effect of the current observation. Answer (d) is incorrect because it assumes a linear relationship.

Questions 70 through 74 are based on your examination of last year's financial statements of MacKenzie Park Co., which manufactures and sells trivets. You wish to analyze selected aspects of the company's operations. Labor hours and production costs for the last four months of the year, which you believe are representative for the year, were as follows:

Month	Labor Hours	Total Production Costs
September	2,500	$ 20,000
October	3,500	25,000
November	4,500	30,000
December	3,500	25,000
Total	14,000	$100,000

Based upon the information given and using the least squares method of computation with the letters listed below, select the best answer for each question.

Let a = Fixed production costs per month
b = Variable production costs per labor hour
n = Number of months
x = Labor hours per month
y = Total monthly production costs
Σ = Summation

70. The equation(s) required for applying the least squares method of computation of fixed and variable production costs could be expressed as

a. $\Sigma xy = ax + b\Sigma x^2$
b. $\Sigma y = na + b\Sigma x$
c. $y = a + bx^2$
   $\Sigma y = na + b\Sigma x$
d. $\Sigma xy = a\Sigma x + b\Sigma x^2$
   $\Sigma y = na + b\Sigma x$

The correct answer is (d). *(CPA 570 P-1)*
REQUIRED: The equation(s) expressing the relationship between fixed and variable costs.
DISCUSSION: The least squares method of computing fixed and variable production costs minimizes the sum of the squares of the vertical deviation from the points to a line depicted on a scatter diagram. The least squares equation minimizes the deviation from the expected linear relationship to provide the closest approximation of the relationship of fixed and variable production cost.

71. The cost function derived by the simple least squares method

a. Would be linear.
b. Must be tested for minima and maxima.
c. Would be parabolic.
d. Would indicate maximum costs at the function's point of inflection.

The correct answer is (a). *(CPA 570 P-2)*
REQUIRED: The characteristic of the cost function derived by the least squares method.
DISCUSSION: The cost function derived by the least squares method is linear, containing both fixed and variable elements. Although it is useful over the relevant range, it is probably not completely accurate.
Answer (b) is incorrect because the minima and maxima test would not be appropriate in a linear function. Answer (c) is incorrect because the function is not curvilinear. Answer (d) is incorrect because it describes curvilinear relationship defining maximum costs on a total cost function.

72. Monthly production costs could be expressed

a. $y = ax + b$.
b. $y = a + bx$.
c. $y = b + ax$.
d. $y = \Sigma a + bx$.

The correct answer is (b). *(CPA 570 P-3)*
REQUIRED: The equation expressing monthly production costs.
DISCUSSION: The least squares method of computation results in an equation with a dependent variable y, a constant coefficient a, plus a variable coefficient and an independent variable known as x. Thus, $y = a + bx$ expresses total monthly production cost y in terms of fixed cost a plus the variable cost b times the activity level x.

73. Using the least squares method of computation, the fixed monthly production cost of trivets is approximately

   a. $10,000.
   b. $9,500.
   c. $7,500.
   d. $5,000.

The correct answer is (c). *(CPA 570 P-4)*
REQUIRED: The fixed monthly production cost using the least squares method.
DISCUSSION: Using the least squares method of computation, the fixed monthly production cost of trivets is the constant coefficient. It can be calculated by substituting into the least squares equation.

$$\Sigma y = na + b\Sigma x$$
$$\Sigma xy = a\Sigma x + b\Sigma x^2$$

or

$$b = \frac{\Sigma xy - n\bar{x}\bar{y}}{\Sigma x^2 - n\bar{x}^2}$$
$$a = \bar{y} - b\bar{x}$$

x	y	xy	x^2
2,500	20,000	50,000,000	6,250,000
3,500	25,000	87,500,000	12,250,000
4,500	30,000	135,000,000	20,250,000
3,500	25,000	87,500,000	12,250,000
14,000	100,000	360,000,000	51,000,000

$\bar{x} = 3,500$; $\bar{y} = 25,000$; $n = 4$

$$b = \frac{360,000,000 - 4(3,500)(25,000)}{51,000,000 - 4(3,500)^2} = 5$$

$$a = 25,000 - 5(3,500)$$
$$= 25,000 - 17,500$$
$$= 7,500$$

74. Using the least squares method of computation, the variable production cost per labor hour is

   a. $6.00.
   b. $5.00.
   c. $3.00.
   d. $2.00.

The correct answer is (b). *(CPA 570 P-5)*
REQUIRED: The variable production cost per labor hour.
DISCUSSION: The variable production cost per labor hour utilizing the least squares method of computation is the value of b in the least squares equation, or $5.00. Using the values calculated in Q. 73, the least squares line is

$$\hat{y} = 7,500 + 5x$$

75. There are four components to time series data: an irregular movement, a seasonal variation, a cyclical variation, and secular trend. Sometimes, it is important to look at data after removing their seasonal components. In order to deseasonalize data, the original data can be

   a. Divided by the seasonal factor.
   b. Reduced by the seasonal factor.
   c. Multiplied by the seasonal factor.
   d. Multiplied by the irregular, cyclical, and secular components.

The correct answer is (a). *(CIA 1187 III-49)*
REQUIRED: The means of deseasonalizing data in time series analysis.
DISCUSSION: Time series analysis or trend analysis relies on past experience. Changes in the value of a variable (e.g., unit sales of a product) may have several possible components. In time series analysis, the dependent variable is regressed on time (the independent variable). The secular trend is the long-term change that occurs in a series. It is represented by a straight line or curve on a graph. Seasonal variations are common in many businesses. A variety of methods include seasonal variations in a forecasting model, but most methods adjust data by a seasonal index. Cyclical fluctuations are variations in the level of activity in business periods. While some of these fluctuations are beyond the control of the firm, they need to be considered in forecasting. They are usually incorporated as index numbers. Irregular or random variations are any variations not included in the three categories above. Business can be affected by random happenings, e.g., weather, strikes, or fires.
Answers (b) and (c) are incorrect because dividing by the seasonal norm removes the seasonal variation. Answer (d) is incorrect because the other components are not the basis for any adjustment for seasonality.

Questions 76 through 83 are based on Armer Company, which is accumulating data to be used in preparing its annual profit plan for the coming year. The cost behavior pattern of the maintenance costs must be determined. The accounting staff has suggested that linear regression be employed to derive an equation in the form of y = a + bx for maintenance costs. Data regarding the maintenance hours and costs for last year and the results of the regression analysis are as follows:

	Hours of Activity	Maintenance Costs
January	480	$ 4,200
February	320	3,000
March	400	3,600
April	300	2,820
May	500	4,350
June	310	2,960
July	320	3,030
August	520	4,470
September	490	4,260
October	470	4,050
November	350	3,300
December	340	3,160
Sum	4,800	$43,200
Average	400	3,600

Average cost per hour (43,200 ÷ 4,800) = $9.00

a coefficient	684.65
b coefficient	7.2884
Standard error of the a coefficient	49.515
Standard error of the b coefficient	.12126
Standard error of the estimate	34.469
r^2	.99724
t-value a	13.827
t-value b	60.105

t-table for
Single-Tailed Values of t

Degrees of Freedom	t.100	t.05	t.025	t.01
8	1.40	1.86	2.31	2.90
9	1.38	1.83	2.26	2.82
10	1.37	1.81	2.23	2.76
11	1.36	1.80	2.20	2.72
12	1.36	1.78	2.18	2.68
13	1.35	1.77	2.16	2.65
14	1.35	1.76	2.15	2.62

76. The statistic used to determine if the estimate of the slope is significantly different from zero is the

a. Coefficient of determination.
b. Standard error of the a coefficient.
c. Standard error of the estimate.
d. t-value of b.

The correct answer is (d). *(Publisher)*
REQUIRED: The statistic used to determine if the slope is significantly different from zero.
DISCUSSION: The t-value of b (the slope of the line of the equation) states how far the estimate of b is away from zero in terms of standard deviations, under the assumption that the true value of b is zero. The more standard deviations the estimate of b is away from zero, the greater the probability that zero is not the true value.
Answer (a) is incorrect because it is the portion of total variance explained by the independent variable. Answer (b) is incorrect because it describes the variance of the constant term a. Answer (c) is incorrect because it describes the variability of the actual values around the least squares line.

77. If Armer Company uses the high-low method of analysis, the equation for the relationship between hours of activity and maintenance cost would be

a. y = 400 + 9.0x.
b. y = 570 + 7.5x.
c. y = 3,600 + 400x.
d. y = 570 + 9.0x.
e. None of the above.

The correct answer is (b). *(CMA 681 5-17)*
REQUIRED: The equation for the relationship based on the high-low method.
DISCUSSION: The high-low equation compares the highest and the lowest activity levels with the highest and lowest maintenance costs. The high activity level occurred in August and the low activity occurred in April. The difference in the high activity level and the low activity level establishes the variable coefficient. In this case, 520 - 300 = 220, 4,470 - 2,820 = 1,650. 1,650 ÷ 220 = 7.5, which is the variable coefficient. Substituting 7.5 back into the equation using either the high or low activity, the fixed element is calculated as 570.

78. Assume the t-value of b is 2.0, and we expect maintenance costs to increase as hours of activity increase. Is the estimate of b significantly different from zero?

   a. No, with 95% confidence.
   b. Yes, with 99% confidence.
   c. Yes, with 95% confidence.
   d. Yes, since our estimate of b is positive.

The correct answer is (c). *(Publisher)*
   REQUIRED: The correct interpretation of the t-value.
   DISCUSSION: Under the assumption that the true value of b is zero, a t-value tells how much the observed estimate of b differs from zero in terms of standard deviations. The formula for this t-value is

$$\frac{\hat{b} - 0}{\text{standard deviation of b}}$$

The greater the number of standard deviations, the less probable it is the true value of b equals zero. If we wish some required level of confidence or probability, we use a t-table to check how large a t-value is needed to assure a set amount of confidence. The absolute value of the t-statistic (derived by formula) must be equal to or greater than the value taken from the t-table to be at least that confident (or insure that level of probability). If we wish to be 95% confident, we look at the values in the table of single-tailed values of t under the column for .05 and degrees of freedom, n - 2 = 10, to get the value 1.81. Since 2 (the given t-value) is greater than 1.81 we can be at least 95% confident that the estimate b is different from zero.

79. Based upon the data derived from the regression analysis, 420 maintenance hours in a month would mean the maintenance costs would be budgeted at

   a. $3,780.
   b. $3,461.
   c. $3,797.
   d. $3,746.
   e. None of the above.

The correct answer is (d). *(CMA 681 5-18)*
   REQUIRED: The budgeted maintenance cost at 420 maintenance hours.
   DISCUSSION: The budgeted maintenance cost at 420 hours in a month (or at any other activity level within the relevant range) is the a coefficient plus the b coefficient times the activity level. Here, the resulting equation is $684.65 + (7.2884 × 420) = $3,746.

80. The coefficient of correlation for Armer's regression equation for the maintenance activities is

   a. 34.469/49.515.
   b. .99724.
   c. $\sqrt{.99724}$.
   d. $(.99724)^2$.
   e. None of the above.

The correct answer is (c). *(CMA 681 5-19)*
   REQUIRED: The coefficient of correlation for the maintenance activities.
   DISCUSSION: The coefficient of correlation determines the relative strength of the relationship between two variables. This relationship may vary from zero (indicating no correlation) to plus or minus one (indicating positive or negative correlation). The coefficient of correlation is equal to the square root of r^2. Since r^2 is given as .99724, the coefficient of correlation is $\sqrt{.99724}$.

81. The percent of the total variance that can be explained by the regression equation is

   a. 99.724%.
   b. 69.613%.
   c. 80.982%.
   d. 99.862%.
   e. None of the above.

The correct answer is (a). *(CMA 681 5-20)*
   REQUIRED: The percent of total variance that can be explained by the regression equation.
   DISCUSSION: The percent of total variance that can be explained by the regression equation is r^2, or the coefficient of determination. It is expressed as the percent of the total variance which is equal to one minus the proportion of the total variance not explained. Here, r^2 is given as .99724, or 99.724%.

Questions 82 and 83 are based on the information presented on page 596.

82. Armer can be 95% confident that the true value of the marginal maintenance cost will fall within what range?

   a. $7.02 - $7.56.
   b. $7.17 - $7.41.
   c. $7.07 - $7.51.
   d. $6.29 - $8.29.
   e. None of the above.

The correct answer is (a). *(CMA 681 5-21)*
REQUIRED: The 95% confidence interval for the marginal maintenance cost.
DISCUSSION: Marginal maintenance cost is the variable coefficient factor, or 7.2884. The 95% confidence interval would extend within a two-tailed test at the .025 single value of t. It is two-tailed because we are concerned with both ends of the possible range. The value of t is .025 because the confidence interval is two-tailed (.05 ÷ 2 = .025). The .05 is 100% - 95% confidence level. The degrees of freedom would be 10 [n - 2, where n = the number of time periods, or 12, and 2 is the number of parameters that were estimated (a and b) in the least squares equation], resulting in a 2.23 standard deviation (see t-table) times the standard error of the b coefficient. The standard error of the b coefficient is .12126. .12126 x 2.23 = .2704098. When this result is both added to and subtracted from the $7.28884, the confidence interval is $7.02 to $7.56.

83. At 400 hours of activity, Armer management can be approximately two-thirds confident that the maintenance costs will be in the range of

   a. $3,550.50 - $3,649.53.
   b. $3,551.37 - $3,648.51.
   c. $3,586.18 - $3,613.93.
   d. $3,565.54 - $3,634.47.
   e. None of the above.

The correct answer is (d). *(CMA 681 5-22)*
REQUIRED: The 66 2/3% confidence interval for actual average maintenance costs.
DISCUSSION: A confidence interval with approximately 66.6% probability can be established by adding and subtracting one standard deviation of the estimate to/from the predicted value of maintenance costs. When activity is 400 hours, the predicted maintenance cost is $684.65 + $7.2884 (400) = $3,600. The standard error of the estimate is given as $34.469. The 66.6% confidence interval is thus $3,600 ± $34.469, or $3,565.54 to $3,634.47.

CHAPTER TWENTY
LINEAR PROGRAMMING

> 20.1 Concepts .... (14 questions) 599
> 20.2 Graphs .... (12 questions) 603
> 20.3 Formulation .... (22 questions) 606
> 20.4 Calculations .... (36 questions) 613

This chapter focuses on linear programming and the characteristics of linear programming functions. Some emphasis is placed upon graphical solutions and formulation of the objective function and the constraints. Note that linear programming (LP) has received decreased emphasis on the professional examinations in recent years.

20.1 Concepts

1. A quantitative technique used for selecting the combination of resources that maximizes profits or minimizes costs is

   a. Nonlinear analysis.
   b. Queuing theory.
   c. Dynamic programming.
   d. Linear programming.

The correct answer is (d). *(CPA 574 P-18)*
REQUIRED: The quantitative technique to select optimal resource combinations.
DISCUSSION: Linear programming is a mathematical technique used to maximize revenue (profit) functions or to minimize cost functions subject to constraints. Linear programming is often used to plan resource allocations. Managers need to select the most profitable or least costly way to use resources.
   Answer (a) is incorrect because LP assumes a linear relationship. Answer (b) is incorrect because it is a technique used to calculate the costs of waiting lines. Answer (c) is incorrect because dynamic programming solves problems involving time-staged decisions with few variables, e.g., inventory reordering.

2. Linear programming is an operations research technique that allocates resources. Mathematical expressions are used to describe the problem. The measure of effectiveness that is to be maximized or minimized is called

   a. The constraints.
   b. The decision variables.
   c. The objective function.
   d. The derivative of the function.
   e. The nonlinear function.

The correct answer is (c). *(CMA 1278 5-25)*
REQUIRED: The measure of effectiveness to be maximized/minimized.
DISCUSSION: The objective function in a linear programming model symbolically represents the revenues (profits) or costs being maximized or minimized, respectively.
   Answer (a) is incorrect because constraints are the conditions under which the objective function is optimized. Answer (b) is incorrect because they are the values used to construct the objective function and the constraints. Answer (d) is incorrect because it is an irrelevant calculus term. Answer (e) is incorrect because this technique requires linear functions.

3. A 200-bed hospital serves 500 meals per day. An analytic tool which would help them plan meals to meet nutrition goals at minimum cost is

   a. Monte Carlo simulation.
   b. Linear programming.
   c. Material requirements planning.
   d. Markov analysis.

The correct answer is (b). *(CIA 1186 III-38)*
REQUIRED: The technique that would help meet goals at minimum cost.
DISCUSSION: Linear programming is a technique used to maximize a revenue or profit function, or minimize a cost function, subject to constraints, e.g., limited (scarce) resources or minimum/maximum levels of production, performance, etc. In business, linear programming is used for planning resource allocations. Managers are often faced with problems of selecting the most profitable or least costly way to use available resources.
Answer (a) is incorrect because the Monte Carlo method is used in simulation to generate values of a random variable. Answer (c) is incorrect because MRP is an inventory control method. Answer (d) is incorrect because Markov processes are useful in decision problems in which the probability of occurrence of a future state depends on the current state.

4. A manufacturer has developed four new products and must decide how much of each should be manufactured to maximize profit. The constraints for each product include a fixed limit to the amount of Chemical A that can be used per run and the amount of each product that can be successfully marketed. To determine optimum production, which of the following mathematical models should be used?

   a. Linear programming.
   b. Minimum-spanning tree.
   c. CPM.
   d. Monte Carlo simulation.

The correct answer is (a). *(CIA 586 III-17)*
REQUIRED: The model for determining optimum production.
DISCUSSION: Linear programming is a technique to maximize a revenue or profit function or minimize a cost function subject to any constraints (e.g., the amount of Chemical A that can be used per run).
Answer (b) is incorrect because minimum-spanning tree refers to the shortest route in a network, i.e., the minimum spans between nodes in a network. Answer (c) is incorrect because the critical path method is a network of time relationships such that the completion time of a complex project can be determined and controlled. Answer (d) is incorrect because the Monte Carlo technique generates individual values for a random variable.

5. An internal auditor for a wood-products company is reviewing a linear programming model. Which of the following would not be in the model?

   a. Independent variables.
   b. Networks.
   c. Dependent variables.
   d. Constraints.
   e. Slack variables.

The correct answer is (b). *(CIA 579 II-5)*
REQUIRED: The element not found in linear programming models.
DISCUSSION: Linear programming (LP) is a mathematical technique used to maximize revenue/profits or to minimize costs. Solving LP problems requires the use of independent variables, dependent variables, constraints, and slack variables. Network diagrams are used to solve optimization problems of a special nature, e.g., applying PERT (program evaluation and review technique), a management control method for complex projects.

6. Which of the following is not an essential step in using a linear programming model?

   a. Quantify the maximization coefficient inflows.
   b. Determine the objective function.
   c. Establish the basic relationships between the variables and the constraints.
   d. Identify the feasible alternatives.
   e. Solve the equations to find the optimal alternative.

The correct answer is (a). *(CIA 976 IV-12)*
REQUIRED: The step not essential in an LP problem.
DISCUSSION: LP is a mathematical technique used to maximize revenues/profits or to minimize costs subject to given constraints. The following steps must be taken: (1) establish the basic relationships between the variables and the constraints, (2) identify the feasible alternatives, (3) determine the objective function, and (4) solve the equations to find the optimal alternative.

7. The objective of the transportation model is to minimize the cost of transporting resources from one location to another. This model is a specific application of

    a. Dynamic programming.
    b. Queuing theory.
    c. Game theory.
    d. Linear programming.
    e. Regression analysis.

The correct answer is (d). *(CMA 1278 5-26)*
REQUIRED: The category of quantitative methods to which transportation models belong.
DISCUSSION: A transportation model is a special kind of LP problem in which the costs of receiving supplies from several sources are described. The model attempts to minimize costs by allocating the outputs of the supply points to various destinations.
    Answer (a) is incorrect because dynamic programming solves problems involving time-staged decisions with few variables, e.g., inventory reordering. Answer (b) is incorrect because it is used to evaluate the costs of waiting lines. Answer (c) is incorrect because game theory is a mathematical approach to decision making given an opponent's behavior (i.e., given competition). Answer (e) is incorrect because it is used to describe the strength and direction of relationships between variables.

8. Of the following methods, the one that would not be appropriate for analyzing how a specific cost behaves is

    a. The scattergraph method.
    b. The industrial engineering approach.
    c. Linear programming.
    d. The high-low method.
    e. Statistical regression analysis.

The correct answer is (c). *(CMA 1285 5-28)*
REQUIRED: The method not appropriate for analyzing how a specific cost behaves.
DISCUSSION: Regression analysis assumes that a change in the value of a dependent variable is related to the change in the value of an independent variable. Regression analysis attempts to find an equation for the linear relationship among variables. Statistical regression analysis is thus a useful means of determining how costs are affected by certain variables. The scattergraph and high-low methods are less scientific means of correlation analysis. Engineering estimates could also be used when there is no past experience upon which to base a regression. Only linear programming could not be used to analyze cost behavior. Linear programming is used to determine the means of maximizing profits or minimizing costs given certain constraints.

9. Long Corporation uses linear programming in its production mix. One alternative they are considering is expansion of production facilities, thereby relaxing a binding constraint. The increase to the contribution margin that would result from increasing the capacity by one unit is referred to in linear programming as the

    a. Shadow price.
    b. Production cost.
    c. Capacity price.
    d. Market price.
    e. Sunk cost.

The correct answer is (a). *(CIA 1182 IV-16)*
REQUIRED: The increase in CM resulting from a one-unit increase in a constraint.
DISCUSSION: The shadow price of a constraint is the amount by which the contribution margin will increase as a result of relaxing that constraint in an LP model by one unit. The calculation of shadow price is a simple example of sensitivity analysis, which is a procedure designed to test the responsiveness of an alternative decision or variable to changes or errors in the decision model.
    Answer (b) is incorrect because it is the cost associated with the production of an item. Answer (c) is incorrect because it is the amount paid to develop the capacity of a firm or a plant. Answer (d) is incorrect because it is the going rate charged for an item. Answer (e) is incorrect because it is a past cost not relevant to future decisions.

10. In a system of equations for a linear programming model, what can be done to equalize an inequality such as $3X + 2Y \leq 15$?

a. Nothing.
b. Add a slack variable.
c. Add a tableau.
d. Multiply each element by -1.

The correct answer is (b). *(CPA 576 P-28)*
REQUIRED: The proper method of equalizing an inequality in a system of LP equations.
DISCUSSION: Linear programming equations are sometimes stated as inequalities. To solve LP models, slack variables must first be added to the equations to result in equalities.
Answer (a), (c) and (d) are incorrect because none changes the form of the linear programming constraint from an inequality to an equality.

11. Which of the following is not an application of linear programming techniques?

a. Scheduling flight crews to various flights to minimize costs.
b. Routing production to minimize costs.
c. Determining the optimum trade-off between time and costs to maximize profits.
d. Deciding which warehouses will service which customers to minimize total shipping costs.

The correct answer is (c). *(CPA 1176 P-28)*
REQUIRED: The decision to which linear programming (LP) techniques do not apply.
DISCUSSION: LP techniques are used to maximize revenues/profits or minimize costs by determining the best allocation of resources, e.g., scheduling, routing, and transportation algorithms. Minimizing cost functions is usually an application of differential calculus because costs usually contain fixed and variable portions. The result is a nonlinear total cost function.

12. What is the simplex method of linear programming?

a. A general procedure of linear programming that will solve only two variables simultaneously.
b. A means of determining the objective function in the model.
c. A means of determining the constraints in the model.
d. A general procedure for solving linear programming models.

The correct answer is (d). *(CPA 577 T-44)*
REQUIRED: The simplex method of linear programming.
DISCUSSION: The simplex method is the technique most commonly used to solve LP problems. It is an algorithm used to move from a possible solution to a better solution. The mathematical constraint equations are arranged in a matrix of coefficients and manipulated as a group by means of matrix algebra. The simplex method is used primarily with computers.
Answer (a) is incorrect because the simplex method may be used to solve equations with many variables. Answers (b) and (c) are incorrect because it is necessary to know the objective function and the constraints of the model in order to use the simplex method.

13. Given the basic equations for the maximization of profits in a linear programming model, what quantitative technique would generally be employed to arrive at an optimal solution?

a. Regression analysis.
b. Markov analysis.
c. Monte Carlo analysis.
d. Simplex method analysis.

The correct answer is (d). *(CPA 1174 Q-19)*
REQUIRED: The most generally used method of solving linear programming problems.
DISCUSSION: The simplex method is the technique most commonly used to solve linear programming problems. It is an algorithm used to move from a possible solution to a better solution. The mathematical constraint equations are arranged in a matrix of coefficients and manipulated as a group by means of matrix algebra. The simplex method is used primarily with computers.
Answer (a) is incorrect because regression analysis measures the relationship between two or more variables. Answer (b) is incorrect because Markov analysis is used in decision problems in which the probability of the occurrence of a future state depends only on the current state. Answer (c) is incorrect because the Monte Carlo technique is used in a simulation to generate random values for a variable.

14. Given below is the final solution for which type of problem?

X_1	8	0	1	.5	-.055	0
X_2	4	1	0	-.5	.111	0
C_j-Z_j:		0	0	-20	-6.67	0

    a. Linear programming.
    b. Markov absorbing chain.
    c. Material requirements planning.
    d. Two-line, three-server queuing system.

The correct answer is (a). *(CIA 1187 III-34)*
REQUIRED: The type of problem that the given solution represents.
DISCUSSION: The matrix given is the final solution of a simplex tableau. The simplex method is the technique most commonly used to solve linear programming problems. It is an algorithm used to move from a possible solution to a better solution. The mathematical constraint equations are arranged in a matrix of coefficients and manipulated as a group by means of matrix algebra. The simplex method is used primarily with computers.
Answer (b) is incorrect because a sequence of events (a Markov chain) is an absorbing chain if it can reach a state that will never change. An example is the completion of a project. Answer (c) is incorrect because MRP is an inventory management technique that treats inventory as directly dependent upon short-term demand for the finished product. Answer (d) is incorrect because queuing theory is used to minimize the costs of waiting lines.

20.2 Graphs

15. The graphic method as a means for solving linear programming problems

    a. Can be used when there are more than two restrictions (constraints).
    b. Is limited to situations in which there are two restrictions (constraints).
    c. Is limited to situations in which there is one restriction (constraint).
    d. Cannot be used if there are any restrictions (constraints).

The correct answer is (a). *(CPA 1180 T-41)*
REQUIRED: The true statement about constraints in graphic solutions of linear programming problems.
DISCUSSION: Linear programming (LP) problems assume linearity of relationships; the solutions may be examined by plotting a solution region on the graph. The solution region is formed or bounded by the constraint lines. The objective function is also a linear relationship which may also be used on the graph. Thus, multiple relationships and multiple constraints may be examined.
Answer (b) is incorrect because more than two restrictions (constraints) are possible. Answer (c) is incorrect because no graph is needed if only one restriction exists. The optimal solution is either all of one product, item, etc., or all of another unless the slope of the constraint line equals the slope of the objective function. Answer (d) is incorrect because all LP problems by definition have constraints.

16. When using the graphic method of solving a linear programming problem, which of the following would be depicted on the graph?

	Line of Best Fit	Optimum Corner Point
a.	No	No
b.	No	Yes
c.	Yes	No
d.	Yes	Yes

The correct answer is (b). *(CPA 584 T-50)*
REQUIRED: The element(s) of a linear programming graph.
DISCUSSION: The graphic solution to a linear programming problem depicts the area of feasible combinations of activity given the constraints. Any point along a constraint line will have the same characteristics; thus, a point represents the line. By moving to the extreme point of the feasibility region, one finds the optimal solution. The line of best fit is found when using the least squares method.

17. When using the graphic method of solving a linear programming problem, which of the following would be depicted on the graph?

    a. Coefficient of correlation.
    b. Line of best fit.
    c. Critical path.
    d. Constraint.

The correct answer is (d). *(CPA 582 T-48)*
REQUIRED: The elements of a linear programming graph.
DISCUSSION: A linear programming graph contains the constraint lines and an objective function line. The combination graphically depicts what is essentially a feasibility space. See the diagram accompanying the next questions.
Answer (a) is incorrect because it is the measure of relationships between variables. Answer (b) is incorrect because it is the term used in the least squares graphic method. Answer (c) is incorrect because it is used when PERT/CPM is used.

Questions 18 through 25 are based on Hale Company, which manufactures products A and B, each of which requires two processes, polishing and grinding. The contribution margin is $3 for Product A and $4 for Product B. The graph below shows the maximum number of units of each product that may be processed in the two departments.

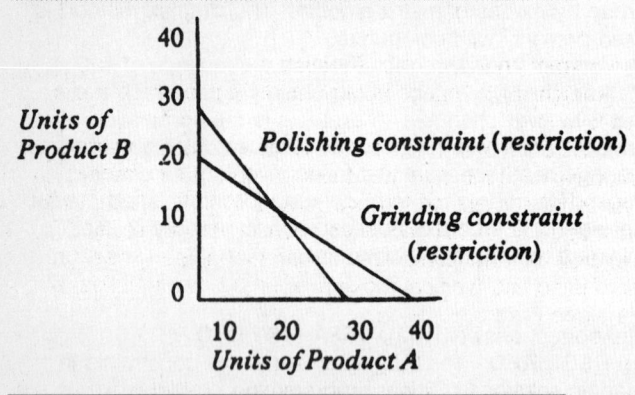

Units of Product B — Polishing constraint (restriction), Grinding constraint (restriction), vs. *Units of Product A*

---

18. Considering the constraints (restrictions) on processing, which combination of products A and B maximizes the total contribution margin?

 a. 0 units of A and 20 units of B.
 b. 20 units of A and 10 units of B.
 c. 30 units of A and 0 units of B.
 d. 40 units of A and 0 units of B.

The correct answer is (b). *(CPA 1177 P-33)*
REQUIRED: The profit maximization point in the graph.
DISCUSSION: To determine the profit maximization point on an LP graph requires the examination of each of the corner points on the feasibility space. At the point where 0 units of A and 20 units of B are produced, the contribution margin is $80 (20 units x B's $4 CM). At 20 units of A and 10 units of B, the CM is $100 ($60 UCM for A + $40 UCM for B). At 30 units of A and 0 units of B, the CM is $90 (30 units x A's $3 CM). Thus, the revenues for the product mix at 20 units of A and 10 units of B are maximized. Forty units of A and 0 units of B lie outside the feasibility space.

19. What is the polishing constraint if A requires 2 hours of both grinding and polishing and B requires 4 hours of grinding and 2 hours of polishing?

 a. $2A + 4B \le 80$.
 b. $2A + 2B \le 60$.
 c. $20A + 10B \le 100$.
 d. $30A + 30B \le 30$.

The correct answer is (b). *(Publisher)*
REQUIRED: The equation of the line representing the polishing constraint.
DISCUSSION: The polishing constraint on the graph consists of a line from 30B to 30A. Thus, the limitation imposed by polishing is 30A, 30B, or some combination of the two. Since A and B both require 2 hours of polishing, there must be 60 hours of polishing capacity available. Thus, $2A + 2B \le 60$.

20. What is the grinding constraint if A requires 2 hours of both grinding and polishing and B requires 4 hours of grinding and 2 hours of polishing?

 a. $3A + 4B \le 20 + 40$.
 b. $2A + 4B \le 80$.
 c. $30A + 20B \le 50$.
 d. $2A + 2B \le 60$.

The correct answer is (b). *(Publisher)*
REQUIRED: The equation of the line depicting the grinding constraint.
DISCUSSION: The grinding constraint is a line from 20B to 40A. Thus, if only B is produced, only 20 units can be produced. If only A is produced, 40 units can be produced. Also, note that A requires 2 hours of grinding and B requires 4 hours of grinding. Only 80 hours of grinding capacity are available since, at one end of the constraint, only 20 units of B can be produced at 4 hours each. Thus, the constraint is $2A + 4B \le 80$.

Module 20.2: Graphs

21. What is the slope of the polishing constraint?
    a. 1/1.
    b. 4/3.
    c. 1/2.
    d. -1/1.

The correct answer is (d). *(Publisher)*
   REQUIRED: The slope of the polishing constraint.
   DISCUSSION: The slope is rise (change in vertical distance) over run (change in horizontal distance). As one follows the polishing constraint line, it decreases by 1 vertically as one moves to the right (increases) horizontally by 1. Thus the slope is -1/1. Note that the slope of the constraint and objective functions in linear programming is usually negative.

22. Constraint lines in linear programming usually have a negative slope. Which is an example of a constraint line that is not a negative slope?
    a. $2X + 7Y \le 40$.
    b. $7X + 2Y \le 40$.
    c. $X + Y \le 40$.
    d. $Y \le 40$.

The correct answer is (d). *(Publisher)*
   REQUIRED: The constraint line that does not have a negative slope.
   DISCUSSION: Each of the constraint lines given as answer choices is downward sloping (i.e., they connect between the Y axis and X axis) except $Y \le 40$ which, when the inequality is changed to an equality, is graphically depicted as a horizontal line. Given that slope is rise/run, there is no rise (vertical movement) in a horizontal line, so the slope is zero.

23. What is the slope of the grinding constraint?
    a. -3/4.
    b. -1/2.
    c. -2/1.
    d. -4/3.

The correct answer is (b). *(Publisher)*
   REQUIRED: The slope of the grinding constraint line.
   DISCUSSION: The grinding constraint line goes from 20B to 40A, decreasing 1 vertically for every 2 moved horizontally. Accordingly, the slope is -1/2.

24. What is the slope of the objective function?
    a. -2/4.
    b. -3/3.
    c. -3/4.
    d. -4/3.

The correct answer is (c). *(Publisher)*
   REQUIRED: The slope of the objective function.
   DISCUSSION: The objective function consists of a series of parallel lines outward from the origin which have the same profit potential. Since each A generates $3 of CM, and each B produces a $4 UCM, the company would be indifferent between producing 4A and 3B. On this graph, such a line would run from 30B to 40A. The rise would be $3 vertically downward for every $4 horizontal increase, for a slope of -3/4.

25. Which combination of A and B lies on the same objective function line?

	A	B
a.	40	20
b.	20	40
c.	30	30
d.	40	30

The correct answer is (d). *(Publisher)*
   REQUIRED: The combination of A and B to provide the same profit.
   DISCUSSION: Recall from Q. 24 that the company should be indifferent between producing 4A and 3B, which combination can be provided by 40A or 30B. Each combination provides a contribution margin of $120.

26. An internal auditor is reviewing the following linear programming model for expected output of a production department:

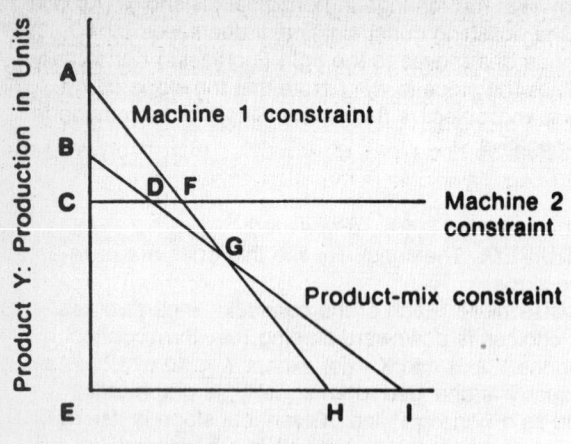

The feasible production area is described by

a. A E I G F
b. C D G H E
c. C D G I E
d. C F G I E
e. B D G H E

The correct answer is (b). *(CIA 580 II-3)*
REQUIRED: The feasibility space in a linear programming problem.
DISCUSSION: Feasible production surrounded by the area on the graph gives production possible given three constraints: Machine 1 constraint, Machine 2 constraint, and product mix constraint. All prevent production from occurring above their lines. Accordingly, the feasible area of production is bounded by points C D G H E. Of course, at point E, the point of origin, there is no production of either X or Y.

20.3 Formulation

27. The term "constraints" in a linear programming model generally describes

a. The objective function.
b. Costs.
c. Scarce resources.
d. Dependent variables.
e. Inefficiencies.

The correct answer is (c). *(CIA 581 IV-15)*
REQUIRED: A description of constraints.
DISCUSSION: LP models are mathematical techniques in which an objective function is maximized or minimized subject to constraints. These constraints must be fully specified before a linear programming problem can be solved.
   Answer (a) is incorrect because the objective function is to be maximized or minimized. Answer (b) is incorrect because they are included in the objective function. Answer (d) is incorrect because the constraints are given and are independent. Answer (e) is incorrect because they are not contemplated by the LP model.

28. Boaz Co. manufactures two models, medium (X) and large (Y). The contribution margin expected is $24 for the medium model and $40 for the large model. The medium model is processed 2 hours in the machining department and 4 hours in the polishing department. The large model is processed 3 hours in the machining department and 6 hours in the polishing department. If total contribution margin is to be maximized, using linear programming, how would the objective function be expressed?

a. 24X(2 + 4) + 40Y(3 + 6).
b. 24X + 40Y.
c. 6X + 9Y.
d. 5X + 10Y.

The correct answer is (b). *(CPA 1184 Q-12)*
REQUIRED: The objective function.
DISCUSSION: The objective function is the function that is to be maximized or minimized. The UCMs are $24 and $40, respectively, for X and Y. The function to be maximized is therefore $24X + $40Y. The processing times are reflected in the constraints, not the objective function.

Module 20.3: Formulation

29. Among its other products, Ammer Company manufactures two model doodads, X and Y. Model X is processed 4 hours in the machining department and 2 hours in the polishing department. Model Y is processed 9 hours in the machining department and 6 hours in the polishing department. The available time for processing the two models is 200 hours a week in the machining department and 180 hours a week in the polishing department. The contribution margins expected are $10 for Model X and $14 for Model Y. How would the restriction (constraint) for the polishing department be expressed for these two models?

   a. $2X + 6Y \leq 180$.
   b. $6X + 15Y \leq 180$.
   c. $2(10X) + 6(14Y) \leq 180$.
   d. $10X + 14Y \leq 180$.

The correct answer is (a). *(CPA 1179 T-40)*
REQUIRED: The constraint equation for two products in one department.
DISCUSSION: A constraint equation of a linear programming problem depicts the constraint of production by limiting total available hours or other resources, assuming that those hours or other resources may be used on either or both the products. In this case, 2 polishing hours of X plus 6 polishing hours of Y must be less than or equal to the total 180 hours available in that department.

30. Referring to Q. 29, how would the constraint for the machining department be expressed?

   a. $2X + 6Y \leq 180$.
   b. $6X + 15Y \leq 200$.
   c. $4X + 9Y \leq 200$.
   d. $10X + 14Y \leq 200$.

The correct answer is (c). *(Publisher)*
REQUIRED: The constraint equation for making two products in the other department.
DISCUSSION: A constraint equation of an LP problem depicts the constraint of production by limiting hours or other resources available in total. It assumes that those hours or other resources available may be used on either or both the products. In this case, 4 hours of X plus 9 hours of Y in the machining department must be less than or equal to the total 200 hours available in that department.

Questions 31 and 32 are based on the following. Pleasant Valley Company makes two products, ceramic vases (V) and ceramic bowls (B). Each vase requires 2 pounds of material and 3 hours of labor. Each bowl requires 2 pounds of material and 1 hour of labor. During the next production week, there will be 100 pounds of material and 60 hours of labor available to make vases and bowls. Each pound of material costs $4 and each hour of labor costs $10. All factory overhead is fixed and is estimated to be $200 for this production process for a week. Pleasant Valley sells vases for $50 each and bowls for $35 each.

---

31. The objective function for Pleasant Valley would be

   a. Maximize $Z = \$50V + \$35B$.
   b. Maximize $Z = \$12V + \$17B$.
   c. Minimize $Z = \$38V + \$18B$.
   d. Maximize $Z = \$12V + \$17B - \$200$.
   e. Some function other than those given above.

The correct answer is (b). *(CMA 687 5-18)*
REQUIRED: The objective function in a linear programming problem.
DISCUSSION: The objective is to maximize contribution margin. Since each bowl requires $8 of material and $10 of labor, its total variable cost is $18. Given a selling price of $35, the unit contribution margin is $17. Each vase requires $8 of material and $30 of labor, a total variable cost of $38. At the $50 selling price, the unit contribution margin is $12. Thus, the objective function is to maximize $12V + $17B.

32. One of the constraints on Pleasant Valley's objective function would be

   a. $2V + 2B \leq 60$.
   b. $2V + 2B \leq \$400$.
   c. $3V + B \leq 60$.
   d. $V + 3B \leq 100$.
   e. $\$8V + \$8B \leq \$600$.

The correct answer is (c). *(CMA 687 5-19)*
REQUIRED: The linear programming constraint.
DISCUSSION: Given 100 pounds of material, the material constraint requires that 2 pounds per vase plus 2 pounds per bowl be less than or equal to 100. The labor constraint is 3 hours per vase plus 1 hour per bowl, which must be less than or equal to 60 hours.

Questions 33 through 38 relate to the terminology and techniques used in linear programming and are based on the following information. Linear programming is a mathematical technique that is designed to assist an organization in allocating its resources. A linear programming problem takes the form presented in the next column.

$$f = A_1X_1 + A_2X_2 + \cdots + A_nX_n$$

subject to

$$B_1X_1 + B_2X_2 + \cdots + B_nX_n \leq C_1$$

33. The following function is referred to as the

$$f = A_1X_1 + A_2X_2 + \cdots + A_nX_n$$

   a. Revenue function.
   b. Cost function.
   c. Constraint function.
   d. Linear function.
   e. Objective function.

The correct answer is (e). (CMA 1286 5-25)
REQUIRED: The correct identification of the function given.
DISCUSSION: Linear programming is a mathematical technique used to maximize revenue (profit) functions or to minimize cost functions subject to constraints. Here, the function f is the objective function. The objective function in a linear programming model symbolically represents the revenues (profits) or costs being maximized or minimized, respectively.
Answers (a) and (b) are incorrect because revenue and cost functions are specific kinds of objective functions. Answer (c) is incorrect because the constraint functions are the conditions under which the objective function is to be maximized or minimized. Answer (d) is incorrect because it is a nonsense answer.

34. The following function is referred to as the

$$B_1X_1 + B_2X_2 + \cdots + B_nX_n \leq C_1$$

   a. Variable function.
   b. Constraint function.
   c. Linear function.
   d. Slack function.
   e. Objective function.

The correct answer is (b). (CMA 1286 5-26)
REQUIRED: The correct identification of the function given.
DISCUSSION: The constraint functions are the "subject to" functions; i.e., they state the limits on production imposed by scarce resources.
Answers (a), (c), and (d) are incorrect because none is meaningful in this context. Answer (e) is incorrect because the objective function is to be maximized or minimized subject to the constraints.

35. In order to solve a linear programming problem, slack, surplus, and artificial variables must be employed. A slack variable represents

   a. Opportunity costs.
   b. Unused capacity.
   c. Outside variables with high cost.
   d. The variable with the most negative value.
   e. The variable with the greatest profit.

The correct answer is (b). (CMA 1286 5-27)
REQUIRED: The definition of a slack variable.
DISCUSSION: A slack variable represents unused capacity. Since linear programming formulations are often stated as inequalities, there is a possibility of unused capacity even at the optimum production level. To convert inequalities to equalities, slack variables are introduced to account for this unused capacity.

36. The procedure employed to solve linear programming problems is

   a. Differential calculus.
   b. Integral calculus.
   c. Simulation.
   d. Expected value.
   e. Matrix algebra.

The correct answer is (e). (CMA 1286 5-28)
REQUIRED: The procedure used to solve linear programming problems.
DISCUSSION: Matrix algebra is a method of manipulating multiple linear equations. It is used to solve linear programming problems (assuming that a computer is not available). The use of matrix algebra to solve such problems is called the simplex method.

Module 20.3: Formulation

37. Shadow prices in linear programming measure the

  a. Contribution of acquiring an additional unit of a scarce resource.
  b. Contribution of a product.
  c. Cost of the optimum solution.
  d. Profitability associated with the optimum solution.
  e. Cost of acquiring an additional unit of a scarce resource.

The correct answer is (a). *(CMA 1286 5-29)*
  REQUIRED: The item that is measured by shadow prices.
  DISCUSSION: The shadow price of a constraint is the amount by which the contribution margin will increase as a result of relaxing that constraint in a LP model by one unit. The calculation of shadow price is a simple example of sensitivity analysis, which is a procedure designed to test the responsiveness of an alternative decision or variable to changes or errors in the decision model. The shadow price is essentially an opportunity cost.

38. In reality, a shadow price is a type of

  a. Incremental cost.
  b. Variable cost.
  c. Artificial cost.
  d. Opportunity cost.
  e. Incremental revenue.

The correct answer is (d). *(CMA 1286 5-30)*
  REQUIRED: The true statement about a shadow price.
  DISCUSSION: The term opportunity cost refers to the benefit (e.g., profit) forgone because of the choice of a given action. Opportunity costs are considered when determining the most profitable utilization of resources. Since a shadow price is the contribution that would be provided if one additional unit of a scarce resource were available, it is essentially the opportunity cost of not adding the additional unit.
  Answers (a), (b), and (c) are incorrect because the shadow price is not a cost in the usual sense. Answer (e) is incorrect because the shadow price is an increase in contribution margin (selling price - variable cost), not incremental revenue (selling price of one additional unit).

39. Johnson, Inc. manufactures product X and product Y, which are processed as follows:

	Type A Machine	Type B Machine
Product X	6 hours	4 hours
Product Y	9 hours	5 hours

The contribution margin is $12 for product X and $7 for product Y. The available time daily for processing the two products is 120 hours for machine Type A and 80 hours for machine Type B. How would the restriction (constraint) for machine Type B be expressed?

  a. $4X + 5Y$.
  b. $4X + 5Y \leq 80$.
  c. $6X + 9Y \leq 120$.
  d. $12X + 7Y$.

The correct answer is (b). *(CPA 1180 P-30)*
  REQUIRED: The constraint equation in a linear programming problem.
  DISCUSSION: A constraint equation of a linear programming problem depicts the constraint of production by limiting hours or other resources available in total. It assumes that those hours or other resources available may be used for either or both the products. In this case, 4 hours of X on the Type B machine plus 5 hours of Y must be less than or equal to the total 80 hours available for processing these products.

40. Referring to Q. 39, how would the constraint for machine Type A be expressed?

  a. $4Z + 5Y$.
  b. $4X + 5Y \leq 80$.
  c. $6X + 9Y \leq 120$.
  d. $12X + 7Y$.

The correct answer is (c). *(Publisher)*
  REQUIRED: The constraint equation for making two products on the other kind of machine.
  DISCUSSION: A constraint equation of an LP problem depicts the constraint of production by limiting hours or other resources available in total, assuming that those hours or other resources available may be used for either or both the products. In this case, 6 hours of X on the Type A machine plus 9 hours of Y must be less than or equal to the total 120 hours available for processing these products.

Questions 41 through 43 are based on the following information. Belmont Company manufactures and sells two products - shirts and gloves - in its two-department plant. Belmont employs linear programming to determine its optimum product mix. Economic data pertaining to the two products are presented in the next column.

	Shirt(S)	Gloves-Pair (G)
Selling price per unit	$22	$40
Cost data per unit		
Variable manufacturing cost	8	12
Variable selling expense	2	4
Fixed manufacturing cost	5	9
Fixed selling expense	1	2

Direct Labor Data

	Cutting	Finishing
Shirt(S)	10 min.	15 min.
Gloves-pair(G)	6 min.	30 min.
Monthly capacity	960 hrs.	1,920 hrs.

41. The algebraic formulation of Belmont's objective function is

   a. MAX Z = 10S + 16G.
   b. MAX Z = 14S + 28G.
   c. MAX Z = 12S + 24G.
   d. MAX Z = 7S + 15G.
   e. MAX Z = 6S + 13G.

The correct answer is (c). (CMA 1285 5-9)
REQUIRED: The algebraic formulation of the objective function for a linear programming problem.
DISCUSSION: Linear programming is a mathematical technique used to maximize revenue (profit) functions or to minimize cost functions subject to constraints. The objective function in a linear programming model symbolically represents the revenues (profits) or costs being maximized or minimized, respectively. The contribution margin from production of the combination of shirts and pairs of gloves is to be maximized. The contribution margin from shirts is $12 ($22 - $10 variable unit costs). The contribution margin from gloves is $24 ($40 - $16 variable unit costs). Thus, the objective is to maximize 12S + 24G.

42. The algebraic formulation of Belmont's monthly direct labor constraints is

   a. $10S + 6G \leq 960; 15S + 30G \leq 1,920$
   b. $10S + 15S + 6G + 30G \leq 2,880.$
   c. $1/6 S + 1/4S + 1/10G + 1/2G \leq 2,880.$
   d. $1/6S - 1/10G \leq 960; 1/4S - 1/2G \leq 1,920.$
   e. $1/6S + 1/10G \leq 960; 1/4S + 1/2G \leq 1,920.$

The correct answer is (e). (CMA 1285 5-10)
REQUIRED: The algebraic formulation of the monthly direct labor constraints.
DISCUSSION: A constraint equation of a linear programming problem depicts the constraint of production by limiting total available hours or other resources, assuming that those hours or other resources may be used on either or both the products. The cutting labor time available is 960 hrs. per month. The finishing labor constraint is 1,920 hours. Since each shirt requires 10 minutes (1/6 hr.) of cutting time, and each pair of gloves requires six minutes (1/10 hr.), the cutting constraint is that 1/6S + 1/10G must be less than or equal to 960. Since each shirt requires 15 minutes (1/4 hr.) of finishing time, and each pair of gloves requires 30 minutes (1/2 hr.), the finishing constraint is that 1/2S + 1/2G must be less than or equal to 1,920.

43. The algebraic formulation of the monthly nonnegativity constraints is

   a. $S, G > 0.$
   b. $S, G < 0.$
   c. $S, G \leq 0.$
   d. $S, G \geq 0.$
   e. $S + G \geq 0.$

The correct answer is (d). (CMA 1285 5-11)
REQUIRED: The algebraic formulation of the monthly nonnegativity constraints.
DISCUSSION: Production cannot be negative, but it can be exactly zero. Thus, the nonnegativity constraints are that production of S and G must be greater than or equal to 0.

Module 20.3: Formulation

44. The Sanch Company plans to expand its sales force by opening several new branch offices. Sanch has $5,200,000 in capital available for new branch offices. Sanch will consider opening only two types of branches: 10-person branches (Type A) and 5-person branches (Type B). Expected initial cash outlays are $650,000 for a Type A branch and $335,000 for a Type B branch. Expected annual cash inflow, net of income taxes, is $46,000 for a Type A branch and $18,000 for a Type B branch. Sanch will hire no more than 100 employees for the new branch offices and will not open more than 10 branch offices. Linear programming will be used to help decide how many branch offices should be opened. In a system of equations for a model, which of the following equations would not represent a constraint (restriction)?

   a. $A + B \leq 10$.

   b. $10A + 5B \leq 100$.

   c. $\$46,000A + \$18,000B \leq \$64,000$.

   d. $\$650,000A + \$335,000B \leq \$5,200,000$.

The correct answer is (c). *(CPA 1177 P-39)*
REQUIRED: The constraint equation not called for by the LP problem.
DISCUSSION: Constraint equations of linear programming problems represent the amount of scarce resources available. This problem has or two types of resources, Type A and Type B branch offices. Type A + Type B must be less than or equal to 10. No more than 100 employees will be hired, so 10A + 5B must be less than or equal to 100. Minimizing the cost of cash outlay, Type A and Type B branches require that $650,000 A + $335,000 B must be less than or equal to the $5,200,000 total capital available to branch offices. Thus, there are three constraint equations for this problem.

$$\text{Branches } A + B \leq 10$$
$$\text{Employees } 10A + 5B \leq 100$$
$$\text{Capital } \$650,000A + \$335,000B \leq \$5,200,000$$

Note that the objective function is $\$46,000A + \$18,000B$.

45. An internal auditor developed the following data for a linear programming model for its southern plant:

	Product		
	X_1	X_2	X_3
Selling price	35	90	20
Costs:			
Material	15	30	10
Labor	15	30	3
Variable Overhead	2	5	1
Fixed Overhead*	5	10	1
Profit/(loss) per unit	(2)	15	5

*Allocated to products based on labor hours.

Based on the data above, which of the following should the internal auditor select as the correct function to maximize profit from that plant?

   a. $35X_1 + 90X_2 + 20X_3$
   b. $-2X_1 + 15X_2 + 5X_3$
   c. $15X_2 + 5X_3$
   d. $3X_1 + 25X_2 + 6X_3$
   e. $5X_1 + 30X_2 + 7X_3$

The correct answer is (d). *(CIA 582 II-23)*
REQUIRED: The objective function for maximizing profits.
DISCUSSION: Linear programming problems are a mathematical technique used to maximize profit. Profit maximization is concerned with the contribution margin (selling price - variable costs).

		X_1	X_2	X_3
SP	UCM	35	90	20
M	UCM	-15	-30	-10
L	UCM	-15	-30	-3
VOH	UCM	-2	-5	-1
		3	25	6

The objective function is an expression of the combined CM to be maximized:

$$3X_1 + 25X_2 + 6X_3$$

46. Watch Corporation manufactures products A, B, and C. The daily production requirements are shown below.

Product	Profit per Unit	Hours Required per Unit per Department		
		Machining	Plating	Polishing
A	$10	1	1	1
B	$20	3	1	2
C	$30	2	3	2
Total hours per day per department		16	12	6

What is Watch's objective function in determining daily production of each unit?

  a. A + B + C ≤ $60.
  b. $3A + $6B + $7C = $60.
  c. A + B + C ≤ Profit.
  d. $10A + $20B + $30C = Profit.

The correct answer is (d). *(CPA 576 P-37)*
REQUIRED: The profit-maximizing objective function of an LP problem.
DISCUSSION: Profit is expressed as the sum of the individual UCMs times the number of individual units sold. Thus, $10A + $20B + $30C = Profit.

47. The Beauty Company produces a cosmetic product in 60 gallon batches. The basic ingredients used are material X, costing $7 per gallon, and material Y, costing $17 per gallon. No more than 18 gallons of X can be used, and at least 15 gallons of Y must be used. How would the objective function (minimization of product cost) be expressed?

  a. 7X + 17Y.
  b. 17X + 7Y.
  c. 18X + 15Y.
  d. 18X + 42Y.

The correct answer is (a). *(CPA 580 P-36)*
REQUIRED: The objective function of an LP problem.
DISCUSSION: Cost minimization occurs when the cost per unit is used as the coefficient of each item in the objective function. 7X + 17Y thus equals the objective function. Note that the information about numbers of gallons would be used to formulate the constraint equations, not the objective function.

48. Referring to Q. 47, which is not a constraint of the Beauty Company?

  a. X ≤ 18.
  b. X + Y ≤ 60.
  c. Y ≥ 15.
  d. X ≥ 0.

The correct answer is (b). *(Publisher)*
REQUIRED: The irrelevant statement of a constraint.
DISCUSSION: The Beauty Company's production is in 60 gallon batches. Accordingly, X + Y must at least equal 60, i.e., cannot be less than 60. The maximum limit for X is 18 gallons, and the minimum limit for Y is 15 gallons. Since X gallons must be no more than 18, but they must also be greater than 0, a negative amount of X cannot be used.

20.4 Calculations

49. Patsy, Inc. manufactures two products, X and Y. Each product must be processed in each of three departments: machining, assembling, and finishing. The hours needed to produce one unit of product per department and the maximum possible hours per department follow:

Department	Production Hours Per Unit X	Y	Maximum Capacity in Hours
Machining	2	1	420
Assembling	2	2	500
Finishing	2	3	600

Other restrictions follow:

$$X \geq 50$$
$$Y \geq 50$$

The objective function is to maximize profits where profit = $4X + $2Y. Given the objective and constraints, what is the most profitable number of units of X and Y, respectively, to manufacture?

a. 150 and 100.
b. 165 and 90.
c. 170 and 80.
d. 200 and 50.

The correct answer is (c). *(CPA 1175 P-23)*
REQUIRED: The optimum values in a linear programming problem.
DISCUSSION: LP is a mathematical technique used to optimize objective functions, either cost minimization or profit maximization, subject to constraints. The optimum point occurs at a corner solution on a graph of the constraint equations and the objective function. The corner points define the feasibility space. Assuming the alternative answers contain the optimum solution, each alternative should be evaluated by plugging in the appropriate number of hours to eliminate the nonfeasible choices.

Constraints:
150(2) + 100(1) = 400
150(2) + 100(2) = 500
150(2) + 100(3) = 600

165(2) + 90(1) = 420
165(2) + 90(2) = 510 (answer b)*
165(2) + 90(3) = 600

170(2) + 80(1) = 420
170(2) + 80(2) = 500
170(2) + 80(3) = 580

200(2) + 50(1) = 450 (answer d)*
200(2) + 50(2) = 500
200(2) + 50(3) = 550

*Not feasible because they exceed capacity.

Finally test the maximizing CM function for alternatives given in (a) and (c) and select the alternative that gives the higher CM:

150(4) + 100(2) = 800
170(4) + 80(2) = 840

50. How many constraints exist in Patsy's LP problem?

a. 2.
b. 3.
c. 4.
d. 5.

The correct answer is (d). *(Publisher)*
REQUIRED: The number of constraints in the LP formulation.
DISCUSSION: Each of the three departments, Machining, Assembling, and Finishing, has a constraint. Additionally, there are constraints that each X and Y must be greater than 50. Accordingly, there are 5 constraint equations.

> Questions 51 and 52 are based on the following information. Your client, Globe Manufacturing, has several plants in different cities and serves customers in various other cities. Globe wants to know the best way to schedule shipments from various plants to various customers. You advise Globe that the problem can be solved by using the transportation method of linear programming.

51. In a transportation minimization problem, what are the usual coefficients of the objective function?

  a. Usage rates for transportation facilities.
  b. Restrictions on transportation facilities.
  c. Shipping costs.
  d. Time estimates for the critical path.

The correct answer is (c). *(CPA 1175 P-24)*
REQUIRED: Coefficients of the objective function in a transportation LP problem.
DISCUSSION: Linear programming is a mathematical technique used to optimize objective functions, either cost minimization or profit maximization, subject to constraints. To find the "best" way to schedule shipments, shipping costs must be minimized.
Answer (a) and (b) are incorrect because they are coefficients for the constraints. Answer (d) is incorrect because it refers to CPM/PERT.

52. If the number of units at supply points exceeds the number of units demanded at destinations, what action should be taken concerning this inequality of supply and demand?

  a. Include a "dummy" demand equal to the excess supply.
  b. Consider the excess supply to be a "dummy" supply.
  c. Eliminate the excess supply.
  d. Proceed without modification.

The correct answer is (a). *(CPA 1175 P-25)*
REQUIRED: The appropriate use of slack variables.
DISCUSSION: Constraint inequalities are usually restated into equalities. A slack variable (dummy variable) is added to make each inequality into an equality.

Module 20.4: Calculations

> Questions 53 through 68 are based on Milligan Company, which manufactures two models, small and large. Each model is processed as follows:
>
> | | Machining | Polishing |
> |-----------|-----------|-----------|
> | Small (X) | 2 hours | 1 hour |
> | Large (Y) | 4 hours | 3 hours |
>
> The available time for processing the two models is 100 hours a week in the Machining Department and 90 hours a week in the Polishing Department. The contribution margin expected is $5 for the small model and $7 for the large model.

53. How would the objective function (maximization of total contribution margin) be expressed?

  a. 5X + 7Y.
  b. 5X + 7Y ≤ 190.
  c. 5X(3) + 7Y(7) ≤ 190.
  d. 12X + 10Y.

The correct answer is (a). *(CPA 1178 P-30)*
  REQUIRED: The objective function for the two models.
  DISCUSSION: The objective function is the formula for the maximum total contribution margin. Since each X produces a $5 CM, and each Y produces a $7 CM, the total CM will be 5X + 7Y.

54. How would the restriction (constraint) for the Machining Department be expressed?

  a. 2(5X) + 4(7Y) ≤ 100.
  b. 2X + 4Y.
  c. 2X + 4Y ≤ 100.
  d. 5X + 7Y ≤ 100.

The correct answer is (c). *(CPA 1178 P-31)*
  REQUIRED: The constraint equation for the Machining Department.
  DISCUSSION: The Machining Department has a total of 100 hours available each week. Each X requires 2 hours of time from that department, and each Y requires 4 hours. Accordingly, the total Machining Department time taken by production is 2X + 4Y, which must be equal to or less than the 100 hours available.

55. How is the restriction (constraint) for the Polishing Department expressed?

  a. 5X + 7Y.
  b. 5X + 7Y ≤ 90.
  c. 2X + 4Y ≤ 90.
  d. X + 3Y ≤ 90.

The correct answer is (d). *(Publisher)*
  REQUIRED: The constraint equation for the Polishing Department.
  DISCUSSION: The Polishing Department has a total of 90 hours available each week. Each X requires one hour of time, and each Y requires three hours of time. Thus, the constraint for this department is that X + 3Y must be equal to or less than 90.

56. How many slack variables are needed for the simplex tableau?

  a. 0.
  b. 1.
  c. 2.
  d. 3.

The correct answer is (c). *(Publisher)*
  REQUIRED: The number of slack variables necessary to construct a simplex tableau.
  DISCUSSION: The simplex method requires a slack variable to transform each inequality constraint into an equality. Therefore, two slack variables are needed, one for each of the two inequality constraints.

57. What are the constraint equations in Qs. 54 and 55 as transformed to equalities?

  a. 2X + 4Y = 100; X + 3Y = 90.
  b. 2X + 4Y + 1S_1 + 0S_2 = 100;
     X + 3Y + 0S_1 + 1S_2 = 90.
  c. 2X + 4Y + 1S_2 = 100; X + 3Y + 1S_1 = 90.
  d. Undeterminable from the data given.

The correct answer is (b). *(Publisher)*
  REQUIRED: The constraint equations expressed as equalities.
  DISCUSSION: The machining constraint is 2X + 4Y ≤ 100 (Q. 54), which can be transformed into the equality 2X + 4Y + 1S_1 = 100 or 2X + 4Y + 1S_1 + 0S_2 = 100. The polishing constraint (Q. 55) is also transformed by adding slack variables: X + 3Y + 0S_1 + 1S_2 = 90.

Questions 58 through 68 are based on the following initial simplex tableau (in its most common format) from the Milligan Company's LP problem that began with Q. 53. Remember that "rows" run horizontally and "columns" run vertically.

C_j	5	7	0	0	RHS
Variables / CB	X	Y	S_1	S_2	
0	2	4	1	0	100
0	1	3	0	1	90
Z_j	0	0	0	0	0
$C_j - Z_j$	5	7	0	0	

58. How many basic variables are there in the above tableau (solution)?

a. 0.
b. 1.
c. 2.
d. 3.

The correct answer is (c). *(Publisher)*
REQUIRED: The number of basic variables in the tableau.
DISCUSSION: There are as many basic variables as there are constraints to the problem. Basic variables are the variables that exist in the current tableau as a possible solution (not necessarily optimal), e.g., S_1 is equal to 100 and S_2 is equal to 90. Nonbasic variables are the variables that are equal to zero in the current solution, e.g., X and Y.

59. Which row is constructed first in the simplex tableau?

a. S_1, S_2, X, Y.
b. X, Y, S_1, S_2.
c. $Z_j, C_j - Z_j$.
d. CB, C_j.

The correct answer is (b). *(Publisher)*
REQUIRED: The first step in constructing the simplex tableau.
DISCUSSION: After converting the constraint equations to equalities, build the tableau by beginning with the variables row, which consists first of the constraint variables (X and Y) and then the slack variables (S_1 and S_2). It is essentially a row of labels.

60. What are the basic variables in the current (initial) solution?

a. X, Y.
b. The slack variables.
c. X, S_1.
d. S_1, S_2.
e. Both (b) and (d) above.

The correct answer is (e). *(Publisher)*
REQUIRED: The basic variables for the initial tableau.
DISCUSSION: The basic variables are those that form an identity matrix. That is, they have one entry of 1, and the others of 0 in their corresponding variable columns. The variable columns are those beneath each variable, e.g., X, Y, S_1, S_2. Referring to the sample tableau, you see that S_1 has 1, 0, 0, 0 in its column, and S_2 has 0, 1, 0, 0. Note that in this tableau, the basic variables happen also to be the slack variables. The basic variables may not necessarily be next to each other in the tableau.

61. What are the values of the basic variables in this simplex tableau (solution)?

a. $S_1 = 0; S_2 = 1$.
b. $S_1 = 1; S_2 = 0$.
c. $S_1 = 100; S_2 = 90$.
d. $S_1 = 90; S_2 = 100$.

The correct answer is (c). *(Publisher)*
REQUIRED: The values of the basic variables in the simplex tableau.
DISCUSSION: The values of the basic variables are given in the right-hand side (RHS) column of the tableau. Since the entry 1 for the S_1 variable is on the first row, the value of S is given in the first row of the RHS, or 100. Since the entry of 1 for S_2 is in the second row, its value is found in the second row under RHS, which is 90. Note that the 100 and 90 come from the right-hand side of the constraint equations as found in Qs. 54 and 55, respectively. Thus, the RHS values are also the amount of available resources.

Module 20.4: Calculations

62. The C_j row (the top row) in the simplex tableau consists of

a. The payoff coefficients of the variables, which are the coefficients in the objective function.
b. The amount of available resources.
c. The index row.
d. The resource coefficient row.

The correct answer is (a). *(Publisher)*
REQUIRED: The true statement about the C_j (or top) row in the simplex tableau.
DISCUSSION: The C_j row lists the negative of the payoff coefficients for a profit-maximization problem (or the cost coefficients for a cost-minimization problem), given by the coefficients of the objective function. Note that the slack variables have payoff/cost = 0. Thus, here, the C_j row consists of the negative of the coefficients from the objective function (which was 5X + 7Y, as expressed in Q. 53) and the slack variables payoff values of 0 and 0. The C_j row is -5 -7 0 0.
Answer (b) is incorrect because it is given by the RHS column. Answer (c) is incorrect because the index row is the last (bottom) row. Answer (d) is incorrect because it is given by the constraint rows.

63. What are the machining and polishing constraint rows?

a. 2, 4, 1, 0; 100 and 1, 3, 0, 1; 90.
b. 2, 1, 0, 5 and 4, 3, 0, 7.
c. 5, 7, 0, 0 and 2, 4, 1, 0.
d. X, Y, S1, S2 and 5, 7, 0, 0.

The correct answer is (a). *(Publisher)*
REQUIRED: The machining and polishing constraint rows in the simplex tableau.
DISCUSSION: As found in Q. 57, the constraint equalities are

$$2X + 4Y + 1S_1 + 0S_2 = 100$$
$$X + 3Y + 0S_1 + 1S_2 = 90$$

Using these coefficients, the constraint rows are

```
2  4  1  0    100
1  3  0  1     90
```

These are also known as the resource coefficient rows. There must be as many resource coefficient rows as there are constraints to the problem.

64. What is the CB column?

a. The cost column.
b. The payoff column.
c. The payoff column of basic variables.
d. Always zero.

The correct answer is (c). *(Publisher)*
REQUIRED: The true statement about the CB column in the simplex tableau.
DISCUSSION: The CB column consists of payoff (cost) coefficients of the basic variables in profit-maximization (cost-minimization) problems. The column thus consists of as many numbers as there are basic variables (i.e., two for this tableau). Note that the numbers to enter are the same payoff numbers for the basic variables as are found in the C_j row, or 0 and 0. Note also that the Z_j and $C_j - Z_j$ are not part of the CB column.
Answer (a) is incorrect because the problem involves profit maximization so it is the payoff column, not the cost column. Answer (b) is incorrect because C_j is the payoff column of all the variables. Answer (d) is incorrect because the CB entries are not always zero, although, here, the basic variables are the slack variables, for which the payoff is zero.

65. The index row is

a. The C_j row.
b. The Z_j row.
c. The $C_j - Z_j$ row.
d. None of the above.

The correct answer is (c). *(Publisher)*
REQUIRED: Identification of the index row.
DISCUSSION: The index row is the last (bottom) row. It provides a measure of the direction of improvement of the objective function value for a corresponding change in the tableau. It is obtained by subtracting the Z_j row from the C_j row.

Questions 66 through 68 are based on the data presented on pages 615 and 616.

66. The Z_j row is

a. Found by multiplying each element of the CB column by elements of subsequent columns and adding the products.
b. Always zero.
c. The index row.
d. None of the above.

The correct answer is (a). *(Publisher)*
REQUIRED: The true statement about the Z_j row in the simplex tableau.
DISCUSSION: The first element of the Z_j row is the sum of the products of multiplying each element in the CB column by each element in the first column: (0 x 2) + (0 x 1) = 0. The subsequent elements are obtained by multiplying each element in the CB column by each element in the next column and adding the products. For example, the third element in the Z_j row is (0 x 1) + (0 x 0) = 0.
Answer (b) is incorrect because the Z_j row does not always equal 0, although it does in this case because the CB entries equal 0. Answer (c) is incorrect because the index row is the last (bottom) row. It provides a measure of the direction of improvement of the objective function value for a corresponding change in the tableau. The index row comes from the Z_j row.

67. The current objective function value in this problem is

a. Given by the Z_j element in the RHS column.
b. Always zero.
c. Equal to 100.
d. Equal to 90.

The correct answer is (a). *(Publisher)*
REQUIRED: The current objective function value to this simplex problem.
DISCUSSION: The current objective function value is obtained by multiplying the CB column times the RHS column and adding the products. The result, which is the current objective function value, is found in the far right column (RHS) in the Z_j row, which here is zero.
Answer (b) is incorrect because the current objective function value does not always equal zero, although it does in this case because CB = 0. Answer (c) is incorrect because it is the amount of available resources for the machining constraint. Answer (d) is incorrect because it is the available resources for the polishing constraint.

68. The solution to this LP problem is not optimal because

a. The index row has negative elements.
b. The index row has zero elements.
c. The Z_j row is equal to zero.
d. The solution is equal to zero.

The correct answer is (a). *(Publisher)*
REQUIRED: Why the solution is not optimal.
DISCUSSION: Negative elements in the index row for a linear programming problem indicate that the solution could be improved.

Questions 69 through 72 are based on the Ball Company, which manufactures three types of lamps -- A, B, and C. Each lamp is processed in two departments -- I and II. Total available man-hours per day for Departments I and II are 400 and 600, respectively. No additional labor is available. Time requirements and profit per unit for each lamp type are presented below.

The company has assigned you as the accounting member of its profit-planning committee to determine the numbers of types of A, B, and C lamps that it should produce in order to maximize its total profit from the sale of lamps. The following questions relate to a linear programming model that your group has developed.

	A	B	C
Man-hours required:			
Department I	2	3	1
Department II	4	2	3
Profit per unit (Sales price less all variable costs)	$5	$4	$3

69. The coefficients of the objective function are

   a. 4, 2, 3.
   b. 2, 3, 1.
   c. 5, 4, 3.
   d. 400, 600.

The correct answer is (c). *(CPA 573 P-23)*
   REQUIRED: The coefficients of the objective function.
   DISCUSSION: The coefficients of the objective function are the amount of contribution margin (sales price less all variable costs) for A, B, and C, respectively. These are given as $5, $4, and $3.

70. The constraints in the LP model are

   a. 2, 3, 1.
   b. 5, 4, 3.
   c. 4, 2, 3.
   d. 400, 600.

The correct answer is (d). *(CPA 573 P-24)*
   REQUIRED: The right-hand sides of the constraints in an LP model.
   DISCUSSION: The constraints in the LP model are the available man-hours per day for Departments I and II, which are given as 400 and 600, respectively.

71. The constraint imposed by the available man-hours in Department I can be expressed as

   a. $4X_1 + 2X_2 + 3X_3 \leq 400$.
   b. $4X_1 + 2X_2 + 3X_3 \geq 400$.
   c. $2X_1 + 3X_2 + 1X_3 \leq 400$.
   d. $2X_1 + 3X_2 + 1X_3 \geq 400$.

The correct answer is (c). *(CPA 573 P-25)*
   REQUIRED: The constraint equation for man-hours in Department I.
   DISCUSSION: In Department I, each A requires 2 hours, each B requires 3 hours, and each C requires 1 hour. Accordingly, the total hours to be utilized in Department I are

   $$2X_1 + 3X_2 + 1X_3$$

   which sum must be equal to or less than 400.

72. The most types of lamps that would be included in the optimal solution would be

   a. 2.
   b. 1.
   c. 3.
   d. 0.

The correct answer is (c). *(CPA 573 P-26)*
   REQUIRED: The maximum number of variables in the optimal solution.
   DISCUSSION: In the solution, it is possible that all 3 lamps could be manufactured in some amount. The presumption is that at least 1 type of lamp will be produced, but probably more than 1. Since there are only 3 types of lamps available to be produced, there could not be more than 3 types manufactured.

Questions 73 through 76 are based on the following information and should be treated as being completely independent of one another.

The Marlan Metal Products Company has just established a department for the production of two new products -- metal trays and storage devices. This department is ready to begin operations with five metal-forming machines and five metal-cutting machines which have been rented for $300 each per month from a local machine company. Both products require production time on both machines. Each of the machines is capable of 400 hours of production per month. No additional machines can be obtained.

Linear Programming Formulation

Maximize $Z = \$4T + \$7S$

Subject to:

$T + 2S \leq 2{,}000$

$2T + 2S \leq 2{,}000$

$T \leq 800$

$T, S \geq 0$

Where T = number of trays produced
S = number of storage devices produced
Z = contribution margin

Machine hours per unit

	Trays	Storage Devices	Total Available Machine Hrs./Mo.
Metal-cutting machines	1	2	2,000
Metal-forming machines	2	2	2,000

The controller's department has summarized expected costs and revenues as follows:

	Trays	Storage Devices
Selling price per unit	$18.00	$27.00
Variable cost per unit	14.00	20.00

Demand for the storage devices is unlimited but Marlan believes that no more than 800 units of the trays can be sold per month.

The following linear programming formulation and accompanying graph represent the facts described above. Marlan must operate within the specified constraints as it tries to maximize the contribution margin from this new operation. Marlan intends to operate at the optimal level which it has determined to be the point labeled "OP" on the graph below.

Graphical Presentation

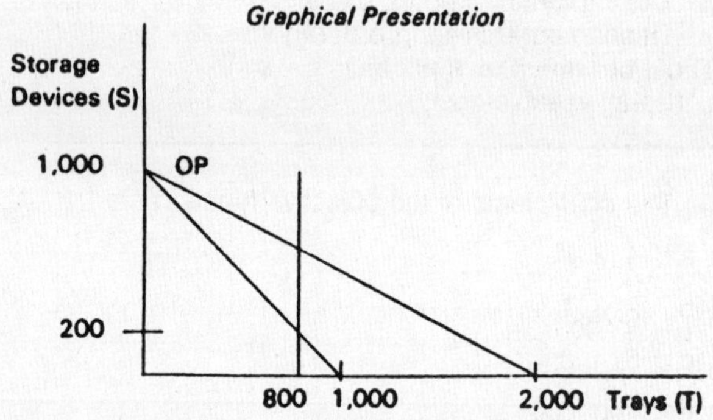

73. If the selling price of storage devices is lowered from $27 to $23, the maximum total contribution margin Marlan could earn would

  a. Decrease by $3,800.
  b. Decrease by $4,000.
  c. Increase by $4,000.
  d. Decrease by $3,200.
  e. Not be expected to change.

The correct answer is (d). *(CMA 1277 5-16)*
REQUIRED: The change in total CM given a change in selling price.
DISCUSSION: At the optimum point (point OP on the graph), Marlan is producing 1,000 storage devices which results in CM of $7,000 ($7/unit times 1,000 storage devices). Lowering the price of storage devices reduces the UCM to $3 ($23 - $20), and the maximum number (800) of trays will be produced because their UCM is $4 ($18 - $14). The remaining 200 units will be storage devices.

```
800 trays x $4      =   $3,200
200 storage devices x $3 =     600
                            $3,800
```

The total CM drops from $7,000 to $3,800, for a $3,200 decrease. Note that no more than a total of 1,000 trays and storage devices can be produced.

74. The maximum amount Marlan should be willing to spend on advertising in order to increase the demand for trays to 1,000 units per month is

  a. $0.
  b. $600.
  c. $1,400.
  d. $5,400.
  e. $7,000.

The correct answer is (a). *(CMA 1277 5-17)*
REQUIRED: The maximum amount to spend on advertising to generate targeted demand.
DISCUSSION: If the optimum point is 1,000 storage devices and zero trays per month, it would not pay Marlan to produce any trays.

75. If one metal-forming machine is returned to the rental agency and the rent can be avoided on it, Marlan's total profit would

  a. Be unaffected.
  b. Increase by $300.
  c. Decrease by $1,100.
  d. Decrease by $1,400.
  e. Decrease by $4,300.

The correct answer is (c). *(CMA 1277 5-18)*
REQUIRED: The impact on total profit of returning one machine.
DISCUSSION: Each metal-forming machine provides 400 hours of production per month, which generates 200 storage devices. Returning one machine thus means that CM will be reduced by $1,400 (200 units x $7). On the other hand, cost will be reduced by the $300 rent savings, so total profit would decrease by $1,100.

76. Marlan has just realized that a material needed for the production of both products is in short supply. The company can obtain enough of this material to produce 1,200 trays. Each tray requires 2/3 as much of this material as the storage devices. Which of the following constraints will incorporate completely and correctly this additional information into the formulation of the problem?

  a. $T \leq 1,200$.
  b. $2/3\ S \leq 1,200$.
  c. $T + 2/3\ S \leq 1,200$.
  d. $2/3\ T + 1\ S \leq 800$.
  e. $T - 3/2\ S = 0$.

The correct answer is (d). *(CMA 1277 5-19)*
REQUIRED: The constraint required to express the change in available material.
DISCUSSION: Recall that the fact situation said to treat each question independently. Thus, the decision to produce no trays (Q. 74) is irrelevant here. This material constraint will limit both trays and storage devices. Either 1,200 trays or 800 (1,200 x 2/3) storage devices or some combination can be produced. Thus, $2/3T + 1S \leq 800$.

Questions 77 through 79 are based on the final tableau for a linear programming profit maximization problem presented below.

	X_1	X_2	X_3	S_1	S_2	
X_1	1	0	4	3	-7	50
X_2	0	1	-2	-6	2	60
	0	0	5	1	9	1,200

77. If X_1, X_2, and X_3 represent products, S_1 refers to square feet (in thousands) of warehouse capacity and S_2 refers to labor hours (in hundreds), then the number of X_1 that should be produced to maximize profit is

a. 60.
b. 50.
c. 1.
d. 0.
e. None of the above.

The correct answer is (b). *(CPA 1171 P-21)*
REQUIRED: The number of X_1 to produce to maximize profit.
DISCUSSION: X_1 and X_2 are products that will be produced: $50X_1$ and $60X_2$ for a profit of $1,200. Product X_3 is not included because its column does not have a 0 and 1 as there are for X_1 and X_2. Thus, X_3 is not a basic variable.

78. Referring to Q. 77, the contribution to profit of an additional 100 hours of labor would be

a. 9.
b. 2.
c. 1.
d. -7.

The correct answer is (a). *(CPA 1171 P-22)*
REQUIRED: The contribution to profit of an additional 100 hours of labor.
DISCUSSION: Remember that the units of labor are in 100 hours as the units of square feet are in 1,000. The numbers 1 and 9 below the line in the S_1 and S_2 columns represent the amount of additional profit that would be available to the process. For instance, if we were able to add one unit of S_2 (100 hours of labor), we would decrease production of X_1 by 7 and increase production of X_2 by 2 units, with a net increase in profit of $9.

79. Referring to Q. 77, an additional 1,000 square feet of warehouse space would

a. Increase X_1 by 3 units and decrease X_2 by 6 units.
b. Decrease X_2 by 6 units and increase X_1 by 2 units.
c. Decrease X_1 by 7 units and increase X_2 by 2 units.
d. Increase X_1 by 3 units and decrease X_2 by 7 units.

The correct answer is (a). *(CPA 1171 P-23)*
REQUIRED: The effect of an additional 1,000 square feet of warehouse space.
DISCUSSION: Continuing the explanation to Q. 78 above: If we add an additional unit of S_1 (1,000 sq. ft. of warehouse space), we will increase profit by $1 because we can decrease production of X_2 by 6 and increase production of X_1 by 3.

Module 20.4: Calculations

80. Assume the following data for the two products produced by Wagner Company:

	Product A	Product B
Raw material requirements (units)		
X	3	4
Y	7	2
Contribution margin per unit	$10	$4

If 300 units of raw material X and 400 units of raw material Y are available, the set of relationships appropriate for maximization of revenue using linear programming would be

a. 3A + 4B ≥ 300
    7A + 2B ≥ 400
    10A + 4B   MAX

b. 3A + 7B ≥ 300
    4A + 2B ≥ 400
    10A + 4B   MAX

c. 3A + 7B ≤ 300
    4A + 2B ≤ 400
    10A + 4B   MAX

d. 3A + 4B ≤ 300
    7A + 2B ≤ 400
    10A + 4B   MAX

The correct answer is (d). *(CPA 1171 P-20)*
REQUIRED: The set of relationships appropriate for maximization of revenue using LP.
DISCUSSION: The constraint equation for X is that 3 times the number of A units produced plus 4 times the number of B units must be less than or equal to the 300 units of X available. The constraint equation for Y is that 7 times the number of units of A plus 2 times the number of units of B must be less than or equal to the 400 units of available Y. The contribution margin is defined as $10 times the number of units of A plus $4 times the number of units of B, which Wagner wishes to maximize.

81. Acme Drug Company produces product A and product B. Each product is made from the same chemicals but mixed in different proportions. Product A uses two ounces of Xon and two ounces of Wyanide, while product B uses four ounces of Xon and two ounces of Wyanide. Acme decides to use linear programming to determine how many of each product it can produce by exactly utilizing its inventory of 400 ounces of Xon and 300 ounces of Wyanide. The initial tableau would be

a. 2 2 | 400
    4 2 | 300

b. 2 4 | 400
    2 2 | 300

c. 300 | 2 2
    400 | 2 4

d. 2 4 | 0
    2 2 | 0

e. 1 0 | 400
    0 1 | 300

The correct answer is (b). *(CIA 581 IV-18)*
REQUIRED: The initial tableau of a linear programming problem.
DISCUSSION: The constraints are 400 ounces of Xon and 300 ounces of Wyanide. Product A requires two ounces of Xon and two ounces of Wyanide. Product B requires four ounces of Xon and two ounces of Wyanide. For Xon, 2A + 4B must be less than or equal to 400. For Wyanide, 2A + 2B must be less than or equal to 300. These inequalities produce the following initial tableau:

    2 4 | 400
    2 2 | 300

Note this initial tableau consists of the coefficients of the constraints (but usually contains slack variables for each), e.g.,

    2 4 1 0 | 400
    2 2 0 1 | 300

82. The following is the final tableau of a linear programming profit maximization problem:

	X_1	X_2	S_1	S_2	
X_1	1	0	-5	3	125
X_2	0	1	1	-1	70
	0	0	5	7	500

The marginal contribution to profit of 5 for each added resource unit S_1 can be maintained if the added resource units do not exceed

a. 125.

b. 100.

c. 70.

d. 25.

The correct answer is (d). *(CPA 1171 P-24)*
REQUIRED: The number of resource units that cannot be exceeded.
DISCUSSION: As we add additional S_1, we will decrease production of X_1 by 5 units for each unit of S_1 made available. Since the production of X_1 is currently slated at 125, we can only add 25 units of S_1 before we bring X_1 production to zero. We can continue to make S_1 available beyond 25 units, but we will not be able to add $25 to our contribution margin thereafter.

83. Referring to Q. 82, what is the shadow price of the first constraint?

a. 5.

b. 7.

c. 125.

d. 70.

The correct answer is (a). *(Publisher)*
REQUIRED: Shadow price of the first constraint.
DISCUSSION: Shadow prices are the amount one could pay for an additional unit of a constraint resource without decreasing the objective function. Conversely, it is the improvement in the objective function caused by increasing the constraint resource by one unit. The shadow price of the first constraint is 5. Shadow prices for constraint resources appear under the slack variable in the index row ($C_j - Z_j$) of the final (optimum) tableau.

84. When using the simplex method to solve a linear programming problem for the maximization of contribution margin, the optimum solution has been reached when the values in the index row of the matrix are

a. All zero.

b. All positive or zero.

c. Equal to zero when added across.

d. Equal to a positive value when added across.

The correct answer is (b). *(CPA 1178 T-46)*
REQUIRED: The values in the index row when the optimum solution is found.
DISCUSSION: The index row ($C_j - Z_j$) gives a measure of reduction in objective function value by a corresponding change in the tableau. If the index row has positive or zero elements (i.e., nonnegative), the solution cannot be improved. In this maximization problem, the values in the index row are all positive or zero, so another step in the algorithm will not improve the solution.
Answer (a) is incorrect because $C_j - Z_j = 0$ is only for basic variables. The other variables, those not in the solution, have positive or negative values. Answers (c) and (d) are incorrect because each has a possibility of a negative number.

CHAPTER TWENTY-ONE
OTHER QUANTITATIVE APPROACHES

21.1 Simulation and Sensitivity Analysis . . . . (16 questions) 625
21.2 Queuing Theory . . . . (6 questions) 630
21.3 Network Models . . . . (16 questions) 632
21.4 Learning Curves . . . . (12 questions) 638
21.5 Matrix Algebra . . . . (5 questions) 641
21.6 Calculus . . . . (12 questions) 643

This chapter provides an overview of some other quantitative approaches which have received attention on the professional examinations and which are increasingly covered in cost and managerial accounting textbooks. Interpretations of the results and assumptions underlying these quantitative approaches are emphasized. It is unlikely that there will be increased attention to computational problems on the professional examinations.

21.1 Simulation and Sensitivity Analysis

1. Quantitative methods are important to the management accountant for all except which of the following reasons?

a. Familiarity with quantitative methods will permit the management accountant to recognize possible applications.

b. Quantitative methods utilize accounting data. The management accountant needs to be able to make an appropriate judgment regarding the use of accounting data.

c. The management accountant can use quantitative methods to make subjective decisions about employees.

d. Quantitative methods may significantly reduce the cost of decision making within the firm.

The correct answer is (c). *(Publisher)*
REQUIRED: The statement not a reason for the importance of quantitative methods.
DISCUSSION: The management accountant must recognize the importance of quantitative methods in the organization. By being familiar with these methods and their uses, the management accountant can recognize possible applications within the firm and advise management on their use. The management accountant can also judge whether the accounting data are being used correctly in the quantitative methods. Finally, quantitative methods can reduce the cost of obtaining information concerning the operations of the business and aid in forecasting business operations. They should not, however, take the place of qualitative decision making, which must take intangible data into account.

2. Which of the following is not an advantage of using mathematics in quantitative data analysis methods?

a. To permit repetition of rational decisions.

b. To discover solutions that support casual observation and/or in contrast to casual observation.

c. To provide understanding in complex issues.

d. To quantify the decision making factors.

e. None of the above.

The correct answer is (e). *(Publisher)*
REQUIRED: The item not an advantage of using mathematics in quantitative methods.
DISCUSSION: Each item listed is an advantage of using quantitative methods. The decision process is improved by the precision of the quantitative method approach. Rational decisions can be modeled and replicated, usually using a computer. Increased understanding of complex problems is also facilitated.

3. Which is the false statement about quantitative methods?

   a. Quantitative models are generally oversimplifications.
   b. It is impossible to include all relevant variables in each model.
   c. The techniques may not be justifiable on a cost/benefit basis.
   d. Every decision may be modeled mathematically and will always permit a deterministic solution.
   e. Behavioral considerations should not be taken into account in analyzing quantitative methods.

The correct answer is (e). *(Publisher)*
REQUIRED: The incorrect statement about quantitative methods.
DISCUSSION: It is virtually impossible to include all relevant variables in a mathematical model. Thus, the model must be reviewed in light of behavioral considerations as well as other considerations.
Answer (a) is incorrect because mathematical models are generally oversimplifications of the real world; to perform the calculations, assumptions must be made. Answer (b) is incorrect because some relevant variables may not be quantified and would therefore not be included. Answer (c) is incorrect because the techniques can be very complex and costly. Thus, cost/benefit analysis may not justify the use of some quantitative methods. Answer (d) is incorrect because every real-life decision situation may be modeled mathematically under certain assumptions, and a deterministic solution may be achieved.

4. A decision model designed to help its user find the best alternative or decision rule according to some criteria is said to be

   a. Bayesian.
   b. Probabilistic.
   c. Satisficing.
   d. Optimizing.

The correct answer is (d). *(CPA 1174 Q-18)*
REQUIRED: The design quality of helping to find the best alternative.
DISCUSSION: Optimizing is a technique used to find the most valuable or best solution given a set of alternatives.
Answer (a) is incorrect because it is a technique used to revise prior probabilities. Answer (b) is incorrect because it is a result based upon the relative probabilities of the states that may occur. Answer (c) is incorrect because it describes suboptimizing behavior.

5. The accountants for OEM Inc. have proposed that sensitivity analysis be incorporated into the company's capital budgeting program. This proposal is based on the fact that the major contribution of sensitivity analysis will be the determination of

   a. A measure of the probabilistic distribution of cash outflows.
   b. A financial measure of the new investment from alternative values for the parameters.
   c. A financial measure of the value of the new investment.
   d. A measure of the probability of the calculated outcome.
   e. A measure of the probable maximum rate of return.

The correct answer is (b). *(CMA 1278 5-9)*
REQUIRED: The major contribution of sensitivity analysis.
DISCUSSION: Sensitivity analysis allows evaluation of the effect of changes in variables. In this case, the company's capital budgeting program will produce results that can be evaluated subject to the sensitivity of certain parameters. Thus, sensitivity analysis permits "what if" questions to be examined.
Answer (a) is incorrect because sensitivity analysis assumes a deterministic distribution of cash outflow. Answer (c) is incorrect because sensitivity analysis is concerned with the change in the value of the investment given changes in the values for the parameters of the model. Answers (d) and (e) are incorrect because sensitivity analysis utilizes a deterministic approach.

Module 21.1: Simulation and Sensitivity Analysis

6. A manager wants to know the effect of a possible change in cash flows on the net present value of a project. The technique used to do this is

a. Sensitivity analysis.
b. Risk analysis.
c. Cost behavior analysis.
d. Variance analysis.
e. Return on investment analysis.

The correct answer is (a). *(CMA 1286 5-4)*
REQUIRED: The technique for measuring the effect of a change in cash flows on NPV.
DISCUSSION: Sensitivity analysis is a technique to evaluate a model in terms of the effect of changing the values of the parameters. It answers "what if" questions. In capital budgeting models, sensitivity analysis is the examination of alternative outcomes under different assumptions.
Answer (b) is incorrect because probability (risk) analysis is used to examine the array of possible outcomes given alternative parameters. Answers (c) and (d) are incorrect because cost behavior (variance) analysis concerns historical costs, not predictions of future cash inflows and outflows. Answer (e) is incorrect because ROI analysis is appropriate for determining the profitability of a company, segment, etc.

7. If a firm wishes to assess the effect of changing the contribution margin of product Z upon its optimum product mix and profitability, the most relevant quantitative technique is

a. Correlation analysis.
b. Cost/volume/profit analysis.
c. Queuing analysis.
d. Sensitivity analysis.
e. Time series or trend regression analysis.

The correct answer is (d). *(CPA 572 T-34)*
REQUIRED: The most relevant quantitative technique to evaluate a change in contribution margin.
DISCUSSION: Sensitivity analysis permits the examination of a variety of outcomes depending on a change in parameters for chosen assumptions. Changing the contribution margin of product Z in performing cost/volume/profit analysis is an example of sensitivity analysis.
Answer (a) is incorrect because it is a technique that quantifies relationships between two or more variables, i.e., the amount of change in one variable explained by change in another variable. Answer (b) is incorrect because it analyzes the relationships between cost and profit in terms of level of activity. Answer (c) is incorrect because it minimizes the sum of costs of servicing waiting lines plus the costs created by waiting lines. Answer (e) is incorrect because it denotes the relationship between a dependent variable and time (the latter being the independent variable).

8. Proxy Company is a foundry which specializes in custom orders. The company employs a job shop manufacturing facility. Due to the nature of its business, Proxy seldom does the same job more than once and each job has a separate set and sequence of operations. The company has to consider the cost of idle machine and labor capacity, the cost of carrying in-process inventory, and the importance of meeting specified order-completion due dates. Proxy management wants to develop a model which incorporates the operating characteristics of the job-shop, including random events and occurrences that affect operations. The methodology Proxy would find most useful is

a. Dynamic programming.
b. Linear programming.
c. Simulation techniques.
d. Cost/volume/profit analysis.
e. Markov analysis.

The correct answer is (c). *(CMA 1280 5-4)*
REQUIRED: The quantitative method most useful in predicting the future under uncertainty.
DISCUSSION: Simulation techniques would be most useful in this situation because they can be used to develop a quantitative model of business as well as to answer "what if" questions about possible outcomes. Simulation models can then be used to evaluate various outcomes if functions are changed by trial and error.
Answer (a) is incorrect because it is a method of solving a series of selected problems to maximize overall effectiveness. Decision trees are an example of dynamic programming. Answer (b) is incorrect because it is a method of solving optimization problems under constraints. Answer (d) is incorrect because it analyzes the relationships between cost and profit in terms of level of activity. Answer (e) is incorrect because it is used to predict future behavior of a variable in terms of its present behavior, e.g., consumer brand switching.

9. Computer simulation has been advocated as an important tool to assist management in decision making. Which of the following is not a correct assessment of computer simulation?

   a. It can only be used on large computers.
   b. It can be used to ascertain the sensitivity of an outcome to changes in components.
   c. The relationships of variables in the computer model can be changed over time.
   d. The models can be refined as more evidence from results becomes available.
   e. It can be used for both production and finance problems.

The correct answer is (a). (CIA 1182 IV-20)
REQUIRED: The incorrect assessment of computer simulation.
DISCUSSION: Computer simulations are used to examine "what if" situations. Variables may be changed, assumptions modified, and models refined. Computer simulations may be used in various types of problems, including production and financial models. Simulation techniques can be used on microcomputers as well as larger installations.

10. ZorbaCo has developed a comprehensive budget using a microcomputer spreadsheet. ZorbaCo's sales manager wishes to study the effects of: (1) decreasing selling price in order to increase sales volume, and (2) putting salespersons on commission instead of fixed salaries. These options can best be studied on the microcomputer by using

   a. Linear programming.
   b. Decision tree analysis.
   c. Simulation.
   d. Expected value analysis.
   e. Markov analysis.

The correct answer is (c). (CMA 1285 5-23)
REQUIRED: The technique that can be used to study the effects of decreasing selling prices and putting salespersons on commission.
DISCUSSION: Simulation analysis is appropriate. Simulation involves developing an environment (economy) in mathematical form. Changes in assumptions can then be made and the results will flow through the model economy.
Answer (a) is incorrect because linear programming is used to maximize or minimize an objective function given a number of limiting factors. Answer (b) is incorrect because decision tree analysis is used to study the results of various decisions that have a number of outcomes, all with different risks. Answer (d) is incorrect because expected value analysis is used to find an optimum value given a number of probabilities. Answer (e) is incorrect because Markov analysis is useful when a problem involves a variety of states of nature and the probability of moving from one to another depends only upon the current state.

11. A construction firm is in the process of building a simulation model for cost estimation purposes. They have identified all relevant variables and relationships and have gathered data on past projects. Their next step should be model

   a. Implementation.
   b. Design.
   c. Validation.
   d. Experimentation.

The correct answer is (c). (CIA 1186 III-41)
REQUIRED: The next step in developing a simulation model.
DISCUSSION: The first step to build a simulation model is to define the objectives of the project. The next step is to formulate the model, that is, to determine the variables to be included, their behavior, and their interrelationships in precise logical/mathematical terms. The third step is to validate the model. Some assurance is needed that the results of the experiment will be realistic. This assurance requires validation of the model, often with historical data. If the model gives results equivalent to what actually happened, the model is historically valid. There is still some risk, however, that changes could make the model invalid for the future.
Answer (a) is incorrect because implementation of the simulation follows validation. Answer (b) is incorrect because the model has already been formulated (designed). Answer (d) is incorrect because experimentation is sampling the operation of the model after validation and before full implementation.

Module 21.1: Simulation and Sensitivity Analysis

12. Probability (risk) analysis
    a. Ignores probability weights under 50%.
    b. Is only for situations in which there are three or fewer possible outcomes.
    c. Does not enhance the usefulness of sensitivity analysis data.
    d. Is an extension of sensitivity analysis.

The correct answer is (d). *(CPA 1181 T-58)*
REQUIRED: The correct description of probability (risk) analysis.
DISCUSSION: Probability (risk) analysis is used to examine the array of possible outcomes given alternative parameters. Sensitivity analysis answers "what if" questions when alternative parameters are changed. Thus risk (probability) analysis is similar to sensitivity analysis: both evaluate the probability and effect of differing inputs or outputs.
Answer (a) is incorrect because, if there are more than two variables, most probabilities are less than 50%. Answer (b) is incorrect because it can be used when there are many possible outcomes. Answer (c) is incorrect because it enhances the usefulness of sensitivity analysis data.

13. Practical use of most mathematical decision models requires the estimation of one or more parameters in the model. A technique which helps the decision maker understand the extent to which the outcome described by the decision model depends on the parameter estimates is
    a. Parametric statistics.
    b. Differential calculus.
    c. Nonparametric statistics.
    d. Dynamic programming.
    e. Sensitivity analysis.

The correct answer is (e). *(CMA 1277 5-7)*
REQUIRED: The quantitative method used to estimate the effects of changes in parameters.
DISCUSSION: Sensitivity analysis examines "what if" questions when changes are made to basic assumptions or parameters. Sensitivity analysis thus demonstrates the responsiveness of final results to the changes in one of the model parameters.
Answer (a) is incorrect because it uses traditional cardinal scales of measurement. Answer (b) is incorrect because it is a technique used to determine the maxima and minima of nonlinear functions. Answer (c) is incorrect because it uses ordinal measuring scales (items can only be rank ordered, not measured). Answer (d) is incorrect because it is a method of solving a series of selected problems to maximize overall effectiveness.

14. Parker Company is concerned about customer loyalty and has accumulated data on the extent that customers switch among brands. Parker can best analyze the data on brand switching by using
    a. Linear programming.
    b. Queuing theory.
    c. Differential calculus.
    d. Markov analysis.
    e. Decision tree analysis.

The correct answer is (d). *(CMA 1285 5-22)*
REQUIRED: The technique that can be used to analyze the data on brand switching by customers.
DISCUSSION: In a Markov chain, the probability of an event is conditioned upon the previous event. Many card games reflect the Markov process because the probabilities are altered by the cards already played. Markov analysis is thus an appropriate technique for forecasting consumer buying habits because it relies on recent evidence rather than on an average of all evidence.
Answer (a) is incorrect because linear programming is used to maximize (or minimize) an objective function given a variety of limitations. Answer (b) is incorrect because queuing theory is used to optimize waiting line situations. Answer (c) is incorrect because differential calculus is used to find derivatives of functions and to determine the points of maximization or minimization. Answer (e) is incorrect because decision trees are diagrams used to analyze sequences of probabilistic decisions, the events that may follow each decision, and the possible outcomes.

15. The branch of decision theory which deals with decision making when facing a live opponent is called

    a. Catastrophe theory.
    b. Negotiation theory.
    c. Game theory.
    d. Conflict theory.

The correct answer is (c). *(CIA 587 III-47)*
REQUIRED: The branch of decision theory that deals with facing a live opponent.
DISCUSSION: Game (or decision) theory is a mathematical approach to decision making when confronted with an "enemy" or competitor. Games are classified according to the number of players and the algebraic sum of the payoffs. In a two-person game, if the payoff is given by the loser to the winner, the algebraic sum is zero and the game is called a zero-sum game. If it is possible for both players to profit, however, the game is a positive-sum game. Mathematical models have been developed to select optimum strategies for specific simple games.
    Answer (a) is incorrect because catastrophe theory concerns the breakdown of stability in mathematical models. Answers (b) and (d) are incorrect because negotiation theory and conflict theory, as used in the management science literature, describe certain aspects of game theory.

16. A firm wishes to compare the effects of using a new labor-saving machine with present direct labor methods. These comparisons will be made over a wide variety of operations on several typical days. The demands placed upon each operation as well as the sequence of individual operations can be described by probability distributions. The most relevant quantitative technique is

    a. Cost/volume/profit analysis.
    b. Monte Carlo simulation.
    c. Program evaluation and review technique (PERT).
    d. Statistical sampling.
    e. Time series or trend regression analysis.

The correct answer is (b). *(CPA 572 T-33)*
REQUIRED: The most relevant quantitative technique to compare proposed and present labor methods.
DISCUSSION: Monte Carlo simulation is used in conjunction with random number tables to simulate a process or project upon which data are unavailable or for which the cost of test runs would be prohibitive.
    Answer (a) is incorrect because it analyzes the relationships between cost and profit in terms of level of activity. Answer (c) is incorrect because it is a technique used to examine complex projects and help complete the projects in the minimum amount of time. Answer (d) is incorrect because it involves selection of items from a population when every item in the population has an equal chance of being chosen. Answer (e) is incorrect because they describe the strength and direction of the relationship between two or more variables.

21.2 Queuing Theory

17. A quantitative method that deals with the problem of supplying sufficient facilities to meet the needs of production lines or individuals that demand service unevenly is

    a. Regression analysis.
    b. PERT.
    c. Queuing theory.
    d. Nonlinear analysis.

The correct answer is (c). *(CPA 574 P-14)*
REQUIRED: The quantitative method that deals with supplying facilities to meet uneven service demand.
DISCUSSION: Queuing theory examines the cost of waiting in lines and costs of servicing waiting lines. It is useful whenever units or variables randomly arrive at a point in the process where service is sequential. To minimize total cost, queuing theory balances the costs of waiting (e.g., wages for an employee standing idle while waiting for the copy machine) against the costs of providing the service (e.g., providing a second machine).
    Answer (a) is incorrect because it examines the relationships between variables. Answer (b) is incorrect because it is used to examine complex projects and identify critical processes. Answer (d) is incorrect because it deals with models having nonlinear relationships. An example is differential calculus.

Module 21.2: Queuing Theory   631

18. A bank has changed from a system where lines are formed in front of each teller to a one-line, multiple-server system. When a teller is free, the person at the head of the line goes to that teller. Implementing the new system would

   a. Decrease the bank's wage expenses since the new system uses fewer tellers.
   b. Decrease time customers spend in the line.
   c. Increase accuracy in teller reconciliations at the end of the day due to fewer customers per teller.
   d. Improve on-the-job training for bank employees since each teller would perform different duties.

The correct answer is (b). *(CIA 586 III-15)*
REQUIRED: The effect of implementing the new queuing system.
DISCUSSION: When all customers must wait in a single queue, it is possible to decrease waiting time if there are multiple servers. This would have the added effect of increasing customer satisfaction.
Answer (a) is incorrect because it is unlikely that the number of employees would change due to the new system. Answer (c) is incorrect because, assuming a Poisson process, the number of customers per teller would not change. Answer (d) is incorrect because tellers' duties would not change, so on-the-job training would not improve.

19. The drive-through service at a fast-food restaurant consists of driving up to place an order, advancing to a window to pay for the order, and then advancing to another window to receive the items ordered. This type of waiting-line system would be called

   a. Single channel, single phase.
   b. Single channel, multiple phase.
   c. Multiple channel, single phase.
   d. Multiple channel, multiple phase.

The correct answer is (b). *(CIA 1187 III-39)*
REQUIRED: The type of waiting-line system described.
DISCUSSION: The drive-through represents a single queue (channel). Since this waiting line has three services in series, it may be said to be multiple phase. Another example is the typical factory assembly line. This terminology (channel, phase), however, is not used by all writers on queuing theory.
Answer (a) is incorrect because service by a one ticket-seller at a movie theater is an example of a single channel, single phase system. Answer (c) is incorrect because supermarket checkout lines are a common example of multiple single phase servers servicing multiple lines. Answer (d) is incorrect because an example of a multiple channel, multiple phase system is a set of supermarket checkout lines each of which is served in sequence by a cashier and a person who packs grocery bags.

20. A post office serves customers in a single line at one service window. During peak periods, the rate of arrivals has a Poisson distribution with an average of 100 customers per hour and service times that are exponentially distributed with an average of 60 seconds per customer. From this, one can conclude that the

   a. Queue will expand to infinity.
   b. Server will be idle one-sixth of the time.
   c. Average rate of service is 100 customers per hour.
   d. Average customer waiting time is 2.5 minutes.

The correct answer is (a). *(CIA 584 IV-34)*
REQUIRED: The conclusion that can be reached about a queuing model.
DISCUSSION: One hundred customers arrive in line per hour and only 60 are serviced per hour. Accordingly, the queue will expand to infinity during peak periods.
Answers (b) and (d) are incorrect because insufficient information is given to determine overall idle time or average customer waiting time. The question only gives peak period data. Answer (c) is incorrect because it is unlikely that the overall average rate of service is 100 customers per hour given peak customer service of only 60 per hour.

21. A highway department plans to open a newly constructed toll bridge. Determining how many toll booth attendants should be on duty at different hours of the day requires the application of

a. Statistical sampling.
b. Correlation analysis.
c. Operations research.
d. Queuing theory.
e. Variance analysis.

The correct answer is (d). *(CIA 580 II-20)*
REQUIRED: The quantitative method to determine how many attendants should be on duty.
DISCUSSION: Queuing theory is useful whenever an item randomly arrives at a point in a process where items are serviced one at a time. To minimize total cost, queuing theory balances the cost of waiting against the cost of providing service.
Answer (a) is incorrect because it is used to select a sample from a population so every population item has an equal chance of being chosen. Answer (b) is incorrect because it is used to describe the relationship between variables. Answer (c) is incorrect because operations research is a general term describing quantitative analysis of organizational operations and decision making. Answer (e) is incorrect because it describes the process of examining deviations from expected results.

22. A company is designing a new regional distribution warehouse. To minimize delays in loading and unloading trucks, an adequate number of loading docks must be built. The most relevant technique to assist in determining the proper number of docks is

a. Correlation and regression analysis.
b. Cost/volume/profit analysis.
c. PERT/CPM analysis.
d. Linear programming.
e. Queuing theory.

The correct answer is (e). *(CMA 1280 5-7)*
REQUIRED: The technique to assist in determining the proper number of docks.
DISCUSSION: Queuing theory minimizes the total cost of providing services against the cost of additional capacity for work flows that arrive randomly at the service facility.
Answer (a) is incorrect because they are used to describe the relationships among variables. Answer (b) is incorrect because it is used to examine a relationship between cost and profit in terms of activity level. Answer (c) is incorrect because it is used to determine critical paths or processes in completing a project. Answer (d) is incorrect because it minimizes cost or maximizes profit within constraints.

21.3 Network Models

23. The technique used to obtain a probabilistic estimate of the completion time for a project is

a. A GANTT chart.
b. The critical path method (CPM).
c. A time-cost-performance chart.
d. The program evaluation review technique (PERT).
e. The Markov chain.

The correct answer is (d). *(CMA 1286 5-9)*
REQUIRED: The technique used to determine a probabilistic estimate of the completion time for a project.
DISCUSSION: PERT is used to obtain a probabilistic estimate of the completion time for a project. The PERT method is sometimes known as the 1-4-1 three-estimate method because the most optimistic and pessimistic estimates are each weighted by one and the most likely estimate is weighted by four. The sum of these three weighted estimates is then divided by six to arrive at the probable completion time.
Answer (a) is incorrect because a GANTT chart is a bar chart used to keep a record of the steps in a project that have already been completed. Answer (b) is incorrect because CPM is similar to PERT, but uses deterministic estimates of time. Answer (c) is incorrect because it includes cost. Answer (e) is incorrect because Markov analysis is useful when a problem involves a variety of states of nature and the probability of moving from one to another depends only upon the current state.

Module 21.3: Network Models

24. The most appropriate technique for determining the longest time required to complete a particular project would be

    a. Regression analysis.
    b. Integer programming.
    c. Game theory.
    d. Queuing theory.
    e. Program evaluation and review technique (PERT).

The correct answer is (e). *(CIA 1182 IV-15)*
REQUIRED: The technique to determine the longest time to complete a project.
DISCUSSION: PERT is used for analyzing, planning, and scheduling large, complex projects by forecasting the time of completion, monitoring progress, and identifying parts of the project critical for the project to be completed on time.
    Answer (a) is incorrect because it finds an equation which explains the relationship among variables. Answer (b) is incorrect because it is an LP technique where variables and solutions are in integers, i.e., no fractions are considered. Answer (c) is incorrect because it is used to evaluate alternatives under competition. Answer (d) is incorrect because it minimizes the sum of the costs of waiting lines and the costs of providing service.

25. Program evaluation and review technique (PERT) is a system which uses

    a. Least squares method.
    b. Linear programming.
    c. Economic order quantity formula.
    d. Network analysis and critical path methods (CPM).

The correct answer is (d). *(CPA 1179 T-38)*
REQUIRED: The method(s) used in a program evaluation and review technique system.
DISCUSSION: A PERT system shows the interrelationship of a complex time network of activities and identifies any critical paths. The critical path (the longest path through the system when completing a total project) is dependent upon completing various subunits at specific times to enable the work to progress.
    Answer (a) is incorrect because it is a statistical tool for fitting a straight line to a series of data observations. Answer (b) is incorrect because it is a mathematical approach to maximize profits or minimize costs subject to constraints. Answer (c) is incorrect because it minimizes the sum of inventory order costs and inventory carrying costs.

26. In a program evaluation review technique (PERT) system, activities along the critical path

    a. Follow the line of best fit.
    b. Have a slack of zero.
    c. Have a positive slack.
    d. Intersect at a corner point described by the feasible area.

The correct answer is (b). *(CPA 1184 T-58)*
REQUIRED: The characteristic of a critical path in a PERT system.
DISCUSSION: A PERT system shows the interrelationship of a complex time series of activities and identifies any critical paths in those series of activities. The critical path is the longest path through the network and therefore includes no slack time. Reducing the critical path through the system is the only way to reduce total time.
    Answer (a) is incorrect because it concerns regression analysis. Answer (c) is incorrect because it indicates that time may be wasted without affecting the completion date. Answer (d) is incorrect because it concerns a linear programming concept.

27. What is the appropriate technique for defining the critical path when the completion of a total project is dependent upon the completion of various subunits at specific times to enable the work to progress?

   a. Linear programming.
   b. Multiple regression analysis.
   c. Program evaluation and review technique.
   d. Queuing theory.

The correct answer is (c). *(CPA 1180 T-42)*
REQUIRED: The technique for defining the critical path in a complex job.
DISCUSSION: PERT shows the interrelationship of a complex time series of activities and identifies any critical paths in that series. The critical path is the longest path through the system when the completion of a project is dependent upon the completion of various subunits at specific times to enable the work to progress.
Answer (a) is incorrect because it is a mathematical approach that maximizes profits or minimizes costs. Answer (b) is incorrect because it is a tool for measuring the change in the dependent variable associated with the change in two or more independent variables. Answer (d) is incorrect because it is a method of studying the costs of waiting lines and the cost of servicing the waiting lines.

28. Owens University is planning to install a microcomputer laboratory for use by faculty and students. Project steps include needs assessment, remodeling a classroom to accommodate the facility, system selection, purchasing hardware and software, and recruiting and training laboratory staff. Owens can best schedule the microcomputer laboratory project by using

   a. Critical path analysis.
   b. EOQ modeling.
   c. Decision tree analysis.
   d. Linear programming.
   e. Markov analysis.

The correct answer is (a). *(CMA 1285 5-19)*
REQUIRED: The best method to use to schedule the steps in installing a new computer lab.
DISCUSSION: A PERT system (program evaluation and review technique) is a formal diagram showing the interrelationships of a complex time series of activities and the critical paths in that system. The critical path is the longest path through the system given that completing a total project is dependent upon completing various subunits at specific times to enable work to progress.
Answer (b) is incorrect because EOQ is used to determine optimum inventory purchase sizes. Answer (c) is incorrect because decision tree analysis is used to evaluate a variety of decision possibilities and their associated risk levels. Answer (d) is incorrect because linear programming is used to maximize or minimize an objective function (such as profits or costs) given certain constraints. Answer (e) is incorrect because Markov analysis is a decision tool that predicts future states of nature based on the current state of nature. Past states are not as important as the current state.

29. The use of PERT or CPM might apply in the case of planning for

   a. The construction of a new office building.
   b. The installation of a new computer system.
   c. The development of a new product.
   d. All of the above.
   e. None of the above.

The correct answer is (d). *(CIA 577 IV-9)*
REQUIRED: The situation(s) in which PERT or CPM might apply.
DISCUSSION: Both PERT (program evaluation and review technique) and CPM (critical path method) are useful in the planning and control of a large system or process. PERT and CPM both construct a network of time relationships between each subunit or subproject to identify the subprojects that have a direct effect on the completion date of the project.
Answers (a), (b), and (c) are incorrect because each is a complex project suitable for application of PERT or CPM.

30. Critical path method (CPM) is a technique for analyzing, planning, and scheduling large, complex projects by determining the critical path from a single time estimate for each event in a project. The critical path

   a. Is the maximum amount of time an activity may be delayed without delaying the total project beyond its target time.
   b. Is the earliest starting time that an activity for a project can begin.
   c. Is the pessimistic time estimate for an activity of a project.
   d. Is the shortest time path from the first event to the last event for a project.
   e. Is the longest time path from the first event to the last event for a project.

The correct answer is (e). *(CMA 1278 5-27)*
   REQUIRED: The correct description of a critical path.
   DISCUSSION: The critical path is the longest time path from the first event to the last event for a project. If there are any delays on the critical path, the total time for the entire project will increase.
   Answer (a) is incorrect because it defines the slack time. Answer (b) is incorrect because the starting time does not affect the total time required to finish a project. Answer (c) is incorrect because the pessimistic time estimate is the longest time considered possible to complete the project. Answer (d) is incorrect because it is the path with the most slack time in the project. Slack time is the amount of extra time which could be used on that path without extending the completion time of the project.

31. Ridgefield, Inc. is considering a three-phase research project. The time estimates for completion of Phase 1 of the project are

Optimistic	4 months
Most likely	8 months
Pessimistic	18 months

The formula for the expected time of a particular project is

$$\frac{A + 4M + B}{6}$$

where A = Optimistic estimate
      B = Pessimistic estimate
      M = Most likely estimate

Using the program evaluation and review technique (PERT), the expected time for completion of Phase 1 should be

   a. 8 months.
   b. 9 months.
   c. 10 months.
   d. 18 months.

The correct answer is (b). *(CPA 1181 P-29)*
   REQUIRED: The expected time for completion using PERT.
   DISCUSSION: PERT is a technique to identify the paths to complete a complicated process. The critical path is the longest path from the beginning to end.

Expected time of completion = $\frac{4 + 4(8) + 18}{6} = 9$

32. PERT is widely used to plan and measure progress toward scheduled events. PERT is combined with cost data to produce a PERT-Cost analysis in order to

   a. Calculate the total project cost inclusive of the additional slack time.
   b. Evaluate and optimize trade-offs between time of an event's completion and its cost to complete.
   c. Implement computer-integrated manufacturing concepts.
   d. Avoid the problem of time variance analysis.
   e. Calculate expected activity times.

The correct answer is (b). *(CMA 1287 5-26)*
   REQUIRED: The true statement about PERT-Cost analysis.
   DISCUSSION: Combining PERT with cost data permits decisions as to whether the benefits of earlier completion of a project are justified in terms of the additional costs of completion. For this purpose, activity times and costs must be estimated for both normal and crash efforts.
   Answer (a) is incorrect because slack time is an inherent part of the noncritical paths on PERT projects. Answer (c) is incorrect because PERT-Cost can be used without computerization. Answers (d) and (e) are incorrect because costs are not needed for these calculations.

33. A PERT diagram was drawn showing the fifteen activities required for the implementation of a new computer system at a particular firm. With activities identified by letters, the five paths through the network and their lengths were:

Path 1: A-C-G-M   10 weeks
     2: B-D-F-N   15 weeks
     3: A-H-I-J-K-O   12 weeks
     4: A-E-J-L-N   10 weeks
     5: A-C-K-L-M   13 weeks

The critical path(s) is(are)

a. Path 1 and Path 4.
b. Path 2.
c. Path 3.
d. Path 5.

The correct answer is (b). *(CIA 587 III-46)*
REQUIRED: The critical path(s) based on a PERT analysis.
DISCUSSION: The critical path (path 2) is the longest path in time through the network. It is critical in that if any activity on the critical path takes longer than expected, the entire project will be delayed. Every network has at least one critical path. Some have more than one.

34. Red Company has bid on a contract to build a prototype personal computer for Black Company. Parts for this prototype will be obtained from outside vendors. The table below presents the activities involved in this project and the various number of days involved in each event.

Event	Optimistic Time	Most Likely Time	Pessimistic Time
1. Bid awarded	--	--	--
2. Order parts	4	5	12
3. Prepare space for production	3	8	13
4. Receive and inspect parts	10	14	24
5. Assemble prototype	7	10	19
6. Quality assurance testing	3	5	7
7. Ship to customer	--	--	--

How much time is the total project expected to take?

a. 34 days.
b. 37 days.
c. 42 days.
d. 45 days.

The correct answer is (b). *(CIA 1185 III-3)*
REQUIRED: The time the total project is expected to take.
DISCUSSION: Preparation (8), receipt and inspection of parts (14), assembly (10), and testing (5) is expected to take 37 days. Ordering can be accomplished after preparation of space for production has begun. Note that this planning method totals the most likely time estimates rather than the pessimistic or optimistic estimates.

35. The following diagram represents various project activities and the sequencing requirement in days. Define the critical path.

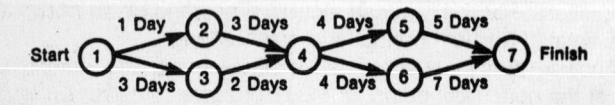

Start ① →1 Day→ ② →3 Days→ ④ →4 Days→ ⑤ →5 Days→ ⑦ Finish
      ① →3 Days→ ③ →2 Days→ ④ →4 Days→ ⑥ →7 Days→ ⑦

a. Path 1-2-4-5-7.
b. Path 1-2-4-6-7.
c. Path 1-3-4-5-7.
d. Path 1-3-4-6-7.

The correct answer is (d). *(CIA 1187 III-43)*
REQUIRED: The critical path through the diagram.
DISCUSSION: The critical path is the longest path. Path 1-3-4-6-7 is the critical path because it requires 16 days (3 + 2 + 4 + 7).
Answer (a) is incorrect because it takes 13 days. Answer (b) is incorrect because it takes 15 days. Answer (c) is incorrect because it takes 14 days.

Questions 36 and 37 are based on the following information. During an operational audit, an internal auditing team discovers the following document, entitled Project Analysis.

Project Analysis

Activity	Time in Weeks	Preceding Activity
A	3	-
B	3	A
C	7	A
D	4	A
E	2	B
F	4	B
G	1	C,E
H	5	D

Using the Project Analysis document, the audit supervisor prepared the following diagram:

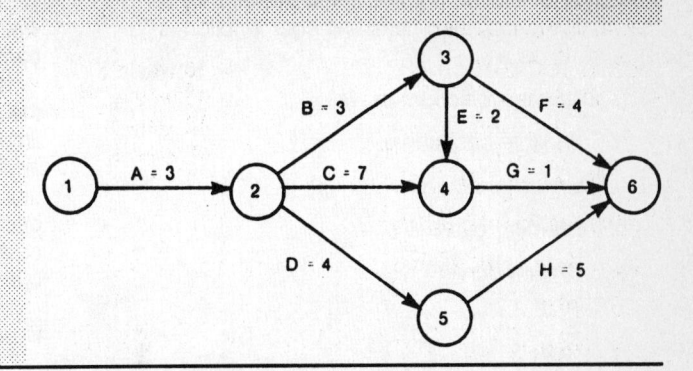

[Network diagram: Node 1 →(A=3)→ Node 2; Node 2 →(B=3)→ Node 3; Node 2 →(C=7)→ Node 4; Node 2 →(D=4)→ Node 5; Node 3 →(E=2)→ Node 4; Node 3 →(F=4)→ Node 6; Node 4 →(G=1)→ Node 6; Node 5 →(H=5)→ Node 6]

36. What is the earliest completion time that is indicated by the project analysis?

a. 9 weeks.
b. 10 weeks.
c. 11 weeks.
d. 12 weeks.

The correct answer is (d). *(CIA 1186 III-49)*
REQUIRED: The earliest completion time that is indicated by the project analysis.
DISCUSSION: The critical (longest) path through the diagram provides the estimate of the earliest completion time, assuming all activities must be completed. The critical path is thus 1-2-5-6 (path ADH), which requires 12 weeks.

37. What is the earliest time by which Node 4 would be reached?

a. 6 weeks.
b. 7 weeks.
c. 8 weeks.
d. 10 weeks.

The correct answer is (d). *(CIA 1186 III-50)*
REQUIRED: The earliest time by which Node 4 would be reached.
DISCUSSION: The network diagram contains two paths leading to Node 4: 1-2-3-4 (path ABE) and 1-2-4 (path AC). The former requires 8 weeks and the latter 10 weeks. Accordingly, the earliest time by which all activities preceding Node 4 can be completed is 10 weeks. Thus, the critical path to Node 4 is 1-2-4 (path AC).

38. The Gantt chart below shows that the project is

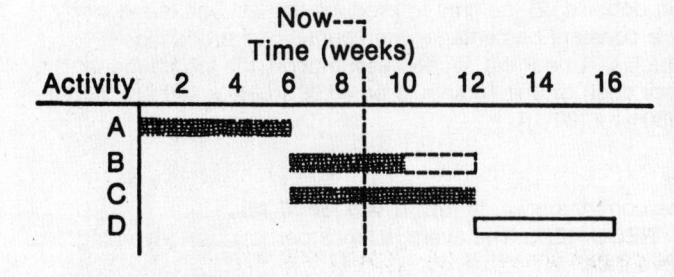

[Gantt chart: Now line at week 9. Activity A: weeks 0-6 shaded complete. Activity B: weeks 6-11 shaded, extending to 12 unshaded. Activity C: weeks 6-11 shaded, extending beyond unshaded. Activity D: weeks 12-14 unshaded (not started).]

a. Complete.
b. Ahead of schedule.
c. On schedule.
d. Behind schedule.

The correct answer is (b). *(CIA 586 III-23)*
REQUIRED: The status of a project according to the Gantt chart.
DISCUSSION: Assuming that each of the bars represents the expected time necessary to complete an activity and that the shaded regions represent the portions completed, it can be seen that activity A has been completed as scheduled and activities B and C are ahead of schedule. Therefore, the project is ahead of schedule.
Answers (a), (c), and (d) are incorrect because the project is ahead of schedule, but activity D has not yet been started, much less completed.

21.4 Learning Curves

39. If a cost function behaves such that the average costs per unit of output decline systematically as cumulative production rises, the cost function is referred to as a

a. Quantity discount curve.
b. Variable cost curve.
c. Linear cost curve.
d. Learning curve.
e. Growth curve.

The correct answer is (d). *(CMA 1286 5-8)*
REQUIRED: The term referring to a cost function in which average cost per unit declines systematically as cumulative production rises.
DISCUSSION: The learning curve effect occurs during the early stages of production. It reflects the decrease in time needed to perform tasks as workers gain experience and economies of scale are achieved. The average cost per unit and the time required to produce one unit both decrease. For example, an 80% learning curve means that each time cumulative production doubles (up to a point), cumulative average costs will decrease by 20%.
Answers (a), (b), (c), and (e) are incorrect because none is meaningful in this context.

40. Robinson Company began manufacturing a new product at one of its plants last year. An analysis of production information indicated that the time spent to produce a unit of this product was considerably more than standard but kept decreasing steadily until it reached standard. After that, there was little change. This pattern was probably due to

a. The standards being too tight.
b. The standards being too loose.
c. A favorable labor efficiency variance.
d. The learning curve effect.
e. A favorable labor rate variance.

The correct answer is (d). *(CIA 1182 IV-12)*
REQUIRED: The cause of decreasing time spent on producing a product.
DISCUSSION: The learning curve states that, as production increases, the time it takes to complete each product will decrease due to economies of scale and experience of the production personnel. The learning curve is exponential in form; it drops sharply and then changes very little.

41. A learning curve of 80% assumes that production unit costs are reduced by 20% for each doubling of output. What is the cost of the sixteenth unit produced as an approximate percent of the first unit produced?

a. 30%.
b. 40%.
c. 50%.
d. 60%.

The correct answer is (b). *(CIA 1187 III-41)*
REQUIRED: The cost of the last unit produced given a learning curve.
DISCUSSION: A learning curve model is based on one of two assumptions: 1) cumulative average time per unit is reduced by a constant percentage when cumulative production doubles; 2) the time to produce the last unit is reduced by a constant percentage when cumulative production doubles. Under the second assumption, the labor time (and labor cost) of unit 16 should be 40.96 [(80% x 100%) x (80%) x (80%) x (80%)].

42. A 75% learning curve is applied to the following consecutive lots as follows:

Number of Units	Average Time/Unit
A. 50	6.0
B. 100	?
C. 200	?
D. 400	?

The average time per unit for lots B through D is

a. 4.5, 3.4, 2.5.
b. 4.5 each.
c. 6.0 each.
d. 7.5 each.

The correct answer is (a). *(CIA 1186 III-46)*
REQUIRED: The average times per unit using learning curve data.
DISCUSSION: Learning curves reflect the increased rate at which people perform tasks as they gain experience. The time required to perform a given task becomes progressively shorter. This technique is only applicable to the early stages of production or of any new task. Usually, the curve is expressed in a percentage of reduced time to complete a task for each doubling of cumulative production. The average time per unit of lot B should thus be 4.5 (.75 x 6.0), the average unit of time for C is 3.4 (.75 x 4.5), and the average unit of time for D is 2.5 (.75 x 3.4). This calculation assumes that the "Number of Units" column in the problem statement is for cumulative units.

Module 21.4: Learning Curves

43. If a firm is considering the use of learning curve analysis in the determination of labor cost standards for a new product, it should be advised that this technique generally is most relevant to situations in which the production time per unit decreases as additional units are produced and the unit cost

a. Decreases.
b. Does not change.
c. Increases or decreases in an unpredictable manner.
d. Increases slightly.
e. Increases substantially.

44. A company has developed a learning (improvement) curve for one of its newer processes from its accounting and production records. Management asked internal audit to review the curve. Which of the following events would tend to mitigate the effects of the learning curve?

a. Labor costs incurred for overtime hours were charged to an overhead account.
b. The number of preassembled purchased parts used exceeded the plan.
c. The number of skilled, higher-paid workers used in production exceeded the plan.
d. Newly developed processing equipment with improved operating characteristics were used.
e. All of the above.

45. A construction company has just completed a bridge over the Mississippi River. This is the first bridge the company ever built and it required 100 weeks to complete. Now having hired a bridge construction crew with some experience, the company would like to continue building bridges. Because of the investment in heavy machinery needed continuously by this crew, the company believes it would have to bring the average construction time to less than 1 year (52 weeks) per bridge to earn a sufficient return on investment. The average construction time will follow an 80% learning curve. To bring the average construction time (over all bridges constructed) below 1 year per bridge, the crew would have to build approximately

a. 2 additional bridges.
b. 3 additional bridges.
c. 7 additional bridges.
d. 8 additional bridges.
e. 15 additional bridges.

The correct answer is (a). *(CPA 572 T-35)*
REQUIRED: The unit cost behavior when using the learning curve approach.
DISCUSSION: The learning curve is a cost function which shows that the average cost per unit and time required to produce one unit both decrease as production rises.
Answers (b), (d), and (e) are incorrect because as production increases, efficiency also increases, resulting in lower unit costs. Answer (c) is incorrect because the unit cost decreases in a predictable manner.

The correct answer is (e). *(CIA 582 II-22)*
REQUIRED: The event(s) that would tend to mitigate the effects of the learning curve.
DISCUSSION: The learning curve is developed with a plan of all the factors of production. Any changes in the skill level of workers, processing equipment, parts used, or method of labor cost allocation will make the predesigned learning curve less useful.
Answers (a), (b), (c), and (d) are incorrect because each would change the results of the learning curve.

The correct answer is (c). *(CMA 1277 5-10)*
REQUIRED: The number of bridges to bring average construction time below 1 year per bridge.
DISCUSSION: An 80% learning curve means that the average production time will be 80% of the previous average each time production is doubled. Thus, to lower the time per bridge below 1 year, calculate the per bridge time savings as follows:

First bridge	(given)	=	100 weeks
Second bridge	(100 x .8)	=	80 weeks
Fourth bridge	(80 x .8)	=	64 weeks
Eighth bridge	(64 x .8)	=	51.2 weeks

Therefore, seven additional (since one bridge has already been built) bridges would have to be built to get the average construction time below 1 year.

46.
You are performing an internal audit in a factory which has established an improvement (learning) curve of 70%. Unit number one of the current model being produced required 8,000 labor hours to construct. How many cumulative average labor hours per unit should be required to construct eight units?

a. 3,920.
b. 7,250.
c. 1,921.
d. 2,744.
e. 5,600.

The correct answer is (d). *(CIA 579 II-26)*
REQUIRED: The average labor hours needed to construct units given a learning curve.
DISCUSSION: The 70% learning curve means that every time production is doubled, the cumulative average time per unit required for production will be 70% of the average time required for the prior production level. To determine the cumulative average number of labor hours to construct eight units requires the calculation of the average time to construct units two, four, and eight.

Unit			Cumulative Average Hours
1	(given)	=	8,000
2	(8000 x .7)	=	5,600
4	(5600 x .7)	=	3,920
8	(3920 x .7)	=	2,744

47.
Which of the following may be scheduled in production planning by the use of learning curves?

a. Labor assignments.
b. Purchases of materials.
c. Subassembly production.
d. Delivery dates of finished products.
e. All of the above.

The correct answer is (e). *(CIA 580 II-10)*
REQUIRED: The use(s) to which learning curves may be put.
DISCUSSION: Learning curves are used to describe the increase in production efficiencies resulting from experience. Answers (a) through (d) are all activities which would be more efficient as experience increases. Labor assignments would benefit from applications of learning curves to labor-hour budgets. Materials purchases would result in efficiencies in the EOQ if the adjustments in production efficiency, as shown by the learning curve, were used in ordering. Subassembly production and delivery dates of finished products could each be more efficiently scheduled if learning curve efficiencies were taken into account during the planning process.

48.
Mori Company plans to begin production of a new product on July 1. An 80% learning curve is applicable to Mori's manufacturing operations. If it is expected to take 1,000 direct labor hours to produce the first unit, how many direct labor hours should it take to produce the third and fourth units?

a. 640.
b. 960.
c. 1,600.
d. 2,560.

The correct answer is (b). *(CPA 1182 Q-34)*
REQUIRED: The total production time for the third and fourth units given a learning curve.
DISCUSSION: The 80% learning curve means that every time production is doubled, the average time required for production will be only 80% of the time required for the prior production level. As shown below, the average time to produce the first two units is 800 hours, so the total time is 1,600 hours (2 x 800). After four units are produced, the average is 640 hours, a total of 2,560 hours (4 x 640). The time to produce units three and four should be 960 hours (2,560 - 1,600).

Units	Average time/Unit
1	(given)
2	800 (80% x 1000)
4	640 (80% x 800)

Module 21.5: Matrix Algebra

49. The forecasting procedure known as exponential smoothing is a special kind of weighted moving average in which the assignment of weights is based on the same mathematical process which is the basis for describing the growth of an amount invested at a fixed interest rate with annual compounding. This mathematical process is known as the

   a. Markov process.
   b. Bernoulli process.
   c. Geometric progression.
   d. Poisson distribution.
   e. Arithmetic progression.

The correct answer is (c). *(CMA 1277 5-8)*
   REQUIRED: The mathematical process used in exponential smoothing which describes the growth of an amount invested at a fixed interest rate with annual compounding.
   DISCUSSION: Geometric progression means that each term in a series is a multiple of the previous term. In a compound interest calculation, the amount of money is calculated by taking the amount at the end of the last period and multiplying it by the current interest rate plus one. In exponential smoothing, the procedure is reversed in that the effect of events in the past is discounted based upon a multiple (the more time that has elapsed since a given event, the less effect it has on the current figure). It thus constitutes a moving average of the figures.
   Answer (a) is incorrect because it is a process in which the probability of a variable's moving to one of several states is dependent only on the current state. Answer (b) is incorrect because it is a process in which there are only two alternatives. Answer (d) is incorrect because it is a process in which the probability of the occurrence of an event is independent of what has happened immediately proceeding the present observation. The Poisson process is used in the queuing theory. Answer (e) is incorrect because it is a progression in which the differences between each of the terms in the progression is a constant.

50. Operations research is a

   a. Discipline using quantitative methods oriented to planning.
   b. Set of generally accepted manufacturing methods.
   c. Review of operating techniques within an industry.
   d. Method used to analyze financial data.
   e. Term describing an area of pure research.

The correct answer is (a). *(CIA 578 IV-6)*
   REQUIRED: The definition of operations research.
   DISCUSSION: Operations research is a quantitative method oriented to planning.
   Answers (b) and (d) are incorrect because operations research is not concerned only with manufacturing methods and/or financial analysis; it is a broader discipline. Answer (c) is incorrect because operations research may be applied within a firm, an industry, or many other production systems. Answer (e) is incorrect because operations research is applied rather than pure research.

21.5 Matrix Algebra

51. A manufacturing company allocates the cost of its service departments to the producing departments. The service departments provide services to each other as well as to the producing departments. The allocation technique which will charge each service department with the cost of the service received from other service departments as well as charge the producing departments for the total incurred costs of all service departments is

   a. Matrix algebra.
   b. Boolean algebra.
   c. Simulation techniques.
   d. Dynamic programming.
   e. Learning curve techniques.

The correct answer is (a). *(CMA 1280 5-13)*
   REQUIRED: The allocation technique that will charge both (1) intradepartmental service costs, and (2) each producing department for the service received from every service department.
   DISCUSSION: Matrix algebra can be used to solve the system of simultaneous equations that result from the description of cost for each department. The equations are simultaneous because the costs are simultaneously allocated between service departments and producing departments.
   Answer (b) is incorrect because Boolean algebra is a technique to solve problems in logic or binary arithmetic. Answer (c) is incorrect because the simulation technique model is a process to permit analysis of the effects of changing one or more variables. Answer (d) is incorrect because dynamic programming is a method of solving a series of selected decision problems, usually involving only a few variables. Decision trees are an example of dynamic programming. Answer (e) is incorrect because learning curve techniques describe the increases in efficiency due to increasing expertise by production people.

52. A set of simultaneous equations reads:

$$6X_1 + 3X_2 = 49$$
$$12X_1 + 2X_2 = 17$$

If the equations were placed in a matrix format it would be

a. $\begin{pmatrix} X_1 \\ X_2 \end{pmatrix} \begin{pmatrix} 6 & 3 & 49 \\ 12 & 2 & 17 \end{pmatrix}$

b. $\begin{pmatrix} 6 & 3 \\ 12 & 2 \end{pmatrix} \begin{pmatrix} X_1 \\ X_2 \end{pmatrix} \begin{pmatrix} 49 \\ 17 \end{pmatrix}$

c. $\begin{pmatrix} 6 & 3 \\ 12 & 2 \end{pmatrix} \begin{pmatrix} 49 \\ 17 \end{pmatrix} \begin{pmatrix} X_1 \\ X_2 \end{pmatrix}$

d. $\begin{pmatrix} X_1 \\ X_2 \end{pmatrix} \begin{pmatrix} 6 & 3 \\ 12 & 2 \end{pmatrix} \begin{pmatrix} 49 \\ 17 \end{pmatrix}$

The correct answer is (b). *(CIA 1187 III-45)*
REQUIRED: The proper matrix format for the equations.
DISCUSSION: Systems of linear equations can often be more conveniently manipulated by using matrix notation and matrix algebra techniques. In this format, the ordered numerical coefficients of the unknowns are presented in a matrix (in this case, two rows by two columns). The variables are described by a row or, in this problem, a column vector. Finally, the right side of the system is described by a vector (here, a column) of constants.

Answer (a) is incorrect because 49 and 17 are constants, not coefficients. Answer (c) is incorrect because the variables vector and the constants vector are misplaced. Answer (d) is incorrect because the coefficients matrix and the variables vector are misplaced.

53. The Apex Fertilizer Company is planning a new formulation to appeal to the increasing market of herb growers. Each unit of the product will require 3 pounds of chemical A, 1 pound of chemical B, and 4 pounds of chemical C. The per-pound costs of chemical A are $7.95; chemical B, $3.28; and chemical C, $6.14. Which of the following matrix algebra formulations will lead to the cost of one unit of the new fertilizer?

a. $\begin{bmatrix} 7.95, & 3.28, & 6.14 \end{bmatrix} \begin{bmatrix} 3 & 0 & 0 \\ 0 & 1 & 0 \\ 0 & 0 & 4 \end{bmatrix}$

b. $\begin{bmatrix} 7.95 \\ 3.28 \\ 6.14 \end{bmatrix} \begin{bmatrix} 3, & 1, & 4 \end{bmatrix}$

c. $\begin{bmatrix} 7.95 \\ 3.28 \\ 6.14 \end{bmatrix} \begin{bmatrix} 3 \\ 1 \\ 4 \end{bmatrix}$

d. $\begin{bmatrix} 3, & 1, & 4 \end{bmatrix} \begin{bmatrix} 7.95 \\ 3.28 \\ 6.14 \end{bmatrix}$

e. $\begin{bmatrix} 3, & 1, & 4 \end{bmatrix} \begin{bmatrix} 7.95, & 3.28, & 6.14 \end{bmatrix}$

The correct answer is (d). *(CIA 581 IV-25)*
REQUIRED: The matrix algebra formulation to determine unit cost of fertilizer.
DISCUSSION: The objective is to multiply the number of pounds of each material times the cost of each material and sum the answers. This matrix appears in answer (d).

$$(3 \times 7.95) + (1 \times 3.28) + (4 \times 6.14)$$

When multiplying two matrices together, multiply the items in each row (horizontal) of the first matrix times each item in the second matrix's column (vertical), and then add the products. Here, a 1 by 3 matrix is multiplied by a 3 by 1 matrix, resulting in a 1 by 1 matrix representing the cost. Thus, the dimensions of the matrix resulting from multiplying 2 matrices together are equal to the number of rows in the first and the number of columns in the second.

Answer (a) is incorrect because a 1 by 3 matrix times a 3 by 3 matrix results in a 1 by 3 matrix, i.e., 3 separate numbers. Answer (b) is incorrect because a 3 by 1 matrix times a 1 by 3 matrix results in a 3 by 3 matrix, i.e., 9 numbers. Answer (c) is incorrect because a 3 by 1 matrix times a 3 by 1 matrix results in a 3 by 1 matrix, i.e., 3 numbers. Answer (e) is incorrect because a 1 by 3 matrix times a 1 by 3 matrix results in a 1 by 3 matrix, i.e., 3 numbers.

Module 21.6: Calculus

54. Presented below is a system of simultaneous equations.

$S_1 = 98{,}000 + .20S_2$ or $S_1 - .20S_2 = \$98{,}000$
$S_2 = 117{,}600 + .10S_1$ or $S_2 - .10S_1 = \$117{,}600$

This system may be stated in matrix form as

a. $\begin{matrix} A \\ \begin{bmatrix} 1 & -.20 \\ -.10 & 1 \end{bmatrix} \end{matrix} \begin{matrix} S \\ \begin{bmatrix} S_1 \\ S_2 \end{bmatrix} \end{matrix} = \begin{matrix} b \\ \begin{bmatrix} \$98{,}000 \\ \$117{,}600 \end{bmatrix} \end{matrix}$

b. $\begin{matrix} A \\ \begin{bmatrix} 1 & \$98{,}000 & 1 \\ -.20 & \$117{,}600 & -.10 \end{bmatrix} \end{matrix} \begin{matrix} S \\ \begin{bmatrix} S_1 \\ S_2 \end{bmatrix} \end{matrix} = \begin{matrix} b \\ \begin{bmatrix} \$98{,}000 \\ \$117{,}600 \end{bmatrix} \end{matrix}$

c. $\begin{matrix} A \\ \begin{bmatrix} 1 & S_1 & 1 \\ -.20 & S_2 & -.10 \end{bmatrix} \end{matrix} \begin{matrix} S \\ \begin{bmatrix} S_1 \\ S_2 \end{bmatrix} \end{matrix} = \begin{matrix} b \\ \begin{bmatrix} \$98{,}000 \\ \$117{,}600 \end{bmatrix} \end{matrix}$

d. $\begin{matrix} A \\ \begin{bmatrix} 1 & 1 & S_1 \\ -.20 & -.10 & S_2 \end{bmatrix} \end{matrix} \begin{matrix} S \\ \begin{bmatrix} S_1 \\ S_2 \end{bmatrix} \end{matrix} = \begin{matrix} b \\ \begin{bmatrix} \$98{,}000 \\ \$117{,}600 \end{bmatrix} \end{matrix}$

The correct answer is (a). *(CPA 1170 Q-29)*
REQUIRED: The matrix form of the simultaneous equations.
DISCUSSION: The requirement is to multiply matrix A times matrix S to equal matrix B. In matrix multiplication, one multiplies rows by columns. In answer (a), for example, multiplying the first row of A times the first (and only) column of S results in

$1 \cdot S_1 + -.20 \cdot S_2$

Multiplying the second row in A times the only column in S gives

$-.10 \cdot S_1 + 1 \cdot S_2$

The result is the original equations:

$S_1 - .20S_2 = \$98{,}000$
$S_2 - .10S_1 = \$117{,}600$.

55. For the correct matrix A in Q. 54, there exists a unique inverse matrix A^{-1}. Multiplication of the matrix A^{-1} by the matrix A will produce

a. The matrix A.
b. Another inverse matrix.
c. The correct solution to the system.
d. An identity matrix.

The correct answer is (d). *(CPA 1170 Q-30)*
REQUIRED: The product of multiplying a matrix by its inverse matrix.
DISCUSSION: In matrix operations, division is not possible as we usually know it. In lieu of division, we multiply by an inverse matrix. By definition, a matrix times its inverse will give us a "1 type" inverse, known as an identity matrix. This operation is similar to dividing one number or one variable by itself and obtaining one. An identity matrix is a matrix with zeros in all elements except the principle diagonal, which contains ones.

21.6 Calculus

56. Financial statements of a number of companies are to be analyzed for potential growth by use of a model which considers the rates of change in assets, owners' equity, and income. The most relevant quantitative technique for developing such a model is

a. Correlation analysis.
b. Differential calculus.
c. Integral calculus.
d. Program evaluation and review technique (PERT).
e. Statistical sampling.

The correct answer is (b). *(CPA 572 T-29)*
REQUIRED: The quantitative method for analyzing rates of change.
DISCUSSION: Differential calculus is used to identify the maxima or minima of nonlinear functions, which, in business and economics, are the points of revenue (profit) maximization or cost minimization. The derivative of a function measures the slope or rate of change of that function. Maxima or minima occur where the slope is equal to zero. Thus to measure rates of change, differential calculus is the appropriate technique.
Answer (a) is incorrect because it is the technique used to measure relationships between two or more variables. Answer (c) is incorrect because integral calculus is usually used in business applications to identify the area under a probability curve. Answer (d) is incorrect because it examines complex projects for processes which are critical to the timely completion of the entire project. Answer (e) is incorrect because it measures a population by examining selected items from the population.

57. The calculus operation of differentiation is used in business to

   a. Find maxima and minima.
   b. Compute the area under a curve.
   c. Separate exogenous variables.
   d. Predict product mix.

The correct answer is (a). *(CIA 587 III-48)*
REQUIRED: The use in business of the calculus operation of differentiation.
DISCUSSION: The primary business application of differential calculus is to identify the maxima and minima of curvilinear functions. In business and economics, this is the point of revenue or profit maximization (maximum) or cost minimization (minimum). Maxima or minima occur when the slope equals zero.
   Answer (b) is incorrect because it states the function of integral calculus. Answers (c) and (d) are incorrect because they are not meaningful in this context.

58. Ortega Industries has developed its sales function and its cost function for use in profit planning. Ortega can best apply these functions to profit maximization by using

   a. Markov analysis.
   b. Differential calculus.
   c. Decision tree analysis.
   d. Simulation.
   e. Regression analysis.

The correct answer is (b). *(CMA 1285 5-25)*
REQUIRED: The technique that can be used to determine profit maximization given sales and cost functions.
DISCUSSION: Differential calculus is used to identify the maxima or minima of nonlinear functions, which, in business and economics, are the points of revenue (profit) maximization or cost minimization. The derivative of a function measures the slope or rate of change of that function. Maxima or minima occur where the slope is equal to zero.
   Answer (a) is incorrect because Markov analysis is used to predict future states of nature given the current state. Answer (c) is incorrect because decision tree analysis is used to evaluate decisions that are subject to differing degrees of risk. Answer (d) is incorrect because simulation involves developing a quantitative model. Answer (e) is incorrect because regression analysis is used to find relationships among variables. In fact, regression analysis might have been used to determine the sales function and the cost function mentioned in the question.

59. The mathematical notation for the total cost function for a business is $4X^3 + 6X^2 + 2X + 10$, where X equals production volume. Which of the following is the mathematical notation for the average cost function for that business?

   a. $2(2X^2 + 3X + 2)$.
   b. $2X^3 + 3X^2 + X + 5$.
   c. $.4X^3 + .6X^2 + .2X + 1$.
   d. $4X^2 + 6X + 2 + 10/X$.

The correct answer is (d). *(CPA 1174 Q-20)*
REQUIRED: The formula for average cost function.
DISCUSSION: The average cost function equals the total cost function divided by production volume. The total cost function is $4X^3 + 6X^2 + 2X + 10$. X is the production volume. Dividing the total cost by X equals $4X^2 + 6X + 2 + 10/X$.

Module 21.6: Calculus

60. To find a minimum-cost point given a total-cost equation, the initial steps are to find the first derivative, set it equal to zero, and solve the equation. Using the solution(s) so derived, what additional steps must be taken, and what result indicates a minimum?

a. Substitute the solution(s) in the first derivative equation; a positive solution indicates a minimum.

b. Substitute the solution(s) in the first derivative equation; a negative solution indicates a minimum.

c. Substitute the solution(s) in the second derivative equation; a positive solution indicates a minimum.

d. Substitute the solution(s) in the second derivative equation; a negative solution indicates a minimum.

The correct answer is (c). *(CPA 576 T-26)*
REQUIRED: Subsequent steps in differential calculus and interpretation of results.
DISCUSSION: The steps in differential calculus are to (1) calculate the first derivative, (2) set the first derivative equal to zero and solve the equation, and (3) calculate the second derivative to determine whether it is positive or negative. If the second derivative is positive, it is a minimum. If the second derivative is negative, it is a maximum. The second derivative of a function is the derivative of the first derivative of a function.
  Answers (a) and (b) are nonsensical repetitions. Answer (d) is incorrect because a negative solution indicates a maximum.

61. The mathematical notation for the average cost function for a business is $6X^3 + 4X^2 + 2X + 8 + 2/X$, where X equals production volume. What would be the mathematical notation for the total cost function for the business?

a. The average cost function multiplied by X.

b. The average cost function divided by X.

c. The average cost function divided by X/2.

d. The first derivative of the average cost function.

The correct answer is (a). *(CPA 1176 P-30)*
REQUIRED: The formula for the total cost function.
DISCUSSION: Total cost is average cost times production volume. The average cost function is $6X^3 + 4X^2 + 2X + 8 + 2/X$. Production volume = X. Multiplying the given average cost function by X thus results in the total cost function:

$$X(6X^3 + 4X^2 + 2X + 8 + 2/X)$$

62. The mathematical notation for the total cost for a business is $2X^3 + 4X^2 + 3X + 5$, where X equals production volume. Which of the following is the mathematical notation for the marginal cost function for this business?

a. $2(X^3 + 2X^2 + 1.5X + 2.5)$.

b. $6X^2 + 8X + 3$.

c. $2X^3 + 4X^2 + 3X$.

d. $3X + 5$.

The correct answer is (b). *(CPA 1175 P-33)*
REQUIRED: The formula for the marginal cost function.
DISCUSSION: The total cost function is $2X^3 + 4X^2 + 3X + 5$. Production volume = X. The marginal cost function notation is determined by taking the first derivative of the total cost function notation. The derivative of a function is found using the formula nx^{n-1}; multiply the coefficient of the term by the exponent and reduce the exponent by one. All constants are dropped. The marginal cost function is thus $6X^2 + 8X + 3$.

63. A second derivative that is positive and large at a critical point (i.e., within the relevant range) indicates

a. An important maximum.

b. An unimportant maximum.

c. An important minimum.

d. An unimportant minimum.

e. None of the above.

The correct answer is (c). *(CPA 1171 P-33)*
REQUIRED: Interpretation of a large positive second derivative at a critical point.
DISCUSSION: A positive second derivative indicates that the function is at a minimum. The critical point implies an important minimum, i.e., the point is critical from the context of the problem, not from a math context.

Module 21.6: Calculus

> Questions 64 through 67 are based on MacKenzie Park, which sells trivets for $.25 per unit and during the year reported net sales of $500,000 and net income of $35,000. Production capacity is limited to 15,000 trivets per day and trivets are produced 300 days each year. Variable costs are $.10 per trivet. The company does not maintain an inspection system but has an agreement to reimburse the wholesaler $.50 for each defective unit the wholesaler finds. The wholesaler uses a method of inspection which detects all defective units. The number of defective units in each lot of 300 units is equal to the daily unit production rate divided by 200. Let X equal daily production in units.

64. The number of defective units per day could be expressed as

a. X/60,000
b. (200/X) x (X/300)
c. X/500
d. X^2/60,000

The correct answer is (d). *(CPA 570 P-11)*
REQUIRED: The expression of the number of defective units per day.
DISCUSSION: The number of defective units per day is equal to the number of production lots which is (X/300) times the daily unit production divided by 200 which is (X/200), or X^2/60,000.

$$\frac{X}{300} \times \frac{X}{200} = \frac{X^2}{60,000}$$

65. The equation to compute the maximum daily contribution to profit, including the reimbursement to the wholesaler for defective units, could be expressed as

a. .25X - .10X - .50X/60,000
b. .25X - .10X - .50X^2/60,000
c. .25X - .10X - $\frac{X^2}{60,000}$ - $\frac{125,000}{300}$
d. .25X - .10X - X/60,000 - 125,000

The correct answer is (b). *(CPA 570 P-12)*
REQUIRED: The equation to compute the maximum daily contribution to profit.
DISCUSSION: The daily contribution to profit (thus ignoring fixed cost) would be sales minus variable costs. Sales equals $.25 times the number of units produced. Variable cost is $.10 per unit produced. The cost of defective units is $.50 times the number of daily defective units (X^2 divided by 60,000 from Q. 64). Thus the answer is

.25X - .10X - .50X^2/60,000

66. The first derivative of the equation to determine the number of units to maximize daily profits could be expressed

a. .25 - .10 - X/60,000
b. .10 - .25 - X^2/60,000
c. X^2/60,000
d. X/(200)(300)

The correct answer is (a). *(CPA 570 P-13)*
REQUIRED: The equation for the number of units to maximize daily profits.
DISCUSSION: The first derivative measures the slope or rate of change of a function. Setting the first derivative equal to zero determines a maxima or minima. Thus, given a cost or profit function (the independent variable being production or sales), one can determine the activity level to maximize profit or minimize costs. You find the derivative of a function with the formula nx^{n-1}; i.e., you multiply the coefficient of the term by the exponent and reduce the exponent by one. All constants are dropped, e.g., the derivative of 3 + X^6 is 6X^5.
The notation for derivative is f'(X).

$$f'(.25X) = .25$$
$$f'(-.10X) = -.10$$
$$f'(.50X^2/60,000) = 2(-.50X^{2-1}/60,000)$$
$$= -X/60,000$$

67. The second derivative of the equation to determine the number of units to be produced daily to maximize profits would be

a. 1/(200)(300)
b. $.25 - $.10 - 1/60,000 - $125,000
c. $125,000/60,000
d. -1/60,000

BLANK PAGE

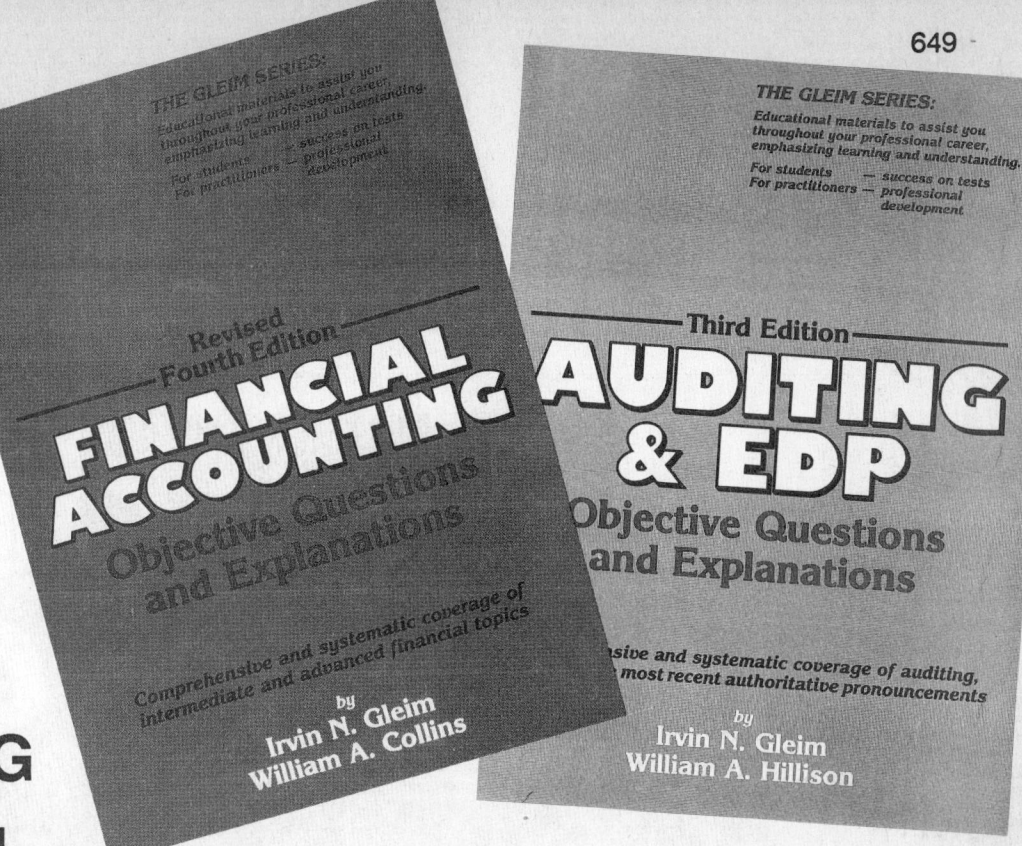

SUCCESSFUL CAREERS IN ACCOUNTING BEGIN WITH THE GLEIM SERIES OF OBJECTIVE QUESTIONS AND EXPLANATIONS . . .

... AND CONTINUE THROUGH
MULTIPLE CERTIFICATION PROGRAMS

BOOKS AVAILABLE FROM ACCOUNTING PUBLICATIONS, INC.

THE GLEIM SERIES

OBJECTIVE QUESTIONS AND EXPLANATIONS STUDY BOOKS

To help accounting and business law students and professional accountants, we have developed a series of five objective question study manuals. The books in the series cover

**AUDITING & EDP • FINANCIAL ACCOUNTING • FEDERAL TAX
MANAGERIAL ACCOUNTING • BUSINESS LAW/LEGAL STUDIES**

Each manual is a comprehensive, carefully organized compendium of 1,900 to 2,200 objective questions taken from past CPA, CIA, CMA, and other professional certification exams. Where appropriate, questions have been modified to reflect changes in the law, authoritative pronouncements, etc. Hundreds of author-developed questions have been added to each book to assure complete coverage of the topics, not just what has been tested on previous professional exams.

Our exclusive answer explanations (why the right answer is correct; why the wrong answers are incorrect) appear to the immediate right of the questions to eliminate the wasted effort of turning pages back and forth. Because the questions are so comprehensive, each book provides "programmed learning." In addition to helping you learn faster and more easily, these books help you improve your college examination scores and look ahead to professional examinations.

The questions in each book are organized by topic in "modules" within each chapter. The tables of contents of most related textbooks are presented and cross-referenced to the modules in each respective *OBJECTIVE QUESTION AND EXPLANATION* book. As you study a particular chapter in your own text, you know exactly where relevant questions appear in your *OBJECTIVE QUESTION AND EXPLANATION* book. Additionally, each book has a detailed index to assist you in locating questions relevant to the particular topic you are studying.

OTHER BOOKS

CIA EXAMINATION REVIEW, *CMA EXAMINATION REVIEW,* and *CPA EXAMINATION REVIEW* are each two-volume, comprehensive study programs designed to prepare you to pass the CIA (Certified Internal Auditor), CMA (Certified Management Accounting), and CPA (Certified Public Accountant) examinations.

Each set of books contains structured, point-by-point coverage of all material tested, and clear and concise phraseology to help you understand and remember the concepts. They also explain the respective certification programs, introduce you to examination preparation and grading procedures, and help you organize your examination strategy. In addition, these books contain past exam questions (the multiple-choice questions are, of course, accompanied by our exclusive answer explanations).

HOW TO ORDER THESE BOOKS

Any of the books described above can be obtained by completing the order form on page 652 and mailing it to us. All prepaid mail orders are shipped postpaid (i.e., we pay postage) within one day of receipt.

ACCOUNTING PUBLICATIONS, INC. • P.O. Box 12848 • Gainesville, FL 32604 • (904) 375-0772

"THE GLEIM SERIES" OBJECTIVE QUESTION AND EXPLANATION BOOKS

AUDITING & EDP	(720 pages • 1,847 questions)	$14.95	$_____
BUSINESS LAW/LEGAL STUDIES	(800 pages • 1,928 questions)	$14.95	$_____
FEDERAL TAX	(768 pages • 2,380 questions)	$14.95	$_____
FINANCIAL ACCOUNTING	(736 pages • 1,835 questions)	$14.95	$_____
MANAGERIAL ACCOUNTING	(672 pages • 1,967 questions)	$14.95	$_____

CIA EXAMINATION REVIEW (3rd Edition, published February 1989)

VOLUME I: Outlines & Study Guides	(784 pages)	$21.95	$_____
VOLUME II: Problems & Solutions	(776 pages)	$21.95	$_____
1990 CIA UPDATING EDITION	(304 pages)	$15.95	$_____
All three of the above CIA books	(save $9.95)	$49.90	$_____

CMA EXAMINATION REVIEW (4th Edition, available August 1990)

VOLUME I: Outlines & Study Guides	(800 pages)	$23.95	$_____
VOLUME II: Problems & Solutions	(800 pages)	$23.95	$_____

CPA EXAMINATION REVIEW (published by John Wiley & Sons, Inc.)

TWO-VOLUME SET *(17th Edition, published June 1990)*

Volume I: Outlines & Study Guides	(1,398 pages)	$35.95	$_____
Volume II: Problems & Solutions	(1,154 pages)	$35.95	$_____

THREE-VOLUME SET *(published January 1990)*

Auditing	(622 pages)	$24.95	$_____
Business Law	(570 pages)	$24.95	$_____
Theory and Practice	(1,472 pages)	$34.95	$_____

Florida Residents must add applicable sales tax .... $_____
Foreign Surcharge (call or write for charges) .... $_____
Payment must be in U.S. dollars and payable on a U.S. bank .... TOTAL $_____

---

1. We process and ship orders daily, generally 1 day after receipt of your order.

2. Please PHOTOCOPY this order form as necessary.

3. No CODs. All mail orders from individuals must be prepaid and are protected by our unequivocal refund policy.
   Library and company orders may be purchased on account.
   Shipping charges will be added to telephone orders and to orders not prepaid.

4. Accounting Publications, Inc. guarantees immediate, complete refund on all mail orders if resalable texts are returned in 30 days.

NAME (please print) _____

ADDRESS _____

CITY _____ STATE ___ ZIP _____

___ MasterCard   ___ VISA   ___ Check/Money Order

MC/VISA No ____ - ____ - ____ - ____

Exp. Date ___/___ Mo. / Yr.

Signature _____

Accounting Publications, Inc.

(904) 375-0772
Post Office Box 12848
University Station
Gainesville, Florida
32604

Gleim's
Continuing Professional Education
TWO NEW SELF-STUDY FORMATS

WHY: To provide an alternative to conventional CPE delivery:
- Interactive
- Programmed learning
- Effective
- Challenging
- Easy-to-use *(see p. 654)*
- Broad coverage

WHERE: Wherever you can carry two books weighing less than 4 lbs. - home, office, train, plane, etc. No inconvenient out-of-town travel and expense.

WHEN: Whenever you have available time. Study may be completed at your own pace in any time segments, long or short.

COST: A few dollars per CPE credit hour.

PRESENTATION METHODS: *Objective Question "Quizzer" Format* -- for review and reinforcement of basic-intermediate knowledge, completely updated to reflect the most recent authoritative pronouncements, tax law, etc.
Outline - Illustration - True/False Study Question Format -- for new topics such as tax law revisions and new authoritative pronouncements.

APPROVED CPE: Our certificate of completion is accepted by all boards of accountancy, the Accreditation Council for Accountancy, the U.S. Department of Treasury, California and Oregon Tax Preparer Programs, Institute of Internal Auditors, Institute of Certified Management Accountants, and others. We currently interact with 60 accounting related agencies that require CPE in the U.S.

VARIOUS CPE RULES: Most of the 60 agencies have their own rules regarding what types and topics of CPE are acceptable, and also how to measure them. Not all agencies accept all of our courses. Call us for assistance:
(800) 87-GLEIM.

AUTHORS: Irvin N. Gleim, Terry L. Campbell, William A. Collins, Dale Flesher, Holger D. Gleim, William A. Hillison, Sandra S. Kramer, Jordan B. Ray. All are professional educators.

NO RISK: Order a program today -- look it over carefully; return it for a refund if you are not completely satisfied.

SATISFACTION GUARANTEED: Unequivocal, immediate, complete refund if resalable course materials are returned in 30 days.

EXPIRATION DATE: One year or 30 days after you are notified of program retirement by first class mail, whichever occurs later.

FIVE CPE PROGRAMS
USING OBJECTIVE QUESTION FORMAT

These CPE programs constitute a totally new approach to CPE. The courses are based on self-diagnosing objective questions. They are designed to meet the needs of practitioners by providing low-cost, easy-to-use, effective CPE.

All of these programs provide you with an opportunity to review and study a wide range of topics.

- First, they provide a self-diagnosis of your knowledge.

- Second, they constitute a review and study of the professional and technical standards that have come to be the basic proficiency package expected of CPAs. As such, each individual course is a formal program of learning that contributes directly to your professional competence.

- Third, they are interactive in the sense that you must continually respond to multiple-choice or true-false questions. Thus, you challenge yourself to do well. When you have difficulty, a thorough, easy-to-understand explanation is provided.

- Fourth, these courses are organized in a programmed learning format through a careful ordering of questions, i.e., from general to specific, easy to difficult, etc.

EASY TO USE

With each program, you receive:

1. Objective Question and Explanation Study Book
2. CPE Book of final exam questions
3. Machine-readable final exam answer sheet *
4. Complete, easy-to-follow instructions

- You study the questions and explanations in the Objective Question and Explanation Study Book when and where you want.

- Then, you take a final exam (open book) using our machine-readable answer sheet.

- Lastly, you return the answer sheet to use for grading, and if you score 70% or above, we will send you a certificate of completion.

* In each program, you have the option of taking all of the courses, just one course, or any combination of courses. All of the courses in a single program can be completed at no additional charge by using the one answer sheet provided with each program. If you want to obtain CPE credit for a few courses at a time, there is a $15 grading fee (additional answer sheet) for each subsequent submission.

AUDITING & EDP CPE **$75**
8 separate courses with up to 46 CPE hours
1. Audit Environment, Standards, and Ethics 7
2. Internal Control 5
3. Audit Evidence and Procedures 8
4. Electronic Data Processing 8
5. Statistical Sampling 3
6. Audit Reports 7
7. Special Reports and Other Reporting Issues 3
8. Internal Auditing 5

BUSINESS LAW CPE **$60**
11 separate courses with up to 48 CPE hours
1. Our Legal System and Environment 5
2. Torts, Consumer Law, and Accountants' Liability 4
3. Contracts 5
4. Sales, International Law, and Ethics 4
5. Commercial Paper and Antitrust 4
6. Property and Computer Law 5
7. Assurance of Creditors' Interests 4
8. Corporations and Securities Regulation 5
9. Insurance and Bankruptcy 4
10. Estate Planning, Employment Regulation, and
    Environmental Law 4
11. Agency and Partnerships 4

FEDERAL TAX CPE **$95**
16 separate courses with up to 57 CPE hours
1. Gross Income and Exclusions 4
2. Business Expenses and Losses 3
3. Investment and Personal Deductions 4
4. Individual Loss Limits, Tax Calculations, and Credits .. 4
5. Property I 4
6. Property II 4
7. Partnerships 4
8. Corporate Formations and Operations 5
9. Advanced Corporate Topics 4
10. Accounting Methods and Employment Taxes 4
11. Estates, Trusts, and Wealth Transfer Taxes 4
12. Tax Preparer Rules, Process, and Procedure 3
1988 Tax Law Changes
13. TAMRA: Individuals 3
14. TAMRA: Losses, Depreciation, Credits, Accounting Changes .. 3
15. TAMRA: Trusts and Estates 2
16. TAMRA: Corporations 2

FINANCIAL ACCOUNTING CPE **$75**
13 separate courses with up to 46 CPE hours
1. Basic Concepts and the Accounting Process 4
2. Current Assets 4
3. Noncurrent Assets 4
4. Current and Noncurrent Liabilities 3
5. Present Value, Pensions, and Leases 4
6. Shareholders' Equity and EPS 4
7. Income Tax Allocation, Accounting Changes, Error Corrections .. 2
8. Financial Statements and Disclosures 3
9. Statement Analysis, Interim Statements, and Segment Reporting .. 4
10. Equity Method and Business Combinations 5
11. Price-Level Changes and Foreign Exchange 2
12. Government and Nonprofit Accounting 4
13. Specialized Industry and Partnership Accounting 3

MANAGERIAL ACCOUNTING CPE **$60**
11 separate courses with up to 43 CPE hours
1. Cost Accounting Overview and Job Order Costing 4
2. Process Costing; Spoilage, Waste, & Scrap 4
3. Joint Products and By-Products 2
4. Service Cost Allocations and Direct Costing 3
5. Cost-Volume-Profit Analysis 5
6. Budgeting and Responsibility Accounting 4
7. Standard Costs 6
8. Nonroutine Decisions and Inventory Models 4
9. Capital Budgeting 4
10. Probability and Statistics; Regression Analysis 4
11. Linear Programming and Other Quantitative Approaches .. 3

FIVE CPE PROGRAMS USING OUTLINES, EXAMPLES, AND TRUE/FALSE STUDY QUESTIONS FORMAT

PASSIVE LOSS RULES CPE $50
4 separate courses with up to 8 CPE hours

- Course 1 - Passive Activities, Taxpayers, Material Participation
  Course 2 - Passive Activity Income and Loss
  Course 3 - Loss Limitations, Carryovers, and Credits
  Course 4 - Rental Activities

- Limitations on the deduction of losses from passive activities are a result of the Tax Reform Act of 1986. The IRS has issued some 70 pages of regulations which go beyond and contain far more detail than discussed in the Code, Committee Reports, or even the explanation prepared by Staff of the Joint Committee on Taxation.

- Now you can master the requirements of this complex labyrinth of law and regulation with easy-to-read outlines and hundreds of clear and concise examples. These outlines do NOT follow the confusing format of the regulations. They are organized to take you from beginning concepts right through to ultimate use of disallowed losses in an easy-to-follow modular breakdown.

- DO NOT be fooled. The passive loss rules apply to much more than tax shelters. You need to know how they apply and how to use them for any taxpayer who rents property, is a sole proprietor of a business, is a partner, or is a shareholder of an S corporation, personal service corporation, or closely held corporation.

- A detailed index is provided.

1988 TAX LAW (TAMRA) CHANGES
These are courses 13-16 in FEDERAL TAX CPE (see opposite page)

The Technical and Miscellaneous Revenue Act of 1988 (TAMRA) is presented in outline format for ease of understanding this new tax law. Also included are the relevant areas of the Family Support Act of 1988 and the Medicare Catastrophic Coverage Act of 1988.

SAS 52-61 UPDATE CPE $50
2 separate courses each with 4 CPE hours

- Course 1: SASs 52, 53, 54, 55, 56
- Course 2: SASs 57, 58, 59, 60, 61
- These are the new "expectation gap" standards issued in the Spring of 1988 with effective dates of January 1989, except SAS 55, which becomes effective January 1990.

CMA CPE $125
Tentative course listing; total hours approximately 88

- **BROADEN YOUR BACKGROUND:** Comparable to a mini-MBA program, this will assist you both in your own business endeavors and with your clients. It is more user-oriented with respect to financial statements instead of preparer-oriented.

- **BECOME A CMA:** CMA stands for Certified Management Accountant. This CMA CPE program will thoroughly prepare you for the CMA exam as you earn CPE credits.

33. *The CMA Examination: Exam Grading and Self-Study

PART 1: ECONOMICS, FINANCE, AND MANAGEMENT
1. Microeconomics
2. Macroeconomics
3. International Economics
4. Institutional Environment of Business
5. Working Capital Finance
6. Capital Structure Finance
7. Organization Theory
8. Motivation and the Directing Process
9. Planning and Budgeting
10. Communication
11. Ethics and the Management Accountant

PART 2: FINANCIAL ACCOUNTING AND REPORTING
12. Financial Accounting: Development of Theory and Practice
13. Financial Statement Presentation
14. Special Financial Reporting Problems
15. Ratio Analysis
16. The SEC
17. Internal Control
18. External Auditing
19. Income Taxes

PART 3: MANAGEMENT REPORTING, ANALYSIS, AND BEHAVIORAL ISSUES
20. Process and Job Order Costing
21. Direct (Variable) Costing
22. Budgeting and Responsibility Accounting
23. The Controlling Process
24. Standard Costs and Variance Analysis

PART 4: DECISION ANALYSIS AND INFORMATION SYSTEMS
25. Incremental Costing
26. Cost-Volume-Profit Analysis
27. Capital Budgeting
28. Decision Making Under Uncertainty
29. Inventory Models
30. Quantitative Methods
31. Information Systems
32. Internal and Operational Auditing

*Course 33 covers Chapters 1 through 4 of Volume I of CMA EXAMINATION REVIEW. It should be completed before any of the other courses are taken.

WHY SELF STUDY ?

COST/BENEFIT: Formal correspondence courses have the greatest potential to help participants learn more (and with better results) at a lower cost. Travel is expensive. So are rooms and good lecturers.

MORE EFFICIENT

1. The cost of formal correspondence course preparation and delivery is largely fixed. Once a course is developed into textual, audio-video, CBI, etc., the cost of incremental courses is negligible. We produce interactive correspondence courses for most "general" CPE courses so as to cost participants $6 or less per credit hour. CBI prior to widespread use of laser disks will be slightly higher, e.g., $10 per credit hour.

2. Travel costs (including travel time) are eliminated by formal correspondence courses.

3. Formal correspondence courses are convenient -- they can be undertaken when and where the participant desires. This flexibility can save practitioners many billable hours and also results in better (and more timely) service to clients.

4. Textual self-study CPE materials should constitute excellent reference books (ours do!) at no additional cost.

5. Most CPAs relied heavily on self-study to prepare for the CPA exam (even if they took a review course) and thus are experienced at using self-study textual material.

MORE EFFECTIVE

1. Formal correspondence courses require individual study and effort in contrast to merely being "in attendance."

2. When formal correspondence courses are interactive, they provide more opportunity for individual participation than most seminars and professional conferences. We use true/false study questions to ask participants questions that they need to be asked. We also include questions that participants should be asking and then answer them.

3. The AICPA Standards for CPE Reporting require self-study programs to provide evidence of completion (e.g., completed workbook or examination) and a certificate of completion supplied by the sponsor.

The existence of a "final examination," whether in workbook or exam mode, is excellent motivation for participants to study and learn versus simply becoming familiar with the subject matter, as occurs at many CPE seminars and professional conference CPE programs.

.... Detach and order today -or- Call (800) 87-GLEIM ....

Accounting Publications Inc

Post Office Box 12848
University Station
Gainesville, Florida 32604
(800) 87-GLEIM

CPE Programs Available

AUDITING & EDP .... @ $75.00 $ _____

SAS 52-61 UPDATE .... @ $50.00 _____

BUSINESS LAW .... @ $60.00 _____

FEDERAL TAX .... @ $95.00 _____

PASSIVE LOSS RULES .... @ $50.00 _____

FINANCIAL ACCOUNTING .... @ $75.00 _____

MANAGERIAL ACCOUNTING .... @ $60.00 _____

CERTIFIED MANAGEMENT ACCOUNTANT .... @ $125.00 _____

Add applicable sales tax for shipments within Florida .... $ _____

TOTAL $ _____

Please type or print legibly. This information is used to establish a permanent record for maintaining your progress and mailing certificates of completion.

NAME *(please print)* _____

Social Security No. ___ ___ ___ - ___ ___ - ___ ___ ___ ___
(for CPE record keeping purposes only)

Address _____

_____

City _____ State _____ Zip _____

Check enclosed ___   Credit Card ___   Bill Me ___   *(add $5 S & H)*

MasterCard/VISA #   Exp. Date ___/___ *(Month/Year)*

___ ___ ___ ___ - ___ ___ ___ ___ - ___ ___ ___ ___ - ___ ___ ___ ___

Signature _____

No CODs. We pay the shipping costs on prepaid mail orders. Shipping and handling charges will be added to telephone orders and to orders that are not prepaid. Accounting Publications guarantees the immediate, complete refund on all mail orders if resalable materials are returned within 30 days.

INDEX

Abbreviations in this book 7
Absorption
   Costing 58, 62
   Manufacturing costs 221
   vs. variable costing 207
Acceptance sampling 543
Accounting rate of return 469
Activity bases, overhead 78
Additional processing costs, joint products ... 188
After-tax cash flow 476
Algebra, matrix 641
Allocation, joint cost 163
American Institute of CPAs 25, 34
Anderson and Lievano 2, 18
Annual
   Overhead application rate 78
   Profit plan 290
Answering technique, multiple-choice 21
Applications, spoilage 145
Arithmetic progression 641
Attribute sampling 543
Auto correlation 583
Avoidable costs 65

Bail-out payback period 506
Basic
   Standards 333
   Variables, simplex tableau 616
Bayesian statistics 589
Bernoulli process 641
Bierman, Bonini, Hausman 2, 18
Bimodal distribution 568
Binomial distribution 546
Boolean algebra 641
Bottom-up budgeting 404
Breakeven
   Equation 223, 227
   Problems, basic 231
   Multiproduct 250
Budget
   Definitions 289
   Director 292
   Master 289
   Operating 291
   Participation 290
   Variance, fixed overhead 339
Budgetary accounting 399
Budgeting 45, 289
   Computations 297
   Zero-base 293
Budgets, not-for-profit organizations 289
Budnick, Mojena, Vollmann 3, 19
Byproducts 161

Calculations
   Cost allocation 195
   Variable costing 212
Calculus 643
Capacity price 601
Capital
   Budgeting 467
   Intensive industry 78
   Turnover 407

CASB 70
Cash
   Collection budgeting 301
   Disbursement budgeting 301
   Discounts 50
   Flow calculations 495
CB column, simplex 617
C chart 545
Central
   Limit theory 549
   Tendency 537
Centralization 404
   vs. decentralization 409
Certification
   Cost 35
   Exams 23
   Programs 25, 26
   When to take 36
Chapter cross references 7
Chi-square 546
CIA
   Certification program 25
   Exam content 27
   Examination registration 36
   Examination Review 38
   Pass rates 32
   Student exam fee 37
C_i row, simplex 617
CMA
   Certification program 25
   Exam content 27
   Examination registration 37
   Examination Review 38
   Pass rates 32
   Student exam fee 38
Coefficient of
   Correlation 582, 590
   Determination 584
Committed costs 66
Common costs 67
CPA
   Certification program 25
   Exam content 27
   Examination Review 38
   Requirements, state 40
CPE requirements, CIA, CMA, CPA 35
CPM 515
CVP
   Analysis 223
   Assumptions 228
   Capital budgeting 497
   Comprehensive 265
   Concepts 223
   Equation 227
   Problems 265
   Spoilage 152
   Standard costs 379
   Variables, changes in 236
Computational problems 6
Computations, inventory control 526
Computer simulation, CVP 230
Conditional
   Cost 560
   Probability 535

657

Index

Confidence interval 542
    Regression 584
Constant
    Order-cycle system 516
    Variance, regression 584
Constraint function
    Formula 608
    Slope, LP 605
Constraints 599
Continuous
    Distribution 546, 568
    Profit plan 296
Contribution
    Margin 62, 209
    Margin ratio 227
    Margin volume variance 361
    To profit, CVP 234
Control
    Accounting 399
    Loop 45
    Systems 45, 47
Controllable
    Costs 63, 65, 399
    Variance 341
Controllers 47
Conversion costs 52, 59, 110, 133
Correlation
    Analysis 627
    And regression analysis 545
Cost
    Allocation 189
    Allocation base 191
    Behavior 400
    Benefit accounting 399
    Benefit ratio, capital budgeting 483
    Definitions, other 62
    Flow between accounts 74
    Objectives 190
    Of capital 478
    Of capital, weighted average 478
    Of financing 479
    Of goods manufactured 48
    Of goods sold 48, 88
    Of production report 160
    Pools 190
    Transferred out 105
Cost Accounting
    Standards Board 70
    Terminology 43
    Texts 2, 7
Cost vs. managerial accounting 43
Cost/volume/profit analysis 223
Costing, process 109
Critical path method 515, 632
Cross references, chapters 7
Cross-sectional
    Analysis 544
    Data, regression 586
Cumulative cash flow 476
Currently attainable standards 333
Curvilinear relationship 580

Davis and McKeown 3, 19
Deakin and Maher 2, 8
DeCoster and Schaefer 2, 7
Decentralization 409
    vs. centralization 409
Decentralized company 411

Decision
    Model 626
    Tree analysis 571, 644
Defective units 145
Definitions
    Probability and statistics 535
    Spoilage 141
Degrees of freedom 553
Departmental performance 404
Dependent variable 573
Descriptive statistics 538
Differential
    Calculus 545, 643
    Costs 68
Direct
    Costs 46, 58, 69, 203
    Labor usage variance 368
    Manufacturing costs 221
    Materials price variance 324, 366
    Materials purchased 88
    Method, cost allocation 191
Discontinuing departments 406
Discounted cash flow techniques 470
Discovery sampling 543
Discrete vs. continuous distribution 550
Discretionary costs 66
Dispersion 538
Divisional ROI 408
Dominiak and Louderback 2, 8
Dynamic programming 578, 599

Earnings reinvestment 473
Education requirements, CIA, CMA, CPA 35
Efficiency variance 317, 345
Ending work-in-process inventory 102
Engineering standards for OH allocation 318
Engler 2, 9
EOQ formula 521
Equivalent units of production 115
Error term, regression 575
Essay questions 6
EUP 115
    Analysis 115
    Formula 120
Examination pass rates 32
Excess
    Capacity 64
    Present value index 513
Expected
    Annual capacity 79
    Costs 560
    Value 432, 555
Exponential smoothing 593

Factory overhead 52, 57, 60, 77
    Applied 80
    Closing entries 84
    Control 80
Feasible production area, LP 606
Feedback 44
    Report, responsibility accounting 401
FIFO
    EUP calculation 123
    vs. weighted average EUP 118
Financial
    Accounting 43, 49
    Analysis 441
    Budget 291

Index

Financing cost 479
First derivative, calculus 645
Fischer and Frank 2, 9
Fixed
    And variable costs separation 588
    Budget 294
    Costs 52
    Costs, service department allocation 193
Flexible
    Budgeting 294, 399
    Budget variance 317
Forecasting 292
Formula, EUP 120
Formulation, linear programming 606
Full
    Absorption costing 207
    Cost 53
    Cost based transfer price 411
    Direct labor costs 102
Future value 468

Game theory 576
Garrison 2, 9
General
    Concepts, capital budgeting 467
    Overhead/operating departments 191
Geometric progression 641
Goal congruence 404, 411
Goals and objectives 290
Graphs, linear programming 603
Gross profit method 50
Gross margin 207

Hartley 2, 10
Heteroscedasticity 586
High-low calculations, CVP 230
Hirsch and Louderback 2, 10
Homoscedasticity 586
Horngren and Foster 2, 11
Hurdle rate of return 481
Hypergeometric distribution 546
Hypothesis testing 538, 551

Ideal standards 333
Idle capacity variance 346
Immaterial variance, treatment 321
Imposed budgeting 404
Imputed costs 55, 65
Incremental costs 55
Independence of error terms, regression 585
Independent
    Events 536
    Variable 573
Indirect costs 69
Inferential statistics 538
Input/output
    Analysis 588
    Variance analysis 319
Inspection point, spoilage 149
Institute of
    CMAs 35
    Internal Auditors 34
Internal rate of return 490
Integral calculus 643
Inventoriable costs 57

Inventory
    Carrying costs 518
    Costing policy 516
    Obsolescence costs 518
    Planning and control 515
    Turnover ratio 517
Investment center 400
Irrelevant costs 435
IRR model 474

JIT costing system 72
Job
    Balancing ABC system 515
    Cost sheet 73
    Order costing 71, 100
Joint
    Costs 68
    Cost allocation 163
    Probability 535
    Product profitability 178
    Products 161, 184
Journal entries
    Job order 99
    Joint products 179
    Spoilage 150
    Standard costs 372
Just-in-time 71, 74

Kellough and Leiminger 2, 12

Labor
    Efficiency variance 330, 383
    Intensive industry 78
    Mix variance 337
    Price variance 383
    Quantity variance 383
    Rate variance 394
    Standard costs 331
    Variance formula 331
    Yield variance 337
Lead times for orders 515
Learning curves 542, 638
Least squares
    Formula 592
    Method, CVP 230
Levin, Rubin, Stinson 3, 19
Linear
    Algebra 471
    Programming 519, 599
    Programming graphs 603
Longest-time path, CPM 635
Loss, spoilage 147
LP concepts 599

Make or buy 427
Management
    Accountants 44
    By exception 45, 293, 401
    Process, basic 44
Managerial
    Accounting 43
    Accounting texts 2, 7
    Effort 410

Index

Manufacturing
- Account 43, 48
- Costing, direct 221
- Costs, absorption 221

Margin of safety 225

Marginal
- Costs 54
- Revenue per unit 237

Market
- Price 601
- Share variance 360

Markland and Sweigert 3, 20

Markov
- Analysis 600, 627
- Chains 540, 632

Master budget 289

Material
- Requirements planning 515, 600
- Usage variance 325

Materials
- Mix variance 330
- Price variance 321
- Quantity variance 381
- Standard costs 322
- Yield variance 330

Matrix algebra 555
Maxima, calculus 643
Maximum efficiency standards 333
Mean 536
Median 536
Minima, calculus 643

Mix
- Costs 161
- Variance, labor 337
- Variance, materials 330
- Variance, sales 359

Mode 536
Modules 3
Monte Carlo simulations 540
Moore, Anderson, Jaedicke 2, 12
Moriarity and Allen 2, 13
Morse and Roth 2, 14
Morse, Davis, Hartgraves 2, 13
Moscove, Crowningshield, Gorman 2, 14
Motivation 411
Moving average 593

Multicollinearity 583
- Regression 583

Multiple
- Calculations, regression 592
- Regression 576, 583

Multiple-choice
- Answering technique 21
- Exams 23

Multiple-step income statements 400
Multiproduct breakeven 250
Mutually exclusive events 535

National Association of Accountants 47

Net
- Present value 480
- Realizable value, joint products 175

Network 600
- Problem models 632

Nonmanufacturing organization, cost process . 72
Noncontrollable costs 399
Nonfinancial issues 441

Nonlinear
- Analysis 599
- Relationship 573

Nonparametric statistics 538, 629
Nonroutine decisions 427

Normal
- Capacity 79
- Capacity for OH allocation 318
- Distribution 546
- Spoilage, inconsistent 143

NPV method 474
Null hypothesis 551

Objective
- Distribution 568
- Function 599
- Function slope, LP 605
- Questions answering technique 21
- Questions sources 3
- Questions uniqueness 5

One-tailed test 551
Operating budget 291
Operation costing 112
Operations research 632
- Accounting 399

Opportunity cost 55, 64, 433
Optimal capital budget 473

Order
- Filling costs 515
- Getting costs 515
- Of questions 4
- Placing costs 519
- Point, inventory 518

Other applications, probability and stats. .. 566
Out-of-pocket costs 54, 64, 68
Overapplied factory overhead 80

Overhead
- Application rate 77
- Rate 150
- Spending variance 346
- Standard costs 340
- Volume variance 365

Overview of certification program 25

Parabolic 580
Parameter 536
Parametric statistic 629
Participative budgeting 405
Pass rates, examination 32

Payback
- Capital budgeting 474
- Method 470
- Reciprocal 507

Payoff
- Matrix 558
- Table 558

P chart 545
Perfect information, value of 539

Performance
- Analysis 289
- Evaluation 402

Period costs, expense 51, 57, 203
Perpetual inventory methods 69
PERT 519
PERT/CPM analysis 555
Pessimistic time estimate, CPM 635

Index

Planned activity level 343
Planning 293
    Calendar, budgeting 290
Plant-wide overhead rates 191
Poisson 546
    Analysis 576
    Distribution 546, 641
Polimeni, Fabozzi, Adelberg 2, 15
Pools, cost 190
PPBS 294
Practical capacity 79
Predetermined overhead rate 55, 111
Present value 468
    Method 470
    Tables 493
Price variance 317
Prime
    Costing 204
    Costs 52, 59
Probabilistic 580
Probability
    And statistics 535
    Distributions 546
    Theory 540
Process costing 109, 132
Processing decisions, joint products 177
Product
    Costing 164, 203
    Mix 223
    vs. period costs 57
Production
    Cost report 113
    Report, cost of 160
    Report, quantity of 160
    Volume variance 345
Profit
    Center 400
    Plan, continuous 296
    Volume chart 226
Profitability index 482
Program
    Budgeting 399
    Evaluation review techniques 519
    Planning and budgeting system 294
Project selection 469

Quality control standards 143
Quantitative
    Approaches, other 625
    Method texts 2, 7, 18
Quantity
    Of production report 160
    Variance, sales 359
Question order 4
Queuing theory 471, 519, 542, 576, 630

Random sampling 544
Ratio sampling 543
Rayburn 2, 15
R chart 545
Reciprocal method, cost allocation 191
Regression
    Definitions 573
    Interpretation 589
    Relationships 578
Relative
    Profitability by product 223
    Sales value 165
    Sales value/joint costs 168

Relevant
    Costs 54, 63, 68, 204, 431, 433
    Range 52
Reorder points 524
Residual income 409
Responsibility accounting 399
Return on investment 407
Revisions of standards 441
Rework costs 148
Reworked products 143
Ricketts and Gray 2, 16
Risk 468
    Averse behavior 544
    Analysis 629
    Neutral behavior 541
    Seeking behavior 544
ROI formula 407

Safety
    Margin of 225
    Stock 524
Sales
    Mixed variance 359
    Price variance 360
    Quantity variance 359
    Value, relative 165
    Value, split-off point 170
    Volume variance 361
    Volume, master budget 291
    Volume, standard costs 361
Sell/process decisions 176
Scattergraph method 588
Scrap 141, 165
Second derivative, calculus 645
Segment of an organization 401
Semivariable costs 61
Sensitivity analysis 541, 626
Separating fixed and variable costs 588
Service
    Cost allocation 189
    Level, inventory quantities 521
Shadow price, LP 601, 624
Shrinkage 145
Simple regression 573
Simplex
    Method 588
    Tableau 603
Simulation 625
    Techniques 471, 545
Single-step income statements 400
Single-valued test 551
Skewed distribution 568
Slack variable 600
Smith, Keith, Stephens 2, 16
Special orders 435, 450
Specification errors, regression 585
Spending variance 345
Split-off point 162
Spoilage 107, 141
    Abnormal 141
    Comprehensive 152
    Loss 147
    Normal 141
Staff vs. line 46
Standard
    Costs 63, 315
    Deviation 537
    Deviation of the mean 549
    Error of the estimate, regression 584
Standards, revisions 441

State CPA requirements 40
Static budget 294
Statistics 535
Step-down method, cost allocation 191
Stockout cost 524
Stockout costs, inventory 520
Stop-or-go sampling 543
Storage costs 518
Straight-line depreciation 55
Stratified random sampling 544
Student exam fee
    CIA 37
    CMA 38
Student's t distribution 546
Study for undergraduate examinations 5
Subjective distribution 568
Suboptimization 404
Sunk costs 434
Symmetric distribution 568

T-
    Test 539
    Value, regression 597
Tableau, simplex 603
Targeted profit, CVP 242
Tax shield effect of depreciation 500
Texts
    Cost/managerial accounting 2, 7
    Quantitative methods 2, 7, 18
Theoretical capacity 80
Three-variance overhead method 345
Tight standards 319
Time
    Adjusted rate of return 470
    Series analysis 545
    Value of money 468
Top-down budgeting 404
Total
    Manufacturing costs 103
    Materials variance 320
Transfer pricing 91, 409
Transferred-in costs 91, 113
Transportation models 601
Treasurer 47
True-false questions 23
Two-bin inventory system 516
Two-tail test 551
Two-way analysis of overhead variance 341

Uncertainty 471
Undergraduate examination study 5
Unfavorable
    Material purchase price variance 325
    Materials usage variance 320
    Price variance 323
Uniform distribution 546
Unimodal distribution 568
Uniqueness of objective questions 5
Unit conversion costs 133
Units started 127
Usry, Hammer, Matz 2, 17

Variable
    And fixed costs, separating 588
    Budget 294
    Costing 203
    Costs 52
    Costs, service dept. allocation 193
    vs. fixed costs 52
Variance investigation 319
Volume variance, sales 317

Warren and Fess 2, 17
Weighted average
    Cost of capital 479
    EUP 125
Work-in-process account 50, 89
Working backwards, CVP 257

X bar chart 545

Y-axis intercept 574
Yield variance
    Labor 337
    Materials 330

Zero-base budgeting 293

Please forward your suggestions, corrections, and comments concerning typographical errors, etc. to **Irvin N. Gleim • c/o Accounting Publications, Inc. • P.O. Box 12848 • University Station • Gainesville, Florida • 32604**. Please include your name and address so we can properly thank you for your interest.

1. _____

2. _____

3. _____

4. _____

5. _____

6. _____

7. _____

8. _____

9. _____

10. _____

11. _____

12. _____

13. _____

14. _____

15. _____

16. _____

17. _____

18. _____

19. _____

20. _____

21. _____

22. _____

23. _____

24. _____

Name: _____

Company: _____

Address: _____

City/State/Zip: _____